ANNE CATHERINE EMMERICH

LIFE

OF

ANNE CATHERINE EMMERICH

VERY REV. K. E. SCHMÖGER, C.SS.R.

VOL. I.

TAN BOOKS AND PUBLISHERS, INC.
Rockford, Illinois 61105

APPROBATION.

The first volume of the work entitled "Life of Anne Catherine Emmerich," by Father Schmöger, C.SS.R., presented to us in manuscript, contains nothing contrary to the teachings of the Catholic Church, either as to dogma or morals, and, as it seems conducive to faith and piety, we cheerfully give it the approbation solicited by the author.

✠ PETER JOSEPH,
Bishop of Limbourg.

Limbourg, Sept. 26, 1867.

Reprinted from the 1968 edition of Maria Regina Guild, Los Angeles, California, itself reprinted from the English edition of 1885.

ISBN: Volume 1—0-89555-059-8
Volume 2—0-89555-060-1
The Set—0-89555-061-X

Printed and bound in the United States of America.

TAN BOOKS AND PUBLISHERS, INC.
P.O. Box 424
Rockford, Illinois 61105

1976

DEDICATION

To the Immaculate Heart of the Virgin Mary, Mother of God, Queen of Heaven and Earth, Lady of the Most Holy Rosary, Help of Christians, and Refuge of the Human Race.

CONTENTS

OF VOL. I.

Contents.

PREFACE TO THE ENGLISH EDITION.

The life of Anne Catherine Emmerich is already well known to thousands in Germany, Italy, and France. Its publication in those countries was hailed by numbers who have profited by its perusal. It will be no small recommendation in its favor to state that His Holiness, Pius IX. of blessed memory, ordered the Italian translation to be made from advanced proof-sheets of the German. The French, also, as we are told by Canon de Cazalès in his preface, was taken from the original proofs furnished by the author himself, Very Rev. Carl Erhard Schmöger, C.SS.R.

The present translation from the edition of 1870 was undertaken in the conviction, that the work is calculated to edify English readers not less than those of other nationalities. We were likewise actuated by the persuasion that it would be pleasing to Almighty God to publish the wonders of His workings in chosen souls; for if it is good to hide the secret of the king, it is also honorable to confess the works of the Most High (Tob. xii. 7).

The disciples of Antichrist never weary of publishing book after book, each more pernicious than the preceding, with the design of perverting the mind and corrupting the hearts of millions; they employ every effort, every stratagem to spread around by means of the press and in every possible form the deadly poison of hell.

Should the children of Holy Church, they who have it in their power to counteract these diabolical designs by the publication and circulation of good books, remain idle ? Should they fancy themselves exonerated from further efforts in a contrary direction by the mere utterance of useless lamentations whilst, at the same time, they behold the tide of evil gaining fresh strength as it sweeps along bearing with it innumerable souls to ruin ? Can too much be done to stem the torrent, to avert the danger before it is too late ?

May we not, also, whilst offering an antidote to the deadly effects of so much of our current literature, supply the spiritual wants, and gratify the varied tastes of many souls hungering for fresh and more suitable nourishment ?

Much has already been done in English Catholic literature, both in defence of Catholic principles and to lay before the public the lives of numerous saints and servants of God. But much still remains to be done, and it ought to be accomplished as carefully, as conscientiously as so noble an object deserves.

As every bad book tends to mislead the mind and corrupt the heart of its reader; so every good book is a cherished companion, a faithful teacher, whose lessons are often more telling on the interior life than the most eloquent sermons.

Should we have to-day a St. Ignatius Loyola had he, when convalescing after his wound at Pompeluna, been supplied with novels by way of entertainment instead of the legends of the saints ? Where would be our great St. Teresa had she continued her secret perusal of those dangerous ro-

mances which she found in the paternal home ? Should we
be called upon to lament the spiritual ruin of so many of
our young people, had they not imbibed principles of infidelity and licentiousness from the pages of those miserable
publications whose only aim is to depict vice in its most
vivid colors, and to spread it broadcast throughout the land ?
Earnest Catholic parents, good Catholic schools, zealous
priests, are indeed rich blessings for our Catholic youth;
but let some dangerous book fall into a child's hands, and the
efforts of parents, teachers, and priests will soon be frustrated.

May the present work, the "Life of Anne Catherine
Emmerich," open in the future, as it has done in the past,
a source of multiplied graces to its readers ! May its perusal prepare them for that of another most intimately
connected with it; viz., the "Life of Our Lord Jesus
Christ and His Blessed Mother," compiled from the revelations made to this holy religious !

If some of our readers find it difficult to lend credence to
the extraordinary favors conferred upon this privileged
spouse of Christ, let them remember that they are facts not
met in every-day life, consequently, facts to the contemplation of which the mind must be gradually trained as to any
other subject of thought and reflection. Let them understand that *the arm of the Lord is not shortened :* that He who
bestowed so many extraordinary favors on His servants both
of the Old and the New Law, has the same power, the same
freedom to show forth in our own day for the benefit of mankind His marvellous gifts in those whom He has selected
and prepared for them.

To those of our readers who may feel an interest in the
opinion of theologians concerning the present biography,
we can afford evidence not to be lightly put aside.

Even in her lifetime, after she had been subjected to the
test of a most rigid examination, sound theologians approved Anne Catherine Emmerich's supernatural state;
after her death sound theologians wrote and examined her
life, and distinguished ecclesiastical authorities set their
seal of approbation upon it.   Among the first class, we may
mention Mgr. Clemens Auguste, Count von Droste-Vischering, Coadjutor-Bishop of Münster, later Archbishop of
Cologne, who suffered so much, even two years' imprisonment, for defending and upholding the rights of the Church
against the encroachments of the government.   We mention the renowned Bishop Michael Sailer, of Ratisbon, and
his coadjutor, the saintly Bishop Wittman, (1) one of the
greatest prelates of our age.   Some hours before the death
of the latter, as we read in *Schmöger's Lebensbild*, he earnestly exhorted the Pilgrim (Brentano) to publish his manuscripts relating to the servant of God.   "O my beloved
friend," said he, "labor faithfully, labor faithfully for the

(1) Mgr. Wittman (1760-1833) was during the greater part of his life Director of the
Seminary at Ratisbon, Bavaria.   He was a man of extraordinary learning, eminent
holiness, and untiring activity.   Besides his position as Director of the Seminary and
professor in several branches, for twenty-five years the administration of the Cathedral
parish was intrusted to him.   In this capacity, he gave thirty-seven hours catechetical
instructions weekly, preached generally twice on Sundays, visited the hospitals, the
prisons, and the poor-house every week, breaking to the afflicted inmates the Word of
God and affording them spiritual consolation.   Five o'clock every morning found the
good priest in his confessional, where he often had an opportunity to exercise the
peculiar facility bestowed upon him to reconcile inveterate enemies.   Amid all these
labors he still found time to compose a number of excellent works particularly
adapted to the use of the clergy.   His day was divided as follows : seven hours of
prayer; seven hours of study ; seven hours' work; and three hours' sleep taken on a
plank with a book for his pillow   He died in his seventy-third year, lying on the floor
under a crucifix, as preconized Bishop of Ratisbon.   His death was lamented by all
that knew him, but most of all by the poor, to whom he was a real father and benefactor.   His name is held in veneration by the Catholics of southern Germany.—Taken
from Herder's Lexicon.

honor of Jesus Christ! Go on courageously!"—So spoke he dying Bishop as he blessed Brentano, and congratulated him in the hearing of all around upon having noted down the visions of Anne Catherine, to the publication of which he had in their very first interview urged him. Nor must we omit Sister Emmerich's extraordinary confessor, the pious and learned Dean Overberg, for a time Director of the Seminary at Münster. We shall often meet his name in the following pages. To the foregoing illustrious names may be added those of Count von Stolberg and Joseph Goerres who, though not in the ranks of the priest-hood, so excelled in theological learning and sound judgment that their words were received as oracles in their time

All these distinguished men knew Anne Catherine Emmerich personally and, like innumerable other witnesses of her life, pronounced her a true spouse of Christ, a chosen soul endowed with extraordinary graces and privileges.

Let us now turn to the second class of witnesses, to the sound theologians that wrote and examined her life at a later period The notes taken by Clement Brentano at the bedside of the ecstatica during his six years' stay in Dülmen, were at his death bequeathed as a precious legacy to Christian Brentano, his brother. The latter handed them over to the Abbot Haneberg, later Bishop of Spires, with the understanding that they should at some future day be arranged and published But the pious Abbot, a sincere admirer of Sister Emmerich and fully conscious of the treasure in his possession, could not find the time necessary for the accomplishment of so great a work ; viz., the publication of the Life of Christ with that of the venerable Sister herself.

Almighty God called another to undertake the task, one eminently competent, one who united deep learning with solid piety. This man was Very Rev. Carl Erhard Schmöger, C.SS.R., who had in 1850 entered the Congregation of the Most Holy Redeemer as a secular priest of more than ordinary learning. His Superiors soon discovered his extraordinary talents and uncommon love for the study of theology. He was, consequently, engaged for years as professor in its different branches, dogmatic, hermeneutic, and exegetic, besides which he for some time taught philosophy. As he was constantly enriching his mind by the reading of the Holy Fathers, his keen eye could detect at a glance the least inaccuracy in any author respecting Catholic faith or tradition. This was an excellent preparation for Father Schmöger's later providential mission.

Gladly and with noble generosity, Abbot Haneberg delivered Brentano's manuscripts to such a man, to one whom he considered so well qualified for the work, and by whom that rich treasure of God's mercy was to be opened to the faithful. Meanwhile, Divine Providence favored the undertaking. Father Schmöger found access to many documents concerning the civil and ecclesiastical trials to which Sister Emmerich had been subjected, and this enabled him to give a still more correct picture of her interior and exterior life. The task was begun in obedience to the command of Superiors. Encouraged by men like Abbot Haneberg and Very Rev. Frederic Windischmann, Vicar-General of Munich, and supported by the prayers of many pious souls, Father Schmöger continued and accomplished t only after years of hard and oft-interrupted labor ; or during the latter part of his life, he held the office of Provincial of his Congregation in Bavaria. Although himself a renowned theologian, he never failed to submit the result of his careful researches to other theologians and authorities upon whose learning and solidity he could safely rely. And so the Life of Anne Catherine Emmerich was published for the first time in 1870, with the approbation of the Bishop of Limbourg and the permission of Father Schmöger's Superior, the General of the Redemptorists at Rome.

The fact that not one voice was raised against his works after their publication by the Catholic press ; the fact that his books found their way unmolested into the houses of thousands, as the "Dolorous Passion," the only compilation from Sister Emmerich's revelations published during Brentano's lifetime, had previously done ; the fact that the Life of the Stigmatisee was immediately translated into French and Italian with the approbation of orthodox Bishops ; the fact that in Germany a second edition of the said Life soon followed the first, and that new demands now render a third necessary—these facts might, we think, be accepted as sufficient proofs of God's blessing on the work.

But when great men like Dom Guéranger, Abbot of Solesmes, and Very Rev. F. Windischmann of Munich, whose names are known throughout the Catholic world, speak in the highest terms of it, have we room to fear not being in harmony with Catholic faith and teaching if we lend to it our meed of praise? Dom Gueranger (whose word, as Rev. Frederic Windischmann tells us, is of more weight with him than that of a thousand others) expresses his conviction that Anne Catherine Emmerich had a mission from God and that she faithfully fulfilled the same; otherwise God never would have lavished so abundant and so extraordinary favors upon her. It was hers to bring before the mind of the German nation the Gospel in its most minute details just at a time when the Divinity of Christ and the Gospel truths were most strenuously denied by the philosophers so-called of the day. And here the learned Abbot expresses his astonishment at the way in which she fulfilled her mission. That a poor, uneducated peasant-girl in the heart of Europe should describe in their smallest details the various characters and languages, manners and customs of different and far-off countries; that she should do all this with perfect accuracy with respect to the varied circumstances of geography, topography, and archæology of times long passed, is certainly sufficient to astound even the most prudent and learned.

Rev. F. Windischmann, himself a warm friend of Father Schmöger, considers it something very wonderful that in all Sister Emmerich's descriptions of the various circumstances and situations in which the Sacred Person of Our Lord figures; viz., at meals, at marriage-feasts, on journeys, etc., we find not the least trace of anything unworthy of Him. All and everything He does or says is animated by a certain nobleness indicative of His Divine Personality. This, he concludes, Anne Catherine could never have done had her work been a mere human invention.

These facts would seem proof sufficient to establish the truth of Sister Emmerich's revelations. But we have still some others to bring forward.

Rev. Alban Stolz, Professor in the Seminary of Freiburg, and a famous German author, mentions in the description of his journey to Jerusalem that a certain Franciscan, Father Wolfgang of Jerusalem, told him that for six years he had made the statements of Anne Catherine Emmerich respecting the Holy Land, as given in Brentano's "Dolorous Passion," a point of special study. The result of his observations was, that they are perfectly correct in all their details. Rev. Stolz tells us on the same page that one Professor Hug, a man known to be not over-credulous on the subject of visions or revelations, one day expressed to his pupils his surprise that the statements of the nun of Dülmen agree so exactly with those of the Jewish historian Josephus. (1)

Rev. Anton Urbas, Parish-priest and Canon of the Cathedral of Laybach, Austria, published a book in 1884, entitled *"Die Reiche der Heiligen Drei Könige."* He mentions in the preface that he had read Anne Catherine Emmerich's Life, Visions, and Revelations for a considerable time without being able to harmonize many points that he found therein. Some things seemed to him very beautiful, useful, and correct; but others were hard to accept. Instead

(1) See "Sem. Cham. and Japhet," by Alban Stolz.

of denouncing the whole as the pious dream of a good nun,
he set himself to the task of studying the geography of Asia
in all its details.   As he studied he compared his researches with the statements of A. C. Emmerich.   The result of
his earnest and honest investigation was, that he publicly acknowledged Sister Emmerich to be the most correct geog-
rapher, topographer, and archæologist in the world, and
that his first difficulties were to be attributed rather to a
want of knowledge on his own part than to any fault on that
of the wonderfully enlightened Sister.

St. Paul writes to the Corinthians (I. Cor. i. 28, 29), " God
has chosen the foolish things of the world that He may confound the wise, and the weak things of the world God has
chosen that He may confound the strong . . . . . that no flesh
should glory in His sight."   Are not these words here literally verified ?

Canon Urbas says, moreover : " The works of Sister Emmerich are a rich mine.   Some few remarks often throw
much light on certain subjects.   Like cross-road signs,
they point out the right way.   Their power to move and
vivify the soul is especially noticeable.   Here, as in no
other book outside the Holy Scriptures, do we find words
of eternal life."

But coming nearer home, we could cite many distinguished ecclesiastics as stanch supporters of Sister Emmerich and her revelations.   We shall limit ourselves to
two whose rank in the sacred hierarchy lends greater
weight to their authority ; viz., the saintly John N. Neu-
mann, Fourth Bishop of Philadelphia, and the lately de-

ceased Bishop Tœbbe, of Covington, Ky. That the former favored her works, may be seen by a reference to his Life. In it we read that among others books which he imported from Europe in the early days of his ministry, he called particularly for those of A. C. Emmerich ; the latter, Bishop Tœbbe, showed his appreciation of the same by heartily approving the new edition of the " Life of Jesus," compiled from her revelations. (1)

But as some critic may object that even great theologians may be deceived in such matters, we shall refrain from arguments of our own in its defence, referring our readers to the rules of Pope Benedict XIV. which Rome follows in the canonization of such souls as were favored in life with visions and revelations. By the application of these rules (which may be found in the author's preface) any fair-minded Catholic may judge whether such visions and revelations are from God or not.

If the life of Anne Catherine Emmerich may be tested by these rules, we may safely conclude that her extraordinary gifts were indeed from God ; for what is considered by the Holy Father and his Cardinals a sufficient guaranty of truth in the process of canonization, ought to be sufficient also to satisfy the inquiries of the severest critic. Let the reader study without prejudice the Life of this favored soul, let him apply to it the aforesaid rules, and then only let him form his judgment of the same.

In conclusion, we beg leave to state that the translation

(1) " Das arme Leben und bittere Leiden unseres Herrn Jesu Christi und seiner heiligsten Mutter Maria," published by Fr. Pustet & Co.

of the present work was undertaken with the sole view to extend the reign of Jesus Christ in hearts and to further the coming of His kingdom upon earth. Our aim has been to reproduce carefully and conscientiously from the original every word that fell from the lips of the stigmatisée ; whilst, to suit the taste of English readers, the accompanying matter has been somewhat condensed, though not to the detriment of the author's meaning. Like the original it has been submitted to the judgment of competent persons and been thoroughly revised by an able theologian.

February 5, 1885.

PREFACE TO THE SECOND EDITION.

One of the hopeful signs of our times, despite a spirit of worldliness and polite sensualism, is the growing interest which is being manifested in the study of the lives of the mystics. It is evidence of how far the Church of God has lifted society out of the dross of materialism, when her great heroes and heroines of virtue, whose hearts were so unreservedly and passionately set upon things not of this earth, and never appealing to anything but the highest and noblest in their fellow men, are receiving a recognition so sincere and so profound. Nor is this recognition confined to the children of the " household of the faith." The " mystical " literature of the Catholic Church is read by a great number of non-Catholics who are engaged in a sincere search after truth. The writer has in mind the testimony of more than one devout convert, who owes the first dawning of the Light to the reading of the life of a saint. And this is but natural. The blending of the potential perfections of heaven with the actual experiences of earth, so impressively illustrated in the lives of the saints, brings the well disposed mind into such close touch with the supernatural, that all worldly concerns appear dwarfed and pale. The tree is judged by its fruit, and the conclusion is, that a church which can produce such exalted characters must have within her the divinity of the Gospel and the truth as it has been revealed by Jesus Christ.

Considering these facts, it is with joy and edification we hail this second English edition of the life of Anne Catherine Emmerich. Already her name is well known to the whole Catholic world. When the record of the wonderful

visions accorded her first appeared, it provoked a great deal
of adverse criticism. But time, which is the one great test
of genuineness, has caused that adverse criticism to disappear and to give way to the highest approval. An illustrious evidence of this fact is shown by the following letter from
a canon of the Cathedral of Loybach, Bavaria : "At first
I did not believe Catherine Emmerich's statements. I
wondered how the Bishop of Limbourg could approve the
publication of such a book. I went to work to find out all
the falsehoods she was telling, and to my surprise, I found
that in the light of tradition, geography, topography, and history, Anne Catherine Emmerich knew more than all our
so-called savants. After Holy Scripture, there is no book
that contains so many words of eternal truth and life than
the revelations of A. C. Emmerich."

To this we must add the testimony of the eminent theologian, Dr. Rohling, who writes in an Appendix to his
Medulla Theologiæ Moralis : " I cannot refrain from
adding my voice of commendation to that of all who have
written on the life and visions of Anne Catherine Emmerich, and I earnestly commend them. I desire to mention
in particular her visions on the Life and Passion of Our
Lord, since I am convinced that every priest who studies
them will be so inflamed with zeal for souls and longing
for his own salvation, that it will be impossible for him to
be lost. He will find Our Lord therein portrayed in colors
so lively, and he will receive so clear a perception of His
goodness, that he will gladly renounce all worldly pleasure,
and daily participate in a new outpouring of God's Holy
Spirit, thus becoming ever fitter to move the hearts of
worldlings and lead them to penance."

A perusal of the Life of Catherine Emmerich makes one
appreciate these impressive words of Dr. Rohling. Her

visions bring before the mind so vivid a realization of the mission and Passion of Our Redeemer that, when the reader finishes his study of them, he feels conscious of having undergone an unusual influence, and he is moved to voice his feelings in the exclamation of the two who met the Saviour on the way to Emmaus : " Was not our heart burning within us whilst He spoke in the way, and opened to us the Scriptures ? "

To learn the life of Our Divine Lord, is the chief study of every Christian. Catherine Emmerich is a notable aid to the performance of this duty. It was a commendable thought of the translator to place this work at the disposal of English readers, for whatever tends to bring the soul into close union with the Saviour is of supreme value. We read in the Gospels that a diseased woman once pressed through the crowd, touched the hem of the Master's garment, and by the power of her faith was immediately healed. Is not the loyal disciple, who gets still near enough to touch Him in spirit and draw forth the inspiring virtue He delivers, made spiritually whole ? This is the mission of Catherine Emmerich—to bring souls into touch with Christ. And in a day like ours, when so many hearts are waxing cold, and a spirit of irreligion seems to sway the minds of multitudes, who will deny that the mission of Anne Catherine Emmerich is a blessing to the world ?

All admirers of this great servant of God received with grateful hearts the blessed tidings that the process for her Beatification had actually begun in Rome. We pray that the day is not far distant when the Church will enroll her name in the list of saints. One thing is certain : we may safely venture the opinion that the influence she has had upon the history of the Church in the nineteenth century will increase as the years roll by, and continue till time is no more. Despite all that the haters of the Christian religion may say—and they are saying much that is blasphemous—the memory of Jesus and His Passion will endure to the end. Ah, how little did Pilate dream, as he led Him out, bleeding from the degradation of the scourge, and said to the multitude, "Behold the man!"—how little did the infuriated mob dream that the voice of that silent sufferer would thrill the world forever, and the image of Him crucified would melt the heart of all posterity. Animated by a very different spirit from that which filled the soul of the worldly-ambitious Pilate, Anne Catherine Emmerich cries out to us, "Behold the Lamb of God that taketh away the sins of the world!"

This work will no doubt, now and then, meet with half-veiled sneers and cynical warnings from those that cannot appreciate its merits. But it is comforting to know that such criticism will in no way lessen its effect upon those elect souls who are seeking encouragement and enlightenment in a life of prayer. And He who, while on earth, breathed such divinity of tenderness, such inexhaustible magnanimity of forbearing pity and love toward all men; who from His throne in Heaven is now willing to give the pearl of great price purchased with His Precious Blood to the lowest child of humanity; who in the agony of death on Calvary's Cross yearned over the broken malefactor by His side with the promise of Paradise, will not fail to bless and enlighten all who, in a rightful spirit, study the life and revelations of Anne Catherine Emmerich.

A word, in conclusion, as to the work of the translator. She has succeeded in producing a work that reads as if it had been originally written in English. One may say that she has literally put her heart into it. It ranks among the most valuable productions of the Catholic press, and none will read it without profit.

T. A. D.

Feast of St. Monica,—1903.

INTRODUCTION

The author of the present biography published eight years ago the last volume of the " Life of Our Divine Saviour," compiled from the visions of Anne Catherine Emmerich. He purposed issuing, as a supplement to the same, the life of the servant of God drawn from the most authentic sources; but the duties of his ministry, sickness, and the difficulties attendant on the undertaking itself, retarded its publication until the present.

If Clement Brentano, (1) who resided at Dülmen from the

---

(1) Clement Brentano, whose name will appear so often in the course of this biography, was born September 8, 1778. He was a poet of the highest genius. What others acquired only by long and hard study, he learned with ease. He was perfectly at home with the Greek and Latin authors, with Calderon, Dante, and Shakespeare, as well as with those of his own tongue. His wit and humor, his brilliant talents and exquisite poetical productions won for him the love and admiration of all who came in contact with him, and opened to him access to the highest literary circles. His religious education had been very much neglected ; still he believed in the existence of God as a remunerator of good and evil, and in Jesus Christ as a divine mediator. He was charitable to the poor. Like Solomon he saw the vanity of all created things, and like the great Augustine he longed for something higher than earthly glory and knowledge. His restless heart at last found peace in God in a general confession, 1817. A new world was now opened up before him, new friends gathered round him ; his religious fervor was great, although wanting in prudence and needing direction. This he found by the bedside of the poor and suffering Anne Catherine Emmerich, to whom Divine Providence had sent him in 1818. So attracted was he by the heroic virtue he there witnessed that the former idol of the fashionable world resolved to bury himself in the little town of Dülmen, and warm his heart at this furnace of divine love. But nòt for himself alone were the graces he there received. Brentano was to be the instrument for the accomplishment of God's design that the revelations with which the ecstatica was favored should be recorded for the benefit of mankind. Ardently desirous of doing something for the glory of God, and thereby to atone for the shortcomings of the past, Brentano readily accepted the pressing invitation of Dean Overberg to become the amanuensis of the favored stigmatisée. For nearly six years, despite the jeers and mockery of his friends, he daily committed to writing what he learned in that school of Christ Crucified. When A. C. Emmerich died, Brentano returned to his friends, not now to entertain them by his talents, but to astound them by his ardor in the service of God and his neighbor. The large sums realized from his literary productions were all devoted to this noble purpose. Catholic literature felt a new impulse,

fall of 1818 till the spring of 1824, daily making notes of his observations, shrank from the task of compiling this life, so simple in the exterior, so little calculated to strike the senses, and yet so rich, so wonderful in its interior signification, the writer of these lines may surely believe himself entitled to the indulgence of his readers for withholding it so long. He deemed the sketch of Sister Emmerich's life prefixed to the first edition of " The Dolorous Passion," published by Clement Brentano, in 1833, sufficient, until his friend Dr. Krabbe, Dean of the Cathedral Münster, procured him access to the original " Acts of the Ecclesiastical Inquiry of 1813," and also accompanied him to Dülmen, Coesfeld, and Flamske, to collect among her few surviving contemporaries some circumstances of her life, which led to the present work. Gratitude demands the mention of the late Herr Aulike, Privy-Councillor at Berlin, who kindly forwarded to the author the notices given to the public at intervals from the year .1813 to that of her death, 1824. The above-named gentlemen regarded her with deep veneration, and eagerly awaited the publication of her biography, which, however, neither lived to see.

Owing to the conscientious record of the Acts of the In-

good books were translated and circulated, sculpture and painting were raised to new life by his religious energy. Encouraged by the pious and learned of his time, and we may add in the very home of the famous Diepenbrock, afterward Cardinal-Archbishop of Breslau, he published in 1835 the " Dolorous Passion of Christ," the first work compiled from the revelations of A. C. Emmerich. One edition succeeded another and quickly prepared the public mind for other works from the same source. Brentano died holily in 1842. With him a great and noble soul passed from earth to heaven. His early failings he had long before blotted out by torrents of contrite tears. If charity covers a multitude of sins, certainly his heroic love for God and his neighbor more than atoned for the wanderings of his early career, wanderings that sprang rather from ignorance than malice. His death was followed by the conversion of some noble souls to whom in life he had earnestly pointed out the Catholic Church as the only secure refuge, the only safe harbor of salvation.—*Taken from " Sketch of Clement Brentano,"* by REV. F. DIEL, S. J.

vestigation, wholly unknown to Clement Brentano, the author has been enabled to support this history on testimony so weighty that none more conclusive can be found in the life of any saint favored by similar graces, whilst the rich materials they afford give a clearer understanding of Sister Emmerich's mission. In them we behold a fact whose significance is universally acknowledged by the Church, a fact known and appreciated in every age ; viz., that Almighty God at all times chooses certain souls, who, either secluded from the world or amid the hurry of secular life, serve as instruments in suffering and combating for the Church. The life and sufferings of such chosen ones are often widely dissimilar : for instance, Lidwina of Schiedam, or our own Domenica Lazzari appear as victims in the body, like the early virgin-martyrs ; whilst others, such as Magdalene di Pazzi, or Colomba di Rieti, combat and suffer for the Church spiritually ; though, inasmuch as their life is a perpetual sacrifice, a course of uninterrupted endurance in perfect abandonment to the will of God, they closely resemble one another. They expiate the faults committed in the bosom of the Church and repair the wrongs she endures from her own children, or they atone for actual guilt, doing penance for the guilty. By prayer, or rather by an extraordinary gift which converts prayer into action, they avert impending dangers from the Sovereign Pontiff and the clergy ; they obtain conversion for sinners ; an increase of faith for the weak ; zeal and intrepidity for pastors ; and, lastly, they wrestle for souls in danger of being lost through the negligence of others, chiefly of those entrusted with their spiritual guidance. Besides this duty of prayer and expiation, there is, moreover, the task militant, to be undertaken by some privileged souls, and which consists in actually embracing corporal and spiritual dangers, diseases, temptations, and evil inclinations. Here it is no longer simple suffering or sacrifice, the fruits of which are reaped by others; but there is question of exposing one's self, really and personally, to all the perils that menace the neighbor, of taking upon one's self sickness or temptation exacting of the substitute a real struggle, the fruits of whose victory are to be made over to another. One of the most sublime instances of such a task is found in Judith confronting Holofernes and his army to prevent the profanation of the Sanctuary and the opprobrium of God's chosen people. It may seem, perhaps, that prayer must be the only or. at least, the chief duty of these victims; but such is not exclusively the case, since the martyrdom of penance undergone by the innocent is precisely that which gives to prayer its efficacy and draws down upon the Church the richest benedictions. The expiatory task is never separated from that of combating, and both united to prayer are found to an extraordinary degree in the life of Sister Emmerich who, from her very infancy, had been prepared for her mission, her communications with her angel, her intuitive perception of the unseen, and the gift of contemplation bestowed at her birth contributing thereto.

Three great evils menaced the Church at the epoch in

which she lived : the profanation of sacred things, the dis-
semination of false doctrines, and the corruption of morals,
to meet which with the weapons of prayer and expiation
was Sister Emmerich's mission, to struggle in defence of
the Church delivered over, as it were, to the will of her enemies. It will, in no small degree, animate the pious reader
to renewed confidence in God when he finds in this biography so many proofs of His merciful protection over His
Church during those troubled times, and beholds the instrument employed for that end in the person of the poor little
shepherdess of Flamske. This was the consideration that
encouraged the author to resume his oft-interrupted task,
and to spare no trouble in the study of her life, diligently
comparing for this end the facts contained in it with those
presented in the biographies of others similarly favored by
Heaven.

They who are familiar with the rules laid down by Benedict XIV. and the great theological authorities to whom he
constantly refers in his work, *"De Servorum Dei Beatifica-
tione,"* will understand the author's anxiety in elaborating
a history like the one under consideration, and agree with
him in declaring Sister Emmerich's life a striking exempli-
fication of the virtues exacted by the Church as proofs of
the truth wherever there is question of the supernatural (1).

To be able prudently to pronounce upon so delicate a
question, consideration must be had on the one side to the

---

(1) The following lines, taken from Father Schmöger's Introduction to the " Life of
Christ," seem so suitable to the subject here treated that, conforming to the advice of
certain capable persons, among them a holy confrère of the author himself, we take
the liberty of incorporating them in this Introduction to the Life of Sister Emmerich.

virtue of the person under examination, and on the other to her manner of conducting herself both in and out of vision ; for which latter point, Benedict XIV., with the most distinguished doctors and theologians, has laid down twelve marks deserving special attention :—

I.—Has the person in question ever desired visions ; or, on the contrary, has she begged of God the grace of being conducted in the ordinary ways ? Has she received such visions only in the spirit of obedience ?—" To desire such favors," says St. Vincent Ferrier, " would be to nourish secret pride or reprehensible curiosity ; it would be a sign of weak, imperfect faith."

II.—Has she received from her confessor an order to communicate her visions to holy and enlightened persons ?

III.—Has she always shown absolute obedience toward her spiritual guides ? Has she in consequence of her visions made rapid progress in the love of God and humility ?

IV.—Has she willingly conferred with persons disinclined to credit her, or who tried and contradicted her ?

V.—Does she habitually experience peace and tranquillity of conscience ? Is her heart always inflamed with ardent zeal for perfection ?

VI.—Were her spiritual directors ever obliged to reproach her with imperfections ?

VII.—Has she received from God a promise to hear all her lawful and reasonable petitions ? Has she by her prayers obtained great favors from Him ?

VIII.—Have those who live with her, supposing their own

perversity no obstacle to her virtuous influence, been incited to piety and the love of God ?

IX.—Have her visions been vouchsafed her after fervent prayer or Holy Communion ? Have they excited in her a desire to suffer for the glory of God ?

X.—Has she crucified her flesh ? Has she rejoiced in trials and contradictions ?

XI.—Has she loved retreat ? Has she fled the society of creatures ? Is she despoiled of every natural attachment ?

XII.—Has she preserved serenity of soul as well under adverse as under prosperous circumstances? Finally, have learned theologians found nothing in her visions contrary to the rules of faith, or which might appear reprehensible, viewed in any light whatever ?

These twelve points laid down by Benedict XIV., fruits of the experience of the most holy and enlightened Doctors, furnish sure and infallible rules in such cases ; and the more closely a soul endued with the gift of vision is conformed thereto, the more motives are there, according to the holy pontiff, for accepting her testimony and visions as true and real. Now, the reader will, without doubt, be no less gratified than we in tracing the perfect and truly surprising correspondence between these rules and the whole life of Sister Emmerich. He will agree with us in declaring that to find these different characteristics united in the same degree in any one soul, he would be obliged to search the lives of the most illustrious saints of the Church. In the first place, Sister Emmerich never desired such fav-

ors. They entailed upon her so many trials and contradictions that she frequently conjured God to deliver her
from them. Again, the age at which she first received them
permits us not to suppose she could have desired them, for
when she did begin to speak of them, it was with the simplicity of a child ignorant of the precise meaning of what it
says. Secondly, she could be induced to communicate
her visions only by the reiterated instances of her angelic
guide, and not till the last ten years of her life did she find
any one willing to listen to them. Thirdly, as her confessors
suspected her visions and took the trouble not even to examine them, she did all in her power to hide them, to
stifle them, so to say, in her own breast. The struggle
thence arising with her invisible guide, who ceased not to
urge her to reveal them despite her confessor's aversion,
caused her indescribable suffering. Still she continued to
address herself to the same directors from whom, however,
she had naught to expect but stern rebuffs and bitter humiliations. She left to God the care of enlightening them
in His own good time upon the origin and character of
her supernatural gifts ; and she rejected, as far as in her
lay, all that could modify or ameliorate her painful position, testifying only charity, patience, and sweetness
toward the authors of her trials.

Passing over the other points, we shall limit ourselves to a
glance at the twelfth and last: viz., the conformity of Sister Emmerich's visions with the teachings of faith—a circumstance
of the utmost importance in visions containing revelations.

Benedict XIV. here supports his opinion chiefly upon Suarez, who establishes **as an incontestable** principle that, **in the study of revelations, it is chiefly to be considered whether they are in** perfect accordance with the rules of **Faith and sound morals,** rejecting as illusory and diabolical every pretended revelation in contradiction with Holy Scripture, tradition, the decrees of Councils, and the unanimous teachings of the Fathers and theologians. Even those revelations which, without contravening the Faith, contain evident contradictions and serve but to satisfy vain curiosity, which appear to be the result of a purely human activity, or which, in fine, are opposed to the wisdom of God or to any other of His divine attributes, are to be suspected.

And here the illustrious pontiff asks what should be thought of revelations containing statements apparently opposed to the common opinion of the Fathers and theologians, revelations which on some particular point, give details quite new, or which affirm as certain what has not as yet been pronounced upon by the Church ? Resting upon the most solid authority, he answers that this motive suffices not to reject without further examination revelations in which such things are found ; for, 1st, a fact which at first sight appears opposed to the common opinion may, if submitted to an earnest and conscientious examination, evoke in its favor weighty authority and excellent intrinsic reasons for belief; 2d, a revelation should not be condemned as false merely on account of its containing circumstances in the

Life of Our Lord, or that of His Blessed Mother, of which no mention is made in the Sacred Writings, in tradition, or in the Holy Fathers ; 3d, a revelation may, without militating against the decisions of the Church, the Fathers, and theologians, explain a point unexplained by them or make known some detail on which they are silent ; 4th, it would be to place arbitrary limits to the almighty power of God to suppose that He cannot reveal to a private individual a point which, not yet pronounced upon by the Church, is still a subject of controversy.

If the reader desires to apply the foregoing rules to the revelations contained in this work (1), he will find therein absolutely nothing wounding to the principles of Christian faith ; on the contrary, he will be fully satisfied that there are few books which enable the soul to penetrate so easily into the mysteries of our holy religion, or which impart so speedily even to ordinary minds the knowledge of that *art of arts* which, according to the author of the *Imitation,* consists in the meditation of the Life of Our Lord Jesus Christ, *In vita Jesu Christi meditari* (2).

As impostors and hypocrites are often met in these our days who vaunt themselves the favored recipients of Heaven's special favors, and who occasionally gain credence with some, the author has given faithfully and in detail the investigations made on Sister Emmerich's case as he found them in the original documents.

(1) "*Life of Our Lord Jesus Christ.*" The above remark is equally applicable to many points in Sister Emmerich's own life.

(2) Extract from Introduction to *Life of Our Lord,* Schmöger.

Clement Brentano's friend, Edward Steinle, painted the portrait from which the engraving prefixed to this volume was taken. His models were the drawings sketched by Brentano himself at various periods of his sojourn in Dülmen. They who knew Sister Emmerich best testify to its fidelity.

In conclusion the author declares his unreserved submission to the decrees of Pope Urban VIII. of March 13, 1625, and June 5, 1634, in consequence of which he claims for whatever is extraordinary in this book but a purely human origin.

P. SCHMÖGER, C.SS.R.

CONVENT OF GARS, ON THE INN, BAVARIA,
        September 17, 1867.

– LIFE –

OF

ANNE CATHERINE EMMERICH.

CHAPTER I.

Manners and Customs of Westphalia at the Commencement of the Present Century.

The baptismal register, St. James, Coesfeld, contains the following record:—"On September 8, 1774, was baptized Anne Catherine, daughter of Bernard Emmerich and Anne Hillers his wife, God-parents, Henry Hüning and Anne Catherine Heynick, née Mertins." The day of little Anne Catherine's baptism was also that of her birth. She was the fifth of nine children, six sons and three daughters. Gerard, the youngest brother, never married. He was still living in September, 1859, when the author visited the little hamlet of Flamske, near Coesfeld, the birthplace of the subject of this biography. Gerard had little to say of his sister, excepting that she was of a remarkably sweet disposition, that she had been a lifelong sufferer, and that he had often gone to see her at Dülmen after she became a religious. "She was so kind and affectionate to us," he added, "that it was a great pleasure to her family to visit her."

The venerable pastor of the church of St. James, Rev. F. Hilswitte, was also alive and remembered having seen Anne Catherine for the last time in 1812. He testified to her reputation for piety, but the particulars of her life were un-

known to him. " The period in which she lived," he remarked, " was not capable of either understanding or appreciating such a case as hers, and few, even among the
clergy, interested themselves in her; consequently, she
was more quickly forgotten in her native place than elsewhere. In distant cities she was better known through
Bishop Wittmann and Clement Brentano. The latter, after
his visits to Dülmen, excited public interest in her by the
account of the marvels he had seen."

Long before her death, Sister Emmerich had uttered the
following words : " What the Pilgrim (1) gleans, he will bear
away, far, far away, for there is no disposition to make use
of it here; but it will bring forth fruit in other lands, whence
its effects will return and be felt even here."

The humble abode in which she was born was yet standing, in 1859, in the same condition in which Clement Brentano had found it forty years before. It was a little old
farm-house, or rather a barn in which man and beast dwelt
peaceably together. The worm-eaten door opened into a
small room whose only floor was the well-trodden ground;
this was the common room of the family. To the left were
spaces cut off from the main room by rough board partitions,
and strewn with the hay and grain scattered by the cattle ;
these were the sleeping apartments. The chimney-place,
rude and primitive, consisted of a stone slab or iron plate
cemented into the ground; on it glowed the fire, and above
it hung the kettle from an iron bar. The smoke, after depositing its soot upon the rough beams and dingy chairs
and table, the handiwork of preceding generations, escaped
as best it could by any chink in the roof or walls. The
rest of the dwelling was given up to the cows, which were
separated from their owners only by a few stakes driven

(1) " The Pilgrim"—it was thus Sister Emmerich always designated Clement Brentano. We shall retain the title throughout this work.

into the gronnd. At a later period a small addition of two
bedrooms was annexed to the principal building. In front
of this humble abode stood some aged oaks, beneath whose
shade the wonderful little girl of whom we write often sported
with her village companions.

Clement Brentano paid a visit to Sister Emmerich's birthplace during her lifetime. And the following are his impressions of the customs of that period in the country of Münster:—

"I went three leagues from Dülmen to the hamlet of
Flamske,to visit Anne Catherine's early home, then occupied
by her eldest brother Bernard and his family. Dülmen
belongs to the parish of St. James, Coesfeld, a city about
half a league distant. I longed to see the place of her
birth, the cradle of her infancy. I found it an old barn,
with mud walls and a moss-covered thatched roof. The
rickety door stood invitingly open, and I entered to find
myself in a cloud of smoke through which I could scarcely
distinguish a step ahead. A look of surprise from Bernard
Emmerich and his wife greeted my unceremonious entrance.
But when I introduced myself as the bearer of messages
and compliments from their sister, they received me most
cordially, and the little ones, shy at first, came forward on
a sign from their father and kissed their tiny hands in welcome. I saw no other room than the one I had entered, a corner of which was partly partitioned off. In it stood a
rude loom belonging to one of the brothers. Several old
chests blackened by smoke displayed when opened the
novel sight of straw beds furnished with feather pillows.
Opposite this room was the still more novel spectacle of the
cows behind their stacks.

"The furniture was scanty enough. Cooking utensils
garnished the walls and from the rafters hung straw, hay,

and tow black with soot. Here in this dingy atmosphere, in this disorder and poverty, was born and reared that favored child, so pure, so enlightened, so surpassingly rich in intellectual gifts; here was her baptismal innocence preserved untarnished. It recalled to my mind our Saviour's crib at Bethlehem. From a wooden block before the door, which served as a table, I ate a slice of brown bread and drank a mug of milk whilst conversing with Bernard Emmerich, whose genuine piety shone forth in his words, his favorite expression being, ' With God's help !'

" An old discolored picture of Our Lady hung over the spot in which Anne Catherine used to take her rest.   With the owner's leave I replaced it by another, and took it with me along with some acorns from the old oaks before the door as a memento of my visit.   On bidding farewell to these good people, they told me that I was the first who had ever taken so much interest in their sister's birthplace. Thence I went half a league further to Coesfeld, to visit the church in which she had received the marks of the Crown of Thorns.   It was here, in the parish church of St. James, that she had received holy Baptism, September 8, 1774, which day, the Feast of Mary's Nativity, was also that of her birth (1). My visit to this beautiful old church filled me with the sweetest impressions. From it I went to see the old pastor, Father Hartbaum, whom I found still quite vigorous, despite his years.   He did not seem fully to appreciate his former parishioner, and he expressed surprise at the interest manifested in her. He struck me as one of those who would willingly see things remain always the same, who care not to deviate from their daily routine, whose horizon extends not beyond the range of their own intellectual vision.

(1) Clement Brentano himself was born Sept. 8, 1778.

"I next visited St. Lambert's, the principal church, wherein is preserved the miraculous crucifix, known as the 'Crucifix of Coesfeld,' before which when a child Sister Emmerich used to spend long hours in fervent prayer, receiving in return abundant graces. It is forked like that which, at a later period, was imprinted upon her own breast. Tradition says it was brought from Palestine in the eighth century. Here it was that Sister Emmerich received the Sacrament of Confirmation. I afterward went to the Jesuit church in which, at the age of twenty-four, probably in 1798, the Crown of Thorns was laid upon her brow by her Heavenly Spouse, as she prayed toward mid-day before a crucifix in the organ-loft. It saddened me to think that this beautiful church had partly fallen into Protestant hands since the Count von Salm's residence here. The so-called communion-table stood in front of that altar from whose tabernacle had issued the apparition of the Saviour to Anne Catherine; the feast of the Reformation, that triumph of apostasy, is here annually announced from the pulpit; and the grand old organ, near which she prayed at the time of the miraculous favor, has been replaced by one of more recent make. At present, the church is used by both Catholics and Protestants, and I was told that the Countess von Salm, as if she were sole mistress, had tried to deprive the former of their right to worship in it. She also arrogated to herself the privilege of quartering her people on the Capuchins whose monastery is not far off, and she loudly complained of the annoyance caused her by the sound of the morning bells calling the faithful to Holy Mass. This church, capable of seating two thousand, is one of the most devotional I have ever seen. The whole interior is in perfect harmony, the carving of the altar, the communion rail, and the

furniture most elegant and elaborate. Some might wish it
a little more lofty, but that is its only defect. The beautiful
floor looks as if covered with a rich carpet. As soon
as it shall have passed entirely into the hands of the Protestants, they will destroy its richly carved altars as too suggestive, perhaps, of the honor once paid the God of the
Eucharist.

"Coesfeld was little Anne Catherine's Jerusalem. Here
she daily visited her God in the Blessed Sacrament. Thither
she lovingly turned whilst working in the fields, tending her flocks, or praying by night in the open air; and
from Coesfeld it was that the bells of the little convent of
the Annonciades struck upon her ear, awakening in her
soul a longing desire for the cloistered life. This same
convent now stands dismantled and deserted.

"For several years, Sister Emmerich lived at Coesfeld
with a pious mantua-maker, and for three more in a choir-
master's family with a view of learning to play on the organ,
hoping by this means to facilitate her entrance into some
convent; finally, it was from Coesfeld that she went to accomplish her pious design. It is not surprising, therefore,
that she took a lively interest in the little city, and that she
was deeply afflicted at the decay of Catholic piety, even
among its clergy, owing to Protestant influence and the
diffusion of the so-called enlightenment of the age. Piety
and morality still prevail, however, throughout the country of
Münster, preserved among the youth less by the education
they receive than by the frequent use of the Sacraments.
The Holy Scriptures are not, indeed, found in every family,
nor are quotations from them common, but the practice of
their sacred lessons is plainly visible. Instruction for the
people adapted to the wants of the age, began with the
present generation, the teachers both male and female

having been formed in the school of Dean Overberg (1), who
is everywhere honored as a saint and the common father of
all. His praises are heard on all sides and his zeal and simplicity shed a blessing over all his undertakings ; yet none
dare affirm that his efforts have rendered them more pious
and faithful than their forefathers. Though Sister Emmerich
entertained the greatest veneration for him, yet she
often declared her opinion, corroborated by her visions,
that the poor old village schoolmasters, sometimes obliged
to follow also the trade of tailoring to gain a sufficient support, received more abundant helps from God as pious in-
structors of youth than their modern co-laborers puffed up
by successful examinations. Every work bears its own
fruit. When the teacher takes complacency in his labors,
when he finds therein a certain personal gratification, he consumes, so to say, the best part of the blessing accorded him
for his task. This is the case nowadays when teachers say :
' We teach well; ' pupils, ' We learn well; ' and parents
glory in their children's talent and education, whilst in all
is engendered a seeking for empty show. Our people do,
indeed, read and write much better than their forefathers ;
but with their improvement the devil daily sows bad seed
in the way which springs up to choke piety and virtue. I
feel convinced that the real source of the morality and piety
still to be seen among the people of Münster lies more in their
firm adherence to the traditions of faith and the customs of
their religious forefathers, in the great respect for the priest
and his benediction, in their fidelity to the Sacraments, than
in the rapid spread of modern education. Early one
morning, as I was passing along by a hedge, I heard a

(1) Dean Overberg (1754-1826) was a renowned priest, a great catechist, and an experienced confessor. He was the tutor of the Countess Gallitzin, and in 1809 held the
position of Director of the Seminary of Münster. He wrote many books on Christian
Doctrine for the use of both teachers and pupils. Dean Overberg lived and died loved
and venerated by all.

child's voice. I drew near softly and peeping over I saw
a ragged little girl about seven years old driving a flock
of geese before her, a willow switch in her hand. With
an inimitable accent of piety and innocence she exclaimed :
' Good morning, dear Lord God ! Praise be to Jesus
Christ ! Good Father, who art in heaven ! Hail Mary,
full of grace ! I want to be good ! I want to be pious !
Dear saints of paradise, dear angels, I want to be good !
I have a nice little piece of bread to eat, and I thank you
for it. O watch over me ! Let not my geese run into the
wheat ! Let no bad boy throw a stone and kill one !
Watch over me, for I want to be a good girl, dear Father
in heaven !'—Doubtless, the innocent little one composed
her prayer from some old family traditions, but our modern school-mistresses would scarcely tolerate it. When I
reflect on the scanty education, the rusticity of many
among the clergy ; when I behold so little attention given
to order and neatness in many of the sacred edifices, even
in what directly appertains to the service of the altar ;
when I recall the fact, that the people all speak the Low
German, whilst sermons and instructions have been for
years delivered in the language of upper Germany ; and
when, notwithstanding, I daily perceive the purity, the
piety, the good sense of even the humblest of these people,
their aptitude for the truths of religion, I am forced to exclaim that the grace of Our Lord is more active in His
living members than in speech or in writing. It dwells
with creative force in the divine Sacraments, perpetuated
from age to age by the marvellous power attached to the
sacerdotal consecration. The Church herself is there with
her benediction, her salutary influence, her authority, and
her miracles. She has existed from all ages and she will
continue te exist to the end, for she is the work of God

Himself, and all that believe in Jesus and His Church
share in her sublime gifts.

" The population of this district is scattered over a wide
extent of country, a fact which greatly contributes to the
preservation of morality, as well as of national character ;
for the people do not mutually entice one another to sin as
happens in crowded cities. Each family, of which the
cattle always form a part, has a house surrounded by clus-
tering oaks which shelter it from the storms, and broad
fields enclosed by hedges or embankments. Distant about
a quarter of a league is another homestead similar in its
surroundings, though perhaps of greater or less size. A
certain number of these farms constitutes a hamlet, and several hamlets, a parish. Charming clumps of trees, verdant hedges, shady nooks lie scattered all around. As I
journeyed from house to house through the green meadows,
I could not restrain the exclamation : What sweet scenes
for childhood's innocent years ! What solitary nooks !
What lovely bushes and luscious berries !—The household
of the peasants and indeed that of the gentry also, in some
degree, presents a character altogether patriarchal. It
centres, so to say, around the fire in which quarter the
very best arrangements in the house are to be found. The
outer door opens directly into the kitchen, which serves
also as the family sitting-room, in which is passed the
greater part of their life. The beds occupy recesses in the
walls, the doors of which are kept closed during the day.
Sometimes in the kitchen itself, but oftener in an adjoining area, are seen to the right and left the cows and horses
upon a ground floor, a few feet lower than that of the
main building, their mangers being on a level with it ; in
feeding their heads often protrude beyond the stakes of
their enclosure into the family room. A movable iron or

wooden trough conducts water from the pump to the huge kettle over the fire, in which the food is prepared.   In one house I saw a child turning round and round in a hole cut in one end of a board, the other being fastened to a post by a transverse rod —a primitive arrangement to prevent the little one's falling into the fire.   At the further end of the apartment, shut off by a gate, is a large open space in which the wheat is threshed or the flax hatchelled ; overhead are stored hay, straw, and grain.   The good wife can attend to her culinary duties at the fireplace, and at the same time command a view of the whole establishment.

" The narrow window panes are adorned with pictures of events of olden times, pictures of the saints, of heraldry, and other devices.   Goffine's 'Familiar Instructions,' Overberg's Catechism, and a volume of sacred history are either displayed to advantage on a wooden shelf, or carefully stowed away in a chest with the Sunday clothes, to which a couple of mellow apples are added for the sake of their sweet perfume.   The cottage is guarded without by stately old oaks, through whose boughs the wintry winds whistle unheeded by the pious, simple-hearted occupants within, who are ever ready to extend hospitality to the wayfaring stranger.

" A degree of what one might call elegance is noticeable in the household arrangements of the rich.   In summer an enormous bouquet replaces the blazing fire on the hearth, and little porcelain plates are ranged around as an additional ornament.   Among the poor all is plainer and simpler, yet stamped with the seal of domestic life and local custom. One feature in their homes, which is however gradually dying out, is the absence of a chimney.   In rainy weather the smoke fills the dwelling like a dense vapor."

Such is Clement Brentano's account of his visit to Flamske and the surrounding district.

CHAPTER II.

ANNE CATHERINE'S BAPTISM AND INFANCY.

Bernard Emmerich's little girl could like St. Hildegarde say : "From the dawn of existence when God awoke me in my mother's womb, breathing into me the breath of life, He infused into my soul the gift of contemplation. Before my frame with its nerves and fibres was knit together, my soul enjoyed uninterrupted visions "—for she, too, had been endowed with gifts so sublime that from her very infancy she had the use of her intellectual faculties. A few hours after her birth she was taken to Coesfeld to receive holy Baptism in the Church of St. James, and the various impressions made upon her by the persons and objects met on the way never faded from her mind. Besides the gift of sanctifying grace and the theological virtues, the light of prophecy was so abundantly infused into her soul by Baptism as to find a precedent in the Church's calendar only in a very small number of privileged souls. Toward the close of her life she alluded to it in the following words :—

"I was born on the 8th of September and to-day (Sept. 8, 1821) being the anniversary of my birth, I had a vision of the same, as also of my Baptism. It produced upon me a most singular sensation. I felt myself a new-born babe in the arms of my god-mother going to Coesfeld to be baptized, and I was covered with confusion at beholding myself so small, so weak, and at the same time so old! All the impressions I had experienced as an infant I now again felt, yet mingled with something of the intelligence of my present age. I felt shy and embarrassed. The three old women present, so also the nurse, were displeasing to me. My mother inspired very different sentiments, and I willingly took her breast. I was fully conscious of all that passed around me. I saw the old farm-house in which we dwelt with all its appurtenances, and some years later I could recognize the changes that had been made in it. I saw how the various ceremonies of Baptism -enriched my soul with the graces which they symbolized, and my eyes and heart were miraculously enlightened and touched. The Mother of God was present with the little Infant Jesus, to whom I was espoused with a ring. I saw also my angel-guardian, and my holy patronesses Sts. Anne and Catherine.

" All that is holy, all that is blessed, all that appertains to the Church, was as perfectly intelligible to me then as now, and I saw marvellous things of the Church's essence. I *felt* the presence of God in the Most Blessed Sacrament. I saw the relics shining with light, and I recognized the saints who hovered above them. I saw all my ancestors back to the first one that had received Baptism ; and, in a series of symbolic pictures, I beheld the dangers that menaced me through life. The whole time I had most singular impressions of my god-parents, my relatives present, and above all of those three old women who were always a little repulsive to me. I saw how my ancestors had branched off into different countries. The first one baptized lived in the seventh or eighth century. He built a church. Several others became religious, and there were two who received the stigmata, but lived and died unknown to the world. Among them was a certain hermit,who had once held a high position and had had several sons. He retired into solitude and lived the life of a saint.

" On our way home through the cemetery, I had a lively perception of the state of the souls whose bodies lay there, and I was filled with veneration for some which shone with great brilliancy."

As other children experience heat and cold, pain, hunger, and thirst, so did this blessed little child perceive the relations and influences of the superior order into which holy Baptism had admitted her ; that is, the Church, the Communion of Saints, the mystical Body of Jesus. All was realized by her in the most perfect manner and, leaning from the nurse's arms, she dipped her tiny hands into the holy-water font to appropriate to herself its beneficial effects. Her dignity as child of the Church was as palpable to her as the existence of her own members and, before she could articulate, she understood the signification of feasts and of the pious customs and practices that regulated the life of her good parents, all which she observed as far as the weakness of infancy would permit. Her understanding was developed, her mysterious life regulated by her angel, who taught her to serve the triune God by the practice of the infused virtues, faith, hope, and charity. The first movements of her soul were directed toward its Creator, who took entire possession of her heart before any created good could claim it. In the splendor of baptismal innocence she belonged to that Spouse who had chosen her heart to be conformed to His own in purity, charity, and suffering. The Holy Spirit animated all the powers of her soul and directed its rapturous elevations on high. In her second year when able to pronounce a few words, she began the practice of vocal prayer with all the fervor of one long used to the exercise. Her pious father eagerly awaited the moment in which his little girl would utter her first words and, thanks to his watchfulness, they were those of the petitions of the Lord's prayer. Even in the last years of her life she gratefully recalled this fact.

"My father," she said, "took great pains with me teaching me how to say my prayers and make the sign of the Cross. He used to put me on his knee, close my hand, and teach me first the small sign of the Cross, then opening it he would guide me in making the large sign. When I was too young to say more than half the *Our Father*, I used to repeat the little I knew over and over, until I thought I had said the equivalent of the whole prayer."

To this interior light belongs the angelic virtue, holy purity, which was bestowed upon little Anne Catherine at Baptism and whose effects were shown forth even at her mother's breast. Never was she heard to cry, never was she seen in a fretful humor, but like Maria Bagnesi of Florence, or Colomba di Rieti, she was ever gentle and amiable. Her parents found their delight and consolation in their affectionate little girl, who soon became the darling of the simple-hearted peasants among whom her lot was cast. St. Catherine of Sienna's friends used to vie with one another for the possession of her when an infant, for the sight of her charmed all hearts; and Maria Bagnesi was so attractive a child that, when she was taken to see her sisters in the convent, the religious could not bear to let her leave them. It was the same with the poor little peasant-girl of Flamske; she was the joy of all around her. The lustre of purity which beamed in her whole person lent an irresistible charm to every glance, to every motion, to every word of the timid child. As she advanced in age it clothed her with a sacred character which, unknown to herself, exercised a sanctifying influence upon all that came in contact with her. When later she entered upon the most painful portion of her task of expiatory suffering, this purity of soul shone exteriorly in proportion as her pains increased; and the nearer she drew to the end of her mission, the more sensible became the mysterious power that emanated from her. When her stigmata were subjected to investigation, the ecclesiastics and physicians engaged in it rendered this same testimony ; and the strongest impression received by Count Frederic Leopold von Stolberg (1) on his first visit to her, was that of her angelic innocence.

One result of this purity was that Anne Catherine preserved till death the naive simplicity of an humble, innocent child knowing nothing of herself or of the world, because her life was wholly absorbed in God. This simplicity was so pleasing to Him that it is shown us as the end of the wonderful operations of grace wrought in her soul. Her Divine Spouse ever treated her as a child and, in His wisdom, so ordered it that in the full light of supernatural knowledge flooding her soul she was always the docile pupil. With the heroism that sighed continually after fresh struggles, she evinced the most attractive timidity ; in a word, her grand and arduous mission in life found her— in its accomplishment as at its commencement— a shrinking, artless child. With eyes still suffused in tears she would in an instant regain the joyousness of that age which knows not sorrow because it knows not sin, as soon as a ray of consolation mitigated the torments which like furious waves were unchained against her. These sunbeams were often pictures of her own infancy presented to her soul by the God of all goodness. Then she became once more a little

(1) Count von Stolberg was renowned in his day for the nobility of his family, the high position he held under government, his great talents and learning, and his numerous literary productions. In 1800, being then in his fiftieth year, he resigned all his offices of honor, renounced Protestantism, and became with almost all the members of his family a fervent Catholic. He was a noble champion of the faith in Germany, and with some others of his own stamp he gave new impulse to Catholic life throughout the country. He died in 1819. Among his most noted works are the following : A Translation of the Works of St. Augustine; The True Religion ; The Practices of the Catholic Church ; History of the Religion of Jesus Christ (in 15 vols.) : History of Alfred the Great ; and Meditations on the Holy Scriptures.—(Herder.)

child, a little peasant-girl in her father's house, light hearted and loving. She drew from the sight fresh energy and fortitude to push on in the way of the Cross, at every step more steep and rugged.

Although the gift of purity had been bestowed upon Anne Catherine in Baptism, yet she had to purchase its possession by mortification and penance; and, as its preservation and increase demanded an unrelenting struggle against self, the practice of patient suffering was the exercise she was destined to undertake even in the first year of her life.

" I remember," she said, " a heavy fall that I got in my first year. My mother had gone to Coesfeld to Church; but feeling that something had happened to me, she returned in great haste and anxiety. One of my limbs had to be stretched and bandaged so tightly that it became quite shrunken. I was unable to walk for a long time. It was not till my third year that I was cured."

The remembrance of this accident, as well as some of the consequences of it, Anne Catherine preserved all her life, which proves how perfect must have been her mental development at the time it happened. Guided as she was by her angel-guardian, we may presume that it was with her as with Maria Bagnesi whom she closely resembled in many particulars. Maria, too, whilst yet a tender infant, began her task of suffering by enduring the cravings of hunger. Entrusted to an unprincipled nurse, who gave her neither milk nor other nourishment, the poor child was often seen picking up with her tiny fingers the scanty crumbs that fell to the floor. She then laid the foundation for that life of wonderful mortification and suffering which rendered her, like our own little child, a source of benediction for innumerable souls.

As soon as she was able to refuse a gratification, impose

a penance, or gain a 'victory over self, Anne Catherine began so to exercise herself as far as her age permitted,
following in this the never-failing direction of her angel
with astonishing prudence and constancy. She had hung
up in a corner a picture of the Blessed Virgin and the Infant Jesus, and put before it a block of wood for an altar.
On this she laid the trifles given her from time to time,
those little nothings that make children so happy. She
firmly believed that these small sacrifices were highly pleasing to the Holy Infant, and she joyfully renounced in His
favor every gift she received. She did it so simply and
quietly that seeing nothing to remark in these apparently
childlike actions, no one ever interfered in her little arrangements. As her offerings frequently disappeared, she had
the happy assurance that the Infant Jesus had, indeed,
taken them for Himself. The more her sacrifice had cost
her, the greater was her joy on such occasions ; for with
all her wonderful gifts of grace, she was still a child capable,
like others of her age, of being tempted with fruit, cakes,
etc. Flowers, pictures, ribands, wreaths, rings, toys, and
such things of value in the eyes of a child, all had to be
immolated to the holy rapture of her heart.

By such practices of mortification her purity of soul so increased that, in her third year, she offered to God this
fervent prayer : "Ah ! dear Lord, let me die now, for
when children grow up, they offend Thee by great sins ! "

And did she step out of her father's cottage, she earnestly
exclaimed :

"Rather let me fall dead on this threshold than live to
offend my God ! "

When she grew older and began to associate with children
of her own age, she gave them, for the love of God, all that
of which she could dispose ; and, if she showed a preference,

it was for the poorest.   A child herself of needy parents,
she was bountiful in her gifts.   She had not completed her
fourth year when she was accustomed to deny herself at her
meals, taking the worst of everything and eating so sparingly
that her family wondered how she lived.

"I give this to Thee, O God," she said in her heart,
"that Thou mayst divide it among those poor souls that
have the most need of it."

The poor, the suffering, had so strong a hold on her affections that her first sorrows in life sprang from her great
compassion for them.   If she heard of any misfortune, she
was so overcome that she sank down like one about to
faint.   Her parents' anxious questions as to the cause of
her strange emotion recalled her to herself ; but the desire to
relieve her neighbor became so ardent that she offered herself to God, earnestly begging Him to lay upon her the miseries of others.   If a beggar passed, she ran after him,
calling out : " Wait, wait, I will run home and get you a
piece of bread."   And her good mother never refused her
an alms for the poor.   She even gave away her own clothing.   Once she pleaded so earnestly that she obtained permission to bestow her only remaining undergarment on a poor
child.

She could not see a child crying or sick without begging
to suffer in its stead, and her petition was always heard ;
she endured the pain, and beheld the little sufferer relieved.
Her prayer on such occasions ran thus : " If a poor beggar
asks not, he receives not.   And Thou, O my good God,
Thou dost not help him who prays not and yet is unwilling
to suffer !   See, I cry to Thee for those that do it not for
themselves ! "

If she knew of a child that committed faults, she prayed
for it ; and to insure being heard, she imposed some punish-

ment on herself. Years after, when asked to say how it was that at so tender an age she had thought of such things, she answered :

" I cannot say who taught me. Pity prompted it. I have always felt that we are but one single body in Jesus Christ, and my neighbor's pain is as sensible to me as if it were in one of my own fingers. I have always asked for the sufferings of others. I knew that God never sends affliction without a design; there must be some debt to be paid off by it. And if these afflictions weigh so heavily upon us at times, it is because, as I reasoned with myself, no one is willing to help the poor sufferer to pay off his debt. Then I begged to be allowed to do so. I used to ask the Infant Jesus to help me, and I soon got what I wanted."

" I remember," she said on another occasion, " my mother had erysipelas in her face. She was lying in bed, her face all swollen. I was alone with her and greatly distressed at seeing her in such a state. I threw myself on my knees in a corner and prayed with all my heart. Then I bound a piece of linen round her head and prayed again. Soon I felt an intense toothache and my face began to swell. When my father and brothers came home, they found my mother entirely relieved, and I also soon got well."

" Some years later I again endured intolerable pains. My parents were both very ill. I knelt down by their bed near the loom and invoked Almighty God; then I saw my hands joined over them and still praying, I was impelled to lay them upon them that they might be cured."

If she heard sin mentioned or saw it committed, she burst into tears. When questioned by her parents, she could give no satisfactory reason for her grief; consequently, she was often rebuked for her unaccountable behaviour.

This did not, however, cool the ardor of her loving heart; she still continued to pray and do penance for her dear neighbor.   One day, in her fourth year, she stood by the crib of a sick child, its mother by her side.   The father, in a fit of drunken rage, hurled at his wife an axe which would have cleft the child's skull, had not Anne Catherine skilfully intercepted the blow, the axe grazing her own head as it shot by the crib.   The child was saved, and the terrible consequences of the furious act prevented.

On another occasion, Anne Catherine saw some children violating modesty in their sports.   She was stung to the quick, and threw herself among the nettles, begging God to accept that act in expiation.

She deeply compassionated the Jews.

"When I was a little girl," she said, "my father often took me with him to Coesfeld to make his purchases at the store of a Jew.   The poor man always filled me with compassion.   The thought of this hardened race, so obstinate in rejecting salvation, often brought the tears to my eyes.   Ah! how much they are to be pitied!   They have no idea of the holy Jews of olden times such as I see.   The Jews of the present day are the descendants of the Pharisees.   Their misery and blindness have always grieved me; yet, I have often noticed that one can speak very well to them of God.   Poor, poor Jews!   They once had among them the living germ of salvation, but they did not recognize the fruit; they rejected it, and now they do not even seek it."

But the most astonishing of all Anne Catherine's mortifications was the practice of nocturnal prayer, begun in childhood and never after omitted.   She commenced from her fourth year to curtail her hours of sleep in order to devote them to prayer.   When the family was buried in

slumber, she arose from her little bed and prayed with her
angel two or three consecutive hours, sometimes even till
morning. She loved to pray in the open air. When the
weather permitted, she used to slip out to a little hill in
front of the house. There she felt nearer to God, and
there she knelt in prayer, her arms extended, her eyes
turned toward the church at Coesfeld. We cannot suppose the child would have undertaken such a practice save
through an inspiration of her angel guardian and in accordance with the designs of Almighty God who, desiring to be
glorified by the prayer of so pure a creature, imparted to
her the strength necessary. We must not, however, imagine that by reason of the special helps of grace bestowed
upon her the practice was easy and, as it were, self-sus-
taining. Not at all! It was quite the contrary. It is a
peculiar characteristic of such souls that they are forced to
acquire little by little the perfection to which they are
called, by a faithful co-operation with grace and a perpetual
struggle against the weakness of nature. By virtue of this
law, Almighty God permitted the latter daily to assert its
rights over Anne Catherine ; her delicate frame imperiously
exacted the repose indispensable to growth and strength.
But the heroic little girl promptly obeyed the angel's
call to prayer in spite of the involuntary shrinking of nature, in spite even of the hot tears that flowed from her
eyes. She even had the courage to devise means for facili-
tating her rising at any hour of the night. She found
none more efficient than the sharp chips and hard cords
strewn on her bed purposely to render her rest uneasy,
besides which she bound her waist with knotted cinctures
woven by herself. It was from an increase of voluntary
suffering she drew that strength which nature was not allowed to supply. God recompensed her generous efforts.

She gradually arrived at a state in which she was able to
deny rest to her weary body and, up to the last moment of
her life, she served her Lord, by day and by night, without
repose or intermission.

Many will, perhaps, be more surprised at the fact of a child's
being able to prolong her prayer two or three consecutive
hours, at the tender age of four, than even at her power to
deprive herself of sleep. They will ask, " What, then, was
the subject of this protracted prayer ?" The subject was as
varied as were the objects for which God willed the child's
petitions to be offered. She was shown in a vision every day
the task to be accomplished by prayer. In a series of tableaux she beheld the corporal and spiritual miseries which
she was to avert. She saw the sick impatient, captives dejected, the dying unprepared ; she saw travellers wandering or shipwrecked ; she saw her fellow-creatures in distress and despair, trembling on the brink of the abyss ; and,
moreover, she saw that Almighty God in His mercy was
ready to give them at her request help, consolation, salvation. She understood that, if she neglected penance
and supplication, these souls in so great need would perish
for want of assistance. Her angel sustained her in her
prayer, and her burning love for her neighbor made her
so confident, so eloquent, so persevering in her petitions that
the hours seemed rather short than long.

At the breaking out of the French Revolution, her visions became especially varied and frightful. She was carried in spirit to the prison of Marie Antoinette, Queen of
France, and told to beg strength and consolation for her.
The impression she retained of this visit was so strong that
she related to her family the queen's distress, and begged
them all to pray for the unfortunate lady. But her friends,
as might be supposed, could not understand her. They

thought her dreaming, and told her quite plainly that a person who could be in two different places at one and the same time or who could see all that is going on at a distance, could be none other than a witch. Anne Catherine was so appalled at this information that she ran to confession to regain her peace of mind. She assisted, also, at many executions—helped and consoled the poor victims by her prayers. She was present in this way at the execution of the unfortunate monarch, Louis XVI.

" When I beheld the king and many other noble victims meeting death so calmly, so resignedly, I said to myself : Ah ! it is well for them to be taken from the midst of such abominations. But when I mentioned what I had seen to my parents; they thought I had lost my senses. I often knelt and with tears begged God to save such or such a person. I then saw that dangers, either impending or still remote, may be averted by the prayer of faith."

Some years later, when Anne Catherine was called upon to render to Dean Overberg, her director, an account of the prayer of her childhood, she said :—

" I always prayed less for myself than for others, that they might not sin, might not be lost. There was nothing I did not ask of God, and the more I obtained, the more I asked. I never had enough. I said confidently to myself : All things belong to God, and nothing pleases Him so much as to see me begging Him for something with my whole heart."

Dean Overberg tells us what purity of heart this wonderful little child attained by such practices. He says : "From her sixth year Anne Catherine knew no other joys than those she found in God, no other sorrows than those that pierced her heart at the thought of His being outraged by men. When she began to practise mortification of the senses, the love of God was enkindled in her heart with such intensity that she often cried out in the midst of her prayer: ' Were there no heaven, no purgatory, no hell, I would still love Thee, O my God, with my whole heart and soul !' "

The poor sufferers in purgatory shared largely in her spiritual alms, and they often appeared to her, claiming her pity. Even in winter she arose at night and went out in the snow to pray with extended arms for their relief, until frozen stiff with cold. Sometimes she knelt on a triangular block of wood whose sharp edge cut deep into her knees; or, again, she forced her way through stinging nettles to discipline her innocent flesh, that penance might lend efficacy to her prayer. In return for her charity, she often had the consolation of receiving the thanks of the souls that she had delivered.

"When I was a little child," she says, "I was taken by a person unknown to me to a place which appeared to be purgatory. I saw crowds of souls in excruciating torments who earnestly begged for prayers. I thought I was in a deep abyss. I saw a great, broad space, frightful, pitiable to behold. In it were the poor souls, silent and afflicted, yet not without joy and hope in the mercy of God. I saw no fire, but I felt that the souls were racked by the most intense interior sufferings."

" Whilst praying for them, I often heard voices around me, saying : 'Thank you ! thank you !' Once, on my way from church, I lost a little bag that my mother had given me. I was very much concerned at my carelessness, and I forgot that evening to offer my accustomed suffrages for the dear souls. I had to go to the shed for wood, and as I went along a white figure covered with black spots, appeared before me, saying : ' Thou art forgetting me !'—

I was very much frightened, and began right off to say some prayers. The next day I prayed hard and found my bag in the snow.

" When I grew older, I used to go very early in the morning to hear Mass at Coesfeld. I always chose a lonely road, that I might pray without distraction for the suffering souls. When it was still dark, I used to see them floating before me two by two, like fiery sparks in a dull flame. The way was lit up before me and I rejoiced in their presence, for I both knew and loved them. They often came at night to beg help in their pains."

CHAPTER III.

When little Anne Catherine began to talk, the wonders revealed by infused light to her soul were soon made known to all around. Her father's favorite recreation, as he sat by the fire after his day's toil, was to take his little daughter on his knee and listen to the marvellous things she would relate at his bidding. " Anne Kathrinchen," he would say, "now here we are! now tell me something!" (1) Then she would describe to him the pictures shown her from the Old Testament, until the good man would exclaim, with tears in his eyes : " But, child, where did you get all that ?" (2) And the little one would answer earnestly : " Father, it is all true! That is the way I saw it !" Whereupon the astonished father would become silent and forbear to question further.

No special time was chosen for the unveiling of these pictures before the eyes of her soul—all hours of the day, all occupations were the same. Anne Catherine thought that every one had visions, as well as herself; consequently, she used to speak of them quite freely. But when her little playmates contradicted or ridiculed her on the subject, she became pensive and silent. Once it happened that a hermit, who wanted to impress his hearers with the belief that he had been in Rome and Jerusalem, spoke of the Holy Places, but in a manner altogether incorrect. Anne Catherine, who had been silently listening by the side

(1) "*Anna Kathrinchen, nun bist du in meinem Kämmerchen, nun erzähle mir etwas!*"

(2) " *Kind, woher hast du das?*"

of her parents, could not long restrain her indignation. She boldly taxed the man with falsehood, describing the Holy Places herself as if perfectly familiar with them, until her parents checked her vivacity and she became silent.

Anne Catherine went to the village school taught by an old peasant. One day she described the Resurrection of our Lord as she had seen it in vision, for which she received a severe reprimand and an injunction never again to indulge such imaginations. This treatment sealed the lips of the frightened child, who ever after refrained from communicating what passed in her interior. Her visions, however, were not discontinued. The truths and mysteries of holy faith, linked together in grand historic pictures, passed in still greater numbers before the eyes of her soul; wherever she chanced to be, they formed the subject of her contemplation.

The Twelve Articles of the Apostles' Creed were presented to her during the course of the ecclesiastical year. She contemplated the creation of heaven, the fall of the angels, the creation of the earth and Paradise; she beheld Adam and Eve and their fall. In successive visions, she followed, through ages and generations, the development of the holy mysteries of the Incarnation and the Redemption. The scenes of Sacred History and the personages of the Old Testament were better known to her than those of her own life; and those saints who, by their relationship to the Sacred Humanity of Jesus Christ, appear more closely connected with the faithful, were shown her in vision as communicating directly with her. Among them were the holy families of Joachim and Anne, of Zachary and Elizabeth, with whom she kept up the most familiar and affectionate intercourse. With them she celebrated the feasts of the time of Promise, made pilgrimages to Jerusalem and other holy places, sighed for the Saviour's coming, hailed His advent, and adored Him at His birth.

The Temple of Jerusalem (1), the splendor and magnificence of the worship there offered to the Most High, the Ark of the Covenant and all it contained, the mysteries of the Holy of Holies, understood by so few, the chanting of psalms, the numerous ceremonies and observances of the Old Law, all were perfectly familiar to her even in their slightest details. She understood, likewise, the pious customs and traditions of the faithful Israelites in the fulfilment of the law and the government of their family.

These contemplations were not for her a vain show; she actually lived among the scenes and associated with the actors of a thousand years ago. In this she resembled St. Catherine of Sienna, who also had been prepared by visions for the important part she was to play in the history of the Church. Her abstraction of soul from the things of this life, her recollection in God were so great that even when surrounded by the tumult of the world, in the midst of Popes and princes, she was as inaccessible to every distraction as if in the sanctuary of her own cell. She had acquired this power in the school of the penitents of the Thebaid whom she contemplated for many years in so real a way that with them she wove baskets and mats, chanted psalms, fasted, performed penances, observed silence; in one word, practised with them those mortifications which elevated her

(1) The history of Jerusalem from the date of its foundation was unfolded before her in successive pictures ; in her childhood she knew of the Knights-Templars. " The first time that I saw some soldiers passing through our country," she said, " I thought they surely must be the same that I had seen in vision, and I scanned them closely to discover some belonging to a religious Military Order. I would have known them by their dress, a white habit ornamented with crosses, and a sword hanging from a little belt. I saw some of them far, far away among the Turks. They had secret practices like the Free-Masons, and I saw that many perished at their hands. I was surprised at not seeing any such soldiers among the troops marching by, and I found out afterward that they for whom I looked in vain were the Knights-Templars, and that the Order had long ceased to exist.

to perfect union with God. St. Paul, St. Antony, St. Pacomius, St. Hilarion, were her models and teachers. She communicated as intimately with them as Anne Catherine with St. Joachim, St. Anne, and their holy predecessors.

Although Anne Catherine celebrated in spirit the feasts of the Old Law as if really contemporary with them, yet she was, at the same time, a child of our holy Catholic faith; since in these prophetic figures and mysteries, she contemplated their fulfilment, seeing in them both their actual celebration and the historical events that gave rise to them. Her marvellous intuition embraced the whole plan of Redemption. These were the visions of her early years; they were succeeded by others, no less comprehensive, on the life of our Holy Redeemer. This order was in conformity with the task imposed upon her. She was called to suffer for the faith at a time in which men, in their insensate malice, questioned even the possibility of divine revelation, denied the mystery of the Incarnation and Redemption, and blasphemed the prophets, the Apostles, and the saints with diabolical rage; a time in which the enemies of God daily gained fresh recruits even from the ranks of the priesthood. At this terrible epoch it was that God gave to Anne Catherine full and clear knowledge of the truths of religion. He called upon her to bear witness to the accomplishment of His eternal decrees, and the purity and ardent love of her heart indemnified Him in some degree for the outrages offered to His mercy.

Our Saviour Himself deigned to be her guide through the immense circle of visions granted her, and He communicated to her the light to understand His hidden mysteries. With Him she visited the places sanctified by His presence, and learned from His own lips the mysteries there enacted for the salvation of fallen humanity. His never-failing assist-

ance gave her the strength to support the infinite variety
of her visions, and to maintain her interior and contemplative life in harmony with the exterior. For whole days
she was lost in contemplation, her soul perfectly abstracted
from the things of sense ; but, in spite of this, the duties
imposed upon her by her parents were as promptly and
carefully fulfilled, as if she had no thought beyond. It was
proper that no exterior affair should disturb her contemplation ; therefore, God bestowed upon her wonderful aptitude for manual labor and domestic duties. As soon as she
opened a book, she could read its contents ; whatever work
she undertook, either in the house or field, instantly succeeded; it appeared as if her very touch imparted a blessing even to things inanimate. Her friends were so accustomed to her taking part in the most painful labors and
accomplishing them well, that they respected her interior
recollection, and never intruded upon her by inquisitive
questioning.

The embarrassing task of rendering an account of her
visions had not yet been imposed upon Anne Catherine ;
she had not yet been called upon to confine in the narrow
compass of human language the spiritual riches lavished
upon her. She herself could gaze upon them only by the
prophetic light shed upon her soul; she saw them not under
a form capable of being clothed in words. Although pain
and suffering were - her constant companions, yet they
could not ruffle the profound peace and recollection in which
her days glided by. In after years she often sighed for
the silence and solitude of her childhood. She used to say :
" When I was a little girl, I was continually absorbed in
God. I performed all my duties without interfering with
this abstraction. I was always in contemplation. Working
with my parents in the fields, or engaged in any other

labor, I was, as it were, lifted above the earth. Exterior things were like a confused and painful dream, within all was heavenly light and truth."

Our Lord deigned to be her teacher not only in the regions of contemplation, but also in the practice of piety. He played with her as a little child that He might lead her step by step to perfection, to the highest conformity with Himself. Sometimes He appeared to her as a child of her own age, a cross on His shoulders. He would stand and gaze at her in silence until she, in her turn, would snatch up a heavy log of wood and carry it after Him as far as she could, praying all the time; or again, she beheld Him in tears at the treatment He endured from disobedient children, and at this sight, she would throw herself among the nettles to console Him by her own penance. When she made the Way of the Cross, He used to lay His own cross upon her shoulders. When she kept the cows in the fields, which she did when only five years old, He came to her under the appearance of a child looking for its little companions, eager to share their sports and labors. He wished thereby to teach her by word and example to turn all her actions to God. He endued her with intelligence to act only for His glory, and taught her to sanctify even her little amusements.

In connection with this subject, she used to relate some very pleasing little incidents.

"When I was a child," she said, "the Little Boy used to come and work with me. At the age of six I did just what I now do. I knew, though I cannot say how, that I was soon to have a baby brother, and I wanted to make my mother something for the child; but I could not sew. The Little Boy came to my aid and showed me how to make a little cap and other things necessary for infants.

My mother was astonished at my successful attempts, and she gladly made use of the articles."

" When I first began to mind the cows, the Little Boy used to meet me in the fields, and so arranged matters that my cows took good care of themselves. Then we used to talk together about all kinds of holy things, that we wanted to serve God and love the Infant Jesus, and that God sees all things. These encounters often took place, and nothing appeared impossible to me when I was with Him. We sewed, we made caps and stockings for poor children. I could do whatever I wanted, and I had everything necessary for my work. Occasionally some of the nuns of the ' Annunciation of the Blessed Virgin' (1) joined us. There was one thing that puzzled me : I always thought that I myself was managing everything, whereas it was, in reality, the Little Boy who was doing it all."

The blessing emanating from such intercourse was communicated by Anne Catherine to all with whom she came in contact ; but it was chiefly among children of her own age that she practised the teachings she had received. She spoke to them so charmingly of the presence of God, of the Infant Jesus, and of their angel-guardian, that the little ones listened with delight. When she went with them to gather stubble along the roads, she arranged them in procession, reminding them of their holy angels who also were present.

" We ought," she said, " to imitate the blessed in heaven. We should do nothing bad ourselves and, when we can, we ought to keep others from doing it. If, for instance, we come across traps or nets set by idle boys to catch hares or birds, we ought to remove them, that such petty thefts may be prevented. We ought to begin, little by little, to lead a new life, a life of heaven upon earth."

(1) The Annonciades.

If she played in the sand with other children, her skilful hands piled it up in imitation of the Holy Places of
Jerusalem such as she had seen in her visions. She afterward said in allusion to this : " If I had had some one to
help me, I could have made models of most of the roads and
places of the Holy Land. They were always before my
eyes; no locality was better known to me. When playing
with my companions in the moist sand, I used to build up
a Mt. Calvary, lay out a garden, and hollow out a sepulchre
in it ; then I formed a brook with a bridge over it and
houses on either side. I can remember how I joined the
square houses and cut with a chip strange looking openings
for windows. Once I was about to make figures to represent our Saviour, the Blessed Mother at the foot of the Cross,
and the two thieves, but I gave up the idea as irreverent.
One day two children and myself were playing in the fields.
We wanted a cross for the little mud-chapel we had built, to
say our prayers before it, but we knew not where to get one.
At last, I cried out : 'I know, I know ! Let us make a
wooden one and then press it down into the soft clay until
it leaves a deep mark. I can get an old pewter lid we have
at home. We'll melt it, pour it into the mark, and when it
cools, we'll have a beautiful cross.' I ran to the house to
get the lid and fire to melt it. But just as we were ready to
begin our work, my mother made her appearance and I
was punished."

St. John the Baptist also shared Anne Catherine's innocent amusements, appearing to her as a child such as he was
when he dwelt in the desert under the guardianship of the
angels, irrational creatures his only companions. When she
went out with the cows, she used to call him : " Come, little
John ! I want little John in his sheepskin," and he came immediately to keep the child company. His life in the desert

was shown her in detailed visions, and he taught her to imitate that ineffable purity and simplicity which had rendered him so pleasing to God. Whilst celebrating with him the marvels of his birth, she was conducted into his paternal home, and introduced to the wide circle of his relatives. She knew them all well; she felt more at home among them than even in her father's house.

To what an extent this mysterious intercourse with the characters of Sacred History was interwoven with the outward life of the child, we may glean from her own words. When, shortly before her death, she related her visions on the life of Our Lord, she gave the following account of what passed within her respecting them:

"Every Advent since my childhood I have accompanied St. Joseph and the Blessed Virgin from Nazareth to Bethlehem. The solicitude I felt for the holy Mother of God, and my share in all the difficulties of the journey, were as real for me as any other incident of my life. I took a far greater interest in it all, I was more affected by it than I could possibly be by anything that might happen to myself; for Mary was the Mother of my Lord and my God; she bore in her womb my salvation. The feasts of the Church were for me not only simple commemorations or subjects of attentive consideration; my soul actually took part in them, as if the mysteries they celebrated were under my very eyes. I saw them, I felt them, as if present before me."

So lively an intuition could not lie dormant in her soul; its influence marked her every action. Filled with tender love for Mary, she did with childish eagerness all she would have done had she really lived with the Holy Family; for instance, if she beheld Mary and Joseph journeying toward Bethlehem, she joined them in spirit; if she went out to pray by night, she waited on the road for Mary, and she deprived herself of food that she might have something to offer the holy travellers wearied by their long journey. She took her own short repose on the bare ground, that her little bed might be free for the Mother of God; she ran out on the road to meet her, or waited for her in prayer under a tree, because she knew that Mary would rest beneath its shade. On Christmas Eve she had so distinct a perception of the Blessed Virgin's arrival in the grotto of Bethlehem, that she lit a fire to warm her and to enable her to prepare some food. All that she had to dispose of, she held in readiness to offer to the Divine Mother.

" Almighty God," she said one day, " must have been pleased with this good-will of a child, for, from my infancy to the present time, He has shown me every year during Advent all the circumstances of His coming, and always in the same way. I am always seated in a little corner from which I can see everything. When a child I was free and unrestrained with Him ; but, when I became a religious, I was much more timid and reserved. At my earnest request, the Blessed Virgin often laid the Infant Jesus in my arms."

These tender and intimate relations with God and His saints awoke in the child's heart a desire, or rather an insatiable thirst for purity and penance which suffering alone could allay. The visions that nourished her soul wonderfully increased her exquisitely delicate perception of all that is pure and holy, and filled her with horror of sin and everything leading to it. This instinct was an infallible guide on which she could rely as unerringly as upon her angel-guardian. It increased in delicacy and power in proportion to her fidelity in following the impulse of the Holy Ghost, urging her to watch scrupulously over her senses and conscience by virtue of the abundant graces that enriched her soul. Before the world's corruption could sully her sight, her eyes had gazed in vision on the splendors of sanctifying grace and innocence as existing in paradise. She knew the infinite value of the merits of the Redeemer, who deigned to restore fallen man to his pristine purity, even before he was conscious of the dangers menacing his soul. Her love of purity was like a consuming fire ; it destroyed whatever could sully her soul before it had the power to touch her. Her director, Dean Overberg, renders the following testimony:—

"Anne Catherine never experienced a movement of sensuality, never had to accuse herself of even a thought against holy purity. When questioned as to this perfect exemption from every temptation to the opposite vice, she answered in obedience that she had been shown in a vision that her nature would have inclined her thereto; but that, owing to her early mortification, her efforts to repress her desires and to surmount all other vicious inclinations, she had rooted out these evil propensities even before they had made themselves felt.

This unerring instinct was manifested in her childhood in a singularly touching manner, as may be seen by the following communication made whilst relating her visions of paradise :

"I remember that when I was about four years old, my parents took me one day to church, where I was sure I would see God and meet people very different from any I knew. I thought they would be far more beautiful, indeed quite resplendent. I looked all around the church as I entered, but saw nothing of what I had pictured to myself. 'The priest there at the altar,' I said to myself, 'may, perhaps, be God, but where is the Blessed Virgin Mary ?' I expected, too, the whole heavenly court to be in attendance ;

but alas! I was disappointed. After awhile I saw two
pious-looking women, who wore beads and appeared more
devout than their neighbors. I thought, perhaps, they
were those for whom I was looking; but no, they were
not. I used to think that Mary wore a white robe, a sky-
blue mantle, and a white veil. I had had before this the
vision of paradise, so I now looked through the church for
Adam and Eve, hoping to see them as beautiful as they
were before their fall; but disappointed in this also, I said
to myself: 'Wait till you have been to confession, then
you will find them.' But alas! even then I found them
not. I saw a pious noble family in the church, the daughters all in white. I felt that they came a little nearer to
those whom I sought, and I conceived very great respect
for them. Still I was not satisfied. I felt that what I had
once seen so beatiful had now become sullied and deformed.
I was so taken up by these thoughts that I forgot to eat.
I often heard my parents say: 'What is the matter
with the child? What has happened to little Anne
Catherine?' Sometimes, too, I would complain to Almighty
God that He had done such or such a thing. I could not
understand how He, who is all powerful, could have allowed
sin to enter the world; and the endless duration of hell
torments seemed to me incompatible with His attribute of
mercy. Then I was instructed in visions on the infinite
goodness and justice of God, and I was soon convinced
that, if things were according to my ideas, they would
be very miserable."

After what we have thus far seen of little Anne Catherine,
we may lawfully apply to her the words of Prof. Sebastian of
Perouse, when speaking of Blessed Columba di Rieti:

"This child was born for a life elevated above the
senses; she was to be liquified in the fire of charity, to be

inflamed with the love of God and the neighbor. She was
so well grounded in her holy vocation that she could not be
disconcerted by the insinuations of the evil one, troubled
by pride, nor attacked by the sting of the flesh." And
how, indeed, could Anne Catherine's soul receive such illumination, did it dwell in a body which was not as pure
as a lily, in a body which knew no other law than that
which subjecꞇd it wholly to God ?

CHAPTER IV.

EARLY TRAINING AND EDUCATION.

A closer acquaintance with the thrice-happy parents to whose care Almighty God had confided so precious a treasure, affords a fresh proof of the wonderful vigilance of Divine Providence in arranging even the least details connected with His chosen ones, that all things may concur in the fulfilment of the mission assigned them.

Anne Cathèrine was the child of truly pious souls who, contented in their poverty because it was consecrated to God, found a rich indemnification for the want of material goods in the heavenly blessings shed upon them. Their whole life presented to the child a perfect model of Christian faith, and she received, thanks to their gentle firmness, an education best suited to her high vocation. Her father's house was a school of piety for his children; even in her last years, Anne Catherine gratefully recalled the advice given her by her good parents and the pious and regular habits to which they had trained her. She loved to speak of them. Their whole life might be written from the words of their child.

"My father was very pious and upright, of a serious disposition, but by no means morose or inclined to sadness. His poverty obliged him to hard labor, but he was not actuated by the love of gain. He had a childlike trust in God and performed his daily toil like a faithful servant without anxiety or cupidity. His conversation was full of beautiful, homely proverbs, interspersed with pious, simple expressions. One day he told us the history of a great man named Hun,

who travelled all over the globe. That night I dreamed
that I saw this great man wandering over the earth and
turning up with an immense spade good and bad soil.   As
my father was very laborious himself, he taught me to work
hard even in my childhood.   Summer and winter, I had
to go out to the fields before daybreak to catch a vicious
horse which kicked and bit and used to run away from my
father.   The vicious creature used to let me catch him; indeed, he sometimes came himself to meet me.   I used to
climb on a stone or mound, get on his back, and ride home
in triumph.   If he took a notion to turn his head to bite,
I would give him a blow on the nose, which made him trot
on quietly as before.   I used to haul manure and produce
with him.   I cannot now understand how I managed
him at all.

"We often went into the fields before daybreak. At the
moment of sunrise my father used to uncover his head and
say some prayers; then he would speak to me of the great
God who made His sun rise so gloriously above us.   He
often said it was a shameful thing to lie in bed whilst the
sun rose high in the heavens, for it leads to the ruin of
whole families, countries, and nations. Once I replied: 'Yes,
but that does not mean me, for the sun cannot get near my
little bed!' and he answered: 'Even if you cannot see the
rising sun, he sees you—he shines everywhere.'   I thought
over these words a long time.

"On another occasion, he said to me: 'See, no one has
yet trodden in the dew! We are the first and, if we pray
devoutly, we shall draw down blessings upon the earth.   It
is good to walk on the morning dew before any one else has
touched it.   There is a blessing upon it then, entirely fresh.
No sin has yet been committed in the fields, no bad word
has been spoken.   When the dew has been trodden under

foot, it seems as if the freshness and beauty of morning
had flown.'

" Although very small and delicate, yet I always had
to work hard, either around the house or out in the fields
with my brothers and sisters. Once I had to load a cart
with about twenty sacks of corn. I did it without stopping
to rest, and more quickly than a strong boy could have done
it. In the same way I used to reap and mow.

" Sometimes I led the horse for my father, sometimes I
harrowed the ground. I did all kinds of field labor. Occasionally when we paused a moment to rest, my father would
exclaim: ' Ah ! how fortunate ! Look ! We can see straight
ahead to Coesfeld. There is the church ! We can adore
Our Lord in the Blessed Sacrament. He watches us and
blesses our work.' When the bell rang for Mass, he would
take off his hat and say a little prayer. Then he would
say : ' Now we must follow the Holy Mass,' and still
continuing his work, he would utter a few words from time
to time, such as : ' Now the priest is at the Gloria, now the
Sanctus—we must say such or such a prayer and
make the sign of the cross,' and sometimes he would sing
a verse from the Holy Scriptures, or whistle a tune. Whilst
I went on harrowing, he would say : ' They make great
account of miracles, and yet we live only by miracles and
the pure goodness of God. See the grain of wheat in the
ground ! There it lies and sends up a long stalk that re-
produces it a hundred-fold. Is not that a great miracle ?'

" On Sunday afternoons he used to rehearse the sermon of the morning for us, commenting upon it in the most
edifying manner, and end by reading aloud an explanation
of the Gospel."

Anne Catherine's mother was equally good and pious.
In twenty-one years of married life she had given birth to

nine children, the first in 1766, the last in 1787. She was
a happy, contented, and faithful wife. Her life of incessant
care and toil had stamped her countenance with rather a
grave expression, without, however, embittering her heart;
that was kind and gentle toward all. The incessant struggle to procure a suitable maintenance never brought a complaint to her lips ; on the contrary, in a spirit of prayer, she
looked upon the necessity to labor as a favor from Heaven,
and thought only of being in the eyes of God a faithful
stewardess. In after years, Anne Catherine thus spoke of
her :

" It was my mother who gave me my first lessons in
Catechism. Her favorite ejaculations were : ' *Lord, give me
patience,* and then strike hard !'—' Lord, may Thy will, not
mine, be done !' I have never forgotten them. When I
played with my young companions, my mother used to say :
' If children play together innocently, the angels join them;
sometimes even the little Infant Jesus comes, too.' I
looked upon this as literally true, and it did not in the
least astonish me. I often cast a searching glance up at
the sky to see if they were coming. I sometimes imagined them present, although we could not see them.
That they might not fail to come, we always played innocent games. My mother taught me to walk last and to say
my prayers on the way when I went out with other children to church or elsewhere. She said that by doing so I
should neither hear nor see anything bad. When I made
the sign of the cross on my forehead, lips, and breast, I
said to myself that these crosses were the keys to lock up
my heart against everything hurtful, and that the Infant
Jesus alone should hold them. All goes well when He has
charge of them."

Anne Catherine saw nothing in the whole life of her

parents that was not in accordance with the commandments of God and the Church. The only joys that
lightened their labors were those they found in the celebration of her festivals. These simple souls were well suited for
such happiness; for never was their work so pressing,
their fatigue so great, as to prevent their making any
sacrifice for the good of their neighbor. Bernard Emmerich after his long day's toil never neglected to remind
his little ones, as night closed in, to pray for travellers,
for poor soldiers, for their fellow creatures in distress, he
himself saying particular prayers for such intentions. During the three days of Carnival, the mother accustomed her
children to prostrate and with extended arms to say four times
the *Our Father,* in order to avert all attacks upon innocence during those days : " Children," she used to say to
them, " you do not understand it, but I know it well.
Pray !"

The following incident shows how God blessed the
words and example of these good parents :—

" When we were very small, my eldest brother and I
slept in the same room. He was very pious, and we often
prayed together, kneeling by our little beds, our arms extended in the form of a cross. I often saw the room
all lighted up. Sometimes, after kneeling a long while in
prayer, I was suddenly jerked up with violence by some
invisible force, and a voice cried : ' Go to bed ! Go to
bed !' This used to frighten my brother very much, but
its only effect upon me was to make me pray the longer.
My brother himself did not escape these attacks of the evil
one who often tried to trouble him during his prayers.
My parents once found him kneeling with his arms extended, perfectly stiff with the cold."

As these good people were too humble to look upon the

unremitting practice of their Christian duties as anything
extraordinary, so neither did the phenomena they witnessed
in their child arouse in them feelings of pride. They beheld with grateful emotion the gifts of grace with which she
was endowed; but they concealed their wonder and continued to treat her as they did their other children. The
mother chided her little Anne Catherine as severely for her
faults as she did her brothers and sisters, and, even in her
babyhood, she was not exempt from her share in the family
duties. She was thus kept in happy ignorance of herself.
Her simplicity and humility were never endangered by
praise, admiration, or indiscreet curiosity. Her rich interior life remained hidden and unknown, expanding with
ever-increasing beauty under the conduct of her angel-
guardian, who regulated all her sentiments, thoughts, and
words, and restrained her ardent nature by the constant
practice of obedience.

Her parents, it is true, felt more than ordinary affection
for this child, but it was contrary to their nature to manifest
it by exterior marks or caresses. It was almost a necessity
for Bernard Emmerich to have his winning, discreet little
girl near him when he worked in the fields. Her childish
remarks, her answers to his questions, her whole demeanor
were so pleasing to him that he could not bear to have her
absent from his side. Her mother was too much occupied
with the care of her younger children to give as much of
her attention to Anne Catherine as her husband. The
father's sprightly disposition had been inherited by the
child, who cheered his daily toil by her innocent sportive-
ness. She was naturally gay, as might be expected of one
admitted to so familiar intercourse with God and His saints.
Her forehead was high and well-formed, and the sweet
light of her clear brown eyes shed an air of serenity over

her whole countenance. Her dark hair was thrown back
either in braids or coils around her head, and her silvery
voice and vivacity of expression revealed the intelligence
of her mind. She spoke with ease and fluency of things
that seemed mysterious and unintelligible to her hearers ;
but her modest and humble reserve soon dispelled the impression produced by these unexpected flashes of superior
gifts. She was so sweet, so kind, her eagerness to be of service to others was so charming that young and old flocked
to little Anne Catherine to receive assistance and advice.
Although ignorant of her high gifts, none could help loving
her. These simple peasants knew well that there was no
sacrifice that she would not make for their good, and they
were as much accustomed to the blessings that emanated
from her as to the perfume of the rosemary in their own
gardens.

"When I was a child." she said, " the neighbors used
to come to me to bind up their wounds, because I tried to
do it carefully and gently. I was skilful at such things.
When I saw an abscess, I used to say to myself : ' If you
squeeze it, it will get worse ; the matter must, however,
come out in some way.' Then I sucked it gently and it
soon healed. No one taught me that. It was the desire
of rendering myself useful that led me to do it. At first, I
felt disgust, but that only made me overcome myself, for
disgust is not compassion. When I promptly surmounted
the feeling, I was filled with tender joy. I thought of Our
Lord who did the same for all mankind."

Sometimes her color changed from a bright red to a livid
pallor, her sparkling eyes grew suddenly dim, her simple
gayety was exchanged for gravity, and a shade of inexplicable sadness passed over her countenance —she was hardly
recognizable. Her parents anxiously questioned each other :

' What is the matter with the child ?" The cause of this sudden change lay in the sad sight of the miseries of mankind presented to her mind. As she could not hear the name of God or a saint without falling into contemplation, so neither could mention be made in her presence of any accident or misfortune, without her soul's being irresistibly borne to the scene of suffering by her desire to relieve it at any cost. Her friends, as may be supposed, could not account for her singular conduct, and her mother's uneasiness soon gave way to displeasure on beholding the child's languor disappear as quickly as it had come. She ascribed these unaccountable changes to caprice, and thought reproofs and punishments the best remedy to apply to them ; therefore she sometimes chastised the little girl severely when the latter, overwhelmed by interior sufferings, was scarcely able to stand. But the undeserved treatment was received with such patience and submission, the child was still so bright and loving, that the father and mother gazed at each other in amazement, saying: " What a strange child ! Nothing ever appears to intimidate her. What will become of her !" It was not only the angel's admonitions that influenced Anne Catherine to bear this harsh treatment for the love of God, it was her own conviction that she deserved all kinds of punishment.

"In my childhood," she says, "I was irritable and whimsical, and I was often punished on that account. It was hard for me to repress my capricious humor. My parents often blamed and never praised me; and, as I used to hear other parents praising their children, I began to look upon myself as the worst child in the world. What disquieted me most was the fear of being an object of abhorrence in the sight of God also. But one day I saw some children very disrespectful toward their parents, and, though pained at the sight, yet I felt somewhat reassured, as I thought I might still hope, for I could never do so bad a thing as that."

Anne Catherine found the greatest difficulty in repressing her vivacity, crushing self-will, and submitting entirely to that of others. Her tender heart, her exquisite sensitiveness, ever alive to a thousand things which others would pass over unheeded, her ardent zeal for the glory of God and the salvation of her neighbor, obliged her to repeated efforts to acquire meekness founded upon self-forgetfulness and obedience so perfect that the first movements of resistance were stifled in their birth. Her courageous soul gained the victory, however, and her fidelity was so freely recompensed that she could say in later years : —

" Obedience was my strength, my consolation. Thanks to obedience, I could pray with a peaceful, joyous mind. I could commune with God—my heart was free."

She not only thought herself the least and last of creatures, she actually felt herself such and regulated her whole conduct by this inward conviction. Her angel tolerated no imperfection ; he punished every fault by reprimands and penances. In her fifth year, she one day saw through a garden-hedge an apple lying under a tree, and felt a childish desire to eat it. Scarcely was the thought conceived when her contrition for this covetousness was so great that she imposed upon herself as a penance never again to touch an apple, a resolution to which she ever faithfully adhered. On another occasion, she felt a slight aversion for a woman who had spoken disparagingly of her parents, and she resolved not to salute her the next time she met her. This resolve she acted on, though not without an effort. The next moment she was so contrite that she instantly turned back and begged pardon for her rudeness.

When she began to approach the Sacrament of Penance, her delicate conscience gave her no peace after faults of this kind until she had bitterly accused herself of them to her confessor and received penance and absolution.

That these early interior sufferings and her penitential life might not banish the innocent gayety of childhood from her heart, God in His goodness amply indemnified her by the joy she derived from the uninterrupted contemplation of the greatness and magnificence of creation and by her constant intercourse with irrational creatures. When alone in the woods or fields, she would call the birds to her, sing with them the praises of their Maker, and caress them as they perched familiarly on her shoulder. If she found a nest, she peeped into it with beating heart and spoke the sweetest words to the little ones within. She knew where the earliest flowers bloomed, and gathered them to weave into garlands for the Infant Jesus and His Mother. But her eye, enlightened by grace, saw far beyond the senses. Other children are amused by picture-books. They take more delight in painted flowers and animals than in the glowing colors of animated nature. But for Anne Catherine creatures were themselves the pictures in which she exultingly admired the wisdom and goodness of the Creator. She knew their nature and varied properties, as she intimates in her account of her visions of St. John the Baptist:—

" What John learned in the desert of flowers and animals never surprised me ; for, when I myself was a child, every leaf, every tiny flower, was a book which I could read. I perceived the beauty and signification of color and form ; but when I spoke of it, my hearers only laughed at me. I could entertain myself with everything I met in the fields. I understood everything, I could even see into the flowers and animals. O how charming it all was! I had a fever when

I was young which, however, did not prevent my going
about. My parents thought I would die, but a beautiful Child came and showed me some herbs which
would cure me if I ate them. He told me also to suck the
sweet juice of the bind-weed blossom. I did both, and I
was soon quite well. I have always been exceedingly fond
of camomile flowers. There is something agreeable to me in
their very name. Even in my childhood I gathered them
and kept them in readiness for the sick poor who came to
me in their ailments. I used to think of all sorts of simple
remedies for them."

The beauty of the sacred discipline of the Church was
also manifested to her, as the following lines will prove :—

" The sound of blessed bells has always been to me like
a ray of benediction which banishes hurtful influences
wherever it reaches. I think such sounds terrify Satan.
When I used to pray at night in the fields, I often felt and,
indeed, saw evil spirits around me ; but, as soon as the bells
of Coesfeld sounded for matins, they fled. I used to think
that, when the voices of the clergy were heard at a great
distance, as in the early ages of the Church, there was no
need of bells ; but that now these brazen tongues were
necessary. All things ought to serve the Lord Jesus, pro-
mote our salvation, and protect us against the enemy of our
soul. God has imparted His benediction to His ministers
that, emanating from them, it may penetrate all things and
make them subservient to His glory. But when the Spirit
of God withdraws from the priests and the bells alone diffuse
His benediction and put the evil one to flight, it is like a
tree which appears to flourish. It receives nourishment
through its bark, but the heart-wood is rotten and dry. The
ringing of blessed bells strikes me as essentially more
sacred, more joyous, more animating, and far sweeter than

all other sounds, which are in comparison dull and confused ; even the music of a church organ falls far short in fulness and richness."

The language of the Church made a still more lively impression upon her. The Latin prayers of Mass and all the ceremonies of the divine service were as intelligible to her as her mother-tongue, and it was long before she discovered that all the faithful did not understand them as well as herself.

" I was never conscious of any difference," she said, " between my own language and that made use of by the Holy Church. I understood not only the words but even the various ceremonies themselves."

She had so keen a perception of the power and beneficent influence of the priestly benediction, that she could tell when a priest was passing the house. She felt herself involuntarily drawn to run out and get his blessing. If she happened to be minding the cows at the time, she quickly recommended them to her angel-guardian, and set off in pursuit of the priest.

She always wore around her neck, in a little bag, the Gospel of St. John. On this point she says :

" The Gospel of St. John has ever been for me a source of light and strength, a real buckler. When frightened or in any danger, I used to say confidently : *And the Word was made flesh and dwelt among us.* I never could understand how some priests could call these words unintelligible, and yet I have really heard them say so."

As Anne Catherine was keenly alive to whatever had received the blessing of Holy Church, she was, on the contrary, seized with horror at the approach of anything evil or accursed. She was immediately impelled to prayer and penance on such occasions. She relates the following incident of her youth :

" At a short distance from our house, lying in the midst of a fertile field, was a little piece of ground where nothing would grow, When I was a child, I never crossed it without a shudder. I used to feel myself pushed by some invisible power, and sometimes I was even thrown down. Once I saw two black shadows wandering about, and I noticed that the horses became uneasy at their approach. I felt that there was something sinister about the place and I tried to get information concerning it. Fearful stories were told of it, and many pretended to have seen strange sights there; but this was all false. At last my father told me that at the time of the ' Seven-Years' Wars,' a Hanoverian soldier had been condemned by a military tribunal and executed on that spot. The poor man was innocent; two enemies had been the authors of his misfortune. I did not hear this till after my First Communion. I went by night to pray there with my arms extended. The first time I had to force myself, I was so afraid; the second time a horrible phantom appeared to me in the form of a dog. It stood at my back resting its head on my shoulder. If I turned my head, I could see its snout and flaming eyes. I was terror-stricken, but I tried to hide my fear. I said in my heart: ' Lord, when Thou wert in agony on the Mount of Olives, Thou didst pray the longer! Thou art by me !' The evil spirit could not harm me. I began to pray and the horrible figure disappeared. On another occasion, whilst praying in the same place, I was lifted up violently as if about to be cast into the ditch close by. I renewed my confidence in God, and exclaimed : ' Satan, thou canst not harm me !' He ceased his attacks, and I went on with my prayers. I never again saw the two shadows, and from that time all appeared quiet.

"I often felt repugnance for places in which there had once

been pagan graves, although I had never heard anything about them. A short distance from home there was a sandhill in the middle of a meadow. I never liked to keep my cows there, for I always saw a black, ugly-looking vapor, like the smoke of smouldering rags, creeping over the ground. A strange obscurity hung over the spot, and sombre figures, enveloped in darkness, moved here and there and, at last, disappeared underground. I used to say to myself, child that I was, 'It is well the thick grass is above you, for that keeps you from hurting us!' When houses are built over such places, a curse issues from the pagan bones resting beneath them, if their occupants do not lead lives sanctified by the benediction of the Church and so counteract its baneful effects. If they should happen to make use of superstitious means condemned by the Church to rid themselves of the curse, they enter, though without knowing it perhaps, into communication with the powers of darkness, which then acquire fresh strength. It is hard for me to make this understood. I see it really, with my bodily eyes, but my hearers can only see it in thought. It is far more difficult for me to comprehend how it is that so many people see no difference between the holy and the profane, the believer and the unbeliever, the pure and the impure. They see only the external appearance. They do not trouble themselves as to whether it is lawful to eat certain things or not, whether they may turn them to profit or not; but I see, I feel quite differently. That which is holy, that which is blessed, I see all luminous, diffusing light and benediction ; while that which is profane, that which is accursed, I see spreading around darkness and corruption. I behold light or darkness springing like corporeal things from what is good or bad, each producing its own fruits. Once, on my way to Dülmen, I passed the hermitage near the grove in which the peasant H— dwelt. Before it stretches a heath. As I drew near with my companion, I saw rising from it a vapor which filled me with horror and disgust. In the middle of the heath several such currents arose and floated in waves over the ground, but I could see no fire. I pointed them out to my companion, saying : ' What smoke is that over there ? I see no fire.' But she could see nothing. She seemed astonished at my question ; she thought something was the matter with me. I said nothing more although I still saw the vapor and felt my terror increasing. As we approached nearer the spot, I distinctly saw a similar vapor rising from the opposite side. Then I understood that unhallowed bones were interred there, and I had a rapid view of the abominable, idolatrous practices that had formerly been carried on in the place."

CHAPTER V.

ANNE CATHERINE MAKES HER FIRST COMMUNION.

About the seventh year of her age, Anne Catherine went with the other school children to make her first confession for which she had prepared most earnestly. Her contrition was so great that, on her way to Coesfeld, her strength gave out, and her little companions had to carry her to the church. Her conscience was burdened not only by some childish transgressions long before expiated, but also by her uninterrupted visions, for which she had so often been reproached as for "imaginations and dreams." As her mother was incessantly warning her against idle fancies and superstition, her anxiety on the subject was proportionately great, and she laid these "day dreams" clearly and fully before her confessor to receive his advice and direction. Here let us pause to admire the designs of Almighty God. Having given Anne Catherine the gift of contemplation for the good of the Faithful, He now willed to submit this gift to the decision, to place it under the guardianship of the Church. Whilst examining her conscience before confession, Anne Catherine feared above everything else that self-love or false shame would lead her to conceal or palliate her sins. To encourage herself, she often repeated these words : " What the devil has taken he may keep. If he took away shame before sin, he may keep it now. I will not take it back before confession."

She dreaded self-love more than the demon himself, for she

had seen in vision that Adam would not have fallen so low, had
he not cast the blame on Eve who, in turn, threw it on the
serpent ; consequently, she accused herself with intense
sorrow, looking upon her offences as mortal and unwilling
to accept any extenuation from the lips of her confessor.
She had once quarrelled with a playmate and replied to another by a sarcastic speech, which faults she thought mortal,
since the school-master had told his pupils that God commanded us, if struck on one cheek, to turn the other.

Dean Overberg states that it was her greatest delight to
be able to testify her affection to one who had offended her.
She confessed her so-called mortal sins, therefore, with
hearty contrition, trembling lest the priest would refuse
her absolution. The Father said to console her : " My
child, you are not yet capable of mortal sin," whereupon
she burst into tears and had to be taken from the confessional. Her parents had given her seven pence to buy
white bread, as the children were accustomed to do after
their confession ; but she gave them all in alms that God
might pardon her sins. Her parents always allowed her
the same sum and for the same purpose when she went to
confession. She used to make the little purchase, but not
for herself; she took it all home to those dear parents. On
another occasion, she was much troubled when approaching the tribunal of penance. She had heard her mother
talking to one of her friends of a certain deceased person
whose soul, she said, was not at rest. This news touched
her with pity. She constantly thought of the poor, uneasy
soul and almost involuntarily sought other intercessors
for it. One day she was on the point of communicating what
she had heard. She began : " The poor woman has no
. . . .," when she became so terrified that she could
not utter another word. The thought had suddenly

presented itself that she would be unable to repair this sin of detraction, that she could not ask pardon of the dead, and she could get no peace until she had confessed her inadvertence. This fright of hers was no exaggerated scruple, but the effect of great purity of conscience. The following fact will bear witness to this :—

" When she began to read," says her father, "she loved to sit on the ground near the fire and, gathering together the burning embers, read her prayer-book by their light. Once I was repairing a bench for a neighbor and using for the purpose a piece of new wood. Anne Catherine gathered up the shavings for the fire, but only those from the new wood. I asked her why she did not take the old wood, too. She answered : ' I only pick up the new, because the old chips that fall from the bench do not belong to us.' I was struck at her words and, turning to her mother, I said : ' She is, indeed, a most singular child !' "

When her parents had retired for the night and the fire was smouldering on the hearth, the little girl sometimes hunted up the ends of candles by which to read her prayer-book. She saw no harm in it at the time, but she confessed it later with true contrition, and never again made use of the least thing without permission.

Anne Catherine was in her twelfth year when she made her First Communion. From the day of her Baptism, she had been powerfully attracted toward the Most Blessed Sacrament. When before It, her joy shone exteriorly. She never entered the church without her angel-guardian who taught her by his own example the homage due to the Eucharistic God. Our Lord Himself had made known to her in vision the grandeur and magnificence of His mysteries. This inspired her with such reverence for the priesthood that no dignity appeared to her com-

parable to it. We shall see later on that there were no offences expiated more rigorously by her than those committed
by the ministers of the altar. When kneeling in church, she
dared not look either to the right or to the left ; her heart
and eyes were fixed upon the Most Blessed Sacrament.
The silence of the holy place was equalled only by the
profound recollection of her soul. She spoke to Jesus in
the Eucharist with confidence and fervor, and on feast days
she sang to Him the hymns of the liturgy ; but as she
could neither go to church as often as she desired nor when
there remain as long as she wished, she turned almost involuntarily in her nocturnal prayer in the direction of the
nearest tabernacle.

Even in her babyhood she knew how to make spiritual
communion ; but when the time came for actually receiving the Holy Eucharist, she thought she could never do
enough. Her desires were equalled only by her efforts to
make ready the poor house of her soul for the coming of
her Celestial Guest. She reviewed her short life over and
over in her anxiety to appear pure in the eyes of her God.
She feared now even more that at her first confession, having some stain on her soul, and she was tormented by the
thought of not having confessed as fully and sincerely as
she should have done. She looked upon herself as the
worst child in the world, and earnestly begged her parents
to help her examine her conscience, saying :

" I want no secret, no fold in my heart. Could I discern the slightest concealment in an angel, I should not
hesitate to declare that he had dealings with the evil one
who lurks in the by-places of hearts." She kept her eyes
closed going to church on the day of her Communion, that
she might see nothing to disturb the recollection of her
soul, and she repeatedly offered herself as a sacrifice for the

salvation of others. Dean Overberg says on this point :
" Anne Catherine did not ask for many things at her First
Communion. She begged Our Lord to make her a good
child, such as He Himself desired to see her, and she devoted herself to Him entirely and unreservedly."

We may judge of the child's earnestness and of God's
pleasure in the same by the surprising effects the Holy
Eucharist produced in her heart. She was all on fire with
the love of her God. It impelled her so powerfully that she
began at that early age a life of mortification and renunciation such as the most rigorous rule never prescribed to a penitent in the cloister or a monk in the desert. Did we possess no other testimony than Dean Overberg's on the effect of
her First Communion, it alone would suffice to prove something truly extraordinary in the inspiration, the heroic energy,
and the ardent love of this child, who, in her twelfth year,
without direction, under the blessed influence alone of the
Divine Sacrament, could impose upon herself so entire a
renunciation, could persevere in it as unflinchingly as did
Anne Catherine. She closed her senses against everything
that might allure her from God. He alone who had
deigned to enter her heart, He alone should possess and
govern it. Dean Overberg says :—

" From the day of her First Communion, her efforts to
mortify and renounce self became even more persevering
than before. She was convinced of the truth that without
mortification it is impossible to give one's self entirely to God·
Her love had taught her this. She used to say : ' The love
of creatures impels men to great and difficult undertakings.
Why, then, should not the love of Jesus lead us to the
same ?' " She mortified her eyes, turning them away from
curious or beautiful objects ; in church especially she
kept them under continual restraint, addressing to herself

these words : ' Do not look around. It would distract you, or be, perhaps, too much of a gratification. And why would you indulge your sight? Restrain it for the love of God.' If an occasion presented itself of hearing something strange or amusing, she would say : ' No, I have no ears for that. I will be deaf to it for the love of God.'

" She mortified her tongue, imposing silence upon it when she wished to speak. She ate nothing pleasing to her taste. When her parents noticed this, they ascribed it to caprice and insisted upon her eating. She mortified her feet when inclined to go where duty did not call her. ' No,' she said, ' I will not go there. It will be better to stay away for the love of God. If I went, I might have cause to regret it.' It was customary with her to make the long Way of the Cross at Coesfeld barefoot. She refused herself many little pleasures she might have innocently enjoyed. She disciplined her body with nettles, she wore penitential cinctures, she slept on a wooden cross, or on a kind of frame formed of two long beams with two shorter transverse pieces."

After Holy Communion, the child had a vision in which she assisted at the Sacred Mysteries in the Catacombs in company with St. Cecilia.

" I knelt," she said, " in a subterranean hall which seemed to be cut out in a mountain. Many people were kneeling around on the bare ground. Flambeaux were fastened to the wall, and there were two upon the stone altar which had a tabernacle, likewise of stone, and a door. A priest was saying Mass, all the people answering. At the end of it he took a chalice from the tabernacle. It looked like wood, and from it he distributed the Blessed Sacrament to the people, who received it on little white linen cloths spread carefully on their breast. Then they all dispersed."

This vision was a pledge that God had heard her and had accepted the sacrifice of her whole being. Her purity of heart and austerity of life rendered her worthy of figuring in the sacred cohort of early Christians who had drawn from the Most Blessed Sacrament their strength in the midst of torments. Her own life was to be a perpetual martyrdom and she, too, was to draw strength and courage from the same divine source. Like St. Cecilia she was to suffer for the Faith at a time of persecution, unbloody, it is true, but not the less dangerous to the Church. She, too, with heroism not inferior to that of the virgin-martyrs, was to confess her Redeemer denied and abandoned by the multitude.

Dean Overberg tells us that the little girl divided the time between her Communions into two parts : preparation and thanksgiving. She intreated the saints to join their prayers to hers, and conjured Almighty God, by His love for Jesus and Mary, to prepare her heart for His well-beloved Son. On the morning of her second Communion, a little incident occurred which seemed to indicate her own intimate communication with the Blessed Sacrament and the graces received from It for herself and others. She was to set out with her mother before daylight for Coesfeld. Her best clothes were carefully kept in the family chest. When she went to get them, she found it filled with fine white loaves so numerous that she could not count them without taking them out. At first she thought her mother had put them there to try her. She had scarcely time to replace them when her mother, impatient at the delay, came after her and hurried her off so quickly that she forgot her neckerchief. She did not miss it until some distance from home. She dared not return for it, but ran on after her mother, in dread all the time of being discovered, and praying earnestly to God to help her out of her difficulty. At last they came to a muddy crossing and, just as the mother turned to help her over, the child felt a kerchief placed by invisible hands around her neck. Anne Catherine was so agitated at this speedy answer to her prayer as to be scarcely able to follow her mother, who chided her a little for her strange conduct. When she reached the church, she tearfully confessed the curiosity that had led her to take the loaves from the chest. Her longing for the Holy Communion became like a flame; her breast and tongue seemed to be on fire. In her humility she looked upon this as a punishment for her curiosity, and the thought almost deprived her of consciousness. To get some relief, she touched her tongue with a little picture of the Five Wounds. When she approached the Holy Table, she distinctly beheld the Sacred Host fly toward her under a luminous form and enter her breast, whilst, at the same moment, the priest laid another Host on her tongue. Again did the divine fire burn more intensely than before, and she tried to cool her parched mouth as she returned home by pressing to it her cold gloves. At the spot on which she had miraculously received the neckerchief, her former uneasiness returned on noticing for the first time that it was much more beautiful than her own : " It has fringe !" she cried in trepidation. " What will my mother say !" When she reached home, she took it off tremblingly and laid it on her bed ; but, on turning again to look at it, it was gone ! She was greatly relieved at its having escaped her mother's eye.

The little loaves, visible only to Anne Catherine, were symbolical of the rich gifts she was to receive as a reward for her fervent preparation for Holy Communion and which she was to distribute as spiritual nourishment to the needy. They were hidden under her apparel as a sign that she was herself to multiply and distribute them. The greater part she gave to the most necessitous, the suffering souls in purgatory, for whom she offered all her actions; in return they testified their gratitude by prayers and assistance. It was to them she was indebted for the neckerchief so opportunely presented.

Her confessor at this time was a venerable old Jesuit of Coesfeld, Father Weidner. She says:

" My confessor was Father Weidner who lived with his two sisters at Coesfeld. I used to go to the first Mass on Sundays and then attend to the cooking, so that the rest of the family might go to church. Coffee was not so common then; and, when I had a couple of stivers, I used to go after early Mass to Father Weidner's sisters, pious girls who sold coffee. I liked to go there, the old gentleman and his sisters were so good and kind. When my parents returned from church and found the coffee ready for them, they were greatly pleased."

CHAPTER VI.

SNARES OF THE EVIL SPIRIT.

As soon as Anne Catherine had become sufficiently strong
to resist the open attacks of Satan, Almighty God allowed
her to be tormented by him. But the evil one tried in vain
to draw her from the path of perfection along which she was
walking so courageously. She despised his cunning, his
malice, and his power. The more humble she became, the
more difficult was it for her to comprehend how he could intimidate a soul. His first attacks were directed against her
life. She tells us herself :—

" When a child my life was repeatedly in danger, but by
the help of God I was always saved. I knew very well
that these perils were not accidental ; I knew they came from
the evil spirit. They generally happened when I was not
thinking of the presence of God, or when I had negligently
committed some fault. I never could attribute them to
chance. God always protects us if we do not wander from
Him. His angel is ever at our side, but we must render
ourselves worthy of His care. Like grateful children, we
ought never to leave Him. We ought constantly to beg His
assistance, for our enemy lies in wait to destroy us. When
I was only a few years old, my parents went out one day
and left me at home alone, my mother charging me to stay
in and mind the house. Presently an old woman came in
who, for some reason or other, wanted to get rid of me for
awhile. ' Run,' she said ; ' run get some pears off my tree !
Run fast before your mother comes back !' I yielded to the

temptation, forgot my mother's orders, and ran to the old woman's garden in such haste that I stumbled over a plough half-hidden in the hay and, striking my breast violently against it, I fell unconscious to the ground. My mother found me in this state, and brought me to by a smart correction. I felt the effects of this accident a long time. Later I was shown that the devil had made use of the old woman to tempt me to disobedience through gluttony and that, by yielding to the temptation, I had endangered my life. This gave me horror for the latter vice, and I saw how necessary it is for man to deny himself."

When Anne Catherine began her nocturnal vigils, the attacks of the evil spirit became bolder and more frequent. He tried to frighten her from her prayers by terrible noises and apparitions, even by blows. She often felt icy-cold hands grasping her by the feet, casting her to the ground, or lifting her high in the air; but, though terror-stricken, the child never lost countenance. She continued her prayer with redoubled fervor till Satan was forced to withdraw. She even returned to the place in which she had been maltreated, saying : " Miserable wretch ! thou shalt not chase me away. Thou hast no power over me ! thou shall not hinder my prayer ! "

These attacks were renewed whenever she prayed for the souls in purgatory or performed penances. But as she was always instructed how to resist the enemy, and the beloved souls were often visible thanking her for the relief she gave them, they served but to animate her courage and nerve her to fresh exertions.

Sometimes she went at night to pray before a rustic Crucifix which stood toward the middle of the hamlet. The road was crossed by a narrow by-path upon which there often stood facing her a horrible beast like a dog with an enormously large head. At first she used to shrink back some steps in horror ; but quickly summoning courage, she would say to herself : " Why flee before the enemy ?" Then with the sign of the cross, she would boldly push by the monster. But she trembled violently, her hair stood on end, and she flew rather than walked over the road that led to the crucifix, the brute running along by her side, sometimes even brushing up against her. However, she speedily surmounted her fear, and walked on bravely by her enemy who, unable to endure his own discomfiture, soon took to flight.

As the devil could not force her by apparitions to desist from penance, he instigated a wretch to attack her near the crucifix ; but, aided by her angel, she courageously defended herself and forced him to retire. Owing to the angel's protection, she was delivered from innumerable dangers. Once the evil spirit tried to hurl her down a ladder ; again he pushed her into a deep ditch, plunging her repeatedly to the bottom in order to drown her. But her angel drew her out and placed her on the brink safe and sound. These attacks have a deep signification which may not, perhaps, be understood at first. We discover in them not only the rage and malice of hell aiming at the destruction of God's chosen instrument, but also an essential part of the mission assigned her. This was, indeed, to draw upon herself hell's fury, to expose herself to its assaults, thus to avert them from certain other souls whose sins rendered them powerless to resist. She took the place of those who had incurred chastisement ; she suffered for those who exposed themselves to the danger of being lost ; and she paid off their debt by her own combats. As she took upon herself the corporal maladies of her neighbor in order to deliver him from them, so also did she bear for him the attacks of the demon, sustain the struggle in his stead, and gain for him the victory. She not only took the place of the members of the Church, but she also guarded the treasures that had been confided to her pastors, and which were now exposed to the fury of hell. Her painful exercises, her vigils, etc., were not dependent on her own will; they were all regulated by her angel, by instructions received in vision. Her own choice does not move her to make the long Way of the Cross at night, or to pray in the open fields—all forms part of the task marked out for her. Its accomplishment demands that she should traverse the lonely road that led to the centre of the hamlet to expiate the negligence of a slothful pastor who sleeps whilst the wolf breaks into the sheepfold ; she must struggle with the rapacious animal and prevent his devouring the flock. Is she dashed from a ladder, or thrown into a ditch ?—it is for a soul in mortal sin whom she snatches from the demon at the moment in which he thinks himself sure of his prey. If frightful visions and phantoms fill her soul with horror, they are the terrors from which she delivers the dying, that they may prepare in peace for the hour of death.

These attacks of Satan were redoubled whenever her prayers confounded the efforts of his malice, or disconcerted his plans.

"Once," she said, " I was going to church in the dark when a great dog passed me. I stretched out my hand, and received so violent a blow in the face that I staggered. My face and hand swelled up in church and both were covered with blisters. When I reached home I was unrecognizable. I was cured by bathing with baptismal water. On the road to the church was a hedge over which I had to climb. When I came to it early on St. Francis's day, I felt a great black figure pulling me back.

I struggled and succeeded in crossing. I was not frightened. He, the demon, used to station himself in the middle of the road to force me to turn aside, but he never succeeded."

The devil now sought to perplex her by more artful and subtle attacks. The mortification of her early years which had acquired for her such strength to resist, was hateful to him. He tried to tempt her to some little self-indulgence, but she only redoubled her austerities as soon as she discovered the artifice. Then, taking the opposite course, he urged her to carry her penances to excess; but she with the advice of her director immediately moderated them.

It will be seen further on that although Satan never desisted from tormenting Anne Catherine in every conceivable way, yet he could never excite in her the slightest movement opposed to perfect purity. He dared not present this temptation to a soul endowed with the gift of prophecy and confided to the visible guardianship of her angel. Hers was, indeed, to be a way of sorrows, but no stings of concupiscence were to spring up in her path. He did, it is true, sometimes place impure objects before her imagination, but never could he lead her to cast a glance upon them. He did, indeed, instigate his wicked slaves to attempt violence against the young virgin; but, with the courage of a lioness, she struck the wretches to the ground. " My Lord and my God does not abandon me !" she said. " He is stronger than the enemy !" This confidence in divine protection was her buckler, the shield that warded off every attack.

CHAPTER VII.

Her Communications with Her Angel.

The familiar intercourse that existed between Anne Catherine and her angel-guardian ever visible to her, is but a repetition of what all souls enjoy who have been raised to high contemplation. The gift of supernatural intuition is for man so weighty a burden, it is exposed to such risks in his possession, it exacts so great purity of soul that, for him to use it rightly, special assistance is necessary. He must follow a guide in the boundless spheres unveiled to the eye of contemplation. From his birth every man without exception is attended by an angel who watches over him, who directs him in the good use of the graces assigned him by the eternal decrees of the Almighty; that, by so doing, he may become a child of faith and in the end attain heavenly beatitude. The soul's capability of profiting by the angelic influence increases with its own purity and perfection. But nothing brings it nearer to its angel, or renders it more deserving of communication with him than the unsullied splendor of baptismal innocence. This was the surpassing, the indescribable charm in Anne Catherine that made the heavenly spirit, although belonging to the highest ranks of the celestial hierarchy, look upon his duty of enlightening and conducting her as a commission well suited to his high dignity. A child still in years and experience, she was however ripe for the understanding of eternal truths, and ready to become the depository of divine secrets.

The angel's first care was to instruct his charge in the Catholic faith, by intuition and symbolical images. She thus acquired an incomparably clearer view, a deeper knowledge of its mysteries than human teaching and reflection could bestow. To the light of faith was added the practice of the love of God which kept her in constant union with Him. It became, so to speak, a necessity for her to seek God in all things, to refer all to Him, to see all in Him. He was the first good that attracted her soul, and He possessed her so entirely that no creature could separate her from Him. The splendor emanating from the angel enshrouded her from the first moment of her existence, constituted the very atmosphere she breathed, and hid from her those seductions which engross and dissipate the affections of man. Her soul confirmed in charity regarded creatures but in God. Every look of the angel was a ray of light, a breath which fanned the flame of divine love, an impulse on to God. All the powers, all the movements of her soul were so well regulated that no wave of passion could ruffle its peace. She calmly endured the most intense bodily sufferings, and her soul, despite the keen sensitiveness of her sympathetic nature and the timidity consequent on childhood, was possessed of so great energy that she could instantaneously surmount terror or pain. The angel's jealous watchfulness suffered not the smallest attachment in her to anything earthly.

She felt that her whole being was laid open to his gaze, that he penetrated the inmost recesses of her heart; therefore she watched unceasingly to keep the mirror of her soul untarnished. She was all her life a child of wonderful simplicity and candor. Her artlessness alone would have sufficed to prove the origin of her extraordinary gifts, for even the gift of contemplation is of less value than that spirit of humility which hid the riches imparted to her. She never dreamed of her high privileges, the thought of self filled her with confusion and disquietude. Such an estimation of one's self can proceed neither from nature nor from the evil one, but only from a high degree of grace and extraordinary fidelity.

The angel's direction had been given Anne Catherine as a talent which she was to increase by the good use she made of it. The more she strove to become worthy of so great a favor, the more abundant light did she receive, the firmer and closer grew the bond that united her to her angelic protector. Now, this bond could be none other than obedience springing from the love of God; for there is none higher, none more meritorious. It is, in truth, the very one which unites the angel himself to God. From her earliest years Anne Catherine was exercised in perfect abnegation of her own will in the sacrifice of every power of soul and body to God. It was in this way she perpetually offered herself for others. God accepted her offering and so regulated her life through the ministry of her angel, that every action, even in the smallest detail, became a meritorious act of obedience for her. She abandoned her will to her angel that he might govern it, her understanding that he might enlighten it, her heart that he might keep it for God alone, pure and free from every earthly attachment. Docile to his interior instructions, she refused herself sleep and nourishment, chastised her body severely, and petitioned only for the pains and maladies of others. Her perseverance in such a course attracted upon her the blessings of heaven, which richly indemnified her for all the privations attendant upon it.

In consequence of her great charity for her neighbor, she acted as substitute for those who could not endure their sufferings, and she aided others who sued for mercy. It was the angel who conducted her where she was most needed. As the flame borne by the breeze first to one side then to the other, her loving soul followed the angel's call when he led her to the abodes of misery and sin. Guided by him she was ever ready to succor the needy, to go wherever the irresistible impulse of pity impelled, for compassion knows neither time nor space ; no bounds can arrest the desires of the soul. Like a flame mounting on high, enlightening all things far and near, her charity penetrated the whole body of the Church, bearing help and succor wherever her angel led her. She said once, speaking on this subject :

" The angel calls me and I follow him to various places ; I often journey with him. He takes me among persons whom I know either well or slightly, and again among others who are entire strangers to me. We cross the sea as quickly as thought travels. I can see far, far away ! It was he who took me to the Queen of France (*Marie Antoinette*) in her prison. When he comes to take me on a journey I generally see first a glimmering of light, then his luminous form appears suddenly before me like a flash from a lantern opened in the dark. As we journey along in the darkness, a faint light floats over our path. We pass over countries familiar to me to far distant regions. Sometimes our way lies over roads; sometimes across deserts, mountains, rivers, and seas. I travel always on foot, and I often have to climb rugged mountains. My knees ache from fatigue, and my bare feet burn. My guide is sometimes ahead of me, sometimes at my side. I never see his feet move. He is silent, he makes few motions, but sometimes he accompanies his short replies by a gesture of the hand or an inclination of the head. O how bright and transparent he is ! He is grave but very kind. His hair is smooth, flowing, and

shining. His head is uncovered, and his robe long and dazzlingly white like that of a priest. I address him freely,
but I can never look him full in the face. I incline before
him. He gives me all kinds of signs. I never ask him
many questions ; the satisfaction I take in being near him
prevents me. He is always very brief in his words. I
see him also in my waking moments. When I pray for
others and he is not near, I call to him to go to the angel of
those for whom I am praying. I often say to him when he
is by me : ' Now I shall stay here, but do thou go to such or
such a place where thy help is needed,' and I see him going.
When I come to broad waters and know not how to cross,
I find myself all at once on the other side, and I look back
in wonder. We often soar above cities. I left the
church of the Jesuits at Coesfeld late one winter evening
in a heavy storm of snow and rain to return home over the
fields to Flamske. I was frightened, and I began to cry to
God. Suddenly I saw a light like a flame on before me. It took
the form of my guide in his robe. The ground under my
feet became dry, it cleared overhead, neither rain nor snow
fell upon me, and I reached home not even wet."

Anne Catherine's communications with the souls in purgatory were also carried on through her angel who took her
into that prison of mercy that she might refresh the dear
captives with the fruits of her penance.

"I was with my guide," she says, " among the poor souls
in purgatory. I saw their desolation, their inability to help
themselves, and the little assistance they get from the living.
Ah, their misery is inexpressible ! Whilst contemplating
their state, I saw that a mountain separated me from my
guide. I sighed for him like one famished, I almost swooned
with desire. I saw him on the opposite side, but I could
not reach him. He said to me : ' See, how thou sighest

for help ! The poor souls are always in the state in which
thou now art ! ' He often took me to pray before caverns
and prisons. I prostrated, I wept, my arms extended, and I
cried to God for mercy. My angel encouraged me to offer
all kinds of privations for the poor souls. They cannot help
themselves, they are cruelly neglected. I often sent him
to the angels of certain persons in suffering, to inspire them
to suffer their pains for them. They are instantly relieved
by such offerings ; they become so joyous, so grateful !
Whenever I do something for them, they pray for me. I
am terrified to see the riches the Church holds out in such
abundance neglected, dissipated, so lightly esteemed,
whilst the poor souls are languishing for them."

From her earliest childhood, Anne Catherine had always
begged God to keep her from sin, to treat her as a loving
father treats his little child, to teach her to know and fulfil
His holy will. And Almighty God mercifully heard her
prayer. He guarded and enlightened her through the ministry of her angel in her long journey through a life of toil
and suffering. He showed her all that was in store for her
in symbolical pictures, that she might be ready for any
emergency. He prepared her for sufferings, that she might
ask for strength to embrace them. Every incident, every
encounter which was to happen, either to herself or those
connected with her, was shown to her in advance. She received precise instructions as to her behavior toward all
with whom she came in contact, whether she was to treat
them with frankness or reserve. The angel even prescribed,
at times, the words she was to use.

She lived in two worlds : in the external, visible to the
senses, and in the invisible and hidden one. She acted in both
and for the good of both. The immense task imposed upon
her by Almighty God, demanded that she should fulfil per-

fectly all the duties of the common life, in the midst of difficulties and sufferings sufficient of themselves to fill a whole
lifetime ; and to this was added her interior action for the
good of the universal Church. The sufferings of Christianity, the dangers threatening the faith, the wounds endured,
the sacrilegious usurpation of church property, the profanation of holy things—all were placed before her, and she
was so absorbed by the labors resulting therefrom, that days
and weeks passed in this state of spiritual abstraction. She
retained, meanwhile, entire control over her senses and faculties, that she might fulfil the duties of everyday life in that
world from which she was daily more and more removed.
How would she have been able to satisfy its demands,
how would those with whom she lived have been able to endure her, had not the angel watched over this double life, had
he not aided her in such a way that all she did received a
blessing, had he not, in fine, harmonized these diversified
operations ?

Whilst yet too young to fall under the direction of the
pastors of God's flock, her angel was her only guide. But
when she began to approach the Sacraments, the respect
and submission paid by her to the angel then became the
rule of her communication with the priest, the angel himself
setting her the example by submitting his own direction to
that of the minister of God. He now was, as it were,
merely the treasurer and dispenser of the gifts granted his
pupil for the benefit of the faithful. Whilst the Church, in
the person of her priests, assumed the guidance of Anne
Catherine, she was herself to work out her salvation by
means common to all the faithful. God's wonderful gifts
were not to form the end of her life, but only a means of
fulfilling her mission of expiatory suffering for the Church ;
consequently, these gifts were to fall under the judgment

and decision of her Ecclesiastical Superiors. The immense power of the priesthood is hereby undeniably proved, since we see the angel himself bowing to the decisions of lawful authority. It was the angel who transmitted to her the word of obedience from her confessor or superiors when, transported in spirit to other worlds, she lay like one dead, wholly insensible to every outward impression. One word from either was sufficient at such moments to recall her instantaneously to consciousness.

Once she said: " When in contemplation, or in the discharge of some spiritual labor, I am often suddenly recalled into this world of darkness by a sacred and irresistible power. I hear the word ' *obedience*,' as if uttered from afar. It is a sad sound to me at such moments, but obedience is the living root of the tree of contemplation."

Nevertheless, the confessor's voice could not have reached her but for the angel who regarded the practice of obedience as more meritorious for his charge than the highest flights of contemplation. Although his unexpected and peremptory order pierced her soul like an arrow, yet he never delayed to recall her to consciousness at the word of her superiors.

We shall see, further on, the priest's direction opposed in many instances to that of the angel; but never shall we see the least departure from the order prescribed by God for the preservation of faith in its purity—an order by which no vocation, no privilege can exempt a soul from submission to superiors. No grace, no degree of sanctity surpasses in intrinsic dignity and grandeur the sacerdotal character. Between God, the invisible Head of the Church, and the faithful there exists no other mediator than the priest ; hence the treasures of mercy bestowed upon the Church in the persons of His chosen ones must fall under the supervision of the priesthood, must be received by them in trust for the wants of the faithful at large. Thus it was with Anne Catherine Emmerich. Her angel omitted nothing to make her a source of benediction to the Church. This benediction was to be diffused only by God's minister, and according to the use made of this power was to be its fruit.

CHAPTER VIII.

Anne Catherine's Vocation to the Religious State. She is Prepared by Special Direction.

The desire of living for God alone went on increasing in the heart of the wonderful little child. She dreamed but of the state which would most surely lead her to its fulfilment. For a long time she entertained the thought of secretly quitting her home to seek in some distant land a spot in which she might, unknown to all, lead a life of penance. Her parents, her brothers and sisters were the only objects that shared her love with God ; yet she looked upon herself as wanting in fidelity as long as she remained in her native place. Her project was impracticable to one in her position; but the greater the obstacles that presented themselves, the more earnestly did she sigh after the contemplative life. The thought of it pursued her constantly, it formed the supreme end of all her youthful aspirations. She was unable to control her emotion at the sight of a religious habit, though she hardly dared hope for the happiness of ever being clothed in a similar manner.

Almighty God, who inspired her with this ardent longing, deigned Himself to guide her to the wished for term. If we consider the intrinsic character and exterior circumstances of this direction in connection with the situation in which the Church was at the time, we shall not fail to discover in it something very remarkable. We shall find therein the mysterious ways by which Almighty God aids the Church in her trials, and a consoling and encouraging proof that the miracles of His Almighty power are never wanting to her, even when her own members league with her enemies for her destruction. When Anne Catherine was called to the religious state there to exercise a most exalted influence, events had transpired which made such ravages in the vineyard of the Church that she could not, like a St. Colette, restore conventual discipline nor establish new communities. There remained to her only the far more arduous task of serving God as an instrument of expiation, as did Lidwina of Schiedam at a time equally disastrous. She was to satisfy for the sins of others, to take upon herself the wounds of the body of the Church, and thus apply a remedy.

God directed the child in accordance with her immense task. He condescended to woo her as His betrothed, and thus to fit her for the highest perfection. The Church regards every soul that makes the triple vows of religion as contracting thereby a spiritual betrothal with God; but the extraordinary vocation of this child, the multiplied favors bestowed upon her, her wonderful fidelity to grace, are proofs that her dignity was unparalleled, that she was specially chosen to repair the innumerable outrages offered to the Celestial Spouse of souls. God in His liberality ever holds in reserve a superabundance of spiritual favors for His elect; but, when His graces are despised or squandered, justice demands their withdrawal. This would follow as a necessary consequence, did He not in His mercy prepare some souls in whom to store these slighted treasures till more favorable times. Now, God wills that this guardianship of His graces should be meritorious; consequently, He qualifies their custodian to acquire by labor and suffering more than is sufficient to discharge the debts contracted by the levity, the sloth, the infidelity, or malice of others. These instruments of God's mercy have never been wanting to the Church in any age ; and they are so much the more needful to her as the zeal of her priesthood, the mediators between God and His people, grows weak. The Church had never been so oppressed, the scourge of incredulity had never produced ravages so great, the enemies of the faith and their machinations for its destruction had never met with so little resistance as at the period in which Almighty God chose Anne Catherine for His betrothed. Poor, weak, lowly child ! she was called to war against powerful enemies. God placed in her hands the arms with which He Himself, in His most holy Humanity, had conquered hell, and He exercised her in that manner of combating which secures the victory. We see her led, not by the way of human prudence and foresight, but by that marked out by the impenetrable wisdom of Divine Providence.

She was in her fifth or sixth year when she received her first call to the religious state. She says on the subject :—

" I was only a tiny child, and I used to mind the cows, a most troublesome and fatiguing duty. One day the thought occurred to me, as indeed it had often done before, to quit my home and the cows, and go serve God in some solitary place where no one would know me. I had a vision in which I went to Jerusalem, where I met a religious in whom I afterward recognized St. Jane of Valois. She looked very grave. At her side was a lovely little boy about my own size. St. Jane did not hold him by the hand, and I knew from that that he was not her child. She asked me what was the matter with me, and when I told her, she comforted me, saying : ' Never mind ! Look at this little boy ! Would you like him for your spouse ?' I said : ' Yes !' Then she told me not to be discouraged, but to

wait until the little boy would come for me, assuring me
that I would be a religious, although it seemed quite un-
likely then. She told me that I should certainly enter the
cloister for nothing is impossible to my affianced. Then I
returned to myself and drove the cows home. From that
time I looked forward to the fulfilment of her promise. I
had this vision at noon. Such things never disturbed me.
I thought every one had them. I never knew any difference between them and real intercourse with creatures."

Some time after another incident happened which encouraged her to make a vow to enter religion. She relates it
herself:—" My father had vowed to give every year a calf
to the nuns of the Annunciation of Coesfeld, and when he
went to fulfil his vow he used to take me with him. The
nuns used to play with me, whirling me round in the turn,
giving me little presents, and asking me if I did not want
to stay with them. I always answered : ' Yes,' and I never
wanted to leave them. Then they would say : 'Next time
we'll keep you ! Next time !'—Young as I was, I formed
an affection for this house in which the Rule was still strictly observed, and whenever I heard its bells, I used to unite
with the good nuns in prayer. In this way I lived in close
union with them.

" Once, about two o'clock, on a sultry summer day, I
was out with the cows. The sky grew dark, the thunder
rolled, a storm was at hand. The cows were restless from
the heat and flies, and I was in great anxiety as to how
I should manage them, for there were about forty
and they gave me no little trouble running into the copse.
They belonged to the whole hamlet. As many cows as
each peasant owned, so many days was he obliged to herd
them. When I had charge of them, I always spent my time
in prayer. I used to go to Jerusalem and Bethlehem. I was

more familiar with those places than with my own home. On the day in question, when the storm burst I took shelter under some juniper-trees that stood behind a sand-hill. I began to pray, and I had a vision. An aged religious clothed in the habit of the Annonciades appeared and began to talk to me. She told me that to limit the honor we pay the Mother of God to adorning her statues, to carrying them in procession, and to addressing fine words to her, is not truly to honor her. We must imitate her virtues, her humility, her charity, her purity. She said also that, in a storm or in any other time of danger, there is no greater security than to fly to the Wounds of Jesus; that she herself had had profound devotion toward those Sacred Wounds; that she had even received their painful impression, but without any one's ever knowing it. She told me that she had always worn on her breast a hair-cloth studded with five nails and a chain around her waist, but that such practices ought to be kept secret. She spoke, too, of her particular devotion to the Annunciation of the Blessed Virgin. It had been revealed to her that Mary from her tender infancy had sighed for the coming of the Messiah, desiring for herself only the honor of serving the Mother of God. Then she told me that she had seen the Archangel's salutation, and I described to her how I had witnessed it. We soon became quite at home with each other, for both had seen the same things.

"It was about four o'clock when I returned to myself; the bell of the Annonciades was ringing for prayer, the storm was over, and I found my cows quietly gathered together. I was not even wet from the rain. Then it was that I made a vow to become a religious. At first, I thought of the Annonciades; but on further reflection, I concluded that it would be better to be altogether separ-

ated from my family. I kept my resolution secret. I
found out later that the religious with whom I had conversed was St. Jane. She had been forced to marry. I
often saw her in my journeys to Jerusalem and Bethlehem.
She used to go with me, as did also St. Frances and St.
Louisa."

From this time Anne Catherine was firmly resolved
to enter a convent. She saw no human possibility of fulfilling her vow, still less had she any idea as to where she
would apply for admittance; but strong in the remembrance of what had been promised her, she felt sure that
God would perfect in her what He had begun, that He
Himself would be her guide. She tried, in her own way,
to begin at once the life of a religious as far as circumstances permitted. Her parents and teachers she looked
upon as her Superiors and she obeyed them most punctually.
The mortification, self-renunciation, and retirement prescribed by conventual rules, she observed as perfectly as
she could.

One of her companions, Elizabeth Wollers, deposed
before ecclesiastical authority, April 4, 1813:—

"I have known Anne Catherine Emmerich from childhood. We were much together; in fact, we lived for a
time under the same roof. Her parents were strict, but
not harsh. She was of a good disposition, very fond of
her family, prudent and rather reserved. Even when she
was a little girl she wanted to be a nun, having always an
attraction to piety, caring nothing for companions or amusements. She generally left them and went to church. She
was recollected, sparing of her words, active, laborious,
cordial and affable toward all. Her winning ways often
gained her little presents. She was good-hearted, but sometimes a little quick and impetuous, which gave her cause

for regret. She was not fastidious about her dress, though she was very clean and neat."

In her twelfth year she entered upon service in the family of one of her relatives also named Emmerich. His wife made the following deposition, April 18, 1813 :—

" When Anne Catherine was twelve or thirteen years old, she came to my house and kept the cows. She was kind and respectful to every one; no fault was ever found with her; our intercourse was always agreeable. She never went to any assembly of pleasure. She preferred going to church. She was conscientious, industrious, and pious; she spoke well of every one; she was indifferent to the things of this world. Next to her person she wore a rough woollen garment. She used to fast continually saying that she had no appetite. When I advised her to give up the idea of becoming a nun, since she would have to sacrifice everything to do so, she used to say : ' Don't speak that way to me or we shall fall out. I must be a religious, I am resolved to be one !' "

Anne Catherine met in this new home certain well-to-do peasants, a circumstance very pleasing to her parents, who hoped that, by being thrown more with others, she would gradually become less silent and reserved. They could not understand such aversion to the world in so young a child, and they feared besides that her retired life would injure her future prospects. But the more Anne Catherine saw of the world, the more did her disgust for it increase. She was always in contemplation, even in the midst of those exterior occupations which she knew how to discharge so skilfully. When at work in the fields, if the conversation turned on God, she would utter a few short words; otherwise, she kept silence performing her share of the labor promptly, calmly, and systematically. If she were

addressed suddenly, she either did not hear at all or, like
one waking out of a dream, gazing upon her questioner with
eyes whose expression made even her simple-minded
companions suspect that they were not turned upon things
of sense, she gave an answer irrelevant to the subject.
But her winning artlessness, her cordial willingness to
oblige, soon dispelled the impression produced by her
manner.

After three years spent in the family of her relative she
was placed with a seamstress, her mother thinking this
would suit her delicate constitution better than hard labor.
Before she began her apprenticeship, however, she returned
home for awhile to help with the harvest. An incident occurred about this time which led to the disclosure of
her long-cherished design to enter the cloister. They
were all at work in the fields one afternoon when
the bell of the Annonciades rang for Vespers. Anne
Catherine had often heard it before, but this time the
sound so moved her soul that she almost lost consciousness.
It was like a voice calling to her : " Go to the convent !
Go at any cost !" She was unable to continue her work
and had to be taken home.

" From this moment," she relates, " I began to be sick.
I had frequent vomitings, and I was very sad. As I went
about languid and sorrowful, my mother anxiously begged
me to tell her the cause. Then I told her of my desire to
enter a convent. She was greatly vexed, and asked me
how I could think of such a thing in my poverty and state
of health. She laid the affair before my father, who
immediately joined her in trying to dissuade me from
the thought. They said that such a life would be a most
painful one for me, as a poor peasant-girl would only be
despised by the other religious. But I replied : ' God is

rich, though I have nothing. He will supply.' My parents' refusal grieved me so that I fell sick and was obliged to keep my bed.

"One day about noon, the sun was shining through the little window of my room, when I saw a holy man with two female religious approach my bed. They were dazzling with light. They presented me a large book like a missal and said: 'If thou canst study this book, thou wilt see what belongs to a religious.' I replied: 'I shall read it right away,' and I took the book on my knee. It was Latin, but I understood every word, and I read it eagerly. They left it with me and disappeared. The leaves were of parchment, written in red and gold letters. There were some pictures of the early saints in it. It was bound in yellow and had no clasps. I took it with me to the convent and read it attentively. When I had read a little, it was always taken away from me. One day it was lying on the table when several of the Sisters came in and tried to take it off with them, but they could not move it from its place. More than once it was said to me: 'Thou hast still so many leaves to read.' Years after when I was rapt in spirit to the Mountain of the Prophets, I saw this same book among many other prophetic writings of all times and places. It was shown me as the share I was to have in these treasures. Other things which I had received on various occasions and which I had kept for a long time, were also preserved here. At present, Dec. 20,1819, I have still five leaves to read; but I must have leisure for it, that I may leave its contents after me" (1).

This mysterious book was not merely symbolical, it was a real book, a volume of prophecies. It formed a part, as will be seen further on, of the treasure of sacred writings

(1) Sister Emmerich died in 1824.

preserved upon what Anne Catherine calls the "Mountain of the Prophets." These writings are transmitted miraculously to those who, by the infusion of prophetic light, have been rendered capable of reading them. The book in question treated of the essence and signification of the religious state, its rank in the Church, and its mission in every age; it also taught those to whom such a vocation was given what service they could render to the Church in their own time. What Anne Catherine read in this book was afterward unfolded to her in a series of pictures. When she recited a psalm, the Magnificat, the Benedictus, the Gospel of St. John, a prayer from the liturgy, or the Litany of the Blessed Virgin, the words unfolded, as it were, like the ovary which contains the seed, and their history and meaning were presented to her contemplation. It was the same with this book. In it she learned that the chief end of the religious life is union with the Heavenly Bridegroom, and in this general view she distinctly perceived her own duty with the means, the obstacles, the labors, pains, and mortifications which would further its accomplishment. All this she saw not only in what referred to her own sanctification, but also in what related to the situation and wants of the whole Church. She had not received the grace of religious vocation for herself alone. She was to be, as it were, a treasury for this grace with all the favors attached thereto, that she might preserve it to the Church at a time in which the Lord's vineyard was being laid waste; therefore, all that she learned in the prophetic book, and all that she did in accordance with its teachings, bore the stamp of expiation and satisfaction for the failings of others. Her spiritual labors were performed less for herself than for her neighbor; they were a harvest, a conquest, whose fruits and spoils were for the good of the whole Church.

The more closely Anne Catherine studied this mysterious book, the more extended became her visions, the more did they influence her whole inner and outer life. She saw the harmony of the pictures presented to her soul, whether with one another, or with her own mission; she saw that they embraced in their entirety the history of a soul seeking her Celestial Spouse. She sighs after Him, she tends toward Him, she prepares all that is needful for her espousals; but she is continually delayed and perplexed by the loss or destruction of many necessary articles, and by the malicious efforts of others to thwart and annoy her. From time to time impending events were shown her in symbolical pictures, which never failed to be realized. She was warned of the hindrances caused by her own faults and by her too great condescension to others; but this foreknowledge never removed difficulties from her path. It did, indeed, strengthen and enlighten her, but the victory was still to be won by many a hard struggle.

Anne Catherine's labors in vision bore reference to the nuptial ornaments of a maiden betrothed to a royal consort. All that a careful, judicious mother would do to prepare her child for such an affianced, was precisely what she did in her visions. She got all things ready as in common and ordinary life, but with a far more elevated significance and altogether different results. She prepared the soil, sowed the seed, rooted out the weeds, gathered the flax, soaked, hatchelled, spun, and wove it; lastly, she bleached the linen destined for the bride. After this she cut out, made, and embroidered the numerous pieces according to their varied signification. These spiritual labors were typical of the weariness, mortification, and self-victories of her daily life. Every stitch was symbolical of some pain patiently borne which increased her merits and helped her on to her end.

An imperfect act of virtue appeared in her vision as a defective seam or a piece of embroidery that had to be taken out and done over. Every act of impatience or eagerness, the slightest failings appeared in her work, as defects that had to be repaired or removed by redoubled exertions. Year by year these labors advanced from the simplest article of apparel to the festal robe of the bride. Each piece was finished off by some sacrifice and carefully laid away until the time of the marriage. The vision relating to this end became daily more extended. All the circumstances and influences that bore upon the Church at this epoch were therein depicted. All persons throughout the whole world, whether ecclesiastics or seculars, who either opposed or supported the Church's interests, were shown most clearly with their unanswered petitions, their unsuccessful enterprises, and their baffled hopes.

Anne Catherine's spiritual labors blended simply and naturally with her exterior life ; one never interfered with the other, and she herself was conscious of no difference between the two actions. They were but one and the same for her, since similar views and intentions ruled both, and both were directed to the same end. Her spiritual labor preceded her exterior actions as prayer those of a pious Christian. He offers his works to God for His greater glory and the acquisition of some virtue. As he is accustomed to renew his intention during the course of the day, to strengthen himself in his good dispositions and designs, so too was it one and the same thing for Anne Catherine to obey her mistress or her parents and to follow the instructions received in vision. Once she explained it, as follows :—

" I cannot understand how these visions are connected with my actions ; but it is in accordance with them that I either punctually perform, or carefully shun whatever occurs in the course of everyday life. This fact has always been very clear to me, although I have never met any one who could comprehend it. I believe the same happens to every one who labors zealously to attain perfection. He sees not the guidance of Almighty God in his own regard, though another enlightened from above may do so. This I have often experienced in the case of others. But, though the soul sees not the divine direction, yet she fails not to follow it as long as she obeys the inspirations of God made known to her by prayer, by confessors, Superiors, and the ordinary events of life. On whatever side I look, I see that humanly speaking my entrance into a convent is impossible; but, in my visions, I am ever and surely conducted thereto. I receive an interior assurance which fills me with confidence that God, who is all powerful, will lead me to the term of my desires."

When Anne Catherine had recovered from her illness, she went to a mantua-maker of Coesfeld, Elizabeth Krabbe, her good mother anxiously hoping that this contact with people of all classes would distract her a little and wean her from her desire of the conventual life. But God so ordered it that this very period of about two years should be the most tranquil of her life. She did not have to begin by learning. As she had formerly acquitted herself creditably of all her duties without prejudice to contemplation, so now her skilful fingers plied the needle, her mind turned toward other things. She could accomplish the most difficult tasks without the least mental application, her fingers moving mechanically. She at first took her place at the work-table with uneasiness, knowing well that it would be impossible to resist the visions that so suddenly came upon her; she was tormented by the dread of attract-

ing the attention of her companions. She begged God's
assistance, and her prayer was heard. The angel inspired
her with the proper answers when unexpectedly addressed,
and watched over her fingers to prevent her work from
falling. She soon became so skilled in her trade that to
the close of her life she was able to consecrate her nights
of suffering not only to prayer and labor purely spiritual,
but also to sewing for poor children and the sick without
applying either mind or eyes to the work.

We can readily believe that the rough field-labors of her
younger days demanding, as they did, greater physical
exertion, rendered it much easier for her to resist a profound absorption in vision than when quietly seated at a
table employed in things which cost little effort or attention.
Her whole soul was now rapt in her contemplations. They
seized upon her more vehemently than did the scenes from
Sacred History, since their subject was almost always her
own life and the task she was to accomplish. God showed
her what great things He operates in a soul called to
the religious life, and the grace needful to a weak, incon-
stant creature to arrive at her sublime end in spite of failings and infidelities. Filled with gratitude, she praised
the touching bounty of God, who lavishes His inestimable
gifts on certain chosen souls, and the greater became her
sorrow at the sad situation of the Church, in which the religious state with its holy vows seemed fast dying out.
This was all shown her to animate her to prayer, suffering,
and sacrifice for the preservation of these graces to the
Church ; to rouse her to greater ardor in following her own
vocation and offering herself as a perpetual victim to atone
for the ingratitude and contempt with which it was everywhere treated.

The Saviour showed her all He had done and suffered to

confer upon His Church the jewel of the religious state. He had placed it under the patronage and special care of His most pure Mother ; and, to enhance that Mother's glory, He had delegated to her the privilege of planting the different Orders in the vineyard of the Church and of re- forming them when necessary. It was to Mary that Anne Catherine presented one by one the nuptial garments as she finished them, to receive her approval or correction. When we recall Anne Catherine's custom of disciplining herself with thorns and nettles even in her fourth year when she saw little children offending God, we may perhaps form some slight idea of that love which now led her to indemnify Him for the infidelity of His unfaithful spouses. This desire increased in proportion as she more clearly understood the high dignity of the religious vows. When she reflected upon the merit and perfection communicated by vows to the most insignificant actions, she longed for the privilege of making them. She deemed a lifetime of labor and suffer- ing insufficient to purchase so high a favor ; therefore, the utter impossibility of at once accomplishing her desire had no power to daunt her noble soul, though her physical strength gave way under the constant pressure of interior suffering, and she became so ill that she was forced to give up her apprenticeship.

Her mistress, the mantua-maker, deposed the following before ecclesiastical authority, April 14, 1813 :

" I first knew Anne Catherine Emmerich when she was only twelve years old. She lived with her relative, Zeller Emmerich, in Flamske, parish of St. James, Coesfeld. It was from that situation she came to me at the age of fifteen to learn mantua-making. She was with me only about two years, as she fell ill, and before being quite recovered went to Coesfeld where she remained.

" Whilst in my house she conducted herself in the most exemplary manner. She was very industrious, silent, and reserved, always ready to do what she was told. She stayed with me only on work-days, Sundays and holy-days being spent at home. I never saw any fault in her, unless, perhaps, that she was a little particular in her dress."

When Dean Overberg, April 21, 1813, asked Anne Catherine if it were true that in her youth she had been particular about her dress, she answered :—

" It is true I always wanted to be dressed properly and neatly, though not to please creatures ; it was for God. My mother was often unable to satisfy me on this point. Sometimes I used to go to the water or before a looking glass to arrange my dress. To be clothed decently and neatly is good for the soul. When I went very early to Holy Communion I used to dress as carefully as if it were broad day; but it was for God, and not for the world."

CHAPTER IX.

ANNE CATHERINE FROM HER SEVENTEENTH TO HER TWENTIETH YEAR AT COESFELD.

Up to the present, Almighty God had directed Anne Catherine by extraordinary means to the religious state. Now she was to follow the ordinary way, to overcome those difficulties against which all that are so called have more or less to struggle. As long as her soul was immersed in the contemplation of the supreme excellence and dignity of that state, her desire of embracing it was equalled only by her sorrow at beholding its lamentable decadence and the efforts of its enemies to destroy it. Her interior trials consisted, for the most part, in her painful attempts to control her ardent desire and her ignorance as to how she could triumph over obstacles apparently insurmountable. God willed that she should experience the weakness of a soul thrown upon its own resources, that she should prove her fidelity amid darkness, aridity, and contradictions.

At the age of seventeen a new period began in her direction which lasted till her twentieth year. She resided at Coesfeld, working at her trade of mantua-making, hoping by strict economy to lay up a sum sufficient to gain her admittance into a convent. But this plan was never realized. Her small weekly earnings were often disposed of the very day they were received, for all that she made belonged to the poor. Her desire to enter a convent, though truly intense, equalled not her love for the needy for whom she never hesitated to despoil herself. One day she met an old woman in rags. Without a thought she took off one of her garments (the only one of the kind she possessed) to clothe the beggar. The more painful the privation in her neighbor's behalf, the more readily she embraced it, hoping by this to regain the fervor she feared she had lost during her sojourn at Coesfeld. The consolations she had once tasted in her devotions had been withdrawn, and she fancied that she had grown cold in the love of God. This thought greatly tormented her, especially when she found her usual practices of piety become difficult and painful. She attributed it to her own infidelity, and esteemed herself wholly unfit for the religious vocation. No penance, she thought, could expiate her faults, and, notwithstanding her repugnance, she multiplied her austerities and devotions. In confession she could not accuse herself of even the least negligence or consent to her sudden antipathy to spiritual things, yet her feeling of guilt was so great that she dared not approach the Holy Table as often as usual, a positive command from her confessor being necessary to overcome her dread. Thus did she struggle for three years, when God again inundated her mind with light, her heart with peace and joy.

Her family at this time annoyed her in many ways in their efforts to divert her from entering a convent. The mantua-maker, at whose establishment she worked, formed such an affection for her that several times she offered to remain single and share all she owned with her if she would only promise never to leave her, if she would lead with her a life wholly dedicated to the service of God. She never embarrassed her young work-woman by indiscreet curiosity nor restrained her in anything. She was pleased when other young girls came to ask her advice in their practices of piety, hoping that Anne Catherine would look more favorably on her proposal when she saw in it an opportunity of doing good. But the latter could not be won over. She declined her benevolent offers with arguments so sweet and persuasive that the good understanding existing between them was never wounded.

It was more difficult to resist her parents who imagined she would lose her desire of the religious life if they could prevail upon her to take part in worldly amusements. Anne Catherine had always found it hard to refuse anything to her neighbor, and how could she continually repulse those good parents when they urged her to go to a dance or elsewhere with her brothers and sisters ? Twice she yielded a reluctant consent hoping by this concession to secure herself from further remonstrances on the subject. She says :

" Once my eldest brother insisted on my going with him to a dance. I refused. He fell into a passion and left the house. But he soon returned weeping bitterly and knelt down in our parents' presence to ask pardon. We never disagreed before nor since.

" But one day when I had allowed them to persuade me to go to such an assembly, I became so sad that I was almost in despair. My heart was far from the gay scene. I endured the torment of hell, and I was so strongly urged to quit the place that I could scarcely control myself. I remained only through fear of attracting attention. At last I thought I heard my Divine Spouse calling me, and I fled from the house. I looked around, and there I saw Him standing under a tree, sad and displeased, His face pale and bloody. He said to me : ' How unfaithful thou art ! Hast thou forgotten Me ? How hast thou treated Me ! Dost thou not recognize Me ?' Then I implored pardon. He told me what I should do to prevent sin ; viz., to kneel and

pray with extended arms, and to go where my presence would
hinder its commission.

"On another occasion I went, though reluctantly, to
the same kind of a gathering. But again I was drawn
away by an irresistible power, and I fled in spite of my
companions who tried to detain me. I thought the earth
would swallow me up. I felt as if I should die of grief.
Hardly had I passed the city gate, when a majestic lady appeared before me and in a severe tone thus addressed me:
' What hast thou done? What conduct is this? Thou
wast betrothed to my Son, but thou no longer deservest that
honor!' Then the youth approached, pale and disfigured.
His reproaches pierced my heart, when I reflected in what
company I had been whilst he was awaiting me, sad and
suffering. I thought I should die. I begged His Mother
to intercede for me, and I promised never to yield again.
She did so, I was forgiven, and I resolved never more to
allow myself to be enticed to such places. After accompanying me some distance, they disappeared. I was wide
awake, with full consciousness. They had spoken with me
just like ordinary people. I returned home sobbing, sad
unto death. The next day my friends reproached me for
having left them, but they never again pressed me to attend such amusements. About the same time, a little
book fell into my father's hands in which he read that parents are wrong in forcing their children to such places. He
was so troubled that he shed tears, saying: ' God knows
my intention was good!' I consoled him." Her parents'
opposition did not, however, cease; indeed, it became only
the more obstinate. At first sight it seems strange that
these poor peasants, who could entertain no hope of ever
seeing their daughter occupying other than a very humble
position in life, should have so strongly opposed her becom-

ing a religious; but when we reflect what a treasure she was to them, we can no longer be surprised. She was their joy and consolation. They had recourse to her in every doubt. Her wisdom and intelligence guided them in every emergency, they could not do without her. All that she undertook received a blessing; nothing succeeded so well when their favorite child was absent, and there was something so attractive about her that they could not bear to be separated from her for any length of time. She was attentive to their wants, she sought to gratify their every desire. They looked upon her as the support of their old age. Although she had for some years been from under the paternal roof, yet it was at so short a distance that daily intercourse had not been interrupted; but the cloister once entered would deprive them of her presence altogether. They knew her too well not to feel confident that, even were she in a relaxed community, she would live as a perfect religious, scrupulously observing her Rule. They would have been more pleased to discover in her an inclination for the married-state, as that would not preclude their frequent communication with her. They also feared that her poverty would be made a subject of reproach to their child in the miserable condition to which convents were then reduced. Actuated by these considerations, they implored her with tears, reproaches, and entreaties to abandon a design which they represented as the effect of caprice and presumption, or as a desire of escaping a life of poverty in the world. Her affectionate heart was crushed by such arguments, and often she knew not what to reply. Her only resource was prayer, from which she drew the strength and light necessary to carry out her resolution.

"My parents," she said to Dean Overberg, "spoke of marriage, for which I felt the greatest repugnance. Sometimes

I thought that my distaste to it arose from a dread of the duties it imposes. ' If it be the will of God that I should marry,' said I to myself, ' I ought to be willing to bear the burden.' Then I begged God to take from me that feeling of dislike, if it were His will that I should conform to my parents' desires. But my longing for the convent only increased.

" I laid my trouble before my pastor and my confessor, and begged their advice. Both told me that if there were no other children to take care of my parents, I ought not to enter religion against their wishes ; but that, as they had several sons and daughters, I was free to follow my vocation. So I persevered in my resolution."

It was a very remarkable fact that, although Anne Catherine had so often received in vision a positive call to the religious state, yet she had to recur to ordinary means for a confirmation of what had been extraordinarily communicated. As obstacles did not disappear miraculously, as they had to be surmounted by her own efforts, so neither did her supernatural illumination dispense her from the obligation of proving her vocation by the usual methods. She was called to religion for the good of the Church, she was to serve as a model for all in it, she was to show forth at a time in which the religious state was in absolute decadence, what fidelity a soul can practise who has chosen God for her spouse. For this it was that she was sent to the representatives of God, the priesthood of the Holy Church. Like the ordinary Faithful, her life was to be regulated by their judgment and decision, and by this way open to all, she was to attain the end marked out for her by God. This submission to the guidance and discipline of the Church was precisely the surest test of the truth of all that was extraordinary in her. We shall meet in her life numer

ous facts which prove that the graces bestowed upon
her were all destined to be placed under the guidance
of ecclesiastical Superiors to receive from them their seal
of authenticity.

She was in her eighteenth year when she received the
Sacrament of Confirmation from the hands of Gaspard Max
von Droste-Vischering, then suffragan Bishop of Münster.
This sacred ceremony was performed during the period of
her interior desolation ; hence, the call to receive the Sacrament was to her like a voice from heaven. She prepared
for it most carefully, trusting through its efficacy, to regain
that spiritual strength and joy for which she thought she had
been striving uselessly during the past year. At her
First Communion she had begged to be a good and docile
child ; now she asked for fidelity and love that she might
suffer until death for God and her neighbor. Again she
felt rise in her soul her former desire of burying herself in
some distant land to serve God unknown and alone. One
day, as she was conversing with an intimate friend, she said
that a true imitator of Jesus Christ ought like the saints
to quit all things for Him. These words made so deep an
impression on her hearer that she declared her readiness to
follow wherever she might lead in imitation of those servants
of God. Anne Catherine joyfully accepted the offer and together they planned their flight into solitude; but they soon
discovered that their pious design was not feasible.

The following is Anne Catherine's own account of her
Confirmation :—

" I went to Coesfeld with the children of our parish to
be confirmed. Whilst I stood at the church door with my
companions waiting my turn, I had a most lively sentiment of the sacred ceremony going on inside. I saw those
who came out after receiving Confirmation interiorly

changed, but in various degrees. They bore an exterior mark. When I entered, the Bishop seemed to me to be all luminous, a band of heavenly spirits around him. The chrism was resplendent and the forehead of the confirmed shone with light. When he anointed me, a fiery dart shot from my forehead to my heart, and I felt the strength emanating from the sacred chrism. I often saw the suffragan Bishop after, but I would scarcely have known him."

We can judge of the effects of this Sacrament in Anne Catherine's soul from her own words. She declares that from this time she had to endure frightful apparitions and chastisements from invisible agency for the faults of others. This expiation was often performed under circumstances apparently accidental : for instance, she was sometimes thrown down, wounded, bruised, or scalded by the awkwardness of a companion ; or, again, she was suddenly seized by some unaccountable malady which every one ridiculed. She bore their bantering with patient sweetness, she silently endured contradiction, blame, harsh words, and unjust accusations. Naturally hasty, the interior struggle to control her feelings, pardon her persecutors, and, at the same time, to bear the chastisement due to them, was great. In the Sacrament of Confirmation, she received the strength to fulfil her mission. We shall see later on how rapid was her progress in perfection.

The corporal maladies that from this epoch unceasingly attacked her, bore the characteristic stamp of expiation under the most varied forms. They had a special reference, known to God alone, to the offences for which they atoned. The more faithful Anne Catherine was to the direction given in her great vision, the more worthy was she of holding before God the place of the Spouse *par excellence*, the Church; but by the impression of the Sacred Stigmata of

Jesus Christ, her quality of representative reached perfect assimilation with her Beloved.

As in the sight of God she held the place of Holy Church, she was to bear the same wounds, incur the same dangers, undergo the same persecutions that menaced either the whole body or its individual members. At the age of four, she had intercepted the murderous axe hurled at the sleeping infant; now as a substitute she was to endure whatever threatened the Pope, ecclesiastics, or other influential personages, whose well-being in any way affected that of the Church. She expiated the spiritual maladies of such members by unspeakable sufferings; and she atoned by patience for those whose infidelity, negligence, or immorality would have drawn down upon the Church the chastisements of Divine Justice if not appeased by some such offering.

In Anne Catherine was wrought the same marvellous change as in the Apostles on the day of Pentecost when, as the catechism teaches, " They were so filled with the power of the Holy Spirit that they esteemed themselves happy to be judged worthy to suffer stripes, imprisonment, and even death for the name of Jesus Christ." One day she revealed the secret of her strength in the following words: —

" After my Confirmation, I could not refrain from petitioning to bear the punishment of every sin."

What a high idea of the sanctity and justice of God, what reverence for the Precious Blood, what horror of sin, what compassion for sinners, must have found a place in that heart which lived but to atone for its neighbor's faults!

Her love of penance ever increased. Her days were spent in labor, her nights in prayer and penitential exercises. From her infancy, though hiding it as much as possible from her family, she had been accustomed to the same; even now humility forbade her revealing all these prac-

tices to her confessor. Her mistress, the mantua-maker,
had however informed him of it. When he questioned
Anne Catherine upon the subject, she was covered with confusion ; she acknowledged all and afterward followed his advice
most exactly. He again declared to her that she was called
to the religious state. When she expressed her fear of
not being received into any convent without a dowry, he
recalled to her the power and goodness of God, and promised
to interest himself for her with the Augustinians of Borken.
He did so, and soon announced to her the welcome news that
she might present herself to the Superioress of the Borken
community, who was disposed to admit her on his recommendation. The Superioress did, it is true, receive her
most kindly ; but Anne Catherine was suddenly overcome
by mental anguish, tears choked her utterance. The sight
supernaturally revealed to her of the spiritual state of the
community, the Founder of the Order and even their holy
Rule being almost entirely unknown to the religious, overcame her. The Superioress in surprise asked the cause
of her tears, to which question Anne Catherine answered
truthfully, but evasively : "I weep over my want of veneration for St. Augustine. I am not worthy to become an
Augustinian ! " She took leave, saying that she would reflect on the matter ; but she could never resolve to return.

Dean Overberg speaks thus of her mortifications at this
time :—

" Anne Catherine practised more austerities in the world
than she did after entering the convent. She knew not at the
time that for such things her confessor's leave was necessary.
She wore chains and cords and a rough undergarment
which she had made herself of the coarsest material she
could find."

Among her other penances was that of the Stations of the

Cross, erected upon the confines of Coesfeld. It took at least two hours, pausing only a few moments at each station, to perform this devotion, since they were at a great distance apart, separated by intervening groves of fir-trees. Her labor began at daybreak and lasted till late in the evening; consequently, it was only at night she could make this exercise. She used to begin a little after midnight and, when the city-gates were closed, she had to climb over the broken wall. She was naturally timid and her retired life made her still more so. This nocturnal expedition was a very formidable undertaking for her, yet she never failed to perform it at the instance of the souls in purgatory, or on a command received in vision. No inclemency of the weather could prevent her. She was sometimes accompanied by a friend who shared her pious sentiments.

"Once," she says, "I went with my friend, about three o'clock in the morning, to make the Way of the Cross, and we had to climb the broken wall. On our return, we stopped awhile outside the Church to pray, when I saw the cross with all the silver offerings suspended from it leave its place and draw near to us. I saw it clearly and distinctly; my companion did not see it, but she heard the clinking of the silver objects. After this, I used to go behind the main altar to pray before the miraculous crucifix there, and I often saw the Saviour's figure inclining toward me. It made a strange impression on me."

On one occasion, she performed this devotion to ask for peace in a certain household.

"The hatred existing between a husband and wife at Coesfeld," she says, " afflicted me greatly. I often prayed for the poor people. On Good-Friday, after leaving the Holy Sepulchre, about 9 o'clock in the evening, I made the Way of the Cross for them. The evil spirit in human

form attacked me and tried to strangle me, but I cried to
God with my whole heart and the enemy fled. After
this the husband treated his wife less harshly."

She often experienced similar opposition from the demon.
She says :—

"I felt great compassion for a poor girl who had been
deceived by a young man, who afterward refused to make
her his wife. This great sin against God grieved me to
death. I formed a little plan with two companions to make
on Easter-night fifty-two turns around the cemetery of
Coesfeld for the souls in purgatory, begging them to help
the poor girl. The weather was bad, the night dark. We
went barefoot, I between my two companions. As we were
praying earnestly, the evil one in the form of a young man
rushed upon me and dashed me several times from side to
side. But I went on praying all the more fervently, for I
knew that prayer is hateful to the demon. I know not
whether my friends saw what I did, but they both screamed
with terror. When we had finished our rounds, we were
so exhausted that we could go no further. As we
returned home, the same apparition cast me head foremost
into a tan-pit twenty feet deep. My companions thinking
I was surely killed, again screamed, but I fell quite gently. I cried out to them : 'Here I am !'—and, on the instant, I know not how, I was drawn out of the pit and
placed on the ground. We began our prayers once more,
and now went on unmolested. On Easter Tuesday the
girl came full of joy to tell me that the young man had
consented to marry her. He did so in effect. Both are
still living (1818).

Another time, as a friend and myself were crossing a field
before daybreak in order to go pray, Satan under the appearance of a huge black dog came bounding toward us on a little

path we had to cross. He wanted to prevent our going any further. Every time that I made the sign of the Cross he re-
treated a short distance and stood still. He kept this up
full fifteen minutes. My friend was trembling with fright.
She caught me and tried to hold me back. At last I went
boldly forward, saying : 'We will go in the Name of Jesus!
We have been sent by God and what we are going to do is
for God! If thou wert of God, thou wouldst not try to hinder
us. Go thy way, we will go ours!' At these words, the
monster disappeared. When my friend recovered from her
fright, she exclaimed : 'Ah! why did you not speak that
way at first?' I answered : 'You are right, but I did not
think of it.' We then went on in peace.

"On another occasion, I was praying earnestly before the Blessed Sacrament, when the evil one threw
himself down so violently beside me on the kneeling bench
that it cracked as if split asunder. Cold chills passed over
me, I was so frightened ; but I continued praying, and he
soon left me."

For three long years, as before stated, Anne Catherine
patiently endured spiritual dryness. At the end of that
time the sun of consolation again shone upon her soul and
her intimate communication with the Celestial Spouse was
never afterward interrupted. Without such support she
would have been unable to fulfil the terrible expiatory task
of her life. O the mysterious ways of Divine Providence!
Anne Catherine now beholds her Redeemer almost constantly! She is enlightened, strengthened, consoled by
Him, the invisible Head of the Church! She receives
from Him the promise of assistance—but, at the same time,
all her efforts to enter a convent are futile! For three
years she had toiled to put by a sum for a dowry, and at
the end of that time she finds herself as poor as before,

for her Heavenly Betrothed sent her so many occasions of relieving the wants of her neighbor, that she could keep nothing for her own needs. But a still more serious obstacle stands in the way, one well calculated to crush her hopes, and that is her continued ill-health. She saw, indeed, in her visions, what she had to suffer and why she suffered; but the knowledge of these hidden causes was poor compensation for a life of daily sacrifice, for sickness so real, so sensible as to exhaust her vital energies. She could now with difficulty perform her usual duties; and when, after her unsuccessful attempt at Borken, she begged her confessor to speak for her to the Trappistines, of Darfeld, his reply was that he could not encourage one so weak and sickly as she to enter so severe an Order. On beholding her distress at this declaration, he consoled her by promising to ask admittance for her among the Clares, at Münster. These religious gave a favorable answer to his application, and Anne Catherine went to present her petition in person. But they informed her that, as their convent was poor and she could bring no dowry, they would admit her only on condition that she would learn to play the organ, and thus become useful to the community. She agreed to this, but her increasing debility made it necessary for her to return home awhile before beginning her new study.

The friend who accompained her to Münster on this occasion, made the following deposition before ecclesiastical authority, April 8, 1813 :—

"My name is Gertrude Ahaus, of Hammern, parish of Billerbeck. I have known Anne Catherine Emmerich for fourteen years. I became acquainted with her at Coesfeld, and we were very intimate. She told me of her desire to become a nun, and I went with her to the Clares at Mün-

ster in which community I had two relatives. Her desire
was so great that, when I represented to her that
these houses would soon be everywhere suppressed,
she replied that if she could enter one although
with the certainty of being hanged eight days after, she
would still be too happy to do so. The most severe Order
was her attraction. I never saw any fault in her; she was
pious and upright. I had the greatest confidence in her.
Our conversations were always upon piety, and she instructed me in many things concerning the duties of a Christian,
relating traits from the lives of holy religious, St. Matilda,
St. Catherine, St. Gertrude, St. Clare, etc.

"She communicated on Sundays and feasts. When
she worked at our house, she used to kneel long in prayer
every evening. She had a particular devotion to the Five
Wounds of Jesus and to the three upon His Shoulder, from
which He suffered more than from all the others.

"She wore a red garment next her person. On Fridays
she fasted till mid-day, and if she could escape notice she
took nothing in the evening. She often went at night to
make the Way of the Cross and she spent Sundays and holy-
days in prayer.

"Her patience was wonderful. If I were sick, she consoled
me reminding me of the sufferings of Christ. Some said
it was through pride that she wanted to be a nun. But
Anne Catherine answered that she was pleased to be thus
spoken of, for her innocent Saviour also had been calumniated. She was prepossessing, kind to all, and very diligent.
She always worked hard at our house, and her conversation
did me much good. She was so generous that she gave away
all she had. She was frank and sincere in her words, although with most people she spoke but little."

We shall here give some other depositions made by Anne

Catherine's early companions concerning the period which forms the subject of the following chapter. They were made before Ecclesiastical Superiors in 1813 when the details of her life were collected. Their simplicity and truthfulness not only prove the wonderful benediction emanating from her, but they also present a striking and faithful picture of her. We shall give that of her eldest brother first, taken April 11, 1813 :—

"Anne Catherine Emmerich is my sister, and I am the eldest of the surviving children. She lived some years out of the family, but only at a short distance so that we saw her often. I always got along with her, although her disposition was like my own a little hasty ; but her earnest efforts to correct this defect were soon perfectly successful. She was by no means vain, though she liked to be well dressed. She kept aloof from parties and amusements of all kinds, and she was always respectful and affectionate to our parents.

"She spoke little on worldly things, but she was always glad to be able to instruct others on points of faith and morals. She often repeated the sermons she had heard or the lives of the saints, and tried by all means to make us love virtue. She was so kind-hearted that she gave away all she earned. She never allowed us to speak of our neighbors' defects, but often gave us sound admonitions on this score. When any one found fault with her, she said it was all true ; and, when we asked her how she could endure such injuries so sweetly, she used to answer : ' That is only what I ought to do. You can do the same if you try.' Much of her time was given to prayer. Long after the family had retired, she was still up reading or praying on her knees, her arms extended, and even when she worked she prayed.

"She fasted often, especially on days consecrated to the Sacred Passion. When we begged her to eat on account of her weak health, she replied that it was not necessary. She mortified herself in every way, and wore next her a robe of rough material. She strewed her bed with chips or thistles to do penance whilst she slept."

April 7, 1813, Clara Soentgen deposed :—

"Anne Catherine so distinguished herself among the other children at school that the master often told her parents that there was no question he could ask her which she could not answer, although she attended regularly only four months. She used to study during her leisure moments and whilst tending the cows. When the other children were playing, she sat off by herself with a book.

When she grew older she had to share the hardest labors; and even then, though worn out after the day, she often spent half the night reading pious books after her parents had retired. Sometimes they had to order her to bed. She used to instruct the girls among whom she worked as seamstress telling them the beautiful things she had read. She was sought after by many, but chiefly by the young who confided to her their secrets and asked her advice. On Sunday afternoons she used to persuade them, especially when she knew they were wandering a little from the right path, to make the Stations of the Cross with her, she saying the prayers aloud. She often rose at night, slipped barefoot from the house, and made the Way of the Cross. When the city-gate was closed, she used to climb the wall. Sometimes she fell, but she never received any injury. Sunday was her joyous day, the day on which she could confess and communicate. When several feasts followed in succession, her confessor allowed her to receive Holy Communion on each. She fasted the last three days of Holy Week, touching nothing until dinner on Easter Sunday. But even when fasting, she performed the most fatiguing labor."

Anne Gertrude Schwering, St. Lambert's, beyond Coesfeld, deposed, April 16, 1813:—

" I have been intimate with Anne Catherine Emmerich for about fifteen years, and I always saw in her great virtue. She was very pious, her conversation always turning upon the Holy Scriptures, the lives of the saints, or the truths of faith. She never spoke of the defects of others or of worldly things. She was assiduous in her employment, and knelt long every evening in prayer. She was indulgent toward all, generous as far as her means would allow, and she never complained. I never saw any fault in her."

Mary Feldmann, St. James's, district of Flamske, beyond Coesfeld, deposed as follows, April 11, 1813 :—

" At the age of fourteen I went to Anne Catherine to learn to sew, and we were on as intimate terms as the difference in our age permitted. I was with her over two years and I loved her much because she was so good. She taught me so patiently, in spite of my dulness. I judged of her piety by the numerous prayers she said during the day, and by her quiet and retiring manners. She was already up and praying when I awoke in the morning, and at night when I fell asleep she was still on her knees, her arms extended in the form of a cross. I often saw little pieces of wood lying crosswise on her bed. She used to speak frequently of the Offices of the Church and instruct me in my faith. She never talked about her neighbor and always told me never to say anything uncharitable of any one and to return good for evil. She gave all she had to the poor. She rarely had any money since it all went as fast as it was earned. She never attended assemblies and only went out on business."

CHAPTER X.

ANNE CATHERINE'S ATTEMPT TO LEARN THE ORGAN—
THREE YEARS AT THE HOUSE OF THE CHOIR-LEADER.

When Anne Catherine had regained strength sufficient
to resume her occupations, she made every effort to earn
enough to cover the first expenses that her project of
learning the organ would entail. The needle never left
her fingers during the day, and at night she plied the distaff
to be able to take at least some linen with her to the convent. God blessed her efforts. In the course of a year,
she put by twenty thalers (about 15 dollars) earned by
her sewing, and a good supply of fine linen. This appeared to her so enormous a sum that she would not have
dared to keep it for any other purpose than that of entering religion. Her parents, meanwhile, renewed their entreaties to dissuade her from leaving them, her mother tearfully
representing to her that, being almost constantly sick, she
could not hope to discharge the numerous and painful duties to which her poverty would expose her.

"My dear mother," would she reply, "even if things
turn out as you say, even if I do have to work as you pre-
dict, still I shall escape the dangers of the world."

But the good woman understood not such reasoning, since
her child was even then so estranged from the world that
she could hardly imagine a more complete separation possible. She ceased not, therefore, her earnest entreaties ;
but her daughter replied so sweetly, so tenderly, and yet
so firmly, that the poor mother had no words in return.

She desisted from seriously opposing her when she saw her settled in the family of the organist Soentgen, at Coesfeld.

A very important witness whom we shall often meet in the course of our narrative, Dr. Wesener, of Dülmen, tells us the following on this point:—

" I attended Anne Catherine's aged mother in her last illness. She often told me with tears that she had, even in infancy, perceived something extraordinary in her daughter, and had always loved her with particular affection. It was a great affliction to her that Anne Catherine, the eldest of her daughters, who should have been the consolation of her old age, desired so ardently to enter a convent. ' That was,' she said, ' the only grief she ever caused me. I cannot say the same of my other children !' When Anne Catherine was eighteen she was sought in marriage by a young man, the son of parents in easy circumstances. They greatly desired Anne Catherine's consent, for they knew her worth and skilful industry in spite of her delicate health. ' But,' said her mother, ' I could not part with her then. Her father's health was bad and two of my other children gave me much anxiety. I did not press her on that occasion. Some years later a still more eligible proposal was made her, and her father and I were very desirous that she should accept. It seemed to us highly advantageous. But she pleaded so earnestly against it that we had to yield assuring her, however, that we should never give her anything toward entering a convent. She had put by some pieces of linen, thinking that would facilitate her design ; but she was everywhere refused as too delicate. Then she obtained a situation at the organist Soentgen's of Coesfeld to learn the organ, hoping such an accomplishment would open to her the door of a convent. Soon, however, she saw her mistake, for she found in this family such poverty and distress that she sacrificed her little all to relieve them. She gave them her linen, seven or eight pieces worth about twenty-four dollars. After she had lived with them some time, Clara, the organist's daughter, also began to think of beco ning a nun." Let us hear Anne Catherine's own remarks on the subject :—

" As to learning the organ," she said to Dean Overberg, " there was no question of such a thing. I was the servant of the family. I learned nothing. Hardly had I entered the house when I saw their misery, and I sought only to relieve it. I took care of the house, I did all the work, I spent all I had saved, and I never learned to play."

She could, however, have learned most readily. Her ear was so delicate, her appreciation of musical harmony so keen, and her fingers so skilful that she could find nothing difficult. Sometimes she would say :

" When I listened to singing or the tones of an organ, nothing moved me so much as the consonance of the different notes. How charming, I cried, is perfect harmony ! Since inanimate creatures accord together so sweetly, why do not all hearts do the same ! Ah, how sweet this world would be if it were so !"

But God wished to initiate His chosen servant into harmony of a more exalted order than that of the musical world, into perfect conformity with His own most holy will. She was now to walk by paths very different from those for which her heart sighed. Her plan, so carefully matured, so well carried out, proved a failure with respect to her study of music. The idea as we have seen, was abandoned even before it was put into execution.

" Ah ! I learned in that house what hunger is ! " did she once say. " We were often eight days together without bread ! The poor people could not get trust for even seven pence. I learned nothing, I was the servant. All that I had went, and I thought I should die of hunger. I gave away my last chemise. My good mother pitied my condition. She brought me eggs, butter, bread, and milk which helped us to live. One day she said to me : 'You have given me great anxiety, but you are still my child! It breaks my heart to see your vacant place at home, but you are still my child!' I replied : 'May God reward you, dear mother! I have nothing left, but it is His will that I should help these poor people. He will provide. I have given Him everything, He knows how to help us all!' Then my good mother said no more."

In the most austere Order, Anne Catherine would not have practised poverty so rigorously as she did in the Soentgen family. The more she relieved their wants, the further did she remove from the end in view, the more was her hope of arriving thereat disappointed and crushed. She spent her small savings, she served without wages, she was in absolute want ; and yet it all led to nothing. No attempt was made to teach her anything ; but her confidence in God remained unshaken.

Speaking of this period, she says : "I used often to say to myself : ' How can I enter a convent now ? I have nothing, everything works against me!' Then I would turn to God and say : ' I know not what to do ! Thou hast ordained it all! Thou alone canst free me from it!'"

She was then shown in a vision what a rich increase her bridal ornaments had received from all these trials and unsuccessful efforts. She saw the fruits of her self-victory, patience, and devotedness wrought into garments of exquisite beauty ; she saw them daily enriched by her renunciation and charity ; and she was told that her prayers and tears, her struggles and privations, emitted sounds more agreeable to God than the organ's most harmonious strains. But was it in accordance with the dignity of her Betrothed that she should attain to the nuptial union by such means ? At this period, no attention was paid in convents to the signs of a supernatural vocation. Worldly advantages, external qualities, personal considerations decided everything, whence it followed that true religious were rarely met. It was this very indignity to the Divine Spouse that Anne Catherine was called upon to expiate. She had to open for herself in the most painful and humiliating manner access to a religious community in atonement for the slight put upon the religious vocation.

The organist Soentgen was grateful for Anne Catherine's disinterested charity and devotedness, and he promised to do all in his power to further her designs. He had a daughter of the same age, a skilful musician, who would be received anywhere. He resolved, therefore, to allow her to enter that convent only into which Anne Catherine would also be received, and his solicitude for his daughter's welfare gave strength to his resolution. He used to say to Anne Catherine: " My Clara shall not enter a convent without you. Convents are not so strict now as they used to be ; but if you are with Clara, you will keep her up to her duty."

The two young girls applied to several religious houses, but in vain. Some refused on account of their want of dowry, some would receive Clara alone. This was the case with the Augustinians of Dülmen who were in need of an organist. But Mr. Soentgen was true to his word. He would not permit his daughter to enter without Anne Catherine; so, at last, the religious reluctantly consented to receive her, too.

April 7, 1813, Clara Soentgen deposed, as follows, at

the request of the Vicar-General, Clement Auguste von Droste-Vischering (1):—

" Anne Catherine Emmerich lived with us nearly three years, and I noticed at meals that she always took what was most indifferent. She wore a coarse woollen garment next her person and under it a rough cincture, twisted and knotted, which she bound so tightly around her waist that the flesh became inflamed and swollen. When her confessor heard of it he forbade her to wear it. She told me that after obedience had deprived her of this cincture, there remained imprinted on the skin a mark like a red band. She used to go out alone in the evening to pray and on her return I noticed her skin all torn as if by briers. On being questioned, she was forced to acknowledge that she had disciplined herself with nettles. She once told me that a huge black beast often rushed upon her to frighten her from her prayer ; but she took no notice of him. Then he would hang his head over her shoulder, glare in her face with fiery eyes, and disappear. The same apparition appeared to her one morning on her way home after Holy Communion."

With regard to this incident and others of the same nature, we shall give Anne Catherine's own words :—

" Whilst at the Soentgen's I kept up my old habit of praying

---

(1) Clement Auguste von Droste-Vischering, Archbishop of Cologne, was borne in 1773 and died in 1842. He was ordained to the priesthood in 1797 and later became Coadjutor and Vicar-General of the diocese of Münster. In 1835 he was appointed to the Archbishopric of Cologne. His opposition to the Prussian laws respecting mixed marriages, his condemnation of writings favoring heretical tendencies. and his disavowal of certain professors of theology infected by heresy, aroused the animosity of the government against him. He was, accordingly, declared guilty of 'obstinacy and rebellion. Without formal process or investigation, the Archbishop was conducted by a military force to the fortress of Minden as States-prisoner, Nov· 20 1837. This proceeding roused the just anger of all good Catholics throughout Germany. In an able article, called " The New Athanasius," the great Goerres vindicated the rights of the Archbishop.

After an imprisonment of two years, Clement Auguste was honorably released. He resigned his position as Archbishop of Cologne and found at Rome, in the arms of the Holy Father, ample indemnification for the wrongs he had suffered. He repeatedly frustrated the intention of His Holiness to create him Cardinal. His death was announced to the Catholic world by Pope Gregory XVI. with a becoming eulogy.

Mgr. Clement Auguste was a hero of the faith who, by the splendor of his virtues, became a spectacle to men and angels. He formed one of the literary circle of Münster in the time of the Princess Gallitzin.—(Herder's Kirchen-lexicon·)

by night in the open air. As usual, Satan tried to frighten me from it by horrible noises; but, as I only prayed the more fervently, he used to come behind me under the form of a hideous beast, an enormous dog, and rest his head upon my shoulder. I kept calm, by the grace of God. I stirred not from my position, but I said: ' God is more powerful than thou ! I am His, I am here for His sake. Thou canst do me no harm !' I no longer felt afraid and the fiend vanished. He often seized me by the arm and tried to drag me out of bed, but I resisted with prayer and the sign of the cross. Once when I was ill, he attacked me furiously, opening his fiery jaws at me as if about to strangle me or tear me to pieces. I made the sign of the cross and boldly held out my hand to him : ' Bite that !' I said, and he instantly disappeared.

" One evening, Clara and I were praying for the poor souls. I said, ' Let us say some *Our Fathers* for your mother in case she needs them.' We did so earnestly. After each *Pater*, I said : 'Another, another !' As we went on in this way, the door opened and a great light streamed in. Several blows were struck upon the table, which frightened us both, especially Clara. When Mr. Soentgen came home, we told him of the circumstance, and he shed many tears."

" Often," continues Clara in her deposition, " after we had finished our prayers, never before, a pillow used to be pressed down upon our faces, as if to smother us, and re-peated blows were struck with the fist on Anne Catherine's pillow. Sometimes impatient at this annoyance, she would run her hands over the pillow, but discover nothing. No sooner had she again settled herself to sleep than the noise recommenced. This was often kept up till mid-night. Sometimes she arose and ran out into the garden

to see if she could discover any clue to the noise, but in vain.
It happened not only at our house but also in the convent
where, at first, I occupied the same cell with her.

" After we retired to rest we used to pray for the souls
in purgatory and once, as we finished our devotions, a
brilliant light hovered near our bed. ' See! see! the bright
light!' cried Anne Catherine to me joyously. But I was
afraid, I would not look."

Reverend James Reckers, Professor at the Latin School,
Coesfeld, was Anne Catherine's confessor. He deposed,
as follows:—

"I was for about nine months, just before her entrance
into the convent, the confessor of Anne Catherine Emmerich. She came to me sometimes out of confession to ask my
advice with regard to her vocation. She appeared to me
to be a person of great simplicity, uprightness, and goodness
of heart. I know nothing unfavorable of her, except that
her charity toward the poor sometimes led her to purchase
what she could not immediately pay for. I must say in her
praise that when able she assisted every morning at the
Holy Sacrifice, confessed and communicated on Sundays
and feasts, and that she was thought to be a very good, pious
person. On several occasions, when her hopes of being admitted into a convent were frustrated, she showed unvarying and edifying submission to the will of God."

CHAPTER XI.

ANNE CATHERINE RECEIVES THE CROWN OF THORNS.—
HER ENTRANCE AMONG THE AUGUSTINIANS, OF DÜLMEN.

When Anne Catherine had completed her bridal outfit by the practice of the most abject poverty and self-abnegation, the Heavenly Bridegroom Himself added to it the last and most precious jewel, the Crown which He had Himself worn on earth. One day about noon, during the last year of her residence in the Soentgen family, she was kneeling near the organ in the Jesuits' Church, at Coesfeld. Clara was by her side. Immersed in contemplation, she beheld the tabernacle door open and her Divine Betrothed issue from it under the form of a radiant youth. In His left hand He held a garland, in His right a Crown of Thorns, which He graciously presented to her choice. She chose the Crown of Thorns. Then Jesus laid it lightly on her brow; and she, putting up both hands, pressed it firmly down. From that instant, she experienced inexpressible pains in her head. The apparition vanished, and Anne Catherine awoke from her rapture to hear the clicking of the sacristan's keys as he closed the church. Her companion was wholly unconscious of what had happened. They returned home. Anne Catherine, suffering acute pains in her forehead and temples, asked Clara if she could see anything. The latter answered in the negative. But the next day, the forehead and temples were very much inflamed, although there was, as yet, no appearance of blood. That began to flow only in the convent where she tried carefully to conceal it from her companions.

As St. Teresa in her waking moments saw herself adorned with the jewels, the ring, and the girdle, received in vision, so too on days dedicated to the Sacred Passion the Thorny Crown was visible to Anne Catherine. She described it as composed of three different branches : the first was of white flowers with yellow stamens ; the second like the first, but with larger leaves ; the third was like the wild eglantine, or sweet-brier. In the fervor of her prayer, she often pressed it down upon her head, and each time she felt the thorns penetrating more deeply. The wounds began to bleed in the convent and, at times, the red punctures were visible through the soaked bandages. The religious thought them mildew stains on the linen, and asked for no explanation. Once only did a sister surprise her wiping the blood from her temples, but she promised secrecy.

The moment was approaching for Anne Catherine to attain the long-desired end. The circumstances attending it were, in the sight of God, the most suitable termination to her persevering and laborious efforts, a proof of the fidelity with which the Bridegroom had waited for the bride. Some days before she bade adieu to the world, she repaired for the last time to Flamske to take leave of her parents. She thanked them with tears for their affection toward her, and begged their pardon and that of the rest of the family for the pain she gave them in following her vocation. Her mother replied only by tears. Her father, usually so indulgent, was quite overcome at the prospect of losing his child. When she humbly asked a little money for her journey, he answered bitterly: " Were you to be buried to-morrow, I should willingly defray the expenses of your funeral; but you shall get nothing from me to go to the convent."

In tears, poor, despoiled of everything, but interiorly

joyful, she quitted Flamske to follow the call of God. Next
day she and Clara were to start for Dülmen some leagues
distant from Coesfeld. But, at the last moment, fresh difficulties arose. The organist Soentgen needed ten dollars
and he could get the loan of this sum only on condition of
Anne Catherine's going his security. He explained his
embarrassment to her and ceased not his importunities until
she, trusting to Divine Providence, gave her signature for
the required amount. She had no money and only what
was absolutely necessary in the way of clothing. This with
her scanty bedding was packed in a wooden chest into
which her mother had secretly slipped a piece of linen for
her beloved child. When the latter discovered it, she would
not keep it, but gave it to Clara Soentgen in gratitude for her
admission to the convent. This generous act was richly rewarded. The mysterious book of prophecies was restored to
her, and she took it with her to Dülmen.

Never since its foundation had there entered this convent a maiden so poor in earthly goods, so rich in spiritual
treasures. She humbly begged the Reverend Mother to receive her as the last and least in the house and to employ her
in whatever she saw fit; but her gentle and retiring manners
could not calm the general discontent at the reception of a
subject so poor and, besides, in bad health. The very fact
of her asking such a favor proved, as was thought, her
audacity. Agnetenberg, the Augustinian convent of Dülmen, founded toward the middle of the fifteenth century (1)

(1) The Act of Foundation, still extant, runs as follows: "In the year of Our Lord
Jesus Christ, 1457, Hermann Hoken and Margretta, his lawful wife, gave this house and
its dependencies to be forever a house of religious Sisters. In consequence thereof the
Burgomaster and City-Council of Dülmen wrote to the Sisters of Marienthal, Münster,
to beg their acceptance of the above-named house and to send hither three religious to
begin the work. Margretta Mosterdes was sent as Superioress, and with her came Gertrude Konewerdes and Geiseke Tegerdes. Hermann Hoken and his wife Margretta,
named above, gave the house as a free gift to them and their successors that it might
be forever a house of religious, to the glory of God and the honor of Mary, His Mother.
The donors, with their respective parents, as also Mette, deceased first wife of the aforesaid Hoken, are to share in the good works performed therein at all times, especially
on the anniversary of the death of each of the aforesaid persons. Their patronal feasts

had received its first religious from the convent of **Marien-thal**, Münster. It remained up to the time of its suppression, under the spiritual direction of the Augustinian Canons of Frenswegen, and toward the last it was under the Canons of Thalheim, near Paderborn. It had always been in very straitened circumstances, and during the Seven Years' War it was in great distress. The community would have been forced to disperse, were it not for the alms of the people of Dülmen. Their circumstances did not improve with time. The convent was never again able to provide for the wants of its inmates, or to restore community life in its perfection. The religious supported themselves individually, some by their dowry, others by their labor. They who had not these resources, or who received no help from strangers, fared badly enough.

Under the spiritual direction existing at the time of Anne Catherine's entrance, the convent of Agnetenberg shared the same fate as most of the poor female cloisters throughout the whole country of Münster at that period. The Rule was no longer punctually observed, in truth, it was almost forgotten. The cloister, once so rigorously closed, was now thrown open to all visitors without distinction; the peace and silence of a religious house no longer reigned. The Sisters lived as persons whom chance had thrown together, each as best she could, rather than as members of a religious community strictly bound by vows and rules to a life of perfection. Custom and necessity indeed still kept up a certain order and regularity; but it was the habit

are, likewise, to be kept with the Masses and vigils as they occur in the calendar. In the year of Our Lord, 1471, the Saturday in the octave of St. Servias, Bp., the above-named religious house was solemnly cloistered according to the Rule of their holy Father and Patron, St. Augustine. The above-mentioned Margretta Mosterdes, Mother Superioress, and five other Sisters received the Rule and bound themselves to enclosure, to serve God, the Author of salvation, in all purity and the observance of the Commandments and doctrines of Jesus Christ, Our Redeemer. On the same day and year, four other Sisters were admitted to live outside the enclosure according to the Rule.

alone and not the spirit of religion that distinguished the inmates from their fellow-Christians in the world. Anne Catherine was introduced by Almighty God into the midst of this relaxation that she might attain the highest religious perfection ; but these unfavorable surroundings were to be no more an obstacle to that end than the fruitless attempts she had hitherto made to effect her entrance. Her expiatory mission had this one peculiar characteristic : all that might be for another an occasion of sin and damnation, became for her a means of proving her fidelity to God. The decadence of conventual discipline, the loosening of the bond of obedience, the absence of enlightened direction, in a word, all the miseries of communities at this period, miseries which called down the sentence of universal suppression upon them, became for Anne Catherine so many means of reaching perfection ; they did but arouse her zeal in the service of her God.

We now turn to a new page in her prophetic book. The vision of the espousals familiar to her from her sixteenth year and by whose direction she labored at her spiritual dowry, takes a new character. She sees herself in the house of the Bridegroom or, as she was accustomed to express it, in the Nuptial House, and thither also her bridal outfit was removed. She entered the convent with an empty purse and a scanty wardrobe, and her poverty, though dear to God, drew upon her the contempt of the nuns at large, who little knew that by this very treatment they were opening for the poor peasant-girl the door of the inner chamber of the Spouse. She no longer lives in the symbolical pictures which hitherto guided her, but really in a house of God, a religious house, in the midst of which He Himself dwells in the Most Holy Sacrament. From the tabernacle He calls upon the religious to serve Him by day and by

night, in the holy Office and ceremonies of the Church;
thence He regulates by the monastic constitutions not
only their various practices of piety and mortification, but
even their daily occupations. He notes every step, every
look, every gesture, in a word, their whole life, upon which
He stamps the seal of consecration to His service. Anne
Catherine saw all this most clearly. The higher her estimation of the incomparable dignity of such a life, the more
sensitive was she to each infraction of the Rule, every indi-
cation of indifference, indolence, or worldliness; and in
corresponding proportion did she deem herself unworthy
of so great a dignity. She indulged in no figure of speech
when, on her entrance, she asked the Superioress to be
treated as the last and least of all. We shall see that, by
Almighty God's permission, her petition was fully granted.

CHAPTER XII.

ANNE CATHERINE'S NOVITIATE.

Anne Catherine passed her first months in the convent as a postulant in the secular dress, she and Clara Soentgen occupying the same cell. She had no security of being permitted to remain in the community, but God gave her during this time strength sufficient to render herself useful. She earned, besides, by her needle sufficient to supply her few necessities and to defray the expense of her reception to the habit. She thus escaped being sent away under the plea of uselessness, and on Nov. 13, 1802, she was clothed with the habit of the Order and formally admitted to the novitiate. The worst cell in the house was assigned her. It had two chairs, one without a back, the other minus a seat; the window-sill served as a table.

" But," she declared years after, " that poor cell of mine appeared to me so well furnished, so grand, that it was to me a perfect heaven !"

We can readily imagine what the spiritual training of novices would be in a community in which the exercises employed in happier times for this end had fallen into disuse. Anne Catherine sighed for the humiliation and obedience prescribed by the Rule, but there was no one to impose them. She knew that the humility that springs from obedience is infinitely more efficacious and meritorious than self-imposed penance. But such occasions of meriting would never have been hers had not her Divine Betrothed intervened as Master to conduct His pupil to the highest perfection, and this He did precisely by those very circumstances which seemed so unfavorable to spiritual progress. Everything was to be a means of attaining this end and, in the same measure, a means of advancing the glory of God and the good of His Church. A prudent mistress, one experienced in the spiritual life, would soon have discovered her novice's sublime vocation and would have directed her in accordance with it, tolerating in her no imperfection, no defect. Anne Catherine was naturally hasty. She had a keen sense of injustice, and resented it accordingly ; but to the mortification of these dispositions she could not attain without proper direction. Almighty God, however, furnished the occasions for self-victory in these very points. From the beginning of her novitiate, He permitted her to be unjustly suspected, accused, reprimanded, and penanced, all which she bore without murmur, excuse, or reply.

We shall cite one instance among many of the kind. The convent possessed but a slender revenue from its lands ; and in order to increase its funds, it boarded for a trifling sum a few poor French nuns, émigrées, and an old gentleman, the brother of the Superioress. The nuns, learning by chance that the old gentleman paid less than they, grew dissatisfied and accused the Superioress of injustice. Then the question arose as to how the nuns had come by this information. No Sister, of course, acknowledged herself guilty, and so the blame fell on the unfortunate novice, who was known to take a lively interest in the destitute religious banished on account of their profession. Anne Catherine could say most truthfully that she knew not what either party paid and, consequently, she had nothing to reveal on the subject. But this was of little moment in the estimation of her accusers. She was reprimanded by the Superioress in full Chapter and she underwent the penance imposed. At once there arose loud complaints in the community against the galling ingratitude, as they styled it, of this miserable peasant-girl. The innocent victim of all this clamor had to bear not only unjust suspicion and severe punishment, but she endured also the bitterness of having been, although involuntarily, the cause of such uncharitableness. There was no one in the house to whom she might unburden her heart, no one to pour into her wound one drop of consolation. She overcame her feelings so far as not only to forgive them who had injured her, but also to render thanks to God for what she tried to look upon as a merited chastisement. The effort was, however, too trying on her delicate sensibilities. She fell seriously ill and recovered but slowly.

About Christmas, 1802, she felt around her heart acute pains which prevented her attending to her customary duties. In vain did she struggle against her sufferings, they did but increase ; it was as if she were being pierced by sharp arrows and she was, finally, obliged to keep her bed. In her humility, she dared acknowledge neither to herself nor to others the real cause of her malady, although she knew it from a vision vouchsafed her at the time of her clothing. The signification of the ceremony, as well as of every article of the religious dress, had been shown her. She had, in consequence, received it with deep respect and gratitude. St. Augustine, patron of the Order, had shown her his heart burning with love, had clothed her with the habit, accepted her for his daughter, promised her his special assistance. At this sight so great a fire was enkindled in her breast that she felt herself more closely united to the community than with her own blood-relations. The significance of the religious dress became then as real to her as the dress itself. She was actually conscious of the spiritual union it established between her and the rest of the sisterhood. It was like a current flowing through the whole body, but ever returning to herself as to its source. Her heart had become, so to say, the spiritual centre of the community. Hers was the terrible mission of enduring the wounds inflicted upon the Heart of the Bridegroom by the sins and imperfections of its members. She could advance but slowly in this way, for love did not render her insensible to pain and sorrow, and every infraction of vows or rules pierced her heart like a burning dart.

No one understood her state. The physician of the convent was called in. He pronounced her sufferings purely physical. It was the first time in her life that she had been subjected to medical treatment. In her own home certain simple herbs, of whose virtues she herself possessed the knowledge, and a little repose quickly wrought a cure; no one thought of having recourse to medicine. Now it was very different. The Rule imposed it as a duty to declare herself sick and to receive the care of the physician appointed. Although knowing her illness to be purely spiritual, to be relieved only by spiritual means, yet, as an obedient novice, she could refuse no remedy offered her. She quietly allowed herself to be treated, happy in having an occasion to practise obedience.

That her submission might be still more perfect, Almighty God permitted the evil spirit to lay all kinds of snares for her. He appeared as an angel of light, and exhorted her to return to the world. It would be sinful, he reasoned, to desire longer to bear a burden above her strength, and he pictured to her what she would have to endure from the Sisters, etc. But the sign of the cross put the tempter to flight even before he had finished his wily speech.

Again he sought to rouse her resentment and make her
murmur against Superiors, or he tried to inspire her with
such fear of them as to force her to leave the convent. One
night he threw her into an agony of terror. It seemed to
her that the Superioress and the Novice-Mistress suddenly
entered her cell, reproached her in unmeasured terms,
declared her absolutely unworthy of their holy vocation,
and ended by saying she should be expelled from the community. Anne Catherine received their rebukes in silence,
acknowledged her unworthiness, and begged them to be
patient with her. Then the angry nuns left her cell, abusing her as they went. The poor novice wept and prayed
till morning, when she sent for her confessor, told him
what had occurred during the night, and asked him what
she should do to appease the Superioress. But on inquiry,
it was proved that neither the Superioress nor any other
Sister had entered her cell at the time specified. The confessor saw in it an attack of the evil one, and the novice
thanked God for the deep feeling of unworthiness by which
she had overcome the tempter.

After some weeks the physician's visits were discontinued.
The community thought her cured; but, in reality, it
was not so. She was so weak and infirm that again the
hue and cry was raised against the convent's burdening itself by the profession of such a member. "Send her away
at once," they said; "do not incur the obligation of keeping
her altogether." These whispers, although perhaps at the
other end of the building, were heard by the poor invalid
as if spoken in her cell. All the little plots, all the thoughts
of her Sisters against her, pierced her soul like so many
fiery sparks, like so many red-hot spears, wounding her to
the quick. The gift of reading hearts which she possessed
from her infancy, but which had never given her pain

among the simple peasants, who all loved and reverenced her, now became for her a source of exquisite suffering. All this was in accordance with the designs of God. He willed that only by the perfection of virtue, should she surmount the obstacles she was to meet in her task of expiation. She saw the passions of her fellow-sisters, inasmuch as she had to struggle against them by her own prayer and mortification ; and by humility, patience, and charity she had to disarm those who opposed her making the religious vows. If a word of complaint, a sign of dissatisfaction escaped her, she tearfully implored pardon with expressions of sorrow so touching that the Sisters became more kindly disposed toward her. Then she would run before the Blessed Sacrament and beg for strength to perform her duties. "She redoubled her efforts to render herself useful and stilled the anguish of her heart with these words : "I will persevere, even if I should be martyred !"

On a certain Friday in February, 1803, as she was praying alone before the Blessed Sacrament, there suddenly appeared before her a cross, eight inches in length, on which hung an image of the Saviour covered with blood.

"I was," she says, "greatly agitated by this apparition. I flushed and trembled, for I saw everything around me and the bloody crucifix before me. It was not a vision, I saw it with my bodily eyes. Then the thought struck me that by this apparition God was preparing me for extraordinary sufferings. I shuddered!—but the pitiable sight of my blood-stained Jesus banished my repugnance, and I felt strong to accept even the most fearful pains if Our Lord only granted me patience to bear them."

The presentment was soon realized. The gift of tears was bestowed upon her that she might weep over the out-

rages offered her Divine Betrothed and find in it for herself a fruitful source of humiliation. Whenever anything
was presented either to her corporal or mental sight which
called for supernatural sorrow, it was impossible for her to
restrain her tears. When she considered the sufferings
and tribulations of the Church, when she saw the Sacraments conferred or received unworthily, her heart was so
wounded that torrents of bitter tears flowed from her eyes.
If she beheld spiritual blindness, false piety veiling evil
dispositions, grace despised or obstinately resisted, the truths
of faith set aside, her tears flowed involuntarily, bathing
her cheeks, her neck, her breast almost unknown to herself. In the chapel, at Holy Communion, at meals, at
work, at community exercises, her tears would gush forth
to the extreme displeasure of the religious. During Mass
and Holy Communion, all eyes were turned upon her.
This was all the notice she received, at first ; but, as her
tears became more abundant, she was taken aside and reproached for her singular behavior. She promised on her
knees to correct ; but soon, next day perhaps, it was remarked that during Mass even the kneeling-bench was
wet with her tears, a fresh proof as it was thought that
the novice was still indulging wounded self-love. Again was
she reprimanded, again was she penanced ; but her humility and submission were such that the Superioress was
forced to acknowledge the poor novice's tears a greater
mortification to herself than to others. They were, in the
end, ascribed to constitutional weakness and not to discontent or caprice. As to Anne Catherine, so far from looking upon them as supernatural, she anxiously examined
whether they did not proceed from some secret aversion to
the Sisters. She dared not decide for herself, and disclosed
her fears to her confessor, who quieted her with the assurance

that they sprang not from hatred but from compassion.

She hoped that time would mitigate the intensity of her feelings and that her tears would cease to flow. But this was not the case; they rather increased than diminished. In her distress she applied to the other confessors appointed for the religious, but from all she received the same answer.

Dean Overberg says on this point :—

" Anne Catherine so tenderly loved her Sisters in religion that she would willingly have shed her blood for them individually. She knew that several were against her, yet she did all in her power to propitiate them and rejoiced when any one asked her assistance. She hoped by kindness to win them over to their duty.

" God permitted that she should not be appreciated by the Superioress and Sisters who saw in all that she did either hypocrisy, flattery, or pride, and they failed not to reproach her openly. At first she tried to justify herself; but afterward she merely replied that she would correct. She wept over the deplorable spiritual destitution of the religious; for whether at exercises of piety or other conventual duties, it was ever before her eyes.

" The tears she shed during the Holy Sacrifice were particularly displeasing to the nuns, and they held little whispered councils as to the most effective means of curing her of what they termed her sloth and caprice. All this added to her desolation, since she clearly knew what was passing in their inmost thoughts.

" She assured me that she knew all that was said or planned against her. ' I saw then even more clearly than I do now.' she said (April 22, 1813), ' what passed in souls, and sometimes I let them see that I knew it. Then they wanted to know how I came by the knowledge, but I dared not tell them, and they straightway imagined that some one had told me. I asked my confessor what I should do. He told me to say that I had spoken of it in confession and to give no explanation on the subject."

On another occasion, she again alluded to her gift of tears :—

" I would willingly have given my life for my sister-re-ligious and, therefore, my tears could not be restrained when I saw them so irritated against me. Who would not weep at seeing himself a stumbling-block in the house of peace, among the chosen of God ? I wept over the poverty, the misery, the blindness of those whose hard hearts languished amidst the superabundant graces of our Holy Redeemer."

When, in 1813, Ecclesiastical Superiors demanded the tes-timony of the community of Agnetenberg concerning Anne Catherine, the Superioress, the Novice-Mistress and five of the other religious unanimously deposed as follows :—

" Anne Catherine was affable and cordial, very easy to deal with, humble, condescending, and exceedingly pre-venting. In sickness she was admirable, ever resigned to the will of God. She quickly and cheerfully forgave every offence against her, always asked pardon if she herself were in fault, never harbored ill-will, and was always the first to yield."

And Clara Soentgen told Dean Overberg :—

" Anne Catherine was never so happy as when serving the Sisters. They might ask what they pleased, she never refused; she gladly gave them even what she needed most herself. If she had a preference, it was only for those that she knew disliked her."

Dean Rensing of Dülmen deposed, April 24, 1813 :—

" I had been told of Anne Catherine's having rendered great services to one of the Sisters during an illness, and I asked her why she did it. She answered :—' The Sister had sores on her feet and the servants did not like to wait on her as she was hard to please. I thought it a work of mercy, and I begged her to let me wash her blood-stained bandages. She had the itch, too, and I used to make up her bed, as the servants were afraid of catching her disease. But I confided in God and He preserved me from it. I knew that this whimsical Sister would not thank me when she got well, that she would again treat me as a hypocrite as she had often done before. But I said to myself, ' I shall have so much the more merit before God,' and so I went on, washing her linen, making her bed, and taking the best care I could of her."

Anne Catherine understood so perfectly the signification of the religious vows, she so ardently longed to practise obedience in all things, that the fact of not being exercised in it by the commands of Superiors was a very grievous trial to her. She often begged the Reverend Mother to command her in virtue of obedience that she might practise her vow. But such requests were looked upon as singular, the effects of scruples, and she received no other reply from the weak and indulgent Superioress than : " *You know your duty*," and thus she was left to herself. This want of training afflicted the novice even to tears. It seemed to her that the blessing attached to the religious state was not for her, since blind obedience to Superiors, so pleasing to her Divine Betrothed, was not permitted her.

In 1813, the Superioress deposed as follows :—

" Sister Emmerich cheerfully and eagerly fulfilled the injunctions of obedience, especially when enjoined upon her individually."

The Novice-Mistress says :—

" She practised obedience perfectly. Her only regret was that Reverend Mother laid no commands upon her."

If occasions of practising obedience were for the most part wanting, she tried to supply the loss by her interior submission and untiring attention to regulate all her actions according to the spirit and letter of the Rule. She would not live in religion in the mere practice of the still existing observances; she aimed at moulding her whole interior and exterior life by its animating principle. With this view she made it a careful study, and so great was her respect for it that she read it only on her knees. Sometimes whilst thus engaged, the light by which she was reading would be suddenly extinguished and the book closed by an invisible power. She knew well by whose agency this was affected so, quietly relighting her candle, she set to work more earnestly than before. These attacks of the demon grew more sensible and violent, and amply indemnified her for the want of other trials. If he maltreated her for seriously studying her Rule, she applied thereto more assiduously ; if he excited a storm against her in the community, it only gave her an occasion to practise blind and humble obedience as the following incident will prove :

A rich merchant of Amsterdam had entered his daughter as a boarder in the convent. When about to return home, the young lady presented a florin to each of the nuns. But to Anne Catherine, for whom she had a special affection, she gave two, which the good novice immediately handed over to her Superioress. A few days after the whole house was up in arms. Anne Catherine was cited before the Chapter, accused of having received five thalers from the young Hollander, of giving only two to the Reverend Mother, and of having handed over the other three to the

organist Soentgen, who had just paid a visit to his daughter.   They appealed to her conscience, and Anne Catherine truthfully declared all that had passed.   The nuns redoubled their accusations, but she firmly denied having received five thalers.   Then sentence was passed upon the
poor novice.   She was condemned to ask pardon on her
knees of each Sister.   She gladly accepted the undeserved
penance, begging God to grant that her Sisters might pardon not only this imaginary fault, but all they saw displeasing in her.   Some months after the merchant's
daughter returned, and the novice asked the Superioress to
inquire into the affair.   But she received for answer to think
no more of what was now forgotten.   She obeyed and reaped
the full benefit of the humiliation.

   We see by this circumstance how prone these imperfect
religious were to dislike and suspect their innocent companion, and also how quickly the storm was lulled even
when at its height.   Their novice's demeanor produced
impressions so varied upon them that we can scarcely wonder that, in their inexperience, their obtuseness to all beyond their every-day existence, they sometimes went astray.   And, although Anne Catherine's sweetness and
patience under such trials, her earnestness in begging pardon, could not fail to soften even the most exasperated,
yet new suspicions, fresh charges soon arose against her.
There was in the richness of her supernatural life, in the
varied and wonderful gifts imparted to her, in a word, in
her whole being something too striking to remain hidden,
or to allow her to tread the beaten paths of ordinary life
like the other religious.   However great the simplicity and
modesty of her bearing, there shone about her a something
so holy, so elevated, that all were forced to feel, though
they might not acknowledge her superiority; consequently,

they regarded her as singular, tiresome, and disagreeable.

Anne Catherine was drawn to the Blessed Sacrament by an irresistible force. When some errand took her through the church, she fell as if paralyzed at the foot of the altar. She was ever in a state of contemplation and interior suffering which, in spite of every effort on her part, could not be wholly concealed. To all around her she was simply a mystery, to some quite insupportable.

Clara Soentgen deposed on this point as follows :—

"Anne Catherine did her best to conceal the attraction which impelled her to extraordinary devotion ; but nothing could escape me, I knew her so well. I often found her in the chapel kneeling or prostrate before the Blessed Sacrament. She was so powerfully attracted to contemplation that, even in the company of others, I could see that she was quite abstracted. She was much given to bodily mortification. At table I used to notice that she took the worst of everything, leaving dainty dishes untouched, or passing her share to her neighbor, especially if the latter had any ill-will toward her, and she was so pleased when a chance presented itself to do this that I was filled with astonishment."

The Novice-Mistress says :—

"Several times during Anne Catherine's novitiate, I removed little pieces of wood from her bed. She had put them there to render her rest uncomfortable, for she was much given to corporal mortification. I was sometimes obliged to make her leave the chapel at ten o'clock in winter and send her to bed ; otherwise she would have remained too long."

On various occasions, Anne Catherine herself spoke of her early days in the convent. Clement Brentano, who carefully collected all her communications and reduced them to writing, gives us the following :—

" From the very beginning of my novitiate I endured incredible interior sufferings. At times my heart was surrounded by roses and then suddenly transpierced by thorns, sharp points, and darts, which arose from my perceiving much more clearly than I do now every injurious thought, word, or action against me. Not one with whom I lived, no religious, no confessor, had the least idea of the state of my soul or the particular way by which I was led. I lived wholly in another world of which I could make nothing known. But, as on some occasions, in consequence of any interior direction, things appeared in me not in conformity with everyday life, I became a cause of temptation to many, a subject for injurious suspicion, detraction, and unkind remarks. These mortifying opinions and speeches entered my soul like sharp arrows. I was attacked on all sides, my heart was pierced with a thousand wounds. Exteriorly I was serene and cordial, as if ignorant of their cruel treatment ; and, after all, I really did not know much from without, for the suffering was all within. It was shown me in order to exercise my obedience, charity, and humility. When I failed in these virtues, I was interiorly punished. My soul appeared to me transparent ; and, when a new suffering assailed me, I saw it in my soul under the appearance of fiery darts, red and inflamed spots, which patience alone could remove.

" My condition in the convent was so singular, so perfectly abstracted from outward things that my companions can hardly be blamed for their treatment of me. They could not understand me, they regarded me with distrust and suspicion ; however, God hid many facts from them that would have perplexed them still more. As for the rest, in spite of these trials, I have never since been so rich interiorly, never so perfectly happy as then, for I was at peace with God and man. When at work in the garden, the birds perched on my head and shoulders and we praised God together.

" My angel was ever at my side. Although the evil spirit raged around me, although he heaped abuse upon me in the quiet of my cell and sought to terrify me by frightful noises, yet he could never harm me; I was always relieved in good time.

" I often thought I had the Infant Jesus in my arms for hours at a time ; or, when with the Sisters, I felt Him by my side and I was perfectly happy. I beheld so many things which roused feelings of joy or pain, but I had no one to whom I could impart them, and my very efforts at concealing these sudden and violent emotions caused me to change color frequently. Then the sisters said that I looked like one in love. They were, indeed, right for I could never love my Affianced enough, and when His friends spoke well of Him or of those dear to Him, my heart beat with joy."

CHAPTER XIII.

The year of novitiate drew to a close, but the community had not yet decided upon admitting the novice to her holy profession. The Novice-Mistress could in all truth render the following testimony of her charge : "I remark in her constant submission to the will of God, but she is often in tears. She will not say why, because she dares not; otherwise I see nothing in her that deserves censure."

This testimony in her favor did not, however, satisfy the community. When the Chapter deliberated as to whether she should be sent away or allowed to remain, no other reason could be assigned for her dismissal than that she would soon become incapable of labor, a burden on the house ; yet the Reverend Mother was forced to acknowledge that the novice was very intelligent, that she possessed skill and aptitude, and that she would certainly be of great use ; a declaration which drew from her opponents the avowal that she always comported herself as a good religious and that, after all, there was not sufficient reason for sending her home.

These obstacles removed and the day appointed for the ceremony, a new difficulty arose on the part of the novice herself. She had not yet redeemed the security given to the organist Soentgen for ten thalers, and she had good reason to fear being held responsible for the debt. She explained her embarrassment to the Reverend Mother, who applied to the gentleman in question. But he declared his inability to release Anne Catherine from her obligation, as he was unable to discharge his indebtedness. The community resolved not to allow the novice to make her vows until she had freed herself from her engagement. What was now to be done? Anne Catherine turned to God. We shall give her own words on this subject:—

"I had not a single cent. I applied to my family, but no one would help me, not even my brother Bernard. All reproached me as if I had committed a crime in going security. But the debt had to be cancelled before I could make my vows. I cried to God for assistance and, at last, a charitable man gave me the ten thalers. My brother used to shed tears at a later period over his hard-heartedness toward me.

"This obstacle being happily removed and the preparations for the profession almost completed, another difficulty sprang up. The Reverend Mother told Clara and myself that we were still in need of something for which we should have to send to Münster, entailing an expense of three thalers each. I had no money, and where was I to get any? In my distress, I went to Abbé Lambert, who kindly gave me two crowns. I returned joyfully to my cell where, to my great delight, I found six thalers lying on the table. I ran with the two crowns to my friend who, like myself, had nothing and knew not where to procure her three thalers.

"Three years after I was again in need of money. Each Sister had to provide her own breakfast, and I had nothing at the time to procure mine. One day I entered my cell, which was locked, and found two thalers lying on the window-sill. I took them to the Superioress, who allowed me to keep them.

"Eight days before the Feast of the Presentation of the Blessed Virgin, 1803, on the same day on which one year before Clara Soentgen and I had taken the habit, we made

our profession as Augustinians in the convent of Agnetenberg, Dülmen, and from that day we were consecrated
spouses of Jesus Christ under the Rule of St. Augustine.
I was in my twenty-eighth year. After my profession my
parents became reconciled to my being a religious, and my
father and brother came to see me and brought me two
pieces of linen."

The Abbé John Martin Lambert, whom we now meet for
the first time, formerly a vicar in the parish of Demuin,
diocese of Amiens, had been like many other good priests
forced to leave his country on refusing to take the famous
oath of the Constitution. With recommendations from the
Archbishop of Tours and the Bishop of Amiens, he went
in 1794 to Münster, obtained faculties from the Vicar-General von Fürstenberg and was appointed confessor with a
small allowance to the house of the Duke von Croy, who resided in Dülmen. In the convent of Agnetenberg, which
had its own confessor, the Abbé held also the office of chaplain, a post which conferred upon the possessor the right
of a lodging within the convent grounds. When Sister
Emmerich had charge of the sacristy she became acquainted with him; his piety and deep recollection in saying holy
Mass impressed her favorably and she conceived great
confidence in him.

The unsisterly treatment she experienced from her companions distressed her sorely and failing to make herself
understood by the ordinary confessor, she resolved to open
her heart to the Abbé and ask his advice and assistance.
But, as the good father knew little German, their communications were, at first, necessarily very restricted.
Nevertheless, the pious and enlightened priest soon acquired
an insight into his penitent's state, and felt bound in consequence to help as far as possible a soul so highly favored

by God. He engaged the confessor to permit her to communicate more frequently, even to command it when
through humility she wished to abstain. And he it was
who at dawn of day held himself in readiness to administer to her the Adorable Eucharist when her desire of the
Heavenly Manna made her almost swoon away. Though
very poor himself, he was ever willing to assist her when her
distress made her consent to accept an alms from him, and
on her side she honored him as her greatest earthly benefactor. Later on we shall see her returning, as far as she
was able, his unvarying kindness.

We may readily conceive Anne Catherine's sentiments
when pronouncing at the foot of the altar the solemn vows
to which she had so long aspired. The same zeal, the same
desire with which sixteen years before she had prepared
for her First Communion, marked her preparation for this
solemn occasion. Multiplied prayers and penances, trials
and anxiety had exhausted her strength during the days
immediately preceding her profession; yet upon the
joyful day itself, she appeared to be endued with new
vigor. The joy of her soul manifested itself in her exterior;
she was, as it were, all luminous. She understood the real
signification of the ceremony, she perceived the meaning of
the trials that had beset her path since her first call to the
religious state, and her heart overflowed with gratitude for
all that God had operated in her and by her up to that
moment. She saw herself clothed in the festal robes and
bridal ornaments over which for years she had untiringly labored according to the directions given in her great visions ;
every step, every self-victory, every sigh, was therein represented as a precious stone or an exquisite piece of embroidery. Now she saw how necessary all these trials had
been to prepare her for the nuptials at which her Divine

Betrothed assisted visibly with the saints of the Order of St.
Augustine.

As at baptism she had seen herself espoused to the Infant
Jesus by His holy Mother, so now it was by the Queen
of Virgins she was presented to her Betrothed. Whilst
her lips pronounced the words of holy profession, she
beheld her solemn consecration to God ratified in a
twofold manner. The Church Militant received her and
the Heavenly Bridegroom deigned to accept her from the
hands of Mother Church, sealing His acceptance by bestowing upon her His most magnificent gifts. She saw the exalted position in the Church to which the vows elevated
her; she highly appreciated the abundant graces bestowed
upon her and the dignity with which her quality of spouse in-
vested her, a dignity which she ever after regarded in herself with respect. The same thing happened to her as to a
pious candidate for Holy Orders. At the time of his ordination, his own soul became visible to him in all the splendor communicated to it by the indelible mark of the priesthood. Anne Catherine felt in what way she henceforth
belonged to the Church, and through the Church to her
Heavenly Bridegroom; as a consecrated gift she was
offered to God body and soul. Like Columba di Rieti,
Lidwina of Schiedam, and Blessed Colette, she understood the
spiritual signification of her different members, as a spouse
of God, and also their symbolical relation to the body of
the Church.

No inmate of Agnetenberg had the slightest suspicion of
these marvels, yet God willed that this day of spiritual nuptials should be for all supereminently a day of joy and peace.
Anne Catherine, though in blissful tears that would not be
kept back, exerted a gladdening influence on all her Sisters;
and her reiterated thanks for admitting her irrevocably

among them won even the most obstinate to smile upon her for that one day at least. A repast awaited the guests in the convent refectory, to which her beloved parents were invited after High Mass. The opposition of these good people and the suffering it had brought upon their daughter had had no other effect upon the latter than that of caus- ing her to pray most earnestly that God would grant them the grace to make the sacrifice He demanded of them. Her prayer was heard at last. They were so deeply affected by the sight of their child on this day, the day of her espousals, that, uniting in her sacrifice, they gave her to God with all their heart. They testified their joy in so many ways and showed so much affection for her that, to the end of her life, the remembrance of this solemnity was always one of the sweetest.

The year 1803 opened most disastrously for the Catholic Church in Germany. It would, doubtless, have been utter- ly annihilated were its founder and defender other than God Himself. As formerly He had permitted the destruction of His holy city and temple as a punishment for the infi- delity and apostasy of His people, so now the Church's powerful enemies were to be for her the instruments to separate the good from the bad grain. Whilst this sentence was being executed, whilst the " abomination of desolation" lasted, the Lord hid the holy things of His Church, as the priests of the Temple the sacred fire, until crime being ex- piated, it might be enkindled with greater brilliancy than before. The pits in which the sacred fire of the Christian Church was preserved were holy souls, few in number at this period. They hid 'neath the waters of tribulation those treasures which formed of old the delight and ornament of the Bride of Christ; treasures which were now abandoned by their custodians, pillaged and dissipated by those that ought to have guarded and defended them. Anne Catherine shared this task with a small number of faithful servants. The Lord made use of the fire of sufferings and the mallet of penance to make of her a vase, pure, strong, and sufficiently capacious to receive the incommensurable riches of the Church until the time for their restoration.

What now was the life that awaited Sister Emmerich in the convent ? The favorable impression of the festal day was soon effaced from the hearts of her Sisters, and the poor child became once more what she had ever been, the unwelcome intruder among them. Almighty God had, as it were, procured her an entrance into this convent by force ; and from the very first she had contracted in the eyes of the religious, by her poverty and ill-health, a debt she could never discharge. The habit had been given her in the midst of dissatisfaction, and now she had taken her vows almost in spite of general opposition. A vessel of election, God's chosen instrument, she is forever to be a stumbling-block, an object of aversion to those for whom she entertained so warm an affection. This she knew and felt at every moment, owing to her gift of reading hearts, and thus she was in her own person treated precisely as the religious state itself was treated at that epoch by too many of its members. She had, moreover, not the faintest hope of being able to restore the strict discipline of former times by training active young members to it; for, after her entrance, the novitiate was closed forever. She was the last to make the religious profession in the convent of Agnetenberg, and she knew both from the political aspect of the day and her own visions, that this spiritual family would shortly be dissolved never again to be reunited. How admirable are the ways of God! How contrary to those of the world! How different are the means that He employs from those of men! Anne Catherine combined, in a human view, qualifications eminently suited for rendering the highest services to the Church; but God demands of her no dazzling marks of loyalty. Incalculable sufferings, years of obscurity and humiliation, were the only remedies she was to apply to the deep wounds of His Spouse on earth. The further she advanced in her mission, the greater became her sufferings. We could scarcely support the frightful spectacle if her sweet, childlike simplicity came not as a gleam from Paradise to light up the dark sea of sorrows which bore her storm-tossed bark to the haven of rest.

CHAPTER XIV.

CORPORAL SUFFERINGS.

"I gave myself to my Heavenly Spouse and He accomplished His will in me. To suffer in repose has ever seemed to me the most enviable state in this world, but one to which I never attained." In these words Sister Emmerich summed up the mystery of her whole life both in the convent and out of it, for sufferings never failed her. She accepted them gratefully from the hands of God, she welcomed them as a precious gift, but never was repose in suffering hers, never did a peaceful, hidden life fall to her lot. She was to arrive at perfect conformity with her Spouse. He consummated His mission amidst contradictions, tribulations, and persecutions—His servant was not to accomplish hers otherwise. From her infancy she had suffered for others; but now these sufferings assumed a more elevated, a more extended character. The wounds of the body of the Church, that is the falling off of whole dioceses, the self-will and negligence of ecclesiastics, the deplorable state of society —all was laid upon her to be expiated by varied and multiplied sufferings. Her infirmities resulted from spiritual wounds entailed upon the flock of Christ by the sins of its own members. In this she may be compared to Blessed Lidwina of Schiedam who together with Christina of Saint-Trond (*Christina mirabilis*) is, perhaps, the most wonderful instrument of expiation ever made use of by Almighty God for the good of the Church. A glance at her life will give us a clear insight into Sister Emmerich's mission (1).

(1) Blessed Lidwina's life was compiled by a contemporary, Brother John Brugmann, Provincial of the Friars Minor, in Holland, who died in the odor of sanctity. Communications were made for this end by Lidwina's confessor, Walter von Leyden, and John Gerlach, his friend. The Burgomaster and Council of Schiedam testified thereto, as also the blessed Thomas à Kempis.—See Acta Sanctorum, April 14th.

Lidwina, the daughter of a poor watchman of Schiedam, was born some weeks previously to the death of St. Catherine of Sienna and, by a special privilege, dedicated to the Mother of God to receive from her strength to continue the mission of suffering for the Church bequeathed to her by the saint. Catherine had been raised up by God in the fourteenth century, like St. Hildegarde in the twelfth, to aid Christianity by the spirit of prophecy. Her life counted but thirty-three years; for her heart, riven by divine love, could not longer endure the sight of the unhappy divisions in the Church caused by the election of an anti-pope opposed to Urban VI. A schism burst forth two years before her death, and St. Catherine shrank from no sacrifice to restore peace and unity, even imploring Almighty God to permit the rage of hell to be unchained against her own person rather than against the Head of the Church. Her prayer was heard. During the last three months of her life from January 19, 1380, Sexagesima, till April 30, fifth Sunday after Easter, hell did indeed make her its victim, as it had formerly done St. Hildegarde who for three consecutive years wrestled with the infernal cohorts for the good of the Church. On Palm Sunday, 1380, only a few weeks before the death of St. Catherine, Lidwina, the heiress of her sufferings and struggles, was born in Holland. From her very cradle she was a little victim of pain, the intolerable agony of the stone being her portion; yet, in spite of her ill health, she was so beautiful and presented so robust an appearance that her hand was sought in marriage at the early age of twelve. But long before she had consecrated her virginity to God by vow; and now, to free herself from suitors, she begged Him to deprive her of her beauty, a prayer most pleasing to the Author of all beauty. In her fifteenth year she fell ill.

On her recovery she was so disfigured as to be no longer
an object of attraction. In this way she was prepared to be
a vessel of sufferings, and the miseries which at that period
afflicted the Church were laid upon her. Whilst skating
on the ice a companion struck against her. Lidwina fell and
broke a rib of her right side. An internal abscess formed
which no remedies could relieve and from which she endured horrible pains. About a year after this accident,
her father approached her bed one day to soothe and comfort her, when in a paroxysm of agony she threw herself
into his arms. The sudden movement broke the abscess,
the blood gushed violently from her mouth and nose, and
she was in imminent danger of suffocating. From this
moment she grew worse; the suppuration of the abscess
hindered her taking nourishment and if she forced herself to
eat, her stomach refused to retain the food. Burning
thirst consumed her and when she dragged herself out of
bed to swallow a mouthful of water, it was only to throw it
off immediately. Nothing gave her any relief; and, what
was still more deplorable, she was for years deprived of
spiritual consolation and direction. Once a year, at Easter, she was carried to the church to receive Holy Communion, and that was all. Sometimes it seemed to her
as if she could not possibly endure her state of suffering
and abandonment longer; but sickness, even such as hers,
could not at once crush her youthful buoyancy and she was
often seized with a longing desire to be cured. A miserable little room on the ground floor, more like a cave than
an apartment, was the one assigned her and the merry
voices of the young people as they passed the narrow window intensified her feelings of utter abandonment. Three
or four years passed away, and then God sent to her a
holy confessor and director in the person of John Pot, who

taught her how to meditate on the dolorous Passion of Christ, from which exercise she drew fortitude and resignation. She was docile and faithful to his instructions, but perfect relief came to her desolate soul only when the gift of tears was granted to her, which happened one day after Holy Communion. For fourteen days her tears flowed constantly and uncontrollably over her former impatience and tepidity whilst, at the same time, her. soul was inundated with consolation. From that moment she made such progress in prayer that all hours of the day and night found her absorbed in contemplation, and she regulated the time as precisely by her own interior admonition, as if by the sound of a clock. In the eighth year of her sickness, she could say : " It is not I who suffer ; it is my Lord Jesus who suffers in me !" and she continually offered herself as a victim of expiation. Once upon Quinquagesima Sunday she asked for some special pain to atone for the sins committed during the Carnival ; whereupon she was attacked by pains in her limbs so excruciating that she no longer dared to make such petitions. Again she offered herself as a victim to avert the plague from her native city, and instantaneously two pestilential sores appeared on her throat and breast ; she begged for a third in honor of the Most Holy Trinity, and another appeared on her knee.

Soon the entire dismemberment and devastation of the Church were cast upon her. The three-fold havoc made at the time of the great schism by freedom of opinion, immorality, and heresy, was represented in her by swarms of greenish worms that generated in her spine, attacked her kidneys and devoured the lower part of her body, in which they made three large holes. About two hundred of these worms, an inch in length, were daily generated. To protect herself in some degree, Lidwina fed them on a mix-

ture of honey and flour, or with capon fat spread on linen
and laid over the wounds.   This she had to beg as an alms;
and, if it happened not to be fresh, the worms attacked her
instead.   As infidelity, heresy, and schism spring from
pride of intellect and sins against the sixth commandment,
this triple evil had to be expiated in a manner analogous
in its nature, that is by putrefaction and worms.

What remained of the other internal parts of her body
after the action of the purulent abscess, was, at Lidwina's
own desire, buried and the cavity of the abdomen filled up
with wool.   She was attended by the physician of the
Duchess Margarite of Holland.   The agony she endured
from the stone, notwithstanding the decomposition of her
organs, reached at times such a degree of intensity as to
deprive her of consciousness.   This suffering was in
expiation of the abomination of concubinage even among
clerics.   Her kidneys and liver rotted away; purulent
tumors formed on her breasts, because of the milk of scandal
given to multitudes of children, instead of the nourishment
of pure doctrine; and, for the strife and discord that reigned
among Christian theologians, Lidwina endured the most
agonizing toothache, which was often so violent as to affect
her reason.   The unhealthy excitement agitating the body of
the Church was atoned for by a tertian fever that, like a withering blast, dried up her bones or shook her with icy chills.

Lastly, as Christianity for forty years was divided
between popes and anti-popes, so, too, was Lidwina's body
literally separated into two parts.   Her shoulders had to
be bandaged to keep them from falling asunder.   A split
extended vertically through her forehead down to the middle of her nose; her lips and chin were in the same condition; and the blood sometimes flowed so abundantly from
them as to prevent her speaking.

As the Pope could no longer guard the entire flock, Lidwina lost the use of her right eye, and the left was so weak that she could not endure the light. The fire of revolt paralyzed the Sovereign Pontiff's power —and Lidwina's right arm was attacked by St. Anthony's fire ; the nerves lay upon the fleshless bones like the cords of a guitar, the arm itself being attached to the body merely by a tendon. With the use of only her left hand she lay upon her back, heipless and motionless, and for seven consecutive years she could not be moved lest she would literally fall to pieces. Her body, deprived of sleep and nourishment, was like a worm-eaten tree supported only by the bark ; and yet there daily flowed from her mouth, nose, eyes, ears, from all the pores of her body so great a quantity of blood and other fluids that two men would not have been able to carry it away in the space of a month. Lidwina well knew whence came this substitute for the vital sap which had entirely dried up in her frame, for once being questioned as to its origin, she answered : " Tell me whence the vine derives its rich sap which in winter is apparently all dried up ?"— She felt herself a living branch of the true vine, whose benedictions stream to the ground when they find no member to receive them. Lidwina expiated this waste by the blood which flowed from every pore, and which day by day was miraculously replenished. The wonderful vase of her body, notwithstanding its corruption and worms, emitted a most sweet odor. It became at last a victim so agreeable in the sight of Our Lord that He impressed upon it the seal of His Sacred Stigmata.

For thirty-three years Lidwina presented this amazing spectacle of suffering, utterly in contradiction to nature's laws, and which no natural experience could explain. When plied with questions such as these :—" How can you live without lungs, liver, or intestines, and almost consumed by worms ?"—she would quietly answer : "God and my conscience bear witness that I have lost piecemeal what He once gave me. You may well believe this loss was hard to bear, but God alone knows what, in the fulness of His almighty power, He has done in me to replace that loss."

Lidwina's pious biographer, Francis Brugmann, Provincial of the Minorites, throws light upon these inexplicable facts when he says that God, in miraculously preserving the wasted body of His spouse, willed to manifest to all ages the means by which He daily preserves the grace of Redemption to men who persecute the Church, her faith, and her mysteries, as the worms, the fever, and the putrid matter consumed the body of Blessed Lidwina.

That it might be evident to all that Lidwina bore in her own person the wounds of the entire Church, God restored her to her perfect state some time before her demise. When Christianity again acknowledged one Head, Lidwina's task was accomplished, and she received once more all that she had sacrificed for the interests of the Church.

We may now very lawfully inquire how life could possibly be prolonged in a body entirely destitute of vital organs, and we find Lidwina on several occasions alluding to a supernatural nourishment. Her biographer says : " Curiosity impelled crowds to visit the pious virgin, some actuated by laudable intentions, others coming merely to condemn and blaspheme. All saw indeed but a picture of death ; yet the former beheld also in this mutilated vase the balm of sanctification ; in this disfigured image the wonder-working Lord ; in this semblance of death the Author of life, the most lovely among the children of men. Were Lidwina asked in amazement what fever could lay hold of in her, since she took no nourishment, she would answer : " You

are surprised that fever finds anything to feed upon in me—
and I, I wonder that I do not become like a barrel in a
month ! You judge by the cross you see me bearing, but
you know not of the unction attached thereto, you cannot
see the interior."

When holy persons expressed their surprise at seeing
her alive in such a state, saying : " You could not live if
God in His mercy did not preserve you "—she would reply : " Yes, I acknowledge that I do receive, though I am
unworthy of it, a sustenance which God pours out upon me
from time to time. Poor whelp that I am, I could not live
in such a body, if some crumbs from my Master's table fell
not to me ; but it becomes not the little dog to say what
morsels it receives."

Sometimes indiscreet females tormented her with questions as to the reality of her taking no nourishment ; then
she would answer sweetly : " If you cannot understand it,
yet do not join the number of the incredulous, do not despise
God's wonderful operations. He it was who supported
Mary Magdalen in her solitude and Mary of Egypt in the
wilderness. There is no question as to what you think of
me—but do not rob God of His glory."

Lidwina did not mean merely the unction communicated
by the gifts and fruits of the Holy Ghost. She alluded more
particularly to the relief received from the terrestrial
paradise, which invigorated her in a manner altogether
miraculous. The Fathers tell us that paradise still exists
in all its first beauty untouched by the waters of the Deluge.
Here Enoch and Elias were transported to await the coming of anti-Christ, at which time they will reappear upon
earth to announce to the Jews the Word of Salvation. St.
Hildegarde says : " Enoch and Elias are in paradise,
where they have no need of corporal food ; and, in like

manner, a soul rapt in the contemplation of God has no necessity whilst in that state of those things of which mortals make use (1)."

The terrestrial paradise was not created for pure spirits, but for man composed of soul and body ; consequently, it is provided with whatever is requisite not only for his sustenance but also for his *safeguard* against sickness and death, by virtue of the state of original justice in which he was first created. The creatures of this magnificent abode, its animals and plants, belong to a higher order, as much elevated above those of earth as the body of Adam before his sin was superior to his fallen posterity. And as the body of Adam was a real body of flesh and blood, not pure spirit, so, too, paradise is not a celestial or purely spiritual region, but a material place connected with human nature and with the earth itself. This relation between the earth and paradise is clearly indicated in the Holy Scriptures. The manna in the desert revealed to the children of the Old Law the food prepared for man during his earthly pilgrimage. St. Hildegarde says on this subject in her *Scivias*, Lib. I., visio II. :—" When Adam and Eve were expelled from paradise, a wall of light was raised around it, and the Divine Power effaced from it all marks of their sin. It was fortified, as it were, by this great light so that no enemy could reach it; but by this God also testified that the transgression which had taken place in paradise should in time be effaced by His mercy. Paradise still exists, a region of joy, blooming in all its pristine loveliness, and imparting abundant fruitfulness to the sterile earth. As the soul communicates life and strength to the body it inhabits, so the earth receives from paradise her supreme vitality ; the darkness and corruption of sin, which shroud this miser-

(1) Quaestio XXIX. ad Vibertum Gemblacensem.

able world cannot entirely check its beneficent influence."

Man's spiritual bond with paradise is the grace of Redemption, which not only restored him the high gifts possessed by Adam in that abode, but conferred on him besides that superior beauty, dignity, and worth which emanate from the Precious Blood of Christ. By virtue of baptismal innocence, God in every age bestows upon certain chosen souls many of those privileges which Adam received by virtue of original justice. Baptism confers a certain right to those extraordinary gifts, for its innocence is superior to that of paradise. St. Hildegarde wrote to the Cathedral Chapter of Mayence : " God who, by the light of truth leads on His elect to beatitude, has been pleased at various epochs to renew the spirit of faith among them by the gift of prophecy ; by its illumination they may, in a measure, recover that happiness possessed by Adam before his fall."

It is not a matter of surprise, then, that not only the spiritual but also the material favors of paradise, should be bestowed upon God's chosen ones as a recompense for their fidelity ; but such gifts are merited by sufferings and privations.

Man, even whilst living in the flesh, is conducted to paradise and its fruits are brought to him by pain and self-renunciation, and by the good works performed by souls in the splendor of unsullied innocence. The way to these heights is absolute self-denial open only to those who have been, as it were, spiritualized in the fire of affliction. No extraordinary natural faculty, no mysterious malady, no disarrangement between the functions of soul and body, only purity and heroic fortitude fit man though still an exile upon earth to enter the terrestrial paradise.

Rewards and punishments are meted out by Almighty God according to the nature and importance of good or evil works; and so for every pain, every sorrow, for every privation borne upon earth there blooms in Paradise a corresponding production which, as a flower or a fruit, as food or drink, as consolation or relief, is communicated to souls according to their special need, and this not merely spiritually, but really and substantially. This is the wonderful repairer of their corporal life, this explains their miraculous vitality.

It is related of Lidwina (1) that once a woman very virtuous, but a prey to the deepest melancholy, came to implore her help. Lidwina received her with kind words and promised her relief. Some days later the poor sufferer was admitted with Lidwina herself to the earthly Paradise, a favor obtained by Lidwina's prayers; but in spite of the wonders she beheld on all sides, the poor woman ceased not to lament and weep. Then Lidwina led her to a certain locality which seemed to serve as the storehouse of the whole world;—here were perfumes, health-giving spices, and healing herbs, and here the poor sufferer was finally cured and so inundated with celestial consolations that, for several days after, she could not support even the smell of food. As a reward for her docility to Lidwina's advice and directions her melancholy entirely disappeared.

In the life of St. Colette (2), contemporary with blessed Lidwina, it is related that during the whole of Lent, she abstained from food excepting perhaps a few crumbs of bread. On a certain Easter-day God sent her from Paradise a bird resembling a hen, one of whose eggs sufficed her for a long time and, as she had need of some little recreation amid her great labors (she reformed the Poor Clares) there was sent her from Paradise in reward for

(1) Acta SS., die XIV. Aprilis vita post: c. III.
(2) Acta SS., die VI. Martii, Chap. XIII.

her incomparable purity a charming little animal, dazzlingly white and perfectly tame when with her. It used to present itself at the door or window of her cell, as if craving entrance and, after a short time, disappear as mysteriously as it had come. Her sister-religious regarded it with intense interest and curiosity, but they could never succeed in catching it; for, if they happened to meet it in Colette's cell or any place about the convent, it instantaneously vanished (1). Colette entertained the deepest reverence for holy relics and, above all, for the Cross upon which the Saviour died, and as she ardently longed for a little piece of it, her desire was miraculously gratified. A small golden cross, not made by hand of man but a natural production, containing a particle of the True Cross, was brought her from the garden of paradise, and Colette ever after carried it on her person. Again, as she was one day conferring with her confessor on the reform of her Order, a cincture of dazzling whiteness descended from above and rested on her arm.

Lidwina often acknowledged that, without the help of divine consolation, she would have sunk under her accumulation of suffering. Her strength was daily renewed in those hours of rapture which transported her either to heaven itself or to the terrestrial paradise, and the sweetness she then tasted rendered the bitterness of her pains not only supportable but even delightful. Her guardian-angel, ever visible to her, was her conductor on these spiritual journeys. Before setting out, he used to take her to the parish church to an image of the Mother of God, whence after a short prayer they rose swiftly above the earth in an easterly direction until they reached the garden. The first time Lidwina made this aerial journey, she was

(1) Acta SS. die VI. Martii. Ch. IX.

afraid to enter the beautiful gates. It was only on the angel's assuring her that her feet would not hurt the flowery carpet stretching out before her that she ventured in, holding the while her guardian's hand who went on before and gently drew her after him. When, at times, she paused in hesitating wonder at the height and luxuriance of the flowers which seemed no longer to afford a passage, the angel lifted her lightly over the fragrant barrier.

The meadows bathed in light, inaccessible to cold or heat, surpassed Lidwina's powers of description. She ate the luscious fruits presented by her angel, and inhaled their delightful perfume; and when returned to her little chamber, her family dared not approach her from the respect which her appearance inspired. She was wholly embalmed with the glory of another world. Her emaciated frame shone with light; perfumes unlike those of earth breathed around her poor couch; the hand held by the angel on their joyous expedition exhaled a peculiarly delicious odor, and a sensation was experienced by one who approached her such as is produced by aromatic spices. On one occasion, the light surrounding her was so brilliant that her little nephew thinking her in flames ran away in terror.

Lidwina kept near her bed a stalk of dried hemp, light yet firm, with which she could with her left hand open and close the curtain to admit air to her feverish brow. A fire broke out at Schiedam on the night of the 22d of July, and in the confusion this stick was lost. Poor Lidwina was the sufferer, for she was now unable to procure even the small relief of a breath of fresh air. Her angel promised her assistance and, in a short time, she felt something laid gently on the coverlet of her bed. It was a stick about a yard and a quarter long. But in vain did she try to lift it, her poor hand refused its weight, and laughingly she exclaim-

ed : 'Ah ! yes, now, indeed, I have a stick !'—Next
morning she begged her confessor to whittle it for her and
thus render it lighter. He did so or, at least, tried to do
so ; but, even with a sharp knife, he could scarcely cut
away a few chips, which shed around so delicious a fragrance that he dared not whittle any more of the precious
wood. He took it to Lidwina, asking her where she got
it, but she could answer only that she thought her angel
had brought it to her. On August 8th, Feast of St. Cyriacus,
being again conducted to Paradise, the angel pointed out
to her a cedar near the entrance and showed her the bough
from which he had broken a branch for her. He reproved her for not sufficiently honoring the precious gift, which
possessed the power of expelling evil spirits. Lidwina
kept this branch a long time. It lost its fragrance
only in a hand stained by sin. On another visit to Paradise, Dec. 6th, of the same year, she was fed from a date-
palm laden with magnificent fruit whose stones shone like
crystals. We shall mention only one more of the gifts
brought from Paradise to console and strengthen the patient
sufferer.

"She was one day rapt to the choirs of the blessed and the
Mother of God addressed her in the following words : 'My
child, why do you not put on a crown and join these glorious
spirits ? '—to which Lidwina answered simply : 'I came
with my angel; I must do what he tells me.' Then Mary
gave her a beautiful crown with instructions to keep it herself for seven hours and then give it to her confessor, who
was to hang it at Our Lady's altar in the parish church of
Schiedam, whence it would be removed later. When Lidwina returned to earth, she remembered all that had passed ;
but she dreamed not of taking it literally until she felt the
crown of lovely flowers upon her head. When the seven

hours had elapsed, she sent for her confessor at dawn, gave
him the crown, which was hung at Our Lady's shrine according to order, whence it disappeared before full daylight."

After this digression, more apparent than real, we return
to Sister Emmerich whose sufferings were of the same
nature and signification as Lidwina's. Besides her interior
torments, she endured a succession of cruel maladies most
varied in form and opposite in symptoms, since she atoned
both for the whole Church and her individual members. God
had accepted the sacrifice of her whole being, and every
part of her body offered its tribute of expiation, the natural
order of things being entirely reversed in her regard—sickness and pain becoming health and strength to her whilst
she lay consumed in the fire of tribulation. Her body was,
so to speak, the crucible in which the Physician of souls
prepared healing remedies for His people, whilst her soul
was keenly alive to terror, sadness, anguish, dryness, desolation, to all those withering impressions which the passions of
one man can cause another, or by which diabolical malice
can assail its victims. She was burdened with the fears of the
dying, the corruption of morals, with the consequences of
wrath, revenge, gluttony, curiosity; with them she struggled,
over them she gained the victory, the fruits of which she
relinquished in favor of poor sinners. But these pains were
nothing to the anguish she endured at the sight of the unprecedented degradation of the priesthood. The evil one
succeeded in intruding many of his own servants into Holy
Orders, men lost to the faith, members of secret societies
who, with the indelible stamp of ordination upon their soul,
shrank not from the blackest crimes against Christ and His
Vicar upon earth. There was no attack made on the
Church, her rights, her worship, her doctrine, and her
Sacraments, that was not inspired by a Judas from among

her own. The Saviour felt His Apostle's treason more keenly than all His other sufferings; and, in like manner, the
sharpest wounds in the Church's body are ever from one
clothed with the sacerdotal dignity. The impious attacks
of heretics did not call for so grievous expiation as did the
crimes of fallen priests, and the latter were followed by far
more terrible consequences than the former.

If Anne Catherine's corporal sufferings did not seem so
violent, so frightful as Lidwina's, yet they were by no
means less excruciating. Sometimes she saw them as if
endured by another, when she would cry out in compassion:
" Ah! I see a poor little nun whose heart is torn to pieces!
She must belong to our own time, but she suffers more than
I! I must not complain!"

As the blood flows to and from the heart, so Sister Emmerich's pains taking their rise in this source, spread through her
whole person and returned to their point of departure, as if
to gather fresh strength to continue their work of expiation.
The heart is the seat of love. It is into the heart that the
Holy Spirit is poured there to form that sacred bond which
unites all the members of the Church into one body. Never
was love so much vaunted as at this period when both love
and faith were well-nigh dead, when the practice of Christian
piety and the observance of the evangelical precepts seemed
to have totally died out. It was at this time that the most
baneful and hypocritical sect that has ever risen up swept
as a devastating torrent over the vineyard of the Church—
the malicious sect of Jansenism with its so-called lights. Aided
and abetted by the secret societies, whose most zealous disciples were seated even in the ecclesiastical councils, it
sought in its blind hatred of the Blessed Virgin and the
Sovereign Pontiff, to separate irremediably her faithful
children from the heart of the Church by the introduction

of those heterodox elements which, under the cloak of "love and reform," attacked the very principles of faith and abolished those devout practices, those pious customs by whose extinction the most fatal wounds were inflicted upon Christianity. All things combined to further the cause of this diabolical sect : the Church was oppressed by secular power, her property pillaged, bishoprics vacant, religious orders suppressed, and the Pope fettered by Napoleon, whom Sister Emmerich often saw in her visions as an oppressor of the Church.

" Once," she said, " as I was praying before the Blessed Sacrament for the wants of the Church, I was transported into a large and magnificent temple, where I saw the Pope, the Vicar of Jesus Christ, anointing a king, a little yellow man of sinister aspect. It was a great solemnity, but it filled me with sorrow and dismay. I felt that the Pope should have firmly refused to perform the ceremony. I saw what harm this man would do the Holy Father and of what frightful bloodshed he would be the cause. I spoke to Abbé Lambert of this vision and of the fears it awoke in my heart, but he treated it lightly. When, however, we heard the news of Napoleon's coronation, by Pius VII., he said : ' Sister, we must pray and be silent.' "

Such was the epoch in which Anne Catherine bore the Church's sorrows imposed upon her, not as an undefined malady, but according to a certain order, as tasks which it was hers to fulfil perfectly one after another. They were shown her separately under symbolical forms that her acceptance might be for her a meritorious act of love; she was called to labor daily in the vineyard, whilst the father of the family sent the workmen there but seldom. She received the order in vision and executed it without interfering with the regular routine of daily life, being perfectly alive to the hidden signification of her sufferings and their connection with the Church ; but her outer life contrasted so rudely with her inner that it was often more painful to her than the weight of spiritual sufferings that oppressed her. And yet, the former was the necessary complement of the latter ; it formed a part of the task assigned which could be looked upon as fully accomplished only inasmuch as it was fulfilled in the midst of exterior contradictions and interruptions. It was in the patient endurance of tribulations from without and sorrow from within that her merit lay This was the perfume she exhaled to God in an odor of sweetness. If we close our eyes to the economy of Divine Providence in the conduct of souls, her whole existence becomes to us an inexplicable enigma, an unmeaning fact. Many were touched on seeing her purity of soul, her superior supernatural intelligence, who, at the same time, were offended at her poverty and lowliness. They were scandalized at her surroundings, at the crowds of poor that thronged about her, at her helpless and abandoned condition. They understood not that the victim should not fare better than the Church whose wounds she bore, the Church tossed to and fro on the waves of persecution.

She would not have been able to support the trials of her holy Mother did she not also share in her supernatural life. A pilgrim upon earth and, at the same time, the companion of the blessed in heaven, the Church struggles under the pressure of present tribulations whilst bearing in her bosom the salvation of ages. Mourning the departure of her Divine Spouse to His Father, she daily unites herself to Him by the closest union ; and so, too, Anne Catherine, whilst weeping with that holy Mother, arose with her by contemplation above the vicissitudes of time and the bounds of space. The cycle of feasts was ever present to her, ever unveiled and instinct with life, and she perfectly entered into the daily celebration of the mysteries of faith and the truths of religion, which were more intelligible to the eye of her mind than was the exterior world to that of her body. She received from her Divine Spouse with the tasks regulated according to the ecclesiasticial calendar, the strength of soul necessary to fulfil them courageously. Whilst in vision, she was able to understand the connection between her various sufferings and her task of expiation; but, in her waking state, she could not explain it intelligibly. She dared not mention the subject before either the physician or her Sisters, for they would have deemed her delirious, if not quite demented; consequently she submitted silently to all prescriptions, to all attempts of science to cure those sufferings which she well knew to be the very object of her existence.

"Both in and out of the convent," she once remarked, "I suffered intensely from the means employed for my cure, and I was often in danger of death from too violent remedies. I knew the effect they would have, but I took them in obedience. If through forgetfulness I failed to do so, my attendants thought I did it purposely and that my sickness was feigned. The medicines were expensive. A phial which cost a great deal was only half-empty sometimes when another was ordered, and all was charged to my account, I had to pay for all. I cannot understand where I got so much money. True, I sewed a good deal, but I used to give all the proceeds to the convent which toward the end paid half my expenses. I was often so miserable that I could not render myself any service; but if my Sisters forgot me, God helped me. One day I was lying prostrate with weakness and bathed in perspiration, when two female religious appeared, made up my bed, and replaced me gently to my great relief. Shortly after, the Reverend Mother entered with a Sister, and asked me in astonishment who had arranged my bed so comfortably. I thought they themselves had done it, and I thanked them for their kindness; but they assured me that neither they nor any other Sister had entered my cell, and they looked upon what I told them of the two religious as all a dream; however, my bed had actually been made, and I felt better. I found out afterward that the two good nuns, who often rendered me kind and consoling services, were blessed souls who had once lived in our convent."

Clara Soentgen deposed to the above before ecclesiastical authority:—

"Sister Emmerich was very ill and I went one morning to her cell to see how she was. I asked who had made up her bed so early, or if she had had the strength to do it herself. She answered that Reverend Mother and I had come together to see her and that we had arranged her bed so nicely and expeditiously. Now, neither of us had yet been in her cell."

"At another time," says Anne Catherine, "whilst in the same state, I was again lifted gently out of my bed and laid in the middle of the cell by two religious. At the same moment one of the Sisters entered suddenly. Seeing me lying unsupported in the air, she uttered a sharp cry which frightened me so that I fell heavily to the floor. This gave rise to much talk among the Sisters, and one of the old religious tormented me for a long time with questions as to how I could lie thus in the air, but I could give her no explanation. I paid no attention to such things, they all seemed perfectly natural to me." We see by the above that whatever was requisite for her support was supplied by her Spouse from the Garden of Eden, whose products possess the power of dissipating pain and sorrow. Anne Catherine communicated these secrets before her death, either by order of her guide or her confessor. They are, doubtless, short and incomplete, though quite sufficient to prove that she received divine favors similar to those of Lidwina.

" The only remedies that afforded me any relief," she said, " were supernatural. The physician's only increased my languor, yet I had to take them and pay dear for them too. But God always gave me the money, as well as all that I needed in the convent, and I also received much for the house. After I left it the same things often happened to me, and once I was given quite a large sum of which I made use. I mentioned it to Dean Rensing, who told me that the next time this happened I must show him the money ; but from that day I got no more.

" During the second investigation, I gave the nurse two thalers to go on a pilgrimage to Telgten for my intention and to get two Masses for the same. The servant-girl of the house lent me the money, and shortly after I found two thalers lying on my bed. I wondered what it meant and I made the nurse show me the money I had given her. I recognized it at once, and felt convinced that God had repeated the favor I had often received in the past in order that I might pay off my debt to the girl.

" Supernatural remedies were often given me by my angel, by Mary, or the dear saints and even by my Affianced Himself. Sometimes they were in the form of liquids in brilliant phials, or flowers, herbs, or little morsels of food. At the head of my bed was a wooden shelf on which I used to find these marvellous remedies during my visions, or even in my waking moments. Sometimes I found tiny bunches of herbs of exquisite beauty and delicious fragrance laid on my bed or placed in my hand when I awoke from vision;

and by pinching the tender young leaves I knew what use to make of them. Their fragrance at times was sufficient to strengthen me; and sometimes I ate them or drank the water in which they were steeped. After such nourishment I was again ready for my task.

" I also received pictures, statues, and stones from apparitions with directions how to use them; they were either put into my hand or laid on' my breast, and they always relieved me. Some I kept a long time and made use of to cure others, either applying them myself or giving them to those in need; but I never said where I got them. They were all real, but I cannot explain how it was. These incidents did actually take place, and I used the remedies in honor of Him whose goodness had sent them to me.

" Whilst in the novitiate, I was one day kneeling before the Blessed Sacrament, my arms extended, when I felt something slipped into my hand. It was a beautiful little picture of St. Catherine painted on parchment. I kept it a long time and then gave it to a good girl who asked me for a souvenir. She had a great desire to become a religious, but she died before accomplishing her design. The little picture was placed at her own request on the poor child's breast as she lay in her coffin.

" Once my Heavenly Affianced gave me a polished transparent stone shaped like a heart and larger than a thaler, in which there was, as if formed there by nature, a picture of Mary with the Infant Jesus in red, blue, and gold. The picture was exquisitely beautiful; the mere sight of it cured me, for I was ill at the time. I made a little leathern bag for it and wore it a long time when, at last, it was taken from me by the same power that had bestowed it. Again, my Betrothed placed on my finger a ring in which was a precious stone with a picture of His

Blessed Mother engraven on it. I kept that also for a time, when He Himself withdrew it from my finger.

"I received a similar gift from the holy patron of my Order. It was near the hour for Holy Communion. No one dreamed of my being able to rise, but I thought I heard them calling me. I dragged myself to the choir and received the Most Holy Sacrament with the others. Returned to my cell, I fell on the floor fainting. I know not how or by whom, but I was laid just as I was in my habit on the bed. Then St. Augustine appeared and gave me a sparkling stone shaped like a bean, from which arose a crimson heart surmounted by a little cross. I was told that the heart would become as transparent as the stone. When I awoke to consciousness, I found it in my hand. I put it into my tumbler, drank the water off it, and was cured. After awhile it was taken from me.

"There was another gift which I was permitted to retain for seven months during a severe illness. The infirmarian brought me food every day, but I could not touch it. I could take no kind of nourishment and the Sisters wondered how I lived. I had, however, received another sort of aliment from the Mother of God. She appeared to me in vision and when I awoke I found in my hand a large host of dazzling whiteness, thicker and softer than those of the altar, with a picture of Mary and some written characters impressed upon it. I was seized with profound respect, as if before relics or holy things. It was fragrant and, at night, luminous. I kept it by me, hidden in my bed, and every day for seven months I ate a little particle of it, which gave me strength. Then it disappeared to my great disquietude, for I feared I had lost this heavenly manna through my own fault. It had a sweet taste, but not like the Blessed Sacrament.

"One night, I was kneeling before the table in my cell, praying to the Blessed Virgin, when a female resplendent with light entered through the closed door, advanced to the other side of the table, and knelt down opposite to me as if to pray. I was frightened, but I went on praying. Then she placed before me a statue of the Mother of God, about a hand high and dazzlingly white, and laid her open hand on the table for a moment behind the statue. I drew back in fear, when she gently pushed the statue toward me. I venerated it interiorly and the apparition vanished leaving the little image, a mother standing with her child in her arms. It was exquisitely beautiful and, I think, made of ivory. I carried it about with me most respectfully for a long time, when I was interiorly instructed to give it to a strange priest from whom it was withdrawn at the hour of death.

" Once, Mary gave me a marvellous flower which expanded in water. When closed it resembled a rosebud, but when open it displayed leaves of delicate colors which bore a relation to the different spiritual effects it was to produce in me. Its scent was delicious. For more than a month I drank the water in which it was steeped. At last, I was wondering what I should do with this health-giving flower that it might not be profaned, when I was told in vision to have a new crown made for the Mother of God in our chapel and to put the bud into it. I told the confessor and Superioress, who ordered me to save up my money and wait awhile. But I was again commanded in a vision not to delay having the crown made, in consequence of which my confessor gave permission. It was made at the Clares, in Münster, and I myself put the flower in. As the Sisters were not very careful of the ornaments, I saw to the crown myself. The little flower was in it up to the suppression of the convent, when it disappeared and I was shown in a vision where it had been taken.

"My guide once gave me a little flask of whitish balm like thick oil. I used it on a hurt I had received from a basket of wet linen, and with it cured many sick. The flask was pear-shaped with a long narrow neck, about the size of a medicine phial, perfectly clear and transparent. I kept it for some time in my press. Again, some morsels of sweet food were given me which I used and also gave some to the poor to cure their maladies. The Superioress found it one day and reprimanded me for not saying how I had come by it."

In October, 1805, Sister Emmerich was appointed to assist one of the Sisters in carrying the linen from the wash up to the drying-loft. She stood above at the trap-door to receive the rising basket. The Sister below slackened the rope just as Sister Emmerich was about swinging the load over to the floor. The angel seized the rope and saved her from falling with the weight, too great for her strength, on the Sister below. The effort Sister Emmerich made dashed her to the floor, the basket of linen falling heavily on her left hip, crushing the bone in several places and inflicting other injuries which would certainly have been attended with fatal results, had not God miraculously preserved her life. It was soon evident that this accident was destined by God to play as important a part in Sister Emmerich's life as did Lidwina's fall on the ice in her painful career. It increased her expiatory sufferings and afforded her continual and painful humiliations. It now became very difficult for her to ring the convent-bell, her duty in quality of assist-ant-sacristan, and sometimes she was quite unable to do so, a circumstance which drew upon her the accusation of pride and laziness. But, in truth, it was a real privation to her not to be able to ring the bell; for she made of it so earnest a prayer that, whilst thus engaged, she seemed to forget her cruel pains.

" When ringing the blessed bell," she said, " I was full of joy, as if I were spreading around its benediction and calling on all who heard it to praise God. I united my prayers to each stroke to dispel all evil from their hearts and to excite them to glorify the dear God. I would have loved to ring out much longer than the prescribed time."

The furious unbelief of this epoch had proscribed the use of church-bells —and who does not see in this poor nun's tender devotion in the midst of her pains an atonement to God for violence so ignoble?

She could now only with great difficulty, and sometimes not at all, perform her accustomed duties of washing and ironing the church-linen and of working in the garden. God only knew the efforts she had to make; but the following fact shows how her zeal was recompensed. One day, a hot iron fell from her hand on one of the albs. With an invocation to God, she snatched it up and set it on the floor where it burned a hole, but neither the alb nor her hand was hurt. Those poor hands of hers were so emaciated by their constant sufferings that once she remarked :

" I suffered much from my hands whilst in the convent. If I held them up to the sun the rays pierced them like arrows, they were so thin."

The baking of the altar-bread was also very fatiguing for her, on account of the weight of the irons. She looked upon it as a sacred duty, to be performed prayerfully and respectfully. Once, fresh hosts were wanting, and Sister Emmerich lay on her poor bed ill and very sad at not being able to make them. She betook herself to prayer, arose from her bed, dragged herself to the chapel and there implored strength from Our Lord to prepare the hosts. Suddenly she was bathed in perspiration, and strength was, indeed, given her for the work, in which her angel assisted her; but scarcely was it over when she became sick as before, and only with difficulty regained her cell.

After the accident from the linen, she kept her bed till January, 1806. In the spring she had violent pains in her stomach which brought on frequent vomitings of blood. Even whilst at work, her hemorrhages were so copious that the Sisters feared they would prove fatal. But, at last, having seen her quickly recover from such attacks and also from her fainting-spells, so that she could soon return to her duties, they came to the conclusion that they were not very serious after all, and so she received very little atten- tion in her sickness. They rarely thought of her when she was too ill to be among them, and in winter it often happened that the straw of her poor bed froze to the damp wall of her cell, or that, consumed with fever, she sighed in vain for a mouthful of water. A kind-hearted person in Dülmen heard of her distressing condition, and made it known to the Duke von Croy, who immediately caused an infirmary to be fitted up in the convent, furnished it with a stove, and had Sister Emmerich removed to it.

In 1813, the physician made the following deposition:

"The care bestowed by the religious upon Sister Emmerich in her sickness was not always what it should have been. I found her once after a profuse flow of perspiration, trembling in her bed with cold. She had no change of linen, her gown and bed-clothes were frozen stiff. The Sisters complained of the expense of her frequent spells of sickness, and by their murmuring they sometimes turned the Reverend Mother, the infirmarian, and other Sisters against her, although these latter were in general favorably disposed toward her.

"In the beginning of March, 1810, she was seized with a violent nervous fever. She suffered cruelly during this heavy illness, more than two months of which she spent in a cold cell. Profuse sweats, fainting-spells, convulsions, and violent pains succeeded one another more or less frequently the whole time."

When Sister Emmerich was called upon by her Superiors to give an account of how she had been cared for in the convent, she spoke as follows :—

"What struck me on my entrance into the convent was the little care bestowed upon the sick. There was not even an infirmary to receive them. The Duke von Croy, hearing that the sick had to remain in their cell without a fire in the winter season, interested himself in having a suitable room prepared for them and gave a stove for it. In two attacks I was nursed by Sister Soentgen when she was free from her music lessons, and when these prevented, Sister Neuhaus kindly attended to me. As long as these two Sisters extended to me their charity, I had nothing of which to complain ; but their attention to me drew upon them the disapprobation of some others who were not so kindly disposed toward me. Then Sister E— was named infirmarian. She was full of caprice and neglected her duty. When she might have attended to me, she preferred being in her cell. She used to leave me so long in the morning without any regard to my wants that I trembled with cold in my night-clothes soaked with perspiration ; being unable to wait on myself, I endured thirst and many other painful inconveniences. Sometimes I told Reverend Mother not only of Sister E.'s conduct, but of the want of even necessary things. My confessor told me to do so ;

but it did very little good, for Reverend Mother did not care much for me. At times she listened patiently, and again she would tell me the convent was too poor to procure what was necessary for the sick, and that I was never satisfied. I must say, however, in her justification, that she never thought me as ill as I really was. I will add, too, that she took more care of the sick than her predecessors did, as the aged religious testified ; and, on this account, she had to put up with the discontent of many."

The infirmarian mentioned above was the one to whom Sister Emmerich had rendered the most loving services when attacked by a disgusting disease and shunned by all, on account of her cross-grained temper. It was a welcome opportunity to Sister Emmerich to return kindness for neglect and to support fresh trials from the crabbed nun.

The only thing she craved when able to leave her bed, was a little tea or weak coffee. She says in her deposition before Dean Rensing :—

" I often passed several consecutive nights without sleep. Very rarely did I sleep soundly, my rest was usually a light doze often interrupted ; consequently, and especially when I had had heavy night-sweats, I was so weak and sick in the morning that I could not rise for Matins. But, as soon as I had taken a little coffee and had heard Mass, I could attend to my duties. The Sisters did not understand this ; they said my sickness was all put on, or at least greatly exaggerated."

It was customary for each religious to provide her own breakfast. But as poor Sister Emmerich had neither coffee nor money, she used to take her coffee-pot to the kitchen every morning and gather up the grounds thrown away by the other Sisters, from which she made her own little cup which she drank without sugar. Clara Soentgen, who gives

us these details, sometimes compassionately shared her breakfast with her, but not often; for as she ingenuously tells us, she
allowed herself to be too greatly influenced by the remarks of
the Sisters. Assistance, at last, came from another quarter.
One day, on Sister Emmerich's return from the choir to her
cell, which she had left locked, she found two thalers on the
window-sill. She took them at once to the Superioress, who
permitted her to buy a small quantity of coffee with them,
which lasted her a long time.

Clara Soentgen, in her deposition of 1813, gives the following instance of the same nature:—

"I always remarked in Anne Catherine Emmerich the
greatest satisfaction when she had it in her power to give
something to the poor. Both before and after her entrance
into the convent, she gave away all she had. I asked her
once why she did not supply her own needs. ' Ah ! ' she
answered, ' I always receive far more than I give !'—and
indeed I often saw to my astonishment that what she said
was true.

"One morning she had neither breakfast nor money.
She locked her cell door, as usual, and went to the choir ; on
her return, she found some money lying on the window-sill,
at which she was so astonished that she came running to tell
me and I had to go back with her to see it. This happened more than once. She had no greater joy than that of
rendering charitable service to her neighbor. One might
ask her for anything she had ; she gladly gave away even
the most necessary articles and, above all, was she kind
toward those who cared little for her."

One year, on her feast-day, a friend gave her two pounds
of coffee. During a whole year she used it for breakfast without diminishing the little stock, a circumstance which rejoiced her heart. But being attacked by a long illness

during which she received supernatural remedies, this earthly aliment was withdrawn.

"One day," she tells us, "the old Count von Galen insisted on my taking two gold pieces to give to the poor in his name. I got them changed and had clothes and shoes made which I distributed to those in need. God blessed the money, for as soon as all the small pieces were gone, I found the two large ones again in my pocket. I immediately had them changed and used them as before. This went on for a year, and I was thus enabled to help many poor people. The miraculous assistance ceased during an illness, two months of which I lay immovable and most of the time unconscious. This was commonly the case with such favors; for, as others had free access to my cell, God withdrew what might have proved a subject of scandal to them."

By a special dispensation of Divine Providence, all classes of people sought Sister Emmerich's assistance during her stay in the convent, the most abandoned receiving from her the greatest sympathy and relief. Although it was most frequently the poor who applied for help from the sick nun, yet her Sisters in religion also knew with what charity they would be received whenever they were willing to make known to her their wants. The excess of her own sufferings seemed but to increase her tender sympathy for others; the prospect of doing a kind turn for her neighbor seemed to impart fresh vigor and energy to her wasted frame; and she who received so little care and attention herself, could put no bounds to her zeal were there question of relieving another. She possessed a quick perception of what remedies to apply; her prayers and the touch of her gentle hand attracted a blessing upon those for whom she prescribed. She was so patient, so serene, so ingenious in providing relief even when treating with the impatient and irritable, that they lost sight of the fact that she herself was not an instant without intense suffering. Her kindness was irresistible, and she knew so well how to overcome the whims and prejudices of the sick that the physician often sent for her when his own persuasion proved ineffectual.

Among the boarders was a weak-minded girl named K—, a native of M—, who had an abscess in the back of her neck. When the doctor was about applying a bandage, she escaped from his hands and refused to allow him to do anything for her. The Superioress sent for Sister Emmerich, whose presence wrought a magical effect upon the child, who readily took from her hand the medicine prescribed and allowed her wound to be dressed. When the abscess broke, Sister Emmerich sucked it gently, and it soon healed leaving no scar.

A servant-girl had an abscess under her arm. She stole to Sister Emmerich's bedside one night, begging her for the love of God to relieve her. The same charitable service was rendered her and she was cured.

There was a young girl from Amsterdam in the house as a boarder. She had an insupportable temper which burst forth on all occasions. Sister Emmerich was the only one who could calm her, she even won her affections, to the amazement of all.

Speaking of a similar case, she says:—

"The physician of the convent was a little abrupt; one day he scolded a poor woman soundly, because she had neglected to show him her finger which was very sore. The inflammation extended all the way up to the arm which was perfectly black. When he said that he would have to amputate it, the poor creature came running to me, pale with fright, begging me to help her. I began to pray when suddenly the proper way of treating it flashed upon my mind. I spoke of it to Reverend Mother, who permitted me to dress the arm in Abbé Lambert's room. I boiled sage, myrrh, and some of Our Lady's herb in wine and water; to this I added a few drops of holy water and made a poultice which I bound on the woman's arm. It was surely God Himself who had inspired the remedy, for next morning the swelling had entirely disappeared, though the finger was very sore. I made her bathe it in lye and oil. When it opened, I extracted from it a great thorn after which it soon healed."

Upon the nature of the compassion she felt for the sick and the poor, she says :—

" I can never grieve for a person who dies resignedly, nor for a child suffering patiently; for patient suffering is the most enviable state of man. Our compassion is rarely altogether pure; it is most frequently mixed with a certain sentiment of softness and selfishness springing from the horror we ourselves feel for suffering, for all that can wound self. Our Lord's compassion alone is pure, perfectly pure, and no human compassion possesses this quality unless it is united to His. I only pity sinners, poor blind souls, or souls in despair. But alas! I often pity myself too much !"

The following facts will show the blessing attached to her prayers and exertions in behalf of the sick :

"A poor peasant-woman of my acquaintance," she said, "always had very painful and dangerous accouchements. She loved me and told me her trials. I prayed for her earnestly. A parchment band with written characters on it was given to me supernaturally, aud I was told that the woman was to wear it on her person. She did so and was delivered without pain. When dying she requested the band to be buried with her. Such requests are customary among our peasants.

"Once there was great mortality among the cattle. The peasants had to take them to a certain place for treatment, but numbers of them died. A poor mother of a family came to me in tears, begging prayers for herself and the other sufferers. Then I had a vision of the stables belonging to these people. I saw both the healthy animals and those affected by the distemper, as also the cause of the evil and the effect of prayer upon it. I saw that many were attacked as a chastisement from God, on account of the pride and false security of their owners who recognized not that God can give and take away, and that their loss was a punishment for their sins. Then I begged Almighty God to take some other means of bringing them into the right path. Some of these animals were affected by the curse of envious people; they belonged chiefly to men who failed to give thanks to God for His benefits and to beg His blessing on His own gifts. The cattle appeared to me to be shrouded in darkness through which sinister-looking figures passed to and fro. Blessings not only attract the grace of God, but also dispel the evil influence of a malediction. The cattle saved by prayer seemed separated from the others by something luminous. I saw a black vapor escaping from those that were cured and a faint light hovering over others blessed from afar by prayer. The scourge was suddenly arrested, and the cattle belonging to the mother of the family escaped untouched."

Anne Catherine's ill-health prevented her holding any charge in the convent; she was always given as an aid first to one, then to another Sister. She never held authority over any one, but as Clara Soentgen says: "She was the servant of all, but a servant who loved her lowly state. She had the general good at heart, rendered great service to the community, and was always most laborious. Toward the servant-girls and laborers she was not only kind and discreet, but she gave them good advice and instruction."

The Reverend Mother, in 1813, also deposed :—

" In whatever obedience enjoined, Anne Catherine always gave satisfaction. When she had the care of the garden and out-buildings, she labored zealously, every one praised her. She was kind to the servants (as her Mistress testifies), although she exacted from them their duty. She was compassionate toward the poor and was accustomed to make caps for poor children out of the old church things."

CHAPTER XV.

SISTER EMMERICH'S ECSTASIES AND PRAYER.

Among all her privations, none was so painful to Sister Emmerich as the want of proper spiritual direction. She had no one with whom she could confer on her interior, no one to help her bear the burden that weighed her down. " Day and night, " she says, " did I implore God to send me a priest to whom I might lay open my interior, for I was often in dread of being deluded by the evil spirit. This dread made me doubt everything, even what was before my eyes, my sufferings, my consolations, my very existence itself. The Abbé Lambert tried to quiet me ; but, as he knew little German, I was unable to make him understand clearly, and my trouble always returned. All that was going on in my interior and around me I found perfectly incomprehensible, ignorant peasant-girl that I was ! Though it was the experience of my life, it had never before disturbed me. The last four years in the convent were spent in almost uninterrupted contemplation and the incidents consequent upon this state were multiplied. I could not render an account of them to those that were ignorant of such things, they would have thought them simply impossible. Whilst in this state, as I was praying alone in the church one day, I distinctly heard this question : ' Am I not sufficient for thee ? ' The words made a profound impression on me."

It is not astonishing that Anne Catherine left thus to herself was tormented by doubt and anxiety. The gift of contemplation had been imparted to her for the furtherance of

her expiatory mission and, consequently, it entailed upon
her mental sufferings which, like her physical pains, corresponded to the state of the Church at the time. Her
soul gained strength and ripened in her childhood from the
rich contemplations presented to it,contemplations which embraced the whole history of Redemption ;. now, if we may so
express it, the dark side of her visions was to be placed before her, that is the unfolding of the mystery of iniquity,
the combat of the enemy against the Church. She must
now struggle against the malice and cunning of the
evil one who glides into the vineyard whilst the master
sleeps,and sows the bad seed ; she must destroy it before it
springs up and, clothed in the spiritual armor of purity,
humility, and confidence in God, she must wrestle with the
enemy in his attacks on the sacred priesthood. In such
encounters it is not the light of contemplation, but strong
and lively faith that insures the victory. The father of
lies may, indeed, cast her into mental agony, but he cannot shake her faith. Anne Catherine had never wished
for visions and extraordinary favors and, when she first received them, she knew not that they were extraordinary,
she dreamed not of their being peculiar to herself ; but as
soon as the truth dawned upon her, her chief care was to
submit them to the decision of her director. Not her visions,
but her Faith formed the rule of her conduct ; rather would
she have endured a thousand deaths than violate its holy
teachings, and when the tempter cast her into doubt and
fear as to the origin of her supernatural favors, it was by acts
of this virtue that she put him to flight. In his rude and
oft-repeated assaults, Anne Catherine was deprived of spiritual assistance from the ministers of the Church. In this
she resembled the Church herself whose episcopal sees lay
vacant, whose flocks were wandering without pastors to

check the ever-increasing ravages of heresy, and whose Doctors no longer raised a voice against the torrent of evils pouring in upon her on all sides.

We cannot with indifference behold in the midst of this desolation the poor little nun of Dülmen, unfolding like a miraculous flower a beauty equal to any belonging to preceding ages. When Sts. Teresa and Magdalen di Pazzi adorned the Church, the Order of St. Ignatius was in its first bloom. It was rapidly spreading throughout the Church to which it has given more saints and learned men than any religous institute since the time of St. Francis and St. Dominic. When Sts. Catherine of Sienna, Lidwina, and Colette embalmed her vineyard with the fragrance of their virtues, the Church languished, it is true, in a most distressing state ; but beside these saints there arose in all countries holy and learned souls. But no period was more desolate than that in which the Master of the vineyard poured out upon the little shepherdess of Flamske the plenitude of His graces. God gives His gifts only on condition of faithful co-operation; if this be wanting, they are withdrawn and bestowed upon others who will make a better use of them. Thus does He act toward the mass of the faithful. At no period are the power and mercy of God lessened ; but, when vessels are wanting to receive the superabundant riches of His gifts, He displays the wonders of His love in a few faithful souls upon whom he bestows in addition to their own share, the graces slighted by others. It is on this account that Anne Catherine's privileges and sufferings have in them something extraordinary and imposing. St. Magdalen di Pazzi's ecstasies took place in a cloistered community where such things were regarded with respect not unmingled with fear. Being Novice-Mistress she was surrounded by her young pupils, who delighted in speaking of God or His

saints, that they might behold their Mistress rapt in ecstasy.
But Sister Emmerich's raptures often seized her in the
midst of companions who regarded her with uneasiness on
that very account, and to whom she was as insupportable as
was the Church to the gross infidelity of the period, because she dared still to celebrate the grandeur and magnificence of God in His saints.

" I was frequently unable to resist the divine impulse,
and I fell unconscious before my companions. I was in
choir one day, though not singing with the rest, when I
became rigid, and the nuns happening to push against me,
I fell to the ground. Whilst they were carrying me out,
I saw a nun walking upon the highest point of the roof
where no one could go, and I was told that it was Magdalen
di Pazzi, who had borne the marks of Our Lord's wounds.
Again I saw her running along the choir-grate, mounting
upon the altar, or seizing the priest's hand. Her perilous
flights made me reflect on myself, and I took every precaution not to yield to these states. My Sisters understood
nothing of the kind and they, at first, reproached me severely
for remaining in the chapel prostrate, my arms extended.
But as I could not prevent those raptures, I tried to hide
myself from them in a corner. Despite my efforts, however,
I was ravished out of myself, sometimes in one place,
sometimes in another. I lay prostrate, stiff, and immovable, or I knelt with outstretched arms. The chaplain
often found me in this state. I always longed to see St.
Teresa, because I had heard that she had suffered much
from her confessors. The favor was vouchsafed me. I
did see her several times, sick and weak, writing at a table
or in bed. I thought there was a close friendship between
her and Magdalen di Pazzi. It was revealed to me that
Magdalen from her infancy was pleasing to God, on account
of her simplicity and ardent love.

" In my duties as sacristan I was often lifted up suddenly, and I stood on the highest points of the church, on the windows, the carving, and the cornices, cleaning and dusting where humanly speaking no one could go. I was not frightened when I felt myself thus raised and held up in the air, for I had always been accustomed to my angel's assistance. Sometimes when I awoke, I found myself sitting in a large closet in which were kept things belonging to the sacristy ; sometimes I was in a corner near the altar where not a soul could see me, and I cannot understand how I squeezed into it without tearing my habit. But sometimes on awaking, I found myself seated on the highest rafter of the roof. This generally happened when I had hidden myself to weep. I often saw Magdalen di Pazzi mounting up in this way and running over the rafters, the scaffolding, and the altars."

Dean Overberg deposed :—

" Anne Catherine often had ecstasies in the convent, especially during the last four years of its existence. Everywhere, in the cloister, the garden, the church, and her cell, was she accustomed to sink down upon the ground. They came on chiefly when she was alone, though she had slight raptures in the refectory; but she used to beg God not to send them to her there. It seemed to her that the rapture lasted only a moment, though she afterward found that it was much longer.

" I asked her if she knew how to distinguish between ordinary fainting-spells and ecstasies. She answered : ' In fainting-spells from weakness, I am very, very sick as if about to die ; but in the other state, I know not that I have a body. I am often quite joyous, or again sad. I rejoice in God's mercy toward sinners, lovingly leading them back to Himself; or I mourn over the sins of mankind, I am sad at seeing God so horribly offended.

" ' In my meditation I looked up to heaven and there I saw God. When in desolation, I seemed to be walking in a path scarcely a finger in breath, on either side deep, dark abysses ; above me all was blooming and beautiful, and a resplendent youth led me by the hand over the perilous path. I used to hear at this time the voice of God saying to me : " My grace is sufficient for thee !"—and the words were sweet to my soul.' "

Frequently during her ecstasies, Sister Emmerich received from her angel an order to bring the Sisters back to the strict observance of the Rule. Then, still in ecstasy and shedding abundant tears, she would appear in their midst and quote the Rules on silence, obedience, poverty, the Divine Office, enclosure, and others most often infringed; or again, she would cast herself at the feet of a Sister in whose heart she saw aversion or even downright hatred, and beg her to pardon, to be charitable, helping her to resist the temptation, and pointing out the guilt of entertaining such feelings. The religious generally yielded to her persuasions and opened to her their interior, begging her advice and prayers to correct. If, however, they found the former too difficult to follow, they indulged fits of pettishness and mistrust, and hence arose fresh suspicions in those weak souls. They imagined that Sister Emmerich had now ever before her mind their faults and imperfections whilst, in reality, she received such communications as those given her in vision. She guarded their confidence as a sacred deposit with the sole view of rendering glory to God and assistance to souls in need.

" It often happened," she said, " that whilst doing my work or, perhaps, lying in bed sick, I was in spirit among my Sisters. 1 saw and heard all they did and said, and sometimes I found myself in the church before the Blessed Sacrament, though without leaving my cell. I cannot explain how it was. The first time this happened I thought it was a dream. I was in my fifteenth year and absent from home. I had been urged to pray for a giddy young girl that she might not be led astray. One night I saw a snare laid for her. In an agony, I ran to her room and put to flight a servant-man of the house whom I found at her door. When I entered the chamber, she was in a state of consternation. Now, I really had not left my bed, and I thought it was all a dream. Next morning, however, the girl could not look me in the face and she afterwards told me the whole affair and thanked me repeatedly, saying that I had freed her from the tempter, that I had entered her room and saved her from sin. Then, indeed, I regarded the circumstance as something more than a dream. Such things often occurred at a later period. A woman, whom I had never seen, came to me in great excitement, thanked me with many tears, and recounted her fall and conversion. I recognized her as one for whom I had been told in vision to pray.

" It was not always in spirit only, as in the above cases, that I was sent to the assistance of poor tempted souls. I used to go really in body also. The servant-girls of the convent slept in the out-buildings. Once when I was very ill, I beheld at night two persons conversing together apparently on pious subjects, but their hearts were full of evil thoughts. I arose in the dark, but seeing my way clearly notwithstanding, I went through the cloister to separate them. When they saw me coming they fled in affright, and afterward they showed ill-humor toward me. As I returned I awoke. I was only half-way up the stairs that led to the convent, and I regained my cell with great difficulty as I was so weak.

" On another occasion, one of the Sisters thought she
saw me at the kitchen fire taking something away in a
vessel to eat in private, and again, gathering fruit in the
garden for the same purpose. She ran instantly to tell the
Superioress ; but, when they came to inquire into it, they
found me in bed sick unto death. These incidents made
my state a very embarrassing one, and the religious knew
not what to think of me."

From Sister Emmerich's entrance into the convent, no
suffering seemed to her sufficiently great to outweigh the
supreme privilege of dwelling under the same roof with the
Blessed Sacrament, of passing a greater part of her. day
before It. When at work in her cell or elsewhere, she involuntarily turned toward the church, for the sentiment of
the real and living presence of her Lord was never absent
from her heart. Nothing could oppose a barrier to her
loving communings. The very thought of the Blessed
Eucharist threw her into ecstasy and, if untrammelled by
the commands of obedience, she found herself prostrate on
the altar-steps, although corporeally at a distance. In all
that her Rule exacted of her, she discovered something
bearing reference to the Blessed Sacrament and she was,
consequently, as faithful to the least as to the greatest duty.
Her charge of the sacristy she regarded as essentially sacred,
to be attended to at any cost of physical suffering, since it
was the service of the King of kings, a privilege the angels
might well envy. Truly and at all times did she turn
toward Jesus on the altar as a flower to the sun; all her
thoughts and affections were His, all sent up to Him the
sweet odor of love and sacrifice. Her sufferings for the
Blessed Sacrament were great as her love, for no sins cried
more loudly to heaven, none had greater need of expiation
than those directed against faith in the Real Presence.

It was at this period, as we have before remarked, that Jansenism aimed at banishing the Unbloody Sacrifice of the altar and the veneration of Mary, the Mother of God. These abominations filled her soul with anguish as she knelt before the altar and shared with the Heart of Jesus the sorrow occasioned by such outrages. To none other could He turn, since His most cruel enemies were numbered among those whose sacerdotal character gave them unlimited power over this pledge of His love for man. Her ardor led her at night to the church to kneel in the cold before its closed doors, shedding tears of love and desire until daylight gave her admittance, for her only relief was found in the presence of her Saviour. Her sufferings were as varied as the sins of that period against the Blessed Sacrament, and she did penance for every affront offered It, from the tepidity and indifference of the faithful in receiving Holy Communion to the sacrilegious insults of Its greatest enemies. She would have sunk under the weight of this terrible mission, had not God effaced its impressions from her soul and inundated her, at times, with consolation. The more lively her intuition of the grandeur and magnificence of this great Sacrament, the more ardent became her devotion toward It, the greater her veneration. Her reverence for It, joined to the deep feeling of her own unworthiness, sometimes filled her with such fear that it was only obedience could make her approach the Holy Table. She believed herself responsible, on account of her own imperfections, for the numerous infractions of charity and the Rule committed by the Sisters, and this fear prevented her approaching Holy Communion as often as she might have done.

Dean Overberg says :—

" Her confessor wanted her to communicate oftener than

the other religious, and she obeyed for some time; but, from the Purification till Pentecost, she abstained through human respect, because she was accused of mock sanctity and all kinds of remarks were made on the subject. Besides, she looked upon herself as unfit to communicate so often and she fell into a state of sadness. At last, she recognized her fault, and resumed her custom of frequent Communion, though for two years she had to atone for her disobedience on this point, all consolation being withdrawn from her.

"At the end of this time, her peace of soul returned; and so great was her desire for the Holy Eucharist that she could not wait for the usual hour. Her confessor arranged for her to receive before the community arose on days not marked for all to communicate that, being less remarked, the circumstance might create less talk. Early in the morning she used to knock at the Abbé Lambert's door, who kindly went to the church and gave her Holy Communion. But sometimes she presented herself before the appointed hour, and on one occasion, even shortly after midnight, so great was her longing for the Holy Eucharist. Her whole soul was on fire, and so violently was she impelled toward the church that she felt as if her limbs were being torn from her body. The Abbé was not, as might be supposed, any too well pleased on hearing her knock at his door at such an hour; but on seeing the state in which she was, he went and gave her Holy Communion.

"She assisted at Mass with intense devotion. When the celebrant began: 'In nomine Patris,' etc., she contemplated Jesus on the Mount of Olives, and begged for the Faithful the grace of assisting devoutly at the Holy Sacrifice and for priests that of offering It in a manner pleasing to God; lastly, she implored Our Lord to cast upon all as gracious a look as He once cast on St. Peter.

" At the *Gloria,* she praised God in union with the Church Triumphant and the Church Militant, giving thanks for the daily renewal of the Holy Sacrifice, and imploring God to enlighten all men and console the poor souls in purgatory.

"'At the *Gospel,* she asked for all the Faithful the grace to practise fully the evangelical teachings.

" At the *Offertory,* she presented to God the bread and wine with the priest, praying that they might be changed into the Body and Blood of Jesus Christ, and she whispered to her heart that the moment was drawing near for the advent of the Saviour.

" At the *Sanctus,* she called upon the whole world to praise God with her.

"At the *Consecration,* she offered the Saviour to His Father for the whole world, chiefly for the conversion of sinners, for the relief of the souls in purgatory, for the dying, and for her Sisters in religion. She imagined the altar surrounded at this moment by crowds of adoring angels who dared not raise their eyes to the Sacred Host. She said to herself that, although it might be very bold in her, yet she could not deprive herself of the consolation of gazing upon her Lord.

" She often saw a brilliant light surrounding the Sacred Host and in the Host a cross of dark color, never white. Had it been white, she could not have distinguished it. It did not seem to be larger than the Host, but the latter was Itself often larger than usual.

" From the *Elevation* to the *Agnus Dei,* she prayed for the souls in purgatory, presenting Jesus on the Cross to His Father that He might accomplish what she could not. At this moment, she was often rapt out of herself and, indeed, she sometimes fell into ecstasy even before the Consecration.

" At the *Communion*, she reflected on Christ laid in the tomb, and begged Almighty God to annihilate in us the old man and clothe us with the new.

" If at Mass or any other service, she listened to the music, she would exclaim : ' Ah, how sweet is harmony ! Inanimate crea'ures accord so perfectly, why should not men's hearts do the same ! How charming that would be !' —and the thought made her shéd tears.

" Once, during the Christmas Midnight-Mass, she saw the Infant Jesus above the chalice, and what appeared to her strange was that the celebrant seemed to hold the Infant by the feet, notwithstanding which, she saw the chalice too. She often saw an Infant in the Host, but He was very small.

" When she was sacristan, she occupied for a time a place in choir from which she could not see the altar, having given hers up to a Sister who was tormented with scruples when she heard Mass without enjoying that consolation. One day as she was watching to ring the bell for the Elevation, she saw the Infant Jesus above the chalice,—O how beautiful ! She thought herself in heaven. She was about to leap through the grate to get at the Child when suddenly recollecting herself, she exclaimed : ' My God ! what am I going to do !'—She succeeded in restraining herself, but forgot to sound the bell, a frequent omission of hers which drew upon her many a reprimand."

Clara Soentgen says : " When Sister Emmerich received Holy Communion her bodily strength increased. She loved, above all, to communicate on Thursday in honor of the Blessed Sacrament ; but, as this gave rise to remark, she obtained permission from her confessor to communicate in secret. Sometimes she went to receive a little after midnight, sometimes at three or four o'clock in the morning, her ardent desire rendering it impossible for her to wait longer.

" Once I asked her why she wore her best habit on Thursdays, and she answered that it was in honor of the Blessed Sacrament. She rarely made use of a book before or after Communion."

Sister Emmerich herself speaks as follows :—"I very often saw blood flowing from the cross on the Sacred Host; I saw it distinctly. Sometimes Our Lord, in the form of an Infant, appeared like a lightning-flash in the Sacred Host. At the moment of communicating, I used to see my Saviour like a bridegroom standing by me and, when I had received He disappeared, leaving me filled with the sweet sense of His presence. He pervades the whole soul of the communicant just as sugar is dissolved in water, and the union between the soul and Jesus is always in proportion to the soul's desire to receive Him."

Dean Overberg gives the following account of her prayer :—" Before she entered religion, Anne Catherine prayed for sinners and the souls in purgatory. In the convent she prayed also for her companions, rarely for her own wants. Save those prescribed by Rule, she said few vocal prayers, but made use of frequent ejaculations. She spoke to God as a child to its father and generally obtained what she asked.

" Her communing with God ceased neither day nor night, even at table it was not interrupted. She was often unconscious of what was said there, and if the Sisters made remarks about her at such times, she rarely perceived it.

" Abbé Lambert asked her one day at the end of one of the meals :—' How could you listen so quietly to what passed at table ?'— when she answered that she had heard nothing of what was said.

" She had, at one time, the habit of disputing with God
on two points : that He did not convert all the big sinners,
and that He punished the impenitent with everlasting pains.
She told Him that she could not understand how He could
act thus, so contrary to His nature, which is goodness itself,
as it would be easy for Him to convert sinners since all
are in His hand. She reminded Him of all that He and
His Son had done for them ; of the latter's having shed His
Blood and given His life for them upon the cross ; of His
own words and promises of mercy contained in the Scriptures. She asked Him with holy boldness, how could He expect men to keep their word, if He did not keep His ?"

" The Abbé Lambert, to whom she recounted this dispute,
said to her : ' Softly ! you go too far !' and she soon saw
that God is right ; for, if He did convert all sinners or if the
pains of hell were not to last forever, man would forget
that there is a God.

" She had great confidence in the Mother of God to
whom she turned whenever she had committed a fault, saying : ' O Mother of my Saviour, thou art doubly my Mother !
Thy Son gave thee to me for mother when He said to John :
' *Behold thy Mother !*' and then again, I am the spouse of
thy Son. I have been disobedient to Him, I am ashamed
to appear before Him. O do thou pity me ! A mother's
heart is always so good ! Ask Him to forgive me, He cannot refuse thee."

" One day just before the suppression of the convent,
when she had sought in vain for consolation among her
Sisters, she ran weeping to the church and prostrated in
agony before the Blessed Sacrament crying for pardon, for
she was overwhelmed by the thought that she alone was
the cause of all the evil in the house. ' O God, I am the
prodigal child !' she cried ; ' I have squandered my inherit-

ance, I am not worthy to be called Thy child! Have pity
on me! I ask it through my sweetest Mother, who is Thy
Mother, too!'—then the voice of God sounded in her soul
bidding her be at peace, that His grace would suffice for
her, and that she should no more seek consolation from
creatures.

"Often, when begging some favor most earnestly and
making great promises to Our Lord, she heard these words:
—' How canst thou promise great things, when little ones are
so difficult to thee!' "

The following is Dean Rensing's deposition :—

" Sister Emmerich said the prescribed prayers with the
religious, and some other vocal prayers ; but when she prayed interiorly she laid her request before God and in the depths
of her heart begged to be favorably heard. She added an
Our Father or some other short prayer, often going so
far as to dispute the point with the Almighty.

" She loved mental better than vocal prayer. She asked
herself : ' What ought you to be, and what are you ?'—
and then she went on until her meditation had been greatly
prolonged, not knowing herself how she had passed from
point to point."

Clara Soentgen says :—" Sister Emmerich told me that
from the Ascension to Pentecost, her state of contemplation
was uninterrupted. She saw the disciples assembled together praying for the coming of the Holy Ghost, and she
herself was present with them. This had happened to her
even before her entrance into religion. During the ten days
of preparation, she used to receive Holy Communion several
times. I sat by her at table in the convent, and she
was so absorbed at this time that I used to have to remind
her to eat."

Anne Catherine tells us :—

" I cannot use the prayers of the Church translated into German. I find them insipid and tiresome, though in Latin they are full and intelligible; however, I can confine myself to no set form of speech. I was always glad when we had to sing hymns and responses in Latin ; the feast was then more real to me, I saw all that I sang. When we sang the Litany of the Blessed Virgin in Latin, I used to see one after another in a most wonderful manner all the symbolical figures of Mary. It seemed as if I uttered the pictures. At first, it frightened me, but soon I found what a great favor it was, as it excited my devotion. I saw the most wonderful pictures !"

CHAPTER XVI.

SUPPRESSION OF THE CONVENT.—SISTER EMMERICH RECEIVES THE STIGMATA.

On December 3, 1811, Agnetenberg was suppressed and the church closed. Although Sister Emmerich had long foreseen this most painful event to avert which she had offered herself to God to suffer everything, yet she was so affected by it that she thought she would never be able to quit scenes so dear to her. The separation of her soul from her body would have been less agonizing than leaving the hallowed spot in which she had made her sacred vows.

"I became so ill," she says, "that they thought I should surely die. Then the Mother of God appeared to me and said: 'Thou wilt not die! There will yet be much talk about thee, but fear not! Whatever may happen, thou wilt receive help!'—Later I heard in all my sicknesses a voice whispering to me: 'Thy task is not yet finished!'"

The religious quitted the convent one by one, but Sister Emmerich remained till the following spring, so ill as not to be able to leave her bed. Into her cold, damp cell the painful scenes arising from the Sisters' aversion toward her never found their way. She lay alone, abandoned to herself and her sufferings. But the doves and sparrows hopped on her window-sill and the mice scampered familiarly over the coverlet of her bed, playing fearlessly by her and listening to her reproaches when she scolded them for destroying the doves' eggs. If the Abbé Lambert and an old servant-woman had not in pity rendered her the most necessary services, sad enough would have been her condition. The Sisters were too much occupied with their own affairs to think of her; and yet they had scarcely lost sight of her when they forgot their prejudice against her, as well as its cause. To the question put by ecclesiastical authority: "How was it that Sister Emmerich was not loved in the convent and why was she so persecuted?"—they had no other answer than that of the Novice-Mistress: "It is true, she was not much beloved, but I know not why." The Reverend Mother alone tried to assign a reason: "It seems to me that this was the cause: many of the Sisters were jealous of the particular interest the Abbé Lambert took in her, and some thought her ill-health made her a burden on the community."

The Abbé Lambert, an invalid himself and an exile, without a soul upon earth from whom to hope for sympathy in his old age, remained true to Sister Emmerich in her distress. What he had seen in her for the last ten years he had faithfully kept concealed in his own breast. He was the only one to whom she had revealed the wonderful way by which it pleased Heaven to lead her, the only one who had the least idea of her high mission. He felt himself called to guard to the best of his power her person as well as the mystery of her life, regarding her as a chosen instrument, a precious treasure, for which he was to account to God, since to him alone it had been given to know its value. When she could no longer remain in the convent, he accompanied her to the house of a widow named Roters, at Dülmen. She was still so sick that, after dragging painfully through the streets with the assistance of the old servant, she could hardly gain the little front room on the ground-floor which now took the place of the quiet cell whose religious poverty had transformed it into a heaven upon earth.

"I was so nervous and frightened," she said, "when I had to leave the convent, that I thought every stone in the street was about to rise up against me."

She had scarcely reached her miserable lodging, through which the footsteps of the passers-by resounded and into which the curious m ght freely gaze, as it was almost on a level with the sidewalk, when she fell into a deep swoon. Like a flower dragged from its home on the mountain-top and trodden under foot on a dusty highway, she seemed about to fade. Although the strict observance of Rule had fallen into decay, yet the cloister had been for Anne Catherine a consecrated spot, a place sanctified by the prayer and penance of its first occupants in the days of fervor and religious discipline, and where she herself had aimed at the perfect accomplishment of every duty. She had, as it were, identified herself with the conventual exercises still kept up in spite of the inroads of decay. The Divine Office and other religious duties were almost essential to her life, an aliment whose want nothing else could supply; but, above all, the vicinity of the Blessed Sacrament, the house of God open to her at all times, appeared a necessary condition to her stay upon earth, to the accomplishment of her expiatory task. All this was now snatched from her grasp. From the holy asylum in which her life had passed for the last nine years in perfect seclusion, she was cast, so to speak, helpless and friendless, upon the public road there to begin the last and most painful stage of her mission.

That just before the Lent of 1812, a poor sick nun was led through the streets of the obscure town of Dülmen, was an event of little importance, doubtless, in the eyes of the world. And yet, this apparently insignificant circumstance was in strict accordance with the designs of Divine Providence.

On this poor religious woman, worn out by suffering and penance, despised and persecuted on account of her profession, were heaped all the tribulations of the Church at this time scorned and maltreated as never since her foundation. But as the Man-God Himself, "A root out of a thirsty ground" (1), "despised and the most abject of men," "the man of sorrows, wounded for our iniquities, bruised for our sins," willed to work out our Redemption, and would not prevent the word of the Cross from becoming "to the Jews a stumbling-block, to the Gentiles foolishness;" so at all times has He delivered His Church by choosing "the foolish things of the world to confound the wise, the weak to confound the strong, the mean things of the world and the things that are contemptible, and the things that are not, to destroy the things that are" (2). To accomplish this end, incomprehensible to men, sublime in the sight of the blessed, to procure by her means the deliverance of his Church, God now draws His spouse from the hidden retreat in which she had acquired that strength which surpasses all the strength and wisdom of man.

Many religious of either sex had left their cloister without regret to return to that world from which their sacred vows had never wholly detached them; everywhere unworthy monks and priests were met employed by the great ones of the world to spread in the hearts of aspirants to the priesthood the poison of error and revolt against the hierarchy and sacred traditions of the Church. The sanctity and dignity of the sacerdotal character, the graces and privileges attached thereto, were despised and denied even by those that were clothed with it; and the open enemies of the Christian name were not the only ones who confidently looked forward to the speedy destruction of the Church.

(1) Isaias liii. 2-5.   (2) I. Cor. i. 27.

This explains the state to which the poor victim of expiation is now reduced, why she is thrown out, unprotected and proscribed. It is the Church and her Heavenly Bridegroom that suffer and mourn in the person of the helpless little nun of Dülmen.

Sister Emmerich became rapidly worse. All thought her end near, and her former Novice-Mistress sent for Father Limberg, a Dominican priest who, since the suppression of his convent in Münster had resided in Dülmen, to hear the invalid's confession. We shall give his own words on the impressions then received:—

"During the Lent of 1812, my aunt, who had been Sister Emmerich's Novice-Mistress, sent for me to hear her confession. At first I refused, since a special permission is necessary to hear a religious; but, when I was assured that this restriction was no longer in force, I went. She was so weak as to be unable to speak, and I had to question her on her conscience. I thought her dying and delayed not to give her all the Last Rites; but she rallied, and I became from that time her confessor instead of Father Chrysanthe, an Augustinian, lately deceased. She wore a cincture of brass wire and a hair-shirt in the form of a scapular, which I made her lay aside.

" I knew very little of Sister Emmerich before this, having seen her only occasionally. I often said Mass in the convent chapel, and I liked to do so; everything there was so neat. I thus became acquainted with the chaplain, the Abbé Lambert. Sister Emmerich was sacristan, and I used to see her coming and going. Her health seemed to be so miserable that I thought she would soon die. I often said to myself on seeing her : ' What! that poor soul still alive!'"

Sister Emmerich kept her bed the whole of Lent, her

soul the greater part of the time in a state of abstraction which was ascribed to excessive debility.

On the Feast of Easter she went, though not without great effort, to the parish church to receive Holy Communion, and she continued to do so until Nov. 2, 1812, after which she never rose from her bed of pain. In September she made a pilgrimage to a place called the "Hermitage," just outside Dülmen, where an Augustinian had formerly dwelt and near which was a small chapel. She went in the hope of receiving some alleviation to her fearful sufferings. She had hardly reached the spot when she fell into an ecstasy, becoming rigid and immovable as a statue. The young girl who accompanied her was seized with fright, and called out to a woman for help; they thought she had fainted and treated her accordingly. In doing so they discovered upon her breast a bloody cross which she had received on the preceding Feast of St. Augustine, August 28, but which she herself had never seen. When she awoke from her ecstasy, she was so weak that the two women had to help her home.

On December 29, 1812, the daughter of the widow Roters found Anne Catherine again in ecstasy, her arms extended, and blood gushing from the palms of her hands. The girl thought it the effect of an accident and drew her attention to it when she had returned to consciousness, but Sister Emmerich earnestly requested her not to speak of it. On December 31st, when Father Limberg took her Holy Communion, he saw for the first time the bloody marks on the back of her hands.

"I made it known," he writes in his report, "to the Abbé Lambert who resided in the same house. He went immediately to Sister Emmerich's room and, seeing the blood still flowing, he thus addressed her: 'Sister, you must not think yourself a Catherine of Sienna!' But as the wounds bled until evening, he said to me next day: 'Father, no one must know this! Let it rest between ourselves, otherwise it will give rise to talk and annoyance!'"

Father Limberg was fully persuaded of the necessity of such a course. He thought more of treating the affair as of small importance than of seeking any relationship between it and other wonderful things he knew concerning the invalid, nor did he question her on the subject. Sister Emmerich herself rejoiced that the two priests did not pursue the affair and she sought to conceal from all eyes her new and cruel sufferings. Father Limberg did not at the time reduce his observations to writing; but in his ordo he made the following short entries :—

"Jan. 6th, Feast of the Kings, I saw for the first time the stigmata on the palms of her hands."

"Jan. 11th—She sat up in an arm-chair about six o'clock. She was in ecstasy an hour and a half."

"Jan. 15th—She communicated to-day. From seven till nine, stiff and immovable in ecstasy."

"Jan. 28th—Since the 15th, she has been in ecstasy more or less prolonged. To-day, I saw the marks of the wounds on the soles of her feet.

"Her hands and feet bleed every Friday and the double cross upon her breast on Wednesdays. Since the existence of these wounds has come to my knowledge, she has eaten nothing.

"Her state remained secret till February 28, 1813, when Clara Soentgen perceived it and spoke to me of it."

As Sister Emmerich never mentioned her stigmata but, on the contrary, anxiously hid them, we can glean further details on the subject only from the official inquiry to which she was subjected and in consequence of which her state soon became noised abroad.

CHAPTER XVII.

Ecclesiastical Investigations.—Dean Rensing's Report.

Once Clara Soentgen had penetrated Sister Emmerich's secret, the news spread far and wide. Toward the middle of March, 1813, it was the talk of the town. Her case was freely discussed even in the public ale-house and, as might be expected, it soon reached the ears of Ecclesiastical Superiors at Münster (1).

Among those that took part in the discussion mentioned above was Dr. William Wesener of Dülmen, who now for the first time heard such things spoken of, and who saw in the whole affair but the grossest superstition; however, he resolved to visit the invalid that he might be better qualified to judge. He had lost his faith whilst studying at the University; but he was a man of so upright and benevolent a disposition that the mere sight of the patient produced a deep impression upon him. He knew not how to account for the singular facts he witnessed but, trusting to her rare artlessness, he hoped soon to discover their true cause. After a few visits, he offered his professional services, which were willingly accepted (2). Upon close observation he arrived at the conclusion that all suspicion of fraud ought to be discarded though there were, indeed, some facts beyond his comprehension which could neither

(1) The conversation in the public-house had not escaped Sr. Emmerich. After Dr. Wesener's visit to her, her confessor asked her how he knew of her, when she answered: "He was among the gentlemen assembled at the ale-house. He was incredulous, and so he came to see me."

(2) Dr. Wesener kept a journal from his first visit up to 1819, in which he noted down not only his observations and experience with regard to Anne Catherine, but also her exhortations for his return to the faith and the practice of his religious duties.

be denied nor concealed. He consulted with Dean Rensing, the parish-priest, with Father Limberg, and a physician named Krauthausen, upon the measures to be taken
for instituting a proces-verbal respecting the phenomena.
Whilst these gentlemen were discussing at the pastor's
residence the best means to adopt, Almighty God turned
Sister Emmerich's attention toward them, in order to prepare
her for what was to follow. The Abbé Lambert was talking with her when suddenly interrupting him she exclaimed : " What is going to happen to me ? They are holding a council at the Dean's upon subjecting me to an examination. If I mistake not I see my confessor there."

Shortly after these words Dean Rensing entered her
room, and announced that they had decided upon an investigation. It actually took place on the 22d of March,
1813. A report was drawn up of which we shall give one
passage : " On the back of both hands are crusts of
dried blood under each of which is a sore, and in the palms
are similar smaller crusts. The same thing may be seen
on the upper part of her feet and in the middle of the soles.
The wounds are sensitive to the touch, those of the right foot
had just bled. On the right side, over the fourth rib from
below, is a wound about three inches long which, it is said,
bleeds occasionally, and on the breast-bone are round
marks forming a forked cross. A little lower is an ordinary cross formed of lines, half an inch in length which
look like scratches. On the upper part of the forehead
are numerous marks like the pricks of a needle which
run along the temple back to the hair. On her linen binder we saw blood stains."

After this examination, Sister Emmerich said to Dean
Rensing :—" It is not yet over. Some gentlemen are coming from Münster to examine my case. One is a distin-

guished personage, who looks like the Bishop that confirmed me at Coesfeld, and there is another rather older
man with a few gray hairs."

Her words were verified, for on the 28th of March (the
Fourth Sunday of Lent) the Vicar-General of Münster,
Clement Auguste von Droste-Vischering, so celebrated
afterward as Archbishop of Cologne, arrived in Dülmen
accompanied by the venerable Dean Overberg and a medical adviser, Dr. von Druffel. They had come with the intention of rigorously examining into Sister Emmerich's
case. On March 25th, Dean Rensing had addressed to the
Vicar-General an official report upon the invalid's case and
forwarded the statement of the physician. It ran as
follows :—

" Most Noble Baron,
      " Very Reverend Vicar-General :

" With a heart deeply touched and full of religious sentiments, I announce to you, as to my Ecclesiastical Superior,
a fact well calculated to prove that God, at all times admirable in His saints, still operates in them even in our own
days of infidelity, wonders which clearly exhibit the power
of our holy religion, which lead the most frivolous to reflect, the most incredulous to turn from their errors. The
Lord still chooses the weak to confound the strong, still reveals to His little ones secrets hidden from the great. I
have up to the present kept the case secret, being so requested, and also through the deference I believed due to the
favored soul. I feared, too, the annoyances attendant on
its being divulged. But now that God has permitted the
affair to be, so to say, proclaimed from the house-tops, I
deem it my duty to make an official report of it to you. I
shall not longer conceal the secret of the King.

" Anne Catherine Emmerich, Choir-Sister of the Augustinian convent called Agnetenberg, now suppressed, is
the chosen of God of whom there is question, and Clara
Soentgen is the school-mistress of this place. She took the
religious habit on the same day as Sister Emmerich and
with her parents the latter resided just before entering the
convent. Sister Soentgen testifies that from her early
youth Anne Catherine was extremely pious, practising conformity to the will of God in imitation of our Crucified
Saviour. She was sick almost the whole of the ten years
of her conventual life, in bed for weeks at a time, and she
suffered much from the contempt of the other religious who
regarded her as a visionary. Their treatment was not, indeed, very charitable. They disliked her because she received Holy Communion several times a week, spoke enthusiastically of the happiness there is in suffering, performed many good works of supererogation, and thus distinguished herself too much from them. At times, also, they
had reason to suspect her of visions and revelations. Her
state of debility has continued since the suppression of her
convent. She has now been confined to bed for some months
and for the last two she has taken no medicine and no other
nourishment than a little cold water with which for a time
a few drops of wine were mingled; but for the last three
or four weeks she has dispensed with the wine. If she
takes a third or even a fourth part of wine in water, in order to conceal the fact that she lives exclusively upon the
latter, she instantly rejects it. Her night-sweats are so
heavy that her bed linen is perfectly saturated. She is a
living witness to the truth of Holy Scriptures: ' Not by
bread alone doth man live, but by every word that cometh
forth from the mouth of the Lord.' Every evening she falls
into a swoon, or rather a holy ecstasy, which lasts ten hours

and more, at which times she lies stiff and immovable in whatever position she may chance to have been, her face fresh and rosy like a little child's. If the coverlet or even a pillow be held up before her and by stealth, if I may use the expression, and a priest gives her his blessing, she instantly raises her hand which until then had lain immovable as that of a statue, and makes the sign of the Cross. She has revealed to her confessor, Father Limberg, and also to me after these ecstasies, secrets which she could have known only supernaturally. But what distinguishes her still more as the special favorite of Heaven is the bloody crown around her brow, the stigmata of her hands, feet, and side, and the crosses on her breast. These wounds often bleed, some on Wednesdays, others on Fridays, and so copiously that heavy drops of blood fall to the ground. This phenomenon creates much talk and criticism ; therefore, I engaged the physicians of this place to make a preliminary examination that I might be able to draw up a report. These gentlemen were greatly affected by what they saw. The result of their investigation is contained in a statement signed by them, by Father Limberg, by the Abbé Lambert, a French priest, who resides in the same house with the invalid, and by myself.

"I discharge this duty as one I owe to my Ecclesiastical Superior to furnish proper information in so singular an occurrence, and I beg to be informed as to what course to pursue, especially in the event of the decease of this remarkable person. She greatly dreads publicity and particularly the intervention of civil authority. I hope your influence will be able to avert such an annoyance. Should Your Excellency desire to convince yourself of the truth of this statement and of the supernatural character of certain attendant circumstances, which I deem prudent not to com-

mit to paper, I beg you to come to Dülmen with Dean
Overberg and to honor my house by your august presence.

" I should much prefer making this report in person ; but
the sickness of some of my parishioners, catechetical instructions for First Communion, and other affairs prevent my doing so at present. Your Excellency will certainly hold me
excused.

" With profound respect,

" RENSING.

" DÜLMEN, *March* 25, 1813."

CHAPTER XVIII.

First Visit of the Vicar-General to Dülmen.

The report given in the preceding chapter was coldly received by the Vicar-General on March 27th.

"When I read Dean Rensing's report with the official statement of the physicians," he says, "I was very far from regarding the affair as represented by them. As is usual in such cases, I suspected fraud or delusion. I had heard nothing of it before. As it was beginning to be noised about in Dülmen and thinking the truth might be easily tested since it was a question of things falling under the senses, I went the next day to Dülmen. I took them by surprise, as they did not expect me so soon. Dean Overberg and Dr. von Druffel accompanied me, for I was desirous of the latter's opinion; I know him to be clear-sighted and not at all credulous."

Their arrival was not, however, so great a surprise to Sister Emmerich as the Vicar-General supposed. Shortly after, the Vicar Hilgenberg deposed on oath that he had visited Sister Emmerich Saturday evening after the Litanies and, on inquiring how she was, had received for answer: "I have spent a miserable week on account of the medical examination of my wounds; but *to-morrow* and next week I shall suffer still more from new inquiries."

"We arrived about four o'clock in Dülmen," continues the Vicar-General in his notes. "On Sunday, we saw Anne Catherine Emmerich twice and conversed with her in presence of her confessor and the Dean. On Monday morning, the 29th, we had another conversation with her and I spoke also with her friend, Clara Soentgen of Coesfeld.

We left Dülmen about ten o'clock. The case seems to be more remarkable than we expected to find it. "

The 28th of March, 1813, was the Fourth Sunday of Lent and in the diocese of Münster, the Feast of St. Joseph. The Vicar-General caused a special report to be drawn up of the observations made on this day and the following, and Dean Overberg also made notes of what seemed most remarkable in the case The report runs as follows :—

"We visited Sister Emmerich about five o'clock P. M., to assure ourselves of the phenomena said to be displayed in her person. We remarked nothing striking in her counte-nance, nothing that indicated expectancy, no sign of pleasure or surprise. When notified that her Superiors de-sired to examine into her state, she consented unreservedly, and unhesitatingly showed her hands, her feet, and her right side, remarking only that, although such proceedings were painful, yet she desired but to conform to the will of God.

"The lightest touch on her wounds is, as she says, ex-quisitely painful. Her whole arm quivered whenever the wound of her hand was touched, or the middle finger moved.

"Toward nine o'clock that same evening we paid her another visit. Soon after our arrival, she fell into ecstasy, her members becoming rigid, the fingers only remaining flexible. A touch on the wounds or the middle finger excited trembling. Her head could now be raised only with diffi-culty and then the breast, as if following the movement of the head, rose also. The questions put to her by the physi-cians remained unanswered. She gave no sign of life (1). Then the Vicar-General said: 'In virtue of holy obedience, I command you to answer !'—Scarcely were the words pro-

(1) From Dean Overberg's Report.

nounced when, quick as thought, she turned her head, regarded us with a singularly touching expression, and answered every question put to her. Later, she was asked how it was that, although unconscious, she had so quickly turned her head on the Vicar-General's command, and had she heard his voice. She answered: 'No! but when anything is commanded me in obedience whilst in this state, I seem to hear a loud voice calling me.'

"She has begged Our Lord to deprive her of the external signs of His Wounds; but she has always received the answer: 'My grace is sufficient for thee!'— The Vicar-General bade her renew this petition forthwith."

Next morning the visitors returned for the third time and the Vicar-General decided that the surgeon, Dr. Krauthausen, of Dülmen, should wash the wounds in tepid water to remove the crusts of dried blood, apply linen bandages to the hands and feet in such a way that neither the fingers nor toes could move freely, and see that they so remained for eight consecutive days. Sister Emmerich readily submitted to the experiment. She repeated more than once that she would freely consent to any others they might desire to make, only begging them to avoid publicity.

The gentlemen were fully satisfied with her whole comportment especially her acquiescence in the orders of Superiors, although they greatly increased her sufferings. The favorable impression she produced on them appears from the following lines of the report:

"The countenance of the patient during the different interviews was remarkably serene, and one could not help being struck with the frank and benevolent expression of her eye."

"Lastly, the Vicar-General conversed with her in private, telling her that, although it was lawful for us to desire to share in the sufferings of our Divine Redeemer, yet we should not seek external marks of them. To which she replied: 'Those exterior marks form, indeed, my cross!'"

CHAPTER XIX.

Measures Adopted by the Vicar-General.

On returning to Münster, the Vicar-General adopted such measures for the prosecution of the inquiry as clearly proved that the impression made on him personally by Sister Emmerich's demeanor yielded to higher considerations.

"I could not," he remarks in his official report, "conclude from a single investigation that imposture or delusion was impossible. Supposing no deceit whatever in the case, the question as to whether those phenomena can be explained by natural causes, is not my affair. The stigmata are visible to whomsoever looks upon them, the facts themselves cannot deceive. The only question is: Has Sister Emmerich produced them herself, or not? or has some one made them for her? As she has solemnly declared that such is not the case, it remains to be determined whether she is practising deceit or is herself deluded. If the investigation leads to the conclusion that the slightest imposition may reasonably be suspected, there will be no need to push matters further; but to arrive at such a conclusion, we have only to make use of such means as will wound neither justice nor charity."

Clement Auguste von Droste-Vischering united to determination of character so tender a heart that he was often known to purchase birds merely to restore them their liberty. Now, when such a man resolved to regulate his mode of action by principles like those expressed above, we may readily conclude that the sufferings inevitably resulting to the subject of such an examination, would be alleviated as much as possible; yet such alleviation in Sister Emmerich's case was not in accordance with the designs of God. As substitute for the Church, she must endure those pains and trials which alone could draw down pardon on an obdurate world; consequently, in all the Vicar-General's proceedings, his compassion was less consulted than the necessity of satisfying public opinion. The spirit of the times, his own embarrassing position as Administrator of a see long orphaned and exposed to political vicissitudes, imposed obligations to which all other motives stood secondary.

In 1802, Münster had lost its last ecclesiastical ruler, the Prince-Bishop Maximilian Xavier, brother to the Emperor Joseph II., and Prussia had seized on the vacant see. The States-Assembly of 1803 put Prussia in definitive possession of the episcopal city of Münster and the southern portion of the country, the other sections being divided among seven petty sovereigns. Dülmen fell into the hands of the Catholic Duke von Croy, who, at a later period, caused the ancient church and convent of Agnetenberg, the scenes of Anne Catherine's religious life, to be entirely destroyed. Coesfeld and Flamske fell to the Count von Salm. After the battle of Jena, these territories were again wrested from their possessors and united to the Grand-Duchy of Berg, which Napoleon had erected in favor of a child still in the cradle, the eldest son of his sister-in-law, Hortense, Queen of Holland. The year 1810 put an end to this union; and Münster, Coesfeld, and Dülmen were incorporated with the great French Empire until the Congress of Vienna, when the whole province passed into the hands of Prussia.

The Vicar-General's difficult position may now be appreciated. The secular powers were incessantly changing, and the people worn out with the same, daily regretted

the peace and happiness they had formerly enjoyed under
their Prince-Bishops. Besides, Clement Auguste von Droste
belonged to one of the oldest and noblest families of Münster, a sufficient reason for his being looked upon with a
distrustful eye by the strangers then in power. In 1807,
he had been appointed by the Cathedral-Chapter, Administrator of the·diocese vacant since 1802 ; but, April 14,
1813, the Dean of the Chapter, Count von Spiegel, was
named Bishop by a decree of Napoleon, and the Chapter
was forced to deliver over to him the government of the
diocese.   Clement Auguste thus became the Vicar-General
of Count von Spiegel, a proceeding which Rome refused to
tolerate. He resumed, therefore, the Administratorship of
the diocese until 1821, when Münster was provided with a
pastor in the person of Baron von Lüning, formerly Prince-
Bishop of Corvey, who soon, however, fell into a state of
mental weakness which ended in death, 1825.

The Vicar-General von Droste bitterly mourned over
the Church whose servant he gloried in being. He grieved to
see her insulted and despised by the so-called lights of the
age, treated as an institution which no longer had a right
to exist, which was destined soon to fall to pieces ; and he
knew with what a torrent of outrages any sign of life in her
would be pursued, anything which contradicted the opinion
entertained by her enemies, that the extinction of Catholicism was already an accomplished fact.   Nor was this all —
in the ranks of those enemies were her own priests who, by
word and writing, dared to wage open war against her ancient practices of faith and piety.   Let us not, then, be surprised if, in such a situation, a man of his prudence and
foresight should be greatly annoyed at finding himself connected with an affair so extraordinary, so foreign to the
ideas of the times as was that of Sister Emmerich.   He

had hoped promptly to unveil the imposture and prevent reports detrimental to the Church; but now that he
could not look upon the case as such, he felt himself obliged
to pursue inquiries into it as diligently as possible. He was
bound not to expose his authority to a shadow of suspicion,
nor to leave the least room for the charge of censurable
indulgence or carelessness in what might possibly turn out
to be fraud, and which, at all events, could not fail to
exasperate the enemies of the Church.

The Vicar-General's choice of Dean Overberg and Dr.
von Druffel to assist in the examination, was the happiest
that could have been made. Dean Overberg's name is
everywhere pronounced with respect. He was one of the
noblest characters of his time, esteemed throughout Münster as the most enlightened and experienced director of
souls. The Vicar-General fully appreciated his worth;
therefore, he commissioned him to inquire scrupulously into
Sister Emmerich's whole interior and exterior life, prescrib-
ing also to the latter, in virtue of obedience, to give an
exact account of herself to the Dean. The holy old man
found it no difficult matter to gain the invalid's confidence,
and on his very first interview he made the following note :—

" In spirit, she saw me coming and she told me so, though
as she declared to others, she had never seen me in her life
with her bodily eyes. 'I saw you interiorly,' she said to
me, and this made her as confiding as if we had long known
each other."

The childlike candor with which she opened her heart to
the venerable priest enabled him to gaze deep down into
her pious soul, and her interior life soon lay unveiled before
him. Every interview offered him fresh proofs of her extraordinary vocation ; and though multitudes constantly claimed
his advice and assistance, occupying his time and attention

continually, yet he deemed it his duty to undertake the additional task of noting down all he observed in her, even the words that fell from her lips. One might suppose that the Dean's rare kindness would invent some means of mitigating the sufferings attendant on the investigation; but God willed that from no quarter should any hindrance arise to the measures judged necessary to dissipate doubt as to the reality of the phenomena.

Prof. von Druffel, a learned and highly respectable physician, was a man of unbiassed mind who examined the wonders displayed in his patient with the practised eye of an experienced scientist. When he first heard of them, he felt inclined to regard them as fraud; but his very first visit greatly modified these sentiments. Not only did the condition of the wounds and their manner of bleeding convince him that they could not possibly be produced artificially, but Sister Emmerich's whole demeanor forced him to reject absolutely all suspicion of imposture. We may here remark that Dr. von Druffel, as also Drs. Wesener and Krauthausen, had a lively appreciation of the sufferings that would result to the patient from such treatment as the Vicar-General prescribed, and personally they needed no such proof as to the reality of the facts witnessed. The publicity attendant on such an investigation and the interest it aroused, induced Dr. von Druffel to insert a long article signed by himself in the Salzbourg "Journal of Medicine and Surgery," in which he gave a detailed account of his own observations respecting Sister Emmerich. He begins by declaring that he has no intention of trying to explain the phenomena and ends with the bold words:

"As to those that regard the phenomena in question as imposture let them remember that the ecclesiastical investigation was made most strictly. If it be a fraud, it is of a very peculiar nature and very difficult to prove."

Dr. von Druffel, like all who fell under Sister Emmerich's influence, received a great grace from God through her intervention, for she perceived the state of his soul and the danger he was in of losing his faith. After her first interview with him, she confided her discovery to Dean Overberg, allowing him to make use of the information if he thought it advisable. The doctor entertained the highest respect for the holy priest by whom in return he was greatly esteemed. The Dean was amazed, indeed he could scarcely credit what he heard until the doctor himself confirmed Sister Emmerich's statement and gave unequivocal proofs of the benefit he derived from her acquaintance.

The Vicar-General dispatched to Dülmen on the 31st of March, a summary of the rules to be observed in the coming examination. They are a notable proof of this distinguished man's rare firmness, prudence, and foresight. His first step was to nominate Dean Rensing (1) Sister Emmerich's extraordinary director during the process, imposing upon him the obligation of carefully observing the patient's conduct, and of rendering a faithful account to him of the same. The following detailed instructions were also sent to the Dean:—

" It is our duty to investigate these phenomena as strictly as possible, in order to discover their origin : whether produced by sickness, or supernaturally, or in fine by artificial means. There is here no question of private opinion, but only that of verifying what may be possible ; which being premised, it is absolutely necessary not only that all that transpires in the soul and with regard to the soul (without encroaching, in the least, on the secrecy of the confessional) and all that takes place in the person and with regard to the person of Sister Emmerich, should be

(1) " Dean Rensing." he observed, "is a man of sense. It is to him, and to him alone that I venture to confide the direction of this affair."

reported simply and truthfully in writing; besides this, from the day on which Dean Rensing enters upon his charge every physical or mental phenomenon, every bodily change must be recorded in a journal and forwarded to me every eight days. What concerns the soul is confided to Dean Rensing. Dr. Krauthausen has charge of the body. The Dean will say to Sister Emmerich that in obedience to ecclesiastical authority, she will allow Dr. Krauthausen to do all he may judge proper to effect a cure. The patient must, in general, be allowed to perceive as little as possible that the examination has any other end in view than that of her cure. Let no importance be attached to her wounds, let them not be regarded as extraordinary favors. The less the whole affair is spoken of the better. "

The surgeon, Dr. Krauthausen, was charged to make notes of all that he observed respecting the physical phenomena.

" For Dr. Wesener," writes the Vicar-General, " who drew up the report of March 25th, sympathizes too deeply with the sufferer; he must not be engaged for the present. Dr. von Druffel is of opinion that we may unhesitatingly confide to Dr. Krauthausen the treatment of Sister Emmerich's wounds. Under no circumstances must the bandages be removed or even changed, by any other than himself. If he thinks proper, he may remove them at the end of four days provided he replaces them immediately."

The points upon which the weekly report was to turn were also named by the Vicar-General.

Dean Rensing was deputed, on the part of the Vicar-General, to prescribe the following rules to Father Limberg, Sister Emmerich's ordinary confessor:—1. To avoid as much as possible in his conversation with her any allusion to her sufferings; 2. Not to address to her, either during or after her ecstasies, any question upon her interior ; that was, for the present, the exclusive affair of Dean Rensing ; 3. To communicate to the latter all that Sister Emmerich, without any questioning on his part, might tell him either before or after her ecstasies.

Lastly, Clara Soentgen was commissioned to make private reports, " For," says the Vicar-General, " she is known to be a sensible person, absolutely incapable of deceiving. I have asked her to communicate what she observes unknown to the Dean, that by such independent reports I may arrive more surely at the truth."

The order addressed to Sister Soentgen contained the following lines : " In this affair I wish *to know* all—*no thinking, no guessing, but knowing !* What I *know* for certain alone has any weight with me."

The following instructions were given with regard to Sister Emmerich's sister :—" We have no objection to her staying with the invalid ; but if she should attempt to contravene the orders prescribed, let her be instantly dismissed. I may here remark that other measures, infinitely more painful for Sister Emmerich, may be avoided by a scrupulous adherence to those now laid down."

Dean Rensing was authorized to take the depositions of all persons, priests, religious, or laics, who at Dülmen, Coesfeld, and Flamske, had been most nearly connected with the invalid and who could communicate details upon her character, her disposition, and her whole former mode of life.

CHAPTER XX.

SISTER EMMERICH'S WOUNDS ARE BANDAGED.

On April 1, 1813, Dr. Krauthausen applied the bandages to Sister Emmerich's hands and feet. In his report to the Vicar-General he says :—

"In fulfilment of the charge intrusted to me, on Thursday before Passion Sunday, at 8 A. M., I bathed in warm water the spots covered with dried blood in the hands, feet, and head of Anne Catherine Emmerich, formerly an Augustinian religious. I then applied bandages in such a way that neither the fingers nor toes could be moved freely, nor could the said bandages be disarranged, much less removed without my knowledge. The bathing, though performed gently with a fine sponge, and the process of bandaging caused keen suffering for about twenty-four hours. When I had finished the bathing, I perceived on the back of the hands and the insteps an oval wound about half an inch long, which was smaller in the palms of the hands and soles of the feet. They were healthy looking and had no pus."

Some hours after the bandaging Dean Rensing visited the invalid whom he found " weeping from pain produced by the burning heat in her bandaged wounds." He comforted her, and she said : " Gladly, gladly shall I endure it all, if only the dear God gives me strength to bear it without impatience !"

But, when at Vesper-time she began to unite with the Saviour's Passion, her pains became more violent and she was seized with the fear " of not being able to endure them and of failing in obedience to her Superiors."

The Dean calmed her by promising that he and another priest would offer Holy Mass for her next morning to beg God to give her strength to suffer. She replied:—

"I sigh only for that grace, and God will not refuse it if the priests ask it with me."

The night of April 1-2 was so painful that she fainted three times ; it was only in the morning when Mass was said for her that she experienced any relief, though the twitching and smarting of her wounds still continued. On the evening of the 2d, in a hardly audible voice, she said to the Dean :

" There are some others who want to see my wounds; it frightens me! Can you not prevent it ? "

Her words were verified on April 4th. The French Commissary-General, M. Garnier, came officially from Münster to collect information respecting her. He asked her many questions, Abbé Lambert acting as interpreter. M. Garnier, appeared particularly anxious to know if she spoke on politics or uttered predictions. He made Dr. Krauthausen remove the bandages from the right hand that he might see the wound for himself. Sister Emmerich's demeanor produced so deep an impression upon him that, fourteen years after, at Paris, he mentioned this visit to Clement Brentano in the most feeling and respectful terms.

Dr. Krauthausen thus records this removal of the bandages :—" To-day, April 4th, upon an order from M. Garnier, Commissary of Police, of the department of Lippe, I was obliged to unbandage the right hand and, in the afternoon about half-past four, I unbound the left and both feet. The linen was steeped in blood and adhered so tightly to the wounds that it required some time to soften it with warm water before it could be drawn off, and even then the operation caused her acute pain. The wounds were in the

same condition as on the 1st of April. That the bandages
might not again adhere so tightly, and also to relieve the
pain, I put a plaster on the wounds."

The plaster, however, only increased Sister Emmerich's
sufferings and did not hinder the flow of blood. Next day,
April 5th, the bandages were again soaked and the doctor,
at the patient's request, took them off and applied fresh ones.
In removing the plaster, he saw no sign of suppuration.

The following morning the bandages were again wet
with blood, and the sufferings of the patient on the increase.
This went on until the 7th, when she implored the doctor
to unbind her hands and feet, as she could no longer endure the pain. The doctor dared not yield without an express leave from Münster. He was about applying for it
by letter, when the Vicar-General and his companions arrived that same evening in Dülmen.

Upon the doctor's refusal to yield to her entreaties, Sister
Emmerich proposed to herself to be patient one day more,
when she was told in vision to represent to her Superiors
that she desired nothing in this world, neither money, nor
fame, but only solitude and peace, and that they ought not
to subject her patience to so great a trial, since to increase
her sufferings to such a degree was nothing short of tempting God. When, in pursuance of this order, she made
her representations to Dean Overberg, he was, at first,
greatly surprised; for, from what he had seen on his first
visit, he thought he might count upon her ready obedience.
But when she added that she had been ordered to make
this representation, as well as to endure all that obedience
might prescribe, he was satisfied. Later on, we shall see
how perfectly she complied with the injunction received in
vision, in spite of the intense sufferings it entailed.

CHAPTER XXI.

Second Visit of the Vicar-General to Dülmen.

The official statement relative to this visit runs thus :—
" On Wednesday, April 7th, about six P. M., the undersigned visited Sister Emmerich. The patient's countenance appeared the same as on the first visit. The bandages had been removed from her hands and feet by Dr. Krauthausen, each fold of the linen over the wounds having to be moistened that it might be drawn off with less pain, so saturated was it with dark red blood. After their removal, the patient was somewhat relieved, and, with the exception of an expression of pain from time to time, her countenance was sweet and serene as on our first visit. The wounds were healthy, no suppuration nor inflammation." At the last interview that the Vicar-General von Droste had with Sister Emmerich in Dean Overberg's presence, she begged him " to reflect upon what all this must cost her whose life had hitherto been so secluded." She said also :

" These sufferings distract me in prayer. I have had during the past days but very little consolation. I have had to struggle not only with impatience, but also against a feeling of resentment toward those who have made known my state ; however, I am resigned to God's will."

She expressed to the Dean her fear " that her aged mother would hear to what she was being subjected, and that, on account of her age, she would not be able to bear the grief it would cause her." And when the Dean asked her how often she lost the presence of God, she reflected a moment and then answered : " In these eight days (1),

(1) The days of the bandaging. (Dean Overberg's notes.)

oftener than in a whole year !"—A little before his departure she said : " Ah ! how I long to die !" To the question : " Can you, then, no longer bear your pains ?"—she answered : " O yes ! that is not the reason "—and " Her look told me plainly enough," writes the Dean, " why she so longed for death."

The impression Sister Emmerich made on her Superiors at this second visit was as favorable as at the first, and her request that the curious should not be allowed access to her pleased the Vicar-General. He wrote to Dean Rensing, April 9th :—" Sister Emmerich has expressed her gratitude to me for having prohibited useless visits. She has so earnestly begged their discontinuance that, had I no other motives, this alone would decide me to do so. You are at liberty to show this order to both ecclesiastics and laics who may be so indiscreet as to insist on seeing her. Let them understand also that she will receive, in obedience, visits authorized by you ; yet it would be unjust to inflict them upon her unnecessarily."

He expressed also his satisfaction with the Dean's proceedings : " I am convinced that I could not have made choice of any one who would have acquitted himself better of the duty confided to you."

The Vicar-General and his party quitted Dülmen at noon, April 8th. Scarcely had they gone when Sister Emmerich, worn out by the prolonged conversations of the last two days, fell into a state of contemplation on the Passion of Our Lord and the Dolors of His Blessed Mother whose feast it happened to be. At Vesper-time the wounds of her head bled so freely that the blood soaked the bandages and flowed down her face. Whilst in this state, she sent for Dean Rensing to warn him that a visit from the Prefect of the Department had been announced to her which, under the circumstances, could not fail to be very annoying. The Dean asked whether she feared the gentleman would put questions which she could not answer. She said : "No. As to any questions that may be proposed, I feel no uneasiness. I trust in Our Lord's promises to His disciples that He would Himself suggest what they should say."

The Dean noticed that her countenance wore an expression of pain whenever the back of her head touched the pillow upon which she generally allowed only her shoulders to rest. Between it and her head, there was space sufficient for a person's hand. Dr. Krauthausen reported on the same day :

" For about three hours, Sister Emmerich complained of smarting and pains in her head. At a quarter before two, I found the linen which bound her neck and head soaked with blood in several places; it had also run down upon her face. After I had bathed her forehead carefully, I noticed a number of punctures, through several of which the blood again began to ooze.

" On the night of the 8th, her hands and feet bled freely and continued to do so the whole of the 9th. About 8 o'clock P. M. her pulse was so weak that I feared she would die."

Dean Rensing's journal contains a similar report :—

" When I visited her, Friday, 9th, half-past eleven, I was terrified to see her lying pale and disfigured like one in her last agony. When I addressed her, she held out her hand to me complaining in a scarcely audible voice of the frightful pains in her wounds, and I noticed that those of her feet were bleeding so profusely that the bed-clothes were tinged with blood. She told me also that her sick sister had been so ill during the night that she feared she should have to send for her confessor.

" 'This grieved me so,' she said, ' that I complained

earnestly to the dear God of the distress I was in, and I
begged Him to help my sister.   Soon after she was relieved,
and rested a little which gave me such satisfaction that I
forgot my own sufferings.' " Her sister was soon able to
resume her duties.

CHAPTER XXII.

VISITS.—A PROTESTANT PHYSICIAN'S TESTIMONY.

Although the Vicar-General, as we have seen in the preceding chapter, had forbidden visits of mere curiosity and had, at different times, renewed the prohibition, yet the poor sufferer was not secure from intrusion. The Dean found it hard to argue against the reasons of many who insisted on an entrance to her sick room, and some, especially physicians and people of rank, asserted their right to examine the invalid's stigmata.

Such entries as the following were frequently made in his journal:—

" Be not disquieted," she said to me, " even if they are vexed with you on that account. God will reward you for the charity you show me."

The inspection of her wounds was far more painful to Sister Emmerich than the wounds themselves, and though Dean Rensing repeatedly assured her that this mortification would be a source of increased merit, yet such visits never ceased to fill her with dread ; even in her visions she was tormented by the thought of them. She told the Dean that three times already when begging for patience, she had received this reply : " My grace is sufficient for thee !" She added: " I am becoming more and more disgusted at the excitement on my account, though I console myself with the thought that I have given no cause for it."

Dean Rensing writes, April 3d:—

" A visitor presented himself to-day who would take no refusal, a Dr. Ruhfus, of Gildhaus, Bentheim. He was so determined on being admitted that only on my promising

to ask the invalid's consent would he withdraw for a time.
She, at first, objected, but ended by leaving it to my decision and I allowed the doctor to enter. He behaved with
remarkable discretion, examined the wounds carefully, and
asked for such information as he deemed necessary. On
taking leave, he thanked the invalid for her condescension
and expressed himself on the wonders he had just witnessed in a manner that did honor to his candor. As we left
the room, he said to me : 'What I have seen is truly wonderful. There can be no question of imposture in this case.
The religious sentiments of the patient testify to her truth,
as does, likewise, her countenance, which expresses naught
but piety, innocence, and submission to the Divine Will.
The wounds speak for themselves, at least to a man of
science. To ascribe them to natural causes such as imagination, induction, analogy, or similar causes, is simply impossible. The whole affair is, in my opinion, supernatural.'—I have thought it my duty to enter the opinion of
a man so competent and whose impartiality cannot be
doubted. I have given, as far as I remember, the doctor's
own words, since before seeing the phenomena in question, he dropped some jests on the subject at the ale-
house."

As Sister Emmerich's state was a mystery to all around
her, and as she had no one at times to protect her from the
curious, it often happened that they plied her with silly,
indiscreet questions to which she neither could nor would
respond. This prudent silence did not, however, prevent
every word that escaped her lips in contemplation from being eagerly seized upon and construed into an answer,
which when repeated from one to another often gave rise
to all sorts of absurd tales throughout the little town. One
day Dean Rensing mentioned this circumstance to the in-

valid, when she begged him to give her an infallible means
of defence against inquisitive questioners.

" I beg you," she said, " to order me in obedience to
reply to no question dictated by idle curiosity, were it even
my confessor, or one of my Sisters in religion who put it.
Then I will keep silence during my swoons. Then they
cannot say that I have said, ' such or such a one is in
purgatory, such a one is in heaven,' when God knows I have
said nothing of the kind."

With respect to her confessor no such safeguard was
necessary, as he himself was bound by a strict prohibition
from Superiors to put no question to her during her ecstasies. Dean Rensing testifies to the fidelity with which
he observed the command.

" Sister Emmerich told me one morning that she had
fallen into *a swoon* (an ecstasy) the night before and that
she had mentioned it to her confessor, Father Limberg,
but that he had replied she must not say any more about
it, as it was contrary to the will of Superiors ; that, if she
had anything to communicate on the subject, she must
apply to me. ' This,' she added, ' gave me true satisfaction. If he had questioned me, I should no longer have
full confidence in him as my confessor, because he would
by so doing have disobeyed his Superiors.' "

CHAPTER XXIII.

Last Days of Holy Week:—Feast of Easter.

Sister Emmerich prepared to make her Paschal Communion on Holy Thursday, an ardent desire for the Holy Eucharist being enkindled in her breast as was ordinarily the case some days previously. Since the reception of the stigmata, she was incapable of taking any nourishment; but, in preparing for Holy Communion, she experienced a real bodily hunger for the Bread of Life. Wholly absorbed in Its contemplation, she cried out repeatedly: "I am hungry! I am hungry!" And her sister, taking her words literally, gave her two spoonfuls of broth which her stomach instantly rejected. She was so ill after it that the doctor sent for the Abbé Lambert to relieve her by his blessing. All knew well that this result was produced whenever she was forced to eat; but neither the doctor, her confessor, nor her sister desisted from their attempts at making her take nourishment.

Dr. Krauthausen reports, April 11th:—

"Twice I persuaded her to take a spoonful of soup, but she vomited instantly both times, as she had done the day before when by my order a few drops of wine had been given her."

April 14th, eve of Holy Thursday, another trial was made with fish soup. "But," says Dr. Krauthausen, "she could not retain it, vomiting immediately ensued." After she had received Holy Communion, her strength returned for a while and all were struck at the change in her appearance. When the Dean visited her at noon, she was again very weak, as the cross on her breast had been bleeding since the preceding evening; but she was able to make him understand that the consolation she had derived from Holy Communion rendered her sufferings more endurable. She had, during the night, prayed for Clara Soentgen who was very ill.

Although her sufferings by virtue of the Holy Eucharist had become less insupportable, they were by no means diminished; on the contrary, they steadily increased until evening, when their intensity was such as to force from her the avowal that, if it were not otherwise ordained, she should now die of pain.

" On Holy Thursday night, about eleven o'clock," reports Dean Rensing, " all her wounds began to bleed and they were still bleeding when I saw her at eight o'clock next morning. That of her side especially had bled so copiously that I shuddered when I beheld the cloths dyed in blood. I asked her how she had passed the night, to which she answered: ' It did not seem long to me, for I thought at every hour of what Our Saviour had suffered on this night. That gave me consolation, O what sweet consolation ! I had also a short swoon in which I thought that I ought to pray for the marks to be taken from me, but their pains left."

This meditation on the Passion was for Sister Emmerich a real participation in the Saviour's sufferings; therefore, during the days sacred to their commemoration, she endured without intermission the most cruel torments. Every nerve of her body even to her finger ends, was racked with pain, and a burning fever consumed her till midnight between Holy Saturday and Easter-Sunday, April 18th, when relief came about three o'clock in the morning. Her wounds did not bleed on Holy Saturday though the Dean found her very weak. His pious words strengthened her a little, and she was able to answer the questions he asked her. To his question for whom had she prayed particularly during the last days, she answered :—

" For those who recommend themselves to my prayers and, above all, for sinners who know not their own misery. For myself, I pray : Lord, Thy will be done ! Do with me as is pleasing to Thee ! Give me Thy grace to suffer everything and never to sin. Once I could go to church in Holy Week and on the Easter feasts. O what happiness to see there all that recalled the death and resurrection of Our Saviour ! Now I must lie here, but it is the will of God. It is well, I rejoice that it is so ! "

On Easter-Monday the Dean found her brighter than usual, and Dr. Krauthausen remarks on the same day :—

" On the 19th, she was better and more cheerful all day than for the last month. Still, she took no nourishment with the exception of two mouthfuls of water and the juice of half a roasted apple."

When the Dean inquired into the cause of her gayety, she replied :

" It is from my meditation on the Resurrection. I feel now neither hunger nor thirst, but I know not what God has in store for me. It has seemed to me for several days that some gentlemen are consulting about me at the Vicar-General's. There is one in particular who spoke of me, and I think he is coming to see my marks."

After communicating on Holy Thursday, she said : " After Easter I shall have fresh trouble, they will surely try new experiments on me." These words show that she saw as clearly this time as on March 27th and April 15th, when she remarked to the Dean :—" My heart is very heavy, for I still have much to suffer from these gentlemen on account of my wounds."

April 13th, the Vicar-General wrote to Dean Rensing to engage a respectable and intelligent nurse to attend Sister Emmerich day and night for two weeks, observe all that happened and report the same conscientiously.

' When you find one whom you think suitable," added the Vicar-General, " ask Sister Emmerich before proceeding further, if she is satisfied with her. Assure her also that when I order anything disagreeable, it is through a motive of duty and only because I believe it absolutely necessary, and a means of shielding her from greater annoyances. I have to do violence to my own feelings in acting thus."

April 20, Easter-Tuesday, the Vicar-General came again to Dülmen with Dean Overberg. We give an account of this third visit as we find it in the Vicar-General's own notes :—

THIRD VISIT OF THE VICAR-GENERAL AND DEAN OVERBERG.

(From the Official Report of the Vicar-General von Droste.) " April 20, 1813, Dean Overberg and I set out again for Dülmen and arrived about two P. M.

" We had not yet finished dining, when a physician of Stadtlohn, whose name I do not know, came to beg me to allow him to examine Sister Emmerich's case. I think the Dean had refused him some time before ; but as I judge it proper that physicians should examine the phenomena exhibited in her person and as I intended to have all her wounds exposed to me, I promised to take him with me. We were about starting, when a very skilful surgeon of Gescher, whose name also I have forgotten, was announced. He, too, wanted to see for himself. I thought one more or less mattered little since the examination had to be made, so I consented to his being present. The Dean and Dr.

Krauthausen had, likewise, come and I begged the latter to inform the invalid of our visit, as I knew well the presence of strangers would be very disagreeable to her. He went on before to prepare her whilst Dean Overberg, the two physicians and I followed soon after and reached the house about four o'clock. Sister Emmerich was lying in bed as usual.

"The examination began. No blood appeared on the head but only punctures, and her wounds, both the backs and palms of the hands, the insteps and soles of the feet, were as usual, though I think the blood-crust of the right hand had been broken by the bleeding. As I frequently visited the patient during my stay at Dülmen, I cannot say whether I noticed this on my first or on a subsequent visit. I examined the blood-crust of the left hand with a magnifying glass and found it very thin and a little rugose, or plaited like the epidermis when seen under a lens. On one of my visits I examined, if I am not mistaken, the wound in the palm of the left hand through the lens, and under the dried blood I discovered a round hole. (*See plate, fig.* 1.)

"The cross on the breast did not bleed this time, but appeared of a pale red color caused by the blood under the epidermis. I examined also the lines forming a cross, as well as the skin around them, and I could distinctly see that they did not break the skin. The epidermis over the lines and the skin surrounding them to some distance was unbroken and, through the glass, appeared as if peeling off a little.

"I examined also with the lens the grayish speck below the cross, but I could not distinguish it sufficiently well to describe it. Higher up it paled away and disappeared entirely at the centre ; the lower part was longer and a little broader. It was something like this. (*See plate, fig.* 2).

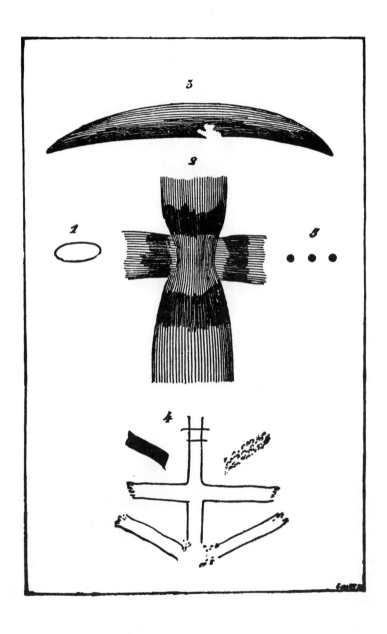

" The wound on the right side was not bleeding, but the upper part of it was encrusted with dried blood of a darker hue, as might be produced by extravasated blood just below the epidermis. It was a little like this. (*See plate, fig.* 3.)

" I used the lens over the parts where there was no blood, but the skin showed no signs of scratches whatever; it may, however, have been of a slightly deeper hue. I cannot remember that distinctly.

"Sister Emmerich consenting (1), Dr. Krauthausen laid on the wound of the left hand a salve of althea and other ingredients spread on lint, and over this he placed sticking-plaster. This was, perhaps, about six P. M. If I do not mistake, she complained that evening when I again visited her that this wound caused her more suffering than the others.

" April 21, Dr. Krauthausen called for me and we went together to see Sister Emmerich. He removed the plaster from the wound, as she complained of intense pain in it which had caused her to pass a sleepless night. The crust that had formed came off with the plaster. I think, however, that a little dried blood remained around it. The wound was clean and bore no trace of suppuration, though a little blood was to be seen and what appeared to be a watery fluid. We prevailed upon her to endure the plaster a little longer upon the same wound, promising to take it off in the evening if she suffered as before.

" I requested Dr. Krauthausen to turn the invalid more to the left that I might see the wound of the right side in a better light than on the preceding day. I examined it again with the glass, but I observed nothing now excepting that the place where a darker shade seemed to betoken extrav-

(1) Dean Overberg says: "After the physicians had examined the wounds, they asked the invalid if she were willing for them to try to cure one of them. She said she was, whereupon a piece of sticking-plaster was applied to the left hand."

asated blood, was less red. At the right of the upper wound, I noticed a few scratches some distance apart, which looked, I shall not say like the scratches of a needle, but rather like the spontaneous cracking of the skin itself.

" The crosses on the breast were red with blood. I washed the upper part and examined it again. Had the skin been broken I should certainly have remarked it. I think there was near the cross a short streak which seemed to be a depression filled with blood. (*See plate, fig.* 4.) Above the left arm of the upper cross and a little to the right, I noticed some scratches like those which I had observed above the wound of the side (1). I asked if the pin in her kerchief had made them, as it might easily have done; but the invalid answered that she always put the pin in so that the point turned out, and she showed me, at the same time, how she did it.

" Another plaster is now on the same wound. I visited the invalid several times to-day and found her in exactly the same state. I find upon examination of one or more of the wounds in the hands and feet that they are, particularly on the upper part, surrounded by a slightly inflamed appearance. Dr. Krauthausen says it is always so.

"Toward noon, I took Mr. Schwelling, of Münster, at his earnest request, to see Sister Emmerich. She consented to receive him on my telling her that he was a very honorable man who asked not to see the wound of her side, the crosses on her breast, nor even, I thought, the wounds of her feet.

" Dr. Krauthausen and I returned about six P. M. I think the invalid slept a little that afternoon. The plaster was removed and found to be saturated with blood. The

(1) "I must hear remark that these things are often as fresh in my memory as if I were really beholding them: then I say, ' It was so and so.' Again, I have but a faint remembrance of them, I cannot speak of them positively, and I express myself as above."--Clem. Droste.

wound evidently had bled **again,** for even supposing the
crust and dried blood had not all come off with the plaster of the morning, so small a quantity could not possibly
have produced such an effect on the second one.   I think
the wound on the back of the right hand also had bled.   As
she complained of the pain, we did not replace the plaster,
for it would be unjust to torture the innocent.

   " Had I commanded it, she would, without doubt, have
submitted ; but she feared yielding to impatience, and I
did not feel that I had any right to impose such a command.
She complained of pain in her head and felt sure that it
was going to bleed.

   " About eight o'clock A. M. on the 22d, Dr. Krauthausen called at my request.   He had just been to see Sister
Emmerich who told him she was under the impression
that her head had been bleeding, or that it would soon do so.
The doctor removed the linen, but saw no signs of blood.
We went together to see her.   I think she had slept a little the night before.   We found that her forehead had, indeed, been bleeding, the blood having run down as far as
her nose where it now lay clotted and dry.   Her cap and the
linen binders being removed, we found large stains in the
back of the former and another large one on the right side
near the temple.

   " Her hair being very thick, it was impossible to examine the punctures around the head.   She consented to have
it cut close, though not so close, however, as to allow the
blood instantaneously to soak her head-dress and the pillow.
She requested this for the sake of neatness.

   " The blood being washed away, a number of fine bloody
marks could be seen with the naked eye scattered irregu-
larly over the forehead and extending from the middle of
it almost to the top of the head. (See plate, fig.5)

"I examined them with the lens and I could see, especially in one of them, some liquid blood. These marks have not the appearance of having been made by a sharp point; they look like little holes. I think I saw distinctly that the one in which there was blood, was indeed a hole.

"Before leaving her, she told me that some one had come from Münster to see her, saying that the Dean had given permission for it. She seemed satisfied when I told her that it was so, and thanked me gratefully for lessening the number of visitors, begging me to remain firm on this point. I reminded her of the prohibition I had given against showing the wounds of her side, breast, and feet; but when I wished to prepare her to allow Drs. Stadtlohn and Gescher to examine them at the end of fourteen days, as they proposed, she answered decidedly: 'No! they shall not see them again!'

"I was obliged to examine the wounds and other phenomena as closely as I did, since Dr. Krauthausen could see nothing through the glass.

"On taking leave of her, I said pleasantly: 'Be sure to let me know when you are going to die'—to which she replied : ' I will!'"

Thus ends the Vicar-General's report.

The poor invalid had no heart for jesting. The preceding days had well-nigh exhausted her ; but her patience and fortitude were proof against every trial, so that Clement von Droste, seeing her peace and calm, seemed to forget for the moment her cruel state.

After this third visit, the Vicar-General addressed the following official communication to the Commissary-General of French Police :—

"Sister Emmerich desires only to be forgotten by the

world that she may be free for spiritual things which alone interest her. She asks nothing, she accepts nothing, she desires not to be spoken of, and I trust the public will soon forget her. I cannot discover the slightest shadow of imposture in her case, yet I shall continue to observe her closely."

CHAPTER XXIV.

Dean Rensing and Dr. Krauthausen Grow Impatient.

As the result of the Vicar-General's observations accorded with the conviction already established among the physicians that the stigmata could neither have been produced nor preserved by artificial means, Dean Rensing confidently hoped that the inquiry would be declared at an end. Dr. Krauthausen thinking the same had discontinued his visits. He had been the attendant physician of the convent and had become so thoroughly acquainted with Sister Emmerich that the thought of imposture never entered his mind. Through respect for the Vicar-General, he had undertaken the medical examination and a daily report of the same. He regarded the stigmata as certain, incontestible facts which, however, baffled his experience and skill, as they could not be healed, and as they daily presented symptoms unknown in natural maladies. Day after day had he witnessed the sufferings they caused the invalid, and it was contrary to his conviction of her innocence, as well as repugnant to his sympathy for her, to behold her longer subjected to such tortures. He had also, like Dr. Wesener, to endure the taunts of his incredulous colleagues who affected pity for his inability to discover the fraud. He heartily wished that Sister Emmerich had known better how to conceal the wonders wrought in her person and so had escaped an examination which resulted, as far as he was concerned, only in fatigue and vexation.

As the Vicar-General had left Dülmen without giving any precise directions, Dr. Krauthausen waited no further orders, but declared in his last report, April 26th, that he considered himself discharged from the duty confided to him. But the speedy termination of the affair, no less desired by Dean Rensing than by the doctor himself, could not yet be effected, for the Vicar-General could come to no decision until Dean Overberg should have finished his notes on the invalid's interior life. Although impressed by what he saw and convinced that extraordinary supernatural favors had been granted, yet he was too prudent, too judicious a man to venture a judgment on the patient before having maturely weighed the reports and conclusions of all engaged in the investigation. Dean Overberg remained in Dülmen some days longer to complete his inquiries as the patient's strength would permit ; and, whilst waiting for the report, the Vicar-General resolved that the project formed on April 13th of placing Sister Emmerich under the surveillance of a confidential nurse should be put into execution. Such a measure he regarded as necessary to avert from himself the reproach of having failed to make use of every means that prudence and foresight could suggest.

Dean Rensing, unable to secure a suitable nurse as speedily as he desired, made a new proposition to the Vicar-General on April 27th, which, he felt assured, would be agreeable to the invalid. It ran as follows— :

"Dr. Krauthausen is beginning to tire of his frequent visits to Sister Emmerich. He informed me yesterday that he would continue his observations and reports till the end of the month only. The patient, too, perceives his weariness of her case and consequently dreads his coming. That she may have some repose of which, in truth, she will enjoy but little whilst in life, and at the same time to satisfy the censorious whom we must consider, the best

way would be to engage two or three physicians to remain
with her day and night by turns for a week and to observe
her closely.   This is also the opinion of the Protestant physician, Dr. Ruhfus, who was here this morning and again
declared to me that the phenomena appeared to him supernatural.   Sister Emmerich will freely assent to such an
arrangement."

The Dean renewed his proposition two days later, petitioning also for full powers of action.   The Vicar-General
replied in very few words : " I still incline to the surveillance of fourteen days by a person of her own sex.   Our
duty demands not that we should place the case so far beyond doubt that they who fear the truth may no longer object to it—such a task would, indeed, be fruitless and
thankless.   What is there really in the body and in the soul ?
Whence has it originated ?   How has Sister Emmerich been
reduced to her present state ?—such are the questions to
be answered to the satisfaction of all reasonable people, not
by isolated facts, but by a combination of circumstances ;
yet in the means employed to such an end, we must not
violate justice and charity. A mere suspicion founded on
possibility deserves not consideration."

We cannot marvel that Dean Rensing earnestly desired
an end to the affair.   It was daily becoming more painful
to him to witness the cruel martyrdom of the poor victim,
without his being able to offer any other assistance or consolation than the bare mention of obedience ; besides, the
visitors to the little town were more numerous now at the
Paschal time and all desired to gratify their curiosity with
regard to the wonderful nun.   Their indiscreet importunities were the occasion not only of vexatious interruptions,
but even of irritating disputes which, to so courteous a man
as the Dean, to one so systematic in his habits, were cer-

tainly most annoying and quite incompatible with his pastoral duties. In his daily visits he scrupulously exacted of Sister Emmerich an account of all that happened to her interiorly and exteriorly, of which he sent a detailed report to the Vicar-General with a multitude of facts which, he was convinced, ought to remove every shadow of doubt regarding the phenomena under consideration. He could consequently see no reason to justify prolonging an inquiry so painful to its object, so wearying to himself. Before pursuing this subject, we shall glance at the Dean's notes, since they contain many facts which throw light on Sister Emmerich and the designs of God over her.

CHAPTER XXV.

Dean Rensing's Testimony.

Dean Rensing had long known Sister Emmerich's sincere piety and her ardent desire of living unknown and hidden from the world. From his very first visit to her he had regarded the truth of the wonders wrought in her as indubitable; but he was timid and cautious, and the objections raised by strangers or enemies failed not to influence him. A specious argument, a suspicion cast upon the freedom of his judgment or the firmness of his character, sufficed to torment him keenly and fill him with distrust. The wisdom and good sense which ordinarily characterized his conduct were not proof against the absurd suspicions raised on all sides as soon as the case was publicly known. Nothing, therefore, was wanting on his part to aggravate the invalid's sufferings; her patience, her confidence in God were subjected to such trials as are imposed only upon chosen souls.

The Dean's favorable opinion of the invalid was first shaken by the idle talk of one of her former Sisters in religion who, about a month before the inquiry began, pretended to have seen her through the key-hole leave her bed and search in her closet for eatables. Two others declared that they had seen the same thing in the same way and that they had once found her lying on the floor with a slice of buttered bread in her hand. Dean Rensing, who had never doubted the invalid's inability to eat, took these words very much to heart. He sent for the persons in question and instituted a proces-verbal upon their reports; but on trying to make observations himself in the same way, he became convinced of the impossibility of commanding from the point indicated a sight of either the invalid's bed or the closet. At last, his informants avowed that they knew for certain Sister Emmerich's inability to leave her bed without assistance; but even then the Dean desisted not from interrogating Sister Emmerich herself, for the bread-and-butter story disquieted him not a little.

"I asked her," he says in his journal, "if she remembered having been found at any time out of bed. 'Yes, certainly,' she answered. 'I lay on the floor by the bed out of which I once fell when I had no one to help me. It may be that I did have a piece of bread in my hand, though I think it more likely that it was on the floor. I had a piece by me for a poor woman whose child I was expecting, and it is probable that it fell to the floor with the coverlet.'"

This quieted the Dean somewhat, but he was not fully reassured till Dean Overberg took upon himself Sister Emmerich's defence. Again was he troubled by a fresh report circulated throughout Dülmen and Münster. It was said that even though Sister Emmerich's sincere piety could not be questioned, yet her stigmata would always be open to suspicion, inasmuch as there could be no certitude that they were not artificially maintained by the Abbé Lambert. Might not this foreign priest be fanatic enough to regard as a good work the assistance given to the simple-minded nun to bear constantly on her person the marks of the Saviour's Passion ?

A priest from Münster on a visit to the Dean informed him of the conjecture. It made all the more impression upon the latter as he had just heard something similar in Dülmen. "This remark has been made here also," he wrote, "not only by judicious Christians, but even by a well-meaning Jew who was struck by the phenomena exhibited in Sister Emmerich's person.

Although Dean Rensing felt morally certain on hearing the formal asseverations of the Abbé and Sister Emmerich, that they were incapable of such a fraud, yet the report gave rise to doubts which haunted him until the invalid herself came to his aid and delivered him from his mental agony. Her penetration discovered his secret uneasiness and, as she knew that he would not explain himself freely, she asked his permission to speak to him of what was on his mind, and she set before him his disquietude and its cause.

"I was," he says, "exceedingly surprised. It was just as she said. I told her it would be better for her to declare her stigmata the result of pious enthusiasm, for then 1 should be freed from many annoyances and she from much suffering—'How could I make such a statement?' she said quietly. 'That would be a lie! Even the smallest lie is a venial sin and so displeasing to God that I would rather suffer any pain than be guilty of it.'"

Dean Rensing's silent reserve was now over. He spoke long of the danger of indiscreet religious zeal; and he conjured the sufferer, for the honor of God and the good of souls, to say whether her wounds were the result of exaggerated piety or not. "But," says his journal, "she protested in the name of all things sacred, that she could truthfully say nothing else about them than what she had already said, that she should be only too well pleased if God would hear her prayer and grant to the physicians the power of effacing them, adding: 'To obtain such a result, I would be willing to be punished as an impostor and despised and mocked by the whole world.'"

Sister Emmerich relieved the Dean in his doubts on another occasion when he had been commissioned by the Vicar-General to interrogate her former Superioress and companions respecting her life in the convent. She clearly foresaw that these women would say many things calculated to perplex his mind and arouse fresh misgivings; and fearing that he would again hesitate to make known his suspicions to her, she herself prepared him for it. "The inquiry you are about to make of my former companions will necessitate your appealing to my conscience in terms the most severe. It will cost you much; but I beg you not to fear. Subject me, as well as those Sisters, to the most rigorous examination. I shall pray God to give you grace and courage to do so."

Sister Emmerich's uprightness and candor rendered the Dean's position toward her less embarrassing. The more he examined, the more convincing became the proofs of the supernatural origin of the favors bestowed upon her, the sublime perfection of her virtue. Her obedience and respect for ecclesiastical authority were unlimited, and her fear of disobeying orders through excessive pain gave her more uneasiness than the sufferings caused by the attempts made to cure her wounds. Sometimes the Dean found her in tears, or a word from him would call forth this touching question: "Have I sinned by my sadness?"—His assurances to the contrary quickly restored her to the innocent light-heartedness of a child, and she would say through her tears:—

"Willingly shall I bear still more, if only the dear God will give me strength to endure my sufferings and not to fail in obedience."

Never did Dean Rensing hear her complain of anything else than of the crowd that flocked to see her. When he prohibited their entrance, she thanked him gratefully. Her tearful pleadings often encouraged him to defend her boldly from the inquisitive throng. Never did he behold in her a sign of impatience or discontent; on the contrary, the serenity of her countenance testified to her resignation and union with God. He says in his journal :—" I found her extremely weak ; but as soon as she saw me, she assumed the air of serenity usual to her." And : " Whilst I chatted with her, her countenance was full of peace ; but I noticed that as often as the back of her head chanced to touch the pillow, her features contracted with pain."

If he reproached her with her stigmata, she took it quietly as if she herself entertained the same sentiments.

" If you had not those singular marks on you," he said to her one day, "you would be free from the pains you now endure from them (1)."

"I have prayed the dear God with all my heart," she replied, " to take them from me, and I am willing to be treated as a hypocrite and impostor, but my prayer has not been heard."

He was often quite overcome at the sight of her sufferings and, not being able to afford her any relief, he desired to withdraw ; but she tried to compose herself and begged him not to deprive her of the solace his presence and benediction afforded. Once he noted the following words in his journal : —" I stayed with her a while longer, deeply affected at seeing the grace of Our Lord so strong in the weak."

Such experience proved to him that the gift of longanimity was attached to the fidelity of her obedience to Ecclesiastical Superiors, the representatives of God; consequently, though not at all enthusiastic, he acquired in spite of himself

(1) When the reality of the stigmata had been unquestionably proved, Dean Rensing changed his tactics and reproached the invalid for having prayed for their disappearance. Dr. Wesener's journal contains the following notes on this subject, Jan. 10, 1815 :—

" To-day, Tuesday, the wounds seemed larger than usual and, on examining them closely, I came to the conclusion that they had bled both on the upper and lower surface. I inquired why this had happened on a *Tuesday* ? The invalid could not say, but she told me the following :—' Dean Rensing was here yesterday. He reproached me for wishing and praying for the removal of these marks. I do not think I did wrong in this, for it was not from any bad intention. 1 am resolved to conform to the will of God, to abandon myself entirely to it. Gladly would I suffer until the Day of Judgment to please God and serve my neighbor !' "

a daily assurance of the power and plenitude of the benediction attached to the sacerdotal character. Whenever she spoke such words as these : "I am not so weak, I am stronger when you stay. What I say to you comes from God, it is for God, and it never tires me," etc.—he always saw them verified by effects.

The Vicar-General had enjoined on her to render to Dean Rensing an exact account of her contemplations and whatever happened to her exteriorly ; therefore, she answered all his questions most carefully. We are thus informed of the fact of her offering all her sufferings for the souls in purgatory and the conversion of sinners. Even during the examination, she spent her nights in prayer and contemplation, often " going out of herself," as she expressed it. On the Dean's first visit, she said in answer to his interrogatories : " Last night I was in purgatory. It seemed to me that I was taken into a deep abyss, a vast region, where I saw, and the sight filled me with sorrow, the poor souls so sad, so silent, yet with something in their countenance which tells that the thought of God's mercy gives joy to their heart. Enthroned in their midst was the Mother of God, more beautiful than I had ever seen her before."—Then she said to him : "Instruct your penitents to pray fervently for the poor souls in purgatory, for they in gratitude will pray for them in return. Prayer for these poor souls is most agreeable to God, as it admits them to His presence sooner."

Some days later she again said : " I had no rest all last night, on account of the sharp pains in my wounds, but I was consoled by an apparition of Our Divine Saviour. I saw how He recalls repentant sinners, how He acts toward them. He was so good, so sweet that I have no words to express it."

She was often strengthened and consoled by this vision at the approach of the Easter solemnities.

"My sufferings have become more endurable," she said one day, "for I have seen in vision that many great sinners will soon return to God. Some have already done so. This gave me strength and filled me with joy."

The week after Easter she again said to the Dean :—

"I have had a short but consoling ecstasy in which I saw how many sinners have returned to God this Easter and how many souls have been released from purgatory. I saw, too, the place of purification, and I noticed on the countenances of the prisoners an air of inexpressible joy which I took as a sign of their approaching deliverance. How glad I was to see them freed from their torments! I knew the souls of two priests who have gone to heaven. They had suffered for years; one for his neglect of little duties, the other for his inclination to jesting."

She saw also the conversion of certain sinners who had relapsed into their evil habits.

"Jesus stood before my eyes. He was maltreated in many ways; but during it all, He was so gentle and loving that His sufferings brought to me a sweet kind of sadness. 'Ah!' thought I, 'every sinner has in this suffering a share, and he would be saved if he only had a little good will!'—I saw also some persons known to me who recognized their faults and corrected them. It was all as clear before me as if I saw it with open eyes. Among them was one who is very pious, who speaks in humble terms of herself; but she knows not at the same time that she thinks too much of herself. It would cost her something to acknowledge her faults. It is not true humility for one to depreciate himself, and yet be unable to endure that another should speak ill of him or be preferred to him."

Again she said: " I was present when God passed sentence upon some notorious sinners. Great is His justice,
but still more inconceivable is His mercy. He damns only
those who are determined not to be converted; they who
have a spark of good will are saved. Some there are who
grieve for their sins, confess them sincerely, and trust confidently in the merits of their Saviour; they are saved and
their sins will no more be remembered. It is true they
go to purgatory, but not to remain long. On the other
hand, many stay a long time in purgatory who, although
not great sinners, have lived tepidly. Through pride they
would take no admonition or instruction from their confessor. The time was when the thought of only one poor
sinner's condemnation grieved me so that I could not get
over it; but on the present occasion, though many were
condemned, I was perfectly calm, for I saw that God's
justice called for it. All was as clear to me as if God
himself had spoken.

" I saw Jesus on a throne, shining like the sun; by Him
were Mary, Joseph, and John, and before Him knelt poor repentant sinners, supplicating Mary to intercede for them.
I saw then that Mary is the true refuge of sinners. All that
fly to her find favor, if they have only a little faith."

The following vision on the value of prayer was afterward vouchsafed to the invalid:

" I was in a great, bright place which extended on every
side as far as the eye could reach, and there it was shown
me how it is with men's prayers before God. They seemed to be inscribed on large white tablets which were divided
into four classes: some were written in magnificent golden
letters; others in shining silver; some in darker characters;
and others, again, in black streaked lines. I gazed with
delight; but, as I thought myself unworthy of such a favor,

I hardly dared ask my guide what it all meant. He told me : ' What is written in gold is the prayer of those who have united their good works to the merits of Jesus Christ and who often renew this union; they aim at observing His precepts and imitating His example.

" ' What is written in silver is the prayer of those who think not of union with the merits of Jesus Christ; but who are, notwithstanding, pious and who pray in the simplicity of their hearts.

" ' What is written in darker colors is the prayer of those who have no peace unless they frequently confess and communicate and daily say certain prayers; but who are, however, tepid and perform their good works through habit.

" ' Lastly, what is written in black, streaked characters is the prayer of such as place all their confidence in vocal prayers and pretended good works, but who do not keep God's Commandments nor curb their evil desires. Such prayer has no merit before God, therefore it is streaked. So also would the good works of a man be streaked who indeed gives himself much trouble to help on some charity, but with a view to the honor or temporal advantage attached to it.' "

Dean Rensing found her one day reciting the Litany of the Saints from a book. He wished not to interrupt her, but she said: "I am not anxious about it. I can take it up again where I left off. I do not think God is so strict. He does not mind where I begin," intimating thereby that she interrupted her prayer, not from carelessness, but as a mark of respect toward her director.

She relates another symbolical vision on prayer:—

"I was kneeling in my accustomed place in church, and I saw by the brilliant light that shone around two beautifully dressed ladies in prayer at the foot of the High Altar. With heartfelt emotion I watched them praying so devoutly, when two dazzling crowns of gold were let down as if by a cord over their heads. I drew near and saw that one crown rested on the head of one of the ladies, whilst the other remained suspended in the air a little above the head of the second. At last, they both arose and I remarked to them that they had been praying earnestly. 'Yes,' replied the second, 'it is a long time since I prayed as devoutly and with as much consolation as I have done to-day.' But the first on whose head the crown had rested, complained that, although she had wanted to pray fervently, yet all kinds of thoughts and distractions had assailed her against which she had to fight the whole time. Now I saw clearly by this that the dear God looks only at the heart in time of prayer."

This vision had been vouchsafed to Sister Emmerich to teach her that her own prayer, so often disturbed and interrupted by the presence of visitors and other annoyances, was now no less agreeable to God than the tranquil devotion formerly hers in the cloister. We may recognize a similar intention in a later vision, simple apparently and of no great significance, but which is a striking proof of God's constant care over His chosen one:—

"I had to cross a narrow bridge. In terror I gazed on the deep waters flowing below, but my angel led me over in safety. On the bank was a mouse-trap around which a little mouse kept running, and running, and at last it slipped in to get the bait. 'Foolish little animal!' I cried, 'you are sacrificing your liberty, your life for a mouthful!'—'Are men more reasonable ?' asked my angel, 'when for a momentary gratification they endanger their soul's salvation ?' "

Her compassion for the poor little mouse was turned by her angel to men blindly rushing to their own destruction, that she might help them from afar by her prayers and supplications. The vision appeared to imply what seemed to her impossible, that the hidden, peaceful life of former years was never to return, and so God willed. That happiness so longed-for was never again to be hers. The time had arrived for the last and most painful part of her mission. As the Church was bereft of her asylums of peace in which piety could be practised unmolested and contemplation sheltered from the vulgar gaze, so was Sister Emmerich torn from that sacred abode in which she had hoped to end her days, a trial which she shared with Holy Church up to the last instant of her life. What it cost her the following pages will tell.

CHAPTER XXVI.

FROM EASTER TO PENTECOST, 1813.

After the Vicar-General's third visit, Dean Rensing had commissioned Sister Emmerich to pray for a certain intention which he did not designate. On May 2d, he found her greatly consoled by an apparition of Mary and the Infant Jesus the preceding night. She said: "I invoked Mary for the intention prescribed; but I have not been heard. I prayed for it three times. I said to Mary: 'I must pray for it, because it has been given to me in obedience;' but I received no answer, and I was so full of joy on seeing the Infant Jesus that I forgot to ask again. I still hope, however, to be heard. I do not pray for myself. I am so often heard when I pray for others, but for myself never, excepting when I ask for sufferings."

Without knowing it, she had this time prayed for herself, Dean Rensing's intention being that the investigation might be speedily concluded. Every one connected with it had almost a greater desire for it than the poor sufferer herself. She often had to tranquillize those from whom she should have received comfort and support. But the suspicions cast upon the good old Abbé Lambert afflicted her more sensibly than her own pains (1). Father Limberg, her confessor, had known her too short a time to be exposed to unjust remarks; yet he knew the exact state of her soul and, in spite of his naturally distrustful disposition, he

(1) Dr. Wesener's Journal, Jan. 26, 1815:—"I was bandaging to-day, in Sister Emmerich's room, an ulcer on the arm of Mrs. Roter's little boy, a child of ten years. The Abbé Lambert, who was present, was so overcome at the sight that he turned his eyes away and began to moan over the little fellow. I expressed my surprise to Sister Emmerich at the old priest's extreme sensibility. She replied: 'You see now what he is! tender-hearted as a child. And yet they say he made my wounds!'"

doubted not the truth of her stigmata. He was a very timid man and easily disconcerted. He trembled in the presence of an illustrious personage such as the Vicar-General; consequently, it is not surprising that he frequently drew upon himself the reproach " of imprudence." Had it been in his power or that of the Abbé Lambert, the wounds would have disappeared as soon as produced, particularly as such a result would have been most conformable to Sister Emmerich's own desires. Both he and the Abbe regarded them as an unavoidable misfortune to be borne as best it could. They utterly rejected the idea that it was the work of God, a distinction granted to few, and the ecclesiastical inquiry with the publicity attending it was annoying in the extreme. All this combined to make the poor sufferer dread losing patience if not soon allowed to return to that life of seclusion and recollection to which she had been accustomed. It was this hope that led her to accede so willingly to Dean Rensing's proposal of a medical surveillance of eight days, and the same hope of freeing herself from further annoyance made her look forward to it with ever-increasing desire.

May 9th, Dean Overberg came for the fourth time to Dülmen on the part of the Vicar-General.

" I went over what she had before recounted to me," he says, " to assure myself that I had understood and noted it down correctly. She gave me to understand that this examination into her past life not a little increased her sufferings ; for it might be thought that she was something, but she herself knew better. I found her cheerful, although she had suffered much the night before and her wounds had bled profusely."

On the second day of his visit, Dean Overberg writes :—

" Sister Emmerich was again very prostrate this morn-

ing and her sister informed me that she had passed an agonizing night, often starting from sleep in dread of a
new examination. She shed tears through her fear of yielding to impatience if not allowed a little rest, and complained
that the investigation had almost entirely deprived her of
recollection. I was not able, nor did I desire to converse
long with her as she was so weak; however, she again confirmed her former statements to me. She was a little better
in the afternoon. She insists upon the eight days' surveillance by physicians and other responsible persons, that her
annoyances may come to an end."

Dean Overberg, Dean Rensing, and Dr. Wesener united
with Sister Emmerich in asking for the surveillance. " She
told me with tears, " writes Dr. Wesener, " how ardently
she sighs for peace. ' Ah!' she said, ' I am willing to do
anything to serve my neighbor. I would allow myself to be
cut to pieces and put together again to save one soul; but
I cannot exhibit myself as a spectacle to the curious. I
think if they watch me for eight days, they will be satisfied
about me. It is not for my own sake that I want the truth
to be known, but for that of my friends, that they may not
on my account be wrongfully accused.' "

After Dean Overberg's departure, Dr. von Druffel came
to Dülmen. Of his visit he writes : " Nothing new dis-
closes itself. The impression produced on me by the invalid is the same. The state of her wounds, the mark in her
side, and the cross on her breast presented no change."

Dean Overberg promised on leaving to gain the Vicar-General's consent to the proposed surveillance and to interest himself in its prompt execution. He succeeded in
the first part of his mission, but failed in the second, as we may
glean from his communication to Dean Rensing :—

" ' Man proposes and God disposes !' Behold a fresh

proof! We cannot find suitable persons to guard our dear Sister Emmerich. The physicians will not be free before the Pentecost holidays, on account of the lectures, and they are desirous that she be removed as soon as possible to a more convenient lodging. Be so good as to console her on the news of this delay, as distasteful to us as to her, and remember me to her." A few days after this letter, there arrived for her bed a leather covering which the good Dean had had made, and with it the following lines : " Dr. Krauthausen told me that our poor sufferer ought to have a leather cover on her mattress, as it is cool and prevents bedsores. I looked for something of the kind and I have been so fortunate as to find one of chamois. I waited several days for an opportunity to send it ; but as none presented itself, I express it to-day that she may have it as soon as possible. Have the kindness to see that it is placed on her bed."

The delay of the surveillance was more grievous to Sister Emmerich than anything she had hitherto endured. She read therein the withering assurance that her hopes were vain, that there was no probability of her ever being able to hide from the public gaze, and escape the manifold annoyances of her present position. She had dared to count on the Feast of the Ascension as the day on which she would recover the only earthly goods she craved, peace and solitude—but now, alas! her expectations were blighted. The Abbé Lambert often heard her sighing : " I am the Lord's instrument! I know not what is in store for me, I only long for rest! " She could not hide from herself the fact that this longed-for rest would never more be hers on earth. Almighty God exacted of her this great sacrifice and she made it unreservedly, but at the cost of complete prostration and great increase of pain.

Dean Rensing's notes, May 17th—" She complained of
having had the night before pains so acute that she was forced
to beg God to lessen them. She was heard, and strength
was given her to suffer patiently. She added : 'Then I
said the *Te Deum laudamus* all through. I had begun it
several times but had never been able to finish on account
of my pain.' The next night she suffered still more. She
said to Dean Rensing :—' I have often begged God for pain
and suffering, but now I am tempted to say : " Lord, enough !
no more, no more ! " The pain in my head was so violent
that I feared I should lose patience. At daybreak, I laid on
it the particle of the True Cross which Dean Overberg had
given me and I begged God to help me. I was instantly relieved. Still greater than my bodily pains are those of my
soul, dryness, bitterness, and anguish ; but I have twice been
restored to peace and sweet consolation after receiving
Holy Communion.' "

As her interior was so little understood by those around
her, no attention was paid to her mental sufferings, and
they often complained before her of her vain expectations.
This made her feel more keenly her want of spiritual assistance, and she fell into such a state of anguish that she
seemed to lose all strength and fortitude. On May 19th,
Dean Rensing found her so prostrate and dejected that he
had not the courage to address her. When he returned in
the evening, he saw that the cross on her breast had been
bleeding profusely; her garments were saturated with blood.
Strength had returned sufficiently for her to tell him that
the evil one, taking advantage of her helplessness, had
troubled her with frightful apparitions on the preceding
night:—

"I endured an agony. My sister was sound asleep, the
lamp was burning, and I was lying awake in bed, when I

heard a slight noise in the room. I looked and saw a hideous figure covered with filthy rags slowly approaching. It stood at the foot of my bed. It drew aside the curtain, and I saw it was a frightful-looking woman with an enormously large head. The longer she looked at me, the more horrible she grew. Then she leaned over me, opening her huge mouth as if to swallow me. At first I was calm, but soon I became greatly alarmed and began to invoke the holy names of Jesus and Mary, when the horrible apparition disappeared."

Father Limberg delivered her at last from her state of desolation. He reproved her a little sharply for complaining, telling her she must calmly await a decision and meditate more attentively on the words: "Lord, may Thy will be done!" Dr. Wesener, who was present at this little scene, made a note of it as follows:—"Sister Emmerich instantly submitted with the best grace in the world, and no more complaints were heard. Father Limberg told me that he thought it his duty to speak to her a little severely, as he knew from experience that the least imperfection was highly prejudicial to her."

Dean Rensing's journal of the following day runs thus:— " I asked her if she had had a vision or apparition the preceding night. 'No,' she answered, 'I was too much afflicted for having been impatient and discontented on account of so many annoyances. I ought to be like clay in the potter's hand, no self-will, no complaints, patiently receiving whatever God sends. That is hard for me, because I still think more of my own peace than of God's will, which tries me; but He knows what is best for me.' In the same way she accused herself before Dr. Wesener of her impatience. 'My attempt to disabuse her of this idea,' he remarked, 'was without effect.' "

God rewarded her humble obedience by sending her fresh consolation. On May 21st, Dean Rensing found her exhausted from suffering and loss of blood. Her wounds had bled so copiously that her head dress and chemise were stiff; but she had tasted great consolation in the midst of her pains, and particularly after Holy Communion.

"One thing gave me great joy," she said. "After Holy Communion, I saw two angels holding a beautiful garland of white roses with long sharp thorns which pricked me when I tried to detach a rose. 'O that these thorns were not here!'—I thought. And then came the answer: 'If you want to have roses, you must suffer the pricks of the thorns.' I shall have to endure much before I attain to joy unmingled with pain."

A short time after she had a similar vision:

"I was taken into a beautiful garden in which I beheld roses of extraordinary size and beauty, but their thorns were so long and sharp that one could not pluck a rose without being scratched by them. 'I don't like that,' I said. My angel replied: 'He who will not suffer shall not enjoy!'."

Joys without suffering were also shown her, but she was given to understand that they were to be hers only at death:

"I saw myself lying in the tomb, and no words can express my joy. It seemed as if I were told at the same time that I should have much to suffer before my death, but that I must abandon myself to God and remain firm. Then I saw Mary with the Child, and it was unspeakable joy for me when that good Mother placed Him in my arms. When I gave Him back, I asked Mary for three gifts which would render me pleasing to her and her Son: charity, humility, and patience."

Her fortitude began to increase from that day, and on
May 26th, eve of the Ascension, she said to the Dean : " O
how I should love to go to heaven with the dear Saviour !
but my time has not yet come. My sufferings increase, I
must still be tried, purified more and more. God's will be
done ! May He grant me the grace to persevere to the end
in patience and abandonment to His good pleasure ! "

On the Feast of the Ascension when she received Holy
Communion, she heard these words :—" Wouldst thou
rather die than suffer longer ?" to which she answered :
"I will still suffer longer, O Lord, if such be Thy good
pleasure." She added, when repeating this incident to
Dean Rensing : " My desire is fulfilled, but in the sense
that I now suffer more intensely than before."

Dr. Wesener declares how numerous and varied were
her pains and how much they were increased by all around
her. On May 25th, he writes :

" I found her this evening very restless and quite beside
herself with pain. Her back is covered with sores. Her
sister had bathed it with brandy, and she had fainted from
pain. She writhed on her bed, moaning : ' Why did you
do that ? I am willing to suffer, but you ought not to do
such things thoughtlessly.' Her face was inflamed, her eyes
full of tears, and her pulse had not varied ; but when Father
Limberg ordered her to be quiet, she lay still instantly and
said no more."

Soon again she had to undergo a similar, though much
greater torment : " I found," says Dr. Wesener, " her
sister by her bedside with a plate of salad swimming in
vinegar-sauce. I asked if the patient had tasted it, and
was told that she had taken a little of the sauce and a
piece of cheese. She lay in a stupor and quite unconscious.
I soon discovered the cause. Her sister had wanted

to bathe her back again with brandy ; and, as the invalid refused, she had left the vessel of liquor by the bed. Its fumes stupefied her and when that stupid, self-willed sister of hers presented the food, she had not the strength to resist. She fell into a pitiable state of nausea, convulsive vomiting, and choking. I feared she would strangle. It was not until nine o'clock that evening that she threw off the food and got some relief. She regretted having taken it, though at the time she knew not what she was doing."

Experience like the above did not, however, disabuse Sister Emmerich's friends nor prevent their ill-advised efforts to relieve her. They still had recourse to brandy as a remedy. Some years after, Mr. Clement Brentano had an opportunity of testing this fact. " I often saw Sister Emmerich,"he says, " reduced to a frightful state by the absurd mania for bathing her bed-sores with brandy. She groaned at the thought of such an operation and refused to submit to it, for the mere smell of the abominable stuff was sufficient to deprive her of consciousness ; but she had not the strength to resist. The use of brandy as a curative is a fixed idea among the lower classes of Münster, and poor Sister Emmerich was forced to endure it. Ah ! the poor thing was often treated more like an inanimate object than a human being !"

One of the chief reasons that awoke Sister Emmerich's longing for a retired life was the crowd of visitors that now began to press around her bed of pain. The disorder it caused afflicted her less than the mental sufferings resulting from it. " She complains," says Dr. Wesener, " of so many visitors. They annoy her exceedingly. She has also other sufferings that she cannot indicate."

What these sufferings were, we may judge from the past. They sprang from her gift of reading hearts and her keen

sense of the moral state of her neighbor. She saw with grief
the sins of those who visited her ; their passions, the intentions that actuated them pierced her like arrows. This truly
terrible gift had been one of her greatest sufferings. But
now that she lay unprotected, as it were, on the public
highway, for the ecclesiastical prohibitions were daily
losing force, it was her greatest torment. She was overwhelmed by crowds of the curious, who gazed upon
her and her priestly guardians with injurious suspicions and haughty contempt. Of what grace, then, had
she not need to insure her against despair, when before her
arose the certitude : " It will ever be thus till the hour of
my death !"

CHAPTER XXVII.

The Vicar General's Fourth Visit to Dülmen.

Dean Rensing had informed Dean Overberg of the painful impression produced by his letter of May 18th upon Sister Emmerich, and of her dissatisfaction with the gentlemen of Münster chosen for the surveillance.

"I hoped," she said, "that the affair would be over by the Feast of the Ascension and that I should then have leisure to prepare for the coming of the Holy Ghost. The time between these two feasts has ever been to me so sacred; but now that consoling hope is gone. If physicians from Münster cannot come, those of our own city could be engaged, especially as they can see all that goes on and are more worthy of confidence than young men still pursuing their studies. Dr. von Druffel assured me that only such persons would be sent as I should approve, but that young men, like R. R., not twenty years old, should sit day and night at my bedside, is what I cannot permit."

Dean Overberg laid this objection before the Vicar-General. He took it into serious consideration, for Sister Emmerich's manner of expressing herself seemed to him little in accordance with the idea entertained of her obedience. He thought it his duty, therefore, to repair at once to Dülmen and have an explanation with her. He wrote to Dean Rensing, reproving him for having mentioned to her the names of the gentlemen chosen for the surveillance, and closed with the following remarks :—" It ought to have sufficed for Sister Emmerich and others concerned to know that the persons in question had the approval of ecclesias-

tical authority. I should not expect so much of every one.
But of those whom God appears to have so highly favored,
I make extraordinary demands ; and when I weigh those
graces in the scale of obedience, I am but imitating the example of the wisest and holiest men."

On June 3d, he arrived in Dülmen. "My intention," he
says in his report, " was chiefly to examine Sister Emmerich's interior dispositions; the inspection of her wounds,
which had recently bled, was but a secondary object.   I
wished to talk to her on her manner of expressing herself
upon the surveillance and the persons chosen for it.   I
found things as usual."

The Vicar-General had scarcely seen the invalid and demanded an explanation of her apparent complaints than he
noted down the following :

" As to the gentlemen from Münster engaged for the surveillance, Sister Emmerich brought forward but one objection, and that was touching their youth.   She was also afraid that they might hear from her lips words which
they would perhaps misunderstand.   Such a fear is not
unreasonable, for she sometimes dreams aloud, and she
knows that she has already been reported to have said:
'Such a one is in heaven, such a one is in purgatory.'   However, she was well-disposed, there was no need of reasoning
with her."

As to her impatience at the delay, the Vicar-General was
equally satisfied.   He says : " Sister Emmerich alleged the
following on this point: 'I have at this season always been
in the cenacle with the disciples, awaiting the coming of the
Holy Spirit.' (Clara Soentgen deposed that at this time she
was always more recollected than usual.)   'This year I
desired the same, and I took it into my head that I ought
not to be prevented ; but now I see that I made a great

mistake. I have also been too presumptuous in praying for sufferings. "To suffer or die," I exclaimed. God has punished me for it. He said to me : ' Dost thou wish to suffer ? thou shouldst be willing then, to suffer what I will that thou shouldst suffer.' "

The Vicar-General recalled to her St. Teresa's device, " To suffer or to die," and that of St. Francis de Sales, " To love or to die," remarking that the former was good for the saints, but the latter suited all. She readily understood the application and expressed her satisfaction.

A few days after the Vicar-General's arrival, Sister Emmerich's mother came to see her. The poor old woman was anxious about her child. We can easily conceive how sad for the good mother was the news that her best loved daughter had been subjected to an ecclesiastical inquiry. The pastor of St. James, Coesfeld, had made a trip to Dülmen for the sole purpose of gaining some information to relieve her mind on the subject ; but on his report of what he had witnessed, she could not longer restrain her desire to see for herself. Clara Soentgen wrote to the Vicar-General :

" The day before yesterday, Sister Emmerich's old mother arrived. Sister Emmerich wished me to be present during the visit, as she felt a little timid before her mother. She had prayed God not to let her mother ask to see her stigmata or make any inquiries on her condition, and her petition was granted ; the old woman's behavior was admirable. She said not a word on the subject of the wounds, but only exhorted her daughter to good. When strangers told her that she ought to rejoice in such a child, that they had never heard of the like before, etc., she replied that such things were not to be spoken of, and that, during the person's lifetime, no importance should be attached to them. Sister Emmerich told me that, having heard such remarks as those given above, she had prayed that if they were addressed to her mother she might answer as she did. Truly her petition was heard."

After the old lady's departure, Sister Emmerich was disturbed by the thought that, although she showed her stigmata to so many strangers, she had concealed them from her own mother. She feared she had been wanting in filial respect. She spoke of it to the Vicar-General, asking him if she should have shown her wounds although her mother had not asked to see them. "I answered her," he wrote in the report, "that if her mother had asked it, she should have obeyed; but that as it was, she had done well in concealing them."

The Vicar-General was highly pleased with this, his fourth visit to the invalid, as his letter on the following day to Dean Rensing proves. The Dean had keenly felt the reproach of having mentioned before Sister Emmerich the names of her custodians, and in this frame of mind, had turned to her disadvantage some trifling remarks that had escaped the Vicar-General. The latter took up her defence as follows :—

"As to her visions, I have never entertained a thought of imposture, but only of the possibility of delusion for which, however, I hold no one responsible. Since my conversation with her, I can conclude but one thing concerning her expressions regarding the surveillance, and that is, that perhaps she has not yet reached the degree of perfection to which she is called." He then gave in writing the following injunctions :

"The project relative to Sister Emmerich must not long be deferred. I should like it begun as soon as possible. As to the choice of persons, I await your advice. Aged men are to be preferred. I approve of Mr. N. N., but his son is too young; neither to him nor to any other of his age must the duty be intrusted."

" When the custodians converse together, it must not be on a subject calculated to aggravate a measure already so painful. I hope you will visit her often and see if she desires a modification of any of the regulations. "

Dean Rensing was soon able to propose twenty gentlemen of Dülmen, all worthy of confidence, who were willing to watch in turn by the invalid under the direction of a strange physician. The Vicar-General approved all, and the surveillance began on the 10th of June. Before proceeding further, we shall notice the reports of the two Deans, Overberg and Rensing, to the Vicar-General on Sister Emmerich's stigmata, since they contribute powerfully toward establishing their truth.

CHAPTER XXVIII.

Dean Overberg's, Dean Rensing's, and Dr. Wesener's Testimony Regarding the Stigmata.

Though from his very first visit the Vicar-General was convinced of the impossibility of imposture with regard to the stigmata, yet he commissioned Dean Overberg to submit the invalid to circumstantial interrogations as to their nature and origin. The Dean began the examination April 8, 1813, and continued it until May 12th. His manner of proceeding consisted in demanding of Sister Emmerich new and detailed explanations upon points already settled, whilst Dean Rensing's and Dr. Krauthausen's daily reports furnished matter for fresh interrogatories to which he insisted on answers. When the report of one of these questionings was forwarded to the Vicar-General, he in turn demanded yet further explanations from the invalid, being satisfied only when by various means he had arrived at conclusions similar to those of the Dean. We find, in his own writing, notes on the report, never contradictory but rather confirmatory of Dean Overberg's conclusions, since they present them in a clearer and more exact style.

The following are faithful extracts of the several reports :—

"I was commissioned," writes Dean Overberg, April 8th, "to inquire of Sister Emmerich if she had made the wounds herself, or allowed others to do so. I represented to her as forcibly as possible that she owed obedience to ecclesiastical authority, and that she was obliged to speak the truth even supposing she had sworn secrecy to the person instrumental in producing the wounds. I impressed upon her that an oath which militates against obedience · to the Church is invalid, and I asked her how she could stand before God's tribunal if she concealed the truth that obedience commanded her to reveal. Being assured that she comprehended the above, I asked :

" 1—' Have you—perhaps, with a good intention—pinched your hands or forced a nail, or something of the kind into them, that you might feel more sensibly the sufferings of Jesus Christ ?'

" Answer.—' No, never !'

" 2—' Have you not applied to those parts nitric acid or lunar caustic ?' Ans.—' I know not what they are.'

" 3—' Has any one, who takes an interest in your spiritual progress and that you may be a lover of Christ's sufferings, made these wounds by pressing, by sticking, by putting something on them, or in any other way ?' Ans.—' Ah, no !'

" During the above questions and answers, her countenance maintained unalterable serenity. She then related what follows :—

" ' I knew not of the wounds at first, it was another who remarked them.' (I think she named the Abbé Lambert.) ' He drew my attention to them, saying : " Do not think that you are now a St. Catherine of Sienna. You have not yet come to that !" '

" When I objected that another could not have remarked the wounds before herself, since we are generally sensible of a wound received, she said : ' That is true ; but having felt the pain three or four years before the wounds appeared, I suspected not the change. When I received the external marks, I had only a little girl to wait on me, and she did not think of washing off the blood. I did not remark it, and so it happened that the Abbé Lambert saw the wounds in

my hands before I did myself.   The pain could not attract
my attention to them, for I had long been accustomed to it
and the external signs made no change in it.'   (Sister Emmerich used to call the pain she felt for many years in the
places where, at a later period, the wounds were formed,
marks, and the wounds themselves she generally denominated
external signs)

" ' The pains in my head I felt for four years before entering the convent.   It is, as it were, encircled by thorns, or
rather, as if all my hair were thorns ; I can never rest on
the pillow without pain.   The pains of the other wounds
are not like ordinary pains, they go to my heart.   A touch
or light pressure upon the cross on my breast is not so
painful outwardly, but inwardly it is as if the whole breast
were on fire.   As to the sign above my stomach, it feels like
a flame of fire.'

" 4—' When did these signs appear on your person ?
Ans.—' The sign on my stomach appeared on the Feast
of St. Augustine ; the lower cross on my breast about six
weeks after; the upper one on the Feast of St. Catherine ;
the wounds of my hands and feet on the last Feast of Christmas ; and that of my side between Christmas and New Year.'

" 5 —' When you first felt these pains and later when the
wounds in your head, hands, and feet appeared, did you
see anything like an apparition, or did you receive special
light on any subject ?'   Ans —' No, I was at the time in
unusual suffering.'

" 6—' Do you not know what the crosses on your breast
signify ?'   Ans.—' No. But when the first appeared on my
stomach, I felt that it was a sign that I should have much to
suffer for Christ.   When, on St. Catherine's Feast, the
second appeared, I felt that my cross would be two-fold;
and the same when the third became visible.'

" She told me again," remarks the Dean, " that she had prayed much to suffer the pains of Jesus, but never for the marks of His Wounds" (1).

" 7—' How must your first declaration (report, March 25th) be understood : " My wounds have not been made by man, but I believe and hope they are from God." '
Ans.—'I said: *I believe,* and not: *1 am sure,* because the Dean and the physicians, as well as their rigorous examination, made me fear that they came, perhaps, from the demon. But the crosses on my breast reassured me, for I said to myself: They certainly cannot have been made by the devil. For the same reason, too, I said, *I hope,* because I do hope that these signs are the work of God and not a delusion of the devil!'

" 8—' And supposing your wounds were healed as Dr. von Druffel thinks possible ? ' Ans.—' I have been permitted to ask for their disappearance, but nothing has been said of their healing. I never thought of that. I understood it this way : that God would not be displeased at my praying for their disappearance, and that their pains would rather increase than diminish. The latter have already much increased.'

The Dean said: " I shall not believe that you have revelations if you cannot prove to me that you know how to distinguish a revelation from a mere remembrance." She replied : "Yes, but how can I prove that ? " He answered : " That I do not know." Then she said : " It may be that I have heard, or seen, or experienced something and that, when I spoke of it, it was misunderstood for a revelation." (' Here she cited an example," says the Dean.) " What we have heard remains in the mind ; but when we suddenly receive the knowledge of something of which we

(1) See Dean Overberg's first visit, March 28, 29.

had never before heard or seen, that cannot be a remembrance ! "

"9—' Do you not know at what time you felt the pains in your hands and feet ?' Ans.—' Four years before the suppression of the convent, I went to Coesfeld to visit my parents. Whilst there, I prayed for two hours at the foot of the cross behind the altar in St. Lambert's Church. I was very much distressed at the state of our convent, so I prayed that we might see our faults and live in peace. I also asked Jesus to make me experience all that He suffered. From that time I have always had these pains and this burning. I used to think it fever and that the pains arose from it. Sometimes I fancied it might be an answer to my petition; but I rejected the thought, deeming myself unworthy of such a favor. I was often unable to walk on account of the pains in my feet, and my hands were so painful that at times I could not perform certain work, such as digging. I could not bend the middle finger, it often felt as if dead.

" ' After I began to feel these pains, I was one day earnestly praying that my Sisters in religion and I might see our faults, that peace might reign, and that my sufferings would cease, when I received this answer : ' Thy sufferings will not decrease. Let the grace of God suffice for thee ! Not one of thy Sisters will die before recognizing her faults !"— After this response, when I felt the *signs,* I consoled myself with the thought that my state would be known only to the Sisters, for it was frightful to think that the world would become cognizant of it.'

10—" To my questions concerning the crosses on her breast, she answered : ' I begged God from my childhood to imprint the cross upon my heart, but I never thought of an external sign.'

" She told me, besides, that the detailed inquiry into her past life was not the least of her sufferings, for reasons stated in a preceding chapter.

11—" On Thursday, May 13th, four P. M., the blood spurted from her head and her forehead. In less than a minute her kerchief was saturated. She became exceedingly pale and weak, and soon after her hands began to bleed. A short time previously she had had violent pains in her forehead and temples as if from the piercing of thorns which she felt even in her eyes. I told her that, if I could, I would draw the thorns out of her head and leave only one, to which she replied : ' I do not want them drawn out, I love their pains.' "

" I asked her what she meant by saying to Dean Rensing that they who believed not would feel ? Did she think that they who did not believe in her stigmata would be punished ?—She answered with a smile : ' Ah, no ! My wounds are not articles of faith. I only meant that they who believe not what the Catholic faith teaches, find no peace ; even on earth they will always feel miserable.'"

Dean Overberg gives an account of a subsequent visit made on Friday, September 15, 1814 : "In the morning, about nine o'clock, I saw the marks on her hands red and swollen, a sure sign of their going to bleed. I expressed surprise that there was no swelling in the palms, upon which Sister Emmerich explained that the wounds in the palms of her hands never swelled before bleeding ; on the contrary, they seemed to contract as if to puff out more on the upper surface.

" The cross on her breast did not bleed, though it was very red, as it invariably is on certain days, even when there is no effusion of blood."

From the first Sister Emmerich carefully sought to conceal her hands from every one. She hid them under the coverlet or, when much inflamed she laid a white cloth over them. This desire possessed her to such a degree that even in ecstasy she perceived any attempt to remove the covering.

Dr. Wesener says : "One day, I took my eldest sister to see Sister Emmerich and found her lying, as was often the case, unconscious. Father Limberg attempted to uncover her hands, but she showed signs of dissatisfaction. He said to her : ' What is the matter ? '—She answered in a low voice and without opening her eyes : ' They want something of me that I must not grant.'—I was wishing in my heart that my sister might be strengthened in her faith by this wonderful sight. Sister Emmerich again said : ' Some one wants signs from me that I must not give.' Then Father Limberg gave her his blessing, when instantly she began, still in ecstasy, to sign herself with her trembling hand, anxiously endeavoring all the time not to let the cloth fall from it."

Something similar occurred to Dean Overberg, Sept. 10, 1813, when he accompanied the Princess Galitzin to Dülmen. He wrote : " I found the invalid very weak. As I sat by her in the evening about six o'clock, she fell into one of her deep swoons (ecstasies). I extended the first fingers of my right hand toward her face. Instantly inclining her head she kissed them respectfully. Then I leaned over to kiss her left hand which lay before me stiff and immovable, but she drew it back frightened. I approached the other, but succeeded no better, so quickly was it withdrawn, although in these swoons her whole body lies stiff as a log."

The Dean had made these attempts through respect for the stigmata, but the patient's humility had become like second nature ; she shrank from such homage even when unconscious. She could not endure a glance animated by such a feeling, as the Pilgrim experienced at a later period. "I was sitting by her bed praying. She was in ecstasy and in intense suffering. I offered to God in union with the Sacred Wounds of Our Saviour, the sufferings of all the martyrs and the pains of all the saints who had had the stigmata and at the same moment I glanced reverently at Sister Emmerich's hands, when quick as lightning she drew them away. The movement surprised me and I asked what was was the matter. From her deep swoon she answered: 'Many things!'"

Dean Rensing was with her once just before the wounds began to bleed, and she complained of the sharp pains that always preceded it. He asked her why she did not uncover her hands, saying that she need not scruple doing so in his presence. "Ah!" she answered, "I cannot myself bear the sight of my signs. They cry out to me of the special favors of which I am not worthy." The Dean adds: "Then she thanked me for having denied admittance to a party of visitors. She wept that these good people gave themselves so much trouble and esteemed her so highly, although before God they were much better than she. She said: 'I must also thank God that He does not hide from me my faults; by them He strengthens me in humility.'"

She spoke of the pain and anxiety such visits gave her and earnestly begged the Dean not to allow her to be seen any more, especially by strange doctors who often inconsiderately wounded delicacy. "It is very hard for me," she said, "to be forced to show my signs so often; but still harder is it when I see that these people seek not the honor of God, but only something to talk about.

"From bodily sufferings I desire not to be free, God will leave them to me. But of what use are these inspections, these investigations? Our Lord Himself did not satisfy all in such a way that they believed and were converted. Some pity me too much. Let them pray for me that I may humbly submit to whatever God ordains through my spiritual Superiors and that I may not lose His grace. God leads every one by a separate way. But what matters it whether we go to heaven by this or that road? Let us only do all that God demands of us according to our state!"

Once Dean Rensing told her that Veronica Giuliani had for a long time around her head the marks of the Crown of Thorns. When it became known, the physicians tried to cure her, which proceeding cost her frightful sufferings. The invalid sighed and said: "I have not yet suffered so much; yet when Ecclesiastical Superiors decided that my wounds should be cured, I felt it very much because I was undergoing such pain. I had the pains of the crown around my head even before my entrance into the convent. I felt them first in the Jesuit church at Coesfeld."

During the first Vespers of St. Catherine of Sienna, Dean Rensing found her wounds bleeding; but on the day itself, April 30th, the flow was much more profuse. He reports as follows: "I visited her at three o'clock. As I entered the room the blood was streaming from her head and hands. I was quite unnerved at the sight, and an expression of admiration at the extraordinary favors bestowed upon her escaped me. She noticed it and said: 'Yes, God grants me more than I deserve. I thank Him for them, but I would rather He would hide these graces from the eyes of men, for I fear they will think me better than I am.' Then we had a conversation which gave me an insight into her pure and humble soul. She related some incidents of her youth which convinced me that the Hand of God had ever conducted her, shielding her from all danger. I was astonished to find one with so little education yet with ideas of God and divine things so clear, so just, so elevated. She told me that Almighty God had asked her the night before: ' Wouldst thou rather be with Me soon, or still suffer more for Me ?'—She answered: ' If thou dost desire it, I will gladly suffer more, if only Thou givest me the grace to do as Thou willest!—God promised me this grace,' she added, ' and now I am right joyful. He also reminded me that, whilst in the convent, I had committed many faults against the perfection to which my vows engaged me. I repented anew of these faults and received the assurance that I had not lost His grace by them, since I had humbled myself before Him and men. I was also reminded that when in the convent, despised by all, I had often prayed that the Sisters might recognize the faults they committed on my account. Often, when thus praying and particularly during the last summer I was among them, I received the consoling promise that all would see their faults before my death. And all have entered into themselves since God has given me these extraordinary signs. This is a joy for which I thank Him in the midst of the intense pains my signs cause me.'

" I asked her once," continues the Dean, " if she had not also a wound upon her shoulder, for I think the Saviour surely had His Sacred Shoulder wounded by the heavy cross. ' Yes, indeed !' she answered, ' the Divine Saviour had a painful wound on His Shoulder from the cross; but I have not the wound, although I have long felt its pain. I have venerated this wound from my childhood, because it is especially pleasing to Our Saviour. He revealed to me in the convent that this Wound of which so little is thought caused Him the greatest pain, and that when one honors it, He is as much pleased thereby as if that person had borne the cross for Him up to Calvary. At six or seven years old, when alone and meditating on the Lord's Passion,

I used to put a log of wood or some other weight on my shoulder and drag it along as far I was able."

During the whole of May, 1813, Dean Rensing noted almost daily the bleeding of the wounds and their increasing pains. Up to the 8th of May, she was forced to lie on her back which was covered with sores. She suffered intensely from it, but she said : "It is nothing compared with my other wounds. Still I am ready to suffer any pain, provided the dear God withdraws not His interior consolation. But I often feel great bitterness of soul now. It is hard, but God's will be done !"

During the octave of the Invention of the Holy Cross her wounds bled daily, her sufferings proportionately increasing. When the Dean saw blood flowing on the morning of the 3d, he did not at once recall the connection between it and the feast of the day. He expressed some surprise, upon which Sister Emmerich replied : "It must be because the Feast of the Invention is kept to-day." She had communicated, but with spiritual dryness, a keener suffering to her than any physical evil. The pains of the Crown of Thorns were simply intense in her forehead, eyes, and temples, and they extended even to her mouth and throat. This state lasted for several days, no consolation being vouchsafed her. The Dean, unable to endure the sight, remained by her side as little as possible.

On May 6th, she exclaimed : "I feel the pains from my feet up to my breast. It seems as if all my wounds communicate their pains one to the other." Her back, as we have said, was raw in several places, and her linen adhered to it; but she declared this nothing when compared with each separate wound. The Dean remarked that she must have had a very bad night. She replied : "No ! my pains are my joy ! I rejoice when I have something to suffer and I thank

God that I am not lying idle in my bed." Once she said
to Dean Overberg that her greatest trial was to have
nothing to suffer; she was never so happy as in suffering
something for the love of God.

On May 9th, her state remained the same, but she had
been consoled and strengthened from on high. She told
the Dean that she felt as if a hair rope were being drawn
through her head, and that she sometimes feared she would
lose her mind. "My suffering is, however, not too great.
God sweetens it by His consolations, although I do
not deserve them. Especially in the convent did I render
myself unworthy of such favors, for I often thought too
much over the faults of my Sisters and what they ought to
do, and too little of what I ought to be myself. That was imperfect and ungrateful; therefore, I am satisfied that God now
lets me suffer. If I knew that by it I could contribute ever
so little to His glory and the conversion of sinners, I would
gladly suffer more and more. God grant me patience!"
Her pains decreased toward evening when the Dean found
her unusually bright.

These effusions of blood were attended by so copious a
flow of perspiration that the bed-clothes were saturated as
if dipped in water. The wounds on her back resulted from
this and prevented her lying down. The wound of her right
side made it impossible to lie upon it, and her left hip-bone
was completely stripped of flesh; consequently she was forced
to remain in a most painful sitting posture. Mr. Clement
Brentano says: "For four years I was in daily communication with Sister Emmerich, and saw the blood flowing
from her head. I never saw her head uncovered or the
blood gushing directly from her forehead, but I saw it running down under her cap in such quantities that it lay in
the folds of her kerchief before being absorbed. Her head,

surrounded by an invisible crown of thorns, could not be rested on her pillow; she balanced it for hours in a sitting posture like a weight of untold pain. Often did I support it for a longer or shorter time on my two fingers placed against the bridge of the nose, the sweat of agony bathing her pallid face. I could not endure the pitiful sight without doing something to relieve her. Whole nights were often passed in this state, helpless and alone."

The absolute impossibility of taking nourishment of any kind coincided with the appearance of the stigmata. Dean Overberg writes, May 12, 1813: "For about five months, Sister Emmerich has taken no solid food, not even the size of half a pea. She can retain nothing, neither chocolate, coffee, wine, nor soup. The only thing she takes occasionally is a tea-spoonful of beef-tea. She endeavors to conceal the fact of her abstinence from food by having a baked apple or some stewed prunes placed by her; but of these she only tastes the juice.

"A little very weak coffee was what she could best take in the convent, but from the early part of last winter she could retain not even this. She then tried weak chocolate, but only for a few days; wine, pure or watered, she could not endure, and, at last, she confined herself to water alone."

We have seen that, in spite of her total inability to eat, she was at times suspected of doing so, a suspicion that was frequently renewed. Dean Overberg reports, Sept. 17, 1814:—"Dean Rensing told me that the widow with whom Sister Emmerich lodges, was very ill for about two months before her death. She had herself carried into Sister Emmerich's room, thinking that she could endure her sufferings more patiently there and better prepare for death. A day or so before she died, she acknowledged that she had once had doubts as to Sister Emmerich's not eating, but now she was convinced that she took absolutely nothing."

Dr. Wesener reports, Oct. 29, 1814, that he was often obliged to defend his patient against such suspicions :—" I had a visit from the Dean von Notteln, who came to find out for himself, as he said, the origin of the report circulating in Münster that Sister Emmerich had been seen out of bed eating some meat. I took him to see the invalid, telling him to watch her closely whilst I repeated the report to her in the plainest terms. She smiled as I told her, saying that such things only made her pity those who invented and propagated them. To render homage to truth, I must here say that I took a great deal of trouble to discover something she could eat without vomiting, but in vain. If I am deceived in her, I must refuse credence to my own senses. She is, moreover, surrounded by people who would be only too well pleased could they find the least thing against her, how equivocal soever it might be. Her own sister, who ought to wait on her, is a perverse, ill-tempered creature, constantly doing something to deserve reprimand both from Sister Emmerich and from me. She has no love for the poor sufferer; she often leaves her the whole day long without even a drink of water. Surely, such a pers n would not keep a fraud secret !"

Father Limberg himself was alive to such suspicions. Fifteen months after the investigation, he was tormented for several days by a stain on the coverlet of Sister Emmerich's bed, which he concluded could have been made only by food eaten in secret. Dr. Wesener and Clara Soentgen reassured him, explaining that it was made by a plaster which the latter had applied to the invalid's hip. Sister Emmerich could not restrain a smile at her confessor's unreasonable doubts. She remarked : " If I could eat, I

know not why I should do it in private!"—She begged
him to communicate to her any suspicions that arose in
his mind and not keep them to himself for entire days.
Later we shall see her suffering greatly from the doctor's
attempts to make her take food.

With regard to her manner of prayer when she received
Holy Communion, Dean Overberg says:—

"Sister Emmerich's immediate preparation for receiving
the Holy Eucharist consisted in begging God, her Saviour,
to give her His own Heart that she might worthily receive
and entertain Him. She represented to Him that it was only
through and with His Heart that she could love and praise
Him as He deserved. Then she offered Him her own,
begging Him to make it pleasing to Himself. After
this she called together all the powers of her soul and
body that she might offer to Him all she possessed —
her eyes, her ears, her members, supplicating Him to
make use of them in His own service and to accomplish by them what she herself could not. Then she
made a contract with Almighty God to praise and thank
Him with her whole being : every thought, every sigh,
every movement of her eyes and hands, every instant
of her sufferings, was to be an act of praise. She begged Mary for some gift from her superabundant treasures, supplicating her to place the Divine Infant in her
arms as she had done to the Eastern Kings. Then turning to the saints she went from one to another, begging for
something of their beauty, their virtues, their ornaments,
that she might prepare better for Holy Communion and
make a more fervent thanksgiving. 'You are so rich,'
did she say to them, 'and I am so poor! Ah, pity me!
I ask for only a mite from your abundance!'

"After Holy Communion, she fell into ecstasy as she
had always done in the convent."

CHAPTER XXIX.

The Surveillance of Ten Days.—End of the Ecclesiastical Investigation.

"On the 9th of June," says Dean Rensing's report, "I informed the invalid that the surveillance would begin the next day. She expressed her satisfaction and readiness to submit to the will of her Superiors. The cross on her breast was bleeding profusely, her garments were quite soaked with blood.

"When I visited her next day to prepare for the coming of the custodians in the evening, she said: 'Would it not be better for the Abbé Lambert to absent himself for the next ten days? He is willing to do so, if you think well of it.' The proposition pleased me, and I spoke of it to the Abbé who set out that very afternoon for the old Chartreuse, three and a half miles from Dülmen. That evening, about eight o'clock, the custodians began their watch."

Not only the Dean, but the Vicar-General also, was pleased with Sister Emmerich's proposal. The latter had earnestly desired the Abbé's absence during the coming days, but he felt a delicacy in proposing it. As late as June 8th, he had written to the Dean: "I beg you, if you can possibly do so, to arrange the Abbé Lambert's absence during the surveillance; at least, do not allow him to visit her. If you cannot effect this, we must commit the affair to God; and if you cannot broach it as coming from the Sister herself, we must give it up. Recommend to Sister Emmerich's prayers an intention which I forgot to mention to her myself."

The Dean replied to the above : " It would certainly be very desirable for the Abbé to go away for some time, but I see no way of effecting it."

The Vicar-General's directions for the surveillance are as follows :

" Her custodians are not to leave Sister Emmerich alone for a single instant. Her sister may be present and render her all necessary services, but under no circumstances must the custodians leave her ; even when she makes her confession, they must be present. Father Limberg will speak to her in a low tone and carefully avoid everything calculated to arouse suspicion that he is in any way accessory to the existence of her wounds. Two custodians must be present at a time and I think it proper that one should, if possible, be an elderly man. They have nothing to do but *to watch*, anything else would overstep the limits of their charge."

On the fifth day the Dean sent the following report to the Vicar-General :

" The custodians have faithfully followed directions, and the invalid is so pleased at their comportment that she has already repeatedly thanked me for having chosen men so discreet for the discharge of a duty necessarily most painful to her.

" N . . . N . . .has withdrawn. He was unwilling to undertake so delicate an affair without the concurrence of his colleagues. Is it not sad to see men, who so often expose their life in contagious diseases, so fearful of the lash of public criticism when there is question of testifying to the truth ?"

The physician alluded to did, however, arrive on the 15th. He spent several nights by the invalid, but his hesitation very nearly frustrated the end proposed. The surveillance had not been undertaken to confirm the opinion of Superiors, but only to avert from them the suspicion of not having investigated the case as rigorously as they should have done ; consequently this physician's withdrawal was a most unpleasant surprise for the Vicar-General. He wrote to the Dean :—

" That we may attain our end in this surveillance, it is necessary for Dr. N. N — to go to Dülmen, direct the affair, and certify to its having been conducted according to prescribed forms. This is an indispensable condition, without which any surveillance over Sister Emmerich will be useless."

The invalid herself was annoyed by the physician's conduct. She prevailed on Father Limberg to go to Münster and make known to the Vicar-General her fears that the present surveillance would be declared defective ; that a new one would be instituted ; and that she would, perhaps, be removed to Münster, from which last proceeding she implored his protection. The Vicar-General, with the severity arising from his upright intentions, sternly reproved her for such a petition which, however, was most justifiable in itself and supported on motives which, as we shall see, were far from groundless. His penetrating, we might even say his mistrustful eye, had never been able to detect in the invalid the least thing not in accordance with her sublime gifts, and what he knew of her past life and present state confirmed his opinion that she was under the special direction of Almighty God ; therefore, he met everything that accorded not with the high idea he had formed of her with rigor as implacable, as he would have shown had a shadow of suspicion attached itself to her wounds. He was impatient at finding her not yet entirely " dead to self-will," still disquieted about her future.

" Say to Sister Emmerich," he wrote to Clara Soentgen,

" with my kind regards, that the proverb runs thus : *Do not worry over unlaid eggs!*—I generally add : *Nor over spoiled ones.* The past is past, the future has not yet come; it may, perhaps, never arrive. To worry about the future is as useless as to grieve over the past; not only useless, but even pernicious, for such anxiety prevents the fulfilment of present duty and ordinarily proceeds from self-will. Tell her from me that all such expressions as these: 'I fear I shall become impatient,' 'We must not tempt God,' etc., appear to me the result of self-love."

If Sister Emmerich's fears called forth such a rebuke from her Superior, what would she not have received had he beheld in her a real fault ? The truth is, he had little need of being convinced of the poor sufferer's sincerity, he needed not the ten days' surveillance to establish the fact of her miraculous state; for, before the prescribed time had expired, he wrote to Dean Rensing as follows:—

" Send me as soon as possible the result of the interrogatories put to Sister Emmerich's companions, that I may close the inquiry without delay."—And some days later, he wrote for the journal of the custodians :—" I am desirous of receiving it by Monday, as it will close the investigation. I beg you, however, to keep me informed on the invalid's condition and to aid her, as far as you can, in the perfect acquisition of the virtue of indifference. St. Francis de Sales says: ' Fear nothing, ask for nothing, complain of nothing.' "

Dean Rensing added the following remarks to the report demanded of him:—

" As Your Eminence is about terminating the inquiry, I should like to know if the duty I have hitherto discharged with regard to visitors is likewise to cease. I greatly desire to be freed from the daily annoyances resulting from it; but,

on the other hand, the poor sufferer will then have not one
hour's rest from morning till night, she will be constantly
assailed by the curious. She told me twice lately that Dr.
Krauthausen has spread the report, both here and in
Coesfeld, that if she herself gives permission there will be
no necessity to apply to me ; and his wife confirmed this
recently by her own example. She was sick, and on last
Thursday, during the afternoon service, she had herself
carried in a chair by two servants to Sister Emmerich's
lodgings, without previous permission from me. I believe it
my duty to inform you of this circumstance, as it has
created much talk and it may be followed by unpleasant
consequences. Several have already asked permission to
visit the invalid to consult her on their bodily infirmities
and other affairs."

The report of the twenty custodians accompanied this
letter. It runs as follows :—

" We,the undersigned, having been invited by Dean Rensing to keep guard over the invalid, Sister Emmerich, and
having been informed orally and by writing of the motives
for the same and the points to be observed in it, went two by
two to her lodgings, June 10, 1813, eight o'clock P. M.,
and entered upon our duty according to the order prescribed, which we continued day and night till Saturday,
the 19th. No one approached the invalid during the aforesaid time, excepting her sister who waited on her, one of
her former companions in the convent, and some visitors who
entered with the Dean, or by written permit from the Vicar-General. No one could speak to her, much less concert
anything with her, without our knowledge. The Abbé
Lambert, who resides in the same house, had removed of
his own accord before the surveillance began, in order to
forestall objections to his presence ; he returned only at its

close. During these ten days, the patient took nothing but clear water ; this she rarely asked for, but drank it when offered either by her sister, the physicians, or the custodians. Once she sucked a cherry, but rejected the pulp. She took also some drops of laudanum from Dr. Wesener one day when she had unusually keen and continued pains.

" Neither she herself nor any one else touched her wounds even slightly. The double cross on her breast began to bleed on the night of the 15th, after she had experienced sharp, shooting pains in it ; the effusion lasted till seven A. M. The other wounds bled early on Friday morning, the 18th, and continued to do so more or less copiously the whole day. Her head bled again for awhile on Saturday morning. Before and during these effusions, she complains of shooting pains in her wounds. We remarked that in the morning until about ten o'clock, she seems brighter and complains less ; before and after this time the blood flows. During the rest of the day, she complains of weakness, fever, and shooting pains in her wounds, head, and eyes. She rarely sleeps soundly. The state which appears to resemble sleep is, as she says, of little benefit to her, and she is generally weaker after it than before. Between ten o'clock and midnight, she falls into ecstasy, speaks aloud, shudders with terror, etc. ; though occasionally she lies as if in deep sleep.

" The foregoing deposition we are willing to repeat before either ecclesiastical or civil authority, and if necessary, attest its truth on oath.

" DÜLMEN, *June* 23, 1813."

The Vicar-General expressed his satisfaction in the following letter to the Dean : " I cannot refrain from expressing to you my gratitude for having conducted the investi-

gation in a manner so entirely conformable to my desires
and instructions. I can give Sister Emmerich no better
advice than to encourage her to the practice of holy indifference with the help of God's grace, which is never wanting to those who ask it. I also advise her to make use of
the means in every citizen's power to rid herself of importunate visitors. I pity Sister Emmerich from my heart,
but I dare not render her further assistance."

These last words refer to an incident which took place
before the close of the examination and which was attended
by ulterior consequences. We shall not pass it over in silence since, four years after, it was made a pretext for attacks upon her through the press.

On June 16th, Dean Rensing received the following directions in writing from the Vicar-General:

" If the wife of the Prefect of the Rhenish Department
of R— with her sister and Professor B— of Münster, should
ask to see Sister Emmerich, do not fail to introduce them
to her and tell her, in virtue of obedience, to allow them
to see all her wounds. It is necessary that the Professor
should see them; he is very incredulous as to their origin."

The above-named visitors arrived that evening. They
first called on Dr. Krauthausen to receive from him an account of his observations. The Professor declared the whole
thing ignorance and illusion and, even before seeing the
invalid, condemned her as an impostor and pronounced the
investigation valueless. On the morning of the 18th of June,
Dean Rensing introduced them to Sister Emmerich who,
in obedience to orders, consented to the inspection of her
wounds, a proceeding highly repugnant to her feelings. The
Professor saw in them only the veriest cheatery. " The
crusts of dried blood were (as he repeated four years after in
a pamphlet) nothing but starch, the cross on her breast was

put on so lightly that it crumbled under his touch, the
wounds had been made with pins and a penknife, and the
blood flowing from them was *paint*." The learned gentleman was, above all, disgusted by the blood oozing from
under her head-dress and trickling down her face. "It
was," he said, "far too gross an attempt to deceive a person of his experience." The invalid herself was, in his
eyes, "a healthy, robust person, wondrously well considering her pretended abstinence from food." So much for
this lynx-eyed Professor, who could see nothing in the invalid's case but sharp instruments, albumen, starch, paint,
and gum water, which important discoveries he imparted
some years later to the astonished public. The Prefect's
lady thought that similar wounds might easily be produced
with a penknife; the ecstasies she described to animal magnetism. She tormented the poor sufferer with innumerable
questions on war, peace, hidden things, and future events,
to all which, however, she received but the short answer :
"Interior peace is all I think about."

The Dean and Dr. Krauthausen were both highly offended, and the former refused them a second visit. This
displeased the Vicar-General, and he expressed his dissatisfaction in the following terms :—

"Under other circumstances it would have been wrong
to permit the repetition of a visit so painful to Sister Emmerich ; but, in this instance, when dealing with people disposed to believe that a pious fraud or, to speak more correctly, that gross ignorance or diabolical charlatanry had
been employed to produce, I know not what effect, the
slightest cause for suspicion should be avoided. Now
to refuse a second visit evidently furnishes such a pretext."

In his pamphlet, some years later the Professor did,
indeed, allude to his having been refused a second visit,

because as he said, " the cross on her breast had not yet been renewed."

The Prefect's wife protested to Dr. Wesener that her only desire was to ascertain the truth for her own and others' satisfaction, begging him, at the same time, to appeal to Sister Emmerich herself for a confirmation of her words. When questioned on the subject, the invalid answered : " The Prefect's lady was the most sincere of the party, yet she did not come with a pure intention. She is too haughty and very far from being a true Christian. I have suffered much from this visit, and I feel that I ought not to be so tormented."

On returning to Münster, the Professor boldly gave out as his opinion that Sister Emmerich was an impostor ; consequently the Vicar-General,though attaching but small importance to the Professor's private opinion, concluded to grant him full powers with regard to the invalid, hoping that prolonged observations would force from him a testimony to the truth, and thus place such an enemy in the impossibility of contesting or denying the real state of affairs. With characteristic boldness, the Professor declared that he could soon cure the wounds, and the Vicar-General took him at his word. In an appendix to the official report the latter expresses himself thus :—

" I stipulated for the experiment's being tried only on one hand, for I knew that it would subject poor Sister Emmerich to much suffering. But as the project would entail his perfect seclusion for some time, the Professor did not even attempt it, although he seemed to be convinced of the reasonableness of trying the experiment on one hand only, for he said : ' If one wound is a fraud, all the others are frauds also.' He declared her abstinence no less an imposture than her stigmata,and that it would all be brought to light were she removed to Münster and placed under the care of six physicians. To this I refused my consent. I would not, by such measures, confirm the suspicions already entertained of the invalid and which I believed utterly destitute of foundation. Such a proceeding would seem to me contrary to justice and charity."

Later, however, Professor B——'s plan was modified : two trusty female nurses were to be chosen by him in Münster and commissioned to watch the invalid as closely as possible ; she was to be removed to other lodgings, receive no visits save those of Dean Rensing, and the Vicar-General was to go himself to Dülmen to make the arrangements.

But the French Prefect opposed the project and ordered the Mayor of Dülmen to forbid a new surveillance. " The civil power," he declared, " ought to protect a subject who had already been subjected to a rigorous examination and of whom so satisfactory a testimony had been rendered to the Commissary of Imperial Police." This declaration was accompanied by the threat to hand over any future inquiry regarding Sister Emmerich to the civil authorities, if it were proved that the ecclesiastical investigation had been insufficient. This threat determined the Vicar-General to abandon the project and leave the Professor to his learned vagaries. It seems a little strange at first sight that the Vicar-General should have paid so much attention to the professor's unworthy proceedings ; but his own words afford the explanation : " I was myself most anxious for him to heal the wounds."

From the beginning, he would willingly have got rid of the stigmata and their bloody effusions even at the cost of great sufferings to the invalid, for they attracted too much attention toward a person whose whole existence was so far removed from the ideas of the age in which she lived. He desired that everything calculated to become for the Church's enemies an occasion of attack should be shunned or ignored; therefore, the publicity given to the invalid's case which appeared to awaken the rage of unbelievers, was in his eyes a most vexatious affair. He himself regarded her stigmata as the work of God alone; but, sympathizing little with any sort of mysticism, he shrank with a sort of fear from further investigation of the mystery and made use of the following argument to dispense himself from it:

"I have aimed at discovering but one thing: *Is Sister Emmerich herself deceived, or does she deceive?* The result of the investigation has convinced me that imposture cannot reasonably be suspected; consequently, I seek nothing further. The stigmata are either natural phenomena of a very rare kind on which I pass no judgment, or they have a supernatural origin difficult to demonstrate."

Viewing it in this light, we can understand how the Vicar-General could entertain the greatest respect for the invalid, could ask her prayers for his own needs and those of the Church, could send to her humble abode the most distinguished personages of his widely-extended circle of acquaintances, and yet at the same time be so anxious to conceal her as much as possible from the eyes of the world.

He wrote to Dean Rensing, July 16th:—"I beg you to present my compliments to Sister Emmerich, and ask her prayers for a special intention. Tell her if the Count and Countess von Stolberg go to Dülmen, to show them all her wounds."

Count von Stolberg arrived in Dülmen with his wife and Dean Overberg, July 22d, one month after Prof. B.'s visit, and remained two days. The following is from the pen of the Count himself, published some time after with a few additions :—

"Dean Overberg announced our coming to Sister Emmerich, and at nine A. M., accompanied us to her lodging. Her little room opens directly on the street, the passers-by can see into it ; in fact, all that goes on in it may be seen outside. It is exceedingly neat, without the slightest disagreeable odor. Though a great trial to the invalid to be seen by strangers, yet she received us most graciously. Dean Overberg asked her, in our name, to uncover her hands. It was a Friday, and the wounds of the crown of thorns had bled profusely. She removed her head-dress, and we saw her forehead and head pierced as if with great thorns. We could distinctly see the fresh wounds partly filled with blood, and all around her head was bloody. Never has the painter's brush rendered so real the Saviour's wounds from the Thorny Crown. The wounds on the back of the hands and the upper part of the feet are much larger than those on the palms and soles, and those of the feet larger than those of the hands. All were bleeding.

"The physicians have been more unreserved than ecclesiastics in pronouncing the case miraculous, as the rules of science furnish more certain data for their judgments. They say that such wounds could not be naturally maintained without suppuration or inflammation ; that it is incomprehensible how the invalid, suffering constantly and cruelly, does not sink under the pressure of pain. She is, on the contrary, full of life, intelligence, and benignity ; she does not even grow pale.

"For sometime it has been optional with her either to refuse or admit visitors, so she declines whenever she can even those from a distance, as she finds such visits very painful. It is only on the recommendation of ecclesiastics or the physician that she consents to make some exceptions. She has enough to do, she says, to beg God for patience in her pains. It is tempting Him to risk it for people who are, for the most part, actuated only by curiosity. 'They who believe not in Jesus Christ,' she says, 'will not believe on account of my wounds.' It must truly be very distressing for a poor, timid, sick religious to be gazed at by a crowd of curious, indiscreet people!

"Anne Catherine, whose childhood passed in labor and the care of flocks, speaks gently, and in an elevated style when touching on religious subjects. This she could not possibly have acquired in the convent. She expresses herself not only with propriety and discretion, but also with superior intelligence. Her glance is full of benevolence, her words kind and affable. Her voice is low, clear, and sweet, and there is nothing forced in her conversation or manners, for love knows no effort. She is a sublime spectacle. The love of God is breathed in her sentiments, words, and actions. She bears with everything, and is charitable toward her neighbor.

"' How happy we are,' she said to Sophie, 'in knowing Jesus Christ! How difficult it was for our pagan forefathers to find God!'—Far from glorying in the external signs of the divine favor, she esteems herself wholly unworthy of them, and carries with humble care the treasure of heaven in a frail earthly vessel."

Mr. Kellermann was the first who took a copy of the foregoing letter for Rev. Michael Sailer,(1) afterward Bishop

(1) John Michael Sailer (1751-1832), Bishop of Ratisbon. Born of humble parents, he was by the providence of God raised to one of the highest dignities in the Church. As a student, he united to rare talents an *iron* industry and zeal together with a spirit of humility and kindliness toward all around. In 1770 he entered among the Jesuits. At their suppression in 1773, he continued his studies at Ingolstadt and was ordained in 1775. He held the professorial chair in pastoral and moral theology in different seminaries for many years. In 1821, he became Bishop of Ratisbon, in which position he accomplished a great amount of good.
For ten years he bore the accusations of his enemies in silence. That he should have

of Ratisbon, who made known its contents to many of
his friends.   It fell into Clement Brentano's hands and inspired him with a desire of knowing more of Sister Emmerich.
Count Stolberg regarded her with deep veneration and
through Dean Overberg maintained a spiritual union with
her till death.   She on her side never forgot the Count
before God ; he was one of those for whom she constantly
prayed and lovingly suffered, the beauty of his great soul
having been shown her.

It was not by an effect of pure chance that, just after the
examination to which she had been subjected, one of the
most eminent men of his day visited the poor stigmatisée
to render open testimony to the wonders of divine power
manifested in her.   His visit was followed by several from the
Princess Gallitzen accompanied by Dean Overberg.

endured his grievous wrongs in the spirit of Christ when he might have defended himself, must excite our admiration.   Bishop Sailer was of a noble character without self-
love or self-interest.   He united piety with cheerfulness and was loved by all that
knew him.   He refused many splendid positions offered him in Wirtemberg, Prussia,
etc., and counted numerous friends among the highest families.—(Taken from Herder's
Kirchen-lexicon.)

CHAPTER XXX.

The Vicar-General's Last Visit to Dülmen.—He Desires to Remove Sister Emmerich to Darfeld.

The Vicar-General was always ready to encourage the visits of men eminent by their position and learning to the stigmatisée of Dülmen. He hoped through their testimony to silence the voice of calumny in her regard. He was accustomed to notify her of such visits and express his desire that she would allow them to see her stigmata. Animated by this laudable design, and intending to make observations as detailed as those of April 21st, he repaired to Dülmen some months after the investigation with a numerous party of friends from among the nobility. Dr. Wesener's journal gives us the following remarks on this visit:

"Thursday evening, August 26th, I met the Vicar-General von Droste and Professor von Druffel by the invalid's bedside. She was very dejected and the Professor inquired of me what her state had been up to this time. He saw no change in her wounds, her countenance and demeanor were about the same as on his last visit. On Friday evening, I found her in a miserable condition, her pulse so weak that we all looked for her speedy dissolution. Father Limberg and her Sister Gertrude accounted for it by telling me that the Vicar-General and his party had wearied her the whole day, repeatedly inspecting the cross on her breast and bathing her wounds in order to examine them better." She had passively yielded to her Superior and uncomplainingly borne these painful inspections; but it was too much for her. She fell into a state of prostration from which she rallied but slowly.

Dr. Wesener deeply compassionated the poor, defenceless invalid, and in a spirited letter complained of the injury done his patient by so protracted an examination :—

" Your Grace desires," he wrote, " to probe this affair to the bottom, and such, indeed, is your duty. So far, so good !—but the investigation should not have been made thus ! The poor creature has been persecuted to death ! Your Grace came with a party of eight or ten and remained by the invalid from eight a. m. till six p. m. I regret that my absence prevented my warning you of the result of such a proceeding. Had I been present she would not have had to endure such an infliction, nor would I have had the grief of finding her in so sad a state. She thought, and she thanked God for it, that her last hour had come. I could not account for your imposing such suffering on her, did I not recall having heard Dr. von Druffel's opinion that such treatment could not harm her ; but I affirm, on my honor, that yesterday's proceedings would without a miracle have cost the invalid her life. If Your Grace continue your examination, the patient will offer no opposition. But, in God's name ! let it be done more leisurely and not at the cost of her already feeble health ! "

Poor Sister Emmerich rallied but slowly. When able to pronounce a few words, she said : "I feel that I ought not to receive such visits or show my signs. I was told so in vision. I was kneeling in spirit in a beautiful chapel before a statue of Mary with the Infant Jesus in her arms. When I invoked her, she descended, embraced me, and said: ' My child, be careful ! Go no further ! Shun visits and remain in thy humility !' "

The Vicar-General's motives excuse his seeming want of consideration for Sister Emmerich. He was seeking to provide her a secure retreat where, hidden from the eyes

of the world, she might accomplish in peace the mission assigned her. After mature reflection, he had decided to prepare for her an asylum on one of the estates belonging to
his family, where her wants would be generously provided
for. But before concluding his arrangements, he thought
that some members of his family ought to see the invalid
and convince themselves of the reality of her extraordinary
state. It was this that had led him to visit her with so
large a party and to subject her to so prolonged an examination. He thought it would be the last inspection of the
kind and that he would amply indemnify her by the advantages he had in store for her. No one at Dülmen was to
know of the project excepting Dean Rensing, who was to
advise her in the matter and, if she accepted the invitation,
accompany her to Darfeld Castle in the Vicar-General's
own carriage.

When the Vicar-General made this offer to Sister Emmerich, he imposed absolute silence on her, even with respect to her confessor, Father Limberg. He was to be informed only at the moment of departure by a sealed letter
which was also to contain a peremptory prohibition to take
any part whatever in the affair. The proposition threw the
invalid into great perplexity which told on her little remaining strength. The greatest, the only earthly advantages to which she aspired, solitude and repose, were now
held out to her, her acceptance seemed almost a duty of
deference and gratitude to her Ecclesiastical Superior, and
Dean Rensing represented to her that the retired asylum of
Darfeld alone could insure her against any attempt at a new
investigation. But, on the other hand, what assurance had
she that, in accepting so generous an offer, she would not
render herself unfaithful to God; that, in seeking a more
tranquil life, she would not pursue a course incompatible

with her mission ? Who would assure her that she did
not contravene her holy religious vows by giving the
preference to a position that would secure her from the
trials consequent on poverty ? Would she then have the
opportunities for works of mercy as she now had ? Would
her door stand ever open to the needy and distressed ?
Again, would not her non-acceptance of so generous an
offer offend her Superior ? Would she not appear ungrateful and capricious ? Her embarrassment was so much the
greater as she had ever been accustomed to absolute dependence on the words of her confessor; now, she was
forbidden to confer with Father Limberg on the subject,
and both the Vicar-General and Dean Rensing carefully
forebore saying a word that could influence her decision.
The acceptance or rejection of the offer was left entirely to
herself. She asked for time to consult God in prayer. After a few days, she dictated the following lines to Dean Rensing to be forwarded to the Vicar-General at Darfeld :—
"Sister Emmerich cannot resolve on a journey to Darfeld.
She is too weak to undertake it without risking her life.
The journey not being *ordered* by Superiors, she fears to
make it, lest by so doing she should tempt God and expose
herself to presumption. She is, moreover, of the opinion
that her sojourn at Darfeld among the Droste family, so
esteemed for their piety throughout Münster, would instead
of putting an end to calumnious accusations, only excite
fresh ones and she is unwilling to expose that noble family
to so disagreeable a result. Prof. B— and others of his
way of thinking would hardly be silenced by such a step;
on the contrary, they, would demand all the more loudly
that she should be removed to Münster and subjected to a
new examination."

Her weakness was indeed so great that she was sup-

posed to be dying several times between September 1st
and 10th. On the 2d, Father Limberg thought her soul
had actually departed and recited by her the prayers for the
dead ; but, when he sprinkled her with holy water, a sweet
expression passed over her face and she slowly returned to
consciousness.

The Vicar-General saw the solidity of her reasoning.
Though pained at the failure of his plan, by which he had
hoped to silence unjust suspicions and crush the calumnies
of unbelievers, yet he read in her non-acceptance of so
advantageous an offer a new proof of her virtue and purity
of intention. Neither his sympathy nor esteem for her diminished ; he kept up constant communication with her
through Deans Rensing and Overberg, and visited her as
often as he could find leisure. A year after the investigation, learning through Clara Soentgen that the invalid's
death was at hand, he wrote as follows to Dean Rensing :—

"I wish to know whether you regard Sister Emmerich's
death as near as some suppose. If you do, let me know,
and tell me also whether you think it will be sudden. I
should be happy to receive a summary of whatever has happened extraordinary since August, 1813. Be so kind as to
present my respects to her."

The Dean replied :—

"I do not, as yet, see anything indicative of speedy
death ; but she herself seems to think her end not far off.
If God reveals anything to her concerning it and she says
anything definite to me on the subject, I shall inform Your
Grace forthwith. The same phenomena are still visible in
her person as were seen a year ago. The blood flows on
Fridays as it did then, but since August nothing new has
appeared. As regards her spiritual life, she has gained in
many points. She has overcome various little imperfections ;

she is more united to the will of God.　What she relates of her ecstasies is frequently of so elevated a character as to excite my admiration; it is, at the same time, accompanied by so much simplicity that one can never suspect deceit. Supposing even that it does not belong to a superior order of things, there is in it, at least, the most beautiful manifestation of a soul pure as the angels, wholly absorbed in God, sighing only for His glory, and the salvation of mankind."

Two months after, the Dean made the following report:—

"Sister Emmerich is a little better; perhaps she will again be well for awhile.　As her existence has so long been at variance with nature, we need not fear that she will die because the symptoms of death appear. Yesterday, in a moment of exhaustion, she told me that she hoped God would give her strength before her death to reveal certain things for the benefit of her neighbors.　She spoke very low, and it was only by an effort that I could understand what she said."

On receipt of the above, the Vicar-General drew up the following ordinance in the event of her death:—

"If the Augustinian religious, Anne Catherine Emmerich, sleeps in the Lord, Dean Rensing shall as soon as possible:—

"1. Send me word by express wherever I may happen to be, and even come himself if he can do so.　If not, let him take the following steps:

"2. Until my arrival, or until further orders from me, let him see that:—

"(a) One or more females, of whose trustworthiness he is assured, watch night and day by the remains.　(I shall defray the expense.)

"(b) Let none other remain near the body, and let permission to see it be given to as few as possible.　If such visits

are too numerous, it would be well for the **Mayor** to interpose his authority for their discontinuance.

" (c) Until my arrival, or further instructions, let the body
remain absolutely untouched. Let no one examine it or
the stigmata in any way whatever.

" 3. Let the Dean take measures for having the death announced to him as soon as possible after its occurrence, and
let him at once invite the Mayor to accompany him to Sister Emmerich's lodgings, not officially, but as a friend. Let
him extend a similar invitation to Fathers Limberg and
Lambert and to Drs. Wesener and Krauthausen. Then, in
presence of all these gentlemen, an official report shall be
drawn up which all shall sign, and which shall consist of the
following points briefly stated :—

" (a) The manner and time of death with any remarkable
circumstances attending it.

" (b) The state of the body ; the different marks on the
hands, feet, side, head, and breast.

" N.B. Between the invitation to the above-named personages and their acceptance of the same, no time must inter-
vene. Let them not go all together to Sister Emmerich's
lodgings, that publicity may be avoided; and only those
mentioned ought to be admitted.

" 4. Lastly : Let the Dean request Fathers Limberg and
Lambert, as also the two physicians, to await my arrival in
Dülmen, if they possibly can, that I may have an inter-
view with them.

" 5. I shall provide for all subsequent steps in good time.
" Clement Auguste von Droste-Vischering,
" Vicar–General.

" Münster, *May* 26, 1814."

CHAPTER XXXI.

SISTER EMMERICH'S LIFE AFTER THE INVESTIGATION.—HER
SURROUNDINGS. —THE ABBÉ LAMBERT.—HER
SISTER GERTRUDE.

To appreciate the closing years of Sister Emmerich's
life, her relations with the outer world must be understood;
for without this it would be impossible to comprehend a
life whose most insignificant incidents were disposed by
Divine Providence for the highest ends. The smallest
events in such a life, though in appearance the veriest trifles,
are of the greatest importance. It was in the midst of the
ordinary occurrences of daily life that Sister Emmerich was
to accomplish her mission and thereby attain sanctity.
Called to labor for the Church in tribulation, her outer life
must be in conformity with her task. Her position had
never yet been regulated by her own choice; it had ever
been subject to direction from on high and, consequently,
in itself a source of virtue and merit. They who influenced
her outer life had not been chosen by her, they had been
gathered around her by causes which sprang not from human foresight.

Let us first consider the effect produced on her life by the
stigmata, whose supernatural origin had been undeniably established by the ecclesiastical investigation. Whilst in the
cloister, she had been able to conceal the bloody effusions of
the crown of thorns from the distrustful curiosity of her
companions, for it did not enter into the divine economy to
disclose at that time the mystery of God's wonderful ways over
His servant. It had, therefore, been allowed her to feel the

pains, but not to bear in her person the visible marks of her
Saviour's Wounds. Without a miracle of divine power, she
could not have endured those excruciating tortures a single
instant; but, thanks to this assistance, she had become so
incorporated with the nature of the vine that, like the branch
around its support, she began to adapt herself to the form of
the cross. Whether sitting or lying, her feet involuntarily
crossed one over the other as closely as those of a crucifix.
When recalled suddenly from ecstasy by her confessor and
unable to rise as quickly as obedience prompted, she would
exclaim beseechingly: "O I cannot! I cannot! Unbind
me! I am nailed." The palms of her hands were pierced
through and through, the middle fingers arose above the
others in an unnatural position, and it cost her intense pain
to make use of them. But scarcely had she left the obscurity of her humble cell to enter an unsympathizing
world, than the exterior signs manifested themselves!
Might she not, poor, sick, abandoned as she was, have hoped
that her expulsion from the convent would, at least, have
formed the culminating point of her sufferings ? Not so !
Now began a life compared with whose austerity and sub-
limity, all that she had hitherto endured sinks into insignificance.

There was still one desire cherished in that poor, suffering
heart, and that was to serve the venerable priest, her benefactor and friend, the only human support ever vouchsafed
her. He had remained with her at Agnetenberg until,
forced to leave, they had both found a miserable lodging
with a widow named Roters. In him she honored not
only her friend and protector, but a confessor of the faith
whose fidelity had condemned him to poverty and exile.
The Abbé Lambert was the only one who treated her kindly during her life in the convent, the only one to whom she

could make known her sorrows. When at an early hour
he went to the sacristy to prepare for Mass, she used to
tell him of the directions received in vision the night before
for her mission of suffering during the coming day, beg his
prayers, and gratefully treasure up his words of encouragement and consolation. They were the most precious boon
she had ever received from any living creature; they were
what even her angel himself could not afford her. Her
heart beat and suffered as sensitively as other human hearts
and for it, as for others, the comforting words of a friend
were a sweet relief, an essential need. And still more—
this *poor nun* had even received alms from the *poor priest.*
He knew that what she earned by her sewing ordinarily
went to the Superioress, and that her trifling wants were
not provided for in return. Sometimes the kind old man
would bring her a little piece of white bread which she had
leave to take, pleased with the thought that from the hand
of him to whom she was indebted for a more frequent reception of the Holy Eucharist, she received likewise the
support of her natural life.

The hope of making some little return for his kindness
by her faithful service, was not to be realized. Her state
not only rendered her incapable of such duties, but even
exacted the charitable services of others, and her ecstasies
were frequent and irresistible. The Abbé had often found
her kneeling rigid and immovable, apparently lifeless. But
he had never dared to recall her by a command given by
virtue of his priestly authority; and consequently, her raptures
had become day by day more frequent and prolonged. His
only anxiety had been to conceal them from all around and
keep this chosen soul in happy ignorance of her state. To
maintain her in humility and divert her thoughts from these
wonders, met but in the lives of the saints, he had absolutely

refused to receive any communication from her on the subject, saying shortly : " Sister, it's nothing ! it's nothing ! it's
only a dream !"—His infirmities made him long for repose,
and he earnestly hoped that his last days in a strange land
might not be troubled by fresh annoyances. The first sight
of her bleeding stigmata had afflicted him deeply, but he
consoled himself with the thought that they would disappear
in the evening, or at least that they might be kept secret.
Soon, however, was the good old man disabused. The
wounds did not disappear, and it added not a little to the
poor victim's sufferings to be obliged to sustain the courage
of her kind father and friend whilst struggling herself to
bear up against her own torrent of affliction.

No event of her life had cost her so much as the appearance of her marvellous signs. As Lidwina of Schiedam,
eaten up by worms and putrefaction, served Almighty God
for over thirty years as an instrument of expiation for the
Church, so now did the stigmatisée of Dülmen bear in her
person the marks of Redemption for the same end. Lidwina, too, had received their imprint ; but her other expiatory sufferings effaced, in a measure, from the mind of the
beholder the impression they would otherwise have produced·
Sister Emmerich's stigmata were precisely the cause of her
being drawn from her retirement and exposed to the public
gaze. At the time in which she lived, such wounds and
sufferings as those of Lidwina could not have been patiently endured by the scoffers at whatever bore a supernatural
character.

Sister Emmerich's miraculous wounds exerted an influence both internally and externally, in consequence of
which the circulation of blood seemed to be entirely changed
from the natural course, each wound being a centre to and
from which the currents flowed. Its very pulsations seemed

changed or, as it were, multiplied, being detected as sensibly at her finger ends as at her wrists. Her hands were pierced through and through, the wounds of her feet were formed on the instep and ran along the soles, and that of her side took an upward direction, as if made by a thrust from below. When they opened and the air blew on them, it cut through like a sharp knife or a scorching flame and caused unspeakable suffering to the poor invalid ; for this reason she usually kept her hands wrapped in soft linen. After years of duration they were as fresh, as sharp, as free from purulent matter as on the first day of their appearance.

Dr. Wesener reports the following, Friday, Sept. 8, 1815 :—

"I found the invalid exceedingly weak but cheerful, her hands and feet bleeding. The wounds on the back of the hands are round and about as large as a small coin, the edges slightly puffed up, but without inflammation. One thing that seemed to me remarkable, though perhaps of little importance to any but a physician, was a slight excoriation at the lower joint of the right fore-finger. This excoriation was inflamed and a purulent liquid had collected under the epidermis in three different places. I asked if she had scratched it with a needle, and she told me that the day before, whilst wiping a tumbler, she had broken the rim and scratched her finger with it. Her skin is easily inflamed and inclined to suppuration. Let science bring this fact to bear on the unchanging condition of her wounds."

Dr. Wesener looked upon the above, as we may infer from his concluding remark, as an evident proof of the supernatural character of the invalid's stigmata ; another **very** striking one is afforded by their bleeding only **on** certain days of the ecclesiastical year. Their effusions

were not confined to Fridays which would make them
fall on fixed and recurring intervals; they happened on all
movable feasts commemorative of the Sacred Passion, independently of the invalid's personal dispositions. Sometimes the only intimation she had of the approach of such
a feast was from the increased sufferings in her wounds.
One year, the annual fair-day held in Dülmen fell on a
Friday; consequently Sister Emmerich was importuned by
visitors, and seeing so many peasants in holiday dress, she
thought surely it must be Sunday. Toward three P. M. she
suddenly grew pale and the blood flowed in four streams from
under her cap, a circumstance for which she could not account
till some one remarked that it was Friday and not Sunday.

The blood always flowed in the same direction as did
that from the Sacred Wounds of Christ upon the cross.
From the palms of the hands it ran toward the inner part
of the forearm; down the feet toward the toes; and from
her forehead and temples it flowed down as far as the nose,
even when her head was not in an upright position. It was
on account of this unnatural course of the blood, that the
Professor of Chemistry hooted at the idea of its reality and
declared it only *paint.* Clement Brentano, some years
later, rendered the following testimony :—

"The flow of blood was visible at the upper part of her
high forehead just below the hair, where it oozed like drops
of perspiration, though no sign of a wound could be seen;
but when it dried up, small red specks like the pricks of a
needle might be distinguished, to which Drs. Wesener and
von Druffel gave a particular name. The quantity that
flowed from her head was, at times, greater or less, and the
same may be said of the other wounds; it seemed, however,
that the flow from some was greater in proportion as that
from the others was less."

Dr. Wesener confirms the last detail, Friday, June 3, 1814 :—

"The blood flowed to-day from noon till about four o'clock, streaming from her head so copiously that she grew frightfully pale and prostrate. Her attendants in alarm tried to stop it by applications of cloths steeped in vinegar."

Friday, Sept. 29, 1815 :—"The Princess Galitzin came this afternoon from Münster to see the invalid, and they conversed together a long time, the Abbé Lambert and Clara Soentgen being present. When the Princess withdrew, the invalid uttered a groan, and Clara Soentgen ran to her bedside to find a stream of clear blood gushing from three small punctures in her forehead ; she caught it in the folds of a linen cloth. Her other wounds began also to bleed, but not so copiously as her head. I must not pass over the Abbé Lambert's exclamation. When he saw the invalid bleeding so profusely, he shed tears and turning to Clara Soentgen, he said : ' *Ma sœur*, now you see *I* did not do it.' "

Six years after, Friday, Feb. 9, 1821, during the obsequies of the old Abbé, Clement Brentano witnessed an effusion of blood, which he noted down with the following remarks :—

" Sister Emmerich has a very high forehead, prominent temples and an abundance of dark brown hair, which, from constant cutting and the pressure of a tight head-dress, has, though naturally soft and fine, become rather coarse. Her headaches have rendered it sensitive to the touch, combing it causes sharp pain ; consequently, it is only when absolutely necessary that she consents to have it cut, though she was forced to submit to it during the first years of her stigmata. Ever watched and suspected, she could hardly keep her door closed long enough to arrange it ; for if any one had been kept waiting, suspicion would have been

aroused. It was very difficult on this account to render
her the most necessary services. When the attempt was
made, it was often with so much hurry and anxiety that it
gave her more suffering than relief. She herself experienced
a kind of reverential fear at the sight of her person impressed
with its marvellous signs. God, who in her early years
had bestowed upon her such aptitude for manual labor,
now gave her such facility and promptitude for whatever
propriety and cleanliness demanded, both for herself and
her surroundings, and this even in contemplation, that
her poor couch of suffering was always as neat and well
arranged as that of the most careful and best attended religious in a convent. And yet it must have been very difficult for her, notwithstanding her dexterity. For years
she could take only a sitting posture in her bed, her head
resting on her knees ; she was often scarcely able to move
her wounded hands with their paralyzed middle fingers ; and
her profuse perspiration made a change of linen necessary
several times a day. But no one ever entered her room, no
matter at what hour, without finding her carefully clothed
and surrounded by such neatness as was pleasant to behold.
I visited her daily and at all hours for four years, and I invariably saw a certain propriety in her and her surroundings which recalled those virtues of which she was truly the
personification : innocence, chastity, and purity of
heart."

We have one fact to prove how little she could expect from
the attention of her friends. In summer, during her ecstatic prayer, swarms of flies sometimes settled on her wounds
and stung them to blood. Dr. Wesener found her in this
state once with none to relieve her. We are also indebted
to him for the information that, chiefly during the octave
of Corpus Christi, the wounds of the Flagellation, bearing

an exact likeness to the cuts of a whip, appeared on her person. They were accompanied by signs of fever.

These marks of the Saviour's predilection were for Sister Emmerich sources of torture, fear, and anxiety, of the deepest and most painful humiliation. But God's grace was sufficient for her. She bore them not as something of her own, not as a mark of distinction, but as the seal of her expiatory mission. The mystery of Redemption had been effaced, so to say, from the memory of man; for perhaps no age made so little account of the Saviour's sufferings as the one of which we write. Apart from the unbelieving, the open enemies of God's holy Church, we are shocked at the small number of those who then comprehended these words of St. Peter : " *Scientes quod non corruptibilibus auro vel argento redempti estis, sed pretioso sanguine quasi agni immaculati Christi.*" (1). It was a period in which perfect silence was kept, both in the pulpit and schools of theology, on the mystery of Redemption, sacrifice and satisfaction, merit and sin ; a period in which good works and miracles had to yield to hollow "theories of revelation ;" a period in which the Man-God, to be at all endurable, had to be presented as the " Friend of men, the Friend of sinners, the children's Friend." His life was, as they said," *a lesson;*" His Passion, " *an example of fortitude;*" His death, "*fruitless love.*" The catechism was taken from the hands of the faithful and replaced by " Bible Histories," in which the absolute want of doctrine was veiled under " *simple language adapted to the understanding of all.*" The books of piety, the ancient formulas of prayer, the time-honored canticles of praise, were exchanged for modern productions as miserable and impious as were those

(1) Knowing that you were not redeemed with corruptible things as gold or silver, but with the Precious Blood of Christ, as of a lamb unspotted and undefiled.—I. Peter. I. 18. 19.

by which the Missal, the breviary, and the ritual were replaced.

This intellectual debasement might pass at first sight for a transient aberration, a false direction of the spirit of the age; but before God it was a direct attack on the faith, imperilling the salvation of numberless souls, an expression of the deepest contempt for His love and justice. All this had to be expiated by an innocent victim who was to be treated not otherwise than Jesus Himself and His work of Redemption. The startling grandeur of His bloody sacrifice and His rigorous satisfaction for sin are a stumbling-block to many; in like manner Sister Emmerich was a cause of offence by reason of her mysterious signs and, even for her nearest friends, she was an insupportable burden. The Abbé Lambert and her confessor ardently desired the disappearance of what deprived them of peace and repose; the pastor of the parish withdrew from her with a feeling of irritation when he found his name associated with her singular case; the Vicar-General, the highest functionary of the diocese, submitted her as an impostor to a most rigorous investigation, in order to spare the world the insupportable spectacle of her wounds; and, finally, this end not being attained, she is abandoned, helpless and defenceless, to the importunate curiosity of a pitiless crowd, suspected and even most cruelly persecuted, as we shall see further on. Her own prayers are, as it were, unheeded by Almighty God. Those loving sighs which draw down torrents of blessings upon others, are powerless in her own cause when she cries to Him to deprive her of her stigmata. "My grace is sufficient for thee!" does she hear, and the mysterious wounds remain. Clement Brentano's beautiful words may here be quoted :—

"Sealed with the Wounds of her Crucified Love, she was driven into the desert of unbelief to render testimony to the truth. What a mission to bear in her own person, to display to the eyes of the world, to the followers of its prince, the victorious insignia of Christ, the Son of the living God, Jesus of Nazareth, King of the Jews! Great courage, special grace were needed for it. To many she was to be an object of scandal and suspicion, to all an enigma. Where the roads of unbelief and superstition, of malice and wickedness, of intellectual pride and foolishness meet, there was she to hang upon the cross, exposed to the curious gaze of the passers-by, subjected to the absurd remarks and criticisms of the vulgar. To live poor and despised, a prey to mysterious maladies, slighted by her nearest friends, often ill-treated, utterly alone amidst the curious throng in which she sees not one who can understand or sympathize with her; to be uniformly patient, affable, meek, discreet; to edify the motley crowd, little considerate in their deportment toward her —this was the task of the outcast religious, the poor peasant-girl, whose only instruction was that found in her catechism."

Never did a word of complaint escape her lips. She saw herself suspected, she heard the absurd calumnies uttered against her, but she was silent; only when looked upon with respect and admiration did she show signs of displeasure. For years she had suffered the pains of the stigmata before their outward marks were vouchsafed to her, regarding it merely as a favor granted to her petition for expiatory sufferings. When she received their visible impress, she still looked upon it as a symbolical vision, not as a real fact; and so, at all times, was she ready to see in them only what obedience bade her behold. She felt her own unworthiness so deeply, she feared the world's praises so greatly that, even in vision, she blushed at herself, she would have been willing to be punished as an impostor.

On Sunday in the octave of the Exaltation of the Holy Cross, 1815, she assisted in spirit at the solemn procession in Coesfeld of the miraculous crucifix; barefoot and adoring, she walked behind the holy cross. As they passed the church of St James, she felt that many of the assistants thought of her and spoke of her mysterious wounds, by which circumstance she was so confused that her efforts to hide them recalled her to consciousness. Sometimes the evil spirit reproached her, saying that she could rise and eat if she wished; that if she began with wine and water, she would soon see that it would be easy to take other nourishment, but that she was a hypocrite, etc. In her humility and forgetful of the tempter's malice, she would reply : " Yes, I am a miserable creature! I deserve to be despised as a hypocrite," and indignant against herself she would try to rise from her bed and call out to the passers-by : " Good people, good people, keep away from me! Be not scandalized at me! I am an unworthy creature!" but falling back exhausted by her efforts, she at last recognized the fiendish impostor.

Friday, August 9, 1816, Dr. Wesener records the following: " She complains of her innumerable visitors. ' I am sad unto death,' sighed she one day, ' on account of this concourse of people, and particularly because I see that many regard what God has done in me, His miserable instrument, with deeper veneration than they feel before the Blessed Sacrament. I could die of shame when good old priests, ten times better than I, ask to see me.' I tried to calm her, saying that God permitted these visits to try her patience, that people came not to see her, but the wonders of God manifested in her; that they did not admire her, but only the incomprehensible decrees of Almighty God. My words consoled and restored her to peace."

No precise knowledge would have been had on her reception of the wounds, if it were not for the visions relative to it which she had at various times during the last years of her life and which she related in obedience to her confessor's order. On Oct. 4, 1820, Feast of St. Francis of Assisi, she had the following vision :—

" I saw the saint among some bushes on a wild mountain in which were scattered grottos like little cells. Francis had opened the Gospel several times. Each time it chanced to be at the history of the Passion, and so he begged to feel his Lord's sufferings. He used to fast on this mountain, eating only a little bread and roots. He knelt, his bare knees on two sharp stones, and supported two others on his shoulders. It was after midnight and he was praying with arms extended, half-kneeling, half sitting, his back resting against the side of the mountain. I saw his angel near him holding his hands, his countenance all on fire with love. He was a slight man. He wore a brown mantle open in front with a hood like those worn at the time by shepherds, a cord bound his waist. At the moment in which I saw him he was as if paralyzed. A bright light shot from heaven and descended upon him. In it was an angel with six wings, two above his head, two over his feet, and two with which he seemed to fly. In his right hand he held a cross, about half the usual size, on which was a living body glowing with light, the feet crossed, the five wounds resplendent as so many suns. From each wound proceeded three rays of rosy light converging to a point. They shot first from the hands toward the palms of the saint's hands ; then from the wound in the right side toward the saint's right side (these rays were larger than the others); and lastly, from the feet toward the soles of the saint's feet. In his left hand the angel held a blood-red tulip in whose centre was a golden heart, which I think he gave to the saint. When Francis returned from ecstasy, he could with difficulty stand, and I saw him going back to his monastery suffering cruelly, and supported by his angel-guardian. He hid his wounds as well as he could. There were large crusts of brownish blood on the back of his hands, for they did not bleed regularly every Friday; but his side often bled so profusely that the blood flowed down on the ground. I saw him praying, the blood streaming down his arms. I saw many other incidents of his life. Once even before he knew him the Pope beheld him in vision supporting the Lateran on his shoulders when it was ready to fall.

"Then I had a vision of myself receiving the wounds. I never knew before how it was. Three days before the new year, and about three o'clock in the afternoon I was lying alone in the little room I used to have at Mrs. Roters', my arms extended. I was contemplating the Passion of Jesus Christ and asking to be allowed to feel His pains. I said five Our Fathers in honor of the Five Wounds. I experienced great sweetness with an intense desire that my prayer might be granted, when suddenly I beheld descending obliquely upon me a great light. It was a crucified body, living and transparent, with extended arms but no cross, the wounds more resplendent than the body, like five circles of brilliant light.

"I was rapt out of myself, and I yearned with mingled pain and sweetness to share my Saviour's sufferings. As my desire grew still more vehement at the sight of His Wounds, it shot, so to speak, from my breast, hands, feet, and side toward them. At the same moment, triple

rays of red light, converging to a point, darted first from
the Hands,then from the Side and Feet of the Image upon my
hands, side, and feet.   I lay for a time unconscious, until
Mrs. Roters' little girl lowered my hands.   She told the
family that I had cut them and that they were bleeding, but
I implored them to say nothing about it.

" I had had the cross on my breast for some time, since
the Feast of St. Augustine when, as I was praying on my
knees, my arms extended, my Affianced signed me with
it.   After I received these wounds, I felt a great change
in my whole person ; my blood circulated toward these
points with a painful twitching sensation.   St. Francis appeared to me that night, consoled me, and spoke of the
violence of interior pains."

That the reader may understand the visions relative to herself, we must enter into some particulars upon their signification.   As an instrument of expiation, all her actions were to
be performed, her sufferings endured in a manner most pleasing to God.   To purify her soul from daily faults, she had
her confessor's direction and the Sacrament of Penance ;
but, when the imperfections committed in vision were to
be effaced, her angel stepped in to impose new efforts and
sufferings.   As her task increased, her visions on the same
became more comprehensive.   Her life was now drawing
toward its close, and it was fitting that every moment of it
should be employed in the accomplishment of its mission.
She had not only to discharge her duty in all that concerned
her personally and repair the faults arising from her own
poor nature, but she was also responsible for those whom
God had associated with her as aids in her work of expiation.   She knew the Vicar-General and Dean Overberg
long before they had heard of her ; and her prayers and
influence were around *the Pilgrim* whilst yet he wandered

far from the Church, careless of God and his own soul.

He had been shown her in vision as the one destined to record her contemplations, for which end she was to gain him to God. The following vision she related to the Abbe Lambert :—

" I was journeying toward the Heavenly Jerusalem with a crowd of people; but I had so weighty a burden to carry that I could hardly get along. I rested awhile under a crucifix around which lay numbers of small straw crosses and little dry branches bound together. I asked my guide what all these crosses meant. He answered : ' These are the little crosses you had in the convent, they were light. But now a real cross is laid on you, bear it !' Then the crowd dispersed and my confessor, whom I saw among them, slipped behind a bush and lay in wait for a hare. I begged him not to lag behind, to come with me ; but he would not listen to my persuasion, and I staggered on alone under my burden. But I feared that I ought not to leave him behind, that I ought to entreat and even force him on to our magnificent destination; so I went back and found him asleep and, to my horror, I heard the howling of wild beasts close by. I awoke him and begged him to continue his journey, but it took all my strength to make him come with me. At last we reached a deep, broad river spanned by a very narrow bridge which I should never have been able to cross without his assistance. We arrived, at last, at our journey's end."

We shall soon see the significance of this apparently simple vision. Father Limberg was a Dominican. The suppression of his monastery afflicted him deeply, and, on returning to the world, he had resolved to regulate his life as strictly as possible by his religious obligations. Sister

Emmerich thanked God for giving her this worthy priest, who held toward her not only the office of confessor and director, but also that of monastic Superiors ; and to him she transferred the respect and obedience which, whilst in the convent, she had paid to the Rule and lawful authority. Almighty God willed that she should still continue the practice of her holy vows ; and, although Father Limberg's superior in intelligence and the spiritual life, she obeyed him blindly, preserving toward him the attitude of a simple child ready to be led and directed in all things. His least word was for her an order from God which admitted neither question nor contradiction. Though sometimes convinced by experience or her angel's warnings that such or such a prescription would be attended by injurious results, she made not the least objection —no pain, no sacrifice counter-balanced in her estimation the merit of obedience. She often saw that his direction aggravated her sufferings ; yet it was for her the order of God who willed that she should accomplish her mission, not by her angel's ministry but by that of His priest. There is one characteristic common to all souls called to a sublime vocation —and that is the sacrifice, the abandonment of their whole being, body and soul, to the will of God, a characteristic which shone out most clearly in Sister Emmerich's whole life, and in no part more than in her relations with her confessor. Obedience was the bond which united her as a living representative to the body of the Church. It was founded on faith which showed her in the person of the priest God's vice-gerent on earth, a faith so much the more meritorious as she saw more clearly in him the weakness of the man. However extraordinary may be the gifts of privileged souls, however elevated may be the task assigned them, they know no other law, no higher direction than the rule of faith such as the Church, the pillar and

ground of truth, lays down. True and pure mysticism
flourishes in no other soil than that of ecclesiastical discipline,
of divine worship, of the Sacraments, and of the devout
practices and usages of Holy Church. It admits no transgression, no dispensation with regard to the Commandments
of God or of the Church, which are binding on all Christians
without exception ; nor does it sanction the omission of
duty under the specious pretext that high spirituality is not
bound by ordinary laws and regulations. They are the
barriers erected by God for the safety of His chosen ones
which the false mystic, the lying pretender to extraordinary
favors, hesitates not to overturn.

When Father Limberg assumed Sister Emmerich's
spiritual direction, he had adopted Abbé Lambert's opinion
as to the necessity of concealing her state. He qualified
her visions as mere dreams. He was of a timid turn of
mind, easily disquieted. It was only after years of intercourse,
that he justly appreciated his penitent's high gifts. He
himself relates the following incident :—

" The invalid lay one afternoon in ecstatic prayer, her
eyes closed, whilst I sat near saying my breviary, which
occupied about an hour. When I had finished, Prof. B.'s
doubts presented themselves to my mind, and I know not
how I conceived the following idea : I remembered that
the Abbé Lambert had that day consecrated two Hosts, reserving one for the invalid's Communion next morning.
May I not, thought I, put her to the test, not through idle
curiosity or any bad intention ? Filled with this thought I
went and got the Sacred Host, placed it in a corporal around
which I folded a stole, and carried It back to the invalid's
chamber. She lay just as I had left her, buried in prayer ;
but no sooner had I placed my foot upon the door-sill, than
she arose hastily though with effort, stretched out her arms,

and fell upon her knees in adoration. ' What do you want ?' I said. 'Ah ! there comes my Lord Jesus to me with the tabernacle !' I allowed her to adore the Blessed Sacrament awhile and then carried It back."

The first time he had found her in ecstasy, he asked for an explanation ; she was greatly confused and begged him not to betray her secret. It was the same with Maria Bagnesi (1) between whom and Sister Emmerich there was a striking resemblance. Maria was once found in ecstasy raised above the ground. On returning to consciousness, she was so affrighted that she hid her face with her hands like a child taken in a fault, not daring to look upon those who had witnessed her rapture.

Father Limberg understood so little of such things that on finding Sister Emmerich absorbed in ecstasy, he would try to arouse her by shaking her roughly, for he said: *"She's raving."* In August, 1814, she took upon herself the sufferings of a poor consumptive to obtain for her patience and a happy death. Father Limberg finding her one day moaning in agony, shook her by the shoulders until she awoke, when she said quietly : "I went to a poor sick woman. On my return, I was so weak that I had to mount the stone steps on my knees (2). It was hard work, my knees are paining intensely."

Her knees were, indeed, blistered and the pain in them continued for some days ; but Father Limberg treated it as a dream until the consumptive, his own sister, begged to be taken to Sister Emmerich, that helped by her prayers she might die by her bedside. He had her carried into Sister Emmerich's room, in whom all the symptoms of consump-

(1) The " Life of Maria Bagnesi," born at Florence, 1514, was written by her confessor, Augustine Campi. It may be found in the Acta S. S., Vol. VI. May.

(2) On Nov. 23, 1813, Sister Emmerich was removed to the house of Mr. Limberg, master-baker and brewer, a brother of Father Limberg. Her room was in the back building looking out upon the garden and church of her loved convent. The Abbé Lambert had a room in the same house.

tion instantly appeared : burning fever, and pains in her
right side so violent that she fainted on being removed from
her bed, whilst the consumptive herself was relieved and
consoled. Dr. Wesener says :—" Sister Emmerich had a
very painful night ; she was maltreated and mocked by some
children who fell upon and beat her. She had to use both
hands to defend herself without, however, being able to escape from them. Father Limberg, who was watching by his
sister, saw Sister Emmerich's gestures, and touched her on the
arm to restrain her. She awoke and, though seeing him by
her, lost not her dread of the children who continued to
ill-treat her. She complained of their having bruised her
and of having tried to make her eat by holding food to her
mouth. She was tormented all the morning with the taste
of it." This vision bore reference to the suspicions that the
dying woman had long nourished and communicated to
others respecting Sister Emmerich's perpetual fast, which
she had looked upon as imposture. The poor invalid expiated this fault by patiently enduring the ill-treatment mentioned above, and obtained for the consumptive the grace of
repentance and a happy death.

Father Limberg was, at last, forced to admit that his
penitent's raptures, etc., were something more than dreams ;
still he remained in obscurity with regard to her state. On
the Vigil and Feast of the Assumption, Sister Emmerich
contemplated the Blessed Virgin's death with its attendant
circumstances. She spoke of her visions whilst still in ecstasy in so clear and animated a style, that even Father
Limberg was compelled to recognize the fact that there was
about her no trace of delirium. He held a little oil-paint-
ing of the Blessed Virgin's death a short distance before her
closed eyes, when her rigid form instantly inclined toward
it ; she bowed her head, took it into her hands, and said, in

allusion to St. Peter who was represented in it —" Ah! the man with the white beard is a very good man!"—Then she fell back, and Father Limberg placed it on her hands which lay crossed on her breast. When returned to consciousness, she said in answer to his inquiries: "I saw the Mother of God dying surrounded by the Apostles and her friends. I gazed on the scene a long while, and then the whole room with all it contained was laid on my hands. O how glad I was! But as I wondered how I could support such a weight, I was told : 'It is pure virtue and that is light as a feather.' All the night before I had visions of Mary's death. I was going to Jerusalem, and that in a strange way, for I was lying in bed neither sleeping nor dreaming, my eyes open. I saw everything going on here in my room, as well as upon the road."

Father Limberg was accustomed to treat her as an ordinary religious. He spoke to her briefly and sternly, and that was precisely what she most appreciated in him. He had been her confessor for two years when, one day Dr. Wesener found her in tears. On asking the cause, he received the following answer: "I fear losing confidence in God, my only helper. Now that I have to lie here, everything afflicts me. I used to have such confidence that no suffering, however violent, could shake it. But lately all is changed and I am now in distress because my confessor is going to look for another position. I value him and prefer him to all others, on account of his severity."

Some years after, she again remarked in the doctor's presence that she felt how beneficial Father Limberg's sternness had been to her, and that nothing would grieve her more than to see him relax in this point. The following characteristic trait is a good illustration of his conduct toward her :—

" One evening," says the doctor, " I found Sister Emmerich apparently dying; her pulse was almost gone, and
she could scarcely articulate a word. I knew not the cause
of her prostration, but I gave her ten drops of opium and
left her. The next morning, to my amazement, she was
bright as usual. I turned to her confessor for an
explanation, and he said : ' Early this morning she
was even weaker than yesterday and, fearing her death,
I gave her Holy Communion as quickly as possible.
Scarcely had she received the Sacred Host upon her tongue
than her face, before like that of a corpse, became rosy,
her pulse grew strong, and she remained over an hour in
adoration. Then I understood the cause of her extraordinary weakness. I had forbidden her Holy Communion for
two days for not allowing her back to be bathed in warm
brandy.' "

This incident affords a true and striking picture of the
invalid's position. The smell of liquor was intolorable to
her, its use as a wash a real torment ; nevertheless, both
physician and confessor ordered it. If her weakness or the
stupor caused by its fumes prevented her rendering this service to herself, she had to commit herself to Gertrude's
hands, who made little account of her delicate sense of modesty ; so, to avoid her summary treatment, the poor sufferer
sometimes failed to make use of the remedy, and this was
the state of affairs in the present instance. The preceding Wednesday, Father Limberg discovered that she had
declined her sister's services. He punished her by depriving her of Holy Communion on Thursday and Friday,
and he would have prolonged the penance, if her state on
Saturday had not aroused fears for her life. The reader
will readily comprehend what benefit ten drops of opium
could be in such a case. But Sister Emmerich was accus-

tomed to receive all such events as punishments merited
by her own failings, for which she never ventured an excuse.
Like Maria Bagnesi, her obedience to the priest's command was perfect. One day when Maria was writhing and
groaning on her bed of pain, her friends sent for her confessor that his benediction might relieve her. He came consoled and encouraged her, and said on leaving: "Now,
Sister Maria, be obedient and lie still!"—Instantly, she
became immovable and stirred not from that position till the
next day when her confessor came and revoked his command. Like Maria, Sister Emmerich also suffered more toward
the close of every ecclesiastical year, because as a faithful
servant, she had to correct the defects of slothful laborers
in the Lord's vineyard. Dr. Wesener relates under date
of Oct. 27, 1815 :—

" She was sick all day, her whole person quivering with
pain. One remarkable feature in her case is her total
deafness which has lasted for several days. Though not
in ecstasy, she could hear nothing excepting what her confessor ordered her in obedience.

" In November she was taken with a severe cough.
Intending to reserve the essence of musk for a last resource
and fearing opium would attack the stomach, I tried rubbing with camphor which, however, only increased the
evil. Fearing the worst, I begged the confessor to stay
by her that night with her sister. Next day she was quite
free from her cough, for which Father Limberg accounted
in these words : 'I watched by her side with her sister
until midnight. Her cough was so violent and incessant
that, not being able to endure it longer, I had recourse to a
spiritual remedy, and I commanded her in virtue of obedience to cough no more. At the sound of the word *obedience* she sank down unconscious and lay quiet till morning.'

Her cough came on again in the evening, but only slightly.

"On Friday, Nov. 10th, we were quite anxious about her as she had endured frightful pains in her stigmata all day. Her hands were clenched and death-like, every limb quivered, and she lay unconscious like one dead. Suddenly she sighed : ' Ah ! if I were only free ! if I could only pray before the Blessed Sacrament !'—Father Limberg replied : 'Do it, you are free !'—These rather indefinite words carried with them no strength to the invalid, and she said supplicatingly : ' May I ? Shall I ?'—I begged him to order her in virtue of obedience. He did so, when she sprang upon her knees and began to pray with extended arms. The sight of her kneeling and praying in such a state had in it something truly impressive. Fearing the consequences of such an effort, Father Limberg bade her lie down, and down she sank without a movement. When returned to consciousness, she said that she felt as if she were dead inside. A poultice steeped in hot brandy was laid on her breast, and at ten o'clock that evening I gave her eight drops of musk."

Her desires for Holy Communion were often most touchingly expressed. One day, her ardor was so intense that she was involuntarily transported in spirit to the church. Kneeling before the tabernacle, she was about to open it and communicate herself, when suddenly seized with terror at the thought of its being an unlawful act, she awoke to consciousness and implored Father Limberg's permission to confess. He dissuaded her, saying it was all a dream ; but it was not without difficulty that he succeeded in calming her.

During the octave of All-Saints, Father Limberg left Dülmen for a few days. Sister Emmerich dared not communicate in his absence, as she feared having yielded to

impatience on her sister's account. In consequence of
this privation, she became, to use Dr. Wesener's words, "so
weak and miserable, her pulse so low, that we feared death."
But when Father Limberg returned and she had confessed
and communicated, she regained her strength and soon was
bright as ever.

Not only in the spiritual life was Sister Emmerich passively obedient to her confessor. In everything without exception, she sought to regulate her conduct by his directions. Her longing for religious obedience had increased with
her inability to practise it. To every creature she desired to
submit for the love of God, and with this view she was ever
perseveringly on the alert to sacrifice her own will in the
daily incidents of life. Her perfect abandonment to God
was not only a burning act of love, it was a fact, a reality
in her existence, and every instant brought her fresh occasions for its heroic practice. Her humble forgetfulness of
self led her friends to look upon her not as sick and requiring special care ; and, as in her early years her visions
and sufferings were never a pretext for dispensing herself
from labor, for rising above her lowly station, so now her actual condition wrought no change in her daily life. Simple,
obliging, and industrious, never did she aspire to notice.
As she could not without assistance superintend the Abbé
Lambert's housekeeping, she had taken her younger sister
Gertrude to help her ; but the latter was so inexperienced
that the invalid had from her bed to teach her everything
appertaining to domestic affairs. Sometimes even, in spite
of her insuperable disgust, she was forced to prepare the
food herself in the way that she knew the infirm old gentlemen could take it. Her skill in household affairs was intuitive, and she exercised it so well that all were accustomed to call on her for different services ; but no word

ever fell from her lips expressive of desire for care or attention toward herself. Renunciation had become her
second nature and the joy she felt in serving others was
her sweet reward. Gertrud from the very first had accused her of keeping her bed through sloth, and of abstain-
ing from food through fastidiousness. What she had to endure from such an attendant, one can readily imagine.
To bear resignedly great sufferings and trials whose cause
lies secret, to maintain patience and serenity in the midst of
bodily pains, is easier than silently and meekly to endure
marks of coldness, explosions of temper, the want of those
trifling cares and attentions which cost so little, but whose
value is priceless to a sufferer. Dr. Wesener gives us the
following details of his first year's attendance on Sister
Emmerich : —

"Gertrude Emmerich is weak-minded and hard-hearted,
a great annoyance to the invalid and myself ; she has little
love and still less respect for her sister, whom she leaves the
whole day long without even a drink of water. If there
were any fraud going on, Gertrude would surely denounce
it. On one occasion, I made some remark to the invalid of
her sister's want of feeling for her. She replied that Gertrude
would, indeed, be the first to witness against her, did she
discover the least hypocrisy, for that she treated her not as
a sister but as an enemy. Gertrude cannot endure her
sister's admonitions. I must say that I cannot put up with
the girl's whimsical and contradictory humor. Sister Emmerich has to help her in every duty. I have often found
her myself preparing on her bed dishes made up of milk,
flour, and eggs. This gives rise to suspicion, and the poor
Abbé Lambert cannot bear to see her attending to such
things ; but if she does not do so, his wants would not be
cared for. She cannot endure the odor of cooking, it is

one of her greatest torments. I found her once coughing convulsively, because her sister had approached her impregnated with the smell of warm bread just taken from the oven. She was generally affected in the same way when the door was left open and the fumes of the kitchen reached her. One morning I found her perfectly exhausted from coughing all the preceding night, Gertrude having blown out a wax candle by her bedside and left the wick smoking."

Six years later, Clement Brentano wrote :—

" One of the invalid's greatest crosses was her sister Gertrude, whom she endured sorrowfully and compassionately. Gertrude had a most unhappy disposition. Her sister strove by suffering, patience, and prayer to obtain for her a change of heart. Day and night was she at the mercy of this creature, and owing to her terrible gift of reading hearts, she saw her interior state, a sight which greatly added to her torment. Not till after her death were Sister Emmerich's prayers answered, and Gertrude became a changed person."

Gertrude had a perfect mania to make her sister eat. Sister Emmerich often suffered for the dying, who had not expiated their sins of intemperance in eating and drinking, and her expiatory pains were then characterized by the physical and moral consequences of this vice. She was sometimes haunted by the savory odor of delicate dishes; again, she was assailed by an irresistible desire to eat ; and, again, she experienced the irritation of an epicure whose craving for dainties cannot be satiated. These inclinations she had to combat in the place of their miserable victims for whom she obtained the grace of a happy death. Sometimes she was consumed by thirst, and if she attempted to drink, strangulation and retching followed which almost cost her her

life. Gertrude, in her stupid indifference, often forced her
to eat when, absorbed in contemplation, the poor sufferer
knew not what she was doing. It was more through
obedience than ignorance that she accepted the food.
Father Limberg's directions to her were that she should
not reject her sister's attentions, and so she passively submitted to Gertrude's whims. Dr. Wesener gives several
instances of this :—

"May 30, 1814—I found the invalid quite unconscious,
in a pitiable state. I suspected that her obstinate sister had
been worrying her, and I was right. Father Limberg
told me that she had forced her to take some sour-krout.
It was not till the following night that she was relieved.

"Sept. 2d—Again Sister Emmerich lay almost dead.
Her pulse scarcely indicated life, and when at last she threw
off some morsels of food, Gertrude explained : ' I made
a ragout for the Abbé and gave her some to taste ; she must
have swallowed a little.'

"Oct. 29th—She was this evening ill unto death—
nauseated stomach, retching and convulsive coughing. This
state came on about noon. On inquiring the cause, I found
that during High Mass whilst she lay absorbed in ecstasy,
Gertrude had made her taste a vinegar-salad. I sat up
with her that night, but I could neither relieve the nausea
nor stop the vomiting until some morsels of the salad came off
mixed with mucus. Next morning she was alive and that was
all. After Holy Communion she rallied a little, but at noon
her sufferings recommenced. She was consumed by thirst,
racked with terrible pains in stomach and throat, and a sip
of water renewed her vomiting. I gave her six drops of
musk but with no effect, and I repeated the dose in the
evening. She reproached herself for having tasted the
salad. I quieted her, telling her that it was not her fault,
but Gertrude's want of judgment.

" May 9, 1815—I found the invalid exceedingly prostrate. Father Limberg and her sister were with her all
night, fully expecting to see her die in one of her violent
spells of vomiting. After Holy Communion next morning
she grew better, though I still noticed in her a convulsive
effort to swallow; at last she vomited a brownish liquid,
the cause of all the trouble. Her eldest brother had visited
her the day before and had offered her some beer of which
she had unconsciously swallowed a few drops."

Sister Emmerich never uttered a word of complaint
against her sister when she caused her such pain; on the
contrary, she blamed only her own imprudence. But when
she saw her turning a deaf ear to her sisterly admonitions;
fulfilling so carelessly the duty of her state; obstinately refusing to acknowledge or correct her faults; above all, when
she beheld her approaching the Sacraments in such dispositions, she became very, very sad. The doctor writes, Sept.
26, 1815 :—

"Sister Emmerich was very sad to-day. When I inquired into the cause, she answered : ' I am ready to endure patiently any pain, for I am in this world only to suffer, I even know why I have to do so ; but the thought, I
may say the conviction, that my poor sister grows worse
near me instead of better, makes me tremble.' I tried to
comfort her, saying that God would never allow her sister
to be lost, that she would surely change after awhile, that
perhaps just now she was the instrument He made use of
to advance her in perfection, etc. My words appeared to console her."

Sister Emmerich had no third person to whom she might
appeal when Gertrude became quite insupportable. The
Abbé was too kind and indulgent and, besides, he knew too
little German to interfere ; Father Limberg was naturally

too timid to assume any kind of authority over the head-
strong girl; and good Dean Overberg saw in her the
touchstone of her sister's humility, the instrument by which
Almighty God willed to purify her soul from every imperfection. So far as her reverend friends were concerned,
she could look to them for no redress, and yet an arbiter
was needed in the daily encounters that took place between
the poor invalid and the perverse Gertrude; so she begged
Dean Overberg to constitute Doctor Wesener judge, since
he knew her domestic affairs and could decide all differences.
The doctor very unwillingly and only in compliance with
her earnest entreaties consented to take upon himself the
thankless office.

"One day," so runs his journal, "I very gently and
cautiously made a few remarks to Gertrude on her ill-humor,
her want of obedience, etc., when she assumed an air of
surprise and wounded feeling, declared it her natural disposition, and that there was no harm in it. I reasoned with
her, recounting some instances of her perversity, but all in
vain. She even seemed to triumph in the fact of having
aroused her sister's indignation." Sister Emmerich regarded the office the docter had accepted as a very serious one,
and she tearfully accused herself to him whenever she thought
she had yielded to impatience. He wrote as follows some
months later to Dean Overberg :—

"If it depended on me, I should long ago have banished
that evil spirit, Gertrude ; but whenever I proposed it, the
invalid would beg me to be patient. ' I alone am to blame !'
she would say. ' It is one of my trials, it is God's will.' I
think, however, that she should be sent away; an angel could
not put up with her. I shall give you, as an instance of her
difficult temper, something that happened lately. Gertrude
had shown ill-humor a whole morning, and the invalid had

meekly borne with her. In the afternoon Sister Emmerich set about mending something for the poor. She asked her sister to help her, showing her at the same time what she wanted done; but Gertrude saw fit to do just the opposite, and recklessly cut away the good part of the garment instead of what she was told. The invalid drew her attention to it and, taking up the scissors, she began to cut away the worn parts; whereupon Gertrude showed such obstinacy and insolence, that her sister took the work from her hands a little quickly, and the scissors fell to the floor. What a triumph for Gertrude ! She picked them up and returned them with a taunting air, intimating that they had been thrown at her. This almost crushed the poor invalid. She became weak as death, and it was only after having confessed and communicated that she regained her strength. Such instances are by no means rare. Something must be done. The Abbé and FatherLimberg are too easy, they let things come and go."

Dean Overberg, on the reception of the above, was ready to consent to Gertrude's being sent away, but Sister Emmerich herself dared not separate from her sister without an express order from her angel. She bore with her daily and hourly annoyances until one year before her death when she was authorized by her guide to send her away. Almighty God generally places those whom He destines for high perfection in such situations as may be for them a school of spiritual renunciation and mortification, in which by constant struggling against their own weakness they acquire the virtues they need most. We see Maria Bagnesi in a situation parallel to that of Sister Emmerich. Her nurse exacted of her the most menial services. Having been for years a servant in her parents' house, she thought herself authorized to claim in her turn the services of their daughter. When scarcely able to endure her pains, Maria was ordered to bring wood and water, get ready the meals, in short attend to all the domestic affairs, whilst the servant herself went gossiping in the neighborhood. Woe to Maria if on her return she found not things to suit her! Then came explosions of rage to which the child opposed only gentle entreaties to be forgiven for the love of Jesus! When forced to keep her bed by fever, or the excruciating pains of the stone, Maria could get not even a glass of water from her hard-hearted nurse, and as she lay parched and dying of thirst, the cats entering by the window brought her meat and cheese, as if compassionating her state. One word from Maria would have rid her of the insupportable woman. But she dared not utter it, knowing well that she could not find a better opportunity for the practice of meekness and patience. These daily trials were for Maria and Anne Catherine what the meadow buds and flowers are to the busy little bee. They drew thence that ineffable spiritual unction by whose means they poured the honey of consolation into the hearts of all that approached them. Their exterior life was, without doubt, humble and commonplace ; but, in the sight of God, grand and magnificent, for it is He Himself who in His chosen instruments labors, suffers, heals, and saves.

CHAPTER XXXII.

Dr. William·Wesener.—Mesmerism,

Let us turn our attention to Dr. Wesener, a man who holds so prominent a place in Sister Emmerich's life, and to whom we owe the knowledge of many interesting facts. As we have seen, the first report of her extraordinary state had drawn him to her bedside, and a more intimate acquaintance with her had won him back to the faith and to the practice of his religious duties. Deeply grateful for the spiritual favors she had obtained for him, he made her case his careful study, noting down not only such facts as proved to him her rare perfection, but also those incidents and conversations which influenced his own progress in virtue. His simple memoranda, like those of Clement Breatano, five years later, show by what means Sister Emmerich gained souls to God. It would be difficult to imagine two individuals more dissimilar in talents and inclinations than the physician of Dülmen and the poet Brentano, so rich in natural gifts ; yet both aver that their connection with the stigmatisée, brought about by apparently fortuitous circumstances, was a most merciful dispensation of Divine Providence in their regard, one most fruitful in happy consequences.

The following are some of the doctor's own words :—

" It was in 1806 that I first heard of Sister Emmerich. I was then practising in Reklinghausen, where the attendant physician of Agnetenberg, Dr. Krauthausen, consulted me upon the inexplicable phenomena displayed in one of its inmates, Sister Emmerich. I had been reading an article on magnetism in "Reil's Archives," and I mentioned to him certain cataleptic cases to which, however, he paid but little attention. He was a stern old man and attended the convent gratuitously ; this was one of the reasons why Sister Emmerich felt obliged to accept his medicines, although at her own expense. He enumerated a long list of her maladies, each marked by its own special character. Scarcely was she cured of one, when she was seized by another. At the moment in which death seemed inevitable, they took a favorable turn, although medical skill seemed to exercise no appreciable influence upon them.

"On March 21, 1813, I visited her for the first time. I had heard her stigmata spoken of in a certain assembly. She lay in bed unconscious ; but on returning to herself, she regarded me with a frank expression, and when the Abbé Lambert introduced me she said smiling, that she knew me well. I thought her remark rather singular, and putting it down as a silly pleasantry, I assumed a grave demeanor. There was however no need for any such proceeding, and as I became better acquainted with her I was convinced of her candor and uprightness. She was a simple, truly Christian soul, at peace with herself and all around her, seeing in everything the will of God, and looking upon herself as inferior to every one. I shall never forget her kindness in calming my fears concerning the war. She often assured me most positively that Napoleon would soon fall and that Dülmen would be spared by the French. Her prediction was remarkably verified. In the French garrison at Minden were numbers of lawless bandits ; they committed many outrages at Dorsten, but passed by Dülmen without even entering the town.

"In our communications I always found Sister Emmerich simple and natural, kind and gracious toward every one, particularly the poor, the sick, and the unfortunate. It is only lately that I have been able to understand her ability to take upon herself the sufferings of others. She possessed in a high degree the gift of imparting consolation as I myself often experienced, for she reanimated my confidence in God, taught me how to pray, and thus lightened in no small degree the heavy crosses which my natural inclination to sadness aggravated Her life was wholly in God. The publicity given to her miraculous state greatly annoyed her. She was constantly employed in relieving the miseries, corporal and spiritual, of the crowds that flocked to her. Her heart was free from creatures; consequently, it is not hard to divine the source whence flowed the consolation she dispensed to her neighbor.

"In our first interview, she exhorted me to confidence. Smiling sweetly, she said: 'God is infinitely merciful! Whoever repents and has a good will finds favor in His sight!' She begged me to help the poor, a work so pleasing to God, saying with a. sigh: 'There never was so little love of the neighbor as at present, although it is so beautiful a virtue, whilst indifference or contempt is so great a vice.' She protested that the Catholic faith alone is true, the only one that leads to salvation, and she spoke warmly of the incom parable happiness of belonging to the Catholic Church: 'Let us trust in God!' she used to say. 'Let us hold to our holy faith! Is there anything more consoling upon earth? What religion or what philosophy could indemnify us for its loss? I pity the Jews above all others. They are worse off, they are blinder than the pagans themselves; their religion is now only a fable of the rabbis, the curse of God rests upon them. But how good is Our Lord to us! He meets us half-way if we have a good will, the abund-

ance of His graces depends only upon our own desire.
Even a pagan may be saved if, sincerely desirous to serve
God, the Sovereign Lord and Creator, he follows the natural light infused by Him, and practises justice and charity
toward his neighbor.'

" Once I turned the conversation upon prayer. I remarked that, according to my ideas, true prayer consisted in
the accomplishment of duty and the exercise of charity
toward the neighbor, and that I felt curious to know how
she could spend entire hours in it, forgetful of all around,
lost, so to speak, in God. She replied. ' Think a moment !
May not a man become so absorbed in a beautiful book as
to be unconscious of aught else ? But if he converse with
God Himself, the Source of all beauty, how is it possible
for him not to be wholly lost in Him ? Begin by adoring
Him in all humility, the rest will come.' I then spoke of
the temptations man has to endure from the evil one, and
she replied :—' True, the enemy tries to hinder prayer ;
the more fervent it is, the more does he multiply his
attacks. Something of this was shown me one day. I was
in a beautiful church in which three females were kneeling
in prayer; behind them stood a horrible figure. It caressed
the first who immediately fell asleep ; it then tried the same
with the second, though not so successfully ; but the third it
struck and abused so cruelly that I was filled with pity. Surprised, I asked my guide what it all meant, and he answered
that it was symbolical of prayer. The first was neither
earnest nor fervent, and the devil easily put her to sleep ; the
second was not so bad, but still she was tepid ; the third
was fervent and therefore she was tempted the most
violently, but she conquered. The prayer most pleasing
to God is that made for others and particularly for the poor
souls. Pray for them, if you want your prayers to bring

high interest. As to myself personally, I offer myself to God, my Sovereign Master, saying : ' Lord, do with me what Thou wilt !' Then I remain in sweet security, for the best, the most loving of fathers can only seek my good. The poor souls suffer inexpressibly. The difference between the pains of purgatory and those of hell is this : in hell reigns only despair, whilst in purgatory the hope of deliverance sweetens all. The greatest torment of the damned is the anger of God. Some faint idea of His wrath may be formed from the terror of a defenceless person exposed to the attack of a furious man.'

"I spoke of man's destiny, and she said : ' Do you know why God created us ? For His own glory and our happiness. When the angels fell, God resolved to create man to fill their places. As soon as their number will be equalled by that of the just, the end of the world will come.' I asked her where she had learned that. She answered simply that, in truth, she did not know. In a little conference on indulgences, I remarked that I looked upon them merely as a remission of ancient ecclesiastical penances. She replied: ' They are more than that, for by them we obtain the remission of the punishments awaiting us in purgatory. To gain an indulgence, it is not enough to say some prayers, or perform some good work ; we must approach the Sacraments with true repentance and a firm purpose of amendment without which no indulgence can be gained. I believe that there is an indulgence attached to every good work. A person's good works are as diverse as their number ; and if upon the least of them there flows some little of the merits of Christ, it acquires great value. What we offer to God in union with these infinite merits, however insignificant it may be, is set down to our account and deducted from the punishment awaiting us. I cannot suffi-

ciently deplore the sad blindness of those for whom our holy
Faith has become a chimera. They live in sin, imagining
they can gain Indulgences by certain forms of prayer.
Many Christians will one day behold Turks and pagans who
have lived according to the law of nature, less rigorously
dealt with at God's tribunal than themselves. We possess
grace, and esteem it not; it is, in a certain sense, forced
upon us, and we cast it away. He who spies a little piece
of money in the dust, runs quickly, stoops, and picks it up;
but if the grace of eternal salvation were lying at his feet,
he would carefully shun it, in order to follow the vain
amusements of the world. Indulgences are of no avail for
such people and, indeed, the religious practices they perform through stupid routine will serve rather for their condemnation.'

" It is to this blind pursuit of worldly goods that the
following vision seems to refer:—' I found myself in a great,
broad field where I could see all around. It was crowded
with people, all striving in different ways to attain their
ends. In the centre of the field stood Our Lord full of
sweetness. He said to me: ' Behold how these people exert
and torment themselves after gain and happiness! They
pay no attention to Me, their Master and Benefactor,
although they see Me here before them. Only a few regard me with grateful feelings and even they thank me only
in passing, as if giving a paltry alms.' Then approached
some priests on whom Our Lord bestowed special attention;
but they threw him something, passed on quickly and mingled with the crowd. One alone went up to Him, but with
an indifferent air. Our Lord laid His hand on his shoulder,
and said : ' Why fly from me ? Why slight me ? I love
you so !'

" ' Then the vision vanished. But I have had many such

on the life of the clergy of the present day which made me
very sad. Owing to the spirit of the world and tepidity,
if the Saviour returned to earth to-day to announce His
doctrine in person, He would find as many opponents as
He did among the Jews.'

" I once heard her relate the following vision upon the
teachings of our times : ' My guide led me to a stately edifice : " Enter, he said, and I shall show you the doctrines of
men." We entered a spacious hall filled with pupils and
professors. A warm dispute was going on ; loud words,
contradictory statements resounded on ɛll sides. I saw into
the hearts of the professors and, to my amazement. I discovered in each a little black casket. In the centre of the
hall stood a female of imposing appearance, who took a
foremost part in the discussion. I paused a few moments
with my guide to listen, when to my surprise I saw the
audience disappearing, one by one. The hall itself began
almost imperceptibly to fall to ruins, the floor was no longer safe. The professors mounted a story higher where
they continued their debate with renewed ardor ; but there,
too, the building began to crumble. I trembled on seeing
myself standing on a worm-eaten plank, and I begged my
guide to save me. He reassured me and led me to a place
of safety. Then I asked him the meaning of the little
black casket. " It signifies," he said, " presumption and the
spirit of contradiction. The female is philosophy or, as they
say *pure reason*, which seeks to regulate all things by its
own formulas. These professors follow her teachings and
not those of truth, the precious treasure handed down by
tradition." Then my guide conducted me into another hall
in which sat several professors in their chairs. All was
very different here ; the clearness and simplicity of their
words charmed me, order and charity reigned and many

who had left the ruined halls took refuge here. My guide said : "Here is simple, unadulterated truth which springs from humility and gives birth to love and all other blessings."'

"One day, I expressed regret at not having a fuller knowledge of the life of Jesus before His public ministry. Sister Emmerich replied : 'I know it, I have seen it even in its smallest details. I know too the history of the Mother of Jesus. I often wonder how I came by the knowledge, since I never read it.' She promised to relate all to me and, once when I got a chance, I reminded her of it. She began by explaining that it had been made known to St. Anne that the Messiah would be born of her posterity. 'Anne had several children,' she said, ' but she knew that the true child of benediction was not yet born ; therefore, she prayed, fasted, and offered sacrifice to obtain the promised blessing. She had no children for about eighteen years, which circumstance rendered her very sad ; but in humility she attributed the non-fulfilment of the promise to her own sins. Joachim went to Jerusalem to offer expiatory sacrifice in the Temple, but he was repulsed. Overwhelmed with sadness, he prayed and received in a dream the assurance that the promise would be fulfilled. At the same time Anne received a similar assurance, and afterward gave birth to the little Mary. Joachim and Anne saw in the child a pure gift from God. They resolved to consecrate her to the Lord in the Temple, which they did in her third year. On reaching the Temple, they attempted to take her little hands to help her to mount the high steps ; but the child ran on alone. She wore a silk robe of sky-blue. She was neither sad nor troubled on taking leave of her parents, but gave herself up quietly to the priests. She was instructed in everything in the Temple, and with the other young girls she spent her time in working for it.

When she had reached her fourteenth year, the priests wrote to her parents to take their daughter home, for the Law did not allow any child to remain over that age. Mary would willingly have stayed in the Temple in a state of virginity, but it was not permitted. Her parents were anxious about choosing a spouse worthy of their admirable child; therefore, they repaired to the Temple to seek light from the Most High. Every youth aspiring to Mary's hand, was directed to bear his staff to the Holy of Holies; but at first no change appeared in any one of them. Prayers and sacrifices were again offered, when a voice was heard saying that the staff of one was still wanting. Search was made and Joseph found. He was of a noble family, but not much thought of by his relatives, because of his simplicity and also on account of his remaining unmarried. His staff was placed in the Holy of Holies. That night it blossomed, and next morning it was surmounted by a white lily. Then Mary was espoused to Joseph, who was filled with joy when she made known to him her vow of perpetual virginity. Mary thought always of the promised Redeemer. In her humility, she prayed to be the handmaid of His chosen Mother. It was on this account that she was so frightened when the angel announced her sublime maternity. She said nothing to Joseph of her visions or of the angel's message.'

"In speaking of alms-giving and of the duties of one's state, Sister Emmerich sometimes alluded to her contemplations. Once she said: 'Use your strength and your means in the service of your patients without, however, wronging your own family; not one only but many of the poor, call upon you for assistance. Their merit lies in their poverty. Faith teaches that it is an enviable condition, since the Son of God chose it for Himself and gave

to the poor the first title to the kingdom of heaven.'
Then she related some singularly beautiful incidents of
Christ's infancy, for instance that Mary some days after the
Nativity, hid herself in an underground cave to escape the
gaze of the curious."

It soon became clear that God had placed the doctor
near the invalid, as later on He did Clement Brentano, to
aid her in the accomplishment of her mission. Under her
direction, he distributed not only his own alms among
his poor patients, but also money and clothing supplied by
her for that purpose. Sister Emmerich received an annual
pension of one hundred and eighty thalers which God so
abundantly multiplied that her alms far exceeded that sum.
Day and night was she occupied in works of some kind for
the needy and, when her own slender resources failed her,
she begged materials from others. Her skilful fingers soon
transformed pieces of old silk, etc., into beautiful little caps
for new-born infants. When in need, she used to invoke
with sweet familiarity the assistance of Lidwina, Magdalena von Hadamar, and other holy virgins who had been,
like herself, marked with the sacred stigmata. Addressing them as if really present, she would say : "Is that you,
little Magdalena? See, it is almost Christmas and there
are still so many children without stockings and caps. You
must keep your promise and bring me some wool and
silk." Never did her petitions go unheeded.

The doctor, convinced by daily experience that she saw
and assisted in spirit every one whom he attended, used to
describe to her the sufferings of his patients. He followed
her advice with the most successful results. He was often
surprised to see unlooked-for recovery, or the alleviation
of maladies. These he ascribed not to his own prescriptions,
but to Sister Emmerich who had taken their sickness upon

herself, either to facilitate their cure or to prepare them for a happy death.

Up to the last he remained a faithful friend and support to the old Abbé Lambert, supplying the remedies his infirmities demanded with such care and charity as could spring only from his deep veneration for Sister Emmerich. This was to her a great consolation. The following incident will prove her interest in the good old priest's welfare, as also her wonderful foreknowledge of approaching danger.

Dr. Wesener's journal, Feb. 15, 1815 :—

"I tried to calm Sister Emmerich's fears for the Abbé, who is suffering from a chronic cough and oppression of the chest. Yesterday he had so severe an attack whilst in her room that he fainted. The confessor was present. He had yielded to her request and remained with her in the afternoon, as she dreaded some approaching danger, and it was fortunate that he did so."

Dr. Wesener's communications with Father Limberg bore very important consequences for the invalid. The timid religious would have abandoned his spiritual daughter at the first sound of the stupid calumnies spread against her, had it not been for the doctor whose experience rendered him deaf and incredulous to all such tales. Father Limberg could not reply coolly and unhesitatingly to the specious arguments and suspicions uttered on all sides. He grew nervous, gave shuffling explanations, and openly declared his desire to withdraw entirely from his connection with Sister Emmerich ; but the doctor's presence always lent him courage. He saw the change produced in the latter by Sister Emmerich's words. The earnestness and fidelity with which he now attended to his religious duties, and his indifference to the world's opinions and judgments greatly encouraged him. His confidence in the doctor made him impose upon his penitent the obligation of simple obedience to every prescription, thus placing her in exactly the same position she had formerly held toward Dr. Krauthausen at Agnetenberg. Again she submitted to all the remedies employed for her cure. Musk, opium, camphor, and above all, hot brandy were, in the doctor's estimation as well as in that of her confessor, the means most conducive to such an end. Truly, they lost sight of the fact that her miraculous body contained not in itself the germ of her singular maladies. They sprang only from the tribulations heaped upon the Church. She never complained even when an aggravation of suffering proved the inefficiency of their remedies. At such times she was even more grateful and docile, so that years passed before the doctor and confessor recognized the uselessness of their prescriptions. We find the following entry in the doctor's journal, May 16, 1814 :—

" The invalid suffers a martyrdom, terrible pains in her breast and loss of hearing. We thought her at the point of death several times. Her sufferings are so horrible, spasms in the throat and stomach, that Father Limberg wants to administer Extreme Unction, which, however, I think not yet necessary ; meanwhile, though convinced that remedies are useless, I can no longer remain a passive spectator of her struggles. She can retain nothing . . . . . I gave her four drops of musk, but she rejected it even before swallowing ; then I diminished the dose but with no better success. She suffered terribly all night, her stomach several times rejected the musk administered ; it was only near morning that she was able to retain five drops. I found her in an alarming state of prostration, and I left expecting never again to see her alive. May 18th, she lay insensible almost all day, at intervals vomiting water with violent retching. I determined to stay by her all night. She grew a little better about midnight, when I read to her from a pious book and spoke to her on religious subjects, which seemed to afford her great relief. On my expressing surprise at this she remarked : ' It is always so. However weak I may be, I am always relieved when God or holy things are spoken of; but if worldly subjects are mentioned, I grow worse.' "

Six years later Clement Brentano witnessed a similar trial of musk of which he highly disapproved. Sister Emmerich said to him : " True, it is particularly disgusting to me, it causes me great suffering. I am always worse after it, but I must take it in obedience to my confessor, although he has often seen what bad effects it has on me."

Shortly after she had a vision of her own past life, of which the following particulars relative to the remedies employed in her case will prove interesting :—"I have had a vision of the sorrowful side of my own life. All that certain persons had ever done to thwart my mission was shown me in pictures in which those persons themselves figured. I had never dared think of them for fear of temptations to aversion. Last night I had to struggle with that temptation, and I had the consolation of hearing it said that I had fought well. The pictures were shown me in various ways; sometimes as if a past trial had actually returned, sometimes people busy among themselves, and again it seemed to be a recital. I saw all I had lost thereby both in my life and spiritual work and what harm such or such a one had done me, although I was not aware of it at the time. What I had only suspected, I now saw for a certainty. It cost me much to endure again the agony of the past, the falsehood and wickedness of men. I had not only to crush every feeling of resentment, but to foster the most sincere affection for my cruel enemies.

" The vision began with my religious profession and all that my parents had done to prevent it. They had tried my patience and secretly hoped to hinder me. The nuns had made me suffer. I saw their great perversity. At first, they abused me ; and, when my state became known, they honored me immoderately, but without refraining from their gossiping. It made me so sad, for I loved them. I saw the physician of the convent, and how hurtful his pre-scriptions were to me. I saw the second physician and his medicines ruinous to my chest. My breast seemed to be quite hollow, and I felt that without care I could not last long. I would have been cured of all my maladies with-out medical treatment, if only the Church's remedies had been applied.

" I saw how wrong it was to expose me to the public gaze, to people who regarded only my wounds without taking other circumstances into consideration, and I saw how I had been forced to show them to curious visitors, a proceeding which had disturbed my recollection without benefiting any one. It would have been much better had they left me in peace. I saw the prayers and entreaties which I made not of myself, but in obedience to an interior warning. All was useless ; and, contrary to my better judgment, I was made a spectacle to the world. The greatest humil-iations accrued to me from it. What I did sorrowfully and only in obedience was cast up to me as effrontery, and they who constrained me to show my signs uttered no word in my defence."

Such contemplations never affected Sister Emmerich's actual position. She endured the same absurd treatment as before, and the physician's remedies remained **unchanged.**

But her soul was enlightened. She recognized in persons and events instruments and means destined by Almighty God to advance her to her end, if she faithfully availed herself of them. Her angel among other instructions ordered her never to refuse remedies, a command in strict accordance with the divine economy. The representative of the Church, she was called upon to expiate the sins of men who, by their principles, their teachings, their baneful designs and measures, sought to exercise over it an influence analogous to that produced upon herself by the musk, the opium, and the brandy lotions. She knew that her expiation would be so much the more efficacious, the more simply and unhesitatingly she submitted to every prescription ; therefore, we detect in her neither resistance nor contradiction. When we reflect upon the waves of destruction that threatened the Church at this period ; when we recall the ravages produced by the unwholesome spirit of philosophy, the factitious exaltation of false mysticism, which generally ended in monstrous depravity, we are involuntarily led to recognize in the opium and disgusting liquor a striking symbol of these false doctrines.

To struggle against the dangers arising from mesmerism formed also a part of Sister Emmerich's task, since both her physician and confessor were the first to resort to it after their vain use of opium and musk. Dr. Wesener tells us :—

" Father Limberg told me that, whilst the invalid lay apparently in a cataleptic state, he tried several mesmeric experiments upon her, but without success. Then I determined to make some myself the first chance I should get. I did so a few days later when she lay rigid in ecstasy. I pronounced a few words on the pit of her stomach and the extremities of her toes ; I laid the tips of the fingers of my right hand upon the pit of her stomach and spoke some words upon the tips of the fingers of her left hand ; I called into her ear, but none of these actions produced the slightest impression upon her. At my request, her confessor made the same experiments, though with no better success; but, when he pronounced the word *obedience,* she trembled, sighed, and returned to consciousness. He asked what ailed her, and she answered : ' I have been called !' "

No further attempts of the kind were made until the following January, when the invalid fell into such a state of misery that neither the confessor nor physician could endure the sight. Daily for weeks she experienced suffocation and convulsive pains around her heart. Death seemed inevitable, and Communion alone enabled her to battle against her frightful pains. Not the poor invalid, but her confessor and physician at last began to lose patience. The doctor reports, January 26th :—

" I was with her this evening ; she was very ill, her pulse low. A kind of trance came on about five o'clock. Her eyes were open, but so void of sensation that I could touch the cornea with my finger without the eyelids closing. The day before she told me that her sight was so wonderfully piercing that, even with closed eyes, she could see. The trance lasted an hour, when she fell into ecstasy, arose on her knees, and prayed with extended arms. I prevailed upon Father Limberg once more to have recourse to mesmerism, to ask her the nature of her malady, and where it was principally seated. He did so several times and insisted upon an answer, but none came. I then begged him to command her in *obedience.* Scarcely had the word escaped his lips than she started and awoke with a sigh. To the question why she appeared frightened, she answered : 'I heard a loud voice calling me.' Again she relapsed into unconsciousness, and I administered twelve drops of musk. Next morning she said she had had vertigo all night from weakness."

There was no human remedy for Sister Emmerich's sufferings, since their origin lay not in physical evils, but in the sins of others. When her convulsions ceased, vomiting ensued and she threw off a watery liquid, although literally unable to swallow a drop of water to slack her burning thirst. Until February 9th, she daily lay for several hours in profound ecstasy which, on that day, was prolonged nine consecutive hours. She gave the following explanation to her confessor, as also to the doctor whose skill was completely baffled :—

"Thursday, Feb. 8th, as I was saying my Hours, my thoughts turned upon our utter unworthiness and God's infinite mercy and forbearance, and I was quite overwhelmed by the reflection that, in spite of His mercy, so many souls are lost forever. I began to beg grace for the unhappy creatures when, all at once, I saw my cross hanging there on the bed-post (1) surrounded by a bright light. I was wide awake, in my senses, and I said to myself : 'Is it not a mere fancy ?' and I went on saying my Office, though the light dazzled me. At last, I knew it was not an illusion, and I began to pray fervently. I asked God, my Saviour, for grace and mercy for all mankind and above all, for poor, weak, straying souls. The cross grew brighter. I beheld a figure attached to it and blood streaming from the wounds, though not falling below the cross. I redoubled my prayers and acts of adoration, when the right arm of the figure stretched forth and described a circle as if to embrace the whole world. I was fully awake and conscious all the time. I noticed certain things around

(1) A little silver reliquary containing two small particles of the True Cross.

me, and I counted the hour every time the clock struck.
The last I heard was half-past eleven, after which I knew
no more, as I fell into contemplation on the Passion of
Christ. I saw it in a picture before my eyes, just as it
had really taken place. I saw the Saviour carrying His
Cross. I saw Veronica consoling, and Simon helping Him.
I saw Him extend His limbs and allow Himself to be nailed
to it. It pierced my inmost soul, though my grief was not
without a sentiment of joy. I saw Our Lord's Mother and
several of her relations. I adored my Lord Jesus, begging
pardon for myself and all mankind. Then He said to me:
' Behold here My love, it knows no bounds! All, all, come
to My arms! I will make all happy!' And then I saw
how most men turn rudely away from His embrace. At
the commencement of this apparition, I begged the Lord
to put an end to the horrors of war, to give us peace, and
again I implored His grace and mercy; thereupon, a
voice said to me: ' The war is not yet over. Many countries will still groan under it! But pray and have confidence!'—And now I firmly believe that Münster and Dülmen will not suffer from it."

The Abbé Lambert and Gertrude say that, during the
whole time the above apparition lasted, from ten a. m. till
about five p. m., she lay quite still. From ten till noon her
eyes were open, her face flushed; but from noon till five
her eyes were closed, and tears flowed down her cheeks.

Feb. 8th was the Thursday before Septuagesima. On
this day she was accustomed to receive her task for the
holy time of Lent, which she accepted eagerly for the salvation of souls. The foregoing details, related to the doctor
on her confessor's command, determined the former to desist for the time being from further experiments in mesmerism. Neither he nor Father Limberg dared mention to her

their unsuccessful attempts which, it was evident, had not in the least affected her ; so they allowed the affair to pass unnoticed. A year later a medical friend of Neeff and Passavant arrived in Dülmen with the express object of making observations on the stigmatisee whom they believed a suitable subject for mesmerism. This physician was something of a fanatic respecting Neeff's theory of somnambulism and mesmerism in which he pretended to have found such confirmation of Christianity as to compel his belief in its doctrines. As he possessed the gift of persuasiveness in no slight degree he found little difficulty in winning Father Limberg and the doctor to his own way of thinking, and both acknowledged that views so elevated had never before been presented to them upon the subject. They were on the point of adopting the mesmeric regime, when a higher wisdom interposed to establish the unerring truth, which facts we glean from Dr. Wesener's journal. He says:—

" Holy Saturday, April 5th, 1817, Dean Rensing announced a visit from a physician of Frankfort with an introduction from the Vicar General. The invalid was so afflicted that she implored me to represent to the Dean how very painful such a visit would be to her. But he paid no attention to her words and reiterated his orders through me. She was distressed, but she soon regained her cheerfulness, saying : ' Well, I submit in obedience ! '—and she begged me to come with the stranger, as she could not talk to him. Some hours after I introduced him to her. He was so struck by her appearance that he fell on his knees to kiss her hand. She withdrew it hurriedly and rebuked him gently for his enthusiasm, saying that she could not understand how a sensible man could bestow marks of respect on one like her—' What temptations I have to endure ! What trials of patience and humility ! But now come others of a different kind.' "

A few days later, Dr. Wesener again records in his journal:—

" Dr. N. has convinced Father Limberg and myself that the science of mesmerism is nothing more than the flowing of certain vital spirits upon the sick. This spirit pervades all nature and the invalid receives it through a spiritual or even corporal communication. It acts upon the recipient according to the nature of the principle from which it springs, enkindling flame which belongs either to the earth or to the higher or lower regions, and operating accordingly either salutary or pernicious effects. This vital principle the Christian can and ought to kindle by religion and the love of God and the neighbor, in such a way as to render it salutary to soul and body."

The doctor knew, however, by repeated experience what possessed the power of inflaming his patient, for shortly before he had noted in his journal the following lines :— " I found Sister Emmerich to-day flushed as if on fire. I asked the cause and received the answer : ' Dean Overberg was here, we spoke only of God ! It excited me, but I do not feel sick.' " But now Dr. Wesener came supported by her confessor and, full of the new discovery, the mesmeric vital principle, explained it to her with so much warmth that she soon perceived the dangerous ground on which they were both standing. She maintained a prudent silence, listened patiently to their arguments in favor of the new science, and answered only when her angel ordered her to do so. It is again from the doctor's notes that we learn the following :—

" On a subsequent visit, the invalid asked me to remain awhile, as she had something to communicate. ' You have seen,' she began, ' how I received what you have all told me about mesmerism. I have not concealed my indiffer-

ence, though I am pleased that you try to present it in its
moral bearing. But now I shall communicate to you what
I have been told in vision for the third time concerning it.
The first vision presented it in an unfavorable light; the
second filled me with terror; and in the third, last night,
my angel showed me that almost everything connected
with mesmerism is an illusion of the devil. I hope to have
the strength to relate it in detail. For the present, I can
only say that, if we desire to imitate the prophets and
Apostles in their works, we must imitate them also in their
life ; then we would have no need of a mesmerizer's manipulations, the holy name of Jesus would be sufficient. There
is no harm in trying to effect a cure by transmitting something from the healthy to the sick ; but the juggling connected with such an attempt is both foolish and unlawful.
The mesmeric sleep which affords a glimpse of distant and
future things comes from the devil, who clothes it with the
semblance of piety to gain adherents and, above all, to ensnare the good.'—She spoke in so impressive a style that I
remarked that perhaps I ought to discontinue the mesmeric
treatment I had begun on a young peasant-girl whose arm
was paralyzed. She inquired how I conducted the operation. I told her that I made certain movements of my
hands, described circles, and breathed upon the affected
part ; that the patient drank mesmerized water and wore
on her lame arm a band of mesmerized flannel. She replied : ' The breathing upon the arm and warming it with
the hands, I think strictly natural remedies; but the passes
and circles I condemn as unreasonable and leading to superstition.'—When I asked her opinion of the strange physician's views, she answered : ' We must beware of intemper-
ate, ill advised zeal in his regard ; but I feel that he will return to the truth, that I shall be of use to him."

The foregoing conversation made so deep an impression upon Dr. Wesener that he forgot his patient's admonition not to make known to Dr. N. her decision too bluntly. He communicated all she had said in the plainest terms, to the stranger's extreme surprise and vexation, as he entertained a high opinion of the piety of a certain somnambulist of Frankfort. Far from losing confidence in his favorite theory, he replied warmly that it could not be thought that men of such consideration as many of its most zealous supporters, had anything in common with the evil spirit. He declared that Sister Emmerich had looked only on the dark side of mesmerism, but that its bright side might be exhibited with her confessor's assistance by the imposition of hands and the sacerdotal benediction, which he denominated the "mesmeric healing process." Although Father Limberg had for years experienced his penitent's wonderful sensitiveness to the blessings and prayers of the Church, yet now, strange to say, he was tempted to ascribe their efficacy to the "mesmeric vital principle." He had been accustomed to use the power conferred on him by Holy Orders only when she was thought to be in extremity; but now, blinded by novelty, he submitted her to the "healing mesmeric process" on every occasion. Sister Emmerich was not a little saddened by proceedings so extravagant and, at last, on a formal command from her angel to that effect, she warned her confessor to desist from such folly. It had been said to her in vision : "God wills that you patiently endure your sufferings. Your confessor must do nothing more than hitherto !" She related the following vision :—

"I was in a spacious hall, like a church, crowded with people. Some grave looking personages were going around and obliging others to leave the church. I was surprised, and on asking why they sent away people who looked so good and knew how to speak so beautifully, one of the grave-looking men answered: 'They have no right here, they are in delusion; and even if they spoke with the tongues of angels, yet their doctrines are false.' The stranger, Dr. N — was among those going to be turned out. I felt very sorry for him and I ran to his assistance. Some persons near tried to prevent me, saying it would not be proper, but I would not be restrained. I said: ' His soul's salvation is at stake'—and I kept him from being expelled."

This vision was very remarkably verified; for, in spite of their seeming inclination toward Catholicism, in spite of their plausible arguments, most of the members of the circle, bewitched by the mesmeric system, died out of the Church. Dr. N. alone, helped by Sister Emmerich's prayers, found another and more solid basis for his faith than mesmerism, to which he had heretofore ascribed the wonders wrought by God in His saints. Father Limberg never after tried any other experiment on his spiritual daughter than that of the Church's blessing, and the doctor also was cured of his enthusiasm for the new theory. His journal contains after this date only the following lines on the subject: "You may make use of the imposition of hands and insufflation when perfectly assured that it will be a cause of temptation neither to yourself nor your patient."

The following are the visions in which Sister Emmerich learned the real nature of animal magnetism, or mesmerism, the degradation into which it plunges the soul, and the dangers thereby incurred.

"The first I heard of mesmerism was from the strange doctor. Whenever he mentioned the clairvoyant and her friends, a feeling of repugnance arose in my soul, I knew not why. This clairvoyant was then shown me, I was en-

lightened with regard to her state. I saw that it was anything but pure or from God. I saw that sensuality
and vanity, though she would by no means acknowledge it,
had the greatest share in it and that without being aware of
it, she cherished too great an affection for her mesmerizer.
Scattered here and there in the distance, I saw as if
through a magnifying-glass other clairvoyants either
sitting or reclining, some having before them a glass with
a tube which they held in their hands. The impression
produced upon me was one of horror which arose, not so
much from the nature of the thing in itself, as from the
temptations it excited and to which its victims almost always yielded. The mesmerizer's jestures before his patient's eyes, his passes, the stroking of the hand, etc., were
so repulsive to me that I cannot express it. I saw the interior of both, the influence of one upon the other, the
communication of their nature and evil inclinations. I
always saw Satan directing the mesmerizer's manipulations
and making them with him.

"In vision these clairvoyants are very different from me.
If on entering into contemplation they have the least impure thought, they see only lies, for it is the demon who
presents their visions to them and glosses all over with a
fine appearance. If a clairvoyant has formed a desire of
saying something to render herself famous, or if she enter-
tains the least sensual feeling, she is instantly exposed to sin.
Some do, indeed, experience bodily relief; but the majority,
unknown to themselves. derive results pernicious to their
soul. The horror these things excite in me can only be compared to that which a certain secret society and its practices
inspire. I perceive the corruption, but I cannot describe it.

" Mesmerism is allied to magic; the only difference between the two is this : in the latter the devil is invoked, in

the former he comes uninvited. Whoever delivers himself
up to mesmerism takes from nature that which can be lawfully acquired only in the Church of Jesus Christ, for the
power of healing and sanctifying is preserved only in her
bosom. Now, for all who are not in living union with Jesus
Christ by faith and grace, nature is full of Satan's influence.
Persons in the mesmeric state see nothing in its essence and
dependence on God ; what they see they behold in an
isolated, separated condition as if through a hole or a chink.
They perceive, as it were, a gleam of things, and God
grant that this light be pure, be holy ! It is one of God's
favors to have veiled us from one another, to have raised
walls of separation between us, since we incline to sin, are
so readily influenced by one another. It is well that we
have to act independently before communicating the con-
tagion of our evil inclinations. But in Jesus Christ, the
God-Man, we have our Head in whom purified and sanctified, we may all become one, one single body without our
sins and bad inclinations infecting the union. Whoever
tries to remove this barrier raised by God unites himself in
a most dangerous manner to fallen nature over which reigns
the author of its ruin, the devil with all his seductions.

" I see that the essence of mesmerism is true ; but there is
a thief unchained in its veiled light. All union between
sinners is dangerous, but the mutual penetration into one
another's interior is still more so. When this happens to
an upright soul, when one becomes a clairvoyant only
through simplicity and inexperience, a prey to artifice
and intrigue, then one of man's faculties possessed before
the fall, a faculty not entirely extinct, is in a certain measure resuscitated, and he lies helpless in a most mysterious
state, exposed to the attacks of the evil one. This state
really exists, but it is veiled, because it is a poisoned source

for all but the saints. I feel that the state of these persons is, in certain particulars, parallel with my own, but springing from another source, tending toward a different end, and followed by very different consequences. The sin of a man in his natural state is an act accomplished by the senses. His interior light is not obscured by it. It stings the conscience, it urges to other acts of the senses, repentance and penance; it leads to the supernatural remedies which the Church administers under sensible forms in the Sacraments. The senses are the sinners, the interior light is the accuser.

" But in the mesmeric state, when the senses are for the time dead, when the interior light both receives and reflects impressions, then that which is holiest in man is exposed to the baneful influence of the evil spirit. The soul cannot fall under such influence by means of the senses subjected as they are to the laws of time and space. In such a state, the mesmeric, it cannot have recourse to the purifying remedies of the Church. I do, indeed, see that a pure soul in God's grace cannot be hurt by the devil even in this state; but I also see that if, before entering it (and it may easily happen, especially to females) the individual has consented to the least temptation, Satan freely carries on his game in the soul, dazzling it with an appearance of sanctity. Her visions are false and if, perchance, she discovers therein a means of healing the body, she purchases her knowledge at the price of her immortal soul; she is sullied by necromantic relations with her mesmerizer."

Females under the influence of mesmerism were often shown Sister Emmerich in vision that she might pray for them and labor to prevent the ulterior consequences of such practices. She was always ready to help them, but never willing to be brought into contact with them either in the natural state or in vision. Once only when Dr. N. was boasting of his clairvoyant's *holy* visions, she said :—

"I wish she were here before me, her fine visions would soon cease, and she would discover by whom she is deceived. I have often seen her in my visions on this subject. I see that, when in the mesmeric state, Satan cast his spells over her whilst she takes him for an angel of light."

On one of his journeys Dr. Wesener met Dr. Neeff, the mezmerizer of the clairvoyant mentioned above. He pointed out to him her danger and the latter resolved to go to Dülmen himself to study the resemblance between Sister Emmerich and his own patient. On his arrival he informed the sister that his clairvoyant could discern remedies for all diseases, that she was in communication with the blessed, that she was conducted by her own angel and the angel of her mesmerizer through worlds of light, and that she received a species of sacrament from "The Holy Grail!" Sister Emmerich shuddered. She tried sweetly and gently to impress him with the immense danger both he and his patient ran (they were Protestants) but she did not succeed. The doctor, completely infatuated by his mesmeric powers, appealed to the good intentions which animated his patient and himself, to the precautions they took before beginning their operations, begging God to preserve them from the snares of the evil one, etc. He declared that his clairvoyant was led by a way that daily became more luminous, more sublime, and he skilfully evaded a closer examination into the nature of his practices. In vain did Sister Emmerich protest against the celestial nourishment and luminous worlds, which she stigmatized as diabolical illusions ; the doctor turned a deaf ear to her warnings and went his way.

"When such persons are shown me," said the invalid, "I see the mesmerizer spinning from the clairvoyant a

thread which he knots and swallows. She holds him bound
by it and leads him around at will. I see this knot in him
like a dark cloud, weighing him down and stifling him.
Sometimes he tries to reject it, but without success."

Certain persons, actuated by curiosity and even by malice, had recourse to a clairvoyant to obtain information concerning Sister Emmerich's own state. During the second
investigation of which we shall speak later, they took her
head-dress to use as a bond between her and a certain clairvoyant of M—, hoping thereby to hear many interesting
things.

"This person," says Sister Emmerich, "was shown me
by my angel, but though she put herself to a great deal of
trouble, she could never find out anything about me. I
always saw the devil with her. When I was released from
imprisonment, I saw my confessor with her, the devil on
one side, another spirit on the other. The devil wanted
the woman to say all sorts of infamous things of me in my
confessor's presence; but, in spite of all her efforts, she
could see nothing. At last, she took Father Limberg by
the hand and said: 'Sister Emmerich is in prayer. She
is very sick. *She* is no impostor, but maybe some of her
friends are.'

"When my confessor returned from M—— and told me
this, I had another vision on this subject. I was seized
with fear at the thought of receiving Holy Communion from
him on the morrow, for I was afraid that he had gone to the
clairvoyant through curiosity; but I was satisfied when I
found that it was not by his own choice that he went. I saw
that she told falsehoods of other people, and that the devil
conjured up visions before her."

During the investigation referred to by Sister Emmerich
when she says, "I was released from imprisonment," an at

tempt was made to put her in communication with a mesmerizer, by making her wear around her neck a magnetic conductor in the form of a little phial covered with silk. So great was the disgust it excited in her that she dashed it from her, indignantly denouncing as a bare-faced lie the assertion that the horrible thing had been sent to her by her director, Dean Overberg.

A woman of Dülmen having allowed herself to be persuaded to consult a fortune-teller of Warendorf, thought she would try her skill by proposing some questions concerning Sister Emmerich. " What is going on near Sister Emmerich ? " she inquired. The fortune-teller shuffled her cards uneasily and answered : " Strange ! All is exceedingly devout there ! There is an aged man quite stout ! There is a younger one ! There is an old woman dying ! " (Sister Emmerich's old mother who died by her). " The person herself is sick !"

The questioner had heard enough, she departed in fright. When Sister Emmerich heard of it, she remarked :

" Not the cards, but their faith in them, makes fortune-tellers see ! They say what they see, but not what the card shows. The card is the image of an idol, but it is the devil who is the idol. He is often *forced* to tell the truth, and then the fortune-teller announces it angrily."

In January, 1821, Sister Emmerich, whilst contemplating the public life of Our Lord, in a vision of the cure of one possessed, saw again the nature and moral effects of mesmerism. The relation between men and the powers of darkness were shown her in three spheres or worlds. The lowest and darkest comprised those that dealt in magic and openly worshipped the demon ; the second those that indulged superstition and sensual desires ; the third was the region of free-masonry and liberalism. These three worlds were bound together by innumerable interlacing threads which, like a ladder, led from the highest to the lowest. In the lowest sphere, as also in the middle one, she beheld mesmerism with its various states and bodily remedies. She understood that it was the most efficient means employed by the demon for the destruction of mankind.

" In the lowest sphere," she says, " I saw certain states and relations which in common life are not regarded as absolutely unlawful. Many individuals therein were under the influence of mesmerism. I saw something abominable between them and the mesmerizer, dark, shadowy figures passing from one to the other. I have rarely, if ever, seen persons mesmerized without discovering sensuality in them. Clairvoyance is produced by the agency of evil spirits. I beheld people falling from the upper and brighter sphere on account of their employing magic under the name of science in the treatment of diseases. Then I saw them mesmerizing and, blinded by their apparent success, they attracted many from the upper sphere. I saw them eager to palm off cures wrought by infernal agency, reflections of the mirrors of hell, as cures from heaven effected by God's favored souls. In this lowest story I beheld very distinguished men, laboring unknown to themselves in the sphere of the **infernal church.**"

CHAPTER XXXIII.

ATTEMPTS TO REMOVE SISTER EMMERICH TO MÜNSTER. DEATH OF HER AGED MOTHER.

In June, 1815, Dean Overberg passed several days in Dülmen. "Not having seen Sister Emmerich for some-time," he wrote,"I visited her to-day, June 8th. She expressed her joy at seeing me, and we spoke almost an hour and a half on her affairs. I determined to remain with her as long as possible. Next morning, at half-past seven, I took her Holy Communion. I stayed by her from the end of her thanksgiving till noon, when I withdrew and again returned at four o'clock. She was weak and tremulous. I asked her the cause and she answered : 'It is from the pain in my wounds, but this pain is sweet.' She says that, even if she lies awake all night, it never seems long to her. She has received the last Sacraments twice since my visit in January. Her attendants thought her dying. She lay without pulse or respiration, her lips livid, her features drawn, her whole appearance more like a corpse than a living being ; but as soon as she had received Holy Communion, life and strength returned. It was her desire for the Eucharist that had reduced her on both occasions to such a state. If through obedience she abstains from communicating, though her desires may be just as ardent, she is able to support the privation ; but, if it is through her own fault, she falls into a death-like state.

"On Friday afternoon, I beheld her in ecstasy. When I stretched out my hand to her, she took the forefinger and thumb, the consecrated fingers, and held them firmly ; after a short time I withdrew them and presented the middle one, when she instantly drew back as if frightened. Then she clasped the thumb and forefinger again, saying : ' These are the fingers that feed me *!* ' "

The Dean made use of his stay in Dülmen to persuade her to allow herself to be removed to Münster for a time to undergo a new investigation by reliable persons, not to convince her Ecclesiastical Superiors of the truth of her case, but only for the silencing of infidel scoffers, for it was thought by many that the first investigation had been too easy, that another was absolutely necessary for the satisfaction of the public. Let her come to Münster, they said, let her submit to a careful medical examination to prove the reality of her stigmata and testify to the conclusions drawn from the first investigation. Dean Overberg was himself convinced that no one could look with an unprejudiced eye upon the invalid without being assured of the truth. On Friday, June 9th, when her wounds began to bleed, he involuntarily exclaimed . " No ! no one could produce such an effect artificially, and she less than any one ! " He hoped that a new investigation would be decisive. He could not understand why Sister Emmerich did not encourage the idea of her removal to Münster, a course so necessary, as he thought, to the general good. Very far from encouraging it, she declared that only on an *order* from Superiors would she undertake a journey physically impossible for her. But the Dean would not give such an order. Her removal must depend wholly upon herself ; consequently, he would not allow Father Limberg to interpose his authority. He did not, however, relinquish the hope of one day realizing the project, and he tried to win over Dr. Wesener to his way of thinking. The doctor, he thought could gain the Abbé Lambert, and all would turn out as he desired. We read in the doctor's journal:—

" Dean Overberg honored me with a visit for the purpose of explaining how necessary it was for the invalid to go to Münster and submit to a rigorous investigation. His arguments were so forcible that, at last, I began to share his opinion. That evening I spoke to the Abbé, who offered no objection. He only said : ' Well, so be it ! If she freely consents to the arrangement, let it be for the sake of the good that may result from it, but I fear my anxiety and her absence will cause my death ! If she does not consent, I shall defend her to my last breath against any violence that may be used to force her to do so. I am ready to make any sacrifice for the good cause, but why persecute her so cruelly in mind and body ? Take a shorter and easier way ! I will leave Dülmen for as long as may be deemed expedient, and then let them examine her as rigorously as possible.' The good old man was so overcome by emotion that the tears sprang to his eyes, and he could only add : ' I know not what good can come from it. It is a frightful thing thus to persecute the poor child !'

" Next day Dean Overberg and myself being together in her room, she herself turned the conversation upon the point in question, and I explained my reasons. After listening quietly for some time, to my great surprise she announced her firm determination never to consent to her removal from Dülmen. ' Dean Overberg,' she said, ' is so good and kind that he is often imposed upon. He is ready to sacrifice me, as he told me himself, to prove to some good people that the phenomena in my person are not the work of human hands. But how can they, his spiritual children, have so little faith in his word ? He is himself convinced of the truth, and he can at any moment bring forward fresh proofs of the same. Could they find a surer, a more reliable witness?' When I remonstrated that something still more formal was necessary to prove her state she replied: ' If five thousand people do not credit ten of acknowledged veracity, twenty millions will not believe the words of hundreds.' I asked if she would not be willing to sacrifice her life for the salvation of one soul? She answered: ' Certainly! But how am I to know whether such can or will result from my removal, since it has not been ordered by the interior voice which has always guided me, and when, besides, my whole soul revolts from the step? I would like to say more, but it is not yet the time. If, in spite of my interior conviction, I undertook the journey and died on the way, would it not be to the prejudice of my soul, would it not be frustrating God's designs over me? And who can assure me that this would not happen, if the interior voice does not? Truly, as soon as my guide says: " You must go!"—I shall be ready to set out on the instant. Dean Overberg says that I ought to go for Professor von Druffel's sake, whose reputation has been attacked on my account. I would do anything in the world for him or any one else unjustly attacked, provided I could do it lawfully. I wish most heartily that he had published nothing relating to me or my wounds. How often have I not begged you yourself not to publish anything during my lifetime! But why should I risk my life and even more than life to secure to any man a little worldly honor? Where are his humility, his patience, his Christian charity? And, after all, the greater number would not be convinced; for sloth, distrust, self-love, incredulity, avarice, and with many the fear of exchanging their own opinion for even a better one, render men blind to truths as clear as day. If so much importance is attached to the verifying of what takes place in me,

those people who are in good health can come to me. I
cannot with impunity go to them. I consent to all
experiments not against my conscience. If others want
to be convinced, let them do what those who already
believe have done, let them take their place by my bedside and watch me. I cannot at the expense of my own
conscience spare the curious the cost and trouble of coming to me. Let those who are able to travel come to see
me. If I went to them they might attribute it to vanity,
presumption, or even something worse, since it is impossible for me to make the shortest journey without risk.
I surely cannot exhibit myself a spectacle to the curious!
Let them send prudent men whom the people esteem. I am
ready to obey their orders in all that is not prejudicial to
my soul; for the rest, I want nothing. I am nothing but a
poor, sinful creature, and I ask for nothing but a little
quiet, so that forgotten by all, I may pray in peace, suffer
for my own sins, and for the salvation of souls. The
Vicar-General has just returned from Rome. Did he
speak of me to the Holy Father? Thank God, he leaves
me now in peace! O be patient, all ye who are good and
faithful! The Lord will show forth His works to you. If
it be from Him, it will endure; if from man, it will vanish!'

" She uttered the above in a firm, animated voice. Her confessor entered at the moment, but took no part one way or
the other. When she made allusion to some words of the New
Testament, he remarked : ' She is thinking of what Gamaliel
said.' "

Dr. Wesener recounted the above to Dean Overberg
who could not but approve Sister Emmerich's reasoning;
consequently, he refrained from pushing the question further. However, eighteen months later, when Prof. B —

published his calumnies accusing her of imposture and treating the ecclesiastical investigation as a lame affair, the Dean again yielded to his friends' solicitations, and expressed a desire for her removal, although he saw that her weakness would render it impossible for her to go to Münster. Meanwhile, regardless of her remonstrances to the contrary, Dean Rensing publicly refuted the Professor's attacks, an attempt which ended as she had predicted. Prof. B —not only repeated his assertions, but even multiplied them; but with all who were not obstinately oblivious to the truth, they bore no weight. Dean Rensing felt hurt that the invalid did not second his efforts in her defence, and from that moment treated her with marked coldness. Although many were of opinion that she ought to submit to a new investigation for the sake of establishing the truth of the first, yet none of her Superiors undertook to give her a formal command to that effect, as they feared the pain and anxiety consequent on it would cause her death. Such was the state of affairs when, in the fall of 1818, Bishop Michael Sailer arrived in Münster and expressed his desire to visit Dülmen. The Dean was highly gratified, as he looked upon the Bishop as a competent judge in such cases. He procured a permit for him and suggested to Father Limberg that his penitent should give a detailed account of her conscience to him, which suggestion Sister Emmerich most willingly obeyed. Bishop Sailer declared her right in refusing to make the journey as it would endanger her life, and he also thought a repetition of the investigation unjustifiable since that of 1813 had been rigorous enough to satisfy all reasonable minds. The poor invalid was grateful for his decision, and clung to it all the rest of her life. She often said that the Bishop's visit had been productive of happy results for her, inasmuch as it had removed her confessor's fears and given him courage to approve the course she pursued with regard to her removal. She was never after annoyed on this subject.

Sister Emmerich's mother had died by her child's bedside, March 12, 1817, aged eighty years. After the suppression of Agnetenberg, she had visited her daughter only once, when the report of the ecclesiastical investigation reached Flamske ; but, when she felt death approaching, she wished to meet it near her favored child. She was taken to Dülmen, Jan. 3, 1817, and her bed of death placed near her daughter's couch of pain. Sister Emmerich had never forgotten her old mother's spiritual interests. She had asked to be allowed to render her in her last moments all that filial love suggests, her only anxiety being lest her own state of suffering would prove an obstacle to the accomplishment of her heart's desire. Almighty God gratified His servant. She had the consolation of her mother's presence and of doing all that lay in her power toward soothing her dying moments. On December 28, 1817, the doctor to his great surprise found his patient sitting up in bed. On asking for an explanation, he received from Father Limberg the following :—

" Last evening after an ecstasy of two hours, she returned to consciousness without a command and asked me, in an animated tone, if she might get up. I answered in the affirmative, when she sat up so briskly that I was frightened. She remained in that position without support until I ordered her to lie down again. She said : 'My guide took me to a place where I saw the massacre of the Holy Innocents and I beheld how magnificently God recompensed those youthful victims, although they did not and could not actively confess the holy name of Jesus. I admired their immense reward and asked for what I might hope, I who had so long patiently suffered pains and opprobrium for the love of my Saviour. My guide answered: "Much has been dissipated in thy case, and thou hast allowed many things to go to waste; but persevere, be vigilant, for great will be thy reward."—This gave me courage, and I inquired if I would recover the use of my limbs and be able to take food again.—"Thy desires will be gratified," he answered, "thou wilt even be able to eat, but be patient!"—"How!" I exclaimed, "may I get up now?"—"Sit up at the word of thy confessor," he replied, "and wait for the rest. What thou sufferest is not for thyself, but for many others and for Dülmen." Then I awoke and was able to sit up.'"

She continued to improve for a week, as Dr. Wesener's journal records :—

"She can sit up alone, she has even been able to leave her bed once and dress without assistance. I am resolved to make her take some nourishment. When I told her so, I added : 'What will Prof. B — say when he hears that you can sit up and eat?' She answered : 'I know not what is in store for me. I care not for the approbation of men. I am indifferent to their opinion, although I pity their blindness. Shall I suffer insults? I am satisfied, provided it glorify God. If, as His unworthy instrument, I am to show forth something, the Lord will confirm it. May His name be praised!'—She still refused to take food without her confessor's order."

On January 16th, he again writes: "She takes daily without bad effects some spoonfuls of milk and water, equal parts. I think she would now be still more improved, did she not devote herself so exclusively to her sick mother. She rejoices that God in His mercy enables her to make some return for the tender care lavished upon her by that good parent. On Friday, Jan. 17, her wounds not having bled, she began to hope that they would disappear entirely ; but her hope was not to be realized.—Toward the close of January, she was able to take at several different times a little thin broth.

" February 14th—She continues bright and cheerful, although she suffers day and night from the sight of her dying mother whose pains she shares.

" February 21st—She is not so well to-day. Her share in her mother's sufferings appears to be the cause of her languor.

" March 12th—Her mother died this evening. Sister Emmerich is much affected. The thought of not having done enough for her good mother distresses her.

" March 20th—She is in as weak and miserable a state as ever, but she expresses the most touching gratitude to God whose merciful hand supported her during her mother's last illness."

CHAPTER XXXIV.

Clement Brentano--Sister Emmerich's Influence on His Spiritual Life.

Dr. Wesener's journal contains a very significant conversation between Sister Emmerich and himself, Sept. 26, 1815. He had found her in a most deplorable condition from the effects of Gertrude's careless ministrations. He tried to console her by saying that God made use of her sister to purify her and that he felt certain Gertrude, with all her faults, would not be lost. Then followed a long conversation during which she expressed herself in these terms :—

" To serve the neighbor, I have always thought a virtue particularly pleasing to God. When a child, I used to beg for strength to be of use to others, and I now know that my prayer was heard. *But I have yet another task to accomplish before my death. I must reveal many things before I die !* I know that I have to do it, I feel it, but I cannot through the fear of drawing praise upon myself. I feel, too, that this very fear is in itself a fault. I ought to say what I have to say in all simplicity, because it is the will of God and for the sake of truth. But I have not yet looked at it in the right light, and *I must lie here until I have learned to overcome myself entirely.*"

The doctor suggested that the prolongation of her incomprehensible life could only be for the increase of her own personal merit ; otherwise it would be a true purgatory for her. She replied : " God grant it ! Yet it is certain that not for myself do I lie here and suffer. I know why I suffer ! Publish nothing about me before my death. What I have, I have not for myself, I am only an instrument in the hand of God. Just as I can put my little crucifix here or there by my own will, so must I abandon myself to everything that God does or wills in my regard, and I do it with joy. I know, indeed, why I lie here, I know it well, and last night I was again informed of it. I have always asked of God, as a particular grace, to suffer and, if possible, satisfy for the erring; but as this city once received me, a poor peasant-girl whom other convents rejected, I have offered myself up especially for Dülmen, and I have the consolation of knowing that God has heard my prayer. I have already averted a threatening danger, and I hope still to be useful to it."

Three years passed, and no one with sufficient zeal or leisure presented himself to take down Sister Emmerich's contemplations. That task was reserved for Clement Brentano, whom an apparently fortuitous circumstance led to Dülmen. Professor Sailer, of Landshut, with whom Brentano corresponded, informed him of his intention of going during the autumn vacations of 1818 to Münster and Sondermühlen, the residence of Count von Stolberg; he invited him to come from Berlin to Westphalia and accompany him. The Professor's other companion was Christian Brentano. He had seen Sister Emmerich the year before and had interested his brother in her singular case. Clement, therefore, embraced this opportunity of making a short visit to Dülmen. The little city could have few attractions for a man like him, and nothing was further from his thoughts than the idea of a prolonged stay. Sondermühlen had been named as the rendezvous; but Clement having arrived before either the Professor or his brother, resolved to proceed to Münster, see Dean Overberg, and go on to Dülmen by himself.

He records in his journal: " Thursday, Sept. 24, 1818, I arrived in Dülmen, about ten o'clock, a. m , and Dr. Wesener announced my approaching visit to the invalid. We had to pass through a barn and some old store-rooms before reaching the stone steps leading to her room. Her sister answered our knock at the door, and we entered the little kitchen back of which is her small apartment. She saluted me graciously, remarking that she would recognize me from my resemblance to my brother. Her countenance wears the imprint of purity and innocence. It charmed me, as did also the vivacity of her manner in which I could detect no trace of effort or excitement. She does not sermonize, there is none of that mawkish sweetness about her which is so disgusting. She speaks simply and to the point, but her words are full of depth, charity, and life. She put me at my ease at once. I understood everything, I *felt* everything."

The secret of Clement Brentano's gracious reception lay in this—Sister Emmerich now beheld before her the one so long desired, the promised amanuensis who was to note down the communications she had been commanded to make. But what the rough forest tree is to the masterpiece of art for which it is destined, was Clement Brentano to the task in store for him. How will she retain by her side one whose tastes and inclinations tend to a far different sphere ? How will she engage this restless spirit, obedient only to impulse and caprice ? this soul whose long and dangerous wanderings have only within a few months led him into the road of salvation ?—At the end of a few weeks, she avowed to him her own surprise at the turn affairs had taken : "I am amazed at myself," she exclaimed, " speaking to you with so much confidence, communicating so much that I cannot disclose to others. From the first glance, you were no stranger to me ; indeed, I knew you before seeing you. In visions of my future, I often saw a man of very dark complexion sitting by me writing, and when you first entered the room I said to myself, ' Ah! there he is!' "

Clement Brentano's first idea was to weave her marvellous life into a narrative more poetical than historical. "I shall try," he wrote in his journal, "to note down what I learn from the invalid. I hope t) become her biographer." In his poetical enthusiasm, he celebrates her praises in his journal and letters to his friends during the first weeks of his sojourn at Dülmen. "She is a flower of the field, a bird of the forest whose inspired songs are wonderfully significant, yes, even prophetic!"—Again, she is his "wonderful, blessed, charming, lovely, unsophisticated, simple, sprightly friend, sick unto death, living without nourishment, altogether supernatural," etc. And again, "A wise, pure, frank, chaste, tried, sensitive soul of good judgment, and yet perfectly naïve, who reminds him, at every instant, in words, manners, and disposition of one most dear to him." Finally, he indulges the hope of improving her exterior situation;—"All might be rendered more endurable for her were there some faithful creature, pious and intelligent, to relieve her of domestic cares and who, seated by her bedside (the most delightful seat in the world!) might ward off everything that could give her anxiety."

Sister Emmerich was kind and patient with Clement Brentano whose whole life and aspirations formed such a contrast to her own. Her confidence won his heart, and he resolved to await the impatiently desired, but long-delayed arrival of Prof. Sailer and his brother, Christian Brentano. Dülmen possessed few charms for him apart from its miraculous "wild flower." He gives his impressions of the little city in the following pleasing words :—

" This place may have attractions for simple souls. It
is a little agricultural town without art, science, or literature;
no poet's name is a household word here and, in the even-
ings, the cows are milked before their owner's doors. The
people wear wooden shocs, and it is to be regretted that
even the servers at Mass do the same. If a respectable
looking person passes through the street, the children run in
front of him, saluting with a kiss of their little hands.
A beggar will promise for an alms bestowed to make the
" Way of the Cross" with all his family that evening for
his benefactor; indeed, on the the vigils of feasts, this
road, with its pictures of Jesus bearing His Cross, is never
without whole families thus united in prayer. The feminine
employments of the gentler sex are carried on in the fields
and gardens, preparing the flax, spinning the thread, bleaching the linen, etc. ; even the daughters of well-to-do citizens
are dressed no better than servants. Not a romance is
here to be found and, to a certain extent, fashion exists not;
clothes are worn, regardless of style, until no longer fit for
use. The mail passes through the place, for it can boast of
a post-office. The Duke von Croy resides here for six
months in the year with a numerous household at least thirty
persons. And yet, we hear of the wonderful progress of Dülmen in the last ten years and its consequent luxury and
corruption ! "

Sister Emmerich's patience and kindness, the permission
accorded by her confessor to visit her several times daily,
the interest she manifested in the recital of his past life—
all concurred to reconcile Brentano to the privations imposed by his stay in Dülmen. Accustomed to act on first
impulses, he was unable to resist the interest shown in his
spiritual welfare. But whilst his only thought was, in his own
poetical words, to lend an ear to the " prophetic strains of the

wild forest bird," Sister Emmerich labored most earnestly
for his soul. She hid her own sufferings and sacrifices under
the veil of gentle sweetness and forbearance lest they
should intimidate this novice in the spiritual life. All her
desires in his behalf tended to one end—to reconcile him
perfectly with God, to renew his interior life by filial submission to the Church. She felt that her visions would be
realized in his regard, only when his lofty intellect should
bend to the yoke of Jesus Christ, when religion should
mould and vivify his every thought and action. Her words
fell like good seed on the soil of his heart. They
germinated unknown to himself. They began to produce their
fruit even whilst he indulged no higher hope than that of
gleaning fresh matter for his poems. The very novelty of
his position proved an attraction to his highly-gifted soul.
It was something new and strange, and it wove its magic
spell around his heart disgusted by indulgence in worldly
pleasures and pursuits. Brentano, or the " *Pilgrim*" (1),
as we shall often style him, seemed led to Dülmen by a
chain of merely fortuitous circumstances. But Sister Emmerich saw therein the direction of Divine Providence, and
it was not long before he was himself convinced that the
unforeseen prolongation of his stay might exercise a most
salutary influence over his life. It is always difficult for a
man to comprehend the call of God, to run counter to his
inclinations, and to free himself from old habits, in order to
respond to it; but for Clement Brentano, with his rich nature, his past life teeming with stirring events, there were
many things which, judging from a human point of
view, seemed to render him in spite of his rare gifts less
proper than another for carrying out the designs of God.
He had just completed his fortieth year on his arrival in

(1) Sister Emmerich used to designate him by this title.

Dülmen. But a very short time had elapsed since his
reconciliation with Almighty God, his whole life having
been spent far away from the Church of whose teachings
he knew but little. A short time before his acquaintance
with the invalid, he had written to one of his friends : " The
forms of Catholic worship are to me as unintelligible, as repulsive as those of the synagogue. I feel that I am not
happy ; but I feel, too, that if I seek peace in Catholicism,
I shall find myself in such perplexity and embarrassment
as to render my position worse than before. When I turn
to the Catholic Church, I meet at every step a thousand
things to disconcert me."—He was, on the contrary, so attracted by the pietism of a Protestant minister of Berlin
that he said :

"The excellent Mr. H.'s church has, for the first time in
my life, impressed me with the idea of a community.
Nothing repulses, all attracts. Although the Catholic Church
no longer has charms for me, yet through a certain reluctance to separate from her, I do not go to Mr. H.'s." This
reluctance for which he could not account, prevented his
taking the final step ; but the following fearful words show
how broad was the abyss which existed between him and
the fold of Christ : " The magical infusion of the spirit of
God by the imposition of hands, has for me no more reality
than the possibility of imposing poetical genius by the crowning of the poet-laureate ; "—and again : " What an abyss
between the Lord's Supper and the Host in our ostensor-
ium !" (1) In these dispositions he set out on his quest
for *truth.* He plunged into the writings of Jacob Böhme
and Saint-Martin ; he expressed his enthusiasm over the
pseudo-mystic sect of Boos and Gossner, in which he
thought he saw " a faithful picture of apostolic times and a

(1) See Brentano's Correspondence, Vol. I., page 180, etc.

manifestation very formidable to the See of Rome;" and,
whilst thus drifting away from the true source, he uttered
the following unjust and bitter words against the Church:
—"Among whom is the teaching of Jesus best seen?
among the Papists, the Protestants, the Reformers, the
Greeks, the Mennonites, the Moravians? Where?—Let
each judge as best he can. If they tell me the Catholics
are right, I answer: Why, then, must the Bible be taken
from them that they may remain Catholic? He that is
right is Jesus! He alone is the Mediator, between Him
and men there is no other. The only knowledge we can
have of Him comes from His own teachings, from nature,
and from man's own heart in relations the most intimate with
Him   It is my duty to shun whatever could disquiet me
or remove me from Him. When an authoritative voice
calls out to me: 'Here, here, this is the right way! You
must do so and so, the true Church commands it!'—I get
perplexed, I undergo a species of torment!"—It is true
that Brentano had, indeed, approached the Sacraments;
but, at the time of his arrival in Dülmen, his ideas of faith
were still very shadowy, and it was only when under the
influence of Sister Emmerich's blessed presence that his
soul found peace. In his wanderings he had involuntarily
uttered a cry for deliverance: "I need a guide, one to introduce me into a region in which I may breathe a divine
atmosphere of piety and innocence; one to lead me like a
blind man, for I cannot trust myself!"—Now, truly, did he
experience the irresistible power of such an atmosphere.
He saw the sufferings imposed upon this innocent victim,
he saw the humble simplicity of her life in God; in her he
beheld the magnificence of the Church, the power and
truth of the Catholic faith. Not her visions, not the communications she made to him, not the supernatural attrac-

tion he himself experienced, made the deepest impression upon him ; but her holiness, her faith whose principles regulated her every action, produced in him an emotion which found utterance in the following words :—" An entirely new world has here opened out before me! How thoroughly Christian is the sufferer! Now for the first time have I an idea of what the Church really is!"—The eighth day after his arrival he wrote in his journal :—

" I have left the post-house at which I first put up, and taken two small rooms in the same house with the invalid. Her apartment is in the rear. It is a tavern and a bakery belonging to her confessor's brother. I have made this arrangement to be able to observe her more closely, and I shall remain here at least two weeks.

" I shall soon be familiar with her exterior life, since it does not require much observation to understand the outer life of one so completely separated from the world. I shall note down my impressions without following any precise order, until I find some determinate point from which I can embrace all.

" The poor invalid's position is embarrassing, no careful female attendance. I see this with sorrow at every instant. Her sister is ignorant and awkward. The invalid has to help her in all the household arrangements, but she never complains, she bears all patiently. One day I found her lying helpless under a pile of damp linen which had been carelessly thrown on her bed. She could not stir under its weight. All this coarse, damp linen had to be examined with her wounded hands before being mangled, her fingers were blue and stiff with the cold. Half the day was often spent in such occupation. If in her life-like contemplations she made a gesture or spoke some word, her rude, ignorant sister treated her as a servant would a sick child in the delirium of fever, roughly bidding her be still.

" Her life, a perpetual martyrdom on account of her horrible bodily and mental sufferings, is besides worn out by indiscreet visitors ; but she is ever kind and gracious, seeing in it all the designs of God to try and humble her. She is most grateful to me for any little effort to relieve her and thanks warmly for it. She is carelessly and negligently attended by those around and even when they have a good will, they are awkward and unskilful ; for instance, in the wall by her bed is a crack which admits a strong current of air. No one thought of stopping it up, although it could easily have been done. I covered it with a piece of oil-cloth, for which she was very thankful.

" In spite of her pitiful situation, I always find her affable and cheerful. From her miserable bed she cannot cast a glance even upon the light of heaven or see the trees before her window in the garden below, she who grew up amid the rural scenes of the paternal cot, she whose relations with nature were so close and intimate !

" On Friday, Oct. 9th, I saw with fright and horror all her wounds. Her confessor wished me to see them that I might be able to testify to their truth. The mark of the lance in the right side produces a most affecting impression. I thought it about two and a half inches long. It reminded me of a pure and silent mouth whose lips are scarcely parted. Besides the double forked cross on her breastbone, there is a Latin one of an inch in breadth on her stomach, the discharge from which is not blood, but water. I saw to-day the wounds of the feet bleeding. It pierces one to the soul to see this poor body signed with so marvellous a seal, this body incapable of movement, saving the hands and feet, which can neither lie at full length nor sit up straight, which is surmounted by a head crowned with the pains of the thorny garland, whose countenance breathes benevolence and affection, and from whose pure lips escape only words of consolation and encouragement, words of fervent and humble prayer. By the couch of this holy soul, taught not by men but by the Lord, His angel, and the saints from her early youth, I learn a thousand things which throw new light on the Church and the Communion of saints. What wonderful, what soul-stirring experiments are daily made upon her by her confessor! What impresses me most is the power of the sacerdotal character over her. If she is in ecstasy and he presents to her the fingers that have received the holy unction, she raises her head and follows their every movement; when they are withdrawn, she sinks down heavily upon her bed. Any priest whatever may exercise the same power over her. Whoever, like myself, has had an opportunity of witnessing this, must feel convinced that the Church alone has priests and that sacerdotal ordination is certainly something more than an empty ceremony. Once I heard her say with tears: ' The consecrated fingers of priests will be recognizable in purgatory; yes, even in hell they will be known and they will burn with a particular fire. Every one will discover the priestly character and load the owner with scorn.'

" How great and touching is her obedience to the priestly command! When it is time for her sister to arrange her bed, her confessor exclaims: ' Sister Emmerich, arise in obedience !'—she awakes with a start, and makes an effort to rise. I asked him to give the command in Latin and in a low tone. He was seated at a little distance saying his breviary. He arose, drew near the bed, and in a tone so low that the words were indistinguishable, said : ' Tu debes obedire et surgere, veni!' (1). Instantly she sprang up, though with difficulty, as if about to throw herself from the

(1) " **Arise in obedience, come !"**

bed. Father Limberg asked in alarm : ' What are you doing ?'—to which she answered : Some one calls me !'—At the order : ' Lie down again !'—she sank down at once.

" This sudden awaking at the priest's command always affects me deeply, and I pity the poor thing snatched without warning from her visions, from the world of light in which alone she truly lives, and cast into this dark, sad region in which everything shocks and wounds her. It fills me with such horror as I might feel on seeing a sick child, playing among the flowers, suddenly caught up on a pitch-fork and flung into a cold, dark dungeon. But suffering is her portion and, although it costs her a struggle, she thanks with a gracious smile for this very suffering. Her obedience is not involuntary and, though there be an irresistible force at work, yet her docile soul is always ready, like a submissive child, to obey. I have heard her say at the moment of awaking : ' I must go ! Yes, I am coming !'—or : ' I cannot ! my feet are nailed ! Loosen my feet !'—referring to the invariable position of her feet which cross one over the other like those of the Crucified. On returning to consciousness it costs an effort to separate them. Then she rubs her eyes, becomes fully awake when sprinkled with holy water, makes the sign of the cross, and takes up her chaplet if perchance it had fallen from her hand during her ecstasy.

" She acknowledged to me once that this sudden returning to consciousness is most painful to her. It is as if in some unexpected way she had fallen among strangers who could neither understand her nor she them. When her friends attempt to relieve her at such moments, their assistance only adds to her pain.

" Again I requested the confessor to give his order in writing, and he dashed off the words : ' Be obedient !

rise!'—She was absorbed in ecstasy, on her head a double head-dress and a linen covering. The paper was laid upon it, she sighed and sat up on the instant. 'What do you want?' demanded Father Limberg. 'To get up! Some one calls me,' she answered. But when he took the writing from her head and bade her 'Lie down!'—she again became immovable. I kept the paper, and I am going to try its effect on her in Father Limberg's absence."

The confessor having given permission for the trial, the Pilgrim made it some days later, as he himself tells us :—

" This evening as she lay in ecstasy, her confessor absent, I laid the written order upon her breast, and as usual she instantly awoke.

" To-day she swooned several times from pain. They gave her musk, which she invariably vomited, and then they rubbed her stomach with opium. Lying like a corpse she submitted to all. I was standing at some distance, distressed at her sufferings. At one time she inclined her head slightly to me. To all that her confessor said, she answered out of her deep swoon: ' Yes! Yes!'—In the midst of this deathlike state, she displayed the most touching obedience and resignation. The other day she said to me : 'I had very much to suffer last night; but when I can suffer in peace, it is sweet! Then it is sweet to think of God. One thought of God is more to me than the whole world. Remedies do me no good, I cannot endure them. Sometimes I am left to languish, and then again all sorts of things are tried on me ; but this also must I bear!' "

It was only by degrees that the Pilgrim understood the deep humility which seemed to have become a part of her nature. His journal says :

" I expressed my desire of procuring an educated person possessed of simple piety and good judgment as a nurse for her. She began to cry like a child, saying that she herself had no education. I replied that she had mis-understood me, the qualifications I had mentioned were not wanting to her, and that it was for her own good I wished her to have such a companion. But she repeated the same words, until, at last, I grew a little impatient. I thought she misunderstood me. In a suppliant tone, she said : ' I do not wish to offend you, I have not those quali-fications ; ·but God is good to me !' "

As Brentano had tested the power of the priest's word, so now did he witness that of his blessing. He writes : "She said to me to-day : ' My bodily and spiritual sufferings and my frightful visions almost kill me. I am parched with thirst and I cannot move to get a drop of water.'— At these words I presented her a drink, having first wet the rim of the glass with holy water, and she exclaimed : ' It is wine ! Wine from the garden of the Church !'

"Once as I was sitting in her room whilst she lay in con-templation, she began to moan. I approached her with a glass that was standing near and which usually held holy water. I was alarmed at her livid paleness and I asked if she would have a drink. She shook her head and answer-ed in a weak voice : ' A little fresh water blessed by the hand of the priest. There are two priests near, they pos-sess the divine power, but they forget me whilst I languish. God wills that I should live upon blessed water. Ah ! will they let me die ?'—I ran to the Abbé Lambert's room close by and there, indeed, was her confessor whom we all thought absent. He blessed some fresh water which she drank saying: ' I feel better !'—Then he said jestingly : ' Come with me in obedience !'—She tried like a dying person to rise, but sank back swooning as the command had not been given seriously. The scene moved me deeply, yet I dared not say a word for fear of giving offence ; but the tears sprang to my eyes at the sight of her uncomplaining endurance of such trials.

" At another time, I heard her utter the following words : ' How sad that the priests of our day are so neglectful of their power, we might even say ignorant of what the sacerdotal benediction is ! Many of them hardly believe in it. They blush at a blessing as if it were a superstitious and antiquated ceremony, whilst some never reflect upon the power given them by Jesus Christ. When they neglect to give me a blessing, I receive it sometimes from God Himself ; but as Our Lord has instituted the priesthood and imparted to it the power to bless, I languish with desire for it. The whole Church is but one body. All must be deprived of what one member refuses to bestow. ' ''

The pilgrim had daily evidence of the above, and he was sorely tried whenever she called for blessed water in her confessor's absence. One day as she lay in a burning fever, her throat parched and dry, he went for a glass of fresh water which, with the best intention in the world, he blessed himself before entering the room. The invalid took it with a smile and the words : " Ah ! why are you not a priest ! "—And, to his amazement, she told him that she had seen him blessing it through the closed door. This made upon him a deep impression which was increased when he suddenly became aware that his inmost thoughts were read by her. Once whilst conversing with her, the thought occurred to him that she would, perhaps, soon die ; and he remembered having read that a certain Pope had had one of the hands of a person favored with extraordinary graces cut off— just at this point, she smilingly interrupted the conversation with the words : " You are thinking of my death, and you want to cut off my hand ! "—We find the following remarks in his journal : " Truly, this obviates the trouble of thinking ! It is very easy to make one's self understood by a person who not only reads one's soul, but who even anticipates the undeveloped thought ! "

Soon there arose in the Pilgrim a desire to profit by the great grace conferred upon him of communicating with this privileged soul. He says : " I have seen her in prayer. Her wounded hands, the middle fingers of which are always in pain, lay joined upon her breast and slightly curved inward. She seemed to smile, and her countenance wore the expression of one who both sees and speaks, although the lips and eyes were closed. The sight affected me. The blessed peace, the deep devotion of her childlike countenance awoke in me a keen sense of my own unworthiness, of my guilty life. In the silent solemnity of this spectacle, I stood as a beggar, and sighing I said in my heart : ' Thou pure soul, pray for me a poor, sinful child of earth who cannot help himself ! '

" I feel that I must stay here, that I must not leave this admirable creature before her death. I feel that my mission is here, and that God has heard the prayer I made when I begged Him to give me something to do for His glory that would not be above my strength. I shall endeavor to gather and preserve the treasures of grace that I have here before my eyes."

This conviction becoming daily more profound, Brentano makes the following significant avowal : —

" The marvels that surround me, the childlike innocence, the peace, patience, and wonderful intuition of spiritual things I behold in this poor, illiterate peasant-girl, by whom a new world has been opened up to me, make me feel keenly the misery of my own life of sin and trouble, as well as the folly of the generality of mankind. I see in another light the value of perishable goods, and I shed tears of bitter repentance over my soul's lost beauty and innocence!. . . .

"She went to confession to-day, fell into ecstasy as soon as it was over, and recited her penance with extended arms. I gazed in rapture on her holy expression. All that I have ever beheld in art or in life representative of piety, peace, and innocence, sinks into insignificance compared with her. On the approach of my next confession, I was seized with intense contrition and I commended myself to her prayers. She consoled me and sent me to the dear Mother of God. 'Ah!' she exclaimed, 'the dear Mother of God! she knows us poor creatures well and she leads us to Jesus, her Child. O what treasures of grace there are in the Church! Be comforted! We have in this treasure wherewith to be encouraged!' . . . . I feel again that the Church is for her something that I, in my blindness, cannot yet comprehend; and I ponder over all that I have here received, upon all that I have learned for the first time. I compare with it my past disorderly life, and a new longing for conversion is aroused in my soul. In this frame of mind, I penned a letter to her, telling her of my sadness and begging her prayers for my conversion. She received it kindly. I did not see her read it, but she knew well all it contained and, perhaps, much more besides . . . . . .

"The kindness and confidence shown me by this privileged creature encourage me, do me the greatest good, for she is so truly, so sincerely Christian. None ever knew as she the misery of my soul, the enormity of my sins. I myself know them not as they really are; but she knows them, she weighs and measures with a clear-sightedness unknown to me. She consoles and helps me . . . . .

"Now I understand the Church. I see that she is infinitely more than an assemblage of individuals animated by the same sentiments. Yes, she is the body of Jesus Christ who, as her Head, is essentially united to her, and who maintains with her intimate and constant relations. And now, too, do I see what an immense treasure of gifts and graces the Church has received from God who communicates Himself to men only in and by her."

These last remarks refer to a conversation held with the invalid in which she had unquestionably established the purity and truth of the Catholic faith. Ruled by false mysticism, which made him look upon the Church "as a community of the children of God without distinction of outward profession," Brentano had one day shortly after his arrival expressed himself in glowing terms " of brethren separated in body but united in soul, since all belong to the universal Church." He was not a little surprised to receive the following grave and conclusive reply : " The *Church* is only one, the Roman Catholic ! And if there were left upon earth but one Catholic, he would be the one, universal Church, the Catholic Church, the Church of Jesus Christ against which the gates of hell shall never prevail."—When he objected that all that believe in Jesus Christ are sons of God, she replied ; " If Jesus Christ declares that the children of God should love and honor Him as their Father, they should also call the dear Mother of God their mother and love her as their mother. The *Our Father* is for him who does not understand this, who does not do it, simply a vain formula; he is far from being a child of God." – Then, returning to the subject of the Church, she continued : " The knowledge of the greatness and magnificence of this Church in which the Sacraments are preserved in all their virtue and inviolable sanctity is, unhappily, **rare in these**

our days, even among the clergy. It is because so many
priests are ignorant of their own dignity that so many of
the faithful forget theirs and comprehend not the expression
to belong to the Church! That no human power may ever
destroy it, Almighty God has attached an indelible character to Holy Orders. Were there but a single priest on earth
rightly ordained, Jesus Christ would live in His Church
as God and Man in the Most Holy Sacrament of the altar ;
and whoever would receive this Sacrament, after being ab-
solved by the priest, would alone be truly united to God.

" It is something grand but, at the same time, something
impossible without true interior light, without purity and
simplicity of heart, to live in accordance with the faith of
this Holy Church ; to celebrate with her the divine worship
and thereby participate in the infinite treasure of grace and
satisfaction she possesses in the merits of her Divine Head ;
and, through His merits, to share in the blood of her innumerable martyrs, in the penance and sufferings of her saints, in
the prayers and good works of the devout faithful. This treasure she communicates without diminishing to all in union
with her, to all her true children. It is from it that she
draws wherewith to satisfy the justice of God, to liquidate
for the living as well as for the souls in purgatory, the debts
which they themselves could never cancel. Every hour
has its own particular grace ; he who rejects it, languishes
and perishes. As there is an earthly year with its seasons,
an earthly nature with its creatures, its fruits and its peculiar properties ; so also does there exist an economy of a
higher order for the restoration of our fallen race. It has innumerable graces and means of salvation all linked together
in the course of the spiritual year which, too, has its different seasons. Each year, each day, each hour ripens these
fruits for our eternal salvation. The children of the Cath-

olic Church that piously celebrate the spiritual year with its
feasts and ceremonies, that regulate their life according to its
prescriptions, that recite the holy Canonical Hours, alone
are faithful laborers in the vineyard, they alone will reap
abundant benedictions.   It is sad to behold in our times so
few that understand this economy of divine grace and conform their life thereto. But a day will come on which, con-
science-stricken, they will at last comprehend what the ecclesiastical year is, with its feasts and seasons and days consecrated to God, its public and private devotions, its Canonical
Hours, its breviary recited by priests and religious.   It is
the Divine Saviour Himself who abides with us in this order
of things, who gives Himself to us at all times as food and victim, that we may become *one* with Him.   How strikingly do
not His untiring mercy and solicitude for us shine forth in
the thousands of Masses in which the propitiatory sacrifice,
His bloody death upon the cross, is daily renewed in an
unbloody manner and offered for us to the Heavenly Father!
This sacrifice of the cross is an eternal sacrifice, a sacrifice
of infinite efficacy, unalterable and ever new. But men must
profit by it in time which is finite and during which all things
are taken into account.   In accordance with the precept
of the Son of God made man, this thrice holy Sacrifice
shall be daily renewed until the account is filled up and
the temporal existence of the world shall reach its term ;
for it is Jesus Christ Himself who, by the hands of lawfully
ordained priests (even were they otherwise unworthy) offers
Himself to His Heavenly Father under the species of bread
and wine for our reconciliation."

When Sister Emmerich held such conversations with the
Pilgrim, she profited by the opportunity to exhort him to
prayer, to the practice of penance, to Christian charity, to
self-victory and renunciation, and all in so simple and natural

a manner that her remarks penetrated his soul less as words
of exhortation than of consolation, or as the necessary consequence of what she had previously said and which he had
recognized to be true.

When unable to hold long conversations, she begged his
prayers as a spiritual alms for herself or some intention
recommended to her, or prescribed to him certain pious exercises, certain prayers, encouraging him to hope in God and
thus unite himself more closely with the Church. She
would use arguments like the following :—" We enjoy the
goods left us by our parents and ancestors, but we forget
what we owe them in return How they sigh for our gratitude! How much they need our help ! They cry : 'Suffer, pray, give alms for us ! Offer the Holy Mass for us ! '"
When he asked what he could do for his deceased parents,
she advised him, besides prayers and alms-giving, to impose
upon himself for a certain time determinate practices of
self-renunciation, patience, sweetness, and interior mortification.

The Pilgrim could not, indeed, resist the force of Sister Emmerich's words. But there was one opinion dear to
his heart and of which he scarcely wished to be disabused :
viz., the possibility of practising piety, of being very agreeable to Almighty God even without actual and exterior union
with the Church. He alleged as a proof of this that, numbers
of non-Catholics are better than some Catholics living in
communion with the Church, whose sad state in many
countries he painted so eloquently that Sister Emmerich
dared not reply. She saw plainly that her arguments
would have no effect upon him at the time. One day she
herself turned the conversation on this point:

" My spiritual guide has reproached me severely for having listened with too much complaisance to your eulogy of

pious heretics. He asked whether I had forgotten who I
am and to whom I belong. He says that I am a virgin of the
Catholic Church, consecrated to God and bound by holy
vows; I ought to praise God in the Church and pray with
sincere pity for heretics. I know better than others what
the Church really is, and I ought on that account to praise
the members of Jesus Christ in the Church, His Body ; as
to those who are separated from this Body and who inflict
cruel wounds upon It, I ought to commiserate them and
pray for their conversion. In praising the disobedient,
one participates in their faults ; such praises are not charitable, since true zeal for the salvation of souls is cooled by
them. It is well for me that I have been reproved on this
head, for we must not be too indulgent when there is question of things so holy. I, indeed, behold many good people among heretics who inspire me with great compassion ,
but I see, also, that they are children whose origin dates
back no further than their own times. They are drifting
about without helm or pilot, and they are incessantly split-
ting up into parties one against the other. A movement
toward piety which at times affects them, emanates
from the Catholic stock to which they formerly belonged ;
but it is soon counteracted by another in an opposite
direction, a spirit of ignorance and indocility which urges
them to rise in rebellion against their common Mother.
They are eager to practise piety, but not Catholicity.
Although they pretend that ceremonies and lifeless forms
are of no importance, and that Almighty God must be served
in spirit and in truth, yet do they obstinately hold to their
own forms which are in reality dead, to forms of their own invention, which are in consequence ever changing.
These forms are not the result of internal development, a
body animated by a soul; they are mere skeletons. It

is for this reason that they who practise them are infected with pride and cannot bend their necks to the yoke. How, in truth, could they possess humility of heart, they who are not taught from their infancy to humble themselves, who confess not their sins and their miseries, who are not accustomed, like the children of the Church, to accuse themselves in the Sacrament of Penance before the representative of God ? Behold, then, why I see even in the best among such people only defects, presumption, obstinacy, and pride. The only heretics that are not in a positively dangerous position, are they who, wholly ignorant of the Church out of which there is no salvation, practise piety as far as they know how ; but as soon as God gives them the least doubt, they should regard it as a call from Heaven and seek to know the truth. Heretics become members of the Church by holy Baptism, if validly administered. They live only by the Church and have, in point of spiritual nourishment, only what falls to them from the Church ; but they do not sit at table with the children of the house, they are outside insulting and boasting, or dying of starvation. When in vision I behold baptized heretics returning to the Church, they appear to come in through the walls before the altar and the most Blessed Sacrament ; whilst the non-baptized, Jews, Turks, and Pagans, are shown to me as entering by the door."

One day she expressed her thoughts by means of the following symbolical picture.

"I beheld two cities, the one on the right, the other on the left. A beautiful avenue of flowering trees led to the city on the left ; but the flowers fell to the ground one after another, no fruit was to be seen. My conductor said to me : ' Notice how much poorer this new city is than the old one on the right.' The city itself was full of windings and streets, but all within was dead. Then my conductor drew my attention to the old city on the right. In many parts it presented a more irregular and dilapidated appearance than the other; but all around arose magnificent trees covered with fruit. In it there were no poor, save those who neglected to gather the fruit or take care of the trees, which were of great age and rose majestically to heaven. The trees on the left appeared neglected, their branches broken, and the fruit fallen; but on the right, they were healthy, vigorous, and laden with fruit."

The Pilgrim was still more disconcerted when he saw how uncompromisingly Sister Emmerich condemned the false mysticism of Boos and Gossner, their secret practices and their adherents. As she herself had once been looked upon as a clairvoyant by the supporters of mesmerism, so now in the early stage of his acquaintance with her, the Pilgrim was tempted to see in her an illustration of his pet mysticism; but a closer study of her demeanor, her purity of faith, her respect for ecclesiastical authority soon led to a more just appreciation. One day he spoke warmly in praise of the sect. She replied: "Yes, I know Gossner. He is abominable to me! he is a dangerous man! The hard, obstinate Boos, too, is abhorrent to me! It would take a great deal to save him." The Pilgrim then spoke of Marie Oberdorfer, one of the foremost in the circle of false mystics, as of a woman highly favored by Heaven, and he supported his opinion upon that of an ecclesiastic whom he greatly esteemed. Sister Emmerich suddenly exclaimed: "Enlightened! What is that?" and upon his explaining that it meant light for the understanding of the Holy Scriptures, she replied: "Such light as you speak of is of no account, but great is the grace of the true children of the Church! They alone, by their sin-

cere and obedient confession of the only true Catholic faith,
by their living communion with the visible Church, are on
the right road to the Heavenly Jerusalem. As to those
who presume to revolt against the Church and her spiritual
authority, who pretend that they alone possess understanding, who call themselves 'the communion of saints,'
they have no real light, for they are not of the faithful;
they wander, sepaated from God and His Churcr. I behold even among the best of them, neither humility, simplicity, nor obedience, but only pride, frightful pride. They
are terribly vain of the separation in which they live. They
speak of faith, of light, of living Christianity, but they con-
temn and outrage the Holy Church in which alone light and
life should be sought. They exalt themselves above the
ecclesiastical power and hierarchy, paying neither submission nor respect to spiritual authority; they presump-
tuously pretend that they comprehend everything better
than the heads of the Church, better than her holy Doctors;
they reject good works but, at the same time, are eager to
possess perfection, they who, with all their so-called light,
deem neither obedience, nor mortification, nor penance, nor
disciplinary rules necessary. I see them straying ever
further and further from the Church, and I see of how much
evil they are productive."

As the Pilgrim was shocked by her severe condemnation,
which grated harshly upon his own opinions, she returned,
again and again, to the same subject:—

"I always see these 'Illuminati' in a certain connection
with the coming of Antichrist; for, by their secrets, by
their injustice, they forward the accomplishment of that
mystery of iniquity."

Brentano dared not contradict her words, but it was long
before he fully understood that they attacked false mysti-

cism in its very essence. No errors entail consequences so disastrous as that pride of intellect which impels men to aim at union with the Divinity apart from the painful road of penance, without the practice of Christain virtue, and with no other guide than that interior sentiment which they regard as an infallible sign of Christ's workings in the soul. " Christ for us! Christ in us!" such is the watchword of these sectaries. They reject the decisions of the Church, they shake off the yoke of faith and the Commandments, and they level every barrier between them and the baneful influence of their theories. Brentano had not, indeed, fully accepted these teachings, but he had looked upon them favorably, and their pet expressions, "Spirit, Love, Light, Way to God, Dwelling in God, Operations of God, the Word of God in us, etc.," held out to him the possibility of attaining their end in the sweetest and easiest way. But in the vicinity of this true servant of God, his delusions vanished. With all the energy of his soul, he now began to cultivate that pure, strong faith which he saw to be the fundamental principle, the essential element whence she herself drew the strength to accomplish the work assigned her.

On October 22d, Bishop Sailer and Christian Brentano arrived in Dülmen. Clement, at first, thought of returning with them to Berlin; but he yielded finally to Sister Emmerich's advice to remain a while longer to continue the work of his spiritual regeneration.

"God is good to me!" he exclaimed gratefully. "Sister Emmerich does wonderful things for me. I have become her disciple!" He truly desired to treat her as his spiritual teacher, to be most submissive to her; but we shall soon see how often his resolution was broken. As his position, attainments, and mental endowments were super-

ior to the invalid's surroundings, so also was his appreciation
of her and her extraordinary gifts clearer and more elevated. Eager not to lose a word that fell from her lips, particularly when in vision, he regarded as time lost every
moment not devoted to himself and such communications.
He aimed at deriving the greatest possible advantage both
for himself and others, and consequently the crowds of
sick and poor who claimed her aid, the time devoted to
the direction of the little household —all annoyed him, all
grieved his impulsive nature, little used to contradiction.
The doctor no longer dared ask advice about his patients,
the confessor speak of his spiritual duties, or the Abbé entertain her with his infirmities ; Gertrude must be removed,
the door must be closed to the few visitors from Flamske ;
and, above all, her old companions of Agnetenberg
must be denied admittance, in order that nothing might
divert her from the one great object—the Pilgrim and the
communication of her visions. His intention seemed to
him most laudable, his demands most just. He assured
her with tears that he would willingly employ his intellect,
spend his life itself in making known to the world the
wondrous favors Almighty God had bestowed upon her,
His chosen instrument of mercy. All Sister Emmerich's
tact was unavailing to restore harmony between her friends
and this impatient, requiring man, unaccustomed to self-
control. No other remedy could be devised than that of
his temporary withdrawal from Dülmen ; and, accordingly
at her earnest request and on the assurance of a gracious
reception at some future day, Brentano left the little city,
Jan., 1819, to be absent until the following May. It,
was long, however, before he attained that liberty of soul
necessary to fulfil the task allotted him by God.

CHAPTER XXXV.

THE PILGRIM'S RETURN.—RUMORS OF A NEW INVESTIGATION.

To leave Dülmen was very painful to the Pilgrim, but Sister Emmerich's kind words reconciled him. "We shall meet again," she said. "You will again taste many consolations and write many things here at my bedside. I would have died long ago, if I had not a special mission to fulfil through you." Father Limberg also had given him the assurance of a kindly reception on his return which, however, was not to be at too early a date and only to be countenanced on the condition that he would not impose his presence on the invalid in such a way as to exclude all others. The good Father, nevertheless, shared the sentiments of the old Abbé and Dr. Wesener. He would have been well satisfied never to have seen Mr. Brentano again, for all knew that, in spite of his protestations, a repetition of the last three months' scenes might lawfully be expected. Such considerations, however, weighed little against the invalid's own conviction that the Pilgrim was destined to the perfect accomplishment of her mission. He, on his side, suspected not how painful it was to her to authorize his return, or what she suffered on his account. On Dec. 2{, 1818, he had written the following :—

"She was very much exhausted this morning from cutting out and making up clothes for poor children, but she bore my questioning with inexpressible patience. She was weak and feverish, and answered with an effort. She asked me afterward if she had not repeated the same thing several times. I did not, at first, remark her great exhaustion. I begged pardon whenever I put a question, to which she invariably replied, 'It is nothing!—'" The Pilgrim, unaccustomed to self-control, could pass from the most joyous mood to one of profound melancholy at the slightest contradiction of his wishes or plans. At such moments the invalid would try to calm him with words like the following :— "Never yet have I confided so much to any one as to you. I have never spoken so freely to any one before, but I have been ordered to do so." Persuaded that no one understood her as well as he did himself, he was too much inclined to attribute her confidence to his own personal influence, and on that account he felt justified in wishing to remove from her vicinity all that could annoy her. Scarcely had he returned to Berlin than he began to take measures for re-establishing himself by the invalid as soon as possible, and to this effect he wrote to Dülmen. The impression produced upon the Abbé Lambert by the news would be difficult to describe. He implored Sister Emmerich with tears to forbid the return of so importunate a guest. She could hardly calm the old priest, usually so gentle and indulgent, but now more persistent in his request as he was supported by Dr. Wesener. Both thought her life drawing toward its close, and wished not to be deprived of the consolation they experienced in their intercourse with her by an intruder, for such they deemed the Pilgrim. His intellectual superiority crushed them, they felt that he thought them incapable of appreciating her high privileges. Various circumstances combined to aggravate the Abbé's uneasiness : the Pilgrim's stay at Dülmen had already attracted attention throughout Münster, and he had also aroused suspicion by his inconsiderate freedom of speech ; in Dülmen itself it was not understood how he, a perfect stranger, could gain so easy and continual access to the invalid ; the most contradictory surmises were circulated on the subject, and it was only his charity to the poor, his piety, and his simplicity of life that disarmed the malevolent.   The Abbé also dreaded a new investigation, and not without reason ; for, by means of the Pilgrim, the report was spread in Münster that since Christmas, 1818, a change had taken place in the bleeding of her wounds.   On Dec. 6th, Sister Emmerich said whilst in ecstasy : " My guide hast said to me : ' If thy wounds are withdrawn from thee, thou shalt suffer greater pains.   Tell this to thy confessor, and do what he says.'   I replied : ' Ah ! I would rather have the sufferings than the wounds ! I am so afraid, I am so ashamed !' "

On the 23d, Dr. Wesener records the following :—

" I have visited her every day since the end of October, but I find no change, nothing new in her physical condition. In the early part of November, we moved her into the little room next the one she was then occupying.   This caus(d some confusion and bustle and gave us a fresh proof of her weakness and nervousness.   She was quite overcome, began to vomit, and lay in this state for two weeks.   Her hands and feet bled as usual on Fridays, her head all the time." From Friday, Dec. 25th, he made the following entries :—

" To-day, Christmas, her head, the cross on her breast, and the wounds in her side have bled more freely than for a long time ; but the skin around the wounds of her hands and feet is white and dry, the crusts of a clear brown.

" Dec. 28th—The crusts fell from her hands and feet. There appeared on the upper part of both a long transparent mark ; and on the opposite surface is a slight induration also of an oblong form. The pain has increased instead of diminishing.

" Friday, Jan. 1st—The wounds of her head and side bled as usual, but not those of her hands and feet.

" Good-Friday, April 9th—The invalid has lain for a week in a state of inexpressible suffering. To the tortures of her stigmata are added bronchial catarrh and cough, pains in the throat and breast. *The wounds of her hands and feet reopened to-day.* I found them bleeding this morning at ten o'clock. Sister Emmerich showed them to me sadly and begged me to say nothing about it. . . . . . The following Friday her hands and feet remained as they have been since Christmas, the wounds closed."

As soon as the report was spread in Münster that her hands and feet had ceased to bleed, the Prussian authorities thought it an opportune moment for executing a project of long standing : namely, that of taking the stigmatisée of Dülmen under their own immediate jurisdiction.

Dr. Wesener says : " Feb. 18th—Sister Emmerich sent for me to-day to advise her on the introduction of two persons : Dr. Rave, of Ramsdorf, and Vicar Roseri, who had arrived with an order from the Chief President von Vinke to inquire into her present state. I advised her to admit them. They called on me that afternoon to inquire about the effusions of blood and many other particulars. I saw that Dr. Rave suspects fraud and that he is resolved to discover it. I begged him to wait until next day when he might witness the bleeding of her wounds for himself.

" Friday, Feb. 19th—The two visitors wearied the invalid all the morning with questions on matters well-known to the public. Instead of waiting until her wounds bled, they left about noon. Toward three o'clock, the cross and her head bled, but not the wound of her side. I sent her headdress stained with blood to Dean Overberg by Father Limberg, after having shown it to the burgomaster Mr.

Moellmann.   Roseri belongs to the so-called *Illuminati* (1)
but he went away with changed sentiments.   It seems as
if God touched his heart (2).   Rave, the physician, is a
worlding, another Bodde; one could read in his eyes his
suspicion of imposture.   He found fault with me for not
having kept the crusts from her hands and feet.   'When
one has the grain,' said I, ' he throws away the husk.   Now
that I understand the most striking features of the case,
unimportant details do not interest me'—but Rave could
not comprehend my meaning.   A few days before this
visit the Abbé Lambert had been called upon to present his
papers of nationality to the burgomaster.   The order was
from the Chief-President and was couched in the following
terms : ' I have been apprised that there is now at Dülmen
a French emigré, a priest, whose position is rather doubtful'—Fancy how such reports must affect the poor invalid
and the old Abbé!   Idle tales and calumnies are rife on
all sides ; but Sister Emmerich confides in God, and we,
her friends, rejoice to suffer for Christ and the truth !"

As Dr. Rave, besides his official statement, had circulated a (3) letter containing his own private opinion on the
subject very unfavorable to Sister Emmerich ; as he revived
the former attacks of Bodde, and threatened to stir up fresh
storms, Dr. Wesener thought it high time to come forward in defence of the innocent, by a memorial addressed

(1) Letter of Dr. Wesener to the Pilgrim.

(2) The doctor was wofully deceived in Roseri, as the sequel will show. The invalid
received information in vision concerning him and his clique. "I saw Rave full of
malice, calumniating me, even against his own conviction, in order to please the followers of the *Eagle*" (the Prussian government.) "I thought Roseri changed, but he
is essentially false and he acts at random. I said to myself : ' How can such a priest help
souls ?—and I received the answer : ' He helps as few as the Good Book does among
the separated. He has no benediction in himself, but he can distribute the Church's
goods without possessing them himself.'—I saw the government of the *Eagle* badly
administered in this part of the country. The Chief-President has a noble heart, he
means well, but he has bad counsellors. If he came to see me himself, I doubt not that
I would be able to gain his good judgment to the truth."....

(3) The Landrath Boenninghausen, of whom we shall hereafter speak more at length,
acknowledged that Dr. Rave, besides his protocol, had privately written to Dr. Borges,
at Münster, expressing his own views *with a little more freedom.*"

to the Chief-President of Münster. But Sister Emmerich was opposed to such a step. She asked Dean Overberg's advice. He replied as follows:—

" How much I have wished to visit my dear friends at Dülmen, among whom you hold not the last place! But such is not the will of God. Sickness and other obstacles prevent. I would like to lay before you my reasons against writing to the Chief-President, but not now, not till I can do so by word of mouth. Neither do I advise you to have the declaration forwarded to me inserted in the journals. Every response is specie payment. We must not buy lead, or what is even of less value, with pure gold. It is written: ' Cast not holy things to the dogs, nor pearls to swine.' I desire to compare no man to dogs or swine. But there must be some deserving of such comparison, else the Saviour, the infinitely wise Son of God, would never have given us this warning . . . . Nothing is so consoling and delightful as to suffer something with Christ! But why attach so much importance to Bodde's pamphlet? why see in it so formidable an attack? I have heard many persons declare that it betrays its spirit too openly to find supporters, it cannot do the least harm."

When Dr. Wesener declared later on that these public attacks ought to be met and refuted for the sake of those concerned, the invalid gravely replied: " Ah! ye good people, I thank you for the interest you take in me. But I must say that one thing in all of you, without exception, afflicts me : that is, that you treat the case with presumption and selfishness and, consequently, with bitterness. Whilst defending the truth, you wish also to defend *your own opinion, your own reputation!* You combat not the *lie* only, but also those who contradict you ; in a word, you seek yourselves and not the glory of God alone ! "

The Vicar-General now thought it his duty again to visit Dülmen, the reports that had reached him being far from satisfactory. It was rumored that access to the invalid was refused by the old Abbé, and that evening re-unions were held around her couch. Sister Emmerich soon gave satisfactory explanations to his inquiries, her irresist-ible candor and simplicity again pleading in her favor. He said to her, half in jest, half in earnest : "I have been a little displeased with you, many things around you shock me ! "—to which she replied : "That distresses me, but you know not my position, and it is not possible to explain it in words."—Then he enumerated certain points : the Abbé's proximity, the Pilgrim's prolonged sojourn, the frequent visits she received, the room in which she was (instead of a more retired one at the back of the house), etc. But when she begged him to point out the remedy for all this, he confessed himself unable to do so. She explained to him the Pilgrim's intentions, the command she had received in vision to make use of him to record her revelations, and begged him to decide, as her Superior, upon what course she was to follow. Whereupon the Vicar-General concluded that Brentano must not be forbidden to fulfil his task. He was, at last, satisfied, or as Sister Emmerich herself expressed it : "It passed off well. We came to the same conclusion ! He went away satisfied and remained so !"

So stood affairs in Dülmen, when the announcement of the Pilgrim's speedy return threw the good people into great agitation Father Limberg said nothing and left to the invalid the care of lulling the storm ; but as this proved no easy task, she had recourse to Dean Overberg for advice. She knew from experience that his decisions were always well received by her little circle, and it was on this account that she had so earnestly desired a visit from him during

the Pilgrim's former stay ; she wished him to explain to her
friends that it was not in her power to dismiss the object of
their dislike, that his coming or going depended not on her
choice. The Abbé and the doctor allowed themselves to
be persuaded to appeal to the Dean, but at the same time,
they wrote to Brentano to dissuade him from returning.
Whilst these negotiations were pending, Sister Emmerich
prayed that the glory of God and the salvation of souls
might accrue from the whole affair.

The Abbé's letter ran thus : "Sir, be not offended with
me, if I desire not your return. I feel that I have not the
strength and courage to undergo a second time what I endured during your last visit to Dülmen. For many years
have Sister Emmerich and I lived in peace, and so we wish
to die. It was very hard for me whilst you were here, to
be forced to see and speak to her, as it were, by stealth. I
cannot consent to your return. No ! No ! my dear sir, no !
What I now write I should have said to you before by word
of mouth, if you had listened to me. I often wanted to
speak to you on this subject, but you would never permit
me."

To the above written in French, the doctor added the
following lines :—"My object in writing is to beg you
not to return. You may smile at this, but your inflexible
will cannot always be a safe guide for your actions. I have
acquainted Dean Overberg with your manner of life here and
your treatment of us all. *Follow his advice!* All Sister Emmerich's friends, both here and in Münster, are of one
opinion —that your return will have most vexatious results.
The fault lies in yourself. You have expressed yourself
in Münster about the clergy of Dülmen, and principally of
one, in terms so free and sarcastic that all declare against
you, not one in your favor. No one is willing to write this

to you; therefore, I do it. I feel obliged to say that the
inconveniences resulting to Sister Emmerich from her relations with you infinitely outweigh the advantages derived ;
consequently, we are resolved, in the event of your return,
not to allow you the free access to her that you enjoyed
before. Sister Emmerich sympathizes with your sad fate
and solid conversion, but she sees, too, with anxiety your
distempered imagination, she dreads your ungovernable
will. If you return, she is resolved to admit you to her
room but one hour a day; and besides, you are not to interfere in her household affairs. Her sister is, in truth, a
miserable creature ; but Sister Emmerich is willing to bear
with her, persuaded that God makes use of this sister to help
her to practise virtue. The good old Abbé Lambert has suffered much from you though, of course, without your intending it. All has not gone so smoothly as you think.
Dean Overberg is of our opinion. Prevail upon him to say
what he thinks of your return."

Dr. Wesener had written, as follows, to Dean Overberg
respecting the Pilgrim :

" Our dear invalid has entreated me to write and give you
some explanation of the Abbé Lambert's letter, and my own
inclinations, as well as my affection for her, urge me to give
you news of her present condition. Mr. Clement Brentano
has visited you ; he has told you marvellous things of the invalid and has spoken to you of her progress in the interior
life. This gentleman, it is true, has been very generous
toward her. He has procured her a convenient lodging
where she can enjoy more quiet; and he has, perhaps, been
of great advantage to the public, furnishing many interesting details by his sagacious observations and researches,
but all at the price of the invalid's domestic peace ! What
do I say ? At the price of her health, her life ! He is in

himself good, his faith is firm, his works noble and Christian; but His poetical genius is out of place among the simple and unlettered. The invalid knows very well that her surroundings are not what they might be, she clearly sees the miseries by which her sister is enslaved, and the sight causes her inexpressible torment; but she is not less firmly persuaded that severity and constraint are not the means to correct and reclaim her. What she cannot cure by the way of charity and peace, she is willing to endure with humility and patience. The invalid has borne with Mr. Brentano and kept silence on all occasions, with the sole intention of being useful to him and to others. She wishes to forget past annoyances, to sacrifice them to God and her neighbor; but she dreads his return. He understands not the way of mildness, he wishes to overcome all obstacles by force. Sister Emmerich is determined not to receive him again unconditionally, not to regard all that he does as right. However, as there is a certain imposing air about him which intimidates some, and as her friends cannot always be near her, she feels unequal to the task of communicating with him directly and she seeks means for ameliorating the evil. He loves and esteems you highly and places in you unlimited confidence; consequently, the invalid entreats you most earnestly to write to him, to represent to him the state of affairs and authorize him to return only upon certain definite conditions."

To this letter, Dean Overberg replied as follows:—

" It is a great satisfaction to me to hear something of our dear invalid from a pen other than that of Mr. Clement Brentano. From his account, I should have conjectured that she was well pleased to have him by her, and perfectly satisfied with his manner of acting. On reading your account, the legal phrase, *Audiatur et altera pars,* recurred to my mind. He also assured me of his intention to return as soon as possible and continue his observations, which I hardly think we can prevent if Almighty God does not oppose some obstacle to his doing so, nor do I see any possibility of persuading him to take up his abode in Münster. That he may comport himself differently toward the invalid and her friends, she must herself assign some hour for his daily visit to her and, moreover, positively decline his interference in her domestic affairs. She must do this *herself,* for if any suggestion to this effect came from me, it would certainly not be adopted for the following reasons :—He is persuaded or wishes to be persuaded that Sister Emmerich is very well pleased to have him near her and that she is satisfied with his proceedings ; he thinks that, at all events, it tends to her greater good. He knows that I cannot go to see her and converse with her upon these subjects ; consequently, he would undoubtedly look upon what I might say of her sentiments concerning him and his manner of acting as suggested by those around her. Now, he might very reasonably suspect that they *wish to remove him from the invalid through motives of envy, jealousy, and the like.* He would then imagine it his duty to espouse her cause so much the more earnestly as he saw that some desired to deprive *her* of the consolation his presence affords her and *him* of the opportunity of securing to her a greater degree of repose by his zealous efforts to keep others at a distance. The arrangement to which I have referred should, as the case demands, be made in your own and Father Limberg's presence, and during the first days of its going into effect, you should watch closely to see if the prescribed time be ob. served. I foresee very plainly that in the beginning the invalid will have difficulty ; but I know no better means to adopt. I hope that if she is firm in the commencement,

Brentano will by degree become less exacting. I must, besides, beg you not to refer him to me for a decision. That
would only render the case more confused and *strengthen
him in the persuasion that the invalid would rather see things
remain as they were heretofore, and that, if she expresses herself differently, it is only through the fear of offending either
party. Her own free will and choice must decide this question.* Mr. Clement Brentano told me something, but only
in a passing way, of the change that has taken place in her
wounds. If you noted the time of this change, I beg you
to send me your account in a day or so. I heard yesterday that she has begun to eat (1). Perhaps God will
raise her up again. Salute her kindly from me. I presume she has received my letter."

The Pilgrim was stung to the quick by the Abbé Lambert and Dr. Wesener's letters and he complained bitterly
of them to his friends (2). But when the first storm was
over, he wrote an answer to the same which unfortunately
has not been preserved. From the doctor's and Father
Limberg's reply, however, it may easily be inferred that
they were deeply touched by his humility and repentance.
The doctor responded : "I have read your letter, and I
thank God that I have done so ! It has moved us to tears,
it has satisfied all ! . . . . . Your intentions were good, you
meant well ; but, under the influence of your impetuous
spirit, you forgot that we are only poor, weak gnats unable
to follow you in your rapid flight . . . . . Were you calm,
gentle, patient, then would you be a sword, a flame in our
Holy Church !"

Of Father Limberg's kind reply, the Pilgrim thus
speaks :—

(1) This refers to Dr. Wesener's attempts to make her take some light nourishment,
such as milk and water, barley soup, or sago. She tried to obey, but without success,
and the doctor was forced to desist from such attempts.

(2) Clement Brentano's Gessammelte Briefe, vol. I., p. 334 and 340.

"From Father Limberg, too, I have received a very beautiful and consoling letter, singularly touching, affectionate, simple, and scriptural. A very elevated spirit, a truly sacerdotal spirit, pervades it. He rejoices at the prospect of my return. I submit, however, to Dean Overberg's decision" (1).

On arriving in Dülmen, May, 1819, Brentano received a most cordial welcome from all, and Sister Emmerich set herself to work to maintain peace on all sides. She exhausted herself in her efforts to keep Gertrude silent in presence of the stranger who seemed insupportable to her; she exacted from Dr. Wesener a renewal of his promise to treat the Pilgrim kindly; and she spared no efforts to make the Pilgrim himself less irritable, less alive to the little weaknesses of his neighbor. One day, after a conversation with her on this subject, he wrote, as follows, in his journal:—
"May the confessor, good and kind as he is, find in me some day a sincere friend! This I desire with all my heart, I really mean it. I have no after-thought in this—may it be so, too, with him! I have no concealments from him. How happy must two men be who trust and warn each other in Christ! God grant that my earnest efforts may earn His love and blessing!"

When he communicated his good resolutions to the invalid, she could scarcely conceal her fears for their constancy. "I saw the Pilgrim," she said, "under a flourishing, but short-lived gourd-vine—it reminded me of Jonas." He understood well the deep significance of her words, though he cared not to acknowledge it even to himself. He remarked in his notes:

"Her strange anxiety troubles me. She wept, and I was distressed, for she could not tell me the cause. May

(1) Letters of Clement Brentano, vol. I., p. 344.

God comfort her, give peace, confidence to all hearts, and to me fortitude and unbounded charity toward all my brethren! The confessor is very good and kind. Does the gourd of Jonas withering so suddenly signify a short-lived peace?"

Yes, without doubt, this vision was to be realized only too soon. The order of the priesthood is, as it were, the channel by which the gifts and graces of God's chosen ones are distributed among the faithful in accordance with His commands; now, in their ranks not one was to be found to secure the fruits of the visions granted Sister Emmerich for the good of her fellow-men. By leading the Pilgrim back to his faith, by preparing him for the duty imposed upon him in the midst of such suffering as it entailed on herself, she supplied for what was wanting in the priestly co-operation and discharged the debt their negligence contracted. Still the accomplishment of her mission was to depend wholly upon ecclesiastical authority. For the Pilgrim's return, she had to gain the consent of her chief Superior, the Vicar-General von Droste. Her director, Dean Overberg not having come to Dülmen as soon as expected, she sent her confessor to Münster to learn from him if it were the will of God that she should communicate her visions to the Pilgrim; and she reminded the Abbé Lambert of the commands so often received to reduce to writing what was shown her of Our Lord's Passion. Dean Overberg could, consequently, on June 6, 1819, unhesitatingly assure her friends that the Pilgrim's employment near Sister Emmerich was in accordance with the will of God. This declaration consoled her, as we glean from the Pilgrim:—

"Dean Overberg has gone. The invalid is so exhausted that she can relate nothing; still she refers with pleasure to her interview with the Dean." Now began a new duty for Sister Emmerich, that of leading the Pilgrim to comprehend that, not being a priest, he possessed neither the sacerdotal power nor authority, and that it was only by his respect and submission to those by whom it was represented, Dean Overberg and her confessor, that he would render himself worthy to receive the communication of her visions. She repeatedly and gravely made use of expressions to him which, at first, seemed strange ; as, for instance, " You are not a priest ! I sigh for Dean Overberg. He has the priestly power that you have not ! You cannot help me, you are not an ecclesiastic ! Were you a priest, you would understand me, etc. !" It was long before he seized the meaning of such words. Only two years before Sister Emmerich's death, he wrote : " Where, then, is the priest who has understood her ? I am reproached in these words : ' Were you a priest, you would understand me and that would spare me many torments'—but *no one* has understood her !" It was only by invincible patience that she by degrees curbed his rebellious spirit, reduced him in some measure to respect for spiritual authority, and enabled him to fulfil his mission with a blessing to others as well as to himself. Superior to good Father Limberg in learning and experience, Brentano saw himself in a position in which he could not approach the invalid for a single word without express leave from the former, and day by day he received convincing proof that strength to communicate her visions was accorded her only by the priest's intervention. He failed not to perceive that this simple and unlettered man, whom he so vehemently accused of not understanding his spiritual daughter, possessed by virtue of his lively faith an influence over her immensely superior to his own ; he could not close his eyes to the fact that he had yet to rid himself of many faults, and acquire many virtues before arriving at a just appreciation of Sister Emmerich and his own relations with her. Sister Emmerich's prudence in aiding him to acquire this knowledge was admirable. If charged by her angel to give him an admonition, she did it only after having adroitly prepared him to receive it well ; and she generally clothed it in parables or striking comparisons which, appealing to his intellectual mind, charmed and attràcted him, forced him, so to say, to accept them in spite of himself. If he expressed disgust at something wounding to his æsthetic tastes, she would say : " One may, indeed, be displeased by bad singing at Mass or an indifferent performance on the organ, whilst others are edified by the same. We ought to banish such sentiments by prayer. He who resists such a temptation in church acquires merit, gains new graces." This simplicity of faith she recalled in words such as these : " He who in his search after truth relies on his own efforts and not on the grace of God, may cling to his own opinion, but he will never dive into the truth."

Some weeks after his arrival, she laid open her soul to him :—

" Every evening I am told to make such or such a meditation. Last night I received an instruction upon myself, and a great deal was said to me about the Pilgrim. Much remains to be corrected in him. I was shown how we can render him better, more easy to deal with, and thereby more useful. As I thought over my manner of acting toward him, asking myself how I could perform his task as well as my own, and by what means we could have a larg er and richer share of merits, I learned that we must be patient with each other in the sufferings that will come upon us, and that he must receive Holy Communion for my intention ; for spiritual union is thereby strengthened. 'Do what thou canst,' was said to me, ' but, for the rest, do not mind the Pilgrim. Many will come to speak with thee. When they present themselves, examine whether it be for their good or not. . . . . . Pray that the Pilgrim may resolve to be humble and patient, for he must overcome his wilfulness. Aim at making him more earnest. Through mistaken condescension, be not deceived by fair words. Do thou resist, be firm, that he may become resolute. Thou art too indulgent, this has always been thy fault. Do not allow thyself to be persuaded into seeing good where, in reality, there is a fault. . . . . . ' My guide told me again that I should have much to suffer, that I must not be frightened, but in the name of God calmly await what is in store for me. He reprimanded me for many faults. He says that I keep silence on many points through false humility which is, in the end, hidden pride; that I ought to receive and to communicate the divine favors as I did in my childhood when I received much more than I do now ; that I ought to speak out boldly on suitable occasions; that I ought to tell my confessor whatever troubles me even if he seemed but little disposed to hear it, for in this way, I should receive his help more frequently. He reproached me for my too great condescension to some, which causes me often to fail in prayer and my duties toward others. He says that I am very unreasonable when I complain of lying in bed unable to act. He knows I would like to wrap in my mantle, go out in the evening, and distribute alms, because of the pleasure it would give me ; but that what God imposes is not agreeable to me. He says that I ought to know that I am not lying here without an object. I must act by prayer and communicate all that I receive. I shall soon have something to impart that will cost me an effort, but I must say it. A great storm is near, the clouds are lowering fearfully ;

there are few who pray, the distress is great, the clergy are sinking lower and lower. I must exhort the good to pray earnestly. He told me that I must be more calm, more collected to meet approaching sufferings, else I might suddenly die. My task is not yet completed. Were I to die now through my own negligence, I should have to undergo the rest of these sufferings in purgatory where it would be much harder for me than here."

Sometimes Sister Emmerich encouraged the Pilgrim by holding out to him the blessings she saw flowing from his labor. She related a vision in which, under the appearance of a garden, she had seen many things of his past life, his present work, and its fulfilment after her own death.

" I saw," she said, " the Pilgrim far away, sad and lonely in his room. He could interest himself in nothing, all was distasteful to him. I wanted to fly to him, to help him, but I could not.

" Then I saw a garden, a large garden divided into two parts by a hedge over which some people were looking, but who were unable to cross it. My guide took me where the vegetation was rich, beautiful, luxuriant, but all over-run with weeds. I saw beans and peas, and there were blossoms and flowers in abundance, but no fruit. Many people were walking about apparently well pleased with themselves.

" My guide said to me as we walked around : 'See, what it means :—beautiful flowers of rhetoric, brilliant but sterile ; abundant, but producing no harvest ; plentiful, but yielding nothing !'—' Ah !' I exclaimed, ' must all the labor be lost ?'—' No !' was the answer, ' nothing will be lost ! It will all be turned under to make manure,' at which I felt glad and yet sorry too.

" The second time we went around, we found standing

in the centre of the path a tent made of the branches of a stunted walnut-tree. It was covered with a cloth. The nuts on these branches were the only fruit in the whole garden. Further on we saw an apple-tree and a cherry-tree around which the bees were gathering honey. The place was desolate enough.

"My conductor said : 'See ! Thy confessor ought to imitate the bees and gather these nuts'—but my confessor feared being stung. I thought to myself his very fear would be the cause of his suffering what he dreaded. If he would go along coolly, the bees would not harm him ; but he ran from tree to tree, he did not even see the nuts.

"When my guide took me the third time, the growth was still luxuriant. I was charmed at seeing the Pilgrim gathering certain strange plants in the corners of the garden which, although partially hidden by others, yielded the most fruit.

"Again I went into the garden where the too luxuriant vegetation was beginning to decay, and at last it was all turned under. I saw the Pilgrim actively digging and tilling.

"When I came again, the garden was all ploughed up and the Pilgrim was setting out plants in beds. It was a pleasing sight. At last he left the garden, and some people entered whom I knew only by sight, I knew not their names. They fell upon me in a rage and abused me terribly, inveighing against my communications to the Pilgrim, complaining that a new sect would arise from it, and asking what they were to think of me! I took it all in silence. Then they broke out against the Pilgrim who, I thought, was within hearing. I rejoiced at being able to bear it all patiently and I ceased not to exclaim : ' Thank

God! Thank God! I can bear it! another, perhaps, might not.'—Then I went and sat down on a stone in a neighboring grove.

"And now a priest came along, an active, energetic man, about as tall as the Prior, robust and florid. He expressed surprise at my not defending myself; but after a little reflection, he said : ' This person endures bad treatment very coolly, and yet she is both intelligent and sensitive! The Pilgrim's conduct is probably very different from what we imagine ; the confessor, too, is a good man who would not permit anything wrong.' As the unknown ecclesiastic continued thus speaking in favor of the Pilgrim, the brawlers began to slink away and I noticed how diligently the Pilgrim had worked and how much the plants had grown and flourished.

"My guide said : ' Make good use of this heavenly instruction. Thou shalt, in truth, endure these injuries and outrages. Be prepared! For awhile thou shalt live at peace with the Pilgrim ; but lose not time, squander not the graces given thee, for thy end will soon come. What the Pilgrim gathers he will bear far away, for here there is no desire to have it. But it will produce fruit where he goes, and that same fruit will one day return and make itself felt even here.' "

The Pilgrim understood the foregoing vision only little by little, as his oft-repeated complaints that the time of peace would never dawn, prove. He thought the words meant freedom from exterior annoyances, whereas they really signified peace of mind, which alone could fit him to receive the visions of *Our Divine Redeemer's Life*. Over a year elapsed before, upon the admonition of her angel, Sister Emmerich began the narration, July, 1820. The Pilgrim had, it is true, planted diligently, but many weeds yet re-

mained to be rooted out. His rich, lively imagination was
as yet too undisciplined for the reproduction of Sister Emmerich's visions in their native simplicity, and it cost him a
struggle not to embellish them with his own poetical ideas.
The interpretations he gave them were infallible in his eyes,
and he hesitated not to introduce them freely without
specifying their origin. This happened principally during
the first year when Sister Emmerich's labors for the Church
formed the greater part of her communications. He had
repeatedly been told that the invalid had asked Almighty
God as a special favor not to be informed for what individuals among the clergy she was called upon to pray and
suffer; yet it was not without difficuty that Brentano
could be dissuaded from introducing the names of persons
to whom he fancied certain visions particularly applicable,
instead of the terms Sister Emmerich herself used; such as
spouse, affianced, pastor, etc. Later on he erased
many of these early notes from his manuscripts, when he
recognized the incommensurable distance between the
highest flights of his own fancy and the pure light in which
this favored soul dwelt ; and then it was that he began to
esteem no trouble too great to reproduce as conscientiously
as possible whatever was transmitted to him for the good
of the faithful.

When we cast a glance at this man of genius, this poet
so admired, the light of the cultivated and intellectual circle
in which he moved, we are forced to admit how slight are
the claims to superiority of all such natural qualities. The
atmosphere which he breathes by the suffering couch of
this poor peasant-girl is far purer, far more elevated than
any he had yet known; her detachment, her patient sufferings,
her voluntary mortifications rendered her inaccessible to any
influence of an inferior order and ever more susceptible of

the sacred light of prophecy. The Pilgrim could, indeed, annoy and afflict her, but to her interior, to her visions he had no access. Nothing could be more absurd than the supposition that his energetic nature had established between the invalid and himself a kind of magnetic communication owing to which he received from her only what he had himself previously dictated. This conjecture loses weight at once when we recall the fact that only one clothed with the priestly dignity could exercise any spiritual influence over her. She endured his presence as she would that of a poor, sick person sent her by Divine Providence to heal and save. He is the debtor, he is the favored one, he is the pupil; she is the dispenser of gifts, she is the teacher, or, in other words, the instrument under God to snatch one of the most brilliant minds of that period from the snares of the world, to win him over to the glorification of His Most Holy Name. No one possessed a more piercing eye with regard to his neighbor's weakness and foibles than did the Pilgrim, a gift he afterward bewailed with bitter tears of repentance. He was the most pitiless, the most acrimonious observer that the invalid and her little circle ever had to endure. When his enthusiasm vanished, and the charm of novelty wore off, woe to Sister Emmerich did he discover, or fancy he discovered the least thing to arouse suspicion or distrust! He was an inexorable judge! Up to the time of her death, his manuscripts teemed with bitter remarks: the words, the gestures, even the steps of her confessor were noted down with tiresome prolixity and interpreted with unsparing rigor. And yet, the only charge that could be brought against the reverend gentleman was that he made little account of the Pilgrim's notes, that he would gladly have dispensed with Sister Emmerich's visions altogether and thus been freed from the obligation of the

aforesaid notes, and that he treated her communications
with freezing indifference. Sister Emmerich herself met
with no greater lenity at the Pilgrim's hands. Let her utter
a word of consolation to the poor and afflicted who flocked
to her for relief, or show the slightest sign of weariness in
relating her visions, and she is instantly rebuked for un-
faithfulness to her mission, for dissipating the graces she received, for injustice to himself. But soon, overcome by her
angelic sweetness and forced to recognize his own unreasonable humor, he records the following words in his journal :
" She is full of goodness and patience ! Yes, she is a
most admirable vessel of divine grace !"

CHAPTER XXXVI.

SISTER EMMERICH IS PLACED UNDER ARREST.—HER PRESENTIMENT OF THIS EVENT.—ITS RESULTS.

From the beginning of the ecclesiastical year, 1818-'19, Almighty God prepared Sister Emmerich for the expiatory sufferings in store for her. The events from which these sufferings were to arise were still future, but the invisible enemy of man had already his powerful engines at work toward their furtherance. The mystery of iniquity which "already worketh," according to St. Paul, was making at that period new and vigorous exertions to sap the foundations of faith in many dioceses, and the weapons used were precisely those which are now about to be turned against the poor invalid herself. As in preceding ages, so was it now: unworthy clerics in the service of anti-Catholic and secret societies, were the inventors and executors of measures which, under the name of " *Fundamental Rules*," " *Ecclesiastical Laws*," " *Conventions*," " *Acts' of Endowment*," etc., were destined to destroy secretly but surely the Church of Jesus Christ. As the struggle drew near, the invalid's visions became more comprehensive, more significant. They were not only prophetic pictures, but real, personal combats, fruitful in results inasmuch as they were a continued development of the great combat of the Church ; she suffered and accomplished in very truth all that she saw in vision. The sentiments and designs of the Church's enemies were made known to her, that she might oppose them by prayer. Her visions were not idle dreams, nor her action in them vain and imaginary, rather was it the confirmation of her own marvellous spiritual life. This life was *one*, having but *one and the same* operations although existing in two different worlds and following a two-fold law, the world of sensible things and that elevated above the senses. In contemplation, she prays, she struggles, she triumphs ; whilst, at the same moment, she suffers in the natural state, or accomplishes her duties of ordinary life. In both cases she is free, in the full possession of her faculties and of all that is requisite, in the natural and supernatural order, to produce meritorious acts. Her external life bears the same relation to her transcendent interior life as the symbol to the thing signified, the similitude to the reality, the shell to the kernel. Her persecutors are, though unconsciously, the representatives of the tendencies of the period. Of these prophetic visions, the invalid was able to recount but a very small part. It is, however, enough to awaken the surprise of the reader, when he beholds how exactly they were realized in all that referred to her own approaching trials.

Advent, 1818.—" I have been warned by my guide to prepare for a severe struggle. I must invoke the Holy Ghost to inspire me what to answer. I do it now all day, and I know what this struggle will be. Artful men will attack me and try to make me contradict myself by their perfidious questioning. It seemed as if my heart would break. But I turned to my Heavenly Spouse and said : ' Thou hast begun the work, Thou wilt also bring it to a close ! I abandon myself entirely to Thee !'—and then when I had put the case into His hands, I felt great strength and peace in God. I said : ' Joyfully will I be torn to pieces, if thereby I can help the world !'—Among my persecutors I saw a physician and some ecclesiastics who came, one after another, to take me away. They pretended to be very friendly, but I saw the deceit in their heart.

" May 19th—I have had a bad night. I was assailed on all sides and torn to pieces, but I remained calm, I rejoiced at what was done to me, and I recognized the instigators of the affair and the chief actors in it. They all talked at once, clamored around me, and ended by tearing me piecemeal. Not one of my friends was present, no one to help me, no priest. I became sad, and I thought of Peter's abandonment of his Lord.

" I saw a party of men assembled to deliberate and exult over their cunningly devised plans to carry me off. They resolved to make use of new means. My guide told me to be calm, that if they succeeded, it would end in their own confusion and be all for the best.

" May 28, 1819—I saw myself alone in my time of trial and, what was worse, my confessor dared not come to me. He seemed forced to go away without bidding good-by. I had a vision in which I found myself alone in a room with only Sister Neuhaus. Then some people came and fell upon me at the right side and foot of my bed, I was utterly defenceless.

" June 6th—I have had a very miserable night. I saw myself abused more than ever, I cannot think of it without shuddering. I was abandoned by all my friends. My bed stood in the middle of the room, and I was tended by strangers. I knew that I was in this miserable state on account of a quarrel between some ecclesiastics and laics, who tore me to pieces to show their mutual contempt. I saw Dean Overberg in the distance sitting sad and silent, and I thought all was over with me.

" July 17, 1819—Again I had visions of my approaching trials. I saw all my old convent companions visiting me, speaking of our past intercourse, and questioning me as to whether I had or had not said when in the convent such or such things of my state, etc. I could not understand what they were aiming at, and I said : 'God knows what they and I have done !'--Then I saw them all going to confession and Communion, after which they came back to me. They were, however, no better than before, and they tried to find something out from me, I know not what. I asked them if they did not know that, long before my joining them, I had had unaccountable pains in my hands and feet; that when with them, I had often made them touch the palms of my hands which were burning hot; and that my fingers had been quite dead, without my understanding what it all meant ? Was I not unable for a long while to take food on account of the vomiting it brought on ? Was not this the case for seven months without my attaching any importance to it ?   Did I not think it a sickness, although it never kept me from my duties, or from prayer, my only delight ? But I found them all hesitating and insincere in their declarations. All sought to clear themselves from blame, all excepting the Superioress and Sister Neuhaus —they alone were honest.   After this came a great many of my acquaintances—they did as they always do, they spoke at random, not one willing to stand up for me. The Abbé Lambert could not help me, they would not listen to him. My confessor was not far off, but he was dejected and weary. Then six ecclesiastics and laics, among them two Protestants, came not all together but one by one, and some were false and malicious to the last degree. The sweetest and blandest among them treated me the worst. Then a man came in saying : 'Whatever is done to this person will also be done to me.' I knew him not, but he stayed by me a long time and was honest and true to me. He saw all that was done, but he could not help me. When the others surrounded me (my bed stood in the middle of the floor) they were

careful not to jostle him. Then they began to put all kinds
of questions, but I made no answer. I had already responded three different times, as recorded in the report, and
I had nothing more to say. The Vicar-General was
near by ; there was some question of him. I saw that
the Dean (Rensing) was interested ; he gave instructions
but he was not for me. Dean Overberg was absent,
but praying for me. The two little nuns Frances and
Louisa comforted me. They repeated continually: ' Have
courage, only courage ! all will be right ! '—My persecutors
began to draw off the skin from my hands and feet. They found
the marks of a deeper red than those on the surface. They did
the same to my breast and discovered the cross more plainly
marked below than on the skin. They were amazed, they knew
not what to say ! In silence they slunk away one after another ; each told his own story, but all were confounded.
Whilst lying there awaiting the operation on my wounds,
I was seized with anguish ; but the two holy nuns encouraged me, promising that no evil would result from it.
Then a marvellously beautiful little Boy in a long robe
appeared to me ; His face shone like the sun. He took
my hand, saying: ' Come, we will thank our dear Father!'—
and raising me up lightly we went into a beautiful
chapel, open in front and only half-finished. It appeared to
be split down the middle. On the altar were the pictures
of St. Barbara and St. Catherine. I said to the little Boy :
' Why the chapel is split !'—and he replied : ' And it is only
half-finished.'—I felt that we were near a magnificent mansion
in which many persons were awaiting me. It was surrounded
by gardens and fields, paths and groves, it was like a
little village. Still it seemed as if it were afar off, and
there did not appear to be any place as yet destined for
me. I know only that I looked into the chapel with the

little Boy and saw the pictures. It was as if I had been caught up in spirit whilst they drew the skin from my wounds, for I felt nothing; I only saw, after it was over, the shreds of red skin. I beheld the amazement of the men when they found the marks penetrating the flesh, and I saw them *scratching behind their ears!* In this confusion of the chapel and the operation, I awoke. The vision of the nuns and the people from the city was obscure. It seemed as if I were informed of an interrogatory to which I was to be subjected. I saw, too, something like a tumult in the city.

"The little Boy said: 'See, now all that troubled and disquieted thee lasted so short a time, but eternity has no end. Take courage! A rude trial is in store for thee, but thou wilt bear it well, it will not be so hard as it seems. Many evils can be averted by prayer, be comforted!' Then he told me to pray in my waking moments at night, for many are in danger of perishing, a great storm threatens. 'Fear not to say it out boldly and urge every one to pray.'"

A few days later, Sister Emmerich had another vision, that of a young virgin-martyr, and the sight strengthened her for her own approaching struggle: — " I was in prayer. Two unknown men came to me and invited me to go with them to Rome to the place in which the martyrs were tortured. There was to be a great combat that day, some of their friends were to engage in it, and they wanted to see them die for Jesus. I asked them why they exposed themselves. They answered that they were Christians in secret, no one would know them and, as they were relatives, a place was reserved for them that the sight of the martyrs' torments might affright them; they desired also to strengthen themselves by the sight and to encourage their friends by their presence. They took me to the amphitheatre. Above the inclosure, facing the entrance to the right of the judge's seat, was a gate between two windows through which we entered a large neat apartment in which were thirty good people, old and young, men and women, youths and maidens—all Christians in secret and assembled for the same purpose.

" The judge, a tyrannical old man, waved a staff right and left and at the signal, the subalterns down in the *circle* began their work. There were about twelve.—To the left before our windows, I saw something like an idol. I knew not what it was, but it made me shudder with horror. On the same side were the prisons. They brought out the martyrs, two by two, driving them forward with iron spears. They were led first before the judge and, after a few words, given over to martyrdom. The whole building was filled with spectators seated in tiers, raging and shouting.

" The first martyr seemed to be about twelve years old, a delicate little girl. The executioner threw her to the ground, crossed her left arm over her breast, and knelt upon it. With a sharp instrument, broad and short, he cut all around the wrist and peeled off the skin as high as the elbow; he did the same to the right arm and then to both feet. I was almost distracted by the horrible treatment of the tender child. I rushed out of the door, crying for mercy. I wanted to share her torments, but the slave pushed me back so violently that I felt it. The child's groans pierced my heart. I offered myself to suffer in her stead, and I had an impression that my turn would soon come. I cannot say what this sight cost me.

" Then the slave bound her hands across and it seemed to me that he was about to cut them off. When I went back into the room (it was semi-circular and there were

square and also triangular stone seats around it) two good people comforted me. They were the little girl's parents. They
said that their child's torments had pierced their soul, but
that she had drawn it upon herself by her excessive zeal.
It was very sad ; she was their only daughter. She used
to go openly to the catacombs to be instructed, and she always spoke out boldly and freely as if courting martyrdom.

"Now the two slaves wrapped her up and laid her on
the round funeral-pile which stood in the middle of the place,
her feet toward the centre ; below was a quantity of little
branches which quickly caught fire, and shot up their flames
through the wood above. The good people, though resigned,
appeared to me quite overcome with grief. A woman
among them opened a roll of parchment as long as one's arm,
fastened in the middle with a large clasp. They read in an
undertone, three or four together, and passed it along from
hand to hand. I understood perfectly what they read. They
were short sentences, how strong and elevating no words can
say. The sense of it was that they who suffer go straight to
God out of this miserable world. I was sure that I could
never forget the words. I still feel them, though I cannot repeat them. The reader often interrupted herself after a short
sentence with the words : ' What think you now ?' The
petitions were addressed to God in most energetic language.
I, too, looked at the parchment, but I could not read a
letter ; it was in red characters.

" During this martyrdom I was in indescribable anguish,
never before had the spectacle affected me so. The little
maiden with the skin hanging loose around her arms and
lower limbs, was always before me and her groanings pierced
my soul. I could not get away, they would not allow us to
cross the arena. Many others were afterward martyred.
They were pushed from side to side with iron points, struck

with heavy clubs and their bones broken, the blood spouting around. At last, there arose wild cries from the spectators and shrieks from one of the tortured. He was the last, and they maltreated him so that he wavered in the Faith. He cursed and yelled at the executioners; despair, pain, and rage made him an object frightful to behold. The good people near me were very sorrowful on his account, for they knew that he had to die. When the others were thrown on the funeral-pile, I grieved over this one, I felt that his soul was not in glory. All was now over, and the good people left me. The bodies were not entirely consumed, and a ditch was dug to receive the bones. I saw coming down from the heavens a shining white pyramid of light into which the souls of the martyrs entered with indescribable joy, like happy children. I saw one fall back again into the fire which now disappeared and in its stead, arose a dark, gloomy place where the soul was received by others. It was the fallen martyr. He is not lost, he went to purgatory—this makes me rejoice. Ah! but, perhaps, he is still there! I always pray for such poor, abandoned souls.

"I have a feeling that this martyr was shown me to animate me to patience in my sufferings, and lately I have seen my own skin peeled from my feet and hands. These old Romans must have been of steel. The tormentors were like the spectators, the martyrs like their friends; but nowadays people are lukewarm, soft, and slothful, they pray to the true God as coldly as the pagans did to their false gods."

From the Feast of the Visitation till the end of July, Sister Emmerich suffered violent inflammation of the chest. A breath of air from the opening of a door, or even a person's approach provoked convulsive coughing; profuse perspiration flowed from her breast, and involuntary dread

of coming events pursued her. On the 2d of August, the
Pilgrim found her sad and nervous. The next day there
arrived in Dülmen a Prussian "Commission of Inquiry," so-
called, the Landrath Bœnninghausen at its head. The other
members were Dr. Rave of Ramsdorf, Dr. Busch of Münster, the Cure Niesert of Velen, Vicar Roseri of Leyden,
and Prof. Roling of Münster. The Landrath went with the
Vicar to announce to Sister Emmerich the " new investigation." She replied that she knew not what they wanted
with an *investigation* since she was ready to give them all
the information they might desire, there was nothing which
had not already been investigated.

" That is of no account," replied the Landrath. " The
investigation has been resolved upon, it must be begun at
once ; therefore Miss Emmerich must forthwith allow herself to be removed to the residence of the Councillor Mersmann."

" If such be the orders of my Ecclesiastical Superiors,"
she replied, " I willingly submit to all demanded of me. I
shall look upon it as the will of God. But I am a religious
and although my convent has been suppressed, I am still a
religious, and I cannot act independently of my Superiors.
The Vicar-General has already proposed a mixed investigation, and if that is what you mean I am ready, for I cannot
but desire to see the truth established !"

The Landrath replied : "Ecclesiastical Superiors are
in this case of no account ; but here are three Catholic
priests." At these words Sister Emmerich turned to the
Vicar Roseri and said : " How can you, a priest, appear here
if ecclesiastical authority is of no account ? You took part in
the last investigation in a manner little becoming a priest,
and I am deeply grieved to see you here again. I have lost
confidence in you." Roseri excused himself, saying that

his presence on the occasion alluded to was only accidental ; but that now it was not only permitted by the Vicar-
General but even desired, and that he regretted not having
with him the document to that effect (1). Sister Emmerich
again declared that she would not consent to her removal,
that her physician would not countenance such a step. The
Landrath withdrew, declaring that she should be conveyed
to Münster whether or not. Dr. Wesener's journal runs as
follows : " Aug. 3d —I found the invalid this evening excited, but not disconcerted. She feared only that the old
Abbé, who was sick, would be neglected.

" Wednesday, Aug. 4th—I found her to-day quite resigned. She saw in a vision last night that they would
make her fine promises, but that she would be reduced to a
most wretched state of weakness in which her confessor
would assist her."

The Pilgrim was indignant and tried to avert the persecution from the poor invalid. On Aug. 3d, he wrote her a
long letter, begging her to propose him to the Commission
as a witness possessed of the necessary qualifications for
assisting at the investigation. But when she presented his
petition to the Landrath, he declared the Pilgrim " *especially excluded.*" Mr Brentano then appealed to the Chief-
President von Vinke, at Münster, who wrote as follows :
" In reply to your letter of the 4th inst., which I had the
honor to receive, I regret my inability to gratify your desire to take part in the investigation instituted with regard
to Miss Emmerich, as I have been expressly enjoined to
remove her from her present surroundings. This is so
necessary for the attainment of the end in view that I cannot neglect the instructions given me on this point. All,

(1) A false statement, as will hereafter be seen in the official acts. Sister Emmerich saw the sad state of the young man's soul, but she could only say that she had no
confidence in him.

however, that you may wish to communicate to the Committee concerning your personal observations will be received with pleasure.

" I am also inclined to think that your presence would prove unpleasant to Miss Emmerich ; for last winter during a certain medical visit paid her, she showed uneasiness at the mention of your name. We have earnestly recommended to the commissioners to treat her with great consideration and all possible kindness, although the choice made of them is sufficient to assure us that such a suggestion was unnecessary.

" I shall be most happy to make the acquaintance of M. Savigny's (1) brother-in-law. My approaching visit to Dülmen will, I trust, procure me that pleasure."

The Pilgrim next applied verbally to the Landrath himself ; but here, too, he met a refusal. Disappointed in his hopes of being placed on the commission, he went, in compliance with the invalid's desire, to the paternal mansion of Cardinal Diepenbrock, at Bockholt, to await the result of the investigation.

Aug. 4th, the Landrath again renewed his persuasions, but Sister Emmerich persisted in her refusal to consent to any change not authorized by her ghostly Superiors. " I demand," she said, " an order from the Vicar-General, officers delegated by him to execute it, and impartial witnesses; then I shall accept whatever happens as coming from God, then I shall have nothing to fear."—The Landrath did not as yet dare to attempt force. His visit was followed by one from Curé Niesert and the Vicar Roseri. The latter began :

"Now, tell us how would you like to be treated ?"

Sister Emmerich answered : " Why do you ask ? Have

(1) M. Savigny, a celebrated lawyer, professor at the Berlin University, who had married Mr. Brentano's sister.

you an order to treat me as I would like ? If so, I ask for
priests lawfully commissioned and for two witnesses to draw
up an official statement which they will read to me, that I
may know what is ascribed to me."

" You ought not to complain," said the Curé ; " you are
lying there comfortably, you seem to be very well."

" How I am," responded the invalid, " God knows !"
then turning to Roseri, she said : " I know now through
the Dean (Rensing) that you have no authorization from
the Vicar-General to be here."

On Friday, Aug. 6th, Dr. Borges of Münster, a Protestant, arrived in Dülmen accompained by a mesmerist.
As soon as they entered the inn, the former boasted that he
would " make short work of the girl, that there would be no
shuffling now !— He would have her removed to Berlin by
the police without its doing her the least harm." The news
of this incident soon spread, and the people became alarmed
lest, indeed, force might be used with the poor invalid.
The liveliest sympathy was manifested by all. An assembly
was held to protest against proceedings so opposed to law
and justice and Commissioner Keus selected to draw up resolutions. These were placed in the Landrath's hands, who
solemnly promised to present them at head-quarters. This
restored calm, and the good citizens hoped they had averted
the threatened blow. Dr. Borges and his companion went
with the Landrath to see Sister Emmerich and urge her once
more to consent to her removal. As the doctor held a high
position among the Freemasons, his presence was particularly
odious to her, and his flattery more disgusting than his abuse.

" How unreasonable in you," he said jeeringly, " to reject
the fine offer made you of being surrounded by the most
distinguished men, and of receiving their attentions in a
place far preferable to this ! "

" The good intentions of these gentlemen," replied Sister Emmerich, "I leave to God. I wish them every blessing, although I have not as yet profited by their good will. If you wish merely to discover the truth, you can examine me here in this room; but I know there is no question for you of the truth, which you could easily discover. If you want the truth, why not seek it *here* by me ? "— As both gentlemen asked what they could do for her during the investigation, she replied : " I demand, being seriously ill, the presence of my physician and confessor, a companion to attend to me, and two priests and two laics as witnesses ; nevertheless, I again protest that I will leave this house only by force." Then she remonstrated against Dr. Rave's having any share in the matter, since, besides his official report in February, he had published another and very different account greatly prejudicial to her. The result of the remonstrance we shall see later on. The mesmerist's discreet and reserved behavior during the interview made it evident that he saw not in SisterEmmerich any marks by which to recognize a medium (1).

Dr. Wesener says: " In the morning I found the invalid tolerably strong, but still opposed to the idea of moving. Dr. Borges tried to persuade me to consent, but when I told him Sister Emmerich was not in a condition to be moved he grew angry, and threatened force. Toward midnight, they did, indeed, intend to remove her, but as there were some assemblies going on, the execution of their scheme was deferred."—

Mr. von Schilgen, an eye-witness, gives the following account of this nocturnal escapade : " Many of the citizens

(1) The **Landrath** himself declared : " There can be no question of mesmerism in Sister Emmerich's case. I may say once for all that I have remarked that she holds it and its adherents, individually and collectively, in abhorrence,"

and myself had made use of the Landrath's acceptance of
our protest to calm the people and persuade them that force
would not be resorted to.   I was so fully convinced of the
truth of what I said that I went quietly to rest; but just
about midnight, J was aroused by one of the police who
came with orders to assemble his comrades, one of whom
lodged in my house.   I was, of course, surprised.   I ran to
the invalid's house where I found quite a number collected
awaiting the issue of the affair.   The police were in motion.
At midnight, Dr. Borges, Landrath Bœnninghausen, and Dr.
Busch made their appearance.   After rapping for some time
at the door leading to Sister Emmerich's lodgings and receiving no answer, they went around to the kitchen and
made Mr. Limberg show them the front room on the lower
floor; but this they did only to ward off suspicion.   They declared it suited to their purpose and went away leaving the
owner, as well as the assembled crowd, under the impression that they would hold the investigation there.   The
people, however, did not disperse till daylight called them
to their various occupations.   It was rumored that at eight
o'clock the next day, the invalid would be carried off by
force.   To be able to give an exact account of the affair,
if it really happened, I went half after seven o'clock to
Sister Emmerich's.   After the usual salutations, I inquired
upon what she had resolved.   She answered : ' I am extremely embarrassed.   The Landrath has appealed to the
Dean to use his influence to gain my consent to being removed and to submit to a new investigation.   He came to
see me for that purpose (1).   I know not what I shall do !'
I remarked that something must be resolved upon, when she
cried : 'No! never will I consent to it !   I persist in my
refusal !' and she implored me to stay and get the police to

(1) Dean Rensing told her that the Landrath had complained bitterly that he would
lose his position if she did not yield to their demands.—(Pilgrim's Notes).

protect her. Just at this moment the Landrath entered and renewed his entreaties. I interfered and reminded him of the protest of the preceding evening, but all to no purpose. He raised her by the shoulders himself, wrapped the bedclothes around her, and a nurse, whom he had brought with him, took her by the feet; thus they carried her down stairs, laid her upon a litter there in readiness, and four of the police bore her away to the house of the Councillor Mersmann, escorted by the Prefect and his men. There was no disturbance, the lookers-on expressing their sympathy only by sobs and tears. I noticed, to my satisfaction, that at the moment they wrapped her in the bed-coverings she fell into the cataleptic state and was, consequently, unconscious of what was being done to her (1)."

We shall now subjoin Sister Emmerich's own account:—

" The afternoon preceding my removal, being fully awake, I saw in vision all that was to take place the following day. The pain it caused deprived me of speech. Dean Rensing wanted me to submit freely, and the Landrath told me that he would lose his position if I did not; but I still refused. When he seized me by the shoulders, my spirit was caught up out of this miserable world into a vision of my youth which I had often had before my entrance into the cloister, and I remained perfectly absorbed until the next day. When I awoke and found myself in a strange house, I thought it all a dream. The whole time of my captivity, I was in a state of mental transport unaccountable to myself. I was frequently gay, and again full of pity for the blind investigators for whom I prayed. I offered all that I endured for the poor souls in purgatory, begging them to pray for my persecutors. I

(1) In Sept., 1859, the author visited the abode of Sister Emmerich at Dülmen, and found the marks of the government seals still visible on the doors of the house. Father Limberg's brother, the owner, was living. He told him that, when the poor Sister was carried off, the cows in the adjoining stable bellowed piteously.

often went down into purgatory and I saw that my sufferings were like those of the holy souls. The more violent my persecutors were, the calmer and even the more content. ed was I, which infuriated the Landrath. God kept me from making any outward demonstration, my graces were silent ones. Without the blessing of a priest or anything holy, I received from God a strength hitherto unknown, as well as every word that I had to say. I had nothing prepared. When my persecutors attacked me on one side, questioning and abusing, I saw on the other a radiant form pouring out strength and grace upon me. He dictated every word that I should say, short, precise, and mild, and I was full of pity. But if I spoke any words of my own, I perceived a great difference; it was another voice, rough, hard, and shrill."

On the Feast of St. Lawrence, I saw his martyrdom. I saw also the Assumption of Mary, and on St. Anne's day, my mother's patroness (1), I was taken up to her in her blessed abode. I wanted to stay with her, but she consoled me, saying: ' Although many evils are before thee, yet terrible ones have been averted from thee by prayer.' Then she pointed out many places in which they prayed for me. 'The heaviest trials thou hast well sustained, but thou hast still much to suffer and accomplish.'

" On the Feast of my Holy Founder, I had a clear view of the position I should have been in, if my enemies' desires had been fulfilled. Some of them were fully confident that, in my person, they had all Catholics in their power, and were about to disgrace them. I saw some ecclesiastics even animated by very evil dispositions. I saw myself in a deep, dark hole, and I thought I was never more to come out ; but, day by day, I rose higher and higher and the light increased. My persecutors, on the contrary, were buried

(1) The Feast of St. Anne falls on August 16th in the Calendar of Münster.

deeper and deeper in darkness; they grew uncertain as to how they should act, struck against one another, and finally, sank to the bottom. St. Augustine, whom I invoked, stood by my bed on his feast-day, and confounded my cruel tormentors. St. John also came to me on his feast and announced my speedy deliverance.

" When my persecutors came, I always saw the wicked enemy standing by. He looked like an assemblage of all the bad spirits: some laughing, weeping, cursing, playing the hypocrite; some lying, intriguing, making mischief. It was the demon of secret societies.

" In this vision my guide led me by the hand like a child. He lifted me out of the window of my father's cottage, led me over the meadow, across the marsh, and through the grove. We went on a long, perilous journey over desert countries, till we reached a steep mountain up which he had to draw me after him. It was strange to think myself a child, although so old! When we gained the summit, he said: 'See, if you had not been a child, I should never have been able to get you up here. Now, look back and see what dangers you have escaped, thanks to the providence of God!'—I did so and I saw the road behind us full of pictures of different kinds. They represented the various snares of sin, and I comprehended how wonderfully I had been preserved by the watchfulness of my angel. What on the way had appeared to me simply as difficulties, I now saw under human forms as temptations to sin. I saw all kinds of troubles which, thanks to the goodness of God! I had escaped. I saw people blindfolded. This signified interior blindness. They walked safely on the edge of the abyss for a time, but at last they fell in. I saw many whose safety I had procured. The sight of these dangers filled me with alarm, and I knew not how I had escaped.

" When my angel had pointed all this out to me, he went on a few steps ahead, and I at once became so weak and feeble that I began to stagger like a child not yet able to walk alone, to cry and lament like a little infant. Then my guide came back and gave me his hand with the words : ' See, how weak thou art when I do not lead thee ! See what need thou hast of a guide in order to pass over such dangers ! '

" Then we went to the opposite side of the mountain and descended, crossing a beautiful meadow full of red, white, and yellow flowers, so thickly crowded that I was in dread of crushing them. There were, too, some rows of apple-trees in blossom and different other trees. Leaving the meadow, we came to a dark road with high hedges on either side. It was muddy and rough ; but I passed over gaily, holding my guide's hand. I did not even touch the muddy path, I only skimmed above it. Then we came to another mountain pleasant to look upon, tolerably high, and covered with shining pebbles. From the top I cast a glance back upon the perilous road, and my guide said that the last road, so pleasant with its flowers and fruits, was typical of spiritual consolations and the manifold action of grace in the soul of man after resisting temptation. My fear of walking on the flowers signified scruple and false conscience. A childlike spirit abandoned to God, walks over all the flowers in the world, without thinking whether it bruises them or not : and, indeed, it does them no harm. I said to him that we must have been a whole year on the journey, it seemed to me so long. But he replied: ' To make the journey thou seest, ten years would be needed ! '—

" Then I turned to the other side to look at the road that lay before me. It was very short. At the end of it, only a little distance from where I stood, I saw the Heavenly Jerusalem. The gloomy, perilous road of life lay behind me, and before me only a little way off was the magnificent city of God shining in the blue heavens. The plain I still had to cross was narrow and beyond it was a road from which, right and left, branched by-paths in different directions, but which finally returned to the main road. By following them the journey would be considerably lengthened. They did not seem so very dangerous, though one might easily stumble on them. I gazed with joy into the Heavenly Jerusalem, which appeared much larger and nearer than it had ever done before. Then my guide took me to a path that led down the mountain, and I felt that danger threatened. I saw the Pilgrim in the distance. He seemed to be carrying something away, and I was eager to go to him. But my guide took me into a little cottage where the two religious, whom I know, prepared a bed and put me into it. I was again a little nun and I slept peaceably in uninterrupted contemplation of the Heavenly Jerusalem until I awoke. On the journey, I gave my hand at several different times to people whom I met, and made them travel part of the way with me.

" The Heavenly Jerusalem I saw like a glittering, transparent, golden city in the blue sky, supported by no earthly foundations, with walls and gates through which I could see far, far beyond. The view was rather the instantaneous perception of a whole than of a succession of parts such as I have here been obliged to present. It had numerous streets, palaces, and squares, all peopled by human apparitions of different races, ranks, and hierarchies. I distinguished whole classes and bodies bound together by ties of mutual dependence. The more I gazed, the more glorious and magnificent did it become. The figures I saw were all colorless and shining, but they were distinguished from one another by the form of their raiment and by various other signs, sceptres, crowns, garlands, croziers, crosses, instruments of martyrdom, etc. In the centre arose a tree, upon whose branches, as if on seats, appeared figures still more resplendent. This tree extended its branches like the fibres of a leaf, swelling out as it rose. The upper figures were more magnificent than those below ; they were in an attitude of adoration. Highest of all were holy old men. Crowning the summit was a globe representing the world surmounted by a cross. The Mother of God was there, more splendid than usual, It is all inexpressible ! During this vision I slept in the little cottage, until I again awoke in time."

CHAPTER XXXVII.

Measures Taken by the Vicar-General.

We shall here interrupt our narrative to say a few words of the ghostly Superiors to whose authority Sister Emmerich so often appealed.

The Vicar General von Droste wrote to Dean Rensing, August 3d—"I hear they are about to institute a new investigation with regard to Sister Emmerich. Inform her of it without delay. Tell her also that they have not consulted me and that I have not authorized any ecclesiastic to take part in it."

The Vicar Roseri received, at the same time, a severe reproof for going to Dülmen without orders. "No ecclesiastic ought to accept an order of the kind from secular authority," wrote the Vicar-General. "He dishonors and forswears his august calling when he allows himself to be employed in police affairs."—Mr. Roseri and Mr. Niesert were, consequently, obliged to quit Dülmen, and the same order was given to Prof. Roling. The latter delayed until the Chief-President and Landrath Bœnninghausen should use their influence for him to remain; but Clement von Droste was not a man to act in contradiction to himself. A second order was despatched to Dean Rensing:

"The Chief-President von Vinke," he wrote, "asks that I should allow some ecclesiastics to take part in this investigation, but I cannot consent. . . . . . I will permit no priest, Prof. Roling no more than any other, to take part in it, especially as Baron von Vinke does not speak of a mixed commission. Once for all, then, until further orders, observe

the instructions I have given you. I trust Prof. Roling will
be not less obedient than Mr. Roseri and Mr. Niesert."

In answer to Sister Emmerich's appeal for assistance and
counsel, the Vicar-General wrote to Dean Rensing. "I
hasten to reply that I can give no particular advice for the
future, as I know nothing respecting the projected investigation. As for the rest, it seems to me that what Sister
Emmerich has done up to the present and what she intends
doing is very proper. Her saying that I ought not to abandon her entirely, shows that she has taken a wrong view of
the case."

When, later on, Sister Emmerich forwarded to the Vicar-
General through Dean Rensing a copy of the protest presented by her to the commission, he sent the following note
from Darfeld: "I have received your communications of
August 5th and 7th, with Sister Emmerich's protest. I shall
reply as briefly as possible. This investigation is *purely
secular*, ordered and directed exclusively by the civil authorities. If ecclesiastics were to take part in it, contrary to
established rules, that fact would not alter its nature ; it
would still remain secular. It is most important that it
should in no way, not even in appearance, assume the
character of a mixed investigation. Therefore, 1st—No
ecclesiastic (yourself included) must take the least share in
it, either for or against ; we must absolutely ignore it. If
Sister Emmerich asks advice of you, Canon Hackram,
or any other priest, it is only right that it should not be refused her ; but neither you nor any other priest must accede
to demands from a commission whose very existence should
be ignored. Act so that all other ecclesiastics may clearly
understand this.

"No. 2—I know not by what right some of Sister Emmerich's friends have laid a protest against the investigation

before the chief tribunals of the country. If such a course is resorted to, it is Sister Emmerich herself who should do it, or at least, her friends should have from her a formal request in writing authorizing them to make such a protest.

" No. 3—It would not be proper for any priest to remain alone with her under the present circumstances, either for counsel or spiritual assistance." This was the only decision to which the Vicar-General could possibly come, since about a year previously the Chief-President had, on some futile plea, positively rejected the proposed idea of a mixed investigation. ":I have," he wrote, " proposed to Baron von Vinke, in accordance with his desire, a commission of investigation, partly secular, partly ecclesiastic, which, however, was not accepted. He assured me that four-persons could not be found (I had expressed a wish that there should be some Protestants among them) who, alternately with four others named by me, would guard Sister Emmerich for eight days at least."

The Chief-President, however, pushed the matter on, designedly eluding the intervention of ecclesiastical authority. He named a commission, the choice of whose members made it plainly visible to the Vicar-General what were its tendencies ; therefore the latter deemed it obligatory upon himself to protect the Church's dignity by forbidding clerics to take part in it. He knew also that he could not hazard any step in favor of persecuted innocence under the then existing government without exposing it to worse treatment ; he looked upon the projected investigation as unworthy of notice, feeling confident (as the invalid had been shown in vision) that, " what was of God would be upheld by God."

Some time before, when Prof. Bodde had published his attacks upon the invalid and, through her, upon ecclesiastical authority, the Vicar-General, to prevent the intervention of the civil authorities, had again seriously thought of removing her from her surroundings and placing her in some peaceful retreat entirely secluded from the world. He was, however, forced to admit that Almighty God, in signing her with the stigmata, had willed to leave her in a position apparently little suited to such a distinction, although he could not be persuaded that the Abbé Lambert and Father Limberg were wholly free from blame in the unsuccessful project of removing her to Darfeld (1). Some years later, owing to the idle talk of one of her former Sisters in religion, it was rumored in Münster that the invalid was going to retire to a place near Dülmen called " The Hermitage." The Vicar-General immediately dispatched an order to Dean Rensing, couched in the following severe terms : " Having learned that Sister Emmerich proposes to go to the *Hermitage* with the Abbé Lambert, or Father

(1) As the venerable old Abbé suffered much in this affair, we think it proper to give here the following letters of Dean Overberg to Dr· Wesener. They testify to the charity and solicitude with which the Dean, the most venerated priest in the country of Münster, interested himself in Sister Emmerich and her little circle.

I.

" Sept. 6, 1818.

" Have the kindness to inform me at your earliest convenience : 1—How much the Abbé Lambert still owes the druggist ; 2—Whether our dear Sister or the Abbé has as yet paid anything, and how much ; 3—Whether our Sister herself still owes anything to the druggist, and how much. I shall try to help them discharge their debt, at least in part. Salute our dear Sister cordially for me, and assure her that I shall write soon, D. V., though I would rather go to see her, if it pleases God to grant me the use of my limbs. I should be much pleased, if you would kindly lend me again for some months your journal of the invalid. I do not write to the Abbé concerning the apothecary, but of the other affair. The position for writing suits not my limbs, it is very fatiguing ; therefore, I must be brief· May God be with us!"

II.

"Sept. 13, 1818.

" I have the honor to send you not only the 8 Thlr. 23 Gr. of the apothecary's bill, but also what is due for the Abbé's medicines, 25 Thlr. We can also count among the medicines, the wine still necessary or, at least, very desirable during convalescence. Let our Sister employ what remains after paying the apothecary in procuring wine or anything else of which she may have need, or wine for the Abbé until he is able to return to his beer. No sick or poor person has suffered by my sending her this sum, but let her remember the donor in her prayers. It is not I. I shall name him to her some time—and yet, there is no reason why you and she should not know him. It is the Prince-Bishop of Hildesheim to whom I wrote about the bill. I leave it to your and our Sister's discretion to let the Abbé know that there is something in reserve to procure him wine. If it please God to cure my limbs so that I can undertake a journey to Dülmen, I shall have the pleasure of seeing all my beloved friends. May God be with us !

" P. S. None of the money is to be returned, even though it should not be expended in wine for the Abbé."

Limberg, or with both, I charge you, Rev. Sir, to inform Sister Emmerich immediately, as well as the two aforesaid ecclesiastics, that, although I cannot forbid her residing at the place named, yet I formally forbid her to allow either one or other of these two priests to accompany her. I also prohibit the latter, under pain of reserved punishment, to lodge at this Hermitage, or even to pass a single night therein, in case Sister Emmerich makes it her abode."

Reports like the above succeeded one another, accusations and threats against the invalid and her friends were addressed to the Vicar-General which aroused in him the fear that it would turn to the prejudice of religion. He resolved therefore, upon an expedient which would insure her removal from Dülmen by placing it out of her own power or that of her friends to object ; an expedient, however, to which spiritual authority ought not to resort. Oct 21, 1817, he wrote to Dean Rensing :—

"I thank you very much for your letter concerning Sister Emmerich. I should have replied the same morning had I not committed to writing and sealed what I propose in her regard, and I look forward to breaking the seal only in your presence. Say to her in my name that as her Superior, I command her to beg God to vouchsafe to her the knowledge in detail of the plan I have formed for her. Tell her also that she can never fail when in obedience. As soon as an opportunity offers, I shall take the liberty to send you a copy of my brother's book on the 'Church and State.' May God command the wind and waves!"

It was, then, upon the hope that his thought would be divined that the Vicar-General rested the execution of his project. He forgot that he was treading on the forbidden ground of divination when he gave such a command. He lost sight of the strict rules of Faith and the very principles that constitute authority in the ascetic life, which alone ought to dictate the measures and trace the limits of an ecclesiastical investigation. His purity of intention, however, was pleasing to God, who granted him the desired satisfaction of seeing the invalid separated for some time from her habitual surroundings. One feature in his project was directly opposed to the will of God, and that was his resolve to sequester her for the rest of her life in an asylum absolutely cut off from the world, for she still had a task to fulfil, that of *relating the Life of Jesus.* Scarcely had Dean Rensing informed her of the above-mentioned command, than she was enlightened by her angel on the Vicar-General's secret project. Next day, Dr. Wesener made the following report:—

"Oct. 25—I found her deathly weak. She had had a miserable night and had seen herself near death. She could not exactly designate the day, but she thought it not far distant.

"Oct. 26—Extreme debility. We resolved to sit up with her last night which she spent miserably. She had three spasmodic attacks in which the muscles of the abdomen were drawn back toward the spine. She announced each attack, saying she *should have to bear this suffering, but that God would give her patience.*"

Her sufferings increased until the first week in November, the doctor and confessor looking upon death as certain. On Nov. 6th, the doctor recorded in his journal: "I found her to-day weak indeed, but cheerful. 'During my last sufferings,' she said, 'I had constant visions. I had to climb a rough mountain with my guide. Right and left on the road, I saw paths leading to precipices and I beheld the distress of the wanderers for whom I had to pray. Half-way up the mountain, I came across a city with a magnificent church; but before I could enter, some holy little nuns of my own Order received me, and clothed me in a shining white habit. I told them I was afraid of not being able to keep it unstained. They answered: 'Do what thou canst. Stains will, indeed, appear, but thou wilt cleanse them with thy tears.' . . . . I had also a conversation with my guide about the secret the Vicar-General had imposed upon me through Dean Rensing, and he told me that I must observe the strictest silence on the subject. I was to tell no one whatever. 'If they push the affair further,' he added, 'God will put an end to it.'"

This absolute silence of the invalid threw the Vicar-General into a state of incertitude. He wrote to Dean Rensing, April 5, 1818 :—

"I have not yet come to any decision, although I have done what I could to fathom the case. Herr von Vinke is responsible for the non-execution of a mixed investigation, under the empty pretext that he could not find four individuals to engage in it. *I think God will take the affair into His own hands!*" . . . And, as if to attest his belief in the invalid's extraordinary vocation and perfect sincerity, he added:—" This letter will be handed you by Prince von Salm Reifferscheid, accompanied, perhaps, by his son and Rev. Herr von Willi. They wish to converse with Sister Emmerich and look upon at least one of her hands. As they are *God-fearing* people, I could not refuse them, and I beg you to escort them to her lodgings. I mention the Prince's son and his venerable tutor merely for the sake of precaution. I know not for certain whether they will go or not."

When Bishop Sailer visited Dülmen in the fall and, conformably to Dean Overberg's wish, received an account of conscience from Sister Emmerich, she revealed to him the Vicar-General's secret and the order she had received in vision. He encouraged her to silence, and the Vicar-General allowed the affair to rest.

CHAPTER XXXVIII

THE CAPTIVITY.

Sister Emmerich was conveyed to Councillor Mersmann's house and placed in a room on the second floor to which there was no access but by one door which opened into an ante-chamber. Her bed stood in the centre of the room, and from the ante-chamber the most minute observations could be made (1). Here two commissioners were to remain constantly six hours at a time, when they were to be relieved by two others; they were not to lose sight of the invalid a single instant. The bed-clothes and linen of the invalid were carefully examined that no sharp instruments or chemical preparations by whose aid, as they imagined, she procured the effusions of blood could be there concealed; her finger nails also underwent inspection lest they should be long enough to tear the skin.

The Chief-President sent from Münster an experienced nurse, a Mrs. Wiltner, on Prof. Bodde's recommendation. She had never seen Sister Emmerich and the commissioners did all they could to prejudice her against the patient, telling her that she was an impostor whose fraud she was to expose. The Chief-President's instructions were that the investigation was to continue until they arrived at a definitive decision. The first day was Sunday, 8th of August. On the preceding evening the invalid had regained consciousness. She perceived the change in her surroundings, but soon relapsed into contemplation which lasted until the

(1) For an account of this investigation, the author has referred to the details published at the time, to the Pilgrim's notes, and especially to Dr. Wesener's. In September, 1819, Sister Emmerich related the particulars of her captivity to the latter, who wrote everything down and daily submitted his notes for her approval.

next morning when she requested her confessor to give her Holy Communion. She offered herself in sacrifice to God, prayed for her persecutors, and drew such strength from the reception of the Holy Eucharist as to look with perfect peace and resignation upon all that might happen to her. The day passed calmly, the watchers often approaching her bed, but most politely. Prof. Roling, of Münster, expressed his amazement at her serenity : " I cannot understand how you can be so self-possessed and serene," he said to her. The nurse, too, testified her astonishment, and Sister Emmerich, noticing the marked attention she paid to her demeanor, to her every word, rejoiced with the thought : " Now the truth will appear !"

That night was a restless one. Her custodians frequently approached her one after another, holding the light in her face and calling her. She said in allusion to this : " Even then I was not left without help. When they came to me with the light, my angel was always present. I obeyed him, I heard him, I answered him. He called out to me, ' Awake !' and when they put insidious questions to me, he told me what to answer."

The following day the interrogatory began, Dr. Rave, to whom she had objected, opening the inquiry. She was obliged to allow him to examine her wounds, which he did in the roughest manner, a proceeding very wounding to her exquisite delicacy. He noted down her answers as she gave them. Perceiving the effort she was obliged to make, he frequently asked her if he should discontinue his questions ; but she begged him to go on. " For," she said, " I am here for that purpose ; I must go through it." From time to time, Dr. Borges and Landrath Bœnninghausen came in, seated themselves at the foot of her bed, and watched her closely. She tried to answer every question as precisely as possible in the hope of establishing her truth and innocence. The interrogatory lasted the whole day and even late in the evening, when completely exhausted she fainted away. Dr. Rave and the Landrath appeared to have concerted together to sound each other's praises; they attributed to each other the best intentions and tried to impress the invalid with the belief that they were her protectors. Dr. Borges's presence was most odious to her. She regarded him as the chief instigator of the injustice done her, and he, on his side, lost no opportunity of wounding her by his coarse and unfeeling remarks. On the third evening, she was informed that neither Father Limberg nor Sister Neuhaus should any longer have access to her, and that Dean Rensing would bring her Holy Communion every week. The night passed with the usual annoyances. She was almost overcome by fear, her custodians continually touching and examining the wounds in her hands; but she kept silence and allowed them to do what they pleased (1).

On Tuesday morning, the 10th, the examination was resumed. Dr. Rave had declared his task finished the preceding evening; yet he began again with Dr. Borges and the Landrath to put differently worded questions on the same points as before, trying to force her to contradict her former statements. He had reported, in February, that she had callosities or painless swellings on her feet, a proof that she really did walk in secret. After he had repeatedly inspected them the invalid said: "What think

(1) Her very patience and silence were for the Landrath a most convincing proof of imposture. "If she, indeed, suffered so much," he reasoned, "she could never have kept silence."—"One single trick," he wrote, "one single act of dissimulation, sufficed to betray the whole affair. We were enlightened sooner than we expected by a seeming trifle. Her friends had united with her in assuring us that the slightest touch on her wounds caused her acute pain, that she even cried out on such occasions; but we found that when engaged in a conversation that embarrassed her, the wounds of her hands might be tightly pressed or even rubbed without her giving any sign of uneasiness. I tested this myself, and so did others."—(Bœnninghausen's Report of the Investigation, 1819).

you, doctor? Can I walk? Do you judge by my feet that I can walk?"—To which he was forced to answer before his companions: " There is no question of it. You are too weak and suffering."

When these interrogatories had continued two hours, all the commissioners were assembled by Dr. Borges for the reading of the official report. This lasted four long hours, from ten A. M. till two P. M.; for each thought himself obliged to test the accuracy of the statements by repeated inspections of her wounds. She was treated with as little consideration by them as if she had been a log of wood. Their savage brutality would not even allow the timid, consecrated virgin to veil her breast. Whenever she tremblingly covered herself, they brutally tore away the linen, answering her plaintive entreaties by cynical railleries. Toward two o'clock they left her, but only for an hour. They all returned at the end of that time and recommenced torturing their victim, who happly fell into contemplation and beheld the martyrdom of St. Lawrence. She remembered only one of the remarks made to her that evening: "Now it is all right. You can go home again on Saturday."

"This day," she said, "was the bitterest of my life. I thought I should die of shame and confusion at what I had to endure, and the words to which I had to listen. I said to myself on the shameful treatment I underwent: 'My soul is in the prison of the body; now is the body itself in prison, and the soul confined to a little space, must deliver up the body of sin. Crucify it, outrage it! It is but a wretched log.'"

On Wednesday, Aug. 11th, they adopted a new plan of action. After the preceding examination, the existence of the stigmata could not possibly be denied; therefore must the invalid be adroitly led to confess that they had been artificially produced by French exiled priests. Dr. Rave undertook to extort from her the avowal. He made his appearance about nine o'clock A. M., assumed an air of extreme kindness, seated himself by her bedside, and expressed the desire " to speak to her heart to heart." The custodians withdrew, and the doctor began in em- phatic terms to praise the intelligence, the virtue, the whole life of the poor invalid. With his hand on his heart, he exclaimed: "Yes, indeed! I feel the most heartfelt compassion for you, sick and suffering as you are! I wish to speak with you in perfect sincerity and assist you as far as I can. Landrath Bœnninghausen, also, esteems and pities you, like myself. He is disposed to serve you, and Chief-President von Vinke is of the same mind ; he wrote to us last evening that he would like to take charge of you and all your family. Confide in us, be perfectly open and sincere with us."—At these words Sister Emmerich inter- rupted him and said :—

"I only wish that you and he could see into my heart, you would find nothing hidden there, nothing bad."

"Yes," he continued, " you may trust me as you do your confessor. I will keep all to myself—even the Landrath shall not know what you confide to me. I shall arrange every- thing for the best, you will soon see an end to this affair."

"I do not understand," she replied, " why you would hide from the commissioners anything concerning me. The commission must and shall know all that I have to say !"

Then he began to run over her life, from time to time putting captious questions to throw her off her guard, such as— " Did you not use the discipline in the convent ?"

"My chief discipline consisted in overcoming myself interiorly and in rooting out my faults and evil inclinations."

" You have always borne great veneration toward the Five Sacred Wounds. Now, it is not an unprecedented thing for pious persons in an excess of love to imprint them visibly upon their person."

" I know nothing of such things. I have already said all that I can of the origin of my wounds."

" Ah ! believe not that I imagine you have made them with a bad intention or through hypocrisy. No, I know you too well. I heard of you from every one as a person given to virtue from your childhood. But there would surely be no harm in wishing to become like to the Redeemer. One might do such a thing out of piety."

" No, not in this way. It would be sinful and unlawful."

" Yes, I think so, too. I esteem you too pious and upright for such a fraud. But I regret that you are now so abandoned by your friends. Do you not wish me to bring your sister or the Abbé Lambert ?"

" No ! I wish no suspicion to rest on them !"

" But you have been visited by other French priests, and you could not know what they did when you were unconscious."

" Just after the suppression of the convent, I had, it is true, long fainting-spells ; but I am certain that no one ever did anything to me. There was only one attendant by me, and she saw the blood flow for the first time."

" It is not possible that such a thing could happen of itself. French priests are very pious, they esteem this sort of thing very highly ; they did it with a good intention, and you allowed it through piety."

" No ! that would not be a good intention nor piety. It would be so great a crime that I would rather suffer death than consent to such a thing."

" Reflect well upon your position ! Let it not come to this, that ecclesiastical authority demand an oath of you."

" What I say I can swear to at any time. Ecclesiastical Superiors may come."

" Then we are all in the dark, and you alone are in the light ! "

" What do you mean by that ? "

" You are so suffering, so full of pains, so tortured on all sides !—Can that be the calling of man ? "

" Ah ! you disquiet and torment yourself still more for the evil things of this world, you live in constant agitation, you perplex your brain over things you cannot understand ; but my sufferings are not so grievous to me, because I know why I suffer."

" No ! I tell you, the wounds come not as you say ! It is impossible l If you have not made them, others have !"

" Now I see plainly what you mean, and what a double game you tried to play last winter !"

" Well, let us remain good friends."

" No ! Friendship cannot exist on such terms. You shall not make me tell a lie !"

Dr. Rave retired and Herr Bœnninghausen entered. Sister Emmerich declared to him her readiness to confirm on oath all that she had stated, whereupon he replied : "O that is nothing! such an oath is of no value ! We would not receive an oath !"—And when she objected that Dr. Rave's duplicity would oblige her to defend herself by sworn testimony, he responded:—

"Dr. Rave has written nothing bad of you, his statement was good. For the rest, he may say and write what and how he pleases, only what is official has weight or truth."

Thursday, Aug. 12th, she was less importuned. She

had violent vomitings all the morning, but they paid little attention to her. One or another made his appearance from time to time, but immediately withdrew. A young man named Busch, hardly yet free from the school-room, was the only one who frequently presented himself, tormenting her with his self-confidence and arrogance.—" Will your wounds bleed to-morrow ?—What! you do not know?—When the blood begins to flow, let me know immediately, etc."—At first, she sought to silence him by her own gravity. But failing in this, she at length addressed him : " Young man, take care ! Do not allow yourself to be drawn into acts of injustice and rash judgments ! It is not so easy to decide upon things of this kind, on which older men than you have suspended their judgment. You are young, and it is becoming in a young physician to be reserved, to judge leisurely." He was moved by these words and said before the nurse : " Sister Emmerich knows how to touch one's conscience. Were she innocent, I might weep tears of blood !" He, however, hardened his heart. He was to the end more insulting than the older members. The nurse could not conceal her sympathy and veneration for the persecuted invalid. That afternoon, Dr. Rave offered her some oatmeal porridge which she declined. He insisted, whereupon she tasted it, when vomiting immediately came on.

August 13th, Friday.—This day had been impatiently awaited by the commissioners. Would there, or would there not be an effusion of blood ? In either case, they had resolved to view it as imposture. Herr von Bœnninghausen and Dr. Rave kept watch the night before and, to give her confidence, as he imagined, the former expressed to her his great desire that the following day would bring an effusion of blood. " Understand," said he, "I do not wish it on my own account, but for Dr. Borges's sake. Only yesterday were we speaking about it, and he assured me that, if he saw the blood flow, he would certainly become a Catholic. He assured me of it."

Sister Emmerich replied indignantly : " On the Day of Judgment, perhaps that man, if he remains what he is, will be dealt with more leniently than they who know the Law, but who do not live conformably to it. It may be that he is not so guilty as you."

The entire night between Thursday and Friday she lay in contemplation, and the dawn of day found her physically stronger. " I begged the nurse," she said, " to give me water to wash. She did so, with these words : ' May God and His holy Mother permit the wounds in your head to bleed ! then these gentlemen will be convinced of your innocence.' I rebuked her for such a wish : ' I hope there will be no blood,' I said. 'Of what use would it be ? These gentlemen would not let themselves be convinced. Still we must commit ourselves to the will of God !' I washed and said in jest, ' My forehead especially I shall wash clean.' Then I took off my cap and the nurse had just spread a clean white linen towel over my head, when in came Dr. Busch with his usual questions. He said : ' You must let the blood flow '—In about a quarter of an hour, he made me take off my binder, and behold it was stained with blood ! It was a most unwelcome sight to me, I had hoped there would be no blood. I did not dare to cover my head, and all the commissioners were called in. They examined my binder and head, and set to work to wash my forehead, first with a warm, then with a cold liquid, which gave me great pain."—The nurse deposed that the invalid's forehead was rubbed first with saliva, then with strong vinegar, and lastly with oil of vitriol. At this application she cried out in pain. "It burns, it burns like fire!" and then, as the nurse said, some red streaks appeared.

"They spent the whole morning in examining, washing, and rubbing my forehead. I fainted from pain. The gentlemen-commissioners showed great embarrassment. The nurse was closely questioned as to how the blood came on my binder. She related all that we had said and how it had happened, but they declared that I had wounded myself. The nurse greatly excited came toward me, wringing her hands : 'O Miss Emmerich, you are betrayed and sold! They say you have put the blood on your bindder yourself! O unhappy woman that I am to be employed by such people! Yet do I rejoice that I now know you and can help you!'—I consoled the woman, telling her that I knew they would act thus, and I exhorted her to trust in God."

Mrs. Wiltner's honest testimony to the truth was exceedingly distasteful to the commissioners, who summoned her before them next day and interrogated her anew. They employed every artifice to make her say that, two minutes before Dr. Busch's arrival, she had left the invalid to empty the basin ; but she firmly refused to tell the falsehood. On the contrary, she declared herself ready to swear solemnly that she had not left the room and that the invalid, after the removal of her binder, had not once raised her hands to her head, but had kept them clasped on her breast the whole time. She forced Dr. Busch to acknowledge that, when he entered the room, the basin of water was still standing on a chair. But her protestations were of no avail. They entered into the report the following words as Mrs. Wiltner's deposition : "Mrs. Wiltner, the nurse, absented herself for two minutes to empty the basin."

Some time after the investigation, the nurse gave her tes-

timony to the public through Dr. Theodore Lutterbeck, of
Dülmen, and offered to repeat it under oath before any
tribunal; upon which the Landrath Bœnninghausen had
the audacity to publish the following : " If Dr. Lutterbeck contests the right of the commission to public confidence, he will find his words received as oracles by few.
I claim it with much more reason for myself, as I have submitted every detail to a minute examination with perfect
impartiality, and a mind free from prejudice. Should more
credit be accorded to a nurse's deposition which, after all,
proves nothing, than to my testimony ? This I leave to
the judgment of the reader. I shall only observe that, from
the first eight days, Mrs. Wiltner manifested a disposition
to talkativeness and a veneration for Sister Emmerich which
led the commission to deliberate whether it would not be
well to supply her place by another, a less bigoted person.
But as she seemed to get on well with the nun, and as it
was very important that the latter should mistrust us as
little as possible, she was retained (1)."

That afternoon the commissioners again met around the
patient's bed, and Dr. Rave experimented on himself to
prove that the effusion of blood had been artificially produced. The Landrath's report is as follows :—

" The circumstance (2) offering the most conclusive proof
of the fraud and which shows that Anne Catherine Emmerich plays not only a passive rôle in it, but that she is
also an active accomplice, happened in the following manner. The fact that the bleeding ceased not entirely in her
head as in the other parts, formed the only basis upon which
it was possible to experiment. The only difficulty was as to
how she made her head bleed, not an easy matter in truth,
since she was never alone and was, moreover, in a position

(1) History and Result of Investigation, 2, p: 46.
(2) History and Result of Investigation, 2, p. 34—39.

that exacted the greatest precautions; besides, a certain one of our members was so inconsiderate as to wish to treat with her candidly and openly, which manner of acting would not, as is evident, have led to the end in view, but would have put her still more on her guard. However, the trial had to be made, and it was announced to her that the commission would not separate until a positive decision had been reached. She informed us herself that her head bled at times, although the other parts had ceased to do so, and the appearance of this phenomenon being all that was required to end the investigation, so painful on both sides, we entreated her to beg God not to delay it. As these words seemed to be pretty well received and, moreover, as we saw that the need of more substantial nourishment began to be felt by our patient, they were again repeated to her with every imaginable mark of sincerity, and lo! that very evening was made the prophetic announcement that, *perhaps the next day, Friday, August* 13*th, a little blood might appear on her forehead!* Now, at last, we had grounds for hope. That she might not be disturbed by too rigorous a surveillance, I took that duty upon myself, and when all were asleep I threw myself gently on the lounge in the ante-room. Toward midnight, I heard a rustling. I arose quietly, peeped through the open door and saw that Sister Emmerich had changed her position. Her back was turned to me and she was in the act of removing the bed-clothes. She caught sight of me; but, as the light did not fall on her face, I could not say whether she was annoyed at being detected or not. Next morning, however, at six o'clock, nothing had as yet appeared on her forehead. I was on the point of giving up hope, when half an hour after, the nurse very much excited brought me the wished for information that Sister Emmerich's head seemed to be bleeding.

The phenomenon was carefully examined by all, and each member was invited to commit his observations to writing. I regard this circumstance as the most important and decisive in the course of the investigation; and I am of opinion, as are also the other members of the committee, that nothing was left undone on the occasion. Our unanimous conclusion is, that the red marks on the invalid's forehead perfectly resemble what might be produced by rubbing or scratching. There were two where the epidermis had evidently been scratched. From them flowed the ordinary lymph which adhered to the head-band, whilst a third had begun to form a crust. This opinion is that of men, unprejudiced, impartial, and of sound judgment; it alone should suffice to convince the most incredulous. Mark well what follows:—to arrive by comparison at still greater certainty, Dr. Rave that same morning scratched his forehead in two places until the epidermis broke and lymph flowed. The result was the same in both cases: the simple red marks made by the rubbing disappeared in two days; in other places the crust formed by the lymph fell off in six days, when the epidermis was renewed, which in both cases took place on the seventh day.

" When we had thus acquired convincing proof that what we had seen was altogether different from the effusions of blood we had heard described —still more that they had been made by the hand of man, and that unskilfully enough, it remained only to be ascertained how far the invalid would carry her denial of the facts. It was easy to see, as is proved by the report that when she was in a state of consciousness, two or three minutes would have sufficed to do the work; and this time she could have had when the nurse left the room with the basin. I exhorted her in presence of some of the members to depose to the report, but she declared that the scratches on her forehead were neither of her own making nor that of any one else, and she offered to take an oath to this effect. A feeling of grief came over me when I heard this declaration on oath of an evident lie, uttered coolly and smilingly by one whose pitiful condition I could not forbear compassionating. She appeared in my eyes as a hardened impostor deserving neither pity nor consideration, one with whom severe measures should be used to bring her to an avowal of her guilt. But the sight of suffering humanity regained its empire over me ; her desolate state effaced my first impression of horror and turned my indignation against the revolting malice of those who had perverted the poor creature."

As some stains had appeared on the invalid's linen, the wound in her side having bled also, an explanation must be found for that. The Landrath said they were merely the stains of the coffee she had vomited. But Mrs. Wiltner declared at the time and afterward to Dr. Lutterbeck that she was ready to swear to the fact that the very weak coffee taken and rejected by the invalid had been received in a blue cloth always at hand, and that not a single drop had fallen on the chemise which had been, besides, protected by a four-double covering. The article was then examined, the stains found to be the red color of blood. After washing it, Mrs. Wiltner showed the water tinged to the commissioners. Still Bœnninghausen clung to his opinion of the coffee stains, and forbade the nurse to show it or the water to Dr. Zumbrink who arrived from Münster the following day. She however disregarded the Landrath's injunction and informed Dr. Z— of all that had passed, offering to confirm what she said by oath (1).

(1) Mrs. Wiltner's deposition was published some time after by Dr. Theodore Lutterbeck, upon which Landrath von Bœnninghausen immediately made the following

In the afternoon they again assembled around her bed to renew the torture of the morning. But Sister Emmerich flatly refused to yield to their wishes; whereupon, the Landrath exhorted her to obedience and patience.

" We must all do our duty," he said. " We are all servants of the State and one must help the other. You, also, must give an account to the State of whatever there is extraordinary in you."

Sister Emmerich replied : " I respect civil authority and I am willing to fulfil my duty ; but I do not recognize all here present as competent judges in this case ! "

They answered by all kinds of persuasive reasoning, but to no purpose. The Landrath exclaimed : " For whom do you take us, then ? "—Instantly in a solemn tone, she answered : " I look upon you all as the servants of the devil !" (1).

These words from the lips of a defenceless female made such an impression upon one of the gentlemen present, Mr. Nagelschmidt, the druggist, that he left the room, exclaiming : " No ! I'll not be the devil's servant ! "—and he refused to take any further part in the iniquitous affair. All were dumbfounded. The Landrath had no answer to make and, one by one, they slipped away, leaving Sister Emmerich in peace.

Dr. Busch came again late that evening, feigning compassion and offering his services. He made the nurse re-

explanation : " The numberless frauds already discovered and the others yet to be disclosed, lead me to suspect that the reddish stains on Sister Emmerich's linen were made by blood from her gums. This assertion is not quite so ridiculous as is the attempts to prove that by capillary attraction it must have flowed from her internal organs ; for the stains were darker outside than inside. I do not, however, affirm that her perspiration was wholly free from blood.'

(1) When Sister Emmerich, in September, recounted this scene to the Pilgrim, she added : " The Landrath was sitting at the right of my bed smoking, near him stood the apothecary The former pretended to pity me because, as he said, my friends had reduced me to so pitiable a state. But, he said. I was not too old to be cured, and so on, and again began to flatter me. I saw the devil behind him. I was too frightened to speak, and the nurse, thinking I was going to faint, brought me some water. Then came the talk about authority, and I said, ' First comes God . . . . . .' "

move the invalid's head-dress, when he poured on the top
of her head some drops of a liquid which deprived her of
consciousness. "Those drops," she said afterward, "gave
me pain through my whole body and took away my senses.
The nurse thought me dead. I lay for a whole hour immovable."

On the morning of Saturday, the 14th, they began
again to rub and to bathe her head. The new physician
from Münster, Dr. Zumbrink, carefully examined everything, but behaved with so much propriety as to gain
Sister Emmerich's confidence. In the afternoon, she had
a chance of convincing herself in an interview with him
that her first impression was not false.

"Before he came," she related, "I had a vision in
which I beheld a tall, dark-complexioned man approach
me and hold out his hand. I thought he was sent from
God to save me and I told my nurse so. He did come, in reality. He was an upright, honorable man; the others were
afraid of him, concerted among themselves, and kept out
of his presence. The chief-officer ironically called him
my doctor; he said that he was of *my* party and asked me
if I were not particularly fond of him. I answered that
I hoped each would do his duty. Dr. Zumbrink was no
flatterer; he was more attentive and more active than
any of the others. He said to me from the first: 'I shall
write whatever I discover, innocence or imposture. Be
not bewildered by anything, neither by fair words nor by
threats. Hold to the truth; with that a person cannot be
worsted (1).'

"The others I saw in vision in the black, filthy, four-

(1) Dr. Lutterbeck declared in his second pamphlet that he had read the opinion
Dr. Zumbrink had given in writing and in which he stated, "Not having seen Anne
Catherine Emmerich for seven years before, he had formed no opinion as to the origin
of her wounds; but that, during the investigation, he had remarked no fraud.
From the impression made upon him at the time by the invalid, he esteemed her
incapable of imposture."

cornered, false church, with a high roof and no turrets; they were very intimate with the spirit that presided therein. This church is full of impurity, vanity, sottishness, and darkness, but scarcely one of those men knew in what obscurity he labored. It is all proud presumption. The walls are high, but they surround emptiness; a stool is the altar, and on the table is a death's head veiled, a light on either side. In their worship they use naked swords, and at certain parts of the ceremonies the death's head is unveiled. It is all bad, thoroughly bad, the communion of the unholy. I cannot say how abominable, how pernicious and empty are their ceremonies. Many of the members know it not themselves. They wish to be one single body in some other than the Lord, and if a member separates from them, they become furious with me. When science separated from Faith, this church was born without a Saviour, good works without faith, the communion of the unbelieving with the appearance but not the reality of virtue; in a word, the anti-Church whose centre is malice, error, falsehood, hypocrisy, tepidity, and the cunning of all the demons of the period. It forms a body, a community outside the Body of Jesus, the Church. It is a false church without a Redeemer. Its mysteries are to have no mysteries and, consequently, its action is temporal, finite, full of pride and presumption, a teacher of evil clothed in specious raiment. Its danger lies in its apparent innocence. It wills differently, acts differently everywhere. In many places its action is harmless, in others it aims at corrupting a few of the learned. But all tends to one end, to something bad in its origin, an action outside Jesus Christ, through whom alone every life is sanctified, and outside of whom every action, every work remains in death and in the demon."

That evening Sister Emmerich reminded the Landrath of his promise to have her conveyed home on Saturday. "It cannot be," he replied. "The case is not closed, we have arrived at nothing definite." The next day, he jested among the other commissioners : "Miss Emmerich shall not escape, though we need not stay by her the whole day, or guard her so closely." Dr. Zumbrink expressed his indignation at such a speech—"What! is this not an investigation of a serious nature? Every one eats, drinks, sleeps, walks, amuses himself. The affair is not conducted as it should be. I do not trust such men!"

On the Feast of the Assumption and the two days following, Sister Emmerich was less tormented than usual. The committee could not agree upon what further experiments to make ; the Landrath went nervously in and out, and spoke of indifferent things. On the 17th, she demanded an end to the investigation, she recounted the torments she had undergone, and asked what they still exacted of her. The Landrath replied that so many new questions had been forwarded from Münster for herself, the Abbé Lambert, and her sister, that he could see no end to it. She responded sadly :

"They have put me off from day to day with vain promises, and the end is still far distant!"

The Landrath grew angry and began to threaten her: "You dare to reproach me, but things will soon be changed! Then you will find your man in me! You yourself and your French priests are the cause of your not being released."

Dean Rensing's entrance at this moment interrupted his invectives. Sister Emmerich turned to him saying : "They exact of me confessions that I cannot make."

The Dean replied : "If there is question of your avowing anything, you can testify to it on oath."

" Truly ! but they tell me that my oath is of no account."

" Who has told you that ? " inquired the Landrath.

" He who said it, ought to know," was her answer.

Thursday, Aug. 18th—This day was spent without special annoyance, excepting the Landrath's menaces and reproaches against her and her absent confessor, to all which she listened in silence.

Drs. Borges and Busch were to watch that night. They hoped that, as the next day would be Friday, they would witness the bleeding of her wounds (1).

Fortunately, Dr. Zumbrink was also present which restrained their brutality. Frightful visions disturbed her rest, and to her great joy the morning brought no effusion of blood. " This circumstance," she says, " seemed to give the Landrath satisfaction, as he looked upon it as a confirmation of his opinion that I am an impostor. Perhaps, too, he hoped to hear something from me. It is only in this way that I can explain his polite attentions, and the flattery with which he loaded me on the following day, forgetful of past scenes. His kindness was more insupportable than his threats."

Dr. Borges was in bad health. The night-watch had greatly fatigued him, and he returned to Münster disgusted at the whole affair.

On Friday evening, Dr. Rave appeared after an absence of a week. He could not conceal the impression made upon him by the invalid's appearance.

" How miserable and suffering you are ! " he exclaimed, and turning to the Landrath, he said : " She is unusually weak, she has fever. I cannot answer for her life much

---

(1) " They gave me that night a small phial," she said "wrapped in a scrap of black silk, saying that Dean Overberg had sent it to me, and that I must lay it awhile on my breast. It inspired me with horror, especially the silk. I felt that it came from an impure being. When they insisted on my putting it on my breast, my heart beat so violently that, in an agony, I dashed it away."

longer !"—When she reminded him that the next day
would be the third Saturday since they brought her there,
he said : "I can do nothing ! I, too, am worn out here.
If you cannot trust us longer, we cannot trust you, etc."

She represented to them their unworthy conduct, saying
sternly : " Which of you can accuse me of falsehood ?"—
but they returned no answer.

On Saturday several of the commission, scarcely knowing
what further·course to pursue, assembled around her. They
spoke of their own weariness of the affair and proposed
bringing it to a close. The nurse ventured the remark:
" What expense this affair has entailed ! And where will
the money come from to pay these gentlemen ? "

" All will be defrayed by the king," answered one.

'· The king is badly served by his subjects," rejoined
Sister Emmerich. " They deceive him to get his gold, which
is steeped in the sweat of the poor peasants ground down to
blood by taxation. Of what use is such an investigation ?
Of what value are all these reports made by men ignorant of
such things, who understand them not, who possess not the
key to them ? Better to distribute the money among the
poor and exact an account of secret prevaricators, of skilful
cheats, for that would do some good and draw down a blessing from God !"

She spoke many earnest words to which the commissioners replied not, though they seemed impressed. The Landrath felt his position as president growing more embarrassing every day ; Dr. Borges had withdrawn in anger at
not being able to persuade the invalid to acknowledge herself an imposter ; Dr. Rave saw all his artifices fall to the
ground, whilst Mr. Nagelschmidt and Dr. Zumbrink had
become her declared friends; the others were wavering. The
president had as yet discovered nothing to substantiate

his private suspicion of fraud, and what report should he make to Baron von Vinke to whom he had promised to bring the case to a definite conclusion? He began to cast around for some escape from his embarrassment, and for three days, from the 21st to the 23d of August, he sought to throw the invalid off her guard by insulting remarks and sudden attacks. He approached her only to irritate and perplex her; for example, he would address her as follows : " There you still lie ! A person in health ought not to lie in bed. You are only feigning. You pray not, you work not, and yet you are so weak and languid ! But you do not impose upon me. It does not escape me that you have strength enough when you wish ! You can speak as loud and as long as you want. I know that at home you were able to sew," etc.

Sister Emmerich full of compassion for the poor man, seldom answered a word. Hearing that his wife had a cancer, she longed to suck the wound and heal her; the certainty that her request would be refused alone restrained her from asking to do so. Sometimes Dr. Busch joined the Landrath in his railleries : " You are pretty well off in this investigation," he would say. " You suffer nothing, you lose nothing." One day as she was in the act of throwing off blood, he, without a word of explanation, suddenly wrenched open her mouth, thrust in the handle of a spoon, and examined her gums. Only from some remarks dropped by the Landrath did she discover what was meant by so violent an action : " Your case," said he, " is somewhat similar to that of an impostor recently unmasked at Osnabruck. She, too, with lips dry and parched, vomited blood ; but it was discovered that she sucked her gums to produce the hemorrhage. You do the same"—then softening his manner a little, he continued : " I pity you though, I do not think you so very guilty. The French priests say you are a patient, good creature willing to do all they tell you. They think they will be able to revive the practices of the Catholic Church and faith in her legends, if they can reproduce in you things of this sort."

Dr. Zumbrink was indignant at the outrages offered the poor invalid, and the nurse wept. " The president," she says, "proclaims you an accomplished cheat."—But Sister Emmerich, consoled and strengthened by God, bore up courageously.

" One day," she afterward related, " an old man with a little Child took me by the arm, led me away, and hid me in a nettle-bush. I was satisfied even to be stung by the nettles ; it was better than the talk of that man. It was St. Joseph and the Infant Jesus who had taken me away. One night the same little Boy that used to help me with the cows, came to me. He was very bright and gay and ran merrily around, a little stick in his hand. I said to Him: ' Ah ! dear Child, it is not now as it used to be in the fields, now I am in prison !' and we talked together joyously and freely. At another time, I had a shining Child by me in a glittering cradle. I rocked Him and cared for Him. He carried a cross, and when I asked what it was, He answered : —' It is thy cross which thou wilt not carry !'

" One day in the third week when I was very sick and longing for the Most Holy Sacrament, I had a vision. I went by a narrow, level, shady path to an island surrounded by walls. And now came two spirits to me, I think they were females, and gave me, for I was very weak, two morsels on a little plate. I remember the nurse was lying near me asleep and, that she might not see them, for they approached from her side, I threw my towel over her head."

August 25th found her so full of courage that she said: "I have lost all fear, all dread. I shall now be strong and cheerful in proportion as my troubles increase." And she begged the Landrath to put to her the questions he had had on hand for several days. But he replied:

"You are too weak and sick! You cannot answer!"—"If I am ordered to answer," she replied, "I can do so. The Lord will give me strength."

After some hours, he returned with Dr. Rave to begin the interrogatory. They had about fifty points to investigate. Dr. Rave felt her pulse at intervals to see how far her strength might be taxed, as he told the nurse (1). Sister Emmerich, alluding to this interrogatory afterward, said: "Before it began I was weak and miserable, but as it went on I grew stronger. But the questions were so singular, so ridiculous that they amused me, sometimes I could not help laughing heartily; for instance, they asked what was done to my wounds when people were kept waiting at the door, etc. When I had responded to all their questions, the report was read to me and I signed it after they had made some changes in it. Then I became again quite prostrate."

On Friday, Aug. 27th, her annoyances recommenced on the part of Dr. Busch. "Your blood must flow," he said, "Yes, make it do so! We are here uselessly, nothing comes of it. What can we say? What have we seen? etc."—"I have not that power," Sister Emmerich replied. "You should have come sooner, if you wanted to see my blood flow. If I could help you in any way with my blood, I should willingly do it; but I have not now as much blood as would satisfy your desire."

(1) He made a note in the report in his own peculiar style: "When Sister Emmerich forgets herself, she can speak very distinctly and at length; otherwise, she speaks in almost a whisper—a proof of her great dissimulation."

Then came the Landrath, impatient at her wounds not bleeding and asking angrily : " What will be the end of all this ? We have as yet found out nothing !"—and he broke out into threats against the invalid for not confessing what he termed *the truth*. At three P. M., he returned, sent the nurse out of the room, and closed the door. His excited appearance alarmed the poor invalid for the moment, but she soon regained her self-possession. He began : " Every day, every hour discovers so many new things that this case becomes more and more serious and complicated. Those Frenchmen's intrigues are now unveiled. Lambert, the old fox, has betrayed himself, but I am more cunning than he ! We now know why he, the Abbé Channes and Father Limberg distributed rosaries. I am now upon Limberg's track. I know that he used to be the exorcist in the parish of Darup. Yes, yes, I tell you, the French made those wounds on you, or you yourself did it. Come now, confess!"

Sister Emmerich replied quietly : " What I have said I hold to. I neither can nor do I wish to say anything else. Father Limberg never was at Darup." In a solemn voice, the Landrath said : " Miss Emmerich, I state the truth to you. It is all a fraud, the work of the French !"

The invalid silently busied herself with her tea. Assuming a gentler tone, the Landrath addressed her : " You shall no longer be annoyed, all will be ended if you only confess. Fear nothing. You and yours will be well cared for ! We wish well to you and to them."

" What you ask I cannot do. It would be a scandalous falsehood !"

" Confess !" he cried in a rage. " If the French did not do it, the Germans did ! But no ! they are not so bad, they are not cheats. But confess, at least, that you made your head bleed the other day !"

" That also would be false. Ask the nurse who saw the blood, ask the commissioners," replied Sister Emmerich. " The nurse is of no account! And your good Dr. Zumbrink? Let him keep out of this affair!" retorted the Landrath.

" Give yourself no further trouble! I understand you. It is useless! You gain nothing!" said Sister Emmerich quietly.

" Ah! you hypocrite! Cunning woman! I know you! I have watched you closely, I have often felt your pulse! You have strength enough when you wish, when it pleases you," said he in a rage.

She was silent—her innocent, peaceful expression only exasperated him, and he began again. " What! you will not answer me?"

" I have nothing to say to you! You do not want the truth. I fear you more than all hell. But God is with me and with all your threats and blasphemies you cannot hurt me!"—answered the Sister.

" It is a fraud, and it will remain a fraud! Confess it! (1) It cannot come from God, and a God, who does such things, I would not have! I offer you *pure wine* (2). What kind of conscience have you? I have something with which to reproach myself, but I would not exchange places with you!"

" It is not *pure wine,* it is gall that you offer me. You would drive me to perdition, but God will protect me. Truth will triumph! I have nothing more to say to you!" and she turned away in silence. The Landrath withdrew, saying : " You shall regret this soon, very soon! Still, I give

(1) Some weeks later, Von Bœnninghausen published the following: "Sister Emmerich must acknowledge that, when the investigation was over, I frankly made known to her my conviction founded upon evident reason." (The afore-named Work, p. 10.)

(2) " Pure wine"—that is the *truth.*

you till to-morrow for reflection. Be reasonable! Allow yourself to be persuaded!"

This scene, which lasted over two hours, the nurse witnessed from the ante-room. When the Landrath withdrew, she entered hastily, weeping and wringing her hands; but the invalid, cool and calm herself, soon restored her peace. When on Nov. 28th she related the affair to the Pilgrim, she said: "The two holy religious who had so often helped me, came and offered to deliver me. But I thought of St. Peter in prison and of his deliverance. I said: 'What am I compared with Peter? I will remain till the end.'"

On August 25th, Dr. Rave paid his last visit. "A curious case," said he, scornfully, "a curious case! I shall have nothing more to do with it! I am going home. I shall not be an obstacle to things turning out well for you!"

As Dr. Rave retired, the Landrath entered to announce a new scene for the evening: "Your affairs go ill," said he. "In the first place, you shall not soon, perhaps you will never return to your lodgings. Still, I leave you till this evening to reflect."

"This evening you shall receive no other answer than that already given," replied Sister Emmerich. Mr. Moellrr an, the burgomaster, came to see her, assuring her of the generous intentions of the Landrath in her regard. He tried to draw from her expressions of satisfaction upon all that had been done in the investigation up to the present moment; but she indignantly repelled his insinuations. About six, the Landrath returned in great excitement, closed the door as on a former occasion, and began:—"Do you remember what I told you?"

"I have no other answer to make," said the invalid.

" Reflect upon what you are doing. Lambert has committed himself. I'll soon catch him," said the Landrath.

" Then hold him fast!" replied Sister Emmerich. " Only take me to my home until he has revealed all, for then I shall have a long rest."

" Will you also confess ?" said he, unmindful of her last remark.

" To be sure," she answered ; " but I can tell you nothing but what I have already told you."

" You are an impostor! You are not sick! You know how to appear so, but I am more cunning than you. I have watched you. I have noticed every pulsation, every breath. You will have to quit Dülmen. Never again shall you see your relations and your good friends, the French. Yes, those French are they who have perverted you, etc., etc. !'"

Two hours were spent in such invectives, during the greater part of which the invalid observed strict silence. At last, her tormentor said : " My patience is worn out. We shall remove you this very evening."

"Have you really the power to do so ?" asked Sister Emmerich. " You have repeatedly said that, as a servant of the State, you would follow your orders closely"—but he interrupted her, saying : " I am now going to write the report. I understand the whole case. You cannot confess your guilt, because you are bound by terrible oaths; but I'll bring all to light ! You must leave Dülmen."

Sister Emmerich replied. " Do without fear or hesitation whatever you will. As for myself, I dread nothing. You call yourself a Catholic Christian, but what is your religion ? You see me receive the Holy Sacrament ! And yet I impress upon myself the signs of the Redeemer ! I

am bound by oaths! I am acting a lie, a horrible crime!
What is your religion?"

He made no answer, and withdrew. In about an hour he
returned with a written paper in his hand, and began:
"Must I send this report? You have yet some time. Reflect seriously!"

"Yes, send it," was the answer.

"I warn you! Think over it well!" said the Landrath
gravely.

"In God's name, take it away!" moaned the poor invalid.

In a solemn voice, he once more inquired: "Again, I
ask you, shall this report be sent? Think of the consequences!"

"In God's name, yes!" she again answered.

He left the room in a rage, returned, renewed the scene,
and left again angrily as before. Sister Emmerich saw
through the farce got up for the occasion. She quieted her
agitated nurse and, the first time since her removal, enjoyed for two hours a calm and refreshing sleep.

"I can say sincerely," she afterward remarked, "that
I was quite calm and more cheerful during this scene than
I had been the whole time previously."

Saturday night, the 29th, passed quietly. At ten the
next morning the Landrath reappeared.

"Now, will you go?" he began.

"O yes! I will gladly go *home!*" answered Sister Emmerich.

"No! not *home,* but out of the city!" repeated the
Landrath.

"I'll not consent to that," said Sister Emmerich firmly.

"How will you return to your home?" inquired her persecutor. "You are too weak!"

"Leave that to me!" answered Sister Emmerich. "You had the care of bringing me here, leave to me that of returning! The servant-girl will take me."

" But it is Sunday ! " he retorted. " You will be seen."

" Let me go at once!" said she. " The people are still at High Mass, the streets are empty."

"Well, let it be so! " he replied. " But before you go, you must promise me something."

" If I can, I will," said the poor invalid.

" You can. Promise to let me know immediately if blood again flows."

She promised, but he was not yet satisfied. He presented a paper, saying: " Here I have written your promise. Sign it, that it may be a pledge of its fulfilment." In her desire to return home, the unsuspecting Sister signed the paper without reading it (1). When he held in his possession the desired signature, he said : " I shall conduct you home myself. As I brought you here, I shall also take you away"—with these words, he seized the coverlet, rolled it round her in spite of her struggles, and carried her down stairs. Here he confided her to a female servant who bore her to her home without attracting much attention, the Landrath following at a distance. She had lost consciousness from the moment he took her into his arms. When she recovered her senses, he said : " I still hold to my opinion, but we shall remain friends ! "—She kept silence, and he withdrew.

Some weeks after, he returned and entered her room unannounced. She was so terrified at the sight of him that she almost swooned away.

(1) Oct. 14th, Von Bœnninghausen published the following :—
" Anne Catherine Emmerich has giving me in writing, signed by her own hand, a solemn promise to inform me immediately of any change that may occur in her physical state ; she has, besides, *expressly authorized* me to contradict all that may be published about her without my knowledge, and to declare him guilty of falsehood who propagates such things."

" But" (she afterward said to the Pilgrim and Dr. Wesener, who both relate this scene), "I turned my thoughts to God and became calm and brave. This man is quite inexplicable to me. He pretends to be very kind, speaks to me with tears of his wife's sickness, makes protestations of friendship, mentions the goodness that he has shown to me, and then says : ' But your wounds have not bled since the investigation, else you would have let me know ?' Then he began to speak of the publications which might be issued. He thought that printed relations of the affair would entail very fatal consequences for me ; and he begged me earnestly, with tears in his eyes, to prevent my friends from publishing anything. I replied : ' Be assured, my nearest friends certainly write nothing for the public. As to what others may do, I know not ; and again, I know not how I could prevent them.' At this he appeared still more affected and said : ' But your position afflicts me greatly. I feel such a desire of befriending you !' ' No,' I replied, ' you mistake on that point, I cannot believe it.' ' I am speaking the truth,' he said.—' I cannot consider it such,' I replied.—' Well, we shall not speak of that,' he said ; ' I have formed my opinion, and I fear not to make it public. However, listen to me, be persuaded! I will give you whatever you ask, your brother also ; but you must leave this place. Your surroundings are prejudicial to you. The French mislead you. You are so upright a person, you have ever been a good child, a virtuous young girl, and a perfect religious. I am acquainted with your whole life, I know it to be exemplary ; but even that excites my pity for the situation in which you now are.' I replied quietly : ' I can neither speak nor act otherwise than I have done. No one around me has had any part in making my wounds. But I am satisfied with my position, I neither wish to accept nor do I demand anything but repose. My brother has no more need than I of your money ; he is happy in his poverty for his heart is content.' Then he spoke to me with great earnestness and gravity. ' Miss Emmerich,' said he, ' you will repent of not having accepted my offer. Reflect seriously upon what you are doing.' ' My resolution,' I replied, ' is firmly taken. I trust in God,' whereupon he left me."

This visit was followed some weeks later by the public declaration of Von Bœnninghausen in which he said : " Anne Catherine Emmerich. as she has herself informed me, will leave this place where she has endured so many sufferings and miseries. She will retire to her brother's cottage in the neighborhood of Coesfeld, as soon as the mildness of spring will permit her to travel. A quiet room in which she may pass the rest of a life which has been rendered miserable by a set of impostors, has already been prepared for her. Who would not desire as I do to see her regain that peace and rest lost partly by her own fault ?" (1)

We may more easily form an opinion of this man with the numberless and strange contradictions manifested in his words and actions, if we consider the firm conviction under which he was even before the inquiry and which he had avowed in these terms : " The phenomena manifested in the person of Anne Catherine Emmerich being diametrically opposed to the best known laws of nature, cannot be natural. There is in the case either a miracle or a fraud." But his want of religion allowed him not to admit the existence of a miracle or of an immediate interposition of Almighty God, as he unhesitatingly declared : " I would not

(1) Work mentioned above, p. 43.

have a God who would do such things." Imposture it must
be, and the only point to be investigated was how far the
invalid was an active or a passive accomplice in it. He
was inclined to decide upon her passive participation ; for,
even in his most violent attacks upon her, he felt that she
was innocent and unjustly persecuted, he bowed to the
mysterious power of her purity and elevation of soul. He
could, in fact, truthfully say in his " History of the Investigation" : " Who could be so hard-hearted as not to
pity her ?   I feel for her, I shall make every effort to draw
her from the snare that holds her captive, the snare of ignorant fanaticism or infernal malice."   Had he presented
to the Chief-President the faintest suspicion of Sister Emmerich's sincerity, he never would have been allowed to
publish such a declaration as the following : " I was authorized by the Chief-President von Vinke to offer pardon and
support to the unfortunate woman, if she would freely confess everything and make known the principal impostors
that have led her astray (1)."

As to solving the question how in one and the same individual could be found diabolical imposition and incomparable purity, the Landrath gave himself no trouble. He
left that to Dean Rensing, whom he had gained over to his
own opinion, though both Dean Overberg and Dr. von
Druffel were more and more strongly convinced of her truth.
The year before Dean Rensing had defended her against
Prof. Bodde's calumnies. "Up to the present," he says,
" I have discovered no reason for supposing the phenomena
in question. (the stigmata) were produced artificially. I
cannot pride myself on having made the natural sciences a
special study ; but I do not subscribe to that love of the
marvellous which sees the supernatural in what is merely

(1) " Report upon the Phenomena Observed in the Person of Anne Catherine Emmerich," by Rensing. Dorsten, 1818.

extraordinary. If I must say what I candidly think, Anne
Catherine Emmerich is not guilty of imposture, although I
refrain from honoring as miraculous the singular manifestations I behold in her. As to explaining her case naturally,
my limited knowledge of nature's forces is inadequate to
such an undertaking, as is also what I have read and heard
on the subject from scientists. No report of any professor
has as yet thrown light upon the case ; consequently, I can
make nothing more out of it than thoughtful Christians do
of the explanations given by commentators on the miracles
mentioned in the Bible."

On May 29th, the Dean addressed a long letter to the
Vicar-General in which he expressed himself, as follows :
" I have been for the last three years and I am still of the
opinion that Miss Emmerich is not an impostor. Trifling
circumstances did, at times, shake my conviction a little ;
but after having submitted them to a severe investigation
by the surest rules of criticism, *the passing doubt ever served
to convince more strongly of the truth.*"

Landrath von Bœnninghausen, however, knew how to raise
a bridge by which the timid Dean might pass from the de-
fensive to the aggressive, and thus escape the dreaded blame
of the new authorities and the disagreeable reproach of cred-
ulity ; this bridge was that of flattery. He was lavish of his
praises. "I must here make honorable mention," he said,
" of Dean Rensing, a man in every way worthy of respect,
but who, on account of a former literary dispute with Prof.
Bodde, has sometimes appeared in a disadvantageous light.
From the first he endeavored to persuade Sister Emmerich
to submit to the investigation, and afterward he did all in his
power to further its ends." This public eulogium, which
classed him among the partisans of the commission, was at
first most disagreeable to the Dean ; he sought to justify

himself with the invalid personally. But this was the last visit he paid her, and from that time he shunned even the appearance of communication with her. Still more, in March, 1821, some weeks after the Abbé Lambert's death, he wrote a dissertation under the title, " *Critical Review of the Singular History of A. C. Emmerich, Religious of the Suppressed Convent of Augustinians, of Dülmen,*" in which referring to the Landrath Bœnninghausen, he actually sought to prove the stigmatisée an impostor (1). All that he had witnessed seven years before, her virtue displayed in the investigation directed by himself, the innumerable testimonies he had collected and forwarded to his superiors together with his own observations—all were of little weight compared with the fear of incurring disgrace with the new government officials. " At present," he says, " the signs of a skilful fraud discovered by the director of the commission, strengthen the suspicion that all may not be exactly as the Sister states ; they have, also, shaken the Dean's faith in her sincerity and truth. He can no longer resist the desire of diving into the mystery, bearing in his hand the torch of criticism." And it was thus that he dicovered, " that at a very early age she was inflamed with an extraordinary love of corporal penance, self-inflicted torture, and voluntary suffering. Now, this strong inclination for exterior penance and mortification affords room for the conjecture of many, who seek

(1) The author would have been silent on this much-to-be-regretted act of the Dean, if after the publication of the first volume of this work, remonstrances had not been addressed to him from Westphalia. After the severe condemnation pronounced by Dean Overberg and Mr. Katerkamp upon his " Critical Review," Dean Rensing kept it shut up in his secretary until his death, 1826. Ten years ago, Dean Krabbe sent the author a literal transcription made under his own supervision. Dean Krabbe, who had known Dean Rensing well, remarked several times to the author that he could not account for the " Critical Review," excepting by attributing it to the influence of Mr. Bœnninghausen's persuasive powers which were very great. He was certain, however, that the Dean had recognized his error and had, consequently, never made his writing public. That this opinion is well-founded we may infer from the fact that three weeks after the invalid's death, Sunday, Feb. 29, 1824, he made in the Pilgrim's presence and of his own accord the following declaration: " *The deceased Sister Emmerich was truly one of the most wonderful personages of this century!*"

the truth with impartial views, that the phenomena exhibited in her person owe their origin rather to a skilful hand than to imagination. Although her piety, her uninterrupted efforts from childhood to lead a life agreeable in the sight of God, and the fact that she has never been unfaithful to her principles, may indeed exonerate her from the charge of a premeditated design to acquire fame, yet we may believe that, either at the suggestion or with the approbation of her French director, she may have allowed those wounds to be made upon her, in order to render the Passion of Our Saviour ever present by the sight of her own bodily marks; and that, desiring to make these signs efficacious for the good of devout souls, she added thereto her abstinence from food, her mysterious cataleptic state, and her imaginary revelations. Having satisfied her conscience by such specious reasons, she decided to play this fanatical part. As she was convinced by her good intentions that she was doing a meritorious work, it was easy to persuade her of the necessity of the most rigorous silence. To this she bound herself by the most frightful oath not to betray her accomplices or her own share in the affair (1), and not to draw contempt upon the religion she aimed at serving. In all this, of course, there would be a detestable abuse of so sacred a thing as an oath, but such an abuse is not unprecedented among fanatics. We know how far certain devout souls can be drawn. Fascinated by their confidence in religious zeal and the superior intelligence of their counsellors, they come, at length, to despise as vain scruples all reproaches of conscience when there is question of co-operating in a work whose end appears to them holy."

(1) Nevertheless, Dean Rensing, in this same dissertation, characterized her accomplice, the venerable Abbé Lambert, as a priest esteemed by all, on account of his great piety.

Dean Rensing, however, had been a witness of Sister Emmerich's docility in submitting to the attempts made for her cure by order of the Vicar-General. He had often been deeply touched at the sight of her sufferings and those bloody effusions surpassing anything of the kind that could be produced in a purely natural manner. And yet, with "the torch of the critic," he went on to discover a new explanation, "the action of the demon."—"Let no one here ask," says he, "how Almighty God could permit a person endeavoring to please Him by a life of virtue from her very childhood, to be so frightfully deceived by the devil. 'God's thoughts are not our thoughts, nor our ways His.' If we refuse to accord to the devil such an agency over men, we subscribe (although unwillingly) to the unbelieving spirit of the age, we spread the reign of the world and of the prince of darkness even whilst protesting most warmly against his power." The "critic's torch" could not, however, preserve so clear-sighted a man from adopting the senseless and revolting opinion that a soul, upright, pious, and faithful to God from her very infancy, could be possessed by the devil and employed by him in his diabolical works. And the light of this *torch* failed to make him perceive that, in expressing himself thus, he blasphemed as much against God and wounded not less the integrity of the faith than did that spirit of the world against which he disclaimed.

We must not omit saying here that this persecution, although stifled in the germ, did not escape the divinely-illuminated intelligence of the invalid, nor must we fail to mention the means employed by an ever-watchful Providence to preserve her from the ulterior consequence of so outrageous a calumny. We read in the Pilgrim's journal, Jan. 24, 1822: "She thanks God for her great sufferings; she rejoices at the thought of the numerous labors she has performed (for the Church) and for what is marked out for her to do this new year, of which task she has already accomplished much. She undertook a new labor last night ; she had a vision of plums which, at first, tormented her greatly. 'I was sitting near a fountain,' she said, ' in the midst of a vast field of wheat where the ears shed their grains in abundance. My confessor ran into the field and saved much of the wheat, he reaped a large part of it. I held his hat, for there were yet many places for him to reap. At every moment, black clouds charged with hail passed over me. I thought they would fall and crush me, but only some few drops fell on me. I saw also a sack full of small plums,which are here called *wichter*,and which I thought were intended for me. They had been gathered and put into the sack for me by people of consideration. They. were injurious fruits, beautiful in appearance but full of falsehood and deceit. There flowed from the tree that bore them a great quantity of gum well enough to look at, but which corroded the tree. The sack was above a ditch, lying half upon heretical ground. I beheld those who busied themselves with it. I knew them, but I do not want to know them (that is, I want to forget their names, to be silent about them). The sack signified the many wicked designs and calumnies that one of them had formed against me. This made me anxious, and I was ashamed of the plums. But I was reprimanded by the soul of a poor woman who had died long before ; she had been employed in the convent and she now came to me, because I had something to do for her. She told me that formerly I would not have paid so much attention to fine large plums as I now did to this miserable fruit that I was dying to eat ! Then the sack was covered with a white cloth by the priest that I might not see it any longer. I saw there

Dean Overberg, Mr. Katerkamp, Father Limberg, and others whom I knew; but I forgot who had prepared these suffer-ings for me, I felt no resentment toward them. The Father's labors in the field had relation to the care he had taken of souls at Fischbeck and of his spiritual children dispersed in other parishes who had come to consult him. I kept his hat as a pledge that he would not leave the field, for I always begged him not to refuse to hear the people even when he was fatigued. The season, the condition of the fields, all was as when Dean Overberg was here."

"Strange thing!" adds the Pilgrim in his recital, "the vision of the plums has reference to a fact which is, as yet, perfectly unknown to her. The Dean, when he went to Münster, circulated a pamphlet in which he declared that he had changed his opinion of her on reading Mr. Bœnninghausen's intelligent report and that he attributed all the blame of the affair to the deceased Abbé Lambert. But by this he, the Dean, only drew upon himself contempt. Dean Overberg, Mr. Katerkamp, and others have pro-nounced against him. Sister Emmerich knew nothing of all that.

"January 31, 1822. Her nephew has come from Mün-ster where the report has spread that she is dangerously ill. He spoke of the Dean's pamphlet against her. She talked with him about it coolly and without bitterness, say-ing that the reports made by one of her old companions of the convent had given rise to something in it. Sister Soentgen reads to every one Dean Rensing's letters in de-fence of his pamphlet."

In this conversation with her nephew, Sister Emmerich related what follows of the time of her captivity: "When I sent word to the Dean to come and hear my confession, he came, but refused to allow me to confess. I fell into a state of contemplation and, wishing to touch a priest's hand, I begged him to give me his. In Landrath Bœnning-hausen's presence he extended to me one finger. I took the whole hand, saying to him: ' Do you refuse me your hand?' He answered: 'You have never yet had it!' I let it go and said. ' I know what will be exacted of this hand.' Then he spoke in a low voice with the Landrath, as the nurse told me afterward."

Sister Soentgen was the chief cause of the susceptible Dean's conceiving an aversion which culminated in the most frightful suspicions of the good and pious Abbe Lambert and even of the invalid herself. After the investigation of 1813, she had repeated to him all that the Abbé, Dr. Wesener, and later the Pilgrim had said, or were supposed to have said. She had laid before him with particular care, "her anxiety and scruples on the invalid's imperfections and her surroundings," whenever she felt herself disposed to complain of either one or all of the above-mentioned personages. It is true the Abbé's welcome of Sister Soentgen to the invalid's bedside was not the most cordial since her indiscreet circulation of the wonders wrought in Sister Emmerich ; he looked upon her as the primary cause of all their troubles, nor was he slow in expressing his sentiments. Sister Soentgen, on the other hand, had become quite an important personage. The Vicar-General had communicated with her during the first investigation, and received from her, by his own orders, secret reports. This and other circumstances of the kind had placed her in a position which she was unwilling to relinquish when her services were no longer required. After the investigation she wrote to the Vicar-General : " I still have something to say in confidence to Your Grace, but I am unwilling to commit it to writing," to which she received the command to forward it by letter without more ado. She replied: " I shall state my reason for wishing to speak privately to Your Grace. For some time I have remarked in Sister Emmerich little imperfections that give me uneasiness, though it would not do to remind her of them. I often thought that I was wrong in observing silence, above all when I heard various interpretations put upon her surroundings. The idea haunts me, and I fear that it may be an obstacle to her perfection. The Dean has remarked the same ; he says he would certainly call her attention to it, *were he her confessor.*" Some months later, she wrote again : " Your Grace will forgive me for again intruding. It is too true that Sister Emmerich has still her daily weaknesses like other people ; but you know, too, her *surroundings.*....and who can say why God permits that she should not perceive the danger herself, or have sufficient courage to free herself from it ? The Dean, I see, keeps aloof, he rarely visits her."

The Vicar-General wished not to understand these insinuations, or to remove the "*surroundings,*" viz., the Abbé Lambert ; so Sister Soentgen, six months later again renewed her communications, though in a different strain : " For a long time I have been urged to write to Your Grace. Truly I am daily charmed by the sight of the sufferings of my dear fellow-religious and at seeing her soul becoming perfect. What a pity she has not the strength to converse !" And again : " The absence of self-will in Sister Emmerich is now much more noticeable than in the past. Many interesting things took place after the Rev. Dean began to absent himself. I often regret his lack of interest in the good cause ; but, even in this circumstance, there may be something which will one day contribute to the glory of God. As I continue to visit her daily, I have a chance of remarking many little things, particularly her interior peace, her progress in perfection. Dr. Wesener has been a little imprudent in reading to her a medical journal in which there was an article about herself. He should not have done it; it only embarrasses the interested party. The Rev. Dean is not aware of my writing." But the Vicar-General desired no further information, and so the matter ended.

Of not less interest to Sister Soentgen were the visits Sister Emmerich received from distinguished individuals. She failed not to be in attendance on such occasions; and, although as little mindful of the poor invalid as the other religious, yet she alway introduced herself as her intimate friend through whose intervention the convent doors had been opened to her. This gave her access to the most distinguished families. But the *"surroundings"* saw through it quite clearly, as the following incident proves : " Sister Soentgen," says Dr. Wesener, " received from different quarters some little presents for the invalid which she exhibited to her with all kinds of indirect remarks and objections, and ended by keeping them for herself. Sister Emmerich does not want to accept presents for fear of giving rise to remarks, so I told her to get them from Sister Soentgen and send them back to the donors.—' Ah,' she said, ' I cannot be so hard on one who is so intimate with me !' ' Certainly,' chimed in the Abbé, ' she knows very well that Sister Soentgen has done wrong, but she will listen to nothing against her !' Then Sister Emmerich begged me to say nothing more about it."

The Abbé and Dr. Wesener always yielded to Sister Emmerich's entreaties not to disturb the peace by their remarks, but not so with the Pilgrim. He thought it an heroic act if, on meeting Sister Soentgen or some other nun in the invalid's room, he managed to keep silence ; but the displeasure depicted in his countenance, the angry glance of his rolling eyes as speedily showed such visitors the door as the plainest words or actions would have done, and this to the deep annoyance of the invalid.

Soon after her deliverance from captivity, Sister Emmerich received the following consoling letter from Dean Overberg : " What personal evils have come upon you of which you can complain ? I address this question to a soul that longs for nothing so much as to become daily more like unto her Heavenly Spouse. Have you not been much better treated than He ? Ought you not to rejoice in spirit that they have helped you to become more comformable to and, consequently, more agreeable to Him ? You have, indeed, had much to suffer with Jesus Christ, but the opprobrium was comparatively little. To the thorny crown were still wanting the purple mantle and the white robe of derision, nor did the cry, ' Let Him be crucified ! ' resound. I doubt not that these are your sentiments."

As soon as his health permitted, he and Dr. von Druffel came to Dülmen. The latter desired to assure himself of the condition of her wounds. The day after their arrival, Dean Overberg took her Holy Communion and spent the morning with her.

" She opened to him her whole heart," wrote the Pilgrim, " and received the consolation that a holy man can impart, even though he says nothing more, nothing different from others who are acquainted with all the details of her life." The Pilgrim did not yet comprehend that the priestly character lent secret unction to the old Dean's words.

" She confided to him all that troubled her, she spoke of the Pilgrim and again received an injunction to tell him everything ; she asked his advice with regard to her sister, and although he gave no decided answer, yet she was consoled and encouraged. He spoke earnestly in her confessor's presence of her gift of recognizing relics and upon the importance he attached to the Pilgrim's recording everything.—Dr. Wesener gave the Dean a detailed account of her state just after the investigation. Before his departure, she related to him many details of her visions to which he listened with emotion and gave her three little sealed packages of relics which she gratefully received."

Dean Overberg sent to the Vicar-General an account of the ill-treatment to which the invalid had been subjected during her imprisonment; whereupon, the latter ordered her to " demand of Mr. Bœnninghausen a copy of the report of the commission, and in the event of a refusal to carry her case before the supreme court. But Mr. von Bœnninghausen knew how to forestall such a claim by declaring in the preface to his pamphlet : " *Gèschichte und Vorläufige Resultate, &c.*" : " All acts reduced to writing during the investigation were sent to the Chief-President and by him forwarded to the Royal Minister " (1).

The inhabitants of Dülmen manifested in various ways their respect and sympathy for the poor sufferer. On the Feast of St. Lawrence they organized a pilgrimage to the Chapel of the Cross, to ask for her speedy deliverance, and on the day of her return home, Mr. von Schilgen announced it in the daily papers :

" This morning, August 29th, a little after ten o'clock,

---

(1) Mr. Krabbe, the Dean of the Chapter, and Mr. Aulike, the Director, put themselves to the greatest trouble to search up the documents relating to the commission, as well at Münster as at Berlin, but without success ; no trace of them could be found. On May 13, 1860, Mr. Aulike wrote to the author at Berlin : "I have searched in every place where there was a probability of finding such papers, for the documents relating to the official proceedings toward A. C. Emmerich. I have not only asked for them as a favor, but I have, as my duty authorized, demanded them officially. On all sides I am told that these acts are not to be found. The oldest archivist attached to the department to which such affairs belong, a respectable old man worthy of belief, remembers very well that these acts were once in existence. " But they assure me," says he, " that they were lost at the house of a high functionary now dead for thirty years," (he mentioned his name) " they could not be found among his papers."

the invalid was carried back to her own home by a servant of Mr. Mersmann.   The joy of those that sympathize with her was unbounded.   All feel that, if this long investigation of twenty-two days had resulted to Sister Emmerich's disadvantage, had proved her either an impostor or the victim of impostors, she never would have been set at liberty."

Not only in Dülmen, but throughout the whole country of Münster, was the publication of the so-called investigation eagerly awaited.   Dr. Theodore Lutterbeck, of Münster, a man of great independence of character, boldly called for it, expressing at the same time the indignation of the community at large at the unheard-of treatment offered an irreproachable female.   " It has been undeniably proved that Anne Catherine Emmerich, now forty-four years old, has led from her infancy a life pure, innocent, peaceable, and retired, nor has she ever drawn, or desired to draw the least emolument from her extraordinary state."

Rev. Mr. Cramer, Archpriest of Holland, says in his pamphlet : " Considerable sums have frequently been offered her which she has always refused.   She never made a spectacle of herself; on the contrary, she withdrew as much as she could from the gaze of the curious.   This being the case, it is incomprehensible that government officials could consider themselves authorized to declare this timid, suffering dove, who interfered not in public affairs, deprived of her lawful right to live in peace, and condemned to imprisonment and an investigation of three weeks such as might have been exacted of an open violator of the laws. We may remark here that all citizens, whether interested in the affair or not, feel their domiciliary rights attacked by such proceedings.   According to the ancient laws of Münster, the courts of justice would have deemed such an imprisonment by order of police officials, an encroachment upon their rights, and would have inveighed against such a commission. When in our own times, some German Vicars wished to submit certain individuals under their jurisdiction to a far less rigorous inquiry (which they had every right to do) what denouncements were not uttered, what measures taken by civil authorities to oppose them! Much less then should secular tribunals busy themselves with a religious living in absolute retirement, asking and expecting nothing from the world; much less should they trouble themselves about the wonders wrought in her person, wonders whose truth had already been sufficiently proved by men of probity, such as Dean Rensing, Count von Stolberg, Dr. von Druffel, Dr. Wesener, and a host of others, some of them citizens of Dülmen, others strangers from a distance. But, as some persisted in suspecting Sister Emmerich's friends of a pious fraud and as suspicion fell principally on Father Limberg and the Abbé Lambert, two most worthy ecclesiastics, it was thought desirable to separate the invalid from her personal and local surroundings, and submit her to a legal investigation. Now, as there was question of inquiring into the culpability or innocence of ecclesiastics, it was, doubtless, in the right and power of the Vicar-General von Droste, by virtue of his high spiritual authority, to demand for such an undertaking representatives chosen and authorized by himself, and not by the head of the police; in a word, a mixed commission alone would have been in accordance with right and justice, whilst the one in question was but a commission of police, not a judicial one entitled to *fidem publicam :* i. e., to the credit of the public. Whatever it may be called, however, the public demand the results obtained; they hereby call upon it to publish its observations."

As the above was accompanied by Mrs. Wiltner's deposition to which she declared herself ready to attest on oath,
Landrath von Bœnninghausen could no longer maintain
silence. The Chief-President ordered him to reply. This
gave rise to the pamphlet, "written from memory," but
which was followed by no official report. The impression
produced by this pamphlet, entitled " *Preliminary Results,*"
may be gathered from the words of Dr. Lutterbeck, who
hesitated not to meet the Landrath's publication with the
following words : " He who openly accuses Sister Emmerich of imposture without supporting his assertion by proof,
may (and the enlightened public will agree with me) put
me in the same category with her. I appeal to the honest
opinion of the public at large."

The Pilgrim notes in his journal, Nov. 14, 1819 : " I
found the invalid to-day unusually cheerful. She had read
the Landrath's publication, she was perfectly reassured."

Dr. Wesener's journal furnishes an account of Sister
Emmerich's physical condition after her inprisonment. He
visited her August 29th, just after the Landrath's departure —" The sight of the invalid alarmed me. She looked
like a skeleton, her eyes dull, her face emaciated and deathly pale ; but her mind was calm and energetic. In speaking of what she had lately gone through, she alluded to
some things that astonished and distressed me."

" Sept. 2d—She is still surprisingly bright, but her pulse
is weak, her hands and feet cold as death ; she is very
much reduced."

" Sept. 3d—I was called to her last night, and I was
sure she was dying although Father Limberg, who arrived
fifteen minutes before me, said that she had rallied a little.
When he first saw her, he thought her dead. At intervals
she vomited a liquid of an offensive odor. I made a poul-

tice of wine and camomile flowers and applied it to her stomach ; it seemed to relieve her. Before leaving I asked her if she forgave every one, and she answered by a sweet smile. I left her fully convinced that she would soon breathe her last. Father Limberg remained to administer Extreme Unction."

" Sept. 4th—The invalid has rallied slightly, and the vomiting has ceased."

" Sept. 5th—She communicated to-day and regained her strength wonderfully. I began this morning to write an account of her sufferings during the last investigation."

The vomiting mentioned in the doctor's journal was the rejection of the decoctions the commissioners had forced her to swallow in spite of the bad effects that always followed (1)."

(1) Von Bœnninghausen wrote on this subject, Oct. 14th : " The vomiting may have arisen from Sister Emmerich's having given up the coarse diet to which she was accustomed.". .. . .

CHAPTER XXXIX.

Close of the Ecclesiastical Year.

Sister Emmerich now resumed her spiritual labors with unabated courage. " Thou art lying there persecuted," said her Divine Spouse to her, " that minds at variance may be united, that many may see their errors." The work begun had to be perfectly fulfilled, and for this end she received all that assistance which a true child of Holy Church derives from the communion of saints: the help of the blessed, the fruits of her own good works, and the prayers and protection of the souls in purgatory. Speaking once of her suffering life, she said : " I can see no end to my pains, they daily become greater ; they increase like the branches of a tree which multiply in proportion as they are pruned. I have often thought over them, as a child in the fields, a religious in the convent garden, and in my own interior ; they will keep on increasing to the end. I have left much behind me, but I grieve that many means of shunning evil have been neglected, many graces rendered useless. It has often been shown me that great harm comes from making small account of the gifts granted me, and from not recording my visions, which show the hidden links of many things. It has often distressed me ; but it is a consolation to think that it is not my own fault. I have also greatly relaxed through condescension."

Her visions now turned upon the views and plots of her enemies. She saw their underhand dealings and their sympathy with the tendencies of the period, tendencies hos-

tile to the Church and Christianity ; against them were
directed her combat of suffering and prayer. "I heard
terrible threats that I was to be carried off again,
whether I would or not. A man stood before me and said :
'Dead or alive, she must go !'—I cast myself into my
Saviour's arms, crying to him piteously. Then came other
pictures : I beheld an informer gathering up all that was
said in the little town ; I saw people coming and going,
tormenting me with questions and raillery ; cunning visitors,
and false friends near me who did me much harm. These
were true torments. The priests I saw in deep sleep ;
whatever they did appeared like a spider's web. I saw on
all sides increasing malice, cunning, and violence which, at
last, frustrated their own designs, failed in their ends, and
completely baffled one another. In terror I beheld myself
abandoned by all my friends. Then I saw a troop of men
in a distant meadow, about a hundred of them with a leader, and I thought to myself that this must be the place in
which Our Lord once fed the seven thousand people. Our
Lord came to meet me. With Him were all His disciples from
among whom He chose twelve. I saw Him looking from one to
another. I recognized them all, the old men full of simplicity, the young robust and sun-burnt. He sent them off in
all directions, following them in spirit to distant nations. I
thought, 'Ah ! what can such a handful do among such
multitudes !'—The Lord answered : 'Their voice sounds
far and near. So also in these days many are sent. Whoever they may be, men or women, they can do the same.
Behold to what multitudes these twelve have borne salvation ! They whom I send in your day will do the same,
no matter how poor or despised they may be!'—I felt that
this vision was for my encouragement."

If she saw in spirit a new attack, she strengthened her-

self for it by prayer. " What can creatures do to me ? "
she said. " If they want to tear this body to pieces, I shall
deliver it up for Thee, my Saviour ! Lord, I am Thy handmaid !"—Then she had a vision in which was shown her
how much good she could do in her state of abandonment.
—"I found myself in a vast region belonging not to earth.
The ground which bore me, or over which I floated, was
like a veil of gauze, and below I saw the earth dark as
night with pictures here and there. Around where I stood
were troops of translucent spirits ranged in choirs; they
were not the saints, but praying souls, who offered petitions
from below and received gifts from on high. They prayed themselves; they offered the prayers of others : they
implored the assistance of the more elevated choirs who
answered such requests, sending more or less help, coming
and going in the light. These elevated choirs were the
saints. They that surrounded me seemed to be souls
whom the Lord willed should see the dangers that menaced the earth and offer prayers to avert them. All pro-
fessions, all stations in life, seemed to have their praying
souls, who exercised a most beneficent influence. I prayed, too, for I saw innumerable miseries. God sent
help by His saints and the effect was instantaneous —obstacles opposed to evil ; undertakings turning out well,
though apparently by chance; changes wrought in souls,
etc. ; the dying converted and admitted to the Sacraments ;
people in danger on land and water—all saved by prayer.
I saw what might prove fatal to certain individuals suddenly snatched out of their path, and all by the power
of prayer. I adored the justice of God ! "

She beheld her own position under the figure of a lamb.
—" I saw a broad country spreading out before me like a
map, with forests and meadows, flocks and shepherds,

Just in front of me was a shepherd with a numerous flock of sheep, and behind them came the shepherd-boys. The former discharged his duties a little carelessly, but the latter were more active. The flock was in good condition. There was one lamb, sleeker and fatter than the others; there was something remarkable about it, the sheep pressed around it. They passed a clump of high trees among which lay a fierce wolf and a second one a little further on; they were wolves, and yet they were like men too. The wolves appeared to understand each other; they often ran together and lay in wait for the lamb. I trembled for the poor little thing, and I could not understand how the shepherd could be so negligent. One of the boys seemed attentive to it, but he could not do much for it, although he was faithful to the portion of the flock intrusted to him. Several times when the wolves attempted to seize it the sheep gathered bleating around it. To my amazement the shepherd made no effort to protect it. Everything seemed to be against it. It was in an exposed position, and once the wolves were on the point of carrying it off; again they caught it by the throat, tore off a piece of its flesh, and were about to strangle it, when the others ran to the rescue. The pity I felt made me understand that there was question of myself   Suddenly there came a man from above, the wolves fled, and I saw that I had the man's bones by me (1). I wondered that his body was in one place, his spirit in another. Then the shepherd's boy came up and brought the lamb back."

The lamb, so little cared for by the shepherds, was helped by some blessed soul who had suffered at a remote period, in the same place and under the same circumstances as Sister Emmerich herself.

(1) Relics.

On October 9th, she related the following : "There was a holy widow by me who had lived at the manor in Dülmen, and who had died in prison. She conversed with me a long time; we have not yet finished our conversation. She spoke of her time and imprisonment, as if in the present; justice and faith were proscribed terms in her day and, therefore, had she suffered. She told me her family name, she was of the house of Galen. She showed me the prisons, partly subterranean, in which she and her relatives were confined. She spoke much of my own history, saying that all things happen according to the designs of God, and that I should never say anything but what is inspired at the moment. 'How wonderfully,' she said, 'hast thou faced the danger! Hadst thou known it beforehand, thou wouldst have died of fright. Other wonders will be effected. Unbelief is at its height, unheard-of confusion will reign; but after the storm, faith will be re-established!'—The lady seemed to know me well. She explained to me many things in my life, consoled and encouraged me, saying that I had nothing to fear. She spoke of the state of the clergy, also of relics. 'It would be well,' she said, 'if they were collected together and deposited in some church. They do, indeed, exercise a beneficent influence wherever they are, but the little respect shown them is very injurious. The dust in which they lie ought to be buried in blessed ground. There are still many relics at Dülmen Manor.'

"The lady wore a robe, open at the neck, crossed in front and falling behind in folds with a train, the sleeves tight with trimming around the wrists gathered and starched, over which fell a part of the sleeve. She died innocent, imprisoned by an association, or secret tribunal which, at that time, was the cause of many evils and inspired great terror.   It was something like the Free-masons, but more violent."

Oct. 21st—" The good lady again appeared to me, conversed a long time, and repeated that she was of the family of Galen.   She does not protect as sacred relics do, but she helps, she warns.   She told me not to mind, for my persecutors fear me more than I do them.   They attack me boldly because nothing is done to oppose them."

" I met a man who also belonged to the time of the good lady of ' The Vehme ' (1).   I saw him in Dülmen Manor, whither he used often to go; but once he stayed too long, which circumstance led to his death.   He was one of the most distinguished men of the country, and one of the heads of the secret tribunal...... He was secretly very pious and good.   He often received warnings on the iniquities and cruelties of the tribunal.   He tried to prevent them by means of the good lady who gave notice to its intended victims and saved as many as she could.   Once he remained too long with her planning projects of this kind.   This roused the suspicions of some wicked men, who plotted to put him to death.

" I beheld secret meetings at night, sinister-looking men introduced into this country, and going furtively from place to place.   Then I had a vision of a castle and garden this side of Münster, an old building with towers.   Here dwelt the good man.   He was in the garden, wrapped in a mantle as if about to set out for the assembly, when three men in disguise fell upon him, stabbed him, and dragged him into an alley.   The blood flowed in streams from his wounds and the men tried to wash away the stains, but in vain.   They filled a sack with the blood-stained earth and carried it to Dülmen Manor with the body.   They deposited

(1) The secret tribunal mentioned above.

them in a vault by the church where were the remains of
many who had been killed in the same way. He belonged to
the Droste family. . . . The lady told me that it was well for
him to die when he did, for he was pious and his conscience
was in a good state. 'Fear not,' she said to me, 'things
must be as they are. Thy persecutors have neither right nor
reason to do thee harm. Let nothing disquiet thee! If
thou art questioned, answer only what comes to thy mind at
the moment !' "

Sister Emmerich in her humility was often occupied
with this thought : " For what have I, poor sinner, deserved
that my persecutors should render themselves so guilty
on my account ?"—and although God had given her the consolation of knowing that she was not responsible, she begged for special sufferings to expiate their offence. From
the last week in October, she was a prey to interior abandonment, whilst her frame was consumed by fever, her
tongue adhered to her palate, and she had not the strength
to reach the water placed at her side ; the pain in her
wounds often drew tears, and sometimes made her swoon
away. These were sufferings she had voluntarily embraced
for the good of her neighbor. In her distress, she was consoled by an apparition of Blessed Nicholas von der Flue, who
said to her : " I shall be thy very good friend, I shall help
thee a little," and he held out to her a little bunch of herbs the
smell of which gave her strength. " Thou sufferest," he said,
"in every member of thy body, because the faults for which
thou dost atone are so manifold."

On the nineteenth Sunday after Pentecost is read the
Gospel of the wedding-feast and the nuptial robe. That
night Blessed Nicholas was her guide in the following
vision:—

"I saw Blessed Nicholas as a great, tall man with hair

like silver. He wore a low notched crown, sparkling with precious stones; his tunic, which descended to the ankles, was white as snow and he held in his hand another crown higher than his own and set with jewels. I asked him why he held that resplendent crown instead of the bunch of herbs. He spoke earnestly and in few words of my death, of my destiny, and said that he would take me to a great wedding-feast. He placed the crown on my head, and I flew with him into the palace which I saw in the air above me. I was to be a bride, but I was so timid and ashamed that I knew not what to do. It was a wedding of wonderful magnificence. I beheld the manners and customs of all classes of society on the occasion of a marriage festival, and the action of deceased ancestors upon their descendants. First of all was the banquet for the clergy. Here I saw the Pope, and Bishops with their croziers and episcopal robes, and many others of the clergy, high and low. Above each one, in an upper choir, were the saints of his race, his ancestors, his patrons and the protectors of his charge, who acted through him, judging and deciding. At this table there were also spiritual affianced of the highest rank. With my crown on my head, I had to join them as their equal, which filled me with confusion. They were all still living, though as yet they had no crowns. Above me stood the one who had invited me and, as I was so abashed, he managed everything for me. The dishes on the table looked like earthly food, but they were not such in reality. I saw through everything, I read all hearts. Back of the banquet-hall were many different rooms filled with people, and there were new arrivals at every moment. Many among the ecclesiastics seated at the banquet were ordered out as unworthy, for they had mixed with worldlings, had served them rather than the Church. The worldlings were

punished first, then the ecclesiastics were banished to other
apartments, more or less remote. The number of the just
was very small. This was the first table and the first
hour.

" The clergy withdrew and another table was prepared at
which I did not sit. I stood among the spectators, Blessed
Nicholas still above me to help me. Emperors, kings, and
sovereign princes placed themselves at table, great lords
served them, and above were the saints reckoned among
the ancestors of each. To my great embarrassment, some
of the kings noticed me, but Nicholas came to my aid and always answered for me. They sat not long at table. They
were all alike, their actions imperfect, weak and inconsis-
tent; if one happened to be a little superior to his fellows
it was not through virtue. Some came not quite up to the
table, and all were sent away in their turn.

" I remember in particular the Croy family. They
must have had among them a holy stigmatisée, for she
said to me, ' See, there are the Croys !'

" Then came the table of the distinguished nobility, and
I saw among others the good Vehme lady hovering over
her family.

" Then came the table of the wealthy citizens, and I cannot describe the frightful state of this class. Most of them
were sent away and cast with those of the nobility who
were as bad as themselves, into a hole like a sewer where
they splashed about in mud and filth.

" After these came a class of a little better standing,
honest old citizens and peasants. There were many good
people here, among them my own family. My father and
mother stood above my other relatives. Then came the
descendants of Brother Klaus (Blessed Nicholas), right good,
strong tradesmen ; but some of them were rejected. Then

came the poor and the crippled from among whom many
pious people were excluded, as well as the bad. I had
much to do with them. Above them I saw numbers of persons and tribunals. I cannot recount all. When the six
tables were over, the holy man brought me back again to my
bed from which he had taken me. I was very weak, quite unconscious; I could neither speak nor make a sign, I seemed
about to die. Klaus signified to me that my life would be
short, without however specifying any particular time for
its close."

November 8th—" Again I had a great vision of persecution and I beheld my miseries increase. I saw my enemies watching that no one should help me, and gathering
up all that was said and done against me. The devil,
furious with me, was rushing with open jaws on certain
persons to confuse them and chase them away ; but what
hurt me most, was that my nearest friends reproached and
tormented me with inconsiderate advice and accusations.
They that were willing to help me were few and they could do
nothing. My persecutors assailed me in my abandonment,
and I was deprived of spiritual and corporal assistance.
My enemies loaded me with trials hitherto unknown. 'Where,'
they asked, ' are your ghostly Superiors ? where your spiritual directors ? Have they ceased to interest themselves in
you ? Who among the clergy are your protectors ?'—Their
words tortured me, drove me almost wild, and the desertion
of my dearest friends afflicted me keenly. When I
was almost in despair Nicholas von der Flue appeared.
He told me to thank God for showing me these things,
to arm myself with patience, and especially to avoid
anger in my replies which should be reserved ; that the
trial would be shorter, if borne well ; and, finally, that I
still had much to suffer from my friends who would injure

me and exact things of me, though not with a bad intention.
If I endured this patiently, I should profit by it.   He promised that the trial would not last long and that he would
help me.   Then he gave me his own little prayer on paper
which I was to say.   I had made use of it from my youth.
It ran thus : 'Lord, detach me from myself,' etc.   He
gave me also a picture about the size of my hand.   On top
was a sun, and underneath the word, *Justice*, from which I
understood that Divine Justice would end my persecution.
At the bottom was a face full of benevolence with the word
Mercy, and this gave me the assurance that I should soon
receive help from the Divine Mercy.   Under the face was a
coffin with four lighted tapers."

Her vision was soon realized.   One week after the
Landrath's injurious pamphlet, her Superiors and friends
urged her to appeal to a higher tribunal, and to lodge a
formal complaint against him and the treatment she had received during imprisonment (1).   The affair was pressed
on all sides ; but Sister Emmerich, in obedience to her
angelic director, declined taking such a step.   She saw
the sufferings now prepared for her under the image
of a thorn-hedge which she had to cross.

"The sight of it terrified me," she said. "but my guide
encouraged me—' How many hast thou not already crossed !
Wilt thou despair at the end ?'—I knelt and prayed and,
by virtue of my prayer, I crossed the hedge, I know
not how.   I felt invisible assistance.   Then I saw three
men coming toward me who tried to make me say
what I would do to the Landrath.   I told them that I would
read his pamphlet to see if it were in accordance with
his character, and that, if my Superiors questioned me, I
should tell the truth.   I was told also that my wounds would

(1) "I see, on account of this writing," she said, " my enemies contending; they separate, they are dissatisfied.   The Landrath stands alone."

bleed next Good-Friday and again on another day; that enemies were waiting for this event; but they would never see it, as they sought not the truth.

" I beheld crowds of children who came from Münster with some grown people to see the *impostor ;* but they were all kind to me, they loved the *impostor* very much. It seemed as if I taught them something. Several saints were round me in this vision and, what pleased me greatly, St. Francis dressed in a long, coarse robe was among them, his forehead very broad, his jaws hollow, his chin large. He consoled me, and told me not to complain, that he, too, had been persecuted. He had kept his wounds very secret, but the blood from his side often streamed down to his feet. Although some had seen his wounds, they did not in consequence believe. It is better to believe and not to see, for seeing does not make them believe who have not the gift of faith. He (St. Francis) was tall, thin, vigorous, his hollow cheeks ruddy as of one interiorly inflamed, and he had black eyes. I saw no beard. He was not infirm, but very winning and sprightly."

When Sister Emmerich was informed of her Superior's desire that she should appeal to a higher court, she suddenly closed her eyes, and fell into ecstasy, her countenance becoming very grave. She afterward said:—" I invoked God, the Father. I begged Him to look upon His Son who satisfies for sinners at every moment, who every moment offers Himself in sacrifice, that He might not be too severe toward that poor, blind Landrath, but to assist and enlighten him for the love of His Son. At the same instant, I saw a vision of Good-Friday, the Lord sacrificing Himself upon the cross, Mary and the disciples at its foot. This picture I saw over the altar at which priests say Mass. I see it at all hours of the day and night. I see, too, the whole parish,

how the people pray, well or badly, and how the priest
fulfils his duties. I see first the church here, then the
churches and parishes all around, as one sees near him a
fruit-tree lit up by the sun, and in the distance others
grouped together like a wood. I see Mass celebrated at
all hours of the day and night throughout the world, and
in some far-off regions with the same ceremonies as in the
times of the Apostles. Above the altar, I see a heavenly
worship in which an angel supplies all that the priest
neglects. I offer my own heart for the want of piety among
the faithful and I beg the Lord for mercy. I see many
priests performing this duty pitiably. Some, mere formalists,
are so attentive to the outward ceremonies as to neglect
interior recollection ; they think only of how they appear
to the congregation, and not at all of God. The scrupulous
ever long to feel their own piety. I have had these impressions since childhood. Often during the day I am absorbed in
this far-off gazing on the Holy Sacrifice; if I am spoken to
my answer comes as from a person who interrupts not his
own work to answer a child's questions. Jesus loves us
so much that He constantly renews His work of Redemption. The Mass is the hidden history of Redemption, Redemption become a Sacrament. I saw all this in my earliest youth and I used to think every one did the same."

That afternoon, still in ecstasy, she said :—"They call
me disobedient, but I dare not do otherwise. They want
me to complain! When it is too late, they will help me! I
see what trouble the wicked enemy gives himself to bring
about a lawsuit; he wants me to lodge a complaint, he cannot harm me in any other way. I see that if there is a
suit, I shall die and all will be hushed up, and that is what
the devil is after. My guide has said to me : ' Thy best
friends want thee to begin a lawsuit, but beware of doing

so ! Forget not that the signs thou bearest are not signs of accusation, but of reconciliation. They have not been given to thee for strife, but for pardon. Write two letters in thy prayer-book, an L. (*liebe, love*) and a V. (*vergiss nicht, forget not*). Let *them* complain, but thou not!"

How faithfully she obeyed her guide's instructions, we see from the Pilgrim's notes, a few days later: "She suffers intensely, she vomits blood, her forehead is inflamed, and the pains of her wounds are so violent that the bed shakes under her quivering limbs. She will not be helped by relics now; she wants to endure her pain for the poor souls and for her enemies."

These poor souls thanked her the following night. "I was the occasion," she said, "of a very great procession of the purified souls. They were known to me, they prayed for me. I took the heavy crucifix from the Coesfeld church, detached the figure, and carried it. I was the only living being there. The souls wore not the clothes of their own time, still all were clothed differently and their countenances were different. They went barefoot, some whiter or grayer than others. I went with the procession out of the gate, and I had much communication with the poor souls. I went to two Jesuits to whom I had confessed in my youth. One lived with his pious sisters who sold coffee, but privately ; it was not a public store. I often bought coffee there after the first Mass. The spirit of the old man pointed out the little house to me and remarked how changed all was now. He told me that he remembered me distinctly, that he had always wished me well, and that he prayed for me. The other also spoke with me."

The evil consequences that would result from any action she might take against the commission were shown her by her angel. She saw that after the unfavorable impression of the commission produced on the public mind by the Landrath's pamphlet, her enemies would willingly carry her off from Dülmen under pretence of a new investigation. All the details of their plans were shown her as if being actually executed; and this made her suffer so much the more acutely as she was forced to bear it in silence. " God alone can help me," she said weeping ; " I have neither consolation nor help beside." She heard in her visions the words : " This is a warning of what they will do," and she beheld the sufferings by which she would avert the dangers.— " Thou mayest ward off the sufferings awaiting thee from thy enemies by prayer ; but they will be replaced by others and by annoyances from thy friends," said her Heavenly Spouse to her one day. "Thou wilt often be almost in despair."—and the very next morning, Gertrude loaded her with reproaches, such as " she gave away to the poor all that they had, she was a spendthrift, their affairs were every which way, and she was ruled by the evil spirit !"

" I found her very weak," says the Pilgrim, " her cheeks stained with tears ; she vomited blood, she was consumed by thirst, and she could not drink. The evil one tormented her. As soon as Gertrude began her reproaches, he showed himself visibly.--' When I was alone and in prayer,' she said, ' I was freed from his presence or, better still, when I took up my relics ; but, if I laid them aside, there he was again ! I struggled with him all day. When the Pilgrim tried to comfort me, the apparition became more frightful. It was the same demon who was always present in Mersmann's house among the commissioners.'—When, at last, the enemy was forced to retire, she saw the road she had yet to travel before reaching the Heavenly Jerusalem. It was a rugged path broken up by precipices over which both friends and enemies had stretched nets to ensnare her; scraps of writing were attached to many of them as if to warn her. She read: ' Be silent! Turn aside! Suffer patiently! Look not back! Look straight ahead! Do not lose sight of Me too often!' which last words gave rise to a conversation with her Spouse from which she gathered charity and patience. ' Yes, I see it!' she exclaimed, ' He shows me what I have already surmounted!'—' And who has guided thee thus far?' said He to her. ' How canst thou complain? O thou forgettest Me too often!'—' Ah! my well-beloved Spouse, I understand all now. All things are for the best. I would rather be despised and ill-treated with Thee than rejoice with the world!'

"Some days after, when I was in distress, the evil spirit again placed before me various pictures of the sufferings in store for me; he showed them as quite unbearable, and I was on the point of yielding. Then I thought, I will make an effort and flee away, but I could not. I sank back, because I was acting on my own light. I was at last worn out with the struggle, and I said, ' Now I will bear my misery with my Lord Jesus!' At the same moment the Lord appeared to me pale and exhausted, dragging His cross up Golgotha and sinking under the weight. I flew to Him, conscious of how I had wronged Him, I acknowledged my sin, and took one end of His cross on my shoulders. Now had I strength and vigor, because I acted for Jesus. He showed me what He endured for me, and my cowardice confounded me; but thanks to Him, I again have courage!"

"On the Feast of St. Cecilia, my cowardice again forced itself upon me and I felt remorse for not having been more patient during the investigation. I invoked St. Cecilia for consolation, and she came to me instantly through the air. O heart-rending sight! Her head half-severed from her body, lay on her left shoulder ! She was short, slight and delicate, black hair and eyes, and a fair complexion. She wore a yellowish white robe, with large heavy golden flowers, the same in which she had been martyred. She spoke as follows :—

" ' Be patient ! God will forgive thy fault, if thou dost repent. Be not so troubled for having spoken the truth to thy persecutors. When one is innocent, he may speak boldly to his enemy. I, too, reproached my enemies. When they spoke to me of blooming youth and the golden flowers on my robe, I replied that I esteemed them as little as the clay of which their gods were formed and that I expected gold in exchange for them. Look ! with this wound, I lived three days and tasted the consolation of Jesus Christ's servants. I have brought thee patience, this child in green. Love him, he will help thee !' She disappeared and I wept with joy. The child sat down by me on the bed and stayed with me. He sat uncomfortably on the edge, kept his little hands in his sleeves,and hung his head with a mournful but kind air, asking for nothing, complaining of nothing. His demeanor touched and consoled me more than I can say. I remember having had the patience-child by me once before. When the people from Holland tormented me almost to death, the Mother of God brought him to me. He said : 'See, I allow myself to be taken on either arm, nursed or put on the floor, I am always satisfied—do thou the same !' Since that time, even in my waking state I see that child, seated near me, and I have *really* acquired patience and peace."

She endured in vision torments equivalent to exterior persecution to satisfy the justice of God.

Nov. 13th—"I saw myself carried by shouting and hooting enemies up a high scaffold which was so narrow

that I could hardly lie on it. I was in danger of falling
and breaking my neck. My enemies were triumphant at
the sight. I lay in agony, until at last the Mother of God
appeared in the form of her statue of Einsiedeln, and made
the scaffold.broad enough for me to walk on it. When I
descended unexpectedly, my enemies were filled with confusion."

Nov. 25th—" I found myself again on an enclosed scaffold in whose centre was an opening through which one beheld a dark prison. All was still, I saw no one and it seemed
as if I were about to perish secretly by falling through the
hole. Then Sts. Frances and Louisa appeared, they who had
so often helped me. They raised a plank and showed me
a ladder which, as soon as I stepped upon it, sank with
me to the ground, and I escaped. Then an old nun of our
convent washed my soiled feet; but the marks of the wounds
were not removed, and I drew my feet away in confusion."

Nov. 27—" That I might see what dangers I had escaped, I was taken by my guide into an empty four-cornered
house like a barn. On one side stood a great cauldron
as large as my room, under which blazed a fire. I was to be
thrown into the kettle. First came all the young people
I knew with sticks and shavings, but their fire soon
burned out. Then came all the married people and old
women I had ever known. They built a blazing fire
with great logs, but it also went out without even catching
all round though some embers lay smouldering. I was
not yet thrown into the cauldron. After them came the
nuns and made a fire in a most ridiculous way. They
heaped up slyly all kinds of trash, reeds, withered leaves,
dry herbs, nothing but hollow worm-eaten things which
they could bring easily and secretly. They were praying
all the time and running into the church. No one wanted

her neighbor to see what she did, and yet all were doing the same thing. It was most amusing to see them making the fire. I recognized each one's peculiar style. I saw in particular Sister Soentgen. She piled up a good deal of wood, so that some of the smouldering sticks were relighted. Then the nuns left the house one after another, and I, too, retired. Soon, however, I returned. Now came people of all sorts in vehicles, among them some doctors, who made observations, setting the cauldron on the fire and feeling again and again if the water was getting hot. Then Sister Soentgen came back, stirred up the fire, and spoke so sweetly that I also ran and brought a log of wood for it. Then came spies, among them the Landrath; they seized me suddenly and threw me into the cauldron. I was frightened to death. I thought I should die. They repeatedly drew me half out and plunged me in again up to the neck, sometimes forcing me down to the very bottom where I awaited my death in agony. Then came my friends, Frances and Louisa, to take me out, but I insisted on remaining till the end. At last, however, they took me under the arms and lifted me out, a proceeding which the *cooks* unwillingly allowed. They went away saying : ' We shall try it in another place, there are too many people here.'—I saw them go to an upper, retired chamber in which they wanted to shut me up, but they did not succeed.

" I thought that, to comfort me in my frightful agony, Blessed Louisa took me to Rome and left me in a great cave, where I saw numerous bones of the saints, bones of the arms and smaller ones arranged in order, and many little pots, urns, and flasks of various shapes, containing dried blood of the saints. I had never before seen such things. I found bones of which I have little particles, and also blood belonging to the saints of whom I have relics. The cave was quite

bright, lit up by these sacred objects. I arranged and venerated them; and I was thinking how I should get out, when
the soul of a woman I had once known appeared to me.
She told me that I must end her sufferings. She had sought
me long and only now found me. During life she had refused
a poor pregnant woman a piece of buttered bread which she
craved and which she might easily have spared her. For
this she was now devoured by insatiable hunger. She begged
me to help her. Then appeared, also, the soul of the other
poor woman entreating me earnestly in behalf of her neighbor. I had once known her too. As I was still in the relic
cave, I knew not where I could get bread and butter,
although I was eager to help the poor soul. Then a beautiful, shining youth appeared and pointed to a corner of the
cave where was what I wanted: an oval loaf, long as my
hand and two fingers thick. It was of a pale yellow color
not like our bread. It looked as if it had been rolled up
in something and baked under the ashes. By it stood a
pot of melted butter and a knife. I tried to spread the
butter thickly on the bread but it always ran back into the
pot ; and, at last, the whole thing fell from my hands into the
dirt. Then the youth said : ' See, that is because you always
want to do too much (1),' and he bade me scrape up the
butter and clean it. When I gave the bread to the woman,
she thanked me, saying that she would soon be in a better
state and then she would pray for me.—Then came another
woman carrying a small bag of salt. She had been a little
niggardly. She told me with tears that she had once refused
a little salt to a poor woman, and now for punishment she
had to beg salt. She asked me to give her some, and the

(1) These souls appeared to Sister Emmerich in a place to which she had been transported in spirit. She could aid them, as she was still living. Weight and measure had
to be observed, since satisfaction must be proportioned to the debt. To give to one soul
more than is necessary is to take away from another. Sister Emmerich participates in
the merits of the holy martyrs which they acquired during their mortal career.

youth showed me where to get it. It was very different from our salt, damp, coarse, and yellow. I took one of the smallest grains to fill up the measure. But every time I laid it on the pile it fell off, and again did I receive the same reproof. When I had given her the salt, she disappeared satisfied, promising to pray for me. Darkness reigned in the cave, the sacred things alone shone brightly. The youth then took me to the place where the martyrs suffered and to a charnel-house, such as I had seen before, to assure me that all was real, and then he brought me back to my bed."

Nov. 28th—"I saw a great conflagration. The Landrath's house was all on fire. Sparks and burning beams flew around wounding people far and near, but not setting anything on fire. I was sorry for the man's misfortune; but I soon found out that I and not he was to be the sufferer. An enormous firebrand, like a burning flitch of bacon, was carried by the wind over my head; but a soul warded it off and it fell to the ground. She said: ' It does not burn me. I have had to undergo a very different fire, but now I am well-off.' Then I saw, to my great joy, that it was the soul of an old peasant-woman who was very fond of me in my childhood, and who had often complained to me of the trouble her daughter gave her. I had shown her affection and cleaned her when covered with vermin. This soul had been thirty years out of the body; she was extraordinarily bright and beautiful. She thanked me with a frank and joyous air, and told me how rejoiced she was to be able to help me now in return for what my prayers had done for her. She bade me be comforted; that I had, it was true, still much to suffer, but that I should accept all quietly and uncomplainingly from God; that she would help and protect me as far as she could. ' And,' she added, ' I am not the only one who helps thee. Ah! thou hast so many protectors! See, all for whom thou hast prayed, whom thou hast assisted—all will help thee in thy need.' Then she pointed to many souls that I knew; they were in various situations, and all were going to protect me. I cannot say enough of the joy and satisfaction I felt on beholding the splendor and beauty of this old woman whom we used to call *Aunty*.

"But I saw all this time the Landrath's house burning more fiercely, and I felt that it was a picture of the consequences of his wickedness, of the ruin and unhappiness in store for him. I pitied him from my heart, and I begged the soul to pray and get prayers that God might not punish him for the evil he had done or still would do me. I begged that he might be treated as if he had loaded me with benefits and, on this condition, I would accept all sufferings. She promised and disappeared.

" Afterward I had to carry the Landrath up a mountain, which greatly fatigued me. I had already had to do this for many others. Long ago, even before he came to see me, I had to carry the Pilgrim in vision, which labor represents the exertion necessary to lead a soul into the way of salvation. When St. Francis Xavier was sent to convert the pagans, he often carried black men on his shoulders in vision."

In the first week of Advent, Sister Emmerich had her last vision relating to her persecutors. " I had to struggle all night, I am worn out with the sad pictures I saw. My guide took me all around the earth through immense black caverns built by the powers of darkness, and filled with people wandering about in sin. It was as if I went over all the habitable points of the globe and saw nothing but sin. I often saw new troops of men falling from on high into the blindness of vice. I saw nothing good. I saw, in general, more men than women, the children were few. Often when I was over-

come by the sight, my guide brought me for a little while out
into the light, into a meadow or beautiful region where the
sun shone, but where there were no people ; afterward I
had to return into the darkness and see again the malice,
blindness, pride, deceit, envy, avarice, discord, murders,
luxury, snares, passions, the horrible wickedness of men—
all plunging them into greater misery, deeper darkness.   I
was under the impression that whole cities were built upon
a thin crust which would soon cave in and precipitate them
into the abyss. I saw people digging ditches for one another's
destruction; but there were no good people here, none falling
into the ditches. All these wicked people were in a great dark
place, running about at random as in a great fair, grouping
together, and enticing one another to sin.   Sometimes the
darkness grew deeper, and the road led down a steep
crag, frightful to behold, extending around the whole earth.
I saw people of all nationalities, all costumes, and all
sunk in crime.   At times I awoke in terror, and saw the
moon shining brightly in at my window. I groaned in anguish, and begged God to send me no more such frightful
pictures ; but I had soon again to descend into those terrible regions of darkness and behold their abomination. Once
I found myself in a sphere so horrible that I thought myself
in hell, and I began to weep aloud.   My guide said : 'I am
by thee, hell cannot be where I am.' Then turning longing-
ly to the poor souls in purgatory, I was transported into the
midst of them.   It seemed like a place near the earth, and
there too I saw inexpressible torments; but they were God-
fearing souls who sinned not, who perpetually sighed,
hungered, thirsted for deliverance. They could all see
what they longed for and for which they had to wait in
patience ; their suffering was full of resignation ; their
acknowledgment of their faults and their utter inability to

help themselves peculiarly touching. I saw all their sins.
They were in different depths, different degrees of abandonment; some up to the neck, some to the breast, etc.,
and they implored aid. After I had prayed for them, I
awoke and again begged God to deliver me from these visions. But scarcely had I fallen asleep than I was lead
once more into the dark regions. Satan threatened me
and placed horrible pictures before me. Once I met an
insolent devil who said something like the following : 'There
was no necessity for your coming down here and seeing
everything—now you'll go up above, boast of your trip,
and write something about it!' I told him to cease his
stupid talk. Once I thought I saw a great, wicked city
being undermined by devils who were already far advanced with the work. I thought as it had so many heavy
buildings, it must now soon fall in. I had often felt that
Paris would sink in, for I see so many caves under it, but
not cut out purposely like those in Rome."

"At last, I reached a large place like one of our own cities.
In it was a little more light, and there I was shown a
horrible sight, Our Lord Jesus Christ crucified! My whole
soul shuddered, for the executioners were men of our own
time, and Our Lord was suffering much more cruelly from
them than He did from the Jews. Thank God, it was only
a picture!--' So would they,' said my guide, ' now treat the
Lord, could He still suffer.'—I saw with horror among His
tormentors men whom I knew, even priests. This place
was connected with the dark regions by many veins and
ramifications. I saw, too, my own persecutors and how they
would treat me, if I fell into their hands ; they would by
torture try to make me confirm their false statements."

The remembrance of this horrible vision made her
heart beat with fright. Nothing could induce her to give it

entire ; she concluded with these words : " My guide said to me, ' Now hast thou seen the horrible blindness and darkness of men. Murmur no more at thy own lot, but pray ! Thy lot is very sweet.'—This vision was followed by that inquietude I so often feel, that of being accountable for something since so many sins are committed on my account. The dread of disobedience haunts me. My guide said : ' It is pride that makes thee think that only good should happen through thee ! And if thou are not obedient, it is my fault and not thine !' "

Some days later, she said : " My persecutors will now leave me in peace. I saw that they had a mind to use violence, but they were suddenly seized with fright and became disunited. I saw it under the picture of a fire breaking out among them. One mistrusts the other and fears being betrayed. My Spouse has told me that I will not yield to impatience. I shall have a little repose to finish reading the last five leaves of my great book. I must have rest that I may leave its contents after me. I have still much, very much to do !"

On Dec. 14th, she had a vision of an ecclesiastical investigation that would be instituted after her death. Whilst in ecstasy, she related to the Pilgrim : " I saw the clergy receiving from Rome letters commissioning them to proceed to an investigation in due form. I saw after this a church in which there were no seats. It seemed to me that it had once been desecrated, but was now restored. It was a solid, angular old building, but beautiful ; no hollow wooden ornaments about it, no sham gold. The clergy entered in silence. With their exception, there was no one in the church but the saints and my own soul. They drew a coffin from one of the vaults, carried it before the altar, opened it as if about to make a trial of something, and left it open whilst they

celebrated High Mass. Then they cut from one of the
hands a consecrated finger, for in the coffin was the body of
a holy Bishop. They laid the relic on the altar and replaced the coffin in the vault. I felt that they were coming
to me with the relic, and I ran off home. They came, and
were very strict and grave. I know not what they did to
me, for I was on high as if in a beautiful meadow, and st ll
at the same time up in the clouds, by the old Bishop whose
finger had been cut off. It was wrapped in red velvet and
one of the clergy carried it on his breast. I was now suddenly united to my body again by the holy Bishop, and I
arose and looked in amazement at all the gentlemen. After
the investigation, I again saw the clergy in the church from
which they had taken the finger. They now put it back into
the coffin under the altar, and a great thanksgiving was
celebrated.—The church was full of people and there were
also many saints and souls present, with whom I sang in
Latin.

"Afterward I had a vision of a new convent. Still it
was as if it all took place after my death. Had I lived
longer, they would have made me undergo a great trial;
so I must die first. The end that they propose can be as
well attained after my death as before. I saw also that after my death, some one will cut off one of my hands, and
here and there changes will be quietly made in the churches in which relics will be more honored and again exposed
for public veneration."

When the Pilgrim mentioned this vision to Sister Emmerich's confessor, he remarked: "She has often enjoined
upon me when she thought herself dying and I carried her the
Sacraments, she being in ecstasy, to cut off one of her hands
after her death. I know not why she said this unless she
intended to intimate that it would retain the power of rec-

ognizing relics.   She often told me that even after death,
she would be obedient to my orders in quality of confessor.
And of the priest's consecrated fingers she says that were his
body fallen to dust and his soul in hell, yet will the consecration still be recognized in the bones of the fingers. They
will burn with an altogether peculiar fire, so ineffaceable is
the mark."

CHAPTER XL.

On the evening of Dec. 15th, as Sister Emmerich lay in
ecstasy, the Pilgrim placed on her breast a little parcel, containing a relic, previously designated by her as belonging to
St. Ludger, and the crusts that had fallen from her own
wounds. She was instantly aware of his action and, without awaking from ecstasy, she exclaimed: "Ah! what a
good shepherd! He has come over the broad waters! His
body lies in the old church in my country. It is he from
whom they took the finger yesterday. But there is another
person! I have not seen her for a long time. Strange!
There is something in it I cannot understand! She has the
stigmata, she is an Augustinian! She is clothed as I used
to be and as I still am, partly as a little nun. It is singular! She must be still alive, she is hidden in some corner.
I cannot understand it! How much she has suffered! I
can take her for a model, for all my sufferings are nothing
to hers! And, strange to say, she is outwardly joyous!
No one knows what she endures. It would seem almost
as if she knew it not herself!

"I see by her so many poor people and children. I think
I know them. Some one must have hidden this person from
me. My friends and acquaintances must know her. Ah! how
her heart is wounded! It is encircled by a crown of thorns

(1) Thus the Pilgrim headed his notes of Dec. 15, 16, 17, 1819. The author retains
it, as he considers the fact of Sister Emmerich's having this remarkable vision just at
the close of the terrible sufferings of this period, most significant.

full of sharp points. She has very curious surroundings, and how many people are secretly spying and calumniating her! How bright and joyous she is under it! She bounds along like a deer! She is truly an example for me. Now I see clearly how miserable I am!"

After these words, the Pilgrim retired leaving the crusts in the parcel! Next morning, she related the following: "I had last night a most wonderful vision which I cannot understand. There must be a person hidden here who is frequently placed in circumstances similar to mine. She had the stigmata, too, but she has now lost them. I watched her all night in her pains. She must have lived in our convent, for I saw around her all the nuns excepting myself. No one ever guessed the terrible secret suffering that oppressed her, as she was always so cheerful. I cannot imagine what it all means. I have never had such graces or such sufferings, and I could not help feeling very much ashamed at my own cowardice. Perhaps, before my time, such a person lived in our convent; but the circumstances are so like unto my own that it puzzles me. I cannot understand it, it is all very strange!"

The Pilgrim here remarked: "Perhaps, it was a picture of yourself, of how you would have supported your sufferings, were you perfect; and you may also have seen graces received of which you may have been unconscious or forgetful."

She thought that this might possibly be the case and, at the Pilgrim's request, she continued the recital of this vision of herself.

"I saw a religious who had been very ill even before her entrance, forced to leave her convent. From the very beginning of her novitiate, she was a prey to indescribable secret sufferings. Once I saw her heart sur-

rounded by roses which changed suddenly to thorns and
tore it cruelly, whilst sharp points and darts entered her
breast. People far and near suspected her, calumniated
her in the most odious manner. All their thoughts
against her, though not passing into deeds, flew toward her
like steel-pointed arrows and wounded her on all sides. Plots
hatched afar entered her flesh like sharp darts, and once I
saw her heart literally cut to pieces. Still was she cheerful,
kind toward all as if unconscious of her wrongs. My compassion for her was so great that I felt her pains in my own
breast. Her soul was perfectly transparent and, when
fresh sufferings assailed her, I saw in her fiery red rays
and wounds, especially in her breast and heart. Around
her head was a crown of thorns of three different kinds of
branches: one of small white flowers with yellow stamens;
the second with flowers like the first, but longer leaves;
the third of roses and buds. She often pressed it down on
her head, and then the thorns penetrated more deeply.

"I saw her at work in the convent, going here and there,
the birds lighting familiarly upon her shoulders. Sometimes she stood perfectly rigid or lay prostrate on the
ground, when a man often came and bore her to her cell.
I could never see into her cell, he seemed to put her in
through the wall. A protecting spirit was ever by her,
whilst the devil constantly prowled around, stirred up
minds against her, raised loud noises in her room, and even
assaulted her person; but she seemed to be always abstracted, her mind elsewhere. I saw her sometimes in the
church, mounting in the most extraordinary manner upon
the altar, clambering up the walls and windows where she
had any cleaning to do. She was raised and upheld
by spirits in places where another could not possibly
stand. On several occasions, I saw her in two places at

once : in the church before the Blessed Sacrament and, at the same time, either up stairs in her cell, in the kitchen, or elsewhere, and once I saw evil spirits maltreating her most cruelly. She used to be surrounded by the saints, and sometimes she held the Infant Jesus in her arms for hours together. When with her sister-religious, He was always at her side. Once I saw her at table and weapons of all kinds being hurled at her ; but she was shielded by the blessed who crowded around her. I saw her at another time making hosts, although quite ill, and a blessed spirit aiding her. Once, when she lay sick and neglected, I saw two of the deceased religious making up her bed and carrying her here and there. They lifted her from her bed and placed her in the middle of the room where she lay on her back without support in the air ; some one entered the room unexpectedly and she fell heavily to the floor. I saw her very often reduced to extremity by the use of natural remedies, and then I saw the apparitions with which she was favored : a beautiful woman all resplendent with light, or a youth like my Celestial Spouse who brought her remedies in little phials, or herbs, or morsels of something which they put on a little shelf at the head of her bed. Once, as she knelt by her table, rigid in ecstasy, she received from an apparition a little statue of Mary; and at another time, her Heavenly Affianced placed on her finger a ring containing a precious stone on which was carved a figure of His Blessed Mother. After some time her Affianced returned and took it away from her. I often saw blessed spirits laying pictures and all sorts of things on her breast when she was ill, and taking them away when she got better ; and I often beheld her miraculously protected from imminent and serious danger. One day she stood by the trap-door of the drying-loft, helping to raise a basket of wet linen, whilst another sister worked the rope below. When the basket had almost reached the top, she made an effort to draw it toward her with one hand, the other grasping the rope. Just then the devil raised a frightful din in the court-yard. The sister below turned her head and slackened her hold on the rope to the imminent peril of the one above who was nearly precipitated, basket and all, upon her companion. Had not God protected her and allowed some one to seize the rope, she would certainly have been killed; as it was, she dislocated her hip from which accident she afterward endured terrible tortures. I saw her wonderfully protected by her angel on many other occasions and under circumstances perilous to both soul and body, and I beheld her driven almost to despair by her persecutors. Once, when sick unto death, she was borne away from her convent by two persons who would never have succeeded in preserving her life during the short journey, had not some more powerful beings come to their aid.

"I saw her when out of her convent dressed as I was at that time, a prey to secret sufferings, but favored by the same graces as before. She was often without assistance and sick unto death.

"Again, I saw her at the hermitage where she fainted. She was brought home to her lodgings by a friend who discovered the cross on her breast. And again, I saw her in two places at one and the same time, lying in bed and walking around her room, several persons keeping watch at the door. I saw her very ill in bed, her whole person rigid, her arms extended, her color brilliant as a rose. A resplendent cross descended from on high toward the right of the bed. On it was the Saviour from whose Wounds shot luminous red rays piercing her hands, feet, and side.

From each wound darted three rays fine as the finest thread, which united in a point as they entered her body. The three from the Wound of the Side were larger and further apart than the others and terminated in a point like a lance. At the instant of contact, I saw drops of bloods spurting from her hands, feet, and right side. When the circumstance became known, the whole town was in excitement, but soon the affair was hushed up and kept secret. I saw her confessor ever true to her, but timid, scrupulous, and suspicious, submitting her to endless trials. An Ecclesiastical Commission was deputed to examine into her case. It was conducted most rigorously, and I rejoiced to see the members soon convinced of her truth. I saw her afterward undergoing the surveillance of some citizens during which she was, as usual, supported by supernatural beings, her angel ever by her side. Later, I saw near her a man writing in secret ; but he was not an ecclesiastic.

" I saw her subjected to another investigation which began with every appearance of good faith and kindness, but the devil was at the bottom of it. She was often in danger of death during it, but she was supported and strengthened by heavenly apparitions. Her persecutors did not want to allow her to return to her friends and there were others expecting her, desiring to have her in other places. She was betrayed and ill-treated. Her heart was torn by men's malice, but she was throughout the whole affair, cheerful, even gay, so much so that even the nurse guessed nothing of what she endured interiorly. I saw her, thanks to supernatural intervention, restored to her own home. I saw her afterward in still greater danger, her enemies assembled for the purpose of carrying her off by force ; but they disputed among themselves and gave up their design. I saw her chief persecutor entering her presence in a rage as if about to attack her, when suddenly, by some interior movement, he became calm and withdrew. Meanwhile her sister, whose hidden malice and perversity were quite in- comprehensible, caused her great anxiety. I saw her spir- itual relations with certain ecclesiastics.

"She excited my pity. I felt her sufferings in my own breast, and I wanted to ask her how she could bear so many afflictions. I inquired of my guide if I might ques- tion her, if I might speak familiarly with her, and he said I might. Then I asked how she could support her secret sufferings so uncomplainingly, to which she answered in these few words : ' *As you do !*'—which greatly astonished me. I saw once that the Mother of God also endured in- comprehensible sufferings in secret.

"Then I saw that this person once lived with a mantua- maker, a good though strict women. I saw her once take off a garment in the street and bestow it upon a poor beg- gar. The devil laid snares for her ; he did not approach her himself, but he sent wicked men, among them a married man; but she understood not the drift of their intentions. Three different times I saw the evil one attempting her life. Twice he tried to hurl her down the ladder which led to the garret in which she slept. She used to rise by night to pray, and twice I beheld a horrible black figure push her to the edge of the landing ; but her angel interposed and saved her. On another occasion, as she was making the Way of the Cross in a lonely place near the river, I saw the enemy trying to cast her into a deep pit near the citadel; but again her angel rescued her. I saw her conversing frequently and lovingly with her dear Celestial Affianced, to whom one day she pledged her troth, though I cannot say whether there was an ex- change of rings or not. Their interviews were full of childlike simplicity. Once I saw her at mid-day absorbed in prayer, languishing with divine love, in the Jesuits' church, Clara Soentgen by her side.—A resplendent youth, her Affianced, issued from the Blessed Sacrament in the tabernacle and presented her two crowns, one of roses, the other of thorns. She chose the latter. He placed it on her head and she pressed it down to her own great pain. She was so absorbed as not to perceive that the sacristan was rattling his keys to attract her attention. Clara Soentgen may have seen something strange in her exterior, but the interior signification was unknown to her. She herself was unconscious of her blood having flowed until one of her companions remarked to her that her binder was stained with iron-mould (1). She hid these effusions of blood until after she entered the convent when they became known to one of the sisters. I saw her at Clara Soentgen's, where she gladly gave all that she earned to maintain the household in peace.

" Again, I beheld her working in the fields. So great was her desire to enter a convent that she fell sick. She firmly resolved to go. She had constant vomitings and went about so sad that her mother anxiously questioned her as to the cause; on learning it she expressed disapprobation, saying that such a project was not feasible on account of her daughter's poverty and delicate health. When she informed her father of it, he also disapproved and reprimanded her severely. But she told her parents that God was rich, He would help her. She fell ill, and I saw her confined to her bed. About noon, one day, when no one was home but her mother, I saw her lying, as I thought, asleep, the sun shining through her little window. A man and two female religious radiant with light entered her room. They approached her bed bearing a large

(1) " Binder," a pointed covering for the forehead, worn by peasants.

book written upon parchment in letters of red and gold, and
bound in yellow with clasps. The frontispiece was a picture
of a man, and there were several other pictures in it.   They
presented it to her, saying, if she would study it, she would
learn all that a religious ought to know. She replied that
she would be only too glad to do so, and she took it on
her knees. It was in Latin, but she understood it all
and read it eagerly.   She took this same book with her to
the convent and often studied it earnestly ; whenever she
had perused a certain portion of it, it was withdrawn from her.
Once I saw it lying on her table whence some of the religious tried to steal it away, but they could not remove it.
I saw her in another part of the convent when the priest
found her in prayer perfectly unconscious of all around, as
if paralyzed.   I saw Our Lord appear to her on the Feast of
St. Augustine, make the sign of the cross on her breast, and
then give her a cross which she pressed to her heart before
returning it to Him.   It was white and soft like wax.
After this she was sick unto death till Christmas, and she received all the Sacraments.   She dreamed that she saw Mary
sitting under a tree at Bethlehem ; she conversed with her
and ardently longed to die and remain with Our Lady.
But Mary told her that she, too, had longed to die with her
Divine Son, but she had to live and suffer many years
after His death.   Then she awoke.

"I saw the luminous cross descending toward her and
her reception of the stigmata. I saw her during the investigation and I understood that she was far advanced in the
reading of her book. I saw her afterward in the house in
which I now am and in Mersmann's house where, too, she
had the book. She was often in danger of death from
which, however, she was always supernaturally saved.
Lastly, I saw her future.   There was an ecclesiastical in-

quiry, and they seemed to be drawing up papers concerning her. (1)"

June 15, 1821.—On this day Sister Emmerich had a vision of St. Ludgarde. She saw a series of pictures drawn from her own life.

"I had also visions of the life of a person who, as I afterward discovered, was none other than myself. Sometimes they were presented in union with those of St. Ludgarde's life that I might note the points of resemblance in God's gifts to each and the manner of their bestowal. From her infancy this person was persecuted by the evil one. She used to pray in the fields in places in which she instinctively felt the influence of a malediction, the presence of the powers of darkness. The devil at such times raged around the child, struck her, and hurled her to the ground ; at first she ran away in terror but soon returned, animating her courage by faith and confidence in God. ' How canst thou chase me away, miserable wretch! There is nothing in common between us. Thou hast never had any power over me, neither shalt thou have it in this place !'—and kneeling down again in the same spot, she continued her prayer until Satan withdrew. Unable to make her relax her fervor, he urged her to weaken and destroy her health by excessive austerities, but the child defied him and redoubled her mortifications. One day, her mother left her alone, charging her to mind the house, and the demon sent an old woman from the neighborhood to tempt her. Having some bad object in view, the old woman said to the child : ' Go get some ripe pears from my garden! Be quick before your mother comes back !'—Off she ran in all haste. A plough half-hidden under the straw lay in her path. She

(1) The Pilgrim was so astonished at her words that he wrote in his journal : " Ah ! If we had not these hateful interruptions ! If we could only get her whole history from her own lips, what a treasure should we possess ! What a faithful portrait of this admirable soul !"

Stumbled and struck her breast so violently against it that she fell senseless to the ground. Her mother returning home, found the child in this condition and brought her to her senses by a sound correction. But the child long felt the effects of the accident.

"I saw how Satan misled the mother. For a long time she had erroneous ideas of her child, and often punished her undeservedly ; but the little girl bore all patiently, offered it to God, and so overcame the enemy.

"I saw her praying at night and the devil inciting a boy to distract her in an unseemly manner ; but she drove him off and continued her prayer.

"I saw the devil cast the child down from a high ladder, but her angel protected her ; and once, as she crept along the narrow edge of a deep ditch, to avoid treading on the wheat he tried to push her in, but again she escaped the danger.—Once Satan threw her into a pond about twelve feet deep and thrust her to the bottom three times, but her angel brought her each time to the surface.

"I saw the child, on another occasion, about stepping into her little bed, her heart raised to God in prayer, when the evil one from under the bed seized her by the ankles with icy-cold hands and tumbled her over on the floor. I remember very well that she was neither terrified nor did she cry aloud ; she remained quite still and, though no one had ever taught her to do so, she redoubled her prayers and conquered her enemy.

"She was always surrounded by suffering souls who were visible to her ; she prayed for them earnestly, notwithstanding the devil's attacks. Last night, during this vision, the soul of a peasant-woman came to me and thanked for her deliverance.

"I saw the child, now arrived at girlhood, attacked by a

young man instigated thereto by the devil; but she was protected by the ministry of two angels.

"I saw her praying in the cemetery of Coesfeld. The devil dashed her from side to side and, as she returned home, he cast her into a tan-pit.

"I beheld all the attacks, all the persecutions levelled against her in the convent. I saw Satan cast her down the trap-door where she remained hanging by both hands in a most wonderful manner. I never saw him rouse in her the least temptation contrary to purity, indeed he never even attempted to do so. I saw the investigation to which she was subjected and Satan taking an active part in the whole affair. I should not have comprehended how she could have endured so much, had I not seen angels and saints constantly by her. I saw, too, the interior dispositions of all the assistants, their continual touching of her wounds, and I heard their discourse. They gave her repose neither by day nor by night, for they were continually approaching her with a light. I saw their rage when they could discover nothing. When the Landrath said to her : 'I have caught Lambert, he has confessed all! You also must now do the same!'—he was truly frightful to behold. He was furious and, at the same time, so pressing, so insinuating, that he was on the point of drawing from her a word that might have served her enemies' purposes ; but I saw a spirit on such occasions laying his hand on her lips. I saw the Abbe Lambert sad unto death, but trying to overcome himself to the great advantage of his soul. I saw that his time of life will be short. I saw the Pilgrim's book from which many things were taken for publication."

CHAPTER XLI.

ADVENT AND CHRISTMAS, 1819.—JOURNEYS IN VISION TO A JEWISH CITY IN ABYSSINIA AND TO THE MOUNTAIN OF THE PROPHETS, *via* THIBET.—LABORS FOR CHILDREN.—MYSTICAL SUFFERINGS.

On the first Sunday of Advent, 1819, a poor old Jewess came begging an alms of Sister Emmerich for her sick husband; she was kindly received and to a few silver pieces Sister Emmerich added words that both touched and consoled her. It was not the first time the poor woman had sought the couch of suffering for relief in her own sorrows, and she had never come in vain. On this occasion, the invalid was seized with such compassion for the poor Jews that she turned to God with ardent prayers for their salvation. She was most wonderfully heard. Shortly after, she related the following vision in which her task was assigned for the beginning of the ecclesiastical year, *prayer* not only for the poor Jewess, but also for her whole race.

"It seemed to me that the old Jewess Meyr, to whom I had often given alms, died and went to purgatory, and that her soul came back to thank me as it was through me that she was led to believe in Jesus Christ. She had reflected that I had so often given her alms, although no one gives to the poor Jews; and she had thereby felt a desire spring up in her heart to die for Jesus, if faith in Jesus were the true faith. It was as if her conversion had already taken place or would take place, for I felt impelled to give thanks and to pray for her. Old Mrs. Meyr was not dead. But her soul had been disengaged from the body in sleep that she might inform me that, if she died in her present sentiments, she would go to purgatory. Her mother, she said, had also received an impression of the truth of Christianity, and she certainly was not lost. I saw the soul of her mother in a dark, gloomy place, abandoned by all. She was as if walled up, unable to help herself or even to stir, and all around her, above and below, were countless souls in the same condition. I had the happy assurance that no soul was lost whom ignorance alone hindered from knowing Jesus, who had a vague desire to know Him, and who had not lived in a state of grievous sin. The soul of the Jewess said that she was going to take me to the native place of her family whence her maternal ancestors had been banished for some crime.

"She would take me also to a city of her people among whom some were very pious, but as they had no one to instruct them, they remained in error. She said I should try to touch their hearts. I went with her willingly. The soul was far more beautiful than the poor old woman who is still living. My angel was at my side and, when the Jewess made little mistakes, he appeared to shine more brilliantly and corrected them. Then she appeared to see him too, for she would ask eagerly, ' Who told you that ? Was it the Messiah ? '—We journeyed over Rome and the sea and through Egypt where I did not see any great waters—only in the middle of the country a great white river which often overflows and fertilizes the soil. All was sand and sand-hills, which the winds scattered around. In this desert are immense stone buildings, high, thick, massive, such as are nowhere else. They are not houses but they are full of great caves and passages where rest numbers of dead bodies. They are very different from the subterra-

nean tombs of Rome. The bodies are all swathed like little infants, hard, stiff, dark brown, and tall ; ungraceful figures
are sculptured on the monuments. I went into one and
saw the bodies, but not one was luminous. We went on
further and further south over sand deserts where I saw
spotted beasts, like great cats, running nimbly, and here and
there round buildings on high hills covered with straw, with
towers and trees above. We went up higher and higher
over white sand and green stone polished like glass, into a
region of steep and rugged mountains. I was surprised to
see so many fertile places among the rocks. At last we
reached a large, strange-looking Jewish city, like nothing
I had ever seen before in the narrowness, obscurity,
and intricacy of its streets and houses. The mountains
and rocks appeared as if about to topple over. The whole
place was pierced with caves, grottos, and fissures over which
one must either climb or go around them. It is less a city
than an enormous group of mountains covered with houses,
towers, square blocks of stone, and it is full of caves and
excavations. We did not touch the earth, though we did
not go over the houses either, but moved between them along
the walls, always mounting higher and higher. It seemed
to me that it was all hollow and might cave in at any moment.
There are no Christians, but on the distant part of the mountain are people who are not Jews. I saw on one side a high
quadrangular stone building with round holes in the top covered with iron bars which I took for a Jewish synagogue.
Here and there were houses with gardens on shelving rocks
lying above and behind them. The soul of the old Jewess
Meyr told me on the way that it was true that in former
times the Jews, both in our country and elsewhere, had
strangled many Christians, principally children, and used
their blood for all sorts of superstitious and diabolical prac-

tices. She had once believed it lawful ; but she now knew that· it was abominable murder. They still follow such practices in this country and in others more distant; but very secretly, because they are obliged to have commercial intercourse with Christians. We entered the city near the gate through a long, narrow, dangerous court between two rows of houses which looked like an open street, but which really ended in an angle full of caves and windings leading into the heart of the rocks. All sorts of figures were cut out in them. I had a feeling that murders had been committed here and that few travellers left them alive. I did not go into them, they were too frightful. I know not how we got out of the court again.

" The soul of the Jewess Meyr said that she would take me now to a very pious, almost saintly family, upon whom the people all looked as upon their hope ; they even expect from them a deliverer, perhaps the Messiah. ' They are very good,' she said, ' and so are all their connections.' She wanted me to see them. We crossed the mountainous city which we had entered at the north, and mounted toward the east, till we reached a level place whence we had a view of the eastern side. There was a row of houses running toward the south at the end of which stood a large, solid building overtopped by mountains and gardens. The soul told me that seven sisters dwelt here, the descendants of Judith. The eldest, still unmarried, was also named Judith, and all the inhabitants of the city hope that some day she will do for her people what Judith did for their ancestors. She dwells in the large stone castle at the end of the place. The soul begged me to be kind to them for they know not the Messiah, and to touch their hearts as I had touched hers. I forgot to say that it was night when we entered the city. I saw men sleeping in the caves and corners, and among them many good, simple-hearted people, very different from our Jews, franker and nobler. They were like gold compared with lead or copper; still there was also a great deal of superstition, crime, horrible filthiness among them and even something like witchcraft.

" We went into the first house at the corner, which belonged to one of the seven sisters. We passed through a round vestibule and entered a square apartment, the bed-chamber of the owner, who had a hooked nose. The soul of the Jewess again praised her excellent qualities ; but, whenever she said anything inexact, my guide drew near, that is he appeared and corrected it. She would then ask, ' Was it the Messiah who told you that ?'—I answered, ' No, His servant.'—As I looked upon Judith's sleeping sister, I suddenly became conscious that she was not good. I saw that she was a wicked adulteress who secretly admitted strangers. She appeared aware of our presence, for she sat up, looked around in alarm, and then arose and went about the house. I said to the soul that now she saw that this woman misbehaved. She was greatly surprised, and asked if the Messiah had told me that too. We went into the houses of the other sisters, who also had hooked noses, but not all equally so, and all were better than the first. I cannot now remember how it was that I found them alone, for all were married and some had children. They wanted for nothing. Their houses were richly carpeted and furnished, beautiful shining lamps hanging in the rooms ; but all lived upon their sister Judith's generosity. The sixth sister was not at home. She was with her mother who lived in a small house just in front of Judith's. We went in by a little round court and saw the mother, an old Jewess at her window. She was complaining angrily to her sixth daughter that Judith gave her less than the others, that she even gave more to her bad sister, and had turned her, her mother, out of doors. It was horrible to see the old Jewess in such a rage.

"We left them quarrelling, and went to see Judith herself in the castle before which stretched a deep broad chasm. I could not look down it steadily. A bridge with an iron railing spanned it, the flooring being only a grating through which at a frightful depth could be seen all kinds of filth, bones, and rubbish. I tried to cross, but something held me back. I could not enter without Judith, so I had to wait; such were my orders. Morning began to dawn, and I saw that the side of the mountain on which we then were, was more pleasant and fertile than the north side by which we had ascended, and I noticed that the castle gate was fastened by a huge beam shaped like a cross. This fact very much surprised me. Suddenly Judith, returning from distributing alms in the city, stood before the bridge. She is about thirty years old, unusually tall and majestic. I never before saw a woman of such vigor and courage, so heroic and resolute; she has a noble countenance, her nose just slightly hooked, hardly enough so, however, to be perceptible. Her whole person, her gestures breathe something elevated, something extraordinary; but, at the same time, she is simple, pure, and sincere. I' loved her from the first. She wore a mantle. Her dress from the neck to the waist was most proper, tight as if laced, especially over the breast; she looked as if she had on a stout corset under her long, striped, many-colored robe. She had something like a gold chain around her neck and large pearls in her ears. A kind of variegated turban was wound around her head, and over it was thrown a veil. A tolerably large basket hung in full view upon her arm, the rods of which were black, the hoops white. She was returning home from one of her nocturnal expeditions when she caught

sight of me on the bridge. She appeared startled, took a
step backward, but did not run. She exclaimed :—' O My
God ! what askest Thou of me ? Whence is this to me ?'—
but soon she recovered herself and asked who I was and how
I came there. I told her that I was a Christian and a religious, that I had been brought thither because of s me
good people sighing for salvation, but who were without instruction. When she found that I was a Christian, she sh w-
ed surprise at my having come so far by a route so dangerous. I told her that curiosity had not impelled me, but that the
soul by me had led me thither, in order to touch her heart.
' This is,' I said, ' the anniversary of the coming of Christ,
the Messiah ; it is a yearly festival.' I added that she
should reflect upon the miserable condition of her race and
turn to the Redeemer, etc. Judith was deeply affected, she
became gradually convinced that she was conversing with
spirits. It seemed to me that she either said or thought
that she would find out whether I was a natural or a supernatural being, and she took me with her to the house. A
narrow path led over the bridge which could, however, be
enlarged. When we reached the huge crossbeam that
barred the gate, she touched something, the gate flew
back, and we passed through a court-yard into which several
gates opened ; all around stood statues of various kinds,
chiefly old yellow busts. We entered an apartment in
which some women were sitting cross-legged on the ground
before a long, narrow table about as high as a foot-stool ;
they were taking something, and Judith thought that she
would now put me to the test. She made me enter first.
I did so and went around behind the women, who did not
appear to see me ; but, when Judith entered, they arose
and passed before her bowing slightly as a mark of respect. Then she took a plate, passed around the women,

and presented it to me, holding it against my breast, for she wanted to find out whether I was a spirit or not. Now, when she saw me decline her offer and that none of the women appeared to see me, she became very serious and went with me into her own room. She acted like a person who half-believes herself alone, who wants to convince herself that it is so, but who at the same time doubts it. She spoke timidly, but not fearfully. She is, in very deed, a Judith, most courageous! Her room was simple, some cushions lying around, and several old busts on the wall. Here we conversed a long time. I spoke of her wicked sister. Judith was exceedingly distressed and desirous of remedying the disorder. Then I mentioned her mother whom I had seen in such a passion, and she told me that, on account of her temper, she had had to build her the little dwelling adjoining the castle; that she was very angry at being sent away, and at her giving more to one than to another, for all shared her bounty, as she, Judith, was not willing that they should live by usury. She took them money every night. Many others of the city lived at her expense, for her father had left a great treasure of which no one living knew but herself. He had loved her tenderly and left her everything. The people built their hopes upon her. Her secret alms made them see in her something superhuman, for they knew not of the treasure. They had once been greatly oppressed by war when she had done all in her power for them ; and so her deceased father (as she called him) left her the treasure. All wished her to marry, hoping that a deliverer would be born from her ; but she instinctively shrank from marriage. My appearance made upon her an impression such as she had never before known, and she felt that the Messiah might, indeed, be already come in Christ. She desired to inquire further into it, and, if she were convinced, she would strive to lead her people to salvation. She knew well that all would follow her, and she thought perhaps that was what they expected of her. After conversing in this strain, she took a lamp, led me into a kind of cave by a secret trap-door in the floor of her room, and showed me the immense treasure. I never before saw so much gold. The whole cave was lined with it and there was, besides, an enormous quantity of precious stones, one could hardly enter without stepping on them. She then took me all over the house. In one room were seated a number of old men, some of them Moors, wearing frontlets and turbans, their robes bordered with fur; they smoked long pipes, and they were drinking like the women in the other room. In another room were both men and women. We went up to the second story and into a large apartment singularly arranged. Around the walls and over the doors were yellow busts of venerable, old, bearded men. The furniture was odd-looking, antique and artistically carved, reminding me of the Jesuit church at Coesfeld, though the carving here was more elaborate. In the middle of the room hung a large lamp and I think seven others around it, and there was also something like an altar with rolls of parchment on it. The whole room was wonderful! Near it was another where lay numbers of decrepit men, as if being cared for. Then we went up on the roof. Back of the house on a terraced slope was the garden with large spreading trees carefully trimmed. We went up on this side and Judith pointed out in the distance a ruined building with crumbling towers, remarking that it had been the boundary of her nation's possessions before they had been conquered by a neighboring people and driven back. They still feared a renewal of their misfortune of which these walls stood as a perpetual me-

morial.   I saw them and water also in the distance.   We
mounted higher across deep ravines and strange buildings,
the rocks at times jutting out over one another as if the trees
and houses on them were about to fall.   We went to
another part of the city where rose a steep rock like a high
wall. Steps were cut in it, and here and there gushed limpid
springs.   Judith told me that there was a tradition of
this city's having suffered extremely from drought.   A
strange man, a Christian, came and struck the rock with
his staff, when water gushed forth.   It used to be conducted by pipes, but they were not now in existence.
All the springs, excepting this one, had ceased to flow.
Judith left me by the fountain ; she returned home and
I continued my journey.   We took no leave of each other.
It was all like a dream to her and she parted from me as if
she no longer saw me.   My road went up, up.   I saw trees
with large yellow fruits lying underneath, fertile fields, beautiful flowers, and bees in hives different from ours.   They
were square, tapering upward, black, and smeared with
something.   I was now far past the Jewish mountain, and I
saw men who lived under large spreading trees like houses.
They had few movables.   Some of them were spinning and
I saw, here and there, a kind of loom.   Their flocks, animals
like those of the Magi, grazed around.   There were also
animals like great jackasses, all very tame.   Some of these
people lived in tents ; but they stayed not long in any one
place, they were continually moving.   Clambering over
bushes and stones, I came to a large subterranean cavern
in good condition supported by short square pillars on which
were all kinds of figures and inscriptions ; in it was something like an altar, a large stone, above it and on either
side great holes like ovens.   I wondered why the people
did not use this beautiful hall.   They are good, simple crea-

tures and they doubt not that their faith is the right one. At last, I crossed the sea and returned home."

June 21, 1820.—"Last night I took another long journey to the high mountain-city and Judith's castle. I did not find her sisters in the houses leading to the castle. I know not where they are. I know that she had promised faithfully to put an end to the disorders of one of them. All the rest was as before, only it was later in the day, and there were numbers of strange Jews up-stairs praying in the synagogue. I went to Judith who was sitting in her room reading a book. There was something about her inexpressibly grand, noble, and touching. I gazed upon her with delight. I have no doubt that she will become a Christian, if God gives her the opportunity, and then the greater part of her people will follow her. I cannot look upon this woman in her beauty, her majesty, her courage, her tenderness of heart, her humility, without great love and hope. I saw her once more in my illness before the last, but I forgot to mention it. I have finished the journey that relates to her."

In the second week of Advent, Sister Emmerich was taken by her angel to the highest peak of a mountain in Thibet, quite inaccessible to man. Here she saw Elias guarding the treasures of knowledge communicated to men by the angels and prophets since the creation. She was told that the mysterious prophetic book in which she had been allowed to read, belonged here. This was not her first visit. She had often been brought hither by her angel, and also to the terrestrial Paradise not far distant. These places seemed to be closely connected, as in both she met the same holy custodians. Her own prophetic light gave her a certain right to participate in the riches preserved in them and she had need of the supernatural gifts there bestowed upon her for the continuance of her expiatory task. She could retain only a general impression of what she saw which she reproduced in very imperfect sketches.

Dec. 9, 1819—"Last night I journeyed over different parts of the Promised Land. I saw it just as it was in Our Lord's time. I went first to Bethlehem, as if to announce the coming of the Holy Family, and then I followed a route already well known to me and saw pictures of Our Lord's public life. I saw Him distributing the bread by the hands of two of His disciples, and then explaining a parable. The people sat on the slope of a hill under tall trees which bore all their leaves on top like a crown. Underneath were bushes with red and yellow berries, like bramble-berries. A stream of water ran down the hill and branched off into other small streams. I gathered some of the grass. It was soft, fine as silk, like thick moss. But when I tried to touch other objects, I could not. I found they were only pictures of times long past, though the grass I really felt. The Lord was, as usual, in a long, yellowish woollen tunic. His hair, parted in the middle, fell low upon His shoulders. His face was peaceful, earnest, and beaming with light, His forehead very white and shining. The two who distributed the bread broke it into pieces which the men, women, and children ran to receive; they ate and then sat down. Behind the Lord was a brook. I saw many other pictures as I passed rapidly from place to place. Leaving Jerusalem I went toward the east, and met several great bodies of water and mountains which the Magi had crossed on their journey to Bethlehem. I came also to countries in which many people lived, but I did not enter them. I travelled mostly over deserts. At last, I reached a very cold region, and I was led up higher and higher. Along the mountain-chain from west to east, was a great road over which troops of men were

travelling. They were diminutive, but very active, and they
carried little standards. I saw some of another race, very
tall; —they were not Christians. Their road led down the
mountain. But mine led up to a region of incredible beauty,
where the air was balmy, and vegetation green and luxuriant—flowers of marvellous loveliness, charming groves,
dense woods. Numbers of animals sported around apparently harmless. No human beings inhabited this region, no
man had ever been there, and from the great road only
clouds could be seen. I saw herds of nimble animals with
very slender legs like young roebucks; they had no horns,
their skin was clear brown with black spots. I saw a short
black animal something like the hog, and others like great
goats, but still more like the roebucks; they were tame,
bright-eyed, and nimble. I saw others like fat sheep with
wigs of wool and thick tails; others like asses, but spotted;
flocks of little yellow nanny-goats and herds of little horses;
great long-legged birds running swiftly; and numbers of lovely
tiny ones of all colors, sporting in perfect freedom, as if
ignorant of man's existence. From this paradise I mounted
still higher, as if through the clouds, and, at last, came to
the summit of the mountain, where I saw wonders! It was
a vast plain, surrounding a lake, in which was a green island connected with the shore by a strip of verdant land.
The island was surrounded by great trees like cedars. I
was taken up to the top of one of them. I held on firmly to
the branches, and saw the whole island at once. There
were several slender towers with a little portico on each as
if a chapel were built over the gate. These porticoes were
all covered with fresh verdure, moss or ivy; for the vegetation here was luxuriant. The towers were about as high
as bell-towers, but very slender, reminding me of the tall
columns in the old cities I had seen on my journey. They

were of different forms, cylindrical and octagonal; the former
built of huge stones, polished and veined with moon-shaped
roofs; the latter, which had broad, projecting roofs were covered with raised figures and ornaments by means of which one
might climb to the top. The stones were colored brown, red,
black, and arranged in various patterns. The towers were not
higher than the trees, on one of which I stood, though they
seemed to be equal to them in number. The trees were a kind
of fir with needle-shaped leaves. They bore yellow fruit
covered with scales, not so long as pine-apples, more like
common apples. They had numerous trunks covered toward
the root with gnarled bark, but higher up it was smoother;
they were straight, symmetrical, and stood far enough apart
not to touch. The whole island was covered with verdure,
thick, fine, and short, not grass, but a plant with fine curled
leaves like moss, as soft and nice as the softest cushion.
There was no trace of a road or path. Near each tower
was a small garden laid off in beds with a great variety of
shrubs and beautiful blooming trees—all was green, the
gardens differing from one another as much as the towers.
As from my tree I glanced over the island, I could see the
lake at one end, but not the mountain. The water was
wonderfully clear and sparkling. It flowed across the island
in streams which were lost underground.

"Opposite the narrow slip of land in the green plain was
a long tent of gray stuff inside of which, at the further end,
hung broad colored stripes, painted or embroidered in all
kinds of figures. A table stood in the centre. Around it
were stone seats without backs; they looked like cushions
and they, too, were covered with living verdure. In the
middle and most honorable seat, behind the low, oval, stone
table, was a manly, holy, shining figure sitting cross-legged
in eastern fashion, and writing with a reed on a large roll of

parchment. The pen looked like a little branch. Right and
left lay great books and parchment rolls on rods with
knobs at either end. By the tent was a furnace in the
earth, like a deep hole, in which burned a fire whose flames
rose not above its mouth. The whole country was like a
beautiful green island up in the clouds. The sky above was
indescribably clear, though I saw only a semicircle of bright
rays, much larger however than we ever see. The scene
was inexpressibly holy, solitary, charming! Whilst I
gazed upon it, it seemed as if I understood all that it signified. But I knew that I should not be able to remember it.
My guide was visible until we reached the tent, and then
he disappeared.

"As I gazed in wonder, I thought, 'Why am I here?
And why must I, poor creature, see all this?'—And the
figure from the tent spoke : ' It is because thou hast a share
in it!'—This only surprised me more, and I descended or
rather I floated down to where he sat in the tent. He
was clothed like the spirits I am accustomed to see, his
look and bearing like John the Baptist or Elias. The books
and rolls were very old and precious. On some of them were
metallic figures or ornaments in relief : for instance, a man
with a book in his hand. The figure told me, or informed me
in some way, that these books contained all the holiest things
that had ever come from man. He examined and compared
all, and threw what was false into the fire near the tent. He
told me that he was there to guard everything until the
time would come to make use of it, which time might have
already come, had there not been so many obstacles. I
asked if he did not feel tired waiting so long. He replied :
' In God there is no time !' He said that I must see everything, and he took me out and showed me around. He said
also that mankind did not yet deserve what was kept there.

The tent was about as high as two men, as long as from here to the church in the city, and about half as broad. The top was gathered into a knot and fastened to a string which went up and was lost in the air. I wondered what supported it. At the four corners were columns that one could almost span with both hands; they were veined like the polished towers and capped by green knobs. The tent was open in front and on the sides. In the middle of the table lay an immense book that could be opened and shut; it seemed to be fastened to the table and it was to this the man referred to see if the others were right. I felt there was a door under the table and that a sacred treasure was kept there. The moss-covered seats were placed far enough from the table to allow one to walk around between them and it; behind them lay numbers of books, right and left, the latter destined for the flames. He led me all around them, and I noticed on the covers pictures of men carrying ladders, books, churches, towers, tablets, etc. He told me again that he examined them and burned what was false and useless; mankind was not yet prepared for their contents, another must come first. He took me around the shore of the lake. Its surface was on a level with the island. The waters at my feet ran under the mountain by numerous channels and reappeared below in springs. It seemed as if all this quarter of the world received thereby health and benediction; it never overflowed above. The descent of the mountain on the east and south was green and covered with beautiful flowers; on the west and north there was verdure, but no flowers. At the extremity of the lake, I crossed over without a bridge, and went all around among the towers. The ground was like a bed of thick, firm moss, as if hollow underneath. The towers arose out of it, and the gardens around them were watered by rivulets which flowed either to or from the lake, I know not which. There were no walks in the gardens, though they were all laid out in order. I saw roses far larger than ours, red, white, yellow, and dark, and a species of lily, very tall flowers, blue with white streaks, and also a stalk as high as a tree with large palm leaves. It bore on the top a flower like a large plate. I understood that in the towers were preserved the greatest treasures of creation, and I felt that holy bodies rested in them. Between two of them, I saw standing a singular chariot with four low wheels. It had two seats and a small one in front. Four persons could easily be accommodated and, like everything else on the island, it was all covered with vegetation or green mould. It had no pole. It was ornamented with carved figures so well executed that, at first sight, I thought them alive. The box was formed of thin metallic open worked figures; the wheels were heavier than those of Roman chariots, yet it all seemed light enough to be drawn by men. I looked at everything closely, because the man said : ' Thou hast a share herein, and thou canst now take possession of it.' I could not understand what share I had in it. ' What have I to do,' I thought, ' with this singular looking chariot, these towers, these books ?' I had a deep feeling of the sanctity of the place. I felt that with its waters the salvation of many generations had flowed down into the valleys, that mankind itself had come from this mountain, and had sunk ever lower, lower, and lower, and I also felt that heaven's gifts for men were here stored, guarded, purified, and prepared. I had a clear perception of it all ; but I could not retain it, and now I have only a general impression.

" When I re-entered the tent, the man again addressed me in the same words : ' Thou hast a part in all this, thou

canst even take possession of it !'—And, as I represented to
him my incapacity, he said with calm assurance: ' Thou wilt
soon return to me !' He went not out of the tent whilst 1
was there, but moved around the table and the books.
The former was not so green as the seats, nor the
seats as the things near the towers, for it was not so
damp here. The ground in the tent and everything
it contained were moss-grown, table, seats, and áll.
The foot of the table seemed to serve as a chest to hold something sacred. I had an impression that a holy body reposed
therein. I thought there was under it a subterranean
vault and that a sweet odor was exhaled from it. I felt
that the man was not always in the tent. He received me
as if he knew me and had waited for my coming. He told
me confidently that I should return, and then he showed me
the way down. I went toward the south, by the steep
mountain, through the clouds, and into the delightful region
where there were so many animals. There was not a single one up above. I saw numerous springs gushing from
the mountain, playing in cascades, and running down in
streams. I saw birds larger than geese, in color like a par-
tridge, with three claws in front of the foot and one behind,
a tail somewhat flat, and a long neck. There were other
birds with bluish plumage very like the ostrich, but rather
smaller. I saw all the other animals.

"In this journey I saw many more human beings than
in the others. Once I crossed a small river which I felt
flowed from the lake above. I followed it awhile, and then
lost sight of it. I came to a place where poor people of
various races lived in huts. I think they were Christian
captives. I saw brown-complexioned men with white kerchiefs on their head, bringing food to them in wicker baskets; they reached it to them the whole length of their

arm, and then fled away in fright as if exposed to danger.
They lived in rude huts in a ruined city. I saw water in
which great, strong reeds grew, and I came again to the
river which is very broad here and full of rocks, sandbanks,
and beautiful green weeds among which it danced. It was
the same river that flowed from the mountain and which,
as a little stream, I had crossed higher up. A great many
dark-complexioned people, men, women, and children in
various costumes were on the rocks and islets, drinking and
bathing. They seemed to have come from a distance. It
reminded me of what I had seen at the Jordan in the Holy
Land. A very tall man stood among them, seemingly
their priest. He filled their vessels with water. I saw
many other things. I was not far from the country where
St. Francis Xavier used to be. I crossed the sea over innumerable islands."

Dec. 22d —"I know why I went to the mountain. My
book lies among the writings on the table and I shall get it
again to read the last five leaves. The man who sits at the
table will come again in due time. His chariot remains there
as a perpetual memorial. He mounted up there in it and
men, to their astonishment, will behold him coming again
in the same. Here upon this mountain, the highest in the
world, whose summit no one has ever reached, were the
sacred treasures and secrets concealed when sin spread
among men. The water, the island, the towers, are all to
guard these treasures. By the water up there are all things
refreshed and renewed. The river flowing from it, whose
waters the people venerate, has power to strengthen; therefore is it esteemed more highly than wine. All men, all
good things have come down from above, and all that is to
be secured from destruction is there preserved.

"The man on the mountain knew me, for I have a share

in it. We know each other, we belong together. I cannot express it well, but we are like a seed going through the
whole world. Paradise is not far from the mountain. Once
before I saw that Elias lived in a garden near Paradise."

Dec. 26th—"I have again seen the Prophet Mountain.
The man in the tent reached to a figure floating over him
from heaven leaves and books, and received others in return.
He who floated above reminded me very much of St. John.
He was more agile, pleasing, and lighter than the man in
the tent, who had something sterner, more energetic and
unbending about him ; the former was to the latter as the
New to the Old Testament, so I may call one John, the
other Elias. It seemed as if Elias presented to John revelations that had been fulfilled and received new ones from him.
Then I suddenly saw from the white sea a jet of water shoot
up like a crystal ray. It branched into innumerable jets
and drops like immense cascades, and fell down upon different parts of the earth, and I saw men in houses, in huts, in
cities all over the world enlightened by it. It began at once
to produce fruit in them."

Dec. 27th, Feast of St. John the Evangelist, Sister Emmerich beheld St. Peter's basilica shining like the sun, its rays
streaming over all the world. "I was told," she said, "that
this referred to St. John's Apocalypse. Various individuals
would be enlightened by it and they would impart their
knowledge to the whole world. I had a very distinct vision,
but I cannot relate it."

During the octave she had constant visions of the
Church, of which, however, she could relate but little. Nor
could she give a clear idea of the connection existing
between them and the Prophet Mountain, but we may
infer from the Pilgrim's notes that they formed a cycle of
visions singularly grand.

" I saw St. Peter's. A great crowd of men were trying to pull it down whilst others constantly built it up again. Lines connected these men one with another and with others throughout the whole world. I was amazed at their perfect understanding. The demolishers, mostly apostates and members of the different sects, broke off whole pieces and worked according to rules and instructions. They wore white aprons bound with blue riband. In them were pockets and they had trowels stuck in their belts. The costumes of the others were various. There were among the demolishers distinguished men wearing uniforms and crosses. They did not work themselves, but they marked out on the wall with a trowel where and how it should be torn down. To my horror, I saw among them Catholic priests. Whenever the workmen did not know how to go on, they went to a certain one in their party. He had a large book, which seemed to contain the whole plan of the building and the way to destroy it. They marked out exactly with a trowel the parts to be attacked, and they soon came down. They worked quietly and confidently, but slyly, furtively, and warily. I saw the Pope praying, surrounded by false friends who often did the very opposite to what he had ordered, and I saw a little black fellow (a laic) laboring actively against the Church. Whilst it was thus being pulled down on one side, it was rebuilt on the other, but not very zealously. I saw many of the clergy whom I knew. The Vicar-General gives me great joy. He went to and fro, coolly giving orders for the repairing of the injured parts. I saw my confessor dragging a huge stone by a roundabout way. I saw others carelessly saying their breviary and, now and then, bringing a little stone under their cloak or giving it to another as something very rare. They seemed to have neither confidence, earnestness, nor method. They hardly knew what was going on. It was lamentable! Soon the whole front of the church was down; the sanctuary alone stood. I was very much troubled and I kept thinking, 'Where is the man with the red mantle and white banner whom I used to see standing on the church to protect it?' Then I saw a most majestic lady floating over the great square before the church. Her wide mantle fell over her arms as she arose gently on high, until she stood upon the cupola and spread it over all the church like golden rays. The destroyers were taking a short repose, and when they returned they could in no way approach the space covered by the mantle. On the opposite side, the repairs progressed with incredible activity. There came men, old, crippled, long-forgotten, followed by vigorous young people, men, women, children, ecclesiastic and lay, and the edifice was soon restored. Then I saw a new Pope coming in procession, younger and far sterner looking than his predecessor. He was received with pomp. He appeared about to consecrate the church. But I heard a voice proclaiming it unnecessary as the Blessed Sacrament had not been disturbed. The same voice said that they should solemnly celebrate a double feast, a universal jubilee and the restoration of the church. The Pope, before the feast began, instructed his officers to drive out from the assembled faithful a crowd of the clergy both high and low, and I saw them going out, scolding and grumbling. Then the Holy Father took into his service others, ecclesiastic and lay. Now commenced the grand solemnity in St. Peter's. The men in white aprons worked on when they thought themselves unobserved, silently, cunningly, though rather timidly."

Dec. 30th—"Again I saw St. Peter's with its lofty copola on whose top stood Michael shining with light. He wore a blood-red robe, a great banner in his hand. A desperate struggle was going on below—green and blue combatants against white, and over the latter, who seemed to be worsted, appeared a fiery red sword. None knew why they fought. The church was all red like the angel, and I was told that it would be bathed in blood. The longer the combat lasted, the paler grew the color of the church, the more transparent it became. Then the angel descended and approached the white troops. I saw him several times in front of them. Their courage was wonderfully aroused, they knew not why or how, and the angel struck right and left among the enemy who fled in all directions. Then the fiery sword over the victorious whites disappeared. During the engagement the enemy's troops kept constantly deserting to the other side; once they went in great numbers.

" Numbers of saints hovered in the air over the combatants, pointing out what was to be done, making signs with the hand, etc., all different, but impelled by one spirit. When the angel had descended, I beheld above him a great shining cross in the heavens. On it hung the Saviour from whose Wounds shot brilliant rays over the whole earth. Those glorious Wounds were red like resplendent door-ways, their centre golden-yellow like the sun. He wore no crown of thorns, but from all the Wounds of His Head streamed rays Those from His Hands, Feet, and Side were fine as hair and shone with rainbow colors; sometimes they all united and fell upon villages, cities, and houses throughout the world. I saw them here and there, far and near, falling upon the dying, and the soul entering by the colored rays into the Saviour's Wounds. The rays from the Side spread over the Church like a mighty current lighting up every part of it, and I saw that the greater number of souls enter into the Lord by these glittering streams. I saw also a shining red heart floating in the air. From one side flowed a current of white light to the Wound of the Sacred Side, and from the other a second current fell upon the Church in many regions; its rays attracted numerous souls who, by the Heart and the current of light, entered into the Side of Jesus. I was told that this was the Heart of Mary. Besides these rays, I saw from all the Wounds about thirty ladders let down to the earth, some of which, however, did not reach it. They were not all alike but narrow and broad, with large and small rounds, some standing alone, others together. Their color corresponded to the purification of the soul, first dark, then clearer, then gray, and, at last, brighter and brighter. I saw souls painfully climbing up. Some mounted quickly, as if helped from above, others pressed forward eagerly but slipped back upon the lower rounds, whilst others fell back entirely into the darkness. Their eager and painful efforts were quite pitiful. It seemed as if they who mounted easily as if helped by others, were in closer communication with the Church. I saw, too, many souls of those that fell on the battle-field taking the path leading into the Body of the Lord. Behind the cross, far back in the sky, I saw multitudes of pictures representing the preparation begun ages ago for the work of Redemption. But I cannot describe it. It looked like the stations of the Way of Divine Grace from the Creation to the Redemption. I did not always stand in the same place. I moved around among the rays, I saw all. Ah, I saw inexpressible, indescribable things! It seemed to me that the Prophet Mountain drew near the cross whilst at the same time it remained in its own position, and I had a view of it as in the first vision. Higher up and back of it were gardens full of shining animals and plants. I felt that it was Paradise.

" When the combat on earth was over, the church and the angel became bright and shining, and the latter disappeared ; the cross also vanished and in its place stood a tall, resplendent lady extending over it her mantle of golden rays. There was a reconciliation going on inside, and acts of humility were being made. I saw Bishops and pastors approaching one another and exchanging books. The various sects recognized the Church by her miraculous victory and the pure light of revelation they had seen beaming upon her. This light sprang from the spray of the fountain gushing from the Prophet Mountain. When I saw this reunion, I felt that the kingdom of God was near. I perceived a new splendor, a higher life in all nature, and a holy emotion in all mankind as at the time of the Saviour's birth. I felt so sensibly the approach of the kingdom of God that I was forced to run to meet it uttering cries of joy (1).

" I had a vision of Mary in her ancestors. I saw their whole stock, but no flower on it so noble as she. I saw her come into this world. How, I cannot express, but in the same way as I always see the approach of the kingdom of God with which alone I can compare it. I saw it hastened by the desires of many humble, loving, faithful Christians. I saw on the earth many little luminous flocks of lambs with their shepherds, the servants of Him who, like a lamb, gave His Blood for us all. Among men reigned boundless love of God. I saw shepherds whom I knew, who were near me, but who little dreamed of all this, and I felt an intense desire to arouse them from their sleep. I rejoiced like a child that the Church is my mother, and I had a vision of my childhood when our school-master used to say to us : ' Whoever has not the Church for his mother,

(1) **This she** really did in her vision, praying in a loud voice.

looks not upon God as his father!'—Again I was a child, thinking as then, 'The church is stone. How, then, can it be thy mother! Yet, it is true, it is thy mother!'—and so I thought that I went into my mother whenever I entered the church, and I cried out in my vision, 'Yes, she is, indeed, thy mother!'—Now I suddenly saw the Church as a beautiful, majestic lady, and I complained to her that she allowed herself to be neglected and ill-treated by her servants. I begged her to give me her son. She put the Child Jesus into my arms, and I talked to Him a long time. Then I had the sweet assurance that Mary is the Church; the Church, our mother; God, our father; and Jesus, our brother—and I was glad that when a child I had gone into the stone mother, into the church, and that, through God's grace, I had thought: 'I am going into my holy mother!'—"Then I saw a great feast in St. Peter's which, after the victorious battle, shone like the sun. I saw numerous processions entering it. I saw a new Pope, earnest and energetic. I saw before the feast began a great many bad Bishops and pastors expelled by him. I saw the holy Apostles taking a leading part in the celebration. I saw the petition: 'Lord, Thy kingdom come,' being verified. It seemed as if I saw the heavenly gardens coming down from above, uniting with pure places on earth, and bathing all in original light. The enemies that had fled from the combat were not pursued; they dispersed of their own accord."

These visions upon the Church were soon absorbed in one great contemplation of the Heavenly Jerusalem.

"I saw in the shining streets of the city of God brilliant palaces and gardens full of saints, praising God and watching over the Church. In the Heavenly Jerusalem there is no Church, Christ Himself is the Church. Mary's

throne is above the city of God, above her are Christ and
the Most Holy Trinity, from whom falls upon Mary a
shower of light which then spreads over all the holy city.
I saw St. Peter's basilica below the city of God, and I ex-
ulted at the thought that, in spite of all men's indifference,
it ever receives the true light from on high. I saw the
roads leading to the Heavenly Jerusalem and pastors conducting therein perfect souls among their flocks ; but these
roads were not crowded.

"I saw my own way to God's city and I beheld from it,
as from the centre of a vast circle, all whom I had ever
helped. There I saw all the children and poor people for
whom I had made clothes, and I was surprised and amused
to see what varied forms I had given them. Then I saw
all the scenes of my life in which I had been useful, if only
to a single person, by counsel, example, assistance, prayer,
or suffering ; and I saw the fruit they had drawn from it
under the symbol of gardens planted for them which they
had either cared for or neglected. I saw every one upon
whom I had ever made an impression and what effect it
produced."

The fact of Sister Emmerich's retaining the liveliest remembrance of those actions most dear to her in her natural
state, is quite characteristic of her, so simple and yet so
heroic. Her labors for the sick and the poor ever constituted her greatest delight. Day and night, awake or in vision,
in the midst of her sufferings, she was constantly occupied
in works of this kind, and great was her delight when she
finished some pieces of clothing for her needy clients. We
shall give the Pilgrim's remarks on this subject just as they
fell from his own pen :—

"Nov. 18th—I found her mending some coarse woollen
stockings to be given away. I thought it all a waste of time

and I said so to her, whereupon she gave me a beautiful instruction on the way to perform charity."

" Dec. 12th—She was unusually gay this morning, working away at little caps and binders, made out ot all kinds of scraps, for poor women and children at Christmas. She was enchanted with her success, laughed and seemed perfectly radiant. Her countenance shone with the purity of her soul; she even looked a little mischievous as if about to introduce some one who had lain concealed. She says she is never so happy as when working for little children. This joyousness was, however, accompanied by a peculiar sensation—she was, as it were, absent and beholding an infinity of things against her will. She recollected herself repeatedly, glancing around her little room as if to assure herself that she was really there ; but soon it all disappeared again and she was once more surrounded by strange scenes."

Dec. 14th—" Last night I saw a woman of this place who is near her accouchement. She confided to a friend her destitute condition, not having clothes in which to wrap the child. I thought, ' Ah ! if she would only come to me !'— Her friend said to her, ' I shall see if I can get you something,' and to-day she came to tell me of the poor creature's distress. I was so glad to be able to provide for her wants."

We turn again to the Pilgrim's journal and find the following:—

" Dec. 13th—She was very bright again to-day, making clothes for poor infants. Nothing pleases her more than to receive some cast-off garments and old scraps for this purpose. Her money has also been again miraculously multiplied. For two days she knew not what to do, having only four thalers left. She recommended the affair to God when, all at once, she found ten in small change. She thinks their being in small change signifies that she should make use of them right away. She is surprised at the quantity of work she has finished. Her scraps and old pieces are dearer to her than the most costly treasures, though she is so rapt in contemplation during her work that she sees the scissors moving as if in a dream, and she often thinks she is cutting up the wrong thing."

" Dec. 18th—When I entered she was talking to her little niece about poor children; she was quite bright, although suffering a good deal. She said to the child : 'Last night I saw a child in a new jacket, but it had only one sleeve.'— ' Yes,' replied the child, ' it was little Gertrude. You gave her some stuff for a jacket, but there was not enough for both sleeves ; she told me so in school to-day.' Tears sprang to the invalid's eyes, and she told me that she always felt such consolation in speaking to the innocent child that she could hardly restrain herself ; she was sometimes obliged to send her away that she might not witness her emotion."

" Dec. 20th—She finished her work to-day with great effort and the help of God. She put herself to much trouble, she has everything in perfect order. 'I have nearly all my gifts ready,' she said, ' for mid-winter, then I shall have to begin again. I am not ashamed to beg for the poor. Little Lidwina used to do it. I have seen her in her room on the ground-floor ; it was about twice as large as mine, the miserable walls of clay, all was very poor. On the right of the door stood her bed around which hung a black woollen cloth like a curtain. Opposite the bed were two little square windows with round panes opening upon a court, and against the wall, between the windows, stood a kind of little altar with a cross and ornaments. Good Lidwina lay patiently in the dark corner with no feather bed, only a heavy, black quilt. She wore a black mantle which covered her all over even her hands, and she looked very sick, her face was full

of fiery red marks. I saw her little niece by her, a remark-
bly good and amiable child, about as large as my niece.
She waited on her so compassionately! Lidwina sent her
to beg some meat for the poor, and she brought back a
shoulder of pork and some pease; then I saw her in the ¢orner
to the left of the door, where the fireplace was, cooking
both in a great pot or kettle. Then I had another picture,
Lidwina looking for her Heavenly Spouse whom she saw
coming. I saw Him, too, He was mine also. But a man
who had hid len himself between the door and her bed distracted her, and she was so worried that she began to weep.
1 had to laugh, for the same thing often happened to me
too. I saw that her lips were greatly swollen."

Dec. 21st—" When I felt the cold last night, I thought
of the freezing poor, and then I saw my Spouse who said :
' Thou hast not the right kind of confidence in me. Have
I ever let thee freeze ? Why dost thou not give thy extra
beds to the poor ? If thou hast need of them again, I shall
give them back to thee.'—I was ashamed of myself and I
resolved, in spite of Gertrude, to give away the beds not in
use."—That very evening she did so, saying : ' If my relations want to visit me, they may sleep on straw, or stay at
home.' "

Dec. 22d—" She cried out in ecstasy : ' There I see all
the children for whom I have ever made anything ! They
are so merry, they have all the things, they all shine—my
little Boy is there, too. Come here, dear little one. sit there,'
and she pointed to a seat. 'O how I thirst for my Saviour !
It is a burning thirst, but it is sweet—the other thirst is
disgusting. O what thirst Mary must have had for her
Child ! Still she had Him only nine months under her heart,
and I can receive Him so often in Holy Communion ! Such
food is upon earth, and yet many die of hunger and thirst !

The land in which this blessing is given to man is just as desolate and poor as the rest of the world! But the blessed let nothing go to loss. Wherever a church once existed, it still exists. O how many churches I see around Bethlehem and in the whole world, floating in the air above the places on which they formerly stood! Feasts are still celebrated in them. There is the church in which Mary's Conception was so magnificently celebrated. Mary's spotlessness consists in this that she had in her no sin, no passion; her sacred body never endured sickness. She possessed, however, no grace without her own co-operation, excepting that by which she conceived the Lord Jesus."

After this she had a vision of how the "Little Boy," had been the constant companion of her life :—

"What I now saw in vision, once really happened; for the little Boy used to work with me when I was a child (1).

"When I was ten years old, He said to me : 'Let us go see how the little crib looks that we made years ago !'—'Where can it be?' I thought. But the little Boy said I had only to go with Him, we should soon find it. When we did so we saw that the flowers (2) of which we had made it, had formed garlands and crowns, some only half-finished. The little Boy said, 'The pearls are still wanting in front.' Only one small circlet of pearls was entirely finished and I slipped it on my finger. But, to my great distress and fright, I could not get it off. I begged the little Boy to do so, for I was afraid I should not be able to work with it on. He succeeded, and we put everything back again. But I think it was only a picture, I do not remember it as a real event. After I had grown up I got sick. I wanted to go to the convent; but as I was so poor, I became sad. The little Boy

---

(1) The particulars are given in one of the first chapters.

(2) Symbols of suffering.

said that that was nothing, His Father had enough, the Christ-Child had nothing either, and that I should one day enter a convent. I did, indeed, enter; it was a joyful time! As a nun, I was sick and in distress because I had nothing. I used to say, ' Now, see how it is! Thou wast to have care of all, I was always to have enough; and now Thou stayest away, and I get nothing!'—Then the little Boy came that night with gold, pearls, flowers, and all kinds of precious things. I knew not where to put them all. Twice again I received such things in vision, but I know not what has become of them. I think they were symbolical of the gifts I was to receive and which were miraculously multiplied; as, for example, Herr von Galen's present and the coffee on St. Catherine's day. I used to be sick all the time; well for a couple of days, then sick again, and in this state I saw many things with the Child Jesus and many cures. Then I was out of the convent very ill, often in intense agony and distress; but the little Boy always came with help and advice. Lastly, I had a vision of the future. The little Boy took me again to see the garlands and flowers of the crib in a kind of sacristy, where they lay in a casket, like golden crowns and jewels. He again said, ' Only some pearls are wanting, and then all will be used in the Church.'—I understood that I am to die, as soon as all the pearls will have been added."

In Advent she had her usual visions of Mary and Joseph journeying from Nazareth to Bethlehem:—

Nov. 27th—"I went to Bethlehem, and thence I journeyed a good distance to meet the Mother of God and Joseph. I knew they would go into a stable, and I hurried on joyously to meet them. Again I saw them coming with the ass, as peaceful and calm, as lovely as ever, and I was so glad to see it all once more as I had done in my childhood.

I went a long way back and found the stable, and on looking behind I saw Joseph and Mary far away with the ass,
shining with light. It seemed as if a luminous disc surrounded the Holy Family as they moved forward in the
darkness. Anne and Joachim had prepared all things
for the holy Virgin's delivery, and they hoped she would come
back in time to make use of them. But Mary knew that she
would not be delivered in her parents' house and with wonderful humility, she took of all that had been prepared but
two pieces, for she had an inexpressible feeling that she
must and should be poor. She could have no outward
show, for she had all within herself. She knew, or felt, or
saw in some unknown way that, as through a woman, sin
had entered the world, so by a woman was the expiation to
come, and it was in this sentiment that she exclaimed, 'I am
the handmaid of the Lord !' She always followed an interior voice which in moments of grace urged her irresistibly. This same voice has often called me to make long
journeys, and never in vain."

Dec. 13th—"Last night I was near Bethlehem in a low,
square hut, a shepherd's hut, occupied by an old couple.
They had partitioned off a corner for themselves on the left
by a slanting black mud-wall. By the fire-place stood
some crooks, and a few plates hung on the wall. The
shepherd came out of his apartment and pointed to another
just opposite, where sat Mary and Joseph in silence on the
ground against the wall. Mary's hands were joined on her
breast; she wore a white robe and veil. I stayed by them
awhile reverently. At the back of the house was a bush."

Dec. 14th—"I went from Flamske to the Promised
Land, as I had often done when a child, and I ran to meet
Mary. I was in such a hurry, so eager for the coming of
the Christ-Child, that I flew through Jerusalem and Beth-

lehem with streaming hair. I wanted to get them a right good lodging for the night, and I found one not far from the first which I met on my entrance. I went into a shepherd's hut back of which was a sheep-fold. The shepherd and his wife were both young. I saw the Holy Family arrive late at night. The shepherd gently reproached St. Joseph for travelling at so late an hour with Mary. Mary sat sideways on the ass on a seat with a resting-place for the feet. She was very near the birth of the Christ-Child. They left the ass at the door, and I think the shepherd took it into the sheep-stable. They were treated kindly. They went into a separate apartment and made some arrangements. They had brought some small fine loaves with them, but I never saw them eat much. I spoke quite simply with the Mother of God and, as I had my work with me, I said to her : 'I know well that thou needest nothing from me, but still I may make something for poor children. Be so good as to point out the most needy.' She told me to go on quietly with my work and that she would do as I requested. Then I went over into a dark corner where no one could see me, and worked away diligently. I finished many things, and watched the Holy Family preparing for their departure."

Dec. 16th—"I journeyed quickly on to Bethlehem although I was quite fatigued, and I hurried to a shepherd's cot, one of the best in sight of Bethlehem. I knew that Mary would arrive there that night. I saw her and Joseph in the distance. She was on the ass and shining with light. The interior of the cot was like the others; on one side of the fire-place all sorts of vessels and pastoral utensils, on the other an apartment in which I thought Mary and Joseph would lodge. There was an orchard near by and back of it the sheep-fold which was not enclosed, the roof supported only by stakes. The shepherd and his wife were young and very hospitable. When I first appeared, they asked what I wanted, and I told them that I had come to wait for Joseph and Mary who would arrive there that day. They replied that that had happened long ago, and that it would never happen again. They were a little short with me. But I said that it happened every year, for the feast was kept in the Church. Then they grew quite clever and obliging. I sat down in a corner with my work. They had to pass me often, and they wanted to give me a light, but I assured them that I needed none, I could see very well. The reason they said that the event was passed and would not again be repeated was that, on entering the house, I, too, had thought : ' How is this ? These people were here long ago, and they are still here ! They cannot still be alive !' Then I said to myself : ' Why, what foolish questioning ! Take things as thou findest them !' This re-assured me, but the people had met my doubt by a similar one. It was like a mirror, reflecting these words : ' What-soever you would that men should do unto you, do ye also unto them.'

" When Joseph and Mary arrived, they were kindly re-ceived. Mary got off the ass, Joseph brought in his bun-dles, and both went into the little room on the right. Joseph sat down on his bundle, and Mary on the ground against the wall. These young people were the first to of-fer them anything ; they set before them a little wooden stool on which stood flat oval dishes. On one were small round loaves, on the other small fruit. Mary and Joseph did not touch them, though Joseph took some and went out with it ; I think there was a beggar outside. The ass was tied before the door. Although they ate not, yet they received the gifts humbly and gratefully. I always wonder-

ed at their humility in taking whatever was given them.
I drew near to them timidly, rendered them homage, and
begged the Blessed Virgin to ask her Son at His birth, not
to let me do or desire anything but His most holy will.   I
spoke of my work, that she might tell me how to do it and
distribute it.   She   bade   me   go on,   soon   all   would   be
right.   Then I sat down timidly in my   little   corner   and
sewed, but I did not stay until the Holy Family   left.

   " My guide took me through a wilderness some distance
from Bethlehem toward the south, and it seemed to be in
our own time.   I saw a garden with   trees   shaped   like a
pyramid, their leaves fine and delicate, and   there   were
lovely green plots with little flowers.   In the centre, on a
column around which twined a luxuriant vine, stood a small
eight-cornered church covered with the vine branches.   At
some distance, only the leaves could be seen, but a   nearer
view disclosed bunches of grapes an ell long.   It was wonderful how the branches supported their weight.   The vine itself was as thick around as a small   arm.   From   the eight
sides of the little church, which had   no   doors   and   whose
walls   were transparent,   ran   pathways.   In the   church
was an altar on which   were   three   pictures   of   the   holy
season (Advent) :   one   was Mary and Joseph's journey to
Bethlehem ; another the Child Jesus in the crib ; the third,
the Flight into Egypt. They seemed to be living representations.   On the eight sides, hovered twelve of the ancestors
of Mary and Joseph who had celebrated these scenes.   My
guide told me that a church once stood here in   which   the
relations of the Holy Family and their   descendants always
celebrated these holy feasts.   It had been destroyed, but the
feast will   continue   to   be   celebrated   in   the   spiritual
church until the   end   of   time.   Then   he   brought   me
back quickly.

" My state on these days is very singular. I seem not to be on the earth. I see around, far and near, people and pictures, men dying of spiritual famine, evils everywhere ; I see people here in our own country, or in the islands, or under tents, or in forests—I see them learning in one place, forgetting in another, but everywhere misery and blindness. When I look up to heaven, how poor and senseless seem these people ! They are sunk in impurity, they interpret everything in a wrong sense. Then I try to push them on to God—it is all dark and obscure, and I feel a deep, deep disgust for life. Everything earthly is abominable, and violent hunger seizes me ; but it is not disgusting, it is sweet. Corporal hunger is so disgusting !"

Dec. 23d—"I met Mary and Joseph near Bethlehem just about dusk. They were resting under a tree by the roadside. Mary got down from the ass and Joseph went alone into the city to seek a lodging in one of the nearest houses. The city had no gate here, the road passed through a broken part of the wall. Joseph hunted in vain for a lodging, for crowds of strangers were in Bethlehem. I stayed with the Mother of God. When Joseph came back he told the Blessed Virgin that he could find no place near, and both returned to Bethlehem, Mary on foot and Joseph leading the ass. They went first to be enrolled. The man made some remarks to Joseph about bringing his wife, saying it was unnecessary, and Joseph blushed before Mary fearing she might think he had a bad name here. The man said also that, as there was such a crowd in this quarter, they would do well to go elsewhere, and they would certainly find lodgings. They went along timidly. The street was rather a country-road than a street, for the houses stood on hills. On the opposite side, where they were far apart, there was a beautiful, widespreading tree, the trunk smooth, the branches forming a shelter. Joseph left Mary and the ass under this tree, and set off again in search of lodgings. Mary leaned at first against the tree, her loose robe falling in full folds around her, a white veil covering her head. The ass stood with his head turned toward the tree. Many passed on various errands, looked at Mary, but knew not that their Redeemer was so near! She waited so patiently, so quietly, so humbly! Ah! she had to wait a long time! At last she sat down, her feet crossed under her, her hands joined on her breast, her head bowed. Joseph returned disappointed, he had found no lodgings. Again he set out in another direction, and again Mary waited patiently; but he was unsuccessful as before. Then he remembered a place near by where the shepherds sometimes sought shelter. They, too, could go there, and even if the shepherds came, they need not mind them. They started and turning to the left, followed a lonely road which soon became hilly. Before a small rising stood a clump of trees, pines or cedars, and others with leaves like box. In the hill was a grotto or cave, the entrance closed by a gate of twigs. Joseph entered and began to clear away the rubbish, whilst Mary stayed outside with the ass. Joseph then brought her in. He was very much troubled. The grotto was but ten feet high, perhaps not that much, and the place where the manger stood was slightly raised. Mary sat down on a mat and rested against her bundle. It was, perhaps, nine o'clock when they entered this grotto. Joseph went out again and came back with a bundle of sticks and reeds, and a box with a handle containing live coals which he poured out at the entrance and made a fire. They had everything necessary for that purpose, as well as various other utensils, though I did not see them cooking or eating. Joseph again went out, and on his return he wept. It must

now have been about midnight. For the first time I
saw the Blessed Virgin kneeling in prayer, after which
she lay down on the mat, her head on her arm, the
bundle for a pillow. Joseph remained humbly at the entrance of the grotto. In the roof, a little to one side, were
three round air holes with gratings. On the left of the
grotto was another apartment cut out of the rock or hill,
the entrance broader than the first and opening on the
road that led to the fields where the shepherds were.
There were small houses on the hills and sheds built of
twigs or branches supported by four, six, and eight posts.

" After this I had quite a different vision. I saw Bethlehem as it now is ; one would not know it, so poor and desolate has it become. The Crib is now in a chapel under the
earth and Mass is still read there ; it is larger than it used to
be, and it is covered with all kinds of white marble ornaments and figures. Above it stands a church like an old
ruined convent. but Mass is celebrated only in the grotto of
the Crib. I saw over it in the air a beautiful spiritual church.
It was eight-cornered and had but one altar. Above it
were choirs of saints. On the altar was a representation of
the Crib before which shepherds knelt, and through the air
came little lambs like little white clouds in the picture.
The officiating priest was a kind looking old man with white
hair and a long beard. He wore a very wide antique vestment,
a cowl over his forehead and around his face. It was Jerome. Incense was used during the ceremony more frequently than with us. Holy Communion was administered, and
I saw, as among the Apostles, a little body, like a tiny body
of light, entering the mouth of the communicants. There
were about six priests performing the ceremony, and when
it was over they ranged before the altar, face to face as in
choir, and chanted. Then the scene changed. Jerome re-

mained alone, and the body of the church was filled with
nuns of different Orders. They ranged in three ranks as in
choir and chanted. I saw the Annonciades among them
and Jane, who told me that, from her childhood, she had
seen these mysteries thus represented and also the great
good resulting from them to mankind. It was for this
reason she had founded her Order. She was now present
with all her faithful nuns to continue the celebration of this
feast almost forgotten by men. She exhorted me to reflect upon what had given birth to her charity and teach it
also to my spiritual children. She told me many more
things of the same kind that I intend to leave after me to
my sisters in religion. May God grant it ! I saw also at the
feast Frances and other nuns whom I knew."

On the evening of Dec. 23d, the Pilgrim and Father
Limberg spent two hours at Sister Emmerich's bedside
whilst she lay in ecstasy (1) The former wrote : "She
experienced violent pains in her limbs and particularly in
her wounds. She bore them joyously, though at times she
was unable to repress her groans ; her hands and feet quivered with pain, the former opening and closing convulsively. She has made all her presents, finished all her work, sorted and put away all the scraps and ends of thread that
were left. When this was done, she sank exhausted under
her pains which were to form her own Christmas gift at the
Infant's Crib. These pains are always shown to her under the

---

(1) The Pilgrim was deeply touched by what he saw and heard. He began his entry
in his journal by these words :—
  " 'Whilst I write, I am saddened at the thought of the miseries by which we are
surrounded. The darkness of our understanding prevents our calmly receiving and
clearly recording the heavenly secrets revealed to us by this simple, childlike soul so
favored by God. I can reproduce very imperfectly mere shadows, as it were, of those
visions which prove the reality, in an ever eternal present, of God's relations with
man obscured by sin. And even this has to be effected hastily and even stealthily. I
cannot express what I feel! They who have for years stifled and mocked at this grace,
they who recognize it and yet persecute her, who know neither how to seek nor how
to appreciate it, will weep with me when the mirror that reflects it shall have been obscured by death !
  "Infant Jesus, my Saviour, give me patience !"

form of flowers. She said : ' Dorothea is going with me to
the Crib, she has come for me. She told me that she had
often been blamed for ornamenting the altar so profusely
with flowers, but that she had always answered : " Flowers
wither. God takes from them the color and fragrance that
He once gave , so, too, may sin wither! May whatever is
good be offered to Him, since it is from Him !' Dorothea
used to be taken to the Crib in spirit, and she offered everything to the Lord in sacrifice. The Pilgrim, too, must
take all his sufferings to the Infant Jesus, all his weaknesses, all his faults, and he must take nothing back. He
must begin all over, and ask the Child Jesus for a burning
love that he may taste the consolations of God. I see also
St. Jerome. He lived here a long time, and obtained from
God such a fire of love that it almost consumed him.'

" O who can tell the beauty, the purity, the innocence of
Mary ! She knows everything. and yet she seems to know
nothing, so childlike is she. She lowers her eyes and,
when she looks up, her glance penetrates like a ray, like a
pure beam of light, like truth itself ! It is because she is
perfectly innocent, full of God, and without returns upon
self. None can resist her glance.

" I see the Crib and above it, celebrating the feast, are
all the blessed who adored the Child Jesus at His birth, all
who ever venerated the Holy Place, and all who have gone
there even only in devout desire. They celebrate in a
wond rful spiritual church the eve of the Redeemer's birth ;
they represent the Church and all who desire the sacred
spot to be honored, the holy season celebrated Thus acts
the Church Triumphant for the Church Militant ; and thus
should the Militant act for the Church Suffering. O how
indescribably beautiful it is ! What a blessed certainty !
I see these spiritual churches all around, far and near, for

no power can destroy the altar of the Lord. Where it is
no longer visible, it stands invisibly cared for by blessed
spirits. Nothing is perishable that is done in the Church
for the love of Jesus! Where men are no longer worthy
to celebrate, the blessed do it in their stead and all hearts
that turn to the service of God are there present. They find
a holy church and a heavenly feast, though their corporal
senses perceive it not; they receive the reward of their
piety.

"I see Mary in heaven on a magnificent throne offering
to her Divine Son, sometimes as a new-born babe, sometimes as a youth, and again as the Crucified Saviour, all
hearts that have ever loved Him, that have ever united in
celebrating His feast. . . . . ."

Here Sister Emmerich was radiant with joy, her speech,
her glance, full of animation, and she expressed herself so
intelligently and with so much ease even upon the most
hidden and sublime subjects that the Pilgrim was lost in
amazement. His words but faintly reproduce those of this
inspired soul, who spoke not so much in glowing colors as
in fiery flames.

" See," she exclaimed, " how all nature sparkles and ex-
ults in innocence and joy! It is like a dead man rising
from the gloom and decay of the grave, which proves that
he not only lives, youthful, blooming, and joyous, but that he
is also immortal, innocent, and pure, the sinless image of his
Maker! All is life, all is innocence and thankfulness! Oh,
the beautiful hills, around which the trees stretch their
branches as if hastening to strew at the feet of their new-
born Saviour the perfumes, flowers, and fruits from Him received! The flowers open their cups to present their varied forms, their colors, their perfumes to the Lord who will
so soon come to tread among them. The springs murmur

their desires, and the fountains dance in joyous expectation, like children awaiting their Christmas gifts. The birds warble notes of joy and gladness, the lambs bleat and skip, all life is filled with peace and happiness. In the veins of all flow quicker, purer streams. Pious hearts, earnest, longing hearts now throb instinctively at the approach of Redemption. All nature is astir. Sinners are seized with sadness, repentance, hope ; the incorrigible, the hardened, the future executioners of the Lord, are anxious and fearful, they cannot comprehend their own uneasiness as the fulness of time draws near. The plenitude of salvation is in the pure, humble, merciful heart of Mary, praying over the Saviour of the world incarnate in her womb, and who, in a few hours, like light become flesh, will enter into life, into His own inheritance, will come among His own who will receive Him not. What all nature now proclaims before my eyes when its Creator comes to abide with it, is written in the books upon the Mountain wherein truth will be preserved until the end of time. As in the race of David the Promise was preserved in Mary until the fulness of time; as this race was cared for, protected, purified, until the Blessed Virgin brought forth the Light of the world ; so that *holy man* purifies and preserves all the treasures of creation and thePromise, as also the essence and signification of all words and creatures until the fulness of time. He purifies all, erases what is false or pernicious, and causes the stream to flow as pure as when it first issued from God, as it now flows in all nature. Why do seekers seek and find it not ? Here let them see that good ever engenders good, and evil brings forth evil, if it be not averted by repentance and the Blood of Jesus Christ. As the blessed in heaven, the pious on earth, and the poor souls work together, helping, healing through Jesus Christ, so do I now see the same in all nature. It is inexpressible! Every simple-hearted man who follows Jesus Christ receives that gift, but it is through the marvellous grace of this season. The devil is chained in these days, he crawls he struggles; therefore I hate all crawling things. The hideous demon is humbled, he can do nothing now. It is the unending grace of this holy season."

Two days after, she related the following:—

"1 saw St. Joseph going out in the evening with a basket and vessels, as if to get food. No words can express his simplicity, gentleness, and humility. I saw Mary kneeling in ecstasy in the same place as before, her hands slightly raised. The fire was still burning, and on a shelf was a little lamp. The grotto was full of light. There were no shadows, but the lamp looked dull like a flambeau in the sunlight, for its flame was material. Mary was alone. I thought then of all I wanted to bring to the Crib of the expected Saviour. I had a long journey to make through places I had often seen in the Life of the Lord, in all of which I saw care, trouble, anguish of soul. I saw Jews plotting in their synagogues and interrupting their service. I went also to a place in the environs where sacrifices were being offered in a pagan temple in which was a frightful idol with wide jaws. They put into it flesh offered in sacrifice, when the monster instantly fell to pieces. Fear and confusion seized the worshippers, who fled in all directions.

"I went also into the country of Nazareth, to Anne's house, just one moment before the Saviour's birth. I saw Anne and Joachim asleep in separate apartments. A light shone over Anne, and she was told in a dream that Mary had brought forth a son. She awoke and hurried to Joachim whom she met coming to her; he, too, had had the same dream. They prayed together praising God, their arms raised to heaven. The rest of their household, likewise experienced something extraordinary. They came to Anne and Joachim whom they found filled with joy. When they heard of the birth, they thanked God with them for the new-born child. They did not know for certain that He was the Son of God ; but they knew that it was a child of salvation, a child of promise. They had an intuitive assurance of it, although they could not express it. They were, besides, struck by the wonderful signs in nature, and they looked upon that night as holy. I saw pious souls here and there around Nazareth, rising up awakened by a sweet interior joy and, whether knowingly or otherwise, celebrating with prayer the entrance of the Word made Flesh into the life of time.

" My whole way on that marvellous night lay through the most varied scenes—people in all countries flocking together, some joyous, some prayerful, others uneasy and sad. My journey was rapid toward the east, though a little more to the south than when I went to the Mountain of Elias. In an old city I saw a large open square surrounded by huge, half-ruined columns and magnificent buildings in which was extraordinary commotion. Men and women flocked together. Crowds were coming in from the country and all were gazing up at the sky. Some looked through tubes about eight feet long, with an opening for the eye, others pointed out something in the air, and all uttered such exclamations as, ' What a wonderful night ! '—They must have observed a sign in the heavens, perhaps a comet, which was, without doubt, the cause of their excitement, though I do not remember having seen anything of it.

" I hastened on to a place where people with their priests were drawing water on the banks of their sacred

river. They were more numerous than before—it seemed
to be a feast. It was not night when I arrived, it was noonday (1). I could not speak to all whom I knew. I spoke
to some who understood me and were deeply moved. I
told them they should no longer draw the sacred water,
but that they should turn to their Saviour who was born.
I know not how I said it, but they were surprised and impressed, and some, especially the most pious and reflective,
were a little frightened, for there were very, very pure
and deeply sensitive souls among them. These latter I
saw going into their temples, in which I could see no idols,
though there was something like an altar; they all knelt,
men, women, and children. The mothers placed their little ones before them and held up their tiny hands as if
in prayer. It was a truly touching sight!

"I was led back to the Crib. The Saviour was born!
The holy Virgin sat in the same place, wrapped in a mantle and holding on her lap the Infant Jesus swathed in ample
bands, even His face was covered. Both were immovable and
seemed to be in ecstasy. Two shepherds were standing timidly at some distance, and some were looking down through
the air-holes in the roof. I adored in silence! When the
shepherds went away, St. Joseph entered with food in a basket and carrying on his arm something like a coverlet. He
set them down, and drew near to Mary who placed the Infant
in his arms. He held It with unspeakable joy, devotion,
and humility. I saw that he did not know It to be the Second Person of the Divinity, although he felt that It was the
Child of Promise, the Child that would bring salvation into
the world, that It was a holy Child.

(1) It must have been, the hour there (India) corresponding to our midnight. Sister Emmerich beheld Christ's birth in Bethlehem at our midnight and all the events
there as night scenes ; but, on arriving in India, the time of Nativity changes in her
vision to the real time, the hour it really was at the Ganges when her soul arrived
here.

" I knelt and begged the Mother of God to lead to her Son all who I knew had need of salvation, and immediately I saw in spirit those of whom I was thinking—my thought was the sign that she had heard my prayer. I thought of Judith on the mountain and, all at once, I saw her in her castle, in the hall in which the lamps hung, and there were many people present, among them some strangers. It looked like a religious reunion. They seemed to be consulting together about something and they were much agitated. I saw, too, that Judith remembered my apparition and that she both desired and feared to see me again. She thought if the Messiah were really come, and if she could be quite sure of what the apparition had said to her, she would do what she had promised, in order to help her people.

" It was day. Mary sat cross-legged in her usual place busied apparently with a piece of linen, the Child Jesus lay at her feet swathed, but His face and hands free. Joseph was at the entrance opposite the fire-place making something like a frame to hang vessels on, and I stood by the ass thinking : ' Dear old man, you need not finish your work, you must soon go.' Now came in two old women from Mary's country who seemed to be old acquaintances, for they were kindly received, though Mary did not rise. They brought quite a number of presents—little.fruits, ducks, large birds with red, awl-shaped beaks, which they carried under their arms or by the wings, some small oval loaves about an inch thick, and lastly, some linen and other stuff. All were received with rare humility and gratitude. They were silent, good, devout woman. They were deeply affected as they gazed down upon the Child, but they did not touch Him. They withdrew without farewells or ceremony. I was looking at the ass; its back was very broad, and I said to myself, ' Good beast, thou hast borne many bur-

dens !'—I wanted to feel it, to see if it were real, and I
passed my hand over its back. It was just as soft as silk,
it reminded me of the moss I had once felt. Now came
from the country of the shepherds, where the gardens and
the balsam-hedges are, two married women with three little
girls about eight years old. They seemed to be strangers,
people of distinction, who had come in obedience to a miraculous call. Joseph received them very humbly. They
brought presents of less size than the others, but of greater
value : grain in a bowl, small fruits, a little cluster of thick
three-cornered golden leaves on which was a stamp like a
seal. I thought how wonderful ! That looks just like the
way they represent the eye of God ! But no ! how can I
compare the eye of God with red earth !'—Mary arose and
placed the Child in their arms. They held Him awhile, and
prayed in silence with hearts raised to God, and then they
kissed the Child. Joseph and Mary conversed with them and,
when they departed, Joseph accompanied them a little distance. They appeared to have travelled some miles and
secretly, for they avoided being seen in the city. Joseph
behaved with great humility during such visits, retiring
and looking on from a distance.

" When Joseph went out with the ladies, I prayed and
confidently laid open my miseries to Mary. She consoled
me, though her answers were very brief; for instance,
three words upon three points. This manner of communicating is very difficult to explain. It is an intuitive perception something like the following : when Mary, for example, wanted to say; ' These sufferings will strengthen
thee spiritually, thou wilt not yield to them, they will make
thee more clear-sighted, will render thee victorious,' I perceived nothing but the meaning of these words under the
figure of a palm-tree which is said to become more elastic,

more vigorous by the pressure of a weight upon it. In the same way, she told me something like the following: 'The struggle with thy sister will be painful, a sharp combat is before thee. Be comforted! With the trial and the suffering thy supernatural strength will increase. The sharper thy sufferings, the more clearly, the more profoundly, wilt thou understand. Think of the profit thou wilt derive from it!'—I received this last instruction under the perception of the principle by which the purity of gold is increased under the hammer, or the polish of a mirror is produced. Then she told me that I must tell all, keep nothing back, even if it seemed to me of small importance. Everything has its end. I must not allow myself to be discouraged by the thought that I do not rightly comprehend. I must tell all even if my words appear useless and unconnected. A change will come over many Protestants after my death, and the conviction of the truth of my state will contribute greatly thereto; consequently I must keep nothing back."

On Christmas-Eve she was shown in a vision new sufferings in store for her. The following is her account of it:—

"There came three holy nuns, among them Frances of Rome, who brought me a clean white robe with a scalloped border; on the left side was a red heart surrounded by roses. I touched them and the thorns pricked me to blood. The nuns threw the robe around me quickly, saying that I must wear it until the new-year when it would be exchanged for a gray one with a heavy iron cross. If at the new-year I returned the present one spotless, the cross on the second one would, perhaps, be much lightened. I thought this referred to my death, and I said, 'Is it true that I am going to die?'—But they answered, 'No, thou hast still much to suffer,' and then they disappeared. My guide announced those bitter sufferings in severe words that cut into my soul like swords. He told me that I should not succumb, that I drew them on myself by undertaking so much for others, that I should be more moderate, not so eager to do so much good, that Jesus alone can do such things. Then sharp pains racked me until two hours past midnight. I lay upon a harrow covered with thorns that penetrated into my very bones."

She had at short intervals three attacks of these same sufferings. On Dec. 29th, the Pilgrim found her quite changed in appearance by physical and mental pain, her features drawn, her forehead knit, her whole frame twitching convulsively. "I have not slept all night," she said, "I am almost dead; still I had exterior consolation. The sweetness of suffering spread itself through my inmost soul, it came from God. The Blessed Virgin also consoled me. I saw her inexpressible sufferings on the night the Lord was seized, and particularly that caused her by Peter's denial. I saw how she lamented it to John; it was only to him that she told her grief. I asked her why my sister's state gave me so much pain, wounded me so deeply, yes, almost distracted me, whilst I supported courageously far worse than it. I was told: 'As thou dost perceive light from the relics of the saints by thy intuition of the union existing among Christ's members, so dost thou perceive more clearly the blindness, the anger, the disunion of thy sister's state, because it comes from the root of thy sinful flesh in fallen Adam, in a direct line through thy ancestors. Thou dost feel their sins in thy flesh through thy parents and earliest ancestors. It is sin proceeding from the share thou hast in the fall.'—I suffered, I watched, I fainted away, I regained consciousness, I counted the hours, and when morning dawned I cried out to my Spouse not to

abandon me.   I saw Him taking leave of His Mother. I saw
Mary's grief. I saw Him upon the Mount of Olives, and He
said to me : ' Dost thou wish to be treated better than Mary,
the most pure, the most beloved of all creatures ?   What
are thy sufferings compared with hers ? '—Then He showed
me endless miseries, the dying unprepared, etc., and my
guide said to me : ' If thou wouldst help them, suffer for
them, else how can justice be satisfied ? '—He showed me
future sorrows, and told me that few pray and suffer to
avert evils.   I became thankful and courageous, I suffered
joyously for I had seen *Him !*   He again said, ' See, how
many dying souls ! in what a state ! '—and showed me a dying priest of my own country, one who had fallen so low
that he could not receive Holy Communion with faith and
purity of heart.   I did not know him.   My guide said,
' Suffer for all these until mid-day '—Then I suffered joyously. I still suffer, but I shall soon be relieved."

" Toward noon her countenance changed, the heart-rending expression faded, her pains seemed to leave her gradually like water evaporating under the sun's rays.   Her
drawn features relaxed and precisely at noon, became
sweet and peaceful as those of a sleeping child—the paroxysm had passed.   Her members became torpid, and she fell
into a state of insensibility exempt from suffering.

" The last evening of the year she was completely absorbed by her journey to the Heavenly Jerusalem, and she occasionally repeated some verses from the Breviary referring
to the City of God.   Once she said : ' I must be trodden
under foot, my garden is too flourishing, it will produce
nothing but flowers.'—She beheld herself in all possible
situations, her heart cruelly lacerated.   She exclaimed : ' O
how much that person afflicts me !   I can hardly endure
the sight of her sufferings ! I beg God to hide them from me !'

"On the night of January, 1820, the three little nuns came again and took off her white robe, which was still spotless. They put on her the promised gray one with the heavy black cross which she was to wash white with her tears. A number of poor souls came to thank her for their deliverance, among them an old woman of her own hamlet for whom she had prayed much. She felt that she had delivered them through the spotlessness of her white robe, and that affected her deeply. ' When I received the gray robe,' she said, ' I saw again all the torments in reserve for me. I had, besides, an apparition of St. Teresa, who consoled me greatly by speaking of her own sufferings. She also reassured me on the score of my visions, telling me not to be troubled but to disclose all; that with her it so happened that the more open she was in this respect the clearer did her visions become. My Spouse also spoke lovingly with me and explained the gray robe.—" It is of silk," He said, "because I am wounded in my whole person, and thou art not to tear it by impatience. It is gray, because it is a robe of penance and humiliation." He told me, too, that when I was sick, He was satisfied with me; but that when I was well, I was too condescending. He said, moreover, that I should tell all that was shown me even though I might be ridiculed for it, for such was His will. Everything is of use. Then I felt as if I were borne from one bed of thorns to be laid on another, but I offered all for the poor souls.' "

January 2d—the Pilgrim found her enduring a martyrdom. "It would be vain," he writes, "to attempt a description of her sufferings. To understand it even slightly, one would have to watch the various phases of her inexplicable state. " The cause of her pains none could divine. Her life glided by in this daily struggle without

sympathy or support. She never appeared to lose the remembrance of her thorny crown; even when the rest of
her person became rigid, she retained command over her
head, supporting it in such a way that the thorns might
not penetrate too deeply. Sometimes her whole body was
slashed and torn with whips, her hands were tied, she was
bound with cords; the torture she endured forced the cold
sweat from every pore, and yet she related all without a sign
of impatience. Suddenly she extended her arms in the form
of a cross with an effort so violent that one would have
thought the distended nerves were about to snap. She
lowered them again, her head gradually sank upon her
breast as if she were dead, her limbs were motionless, she
lay like a corpse. 'I am with the poor souls,' she murmured,
and on returning to consciousness, she related the following
though with an effort :—

" 'I have had three violent attacks, and I have suffered
everything just as my Spouse did in His Passion. When
I was about to yield, when I groaned in agony, I beheld
the same suffering undergone by Him. Thus I went
through the whole Passion as I see it on Good-Friday. I
was scourged, crowned with thorns, dragged with ropes,
I fell, I was nailed to the cross, I saw the Lord descend
into hell, and I, too, went to purgatory. I saw many
detained therein; some I knew, others I knew not. I saw
souls saved who had been buried in darkness and forgetfulness, and this afforded me consolation.

" 'The second attack I endured for all that were not in a
state to bear patiently what falls to their lot, and for the
dying who were unable to receive the Blessed Sacrament.
I saw many whom I helped.

" 'The third attack was for the Church. I had a vision
of a church with a high, elaborate tower, in a great city

on a mighty river (1). The patron of the church is Stephen by whom I saw another saint who was martyred after him. Around the church I saw many very distinguished people, among them some strangers with aprons and trowels who appeared about to pull down the church with the beautiful tower and slate roof. People from all parts were gathered there, among them priests and even religious, and I was so distressed that I called to my Spouse for assistance. Xavier with the cross in his hand had once been all powerful, the enemy ought not to be allowed to triumph now! Then I saw five men going into the church, three in heavy antique vestments like priests, and two very young ecclesiastics who seemed to be in Holy Orders. I thought these two received Holy Communion, and that they were destined to infuse new life into the Church. Suddenly a flame burst from the tower, spread over the roof, and threatened to consume the whole church. I thought of the great river flowing by the city——could they not extinguished the flames with its waters? The fire injured many who aided in the destruction of the church and drove them away, but the edifice itself remained standing, by which I understood that the Church would be saved only after a great storm. The fire so frightful to behold indicated in the first place, a great danger; in the second, renewed splendor after the tempest. The Church's destruction is already begun by means of infidel schools.

" I saw a great storm rising in the north and sweeping in a half-circle to the city with the high tower, and then off to the west. I saw combats and streaks of blood far and wide in the heavens over many places, and endless woes and misery threatening the Church, the Protestants everywhere laying snares to entrap her. The servants of the Church

(1) These details point to Vienna, the Austrian capital.

are so slothful. They use not the power they possess in the priesthood! I shed bitter tears at the sight."—She wept whilst recounting this vision, imploring Almighty God to deliver her from such spectacles. She mourned also over the flocks without shepherds, and counselled prayer, penance, and humility to avert a portion of the impending danger.

END OF VOLUME I.

If you have enjoyed this book, consider making your next selection from among the following . . .

Prices subject to change.

At your Bookdealer or direct from the Publisher.

Toll-Free 1-800-437-5876   *Fax 815-226-7770*
Tel. 815-229-7777   *www.tanbooks.com*

Prices subject to change.

ANNE CATHERINE EMMERICH

LIFE

OF

ANNE CATHERINE EMMERICH

VERY REV. K. E. SCHMÖGER, C.SS.R.

VOL. II.

TAN BOOKS AND PUBLISHERS, INC.
Rockford, Illinois 61105

APPROBATION.

As the second volume of the work entitled, " Life of Anne Catherine Emmerich," by Father Schmöger, like the first, contains nothing contrary to the teachings of the Catholic Church, either in morals or dogma; but which, if read in the spirit of piety, may contribute much to the edification of the faithful, we willingly grant it after a careful perusal the approbation solicited by the author.

✠ PETER JOSEPH,
Bishop of Limbourg.

Reprinted from the 1968 edition of Maria Regina Guild, Los Angeles, California, itself reprinted from the English edition of 1885.

ISBN: Volume 1—0-89555-059-8
Volume 2—0-89555-060-1
The Set—0-89555-061-X

Printed and bound in the United States of America.

TAN BOOKS AND PUBLISHERS, INC.
P.O. Box 424
Rockford, Illinois 61105
1976

DEDICATION

To the Immaculate Heart of the Virgin Mary, Mother of God, Queen of Heaven and Earth, Lady of the Most Holy Rosary, Help of Christians, and Refuge of the Human Race.

CONTENTS

OF VOL II.

Contents.

AUTHOR'S PREFACE.

We advance as a proof of the respect and affection in which the venerable Anne Catherine Emmerich is held by the faithful, the fact that, a short time after the appearance of the first volume of the present biography, it was translated into French (1) and Italian (2) with episcopal approbation. This circumstance, most gratifying to the author, has encouraged him in his efforts to present to the public a faithful history of the servant of God, although he believes himself authorized in saying that few books would be issued, were their publication attended by as numerous and grave difficulties as was that of the present work. Clement Brentano himself, whose journal offers the richest materials for it, shrank from the task of arranging them; the attempts of others came to naught, and the author was often tempted to draw back in discouragement from their labyrinthine maze. The firm conviction that he was rendering testimony to God's wonderful ways in souls, the advice and encouragement of his friend, Rev. Father Capistran, of Kaltern, and the continued prayers of Maria von

(1) "Vie d' Anne Catherine Emmerich," par le P. Schmöger, traduite par E. de Cazalès, Vicar-General and Canon of Versailles.

(2) Vita della serva di Dio, Anna Caterina Emmerich, tradotta dall' Originale tedesco dal *Marchese Cesare Boccella.*

Moerl (1), from 1858 until her blessed death, alone sustained him in his undertaking and enabled him to bring it to a happy conclusion.

Sister Emmerich had herself denominated the Pilgrim's notes, " A pathless, overgrown garden." In March, 1820, she related the following vision, remarkable on account of its fulfilment :—" I was in a garden which the Pilgrim cultivated. A mass of vegetation was springing up thick and green ; but the Pilgrim had planted it so close that there was no room for a path. He took me into a little summer-house around which he had raised bitter-cress (2)." Later on she several times repeated : " I saw the Pilgrim's garden. It is very luxuriant, but it is pathless, it is all over-grown. Still he must go on with his work." Again : " I saw the Pilgrim's garden so overgrown that only he could pick his way through it; others complained of not being able to enter it. It lay blooming and flourishing near a wilder-ness and at the entrance stood a rose-bush covered with thorns. The Pilgrim and others would have wished to pluck the roses, but they pricked themselves with the thorns. I saw one trying to get them ; but they scratched him till he cried out." These pictures could not be more striking. The path which only the Pilgrim could find through his thickly overgrown garden, is symbolical of the seven days of the week during which he wrote down indiscrim-inately what he saw of Catherine Emmerich, what she re-lated to him of her visions, together with his own impres-

(1) The ecstatica and stigmatisée of the Tyrol. 1812-1868.
(2) The fulfilment of this vision is related in Chap. VIII.

sions, his sympathy with or aversion for those who surrounded her or the visitors who flocked to her sick-bed, and in fine, his own private affairs and those of his intimate friends. These miscellaneous materials formed the contents of his manuscripts, from which the author has selected what he deemed necessary for the present biography. The Pilgrim had no other idea at the time, than that of relating as faithfully and circumstantially as possible whatever he observed. Sister Emmerich's interior life was to him a mystery of which she alone could furnish the key, with permission from her spiritual directors, Dean Overberg and Father Limberg; yet he took note of all, as circumstances permitted, reserving what was obscure and unintelligible for a closer investigation at some future time. These the author has reproduced as faithfully as possible in their original form. Sister Emmerich was able to relate and the Pilgrim to write but few visions at one time; consequently, notes, additions, corrections succeeded one another in rapid succession regardless of order or time. The key to some vision was frequently found only after long and wearisome research, and then, perhaps, in some little word of the invalid preserved as if by chance, or in a careful comparison with preceding or following ones. This was particularly the case with the grand vision which she termed the "Nuptial House" (1) and which seems to be the centre to which all her labors tended.

The Pilgrim appears never to have clearly comprehended this vision; but, fortunately, he preserved so many of the

(1) This vision is given in Vol. II., ch. 1.

Sister's communications on the subject as to enable the author to penetrate more deeply into its signification. Then only did he seize the order and import of this privileged soul's immense task of prayer for the Church as a body, as well as for her individual members ; then only did he feel that he might attempt the history of her life.

The first volume has been drawn mostly from Dr. Wesener's notes, as also the Pilgrim's, of whatever they could glean from the invalid herself, from her confessor, her companions, her relatives, respecting her past life. The Pilgrim during his five years' sojourn in Dülmen kept up a large correspondence with his dearest and most confidential friends. These unpublished letters were placed at the author's service, and he has made use of them with the greatest discretion. He looks upon them as one of the greatest proofs of the blessed influence exercised by Sister Emmerich over her amanuensis. Only two of those that were honored by Sister Emmerich's special affection and confidence are yet living (1870) : Misses Apollonia Diepenbrock and Louise Hensel, both of whom kindly aided the author with their communications.

In 1831, the Pilgrim had revised the record of only the first months of his stay at Dülmen ; of this, however, the author has not availed himself, as it does not faithfully accord with the original notes. To avoid copying, the Pilgrim corrected his journal after having recorded some visions ; but he seems to have grown discontented with the task, and abandoned any further attempts of the kind.

His interspersing the above with all sorts of notes and remarks, many of them quite irrelevant, contributed to the greater confusion of the whole. If, for instance, Sister Emmerich were prevented from communicating her visions, complaints filled his journal against her confessor or any one else who had been, according to him, the cause of these intolerable interruptions. These complaints he repeated in his private letters and, as they were published after his death, the author feels that a word of explanation on the subject is necessary. They to whom his letters were addressed were fully aware of his irritable temperament and also of the circumstances attendant on his penning them; consequently, they bore not for them that tone of asperity with which they could not fail to impress the general reader. The author, therefore, feels it a duty to expose clearly, justly, and conscientiously, the true state of affairs, that a correct and unbiased opinion may be formed of Sister Emmerich's position and her surroundings so frequently subjected to the Pilgrim's harsh criticism. The author himself was tempted, at first, to sympathize with the Pilgrim, and it was only after a long and close examination that he was able to discover the truth. In this he feels convinced that he conforms to the Pilgrim's own intentions, since ten years before his death he had nourished the thought of intrusting the arrangement of his notes to some one in whose discretion he might perfectly confide; he thought of handing over to such a person his manuscripts just as they were, without retrenching a single line,

and of allowing him to estimate their contents conscientiously and impartially. As time glided on and the Pilgrim himself began to cast a cooler, more impartial glance upon the
years spent in Dülmen, the more averse did he become to encountering anew the " thorns" that human
frailty had led him to plant around " the roses in his garden." He would then have erased from his journal his
captious remarks, had he not feared that by so doing he
might suppress what was both important and necessary to the clear understanding of Sister Emmerich's position. With rare uprightness and moral courage, he preserved what he had written that even the dispraise thereby
accruing to himself might render its own peculiar testimony
to the chosen of God.

In conclusion, the author submits unreservedly to the
decrees of Urban VIII., and declares that he attributes only
purely human belief to the extraordinary facts and incidents
recorded in the present volume.

P. SCHMÖGER, C.SS.R.

Convent of Gars, Bavaria,
Feast of St. John Baptist, 1870.

— LIFE —

OF

ANNE CATHERINE EMMERICH.

CHAPTER I.

SPIRITUAL LABORS AND SUFFERINGS FOR THE CHURCH.—
THE NUPTIAL HOUSE.—ACTION IN VISION.

In November, 1820, Sister Emmerich remarked : "It is
now twenty years since my Spouse led me into the Nuptial
House and laid me upon the hard bridal bed on which I
still lie ;"—thus did she designate her labors for the Church,
labors imposed upon her from her entrance into Agnetenberg.
No account had ever been demanded of this hidden operation, no director had even been willing to listen to her on
the subject, and it is only now, toward the close of her
career, that she testifies to the ways by which God had led
her for the good of the Church ; now, for the first time,
does she raise the veil which conceals that mysterious action
which, though operated in contemplation, derives its origin
and merit, its importance and results from the divine virtue
of faith. Before her entrance into religion, her principal
task consisted in expiatory sufferings referring to the religious vocation and vows ; but, when she had embraced
the conventual life, her action was extended to the whole
Church. What this task embodied she characterized by
these striking words : " My Heavenly Bridegroom brought

me into the Nuptial House," for such is the relation that the
Church holds with Jesus Christ, her Spouse and Head—a
relation which was shown to Sister Emmerich as an immense sphere, embracing the most varied and opposite
states, for whose individual failings she was to supply by
her sufferings. Jesus is continually renewing His indis-
soluble union with the Church, His Spouse, and that He
may present her spotless to His Father, He incessantly
pours out upon her the torrents of His graces. But every
grace must be accounted for, and few among those who
receive them would be found ready for this, if the Heavenly
Spouse did not at all times prepare chosen souls to gather
up what others waste, to utilize the talents that others bury,
and to discharge the debts contracted by the negligent.
Before manifesting Himself in the flesh, in order to ratify
the New Alliance with His Blood, He had by the Immaculate Conception of Mary prepared her to be the immaculate
type of the Church. He had poured upon her the plenitude
of His graces, that her prayers might hasten the Messiah's
advent, her purity and fidelity retain Him among the
very men who received Him not, who resisted and persecuted Him. When Jesus, the Good Shepherd, began to
gather His flock together it was Mary who cared for them,
particularly for the poorest, the most abandoned, in order to
lead them into the way of salvation ; she was the faithful
stewardess, she was the support of all. After the return of
her Son to His Eternal Father, she remained many years
upon earth to strengthen and protect the infant Church.
And until the second coming of her Son, the Church will
never be without members who, following in her footsteps,
will be so many sources of benediction to their brethren.
It is Mary, the Mother of Mercy, who assigns to these
privileged souls their tasks for the ecclesiastical year; and,

in accordance with this order, Sister Emmerich received, in what she denominates the "*Nuptial House*," her yearly portion of expiation for the Church. Every detail was made known to her, all was to be finished in a certain time, for choice and duration of suffering are at the option of none. This order was indicated by the different parts of the Nuptial House, which had both a symbolical and historical signification. It was the house of Jesse near Bethlehem, the house in which David was born, in which he had been trained by God Himself for his future career as a prophet. It was from this house, also, that the Divine Spouse Himself had sprung in His Holy Humanity. It was the house of the royal race of the Immaculate Virgi ., Mother of the Church, and the paternal house of St. Joseph. It was fitting that Sister Emmerich should contemplate therein the present state of the Church and receive her mission for it, since its former holy occupants had hailed in spirit the advent of the Redeemer, had gazed upon the Church's career through coming ages, and had received their share in the good works that were to hasten Redemption.

This house with its numerous apartments, its spacious surroundings of gardens, fields, and meadows, was a symbol of the spiritual government of the Church; with its various parts, its functionaries, with the intruders who laid it waste, it presented to the soul allowed to contemplate it a perfect representation of the Church in her different relations with the state and the country, with certain dioceses and institutions, in fine, with all the affairs connected with her government. The wrongs done her in her hierarchy, rights, and treasures, in the integrity of her faith, discipline, and morals, by the negligence, slothfulness and disloyalty of her own children; all that *intruders*, that is, false science, pretended lights, irreligious education, connivance with the errors of the day, with worldly maxims and projects, etc., endanger or destroy—all were shown to Sister Emmerich in visions of wonderful depth and simplicity. The scenes of these visions were the Nuptial House and its dependencies, and thither was she conducted by her angel to receive her expiatory mission.

Before considering the details of this action in vision, let us first glance at its hidden nature and signification. We have already remarked that what Sister Emmerich did and suffered in contemplation was as real and meritorious in itself and its results, as were the actions and sufferings of the natural waking state. This double operation sprang from one common source; but for the perfect understanding of it, we must study her gift of contemplation. Her own communications will throw the greatest light upon the question, since they are both numerous and detailed. We can compare them with the testimony of others favored with the same graces, with the decisions of the holy Doctors, and with the principles that guide the Church in her judgment of such phenomena.

Sister Emmerich tells us that the gift of contemplation had been bestowed upon her in Baptism and that, from her entrance into life, she had been prepared in body and soul to make use of it. Once she denominated this preparation, "A mystery of a nature very difficult for fallen man to comprehend, one by which the pure in soul and body are brought into intimate and mysterious communication with one another."

The undimmed splendor of baptismal grace is then according to her the first, the chief condition for the reception of the light of prophecy, for the developing of a faculty in man, obscured by Adam's fall: viz., capability of communicating with the world of spirit without interrupting the harmonious and natural relation of body and soul. Every man possesses this capability ; but, if we may so speak, it is hidden in his soul (1) ; he cannot of himself overleap the barrier which separates the regions of sense from those beyond. God alone by the infusion of superior light, can remove this barrier from the path of His elect; but seldom is such light granted, for few there are who rigorously fulfil the conditions exacted.

We may here remark that, according to the teachings of the great theologians, the principles and theory of contemplation laid down by Pope Benedict XIV. to serve as a basis for the judgment of the Church, there exists no such thing as *natural contemplation.* Pope Benedict in no way requires a *natural disposition thereto* as a favorable condition for the infusion of prophetic light, the light of prophecy (2). There is no such thing as the development of a *natural* faculty into the so-called *clairvoyance.* All phenomena produced in this region are, without exception, either simply the result of morbid perturbations, as in animal somnambulism, and consequently, in themselves something extremely imperfect or even abnormal; or they are an over excitation of the mental powers and, thereby, an extension of the sensible faculty of apperception artificially produced by the action of mesmerism at the expense of the more elevated powers of the soul ; or, in fine, we may recognize in them a demoniacal clairvoyance to which mesmeric clairvoyance necessarily and inevitably tends, since the dangerous illusion and

(1) Secundum quod intellectus humanus ex illuminatione intellectuum separatorum utpote inferior, natus est instrui et ad alia cognoscenda elevari ; et hæc prophetia mo. do prædicto potest dici naturalis.—(S. Thomas in quæst. disp. qu. XII. de veritate, c. 3.

(2) Pope Benedict closely follows the teaching of St. Thomas : "S. Thomas docet quod, sicuti prophetia est ex inspiratione divinâ, et Deus, qui est causa universalis in agendo, non præexigit materiam, nec aliquam materiæ dispositionem sed potest simul et materiam et dispositionem et formam inducere, ita potest simul animam creare et in ipsa creatione disponere ad prophetiam et dare ei gratiam prophetandi."—(*De servorum Dei beatif.*, L. III., Cap XI V., No. 9.)

profound degradation into which the human soul is plunged
by mesmeric influence can have no other result. It is only
in abandoning the truth : viz., the doctrine of the human
soul, as set forth by the great Doctors, upheld and followed
by the Church in her process of canonization, that we can
fall into the erroneous and dangerous hypothesis of *natural
clairvoyance* and support false theories upon facts less certain, less positively attested.

Before considering Sister Emmerich's physical training in
preparation for her action in vision. we shall glance at St.
Hildegarde, that great mistress of the mystical life, since
there exists so striking a resemblance between them. The
latter, being directed by Almighty God to reduce her visions
to writing, heard these words (1):—

"I who am the Living Light enlightening all that is in
darkness, have freely chosen and called thee by My own
good pleasure for marvellous things, for things far greater
than those shown by Me to men of ancient times ; but, that
thou mayest not exalt thyself in the pride of thy heart, I
have humbled thee to the dust. The world shall find in thee
neither joy nor satisfaction, nor shalt thou mingle in its
affairs, for I have shielded thee against proud presumption,
I have pierced thee with fear, I have overwhelmed thee
with pain. Thou bearest thy sorrows in the marrow of thy
bones, in the veins of thy flesh. Thy soul and thy senses
are bound, thou must endure countless bodily pains that
false security may not take possession of thee, but that, on
the contrary, thou mayest regard thyself as faulty in all thou
dost. I have shielded thy heart from its wanderings, I have
put a bridle upon thee that thy spirit may not proudly and
vain-gloriously exalt itself, but that in all things it may experience more fear and anxiety than joy and complacency,

(1) *Scivias*, L. I., *Præfatio.* Edit. Migne.

Write, then, what thou seest and hearest, O thou creature, who receivest not in the agitation of delusion, but in the purity of simplicity, what is designed to manifest hidden things."

Her contemporary and biographer, the Abbot Theodoric renders this testimony (1):—" From her youngest years her purity shone so conspicuously that she seemed exempt from the weakness of the flesh. When she had bound herself to Christ by the religious vows, she mounted from virtue to virtue. Charity burned in her breast for all mankind, and the tower of her virginity was protected by the rampart of humility, whence sprang abstinence in diet, poverty in clothing, etc. As the vase is tried in the furnace of the potter, as strength is made perfect in infirmity, so from her earliest infancy, frequent, almost continual sufferings were never wanting to her. Very rarely was she able to walk and, as her body ever seemed near its dissolution, her life presented the picture of a precious death. But in proportion as her physical strength failed, was her soul possessed by the spirit of knowledge and fortitude ; as her body was consumed, her spiritual fervor became inflamed."

Hildegarde herself laid down as a law established by God, that the prophetic light was never received without constant and extraordinary sufferings (2).—" The soul by its nature tends toward eternal life, but the body, holding in itself this passing life, is not in accordance with it ; for, though both unite to form man, yet they are distinct in themselves, they are two. For this reason, when God pours His Spirit out on a man by the light of prophecy, the gift of wisdom, or miracles, He afflicts his body by frequent sufferings, that the Holy Spirit may dwell in him. If the flesh be not sub-

(1) Vita S. Hildegardis, L. I., C. I.,No. 23.
(2) Loc. cit., L. II., Cap.III., No. 2.

dued by pain, it too readily follows the ways of the world, as happened to Samson, Solomon, and others who, inclining to the pleasures of the senses, ceased to hearken to the inspirations of the spirit; for prophecy, wisdom, and the gift of miracles give birth to delight and joy. Know, O thou poor creature, that I have loved and called by preference those that have crucified their flesh in spirit." St. Hildegarde continues : " I seek not repose, I am overwhelmed by countless sufferings, whilst the Almighty pours upon me the dew of His grace. My body is broken by labor and pain, like clay mixed with water."

And again, " It is not of myself that I utter the following words; the veritable Wisdom pronounces them by my mouth. It speaks to me thus : ' Hear these words, O creature, and repeat them not as from thyself. But as from Me, and taught by Me, do thou declare what follows :'—In the moment of my conception, when God awoke me by the breath of life in my mother's womb (1), He endowed my soul with the gift of contemplation. My parents offered me to God at my birth and in my third year I perceived in myself so great a light that my soul trembled; but unable yet to speak, I could say nothing of all these things. In my eighth year I was again offered to God and destined for the religious life, and up to my fifteenth year I saw many things that I recounted in all simplicity. They who listened asked in amazement whence or from whom I had received them. Then I began to wonder within myself at this that, although seeing everything in my inmost soul, yet at the same time I perceived exterior objects by the sense of sight, and, as I never heard the like of others, I commenced to hide my visions as best I could. I am ignorant of

---

(1) St. Hildegarde, in her beautiful and deeply significant letter addressed to the Chapter of Mayence, uses the same words : " In the light of contemplation poured into my soul by God, the Creator, before my birth, I am forced to write to you, etc.", .

many things around me, on account of the state of constant sickness in which I have lain from my birth to the present moment, my body consumed, my strength utterly wasted. When inundated with the light of contemplation, I have said many things that sounded strange to my hearers ; but, when this light had grown a little dim, and I comported myself more like a child than one of my real age, I became confused, I wept, and longed to be able to keep silence. The fear I had of men was such that I dared not impart to any one what I saw (1)."

How strikingly do not the above words characterize Sister Emmerich ! Her body was from her birth a vessel of sufferings and like Hildegarde, she too was told by the Celestial Spouse why she endured them : " Thy body is weighed down by pain and sickness that thy soul may labor more actively, for he who is in good health carries his body as a heavy burden." And when, during the investigation, the Vicar-General expressed astonishment that she could have received a wound in the breast unknown to herself, she replied simply : " I did feel as if my breast had been scalded, but I never looked to see what it was ; I am too timid for that. From my childhood I have always been too timid to look upon my person. I have never seen it, I never think of it, I know nothing about it." This was literally true, for Sister Emmerich had never thought of her body excepting to mortify it and burden it with suffering. In vain do we strive to understand her great love for penance and mortification. We may form some idea of it as witnessed in a monk in all the vigor of manhood, or in one advanced in years to whom but little sleep and food are necessary, or in the cloistered contemplative ; but in a young and delicate child, lively and ardent, employed in hard labor

(1) Acta S. Hildegarde. Ed. Migne, p. 13, 14.

from her earliest years, having no example of the kind before her, it is truly astonishing! How powerful must have been the strength infused into her young heart by the grace of the Holy Ghost! We are prone to represent the saints to ourselves at immeasurable heights above us, and not amid weakness and miseries such as our own. We see their sanctity, without reflecting on their heroic efforts in its attainment ; we forget that the nature of these valiant conquerors was the same as our own, that they reached the goal only by patient struggling. The practice of heroic virtue was as difficult for Sister Emmerich as for Blessed Clair Gambacorta, of Pisa (1362-1419), who tells us that fasting was so painful to her that once in her childhood she struck herself in the stomach with a stool, in order to benumb the pangs of hunger by pains of another kind. Like all children, she was exceedingly fond of fruit; to abstain from it cost her the greatest efforts. And have we not seen our own little Anne Catherine struggling against nature until penance and renunciation became, as it were, her only nourishment and the gift of angelic purity natural to her? By pain and mortification her body became in a measure spiritualized, dependent on the soul for its support, and endued with the capability of serving the latter as an instrument in the labors accomplished in vision. The following truth cannot be too strongly insisted upon : in those regions, to which intuitive light opens the way, the soul acts not alone as if separated from the body, but soul and body act together, according to the order established by God. This truth flows of necessity from faith, which teaches that man can merit, expiate, suffer for another only as long as he is *a viator* acting in and with the body. Nothing throws more light upon this subject than the facts recorded in the life of St. Lidwina (1) :

(1) Acta SS., die 14 Aprilis, vita prior Cap. 5, vita posterior, Cap. 3.

" When Lidwina," says an eye witness, "returned from visiting the Holy Places, Mt. Olivet or Mt. Calvary, for instance, her lips were blistered, her limbs scratched, her knees bruised, her whole person bore not only the wounds made by her passage through briers, but even the thorns themselves remained in the flesh. Her angel told her that she retained them as a visible, palpable proof that she had been to the Holy Places not merely in dreams or in imagination, but really and truly bearing with her the faculty of receiving sensible, corporeal impressions. Once in vision she had to cross a slippery road on which she fell and dislocated her right limb and, when returned to consciousness, she found one eye bruised and inflamed. The pain in the limb and other members was violent for several days. In these far-off journeys she wounded sometimes her hands, sometimes her feet, and the marvellous perfume exhaled by her person betrayed to her friends whither she had been conducted. By a divine dispensation her soul not only communicated to her body the superabundant consolations it experienced, but it also employed the latter as an instrument, as a beast of burden in its journeys, and made it a sharer in the fatigue and accidents resulting therefrom. The soul of the saintly virgin struggled in her body, and her body struggled conjointly with her soul up to the moment of her last agony. They ran together the same career; they endured together the same hardships, like companions under the same roof. We must not, then, be surprised if they journey together, rejoice together in the Lord and, during the pilgrimage of this earthly life, receive together a foretaste of the glory that is to come, the first fruits of the Spirit, the abundant dew that falls from heaven.

" In all her supernatural journeys the angel was her companion and she treated with him as a friend with a

friend. He constantly appeared to her surrounded by a
wonderful light which surpassed the brilliancy of a thousand
suns. On his forehead shone the sign of the cross, that Lidwina might not be deceived by the evil one, who often appears as an angel of light. At first she used to experience
so great an oppression on her chest that she thought herself dying ; but the feeling passed as she became accustomed
to the ecstatic state. She lay like a corpse perfectly insensible to external impressions whilst her spirit obeying the
angelic voice, after a short visit to the Blessed Virgin's altar
in the parish church of Schiedam whither the angel always
led her first, set out on the journey imposed upon her. Now,
Lidwina's sufferings were such as never to allow her to
leave her bed ; and yet many circumstances combined to certify to the truth of her spiritual and corporal ravishment. She
tells us that more than once she was raised, bed and all, to
the ceiling of her room by the force of the spirit ; and the
bruises she bore on her person after her journeys lend
strength to her angel's testimony that her body, as well as
her soul, had shared in the rapture. How this was effected the angel alone knew."

There can, however, be no question here of the material
body, no question of the pious virgin's being caught up in
her state of ordinary life. The angel only intended to say
that her soul in its flights or, as St. Hildegarde expresses it,
when it flashed through the realms of space like a ray of
light, separated not from the body, ceased not its communication with that infinitely subtle fluid which we term the
vital spirits which, in truth, belong to the body, but which
are at the same time so closely connected with the nature of
the soul as to form the first and chief instrument of its vital activity. The more spiritualized the physical organism
of God's chosen ones becomes (a result which follows extra-

ordinary mortification), the more penetrating become also the *vital spirits*, like unto fire and, consequently, the nearer do they approach to the nature of the soul ; so that the latter, the soul, acting in vision as if out of the body and without the body, is rendered capable of communication with the world of spirit without really separating from the body, without actually loosening the natural and necessary bond that holds them together. It may be said, therefore, to act in a *corporal* manner. Freed from the confines of space and the obstacles opposed to it by the weight of the body, it can act in and with the body, effect that for which the senses serve as instruments and receive impressions through their medium. The interior senses, now become spiritualized, no longer offer resistance to the workings of the soul, but follow it whithersoever it leads. Thus, the whole man, body and soul, acts in contemplation, suffers and operates, although the exterior organs of sense remain inactive and, as it were, closed, and the body, owing to its weight, cannot really follow the soul into the far-off regions through which it journeys. We entirely reverse the natural relation existing between the soul and the body when we fancy that the former can receive without the intervention of the latter, impressions of material objects, impressions so powerful that they are forced, so to speak, to find an exit out of it into the body on which they exercise an action wholly new.

If we now consider the spiritual and supernatural preparation of a soul to dispose her for the reception of prophetic light, we shall see that, besides sanctifying grace, it is the infused virtue of *faith* that renders her capable of receiving and making use of this gift. And yet, infused faith is not a simple condition, it is the proper cause and end, by virtue of which God bestows the gift of contemplation. For

man to attain beatitude, the first, the most necessary of God's
gifts, is the light of faith. All extraordinary gifts of grace
relate to faith as the inferior to the superior, the means to the
end, although the visible effects of these gifts are often more
striking, more wonderful than the invisible, which are, however, incomparably more elevated. Faith, and not visions,
is the source, the root of justification. No one can draw
near to God or be pleasing to Him without faith. It is
by faith that Jesus Christ dwells in the heart, and it is
faith, and not visions, that seizes upon and appropriates the
salvation offered with Him. St. Paul, in his epistle to the
Hebrews, calls faith the *substance*, that is the real and essential possession of things hoped for, the real sign of invisible goods. Although faith gives not a clear, precise
intuition of the facts and mysteries of our Redemption, yet
it excludes even the possibility of error or doubt, and enables the believer to acquire the immense treasures contained in God's revelations and promises to His infallible
Church. The believer by virtue of his faith, possesses actually
the goods acquired for him by the Redemption, however
multiplied or admirable they may be; but, owing to his
imperfect intelligence they are veiled from him just as the
appearance and form of the future plant are concealed in
the germ. To arrive at a clear perception of his treasures,
to appreciate them as they deserve, he needs light to penetrate what is hidden, to read at a glance the history of
by-gone ages, or the unfulfilled promises of the future (1).
This Almighty God communicates by the angel-guardian of
the soul, who sustains its weakness and renders it capable of supporting its brilliancy (2). The angel's assistance

(1) Cum prophetia pertineat ad cognitionem, quæ supra naturalem rationem existit,
consequens est ut ad prophetiam requiratur quoddam lumen intellectuale excedens lumen naturale rationis.—(St. Thomas, 2, 2æ, quæst. 171, art. 2.)
(2) Ipsum propheticum lumen, quo mens prophetæ illustratur, a Deo originaliter pro-
cedit : sed tamen ad ejus congruam susceptionem mens humana angelico lumine con-

is necessary; without it, the soul could never rise to the marvellous regions of contemplation. The first effect of the angelic teaching is an awakening to the practices of the theological virtues; for the soul receives this light, not to find in it a source of joy, but an increase of intelligent faith. Therefore, in Sister Emmerich faith was never inactive. From her very Baptism, it manifested itself in uninterrupted acts of love, so much the more perfect as her soul never rested on sensible goods. St. Thomas teaches that faith holds the first rank in the spiritual life, since it is by faith alone that the soul is bound to God, the foundation and source of its life. As the body lives by the soul, the soul lives by God, and that which gives life to the soul is that which binds it to God, namely, faith. This light made known to Sister Emmerich through the angel the signification of the Twelve Articles of the Creed, which is a summary of the mysteries of salvation hidden in God from all eternity, revealed first as a promise and, in the fulness of time, accomplished in Jesus Christ. The whole history of Redemption, with all its circumstances of time, place, and actors, passed before her soul in pictures. Thousands of years could not separate her from these different events. She saw all by faith and penetrated into the interior and mutual relation between the most remote and the most recent facts connected with our Redemption, standing face to face with one another, the promise and the fulfilment. Every outward sign of faith renewed its effects in her soul. Did she witness the adminstration of a Sacrament, its supernatural effects were revealed to her by floods of light which either flowed in upon the soul of the recipient

fortatur et quodammodo præparatur. Cum enim lumen divinum sit simplicissimum et universalissimum in virtute, non est proportionatum ad hoc quod ab animâ humanâ in statu viæ percipiatur,nisi quodammodo contrahatur et specificetur per conjunctionem ad lumen angelicum quod est magis contractum et humanæ menti magis proportionatum.—(S. Thomas, Quæst. XII. de veritate, art. 8.)

or were repelled in their course, thus making known to her his spiritual disposition. Were a pious picture placed under her eyes, she instantly perceived a representation infinitely more faithful than the one before her, since faith awakened in her soul a perfect image of the original. Pious reading, holy conversation, the breviary, the chanting of psalms, everything, in fine, connected with religion, awoke in her emotions so strong and lively that, to resist absorption in vision, she was often obliged to use violence with herself.

Sister Emmerich tried several times to give the Pilgrim some idea of her contemplation, but in vain; she could never satisfactorily explain the spiritual activity of her visions. We quote what the Pilgrim was able to write on different occasions :—

"I see many things that I cannot possibly express. Who can say with the tongue what he sees not with the bodily eyes? . . . . . ."

"I see it not with the eyes. It seems as if I saw it with my heart in the midst of my breast. It makes the perspiration start! At the same time I see with my eyes the objects and persons around me ; but they concern me not, I know not who or what they are. I am in contemplation even now whilst I am speaking. . . . . . ."

"For several days I have been constantly between the state of vision and the natural waking state. I have to do violence to myself. In the middle of a conversation I suddenly see before me other things and pictures and I hear my own words as if proceeding from another, as if coming out of an empty cask. I feel as if I were intoxicated and reeling. My conversation goes on coolly and often more animatedly than usual, but when it is over I know not what I have said, though I have been speaking connectedly. It costs me an effort to maintain this double state. I see passing objects dimly and confusedly like a sleeper awaking out of a dream. The second sight attracts me more powerfully, it is clearer than the natural, but it is not through the eyes. . . . . . ."

After relating a vision one day, she laid aside her work, saying : " All this day have I been flying and seeing ; sometimes I see the Pilgrim, sometimes not.   Does he not hear the singing ? It seems to me that I am in a beautiful meadow (1), the trees forming arches over me.   I hear wondrously sweet singing like the clear voices of children. All around me here below is like a troubled dream, dim and confused, through which I gaze upon a luminous world perfectly distinct in all its parts, intelligible even in its origin and connected in all its wonders.   In it the good and holy delight more powerfully since one sees his way from God to God ; and what is bad and unholy troubles more deeply as the way leads from the demon to the demon in opposition to God and the creature.   This life in which nothing hinders me, neither time nor space, neither the body nor mystery, in which all speaks, all enlightens, is so perfect, so free that the blind, lame, stammering reality appears but an empty dream.   In this state I always see the relics by me shining, and sometimes I see little troops of human figures floating over them in a distant cloud.   When I return to myself, the boxes and caskets in which the shining relics lie reappear. "

Once the Pilgrim gave her a little parcel into which without her knowledge he had slipped a relic.   She took it with a significant smile, as if to say she could not be so deceived, and laying it on her heart, she said : " I knew directly what you were giving me.   I cannot describe the impression it produces.   I not only see, I *feel* a light like the will-

(1) A *meadow*, symbol of a *festival.*

o'-the-wisp, sometimes bright, sometimes dull, blowing toward me as if directed by a current of wind. I feel, too, a certain connecting link between the light and the shining body, and between the latter and a luminous world, itself born of light. Who can express it ?—The light seizes me, I can not prevent it from entering my heart; and, when I plunge in deeper, it seems as if I passed through it into the body from which it emanates, into the scenes of its life, its struggles, its sufferings, its triumphs! Then I am directed in vision as is pleasing to God. There is a wonderful, a mysterious relation between our body and soul. The soul sanctifies or profanes the body ; otherwise, there could be no expiation, no penance by means of the body. As the saints whilst alive, worked in the body, so even when separated from it they continue to act by it upon the faithful. But faith is essential to the reception of holy influences.

"Often whilst speaking with others on quite different subjects, I see far in the distance the soul of a deceased person coming toward me and I am forced to attend to it at once. I become silent and thoughtful. I have apparitions also of the saints in the same way......"

" I once had a beautiful revelation on this point, in which I learned that seeing with the eyes is no sight, that there is another, an interior sight which is clear and penetrating. But, when deprived of daily Communion, a cloud obscures my clear inward sight, I pray less fervently, with less devotion, I forget important things, signs, and warnings, and I see the destructive influence of exterior things which are essentially false. I feel a devouring hunger for the Blessed Sacrament and, when I look toward the church, I feel as if my heart were about to escape from my breast and fly to my Redeemer. ....."

" When I was in trouble, because in obedience to my guide's orders I refused to be removed to another abode, I cried to God to direct me. I was overwhelmed with trials, and yet I saw so many holy visions that I knew not what to do. In my prayer I was calm. I saw a face, a countenance approach me and melt, as it were, into my breast as if uniting with my being. It seemed as if my soul becoming one with it returned into itself and grew smaller and smaller, whilst my body appeared to become a great massive substance large as a house. The countenance (1), the apparition in me appeared to be triple, infinitely rich and varied, but at the same time always one. It penetrated (that is, its beams, its regards) into all the choirs of angels and saints. I experienced joy and consolation from it, and I thought : Could all this come from the evil spirit ? And whilst I was thus thinking, all the pictures, clear and distinct like a series of bright clouds, passed again before my soul, and I felt that they were now out of me, at my side in a luminous sphere. I felt also that although I was larger, yet I was not so massive as before. There was now, as it were, a world outside of me into which I could peer through a luminous opening. A maiden approached who explained this world of light to me, directed my attention here and there, and pointed out to me the vineyard of the holy Bishop in which I now had to labor.

" But I saw too on my left, a second world full of deformed figures, symbols of perversity, calumny, raillery, and injury. They came like a swarm, the point directed toward me. Of all that came to me from this sphere, I could accept nothing, for the just, the good were in the pure;

(1) This face, this countenance was the gift of vision, the light of prophecy proceeding from God, by which Sister Emmerich conversed with the saints and angels and received their communications.

luminous sphere on my right. Between these two spheres I hung by one arm poor and abandoned, floating, so to say, between heaven and earth. This state lasted long and caused me great pain ; still I was not impatient. At last, St. Susanna (1) came to me from the luminous sphere with St. Liborius in whose vineyard I had to work. They freed me, and I was brought again into the vineyard which was uncultivated and overgrown. I had to prune the wild, straggling branches on the trellises that the sun might reach the young shoots. With great trouble I worked at a gap in the lattice. I gathered the leaves and decayed grapes into a pile, wiped the mould from others and, as I had no fine cloth, I had to take my kerchief. This labor tired me so that I lay on my bed next morning all bruised and sore ; I felt as if not a bone were left in my body. My arms still ache......"

" The way in which a communication from the blessed is received, is hard to explain. What is said is incredibly brief; by one word from them I understand more than by thirty from others. I see the speaker's thought, but not with the eyes ; all is clearer, more distinct than in the present state. One receives it with as much pleasure as he hails a breeze in summer. Words cannot well express it......"

" All that the poor soul said to me was, as usual, brief. To understand the language of the souls in purgatory is difficult. Their voice is smothered as if coming through something that dulls the sound ; it is like one speaking from a pit or a cask. The sense, also, is more difficult to seize. Closer attention is required than when Our Lord, or my guide, or a saint speaks to me, for their words penetrate like a clear current of air, one *sees* and knows all they say.

(1) Sister Emmerich had this vision Aug. 11, 1821. Feast of St. Susanna, M.

One of their words says more than a lengthy discourse . . . . ."

KNOWLEDGE OF THE THOUGHTS OF OTHERS.

Late one evening in the winter of 1813, Father Limberg returned tired and worn out after a whole day spent in sick-calls. As he sat down in Sister Emmerich's room, breviary in hand, the thought occurred to him: "I am so tired and I have so many prayers to say—if it were no sin, I would let them go." Hardly had he conceived the thought, seated at some distance from her, than she cried out: " O do say your prayers!" He asked: " What prayers do you mean?" " Your breviary," she answered—" Why do you ask?" " This was the first time," remarked the Father, " that I was struck by anything extraordinary in her."

On July 25th, 1821, Sister Emmerich spoke as follows to the Pilgrim: " The Pilgrim has no devotion, he prays nervously, mixing things up quickly. I often see all kinds of bad thoughts chasing one another through his head. They peer around like strange, ugly, wild beasts! He checks them not, he does not drive them away promptly; it is as if he were used to them, they run about as over a beaten path." The Pilgrim remarked: " It is, unhappily, only too true!"

" From the lips of those that pray I see a chain of words issuing like a fiery stream and mounting up to God, and in them I see the disposition of the one who prays, I read everything. The writing is as varied as the individuals themselves. Some of the currents are all aglow, others are dull; some of the characters are round and full, some running, just like different styles of handwriting."

When Sister Emmerich characterized her contemplations as " not seen with the eyes but with the soul, the heart being, so to say, the organ of sight," she intended to indicate not only its beginning and development, but also its supernatural and meritorious character. Every good work originates in the heart; there it is that the faithful soul receives the impulse of grace to produce meritorious acts, either interior or exterior. It is in the heart that the Holy Spirit dwells; there He pours out His gifts; there is formed that bond of charity which unites the faithful together, and binds them to their invisible Head, Jesus Christ, as the branches to the vine. Man's value before God is estimated by the dispositions of his heart, its uprightness, its good-will, its charity, and not by keenness of intellect or extent of knowledge. Thus it was that Sister Emmerich saw in her heart the visions vouchsafed her by her God; there it was that she heard her angel's voice and her confessor's commands, whether expressed in words (1) or only mentally and at a distance. She obeyed instantaneously in either case, returning promptly from ecstasy to consciousness. In her heart also did she hear the distressed cries of those whom she was appointed to succor, even though seas and continents lay between her and them; there too did she feel the agony of the dying whom she was to assist in their last moments by her own sufferings and prayers. It was her heart that warned her of impending danger either to the Church or individuals. She often endured distress of mind long before she clearly understood the cause. In her heart she saw the thoughts, the dispositions, the whole moral character of those with whom she treated either actually or in spirit; there she heard impious words, blasphemy, etc., for the expiation of which God was pleased to accept the torments of His innocent creature; finally, it was in her heart that she heard the voice that called her to ecstasy. She

(1) This was also the case with Maria von Moerl, of Kaltern, Père Capistran's highly favored penitent. No matter at what distance from her, he could, as he more than once assured the author, recall her from ecstasy by his priestly command.

promptly obeyed the call, and collected together all the powers of her soul to accomplish whatever was demanded of her.
She had never known an attachment to perishable goods.
Apart from God and His service, she desired nothing,
knew nothing. Her soul, delighted by heavenly visions,
sought no earthly gratification. Faith and the Commandments were her only measure of created things.

St. Hildegarde informs us what rank the heart holds even
in the natural order (1):

" When by the mysterious order established by the
Supreme Creator, the body is quickened in the mother's
womb, the soul like a fiery globe bearing no resemblance
to the human form, takes possession of the heart, mounts
to the brain, and animates all the members...... It takes
possession of the heart, because glowing with the light
of its deep knowledge, it distinguishes different things in
the sphere of its comprehension (that is, recognizes the
objects that fall under the senses). It takes not the form
of the body, because it is incorporeal and immortal. It gives
strength to the heart which as the fundamental part governs
the whole body, and like the firmament of heaven it holds
together what is below it, hides what is above. It mounts
to the brain, because in the wisdom of God it has the
power to understand not only what is earthly, but
also what is heavenly. It diffuses itself through all the
members, because it communicates vital strength to the
whole body, to the marrow, the veins, to all the different parts
just as a tree transmits sap from its roots to its branches
that they may clothe themselves with leaves."

" The soul dwells in the fortress of the heart, as in a
corner of the house, just as the father of a family takes a
position whence he can overlook and direct affairs for the

(1) Scivias lib. I. , visio IV.

good of his household. He turns toward the east and raises his right arm to give his orders. The soul does the same, looking toward the rising of the sun through the ways (the senses) of the whole body."

" The soul itself is of a fiery nature (1). It penetrates the entire body in which it dwells, the veins with their blood, the bones with their marrow, the flesh with its juices; it is inextinguishable. The fire of the soul rises from the reasoning faculties whence comes the word, the speech. Were the soul not of a fiery nature, it could not vivify the cold mass with its heat nor build up the body with its venous streams. The soul, breathing, burning in the reasoning faculties, distributes its heat throughout the body in proper measure that the latter may not be consumed."

St. Hildegarde's explanation of visions is the same as Sister Emmerich's; they bear testimony to each other :—

" The way in which contemplation is carried on is hard for a man subject to the senses to understand (2). I have my visions not in dreams nor sleep, not in the delirium of fever nor through the instrumentality of the external senses, and not in secret places. I receive them by God's will, in my waking moments, in the untroubled splendor of an unclouded spirit, with the eyes and ears of the inner man, and in places open to all. . . . God works where He will for the glorification of His name, not for that of earthly man. I am in constant dread, because I recognize in myself nothing to assure me ; but I raise my hands to God to be borne by Him like a feather wafted about by the wind. What I see I cannot perfectly comprehend when I am occupied with outward things and my soul not wholly absorbed in contemplation, for then both states are imperfect. From my infancy, when my bones, my nerves, my veins were yet

(1) Explanatio Symboli S. Athanasii, p. 1070. Edit., Migne.
(2) Acta S. Hildegard, p. 17, 18, et p. 98, 99.

without strength, I have had in my soul this light of contemplation, and I am now seventy years old. In vision, as God wills it, my soul soars above the firmament through regions of space, and beholds the far, far distant nations. And, as in this way, I see all these things in my soul, I see also the various strata of clouds and other true creatures. That is to say, this spiritual contemplation is not an empty imagination, but an extension of the soul through the farthest space, and nothing that I meet escapes my observation. I see it not with my outward senses; I hear not with my ears; I create it not from the thoughts of my mind, nor by any co-operation of the five senses, but only through the soul, the eyes of the body being open. The latter never failed me in consequence of ecstasy, for I am in contemplation whilst awake by day, as well as by night.

" The light that I see is not material light circumscribed by place. It is much brighter than the clouds around the sun ; in it I can discover neither length nor breadth, height nor depth. I call it the shadow of the living light. As the sun, moon, and stars are reflected in water, so in this light the writings, the words, the dispositions, the works of men shine out in pictures. What I discover in contemplation I remember long. I see, hear, and know all at once ; I comprehend instantaneously all that I ought to know. What I do not see in contemplation I do not understand, for I have not received a learned education. As for what I have to write in vision, I can trace the words only just as I have seen them, nor can I put them into elegant Latin. I hear them not as flowing from the lips of men ; but they are like a lambent flame, a luminous cloud floating in a clear atmosphere. I can no more recognize a form in this light than I can look steadily at the sun's disc."

" In this light I sometimes see another which is named

to me as the living light, but I do not see it as often as I do the first and still less can I describe it. When I receive it all sadness and sorrow vanish from my mind, so that I am more like a simple child than an old woman. The first light, the shadow of the living light, never departs from my soul. I see it just as I should see a luminous cloud through the starless firmament, and in it I see that which, out of the splendor of the living light, I say."

Whatever may be the effect of this divine light upon the soul, the practice of faith can never be superfluous ; the former never substitutes anything more meritorious than the latter. On the contrary, the prophetic light like that of infused knowledge, serves but to strengthen faith, and confers clearer intelligence upon the points proposed for its exercise. For the mind of man there can be no more elevated, no more perfect acts than those of the infused theological virtues. God has opened for him no other way to eternal happiness than that of faith. The simple faithful, though destitute of the light of contemplation, can by instruction, prayer, and meditation, by the practice of the precepts of faith, penetrate its mysteries and appreciate its inestimable value. He who has been raised to contemplation, looks not upon faith as inferior to this extraordinary gift ; the clearer and more comprehensive his visions, the stronger does it become. St. Catherine of Sienna is a proof of this. Treating of the relation of faith to contemplation, she says in her Dialogues, dictated during ecstasy, that the gift of prophecy can be recognized as true only by the light of faith :—

" O Eternal Trinity, abyss of love, dissolve the cloud of my body ! Thou art the fire that dispels all cold ! With Thy light Thou enlightenest the mind and teachest all truth ! Thou art the light above all light ! From Thy light,

Thou givest light to the understanding ; namely, the supernatural light, in such plenitude and perfection that
thereby the light of faith is increased, faith by which I
know that my soul lives and that in its light I have received *Thy light.* In the light of faith I acquire wisdom in the wisdom of the Word, Thy Son ; in the light of
faith, I am strong, constant, and persevering ; in the light
of faith, I trust that Thou wilt never suffer me to stray
from the right path. The light of faith teaches me the
way that I should follow ; without its light I should wander in darkness, therefore have I prayed Thee, O Eternal
Father, to enlighten me with the light of most holy
faith ! O Most Holy Trinity, in the light (of contemplation)
which Thou hast given me, which I have received through
the workings of the light of most holy faith, I have known
by many admirable explanations the way of true perfection, that I may serve Thee in light and not in darkness !
Why did I not see Thee by the light of most holy, most
praiseworthy faith ? Because the clouds of self-love obscured the eye of my understanding. But Thou, O Most
Holy Trinity, Thou hast dissipated this darkness by Thy
light ! How can I thank Thee for this immense benefit,
for the knowledge of the truth Thou hast given me ? This
instruction (which I have received from Thee by the light
of prophecy) is a special grace (granted only to me) over
and above the general one which Thou dost accord to other
creatures (1)."

Sister Emmerich also was, like Hildegarde, taught by
her angel in infancy how to practise faith as the foundation
of the spiritual life.

"When in my sixth year, I meditated on the First
Article of the Catholic Creed : 'I believe in God, the

(1) Acta SS., die 30 Aprilis. Vita p. III., c. 2.

Father Almighty, Creator of heaven and earth,' pictures of the creation passed before my soul. I saw the fall of the angels, the creation of earth and Paradise, of Adam and Eve, and the Fall of man. I thought everybody saw them just as we see other things around us. I spoke of them freely to my parents, my brothers and sisters, and to my playmates, until I found that they laughed at me, asking if I had a book in which all these things were written. Then I began to be more reserved on such subjects, thinking I ought not to mention them, though why I could not tell. I had these visions by day and by night, in the fields, and going about my different occupations. One day at school I spoke with childish simplicity of the Resurrection, using other terms than those taught us. I thought every one knew the same, I never suspected that I was saying anything strange. The children wondered and told the master, who gravely warned me not to indulge such imaginations. I still had visions, but I kept silence concerning them. I was like a child looking at pictures, explaining them in its own way, without thinking much upon their meaning. These visions represented the saints or scenes from Sacred History, sometimes in one way, sometimes in another. They produced no change in my faith ; I thought them my picture-book. I gazed at them calmly and always with the good thought: ' All to the greater glory of God !' I have never believed anything in spiritual things but what God, the Lord, has revealed and proposed through the Catholic Church for our belief, whether written or not ; never have I believed so firmly what I saw in vision. I looked upon them as I devoutly regard, here and there, the various cribs at Christmas, without annoyance at their different style. In each I adore only the same dear little Infant Jesus, and it is the same with these pic-

tures of the creation of heaven, of earth, and of man. I
adore in them God, the Lord, the Almighty Creator. I
never studied anything from the Gospels, or the Old Testament, for I have myself seen all in the course of my life.
I see them every year; sometimes they are alike, or again
they are attended by new scenes. I have often been present
with the spectators, assisting as a contemporary, even taking part in the scene, though I did not always remain in
the same place. I was often borne up into the air and I
beheld the scene from on high. Other things, mysteries
especially, I saw interiorly. I had an inward consciousness
of them, pictures apart from the outward scene. In all
cases I saw through and through, one body never hid another, and yet there was no confusion. Whilst a child, before I entered the convent, I had many visions principally
from the Old Testament, but afterward they became rare
and the life of Our Lord took their place. I knew the whole
life of Jesus and Mary from their very birth. I often contemplated the Blessed Virgin in her childhood and saw
what she did when alone in her little chamber; I even knew
what she wore. I saw that the people of Our Lord's time
had sunk lower, were even more wicked than those of our
day; still, there were a few more simple, more pious than
now. They differed as much from one another as tigers
do from lambs. Now reign general tepidity and torpor.
The persecution of the just in those days consisted in delivering them to the executioner, in tearing them to pieces;
now it is exercised by injury, disdain, raillery, patient and
constant efforts to corrupt and destroy. Martyrdom is now
an endless torment."

Sister Emmerich's communications with the Pilgrim furnished her many opportunities for combating his religious
errors and prejudices. One day he maintained in

specious arguments that the institution of the Feast of Corpus Christi was unnecessary, since on Holy Thursday and in the daily Mass the Holy Eucharist is celebrated. She listened in silence, but next day she said to him :—

" I have received a severe reproof from my guide. He says I should not have listened to the Pilgrim's words, I should not countenance such talk, it is heretical. All that the Church does, even if there should glide in through human weakness views not altogether pure, is done under the direction of the Holy Spirit of God, and for the wants of the times. The Feast of the Blessed Sacrament had become a necessity, since, at the time of its institution, the adoration due to Jesus therein' was neglected : therefore. the Church proclaimed her faith by public worship. There is no feast, no worship, no article of faith established by her which is not indispensable, not absolutely requisite at the time for the preservation of true doctrine. God makes use of individuals, even with views less pure, to serve His own adorable designs. The Church is founded on a rock ; no human weakness can ravish from her her treasures. Therefore, I must never again listen to such denials of necessity in the Church's decisions, for they are heretical. After this severe lesson, I endured cruel sufferings for my condescension." The Pilgrim here adds a note : " This is a warning to me of how wrong it is to speak lightly of what concerns the Church."

Sister Emmerich again expressed herself as follows, on the " Illuminati," who, rejecting the holy usages of the Church, endeavor to introduce in their stead empty formulas and high-sounding phrases :—

" If the Church is true all in her is true ; he who admits not the one, believes not the other. Whoever attributes things to chance, denies the effects of cause and makes them the result of chance. Nothing is mere ceremony, all is substantial, all acts through the outward signs. I have often heard learned priests say : ' We must not ask people to believe everything at once ; if they only get hold of the thread, they will soon draw the whole ball to themselves.' Such a speech is bad, erroneous. Most people take very fine thread and wind until it breaks, or is scattered in shreds around. The whole religion of either laymen or priests who speak thus is, in my opinion, like a balloon filled with holy things and sent up into the air, but which never reaches the sky. I often see the religion of whole cities floating over them like a balloon.

"I have often been told that God has attached to the holy cross of Coesfeld and to all places in which sacred objects are venerated, the power of resisting evil; but miracles depend on the fervor of prayer. I often see the cross venerated in processions and those that receive with faith the graces flowing from it, preserved from evil, and their petitions heard, whilst their neighbors are shrouded in darkness. I have also been told that lively, simple faith makes all things *real* and *substantial.* These two expressions gave me great light on the subject of miracles and the granting of prayer."

With such words as the above she strove to combat the Pilgrim's inclination to laud the "*piety*" of the Moravians whilst he bitterly decried the "*miseries of the Church.*"

"I was sternly rebuked by my guide when I listened silently to such remarks. He pointed out the rashness of such judgments, saying that one falls thereby into the same faults as the first apostates. He told me that I had to supply what is neglected in the Church, otherwise I shall be more guilty than they to whom it is not given to see what I see. I saw the Moravian settlement. They are as restrained in their movements as a person who tries to avoid waking one who is asleep. It is all so formal, clean, and quiet, they appear so pious, but they are inwardly dead and in a far more deplorable state than the poor Indians for whom I have now to pray. Where there is no struggle there is no victory. They are idle, therefore they are poor ; their affairs go badly enough, in spite of their fine talk and fair appearance. I saw this in the Nuptial House. Under the picture of two invalids, I saw the difference between souls, and their interior state before God. I saw the Moravian community under the appearance of a sick person who conceals her maladies, who is very agreeable and pleasing in the exterior; opposite to her, as in a far-off vision, I saw another invalid covered with ulcers which sparkled and shone like pearls. The bed on which she lay was bright, the floor, the ceiling, the whole room, were dazzlingly white like snow. As the sick Moravian drew near this room, she left stains wherever she stepped though she pretended not to see anything of it."

Sister Emmerich's manner of acting was even more significant than her words. Though so highly privileged ; though in almost continual contemplation of the highest mysteries and truths of religion, the life of our Blessed Lord and His saints ; though admitted to a corporal participation in His Sacred Passion ; yet her greatest happiness, her most earnest desire was to assist at the celebration of the feasts and ceremonies of the Church in company with the faithful. Her infirmities cut her off for years from this consolation, and she felt the privation most deeply ; no ecstasy, no vision could indemnify her for the loss. In this she resembled Maria Bagnesi and Magdalene di Pazzi ; the former of whom begged so ardently to be allowed to visit once more the miraculous statue in the Church of the Annunciation, Florence, that God granted her that favor, the last gratification she had on earth. Maria's sufferings were such as to prevent her moving freely around her little room ; yet she managed, though with great pain, to attend to the altar which it contained and on which Mass was celebrated for her consolation. Magdalene di Pazzi, though in constant communication with her angel-guardian, knew no greater pleasure when a child than to listen to the devout conversation of her mother whom she sometimes embarrassed by her questions ; nothing seemed to her comparable to the happiness of possessing the true faith. As St. Hildegarde could say : " In contemplation I am more like a child than an old woman," so, too, did Sister Emmerich in vision often become again a child of five or six years old (1). This puzzled her, and she once asked her angel what it meant. He replied : " If thou wert not really a child, that could not happen." He wished to imply that, if she were not in soul and body as pure as a flower in the morning dew, she never could return to the innocent simplicity of childhood. When Maria Bagnesi in her eighteenth year was about to pronounce her vows as a Tertiary of St. Dominic, she knew not the meaning of the vow of chastity. She questioned her confessor, who told her that it meant to have Jesus Christ alone for spouse. " O," said Maria smiling, " I have always kept that vow, then, for I have never had any other desire than that of loving Jesus." St. Magdalene di Pazzi also could declare on her death-bed that she had never known anything contrary to purity, nor even in what manner it could be sullied. Here we discover the secret of these privileged souls ; no earthly image ever dimmed

(1) One day, Sister Emmerich lay in ecstasy, when suddenly she began to gesticulate like a little child, stretching out her arms and exclaiming : " Good-day, little mother ! It has been a long time since you came with your child. Oh ! give Him to me ! I have not had Him for so long ! " Returned to herself, she said joyously : " I saw the Mother of God coming to me with the child Jesus. It made me so glad ! I wanted to take the child, but she disappeared, and I called after her."

the mirror of their soul, which should reflect alone the bright beams of prophetic light. And by this, also, we understand why the Church, when passing judgment on extraordinary graces, seeks proofs of their reality in those virtues attained only by constant mortification and detachment. It would be in contradiction with the sanctity of God for the supernatural light of contemplation to dwell in a soul not wholly dead to itself and creatures ; therefore is this gift so rare, for in very few are found that purity and humility which characterized Sister Emmerich. We need no more convincing proof of the latter virtue than the Pilgrim's own testimony. From close observation he had drawn the conclusion that her unaccountable maladies arose from causes in the spiritual order quite foreign to her own physical condition ; and great was his disappointment, not to say disgust, when he saw her attach no importance whatever to their supernatural origin, and pay little attention to their intimate connection with certain evils of the spiritual order which she was called upon to expiate. His journal contains such lines as the following: " All goes to waste, the greatest graces are not understood ! Her carelessness deprives me of the most important revelations concerning the inward workings of her privileged life, etc., etc." And again, when he saw her, regardless of the particular character of her sufferings, accepting and even calling for Dr. Wesener's remedies, his impatience manifested itself.

Jan. 20 and Feb. 3, 1823.--" Her sufferings increase, her courage decreases. She lay all night in one position groaning with pain, until we turned her on the other side. She was also tormented by fearful visions. She thought herself a child pursued by wild beasts, swimming over stagnant pools to escape them, and unable to call for assistance. . . . She endured this state till the vigil of

Candlemas. To the terrible hemorrhages of the last few days succeeded a general swelling of her whole body. 'I am full of pain,' she groaned, ' pain in all my members, even in my heels !' This sudden change began at the sound of the evening-bells of the Purification, and it was completed when they ceased to ring. She was quite courageous, though she neither spoke nor seemed to think of the coincidence. This is her usual manner of acting, whatever be her state. She seems unconscious of anything extraordinary; she even begs for help and seems hurt if we do not try to relieve her. Her mysterious life is neither directed nor governed—hence result loss, confusion, want of harmony."

The Pilgrim failed to reflect that her patient sufferings had obtained for her an increase of fortitude, which proves that her childlike simplicity in receiving them without seeking for a cause, was infinitely more agreeable to God than those around her dared to suspect. Three years previously, when struck by her unalterable peace of soul, the Pilgrim had recorded :—" She is extraordinarily courageous, full of childlike peace and simplicity. She is always in contemplation, although she tries to resist it. She rejoices only in this, that she lives to suffer. It is impossible to repeat her words, her transition from outward realities to the state of vision, her childlike joy, patience, courage, abandonment, the charm and candor of her whole demeanor. Only they who see her can know it. In this state she is the picture of an innocent, trusting child full not of faith, but of that certainty that sight gives. What we believe by God's grace, she knows ; it is as real to her as is the existence of her parents and family. She is, consequently, free from all returns upon self ; she exhibits no discontent, no irritation. She has no enemy ; she is full of peace, of joy, and of love. There is no assumption of false gravity about her. They are

a little disappointed who expect to find in her exterior some
striking confirmation of extraordinary graces. Such persons
attend rather to the emblems of dignity than to the dignity
itself. When the Pilgrim visited her she had a book before
her, though indeed she was not reading ; she made use of
it to prevent her mind's becoming absorbed in vision, but
such efforts were often useless. At times she joyfully
thanked God for letting her live to suffer for her neighbor,
for in eternity she could no longer do so. She knows no
sadness. Many scenes, forgotten during the past days,
have returned to her mind ; for instance, these last cold
nights, she saw all the people in the neighborhood who were
without beds. The sight touched her, and she immediately supplied their need. She saw also a poor widow, her own
relative, in the same want. She turned to her angel, begging him to get her brother's angel to inspire him to send
the poor woman a bed, and next day she had the consolation of learning that her brother had done so."

False sanctity, as we may easily believe, knows no such
consolations, since it turns good into evil and has its root in
spiritual pride. It can aspire only to the recompense offered
by the father of lies ; viz., the satisfaction springing from
gratified vanity, the praise of men, and sensual joys.
True contemplation grounds the soul in obedience and self-
contempt. Its chief characteristic is a disinclination to reveal
the graces received, deference to spiritual authority alone
being able to break the seal of silence in which it shrouds
itself. On the other hand, boasting, vain-glory, and publicity are the marks of a deluded soul ; and, as the effects
of grace are an increase of light, and of all the theological
and moral virtues, so the inevitable consequences of spiritual pride are hypocrisy, heresy, and superstition. One
day Sister Emmerich, overwhelmed by suffering, entreated

Our Lord to withdraw those visions in which she beheld so much that was incomprehensible to her. But she received the following reply :—

"I give thee visions not for thyself, but that thou mayest collect and communicate them. The present is not the time for sensible miracles ; therefore, I give thee visions. I have done the same at all times to show that I am with My Church to the consummation of ages. But *visions alone secure not any one's salvation. Thou must practise charity, patience, and the other virtues.*"

At another time she related what follows :—"I begged Almighty God to withdraw my visions, that I may not be forced to communicate them, but I was not heard. As usual, I was told to relate all that I could recall, even if I should be laughed at or even if I do not see any use in it. I was again told that no one has ever seen all that I have seen or in the same way, but that that is not my affair, it is the Church's. So much being allowed to go to waste will entail great accountability and do much harm. They who deprive me of leisure and the clergy who have no faith and who find no one to take down my visions will have to render a severe account of their negligence. I saw, too, how the demon raises obstacles.

"Long ago I was ordered to tell all, even if I should be looked upon as a fool. But no one wanted to listen to me, and the holiest things that I had seen and heard were so misunderstood and derided that through timidity I shut all up in my own heart, though not without pain. Then I used to see in the distance the figure of a stranger who was to come to write by me. I have found him, I recognize him in the Pilgrim. From childhood I have had the habit of praying every evening for all who are in danger from accidents, such as violent falls, drowning, fire, etc., and

I see pictures of such things turning out happily. If I should happen to omit this prayer, I always see or hear of some great disaster; consequently, I understand by this not only the necessity of special prayers, but also the advantage there may be in making it known, since it may incite others to this loving service of prayer, though they see not its effects as I do. The many, many wonderful communications from the Old and the New Testament, the innumerable pictures from the lives of the saints, etc., have been given me, through God's mercy, not for my instruction alone, for there is much that I cannot understand, but that I may communicate them, that they may revive what is now forgotten. This duty has again been imposed upon me. I have explained this fact, as well as I could, but no one will take the trouble even to listen to me. I must keep it to myself and forget much of it. I hope God will send me what is necessary."

The following communication shows that it was with the shield of faith that Sister Emmerich combated the tempter when he dared approach her in vision :—

"I endured such pain in my wounds that I was forced to scream, I could hardly bear it. The blood flowed in a jerking way toward them. Suddenly Satan stood before me as an angel of light, and said : 'Shall I pierce thy wounds? In the morning all will be well. They will never again give thee pain, thou wilt never suffer more from them.'—But I recognized him at once, and said : ' Begone! I want nothing from thee!—Thou didst not make my wounds! I shall have nothing to do with thee!' Then he withdrew and squatted like a dog behind the cupboard. After awhile he came out and said: 'Do not think thyself so well off with Jesus, because thou dost imagine that thou art always running around with Him. It all comes from

me! I show thee all those pictures. I, also, have a
kingdom!'—I chased him again by my reply.—After a
long time, he came again and said boldly : ' Why torment
thyself with doubts ? All that thou hast, all that thou
seest, is from me. Things are in a bad state, I have thee.
What need of worrying thyself ?'—Again I cried : 'Begone !
I will belong only to Jesus, I will love Him and curse thee !
I shall endure such pains as He wills me to suffer !'—My
anguish was so great that I called my confessor. He blessed
me and the fiend fled. But this morning, as I was saying
my *Credo*, he again appeared and said : ' What use is the
Credo to thee ? Thou dost not understand a word of it;
but I will teach thee all things clearly—then shalt thou both
see and know.' I replied : 'I want not *to know* I want *to
believe.*' Then he recited a passage from Holy Scripture ;
but there was one word in it which he could not pronounce, and I said again and again : ' Say that word,
say it distinctly, if thou canst !' I trembled in every limb,
and, at last, he disappeared. . . . . . "

" When I see the Communion of Saints in the light of
vision, their actions and their love, their interpenetrating
one another, how each is in and for the others, how each is all
and still one in unending brilliancy of light, I feel unspeakable joy and lightsomeness. Then I see far and near the
dark figures of living beings, I am drawn to them by irresistible love, I am urged so sweetly, so lovingly, to pray for
them, to beg God and the saints to help them that my heart
beats with love. I feel, I see more clearly than day that
we all live in communion with the saints, that we are in constant relation with them. Then I grieve over men's blindness and obduracy. I cry out confidently to the Saviour :
' Thou art all-powerful, Thou art all love ! Thou canst do
all things ! Suffer them not to be lost ! Think of Thy

Precious Blood!'—Then I see how He labors for them so
touchingly. 'Only see,' He says, 'How near I am to help
them, to heal them, and how rudely they repulse Me!'—And
then I feel that His justice is full of sweetness and love.

"My guide often takes me in spirit through all sorts of
human miseries : sometimes to prisoners, sometimes to the
dying, to the sick, the poor, to the homes of sin and discord. I see bad priests, I see bad prayers, the profanation of
the Sacraments, and of holy things. I see disdained by miserable creatures, the graces, the helps, the consolations, the
eternal nourishment of the Most Holy Sacrament that the
Lord offers them. I see them turning away, driving the
Lord violently from them. I see all the saints in a sweet,
loving readiness to help them ; but lost to them are the
graces poured upon them from the treasure of Christ's
merits confided to the Church. That afflicts me. I gather up all these lost graces into my heart and thank Jesus
for them, saying : 'Ah ! pity Thy blind, miserable creatures ! they know not what they do ! Ah ! look not at their
offences, keep these graces for poor, blind sinners ! Lord,
give them at another time that they may be helped by them.
Ah! let not Thy Precious Blood be lost to them !'—The Lord
often hears my prayer, and to my great consolation, I see
Him again bestowing His graces.

"When I pray in general for the most needy, I usually
make the Way of the Cross at Coesfeld, and at each station
I pray for a different necessity. Then I have all sorts of
visions which show me in pictures right and left of the station, far off in the distance, the distress, the assistance given,
and the places in which the scenes are enacted. To-day as
I knelt at the First Station, I prayed for those who were going to confession before the feast, that God would grant them
sincere repentance, and the grace to declare all. Then I saw

in various regions people praying in their homes or otherwise occupied, whilst thinking of the state of their conscience. I saw their hearts, and I urged them not to fall
again into the sleep of sin. Then I saw those that would
come to my confessor, and I was directed to say to him,
but in general terms, how to treat this or that person.

"At the Second Station, I prayed for those whom poverty or misery deprived of sleep that God would give them
hope and consolation. And then I saw into many wretched
huts in which the inmates tossed on their straw beds, thinking that morning would find them no better off than the
evening had done, and I saw my prayer procuring them rest.

"At the Third Station, I prayed against strife and
quarrels, and I saw in a cottage a man and wife very angry
with each other. I prayed for them; they grew calm, mutually forgave, and joined hands.

"At the Fourth Station, I prayed for travellers that they
might lay aside their worldly thoughts and go in spirit to
Bethlehem to do homage to the dear Christ-Child. I saw
around me many journeying along with bundles on their
shoulders, and one, in particular, more thoughtless than
his fellows. I prayed for him, and suddenly I saw him fall
over a stone in his path. He exclaimed: 'The devil
put that stone there for me!'—But, recovering himself, he
took off his hat and began to pray.

"At the Fifth Station, I prayed for prisoners who, in
their misery, think not of the holy season and deprive
themselves of its divine consolations. Here, too, I was
consoled. The rest has escaped my memory. . . ."

"As I lay one day thinking: 'In what a miserable
state I am! What a fate is mine! Others can work and do
good, whilst I lie here like a cripple,' I begged God to
give me something that I could do. Then I saw an inn in

which some men were quarrelling. I prayed with all my heart for them to cease their strife. They became calm, and peace was restored. I thought of poor, helpless travellers, and saw a sorrowful-looking man dragging along the road, not knowing where to turn for food or lodging. I was filled with pity. I prayed for him, when there rode up a horseman who, as he passed the poor man, asked whence he came and in what direction he was going. The man mentioned the cities (but I forget the names). The rider gave nim some money and galloped on. The poor man stood in wonder gazing at the money, four whole thalers! He could hardly realize his good fortune; he exclaimed : ' How wonderful is God! Had I reached the city, I should not have received this money.' Then he began to think of all that he would do with it. I can still see him. My guide then took me to about twenty sick people whose ulcers I sucked. When my guide calls me on such errands, I follow blindly. We pass through walls and doors to the sick, and he tells me what I have to do. I see all distinctly and even if there be a crowd around the sick-bed, that does not hinder me, there is always room for me. Whilst I assist the invalids, they seem to sleep or to be unconscious, but they get better. Last night I assisted several at Coesfield. I know one of them, a little fellow twelve years old. I shall make inquiries......."

" I give such assistance only in Christian countries. In far-off infidel lands I float above the darkness, earnestly praying for the inhabitants to be enlightened. I think that every one who prays from his heart for such unhappy creatures, earnestly desirous of helping them all he can, really gives such assistance......."

" I have to heal spiritual maladies also. My guide took me to a spiritual hospital full of sick, of every age

and condition, men and women. There were numbers
whom I knew, others were strangers. I had no help excepting my guide, who blessed the water that I carried in a
little kettle. I had relics also, but I only used them in
secret. All the inmates were sick in soul through sin and
their passions, their maladies appearing exteriorly in the
body. The degree of sin was indicated by their greater or
less poverty, especially shown forth in their beds. The
poorest lay on the ground on straw, others in beds, either
clean or filthy, which bespoke their good or bad surroundings; some were lying on the bare ground, whilst others
were sitting up, etc. I spoke not to them, nor they to me;
but when I bandaged their wounds or sucked their sores,
sprinkled them with the blessed water or secretly touched
them with the relics, they were relieved or cured. They
who had sinned through sloth, had sore or lame hands;
they who were given to theft and such like practices, had
convulsions, cramps in their limbs, and ulcers. Secret
evils had their seat in internal ulcers, which had to be
dissolved by poultices, or drawn out by blisters. Some
were not quite right in their mind from having tormented
themselves with useless researches. I beheld them stag-
gering around and suddenly striking their heads against
something, which brought them to their senses. I had to
attend to many, natives and foreigners, also to Protestants.
There was a girl who was suffering from obstinacy. Hard
and livid welts ran through her whole body like veins;
they looked like the red strokes of a lash. I cured her with
holy water. I also raised the dead. They were in a third
place and differed from the others in this that they lay quite
patient, but utterly incapable of helping themselves.
Among them, also, the evil to be cured manifested itself in
corporal maladies. I bandaged them. . . . . . ."

" Toward the close of my task, I was assisted by some maidens, and then I was brought home by my guide, who gravely reproved me for thinking myself useless ; for, he said, I had done a great deal. God makes use of every one in a different way. . . . . ."

" Again I was taken to a large military hospital. It seemed as if it were under a shed—but where, I know not. Some of the inmates were Germans, and there were others who looked like prisoners who had been brought thither in wagons. Many of the drivers were in rags and wore gray smock-frocks. Some of the sick seemed to be a little elevated in the air; they had moral evils represented, as in the other hospital, by corporal sickness. I went all around relieving, curing, putting on bandages, making lint. Some saints accompanied me, helping me, hiding from my eyes whatever was not decent, and throwing a veil of darkness over many of the unfortunate beings who were quite naked. At last I came to some who had bodily wounds ; they were not suspended in the air, they lay on the ground. The wounds of the morally sick were the most offensive, for their source is in the depths of the heart ; exteriorly they do not seem so hideous, though they are really far more horrible. Bodily wounds are not so deep, they have a more healthful odor ; but they who do not understand such things think them the more frightful. Moral wounds are often healed by patient endurance. I gave all I had, I cut up my bedclothes, used all my white linen, and Abbé Lambert's too ; but the more I gave away the more need there was. I never had enough. Many good people brought me things. There was a room full of officers, and for them something better was necessary. There lay my enemies, and I rejoiced that I could do them good. There was one whom I could not relieve. He wanted a physician according to his own ideas and such could not be found. His state was fearful. Later I had other patients, my own acquaintances, peasants, citizens, ecclesiastics, and also N. N. I had been commissioned a long time before to tell him something; his state grew daily worse. He sought honors and neglected souls.

"'It was given me to see all whom I had cured by sucking their sores, both really and spiritually. My Spouse told me again that such spiritual assistance is *real* assistance, that I do it *in spirit* only because I am now not capable of doing it corporally.

" When I worked as a child in the fields, or as a religious in the garden, I used to feel myself urged to beg God to do for men what I could do only for the plants. I often have a clear idea of the mutual relations and resemblances between creatures which, like emblems, can explain one another; so also in prayer and communion with God one can do really in desire and affection what he could not do actually on account of external hindrances. As a portrait can make me know the original, so can I exercise charity, render services, bestow care upon the picture or image of the object for whom I can do nothing personally and directly. If I do it in Jesus and for Jesus, He transmits it to the person for whom I do it by virtue of His merits; therefore, the merciful God grants to my earnest prayers and longing to assist my neighbor those lively pictures in which I supplicate for the welfare of this or that person. . . .

" I have also been shown how unspeakably good it is in God to give such visions, to accept the labor done in them as a full and perfect work and to reckon it as an increase in the treasury of the Church; but, that it may profit the Church, it must be done in union with the merits of Christ. The needy members of the Church can receive help only from the Church herself. The healing power must be awakened in the Church as in a body, and here it is that the co-operation of her members comes in ; but this is more easily felt than expressed.

" It used to seem strange to me to have to travel so far every night and engage in all sorts of affairs. I used to think : ' When I am on a journey, when I help others in spirit, all seems so real, so natural ! And yet, all the time, I am lying sick and miserable at home !' Then I was told : ' All that a person earnestly desires to do and suffer for Jesus Christ, for His Church, and for the neighbor, *he really and truly does in prayer.* Now thou canst understand !' "

These last communications throw light upon Sister Emmerich's action in spirit, or in the symbolical pictures shown her in vision. It is action by prayer accompanied by suffering and sacrifice, and applied by God to determinate ends. It is always heard, and its fruits applied to him for whom it is offered through the instrumentality of him who suffers and impetrates. Such prayer is infinitely more efficacious than any other, it is certain of success ; it gathers, so to say, fruit already ripe. It is a prayer active, expiatory, and propitiatory in and through Jesus Christ. Sister Emmerich was like to a tree by the side of running waters, upon whose boughs daily hung fresh fruits for the needy ; she was like the nursing mother supplying nourishment to multitudes of spiritual children. She often tried to explain in what such prayer consists. The Pilgrim's journal records, July 7, 1820 :—

" She has suffered intensely for days. Last night she was steeped in perspiration and the wound in her side bled abundantly. She wanted to change her linen herself, so she took a few drops of St. Walburga's oil which gave her the strength necessary for so painful an effort. She looks like a martyr to-day. She acknowledges that her pains were so great last night that she cried aloud to God to help her, not to let her suffer beyond her strength. 'These pains,' she said, 'are my greatest torment, for I cannot bear them in silence, I must groan; and then I always think that, as I have not borne them lovingly, they have not been pleasing to God. It was as if fire had been applied to my person which sent fine currents of pain through my breast, my arms, and my hands.' As she spoke the tears flowed down her cheeks, not so much from her own sufferings, as from those of her Saviour which she constantly contemplated. 'No human intelligence can comprehend what Jesus endured from His birth to His death, even if it were seen as I see it. His infinite love is manifest in His Passion which He bore like a lamb without a murmur. I was conceived in sin, a miserable sinner, and life has ever been a burden to me from the pain sin causes me; but how much more must the incomprehensible perfection of Jesus suffer, insulted on all sides, tormented to death? Last night in the midst of my own pains, I saw again all that He endured from His conception till His death. I saw, also, His interior sufferings, I felt their nature, so intelligible did His grace render them to me. I am so weak, I shall only say what comes to my mind. I saw under the Heart of Mary a glory, and in the glory a bright, shining Child. Whilst I gazed upon It, it seemed as if Mary floated over and around It. I saw the Infant increasing in size and all the torments of the Crucifixion accomplished in Him. It was a frightfully sad spectacle! I wept and sobbed aloud. I saw Him struck, pushed, beaten, crowned with thorns, laid on the cross, and nailed to it, His side pierced. I saw the whole Passion of

Christ in the Child. It was fearful ! As the Child hung on
the cross, He said to me : ' I suffered all this from My conception till My thirty-fourth year, when it was accomplished
exteriorly.' (The Lord died at the age of thirty-three years
and three months). ' Go, announce this to men !'—But
how can I announce it (1) ?"

' ⌐ saw Him, also, as a new-born Babe, and I saw how
many children abuse the Infant Jesus in His crib. The
Blessed Virgin was not there to protect Him. The children brought all kinds of whips and rods, and struck His
face until it bled. He tried gently to parry the blows
with His little hands, but even the youngest children beat
Him cruelly, their parents trimming and preparing the
rods for some of them. They used thorns, nettles, scourges,
switches of all kinds, each had its own signification. One
came with a fine switch like a corn-stalk, which broke
when he tried to strike with it. I knew many of these
children. Some strutted about in fine clothes which I took
away from them. I corrected them soundly.

" Then I saw the Lord walking with His disciples. He
was thinking of all He had endured even in His Mother's
womb, of all that men had made Him suffer in His infancy
and His public life by their blindness and obduracy ; but,
above all, He thought of what He had undergone from the
malice, the envious spying of the Pharisees. He spoke to
His disciples of His Passion, but they understood Him not.
I saw His interior sufferings like colors and heavy black
shadows passing over His grave, sad countenance, through
to His breast, and thence to His Heart which they tore to
pieces. This sight is inexpressible ! I saw Him grow pale,
His whole being agonized, for the sufferings of His soul were

(1) The Pilgrim here remarks : "She forgot that she was even then fulfilling her
commission. Her question reveals the way in which she always acted in such cases.
She has often been directed to tell even what seemed absurd."

far sharper than those of His Crucifixion; but He bore them silently, lovingly, patiently. After this I beheld Him at the Last Supper, and saw His infinite grief at Judas's wickedness. He would willingly have undergone still greater torments could He have kept Judas from betraying Him. His Mother, also, had loved Judas, had often spoken with him, had instructed and advised him. The fall of Judas grieved Jesus more than all the rest. I saw Him washing his feet sorrowfully and lovingly, and looking at him affectionately whilst presenting to him the morsel. Tears stood in the Lord's eyes and His teeth were clenched in pain. I saw Judas approach. I saw Jesus give him His flesh and blood to eat and I heard Him say with infinite sorrow: 'That which thou dost, do quickly.' Then I saw Judas slink behind and soon after quit the supper-room. I saw all the sufferings of the Lord's soul under the form of clouds, colored rays, and flashes of light. I saw Him going to Mt. Olivet with His disciples. He ceased not to weep on the way, His tears flowing in torrents. I saw Peter so bold and self-confident that he thought himself able to crush all his enemies. That distressed Jesus, for He knew that Peter would deny Him. I saw Him leave His disciples, excepting the three whom He loved most, in a kind of open shed near the garden of Olives. He told them to sleep there. He wept all the time. Then He went further into the garden leaving behind the Apostles who thought themselves so valiant. I saw that they soon fell asleep. I saw the Saviour overwhelmed with sorrow, and sweating blood, and I saw an angel presenting Him the chalice. . . . . . ."

"Evening.—She still shudders and trembles with pain; but she is all patience and love, sweetness and gentleness. There is something noble about her in the midst of her pains."

August 30th—"She has been racked by inexpressible sufferings. It was shown her that each has a special signification according to which some particular members are tormented, also that every kind of pain, piercing, tearing, or burning has its own meaning. She knows that each one patiently borne in the name of Jesus, in union with His Passion, becomes a sacrifice for the sins and negligences for which it was imposed. She thereby regains for the Church that of which man's perversity deprives her."

CHAPTER II.

Various Forms of Active Prayer, or Labors in the Nuptial House, etc.

The forms under which Sister Emmerich exercised her action in prayer, or her labors in the Nuptial House, were not optional; they were comformable to the nature of the tasks imposed, which were as varied as the Gospel parables in which Christ's union with the Church is represented. There He shows us the Church as His spouse, His body, His vine, His garden, His field, His flock, whilst He Himself is the Bridegroom, the Head, the Vine-dresser, the Gardener, the Sower, the Shepherd. The priesthood He denominates the salt of the earth, etc. These parables are not empty figures, they symbolize the union existing between Christ, the Saviour, and the objects of His purchase; so also, Sister Emmerich's labors in vision were neither vain nor arbitrary. They were truly necessary, inasmuch as they corresponded to the nature and end of her task. Had she, for instance, to repair the omissions of negligent servants in the Church, the vine of the Son of God, her action in vision partakes of that nature; that is, it has the same form, the same results as labor expended on a real vine. An evident proof that this labor in vision is real, are the physical effects it produces: fatigue, bruises, wounds, etc.

Sister Emmerich relates, June 20, 1820:—"I was taken by my guide to a miserably neglected vineyard west of the Nuptial House. Several of the vines were strong and healthy, but the branches lay unpruned and straggling, the soil was neither dug nor manured. The whole place was

overrun with nettles which grew high and thick where the
stock was most vigorous, though they were not so sharp ;
where the branches hung half-dead, they were almost
buried under small stinging nettles. In the vineyard were
many beautiful houses all in the very best order inside, although on the outside the weeds grew up to
the doors and almost as high as the windows. I saw in
them ecclesiastics, dignitaries of the Church, reading and
studying all sorts of useless books; but no one took the
least care of the vineyard. In the middle of the latter
stood a church with several farm-houses around it ; but
there was no way to get to it, all was covered with rank
weeds, even the church was as it were tapestried with
green. The Blessed Sacrament was in the church, but no
lamp hung before It. As soon as I entered the vineyard,
I felt that the body of St. Liborius was somewhere in the
vicinity ; and, in fact, I found it resting in the church,
though no particular marks of respect were paid to the
sacred remains. The Bishop of the diocese appeared to be
away. Inside the church even there was no clear passage, all was overgrown with weeds. It made me sad. I
was told to set to work, and I found a two-edged bone
knife like a reaping-hook with which to prune the vine,
a hoe, and a basket for manure. The work to be done was
all explained to me. It was hard, at first, but afterward
became easier. I was told how to gather and press the
grapes, but now I have forgotten it. As soon as I began to
work in the vineyard, my sufferings changed. I felt as if
I were being pierced with a three-edged knife. The pain
darted through every member, intolerable shootings in my
bones and joints,even in my finger-tips."

June 22d—" She is," writes the Pilgrim, " constantly engaged in these labors of suffering. In whatever position

she is placed, she feels that she is lying among nettles and thorns.—'I was at work,' she said, 'in the wild vineyard, and besides I was overwhelmed by a swarm of new torments. I knew nothing of what was going on around me. I was worn out, and I felt as if I were lying, not in my bed, but among nettles. Near by was a corner that I had weeded, and I begged to be laid there. My attendants pitied me and said they would put me where there were no thorns and they lifted me to my bed; but I groaned : " Ah ! You have deceived me, you have laid me among still sharper nettles," for so it seemed to me. I thought I was in the vineyard. The tearing up of the stinging nettles was very painful, and I ached all over from pruning the vine with the bone knife. I had already done up to the first house, the wildest part of the vineyard. In my intense pains I made use of the relics of St. Ignatius and St. Francis Xavier and I found relief. I saw the two saints on high. A beam of light from them passed through me like a shock, and I was instantly relieved.' Her sufferings were so great," continues the Pilgrim, " her appearance so changed that, although used to such spectacles, we were all deeply touched. Her hands and feet were scratched, as if from thorns. When she reached the church, St. Frances of Rome appeared to her, haggard and emaciated; she looked like a skeleton. ' See,' she said, ' I also had to labor like you, I was just as miserable as you now are, but I did not die.' Her words encouraged Sister Emmerich. Her pale face began to glow; she looked like one who had received fresh incentive to exertion, and her hands began to clutch and pull, the middle fingers stiff and bent. Suddenly she laughed and exclaimed : ' There, I have hurt my knee ! I struck the bone. I am always so eager, in such a hurry ! I struck it against a great root in the vineyard and the bone knife has hurt my hand.' Her right hand is swollen, her arms covered with scratches."

June 26th—She said : " Now I have only a few days' work before me. Through self-victory my task has doubly succeeded. Now I must grind the weeds to powder. The hardest part of the work was in a presbytery in which a bad servant was the mistress. St. Clare of Montefalco appeared to me and said : ' The worst is over.' " But Sister Emmerich's sufferings were so intense that her confessor thought her dying.

July 2d—" The work in the vineyard is done. Still I have to pray and help with the young shoots. Nettles signify carnal desires. My guide said, ' Thou hast labored hard, thou must have a little rest,'—but I do not think I'll get it !"

July 15th—" Last night I had a labor in prayer. A good man whom I know has for a long time been shown me as having fallen into sin, and I prayed that his heart might be touched. He does not know that I am aware of his state. I have not seen him for some time. Last night I prayed for him earnestly ; he is changed, he will go to confession. This morning he came unexpectedly to see me and I tried to be kind to him. He does not suspect that I have any idea of his state, nor that I have converted him by prayer. He is about to return (*to God*) What I said to him God inspired."

July 29th—" I was in an apple-orchard around which lay hills covered with vineyards, some in the sun, others in the shade. In it was a round building like a storehouse, full of casks and vats, and a great press with holes in the bottom. The little old nun that often helps me took me into the orchard, and I gathered the apples from a high tree until my arms ached. When my apron was full, I emptied it into the press. I was told not to put in any that were unripe and, when I answered that the few I had gathered were hardly worth the trouble, I was shown how much juice they would yield. I understood neither the vision nor its signification, but it is the beginning of a new task."

July 30th—The Pilgrim says: "The vision of laboring under the direction of deceased religious was again repeated. She was wearied with carrying fruit to the press, her arms ached violently."

July 31st—"There is only one large apple-tree in the orchard. I gathered no apples to-day, but I straightened up the plants around the tree, transplanting some, tying up others, pulling up the dead ones, watering and shading the drooping. All has reference to sectarians (false mystics). There are some over-ripe, worm-eaten apples on the tree. The first decayed from an excess of juice, and the worms in the others indicate pride, self-love, and bad company. They fall and crush the plants below, filling them with worms; but when gathered and pressed they yield juice that may be used. They signify teachers in parishes that have gone astray. My companions were the holy old nuns of the convent. Then I had another vision on the state of these people. I saw that most of those that had gone north followed dangerous ways and separated more and more from the Church; and I saw the necessity of importuning God that the proud, exuberant plants may be rooted out of those parishes, in order that the others may not be lost to her."

August 2d—"I worked hard in the garden last night. After I had picked out the specked apples, I had to go to a neighboring vineyard. I had a little tub with me and I gathered bunch after bunch of decayed grapes and threw them into it, that the green ones might ripen and no more be spoiled. When it was full, I emptied it into a press smaller than the apple-press. I prayed all the time, and I had visions of the good resulting from my labor. It refers to the new sect. Only my guide was with me."

August 3d—" For a long time I have gathered and sorted the grapes, filled and emptied the tub, my guide alone with me. I have already accomplished a good deal and I have been told that it bears fruit."

August 5th—" I am very tired, for I worked so hard in the vineyard last night. Some bunches were enormous, almost as large as myself, and so heavy! I knew not how I should carry them. I was told that it was the vineyard of bishops, and I saw the bunch of each one. I had to attend to about ten. I remember our Vicar-General, the Bishop of Ermeland, and one who has not come (*a future one*). I had to pick out the spoiled grapes. I was puzzled how to carry those huge bunches, but I remembered that, when a child, I used to put great bundles of fodder far larger than myself on my head and, bending under their weight, run along with them; so I slipped under the bunch and, and as I was afraid of bruising it, I spread leaves and moss over it. I succeeded in getting it into the tub but, to my dismay, I found that it had not escaped a bruise. I was reassured, however, on being told that it was to be so. I did it all in constant prayer. I was allowed to eat three grapes from three different bunches; the Vicar-General's was one of them, but I know not what it means."

August 8th—" Last night I did some troublesome work on the vines at Coesfeld; they were in a miserable condition, almost all the fruit half-decayed. I found few truly pious Christians, the ecclesiastics were in a tavern. In one place I passed some people who insulted me, though at the same time they sent me to do their work. I saw old N, who is always in the clouds whilst things go to ruin around him."

August 10th—"I had to work hard last night in the vineyard, on account of the want of charity among the clergy. I had to endure the same fatigue as St. Clare of Montefalco in her garden. She was with me and showed me a bed full of plants. In the centre were mignonette and an aromatic plant that flourishes in warm countries; outside were smooth-leaved herbs with long thorns. I knew not how to get across this hedge. Clare told me to dash bravely through it and I should have all the plants in the centre as a reward. She related many incidents of her own life. I saw her as a child kneeling in prayer by a rose-bush. The Infant Jesus appeared and gave her a written prayer which she wanted to keep; but it was taken from her. I know some of this prayer: ' I salute thee, O Mary, through the sweet Heart of Jesus! I salute thee, O Mary, for the deliverance of all the poor souls! I salute thee, O Mary, through all the Seraphim and Cherubim!'— between each of these invocations, she kissed the ground. The last part was beautiful, but I have forgotten it. One of Clare's practices was to kiss her hand when in company, and recall to mind that she was but dust and ashes. I crossed the hedge, but not without scratches; the pain was so acute that I cried aloud. Then Clare left me, and Frances of Rome appeared. She told me what horrible torments she had endured, but as St. Alexis had helped her she was going to help me. Her malady had been the same as that of the Canaanite woman who touched the hem of Our Lord's robe. Alexis threw his mantle over her and bade her read that passage in the Gospel which related to the miracle. She promised that I should soon be relieved."

Sister Emmerich had the following vision of this

wonderful cure at the same hour it had actually been
wrought in St. Frances.

July 17—"I saw," she said, "St. Frances of Rome. She
was married, but still young. She was lying in bed praying,
for she had been ill for a long time; an elderly female
slept near by. It was early dawn, when suddenly her
room was lit up and St. Alexis in the garb of a pilgrim, approached her bed, holding a book like the golden book of
the Gospels which his mother had given him. I am not
certain that it was the same book or only one like it. I
think the latter more probable. The saint called Frances by
name. She started up in bed, and he told her that he was
Alexis and that he had come to, cure her, adding that he
had found salvation in the book he had in his hand. Then
he held it open before her and bade her read. I do not
remember distinctly what followed, but Frances was cured
and the saint vanished. She arose, awoke the woman, who
was amazed to see her up and well, and they went at daybreak to the Church of St. Alexis to bless God in His
saints."

August 11th—"Last night again I lay all alone in the
thorns of the vineyards, which signify priests void of charity.
I awoke, thanks to God, about three o'clock."

August 12th—"Last night I toiled in the vineyard. St.
Clare was there encouraging and consoling me as I lay upon the slanting branches which gave me great pain. She
told me that every sharp knot in them signified the rector
of a parish, and that grapes would grow out of them, if I
lovingly offered for those priests my sufferings in union
with Jesus. Then I saw numerous parishes profiting by it."

Sept. 5th, whilst in ecstasy, she said: "From Mary's
Nativity till the Feast of St. Michael, I shall have to labor
and travel. Angels from all parts have come for me I

am needed in so many places! I was told last night that in many parishes in which I had pulled up the weeds and nettles, tied up and pruned the vine branches, the fruit had begun to ripen, but that robbers and wild beasts were roaming through the vineyards, and that I must enclose them by my labor in prayer. I saw the vintage flourishing by my labor, the grapes ripening, and the red juice flowing to the ground from the wine-presses. That signified that when good people aspire to holiness, they have to struggle and endure persecution and temptation. I was told that I had weeded and manured, but that I must now raise a hedge that they (*these struggling souls*) may not fall a prey to temptation and persecution. It is time for the grapes to ripen, they must be protected. Then I saw innumerable parishes for which I had to do the same between Mary's Nativity and Michaelmas."

Sept. 7th—" I was taken to my vineyard and reproved for not having hedged it in. I carried weeds to the mill and then left. I was so glad to be well again, and I did not continue my prayer. I had to pile up the rubbish and make a hedge with thistles to protect the vineyard. Again I saw the whole vineyard of St. Liborius, with all the gardens that compose it, and also the fruit of my labors; in the villages many conversions, in the city few. The church in which Liborius rests is quite deserted, as if in the hands of Protestants. By prayer I had to enclose the vineyards with dense hedges. God has mercifully shown me the *signification of the vine and its fruits.* The vine is Jesus Christ in us. The wild branches must be pruned in a certain way that they may not absorb the sap which is to become the grape, the wine, the Sacrament, the Blood of Jesus Christ, a Blood which has purchased our sinful blood, which will cause it to rise again, to pass from death to life. This pruning of the vine by certain rules is spiritually the cutting away of superfluities and the mortification of the flesh, that what is holy in us may increase, flourish, and produce fruit; otherwise, corrupt nature will bring forth only wood and leaves. The pruning must be done by rule, because only the superfluous elements of human nature, of which I was shown an almost infinite number, are to be destroyed; anything more would be sinful mutilation. The stock itself is not retrenched. It was planted in humanity in the person of the Blessed Virgin, and it will last till the end of time : yes, eternally—for it is with Mary in heaven. The signification of many other fruits was shown me. I saw a spiritual tree of colored light. The soil on which it stood was like a mountain in the air or a rock of colored crystal. The trunk was a stream of yellow light. The twigs, the branches, even the fibres of the leaves, were threads of light, more or less delicate, of various forms and colors, and the leaves were green and yellow light. It had three rows of branches, one below, one in the middle, and one above, surrounded by three angelic choirs. On the top stood a seraph veiled with his wings, who waved his sceptre in different directions. The highest choir received through the seraph effusions of light and strength from God, like a heavenly, fruitful dew. This uppermost choir and the one below it labored, acted without stirring from their places. They transmitted directions to the lowest choir at the foot of the tree, whose angels bore spiritual gifts into innumerable gardens; for every fruit had its own garden in which it was propagated according to its variety. This tree was the tree of God, and the gardens were the different kinds of fruit produced by it. Below, on the earth, were the same kinds of fruits, but tainted in their fallen nature, more or less poisoned, because the guilty use made of them had subjected them to the influence of the planetary spirits. In the centre of each garden I saw a tree covered with all the varieties of its kind which grew around it. I saw pictures indicating the essence and signification of the plants. *I saw the meaning of their name in universal language.* Wonderful is the saints' influence over plants! They seem to deliver them from the curse and power of the planetary spirits and, by certain religious invocations, render them remedies in sickness. As they become antidotes against diseases which I see as corporal sins in this lower, earthly region, so in the heavenly gardens are they antidotes against faults and sins which I there see as spiritual sickness. In each garden there stood a small house or tent which, too, had its signification. I saw that bees here play an important part. Some were very large, others quite small, their members transparent, as if formed of light, the legs like rays, the wings silver—I cannot describe it. There were hives in the orchards in which they worked—all was transparent. I have received information on the bees, their work and its signification morally and physically, but I have forgotten it. I was taken into several orchards and I saw wonderful things. I knew and understood everything *before I was tormented.* I was told, for instance, that nuts signify combat and persecution in vision, as well as in everyday life; therefore, I often see them growing around the Church and even gathered and given to others. I saw around the nut-gardens visions of strife, single combatants, and whole armies struggling. I saw two men beating each other, neither gaining any advantage until one threw sand into the other's eyes, and so won the victory, though not without a final effort on the part of the vanquished—the whole scene was ridiculous! The men were dressed as at the present day. I knew what it all meant and its relation to the several kinds of nuts. I learned that the mystery of strife and persecution signified by the nuts in the spiritual garden, became after the fall of man and by the power of the evil spirit, the combat of hatred, the origin of homicide. In each garden I was taken into the house, as if I were sick, and I was shown how the nature and secret virtue of fruits gathered in certain states, with certain consecrations, and mingled with other ingredients, were very efficacious in such or such ailments. Unfortunately, I can remember only a little of it: for instance, I understood why, on St. John the Baptist's day, the green nuts should be marked with a cross and allowed to remain on the tree until after a rain when, preserved in honey, they are excellent for weak stomachs. This preparation was explained to me in detail, but I have forgotten it; at the time I understood it all clearly, but now it is incomprehensible to finite intelligence. Again I learned that the oil of nuts is hurtful (her own word " poisonous"), and I knew the reason; but it loses its poisonous qualities, if we cook a morsel of bread in it. I saw a secret relation between it and John the Baptist: the cross made on the nuts, their exposure to the rain, and the power they thus acquire to cure the stomach, refer to the saint's Baptism and his labors as Precursor, the oil to the anointing and sacerdotal consecration. With regard to the baneful influence of the nut-tree's shade, I have had experience of it. I never could stay under the shade of such a tree in our cloister, although the other Sisters could work and wash there quite comfortably. I always had a smothering, oppressive feeling, and I preferred being in the hot sun. I understood all about apples and I saw that like nuts they refer to different things. I saw something about one with six red pips, one of which administered in a certain way and in certain maladies could restore health to the dying. Before the apple-orchard, I had a vision referring to fruit which looked like lemons; perhaps they really were lemons. I saw in Rome a holy person lying ill, and by her one of these fruits. I think she had had a vision on the subject. A slave, for some fault, had been thrown into a pit full of venomous serpents. The saint gave the apple to her physician to give to the poor slave for his cure and, by virtue of the same, he was healed of the serpents' bites. I saw him afterward led before the Emperor. I saw something of the same kind concerning another of these fruits which, cooked in milk and honey, was a cure for the most violent fevers. I saw something about a Feast of the Blessed Virgin, I think the Immaculate Conception, and also the way in which the knowledge of it was spread. I saw something about figs, but I cannot remember what it meant. They are an excellent remedy when used with a certain kind of apple, but by themselves they are hurtful. When so used, the apple must be weighed. The fig and apple hung side by side on the celestial tree which, under the angelic choirs, was covered with all kinds of spiritual fruit. I saw many things concerning the fruit of the tree of original sin in Paradise. The tree had a huge trunk and arose in a sharp, tapering point; but after the fall it inclined toward the earth. The branches took root and sent forth new shoots whose branches did the same, until the tree soon formed a whole forest. In warm, eastern countries people live under them. The boughs have no branches, they bear great shield-like leaves which hide the fruit, growing five together in a bunch; one has to hunt for them. They are tart, not pleasant as they used to be, and yellow, streaked with blood-red veins. I had a vision of peaches. I saw that, in the country to which they are indigenous, they are accursed, deadly poisonous. The people by the aid of witchcraft, extract from them cursed juice to excite lust. They bury them in the ground with dung, then distil them with certain ingredients. I saw that by its use they fall into the most abominable practices, and all who eat of the fruit became raving maniacs, because it is accursed. I saw some unsuspecting strangers entering the country. The Persians offered them some of it in order to destroy them, but God rendered it harmless. I saw these fruits taken to foreign lands for evil purposes, but they were hurtful only in their own country. I saw two kinds, one grew like osiers with delicate branches. I was, also, in a cherry-orchard, and I was shown that cherries signify ingratitude, adultery, and treason, for that is the nature of sweet fruit with a hard, bitter kernel. Of the laurel-tree, I saw that a certain emperor always wore a laurel crown during a storm that he might not be struck by lightning, and I was told, —yes, and I saw it, too, that the perfume of this tree possesses a virtue against storms. I saw some reference to the Blessed Virgin in it ; all was distinct and wonderful. I saw the secret virtue of plants before man's fall; but Adam's sin infected all nature, for plants as well as men then fell under the influence of the planetary spirits. I saw many of the secret properties which paganism used and abused ; but they were afterward regenerated and purified by Jesus Christ and His Church in their struggle against the planetary spirits."

In August and September, 1821, Sister Emmerich's labors introduced her to wheat-fields. One day she said : "I am worn out and bruised by the rough work I have done in the fields of some people I know. I had to sow and plough. I had no horses, and the plough, no handle. They were fields belonging to the Church ; some had grain, others none. I had to gather seeds from the best fields and pre-pare the others to receive it." Then, in the rustic dialect of her country, she described farming and farm utensils, which the Pilgrim could not understand, and she related besides the enemy's attempts to hinder her work:—" Satan struck me so violently, as if with a trowel, that I screamed aloud, and next morning I found my chemise stuck to the wound the blow had made just above the sign on my right side."—She was not discouraged by the enemy's artifices, but boldly undertook a still more severe labor. She had to stow away the harvest in numberless barns, the immensity of the labor being greatly disproportioned to the time allotted for it; and she was obliged to reap the grain so hurriedly that she thought every moment she would sink from fatigue. Still she reached the end of her task. She had to reap, bind, and thresh the wheat, put the grain into sacks, separate the seed-corn from that for present use. She worked fast as if in dread of a heavy storm that would destroy the whole crop. The labor succeeded, but she was too ex-hausted to explain its signification; she only said : " I saw so many ears that had not been reaped, that I ran to help. I saw all clearly, the people, the task imposed, the neglect, all that was wanting. The vision gave me a clea and rapid perception of the case, because I know all about field-labors, having been so engaged when a child. I prayed whilst I worked, for by prayer I knew who were suffering and strug-gling with me, and it seemed as if I often sent my angel to obtain their help. I had visions in which were shown me the cowardly, the slothful, the negligent, the wavering, whose place I had to take. I saw here and there some weak ecclesiastics on the point of spoiling everything, by hesitating *to sign*, to regulate something either good or bad ; and by prayer I had to force them, as it were, to choose the right, to defend the good, to repudiate evil. It was all clear and natural at the time, but now I cannot recall it."

Her task often took the form of repairing and cleaning all kinds of church ornaments. Sometimes she had to gather up the linen from the neighboring parishes, carry it to the cathedral cloister (Münster), and there in the midst of constant interruptions, wash, bleach, iron, and mend it, that it might be ready for the service of the altar. At other times her attention was given to chasubles, maniples, and stoles that had to be made over. " Such a task," she said, " is a symbolical image of prayer for the clergy. It has the same signification, the same effect as these sacred vestments have for the Church and her ministers." At the end of a most painful task of the kind, she received the following instruction upon it :—" I must not wonder at my sufferings. I had a great, indescribable vision of sin, the reparation through Jesus, and the state of the priesthood, and I understood how with infinite toil and pains all that is spoiled, destroyed, or lost must be restored and turned again into the way of salvation. I have had an immense, connected vision of the Fall and Redemption. It would take a year to relate it, for I saw and understood all mysteries clearly and distinctly ; but I cannot explain it. I was in the Nuptial House and I saw in its numerous apartments all forms of sin and reparation. I saw sin from the fall of the angels and Adam down to the present, in its numberless ramifications, and at the same time I beheld all the preparations for its reparation to the coming of Jesus and His death on the cross. I saw His power transmitted to priests in what related to the remedy and how every Christian shares in Jesus Christ. I saw the imperfections, the decay of the priesthood, and their cause, also the chastisements awaiting them and the efficacy of expiatory sufferings, and I felt by my pains the strict bond existing between the fault and its atonement. I saw a future war, many dangers and sufferings in store for me. All these varied instructions and revelations of history, nature, and the mysteries of God's kingdom upon earth, appeared to me in perfect order, following one another, arising from one another clearly and intelligibly. All were explained to me in parables of labor and tasks, whilst suffering, satisfaction, and reparation were shown me under the form of sewing. I have had to rip others' work, as well as my own, and do it over with great pains and trouble. I had to examine what was crooked, see how it had happened, and patiently fix it straight. In the shape of different articles, in the various kinds of sewing, in the trimming, and the careless way in which it was all done, I saw the origin and consequence of every sin; in the repairing of it, I saw the effect of spiritual suffering and labor in prayer. I recognized work belonging to deceased persons, my former acquaintances, work which had actually been done and which was now brought to me to do over again. I had, also, to rip some of my own sewing: for example, an undergarment which I had embroidered too richly to gratify a vain woman, and other things of the kind; but my work for the Church and the poor was good. I went into the Nuptial House as if to a school, and there my Spouse explained everything to me, showing me in great historical pictures all He had done to repair the sin of Adam. I saw all as going on under my eyes; and yet at the same time it seemed as if I beheld it in a mirror, which mirror was myself.

"My Affianced explained to me how all things had deteriorated since the Fall, all had become impure. When the angels fell, innumerable bad spirits came upon the earth and filled the air. I saw many things infected by their malice, and possessed by them in various ways.

" The first man was like heaven. He was an image of
God. In him was unity and his form was a reproduction of
the Divine Model. He was to receive and enjoy creatures,
accepting them from God and returning thanks for
them. He was free and, therefore, was he subjected to
trial. The Garden of Eden with all it contained was a perfect picture of the kingdom of God. So too was the Tree of
Knowledge. Its fruit, on account of its essence, its properties, and effects, was not to be eaten by man since he
would thereby become an independent being, having his
principle of action in himself; he would abandon God to
concentrate himself in himself, so that the finite would compass
the infinite ; therefore was he forbidden to eat its fruit—
I cannot explain how I saw this. When the shining hill
upon which Adam stood in Paradise arose, when was hollowed out the bright flowering vale in which I beheld Eve,
the corrupter was already near. After the Fall, all was
changed, divided, dispersed ; what had been one became
many, creatures looked no longer to God alone, each was
concentrated in self. At first, there were two, they increased to three, and finally, to an infinite number. They
wanted to be one like unto God, but they became a multitude. Separating from God, they reproduced themselves
in infinite varieties. From images of God they became
images of themselves, bearing the likeness of sin. They
entered into communication with the fallen angels ; they
participated in the fruits of the earth already tainted by
these spirits. This indiscriminate blending of things, this
division in man and fallen nature gave birth to endless sins
and miseries. My Spouse showed me all this clearly, distinctly, intelligibly, more clearly than one sees the ordinary
things of life. I thought at the time that a child might
comprehend it, but now I am unable to repeat it. I saw

the whole plan of Redemption from the very beginning. It is not perfectly correct to say that God need not have become man, nor died for us upon the cross, that He could have redeemed us otherwise in virtue of His omnipotence. I saw that He did what He did in His infinite goodness, mercy, and justice. There is, indeed, no compulsion in God. He does what He does, He is what He is!—I saw Melchisedech as angel, as symbol of Jesus, as priest on earth ; inasmuch as the priesthood is in God, he was like an angel, a priest of the eternal hierarchy. I saw him prepare, found, separate the human family and serve them as a guide. I saw, too, Enoch and Noe, what they represented, what they effected ; on the other side, I saw the influence of the kingdom of hell, the infinitely varied manifestations and effects of an earthly, carnal, diabolical paganism, corrupting virtue through a secret, inborn necessity. In this way I saw sin and the foreshadowing, the prophetic figures of Redemption which, in their way, were the images of divine power as man himself is the image of God. All were shown me from Abraham to Moses, from Moses to the prophets, all as symbols of our own time, as connected with our own time. Here followed an explanation why priests no longer relieve or cure, why it is either not in their power, or why it is now effected so differently from what it used to be. I saw this same gift possessed by the prophets and the meaning of the form under which it was exercised ; for instance, I saw the history of Eliseus giving his staff to Giezi to lay upon the dead son of the Sunamitess. Eliseus's mission and power lay spiritually in the staff, which was his arm, the continuation of his arm, that is his power. In connection with this, I saw the interior signification and effects of a bishop's crozier and a monarch's sceptre if used with faith which, in a certain way, binds them together, separating them from all others. But Giezi's faith was weak and the mother thought that her prayer could be answered only by Eliseus in person. Between the power bestowed by God upon Eliseus and his staff, there intervened human doubts, so that the latter lost its efficacy. But I saw Eliseus stretch himself hand to hand, mouth to mouth, breast to breast upon the boy and pray, and the child's soul returned to his body. This form of healing was explained to me as referring to and prefiguring the death of Jesus. In Eliseus, by faith and the gift of God, were all the avenues of grace and expiation opened again in man which had been closed since his fall in Adam : viz., the head, the breast, the hands, the feet. Eliseus stretched himself as a living, symbolical cross upon the dead, closed cross of the boy's form, and through his prayer of faith, life and health were restored. He expiated, he atoned for the sins his parents had committed by their head, heart, hands, and feet, sins which had brought death to their boy. Side by side with the above, I saw pictures of the Wounds and death of Jesus, as also the harmony, the conformity existing between the figure and the reality. After the crucifixion of Jesus I saw in the priesthood of His Church the rich gift of repairing and curing. In the same proportion as we live in Him and are crucified with Him, are the avenues of grace, His Sacred Wounds, open to us. I learned many things of the imposition of hands, the efficacy of a benediction, and the influence exerted by the hand even at a distance —all was explained by the staff of Eliseus. That priests of the present day so seldom cure and bless, was shown me in an example significant of the conformity to Jesus upon which all such effects depend. I saw three painters making figures in wax : the first used beautiful white wax very skilfully

and intelligently, but he was full of himself ; he had not
the likeness of Christ in him, and so his figures were of no
value. The second used bleached wax ; but he was indolent
and self-willed, he did nothing well. The third was unskilful
and awkward, but he worked away earnestly on common wax
—his work was good, a speaking likeness though with coarse
features. And so did I see renowned preachers vaunting
their worldly wisdom, but doing nothing ; whilst many a
poor, unlettered man retains the priestly power of blessing
and curing.

" It seemed all the time as if I were going to the Nuptial
House to school. My Affianced showed me how He had
suffered from His conception till His death, always expiating, always satisfying for sin. I saw it also in pictures of
His life. I saw that by our prayer and suffering, many a
soul who labors not during life, can be converted and saved
at the hour of death.

" I saw the Apostles sent over the greater part of the
earth to scatter benedictions and to cast down Satan's power,
a power which Jesus by His full atonement acquired and
secured forever to such priests as had received or who
would receive His Holy Spirit. The countries in which
they labored were those which had been most con-
taminated by the enemy, and I was shown that the power
of withdrawing various regions from Satan's dominion
by the sacerdotal benediction, is signified by these words :
' *Ye are the salt of the earth.*' It is for the same reason
that salt is put into holy water. That these countries did
not persevere in Christianity, that they are now lying uncultivated, I saw also as a wise dispensation of Divine
Providence. They were only to be blessed, prepared for a
future time, in order that being again sowed they may
bring forth magnificent fruits when other countries shall

lie desolate, when other lands shall lie uncultivated. I saw that David understood the plan of Redemption ; but Solomon did not, for he took too much complacency in his wisdom. Many prophets, especially Malachias, comprehended the mystery of Christianity. I saw innumerable things, all inwardly related, all following one another naturally. Whilst I was thus instructed, I saw about twenty other persons in various positions, some walking, others lying down, who seemed to be taking part in the same instruction. They were all far distant from me and from one another, and there were more women than men. Communicating rays from the pictures fell upon them, but each one received them differently. I wanted to speak to them, but I could not reach them. I thought : 'Now, I should like to know if they receive this light in its purity,' when I saw that, unfortunately, all changed it in something. I thought: ' *I do not mix anything with it,*'—when, on a sudden, a tall female appeared to me, one long deceased, and showed me a garment of her own making. Around the neck and sleeves the sewing was beautiful, but the rest was very badly done. I thought: ' See, what work! No, no, I never sewed like this !'—when I was made to feel that I, too, mixed things up, that I was vain, and that this very work, some parts good, others bad, was symbolical of the manner in which I had received this instruction. The thought troubled me. I saw, too, in this vision, that the punctilios of sensual, worldly life are most scrupulously observed, that the *malediction* (the so-called benediction and miracles in the kingdom of Satan), the worship of nature, superstition, magic, mesmerism, worldly art and science, and all the means employed for smoothing over death, for making sin attractive, for lulling the conscience, are practised with rigorous exactitude even to fanaticism by those

very men who look upon the Church's mysteries as superstitious forms for which any others may be indifferently
substituted. And yet these men subject their whole life and
all their actions to certain ceremonies and observances; it is
only of the kingdom of the God-Man that they make no
account. The service of the world is practised in perfection,
but the service of God is shamefully neglected! Ah!
if souls should ever claim what is owed them by the
clergy, through whose carelessness and indifference they
have lost so much, what a terrible reckoning there would
be!"

The nearer the ecclesiastical year drew to its close, the
more painful and multiplied became Sister Emmerich's
spiritual labors. As each different period approached its
term, the heavier became her task of satisfying for the
offences offered to God by the omissions and negligence of
His servants. This was plainly visible in her increase of
fatigue and suffering, since she had to expiate for the
whole mass of the faithful not only their abuse of the means
of salvation within their reach, but also their culpable loss
of time. There is no created good so lightly esteemed, so
carelessly trifled away by an immense majority of human
beings as the fugitive moments of this short life so rapidly
flying toward eternity. For this blindness Sister Emmerich
did sharp penance, expiating for many who without her aid
would never have attained salvation. The following vision
presents a symbolical picture of the abundant blessings
flowing from her labors in prayer:—

"Last night I was in the Nuptial House. I found
there three wild cows, plunging and raging. I had to milk
them. With immense fatigue I had to draw milk from my
own face, hands, feet, and side, and put it into a large pail
for people of all ranks. I was told: 'These people have

dissipated their gifts, and now they are in want ; but thou hast laid up so many treasures from the Church, that thou canst indemnify them for what they have lost. . . . .'

"I went again with my guide to the Nuptial House, and again I was told to milk the three cows. They had now grown quite gentle, and their litter was so clean that one might have slept on it. I milked first from the middle one and then from the other two three large pails full which I had to carry to a place where it was measured out by priests into small vessels which they counted. Many received it, priests, school-masters and mistresses. It even flowed around outside of the house. I asked my guide why none was kept in the house and why I always had to do the milking. I was told not to ask questions, but to do as I was bid; that I should obey like Isaac whom Abraham answered not when questioned regarding the sacrifice; that the milk will be distributed, because the female sex bears no fruit, it is not fitted for it, it only receives, preserves, fosters; and that the fruits of my labor were to be propagated by the priesthood. 'Thou must milk, and not question. The priests will distribute it, through them it becomes fruitful. . . . .' They brought me a poor, miserable cow which I thought was about to die. It stuck up close to me, I could not get it away. Not knowing what to do with it, I invoked Mary who instantly appeared and said to me : 'Take care of the poor animal. It comes alone, because its keeper, who ought to work and pray for it, demands not for it any one's assistance.' Then she told me with what I should feed it, prayers, sufferings, self-victories, alms, etc., all shown under the form of plants and fruits. I had so miserable a night from colic and other pains that I cried. At last, when quite worn out, I took some blessed oil which relieved me. . . .'

"Again, I had to busy myself in the stable of the Nuptial House, cleaning and feeding the cows; my feet were bare and I dreaded the dirt. The stable was so crowded that I had to push my way through, holding on to the cows; but they did not hurt me, and I had many souls to help me. It was always the Mother of God, however, who gave advice and directions, pointing out this or that herb for this or that cow, and showing me a bitter one for a cow that was too fat. I milked none to-day, but I had, in my bare feet among stones and briers, to gather all kinds of herbs, for all had to be done with suffering and love. When I invoke her the Mother of God always appears as an apparition in the air, tall, majestic, white as snow, her light robe unconfined at the waist and formed from top to bottom of pure rays or folds. Although no corporal figure is visible, nevertheless this apparition impresses one with its majestic, supernatural bearing. . . . . .

"I went into the vineyard of the Nuptial House and found there all the children for whom I had worked, whom I had clothed. They were entwined among the vines and growing with them. The boys were just above the knots of the vine, their hands and feet twisted in the branches, their arms extended in the form of a cross. From them grew branches laden with grapes. The girls bore no grapes, but great ears of wheat. Here I had to work hard ; for, entangled around the wheat and grapes were two kinds of weeds against which the Lord had warned the bridegrooms of Sichar to guard in the cultivation of the fields and vineyards. They can easily be cleared from the vines, but not from the wheat. I took what the girls produced, crushed the grains between my hands, ground them with a stone, sifted the flour, which seemed too coarse, through very fine gauze, and took it to the sacristy of the church along with a whole cask of wine which I had made from the grapes. I was told what it all signified, but my pains were so great that I forgot it. Then I saw religious going out of the vineyard into the different houses of their Order ; among them were many for whom I had made clothes, whom I had prepared for school, for confession and Communion. The girls from whom I had taken the wheat to grind and to make into bread, became nuns : the boys, who bore the grapes for the Church that the wine should be changed into the Blood of the Lord as the bread into His Body, entered the priesthood. Wheat is heavier, more material, and signifies nourishment, it is flesh ; wine is spirit, wine is blood." As Sister Emmerich related the above, she spoke also of the great dangers that menaced the Church, urging the Pilgrim to unite with her in prayer, renunciation, and mortification, and to endeavor to overcome himself, saying : " It often happens that I cannot approach the Pilgrim. I am held back, my soul is restrained. It certainly comes from our sins."

" When later I returned to the Nuptial House, I found in two separate halls the youths and maidens who were to enter different Orders. They were the children of the vine. They had already been replaced by others. In both halls I saw an apparition of the Mother of God seated on a throne. The halls were full of magnificent, shining, heavenly fruits which the future religious took with them when they left the house and scattered throughout the Church. The children of the vine are all those whom I clothed and directed during my life."

Sister Emmerich's labors, as we have already remarked, were accompanied by uninterrupted physical sufferings, the most excruciating and varied. To encourage herself, she used often to say : " Now is a holy time, the new ecclesias-

tical year is approaching, and the old one bears with it
many faults that must be redeemed by suffering. I have
much work to do, and so I must suffer." She often lay
as if at the point of death. One day, feeling a chilly sensation around her heart, she requested her sister to apply
a warm cloth ; but the latter did so only after having steeped
it in hot wine which brought on most painful vomitings.

On November 27th, she awoke from ecstasy with a cry
of pain, the blood gushing from the wound in her side.
" I saw," she said, " high above me a resplendent figure from
which streamed rays of light. They met in a sharp arrow
and pierced my side. I cried out with the pain. For some
days I have constantly had before me a double picture of the
Church, the Church Triumphant treating with the Church
Militant. The former I see as a beautiful, heavenly church
on a mountain of precious stones. In it are holy pastors
and angels making entries on tablets and rolls of parchment,
which seem to be the accounts of the Church Militant, the
faults and omissions of the clergy and the faithful, faults
and omissions which abound everywhere. Then I have
pictures of the innumerable shortcomings of priests and their
neglect of their flocks. I see people ill-prepared kneeling
at the Communion Table. I see others left without consolation in the confessional. I see negligent priests, soiled altar
ornaments. I see the sick not consoled or receiving the
holy Viaticum too late, relics disrespectfully thrown around,
etc. Then I sigh ardently to remedy these evils. I implore God
to satisfy His justice on me, to accept my good will in reparation for the faults of other weak members of the Church,
and I unite my sufferings to the inexhaustible, superabundant sufferings of Christ. I see sin effaced by the angels and
saints, and the omissions of priests in the service of God and
the salvation of souls supplied in most wonderful ways. . . .

" The Mother of God has divided the task among seven persons, most of them females. I see among them the stigmatisée of Cagliari and Rosa Maria Serra, as also others whom I cannot name. I see too a Franciscan in the Tyrol and a priest in a religious house among the mountains ; the latter suffers unspeakably from faults committed in the Church. I, too, received my share. I know my pains, their cause and effect. I shall have to suffer the whole week."

December 2d-—" Till noon to-day," says the Pilgrim, " she suffered intensely throughout her whole person. Her hands were icy-cold, she looked like one who had died on the rack. The pains in her head were the most violent, but she endured all with loving patience. 'Last night,' she said, 'I saw St. Bibiana. She did not help me, but she was so kind and the sight of her sufferings gave me strength for my own. I had a vision of the different kinds of martyrdom. I saw the holy martyrs piling up all sorts of instruments of torture until they formed a high and wonderful tower on the summit of which appeared the cross ; then with the Blessed Virgin Mary at their head they surrounded this trophy of their victories. I saw, too, all who had suffered like myself and all who now, at the close of the ecclesiastical year, are sharing with me the task of expiation. I saw myself pierced from head to foot with thorns. I have constant visions of the two Churches, Triumphant and Militant, and I must labor for three places in which all goes wrong. My last work was to gather honey from thistles, a heavy, painful task. I began by gathering figs from thorns, I ended with honey from thistles. There is a small, white worm in the large ripe thistle heads which possesses virtue against fever and rheumatism, and especially incurable earaches. It is to be bound on the pulse of children, but taken internally by adults."

This worm she had mentioned before. She described it as solitary and not found in all thistles. Toward evening her pains ceased at the same hour they had commenced eight days previously. She fell into a state of utter prostration, and sank as if without consciousness into a light slumber of a few instants. Her whole appearance had in it something singularly sweet, lovely, and childlike. The water which was offered her she refused with a smile, saying " No, I dare not pour water on my pains. They might return. I see them going."

December 3d—She is still exhausted by pain and tormented by domestic cares ; nevertheless she made an effort to relate the following vision which she had had the preceding night :—

CLOSE OF THE ECCLESIASTICAL YEAR.

" I had a great vision in which I beheld accounts settled between the Church Triumphant and the Church Militant. The former was not a building, but an assembly of the blessed. The Most Holy Trinity appeared above them as the living Fountain of all, with Jesus on the right and Mary just below, the choirs of saints and martyrs on the left. Around Jesus were the instruments of His Passion and pictures of His life. The latter related especially to the mysteries of God's mercy and the history of Redemption, whose feasts are commemorated in the Church Militant. I saw Our Lord's temporal and redeeming life as the source of all the graces that flow upon us, inasmuch as the Church Militant mystically celebrating its mysteries, gratefully appropriates them and renews them among her children by the Holy Sacrifice and the Divine Eucharist. I saw the never-failing, outflowing streams of the Most Holy Trinity and the Passion of Christ, and their influence over all crea-

tion. I saw the immense results of Christ's journey through
Arabia before His Passion, when He promised the nations of
the Three Kings that some one should come to baptize them,
and pointed out to them a country to which they should remove, there to become a separate nation. He seemed to
refer to a land in which they should have priests and teachers. I saw the journey they made at a later period toward
the south-west, not the whole nation, but about one hundred
men in separate bands. They bore with them the bodies of
their dead chiefs. I saw them distinctly. They were
clothed with flesh and habited in the style of their country,
the hands and feet bare, the raiment white. The wives of
these Arabs followed them later when they had founded a
settlement. I saw them increase and become a nation.
There was a Bishop among them who had formerly been a
goldsmith. The eagerness of these people to receive his
instructions and the purity of their lives, so different from
those among whom they dwelt, gave him great consolation.
I recognized the descendants of the races that had offered
gold, frankincense, and myrrh.

" I saw all the feasts of Our Lord's life to the descent of
the Holy Ghost. I learned that on this day when her
cycle recommences, the Church receives the Holy Spirit
in her pure and well prepared members in proportion to
each one's desire. Whoever wishes lovingly and zealously
to repair whatever might be an obstacle to the general reception of the Holy Spirit, will endure sufferings for Jesus
and, uniting them to His merits, offer them for this intention. Every one can draw down upon himself the effusions of the Holy Ghost, in such measure as his love and
self-offering participate in the sacrifice of Jesus. I saw
the effusion of the Holy Spirit over the works of the
Apostles, disciples, martyrs, and saints. Suffering gladly

for Jesus, they suffered in Jesus and in His Body, the Church, becoming thereby living channels of the grace flowing from His Passion—yes, they suffered in Jesus and Jesus suffered in them, and from Him sprang the good they rendered to the Church. I saw the multitudes converted by the martyrs. The martyrs were like canals dug out by *pains;* they bore to thousands of hearts the living blood of Redemption. The martyrs, teachers, intercessors, penitents appeared in the Church Triumphant as the substance of all graces profitable to the Church Milliant, which are renewed or of which she takes possession on the feasts of her saints. I saw in these visions their sufferings of short duration ; but their temporal effects, because they proceeded from the eternal mercy of God and the merits of Jesus Christ, I saw working on perpetually for good in the Church, kept alive by her feasts, lively faith, prayer, devotion, and good works. I saw the immense treasures of the Church and the little profit some of her members derive from them. It is like a luxuriant garden above a desert waste. The former sends down thousands and thousands of fertilizing influences which the latter rejects ; it remains a waste, and the rich treasures are prodigally squandered. I saw the Church Militant, the faithful, the flock of Christ in its temporal state upon earth, dark, dark, and desolate ; and the rich distribution of graces from on high received carelessly, slothfully, impiously. I saw the feasts celebrated with such apathy and levity that the graces flowing from them fell to the ground, the Church's treasures were turned into sources of condemnation. I saw all this in a general way and in a variety of pictures. Such negligence must be expiated by suffering; otherwise, the Church Militant, unable to settle accounts with the Church Triumphant, would fall. still lower. I saw the

Blessed Virgin putting everything in order. This was
the end of the task I had begun with her in the Nuptial
House on St. Catherine's day, that tiresome gathering of
fruits and herbs, bleaching of sacristy linen, and cleaning
of church ornaments. It is hard to describe, for nature,
man himself, has fallen so low, is in so constrained a position, man's senses are as it were so tightly bound, that
the visions in which I really act, which I understand, which
never surprise me at the time, appear to me when returned
to consciousness as strange as they do to others. I had, for instance, to press honey from thistles with my bare hands, and
carry it to the Blessed Virgin to pay off the balance of the
Church debt. She boils and refines it, and mixes it with
the food of those who are in need of it. This signifies that
during the ecclesiastical year the faithful have neglected or
squandered grace which a right use would have changed
into multiplied blessings, into sweet strengthening food for
which many poor souls are languishing. The Lord supplied all that was necessary from the Church Triumphant.
The Church Militant must now render an account, must pay
capital and compound interest too. In this account, the
honey had been omitted (God's grace appears in the natural
world under the form of honey) and it should have been represented. In the flowering season it might easily have been
gathered, a little care bestowed on the hives was all that was
needed; but now it can be procured only with suffering and
fatigue, for the flowers have disappeared, and thistles alone
are to be found. The merciful Jesus accepts the pains and
sufferings of some as an expiatory sacrifice for the omissions of
others, and with blood-stained hands had the honey to be extracted from the thistles. The Blessed Virgin, the Mother of
the Church, cooks and applies it where the gifts of grace, which
it typifies, have been wanting during the year. Thus was

my martyrdom accomplished during those days and nights by manifold labors in vision. The two Churches were ever before me and, as her debt was paid off, I saw the lower one issuing from its obscurity.

" I saw the members of the Church Militant as I had seen those of the Church Triumphant. I saw about one hundred thousand great in faith and simple in their actions. I saw six persons, three men and three women, working with me in the Church in the same manner as I do. The stigmatisee of Cagliari, Rosa Maria Serra, and a female laden with great bodily infirmities; the Franciscan of the Tyrol, whom I have often seen united in intention with me, and a young ecclesiastic in a house with other priests in a mountainous country. He grieves bitterly over the state of the Church and through God's grace, he endures extraordinary pains. He prays earnestly every evening to be allowed to expiate all the failings of the Church that day. The sixth of my fellow-laborers is a married man of high rank; he has a wicked, perverse wife and a large household of children and servants. He resides in a great city full of Catholics, Protestants, Jansenists, and Free-thinkers. His house is perfectly regulated; he is very charitable to the poor, and bears most nobly with his bad wife. There is a separate street for Jews in that city, closed at either end by gates. Immense traffic is carried on in it. My labors were mostly in the Nuptial House and garden. The visions in which I drew milk from all my members and which weakened me so, referred to my frequent effusions of blood on those days. Some of my tasks were under the form of washing. I remember one in particular: a so-called devotee who made profession of pious practices, ran to pilgrimages, etc., brought me his bundle. He had often asked why this one or that one did not do as he; consequently, he had a dream in which he saw many of those over whom he had gloried far above him in piety, and he was filled with confusion.

" When I had finished my work, I saw by the Saviour two large tablets on which were recorded all neglects and their expiation. All my labors were shown to me in figures and I saw whatever was lost. On one side were beautiful crowns, ornaments, and flowers, on the other faded garlands, garments slovenly made or only half-finished, and scraps of fruits and vegetables; on one side a pile of the most magnificent of God's gifts, on the other a heap of rubbish and potsherds. I was overcome by sorrow. I prostrated on the ground and wept bitterly for two whole hours. I felt that my heart would break. Then I was shown all this rubbish behind Jesus. He turned his back on it; but I still wept. The loving Saviour approached me and said: ' These tears alone were wanting ! I allowed thee to see all this that thou mightest not think thou hadst done anything of thyself; but now I take all upon My own shoulders!' I saw the six other laborers weeping in like manner and receiving the same consolation. Then I saw the Blessed Virgin extend her mantle over the Church and a crowd of the poor, the sick, and the lame raise it in some way, until it floated in the air clear and shining, where it met and united with the Church Triumphant. Jesus and the Apostles appeared in the upper choir and distributed the Holy Eucharist as a renewal of strength, and numerous souls, among them kings and princes, went from Abraham's bosom into the Church. I saw, above all, many a soul, thought to be among the saints, still in Abraham's bosom, not yet in possession of the vision of God, and I saw others going to heaven after one or two days' purification. I saw purgatory **in this vision as the Church Suffering, a vast, sombre cave** in which souls were paying off their debt. There was a dull glare in it, like candle-light, and a kind of altar. An angel comes several times a year to administer something strengthening to the poor sufferers, but when he retires everything church-like disappears with him. Although the poor souls cannot help themselves, yet they intercede for the Church. When I have visions of the Church as a whole, I always see to the north-west a deep, black abyss into which no ray of light enters, and I feel that that is hell. Afterward I saw a great feast in the Church and multitudes uniting in it. I saw several churches, or rather meeting-houses surmounted by weather-cocks, the congregations, disunited from the Church, running here and there like beggars hurrying to places where bread is distributed, having no connection with either the Church Triumphant or the Church Suffering. They were not in a regularly founded, living Church, one with the Church Militant, Suffering, and Triumphant, nor did they receive the Body of the Lord, but only bread. They who were in error through no fault of their own and who piously and ardently longed for the Body of Jesus Christ, were spiritually consoled, but not by their communion. They who habitually communicated without this ardent love received nothing ; but a child of the Church receives an immense increase of strength.''

December 4th—Sister Emmerich lay prostrate and miserable after her labors and sufferings of the last eight days with continual vomiting of blood, bleeding of her side, and bloody sweats, though she never ceased, day or night, making caps for poor children and lint for the Abbé Lambert. The greater part of several nights she passed in a sitting posture, her head resting on her knees. She was unable to lie down and still too weak to sit upright. Her heart and breast were torn with racking pains and the hot tears flowed copiously from her eyes, greatly aggravating her misery. Another vision showed her the Church after being purified with immense trouble and fatigue, again degraded and dishonored by faithless ministers. St. Barbara appeared and consoled her, reminding her that she, too, had labored and prayed in vain for the conversion of her own father. Then she had a vision on the state of several individuals among the clergy who fulfilled not their duty toward the souls intrusted to them. She saw that they would have to render an account for all the love, all the consolation, all the exhortations, all the instructions upon the duties of religion that they do not give their flock ; for all the benedictions that they do not distribute, although the power of the Hand of Jesus is in them ; and for all that they omit to do in imitation of Jesus. They will have to give a strict account to Jesus for their neglect of souls. For such pastors she had to undergo great trouble and fatigue, carrying them in spirit through water, and praying for such of them as were tempted.

St. Hildegarde and St. Catherine of Sienna often saw the Church under the form of a virgin or a matron, sick, persecuted, struck with leprosy, their spiritual labors assuming an analogous form ; and so, too, did Sister Emmerich find in the Nuptial House and its dependencies the Church symbolized under the form of a matron in various positions. In the last week of Advent, 1819, she related the following : " As I was going to Bethlehem, I found on the road to the Nuptial House an old matron covered with ulcers which she tried to conceal under her soiled mantle. I invoked St. Francis Xavier to overcome my repugnance, and I sucked her sores from which immediately streamed forth rays of light which shed their brilliancy all arou d.

The sucking of these wounds was wonderfully sweet and pleasant. A resplendent lady floated down from on high, took from the matron, who was now almost well, her old, stiff mantle, threw around her her own beautiful, shining one, and disappeared. The matron now shone with light and I took her into the garden of the Nuptial House, from which she had formerly been driven. It was whilst wandering around that she had fallen sick. I have never been able to get her any farther than the garden which I found overrun by weeds and the flowers nearly all dead, because the gardeners were not united. Each one gardened for himself alone. They did not consult the old man placed over them, they gave themselves no trouble about him. The poor old man was sick; he knew not of the spreading weeds until the thistles and brambles mounted up to his very windows. Then he gave orders for them to be rooted out. The matron who had received the mantle from the Mother of God carried a treasure in a box, a holy thing which she guarded without knowing clearly what it was. It is the mysterious spiritual authority of the Church with which they in the Nuptial House no longer want to have anything to do, which they no longer understood. But it will again silently increase, and they who resist will be driven from the house. All will be renewed."

During the above recital, the invalid had assumed a listening attitude as if in expectation of some one's approach. Suddenly she was rapt in ecstasy. She was with her Spouse whom she tenderly conjured to allow her to suffer for the matron and for "those three homeless women, wandering about with their poor children," symbols of the various denominations separated from the Church, wandering out of the sheep-fold.—" There," she exclaimed, still in ecstasy, " there I can suffer no more, there all is pure joy! Ah!

leave me here awhile longer, leave me here to be of service to my neighbor !" At this moment one of her fellow-religious with whom she had previously made an appointment, appeared at the door ; but seeing her in ecstasy, she was about to retire, when Sister Emmerich called out : " Here is a person who wants something. This is for her, and this for her landlady !"—and so saying, she took from the closet near the bed some packages of coffee, and handed them to her former companion. When the latter withdrew, Sister Emmerich began to thank God with signs of delight. " By this alms," she exclaimed,"I have obtained the deliverance of a poor soul from purgatory. I wanted as many as there were grains of coffee ; however, I got *one!*" And she gazed in rapture on the glory of the ransomed soul.

On Christmas, she related the following : " I was in the garden of the Nuptial House. The matron was there still sick, but trying to put things here and there in order. The sheep-fold had become a church, the nut-hedges around the stable were withered, the nuts dried up and empty (1). I saw blessed souls in antique priestly robes cleaning out the church, taking down the spider webs ; the door stood open and all was becoming brighter and brighter. It seemed as if the masters were doing the work of their servants, for the people in the Nuptial House, though making a great bustle, did nothing ; they were disunited and dissatisfied. They all expected to enter the church when in order, but some were to be excluded. The church continued to grow cleaner and brighter. Suddenly there spouted up a beautiful fountain. Its water pure as crystal, flowed out on all sides, through the walls, and into the garden, refreshing everything—all was blooming and joyous.

(1) Nuts signify discord.

Above it rose a shining spiritual altar, a pledge of future increase. The church and everything in it kept growing larger and larger, the saints continued their work, and the bustle in the Nuptial House became greater."

Of separate denominations, Sister Emmerich spoke as follows :—" I came across the house with the weathercock. People were going in and out with books in their hands ; there is no altar in it, all looks bare. I went through it. It is like a public highway, benches and seats thrown here and there—some have been stolen ; the roof is in a bad state, and through the rafters can be seen the blue sky. I saw two mothers covered with ulcers wandering around with two children by the hand, they seemed to be lost ; a third, the most wretched of all, lay with a little child near the dilapidated meeting-house, unable to move. These three women were not very old and not dressed like common people. They wore long, narrow garments which they seemed to draw around them in order to hide their sores. I saw that the children derived no strength from them ; but that, on the contrary, all the mothers' strength came from the children. The mothers were not what they ought to be, but the poor children were innocent. Homeless, they tottered along one after the other, tramping about everywhere, lodging miserably, and thus contracting disease. I saw them again later on in the night. I sucked their sores and bound them up with herbs. I wanted to take them to the church, but they were as yet too timid and they turned away. . . . . These Christians separated from the Church have no place near the Holy Sepulchre, although they now try to introduce themselves into such places. They have lost the priestly ordination and rejected the Holy Sacrifice of the Mass to their own great misfortune. . . . . . ."

" I spoke to the poor wanderers and their children. Surely they will soon be better off! They are like old trees sending up new shoots, for which reason they are not cut down. The children represent souls making efforts to return to the Church and to draw after them their famished mothers who are weak and wholly governed by them. The women nearest the church (the Catholic Church) have each two sprightly children by the hand whose every wish they follow; the third, lying sick on the road near the ruined meeting-house, has only one child, smaller than the others, but it is still a child, and she too will come. . . . . ."

"Again I met the two women with their four children nearer to the Nuptial House. The children would not be quieted. They dragged their mothers after them, but they would not go into the garden; they stood outside timid, frightened, and quite amazed at what they saw; they had never thought of such things. . . . I prayed again before the Crib for the poor mothers that they might, at last, enter the garden of the Nuptial House, and I saw the matron go out to look for them and coax them in. But she behaved so mysteriously, pretending to be only taking a walk; she looked so furtive and timid that I became anxious, especially when I saw that she wanted to go first to a shepherd not of the fold. I feared she had not her box with her, that consequently she was weak and the shepherd would be able to prevent her returning to the Nuptial House. I was so anxious for her to go straight up to the women! I went out to meet her and found, to my great relief, that she had her box with her, but I was sorry to see that she was not quite cured. Some of her wounds had healed too quickly, corruption was still within, and that was what had prevented her giving the invitation to the mothers properly; her timidity proceeded from it. She went not straight on in the name of Jesus. I spoke a

great deal with her, and I found that she was not full of
charity. She was so emphatic with regard to her rights,
her privileges, her possessions that one could easily see
she was not animated by that virtue. I asked her what
she had in the box. She answered: 'It is a mystery,
a holy thing.' She knew not what it was nor what use to
make of it, but kept it locked up. She was displeased at
my not curing her perfectly. I led her past the shepherd to the vagrant mothers whom the four children were
dragging to meet her. She accosted them a little stiffly, at
first, and tried to persuade them to be reconciled with
her and go into the garden of the Nuptial House. The
children wanted to do so, but the mothers insisted on speaking first to the shepherd; so they went all together to see
him. When they found him, the matron addressed him.
I was in dread lest, dissatisfied at not being entirely
cured, she would manage things badly. This really was the
case. She made indiscreet assertions, saying that she
owned everything, all belonged to her, grace, strength,
goods, rights, etc. The shepherd wore a three cornered cap,
and was not very gracious. He said, ' What is in that box
you are carrying around with you ?' She answered that it
was a mystery, and one might readily perceive that it was,
indeed, a mystery even to herself. He replied disdain-
fully : ' Indeed ! If you come again with your mystery, I'll
hear nothing of it. It is on account of your traffic in mysteries that we are separated from you. Whatever will not
bear the light of day, the scrutiny of all, is worth nothing,'
and so they parted. The mothers would not now go with
her, and she and I returned to the garden alone. But the
children could not be prevented from running after us.
They seemed to have a special attraction for the matron and
went with her into the garden when, after examining every-

thing, they ran back to tell their mothers all they had seen. They were very much impressed."

During the last week of the ecclesiastical year, November, 1820, Sister Emmerich saw the result of her labors for the conversion of schismatics. "In my sufferings I invoke the dear Mother of God that all hearts drawing near to the truth may be converted and enter the Church. Mary appeared to me in the Nuptial House and told me that I would have to cook for two hundred and twenty different guests. I had to gather all kinds of fruits and vegetables upon which dew from the heavenly gardens had fallen. My task resembled that of a pharmacist, for I had to prepare mixtures against spiritual evils. It was quite different from ordinary cooking. By the fire of charity something earthly had to be destroyed and the ingredients intimately mixed together —it was a troublesome work. Mary explained to me all I had to do as well as the signification and effect of the various spices which, according to the spiritual state of this or that guest, were to be added to the food. All these symbolical operations in vision were most painful to my earthly nature. During my work, I saw the hard and difficult points in some natures softened; and, according to the different defects of character, was my task more or less difficult. At last, I saw the guests arriving at the Nuptial House and partaking of the food prepared for them and, at the same time, I saw in far-off countries many hurrying with the children of the Church to the Banquet of the Lord."

Conversion of an Ancient Sect (Maronite).

"I went to Bethlehem. I went in reality with great fatigue and rapidity. Near the Nuptial House I met an old woman, so old that one might think she had lived at the birth of Christ. She was so tightly enveloped in a black robe from head to foot that she could hardly walk. She begged my aid and accepted also some alms and clothing; but she persisted in hiding something from me of which, however, I had an instinctive knowledge and which had chiefly attracted me to her. It was an infant which she kept concealed under her mantle as if she were ashamed of it, or feared that I would deprive her of it. She seemed to own nothing but this child, to live for it alone, and she hid it as if she had stolen it; but she had to give it up to me. Ah! it was pitiful to see how tightly and painfully it was swathed; it could not move a limb. I loosened some bandages which were injuring its health, bathed it, and wanted to take charge of it, to which however the old woman would not consent. I thought if the little thing, which loved me and clung to me with its hands now free, were let to run around the Nuptial House, it would grow very fast. I thought, also, that if I had the old woman in the garden of the Nuptial House, she could help me clear away the weeds.

"I told her that I would soon return and that, if I found her behaving more reasonably toward the child, she should receive more help from me. She was something like the obstinate old man with the cross, but she promised everything. The poor, feeble creature is proud of her origin and the perfect preservation of the customs of the primitive Church among her people. It is on this account she is so closely enveloped and so solitary and that the sect live scattered in little isolated groups. She really means nothing bad, but she has become horribly stubborn and ignorant. So it always happens when the wife separates from the husband and wants to preach. She goes apart into the mountains; she swathes her child tightly that it may not grow and she conceals it to preserve its innocence; but, whilst the old swather thinks thus to guard her child, she has nothing

for her pains but her miserable obstinacy, and she helpless-
ly drags herself here and there through the wilderness.
With heart-felt pity and in all charity, I represented to her
her unreasonableness, her poverty, her obstinacy which drove
her even to starvation, her pride, and her misery. Again
and again, I conjured her to have pity on herself, to turn from
her absurd isolation to the source of life, to the holy Sacraments of the Church. But she was hardened in her self-
will. She spurned me haughtily, saying that Catholics
practise not what they teach. I replied that to turn
away from the teacher of truth on account of the faults
of individuals, would be as unreasonable as to abandon
virtue on account of the wicked. She had nothing to reply
though she still persevered in her obstinacy. The poor
woman has been driven from the Holy Sepulchre, to which
she no longer has a right; but in the spiritual church which
I see above the Grotto of Bethlehem, prayer is still offered
for her. It is her good fortune to possess still a living
fibre by which she derives a little strength. Ah! I hope she
will yet return!"

In the Advent of the preceding year Sister Emmerich
had already had dealings with this sect, the Maronites and
their chief. She then received a task which was to continue for the next five years, ending in October, 1822, by a
mission given to bring about their reunion with the Church
of Rome.

"Among those whom I met on my way to the Nuptial
House," she said in December, 1818, "there were more
women than men. This surprised me. They wore long robes,
their heads bound with linen, one end hanging down behind. Near them was one of their priests, a poor helpless
fellow, not like a priest. He scarcely knew how to read or
pray!

" A fiery wild horse was brought to him to tame, but he ran away in fright followed by all his people. Then my guide ordered me to mount the animal. He helped me upon his back himself. I sat sideways, the horse becoming quite gentle. I was ordered to ride five times around the place where the people were gathered, each time widening the circle, to keep off the impure beasts which I had already driven away, but which were doing their best to return. I chased them away at last and, on my fifth round, I discovered a sheep-fold. I thought, ' You must make a turn around it in order to unite it with the Church.' Then I returned to the priest with the horse which had become quite gentle. It had no saddle, only a bridle."

This horse of the desert is a symbol of wild, uncurbed nature which the weak priest could not master; but Sister Emmerich mounted and tamed him to prove that it could be subdued by the discipline of the true Church clothed with strength and authority from God. The five turns on the horse signified the five ecclesiastical years at the end of which the stray sheep would return to the fold.

October 4, 1822, she related the following :—" I have had a tiresome journey to deliver a message, against the accomplishment of which a thousand obstacles arose. I was pursued, maltreated, tormented by evil spirits. I endured hunger and thirst, heat and fatigue ; but, in spite of all, I fulfilled my commission. Under the form of Maleachi, the scout of Moses, I had to go from Jagbeha to an ancient Christian sect ardently sighing for the truth. I was clothed in the habit of Maleachi and accompanied by the prophet Malachias who instructed me what to do. We went through Judea, the wilderness of Sinai, and along the Red Sea. On the whole way I saw the events that had formerly happened there and which bore some reference to our mission. I saw also many circumstances in the life of Malachias himself. The people to whom I was sent dwelt in five establishments under an Ecclesiastical Superior whose decision was law in all religious matters. He was very much attached to the Old Testament and the Mosaic Law, so I had to explain to him some prophecies : for instance, the words, " Thou art a priest forever according to the order of Melchisedech.' I asked him if Aaron had been such a priest ; if Moses on Sinai had received other than an outward, disciplinary law for a people who had believed in an anterior sacrifice of bread and wine ; if this sacrifice was not holier and, properly speaking, the beginning and the end ; if Abraham had not offered Melchisedech bread and wine, paid him tithes, and bowed down before the sacrifice of his Church. I cited texts from the Psalms, such as : ' The Lord said to my Lord,' etc., and passages from Malachias upon the Unbloody Sacrifice. I exhorted him to go to Rome, there to be instructed and to have the above passages particularly explained. After these words, I saw him rise, take a Bible, and consult the texts quoted. These people have no fixed abodes, but they seemed about forming some for they took possession of land, enclosed it with walls, and built mud huts. They seemed to be descendants of the Madianites. Children profit by the good works of their ancestors. He that sins breaks the blessed chain ; he that lives virtuously extends the source of benediction."

Sister Emmerich also described the Greek Schism :—
" On my way from Bethlehem to the garden of the Nuptial House, I met a distinguished looking, gray-haired man, wandering around sick and covered with wounds. I understood that he had lost or wasted something belonging to his family and that he was looking for it, unconscious that it lay quite near him. He appeared to belong to a matron

whom I saw wrapped in a mantle near the garden of the Nuptial House, but he did not want to go to her. He has apparently more repugnance to her than she to him. He always carries with him an old black wooden cross, about as long as one's arm and in shape like a Y. It struck me that he must have had it a long time, for it is well-used and quite polished; he holds on to it most tenaciously. Ah! you dear old man, of what advantage is the wooden cross to you, if it makes you forget your Saviour! The poor man is so hardened, so obstinate, so full of his own ideas; one cannot make him move, and he himself advances not a step. He has been separated from his wife a long time, and he will not be reconciled to her, because she cannot grant him what he demands. I fear great evils will yet follow from their disunion!—I cured something in the perverse old man."

When the Pilgrim heard the above, he expressed his admiration at the merciful dispensations of Almighty God, who deigned not only to relieve the corporal wants of the poor by means of His faithful servant, but also to grant spiritual assistance to the stray children of the Church. Sister Emmerich replied: " It would, indeed, be a matter of astonishment if one lived only in one's self, but the love of Jesus makes all His members one. Every work of mercy performed for His wounded members, goes to the Church as to the Body of Jesus. The perverse old man with the cross has no child. He will not listen to reason, he will never come round, he will yet cause many miseries and troubles. The sick matron with the holy thing in the box has no child either. She is the Church herself with the various diseases existing in her members, and like her she is ill-treated and repulsed by her children. After all, she is now once more in the garden."

Sister Emmerich's visions, as well as her whole mission upon earth, bear a striking analogy to those of St. Hildegarde, as may be seen by a perusal of the magnificent epistle the latter addressed in 1170 to the Provost Werner of Kirchheim. The saint, in obedience to a divine command, had undertaken a journey into Suabia, in order to portray the state of the Church before the clergy of Kirchheim. The impression produced by her words was so powerful that, after her return home, the Provost wrote to her begging in his own name and "that of his fellow-laborers," that they might meditate constantly upon it, a copy of what under the inspiration of the Holy Ghost she had said on the negligence of priests in offering the Holy Sacrifice. The following is a copy of the saint's reply :—

"Confined to my bed by sickness, I had in the year of the Lord, 1170, a beautiful vision of a lady more lovely and attractive than human mind can paint. Her form reached from earth to sky, her countenance shone with splendor, her eyes were fixed on heaven. She wore a shining robe of white silk and a mantle embroidered with precious stones, emeralds, sapphires, pearls, and flowers of gold ; on her feet were shoes of onyx. But her face was soiled with ashes, her robe was torn on the right side, her mantle was stained, her shoes were covered with mud. In a clear, plaintive voice she cried : 'Hear, O ye heavens ! my face is disfigured !—Be afflicted, O earth, for my vesture is rent !— and thou, O abyss, tremble, for my shoes are soiled ! The foxes have holes and the birds nests, but I, I have none to assist or console me, I have no support on which to lean ! —I was hidden in the bosom of the Father until the Son of Man, conceived and born of a virgin, shed His blood in which He espoused me and endowed me with His grace that, in the pure regeneration of spirit and water, I might bring forth those anew whom the serpent's venom had infected. But my nurses, the priests, who should have preserved my countenance resplendent as the aurora, my robe brilliant as the lightning-flash, my mantle glittering as precious stones, my shoes white as snow, have sprinkled my face with ashes, have torn my robe, soiled my mantle, and stained my shoes. They who should have adorned me have allowed me to perish. They sully my countenance when they handle and eat my Bridegroom's Flesh and Blood in spite of the impurity of their life, their fornications, their adulteries, and their rapacity in selling and buying, a thing unlawful for them. Yes, they cover His Flesh and Blood with opprobrium. It is like casting a new-born babe to swine. As man became flesh and blood at the very instant that God formed him from the slime of the earth and breathed into him the breath of life, so the same power of God, at the words of the priest, changes the offering of bread, wine and water upon the altar into the true Flesh and true Blood of Christ, my Spouse; which, however, on account of the blindness occasioned by Adam's fall, man cannot see with his corporal eyes. The wounds of my Spouse remain fresh and open, as long as those of sinful man are not closed. They are outraged by those priests who, instead of preserving me pure and serving me in holiness, seek with insatiable avidity to heap up riches, and benefice on benefice. They tear my vesture by their infidelity to the Law, to the Gospel, to the priesthood. They stain my mantle by their neglect of the precepts laid down for them, instead of fulfilling them joyfully and perfectly by continence like unto the beauty of the emerald, by alms-giving like unto the sapphire, and by the practice of all other good works which honor God as so many precious stones. They soil my shoes by walking not in the right path, the rough and difficult path of justice, and by failing to give good example to their inferiors; but in my shoes I perceive the hidden light of truth among a few. The false priests deceive themselves; they crave the honor attached to their functions whilst dreading the trouble. But it is impossible for them to have one without the other, since to no one who has not labored will wages be given. When God's grace touches a man, it urges him to labor for the reward. God now punishes man by raining evils upon him. He covers the earth with them as with a mist until its verdure disappears and it is clothed in darkness. But the abyss will tremble when He will come in His wrath, making heaven and earth the instruments of His vengeance and man's destruction. Arrogant princes and nations will rise up against you, O ye priests who have hitherto neglected me! They will drive you forth, they will rob you of your wealth, because you have neglected your sacred ministry. They will cry: ' Cast out of the Church these adulterers, these robbers full of iniquity !—' In so doing they think they render God a service, saying that you have polluted His Church; therefore the Scriptures say, ' Why have the nations raged and the people devised vain things?' By God's permission the nations will rise up against you; they will have vain thoughts of you; they will esteem as naught your priestly dignity and consecration. The princes of the earth will unite to cast you down. Your rulers will drive you from their territories, since your crimes have driven the innocent Lamb far from you. And I heard a voice from heaven saying: ' This vision represents the Church—wherefore, O daughter of man, who dost see these things and hear these lamentations, announce it to the priests who have been instituted and ordained to guide and instruct the people, for to them in the person of the Apostles it has been said:

'Go into the whole world and preach the Gospel to every creature.' When God created man, He delineated in him *every creature*, as are written upon a scrap of parchment the seasons and numbers of a whole year ; therefore it was that God named man *'every creature.'* And I, poor woman, saw again a drawn sword floating in the air, one edge toward heaven, the other toward the earth. And it was raised above a spiritual race that the prophet foresaw when he exclaimed in astonishment : ' Who are these, that fly as clouds, and as doves to their windows ?' (Isaias lx. 8) ; for they who are raised above the earth, separated from ordinary men, they who should live holily, showing forth in their actions the simplicity of doves, are evil in their works and manners. And I saw the sword strike the priestly race in many places as Jerusalem was destroyed after the Saviour's Passion ; and I saw, also, that in the time of trib_ulation God will spare many pure and upright priests who fear Him, as He said to Elias that he had left in Israel a thousand men who had not bent the knee to Baal. May the inextinguishable fire of the Holy Spirit be enkindled in you to convert you to better things !" Such are Hildegarde's words.

Sister Emmerich saw in the Nuptial House, not only the state of the Church in general, but also that of individual dioceses. Münster in particular was shown her. In numerous symbolical pictures, she saw its special necessities and how she was to aid it. Her first vision, recounted in December, 1819, clearly tended to the reawakening of piety throughout the country by devotion to the Blessed Virgin and the restoration of religious communities. In one of the chambers of the Nuptial House called the " Bridal Chamber," she had to arrange the dowry and spiritual wedding-garments for those for whom they were destined.

This symbolized the effects of her sufferings and prayers by which she obtained for many souls the grace of vocation to the religious life and the means of corresponding thereto. She had, besides, to avert dangers menacing the faith from foreign influences, to atone for the betrayal of the rights and privileges of the Church, for the cowardice of her children who tried to serve two masters, God and the world, and to wrestle with the consequences resulting therefrom. In this struggle Sister Emmerich held the place of the diocese. She became really and spiritually a mark for the dangers by which it was threatened. The following is what she relates on this point :—

" I went to Bethlehem to meet Mary and Joseph and prepare a lodging for them. I took with me linen and coverings and also my sewing, for I had not yet finished all my work. I entered a house at which I thought they would arrive 'that night. It was like one of the large farmhouses of our own country, the roof not flat. The people were rough and uncouth. They had a large establishment, and when I asked them to prepare lodgings for Mary and Joseph, they answered that there was no room, that they expected many guests ; and, in truth, crowds of young and ill-bred people began to arrive. They set to work to prepare a repast. They spread the table, cooked, and danced about like mad people. Again I asked a lodging for the Mother of God, but all the answer I received was to be trodden upon and pushed from side to side. Then appeared the child in green, *Patience*, whom St. Cecilia had brought to me once before, and with his help I bore their ill-treatment calmly. These rude people did not seem wholly unknown to me ; among them were many Protestants and many who had persecuted me. Whilst they were refusing a lodging to the holy travellers, I had discovered a little unoccupied room which, however, they did not want to let me enter; they seemed to have something hidden in it. But I succeeded in getting in, and I found, to my great surprise, an old woman all covered with spider webs whom they had imprisoned. I brushed her off and took her out to the wedding, but the guests were greatly agitated when they saw her. I reproached them with their treatment of her, when they all fled from the house and the old woman set about preparing another repast. Then I saw other young persons, mostly girls who, I knew, wanted to lead a spiritual life, and I discovered another room which constantly and wonderfully increased in size and brightness. I saw in it the holy deceased of our own country, among them my mother, the lady of Vehme, and their guardian angels. They wore the old Franconian costume, and I kept thinking that my mother in her magnificent dress would never notice me. I prepared the room for the Holy Family. Joseph and Mary arrived, and were received most cordially. But they paid no attention to anything. They retired in the dark and sat down against the wall, when the whole place was instantly flooded with light. I knelt in veneration. Their stay was short. The old people of the house gazed curiously at the holy travellers through the open door and then withdrew, I thought through humility. In the meantime, the old woman whom I had set free had grown quite young and beautiful. She was the most honorable person in the house, indeed she was the betrothed (1). She was very lovely and dressed in the old peasant style. By degrees the whole house turned into a church and where the fireplace had stood, arose an altar."

(1) The old woman typifies the piety and faith of former times, the ancient religion of the country which was to be rejuvenated ; that is, renewed, resuscitated. The costume of the souls referred to the age in which that fervor reigned which was now to be renewed.

" As I went over the sea to the Promised Land, a sudden storm arose and I saw an open boat full of wicked, clamoring people. The thought occurred to me : ' Those people use a boat, for the waters are deep. How does it happen that I can walk over them ?'—and immediately, just like doubting Peter, I sank in the waves up to my neck. But my guide caught me by the arm, bore me to the shore, and reproached me with my want of faith. When I reached the Nuptial House near Bethlehem, I was going to pass it ; but my guide made me go in, and he took me all through it. I saw many strangers in it, men and women. A fine-looking youth in blue uniform seemed to be in command, and there was also a tall, imperious woman strutting around with an important, insolent air. She was attending to everything, and pretending to know everything better than others ; but ecclesiastics seemed to be banished from the premises. Although the Bridal Chamber was locked, still I was able to enter it. I found the walls hung with cobwebs, but the Nuptial robes in good condition. There were four unfinished and twenty finished wax tapers, also twenty full sacks and four empty ones. The youth followed me all over the house, astonished at all I did and said. He showed me a hole into which he and his people had swept, though not without difficulty, swarms of unclean animals, such as toads, etc. He tried to prevent my removing the stone that covered it, saying that I would run a risk in so doing. I replied that I had nothing to fear having often cleaned the place out, and after peeping at the ugly things, I replaced the cover. Then he told me that his people could not cast these reptiles out. I replied that our priests could do it, and I bade him reflect upon it as a proof of their power. I found also a sealed package of writings whose seal, the youth told me, his people were absolutely unable to break, and I again directed his attention to their weakness. He replied that if they were indeed so weak, it was very imprudent in them to drag that great, imperious woman into the house. The latter was very bitter against me and exceedingly displeased at the young man's being with me. She had already tried to quarrel with me, scoffing at the brides, whom she called old maids, and at the woman with the box, etc. ; but, as she feared that the young man would put her out, she began to render herself necessary and important. She gathered up the linen of all in the house and prepared for a grand washing (general confession). But the tub kept tipping over, first on one side, then on the other, so that she could get nothing done ; all had to be taken out again wet and dirty. Then she got ready to bake a batch of bread which, like the washing, was another failure; but, not at all discouraged, she made a great fire, hung over it an enormous kettle containing something to be cooked, and spread herself out before it so that no one could approach, keeping up all the time for my benefit her tiresome prattle on the Pope and Antichrist. Suddenly the pot-hook, the kettle, the whole chimney fell with a crash, the fire flew in all directions, and she and her companions scampered from the house leaving the young man alone. The latter expressed his desire of returning to the church in the garden of the Nuptial House (that is, of becoming a Catholic). He typifies the views (modern pietism) which Protestants entertain of the Church ; his uniform signifies the secular dress ; his authority in the Nuptial House, the pressure of the civil power on the Church in our country ; and the insolent female is symbolical of the old Lutheran leaven. . . . .

" I was in the Nuptial House, and I swept from the room of the stern Superior straw, scraps of charred wood, and some kind of black mould, into a deep hole on the very edge of which I had to stand. The old Lutheran woman stood over in a corner enraged at my return, and doing all she could to annoy me. She scattered, as if in defiance, a quantity of dirty trash around where I was. In sweeping it up my broom happened to touch where she stood. She cried out that I need not sweep near her, she could do it herself. I replied that then she should not have thrown the dirt toward me. Her daughter (shallow rationalism) was always occupied in adorning and beautifying herself, hiding her filthiness so as to catch the eye of the unwary and entice them to her, for she was not chaste. The odious, crafty boy was among the ecclesiastics, but the stern Superior now saw more clearly into his intrigues and labored seriously to baffle them. I swept the filthy room that the Dean occupied when he came there, and he seemed a little confused. The schoolmaster (Overberg) had another bride whom he wanted to hand over to the Protestants. I saw, too, that the stern Superior still wanted to remove me to Darfeld; but I had a vision which showed me how miserable I should have been there lying as if on a bed of state, and that Miss Soentgen would have played a rôle, if I had gone. . . . . . "

Sunday, February 6th, Gospel of the Sowers.—"I saw three gardens or territories: the first was covered with rocks, mountains, and stones; the second, with brushes, brambles, and weeds, here and there flower-beds; the third, which was the largest and best cultivated, was full of seas, lakes, and islands; everything flourished for it was fertile ground. I was in the middle one. First I went, or rather, I gazed into the rocky garden which at the first glance looked like a mere scrap of land, but when considered attentively, turned out like all such pictures to be indeed a little world. Here and there, sprang up good grain among the stones, and the people wanted to transplant it to a bed. But a man came along, saying they should not do so, because without the support afforded the plantlets by the thorns they would fall to the ground. The best land was in the garden on the island. The grain there flourished and produced a hundred-fold, but in some places the plants were entirely rooted up. The seed was in good condition, the little fields fenced in. I recognized in this garden other parts of the world and islands in which I so often see Christianity spreading. In the central garden, the one in which I was, I saw by the weeds, by its neglected condition that its gardeners were slothful. It had everything to make it productive, but it was neglected, choked with weeds, briars, and thistles. I saw in it the state of all the parishes in Europe, and the garden of the Pope was not among the best. In the part symbolical of my own country, I saw a lord filling a deep pit with money, the produce of all the fields. Over the pit sat the devil. I saw, to my amazement, and it made me laugh, a half-dozen sly, nimble little fellows cutting underground passages to the pit and dragging off with the greatest ease all the produce that had been so laboriously stowed away from above. At last, the master spied one stealing off with a sack full of gold. He gazed down into the treasure-pit over which the devil watched so well, and expressed his surprise at seeing it almost empty; but his servants told him that the fields produced no more, that they were badly cultivated, insufficiently manured, etc. In the garden in which I live, I saw many fields attended by gardeners and workmen whom I know and many beds in charge of under-gardeners; but very few of them sowed and cultivated even tolerably well. I saw it all overgrown with weeds, dry, and parched. I went from bed to bed, recognized all, and understood their condition. I saw people in perilous positions, running on the edge of a black abyss, others sleeping, others wasting their labor over crops of empty ears of corn, and among them some men going around like masters, giving orders, etc., although they really had no business there. The poor creatures worked hard, digging and manuring, but with little success. Suddenly they dragged in a child stealthily. The place was shown me as the city of Münster, for I recognized most of the people. There was something repulsive, something that inspired horror about the child. I saw that it was illegitimate; it knew not its father, and its mother had sinned with many. At first it only played around, but it soon showed itself in all its ugliness. It looked old, sick, pale, pock-marked; it was bold, proud, scornful, and servile. It never went to church, but ridiculed everything, dragging itself along laden with books and manuscripts. One ecclesiastic sent it to another. It insinuated itself everywhere, and I saw, to my surprise, some French priests whom I knew letting themselves be cajoled by it. Few opposed it, for it could perform wonders; it was so insinuating, it understood everything, spoke all languages. I saw it aiming chiefly at schoolmasters. The mistresses it either passed by or ridiculed, but it avoided me altogether. I feared it would do much harm, for wherever it went the garden was still more neglected, bearing rank weeds, but no fruit. I saw that the pious schoolmaster (Overberg) would have nothing to do with it; the stern Superior (Droste) let it go its way; another amused himself talking to it; but the Dean gave it a particularly flattering reception, even wanting it to lodge in his house. The child worried me the whole day. It introduced itself so readily everywhere, so quickly extended its influence, that it seemed to me a real pest. It is

always before me with its old, insolent, unchildlike ways.
I know that it signifies the new school-system (rationalistic).
I have had a frightful vision of persecution. I was in the
hands of a masked enemy who tried to drag me away secretly. I was already out of the house and was abandoning
myself to the will of God, when a dove flew around screaming so that it attracted a crowd of other birds. They kept
up such a noise that my enemies hurried me back into the
house. It was a perfect tumult. I recognized the birds
as my old friends : a lark that my confessor had taken
away from me in order to mortify me ; a pigeon which I used
to feed at my window in the convent; and some finches and
redbreasts that used to light upon my head and shoulders
in the cloister garden."

Sister Emmerich's frightful visions were repeated in proportion to the encouragement given to the illegitimate boy
in the diocese of Münster ; for, as the representative of
its spiritual interests now so seriously endangered, she had
to endure the wrong offered to the diocese by the ecclesiastical patrons of the boy. She saw, also, her enemies
forming a project to get possession of her as soon as fresh
effusions of blood should furnish them a pretext to remove
her from Dülmen (at Dean Rensing's instigation), and for
this to arm themselves with the authorization of Ecclesiastical Superiors. The sight filled her with such compassion
for her persecutors that, although in ecstasy, she sprang up
on her knees to say a Rosary for them and, being in a profuse perspiration, she suffered for several days from frequent and violent spells of coughing. Again it seemed to
her that she was lying unprotected in a field and set upon by
dogs, whilst twenty-four children whom she had clothed since
Christmas stood around her, keeping them at bay. St. Benedict also came to her aid and helped her wonderfully.

110 *Life of*

"I had," she exclaimed, "to endure so much that, if it had not been for St. Benedict, I should surely have died. The saint appeared to me, promised me relief, but warned me not to be too discouraged if it were not accorded at once. Then I had a vision in which I saw myself under the form of another, seated on a stool and resting against the wall in a dying state unable to speak or move. Around stood priests and laymen conversing ostentatiously of this, that, and the other thing, but taking no notice whatever of me, that is of the person who represented me. As I gazed on the scene I was filled with pity for the poor creature, when suddenly I saw St. Benedict indignantly making his way toward her through the throng of ecclesiastics (1), and, as he spoke to her, I became conscious that she was none other than myself. He said he would send me Holy Communion. He introduced to me a gentle-looking young priest and martyr in alb and stole, who gave me the Holy Eucharist. Benedict said : ' Be not surprised at the presence of this youth. He is a priest and martyr, my pupil Placidus.'—I felt, I tasted the Blessed Sacrament, and I was saved. The gentlemen seemed to notice by my attitude what had happened, and they became more reserved. A stranger appeared wrapped in a mantle; he addressed them sternly and put them to shame. Benedict said: ' Behold these priests! They strive after offices, but pass by the needy, saying: *I have not time, or: It is not my duty, it is not customary, I have received no order to attend to it.'* Placidus showed me the parable of the Samaritan and how it applied to me—priest and Levite pass by, a stranger comes to my aid."

From Quinquagesima Sunday the pains in her wounds were so violent as frequently to deprive her of conscious-

(1) The apparition of St. Benedict, the great teacher of the West, is connected with Sister Emmerich's sufferings on account of the young schoolboy.

ness, but she received in vision many sweet consolations. All the poor old people to whom she had given alms in her youth passed before her one after another, displaying the gifts they had received from her; even in the midst of her intense pains she could not restrain a smile at the sight of the multifarious articles produced for her amusement. The old people themselves seemed to be rejuvenated whilst the clothes, food, and other alms she had once bestowed upon them, bore no trace of time; indeed they, too, present-ed an improved appearance. Here was an aged woman of Coesfeld, for whose sake she had years ago in a retired corner in broad daylight, deprived herself of a skirt. There was a poor sick man to whom she had sent clothes, a package of the best tobacco, and some cracknels (*bretzeln*), since, being sick herself, she had nothing else in her cup-board. The sight of the cracknels amused her much, for they were over twenty years old. Instead of the tobacco, the old man laid on the table a fragrant bouquet (symbol of suf-ferings). Then came an old woman, now rejuvenated, of whom Sister Emmerich said: "I had almost forgotten her. She had a daughter who turned out badly and whom, as she told me, she could not reclaim. She had vowed, if God would convert her daughter from her sinful life, to make the Way of the Cross on her knees; but it was quite im-possible for her to do so, as she was old and weak. It would have taken three hours to perform the devotion, which would certainly have been too much for her. She told me of her vow and her great anxiety at not being able to fulfil it. I comforted her and promised to make satis-faction for her through the intervention of others. I went on my knees by night several times around a cross in a neighboring field for her intention.

"I went to the Holy Land and saw Our Lord on the

banks of the Jordan. He said, ' Now the time approaches for me to save My sheep. The lambs must be led up the mountain, and the sheep ranged around them ;' and seeing Him so careful of His flock, I thought of my persecutors who were instantly shown me running through a wilderness. Then the Good Shepherd said : ' When I approach them, they injure Me, they maltreat Me,' and I began to pray for them with all my heart; whereupon, I obtained the gift of prayer and I hope it will do some good. I saw that by means of my enemies, I had advanced in the spiritual life. As I prayed for them, I saw, to my great surprise, the Dean engaging in a plot against me (1). . .

"I had to carry many sick, lame, and crippled to a church in which all was in good order. Among them was Rave whom I saved from drowning; the Landrath whom I bore over a swamp; and Roseri whom I found lying all bruised as if from a fall ; he gave me much trouble . . . . . I found myself in vision near a wheat and rye field which lay very high. Around it were ditches, swamps, and deserts, full of wild beasts which lay in wait to tear travellers to pieces, and which had to be fed, in order to keep them out of the fields. For every one of them I had to procure, at the cost of great fatigue and amidst their incessant assaults, a different kind of food, plants, and berries. I had, besides, to carry and feed cats, tigers, swine, and a savage dog. The perspiration poured off of me. These animals signified the passions of the men who tried to get possession of me. I have imposed upon myself a heavy task. I have undertaken to obtain by my prayers this Lent the conversion of my enemies and the liquidation of their debts. I have already obtained this much that they

(1) The Pilgrim added these words : "This seems a little exaggerated."—But from the fact of Dean Rensing's subsequent attempt to brand her as an impostor, we know that Sister Emmerich saw the truth.

will not be punished for what they have hitherto done against me, if they only enter into themselves. I know what it is to bear sins and expiate by sufferings. . . .

"I have averted many dangers by prayer. I received a special instruction on this point, and I saw how much I am indebted to the protection of holy relics, for it is to the saints that I owe the failures of the project formed against me. I was not deceived. I saw for a certainty that it originated with the Dean. Again I was to have been carried off by six men, among them two ecclesiastics, and subjected to a new investigation ; but the Vicar-General would not give his consent."

Sister Emmerich was so confident of her prayer's being heard that she did not hesitate to announce to Dean Rensing the fact of her wounds having bled on the 9th of March. The Pilgrim's notes on this occasion are as follows : " On the evening of March 9th, all her wounds bled, those of her head the most copiously. But she is perfectly calm, in spite of the uneasiness of those around her as to whether or not, or when or how this fact of her bleeding again would be repeated. She lay immersed in contemplation. She knew all that was being done or said about her in different houses even at a distance. Finally, she became ecstatic and looked fresh and young without a trace of age or pain. Her countenance wore a peculiarly bright expression, and she smiled with mingled devotion and gravity.

" On the night of March 9-10, her wounds again bled, and next morning she sent word to the Dean by her confessor. She believed that she had thus discharged her obligation to the Landrath Bœnninghausen. . . . . The bleeding lasted till three P. M., and yet the Dean came not to verify the fact. She had to engage her confessor to inform either the Vicar-General or the Landrath of it."

Good-Friday, March 30th —" Her sufferings up to this time have been steadily on the increase and, although in almost continual contemplation, she has to receive the visits of her friends. But this increase of pain and the terrible violence she endures in the transformation by which she renders testimony to the death of the Man-God, combine to diminish the effects of exterior distractions, and she is entirely absorbed by her task of expiation."—At ten that morning the Pilgrim found her forehead, hands, and feet bleeding. He tried to remove the blood, but with little success, on account of the intense pain any such attempt produced. She was also in dread of some new investigation. She hid the effusions as best she could from both the doctor and Abbé Lambert, fearful of the effect the fact might have upon the latter, himself sick and weak. Dean Rensing was again informed of her state ; but he paid as little attention to the second announcement as to the first, merely sending her word not to trouble herself about the Landrath, that he, the Dean, would take all upon himself (1). She endured intolerable agony up to six P. M., although, as she remarked, Jesus gave up the ghost at about one o'clock. When contemplating the descent from the cross and Mary holding the Body of her Son in her arms, the thought occurred to her : " How strong she is ! she has not fainted once !"—whereupon, she heard her angel's voice, saying : " Well then, do thou feel what she felt !"—and on the instant she fainted away from the violence of her grief, for Mary's sword had pierced her soul. The Pilgrim had placed under her feet some relics wrapped in linen which soon received a few drops of blood from her wounds. That evening he applied the little parcel to her shoulder, from which she was suffering acutely. She exclaimed, though in

(1) And yet, before a year had passed, Dean Rensing accused Sister Emmerich of imposture !

ecstasy : " How strange ! here I see my Spouse alive surrounded by thousands of saints in the Heavenly Jerusalem, and yonder I see Him lying dead in the tomb !—And
what is this ? Among the saints I see a person, a nun,
whose hands, feet, side, and head are all bleeding, and the
saints standing near her hands and feet, her side and
shoulder !"

The following year, 1821, she was told : " Take note,
thou wilt shed thy blood with thy Lord not on the ecclesiastical, but on the real anniversary of His death." Good-
Friday of this year fell on April 20th. The Pilgrim
records :—" What has never before happened since Sister
Emmerich has had the stigmata, occurred to-day. Her
wounds bled not, although it is Good-Friday, and for the
last few days they have even wholly disappeared, a circumstance for which she cannot account. She lay, however, in ecstatic contemplation of the Passion when, at the
instant of the Saviour's Crucifixion, the burgomaster suddenly entered her room, gazed sharply around, asked a few
questions, and took his departure as unceremoniously as
he had come. Strange sight ! the poor, ignorant man and
the helpless ecstatica face to face ! He had come, as he said,
' by orders of Superiors.' "

The Pilgrim's journal of March 30, 1821, explains the
above phenomenon respecting the date of her bloody effusions :—" Sister Emmerich celebrates Good-Friday to-day.
At ten this morning her face was covered with blood and
her whole person bore the marks of the cruel scourging.
About two P. M., the blood gushed from her hands and feet,
but she was then in ecstasy, unconscious of the outer world,
dreading not discovery, wholly absorbed in the contemplation of the work of Redemption."

Sufferings on Account of Mixed Marriages.

" I saw many churches of this country in a sad state as if betokening their future decay, and young ecclesiastics hurrying through their duties negligently.　Entire parishes seemed dying out.　I saw the Nuptial House of Münster. The old woman and her daughter were absent ; but there was an old man in it, a diplomatist, a pettifogger, whom the devil seemed to have raised up, so smooth, so cunning was he.　A sort of council was being held, and I saw the stern Superior and Overberg earnestly acting together on some question of marriage.　It made me sad to see only five others, one a very aged person, standing up for the right with these two men; the rest were all against them.　The gathering was numerous and, to my great alarm, they began to dispute and quarrel.　The Superior's party at once withdrew, leaving the others to side with the Lutherans. But the saddest part of it was that some secretly joined the wicked party again, for instance R. . . . . . , to the great chagrin of Droste and Overberg. . . . . "

" I went again to the Nuptial House which I found crowded with people of two different parties.　Down-stairs were the good around Droste and Overberg and with them the youth in blue uniform who seemed about to be convert- ed.　But he no longer wore his uniform, and seemed to be in high favor with the above-named gentlemen ; they trusted him, he was all in all to them.　Tables stood around with chalices on them.　The young people were sent out, as if on messages, but affairs did not go well. To the upper story they had built an outside staircase up which people were crowding, men and women, ecclesias- tics and seculars, Catholics and Protestants.　All up there was motion, activity, but the people were entirely separated from the Church, quite antagonistic to her. And yet I saw among them several priests whom I knew, siding with the Protestant party against those down-stairs. I saw also several who carried on both shoulders. They ran up and down the whole time betraying the good party. But what alarmed me most was to see that the young man who gave himself out for a convert, whom the Catholic party so implicitly trusted, was an infamous traitor who secretly revealed up-stairs all that went on below. I wept, I wanted to press through the crowd and disclose his treachery, but my guide restrained me, saying: 'It is not yet time. Wait, let him betray himself!'—This spectacle lasted a long while, when something happened up-stairs and the Protestant party were all cast out together. All that had mounted by the outside staircase, that had not entered the sheepfold by the right door, were ignominiously expelled and took to flight. I saw in the garden a flower-bed out of which arose a narrow ladder which reached to heaven. They who had been driven out were not allowed to mount it. I saw people ascending and descending to help up others. I saw some apparently very distinguished people turned away, whilst others mounted the ladder which hung down from heaven. It was guarded by a youth with a drawn sword who repulsed the unworthy."

The preceding vision referred to mixed marriages, from which Sister Emmerich endured lifelong torments. She used to lie for whole days a prey to violent cramps of the bowels, her arms extended in the form of a cross. She saw again in the Nuptial House the Lutheran cook and her project of marrying her illegitimate daughter to the young schoolboy who was now of age. She beheld the clergy open to all sorts of attacks on the score of such marriages now so numerous, and she exerted herself to enlist the prayers of

others in behalf of their members vacillating between right
and wrong ;—all this she saw in pictures back as far as
the Mosaic period, since the Church has never countenanced such unions excepting in cases of absolute necessity.
She saw how detrimental they are to the Church, how
they weaken her influence.

" I saw Moses before reaching Mt. Sinai, separating entirely from the people and sending away some of the degenerate Israelites who had married among the pagans.
They had chosen wives from among the Madianites, I think,
and so lost their nationality. Their descendants had mingled with the Samaritans and these again with the Assyrians,
and finally, had became heretics and idolators. I saw such
marriages contracted out of necessity during the Babylonian
Captivity; but they teemed with fatal consequences. I saw
such unions tolerated in the infancy of the Church, on account of the state of the times and for the propagation of
the faith. But never has the Church consented that the off-
spring should be reared out of her own fold, an event which
happens only by violence. As soon as she was solidly established, the Church positively prohibited such marriages.
I have seen whole countries from which the orthodox faith
has entirely disappeared in consequence of them ; still
more, I have seen that, if the new system of marriage
and education succeeds, in less than a century affairs
will be in a bad state in our own land."

July, 1821.—" For the last week she has writhed on her
bed from the intensity of her sufferings, groaning and
finding relief in no position. She is, however, always in
contemplation and spiritual action, occupied day and night
with the ecclesiastical affairs of Germany whose miseries
she sees far and near. She says it is difficult to converse
with those around her as she is always absent in spirit :—

'I have to go,' she says, 'from place to place, to pastors and statesmen, sometimes individually, sometimes collectively, to suggest such or such things to them; the whole day is often spent in this manner. On entering their council-halls, I see, perhaps, one of the members advocating or subscribing to something useless or prejudicial, and I urge him to desist, not to violate justice. I constantly have visions of schools. I see great boys oppressed by infants yet unborn (but whom I know), and grown girls ruled by little ones. They are pictures of the new systems which spring from the unlawful union of pride and false illumination. All this is purely symbolical, but I generally recognize the fathers of such children, or systems."

One morning the Pilgrim found her in a high fever and convulsed with pain, though in contemplation and utterly unconscious of all around. Whilst he stood regarding her compassionately, Gertrude announced a beggar. The Pilgrim sent her about half a franc in Sister Emmerich's name and unseen by her. Scarcely had the woman received the alms than Sister Emmerich began to smack her lips as if she had just tasted something, murmuring: "How sweet! how sweet! Whence came that morsel you gave me?"— then, although unable to move an instant before, she sat up in her bed and said with a smile, but still in ecstasy: "See, how you have strengthened me with that sweet morsel! It was fruit plucked from a heavenly tree that you gave me!"—The Pilgrim amazed at the incident, recorded the following words in his journal: "How close is the union of this soul with Christ, since the words of the Gospel are so plainly verified in her: *What you do to the least of My brethren, you do unto Me!*"

The Essence of Rationalism.

"I was at the Nuptial House and I saw a large, boisterous

wedding-party arriving in coaches. The bride had around her a crowd of attendants. She was a tall, insolent, extravagantly dressed person, a crown on her head, jewels on her breast. Around her neck hung three tinsel chains and lockets with numberless trinkets shaped like crabs, toads, frogs, locusts, cornucopias, rings, whistles, etc. She was dressed in scarlet, and on her shoulders wriggled an owl whispering first into one ear, then into the other. It seemed her familiar spirit. The woman pompously entered the Nuptial House with her suite and baggage, driving out all whom she had found therein. The old gentlemen and the ecclesiastics had scarcely time to gather their books and papers together, for all had to depart. Some went with disgust, others betraying a little interest in the courtesan (1). They either betook themselves to the church, or scattered around in groops, sauntering here and there. The woman upset everything in the house, even the table with the goblets on it ; only the Bridal Chamber and the apartment dedicated to the Mother of God remained undisturbed. Among her followers was that cunning hypocrite whom I had lately seen serving two masters ; he was all-powerful with her. The learned boy was her son ; he had now grown up and he boldly pushed himself in everywhere. One thing was very remarkable : the woman, her baggage, her books, all swarmed with shining worms, and she bore around her the fetid odor of those sparkling beetles that one recognizes by their smell. The women with her were mesmeric prophetesses who prophesied and supported her. It is well there are such people. They pursue their wickedness until they go too far, when they are discovered and the good are separated from the bad. After upsetting the whole house,

---

(1) " Once I saw this woman's mother in the Nuptial House, preparing from a rank herb with yellow leaves a pottage for the learned who were to increase with the same rapidity as does the herb itself. They often came and ate heartily of it."

she went out into the garden and trampled it under foot; wherever she passed, the flowers faded and died, all turned to worms and infection. But this ignoble bride wanted to marry, and no one would suit her but a pious, intelligent young priest, one of the twelve, I think, whom I so often see doing great things under the guidance of the Holy Spirit. He was among those who had fled from the house on her entrance, but she enticed him back with the sweetest words. When he returned, she showed him everything and wanted to place him over all. He hesitated a little, when she threw off all reserve and used every imaginable artifice to induce him to marry her. The young priest became indignant, solemnly cursed her and her arts as those of an infamous courtesan, and quickly withdrew. Then I saw all her attendants trying to escape, swooning, dying, turning black. The whole house grew dark and swarmed with worms that ate into everything, and the woman herself sank worm-eaten to the ground, all dried up like tinder. I crushed some of the worms lying there dead and shining, and found that they, too, were all dried up, burned to ashes. When everything had fallen to dust and silence reigned around, the young priest returned with two others, one an old man who looked like a Roman legate. He carried a cross which he set up in front of the charred Nuptial House. After having drawn something from the cross, he entered the house and threw open the doors and windows, whilst his companions outside prayed, consecrated, and exorcised. Then a furious storm arose. The wind blew through the house, driving out before it a black vapor which floated toward a great city and hung over it in heavy clouds. The Nuptial House, thus purified, was again occupied by people selected from among the former occupants, and some of the retinue of the unchaste bride, who were now converted, were installed in it. All began again to prosper, and the garden once more flourished."

The Body of the Church.—Labors of the Harvest.

June, 1820.—" I was in the church of the Nuptial House, where a ceremony was being performed, as if preparatory to the setting out of harvesters. I saw the Lord Jesus as a Shepherd, the Apostles and disciples with the saints and blessed in an upper choir, whilst in the nave of the church were crowds of priests and laymen still alive, many of whom I know. The ceremony seemed intended to invoke a blessing on the harvest, to bring laborers to it. Jesus seemed to be inviting them in these words : ' The harvest is great, but the laborers are few ; pray, therefore, the Lord of the harvest to send laborers into his harvest.'— Then He sent the Apostles and disciples forth with blessings and prayers, just as He had done whilst on earth. I, too, went out to the harvest with some of the priests and laics still alive. Some excused themselves and would not go, when immediately their places were filled by the saints and blessed spirits. Then I saw the harvest-field near the Nuptial House and in it a body rising up toward the sky. It was horribly mutilated, the hands and feet cut off, and large holes in many parts of it. Some of the wounds were fresh and bleeding, others covered with decayed flesh, and others were swollen and gristly. The whole of one side was black and worm-eaten. My guide explained to me that it represented the body of the Church, as also the body of all mankind. He showed me in what way each wound referred to some part of the world, and I saw at a glance far distant nations and individuals who had been cut from it. I felt the pain of the amputation of these members as acutely as if they had been cut from my own person.

' Should not one member sigh after another, suffer for another ? Should it not aim at being healed and again united to the body ? Should not one suffer for the welfare of another ?' said my guide. ' The nearest, the most painful amputations are those made from the breast around the heart.'—I thought, in my simplicity, that this must mean brothers and sisters, near relations, and Gertrude came to my mind. But then it was said to me : ' Who are My brethren ? They who keep My Father's commandments are My brethren. Blood-relations are not the nearest to the heart. Christ's blood-relations are they who were once of the same mind, Catholics who have fallen away from the faith.'—Then I saw how quickly the side of the body was healed. The proud flesh in the wounds are heretics, and dissenters form the gangrened part. I saw every member, every wound, and its signification. The body reached to heaven; it was the Body of Christ. The sight made me forget my pains, and I began to work with all my strength to cut, to bind, and carry the sheaves to the Nuptial House. I saw the saints helping from on high and the twelve future Apostles taking part successively in the labor. I saw also some living laborers, but they were few and at great distances apart. I was almost worn out, my fingers ached from binding, and I was drenched with perspiration. I had just one sheaf more of good wheat, but the ears pricked me, I was quite overcome. Suddenly a polished fop with very insinuating manners stepped up to me saying that I must cease working, it was too much for me, and that, after all, it did not concern me. At first, I did not recognize him ; but, when he began to make love and promise me a fine time, I discovered that it was the devil and I repulsed him indignantly. He instantly disappeared. I saw the harvest-field surrounded by an immense vine, and the new Apostles working vigorously at it and calling upon others to do the same. They stood, at first, widely apart. When the harvest was over, the laborers all joined in celebrating a great feast of thanksgiving."

Consoling Symbol of the Effect of Prayer.

" I am still much fatigued from my work, every limb aching. From the harvest-field I went into a large empty barn and found some poor people famishing in a corner. I began to think how I could assist them, when in came crowds of ecclesiastics and laics of all ages and callings, rich and poor, from far and near, known and unknown, all seeking help. My guide told me that I could supply the wants of all, if I worked hard. I expressed my readiness, when he took me over a heath to a large field of wheat and rye, where I set all the people to work at the harvest, binding the sheaves and carrying them away. I directed all. I set the most distinguished to oversee the others. But they were, for the most part, both lazy and awkward; their sheaves would not stand. I had to put one in the centre and lean the others up against it. They carried the wheat to the barn where it was threshed and divided. In the upper story a quantity was stored for the Pope, some for a very pious Bishop whom I did not know, and some for the Vicar-General and our own country. I saw the different parishes and priests receiving their share, some much, others little. The good received most, and the best, more wheat than rye; the bad got nothing at all. Very little came here: the pastor of H— got a very large share ; the confessor, a very small portion, and what remained was distributed to any who wanted it. Sometimes a simple vicar received a portion whilst the pastor got nothing. My guide made the division of it. I am so worn out by this work that I cannot get rested. . . ."

CHAPTER III.

Journeys to the Nuptial House.—Sufferings on Account of the Profanation of the Most Blessed Sacrament.

Daily during the ecclesiastical year did Sister Emmerich travel to the Holy Land under the care of her angel, who chose the route both going and returning. This he determined by the various tasks she had to fulfil for the sick, the dying, the needy, and the souls in purgatory, in accordance with the order laid down by God. No one was excluded from her charitable ministrations, but the Head of the Church received her chief attention when in need of aid to lighten the burden of his pastoral charge. Rome was as familiar to her as the Holy Land. The Vatican, the various churches of the Eternal City, were as well known to her as the Temple, the Palace of David, the Cenacle, and other Holy Places of Jerusalem. On these journeys she visited those places sanctified by the birth, labors and death of the saints, who frequently appeared to her and gave an account of the various details of their life and sufferings. Every day brought its own special tasks, its own particular visions on the mysteries connected with the work of Redemption, so that we must not be surprised at her inability to relate all, weighed down as she was by corporal and mental sufferings. The connection between the Church's calendar and Sister Emmerich's mission was close and real; only the contemplative can understand the multiplicity and variety of action thereby entailed. Although the fragments contained in the following communications are short, they are, nevertheless, most striking and sufficient to convince the reader of the marvellous ways by which this soul was led in the accomplishment of works whose surprising manifestation will redound to the greater glory of God on the Judgment Day.

July, 1820, she related the following:—"I was commanded to travel over the world in order to see its misery. I went through St. Ludger's vineyard to that of St. Peter, viewing everywhere the sad state of mankind and the Church represented by different degrees of cold, fog, and darkness, though here and there I beheld bright spots and people standing in prayer. I had visions of these individuals. Wherever I went, I was taken to the needy, the abandoned, the sick, the persecuted, the imprisoned, for whom I prayed, aiding and consoling them in many ways. Everywhere I saw the state of the Church, the saints of the countries, Bishops, martyrs, religious, and anchorites—all upon whom the grace of God had descended. I saw especially those who had had visions and what their visions were. I saw them appearing in prayer to others and others to them. I saw all that they had done, and I understood that the Church has always had such servants, visions, and apparitions. They existed even in the time of promise, constituting one of her richest graces and contributing largely to her welfare and union. I saw everywhere holy bodies lying in tombs. I saw their influence, their connection with the saints, and the blessing emanating from them through their union with their souls. In this immense vision I had scarcely any other joy than that of seeing the Church founded upon a rock, and of knowing that love follows her and imitates Jesus, from which spring eternal blessings. I was told that in the Old Testament God sent angels to men and warned them in dreams. But, after all, that was not so clear and perfect as the spiritual teaching of Christianity—

and yet, how faithfully and simply the people of the Old Law followed such divine inspirations!—

" When I arrive in any country, I generally see in the chief city, as in a central point, its spiritual state indicated by cold, fog, and darkness. I see the headquarters of corruption and pictures of its greatest perils. I understand all. From them I see streams and pools spreading through the land like poisoned veins, and in their midst pious souls in prayer, churches containing the Blessed Sacrament, countless holy bodies, good works being performed, sin expiated or prevented, assistance given to the needy, etc. When I see the sins and abominations of a nation, their good and evil works; when I have discovered the source of the poison, the cause of their maladies, I see as a necessary result the suffering, chastisement, destruction they entail and a total or partial cure effected in proportion as the good performed by its own people produces salutary effects, or the charitable efforts of others done for the love of Jesus, bring forth streams of grace and salvation. Over some places sunk in darkness I see destruction floating in threatening pictures; over others are strife and bloodshed darkening the air, and from them frequently issues another striking picture with its own signification. These dangers and chastisements do not stand alone. They are connected with the crimes of other countries; and thus, sin becomes the rod that strikes the guilty.

" Whilst all this appears in dark, earthly pictures over these lands, I see above them the good, luminous germs giving rise to other pictures like a world of light, representing what is done for it by its holy members through the treasures of grace they pour out upon it from the merits of Jesus Christ. I see above desecrated churches other churches floating in light, and I see the Bishops, doctors, martyrs, intercessors, prophets and all the privileged souls that once belonged to them; pictures of their miracles, graces, visions, revelations, and apparitions pass before me; and I see their influence far and near, the effects it produced even at the most remote distances. A blessing still lingers over the paths they have trodden, since they are still united with their country and flock through pious souls who keep their memory alive. I see that their bones, wherever they rest, are in mysterious communication with them and become the sources of their loving intercession. Unless supported by God's grace, one could not contemplate such misery and abomination side by side with so great mercy and love—one would die of grief.

"If on the road there are some needy souls for whom the Lord deigns to receive the prayers of a poor creature, I am conducted to them and I behold the cause of their misfortunes. I draw near to their bed if they sleep, I approach them if awake, and I offer to God a fervent prayer for them that He may receive from me in their behalf what they cannot, or know not how to do for themselves. I often have to take upon myself a part of their sufferings. Sometimes they are people who have implored the prayers of others, or even my own, and this is the reason I have to take these journeys; they are all for my neighbor's relief. Then I see the poor creatures turning to God, from whom they receive consolation and all that they need, rarely in a miraculous way, but by ordinary though often unexpected means. This shows that corporal and spiritual distress comes most frequently from man himself who, instead of turning like a child to beg and receive help from the ever-open Hand of God, shuts himself up in himself incredulous and defiant. My intervention, I who have the gift of *seeing*, is in itself the Hand of God that sends to many a blind, closed heart one who *sees*, who is open to the light, who is as a channel for His plenteous mercy. On these journeys I am often directed to hinder sin by intervening to strike terror into, to disconcert some evil-minded person. I have more than once aroused mothers whose infants were in need of them, or in danger of being smothered either by themselves, or drowsy nurses, etc."

" I went over Ludger's vineyard (Münster) where I found things in a miserable state, as usual ; through that of St. Liborius (Paderborn) in which I last labored and which I found improved ; and then by the place where lie Nepomecene, Wenceslas, Ludmilla, and other saints. This place is full of holy remains, but there are few pious priests among the living, and I saw that the good, holy people generally live hidden. I went southward to a great city (Vienna) with a high tower, around which are many streets and avenues ; a broad river flows by the city (the Danube). I turned to the left into a high mountainous district (Tyrol), where dwell many pious souls, especially in the thinly settled parts. Still journeying toward the south, I arrived at a city on the sea (Venice) in which I lately saw St. Ignatius and his companions, St. Mark and other saints ; but great corruption prevails there. I went into Ambrose's vineyard (Milan) and there I saw many visions and graces granted to St. Ambrose, and especially his influence over St. Augustine. I learned many things about him, his knowledge of a person who possessed in some degree the gift of recognizing relics.—I had visions on this point and I think the saint has referred to it in a book. I learned, also, that no one ever had this faculty so fully as God has imparted it to me, and this because of the shameful neglect of relics, and because the veneration of them must be renewed. I saw as I went south an incredible number of churches and saints favored with various graces. I saw clearly the works, visions, apparitions of St. Benedict and his companions ; the two Catherines of Sienna and Bologna, Clare of Montefalco, their visions and apparitions. During my great vision in the diocese of St. Ambrose, it seemed to me that the saint spoke from heaven, for I saw the influence and ministry of women and virgins in the Church through the gift of contemplation, apparition, and prophecy, and he said something on the discernment of true and false visions ; but I cannot repeat his words. I ought to say that in the different countries I generally saw holy Bishops in the first rank, then priests, monks, nuns, hermits, and laics. I saw the apparitions of saints to them in their lifetime and in time of pressing need, when they bore them counsel and consolation from God. I saw in this great country Magdalene di Pazzi and Rita of Cassia, and many of Catherine of Sienna's visions, missions, etc.

"I came to the church of Peter and Paul (Rome) and saw a dark world of distress, confusion, and corruption, through which shone countless graces from thousands of saints who there repose. Could I relate but a portion of what I saw in this central point of the Church, it would furnish material for a lifelong meditation. Those Popes whose relics I possess I saw most distinctly.—I must have some of Callistus I., the seventeenth Pope, which I have not yet found This Pope had many apparitions. I saw John the Evangelist's death and his appearing to Callistus, once with Mary and once with Our Saviour, to strengthen him in time of need. I saw several apparitions made to Xystus, of whom I have a relic, and numberless others of the Apostles and disciples to one another and to their successors, giving them warning in times of distress. In these apparitions I saw a certain order of rank and dignity and their correspondence to the needs of him who received them. The messengers from the Church Triumphant are delegated with due regard to the importance of the occasion on which they are sent, and not in accordance with the blind judgment of the world. With regard to the gift of recognizing relics, I must add that St. Praxedes possessed it to a certain degree.

"I saw the Holy Father surrounded by traitors and in great distress about the Church. He had visions and apparitions in his hour of greatest need. I saw many good pious Bishops; but they were weak and wavering, their cowardice often got the upper hand. I saw the *black fellow* plotting again, the destroyers attacking the Church of Peter, Mary standing with her mantle over it, and the enemies of God put to flight. I saw Sts. Peter and Paul laboring actively for the Church and their basilica greatly enlarged. Then I saw darkness spreading around and people no longer seeking the true Church. They went to another, saying : 'All is more beautiful, more natural here, better regulated' — but, as yet, I have seen no ecclesiastic among them. I saw the Pope firm, but greatly perplexed. The treaty thought to be so advantageous to us will be of no use ; things will go from bad to worse. The Pope shows more energy now ; he has been advised to hold out till death, and this he gained by his late act of firmness. But his last orders are of no account, he enforces them too feebly. I saw over the city terrible evils from the north.

"Thence I went over water in the midst of which lie islands with their good and evil ; the most insolated are the happiest, the brightest. I travelled westward into Xavier's country (Portugal) where I saw many saints and the whole land full of soldiers in red. The master was toward the south beyond the sea. This country was pretty tranquil compared with that of St. Ignatius, which I now entered and found in frightful misery. Darkness lay over the whole land where reposes the treasure of the saint's graces and merits. I was at the central point, and I recognized the place where long before I had had a vision of people cast into a fiery furnace around which their enemies were gathered; but they who had kindled the flames were themselves consumed by them (1). I saw unheard-of abominations spreading over the land, and my guide said to me : ' *This is Babel !'*—I saw throughout the whole country a chain of secret societies with influences at work like those of Babel. They were connected with the building of the tower by a web fine as that of a spider, which extended up through all ages. Its highest blossom was the diabolical woman Semiramis. I saw all going to ruin, sacred things destroyed, impiety and heresy flowing in. A civil war was brewing and a destructive internal crisis was at hand. I saw the former labors of innumerable saints, as well as the saints themselves, of whom I shall mention only Isidore, John of the Cross, Jane of Jesus, and chiefly Teresa, many of whose visions I saw. I was shown the labors of St. James whose tomb is on a mountain. I saw what numbers of pilgrims here find salvation. My guide pointed out Montserrat. He showed me the old hermits who formerly dwelt there, and I had a touching vision of them. They never knew the day of the week. They counted time by dividing a loaf into seven parts of which they ate one part each day. Sometimes when in ecstasy, they made a mistake of a whole day. The Mother of God used to appear and tell them what to announce to men. I saw such misery in this country, so many graces trodden under foot, so many saints

(1) The preceding March Sister Emmerich had seen under the symbol of a burning furnace into which the innocent were cast, the condemnation of the good, the destruction of faith and morals in the country of St. Ignatius ; and she understood that they who prepared the ruin of the innocent should share the fate of their victims.

and their visions, that the thought arose in my mind : ' Why must I, miserable sinner, see all this ? The greater part of it I cannot understand, much less relate'—then spoke my guide : 'Repeat what thou canst ! Thou knowest not how many souls will one day read it and be consoled, reanimated, and encouraged by it. There are numerous accounts of similar graces, but sometimes they are not related as they should be. Ancient things are distasteful to the people of this age, or they are often maliciously misrepresented. What you relate will be published in a better way, and will be productive of blessings far greater than you can imagine.'— This consoled me, as for a few days I had been discouraged and scrupulous.

"From this unhappy land I was taken over the sea, a little toward the north, to an Island in which St. Patrick had been (Ireland) and here I found faithful, sincere Catholics, but very much oppressed. They held relations with the Pope, but very secretly, and there was still much good in the country because the people were united. I had an instruction at this point on the communion of the Church's members. I saw St. Patrick and many of his works. I learned much of his history, and I saw some pictures of the great vision of purgatory he once had in a cave, when he recognized many of the poor souls whom he afterward delivered. The Blessed Virgin used to appear and instruct him what to do.

"From St. Patrick's island I crossed a narrow sea to another large island (England), dark, cold, and foggy, in which I saw, here and there, a band of pious sectarians; but, for the rest, all was great confusion, the whole nation divided into two parties and engaged in dark, disgusting intrigues. The more numerous part was the more wicked. The smaller one had the soldiers on their side and, though

better than the other, yet it was not of much account. I saw
the two parties struggling together and the smaller one
victorious; but there was abominable scheming going on,
every one seemed a spy to watch and betray his neighbor.
Above this land I saw a host of God's friends of former
times, so many holy kings, Bishops, and apostles of
Christianity who left their homes to labor among us in
Germany: St. Walburga, King Edward, Edgar, and St.
Ursula, and I learned that the tradition which makes the
11,000 virgins an army of maidens, is not true. They
were a kind of confraternity like our own charitable associations, and they did not go all together to Cologne for
some of them dwelt widely apart. I saw great misery in
the cold, foggy country, wealth, crime, and ships.

" I continued my journey eastward over the sea into a cold
country in which I saw Sts. Bridget, Canute, and Eric (Sweden
and Denmark). It was poorer, in a more tranquil state than
the last, but it, also, was dark and foggy. It is a land rich in
iron, but not fertile. I do not remember what I did or saw
here; the inhabitants were all staunch Protestants. Then
I passed into an immense dark country subject to great
tempests and full of wickedness. The inhabitants are ex-
cessively proud. They build great churches (Russia) and
think themselves in the right way. I saw them everywhere arming and working; all was dark and menacing.
I saw St. Basil and others. I saw *the fellow* lurking near
the shining palace. I went now on to the south, etc. . . . ."
To China, as we may judge from her description of the country, where she beheld many early martyrs and apostles of
Christianity and the good effected in her own day by the
efforts of the Dominicans. She visited the scene of the
labors and death of St. Thomas, as also that of St. Francis
Xavier and his companions; and she traversed the isles in

which the light of the Gospel is now breaking. One large
island she mentioned particularly, in which the faith is making rapid strides. The people, both Catholics and Protestants, are truly good and gladly receive instruction; the
latter being well-inclined toward Catholicity, the church is
crowded at all public functions. The city is so densely peopled that they are beginning to extend its limits. The native
population are excellently well disposed. They are of a brown
complexion, some of them quite black. They were accustomed to go almost naked, but they now dress as their teachers
prescribe. Sister Emmerich saw their idols which she described—the island seems to be the same for which she had
prayed on Christmas night. In India she met the people
whom, on a former occasion, she had seen drawing the sacred waters of the Ganges and kneeling before a cross;
they were now in a better condition, receiving instruction,
and about to form into a community—it was here she had
a vision of St. Thomas and St. Xavier. Thence she went
into the neighborhood of the Mountain of the Prophets,
traversed the dark country of Semiramis where she met Sts.
Simon and Jude, saw the huge columns of the ruined city,
passed through the land of St. John the Baptist and that
in which the Evangelist John wrote his Gospel, and entered the Promised Land to find ruin on all sides. The Holy
Places are hardly recognizable, though grace still operates
through them. Here her visions became general, portray-
ing the malice of men by frustrating the abundant means of
salvation offered them. On Mt. Carmel she had a vision
of St. Berthold and the discovery of the Holy Lance at
Antioch. She saw many fervent religious, monks and
nuns, still serving God there.

"I saw that my relic of the Knight of Malta is one of St.
Berthold whom the hermit, Peter of Provence, took on the

Crusade. They were together at the seige of Antioch.
When their need was most pressing, Berthold thought: ' If
we had the lance with which Our Lord was wounded, we
should surely conquer'—then he, Peter, and another, though
unknown to one another, severally invoked God's assistance.
The Blessed Virgin appeared to all three separately. She
told them that the lance of Longinus was concealed in the
wall behind the altar of the church, bidding them communicate this intelligence to one another. They obeyed ; they
sought and found the sacred lance walled up in a chest behind
the altar. The iron point was rather short, and the shaft was
broken into several pieces. Victory followed the lance
everywhere. Berthold had vowed to devote himself to the
Blessed Virgin on Mt. Carmel, if the city were delivered ;
he became an anchorite, and later on the Founder and General of the Carmelite Order."

Sister Emmerich then spoke of other holy monks and
hermits whom she had met on her spiritual journey through
the Holy Land, and of many chosen souls who like herself
had been taken there in ecstasy. She found all dark and
dreary in the country in which the Israelites had sojourned,
and she met there some ignorant, but well-meaning monks
belonging to a certain sect. She passed many half-ruined
pyramids belonging to the earliest ages, and saw St. Sabbas
and other saints of the desert. Thence she turned to the
land of St. Augustine and Perpetua, pushed on southward
through frightful darkness, and visited Judith whom she
found pensively planning some way of escape that she
might receive instruction, for she was at heart a Christian.
Sister Emmerich begged God to help her. After this she
crossed over to Brazil where, also, she met saints, visited
the islands, saw many new Christian settlements, passed
through America, found a new impulse given to religion

and met St. Rose and others. She returned over the sea
to Sardinia and found Rosa Maria Serra, the stigmatisée of
Ozieri, still alive to the astonishment of all who knew her,
though old and bedridden. She saw another similarly
favored whom she had met some time previously at Cagliari,
a maritime city of Sicily. The people of this country were
in a tolerably good state. She went on to Rome, thence to
Switzerland, visited Einsiedeln and the abodes of the ancient
hermits, of Nicholas von der Flue, and others. She saw in passing St. Francis de Sales, and St. Chantal's convent; crossed
into Germany where she saw Sts. Walburga, Kilian, the Emperor Henry, and Bonifacius; recognized Frankfort, saw the
infant-martyr (1) and the old merchant in his tomb; crossed
the Rhine and met Sts. Boniface, Goar, and Hildegarde, of
whom she had special visions. She was told that to the latter had been imparted, through the grace of the Holy Ghost,
the power of committing her visions to writing, although
she had never learned to read or write; of calling down
chastisement upon prevaricators; and of prophesying concerning the wicked woman of Babylon. No one ever received so many graces as Hildegarde whose revelations are
fulfilled even in our own day. Sister Emmerich now met
Elizabeth of Schœnau and, on visiting France, saw Sts.
Genevieve, Denis, Martin, with a host of others; but frightful misery, corruption, and abomination reigned in the capital. It appeared to her to be in a sinking condition and
that no stone would be left upon another. Thence she
went to Liege, Belgium, and saw Sts. Juliana and Odilia; in
Brabant, she had visions of St. Lidwina who was wholly insensible to the worms that ate her body, her miserable state
of poverty, or the tears that froze on her cheeks as they
flowed, for Mary stood by her bed extending her mantle

(1) The details will be given later on.

over her. Mary of Oignies she saw in a country still inhabitated by pious Christians, and returning through Bockholt, she found many of the same stamp on the frontiers of Holland. Whilst passing through Saxony, she had seen Sts. Gertrude and Mechtilde. She had visions of their gifts and graces, and of what they had done for the Church. In the country of the infant-martyr, she struck terror into two men who were about murdering a poor courier, in order to seize his papers.

This journey exhausted the poor invalid; its frightful pictures agitated her soul like the waves of an angry sea. Without the support received from on high, she would, as she declared, have been unable to endure the sight of even a small part of the miseries that passed under her eyes. She saw upwards of a thousand saints with the detailed life and visions of about one hundred. But she beheld none of the clairvoyants of the day among them; indeed, she had never seen one of the latter under favorable colors—they all appeared in a suspicious light and in the train of the abominable bride of the Nuptial House. She saw the twelve future Apostles of the Church, each in his own country and present position. The saints of whom she possessed relics appeared to her more distinctly than others. From this fact she inferred that there are among her treasures some of Apostles and disciples which she would discover later.

This extended journey was accompanied by corporal sufferings in expiation of the outrages offered to her Divine Spouse in the Blessed Sacrament of the Altar. She was taken into the various churches she met on her way, there to atone by her fervent prayers for the affronts to which Jesus was exposed from the tepidity, indifference, and incredulity of the age. The first communication on this subject relates to the celebration of Corpus Christi in which she herself took part, 1819. It is given, as follows, by the Pilgrim :—

"All night I went around among the unhappy and afflicted, some known to me, others unknown, and I begged God to let me bear the burden of all who could not approach the Holy Communion with a light and joyous heart. Then I took their sufferings on my own shoulders. I found them so great as to weigh me down almost to the earth. The poor people passed before me in pictures, and from each I took a part or the whole of his burden according as I could get it. I drew it from his breast under the form of fine, flexible rolls, light as a tender switch, but so numerous as to make an enormous package when bound together. My own torments were under the form of a long white leathern girdle, about a hand in breadth, streaked with red. I bound all the rolls together, folded them in two, and fastened the great, heavy package over my cross with the two ends of my girdle. The rolls were variously colored according to the different sufferings they symbolized— if I reflected a little, I should be able to name the colors of many whom I knew. I took the huge bundle on my shoulders and made a visit to the Blessed Sacrament to offer these sufferings for the poor, blind creatures who know not that infinite treasure of consolation. First I went into a chapel, unfinished, unadorned, but in which, notwithstanding, God was waiting on the altar. There I offered my package and prayed to the Blessed Sacrament. It seemed as if this chapel had sprung up merely to give me strength, for I was almost sinking under the burden which I carried on my right shoulder in memory of the wound made on Our Lord's shoulder by the cross. I have often seen that wound, the most painful of all on His Sacred Body. At last I

came to a place in which a procession was being made and
I saw, at the same moment, similar processions in distant
places. In the one in which I took part figured most of
those whose sufferings I bore and I saw, to my astonishment, the same colors issuing from their mouth as they
sang, as were the rolls I had drawn from them. The Blessed Sacrament had the appearance of a little luminous, transparent Infant in the centre of a resplendent sun, surrounded by myriads of angels and saints in great splendor and
magnificence. It is inexpressible ! If the others had seen
what I saw, they would have sunk to the ground unable
from terror and amazement to bear the monstrance further.
I prayed and offered my pack. Then the procession entered into a church which now appeared in the air surrounded
by a garden and cemetery. The graves of the latter were
covered with lovely flowers: lilies, red and white roses,
and white asters. From the east side of the church advanced in unspeakable splendor a priestly figure like unto
Our Lord. He was soon encircled by twelve resplendent
men, and these again by numerous others. I had a good
position, I could see everything. There issued from the
Lord's mouth a little luminous form which gradually increased, took a more definite shape, and then again decreasing
entered the mouth under the figure of a little shining child,
first of the Twelve then of all the others around the Lord.
This was not the historic scene which I see on Holy Thursday, the Lord reclining at table with His Apostles, but it
reminded me of it—all was luminous and sparkling, a divine function, a Church festival. The whole church was
crowded, some sitting, some standing, some hovering
in the air. There were seats raised in tiers, but perfectly
transparent. I saw in the Lord's hands a figure into which
entered the little luminous body that issued from His mouth

and around which appeared a spiritual church highly ornamented—it was the Blessed Sacrament in the monstrance
as It is when exposed for adoration or Benediction. The Lord
repeatedly uttered into It His loving Word, and the Body,
ever one and the same, entered the mouth of all the assistants.

"I laid down my burden awhile and received the Heavenly Manna. When I took it up again, I beheld a troop
of people whose bundles were so filthy that I dreaded to
touch them. I was informed that they were still to be
severely judged and punished according to their works of
penance, but I felt no pity for them. The feast ended, and
it seemed to me as if I had seen some men who would re-
kindle over all the world faith and fervor in the admirable
mystery of the real presence of God. The chapel in which
I had first rested with my burden was in a mountain as,
when a child, I had seen the altars and tabernacles of the
early Christians—it represented the Blessed Sacrament in
time of persecution. The cemetery signified that the altars
of the Unbloody Sacrifice should stand over the tombs and
relics of martyrs, that the churches themselves should be
erected over them. I saw the Church under the form
of a spiritual, heavenly festival. A four-branch candlestick stood before the altar. I saw the Feast of Corpus
Christi, first directly through Jesus, then through the
Blessed Sacrament Itself, the treasure of the Church. I
saw the feast celebrated by numbers of the early Christians, by those of our own times, and by many belonging to the future, and I received an assurance that Its
worship would flourish with new vigor in the Church.

"On the feasts of the holy peasant Isidore, many
things were shown me on the importance of celebrating and
hearing Mass, and I saw how great a blessing it is that so
many are said though even by ignorant and unworthy

priests, as it averts all sorts of dangers, chastisements, and calamities from men. It is well that many priests do not realize what they do, for if they did they would be so terrified as not to be able to celebrate the Holy Sacrifice. I saw the marvellous blessings attached to hearing Mass. It facilitates labor, promotes good, and prevents loss. One member of a family returning from Mass, carries home a blessing to the whole house and for the whole day. I saw how much greater is the advantage attached to hearing a Mass, than to having one said without assisting at it. I saw all defects in the celebration of Mass supernaturally supplied."

The week preceding Pentecost, 1820, Sister Emmerich's sufferings both of mind and body were almost insupportable. These sufferings she had to offer as an atonement for the outrages committed against the Blessed Sacrament. She was assisted by the saints of the day, and particularly by the highly gifted souls who in the past had suffered in the same manner as she now did. "To-day, May 17, 1820," writes the Pilgrim, "I found the invalid in tears, because Clara Soentgen wanted to bring some strangers to see her.—'Every moment I think I shall die of pain,' she groaned, 'and yet they leave me no rest!'—Her malady (retention and a suffocating cough) is intolerable and the shooting pains in her wounded side intense; her longing for the Blessed Sacrament consumes her and her deep sadness makes her shed torrents of tears. Her sufferings of body and soul are pitiful to behold. She begged the child (her niece) to say three Our Fathers to obtain for her strength to live, if it were God's will that she should do so. The little girl prayed with her, and she became calm."

May 18th—"Her desire for the Blessed Sacrament becomes more violent. She languishes, laments the privation of her daily bread, and cries out in ecstasy: 'Why dost

Thou leave me thus to languish for Thee? Without Thee I must die! Thou alone canst help me! If I must live, give me life!"—When she awoke, she exclaimed :—' My Lord has told me that I now must see what I am without Him. Things are changed—I must become His nourishment, my flesh must be consumed in ardent desires.' Her visions at this holy season are sad ; so much distress and misery, so many offences against God! She cannot relate them."

Feast of Pentecost, May 21st.—The Pilgrim, who had witnessed her anguish and tears on the preceding evening, found her this morning radiant as a spouse of Christ, breathing but joy and holiness.

" I have been in the Cenacle with the Apostles, and I have been fed in a way that I cannot express. Nourishment under the form of a wave of light flowed into my mouth. It was exceedingly sweet, but I know not whence it came. I saw no hand, and I began to fear lest, perhaps, having broken my fast, I should not be able to receive Holy Communion in the morning. I was not here, and yet I distinctly heard the clock strike twelve, stroke for stroke. I counted each one. I beheld the descent of the Holy Ghost on the disciples, and how the same Holy Spirit on every anniversary of this feast spreads all over the earth wherever He finds pure hearts desirous of receiving Him. I can describe this only by saying that I saw here and there in the darkness a parish, a church, a city, or one or more individuals suddenly illumined. The whole earth lay in darkness below me, and I saw by a flash of heavenly light here a flower-bed, there a tree, a bush, a fountain, an islet, not only lit up, but rendered quite luminous. Through the mercy of God, all that I saw last night was good; the works of darkness were not shown me. All over the world I saw numberless infusions of the Spirit; sometimes, like a light-ning-stroke, falling on a congregation in church, and I could tell who among them had received the grace; or, again, I beheld individuals praying in their homes, suddenly endued with light and strength. The sight awoke in me great joy and confidence that the Church amid her ever-increasing tribulations, will not succumb; for in all parts of the world I saw defenders raised up to her by the Holy Ghost. Yes, I felt that the oppression of the powers of this world serves but to increase her strength. I saw in St. Peter's at Rome a grand feast celebrated with myriads of lights, and I saw the Holy Father and many others receiving the strength of the Holy Ghost. I did not see the dark church last night (Protestant) which is always a horror to me. I saw in different places the twelve enlightened men whom I see so often as twelve new Apostles or Prophets of the Church. I feel as if I know one of them, that he is near me. I saw the Holy Spirit poured out on some of our own land. I knew them all in my vision, but it is seldom that I can name them afterward. I think I saw the stern Superior. I felt certain that the persecution of the Church here in our own country will turn out well, but great troubles await us."

On Whit-Monday, a painful task of reparation to the Blessed Sacrament was announced to her :—

" I knelt alone with my guide in a large church before the Blessed Sacrament which was surrounded by indescriba-ble glory. In It I saw the resplendent figure of the Infant Jesus before whom since my childhood I have always opened my heart and poured out my prayers. As I presented my petitions, I received an answer to each one from the Blessed Sacrament in the form of a ray which pierced my soul and filled me with consolation. I was, also, gently reproved for my faults. I passed almost the whole night before the tabernacle, my angel at my side." Sister Emmerich's humility would not allow her to give the details of this vision. It was immediately followed by apparitions of St. Augustine and two holy Augustinians, Rita of Cassia and Clare of Montefalco, who prepared her to undergo sufferings such as they themselves had formerly endured for the Blessed Sacrament. She fell into ecstasy and, to the amazement of her confessor and the Pilgrim, who were conversing together in the antechamber, she suddenly stood up on her bed (a thing she had not done for four years), her countenance radiant with joy, her hands raised to heaven, and recited slowly and devoutly in a sweet, clear voice, the whole of the *Te Deum.* Her face was emaciated and slightly sallow, but her cheeks were flushed and a look of enthusiasm beamed from her dark eyes. She stood upright, firm and secure in her position. At certain parts she joined her hands and inclined her head suppliantly, her voice betraying a tender, caressing accent like a child reciting verses in its father's honor. Her ample robe fell below the ankles, giving her a most imposing appearance, and her prayer, repeated in a loud voice, excited in the hearer a feeling of mingled piety and awe.

" St. Augustine stood by me," she said next day, " in his episcopal robes, and O he was so kind ! I was rejoiced to see him and I accused myself of never especially honoring him. He replied : ' Still I know thee. Thou art my child !'—When I asked him to relieve my pain, he presented me a nosegay in which was a blue flower—a feeling of strength and relief instantly pervaded my whole person. The saint said to me : ' Thou wilt never be entirely well, for thy way is that of suffering. But, when in need of help and consolation, think of me. I shall always give them thee. Now rise and say the *Te Deum* to thank the Most Holy

Trinity for thy cure.' Then I arose and prayed. I was perfectly strong and my joy was very great. Afterward I saw St. Augustine in his glory. First, I beheld the Most Holy Trinity and the Blessed Virgin, I can hardly say how. I seemed to see an old man on a throne. From his forehead and breast streamed rays of light in the form of a cross from which, in turn, shot numerous other rays over the choirs and orders of angels and saints. At some distance, surrounded by blessed spirits, I saw St. Augustine's celestial glory. He was seated on a throne, receiving from the cross of the Holy Trinity streams of light which he imparted to the surrounding choirs. Around him were priests in various costumes, and on one side, rising like a mountain one above the other and floating like clouds in the sky, were numerous churches, all of which had emanated from the saint. This was a picture of his heavenly greatness. The light received from the Trinity symbolized his own personal illumination. The choirs around him were the different vessels, the different souls that received light through him. They, in their turn, poured it upon others whilst receiving, also, rays directly from God. The sight of such things is unspeakably beautiful and consoling, and so natural—yes, more natural, more intelligible than the sight of a tree or flower upon earth. In the choirs around the saint were all the priests and doctors, all the Orders and communities which had emanated from him, inasmuch as they are blessed, inasmuch as they have become vessels of God, gushing fountains of living waters whose source is in him. After this I saw him in a heavenly garden, but this picture was a little lower down. The first was a vision of his glory, his place in the starry heaven of the Most Holy Trinity; the second was rather a picture of his actual influence upon earth, his assistance to the Church Militant, to living men. All pictures of the celestial gardens appear lower than those of the saints in God, in glory. I beheld him in a beautiful garden full of the most wonderful trees, shrubs, and flowers. There were many others with him, among whom I remember particularly St. Francis Xavier and St. Francis de Sales. They were not seated in order as for a feast, but going around, distributing the flowers and fruits of the garden, which represent the graces and good works of their life. I saw numbers of the living in the garden, many of whom I knew, and they were receiving gifts in manifold ways. The apparition of the living is something very special, the counterpart, as it were, of the apparition of saints upon earth. They appear in the garden of the saints like spirits under certain, indeterminate forms, and receive all kinds of fruits and flowers. I see some who seem to be raised into this sphere of grace by prayer, and others who seem to receive such favors without conscious effort on their part; they are vessels of election. The same difference exists between these two classes as between one who takes the trouble to gather fruit in a garden, and another who sees it falling at his feet as he walks along, or to whom God deigns to send it by this or that saint.

"After this my guide led me on my own road to the Heavenly Jerusalem, and I saw that I was now far beyond the place where I had seen the little notes of warning (1). I climbed a mountain and reached a garden of which St. Clare of Montefalco had charge. In her hands I saw luminous wounds and around her brow a shining crown of thorns; for, although she had not had the exterior marks of the Wounds, she had felt their pain. Clare told me that this was her garden and that, as I loved gardening, she would

(1) See Vol. I., Chap. 39.

show me how it should be carried on. There was a wall around it, but it was only symbolical, for one could both see and pass through it ; it was built of round, variegated, shining stones. The garden was laid out in eight beautiful beds all verging toward the centre. There were some handsome large trees in full bloom, and a fountain which could be made to water the whole place. A vine was trained all around the wall. I stayed almost all night in the garden with St. Clare. She taught me the virtue and signification of every plant and how to use it. We passed from one flower-bed to another, but I do not now remember where she got the roots. It seemed to be supernaturally in the air, or from an apparition. I worked with her near a fig-tree, though I do not now recollect at what. I only remember that there were beds of bitter-cress and chervil. Clare told me that, if my taste were too sweet, I must take a mouthful of cress, and if too bitter, a mouthful of chervil. I have always been very fond of these herbs. I used to chew them when I was a child, indeed I could have lived on them. The hardest thing for me to understand was Clare's management of the vine, how she trained it, divided it, and pruned it. I could not succeed. It was the last thing she taught me in the garden. During our work the birds flocked round us, perched on my shoulders and were just as familiar with me as they had been in the convent cloister. Clare told me that she had the instruments of the Passion engraven on her heart and that, after her death, three stones had been found in her gall. She spoke, also, of the graces she had received on the Feast of the Holy Trinity, bidding me prepare for a new labor on the coming feast. She looked very thin, pale, and exhausted.

"I saw, too, St. Rita of Cassia. As she prayed one day before a crucifix, she begged in her humility for one single thorn from the crown of her Crucified Saviour, when a ray of light shot from the crown and wounded her in the forehead. She suffered in that spot a lifelong, indescribable pain, matter continually oozing from it which caused her to be shunned by all. I saw also her great devotion to the Blessed Sacrament. She told me many things."

On the eve of the Most Holy Trinity, the task foretold by St. Clare began. Sister Emmerich says: " When I saw the bad preparation of so many persons who were going to confession, I renewed my petition to God to let me suffer something for their amendment ; and then, indeed, my task began. It seemed as if I were being pierced incessantly by fine darts of pain shot at me like arrows, and in the night they became more intense than I had ever felt before. They began around my heart which felt like a furnace of pain tightly bound in flames. Waves of fiery pains swept thence through all parts of my body, through the marrow of my bones, to the tips of my fingers, my nails, and my hair. It was like the regular flow of the tide from my heart to my hands, feet, and head and back again, my wounds being the principal centres. My sufferings increased until midnight when I awoke, steeped in perspiration and unable to move. I had only one consolation—the indistinct idea of the cross formed by the principal centres of my pain which seemed to be grinding me to powder. At midnight I could bear it no longer, for my stupor made me forget its cause ; so I turned like a child to my father, St. Augustine. 'Ah! dear father, St. Augustine, thou didst promise to help me whenever I invoked thee ! Ah! see my distress !'—my prayer was instantly heard. The saint stood before me, telling me most kindly why I was suffering so, but that he could not take away my pains since I was to endure them in union with the Passion of Jesus Christ.

He bade me be comforted although I was still to suffer three hours more. I was greatly consoled though in intense agony, knowing that it was for the love of Christ's Passion and to satisfy Divine Justice for sinners. I rejoiced to be of some use and I threw my whole heart into my pains. I accepted the grace of expiatory suffering with loving confidence in the mercy of the Heavenly Father. St. Augustine reminded me, moreover, that three years ago, on the morning of All-Saints, my Spouse had appeared to me as I lay at the point of death. He had given me my choice either to die and go to purgatory, or to live longer in suffering, and that I had replied : 'Lord, in purgatory my sufferings will be of no avail. If, then, it be not contrary to Thy will, let me live and endure all possible torments if thereby I can aid but a single soul !'—Then, although I had at first asked for death, my Saviour now granted my second request by prolonging my life of suffering. When my Holy Father recalled this circumstance, I distinctly remembered it and, from that moment until the end of the three hours, I calmly and thankfully endured the most cruel tortures. Pain forced from me the bitterest tears and the sweat of death.

" I had another vision of the Most Holy Trinity under the form of a resplendent old man seated on a throne. From His forehead streamed an indescribably clear, colorless light ; from His mouth flowed a luminous stream slightly tinged with yellow, like fire ; and from His breast near the heart, another stream of colored light. These streams formed in the air above the old man's breast a cross which sparkled like the rainbow, and it seemed to me that He laid His hands on its arms. Innumerable rays issued from it. They fell first on the heavenly choirs and then down upon the earth, filling and quickening all things.

A little below the Holy Trinity and to the right, I saw Mary's throne. A ray darted to her from the old man and another from her to the cross. All this is quite inexpressible. But in vision, although dazzling and swimming in light, it was perfectly intelligible: one and three, vivifying all, enlightening all, and most wonderfully sufficing for all. Below the throne were the angels in a world of colorless light; above them the four-and-twenty ancients with silver hair, surrounding the Most Holy Trinity. All the rest of the boundless space was filled with saints who were themselves the luminous centres of shining choirs. At the right of the Trinity was St. Augustine surrounded by his choirs, but much lower than Mary, and all around lay gardens, shining palaces, and churches.—I felt as if I were wandering among the starry heavens. These vessels of God are of every variety of form and appearance, but all are filled with Jesus Christ. The same law governs all, the same substance pervades all though under a different form, and a straight line leads through each into the light of the Father through the cross of the Son. I saw a long line of royal females extending from the Mother of God, virgins with crowns and sceptres, though not earthly queens, souls who had preceded or followed Mary in the order of time. They seemed to serve her as the twenty-four ancients serve the Most Holy Trinity. They were celebrating the feast by a marvellously solemn movement severally and all together. I can compare it only to beautiful music. The angels and saints advanced in one or many processions to the throne of the Most Holy Trinity like the stars in the sky revolving around the sun. And then I saw down on the earth innumerable processions corresponding to the celestial ones, also celebrating the feast—but how miserable! how dark! how full of breaks! To look upon it from above was like looking down into the mire—still there was much good here and there. I saw also our own procession here in Dülmen, and I noticed a poor little ragged child. I know where it lives. I shall clothe it (1)."

On the evening of Holy Trinity Sunday a dance was held in the house in which Sister Emmerich lodged. Next day she spoke of it as follows: "I suffered intensely last night, on account of the indecent dances and games going on in the house. In the midst of the noisy assembly I beheld the devil, a conspicuous figure under a corporal form, urging on certain individuals and inspiring them with all kinds of evil desires. Their angel-guardian called to them from afar, but they turned a deaf ear and followed the evil one. No good came from it; not one went home unharmed. I saw all sorts of animals by their side; their interior was full of black stains. I frequently ran among them, inspiring fear, preventing sin.—To console me I had visions on the life of two saints, Francis de Sales and Frances de Chantal, chiefly upon their spiritual union; the former often received counsel and support from the latter. Once on the occasion of an odious calumny against him, I saw him consoled by Frances who was distressed at seeing him so much afflicted by it. They showed me the foundation, propagation, and dispersion of the Visitation Order and spoke of the restoration of its different houses. Their words came to me as if from a distance. They said that the times are indeed sad; but, after many tribulations, peace will be restored and religion and charity reign once

"It is singularly touching," remarks the Pilgrim, "to see the goodness and compassion of her heart. In the midst of the wonders presented to the eyes of her soul, she pauses to notice the wants of a poor little child, and even to find out its abode. As it passed before her house, she exclaimed:—Ah! how I should love to bring that poor ragged little creature up here and dress it! See, how sadly it walks among the other children in their holiday clothes!'—If one still in the body can see and feel thus, how great must be the compassion of the angels and saints, our brethren in glory, of Mary, of Jesus, of God Himself, who all love us more than those on earth, and who see more clearly! How can one who prays with faith lose courage?"

more among men. Then convents will flourish in the true sense of the word. I saw a picture of this future time which I cannot describe, but in which I saw the whole earth arising from darkness and light and love awaking. I had also numerous pictures of the restoration of Religious Orders (1). The time of Antichrist is not so near as some 'imagine; he will still have many precursors. I saw in two cities some teachers from whose schools they will come."

May 30th—Feast of Corpus Christi, Sister Emmerich's sufferings recommenced as on Holy Trinity :—" Again I felt those pains like fine rays falling upon, piercing me in all directions like threads of silver. Besides, I had to carry, to drag so many people along that I am all bruised; not a bone in my body that is not, as it were, dislocated. When I awoke the middle fingers of both hands were stiff, bent, and paralyzed, and my wounds have pained intensely all night long. I saw in numerous pictures the coldness and irreverence shown the Blessed Sacrament by which I understood the guilt of those who receive It unworthily, negligently, and by routine, and I saw many going to confess in very bad dispositions. At each view, I begged God to forgive and enlighten His creatures. My guide took me into all our own parish churches and showed me everywhere how the Blessed Sacrament is worshipped. I found things best at Ueberwasser, Münster. Around the churches I often saw immense morasses with people sunk in them. I had to draw them out, clean, and sometimes carry them on my

(1) St. Hildegarde, also, describing the actual state of the times, predicts a renewal of life in the Church. After prophesying the partition of the German Empire and the increasing hostility of the secular power toward the Pope, she says : " The Pope will retain under the sovereignty of the tiara only Rome and some unimportant parts of the adjoining territory. The spoliation will be effected partly by the invasion of armed soldiers, and partly by conventions and measures concerted among the people. . . . But after awhile impiety will be vanquished for a time. It will, indeed, try to raise its head again, but justice will be so firmly administered that the people will sincerely return to the faithful practice of the simple manners and wise discipline of their forefathers — yes, even princes and lords, such as Bishops and Ecclesiastical Superiors, may imitate the virtuous example of their inferiors, and every one will esteem in his neighbor only piety and justice."—Liber divinorum operum, pars. III., Visio X., c. 25, 26.

back to the confessional. My guide constantly pointed out new miseries, saying : 'Come, suffer for this one, etc.'— In the midst of my labor I often wept like a child, though I was not wholly destitute of consolation. I beheld the manifold and marvellous workings of grace by means of the Blessed Sacrament as a light shining over all Its adorers.— Yes, even they who think not of It, receive a blessing in Its presence. Lastly I went into our own church and saw the Pilgrim crossing the cemetery and thinking of the dead. The sight pleased me, and I thought : 'He is coming to me (1).' St. Francis de Sales, St. de Chantal, St. Augustine, and other saints consoled me. I saw too that I am instrumental in relieving and healing souls, and that I suffer in union with the Passion of Jesus.

" I had a picture of the Abbé Lambert whose sixty-seventh birthday this is. I saw him in his room, dragging around on his lame foot and apparently growing smaller and smaller, so that several times I lost sight of him altogether. I was told that if he did not become like an innocent little child, he could not enter heaven, and that his sickness is very serviceable to him. Now, as I thought he had already become very small, I suddenly saw a beautiful luminous infant lie down beside him, as if to measure itself with him. But the Abbé was still larger than the infant, and I understood that he had to be exactly the same size as the child, before he could attain beatitude."

In the midst of these sufferings which followed one another in quick succession, she had on Corpus Christi rich and detailed visions upon the institution of the Blessed Sacrament and Its worship down to the present time. But her weakness was so great that she was scarcely able to communicate even what follows :—

(1) About six o'clock A. M. the time the Pilgrim went to Mass. Why should her other visions be less true than this fact ?—(Brentano's Notes).

" I saw a vision of the institution of the Most Blessed Sacrament.—The Lord sat at the centre of the long side of the table. On His right v 1s John ; on His left a graceful, fine-looking Apostle very like to John. Next to the latter sat Peter who often leaned over him. The Lord sat and taught for awhile, then He arose and all the rest with Him. They looked on in silence, wondering what He was about to do. He took up the plate with the bread, raised His eyes, made incisions in the bread with a bone knife, and broke it into pieces. Then He moved His right hand over it as if blessing it, at which moment there flashed from Him into the bread a bright ray of light. Jesus became all resplendent, drowned, so to say, in the splendor which spread over all present. The Apostles now grew more recollected, more fervent. Judas was the only one that remained in darkness, repulsing the light. Jesus raised His eyes, elevated the chalice, and blessed it.—For what I saw passing in Him during this ceremony, I have but one expression : I saw and felt that He was transforming Himself. The bread and chalice shone with light. Jesus placed the morsels on a flat plate like a patena and, taking them one by one in His right hand, He communicated all present, commencing, I think, with His Mother who advanced to the table between the Apostles opposite Jesus. I saw light issuing from the Lord's mouth, and the bread shining and entering into that of the Apostles under a luminous human form. All were filled with light, Judas alone was dark and gloomy. The Lord then raised the chalice by the handle and gave them to drink—and here, again, I beheld a flood of light streaming over the Apostles. After the ceremony, all stood for awhile filled with emotion, and then the picture vanished. The morsels that the Lord gave the Apostles were like two little rolls joined in the middle down which was a furrow."

The above vision was followed by others relating to the changes that have been introduced in the form of the Sacrament, Its distribution and worship, of which Sister Emmerich relates the following : " I saw that in course of time whiter bread was used for the Blessed Sacrament, and the morsels were smaller. Even in the time of the Apostles, I saw St. Peter, at Jerusalem, giving only a morsel to communicants ; at first it was square, but at a later period it was round. When the Apostles dispersed, the Christians having no churches as yet, but only halls in which they assembled, the Apostles kept the Blessed Sacrament at their homes. When they carried It to the place of assembly, the faithful followed reverently, whence originated processions and public veneration. Later on, the Christians got possession of the great pagan temples which they consecrated, and in which was preserved the Blessed Sacrament. When men communicated, they received the Sacred Host in their hand and then swallowed It ; but the women made use of a small linen cloth. Up to a certain time, they were allowed to take the Sacred Species to their homes. They hung It around their neck in a little box, or casket, with a gold drawer wherein It reposed folded in linen. When this custom ceased to be general, it was still permitted to certain very devout persons. I had a vision also of the Holy Communion under two kinds. In the early ages and afterward at certain periods, I saw the faithful very enlightened, full of faith and simplicity ; but later, I beheld them straying, misled, and persecuted. I saw the Church inspired by the Holy Spirit, introducing various changes in her discipline when devotion and veneration toward the Blessed Sacrament had grown weak. Among those that separated from the Church, I saw the Sacrament Itself cease. I saw the Feast of Corpus Christi and public adoration instituted at a time of great coldness. Incalculable graces were thereby bestowed upon the whole Church. Among many other pictures, I saw a great celebration in a city known to me, I think Liege, and in a far-off, warm country, whence come fruits like dates, I saw Christians assembled in church. The priest was at the altar, when a frightful tumult arose outside, and a brutal tyrant appeared riding a white horse. He was surrounded by his followers. He led by a chain a raging wild beast which struck terror into all the beholders. The man's intention seemed to be to force the animal into the church by way of insult, and I thought I heard him say that he would show the Christians whether their God of bread were really a God or not. The people looked on in horror, whilst the priest, turning toward the entrance, gave benediction with the Blessed Sacrament.—Instantly, the furious beast stood spellbound! The priest advanced still holding the Sacred Host, when the animal meekly fell on its knees, and the tyrant and his followers were completely changed. They knelt to adore, and entered the church confused, humbled, and converted.— Last night I endured pain so violent that I often cried out. It passed through all my members, and I was shown pictures which explained to me its cause; viz., sins committed against the Holy Eucharist. I had also a picture which I cannot describe. I learned from it that Our Lord Himself watches over the parishes of bad priests in most wonderful ways and animates the people to piety."

On June 2d the Pilgrim found Sister Emmerich calm but very suffering, retaining but a slight remembrance of her visions of the preceding night. She had again seen St. Clare of Montefalco's garden. St. Clare explained to her that its eight divisions, of which three were already under cultivation, signified the eight days of the octave of

Corpus Christi. She told her the mysterious signification of the plants and what sufferings were indicated by them. In the garden near the fountain is a rose-bush surrounded by thorns.

June 3d—Again Sister Emmerich lay quite unnerved by pain and scarcely able to speak. She begged the Pilgrim's prayers for two very serious cases: one a family in the country in great dread of an impending misfortune, and another in the city in misery brought on by sin. On Sunday in the octave she lay even more prostrate than she had been since the eve of the feast.—" I passed the night, " she said, " awake and in unspeakable torment, my pains interrupted only by visions of people in distress who approached my bed as visitors do in the daytime, recommending themselves to my prayers and recounting to me their needs.— I found myself in a large church surrounded by many parishes. A long Communion Table was prepared in it. I saw both priests and laymen entering the houses around, to call the occupants to receive the Blessed Sacrament; but the latter gave a thousand different excuses. One house was full of young people trifling and amusing themselves, etc. Then I saw the servants sent out to invite the poor, the lame, and the blind whom they met on the streets, and I saw numbers of such entering, the blind led and the lame carried by those who prayed for them. I was almost exhausted. I saw many among the lame whom I know to be perfectly well. I asked a blind citizen how he had lost his sight, for until then I had not thought him blind; but he would not admit that he could not see. I met a woman whom I had known when she was a little girl, and I asked her if it were not by marrying she had become a cripple. But she, too, thought there was nothing the matter with her. The church was far from being full."

That afternoon Sister Emmerich, in obedience to an inspiration, sent for a man who often abused his wife. She exhorted him in words so earnest to treat her kindly, that he was moved to tears. The wife, also, came to be consoled and encouraged by Sister Emmerich's counsel, and the children whom she had clothed for the feast thanked her most gratefully. Then her pains recommenced. Every member was convulsed, the wounds in her hands grew red, the middle fingers contracted, and thus she lay in unmitigated suffering till the evening of June 7th. Once she said whilst in ecstasy that she was now enduring an excruciating trial, that she had reached the fig-tree in the southern end of the garden (St. Clare's) and that she had eaten one fig which contained all sorts of torments. Four beds still remained to be cultivated (four days of the octave). Sister Emmerich had no relic of St. Clare of Montefalco ; but the saint came in virtue of her connection with the Augustinian Order, to which Sister Emmerich belonged, and because their sufferings had been similar. "O that these four days were over !" sighed the Pilgrim, "for her sufferings do but increase !" And yet it was not without regret that the poor invalid saw morning dawn upon her nights of dreadful agony. At night she could at least suffer in peace, whereas day added its burden of vexations and interruptions to her weighty cross.

On June 5th, she had a vision of St. Boniface :—"I knelt before the Blessed Sacrament in a church in the middle of which were high seats, and there I saw the holy Bishop surrounded by people of every age in ancient costume, some even in the skins of beasts. They were simple and innocent. They listened open-mouthed to their holy Bishop. Around him shone a light like rays from the Holy Spirit which fell in various degrees upon his hearers. Boniface was a tall, strong, enthusiastic man.

He was explaining how the Lord marks out His own, imparting to them at an early hour His grace and Spirit.—'But,' said he, 'men must co-operate. They must carefully preserve and make use of such graces, for they are only given that their possessors may become instruments in the hand of God. Strength and ability are given to each member that it may act, not only for itself but for the whole body. The Lord gives vocations even in childhood. He who does not labor to maintain the life of grace and make use of it for his own good and that of others, steals from the body of the faithful something which belongs to it, and becomes thereby a robber in the community. Man should reflect that in loving and assisting a member of the Church, he is loving and assisting a member of one and the same body, a chosen instrument of the Holy Spirit. Above all, should parents look thus upon their children. They should not prevent their becoming the instruments of the Lord for the good of His Body, the Church. They should maintain and develop the life of grace in them and aid them to a faithful co-operation, since they can form no idea of the great injury they do the faithful by a contrary line of conduct.'—It was also shown me interiorly that, despite men's wickedness and the decadence of religion, the Church has had in every age living, acting members raised up by the Holy Spirit to pray and lovingly to suffer for her. Whilst these living members remain unknown, so much the more efficacious is their action.—The present age is no exception. Then I saw shining out through the darkness that envelopes the world, scenes of holy souls praying, teaching, suffering, and laboring for the Church. Of all the pictures that rejoiced and encouraged me in my sufferings, the following did me most good:—I saw in a great maritime city far away toward the south a sick nun in the house of a pious, industrious widow. The nun was shown me as a holy person chosen by God to suffer for the Church and other intentions. She was tall, extremely emaciated, and marked with the stigmata, though it was not publicly known. She had come from a suppressed convent and had been received by the widow who shared her means with her and some priests. The piety of the inhabitants of the city did not please me. They had many exterior devotions ; but they gave themselves up not less ardently, on that account, to sin and debauchery.

" Far away from the last-mentioned city, off toward the west, I saw in an ancient convent lately suppressed, an infirm old lay-brother confined to his room. He, too, was shown me as an instrument of prayer and suffering for his neighbor and the Church. I saw the sick, the poor, and many in affliction receiving consolation and assistance from him. Again I was told that such instruments are never wanting, that they never shall be wanting to the Church of God. They are always placed by Divine Providence where they are most necessary, nearest the centres of corruption."

On Wednesday, June 7th, 9 o'clock P. M., occurred the crisis of Sister Emmerich's present suffering. The pains left her bones, and the intolerable agony she had endured for the last days sensibly abated. She fell into a state of utter prostration, unable to move a limb, utter a sound, or give the least sign of life. Her confessor became uneasy. He put several questions to her which she understood, but to which she could answer only after the lapse of some hours. Then, weeping and stammering like a child, she begged him to pardon her silence, and told him that her pains had ceased. Next morning, Thursday, she lay like a corpse, but without pain. As she herself remarked she had fainted just as she reached the goal, and death seemed inevitable. The doctor spoke of quinine, but she made him understand that she was without fever and that in such paroxysms she generally experienced chilly sensations. "God alone can help me," she exclaimed (1), and then went on to say that Jesus, her Spouse, had sweetly relieved and consoled her; that Clare of Montefalco had appeared to tell her that the work in the garden was finished; the vine was the Blood of Jesus Christ; the fountain, the Blessed Sacrament; that the wine and water had to be mingled together; and that the rosebush near the fountain signified the sufferings in store for her toward the end of her life. She was too weak to give further details, excepting that, at break of day, she had recited the " *Te Deum*" the " Seven Penitential Psalms," and the " Litanies," and now she was to have four days of uninterrupted rest to commune with God alone. When she recalled her pains of the last eight days as well as the mercy of God to her, she could not restrain her tears. Her friends were touched with compassion at her altered appearance. And yet not one of them, not even the Pilgrim, dreamed of taking her words literally and granting the longed-for repose. He writes:

June 9th—"She is pale as a corpse, but she is allowed no rest since no one wards off annoyances from her. After her last martyrdom in union with Christ's Passion, she spoke of three days' repose, as the Body of Jesus had lain that time in the tomb, but she knows not whether she will get it. The doctor wanted to rub her with liquor; but the confessor, who expected her death, would not allow it."— Sister Emmerich could with difficulty ward off the Pilgrim's questioning, because as he says: " From her interior state

(1) " No remedy has ever been able to interpose an obstacle to the designs of God over her. We are blind, blind in everything. Science itself is but specific blindness." —(Brentano's Notes).

and her continued visions, he concluded that the end is not so near, even if the confessor does think so." The latter stood at the bedside and sought to revive her by holding out to her his consecrated fingers. Hardly had he conceived the thought, when she suddenly raised her head and moved toward his hand. As she lay thus, pale and motionless, St. Clare of Montefalco, Juliana of Liege, St. Anthony of Padua, and St. Ignatius of Loyola severally assisted and consoled her. The first-named appeared and said to her:—"Thou hast cultivated the garden of the Blessed Sacrament well and thy work is now over; but thou art exhausted, I must bring thee some refreshment."— "And instantly," continues Sister Emmerich, "I beheld the saint descending toward me resplendent with light. She gave me a three-cornered morsel upon either side of which was an image, and then disappeared. I ate it with relish. I am sure that I have eaten the same before. It was very sweet and strengthened me greatly. New life has been given me through the mercy of God. I live still, I can still love my Saviour, still suffer with Him, still thank and praise Him !. . . . . I saw the eight flower-beds which I have been cultivating these last days in St. Clare's garden. Without the help of God, it would have been absolutely impossible for me to do it. The fig-tree signified search after consolations, weak condescension, too great indulgence. Whenever I worked at the vine, I was bound to it in the form of a cross. . . . . I saw all that I had accomplished in these eight days, for what faults I had atoned, what chastisements warded off, etc. I saw all under the appearance of a procession in honor of the Most Blessed Sacrament, a spiritual festival in which the blessed celebrated the treasures of grace bestowed on the Church during the year by means of the Blessed Sacrament. These graces appeared as costly sacred vessels, precious stones, pearls, flowers, grapes, and fruits. The procession was headed by children in white, followed by nuns of all the different Orders especially devoted to the Blessed Sacrament, all wearing a figure of the Host embroidered on their habit. Juliana of Liege walked first. I saw St. Norbert with his monks and numbers of the clergy, secular and regular. Unspeakable joy, sweetness, and union reigned over all. . . . . .

"I had pictures referring to the defects in divine worship and how they are supernaturally repaired. It is hard for me to say how I saw it, how the different scenes blended and harmonized, one explaining another. One thing was especially remarkable: viz., the failings and omissions in divine worship on earth only increase the indebtedness of the guilty. God receives the honor due Him from a higher order. Among other things I saw that when priests have distractions during the sacred ceremonies, Mass, for instance, they are in reality wherever their thoughts are and, during the interval, a saint takes their place at the altar. These visions show frightfully the guilt of carelessly celebrating the Holy Mysteries. Sometimes I see a priest leaving the sacristy vested for Mass; but he goes not to the altar. He leaves the church and goes to a tavern, a garden, a hunt, a maiden, a book, to some rendezvous, and I see him now here, now there, according to the bent of his thoughts, as if he were really and personally in those places. It is a most pitiful and shameful sight! But it is singularly affecting to behold at this time a holy priest going through the ceremonies of the altar in his stead. I often see the priest returning for a moment during the Sacrifice and then suddenly running off again to some forbidden place. Such interruptions frequently last a long time. When the priest amends, I see it in his piety and recollectedness at the altar, etc., etc. In many parish churches I saw the dust and dirt which had long defiled the sacred vessels cleared away, and all things put in order."

On the night of June 12–13, Sister Emmerich was consoled by visions on the life of St. Anthony of Padua. " I saw the dear saint," she said, " very handsome and noble-looking, quick and active in his movements like Xavier. He had black hair, a nose long and beautiful, dark, soft eyes, and a well-shaped chin with a short, forked beard. His complexion was very fair and pale. He was clothed in brown and wore a small mantle, but not exactly in the style of the Franciscans of the present day. He was very energetic, full of fire, yet full of sweetness too.

" I saw him eagerly entering a little wood on the sea-shore and climbing a tree whose lower branches extended over the water. He sprang from bough to bough. He had hardly seated himself when the sea suddenly rose and inundated the thicket, and an incredible number of fishes and marine animals of all kinds were borne in on the waves. They raised their heads, looked quietly at the saint, and listened to him as he addressed them. After a little while, he raised his hand and blessed them, when the sea receded carrying them back to the deep. Some remained on the shore. The saint put them back carefully into the waters which bore them off. I felt as if I were lying in the wood on a soft bed of moss. By me lay a wonderful marine animal, flat and broad. The head was round as a battle-axe with the mouth underneath ; the back was green streaked with gold. It had golden eyes, and golden spots on the lower part of the body. There it lay floundering from side to side. I tried to drive it away by striking it on the back with my handkerchief, and I also chased off an enormous spider which was running after it. The thicket and the whole country around lay in darkness. St. Anthony alone was bathed in light (1).

" Again I saw St. Anthony in the little thicket by the sea. He knelt facing a distant church, and his whole soul turned toward the Blessed Sacrament. At the same moment I saw the church, the Blessed Sacrament on the altar, and the saint's prayer arising before It. Then I saw a little old hunchback with an ugly face, running up behind Anthony. He carried a beautiful white basket (the edges, above and below colored, made perhaps of brown osiers) full of lovely flowers prettily arranged. The old man wanted to give them to the saint. He shook him to attract his attention ; but Anthony neither saw nor heard anything. He was kneeling in ecstatic prayer, his eyes fixed on the Blessed Sacrament. Then the old man set the basket down and withdrew. I saw the church drawing nearer and nearer to Anthony whilst he prayed. From the Blessed Sacrament there issued, as it were, a little monstrance which, attracted by his burning prayer, approached him in a stream of light and hovered in the air above him. From it came forth a lovely little Jesus dazzling, sparkling with glory, and rested on the saint's shoulder tenderly caressing him. After a little while, the Child re-entered the monstrance which went back again into the Blessed Sacrament on the altar of the far-off church which had drawn near. Then I saw the saint returning to the city, but the flowers remained where the old man had put them.

" Again I saw St. Anthony in a field outside a city near the sea disputing with several persons. One, in particular, a violent, passionate man, argued against the saint in bitter terms. Then I saw that they all agreed on some point and Anthony, fired with holy zeal, stepped

---

(1) The darkness of unbelief, hard-heartedness, and heresy,

forward, his arms under his little mantle, as if affirming
something. After this he pushed his way through the
crowd and left the place. It was a large meadow planted
with trees and surrounded by a wall. It extended from the
city to the shore, and was full of people walking about or
listening to the saint.—Then I had another vision : Anthony
saying Mass in a church, the broad road leading to it from
the city gate filled with an expectant crowd, and the man
who had disputed so hotly with him driving up to the
city an immense ox with long horns. Meanwhile, the
saint having finished Mass, walked solemnly to the church-
door, bearing in his hands a consecrated Host. Instantly,
the ox began to struggle; it freed itself from its master, and
ran rapidly up the street toward the church. The owner
and several others pursued it, the tumult became general,
women and children fell one over the other, but the ox could
not be caught. When, at last, it reached the church, down
it knelt, stretched out its neck, and bowed humbly before
the Blessed Sacrament which Anthony, standing at the
door, held up before it. Its master offered it hay, but the
animal noticed it not, changed not its position ; whereupon,
the whole crowd including the owner prostrated humbly,
praising and adoring the Blessed Sacrament. Anthony re-
entered the church followed by the people. Then only
did the ox arise and allow itself to be led back to the
city gate, where it ate the food presented it.

"I saw a man accusing himself to Anthony of having
kicked his mother, and in another scene I saw the same
man so contrite in consequence of the saint's exhortations,
that he was about to cut off the foot that had done the
wicked deed. But St. Anthony suddenly appeared before
him and restrained his arm."

June 15th—"I turned toward the Blessed Sacrament to

pray, and I was ravished in spirit into the church in which
the Feast of Corpus Christi was celebrated for the first time
upon earth.   It was built in ancient style and adorned with
ancient pictures, but it was not old itself nor did it present
any appearance of decay; on the contrary, all was bright and
beautiful. I knelt before the high altar. The Blessed Sacrament was not in a monstrance, but shut up in a tabernacle
in a high round ciborium, surmounted by a cross.   A vessel
of three compartments could be drawn out of it: the upper
one contained several little vessels which held the Holy
Oils ; the second, several consecrated Hosts ; the lowest one,
a flagon made of shining mother-of-pearl in which there was,
I think, some wine.   Near the church was a cloister of
pious virgins.   On one side of the church stood a small
house occupied by a very devout virgin named Eva.   There
was in her room a little window with a slide through which,
day or night, she could see the Blessed Sacrament on the
high altar. That she was very devout to It, I could perceive
by all her movements. She was dressed respectably, not exactly like a nun, but more like a pilgrim. She did not belong
to the city.   She was of good family, and had moved there
only through devotion, to be able to live near the church.
In the neighborhood of this city, I saw a convent on a
mountain, not built in the usual conventual style, but several
small houses joined together.   One of the religious was
Blessed Juliana who had been instrumental in the institution of the Feast of Corpus Christi.   I saw her walking in
the garden dressed in the gray habit of her Order.   She
seemed to be full of sweet simplicity and often paused in
contemplation before the flowers.   On one occasion I saw
her kneeling near a lily meditating on the virtue of purity,
and I also saw her in prayer when she received the command
to introduce the Feast of Corpus Christi. It gave her great

anxiety, and I saw that another spiritual director was shown her to whom she was to make known the revelation, since the first one had paid no heed to her. Whilst she was in prayer, I saw in the distance a Pope likewise engaged, and near him the number IV. Urged by a vision and in consequence of a certain favor some one had received from the Blessed Sacrament, he resolved to establish the feast in the Church. Between these two pictures, I found myself again in the church before the Blessed Sacrament. I saw come forth from It first a shining finger, then a hand, and lastly, there stood before me a youth resplendent with light and covered with pearls. He said: 'Behold these pearls! Not one is lost, and all may gather them.' The whole world was illumined by the rays that shot from the glorious youth. Then I poured out my soul in thanksgiving for I knew by this picture that the Blessed Sacrament with all Its graces has, at length, become an object of special devotion among the faithful.

" Toward midday I beheld on the horizon over a lovely, fertile plain, five broad, luminous bands, like the sun in color and brilliancy, which united to form a dome overhead. They came from five great, distant cities like the bands of a rainbow in the blue sky. On the dome in indescribable splendor, was enthroned the most Blessed Sacrament in a richly adorned monstrance. Above and below the five arches hovered myriads of angels going to and fro between the cities and the Blessed Sacrament. The pomp attending this picture, the devotion and consolation it inspired, I cannot express. . . . . ."

June 17th—" As I was fainting with desire for the Blessed Sacrament, a dying religious was shown me (Juliana Falconieri). She could not always receive Holy Communion, on account of her frequent vomiting. But to console her, the priest used to lay the Host upon her breast in a corporal, and this relieved her greatly. As her death drew near, they brought the Most Blessed Sacrament to her, and she begged to have It laid upon her breast in a little linen cloth, instead of the stiff corporal. The priest did as she requested, the nuns kneeling around her bed. I saw the dying sister smile sweetly; her countenance became lovely, rosy, and radiant—and she was dead! The priest stooped to remove the Host, but the linen was empty—the Sacred Host had entered her breast leaving the mark of a circle in which was a red cross with the Saviour's figure. I saw crowds flocking to witness the miracle. I longed for a similar favor, but it will not be granted."

" I saw a little chapel standing on a vine whose branches encircled and even entered it. In the centre was a shoot on which stood Jesus, Mary, and Joseph, and around them in prayer were all the saints who had been marked with the stigmata. One among them was conspicuous, a tertiary of the Order of St. Dominic, named Osiana. She did not live in a convent; she lived at home.

" I saw a little person whom I heard called Maria of Oignies. She lived not far from Liege, Juliana's city, which I could see at no great distance. At first I saw a man with her. I knew not before that she was married. She lay at night on the bare boards. Later on I saw her in another place, where the houses were crowded together, and here she served the sick. Then I saw her in another place kneeling all alone at night before the Blessed Sacrament in a church. Again, I saw her lying ill a long time. Those around her were unable to understand her singular malady with its frequent changes, and they scoffed at her abstinence from food. It was shown me how much she had suffered for others, how many poor souls she had helped; and then I saw for my own consolation, a picture of her glory in heaven. The Church has always had such members."

June 18th—St. Ignatius consoles and assists Sister Emmerich :—" During my last great sufferings, I had by me the relic which Dean Overberg sent me. All at once, it became brilliant and, as I prayed to know what relic it was, I saw a resplendent figure surrounded by a white aureola, descending toward me from on high. The light issuing from the relic united, as usual, with that from the apparition, and I heard interiorly these words : ' That is one of my bones. I am Ignatius!' After that I had a long night of horrible torture, of expiatory sufferings. It was as if a knife were being slowly buried in my breast and then turned round and round on all sides, and my wounds pained so intensely that I could not repress my groans and complaints. I cried to our Lord for mercy. I begged Him not to let me suffer beyond my strength, for I feared I should yield to impatience. I gained by my prayers an apparition of Our Lord, under the form of a youth, my Spouse, and I was inexpressibly consoled. In a few words, which I cannot repeat precisely He said :—'I have placed thee on My nuptial couch of pain. I have lavished upon thee the graces of suffering, the treasures of atonement, and the jewels of good works. Thou must suffer, but I shall not abandon thee. Thou art bound to the vine, thou wilt not be lost.'—In such words as these the Saviour consoled me, and I suffered patiently and quietly the rest of the night. Toward morning I had another vision of St. Ignatius. I saw his relic shining. I invoked the dear saint, whom I now knew, and clasped his relic lovingly and reverently. I called to him through the sweet Heart of Jesus. He immediately came as before, the two lights uniting, and

again I heard the words : ' That is my bone !'--He consoled
me, telling me that he had received everything from Jesus.
He promised to stand my friend, to assist me in my labors,
to relieve me in my pains, and he bade me make the usual
devotions in his honor during the following month.   Then
he arose in the air and vanished, after which I saw some
scenes of his life.

  " I thought that I lay on a little bed at the entrance of a
church whose choir was shut off by a grating.   There
were some people in the church, but not many.   In the
choir were about twelve of St. Ignatius's companions, among
whom I recognized Francis Xavier and Favre.   It seemed
as if they were about to start on a journey.   They were not
all priests.   They wore a habit something like that of St.
Ignatius, but not exactly like it.   It was very early, and
still quite dark ; the candles were burning on the altar.   St.
Ignatius, not entirely vested for Mass, a stole around his
neck, and attended by another who carried the holy water,
passed down the church among his companions and gave
the blessing with the asperges.   I, too, prepared to receive
it.   He came, indeed, to my little bed and sprinkled me
abundantly.   At the same instant I experienced a sensation of sweet relief throughout my whole being.   Returning to the sacristy, he came forth again in full vestments
and went to the altar for Mass, during which a flame suddenly appeared over his head.   One of the twelve ran with
outstretched arms to his assistance ; but, when he saw his
countenance all on fire, he respectfully retired.   Then,
when Mass was over, I saw the saint led from the altar by
his companions. He was bathed in tears and so agitated as to
be unable to walk.   His Mass usually lasted an hour,
much longer than our ordinary Masses.

  " After that I saw the men whom I had before seen in

the maritime city, introduced to the Pope. He was in a large hall seated on a magnificent chair before a table covered with papers and writing materials. The Pope wore a short cloak; I think it was red. I know for certain that he wore a red skull-cap. At the door were standing several ecclesiastics. The companions of Ignatius entered. They knelt before the Pope, and one spoke in the name of all. I do not remember distinctly whether Ignatius was there or not. The Pope blessed them and gave them some papers. Then I saw some other pictures of the saint's life. I saw him make so earnest a confession of his past life to a bad priest that the latter burst into tears quite converted. Again, I saw him whilst on a journey, suddenly leave his companions and go to a house in which dwelt a bad man, a slave to his passions. I saw the latter trying to elude the saint who, however, caught him. Falling on his knees before him, he embraced him and implored him to think of his salvation. The man was converted and followed him. I saw the saint in a beggar's garb, journeying alone through a gloomy, mountainous district, and the devil lying in wait for him under the form of a dragon with a thin body and a great, crispy head. Ignatius drove his stick into its neck from which there immediately issued fire. He then pinned him down firmly with a stake, took up his stick, and coolly went on his way."

That evening the Pilgrim found the invalid reciting in a low voice and without a book the Office of St. Ignatius in Latin. When finished, she related what follows:—" I received from Ignatius such comfort and kindness, I saw him so penetrated with ardent love for Jesus, that I turned earnestly and reverently toward him, and his apparition descended from on high in a beam of light, the most holy name of Jesus shining in his heart like a sun. Then

I wanted to make some devotions in his honor, when lo! words and antiphons streamed toward me from him, and I found great sweetness in this gift of prayer." She concluded her devotions with the prayer: "*Oratio recitanda ante imaginem Sancti Ignatii.* A prayer to be recited before the image of St. Ignatius." The following night St. Ignatius again appeared to her and strengthened her to endure her pains. Next day she related the following vision to the Pilgrim :—

"I saw Ignatius and Xavier and their intimate union of heart in Jesus Christ. I saw them shedding around consolation and relief whilst they instructed and served the sick and incurable. As I contemplated their powerful and efficacious action among the people, my heart turned to them with the words :—'If during your life as frail creatures, you so loved and served in the strength God gave you, O how much more efficacious must be your influence now that you revel in light and love! See, here are your sacred relics which once labored so much for your fellow-men! O help us still! Work, pour around grace, O ye perfect vessels of the fountain of grace!'—Then all things earthly vanished, and I saw the two saints in heaven standing together in a sphere of light. St. Ignatius's aureola was perfectly white; Xavier's of a rosy tinge, something like the glory of a martyr. And whilst I gazed upon them, whilst life and light streamed down upon me from them, my soul rose up and gave back as it were in heart-felt, earnest prayer the light and love God shed upon me through them. Just as I received yesterday the prayer to Ignatius, so to-day words of love and joy flowed into my soul, and I called all creatures to praise and to invoke ; my heart swelled and poured itself out in jubilation. I praised and prayed through all the choirs of the blessed, and the whole heavenly court was set in motion. My prayer went up to God through Our Lord Jesus Christ, to Christ through His holy Mother, to the holy Mother through all the saints, and to all the saints through Ignatius and Xavier. It seemed as if I knew exactly what flowers and fruits, what perfumes, what colors, what precious stones and pearls were the purest, the most agreeable to my God; as if from the inexhaustible abundance of these treasures, I had lovingly made and presented to Him a crown, a pyramid, a throne; and as if all precious things streamed down to me in the light from the two saints."— (That afternoon the Pilgrim having read to her an old canticle of Sts. Ignatius and Xavier, in which all creatures are invited to praise them, she exclaimed : "That's it! That is just the way I prayed to them !")

"In this jubilee of prayer and praise and supplication, the vision continued to unfold before my soul; but with this change, I went with the two saints into the Heavenly Jerusalem. What words can describe the joy, the bliss, the splendor that I there beheld ! It was not as when I saw it before with its walls and gates, a city seated on the summit of the mountain of life; but it was an immense world of light and splendor, the streets stretching far and wide in all directions, and all in perfect regularity, order, harmony, and unending love. High up, over the centre of the city, in light incomprehensible, I see the Most Holy Trinity and the twenty-four ancients, and below in a world of glory, the angelic host. I see the saints in their different ranks, bands, and hierarchies, all in their own palaces, on their own thrones, and in their various relations. They with whom I am more particularly connected, whom I honor most frequently, whose relics I have, are more distinct to me, or rather I am nearer to them, and they introduce me to the others.—I have seen, also, their wonderful influence.

When I invoked them, they turned to the Most Holy Trinity from whom streamed rays of light upon them; then they went to some marvellous trees and bushes that stood between the palaces, and gathered fruit, dew, and honey which they sent down upon the earth. I saw the part the angels play. They are swift as lightning, passing quickly to and fro, carrying blessings down to earth and, as it were, multiplying them. I saw Ignatius and Xavier scattering graces over my own land, chiefly on those for whom I had prayed, and sending quantities of dew and honey into far-off countries. I saw in separate pictures sufferers relieved and becoming fervent; people suddenly converted and changing their life; in dark, distant countries light shining out and increasing in brilliancy, and holy souls praying in its brightness. I saw that the saints do indeed dispense graces everywhere, but more especially where their relics repose and where they are invoked. These relics shine with the same light and color as the saints themselves; they always appear as a part of themselves.

"I saw many holy men around Ignatius: Francis Borgia, Charles Borromeo, Aloysius, Stanislaus Kostka, Francis Regis, and numerous others. I saw him, also," she said, pointing to some one who seemed to appear at the moment. The Pilgrim thought, at first, that she meant St. Francis of Assisi, but it was St. Francis de Sales whom she beheld before her attracted by his relic lying near (1). "I saw him not with Ignatius but in a choir of Bishops. I saw multitudes whom I knew, and I drew near many of them by prayer. At first, I dared look only at Ignatius, the others I saw from a distance; but all were so kind and good that after awhile I ventured to go around among them.

(1) "She was in ecstasy, her eyes wide open, and forgetful of our blindness to the spirit world, she spoke to us, as if we could see what she herself saw."-(Brentano's Notes).

" The streets were paved with pearls in all shapes and figures, and some of them also with stars. I thought in my simplicity (for it was stupid nature thinking) : ' Look ! there are the stars that we see above the earth !'—I saw, too, Augustine and his whole Order, and Bishop Ludger with a church in his hand as he is usually represented, and many others with their various insignia, some of whom I recognized, among them St. Joachim and St. Anne. I was quite sure about the last-named, as this is Tuesday, the day on which I always honor holy Mother Anne. Both held a green branch and, as I knew not what it signified, I was given to understand that it was a sign of their ardent desire for the advent of the Messiah who was to spring from them according to the flesh. Then I had visions of their ardent desires, their prayer, mortification, and penance.

" The whole night I was consoled in the midst of my pains by these contemplations. I cannot repeat all the magnificent things I saw, nor their truth and clearness. The figures were not thrown together at random, but they formed one grand whole—one explained another, lived and loved in the other. During this vision my heart beat with joy, my lips sang canticles of praise."

Whilst relating the above, Sister Emmerich, though lying in death-like exhaustion, was full of joyful emotion, and tears flowed down her cheeks.

June 21st—The Pilgrim found her to-day, as the confessor also thought her, nigh unto death, but full of gladness at the remembrance of her last night's vision. She had assisted in spirit at the celebration of the Feast of St. Aloysius : " I was at a grand spiritual festival, a great solemnity with numerous processions : maidens in white with lilies in their hands carried the Mother of God on a throne, and then came St. Aloysius borne by youths also in white. The saint wore over his black habit a white surplice with golden fringe and like his companions, he bore a lily in his hand. There were a great many white banners with gold fringe.

" Aloysius sat on a throne above the altar, and above him again was enthroned the Mother of God to whom he was espoused. The upper part of the church was filled with the heavenly choirs, and around Aloysius were Ignatius, Xavier, Borgia, Borromeo, Stanislaus, Regis, and numbers of other holy Jesuits. Higher up were crowds of other holy religious, and there were countless souls of youths, maidens, and children who by following the example of Aloysius had found favor with the Lord. Only the blessed were in the church.

" When Aloysius had been honored with garlands, crowns, etc., he in his turn honored those who had paid him homage ; for such is the custom at these feasts—the honored one becomes the servant. I cannot describe the splendor of the scene ; it was the feast of chastity and innocence, of humility and love.—Then I saw the saint's life. I saw him still a little boy alone in a large hall whose walls were hung with all kinds of armor, among which was a knapsack. The child seemed to be attracted by it. He unbuckled it, took out a large box which appeared to contain firearms, and carried it away with him. But soon he was seized with remorse. He returned weeping bitterly, and replaced it in the knapsack. He was full of repentance for the theft. Then I saw a tall female enter the hall, go to the child who was leaning against the wall under the knapsack, and try to comfort him. She led him still weeping to his parents who were in a beautiful room, and he confessed his fault with many tears.—I saw him afterward entrusted to a man who was always with him.—I saw him whilst still a child sick in bed for a long time, but so patient that all the servants loved him. I saw them carrying him around in their arms and, in spite of his fever and sufferings, he always smiled on them sweetly.— I saw him in another very grand house. He was always a gentle, earnest boy. Again, I saw him sitting in the midst of ecclesiastics, speaking to them gravely whilst they listened in deep attention, highly edified at his words. They seemed to be preparing him for Holy Communion but, enlightened by God, the pupil taught his masters. He was filled with wonderful devotion and intense desire for the Holy Eucharist. Wherever he was, wherever he went, he always turned toward the Blessed Sacrament in some church. He often drew on the wall of his room a chalice with a Host or a monstrance, before which he prayed with inexpressible devotion, quickly effacing it on the approach of any one. It reminded me of St. Barbara whom I had seen doing the same in her prison. I saw him afterward in a church receiving Holy Communion, the Sacred Host shining before him and, as it were, flying into his mouth. Then I saw him in the convent, his cell so small as to admit of no furniture but a bed. I often beheld him radiant with light when he disciplined himself and prayed. It was told me that his greatest sin had been a distraction for the space of an *Ave Maria* at the end of a prayer which had lasted all day. Aloysius's companions loved him very much. They used to follow him to the door of his cell which, however, he would never allow them to enter for fear of their praising his poverty.

I always saw him, even in infancy, with his eyes lowered. He never looked any woman in the face. It was no affectation in him, but an act of self-renunciation which guarded his purity.—Through God's grace I never knew that necessity, and I often wonder when I read such things in the saints' lives."—

Sister Emmerich wept when the Pilgrim told her that St. Aloysius's father had tried to prevent his entrance into religion.

June 27, 1822—" I had a painful labor to perform in a church in which, through fear of profanation, they had walled up the Blessed Sacrament in a pillar. Mass was said secretly in a cave below the sacristy. I cannot say where this was, but the church was very old and I was in dread of the Blessed Sacrament's being exposed to danger. Then my guide exhorted me to pray and to ask prayers of all my acquaintances for the conversion of sinners and, above all, for faith and perseverance for the clergy.—' For terrible times are approaching, non-Catholics will use every artifice to oppress the Church and snatch from her her possessions. The troubles will ever increase.' "—For several subsequent days Sister Emmerich experienced intense pains in her stigmata. She exhibited all the symptoms of dropsy, the malady of a poor woman living in France and which Sister Emmerich had taken upon herself. During it she was occupied in a labor of prayer that had been imposed upon her. The following is her account : " I was taken by my guide up an immensely high stair-case and I saw people in prayer coming from all directions, drawn, as it were, by threads. I was on the top of the stair-case, but still about five feet below a great, dazzlingly bright city, or rather a world. An immense blue curtain was drawn aside to allow me to gaze into the magnificent scene. Rows of palaces and flower-gardens ran toward the centre where all was so brilliant that one could not look upon it. Wherever I turned my eyes, I beheld hierarchies of saints and angels whose intercession I implored. The virgins and martyrs were the first to present their petitions before the throne of God, and they were followed by the other choirs. The Most Holy Trinity appeared to draw near to them like the sun breaking through the clouds. The angelic choirs were composed of small, delicate forms swimming in light. The cherubim and seraphim were winged spirits, their wings formed of sparkling rays, and I saw the choirs of angels and guardian-angels. Among the holy virgins I saw souls who had lived in the married state, St. Anne and others of early times, St. Cunegundes and other chaste spouses, but not Magdalen. There were no birds or an·imals in the gardens. When I looked down from the steps on which I stood all was gray to right and left—it was blue only behind the curtain. I saw islands, cities, fields, and gardens, earthly regions which appeared in proportion as my thoughts wandered toward them. I saw all sorts of people praying, their prayers mounting like pennants, like written scrolls to the hearts of the blessed from whose countenance they shot in dazzling rays to the throne of God. I saw some of these scrolls turning black and falling down again to earth, and some unfinished ones taken up and offered by others. It was like an exchange between men and between the saints and angels. There was great movement among the latter as they bore aid to the needy and miserable: for instance, to ships in distress. Last night, though very sick, I was carried away by my guide. It was strange how curious I was to know what was behind the blue curtain!—I thought the Mountain of the Prophets lay to the left as I ascended." On July 1st, she added the following:—

"I think my wounds of the Crown must have bled during my great vision on the intercession of the saints, for I saw so much of the Dolorous Passion! Whilst the saints in turn offered before the throne of God their share of compassion for sinners, I saw all Christ's sufferings and the sympathy they excited, all the thorns of the Crown, and other things relating to the Passion."

Toward the close of August, 1820, Sister Emmerich suffered inexpressibly from the continual sight of the tepidity and indifference of both priests and laics toward the Most Blessed Sacrament, and, side by side with the latter, she beheld honest pagans aspiring after salvation. "I saw," she said, "in all places priests surrounded by the graces of the Church, the treasure of Jesus Christ's merits as well as those of the saints ; but they were tepid, they were dead. They taught, they preached, and offered the Holy Sacrifice most slothfully.—Then a pagan was shown me standing on a pillar and addressing a multitude below. He spoke so feelingly of the new God of all the gods, the God of a strange people, that his hearers were seized with the same enthusiasm as himself.—I am assailed day and night by these visions, I cannot get rid of them. Present misery and decadence are always shown me side by side with past good, and I have to pray unceasingly. Mass badly celebrated is an enormous evil. Ah ! it is not a matter of indifference how it is said ! . . . . . I have had a great vision on the mystery of Holy Mass and I have seen that whatever good has existed since creation is owing to it. I saw the *A* and the *O*, and how all is contained in the *O* (1). I understood the signification of the circle in the spherical form of the earth and the heavenly bodies. the aureola of apparitions, and the Sacred Host. The connection between the mysteries of the Incarnation, the Redemption, and the Holy Sacrifice of the Mass was also shown me, and I saw how Mary compassed what the heavens themselves could not contain. These pictures extended through the whole of the Old Testament. I saw the first sacrifice offered and the mar-

(1) The *Alpha* and *Omega*.

vellous significance of holy relics when placed in the altar
on which Mass is said. I saw Adam's bones reposing in a
cavern under Mt. Calvary deep down, almost to water level,
and in a straight line beneath the spot on which Jesus
Christ was crucified. I looked in and saw Adam's skeleton entire with the exception of the right arm and foot and
a part of the right side. Through the latter I could see
the ribs of the left side. In the right side lay Eve's skull
exactly in the spot whence the Lord had drawn it. I was
told that Adam and Eve's resting-place has been a point of
dispute, but they have always lain just where I saw them.
There was no mountain on this spot before the Deluge;
only in consequence of that event did one appear. The
tomb was untouched by the waters. Noe had in the Ark a
portion of their remains which he laid on the altar when
offering his first sacrifice. Abraham did the same at a later
period, the bones of Adam having come down to him through
Sem. The bloody sacrifice of Jesus upon Calvary over the
bones of Adam was a foreshadowing of the Holy Sacrifice
of the Mass over relics placed under the altar-stone.
For it the sacrifices of the patriarchs were but a preparation. They, too, possessed sacred relics by which they reminded God of His promises. The five openings in the
Ark were typical of the Saviour and His Church. At the
time of the Deluge fearful disorders reigned over the earth
and mankind was steeped in vice. They plundered and
carried off whatever they pleased, laying waste their neighbor's houses and lands, and dishonoring the matrons and
maidens. This passage of Scripture : 'The sons of God
saw that the daughters of men were fair,' signifies that the
pure stock, 'born of God, not of the flesh, nor of blood, nor
of the will of men (1),' mingled with impure races, gave

(1) John i. 13.

birth to a powerful people in an earthly human sense, and
so sullied the line from which the Messiah was to spring.
Noe's own relations were corrupt, all save his wife, his sons
and their wives, who dwelt in his immediate vicinity.
They used to build in those early times great stone buildings, and erect around them tents or huts of oiser. The further Noe's family removed from him, the worse they became,
the more corrupt in their morals; they even robbed him
and revolted against him.   It was not that they were rude
or savage, for they lived quite commodiously in well-
arranged households; but it was because they were given
up to vice, to the most abominable idolatry.   They made
idols for themselves out of whatever pleased them best.

"I saw Noe, an artless old man, in a long white robe·
He was walking in an orchard pruning the trees with a
crooked bone knife.   Suddenly a cloud hovered over him,
in it a human figure.   Noe knelt and received the commission to build an ark, as God was about to destroy the world
by a flood.   The news saddened him very much, and I saw
him praying that the punishment might be averted.   He deferred compliance with the order.   The Lord again appeared to him, repeated His command, and told him to begin the
work at once unless he wanted to perish with the rest of mankind.   Then I saw him leaving his home with his family and
going to an uninhabited district where there was plenty of
wood.   He took a great many persons with him, and they all
established themselves in tents.   They had an altar on which
to offer sacrifice and before which they daily prayed at the beginning and close of their labor.   A long time elapsed before
the work was completed, as Noe frequently discontinued it for
years at a time, hoping that Almighty God would relent.
Three times did God warn him to go on with it; each time
Noe engaged more workmen, but again discontinued it.

" I was told that in the Ark, as afterward in the cross, there were four kinds of wood : palm, olive, cedar, and cypress. I saw them felling the trees and fashioning them on the spot. Noe himself carried all the wood on his shoulders to the place of building, just as Jesus afterward carried His cross. The place chosen for the construction of the Ark was a hill surrounded by a valley. First they built the keel of the vessel which was rounded in the back; it was like a trough and was smeared with pitch. There were three stories. The two upper were supported by hollow posts formed from the rough trunks of trees and covered with large leaves, and another kind of wood was used for the light planks. I saw them punching the pith out with some kind of an instrument. When Noe had carried and prepared all the materials, the building was commenced. The bottom was put in and smeared with pitch, then holes made and filled with pitch into which the posts were firmly placed. On these was laid the second floor with another row of posts all around ; and, lastly, the third floor with the roof. The spaces between the posts were inclosed by brown and yellow laths placed crosswise, the holes and chinks filled up with a sort of wool and white moss which grew very abundantly around certain trees. Then the whole was covered with pitch. The roof of the Ark was also rounded. The door was in the middle of one side, a little more than half-way up, with a window on either side, and in the centre of the roof there was likewise a square opening. When the Ark was entirely covered with pitch, it shone like a mirror in the sun. Noe continued to work a long time alone on the compartments for the animals, for all had separate places. There were two passages through the middle of the Ark. Back in the oval part was a wooden altar concealed by hangings, and a little in front of the

altar was a pan of coals ; to the right and left were spaces
partitioned off for sleeping apartments. All kinds of utensils
and chests were taken into it, and seeds, plants, and shrubs
put into earth around the walls which were soon covered
with verdure. I saw vines laden with large, yellow grapes,
the bunches as long as one's arm. No words could express
what Noe endured from the malice and ill-will of the workmen during the whole time of the building. He paid them
well in cattle, but that did not prevent them from cursing,
insulting, and abusing him in every way. They even
called him a fool, for none knew why he was constructing
such a vessel. But he only thanked God, who appeared to
him when it was finished. He told him to take a reed pipe
and call all the animals from the four corners of the globe.
The nearer the day of chastisement approached, the darker grew the heavens. The fear over the earth became very
great, the sun no longer showed his face, and the thunder's
roar was constantly heard. I saw Noe going a short distance north, south, east, and west and blowing his pipe.
Then the animals ranged two by two, male and female, entered the Ark by a plank laid from the door. As soon as
all were in, which was not for several days, the plank was
removed. The large animals, white elephants and camels,
went in first ; they were restless as on the approach of a
storm. The birds flew in through the skylight and perched
under the roof, some of them in cages, and the water-
fowl went to the lower part of the vessel. The four-footed
beasts were in the middle story. Of such animals as are
slaughtered for food there were seven couples. Then Noe
invoking the mercy of God, entered with his wife, his
three sons, and their wives. The plank was drawn in and
the door closed shutting out all the rest of mankind, even
their nearest relations and their little children. Then burst

forth a fearful storm, the lightning played in fiery columns, the rain fell in torrents, and soon the hill on which the Ark stood became an island. The misery was so great that I hope it was itself the cause of many a man's salvation. I saw a black devil of hideous form hurrying to and fro through the tempest and tempting men to despair. The reptiles and serpents sought here and there a hiding-place in the Ark. Of gnats and vermin I saw none; they were sent later to torment man.

"I saw Noe offering incense in the Ark on an altar covered with red and white. Whenever he offered sacrifice he laid upon it Adam's bones which, at a later period, fell into Abraham's hands. I saw the latter lay them on the altar of Melchisedech, of whom he knew and whom he ardently sighed to meet. I saw, also, the sacrifice of Isaac upon Mount Calvary. The back of the altar was to the north. The Patriarchs always placed their altars so, because evil comes from the north.

"I saw, also, Moses praying before an altar on which he had laid the bones of Jacob which he generally carried round him in a box. As he poured out something on the altar, there arose a flame into which he cast incense ; he invoked God by the promise made to those bones. He prayed until he sank down exhausted. In the morning he arose again to pray. Jacob's bones were afterwards placed in the Ark of the Covenant. Moses prayed with arms outstretched in the form of a cross. God resists not such a prayer, for it was thus that His own Son faithfully prayed until death. I saw, also, Josua praying like Moses when the sun stood still at his command. . . . . . .

"I saw the pool of Bethsaida, its five entrances betokening the Five Wounds, and I had many pictures of it at various times. I saw a hill some distance from the first

Temple where in time of danger a pit had been dug wherein to hide the sacred vessels, candlesticks, and censers.
I saw several of the last named with two handles.   In the
centre of the pit was placed the sacred fire of the altar, and
over the top were laid all kinds of beams; the whole was
then covered with earth so that the spot was not noticeable.
The beam which formed the trunk of the holy cross was
found here.   It had formerly been a tree by the brook Ced-
ron.   Its lower branches shot out over the water and came,
at last, to be used as a bridge.   After the hill had been
levelled, it was used for various purposes.   I saw Nehemiah,
when returned from captivity, making excavations around
the pit in which the sacred fire had been buried.   He
found a mass of black mud formed by the swampy earth,
from which he removed the vessels.   When he smeared
the sacrificial wood with it, it immediately burst into flame."

Sister Emmerich's visions now changed from the Mosaic
to the Christian era, and she saw men clothed with the
highest spiritual and worldly dignity vieing with one another in honoring the Most Blessed Sacrament.

"I saw the holy Pope Zephyrinus who, on account of
his zeal for the dignity of the priesthood, suffered much
both from Catholics and heretics.   He was very strict in
the admission of candidates whom he closely examined and
of whom he rejected many.   Once out of an immense
number he chose only five.   I often saw him disputing
with heretics who unrolled parchments, spoke angrily, and
even snatched his writings from him.   Zephyrinus exacted
obedience from priests, sending them here and there, and
silencing them if they would not obey.   I saw him send a
man, not yet ordained, to Africa, I think, where he became
a Bishop and a great saint.   He was a friend of Zephyrinus and a very celebrated man.   I saw the Pope exhorting

the faithful to bring him their silver-plate, when he replaced the wooden chalices of the churches by silver ones. The cruets were of clear glass. Zephyrinus retained the wooden vessels for his own use; but as some were scandalized at it, he had them partly gilded, and all the rest he gave to the poor. I saw him contracting debts for the relief of a poor family, whereupon one of his female relatives reproached him for running into debt for strangers rather than for his own poor relations. He replied that he had done it for Jesus Christ, at which she indignantly withdrew. Now, God had allowed him to see that, if he did anything for this woman, she would be perverted.—I saw that he caused candidates for the priesthood to be examined and ordained in presence of the faithful. He drew up strict rules for their observance when Bishops celebrated, assigning to each his own rank. He also ordained that Christians of a certain age should receive the Blessed Sacrament at Easter in the church. He no longer permitted them to carry It to their homes suspended from their necks in a box, since It was often taken into improper places where feasting and dancing were going on. Zephyrinus bore deep veneration for the Mother of God, and he had many visions of her life and death. He arranged a bed for himself just like the couch on which she had died. He always kept it concealed by a curtain, and with fervent devotion he used to lie down to rest in the same position in which he had seen her die. He also wore secretly under his robe another of sky-blue in honor of Mary's sky-blue mantle.—I saw him receiving again, after their canonical penance, sinners who had been separated from the faithful for adultery and impurity. He had disputes on this point with a learned priest (Tertullian) who was too rigid and who afterward fell into heresy.

"It was shown me how St. Louis of France at the age

of seven prepared by a rigorous fast for his First Communion. He told this to his mother. She had accompanied him
to the church to implore the Mother of God for light as to
whether her son should receive Holy Communion or not.
Mary appeared to her and said that her son must prepare
for seven days and then communicate, that she should receive
at the same time and offer her boy to her (Mary) and she
would ever be his protectress. I saw that all took place as
was directed, and I learned that religious instruction at that
period was both given and received in a different and more
earnest manner than in our day. In all his expeditions
Louis had the Blessed Sacrament with him and, wherever
he encamped, the Holy Sacrifice was offered.—I saw him
on the Crusade. Once during a violent tempest the crew of
his own vessel and those of the other ships, cried to him for
help, begging him to intercede with God for their delivery
from danger. As the Blessed Sacrament was not on board,
the saintly king took up a new-born, baptized infant, went
on deck, and held it up in the storm, begging God to show
pity for its sake. Then, turning slowly around, he gave
benediction with the child and the storm instantly ceased.
He afterward exhorted his grateful people to an increase of
devotion toward the Blessed Sacrament, telling them that,
if God had wrought so great a miracle for the sake of an
innocent baptized child, what would He not do for the sake
of His only Son ?"

Side by side with such scenes as the above, Sister Emmerich beheld others of a different nature intended to animate her to renewed zeal in her task of prayer and expiation.— 'In a certain city I saw over a gay party of ecclesiastics and seculars, men and women who were feasting and
jesting, a heavy black fog stretching off into a region of
darkness. In it sat Satan under a hideous form, and around

him as many devils as there were guests in the assembly
below, all busily engaged in inciting the latter to sin, whispering to them and inflaming their passions. They were in
a dangerous state of excitement and they freely conversed
in a light and wanton strain. The ecclesiastics belonged to the number of those whose motto is, 'Live and
let live!'—who argue thus: 'In our day one must not be
singular, one must not play the misanthrope; rather let
us, *Rejoice with those that rejoice.*'—And in such dispositions
they daily celebrate Holy Mass. I saw but one young
girl in the party still perfectly innocent, and that was owing to her devotion to her patron, a saint whose name is
well known and whom she was in the habit of invoking. I
saw how they bantered her and tried to lead her astray.
But over her appeared a break in the darkness through which
her patron shed light upon her and kept the evil spirits aloof.
Then Satan from his dark circle called out to the saint, asking what he wanted and how he dared encroach upon his
rights; he boasted with a contemptuous smile that all the
priests below were his, since in their present state they
said Mass daily, thereby plunging deeper into his meshes.
The saint bade him retire, telling him that, through the
merits of Jesus Christ, he had no right over the girl whom
he could not even approach. Satan boastingly retorted
that he would yet catch her, that he would make use of a
stranger who had once made an impression upon her, and who
would soon do the work.—Satan's figure was horrible:
short arms with claws, long feet and knees turned outward
so that he could not kneel even if he wished; his face was
human, but cold, wicked, fearful, and he had certain ap-
pendages like wings. He was black and obscure, spreading
darkness wherever he went. As I was surprised to hear
him speaking of his *rights*, I was told that he really did ac-

quire a positive right over every baptized person who, though endued with the power of Jesus Christ to resist him, yet freely and voluntarily delivers himself up to sin.— This vision was most impressive and affecting. I knew the people as well as the girl protected by her patron.

" I went to several dying persons, and one case touched me deeply. A worldly, dissipated woman lay on her death-bed. She would not be converted; she had no faith, she disdained the Sacraments. I made the Stations for her with some souls. Then we prostrated before the crucifix of Coesfeld and prayed so perseveringly that the Saviour detached His hands from the cross and descended. Instantly I found myself again by the dying one before whom stood the Saviour clothed in a mantle which He opened to show His Wounds. The woman was seized with fright, entered into herself, made a contrite confession, and died. . . .

" I went with my guardian-angel into seven churches to pray before the Blessed Sacrament, and to offer the Passion of Jesus Christ in atonement for the injuries and affronts. committed against It by bad priests. The patron of each of the churches was present, and joined in the devotion with my angel. The prayers we said were like litanies. Two of these churches were in distant lands over the great waters; I think the people were English."

On Sunday, August 28th, the Pilgrim found her toward noon still in ecstasy, praying with her arms extended. When returned to consciousness, she was unable at first to recall her surroundings or the hour of the day; but after some time she related the following :—" This morning I had to say prayers enjoined upon me last night. First, I heard a Mass here in our own church, after which I saw the Pilgrim communicate, and this was followed by several other Masses. I saw all the faults and negligence of both priests and seculars, and endured all kinds of sufferings on their account. I offered up all for them, presenting to God in reparation His Crucified Son at each elevation of the Host. I did this not only here, but in all the churches, perhaps a thousand, to which I was transported most wonderfully and rapidly, for I went into all I had ever visited in Europe or elsewhere. What I saw could not be told in two large volumes. I saw here and there, even in our own country some deeply pious people; but, for the most part, tepidity reigns. I saw piety in the Low-Countries, in a district bordering on the sea. In Switzerland I saw some good parishes in the midst of bad ones; and, again, in the north of Germany and the Polish district, where there are priests whom I often see. In Italy I saw many zealously serving God in the old, holy way, and others thoroughly bad and insolent. At the close of this manifold labor of prayer, I had toward noon a picture of St. Peter's which seemed to be floating above the earth in the air. Crowds, great and small, priests and laics, women and children, yes, even old cripples, ran to support it. I was in an agony lest the church would crush them all, for the foundations and the lower part seemed to be crumbling away; but the people put their shoulders under it and held it up. In so doing, they all became of the same height and every one was in his right place, the priests under the altars, laymen under the pillars, and the women under the entrance. Still I feared that its weight would be too much for the supporters, when I saw the heavens open above it and the saints sustaining it by their prayers and helping those below. I was hovering and flying in the air between the two. Then I saw the church borne forward a short distance, and a whole row of houses and palaces in front of it sank into the earth like a wheat-field trodden under foot. The church was

deposited in their place.   Then I had another picture.   I
saw the Blessed Virgin over the church surrounded by Apostles and Bishops, and below a grand procession and solemn
ceremonies.   I saw all the bad Bishops who thought they
were able to act by themselves, who received not for their
labors the strength of Christ through the intercession of their
saintly predecessors, driven out and replaced by others.   I
saw immense blessings descending from heaven and many
changes effected.   The Pope regulated everything.   I saw
numbers of poor, simple-hearted men arise, many of them
quite young.   I saw many aged Church dignitaries who had
entered the service of bad Bishops and neglected the interests of the Church, now on crutches as if lame and paralyzed, led by two persons to receive pardon."

At the close of this labor undertaken that the Unbloody
Sacrifice might be offered in a becoming manner, Sister
Emmerich had another very comprehensive vision.   In it
was shown her the Holy Mass as the line of demarcation
between men both in time and in eternity ; and she saw also
its cessation at the time of Antichrist.

"I had," she says, "a great picture of the Church, but
I can no longer give the details in order.   I saw St.
Peter's surrounded by fields, gardens, countries, and forests;
and I saw multitudes from all parts of the world, many of
whom I knew naturally or by my visions. Some of them were
entering the church and others passing it indifferently.   A
great ceremony was going on. Over the church floated a luminous cloud from which came out the Apostles and holy Bishops and formed into choirs above the altar.   Among them
were Augustine, Ambrose, and all who had labored for the
exaltation of the Church.   It was a grand solemnity and
Mass was being celebrated.   In the middle of the church
on a desk lay a great open book with three seals hanging

from one side and two from the other. I saw the Evangelist John, and I was told that the book contained the rev-
lations he had had at Patmos. Before it was opened something
happened which I have forgotten, and it is a pity there is a
break here! The Pope was not present, he was concealed
somewhere. I think the people knew not where he was,
and I do not remember now whether he was praying, or
whether he was dead. All present, the laics as well as the
clergy, had to lay their hand on a certain passage of the
Gospels. Upon many of them descended as a sign a light
from the holy Apostles and Bishops, but for many others
the ceremony was only an empty form. Outside the church
I saw numbers of Jews who wanted to enter, but could not
as yet. At the close of the ceremony there came a great
crowd, an innumerable multitude ; but the great book was
suddenly shut as if by an invisible power. It reminded me
of the evening in the convent when the devil blew out my
candle and shut my book. All around in the distance I
saw a terrible, bloody combat, and off toward the north a
great battle going on. The whole picture was grand and
imposing. I am sorry I have forgotten the passage in the
book on which they had to put their finger."

CHAPTER IV.

The Souls in Purgatory.—The Angels.—The Heaven-
ly Jerusalem.

We have already spoken of Sister Emmerich's compassion for the souls in purgatory, her unremitting prayers
and sacrifices for them. We shall here give those visions
which refer to them particularly, as also the various good
works undertaken by her for their relief. The first Feast
of All-Souls that the Pilgrim spent in Dülmen, the invalid
noticed in him that general indifference toward the dead,
that comforting assurance with which the living look upon
their deceased relations and friends as no longer in need of
special assistance; consequently, she often repeated with
a sigh: "It is truly sad to think how few help the poor
souls in purgatory. Their misery is so great! They cannot
help themselves, though they may be so easily relieved by
prayers, alms, and suffering offered for them! O how joyful
they then are!—as happy as a thirsty man to whom a cool
drink is given."

When she saw that her words produced a deep impression,
she went on to say how powerful are meritorious works offered
for the poor souls; for example, acts of self-abnegation and
mortification of self-will, victories gained over evil inclinations, acts of patience, meekness, humility, forgiveness of
injuries, etc.—"Ah! how many poor souls are left to suffer in consequence of lukewarmness, want of zeal for God's
glory and the salvation of the neighbor! What can help
them except satisfactory works, acts of those virtues which

they themselves neglected most on earth? The saints in heaven can no longer do penance, they cannot satisfy for them.—Help can come only from the children of the Church Militant. And how the souls long for it! They know that no good thought, no earnest desire to help them is lost; and yet, how few trouble themselves about them! A priest who says his breviary devoutly with the intention of supplying for the failings the poor souls have still to expiate, can procure for them incredible consolation; yes, the power of the sacerdotal benediction penetrates even into purgatory and, like a celestial dew, refreshes the souls to whom it is sent in the spirit of faith. One who could see all this as I see it, would certainly try to relieve them as far as he is able."

Above all, did Sister Emmerich pity the poor souls whose friends send them to heaven at once in reward for natural good qualities, or those to whom relatives bear so soft and foolish an affection as not to be able to endure the idea of their needing the purifying flames of purgatory before their admittance to the enjoyment of God. Such souls she always saw among the most suffering and abandoned. "Immoderate praise," she used to say, "is a theft committed to the prejudice of those upon whom it is lavished."

One day, after a conversation with her on the relations existing between the survivors and the deceased, the Pilgrim wrote down the following, which embodies the most salient points of their discourse:—"All that man thinks, says, or does, has in it a living principle for good or evil. He who sins should hasten to efface his faults by the Sacrament of Penance, otherwise he will not be able to prevent the full or partial consequence of his crime. I have often seen such consequence even in the physical sickness and sufferings of many individuals and in the curse attached to cer-

tain places. I am always told that a crime unpardoned,
unexpiated, entails an infinity of evils. I have seen such
chastisements extending to posterity as a natural and necessary consequence ; for instance, the curse attached to ill-
gotten goods, and I have felt involuntary horror in places
where great crimes were once perpetrated. This is as natural, as necessary as that a benediction should bless and
what is holy, sanctify. I have always had an intuitive
perception of what is sacred and of what is profane, of
what is holy and what unholy ; the former attracts me, the
the latter repels, disquiets, and terrifies me, forcing me to
resist it by faith and prayer. This impression is especially
keen near human remains, nay more, near the smallest atoms
of a body once animated by a soul. The feeling is so
strong that I have always thought there exists a certain
relation between soul and body even after death, for I have
felt the most opposite emotions near graves and tombs.
Near some I have had a sensation of light, of superabundant
benediction and salvation ; by others a sentiment of poverty and indigence, and I felt that the dead implored
prayers, fasts, and alms ; by many others I have been
struck with dread and horror. When I had to pray at
night in the cemetery, I have felt that there brooded around
such graves as the last named a darkness, deeper, blacker
than night itself, just as a hole in black cloth makes the
blackness still deeper. Over them I sometimes saw a black
vapor rising which made me shudder. It also happened
sometimes that when my desire to render assistance urged
me to penetrate into the darkness, I felt something repulsing my proffered aid. The lively conviction of God's most
holy justice was then for me like an angel leading me out
from the horrors of such a grave. Over some, I saw a column
of gray vapor, brighter or darker ; over others, one of light

more or less brilliant ; and over many others, I beheld nothing at all. These last made me very sad, for I had an interior conviction that the vapor, more or less brilliant, issuing from the graves, was the means by which the poor souls made known their needs, and that they who could give no sign were in the lowest part of purgatory, forgotten by everybody, deprived of all power of acting or communicating with the body of the Church. When I knelt in prayer over such graves, I often heard a hollow, smothered voice, as if calling to me from a deep abyss: ' Help me out !' and I felt most keenly in my own soul the anguish of the helpless sufferer. I pray for these abandoned, forgotten ones with greater ardor and perseverance than for the others. I have often seen a gray vapor slowly rising over their empty, silent tombs which by the help of continued prayer grew brighter and brighter. The graves over which I saw columns of vapor more or less bright, were shown me as those of such as are not entirely forgotten, not entirely bound, who by their own expiatory sufferings, or the help of their friends, are more or less consoled. They have still the power to give a sign of their participation in the Communion of Saints, they are increasing in light and beatitude, they implore that help they cannot render themselves, and what we do for them they offer to Our Lord Jesus Christ for us. They remind me of poor prisoners who can still excite the pity of their fellow-men by a cry, a petition, an outstretched hand. A cemetery, such as I have described, with its apparitions, its different degrees of light and darkness, always seemed to me like a garden all parts of which are not equally cultivated, but some allowed to run to waste. When I earnestly prayed and labored and urged others to the same, it seemed as if the plants began to revive, as if the ground were dug and renewed, as if the seed sprang forth under the beneficent influence of the rain and dew. Ah! if all men saw this as I see it, they would surely labor in this garden with far more diligence than I! Such cemeteries speak as plainly to me of the Christian zeal and charity of a parish, as do the gardens and meadows around a village proclaim the industry of its inhabitants.—God has often allowed me to see souls mounting joyously from purgatory to Paradise. But as nothing is accomplished without pain and trouble, so too when praying for the dead, I was frequently terrified and maltreated by lost spirits even by the demon himself. Loud noises and frightful spectres surrounded me. I was pushed off the graves, tossed from side to side, and sometimes an invisible power tried to force me out of the cemetery. But God strengthened me against fear. I never recoiled one hair's breadth before the enemy, and when thus interrupted, I redoubled my prayers. O how many thanks I have received from the poor, dear souls! Ah! if all men would share this joy with me! What a superabundance of grace is upon earth, but forgotten, despised, whilst the poor souls languish for it! In their manifold sufferings they are full of anguish and longing, they sigh after help and deliverance; yet, how great soever their distress, they still praise Our Lord and Saviour, and all that we can do for them is a source of unending bliss."

All-Saints and All-Souls (1819).

"I made a great journey with my guide, how I know not. At such times I neither know who I am nor how I exist. I follow unquestioningly, I look, and I am satisfied. If I happen to put a question and receive an answer, well and good; but if not, still I am satisfied.—We went over the city of martyrs (Rome), then across the sea, and through a wilderness to a place where once stood the house of Anne and Mary, and here I left the earth. I saw innumerable cohorts of saints of endless variety, and yet in my soul, in my interior, they were all only one, all living and revelling in a life of joy, all interpenetrating and reflecting one another. The place was like a boundless dome full of thrones, gardens, palaces, arches, flower-gardens, and trees, with pathways sparkling like gold and precious stones. On high, in the centre, in infinite splendor was the throne of the Godhead.— The saints were grouped according to their spiritual relationship : the religious in their Orders higher or lower, according to their individual merits ; the martyrs, according to their victories ; and laics of all classes, according to their progress in the spiritual life, the efforts they had made to sanctify themselves. All were ranged in admirable order in the palaces and gardens which were inexpressibly brilliant and lovely. I saw trees with little yellow luminous fruits. They who were associated by similar efforts to sanctify themselves had aureolas of the same form, like a supernatural spiritual habit, and they were otherwise distinguished by emblems of victory, crowns and garlands and palms, and they were of all classes and nations. Among them I saw a priest of my acquaintance who said to me : 'Thy task is not yet finished!' I saw, too, legions of soldiers in Roman costume, and many people whom I knew, all singing together. I joined in a sweet song with them. I looked down on the earth which lay like a speck of land amid the waters ; but, where I was, all was immense. Ah ! life is so short, the end soon comes ! One can gain so much—I must not be sad ! Willingly and joyfully shall I accept all sufferings from my God !"

November 2d—" I went with my guide into a gloomy prison for souls, where I consoled on all sides, The souls were buried in darkness, all more or less so ; some to the neck, others to the waist. They were in separate, though adjoining dungeons, some tortured with thirst, others by cold, others by heat, unable to help themselves, sighing in uninterrupted torments. I saw numbers delivered, and their joy was inexpressible. They went forth as gray figures. They received for their short passage to a higher region the costume and distinctive marks of their state upon earth. They assembled in a vast place above purgatory enclosed as with a thorn-hedge. I saw many physicians received by a procession of physicians like themselves and conducted on high. I saw numbers of soldiers liberated, and the sight made me rejoice with the poor men slaughtered in war. I saw few female religious, still fewer judges; but led out by blessed nuns were numbers of virginal souls who had wanted only an opportunity to consecrate themselves to the religious life. I saw some kings of the olden times, some members of royal families, a large number of ecclesiastics, and many peasants, among whom I saw some of my acquaintance and others who, by their costume, seemed to belong to foreign lands. Each class was led on high and in different directions by souls of their own condition in life and, as they ascended, they were divested of their earthly insignia and clothed in a luminous robe peculiar to the blessed. I recognized in purgatory not only my own acquaintances, but also their relatives whom, perhaps, I had never before seen. I saw in the greatest abandonment those poor, dear souls who have no one to think of them. Among those who forget them are so many of their brethren in the faith who neglect prayer ! It is for such souls that I pray the most.—Now began another vision. All at once, I found myself a little peasant-girl just as in my childhood, a band on my forehead, a cap on my head. My guide took me to a luminous troop of blessed spirits coming down from heaven, shining forms with crowns on their heads. Above them hovered the Saviour holding a white staff surmounted by a cross and banner. There were about one hundred spirits, most of them maidens, only one-third of them youths, all in royal robes sparkling with the various colors of their aureolas, and presenting a most lovely spectacle. Among them were some conspicuous by their wounds which shone with a rosy light. I was greatly abashed when my guide led me to them, for I, poor little peasant-girl, knew not how to act before kings and queens. But my guide said : 'Thou canst be like them,' and then, instead of my peasant dress, I was clothed in the white habit of a religious. I saw all around those who had assisted at my clothing in the convent, especially the deceased members of my own community. Then I saw many of the poor souls whom I had known in life, with whom I had had dealings, looking wistfully after me from purgatory, and I understood the difference between true and false sympathy. They followed me with sad eyes, repenting of many things now that I was forced to leave them.—They were citizens of the little city."

Feast of the Guardian-Angels (1820)

"I saw a church on earth and in it many whom I knew. Above were several other churches, higher and higher, like different stories, filled with the angelic choirs ; and higher still was the Blessed Virgin surrounded by the highest order, before the throne of the Most Holy Trinity. Here reigned indescribable order and activity; but below in the earthly church, all was drowsy and negligent to a degree. And this was the more remarkable as it was the feast of the angels who bear up to God with incredible swiftness every word pronounced carelessly and distractedly by the priest in the Holy Mass, and who repair all defects in the service offered to God. At the same time, I saw the guardian-angels discharging their duties with surprising activity, chasing evil spirits from men, suggesting good thoughts, and presenting before them holy imaginations. They long for God's commands, and the prayers of their clients render them still more zealous. I have seen that every man receives at his birth two spirits, one good, the other evil. The good one is heavenly by nature and belongs to the lowest hierarchy; the evil one is not a devil, not yet in torments, though deprived of the vision of God. I always see in a certain circle around the earth nine bodies or spheres like far-off stars. They are inhabited by spirits of different natures, from whom descend beams of light, every ray falling upon some determinate point on the earth with which I have always thought they must have some communication. These nine worlds form three sections, above each of which I saw a great angel enthroned; the first holds a sceptre; the second, a rod; the third a sword. They wear crowns and long robes, and their breast is decorated with ribands. In these spheres dwell the bad spirits who at each man's birth are associated to him by an intimate relation which I clearly understand, which excites my wonder, but which I cannot now explain. They are not lovely and transparent like the angels. They shine it is true, but by an external, unsteady light, as if by reflection. They are either slothful, indolent, fanciful, melancholy, or passionate, violent, obstinate, stubborn, or frivolous, etc., a personification of the different passions. Among them I have remarked the same colors that I see among men in their sufferings and interior struggles and in the aureolas of the martyrs, whose passions purified by torments have been changed into colors of triumph. These spirits have something sharp, violent, and penetrating in their countenance. They attach themselves with extraordinary tenacity to the human soul as insects to certain odors and plants, rousing in them all kinds of thoughts and desires. They are full of stings, of rays, of seductive charms. They themselves produce no act, no sin, but they withdraw man from the divine influence, lay him open to the world, intoxicate him with self, bind him, attach him to the earth in many ways. If he yields, he plunges into darkness, the devil draws near and marks him with his seal;—now some act, some sin, and his separation from God is effected. I have clearly seen that mortification and fasting weaken the influence of these spirits and facilitate that of the angels, whilst Holy Communion is the most effectual means of resisting them. I have seen that certain inclinations and aversions, certain involuntary antipathies, and especially the disgust we have for certain things, such as insects, reptiles, vermin, etc., have a mysterious signification, since these creatures are images of those sins and passions to which, through their connection with these spirits, we are the most exposed. I was told that when one feels disgust for such things, he should recall his sins and evil propensities symbolized by them. I have seen such spirits presenting to people in church all sorts of toys and trinkets, filling their heads with all sorts of thoughts and desires, whilst their angels are busy recalling them to better things. I cannot relate these multiplied pictures. The great ones of the earth are attended by the most powerful both of the good and bad spirits. I have often seen a man receive a higher and more powerful guardian when called to great things.—I myself have had on more than one occasion a different guide. I have seen the angels that protect the fruits of the earth spreading something over the trees and plants and over cities and countries. I have seen angels hovering over them, guarding and defending them, and sometimes abandoning them. I cannot say what myriads of bad spirits I have seen.—Had they bodies, the air would be darkened. Wherever they have most influence, I always see mist and darkness.—I had on my journey a glimpse of Switzerland where I saw the devil laboring in many ways against the Church."

As Sister Emmerich finished the relation of the above, she was suddenly ravished in ecstasy. After a short time, she exclaimed with a sigh: "It is so far away! so far! Those cruel, obstinate, violent spirits there descending, come from an immense distance!" Returned to consciousness, she said: "I was carried up to a great height and from the most distant of the nine spheres, I saw a multitude of those violent, obstinate spirits descending toward a country to which strife and war are approaching. They surround the rulers, making approach to them almost impossible. But I saw, too, a whole army of angelic spirits sent down to earth by the Blessed Virgin; they were led by a great angel burning with zeal and bearing a flaming sword. They will fight against the perverse spirits.

"There are, also, souls neither in heaven, purgatory, nor hell, but wandering the earth in trouble and anguish, aiming at something they are bound to perform. They haunt deserted places, ruins, tombs, and the scenes of their past misdeeds. They are spectres."

Some hours after she cried out in ecstasy: "O who ever saw the like! A great, flaming angel swept from the throne of God down to the city of Palermo where an insurrection rages. He spoke words of chastisement in a voice that pierced through the marrow of my bones, and people fell dead in the city below!"

On another occasion, she said : " I have often understood, in my childhood and later, that three whole choirs of angelic spirits higher than the archangels, fell, but all were not cast into hell ; some, experiencing a sort of repentance, escaped for a time. They are the planetary spirits that come upon earth to tempt men. At the last day they will be judged and condemned. I have always seen that the devils can never leave hell. I have seen, too, that many of the damned go not directly to hell, but suffer in lonely places on earth.

" If men make progress in the spiritual life, they receive guardian-angels of a higher order such as kings and princes have. The four-winged angels, the Elohim, who distribute God's graces, are Raphiel, Etophiel, Salathiel, and Emmanuel. There is much greater order even among the bad spirits and demons than there is on earth. Whenever an angel withdraws, a devil steps instantly into his place and begins his own work. Great order reigns also among the planetary spirits, who are fallen spirits, but not devils. They are very, very different from devils. They go to and fro between the earth and the nine spheres. In one of these spheres they are sad and melancholy ; in another, impetuous and violent ; in a third, light and giddy ; in a fourth, stingy, parsimonious, miserly, etc. They exert an influence over the whole earth, over every man from his birth, and they form certain orders and associations. In the planets I saw forms resembling plants and trees, but light and unsubstantial, like mushrooms. There are, also, waters on them, some clear as crystal, others muddy and poisonous; and it seemed to me that each planet contains a metal. The spirits make use of fruits adapted to their own nature. Some are an occasion of good, inasmuch as man himself directs their influence to good. Not all the heavenly bodies are inhabited ; some are only gardens or storehouses for certain fruits and influences. I see places in which are souls who, although not Christian, yet led good lives on earth. They are now in uncertainty, feeling that some day or other their lot will change; they are without joy or pain. Like the others, they feed upon certain fruits.

"The moon is chilly and rocky, full of high mountains, deep cavities, and valleys. She both attracts and repels the earth. Her waters are constantly rising and falling, drawing up masses of vapor from the earth which like great clouds fill up the hollow places; again they appear to overflow and gravitate so powerfully upon the earth that men become melancholy. I see in her many human figures flying from light into darkness as if hiding their shame, as if their conscience were in a bad state. This I see more frequently in the centre of the moon. In other parts are fields and thickets in which animals roam. I never saw any worship offered to God on the moon. The soil is yellow and stony; the vegetation like pith, fungi, or mushrooms. The moon exerts a wonderful influence over the earth and all nature. Men regard her so wistfully, because one naturally turns to what belongs to him. I often see descending from her huge clouds like masses of poison which generally hang over the sea; but the good spirits, the angels, scatter them and render them harmless. Certain low districts cn the earth are cursed on account of sin there committed, and over them I see falling poison, darkness, fog. The noblest races live in the most highly favored regions.

"The souls that I see hiding in darkness seem to be without suffering or joy, as if imprisoned till the Day of Judgment.—The moon's light is dull, of a bluish white, and the farther from the moon, the brighter it becomes.

"Comets are full of baneful influences; they are like

birds of passage.—Were there not between them and the earth so great tempests and other influences exercised by the spirits, they might easily do the latter much harm. They are the abodes of the passionate spirits. Their tail, that is their influence, follows as smoke from fire.

"The Milky Way is formed of watery globules like crystals. It seems as if the good spirits bathe therein. They plunge in and pour forth all kinds of dew and blessings like a Baptism.—The sun follows an oval path. It is a beneficent body peopled by holy spirits. It has no heat in itself; light and heat are generated only around it. It is white and lovely and full of beautiful colors.

"Many of the heavenly bodies are still uninhabited. They are beautiful regions awaiting a future population, gardens and storehouses of certain fruits. One can understand it only by representing to one's self a state perfectly well-regulated, a city, or a great, wonderful household in which nothing is wanting. Of all these bodies none has the grandeur or the internal force of the earth. The others possess certain special properties, but the earth comprises them all. The sin of Eve made us fall, but we can now become conquerors, for the poorest saint has a higher rank than the highest angel."

Sister Emmerich related the above with the simplicity of a child describing its garden. "When a little girl," she continued, "I used to kneel out in the fields at night in the snow, and look up joyously at the beautiful stars. I said to God : 'Thou art my true Father, and Thou hast so lovely things in Thy house—now, then, show them to me !'—And He took me by the hand, and showed me everything—it all seemed perfectly natural. Full of joy I gazed at everything. I cared for nothing else."

September 2, 1822, she related the following : "I went

up steep heights to an aerial garden. I saw on the north eastern horizon, rising like a sun, the figure of a man with a long, pale face, his head covered with a pointed cap. He was strapped with ribands and had a shield on his breast whose inscription, however, I have forgotten. He bore a sword laced with many-colored ribands. He rose slowly and floated gently over the earth. He waved his sword from right to left and cast the ribands, which interlaced like nets, over some sleeping cities. Upon Russia, Italy, and Spain he scattered pustules and boils, laid a red noose around Berlin, and from there came on to us. The sword was naked. Blood-red streamers like the intestines of animals floated from the hilt, and blood dripped over our land. The figure flew in a zigzag course."

September 11th.—" Off in the southeast rises an angel. In one hand he bears a naked sword, in the other a scabbard full of blood which he pours out on the countries over which he flies. He comes here, too, and pours blood over the cathedral-place in Münster."

St. Michael, the Archangel.

September 29, 1820.—" I had many wonderful visions of the feasts and apparitions of the Archangel, St. Michael. I was in many parts of the world, and I saw his church in France on a rock in the sea. I saw him as the patron of that country. I saw how he helped the pious King Louis to gain a victory. On a command from the Mother of God, Louis had invoked Michael and placed his picture on his standard. He also founded an Order of Chevaliers in his honor. I saw St. Michael take the tabernacle from his church and carry it away, and I also saw an apparition of him in Constantinople and many other places, all of which I cannot now recall. I saw the miracle of the church on

Mount Gargano. A great feast was being celebrated. It was attended by a great concourse of pilgrims, their robes tucked up and knobs on their staves. The angel served at the altar with the others." Here Sister Emmerich recounted the miracle of Mount Gargano pretty much as related elsewhere, adding that the site of the church had been designated by a figure traced on the rock with a chalice in his hand. She continues:—

" Then I went with the Archangel to Rome where there is a church commemorative of one of his apparitions. I think it was built under Pope Boniface and upon a revelation from the Mother of God. I followed him everywhere as he floated above me, grand and majestic, holding a sword and girt round with cords. A dispute was going on in his church. Numbers were engaged in it, most of them Catholics, though not of much account ; the rest were Protestant sectarians. It seemed as if they were arguing some point of divine worship. But the angel descended and scattered the crowd with his sword, leaving only about forty persons who went on with the service very simply. When all was over, St. Michael took up the tabernacle with the Most Holy Sacrament and flew away. My guide ordered me to follow. I did so, flying just below the angel toward the east, until we reached the Ganges, when we turned more to the north. On one side lay the Mountain of the Prophets, and there our road began to descend, becoming colder, darker, wilder, until we arrived at a vast ice-plain. I was seized with terror in this solitude; but some souls appeared to encourage me, among them my mother, Antrienchen, old Soentgen and others.—We came to an immense mill through which we had to pass, and here the souls of my friends left me. The ice kept constantly cracking, the water foamed, and again I was seized with fear;

but my guide gave me his hand and reassured me. The water that turned the mill ran under the ice, and it was warm. The mill was full of great lords and rulers of all nations and periods who were condemned to grind without intermission toads, serpents, and other disgusting and venomous reptiles, as well as gold, silver and all kinds of costly objects which, when thus deprived of their baneful properties, fell into the water and were borne away to shore. The lords took turn about and worked like servants. They had constantly to sweep the horrid things under the millstone; otherwise they would have been much annoyed. The mill appeared to me to be a place of penance for such princes as had involved the affairs of their own and of other states, and had introduced institutions whose pernicious consequences are still felt. Their souls cannot attain beatitude whilst such consequences exist. These consequences now come to them under the form of hideous reptiles whose destruction will prevent their propagation. The warm water in which all was ground flowed back into the world, carrying with it nothing hurtful.—As we passed through, one of the souls approached us and quickly swept the reptiles under the millstone, that we might not tread on them. The soul spoke to me, explained the nature of the place, and expressed his own and his companions' satisfaction at our coming that way, as our footsteps loosened a little of the enormous mass of ice; for, until the whole disappeared, would they have to grind. We left them, crossing the ice-sea through a deep furrow, (it had such cracks here and there) and then for a time ascended an iceberg, glad to leave behind us a tolerably long track for the poor grinders.

" As we mounted I beheld the Archangel Michael floating above me. The sky became clearer and of a more beautiful blue, and I saw the sun and the other heavenly bodies as I had seen them before in a vision. We went around the whole earth and through all the celestial worlds, in which I saw innumerable gardens with their fruits and signification. I hope some time to be allowed to enter, for I want to get medicines and recipes to cure pious sick people. I saw the choirs of the blessed and sometimes, here and there, a saint standing in his sphere with his own distinctive insignia. Still soaring upward, we arrived at a world of unspeakably wonderful magnificence. It was shaped like a dome, like an azure disc, surrounded by a ring of light above which were nine other rings on every one of which rested a throne. These circles were full of angels. From the thrones arose many-colored arches filled with fruits, precious stones, and costly gifts of God, which met in a dome surmounted by three angelic thrones. The middle one was St. Michael's. Thither he flew and placed the tabernacle on top of the dome. Each of the three angels, Michael, Gabriel, and Raphael stood severally over a part of the dome formed by three of the nine angelic choirs, and four great, luminous angels, veiled with their wings, moved constantly around them. They are the Elohim : Raphiel, Etophiel, Emmanuel, and Salathiel, the administrators and distributors of God's superabundant graces, which they receive from the three archangels and scatter throughout the Church, to the four points of the compass.—Gabriel and Raphael were in long, white robes like a priest's. Michael wore a helmet with a crest of rays, and his body seemed encased in armor and girt with cords, his robe descending to the knees like a fringed apron. In one hand he held a long staff surmounted by a cross under which floated the standard of the Lamb ; in the other was a flaming sword. His feet also were laced.

" Above the dome lay a still higher world in which I

saw the Most Blessed Trinity represented by three figures: the Father, an old man like a high-priest, presenting to His Son on His right the orb of the world; the Son who held a cross in one hand; and to the left of the Father stood a luminous winged figure. Around them sat the twenty-four ancients in a circle. The cherubim and seraphim with many other spirits stood around the throne of God hymning incessant praise.

"In the centre above Michael, stood Mary surrounded by innumerable circles of luminous souls, angels, and virgins. The grace of Jesus flows through Mary to the three archangels, each of whom radiates three kinds of gifts upon three of the nine inferior choirs. These in their turn, pour them forth upon all nature and the whole human race.

"As the tabernacle reposed there, I saw it, by the influx of grace descending upon it from Mary and the co-operation of the whole heavenly court, increase in size until it became first a church and then a great shining city which slowly sank to the earth.—I know not how it was, but I saw multitudes of living beings, first only their heads and then the whole figure, as if the earth on which they stood were drawing near to me and, at last, they were suddenly landed in the new Jerusalem, the new city which had descended upon the old Jerusalem, and which had now come upon earth. And here the vision ended. I plunged again into the darkness and directed my way homeward.

"I had a picture of an immense battle. The whole plain was a mass of dense smoke, and the bushes were full of soldiers who kept up an incessant fire. The place lay low, and there were great cities in the distance. When all seemed lost, St. Michael at the invocation of one of the leaders, swept down with a legion of angels and the victory was instantly gained.

Sister Emmerich knew not the time of this battle, although she said it would happen in Italy, not far from Rome, where many ancient things would be destroyed and many holy things, unknown till then, would come to light. She related what follows :—

" As I was once very much disgusted and discouraged, on account of the miseries around me and my own personal pains and troubles, I sighed : ' O that God would grant me even one single day of peace, for I live as if in hell !'— and then came a severe reprimand from my guide: ' That thou mayest no more compare thy state to hell, I shall show thee hell.' and he led me toward the north by the side on which the earth makes a steep declivity. First we mounted high in the air.—I felt that the Mountain of the Prophets was on my right to the east, above which still further eastward I saw Paradise. I was carried northward over steep paths of ice until we reached a horrible region. I felt that we had gone all round the earth, to the steep descents on the north. The way down to hell was wild, dark, and icebound. When I reached the abode of terror, I felt as if I had come to a lower world. I saw a disc, a section of a sphere, and when I think of what I there beheld, I tremble in every limb. I saw everything in confusion : here, a fire, there smoke, everywhere pitchy darkness—a land of unending torments."

September 24, 1820.—"I have had some rough work in the Nuptial House, but I could not finish. With a stiff broom quite unfit for the work, I had to sweep away a quantity of trash ; but I could not succeed. Then my mother came and helped me, as also the soul of her to whom I gave the picture of St. Catherine which I had received in a supernatural manner (1). She wore a little picture on her breast and

See vol. 1., chap XII.

conversed with me a long time. They are not yet in heaven but in a very pleasant place where Abraham and good Lazarus were—a charming place, mild and sweet like dew and honey. Its light is like that of the moon, yet white, more like milk. The vision of poor Lazarus was there given me merely that I might know where I was. Paradise which I again saw, as well as the Mountain of the Prophets, is more joyous, more delightful than Abraham's bosom and full of magnificent creatures. My mother took me to the abodes of the souls. I remember, in particular, a mountain out of which issued a spirit shining with a copper-colored light and bound by a chain. He stood before me. He had been confined here a long time destitute of all assistance, for no one thought of him, no one helped or prayed for him. He uttered but few words, and yet I learned his whole history of which I still remember a part. During the reign of an English king who waged war upon France, he had commanded an English army in the latter country which he frightfully and cruelly laid waste. He had been badly reared through his mother's fault, as I saw; but he had always cherished a secret veneration for Mary. Among other acts of violence, he was accustomed to destroy all the pictures he came across. One day passing a most beautiful statue of the Mother of God, he was about to treat it in like manner when he was seized by a certain emotion that restrained him. He was soon after attacked by a violent fever. He wanted to confess, but he became unconscious and died. His lively repentance obtained for him mercy at the Judgment Seat. He was in a state to receive assistance, but his friends completely forgot him. He told me that he wanted Masses more than all else and that, for a long time past, a very slight assistance would have freed him. He was not in purgatory, for in purgatory proper souls are not tormented by devils. He was in another place of torment and surrounded by dogs, barking at him and tearing him, because he had during life subjected others to the same cruelty. Sometimes he was bound to a block in different positions and drenched with seething blood which ran through all his veins. The hope of deliverance was his only consolation. When he had told me the above he disappeared in the mountain, leaving the grass around him scorched and burnt. This was the third time I had seen him.

"I was afterward transported with several souls whom the Lord had delivered at my petition, into a Franciscan convent in which a lay-brother was struggling in fearful death-agony. The convent was situated in a mountainous district; it had not a large community and there were some seculars among them. The dying man had lived there three years. After a misspent life, he had entered the Order to do penance. It was night when I arrived. I found a troop of evil spirits raising a horrible din around the house. It was swept by a tempest. The tiles were flying from the roof, the trees beating up against the windows, and demons, under the form of crows, other sinister birds, and frightful figures, were dashing around the place and even into the cell of the dying man. Among the assistants at his deathbed, was a holy old monk around whom I saw many souls who had been delivered from purgatory by his prayers. The tumult increased and the monks fled in terror. But the good old man went to the window and adjured the evil spirits in the name of Jesus to say what they wanted. Then I heard a voice demanding why he wished to deprive them of a soul that had served them for thirty years. But the old monk, all the souls, and I myself resisted the enemy until we forced him to withdraw. He vowed that he would enter into a woman with whom the dying man had long sinned, and torment her till her death. I saw the evil one depart and the sick man die in peace."

September 27, 1820.—"Last night I prayed much for the poor souls. I saw many wonderful things concerning their punishments and the incomprehensible mercy of God. Again I saw the unhappy English captain, and I prayed for him. I saw that the mercy and justice of God are boundless, and that nothing of the good still left in man is ever lost; for the virtues and vices of a man's ancestors contribute to his salvation or ruin according to his own will and co-operation. I saw souls receiving by wonderful ways assistance from the treasures of the Church and the charity of her members—all was a real reparation, a full compensation for sin. Mercy and justice, though infinite in God, do not neutralize each ther. I saw many states of purification and especially the chastisement of those indolent, easy-going priests who are wont to say : ' I'll be satisfied with a low place in heaven. I pray, I say Mass, I hear confessions, etc.'—They have to endure unspeakable torments and they sigh after works of zeal and charity. All the souls that once claimed their assistance now pass in review before them whilst they have to sit idle, though consumed by devouring desires to help those in need. Their sloth has become their spiritual torment, their repose is turned into impatience, their inactivity is now a chain which binds them fast.—These chastisements are not imaginary ; they spring clearly and wonderfully from past offences as disease from a germ.

" I saw the soul of a woman deceased some twenty or thirty years. She was not in purgatory, but in a place of more rigorous punishment. She was not only imprisoned, but also punished in inexpressible pain and affliction. In her arms was a dark-skinned child which she incessantly killed, but which always came to life again. The mother was condemned to wash it white with her tears. Souls can shed tears, otherwise they could not weep in the body. The poor creature begged my prayers and related to me her fault, or rather I saw it all in a succession of pictures. She belonged to a Polish city and was the wife of an honest man who kept an inn for the accommodation of ecclesiastics and others of retired life. The wife was thoroughly good and pious and had a very holy relative, a missionary in the Congregation of the Most Holy Redeemer. Her husband being obliged to absent himself from home for a short time, there came to lodge at the inn a stranger, a wicked wretch, who, using violence, forced her into sin. This drove her almost mad. She repulsed the miserable man, but he refused to leave the house even when her husband's return drew near. Her agony of mind became frightful. The fiend suggested to her to poison her seducer, which she actually did, when remorse well-nigh drove her to despair; and, yielding again to the evil one's whisper, she later on destroyed the fruit of her womb. In her misery, she sought a strange priest to whom she might confess. A vagabond disguised as a priest presented himself at the inn. She made her confession to him with unspeakable grief and torrents of tears. Shortly after she died, but God, in His mercy, was mindful of her bitter repentance; and, although unabsolved and without the Sacraments, yet He condemned her to the place of punishment wherein I found her. She must by her own satisfaction complete the years God had destined for her child, before which it cannot attain to light. Such children have a growth in the other world. Five years after her death she appeared to her relative, the priest, during the Holy

Mass. I knew the pious old man ; he prayed in union with me.

"On this occasion I saw many things concerning purgatory, and particularly the state of children put to death before or after their birth; but I cannot relate it clearly, I will pass it over. Of one thing I have always been certain and that is, that all good in soul or body tends to light just as sin if not expiated tends to darkness. Justice and mercy are perfections in God; the first is satisfied by the second, by the inexhaustible merits of Jesus Christ and the saints, and by the works of faith, hope, and love performed by the members of His spiritual Body. Nothing done in the Church in union with Jesus is lost. Every pious desire, every good thought, every charitable work inspired by the love of Jesus, contributes to the perfection of the whole body of the faithful. A person who does nothing more than lovingly pray to God for his brethren, participates in the great work of saving souls."

April 12, 1820.—A young peasant-girl having fallen into sin and dreading her parents' anger, had secretly given birth to a child which died shortly after in consequence of the mother's imprudence. She hid the body away, but it was soon discovered. The affair was deeply afflicting to Sister Emmerich; she suffered and prayed incessantly for the guilty one's repentance. She said : " I know the girl. She came to see me about a year ago, and since Christmas I have often seen her in vision covered up in a mantle. I always had a secret dread of its concealing something bad. I saw her last at the time for her confession, but she was not in good dispositions. I prayed for her and warned her confessor to pay particular attention to her—but she went not near him ! Last night I was occupied with her and greatly distressed at her state. Although she is rather simple, she is not altogether innocent of the child's death. I saw the whole affair and prayed much for her.——Then I remembered the two ex-Jesuits to whom I had gone to confession in my youth, and I thought, 'How piously they lived! How much good they did! Nothing like this ever happened in their time!'——but whilst these thoughts were passing through my mind, the two holy men appeared to me, both in a very good state. One of them led me to his sister with whom he had formerly lived and whom I knew. She was in a very singular place, walled up as it were in a narrow, dark, four-cornered hole in which she could only stand upright; but she was quite content and patient. She had many companions in the same position. Soon I saw her pass to a more roomy prison in front of the other. I could never have imagined that so pious a person would have anything to expiate! She begged me to come oftener to see her. I spoke for some time with the holy old priests and asked them something. . . . . .

"For a long while I have had interior lights on the state of children dying without Baptism, and I have seen the unspeakable blessings, the treasures they lose when deprived of this Sacrament. I cannot express what I feel on beholding their loss! I am so grieved to hear of such a death that I offer to God my prayers and sufferings in satisfaction for the neglect, that the want of charity in some may be compensated for by the body of the faithful, by myself as one of its members; therefore it was that I was so distressed about the child of the unhappy girl. I offered myself to God in satisfaction."

April 10, 1820.——"Last night I had a painful vision, a difficult task. Suddenly there stood beside me the shining soul of a good wife of Coesfeld. She had been deeply devoted to her husband who seemed to be a good, pious man. I had not thought of that couple for a long time. The wife died and the husband married again, but I knew not the second wife. The soul said to me : ' At last I have been permitted by God to come to you. My state is a happy one, but my husband's gives me pain. During my last sickness he had with his present wife very sinful intercourse, and now in marriage he does not live with her in a Christian manner. I fear for his soul and ·that of his wife.' On hearing this I wondered, for I had always thought him so good. She told me much more and begged me to warn her husband, who was coming to see me.—I went with her to Coesfeld. I could see distinctly over the whole road, for she shone like a sun. This greatly rejoiced me. I recognized every turn of the road and found many places changed. She led me into her husband's house in which I had often been before ; in it, also, I found changes. We approached the bed of the married pair who lay asleep. The wife seemed to perceive us, for she sat up. I spoke to her a long time, bidding her reflect on her state and lead her husband to do the same. She promised everything. I think the husband will come to see me and, since the soul has so earnestly begged me to pray for him and give him advice, I feel a little anxious as to how I shall introduce the subject if he does not begin it himself."

LABOR FOR TWO SOVEREIGNS.

October 6, 1820.—" I have had a picture of a pious Franciscan of the Tyrol who foresaw great danger menacing the Church in consequence of a political convention about to be held. He had been commanded to pray unceasingly for her, and I saw him doing so in a little convent on the outskirts of a town. He knelt at night before a miraculous picture of Mary. I saw the demons trying to distract him by raising a great din in the church and dashing violently against the window-panes under the form of crows. But the good monk was not disturbed ; he went on praying with extended arms.—As a consequence of his prayer, I beheld three figures drawing near to my bed : the first was a being like my guide ; the others were souls seeking prayers ; one a Catholic prince of Brandenburg, the other a pious Austrian emperor. They had been sent by the Franciscan's prayer to ask my help, for he had seen the same dangers as I. They petitioned to be raised to a higher state in which they would be better able to influence their present successors on earth. I learned that such souls have more influence over their descendants than others. Something very remarkable now happened to me. Their conductor took my hands himself and held them up. I felt his hand, smooth and soft and airy like down. As often as I allowed my hands to sink, he raised them up again with the words : ' Thou must pray longer ! '—This is all I can remember."

October 8th—" Returning from Rome with my guide, I went again to the Tyrol to see the pious Franciscan to whose prayer I was indebted for the visit from the sovereigns whom I had seen before in the mill (1). He is the same old religious that lately chased the demons from the death-bed of his dying confrère. When I arrived he was praying as usual, his arms extended, to ward off danger from the Church. He held his rosary in one hand. When he retired to rest, he used to hang it around his neck.—I went from here with my guide and a beautiful, resplendent lady (I think Mary), to a charming high mountain on which were all sort of fruits and lovely white animals gamboling among the bushes. Higher up we came to a garden full of magnificent roses and other kinds of flowers. In it were

(1) See page 212, Vol. II

figures walking around. Here I saw the two sovereigns who had been promoted. They approached the gate (for I could not go to them) and again begged prayers that they might mount still higher where they could better influence their descendants for the welfare of the Church.—How I longed for some of those roses! I wanted a whole apronful! I thought if Abbé Lambert's foot were bound up in them, it would surely do him good. But my guide gave me only a few which were of no use."—We see by the above that she asked for expiatory sufferings sufficient to obtain the Abbé's cure; but she received no definite assurance of obtaining them.

FEASTS OF ALL-SAINTS AND ALL-SOULS, 1820.

For some time previously to these feasts, Sister Emmerich suffered in every member for the souls in purgatory, sitting up in bed whole nights, and counting every hour. Like a child, she was unable to help herself. Consumed with thirst yet unable to drink; ardently desirous of assisting the souls, yet feeling herself bound as it were in chains; tortured until she lost consciousness, yet preserving the utmost patience and tranquillity—thus she prepared for the Feast of All-Souls.

On November 1st, she said: "I have had an indescribably great and magnificent vision, but I cannot well express it. I saw an immense table with a red and white transparent cover. It was laden with all sorts of dishes. They were all like gold with blue letters around the rim. Flowers and fruits of every description lay there together, not broken from their stems, but living, growing, and though consumed, eternally renewed—the mere sight of them gave strength. (1) Bish-

(1) That is, one was nourished by merely gazing upon them; but the strength, the nourishment they imparted lay in the interior perception of their essence, in their signification.

ops and all their clergy who had had charge of souls, appeared
at the table as stewards and servers. Around it, seated
on thrones or standing in half-circles were troops of saints
in their choirs and orders. As I stood at the immense table, I thought the innumerable choirs around it were in one
garden ; but on looking more closely, I saw that each choir
was in a separate garden and at a separate table. All received, however, a part of everything on the great table.
And in all the gardens and fields and borders, the plants
and branches and flowers were living as on the great
table. The fruits were not eaten ; they were received by a
certain conscious perception.—All the saints appeared with
their various distinctive characteristics : many Bishops had
little churches in their hands, because they had built
churches ; and others, croziers, as they had only discharged
their duties as pastors. By them were trees laden with
fruits. I wanted so badly to give some to the poor that
I shook them (1). Quantities fell upon certain regions of
the earth. I saw the saints in choirs according to
their nature and strength, bringing materials to erect
a throne at one end of the table, and all sorts of garlands, flowers, and decorations for it. All was done with
indescribable order as is proper to a nature exempt from
defect, sin, and death ; all seemed to spring forth spon-
taneously. In the meantime, spiritual guards watched over
the table. Twenty-four old men now seated themselves on
magnificent seats around the throne with harps and censers praising and offering incense. An apparition like an
old man with a triple crown and widespread mantle descended from on high upon the throne. In his forehead was
a three-cornered light in which was a mirror which reflected everything : every one could see his own image therein.

(1) Her earnest prayers drew down to earth the fruits of heaven.

From his mouth issued a beam of light in which were words. I distinguished letters and numbers quite distinctly, but I have now forgotten them. In front of his breast was a dazzlingly bright Crucified Youth from whose Wounds streamed forth arches of rainbow-colored light, which surrounded all the saints like a great ring, and with which their aureolas mingled and played in unspeakable order, freedom, and beauty. From the luminous Wounds I saw a rain of many-colored drops fall upon the earth, like a shower of precious stones, each with its own meaning. I received then the knowledge of the value, virtue, secret properties, and color of precious stones, as also the properties of all colors in general. I saw between the Crucified and the Eye in the forehead of the Old Man, the Holy Spirit under a winged form, and rays streaming to It from both. Before the Crucified, but a little lower down, was the Blessed Virgin surrounded by virgins. I saw a circle of Popes, Apostles, and virgins around the lower part of the cross. All these apparitions, as well as the myriads of saints and angels in circle after circle, were in constant movement, mingling together in perfect unity and endless variety. The spectacle was infinitely richer and grander than that of the starry heavens, and yet all was perfectly clear and distinct—but I cannot describe it!"

Sister Emmerich at this period, was weighed down by sufferings for the poor souls. Fever produced in her violent thirst which she refused to allay by a drop of water, that by this act of self-denial she might alleviate the pains of those poor sufferers. Although weak and exhausted to a degree, she exerted herself to relate the following:—" I was taken by my guide, I knew not in what direction, but it was over a very difficult road, the ascent becoming steeper, the path narrower, until it led like a bridge of light to an im-

mense height. Darkness lay to the right and left, and sometimes the path was so narrow that I had to go sideways; below was the earth, shrouded in mist and obscurity, and mankind wallowing in misery and mire. Almost the whole
night was passed in this painful ascent. I often fell and I
should certainly have been dashed to pieces, had not my
guide given me his hand and helped me to rise. It may
be that we journeyed toward some point on the globe, for my
guide pointed out certain places on our way wherein were
accomplished various mysteries connected with the deliverance of God's people. I saw the countries over which
the Patriarchs and later on the Children of Israel travelled.
They seemed to spring forth from the darkness and grow
distinct as my guide pointed them out, appearing as deserts,
great ruined towers, huge bending trees, marshes, etc.
He told me that when these countries shall again be cultivated and Christianized, the end of time will draw
nigh. Souls accompanied by their guides floated around
us over the road, looking gray in the surrounding darkness.
They did not come on the path, but fluttered by me and
behind me the whole length of the way. They were souls
lately deceased, for whom I had had to suffer and pray for
some days past. Sts. Teresa, Augustine, Ignatius, and
Francis Xavier had appeared and exhorted me to prayer
and labor, promising that on this day I should know for
what end. My road led to purgatory proper which lay below us, and I saw the souls entering for a purgation of about
eight days, some more, others less. This they owed to my
prayers which I still had to continue for them. I saw the
planetary spirits, not yet damned, teasing and tormenting
the poor souls, reproaching them, trying to make them impatient, etc. The part I entered was an immense, skyless
region covered with foliage as with an arch. There were

indeed some trees, fruits, and flowers, but the place breathed
an air of melancholy; in it there was neither actual suffering nor real happiness. There were innumerable other
sections separated by vapors, mist, clouds, or barriers according to the different degrees of isolation to which the
souls in them were condemned. This region was one between purgatory proper and heaven. On my arrival I
saw a number of souls flying out three by three, each set
accompanied by an angel, to a place on which a glimmering of light descended from on high—all were uncommonly
joyous. They shone with colored light which as they mounted became clearer and brighter. I received an instruction
on the signification of their colors; ardent charity which
they had not practised purely in life, emitted a red light
which tormented them; the white light was that of purity
of intention which sloth had made them neglect; green was
that of impatience to which their irritability had made
them yield; but the yellow and blue I have forgotten.
As they passed me in threes they saluted and thanked me.
I knew many of them, mostly people of the middle class
and peasants. I saw indeed some of the higher ranks, but
only a few. Though one can scarcely speak of rank in
the other world, yet those who have received a more polished education are easily recognized. There is an essential difference between nations as may be detected in
these apparitions. Strength, vigor, decision, distinguish
the male sex; whilst the female may be known by something soft, passive, impressionable—I cannot express it.
There are angels here who nourish the souls with the fruits
of the place. These souls exercise an influence over purgatory and the earth and have, too, a faint consciousness of
heavenly beatitude. This with their waiting for its full attainment forms their last purification. Further on I came to

a brighter region with more beautiful trees. They were angels going to and fro. I was told that this was the abode of the Patriarchs before Christ's descent into hell, and I saw where Adam, Abraham, and John had been. I returned home by a fatiguing road to the left and passed by the mountain where I had seen the man tormented by dogs; but he was no longer there, he was now in purgatory."

November 3d—"Last night I confidently invoked all the saints of whom I had relics. I begged especially my dear blessed sisters, Madeline of Hadamar, Columba of Bamberg, Juliana of Liege, and Lidwina to come with me to purgatory and help out the souls dearest to Jesus and Mary. I had the happiness of seeing many relieved and many delivered."

November 4th—"Last night I went over almost the whole diocese. In the cathedral I saw all the careless-ness and neglect of the clergy under the appearance of a place whose filth is skilfully covered over. I had to carry the dirt and rubbish to a stream which bore it away.—The fatigue was great, and I was almost exhausted. During my task the soul of the daughter of a woman of my country came to beg me to go with her to her mother's assistance. She was in purgatory. I saw the mother, a gossiping epicure sitting alone in a room like a little kitchen, incessant-ly moving and smacking her lips as if tasting and chewing. She implored me to stay with her all night. She, too, passed to a higher, a less painful abode. I accompanied and consoled her.

"The planetary spirits act in purgatory. They reproach the sufferers with their sins. The poor souls are informed by angels of what goes on in heaven and on earth relative to the affairs of salvation, and are visited also by souls from Abraham's bosom. The soul of the daughter who called me to comfort her mother was one of the latter. They cannot act themselves. In purgatory there are no natural productions, no trees, no fruits—all is colorless, brighter or darker according to the different degrees of purification. The abodes are disposed in order. In Abraham's bosom it is like the country, like nature. A soul in Abraham's bosom already possesses the faint colors of its future glory, which become resplendent on its entrance into beatitude.—

"Judgment takes but a very short time. It is held the instant the soul leaves the body and just over the place where death occurred. Jesus, Mary, the holy patron, and good angel of the soul are present. Mary is present even at the judgment of Protestants."

November 6th—" I was thinking this evening that, after all, the poor souls are sure of what they hope for, but sinners are in danger of eternal damnation; and so, I would pray for them rather than for the souls. Then St. Ignatius stood before me, having on one side a proud, independent, healthy man whom I knew, and on the other a man sunk to the neck in mire. This last uttered piteous cries, he was wholly unable to help himself. He reached to me one finger. It was a deceased ecclesiastic, but a stranger to me. St. Ignatius said to me: ' For which will you intercede?--for this proud, wicked fellow who can do penance if he pleases, or for this poor, helpless soul?'—I trembled and wept bitterly. I was then taken by a painful road to purgatory where I prayed for the souls, and afterward into an immense house of correction in my own country. There I saw numbers whom misery and seduction had drawn into crime. I was able to soften their hearts; but the wretches who had ruined them were hardened in their guilt. I went to other similar institutions, also to subterranean dungeons wherein were confined long-bearded men. Their souls were in a good state and they seemed to be doing penance. I consoled them. These places were shown me as terrestrial purgatories.— Afterward I visited some Bishops—one, a very worldly man, was giving a banquet to which even females were invited. I calculated the cost of the feast as well as the number of poor people it would have fed, and held it up before the Bishop. He grew indignant, but I told him that it was all being recorded by an angel holding a book and a rod above him. He replied that it was nothing, that others did still worse.—I saw that this was indeed true, but the chastising angel is everywhere."

In the midst of her painful spiritual labors for the suffering souls, Sister Emmerich had at the close of the octave a consoling vision in which she saw the effects of all the charitable works she had ever performed for them.

"I was again in my father's house, and it seemed to me that I was going to be married. All the souls for whom I had ever prayed came with gifts of various kinds and placed them on the nuptial car. I could not make up my mind to take my seat in the coach and await the moment of departure, for I was confused at the sight of so many things; therefore, I slipped under it and ran on before to the house in which the ceremony was to be performed. But in creeping under the car, I soiled my white dress which, however, I did not perceive until I had reached Martinswinkle. I was dreadfully annoyed when I caught sight of the stain. I knew not what to do. But Blessed Brother Nicholas came to my aid and took it every bit out with a little butter. The house of the marriage was none other than the school-house to which I had gone in my childhood, and which was now greatly enlarged and beautified. The two holy old nuns were to be my bridemaids. Then came my Affianced and the bridal coach.

When I found myself in the school-house, I thought : Here I am for the third time. The first time I was brought as a child to school, and on the way the Mother of God with the little Boy appeared to me, promising that if I studied hard He should be my bridegroom; the second time was when going to the convent I was espoused in a vision in this same house ; and now for the third time, I was come to it for the marriage celebration.—It was now magnificent and full of luscious fruits. The house and garden were elevated high above the earth which lay dark and desolate below. I was told that my creeping under the bridal car signified death incurred by impatience before the completion of my task, and the consequent loss of much merit."

November 9th—" I have had to go into several neglected vineyards and cover up the grapes from the frost. I went also to three vineyards in the neighborhood of Coblentz where I worked hard. As I was thinking of applying to the poor souls for help, nine figures suddenly appeared around me with loads upon their backs, and a tenth laid down his and retired. I had to take on my shoulder and under my arm the long, heavy bundle and mount with the nine toward the east. The road was not an ordinary one ; it shone with light and ran straight on in the midst of fog and darkness. I soon fell, unable to support the load, when a bank suddenly appeared on the roadside whereon I rested it. The bundle contained a great human form, the same that two days previously St. Ignatius had shown me sunk in the mire. I understood by the Elector's cap fastened to his arm that he was one of the last Electors of Cologne. The nine others were his running-footmen. Not being able to keep up with them, the Elector had been dragged along by one of his men who, however, had grown weary of the task and handed it over to me.—Continuing our ascent, we arrived at a large, wonderful place at the gate of which were spirits on guard. The nine entered without difficulty; but after my burden was taken from me and deposited in a safe place, I was shown to the top of a rampart surrounded by trees. I could see all around upon an immense expanse of water full of hills and fortifications on which multitudes of souls were working. They were kings, princes, Bishops, and people of other ranks, principally servants. Some of the kings had their crowns on their arms and others again, the more sinful, had them fastened to their lower limbs. All were obliged to labor at the works, digging, hauling, climbing, etc. I saw some continually falling and climbing up again. The servants drove on their former masters. As far as one could see there was nothing but ramparts and waters, excepting the few sterile trees near me. I saw the Elector whom I had carried, working hard. He was condemned to dig continually under the earth. The nine spoke to me. I had to help them in something, but in what I cannot now remember. There were no females in this place. It seemed to be less dreary than purgatory, for here there were movement and life; here the souls labored, levelling and filling up. I was surprised to see no horizon, only the sky above, the laborers below, and to right and left a boundless expanse of space and water.

" Opposite the last another region, or sphere, was shown me peopled only by females. My guide bade me cross over the water to it, but I knew not how. He said : ' Obey by thy faith !' and at once I began to spread my cloak on the water to cross on it, when lo ! a tiny raft appeared which bore me over without rowing. My guide floated by me just skimming the waves. In the sphere to which I was now introduced, was a huge square dwelling full

of females of all classes, even nuns, some of whom I knew.
They had numerous gardens to cultivate and here, too, the
former mistresses were ordered about by their maids.   The
souls dwelt in bowers, and at the four corners of the abode
floated four spirits on guard; they had little watch-houses
hanging from the branches of high trees.   All kinds of fruit
were cultivated here by the souls; but, on account of the
clouds and fog, it does not ripen. What the souls here gained
was handed over to some little, deformed creatures whom I
saw wandering around in another region among huge icebergs.   Rafts laden with this fruit were sent to them.   They
picked it over and, in their turn, passed on the best of it to
souls in another place. Those on the iceberg were the souls of
barbarians, of nations never Christianized.—The women
asked me what year it was and how affairs were progress-
ing on earth.   I told them and, also, that I thought very
few would join them in the future, on account of the great
sins committed on earth.   I cannot remember what else I
did there.—I returned by a narrow descending path and saw
the Mountain of the Prophets, on which everything seemed
even more flourishing than usual.   There were two figures
occupied under the tent with the books : one laid aside the
fresh rolls of parchment, the other erased certain passages
from them.   As I glanced down I saw the tops of the
highest mountains on the globe, the rivers looking like silver threads, and the seas glistening like mirrors.   I recognized forests and cities.   I descended, at length, near the
Ganges.   The road behind me looked like a slender beam
of light which, like a lambent flame, was soon lost in the
sun's bright rays.   The good Indians whom I saw recently
praying before the cross, had constructed for themselves in
wicker-work a very beautiful chapel covered with verdant
foliage in which they met for divine service.—Thence I

went to Persia, to the place where Jesus taught shortly before His Crucifixion. But nothing remains of it now, excepting some fine fruit trees and the traces of a vineyard which Our Lord Himself had planted. Then I went to Egypt through the land in which Judith dwells. I saw her castle, and I felt that she sighs more ardently than ever to become a Christian.

"I pursued my wonderful journey over the sea into Sicily where I found many places laid waste and deserted. I crossed a mountain-chain not far from Rome, and saw in a sandy plain near a forest of fir-trees a band of robbers about attacking a mill. As my guide and I drew near, one of them was seized with fright and cried out to his companions: 'Such fear comes over me! I feel as if some one were behind us!'—and with that they all took to flight. I am so worn out by this journey, especially with dragging that heavy soul that I am aching all over. I saw and did extraodinary things, but many of them I have now forgotten."

December 31st.—"I settled up accounts with myself for the closing year.—I saw how much I have lost, how much I have to repair. I saw my own misery, and wept bitterly over it! I had also many pictures of the poor souls and of the dying. I saw a priest who died yesterday evening at nine o'clock, a most pious, charitable man who nevertheless went to purgatory for three hours, because he had lost time in jesting. He was to have remained for years, but numerous Masses and prayers had shortened his punishment. I saw his sufferings during the three hours. When he was delivered I almost laughed to hear him say to the angel: 'Now I see that even an angel can deceive. I was to have been here but three hours, and yet I have been so long! so long!'—I know this priest very well."

June 29, 1821, the Pilgrim, unknown to her, attached to the invalid's dress a little parcel containing the hair of a deceased woman and that of her two children, one having died without baptism a few hours after its birth, the other at the age of two months after receiving the Sacrament. Next day Sister Emmerich spoke, as follows :—

"I have seen the life of St. Peter and scenes from that of Maria Marcus. At the same time, I had another picture of some poor souls to whom I was powerfully drawn, but whom I could not reach. I wanted to help a mother and her two children, but I could not. The mother was in a deep abyss to which I could not approach, and she spoke in a hollow, smothered voice scarcely intelligible. The children were in another sphere to which I had access. One was baptized and I could speak to it; it belonged to a higher sphere and seemed to be only on a visit in the place in which I saw it. When I tried to go to the mother, it seemed as if I became too heavy, I sank down unable to move. I tried every means of assisting her by prayer and suffering, but I could not go to her. I saw into a vast, dark region, a world of fog, in which are many spheres. The souls here confined are in restraint, pain, and privation, the necessary consequences of their earthly imperfections and transgressions. Some are in bands, others solitary. Their abodes are dark and foggy, more or less dense, damp or parched, hot or cold, with various degrees of light and color, the whole lit up by a glimmer of morning twilight. The children are nearest the entrance. The unbaptized suffer chiefly from their connection with sin and with the impurity of their parents; the baptized are free and purified. One can approach the souls only by grace, meditation, prayer, good works, the merits of the saints, and sometimes by some good trait in their, the souls' own life on earth. The clearest idea one can form of their state is from those houses of correction which are conducted according to rules of perfect justice, in which the punishments inflicted, the satisfaction demanded exactly correspond to the faults committed. Let us imagine our corporeal separation set aside so that one can act in and for the other, and we may possibly gain some idea of the manner in which one can satisfy for, can deliver another. The poor captive can do nothing but suffer; he is what a diseased or paralyzed member is to the body. But if the veins and nerves that connect it with the body are not entirely dead, the suffering of the affected part awakens a sympathetic chord in the other members which immediately seek to relieve their afflicted neighbor. As one enters such a house only by the intervention of friends and officials, and yet can by his own petitions, labor, payment of debts, etc., obtain pardon and again lead a happy life; as they who are confined in deep dungeons can make their voices heard at a distance, though the sound be dull and muffled; so, in some respects, can the same be done by the poor souls in the other world. On earth all is mingled with sin, lying, and injustice; but in purgatory's abodes of purification, whatever tends to console and assist the poor inmates is executed with the most rigid and impartial justice. There is as much difference between the two as between the currency of earth and that of heaven. I made many attempts to understand the soul and to help her and her children; but, when I thought I was about raising her up, something always prevented. At length, I pursuaded St. Maria Marcus to go with me (for the vision of these souls was always accompanied by another of the Feast of St. Peter and Maria Marcus). She went with me and, by her merits, I was enabled to draw nearer to the poor souls. I received also information respecting a poor unburied child whom I must have interred at the Pilgrim's expense. The woman's soul stands in need of this good work. She told me, also, what else was to be done for her besides continual prayer. I shall notify the Pilgrim of it in good time."

Next day, a poor woman of Dülmen came begging money to bury her child aged three years. The Pilgrim gave the necessary sum and Sister Emmerich furnished the linen, which good work was offered for the benefit of the soul mentioned above.

July 1st—"I was again with the poor mother and her little child, the latter of whom I had to clothe; but it was so weak as to be unable to sit upright. I put on it a little dress given me by a lady, the Mother of God, I think. It was white and transparent and seemed to have been knit in stripes. I felt much ashamed, I know not why, unless it was of those who so neglected the little one. Before this the poor little thing could not stand, but now it went to a feast and played with the other children. The place in which this scene was enacted and in which the mother then was, was better, brighter than the one in which I had first seen them." (This vision took place after the burial of the child above spoken of). "The mother thanked me, but not as we do in this life. I did not hear, I merely felt. Great trouble is necessary to reach such souls, for they can do nothing of themselves. If one of them could spend only a quarter of an hour on earth, it could shorten its punishment by many years."

July 3, 1821.—" I had to work in the cathedral cloister of Münster, washing with great fatigue altar linen brought me by the priests of the whole country around. Clare of Montefalco, Frances of Rome, Louise, and other deceased nuns of our convent helped me. My share of the work was the starching and bluing. As my fatigue was great, I was continually running to look at the clock. Then came a poor soul whom the Pilgrim had recommended to my prayers. She gave me a little hour-glass which she took from her side, saying that she found it frightfully heavy. When I took it from her, she seemed unspeakably relieved and overjoyed to get rid of it. It did not seem to me to be so heavy and I returned to my work thinking I could sell it for the benefit of the poor, when lo ! my washing was all spoiled !—I began to feel impatient, when the soul hastily returned and whispered in my ear : ' Gently, gently ! you have still time enough !'—She begged me earnestly to go on quietly with my work, as if my impatience would do her much harm. She left me, and I contentedly resumed my washing. I made over the spoiled starch so that I was able to use it. Again, I felt my eagerness return and a desire to look at the time, but I repressed it.—The clocks were symbols of time and patience. The poor soul was relieved by my quietly continuing my work and, when I took her hour-glass, her time no longer seemed so heavy."

During the first week of July, 1821, a poor woman of Dülmen, in the pangs of childbirth, sent to implore Sister Emmerich's prayers ; the latter beheld the woman's alarming condition and ceased not her supplications that the unborn babe might receive Baptism. The nurse hesitated but, at last, baptized the child which next day came into the world lifeless; the poor mother died about a week later. The child appeared to Sister Emmerich on the 8th, lovely and radiant with light. It greeted her familiarly, thanked her for its Baptism, and said : " Without it I should now be with the pagans." In consequence of the above incident, the invalid had the following vision :—

July 13, 1821.—" I saw the life of St. Margaret of An-

Life of

tioch. Her father was a very distinguished pagan, a priest of Antioch, who resided in a splendid mansion almost like that of St. Agnes. There was a benediction attached to Margaret's birth, for she came into the world radiant with light. Her mother must have had some connection with Christianity, for I saw her die happily soon after the birth of her babe. She died with a great desire of Baptism and requesting that Margaret might be reared a Christian. The father gave the infant over to a nurse who lived in the country, an unmarried woman, who had had a child and lost it, and who was now a Christian in secret. So impressed was she by the wonderful wisdom of her charge, that she became most pious and virtuous and reared the child in a truly Christian manner. I often saw her mother and the angels bending over Margaret's crib. On one occasion when the nurse took the child into the city to see its father, he wanted to present the little thing before his idols; but she struggled so violently that he had to desist, which circumstance very much provoked him. In her sixth year, I saw her placed by him at a school over which a pagan teacher presided. There were many children in it, boys and girls, with their mistresses. I often saw angelic apparitions and divine direction vouchsafed to Margaret. She learned all kinds of embroidery and how to make stuffed dolls. After a time her master sent her on a visit to her father who tried to make her sacrifice to his idols. She absolutely refused and was severely punished. Her young companions all loved her and aimed at being with her. I often saw her punished, yes, even flogged on account of her Christian tendencies. In her twelfth year I saw her shut up with youths charged to corrupt her, but she was always divinely protected. Once she was called upon to sacrifice in the temple. She refused, and was again severely punished by her father, who set her with some others to guard sheep. A distinguished judge of Antioch, happening to pass, noticed the maiden and asked her of her father in marriage. She was then taken back to the city and, as she declared herself a Christian, she was submitted to trial and torture. Once I saw her in prison all bruised and mangled. As she knelt in prayer, her mother and an angel appeared and healed her, after which she had a vision of a fountain out of which arose a cross. By it she understood that her martyrdom was nigh. The fountain was typical of her Baptism. When her persecutors found her perfectly healed, they attributed the miracle to their gods; but Margaret cursed their idols. I saw her led to execution, burned with torches, and cast into a ditch. She was tied to stakes with several others and sunk so deep that the water rose above her head. Margaret had plunged into the water with an ardent desire of its being to her a Baptism—a luminous cloud in the form of a cross descended upon her and an angel appeared bearing a crown. The miracle was witnessed by many of those around; they immediately confessed Christ, were imprisoned and martyred. But now a mighty earthquake shook the place, the virgin's fetters were severed, and she came forth from the water safe and sound. Then arose a tumult, in the midst of which she was reconducted to her prison. As she stood in prayer, I saw a huge dragon with the head of a lion dart upon her; but Margaret thrust her hand into his jaws, made the sign of the cross, and forced his head into the ground. At the same moment two men with evil intentions rushed into her prison, but the earth trembled and they fled. I saw the maiden again led to a place where an immense multitude was assembled. Around her was stationed a troop of girls for the purpose of intimidating her; but she begged leave to speak and addressed them so feelingly that they confessed Christ aloud and were beheaded with her. This saint is invoked by women in childbed because her own mother died happily whilst giving her birth and, also, because in cruel sufferings she had herself brought forth many daughters to the Lord.

"I had afterward a horrible vision which, at first, I knew not how to connect with St. Margaret. I saw a huge, frightful hog making its way out of a deep marsh. The sight of it made me tremble with horror. It was the soul of a noble Parisian lady who came to tell me not to pray for her, as it could do her no good. She was condemned to wallow in the mire till the end of the world. She implored me to pray for the conversion of her daughter that she might not be the occasion of as many sins as she herself had been. My vision of St. Margaret took place in a little chapel at Paris, the last remains of a ruined abbey, in which a portion of the martyr's arm and skull is still preserved. As I venerated these relics I saw the soul of the unhappy lady and scenes from her life, for her tomb was near the chapel. She was of high rank, and had caused much mischief during the Revolution; through her intervention many priests had been put to death. With all her wickedness she had preserved her youthful veneration for St. Margaret and, through her influence, the saint's chapel had been spared; therefore, was the favor accorded her of being permitted to ask prayers for her daughter and thereby cut off the consequences of her own sins. I saw the daughter leading a worldly life. She was connected with the worst and most dangerous political parties in the country."

August 28th—"All sorts of people, long since deceased and whom I once knew, came to beg my help. They took me to dark corners of fields where they had various tasks to perform, but which they never could finish as certain tools were wanting. All cried to me to help them. With great fatigue I had to do this or that piece of work for them, mostly field-labors, whereby they were relieved. After each task I returned home, but only to set out again for another. I worked, also, for the clergy in their vineyards which were so full of sharp stakes that one could not move without hurting one's self. I slipped and a stake ran into the calf of my leg, which bled profusely,"..... and there did, indeed, appear in the spot specified a large, triangular wound. During these days she was subjected to a special torture as if certain parts of her body were compressed in a vice.

August 30, 1821.—"Last night I worked hard for the poor souls and also for the Jews, both living and dead. My first assistance was given in a case of great misery. The soul of one of my country-women claimed my aid. I saw her being horribly scourged and maltreated, I heard her cries; but I could not go to her. It seems that she had had a good, pious, but rather simple daughter, whom she had been in the habit of abusing cruelly; and for this she was now being punished. I suffered long for her. I must now find some means to rouse up the daughter, who is still alive, to pray for her mother's soul.

" Yesterday, I saw a Jewish wedding, but I cannot now recall it." (There had been one in the city). " Last night the soul of a poor Jewess came and took me around to ex- hort her brethren to be converted and amend their life."— Then Sister Emmerich recounted various scenes in which Jews, living and dead, known and unknown, figured, and whom she visited in far-off lands even in Asia and near Mt. Sinai. She entered the store of a Jewess, of Coesfeld. She was busily arranging her goods, mixing up laces and linen of

inferior quality with the superior in order to deceive cus-
tomers. This fraud Sister Emmerich prevented by perplexing the woman in such a way that she could not find what
she was seeking, could not open the drawers, etc. Greatly
disquieted she ran in tears to her husband who, on hearing
her trouble, decided that she had committed some sin,
yielded to some bad thought perhaps for which she must
do penance. Then Sister Emmerich received a certain
power over her. She spoke to her conscience and made her
feel so sensibly the wrong she was about to do that the
woman cried out to her husband for assistance and consolation. He ran to her, saying: "Now, do you not see that
you did something wrong?"—and the wife resolved to give
a quantity of old linen and other alms to poor Christians in
expiation of her fraud. She thus obtained pardon for
many other sins. "I was taken by the soul of the old
Jewess to the abode of Jewish souls to help and comfort
many poor creatures belonging to Coesfeld, some of whom I
knew. It is an isolated place of purgation, quite separate
from that of Christians. I was deeply touched at seeing
that they are not eternally lost, and I beheld their various
pitiable conditions. I saw a poor, but uncommonly pious
Jewish family who used to trade in old silver and little
crosses as goldsmiths do, and who now had to work incessantly, melting, weighing, and filing. But not having the
implements necessary, they could never finish anything,
something obliged them continually to begin all over again.
I remember making a bellows for them, and I spoke to
them of the Messiah, etc. All that I said the old Jewess repeated and confirmed. I saw some of them swimming in
blood and entrails which produced an ever-abiding loathing; others running without a moment's rest; some dragging heavy loads; others constantly rolling and unrolling

packages; and others, again, tormented by bees, wax, honey—but it is inexpressible!—

" I visited all the Jews of this city. I went by night into their dwellings. The rabbi was perfectly inflexible, petrified as it were. He possesses no bond of grace. I could in no way approach him. Mrs. P — is chained down by the firm, fundamental principle that it is a sin even to *think* upon Christian truths. One must repel such thoughts at once, she thinks. The nearest to Christianity is the big Jewess who sells meat. If she were not such a cheat, she would receive still more grace.—But no one sympathizes with these people. I stood at her bedside and tried to influence her; I told her many things.—She awoke in fright and ran to her husband, saying that she thought her mother had appeared to her. She was in great agony of mind, and she resolved to give an alms to poor Christians.

" I was also among some Jews in a large street where none but their race reside. Very many of them are good and pious. Some are quite rich and distinguished. They have quantities of gold and jewels concealed under their floors. I could do them no good.—I went also to Thessalonica. In another great Jewish city I met many pious Jews whom later I saw assembling together and speaking as if the Messiah had come. They communicated to one another their various emotions and projects. I was also among some Jews who lived in caves near Mt. Sinai and committed numerous robberies and cruelties in the country around. I had to frighten them—perhaps for the sake of the Christian pilgrims as well as for that of the inhabitants of the place."

September 18, 1821.—" I saw a peasant-woman returning from a village fair and a soul approaching and whispering something into her ear. The soul was a gray, sad-looking figure. The woman shuddered, seemed annoyed, and tried to believe it all imagination. She went into a room to speak to her servant, the soul still pursuing her with its remonstrances. Next morning she went again to the fair. Then the gray, sad-looking soul came and addressed me in a hollow, deep voice which sounded as if it came from the depths of a well, but in few words full of meaning. I understood that he was the peasant-woman's deceased husband who was detained a captive, because he had been in a fold in which the sheep went not to true pasturage; they knew not their pastor, they could receive nothing from him. It is a terrible thing to live in such misery and blindness through the fault of one's ancestors, and to see it clearly only after death!—He had been commissioned by God to remonstrate with his wife, and warn her not to follow the advice of false friends and enter into a lawsuit which would only result in the loss of her house and farm and reduce her daughter to poverty. She had married her son to the sister of a widow with whom she had so entangled her affairs that she was about to begin a suit fatal to her credit and property. The soul could find no rest until he had dissuaded her from such a course; but, unhappily, he was in so restrained a state that he was unable to do more than disquiet her by interior reproaches. He continued his efforts but as yet with little success, for his wife attributed her uneasiness to imagination, disclosed it to no one, sought distraction in weddings, baptisms, and festivities, and harkened to domestics cunningly urging her on in her false step, rather than to her honest neighbors. No blessing fell on her household, since she stifled the voice of conscience and confessed not her sins. Grace comes to such a soul only by the way of penance.

" ' For a long time,' said her husband, ' I have disquieted

my unhappy wife, but she yields more and more to the influence of the widow who is leading her to ruin. She will
not listen to me and, when she cannot restrain her anxiety,
she runs to the stable or meadow, visits her flocks, or engages
in some manual labor. Thou hast prayed lately for my
poor wife, thou hast prayed so fervently that God has heard
thee, and, in virtue of the cruel sufferings thou didst offer
for her to-day, I have been allowed to come to beg thee to help
me. I shall now take thee to my son that thou mayest speak
to him, for I am bound, I cannot do it myself. He may
perhaps be able to change his mother's mind, for he is
good and simple-hearted, and he will believe us.'—Then I
accompanied the soul, first to the fair where his wife was
sitting with her companions. He went up to her, whispered
into her ear that she must absolutely free herself from all
connection with the widow and not risk body and soul,
goods and property in an unjust lawsuit. She grew uneasy,
left her companions abruptly, and sought to divert herself
elsewhere. The husband told me that the foolish woman
was on the point of beginning the suit, but that he would
not desist from his efforts, since his sufferings and privation of
light in the other world would be greatly prolonged by his
wife's perversity; for, through his fault, the affairs of the
family had often been very badly administered. Then he
took me to his son by a long dreary way over a broad pool
of raging waters. The danger was great, anguish and peril
encompassed us, and I was worn out by fatigue and alarm.
The soul was at my side, but his voice sounded hollow and
as if far off in the distance. As we passed certain fields and
cottages, he told what danger threatened them and on account of what sins. He urged upon me the necessity of prayer
and told me what to do. When we had crossed the water
the road ran north through a desolate region until we

reached the son's cottage. We entered and went straight
to his room. He was seized with fright (I think he saw his
father's spirit), but he soon recovered himself. I exhorted
him to pray more earnestly and pointed out what he should
do regarding his mother's business affairs. I explained to him
that his father's soul was not at rest, that he, the father,
could not himself actually address his mother, but that he,
the son, should do it and tell her the cause of his father's
disquietude. I told him other important things which I now
forget. The son is a good, simple-hearted young man with
a round face and slightly turned-up nose. He was much
affected, very desirous of doing right, and distressed at his
mother's state.—His simplicity was truly touching. Then
I saw the effect of my words in a far-off picture. The son
called his wife from her spinning and she came, ungraciously
enough, still holding her distaff. He told her what had just
happened, and begged that his mother might be released from
the lawsuit. I heard the wife remark: 'We shall take from her
even the gown on her back!'—whereupon the young husband
went on his knees, begging that they would at least leave
her two fields, or farms, that I saw hanging like islands in the
air. Then I heard the wife reply: 'Since you are so good
and honest, I shall leave your mother one gown if I can.'—
From that moment things took a turn, the widow's affairs inclined to the dark side with herself, and the peasant-woman was
freed from her evil influence. The latter remained poorer
indeed than before, but in far better dispositions among the
peasants of the parish, against which the widow had begun
the iniquitous suit. I shall often have to accompany the
poor soul of the husband in whose distress and unavailing
efforts there was something truly affecting. I could not
approach the woman; she seemed to be surrounded by a lake
in whose waters she was about to be engulfed."

During the first week of October, 1821, Sister Emmerich labored hard and unremittingly for the poor souls, suffering at the same time intense pains in the abdomen. " I was in a dark place with souls of non-Catholics who were in need of something which I had to supply. They entreated me to make and have made for different poor people some articles of clothing, the materials for which I was to beg.— The articles were shown me and I was told where to get materials. At first I declined, but the poor souls were so pressing that I consented. It has proved a very difficult task."—For several days Sister Emmerich was very busy cutting out clothes for the poor in the midst of excruciating pains and incessant interruptions and annoyances from visitors. But she calmly overcame every feeling of impatience as the Pilgrim tells us in his notes: " October 4th—Although suffering intense pains in the abdomen, Sister Emmerich has been all day cheerful, patient, and kind. Visits which could not be declined have greatly fatigued her, without, however, ruffling her serenity. She speaks kindly of all that have wearied and annoyed her." She herself says: " Again, I have been busy with the poor souls, and I know exactly what articles are needed—I have seen their shape and size as well as the materials necessary. I have been told to ask the Pilgrim to contribute to the work.—I went to the poor souls on my journey to the Nuptial House in one of whose fields I had to weed. I found there the big cook with an iron girdle around her waist from which hung spoons, ladles, and other kitchen utensils. My pains were intense, but as my confessor had ordered me to bear them I kept quiet. Toward midnight they became still sharper, and I saw something like a horrible figure casting itself upon me. I sat up in bed and cried with simple faith : ' Be off ! What do you want with me ? I have no need of

you! My confessor has given me my orders!'—Instantly
the pain ceased, and I rested quietly till morning." On
October 10th, the clothing demanded by the holy souls was
finished, and she received instructions regarding its disposal. On October 7th, the Pilgrim had made the following
entry: "The invalid prepared all the articles requested by
the holy souls although she knew not, as yet, for whom
they were destined. When she sent to purchase the materials, she knew exactly where they could, or could not be
procured."

Close of October, 1821.—"For several nights," says the
Pilgrim, "Sister Emmerich has had, on account of the approach of All-Souls, to work hard for the poor souls, some
known, others unknown to her. She is often requested by
them or by their guardian-angels to do such or such a
thing in satisfaction for their shortcomings, and sometimes she is commissioned to exhort the living to certain good works. The soul of a woman appeared to her
begging her to inform her daughter that some of the property she then possessed had been dishonestly acquired by her
grand-parents. To do so Sister Emmerich had to take a
long journey through the snow. She remembers also a
wonderful spiritual church in which she had to serve Mass
and distribute the Holy Communion to some souls. 'I was
very much frightened,' she said, 'although I took the
Host in a linen cloth. I felt that I, a woman, dared not
do it, and even the serving of Mass gave me great uneasiness, until the priest turned around and told me very earnestly that I must do it. In him I recognized the deceased
Abbé Lambert. He was perfectly luminous. I do not remember the vision very well, nor do I understand it.'"

On the morning of October 25th, the Pilgrim found her
greatly distressed and terrified. "Last night," she said,

"I had a frightful vision which still haunts me. As I was praying for the dying, I was taken to the home of a wealthy lady who I saw was about to be damned. I struggled with Satan by her bedside, but in vain; he pushed me back—it was too late! I cannot express my grief on seeing him carry off the poor soul, leaving the body a distorted, frightful carcass, for so it looked to me. I could not approach it. With the angels I could only gaze upon it from on high. She had a husband and children. She passed for a worthy person according to the world; but she had maintained illicit communications with a priest, and this sin of long standing she had never confessed. She had received the last Sacraments. All praised her edifying preparation and resignation; and yet she was in mental agony on account of her concealment in confession. Then the devil sent to her one of her friends, a miserable old woman, to whom she expressed her anxiety; but she urged her to banish such thoughts and beware of giving scandal. The old woman told her not to worry over the past, that she had received the Sacraments to the great edification of her friends, and that she must not now excite suspicion by sending again for the priest, but go in peace to God. After this harangue, the old woman left the room and gave orders that the dying woman should not be disturbed. The unhappy woman, so near her end, still dwelt with pleasure on the thought of the priest, the accomplice of her guilt. As I drew near I found Satan under the form of this priest praying by her. She herself prayed not, for she was dying full of bad thoughts. The accursed one prayed in the words of the Psalms: '*Let Israel hope in the Lord, for in Him is mercy and plentiful redemption,*' etc., etc. He was furious with me. I told him to make a cross over her mouth, which I knew he could not do; but all my efforts were useless—it was too late, no one could reach her, and so she died! It was horrible, Satan carrying off her soul! I wept and cried.—The miserable old woman returned, consoled the relatives, and spoke of her beautiful death. As I was crossing the bridge on my way from the city, I met some people going to see the dead woman. I thought : 'Ah! had you seen what I did, you would fly far from her!'—I am still quite sick, I am trembling in every limb." Scarcely had she finished the above when she begged to be left alone.—They were calling her, she said, she saw something, she must pray—and the Pilgrim, seeing in her countenance that look of abstraction he so well knew, drew the curtain in front of her bed and left her. That afternoon, she related what follows :—" This morning when I asked to be left alone, I saw a dying nun who could not receive Holy Viaticum as the sacristy key was lost. She was in a suppressed convent in which some members of the community still remained, but in secular dress. The others lodged in the neighboring town which had a mixed population of Catholics and Protestants. They often visited their former companions and gossiped and drank coffee at the bedside of the sick one, who now lay at the point of death and longing for the Blessed Sacrament. Divine service was still held in the church of the convent and the Blessed Sacrament kept there. At the time of which I speak, some careless nun had mislaid the key of the sacristy. The priest came to administer to the dying sister, but there was no admittance! The whole house was thrown into confusion, a general search was instituted, the nuns ran talking here and there, and at last the priest went away. I saw it all, and I also saw that the nun was absolutely dying though none knew it. My guide ordered me to pray, and I remember not how, but the key was immediately found in a crevice near the fireplace where a sister had laid and forgotten it. The priest was recalled, the Sacraments administered, and the nun died. I did not know the religious, nor do I now remember where it all took place.

"In the same city in which the unhappy lady died, I attended the deathbed of an author. The good man had written some things against his conscience, but of which he had quite lost sight. He had confessed and received all the last Sacraments, and was now left alone by the advice of some individuals inspired by the enemy of souls. Then Satan suggested to him all kinds of thoughts calculated to drive him to despair, filling his imagination with images of people who reproached him with the harm done by his writings. He fell into an agony of despair, and so was about to die abandoned by all. Then it was that my guide took me to him. I had by my prayers to disquiet his confessor and make him hurry back to the dying man. The latter recognized him, but begged not to be disturbed, as he had business with the people present. The priest seeing that he was delirious, sprinkled him with holy water and made him kiss something that he wore around his neck. The dying man recovered his senses and told the priest the mental anguish that had so suddenly come upon him. This time the accursed one was caught in his own net ; for, had he not driven the man to despair, he never would have recalled what now troubled him. He had his papers hunted up, the priest put them in order before witnesses, and the man died in peace.—I have had also to assist at the deathbed of many young people who had gone astray through love of dancing. They died happily."

On September 21st, a notorious drunkard died suddenly at Dülmen in a state of intoxication. Sister Emmerich saw his horrible state all night, the devils lying around him, suckling him under the form of young dogs.

October 28, 1821. —" Last night, I saw the holy maiden Ermelinda, a most innocent child, who in her twelfth year was introduced to a youth whom her parents intended she should marry. She was noble and rich, and resided in an elegant mansion. One day as she ran to the door to meet the youth, Jesus appeared to her, saying : ' Dost thou not love me more than him, Ermelinda ?'—In transports of joy, she exclaimed : ' Yes, my Lord Jesus !'—Then Jesus led her back into her room and gave her a ring with which He espoused her. Ermelinda at once cut off her beautiful hair, and informed her parents and the youth that she had pledged her troth to God.—I begged the saint to take me to the dying and to the poor souls, and I think I travelled with her through Holland, a most tiresome journey, over water, marshes, bogs, and ditches. I went to poor people who could get no p.iest, so far over the water did they live. I consoled them, prayed for them, assisted them in various ways, and went on further toward the north. I cannot say exactly where purgatory lies. But when going there I generally journey northward for awhile when leaving the earth by a gloomy, difficult road of water, snow, briars, swamps, etc., I descend by dark, aerial paths as if far under the earth to dismal places of different degrees of cold, fog, and obscurity. I go around among souls in higher or lower positions, of more or less difficult access. Last night I went among them all, consoling them and receiving their commissions for various labors. I had to say right off the Litany of the Saints and the Seven Penitential Psalms. My guide warned me to guard carefully against impatience and to offer every vexation for the poor souls. The other morning I almost forgot his admonition and was on the point of yielding to impatience, but I repressed it. I am very glad I did so, and I thank my good angel for helping me. No words can say what immense consolation the poor souls receive from a little sacrifice, a trifling self-victory."

November 2, 1821.—For fourteen days, Sister Emmerich had been constantly occupied with the poor souls, offering for them prayers, mortifications, alms, and spiritual labors, and arranging numerous things to be given away on the Feast of All-Souls. She related the following :—" I went again with the saints to purgatory. The prisons of the souls are not all in the same place, they are far apart and very different. The road to them often lies over icebergs, snow, and clouds ; sometimes it winds all around the earth. The saints float lightly by me on luminous clouds of various colors, according to the different kinds of help and consolation their good works entitle them to bestow. I had to travel painful, rugged paths, praying the while and offering it all for the souls. I reminded the saints of their own sufferings, and offered them to God in union with the merits of Jesus Christ for the same intention. The abodes of the souls differ according to each one's state, yet they all struck me as being round like globes. I can compare them only to those places which I call gardens and in which I see certain graces preserved like fruits ; so, too, are these sojourns of the souls like gardens, storehouses, worlds full of disagreeable things, privations, torments, miseries, anguish, etc., etc., and some are much smaller than others. When I arrive I can clearly distinguish their round form and perhaps a ray of light falling upon some point, or twilight on the horizon. Some are a little better than others, but in none can the blue sky be seen, all are more or less dark and obscure. In some the souls are near one another and in great agony ; some are deeper down, others higher and clearer. The places in which souls are separately confined are also of various forms : for instance, some are shaped like ovens. They who were united on earth are together in purgatory only when they have need of the same degree of purification. In many places the light is colored, that is fiery, or of a dull red. There are other abodes in which evil spirits persecute, frighten, and torment the souls, and these are the most horrible. One would take them for hell, did not the inexpressibly touching patience of the souls proclaim the contrary. Words cannot describe their consolation and joy when one among them is delivered. There are also places for penitential works, as those in which I once saw them raising and storming ramparts, the women on the islands cultivating the fruits which were taken away on rafts, etc. These souls are in a less suffering state ; they can do something for others worse off than themselves. It may be symbolical, but it is symbolical of truth. The vegetation is scanty and stunted, the fruits the same ; yet they afford relief to those still more needy. Kings and princes are often thrown with those whom they once oppressed and whom they now serve in humble suffering. I have seen in purgatory Protestants who were pious in their ignorance ; they are very desolate, for no prayers are offered for them. I saw souls passing from a lower to a higher grade to fill up the vacancies left by some who had finished their purgation. Some can go around giving and receiving consolation. It is a great grace to be able to appear and beg help and prayers. I have also seen the places in which some souls canonized on earth were purified ; their sanctity had not reached its perfection in their lifetime. I went to many priests and churches and ordered Masses and devotions for the souls. I was at Rome in St. Peter's, near noble ecclesiastics,

Cardinals, I think, who had to say seven Masses for certain souls. I know not why they had omitted doing so. Whilst they were being said, I saw the neglected souls, dark and sad, gathered around the altar; they exclaimed, as if hungry: 'We have not been fed for so long, so long!'—I think it was foundation Masses that had been neglected. The confiscation of foundations for Masses for the dead is, as I see, unspeakable cruelty and a theft committed against the poorest of the poor. On my route I saw few if any of the living, but I met souls, angels, and saints, and I saw many of the effects of prayer. During these days, I have had to drag to the confessional and to church many people who otherwise would never have gone."

Sister Emmerich spent the whole day in prayer for the souls and recited for them the Office of the Dead. The wounds in her breast and side bled so copiously that her garments were saturated. When the Pilgrim visited her in the evening, he found her in ecstatic prayer. About half an hour after, her confessor entered the room. Sister Emmerich suddenly left her bed, walked with a sure, firm step to the astonished Father and, prostrating at his feet, attempted to kiss them. Father Limberg drew back in confusion but, at last, yielded to her desires; then kneeling, she begged his blessing for herself and the souls with her. She remained thus in prayer several moments, again asked a blessing for the souls, and rising returned quickly to her bed. Her forehead was bathed in perspiration, but her countenance glowed with joy. She was in ecstasy. The next day when the Pilgrim related to her the scene of the preceding evening, she could scarcely credit what she heard, although she distinctly remembered that some souls, former penitents of Father Limberg, had begged her to kiss his feet and ask him for his benediction. " It was very painful to me," she said, " that he showed so much reluctance and did not rightly understand me ; besides, as he did not give the blessing with firm faith, I still had something to do last night for the souls."

Nov. 2, 1822.—" Last night I had much to do in purgatory. I went northward and, as it seemed, around the pole of the globe. I saw the icebergs above me ; and yet, purgatory does not appear to be at the centre, for I can see the moon. In going around among the prisons, I tried to make an opening that a little light might enter. The outside looks like a shining black wall in the form of a crescent ; inside are innumerable chambers and passages, high and low, ascending and descending. Near the entrance it is not so bad, the souls are free to move around ; but further on they are more strictly imprisoned. Here lies one stretched as it were in a hole, a ditch, there several are together in different positions, higher and lower ; sometimes, one is seen seated on high as if on a rock. The further we penetrate, the more frightful it becomes, for demons there exercise their power. It is a temporary hell in which souls are tormented by horrible spectres and hideous forms that wander around, persecuting and terrifying their victims.

" I see also in purgatory a place of devotion, a sort of church in which the souls at times receive consolation. They turn their eyes wistfully toward it as we do to our churches. The souls are not helped directly from heaven. They receive relief only from earth from the living, who can discharge their debts by prayers, good works, acts of mortification and self-renunciation ; but, above all, by the Holy Sacrifice of the Mass offered to the Judge. Leaving this place, I went northward over the ice to where the earth's circumference decreases (1), and I saw purgatory as one sees the sun or moon very low in the horizon. Then we passed over a cylinder, a street, a ring," (she could not find the right word) " and came to another part of purgatory semi-circular in shape. Some distance to the left is the mill ; to the right are works and intrenchments. I never see any visitor in purgatory, excepting my guide ; but away off on the earth, I behold here and there anchorets, religious, and poor devout people, praying, doing penance, and laboring for the dear souls. This part of purgatory belongs to the Catholic Church. The sects are separated here as on earth, and they suffer much more, since they have no members praying for them and no Holy Sacrifice. The souls of males may be distinguished from those of females only on close examination. One sees figures, some darker, some brighter, the features drawn with pain, but at the same time full of patience. The sight of them is inexpressibly touching. Nothing is more consoling than their gentle endurance, their joy at the deliverance of their fellow-sufferers, their sympathy in one another's pain and for all newcomers. I have seen children there, too.

" Most of the souls are expiating their levity, their so-called small sins, their neglect of trifling acts of condescension, of kindness, and of little self-victories. The connection of the souls with earth is something very sensitive, inasmuch as they experience great relief from even an ardent desire formed by the living to soothe and lighten their pains. O how charitable is he, how much good does he not do who constantly overcomes self for them, who longs ever to help them !"

During this holy season, day and night, was Sister Em-

(1) July 15, 1820.—I saw the earth in darkness, and more like an *egg* than a globe. Toward the north the descent is the steepest ; it seems longest toward the east. The perpendicular descent is always toward the north.''

merich consumed by thirst, but never did she try to allay
the fever that parched her with its withering blast—all for
the poor souls, all for the dear souls !

November 3d—" I have been in a region before purgatory, in the ice country near the mill in which princes,
kings, and rulers have to grind as formerly they made men
and horses do.   They have to grind ice and all sorts of
choice food and precious objects which women bring to the
mill, and which when ground are thrown to the dogs.
Their former servants are now their task-masters."   Sister Emmerich spoke of the road by which she went to purgatory and the countries through which she passed.   She
seems to have travelled through Asia toward the north pole,
passing through the ancient land of Oshemschids into another in which rises a lofty mountain full of monkeys large
and small.   When it is too cold for them on one side of the
mountain, they run to the other.   She afterwards came " to
a land whose inhabitants are clothed in skins.   They are an
ugly, long-haired race who live miserably and are drawn
by dogs whose instincts are so sharp that they may be intrusted with whole sledges of merchandise which they convey in safety to their destination without a driver.   There
are both whites and blacks here, but the latter are not natives.   The inhabitants hunt small, long-bodied animals for
the sake of their fur.   These animals have long ears and
short legs and are not so pretty as these at the foot of the
Mountain of the Prophets.   They are found still further
north.   There is here a region of marshes and deserts,
which is a little warmer, as if the morning sun sometimes
shone upon it.   I saw some of the animals I have just mentioned running around, and here and there miserable looking little people with flat noses.   The vegetation is scanty."
Sister Emmerich went on to describe the country, but not

as inhabited—all is dark and foggy in the black distance. Passing over the metal *street or ring*, as she calls it, she reaches purgatory under which is hell, deep down toward the centre of the earth. "On such journeys," she says, "the moon appears to me very large and full of cavities and volcanoes; but all on it is stony, like coral trees. It both attracts and discharges quantities of vapor, as if absorbing fluids to pour them forth again. I never saw people like ourselves on the moon, or in any of the stars, of which many are like dead, burnt-out bodies. I saw souls and spirits in them, but no beings like men."

November 4th—"I know not where I have been, nor why I had the following vision: I was taken into a beauti- ful mansion in which a lady showed me exquisite pagan statuary belonging to her husband. We descended, pass- ing through doorways so low that we were obliged almost to creep through them. The statues grew uglier and uglier as we descended, becoming at last quite horrible. Then came a gentleman who took me through galleries of the most lovely pictures, each more beautiful than the last. I often thought: 'Ah! If the Pilgrim could only see this!' The longer we stood gazing at them the more exquisite their loveliness became. At last we left the place, and I had another vision. I saw a Protestant with his Catholic wife going through room after room filled with works of art. He pointed out the vaulted halls with their treasures of paintings and curiosities in which he took the greatest de- light. I heard the wife say that he practised idolatry to- ward all these things, that he should rather think upon God and His Church. The husband replied that it was his opinion that God loves every honest man, religion is but a secondary consideration. The wife re- plied that it is not so, adding that when near him she felt her faith weakened, but that one lesson of her youth (here she named it) she had ever carefully practised. Then I saw her take him into a vault in which his ancestors were entombed. The hollow, but powerful voice of one of them now sounded from a tomb containing but mould and dust, and for a long time addressed the husband in broken words. It was in the gentleman's power, he said, to make good what he himself had neglected in life, he had the means, nothing prevented him. Then he spoke of the domain he had forcibly wrested from its rightful owner, of his falling off from the Church, of the numbers who followed his example, and of the misery and confusion it had entailed. Balls, amusements, the fine arts were not the things for his descendants; his people would be given over to the wolves which would tear them to pieces and fatten on their substance; therefore, he should hearken to his commands, restore the true faith, and give back to the Church what belonged to her. If he delayed this work of restitution, he would lose all his wealth and nothing would remain to him but the dust of the tomb.

"During this long discourse, in which the whole family history was set forth, the gentleman swooned repeatedly and more than once tried to make his escape; but his wife held him tenderly in her arms, encouraging him to remain and hear all. I have forgotten what followed and I know not what fruit the exhortation produced. The father of the gentleman, who I think already had two children, was still alive, but imbecile. This son was soon to take entire charge of the family estate. He was fondly attached to his wife, who had great influence over him. I had this vision in the morning and when I was perfectly awake."

Suffering Souls of the Crucified Fanatics, of Wildensbücher near Zürich.

October 19, 1823.—"I have been to purgatory where I saw several members of Mme. Krudener's sect, some of the late martyrs. They were not in the purgatory of Catholics, but in places like ditches below or around it, some at the bottom, others nearer the top. They had been led into error by ignorance. They could speak to the poor Catholic souls whom they earnestly implored to warn their friends on earth of their errors, that thereby they might return to the Church. But the souls replied that they could do nothing, that only the living can pray and work and have Masses said."—(Sister Emmerich seemed to be charged with their deliverance, for she enjoined upon all to whom she gave alms to hear Holy Mass, and she also procured Masses to be said). "I was told how the devil had urged on these people to those frightful murders and crucifixions. He rendered them insensible to pain. I saw that many of them are eternally lost. I learned, also, that a still more subtle sect is about to be formed." (That of Hennhoefer). "I saw that some of the demons whom Christ chained on his descent into hell have been let loose and that this sect was raised up by them. I saw that some are let loose every second generation."

Habitations of the Heavenly Jerusalem.

On January 8, 1820, Dean Overberg had sent to Sister Emmerich by Father Niesing a reliquary in the shape of a tower, which the reverend gentleman carried under his arm from Münster to Dülmen. Sister Emmerich knew nothing of the precious present destined for her, and yet she beheld Father Niesing journeying with a white flame under his arm.

" I was surprised," she said, " that it did not burn him and I could scarcely restrain a laugh at seeing him so perfectly unconscious of the many-colored flames like the rainbow that he was carrying with him. At first I saw only the colored light ; but, as he drew near, I saw the vase also. He carried it past my lodgings and all through the town. I could not understand it, and it made me sad when I thought he was going to carry it away by the other gate. The relics it contained attracted my attention. I felt that there were some very ancient ones and some of a more recent period which, at the time of the Anabaptists, had been removed from their shrines."

The next day, Father Niesing delivered the reliquary to Sister Emmerich. She received it with expressions of joy and gratitude and, on the 12th of January, related the following vision respecting one of the relics it contained : " I saw the soul of a youth approaching me under a luminous form and in a robe something like my guide. A white aureola surrounded him and he told me that he had gained heaven by chastity and victories over nature. It had even been a help to him to refrain from gathering roses which he very much loved.—Then I had a vision in which I saw this youth as a boy of thirteen, playing with his companions in a beautiful large garden. He wore a plaited hat, a tight yellow jacket, open in front, the sleeves trimmed around the wrist. His small-clothes and stockings were all in one and laced tightly up the side with another color; he wore knee-buckles and shoes strapped with ribands. The garden-hedges were neatly trimmed and there were scattered around many rustic ornaments and summer-houses, square outside and round within. There were also orchards and at work in them men clothed very much in the way I used to dress up the shepherds for our Christmas Crib in the convent. The garden belonged to distinguished people of the neighboring city, and was open to the public. The boys went gaily along gathering red and white roses from the numerous rose-hedges ; but the youth, of whom I speak, overcame his desire to do the same. His companions teased him by holding their great, great bouquets under his nose. Here the blessed spirit said to me : ' I was prepared for this little victory over self by one much greater—I had a playmate, a beautiful little girl, one of our neighbors, whom I dearly loved with an innocent affection. My pious parents often took me to hear a sermon and once the preacher warned his hearers against such intimacies. I did violence to my feelings, shunned the company of the little girl, and from this victory I gained strength to renounce the roses.' As he spoke, I saw the little maiden, delicate and blooming as a rose, walking in the city. I also saw the handsome house of the youth's parents situated in a large business-square, in which was a fountain enclosed by a beautiful iron railing artistically wrought in life-size figures. From the centre of the basin arose a figure from which spouted the water. At the four corners of the square were little buildings like sentry-boxes. The city lay in a fertile region bounded on one side by a ditch and on the other by a tolerably large river. I cannot say exactly where it was, but it looked like a German city. It had about seven churches, but no remarkable steeple. The roofs of the houses were slanting, the fronts square with covered archways. The youth's father was a rich cloth and wine merchant. Before his house stood wagons laden with merchandise. I entered and saw the father, the mother. and several children, a pious Christian household The father, a tall, stout man, was elegantly dressed and wore a leathern purse at his side. The mother, a stately lady above the middle height, was dressed in red and brown with a rich, though odd-looking head-dress. Her hair was rolled above her forehead and fastened by a silver clasp; on the back of her head was a pointed cap of broad lace from which hung wide ribands. The youth was the eldest of the children.

" The picture changed, and I saw the youth sent to study in a solitary convent about twelve leagues from the city on a mountain covered with vineyards. He was very industrious and so full of confidence in the Mother of God that, when he found something too difficult in his books, he turned earnestly to his picture of Mary : ' Thou didst teach thy Son,' he would say, ' thou art my mother also. O then, teach me, too !'—and Mary used to appear and help him out of his difficulty. He was full of simpli.ity and confidence. His piety won for him the esteem of all who knew him, but his great humility would not allow him to enter the priesthood. After three years in the convent, the last of which was passed on a sickbed, he died and was buried among the deceased religious. He was only in his twenty-third year. Among his acquaintances was a man about thirty years old, who often fell into sin from the violence of passion. He had great confidence in the deceased and, several years after, he came to pray at his grave. The youth appeared to him, exhorted him to good, and told him to look on his corpse for a certain mark which he gave him as a sign that he had really appeared to him.—The mark was on his finger in the form of a ring which he had received at his betrothal to Jesus and Mary. The friend reported what had happened, the body was disinterred, the mark found, and the finger taken off to be preserved as a relic. The youth has never been canonized. He reminded me very much of St. Aloysius Gonzaga in his ways.

" The youth took me to a place like the Heavenly Jerusalem, for it was all shining and transparent. We went to a great circular place surrounded by beautiful, sparkling palaces. In the centre stood a large table covered with dishes perfectly indescribable. From four of the palaces stretched arches of flowers which united above the table in a magnificent crown around which sparkled the holy names of Jesus and Mary. It was not a production of art, it was all alive and growing, each part producing fruit according to its kind, the arches formed of most varied flowers, fruits, and shining figures. I knew the signification of each and every one, not only symbolically but as a substance, an essence which penetrated and enlightened the mind like sunbeams—but I cannot express it in words. On one side, a little beyond the palaces, stood two octagonal churches; one was Mary's, the other the Christ-Child's. As I approached, there floated from all parts of the shining palaces, even through the walls innumerable souls of deceased children who came to bid me welcome. They appeared at first in the usual spiritual form; but afterward they were shown me as they were during life. I recognized several of my play-fellows long since dead. Among them was little Caspar, Diericke's little brother, a frolicsome, though not a bad child, who had died in his eleventh year after a long and very painful illness. He showed me all around and explained everything. I wondered to see naughty little Caspar now so fine and beautiful. I expressed my surprise at being there, when he said: 'Yes, thy feet have not brought thee here; it was thy good life!'—and this gave me great joy. As I did not recognize him right away, he said: 'Don't you remember how I sharpened your knife once? I overcame myself in that, and it turned out to my own good. Your mother had given you something to cut, but your knife was too dull; you cried, for you were afraid your mother would scold. I was looking on, and my first thought was : Now, let's see what her mother will do to her ! But my second thought was : I'll sharpen the poor little thing's knife. I did it. I helped you, and all for the good of my own soul. Do you remember the day when the children were playing so naughtily ? You said it was a wicked game, they must not play it, and then you went and sat down by the ditch and cried. I went to you, and asked why you would not play with us. You answered that some one had led you away by the arm. I thought over it and resolved not to play such games any more ; and that, too, was for my own good. And do you remember the day we all went together to gather fallen apples ? You said we ought not to do it, but I replied that, if we did not take them, others would. Then you said that we must never give any one a subject for scandal, and you would not touch them. I remarked that also and drew a lesson from it.—One day, I threw a bone at you, but something drew you suddenly aside from the stroke, and that went to my heart,'—and so, little Caspar went on recalling all sorts of incidents by which I saw that we receive for every self-victory, for every good action, a special reward, a certain kind of food which we eat in this sense that we have the full perception of it. It shines in us—but it is inexpressible ! We did not sit down at the table ; we floated from one end to the other, tasting a particular enjoyment for every act of self-renunciation. A voice was heard proclaiming : ' Only he can comprehend this nourishment who partakes of it.'—The food consisted for the most part of marvellous flowers, fruits, sparkling stones, figures, and herbs of quite another, of a more spiritual substance than those here below. They were served in glittering, transparent dishes of indescribable beauty, and they furnished wonderful strength to those who, by such or such an act of renunciation performed on earth, were brought into a certain relation with one or other of them. The table was covered with little crystal, pear-shaped glasses, like those in which I used to receive health-giving beverages, out of which we drank. One of the first dishes was marvellously prepared myrrh. On a golden plate stood a small covered cup on which was a knob surmounted by a delicate little crucifix. Around the rim of the plate were violet-blue letters which I could not make out, but I will understand them after awhile. From the plate grew the most lovely bunches of myrrh, yellow and green, in the form of pyramids, reaching to the top of the cup. There were tiny crisp leaves with blossoms like carnations of uncommon beauty, above which was a red bud surrounded by the most exquisite violet-blue flowers. The bitterness of the myrrh was changed for the spirit into a wonderful aromatic and strengthening sweetness. I shared in this dish, because of the bitterness of heart I had silently borne all my life. For the fallen apples that I would not touch, I now received a whole branch of apples glittering with light, and I had a dish also for the quantities of dry bread I had distributed to the poor. It looked like sparkling colored crystals shaped like loaves of bread. The plate, likewise, was of crystal. For shunning the improper game, I received a white robe. Little Caspar explained everything to me as we went around the table. I saw intended for me a little stone on a plate which I had once received in the convent, and I was told that before my death I should receive a white robe and a stone on which would be inscribed a name which only I could read. At the end of the table, the love of one's neighbor received its reward, white robes, white fruits, great white roses, and all kinds of wonderful dishes and objects of dazzling whiteness. I cannot describe them.

Then little Caspar said : 'Now, you must see here what we have in the shape of cribs, for you always loved to play with them,' and we all went to the churches, first into that of the Mother of God in which the sweetest singing was constantly going on. In it was an altar upon which all the scenes from Mary's life were incessantly succeeding one another, and all around, row above row, were crowds of worshippers. We had to pass through this church to reach the little crib which was in the other church, the church of the Christ-Child. In it, also, was an altar upon which was a representation of His Birth and successive scenes of His life up to the institution of the Blessed Sacrament, as I always see them in vision."

Here Sister Emmerich interrupted her narrative to exhort the Pilgrim to labor more ardently at his salvation, to do what he can to-day, not to put off till to-morrow, for life is so short and judgment rigorous! She continued : "From the church I mounted to a higher region, to a garden full of magnificent fruits, richly ornamented tables, and cases of elegant gifts. On all sides I saw souls floating who, by their studies and writings, had been useful to others. They were dispersed throughout the garden singly and in groups, and they paused at the different tables to receive their respective rewards. In the centre of the garden arose a semicircular structure in tiers. It was laden with the most exquisite objects, and from the front and sides extended arms holding books. The garden opened by a beautiful gate on to a road along which came a superb procession. All the souls crowded over to that side of the garden and ranged in two rows to welcome the new-comers, a troop of souls escorting the lately deceased Count von Stolberg. They advanced in regular order with banners and garlands. Four bore upon their shoulders (but without weight) a litter of state in which the Count half reclined. They who went to meet the procession also had flowers and crowns. Stolberg wore a crown formed principally of white roses, sparkling gems, and stars; it rested not on his head but hovered just over it. The souls all appeared at first under similar forms, like those I saw lower down in the children's heaven; but afterward each assumed the garb that distinguished him on earth. I saw that they were only such as had by their labors and teaching led others to salvation. Stolberg descended from the litter, which then disappeared, and advanced toward the gifts prepared for him. I saw an angel standing behind the semicircular tiers, to whom the surrounding spirits gave books one after another. After he had erased something from them or written something in them, he laid them on two stands at his side. Then he gave to the spirits writings, great and small, which they passed on from one to another. On one side I saw an extraordinary number of little pamphlets circulated by Stolberg. It seemed to be a continuation in heaven of the earthly labors of those souls. Then Stolberg received a large, transparent plate in the centre of which stood a beautiful golden chalice. Around it were grapes, little loaves, precious stones, and tiny crystal flasks. The chalice was not stationary as upon the plate of myrrh. The souls drank from it, as also from the flasks, and they partook of the other things for Stolberg passed them around. In their communication, I often saw the souls giving their hand to one another. Then all went up on high to give thanks. After this vision my guide told me that I must go to Rome, to excite the Pope to greater ardor in prayer, and he explained to me all that I should have to do."

CHAPTER V.

Prayer and Sufferings for Pope Pius VII., for the Ecclesiastical Province of the Upper Rhine, for the Conversion of Sinners, and for the Dying.—Tableaux of Feasts.

I. Pius VII.

The last five years of Pius VII.'s pontificate were a time of trial not less severe than that of former years; viz., his arrest by Napoleon's minions, his imprisonment, and the ill-treatment attending it. We may reasonably conclude that captivity was far less painful to the august and magnanimous sufferer than the network of deceit, treason, and artifice spread by his enemies around the Holy See, to prevent the discharge of his duties as Supreme Pastor toward the Church in Germany. During these two periods of his pontificate, fraught with anxiety and suffering, Sister Emmerich was, perhaps, the most remarkable of the hidden instruments destined by Almighty God to serve the Pope against his adversaries. As at a later period Gregory XVI. and Pius IX. found their faithful auxiliary in Maria von Moerl, so did Sister Emmerich during the whole reign of Pius VII. faithfully typify the apostolic community at Jerusalem earnestly supplicating for Peter imprisoned by Herod (1). The very small part she was able to communicate is quite sufficient to convince us both of the truth of her visions and the vast extent of her mission.

(1) Acts, xxii. 5.

Nov. 15, 1819.—"I had to go to Rome, for the Pope is too yielding to his enemies in weighty affairs. There is a black man in Rome who knows how to attain his ends by flattery and promises. He hid behind some Cardinals. The Pope in the hope of obtaining a certain advantage has consented to something which will turn out to the prejudice of the Church. I saw it under the form of conferences and an exchange of writings. Then I saw the black man proudly boasting to his party : 'Now, I have it ! Now, we'll soon see where the rock is upon which the Church is built ! '—But he was too quick with his boasting. I had to go to the Pope who was kneeling in prayer. I seemed to hover over him.—It was very strange ! I repeated earnestly the message entrusted to me for him, but there seemed to be something between us, and he spoke not. Suddenly he arose, touched a bell, and sent for a Cardinal whom he commissioned to recall the concession that had been granted. The Cardinal looked thunder-struck, and asked whence came this change. The Pope answered that he would give no explanation. 'Let it suffice,' said he, 'that it must be so,' and the Cardinal went away stupefied. I saw many people in Rome deeply saddened by the intrigues of the *black man,* who looks like a Jew.

" I went afterward to Münster to the Vicar-General. He was seated at a table, reading a book. I was charged to tell him that he spoils things by his severity, that he ought to attend more seriously to the particular needs of his flock, and remain at home more for such as wished to see him. It seemed to him that he found in his book a passage suggestive of these thoughts, and he began to feel dissatisfied with himself. —I went also to Dean Overberg, whom I found as usual calm and recollected, advising and consoling women and girls of all classes, and quietly praying in his heart all the time."

January 12, 1820.—"My guide told me I must go to the Pope and stir him up in prayer, and that I should be told all I had to do. I arrived in Rome and, singular thing!—I passed through the walls and stood on high in a corner looking down upon the people below. When I thought of this afterward during the day, it seemed to me very strange, though I am often thus placed with regard to others. I was told to say to the Pope in prayer that he should be more attentive, as the affair then being so artfully negotiated was one of great moment, that he ought to use his pallium more frequently, for then he would be more abundantly endued with strength and grace from the Holy Spirit. There is some connection between this little mantle and the ornament worn by the High Priest of the Old Law when he prophesied. It is thought that the Pope ought to wear it only on certain days, but necessity knows no certain days. He must also solemnly convene the Cardinals oftener. He manages his affairs too quietly, too privately; consequently, he is often deceived, the enemy daily becomes more cunning. There is now some question of Protestants sharing in the government of the Catholic clergy. I had to tell the Pope to invoke the Holy Ghost for three days and then he would act right. Many of those around him are good for nothing. He ought to convict them openly of their want of uprightness and then they would, perhaps, amend."

January 13th—"I was still in Rome with the Pope, who is now firmly resolved to sign nothing. But his adversaries are resorting to more artful measures, and once more I saw the movements of the cringing, cunning *black man.* They often appear to resign what they are sure of gaining later." Sister Emmerich's labor for the Holy Father was accompanied by great sufferings of which the Pilgrim speaks, as follows: "Sister Emmerich is full of courage. She seems to be always in a state of expectancy, eagerly awaiting the moment to give assistance. Once she exclaimed that she saw the two deceased nuns approaching her, and immediately began those tortures she has now endured for a week. Her arms are suddenly jerked up as if by an invisible power, and present the appearance of being fastened to a cross by cords; her feet are closely crossed one over the other; and the tension of the whole body becomes so great that one watches nervously to see it snap asunder. Her feet quiver violently from the pain, her teeth are clenched, and stifled groans escape her. Every member trembles convulsively. Her bones are heard to creak; the upper part of her body is raised; her hands drawn back; her muscles distended.—She is stiff as a wooden statue and light as a hollow paste-board figure. That her state is altogether involuntary that she is acted upon by some external force, is perfectly evident. Her body makes all the movements of a person extended on a cross. This lasted for about ten minutes when the arms suddenly fell; she swooned away and passing into a state of contemplation, she began to say that three unknown persons had bound her to a cross. Then she saw mounting a ladder numbers of holy souls just released through her mediation and who thanked her as they passed. And now her torture recommenced: she was scourged, bound to a cross, and subjected to a repetition of the same cruel sufferings which lasted, like the first, for about ten minutes, the perspiration streaming down her face. She begged the Pilgrim to replace her hands and feet in their natural position, which he did, putting at the same time some relics in her hand. This struggle was endured for all that were then dying unprepared or without the Sacraments, of whom she saw about fifty, most of them young persons and priests. They were all helped in various ways.

She never beheld children among those to whom she was
called upon to render such services.   According to her own
prediction, one   more such crisis was in store for her
to be endured for the Church.   It came, in fact, that same
day with all the circumstances attendant on the preceding
The imposition of her confessor's hands afforded relief.
But when she recovered consciousness, it was found that
she could not speak, her tongue having fallen back paralyzed.   The confessor's blessing in the name of Jesus restored her its use.   She lay perfectly exhausted, though
with the placid, satisfied expression of one who had finished
a painful but meritorious task.   With childlike simplicity
she exclaimed :

"I shall have another weary night all alone ! I will be
thankful if a soul comes to me ; but, in either case, I must
be satisfied."

Next morning the Pilgrim found her all bruised, her
limbs still trembling from the terrible tension put upon them.
Being now able to speak, she explained that the suffering
of the preceding day had been announced to her for the
morning, but that she had begged a respite until the evening instead of enduring it three hours after mid-day, the
time specified by her guide.   She had been a passive
victim during it.   Three unknown persons had bound her
to a cross and scourged her with rods and whips, but the
sight of the miseries for which she suffered rendered all
things sweet and aroused in her a thirst for still greater
pains.   She had seen that night that the Holy Father
yielded not to the wicked and artful proposals made him.
She saw almost all the Bishops sunk in the sleep of indifference.   Soon a new Pope would arise (about 1840-1850),
one who would be more energetic.   She saw the future pontiff
in a city to the south of Rome.   He was not clothed like

a monk, though he wore something like a religious badge. The state of the Church she described as extraordinarily distressing; her enemies subtle and active, her clergy timid and indolent. They neglected the power they held from God, they even aimed at the tiara which, however, they were never to attain. During her martyrdom, she seemed to be lying in a horizontal position, on a mountain, the Mountain of the Prophets far away in the distance. " I still feel," she added, "the sharp pressure of last night's cords. Once I fell, and the cords around my body cut deep into my waist. I felt as if my every vein and nerve had snapped. The first time that I endured such sufferings for my neighbor was after my Confirmation, for before that I had only such as were self-imposed. All my singular accidents and maladies were of the same nature, especially those that befell me in the convent."

February 22, 1820.—" I was in a city beyond Frankfort, in a country of vineyards, and I saw in one of the churches, great disorder occasioned by bad priests. I had to console one old priest who had been misrepresented to his Bishop by his wicked assistants, because he had with the aid of the two sacristans driven them from the confessional and the church which they had presumed to enter after having spent the whole night in carousing. The affair caused great excitement. The old priest said Mass himself, otherwise there would have been no divine service; but he still lies under the accusation. No one will help him but God."

2. St. Mary of the Rotunda and the Chapel of the Protestant Embassy, at Rome.

May 13, 1820.—" Last night, from eleven to three, I had a most wonderful vision of two churches and two Popes and a variety of things, ancient and modern. I shall relate,

as well as I can, all that I remember of it. My angel-guardian came and told me that I must go to Rome and take two
things to the Pope, but I cannot now recall what they were
—perhaps it is the will of God that I should forget them.
I asked my angel how I could make so long a journey, sick
as I was. But when I was told that I should make it without difficulty, I no longer objected.—An odd-looking vehicle appeared before me, flat and slight, with only two
wheels, the flooring red with white edges. I saw no horses.
I was gently lifted and laid on it and, at the same instant, a
snow-white, luminous child flew toward me and seated himself
at my feet. He reminded me of the Patience-child in green,
so sweet, so lovely, and perfectly transparent. He was to
be my companion, he was to console and take care of me.
The wagon was so light and smooth that at first I was
afraid of slipping off; but it began to move very gently of
itself without horses, and I saw a shining human figure going on ahead. The journey did not seem long, although we
crossed countries, mountains, and great waters. I knew
Rome the instant we reached it, and I was soon in the
presence of the Pope. I know not now whether he was
sleeping or praying, but I had to say two things to him, or
give him two things, and I shall have to go to him once
again to announce a third.—Then I had a wonderful
vision. Rome suddenly appeared as in the early ages, and
I saw a Pope *(Boniface IV.)* and an emperor whose name
I knew not *(Phocas)*. I could not find my way in the city,
all was so different, even the sacred ceremonies; but yet I
recognized them as Catholic. I saw a great round building
like a cupola—it was a pagan temple full of beautiful idols.
It had no windows, but in the dome was an opening with a
contrivance for keeping out the rain. It seemed as if all
the idols that ever existed were gathered together there in

every conceivable posture. Many of them were very beautiful, and others exceedingly odd; there were even some of geese which received divine honor. In the centre of the building stood a very high pyramid formed entirely of those images. I saw no idolatrous worship at the time of which I speak, although the idols were still carefully preserved. I saw messengers from Pope Boniface going to the emperor and petitioning for the temple to be changed into a Christian church. I heard the latter declaring distinctly that the Pope should allow the ancient statues to remain, though he might erect therein the cross to which the highest honors should be paid. This proposal, as it seemed to me, was made not wickedly, but in good faith. I saw the messengers return with the answer and Boniface reflecting as to how he might in some measure conform to the emperor's will. Whilst he was thus deliberating, I saw a good, pious priest in prayer before the crucifix. He wore a long white robe with a train, and an angel hovered by his side. Suddenly he arose, went straight to Boniface, and told him that he should by no means accede to the emperor's proposal. Messengers were then despatched to the emperor, who now consented to the temple's being entirely cleared. Then I saw his people come and take numbers of the statues to the imperial city; but still many remained in Rome. Then I saw the consecration of the temple, at which ceremony the holy martyrs assisted with Mary at their head. The altar was not in the centre of the building, but against the wall. I saw more than thirty wagon-loads of sacred relics brought into the church. Many of them were enclosed in the walls and others could be seen through round openings covered with something like glass. When I had witnessed this vision even in the smallest details, I saw again the present Pope and the *dark church* of his time in Rome, It seemed to be a

large, old house like a town-hall with columns in front. I saw
no altar in it, but only benches, and in the middle of it
something like a pulpit. They had preaching and singing,
but nothing else, and only very few attended it. And lo,
a most singular sight!—Each member of the congregation
drew an idol from his breast, set it up before him, and prayed to it. It was as if each man drew forth his secret
thoughts or passions under the appearance of a dark cloud
which, once outside, took some definite form. They
were precisely such figures as I had seen around the neck
of the illicit bride in the Nuptial House, figures of men
and animals. The god of one was short and broad with a
crisp head and numerous, outstretched arms ready to seize
and devour all in its reach; that of another was quite small
with miserable, shrunken limbs; another had merely a
block of wood upon which he gazed with rolling eyes;
this one had a horrible animal; that one, a long pole. The
most singular part of it was that the idols filled the place;
the church, although the worshippers were so few, was
crowded with idols. When the service was over, every
one's god re-entered into his breast. The whole church
was draped in black, and all that took place in it was
shrouded in gloom.—Then I saw the connection between
the two Popes and the two temples. I am sorry that I
have forgotten the numbers, but I was shown how weak
the one had been in adherents and human support, but
how strong in courage to overturn so many gods (I knew
the number) and to unite so many different forms of worship into one; and, on the contrary, how strong in numbers
and yet how irresolute in action was the other since, in
authorizing the erection of false temples, he had allowed
the only true God, the only true religion to be lost among
so many false gods and false religions. It was also shown

me that those pagans humbly adored gods other than themselves, and that they would have been willing to admit in all simplicity the only God, the Most Holy Trinity. Their worship was preferable to that of those who adore themselves in a thousand idols to the total exclusion of Our Lord. The picture was favorable to the early ages, for in them idolatry was on the decrease, whilst in our days it is just the contrary. I saw the fatal consequences of this counterfeit church; I saw it increase; I saw heretics of all kinds flocking to the city (1). I saw the ever-increasing tepidity of the clergy, the circle of darkness ever widening.—And now the vision became more extended. I saw in all places Catholics oppressed, annoyed, restricted, and deprived of liberty, churches were closed, and great misery prevailed everywhere with war and bloodshed. I saw rude, ignorant people offering violent resistance, but this state of things lasted not long. Again I saw in vision St. Peter's undermined according to a plan devised by the secret sect whilst, at the same time, it was damaged by storms; but it was delivered at the moment of greatest distress. Again I saw the Blessed Virgin extending her mantle over it. In this last scene, I saw no longer the reigning Pope, but one of his successors, a mild, but very resolute man who knew how to attach his priests to himself and who drove far from him the bad. I saw all things renewed and a church which reached from earth to heaven. I saw one of the twelve new Apostles in the person of the young

(1) November 17, 1822.—" I saw something very laughable in the *black church*. One of its mighty patrons wanted to do something extraordinarily grand, so he sent word to the preacher that he would give him a white surplice to wear in the pulpit. Then came the preacher, a tall, handsome man with a beautiful tie under his chin. The patron put the surplice on him and sent him into the pulpit. I thought: 'The patron is raising a great, great tree; it will fall into a great, great pool; and there will be a great, great splash!' But it turned out otherwise. The preacher sat in state, carefully showing off his surplice; the congregation waited and waited, but not a word did he utter. And lo! when they looked more closely, they found that their preacher had no head. The surplice covered only a great, great bundle of straw. Many broke out into a laugh, others mocked. but as for the patron—he was perfectly furious."

priest whom the unchaste bride wanted to marry. It was a very comprehensive vision and portrayed anew all that had been previously shown me regarding the Church's destiny. On another occasion, I had a vision of the Vicar-General's stanch resistance to secular power in behalf of the interests of the Church. The affair covered him with glory (1), though upon some other points he was to blame. I was told that I should have to go again to the Pope; but when all this will take place I cannot say."

A NEW CHURCH UNDER THE INFLUENCE OF PLANETARY SPIRITS.

September 12, 1820.—"I saw a fantastic, odd-looking church being built. The choir was in three parts, each raised some steps above the last; and under it was a deep vault full of fog. On the first platform of the choir was a seat; on the second, a basin of water; on the third, a table. I saw no angel helping in the construction, but numbers of the most violent planetary spirits dragging all sorts of things into the vault where persons in little ecclesiastical mantles received them and deposited them in their various places. Nothing was brought from above; all came from the earth and the dark regions, all was built up by the planetary spirits. The water alone seemed to have something holy about it. I saw an enormous number of instruments brought into the church, and many persons, even children, had different tools, as if trying to make something; but all was obscure, absurd, dead! Division and destruction reigned everywhere.—Near by, I saw another church, shining and rich with graces from on high, angels ascending and descending. In it were life and increase, tepidity and dissipation; and yet it was like a tree

(1) An allusion to his vigorous resistance to the Prussian government in the affair of mixed marriages, after he had been raised to the Archbishopric of Cologne.

full of sap compared with the other which was like a chest of lifeless institutions. The former was like a bird on the wing; the latter, like a paper dragon, its tail adorned with ribands and writings, dragging over a stubble-field. I saw that many of the instruments in the new church, such as spears and darts, were meant to be used against the living Church. Every one dragged in something different, clubs, rods, pumps, cudgels, puppets, mirrors, trumpets, horns, bellows—all sorts of things. In the cave below (the sacristy) some people kneaded bread, but nothing came of it; it would not rise. The men in the little mantles brought wood to the steps of the pulpit to make a fire. They puffed and blew and labored hard, but the fire would not burn; all they produced was smoke and fumes. Then they broke a hole in the roof and ran up a pipe, but the smoke would not rise, and the whole place became black and suffocating. Some blew the horns so violently that the tears streamed from their eyes. All in this church belonged to the earth, returned to the earth; all was dead, the work of human skill, a church of the latest style, a church of man's invention like the new heterodox church in Rome."

November 12, 1820.—"I passed over a dark, cold country to a large city, and I saw again the great, odd-looking church with nothing holy about it and innumerable planetary spirits laboring at it. I saw it in the same way that I see a Catholic institution being erected, angels, saints, and Christians all laboring in common; only here the concurrence of the laborers was shown under forms more mechanical. The planetary spirits ascended and descended and shot down rays upon the workmen; but all was done in accordance with human reason. I saw a spirit on high drawing lines and tracing figures, and down below the design, the plan immediately carried out. I saw the influence of the proud, planetary spirits in their relation with the building extending to even the most distant places. All the steps deemed necessary or useful to the construction and maintenance of the church were taken in the most remote countries, and men and things, doctrines and opinions contributed thereto. The whole picture was colored with intense selfishness, presumption, and violence. I saw not a single angel or saint helping in the work. It was an immense vision. Far away in the back ground, I saw the throne of a savage nation, the people armed with boar-spears and a figure saying in mocking terms: 'Build it as solidly as you please, we shall overturn it!'—I went also into a large hall in the city in which a hideous ceremony, a horrible, deceitful comedy was being enacted. The hall was draped in black, and a man wearing a star on his breast was put into a coffin and taken out again. It seemed to be a threat of what would happen to him. In the midst of it all I saw the devil under a thousand forms.—All was dark as night. It was horrible!"

3. St. Henry, Emperor at St. Mary-Major.

July 12, 1820.—" I have had a vision of the Emperor Henry. I saw him last night in a beautiful church kneeling alone before the main·altar. I know the church; there is a beautiful chapel of the Holy Crib in it. I saw it once before on the Feast of Our Lady of the Snow. As he knelt and prayed, a light shone above the altar and the Blessed Virgin appeared alone. She wore a robe of bluish white which shot forth rays, and she carried something in her hand. She covered the altar with a red cloth over which she spread a white one, and deposited upon it a magnificent luminous book set with precious stones. Then she lighted the candles from the sanctuary-lamp. Many other lights in the form of a pyramid burned at the same time. Then she took her stand at the right of the altar. Now came the Saviour Himself in sacerdotal vestments, bearing the chalice and veil. Two angels served Him as acolytes, and two others accompanied Him. Our Lord's head was uncovered. The chasuble was a large, heavy, red and white mantle shining with light and precious stones. The minis tering angels were white. There was no little bell, but there were cruets. The wine was as red as blood and there was also some water. The Mass was shorter than with us and there was no Gospel of St. John at the end. I saw the Offertory and Elevation ; the Host was like ours. The angel read the Gospel and carried the book to Mary to kiss, and then, on a sign from Jesus, to Henry that he might do the same. At first, he dared not obey, but at length gained courage to do so. At the end of the Mass, Mary went to Henry and gave him her right hand, saying that she honored thus his chastity and exhorted him not to grow remiss. Then I saw an angel approach and grasp him by the right side as had been done to Jacob. Henry showed signs of intense pain, and afterward limped a little. During the whole of this ceremony, there were numerous angels in adoration, their eyes fixed upon the altar."

4. Feast of the Scapular.

July 15, 1820.—"I was on Mt. Carmel where I saw two hermits who dwelt far apart. One was very aged and never left his cell, the other, a Frenchman named Peter, visited the old man occasionally and brought him something ; but long intervals sometimes elapsed between his visits. I saw him taking journeys to Jerusalem, Rome, and to our own country, whence he returned with bands of warriors wearing crosses on their clothing. I saw Berthold with him. He was at that time a soldier. Later on, I saw the younger hermit take Berthold to the old man on Mt. Carmel. Berthold had then become a hermit. He was afterward the Superior of the hermits whom he formed into communities, and for whom he erected convents. Then I had another vision. I saw after the hermits began to live in community, a monk on his knees in his cell. The Mother of God appeared to him with the Infant Jesus on her arm. She looked just like the statue that I had seen by the spring on the mountain. She gave him an article of dress in which was a square opening for the head to pass through. It fell in front over the breast. It was shining with light, the colors red and white intermingling, as in the vestment of the High-Priest that Zacharias showed to St. Joseph. On the straps that went over the shoulders were letters inscribed. Mary spoke long to the monk. When she vanished and he returned to himself, he was filled with emotion on seeing himself clothed with the scapular. I saw him assemble his brethren and show it to them.—Then I had a vision of a Church festival on Mt. Carmel. I saw in the choirs of the Church Triumphant as the first of the ancient hermits, and yet separated from them, Elias. Under his feet were the words : ' Elias, Prophet.'—I did not see these pictures one after another, and I felt that a great number of years lay between them, especially between the vision of the reception of the scapular and the feast, for the latter seemed to belong to our own day. Over the spring where once stood Mary's statue, now arose a convent and its church. The spring was in the middle of the latter and above the altar was the Mother of God with the Infant Jesus just as she had appeared to the hermit, living and moving in dazzling splendor. Innumerable little silken pictures hung at her sides attached in pairs by two cords and glancing like the leaves of a tree in the sunshine, in the splendor which radiated from Mary. The holy Virgin was surrounded by the angelic choirs and at her feet, above the tabernacle wherein reposed the Blessed Sacrament, hung the large scapular she had given the hermit in vision. On all sides were ranged choirs of holy Carmelites, men and women, the most ancient in white and brown striped habits, the others in such as are now worn. I saw, too, the Carmelite Order, monks and nuns of the present day celebrating the feast in their several convents, either in choir or elsewhere, but all upon earth."

5. Vision of the Feast of the Indulgence of Portiuncula.

August 1, 1820.—" I had a vision of a feast, but I know not clearly what it signified; however, this is what I can recall:—I saw a great aureola of saints looking like an immense wreath in which they sat, each distinguished by different emblems, such as palms. churches, etc. Below them floated innumerable relics and sacred objects in precious vases; they seemed to belong to the saints above. In the middle of the wreath floated a little church and over it the Lamb of God with His standard. Throned above the altar were the Lord Jesus and His Mother surrounded by myriads of angels. An angel flew into the circle and led St. Francis to Jesus and Mary in the little church, and it seemed as if the saint petitioned for some favor by virtue of the treasure of Christ's merits and those of His holy martyrs, viz., an Indulgence for the little church.—Then I saw Francis go to the Pope, but not in Rome, petitioning for something, an Indulgence, the same that I had seen in the vision.—I saw that the Pope would not grant it at first; but suddenly a light shone upon him, a writing floated before him, and he was inspired to grant what the

saint demanded.   I saw the saint returned from the Pope,
praying that night on his knees.   The devil approached
him under the form of a very beautiful youth, and reproved him for his penances.   The saint recognized the
temptation, fled from his cell, cast off his garments, and
rolled in the thorns until he was all covered with blood,
when an angel appeared and healed his wounds.   This is
all I can remember."

6. Our Lady of the Snow.

"I saw a noble couple in a grand mansion praying at
night in their room before a picture of Mary on the wall.   It
was coarsely embroidered or woven, the robe in some places
striped with red and blue and tapering off round the feet.
Mary was crowned.   She held the infant Jesus in her
arms, His little hands clasping the orb of the world.   Two
lamps burned on either side of the little picture.   The narrow kneeling-bench on which the spouses knelt side by
side, could be turned up before the picture ; it then looked
like a wardrobe, and above it hung a curtain which could
be lowered to hide the picture.   I have seen in olden times
many such woven pictures of Mary.   They could be rolled
up to take on journeys and hung wherever the owner
wished to pray.

" As the couple knelt there, I saw the Blessed Virgin as
represented in the picture, but shining with light.   She
hovered before the picture, between it and the couple, and
enjoined upon them to erect a church in her honor at
Rome upon a hill which they would find covered with snow.
The next morning they related the affair to the Pope, and
went with several ecclesiastics to the hill upon whose summit, the site of the future edifice, lay snow of extraordinary
brilliancy.   I saw them driving stakes as landmarks, when

the snow at once disappeared.—Then I had another vision. I saw the church built and Mass being celebrated in it by a Pope named Martin. Just at the moment of communicating a certain great personage, the Pope was to be assassinated by a man stationed near for that purpose. The assassin had been chosen and instructed for the crime by the nobleman about to receive Holy Communion, and all in obedience to the orders of the Emperor Constantius. I saw the murderer enter the crowded church, but he was instantly struck blind. He ran here and there, stumbling against the pillars and uttering cries. A great tumult was raised. Again, I saw Pope Gregory celebrating High Mass in the church. The Mother of God appeared surrounded by angels, answered *Et cum spiritu tuo,* and served him at the altar. Lastly, I saw in the same church a feast celebrated in our own days. The Mother of God appeared under the same form as she had done to its founders. This is the church in which I lately saw the holy Emperor Henry praying whilst Christ Himself said the Mass. There is a chapel of the Holy Crib in it."

7. FROM AUGUST TO THE CLOSE OF OCTOBER, 1820.

Sister Emmerich's labors at this time were constantly directed to the welfare of the Church which, as usual, she beheld typified by St. Peter's, at Rome. The secret society, with its world-wide ramifications engaged in ceaseless war against the Bride of Christ, was shown her as the empire of Antichrist symbolized by the beast in the Apocalypse rising out of the sea and fomenting attacks upon the flock of Christ. In relating this vision, the Pilgrim makes the following remarks : "It is, indeed, full of breaks, for the invalid saw it under allegorical representations difficult for her to describe. What is most astonishing, is that it touch-

es upon many points of the Apocalypse of St. John, of
which humanly speaking she must have been wholly ignorant, as she has very little knowledge of the Holy Scriptures or of any other book. If, at times, she seems to
read, it is with a mind deeply absorbed in contemplation
and she sees very different things from those discussed in
the volume before her. The vision is, as follows: 'I see
new martyrs, not of the present but of the future, though
even now they are oppressed. I saw the secret society un-
dermining the great church (St. Peter's) and near them a
horrible beast that arose out of the sea. It had a tail like a
fish, claws like a lion, and numberless heads that lay like a
crown around one large head ; its jaws were large and red,
its body spotted like a tiger. It was very familiar with
the demolishers, lying near them whilst they worked, and,
again, concealing itself in a cave. Here and there throughout
the whole world I saw many good, pious people, especially
ecclesiastics, harrassed, imprisoned, and oppressed, and I felt
that at some future day, they would be martyred. When
the church was well-nigh overturned, the choir and altar
alone remaining untouched, I saw the demolishers thronging
into it accompanied by the beast. But they encountered a
tall, majestic female who seemed to be with child for she
walked very slowly. The wretches were filled with affright
on seeing her and the beast lay paralysed, furiously darting
its head toward her, as if to devour her ; but she turned and
fell prostrate on her face. Then I saw the beast fleeing to
the sea, the enemy hurrying off in disorder, and immense
circles of combatants surrounding the church, some on the
earth, others high in the air. The first circle was composed
of youths and maidens ; the second, of married persons of
all classes from royalty down ; the third, of religious ; the
fourth, of warriors, led by a rider on a white horse ; and the

fifth and last was made up of citizens and peasants, many of whom were marked on the forehead with a red cross. As this army drew near, the captives and oppressed were delivered and swelled the ranks, whilst the demolishers and conspirators were put to flight on all sides. They were, without knowing how, gathered together into one confused mass in the midst of a dense fog; they knew neither what they did nor what they ought to do; and they ran pell-mell against one another, as I so often see them. Then I saw the church speedily rebuilt and more magnificent than before, for its defenders brought stones from all parts of the earth. When the most distant circles drew near, the nearest withdrew to make way for them. The former appeared to represent the various labors of prayer; the latter, the soldiers, the deeds of war. I saw among these last friends and enemies of all nations, simply soldiers like our own and dressed like them. They did not form a perfect circle, but a crescent opening toward the north into an immense dark abyss like a chasm, a precipice, like a descent into darkness, like that to which Adam was driven from Paradise. I felt that a region of darkness lay beyond. I saw that some out of these circles remained behind. They would not advance, but stood gloomily huddled together. I saw some also who would one day be martyred for Jesus; but there were many wicked people among them, and another separation was to take place.—The church was completely restored. Above it on a mountain, was the Lamb of God surrounded by a troop of virgins with palm-branches, and five circles of celestial cohorts corresponding to the five circles below. They all arrived together, and all acted in concert. Around the Lamb stood the four mysterious beasts of the Apocalypse."

On the Feast of the Purification, 1822, Sister Emmerich

related the following : " I saw during the last few days marvellous things connected with the Church. St. Peter's was almost entirely destroyed by the sect, but their labors were, in turn, rendered fruitless and all that belonged to them, their aprons and tools, burned by the executioners on the public place of infamy. They were made of horse-leather, and the stench from them was so offensive that it made me quite sick. In this vision I saw the Mother of God laboring so earnestly for the Church that my devotion to her greatly increased."

August 10, 1822.—" I see the Holy Father in great distress. He lives in another palace and receives only a few to his presence. If the wicked party knew their own great strength, they would even now have made an attack. I fear the Holy Father will suffer many tribulations before his death, for I see the black counterfeit church gaining ground, I see its fatal influence on the public. The distress of the Holy Father and of the Church is really so great that one ought to pray to God day and night. I have been told to pray much for the Church and the Pope. . . . . Last night I was taken to Rome where the Holy Father, plunged in affliction, is still concealed in order to elude dangerous exigencies. He is very feeble, quite worn out by distress, anxiety, and prayer. His chief reason for lying concealed is because he can now trust so few. But he has by him a very simple-hearted, pious old priest, his true friend, whom his enemies on account of his simplicity think it not worth while to remove. Now, this good old priest is full of God's grace. He sees, he remarks many things which he faithfully communicates to the Holy Father. More than once I have had to point out to him in prayer traitors and evil-minded men among the Pope's high, confidential officers, that he might give him notice of them. In this way he has been warned against one who was all-influential up to the present; but who will be so no more. The Pope is so feeble that he can no longer walk alone."

August 25.—"I know not now how I went to Rome last night, but I found myself near the church of St. Mary-Major. Around it I saw crowds of poor, pious souls, in great·distress and anxiety on account of the Pope's disappearance and the agitation and alarming reports throughout the city. Led by one common impulse, they had come to invoke the Mother of God. They did not expect to find the church open, they intended only to pray outside. But I was inside, I opened the door and they entered, astounded at the door's opening of itself. I was standing aloof where they could not see me. There was no service, only the chancel-lamps were burning, and the people knelt in quiet prayer. Then the Mother of God appeared. She said that great tribulations were at hand; that the people must pray earnestly with extended arms, if only for the length of three Our Fathers, for it was thus that her Son had prayed for them upon the cross; that they should rise at midnight to pray thus; that they should continue to come to her church which they would always find open; and that they should, above all, pray for the extirpation of the dark church. She said also that the soldiers who were approaching the city would be of no assistance; they would bring only misery and devastation in their train, since the war had been undertaken without prayer or the ministry of priests. She added many other things. She said what is most painful to me to repeat that,if only one priest offered the Unbloody Sacrifice as worthily and with the same sentiments as the Apostles, he could ward off all calamities from the Church. I know not whether the people saw the apparition or not, but they must have been impressed by something super-

natural for, when the Blessed Virgin said they should pray
to God with extended arms, all lifted up their arms.
They were good and pious, but they knew not where to
turn for counsel and assistance. There was no traitor, no
enemy among them, and yet they were anxious and distrustful of one another ; by this we may judge of their
situation. It seemed to be an association of prayer."

From this time Sister Emmerich assisted nightly at the
pious exercises in St. Mary-Major's. On August 31st, she
remarked :

" Prayer is now general and continual, pious souls are
everywhere kneeling at the tombs of the saints and imploring their aid. I have seen the saints whom they especially revere, and I have again seen the Pope—he is in
much trouble. I have had great anxiety on his account
and I have redoubled my prayers . . . . Cardinal
Consalvi's last petition was rejected by the Holy Father ;
he did not approve it, and it has been withdrawn. This
man's influence is at an end for the present."

Sept. 10th—" I saw St. Peter's utterly demolished, all excepting the choir and main altar. St. Michael, girt and
armed, descended into the church and with his sword repulsed several bad pastors who were trying to enter. He
drove them into a corner where they sat looking at one
another. The part of the church that had been demolished
in a few instants was surrounded by light wicker-work so
that divine service could be perfectly celebrated. Then
from all parts of the world came priests and laics, who built
up the walls of stone, for the enemy had not been able to
shake the firm foundation."

Sister Emmerich at this time passed whole nights praying
with her arms in the form of a cross and frequently subjected to the assaults of the devil. The first night he

rushed upon her three times to strangle her. "He re-proached me," she said, "with all the faults of my youth, but I turned a deaf ear to him. I gathered up my relics and opposed him with them ; and, at last, I sat up in bed and made the sign of the cross all around with my relic of the True Cross, when he left me in peace." The following night she struggled with the enemy so victoriously that she sang the *Te Deum* several times. She had constant visions on the state of different dioceses, as we glean from the following entry in the Pilgrim's journal :

September 27th.—"To-day at noon, the invalid entered the state of contemplation in a singularly touching and animated manner. Her eyes were open, she gesticulated and described what she saw, as if in conversation : 'What are they doing in that great, beautiful church ? It is the cathedral (of Münster), and everything has been carried back into the chapel where the silver ship once stood, where Bernard von Galen is interred ! All goes there, all the graces, all, all ! O how beautiful, how wonderful it is ! There stands an empty chalice, and from it issues a ray which rises up to heaven in a great cross of light. On the left of the chalice is a beautiful bride with a church in her hand, and on the right of it, a wonderfully handsome youth who is to be her bridegroom ; they are betrothed. But see ! Outside the church, up in the air, is the Mother of God with the Infant Jesus from whose hands issues a magnificent vine which spreads over all the chapel. Its grapes hang down and discharge their juice into the chalice. Right and left, shoot out beautiful flowers of light and magnificent ears of golden, luminous wheat filling the whole place with splendor. And all the bushes are covered with flowers and marvellous little shin-ing fruits. All is light and beauty ! All is gathered in and preserved there. And behold! there stands, high, high up, a holy Bishop of olden times—it is Ludger! He guards, he takes care of all! And now, what is that? O see, from the whole church, excepting the chapel, shoot forth wild, fiery flames, and in several parts of the city whole rows of houses are destroyed! There in the castle things go badly! But this must be understood only in a spiritual sense. The great church stands intact. Exterior things go on as usual, but the graces are all stowed away in the chapel." As Sister Emmerich recounted the above, she pointed now here, now there, as if her hearers saw what was being unfolded before her own mental gaze. Next day she related what follows : "I have seen yesterday's vision of Galen's chapel all over again. An entirely new church floated in the air above the old one and drew into itself all the beautiful things from Galen's chapel. The church below seemed to grow black and sink into the earth. I thought how nice it would be if the church in the air would only descend just as the other disappeared. This vision was very detailed, but I have forgotten some of it.—I followed a path running back of the cathedral, and found in a field, half-meadow, half-heath, a homeless wandering boy, his feet torn and bleeding from the furze. I wanted to take him to the flower meadow. I told him there were beautiful flowers in it from which he could suck the honey, for I knew not what to do to relieve him. But he told me that it was his destiny, he must suffer and bleed until he had found an asylum. I thought of the youth who espoused the Church yesterday in the Galen chapel."

Sister Emmerich saw, also, at this time a distant diocese falling to decay. It was shown her under the symbol of a desecrated church. "I saw heart-rending misery, playing, drinking, gossiping, even courting going on in the church. All sorts of abominations were committed in it; they had even set up a ninepin alley in the middle of it. The priests let things go their way and said Mass very irreverently ; only a few of them were still a little intelligent and pious. I saw **Jews** standing around the doorways. All this grieved me deeply. Then my Heavenly Spouse bound me as He Himself had been bound to the pillar, and He said: ' So will the **Church** yet be bound. She will be tightly bound before she shall again arise.' "

September 30th—After a night spent in praying with extended arms for the Church, Sister Emmerich vomited blood and endured great pains in the breast. " St. Michael has prescribed for me a seven days' devotion with alms," she said. '' I shall now be sick for seven days," and indeed, the following night verified the prediction. She was attacked by sharp pains, her whole body consumed, as it were, by an internal fire, to allay which she placed her relic of St. Cosmas on her breast and invoked his name aloud. Scarcely had she done so when she fell into a sweet sleep. On awaking, she beheld the saint before her clothed in a long, white mantle resplendent with light. In his hand was a green branch covered with white flowers, and playing around him was a brilliant red aureola which dissolved into a beautiful blue. His younger brother Leontius stood at a little distance, and further back was Damian, the shortest of the three, Cosmas being the tallest. All Sister Emmerich's pains had disappeared. She lay calm and serene, unable to express the marvellous character of her cure which was as sudden and as marked as those previously bestowed through the intervention of St. Ignatius and St. Augustine.

On the evening of October 1st, the Pilgrim found her exhausted and bathed in perspiration from her heavy spiritual labors. She repeated that St. Michael, besides the seven days' task, had prescribed certain alms, pointing out what children were to be assisted and what each one was to receive. " The Church," she groaned, " is in great danger. I must ask every one who comes to see me to say an *Our Father* for that intention. We must pray that the Pope may not leave Rome, for unheard-of evils would result from such a step. We must pray the Holy Ghost to enlighten him, for they are even now trying to exact something of him. The Protestant doctrine, as also that of the Greeks, is spreading everywhere. Two men live at this time who long to ruin the Church, but they have lost one who used to help them with his pen. He was killed by a young man about a year ago, and one of the two men of whom I speak left Germany at the same time. They have their employees everywhere. The little black man in Rome, whom I see so often, has many working for him without their clearly knowing for what end. He has his agents in the new black church also. If the Pope leaves Rome, the enemies of the Church will get the upper hand. I see the little black man in his own country committing many thefts and falsifying things generally. Religion is there so skilfully undermined and stifled that there are scarcely one hundred faithful priests. I cannot say how it is, but I see fog and darkness increasing. There are, however, three churches that they cannot seize : St. Peter's, St. Mary-Major's and St. Michael's. Although they are constantly trying to undermine them, they will not succeed. I help not. All must be rebuilt soon for every one, even ecclesiastics are laboring to destroy—ruin is at hand. The two enemies of the Church who have lost their accomplice are firmly resolved to destroy the pious and learned men that stand in their way."

When the Pilgrim visited Sister Emmerich on October

4th, he found her perfectly worn out by the exertions of the preceding night. That St. Michael's commands were being fulfilled, was very evident. "I have had combats more terrible," she said, "than any I have ever endured, and I am almost dead. I cannot say how fearfully I have suffered. This struggle was shown me long ago under the symbol of a person buffeted by demons, and now I know it was myself. I fought against a whole legion of devils who excite minds against me and do all they can to harass me. I have also undertaken too many prayers. They want to install bad Bishops. In one place they want to turn a Catholic church into a Lutheran meeting-house. I must pray, suffer, and struggle against this, for such is my present task. If the saints did not assist me, I could not endure it. I should be overcome, and that would be most grievous to me! I see the devil using every artifice to put me to shame.—He is continually sending all sorts of people to visit me, to torment and wear me out (1).

"Last night I had a vision of the Pope. I saw St. Francis carrying the church, and the basilica of St. Peter borne on the shoulders of a little man who had something of the Jew in his countenance. It looked very perilous. Mary stood on the north side of the church with her mantle extended over it. The little man was almost bent double. He is, as yet, a laic. I know who he is. The twelve men whom I always see as the twelve new Apostles ought to have helped him, but they arrived too late; however, just as he was about to fall, they all ran up with myriads of angels to his assistance. It was only the pavement and the back part of the church,

(1) The day before, owing to Gertrude's carelessness, a French milliner unceremoniously entered the invalid's little room and spread out her goods on the bed. It was only with the greatest difficulty that Sister Emmerich could rid herself of her importunate visitor, whose loquacity annoyed her so that she could scarcely relate her visions to the Pilgrim, who arrived soon after.

for all the rest had been demolished by the secret society
helped by the servants of the church themselves. They
bore it to another place, and it seemed as if rows of palaces
fell before it like fields of wheat in harvest time.

" When I saw St. Peter's in this ruinous state and so
many ecclesiastics laboring, though secretly, at its destruction, I was so overcome that I cried earnestly to Jesus
for mercy. Then I saw my Heavenly Spouse before me
under the form of a youth. He spoke to me for a long time.
He told me that this translation of St. Peter's signified that
the Church would apparently fall to total ruin : but that,
resting on these supports, she would be raised up again.
Even if there should remain but one Catholic Christian,
the Church would again triumph since its foundations
were not cast in the intellect or councils of men. She had
never yet been without members praying and suffering
for her. He showed me all that He Himself had endured
for her, what efficacy He had bestowed upon the merits
and labors of the martyrs, and He ended by saying that
He would endure it all over again if it were possible for
Him again to suffer. He showed me, also, in numberless
pictures, the miserable aims of Christians and ecclesiastics
throughout the whole world. The vision grew wider,
more extended, until it embraced my own country ; and
then Jesus exhorted me to perseverance in prayer and expiatory suffering. It was an unspeakably great and
sorrowful picture. I cannot describe it !—I was also told
that very few Christians, in the true sense of the term, are
to be found nowadays and that the Jews of our day are
pure Pharisees, though still more obstinate ; only Judith's
people in Africa belong to the ancient Jews.—I am
greatly afflicted at what I saw ! "

October 7th—" I have been on a mission among the

Roman catacombs, and I saw the life of a martyr who with many others lived there concealed. He had made numerous conversions. He lived not long after Thecla's time, but I have forgotten his name. Even when a boy he used to go with holy women to the catacombs and prisons to console the poor Christians. He lay concealed a long time in a hermitage, but afterward endured cruel torments, and ended his life with many others by decapitation. He carried his own head from the place of execution, but I do not remember his history very distinctly. I went with the martyr and St. Frances of Rome into one of the catacombs, the ground of which was covered with shining flowers, the blossoms of his own and his companions' sufferings; for here it was that they had been executed. Conspicuous among them were beautiful white roses, one of which I found all at once sticking in my bosom *(the saint's relic)*. In several other places I saw flowers, the sufferings of those martyrs whose intercession I had implored for the Church in her present tribulations. As I went through Rome with Frances and the saint, we saw a great palace enveloped in flames (*the Vatican*). I was in dread lest the inmates would be consumed, for no one tried to extinguish the fire; but when we drew near, it suddenly ceased and left the building black and scorched. After passing through numerous magnificent apartments, we reached that of the Pope. We found him sitting in the dark, asleep in a large arm-chair. He was very sick and weak, no longer able to walk, and people were going to and fro before his door. The ecclesiastics most nearly connected with him pleased me not. They appeared to be false and lukewarm, and the simple-minded pious men whom I once saw by him were now removed to a distant part of the palace. I spoke long with the Holy

Father, and I cannot express how very real my presence there seemed to be; for I, too, was extremely weak and the people around were constantly obliged to support me. I spoke with the Bishops soon to be appointed, and I again told the Pope that he must not leave Rome, for if he did, all would go to ruin. He thought the evil inevitable and that his personal safety as well as other considerations, would oblige him to go, a measure to which he felt himself strongly inclined and to which also he was advised by his counsellors.—Then Frances spoke to him a long time, whilst I stood by weak and fainting, supported by my companions. Before I left, the Pope gave me a little saucer of sugared strawberries which, however, I did not eat, as I wanted them for a sick person."—Later, she exclaimed still in ecstasy : "Those strawberries have no very good signification.—They show that many ties still bind the Pope to earth."

"I saw Rome in such a state that the least spark would inflame it, and Sicily dark, frightful, abandoned by all that could leave it."—One day whilst in ecstasy, she groaned: "I see the Church alone, forsaken by all and around her strife, misery, hatred, treason, resentment, total blindness. I see messengers sent on all sides from a dark central point with messages that issue from their mouths like black vapor, enkindling in the breast of their hearers rage and hatred. I pray earnestly for the oppressed !—On those places in which some souls still pray I see light descending; but on others, pitchy darkness. The situation is terrible ! May God have mercy ! How much I have prayed ! O city ! O city, (*Rome*) with what art thou threatened ! The storm approaches—be on thy guard ! I trust thou wilt stand firm !"

October 16th—" Last night I made the Way of the Cross

at Coesfeld with a crowd of souls who showed me the distress of the Church and the necessity of prayer. Then I had a vision of many gardens lying around me in a circle, and the Pope's situation with respect to his Bishops. He sat enthroned in one of these gardens. In the others were the rights and privileges of his Bishops and their sees symbolized by various plants, flowers, and fruits. Their mutual connection, their communication and influence, I saw under the forms of threads, of rays extending from them to the see of Rome. In these earthly gardens, I saw the temporal, spiritual authority, and above them in the air I saw their future Bishops ; for instance, I saw above the garden of the stern Superior, a new Bishop with the cross, mitre, and other episcopal insignia, and standing around him Protestants who wished him to ·enter the garden below, but not on the conditions established by the Holy Father. They tried to insinuate themselves· by all sorts of covert means; they destroyed a part of the garden, or sowed bad seed in it. I saw them sometimes here, sometimes there, cultivating the land or letting it lie untilled, tearing up and not clearing away, etc. ; all was full of pitfalls and rubbish. I saw them intercepting or turning away the roads that led to the Pope. When they did succeed in getting a Bishop according to their liking, I saw that he had been intruded contrary to the will of the Holy Father ; consequently, he possessed no legitimate spiritual authority.— Many such scenes were shown me, and it is for me to pray and suffer ! It is very distressing !—I see one who has few claims to holiness about to be installed in the see of a holy deceased Bishop."

Sister Emmerich's sufferings during these contemplations were simply frightful. She felt as if her breast were girded tightly with cords; she had frequent vomitings, and so

lively an impression of a huge, thorny crown that she dared
not rest her head on a 'pillow. The wounds of her forehead and side bled several times. Whilst in this state, she
related the following fragments of a vision of the Sacred
Passion :—

" The crown of Jesus was very large and heavy, and
stood far out from His head. When the executioners dragged His woven tunic over His head, the crown came off
with it. I have an indistinct remembrance of their plat-
ting a smaller one (I know from what thorns) and putting it
on Him by the cross.—The three holes in the latter were too
far apart and, when they had nailed down one hand, they
had to stretch the other with cords to reach the second hole.
The feet also were found to be too high up ; they had to
be stretched in like manner. One of the executioners
knelt upon the Saviour's limbs, whilst the others drove the
nails. The Sacred Body was dislocated in every joint.
One could, as it were, see through it, and below the breast
it was quite sunken and hollow. It was a horrible moment
when they raised the cross and let it fall into the hole prepared for it. The shock was so violent that the Sacred
Body quivered.

" I did not see Jesus go into purgatory ; but, when He
was in limbo, the souls came from purgatory to Him and
all were delivered by Him. I saw the angel gathering and
restoring to His Sacred Body before the Resurrection the
Blood and Flesh lost during the Passion, and then I saw
Him issuing from the tomb in indescribable glory, His shining Wounds so many holy, ineffable ornaments to His
Sacred Body. He did not appear to the disciples in this
radiant glory, for their eyes could not have endured the
sight.

" The Blessed Virgin had some linen stained with the

Blood of Jesus's circumcision and His other Wounds. She gave the Apostles when they dispersed crosses of about an arm's length, made of flexible reeds, which they carried under their mantles. They had also metal boxes for the Holy Eucharist and relics, which were, I think, pieces of the linen that Mary had. I think, too, that the Blessed Virgin wove them robes like that of her Son, for she made many such, sometimes on two needles, or again with a hooked needle."

At the close of this painful task of prayer, Sister Emmerich had a very consoling vision of which she communicated the following:—" I lay on a plank in the midst of thorns which wounded me whenever I moved. In the hedge were numbers of red and white roses and other white flowers. Jesus appeared to me as my Bridegroom and showed me His familiar communications with His brides, Teresa, Catherine of Sienna and Clare of Montefalco whom I saw, one after another, in positions similar to my own : one seated in the midst of thorns, another rolling in them, and the third entirely surrounded by them. I saw how familiarly and confidently they addressed Our Lord. Clare of Montefalco was dragging a cross upon which many of her fellow-religious laid heaps of trifles, little nothings, until it became so heavy that she sank under its weight. Then Jesus reminded her that He, too, had fallen under His cross. Clare exclaimed : " Ah ! then, stretch out to me Thy hand as Thy Heavenly Father did to Thee !'— Jesus showed me also how all who approached my bed pressed upon me, though without intending it, the pricking thorns. I saw too the infirmities, the sufferings, the sorrows, often very grievous, of all these brides. Then Jesus placed before me a shining table and covered it with a snowy cloth. Upon it was immolated by a priest of the Old Law a patient, spotless lamb. I received touching instructions on the purity of the table, the cover, and the lamb, the blood of which did not stain the cover. Then a red cover was placed on the table and over it a white, transparent one, upon which stood bread and a chalice from which the Lord gave me to eat and drink. It was He Himself whom I received—after this He disappeared, leaving me consoled.—Then I saw in a series of pictures an abridgment of His whole Passion, how His friends misunderstood and abandoned Him, and how they would and how they really do treat Him at the present day. I saw Him more truly present in the Blessed Sacrament than He was present on earth during His mortal life, and I saw that His Passion still continues in the patient endurance and offering of their sufferings by His true followers. I saw, too, how many graces are trodden under foot in the mire. I came out of these visions calm and strengthened."

9. Dedication of the Church of St. Saviour at Rome.

" I was in Rome. I saw a very beautiful church, lately finished, delivered into the Pope's hands by the architect, a man clad in ancient style and wearing round his neck a golden chain and collar. The Pope praised the work, but the architect replied boastingly that he could have built it much better had he wished.—Now, they took him at his word and refused him his pay, since he had not made the church as beautiful and magnificent as he could have done. He had, as he himself acknowledged, neglected such and such a piece of sculpturing which would have greatly embellished it. The architect exclaimed : ' O had I only been silent,' and he laid his finger on his lips—' they would have accepted my work as perfect !'—Then he was taken into custody and not released until he had improved his work and sculptured his own likeness on the wall, his finger on his lips. He wrote to the Pope, saying that he would perfect his share in the material construction when the latter would have perfected his own part in its spiritual edification, denouncing at the same time numerous points of ecclesiastical discipline and fraternal charity which greatly disfigured the Church. 'The exterior,' said he, 'needs not to be more perfect than the interior.' On the receipt of this letter the Pope set him at liberty, in accordance with the precept: 'Do not to others what you would not have others do to you.'—Then the church was consecrated with magnificent ceremonies, and I saw an indescribably beautiful church full of saints and angels high up above it in the air. In it was reproduced, but with far more perfection and elegance, all that went on in the church below; for instance, its heavenly choirs responded to all that was chanted in the earthly procession. During this procession, I was suddenly called away to a person dying in a hospital. I had to go over a road covered with snow, and I was afraid that by my footprints it would be discovered that I was barefoot; but on my return I found all traces effaced.— I went again into the new church and stood high upon a wall where I could see the Blessed Sacrament borne processionally in a ciborium. Above it floated a banner of light, and over that again a resplendent Host surrounded by dazzling glory. As It neared me, this supernatural Host flew toward me; but I did not receive It, I only adored It. At the same moment, I saw the consecration of the church going on, and heard the responses sung by the celestial choirs above.—I went up to it and assisted at the celebration of the Feast of St. Martin. I saw many circumstances of his life as also of his death, and the wonderful propagation of his spiritual

influence. This was represented by bands of light streaming from the church which he held in his hand. From their
extremities sprang forth other churches which likewise propagated the faith and bore similar fruits.

"Then my guide took me up to the top of the spiritual
church which appeared to increase in size until, finally, it
became a tower full of luminous, transparent sculpturing.
From it he showed me the earth spread out like a map.
I saw and recognized all the countries in which I have so
often been. I saw the Ganges and spots where lay piles of
sparkling precious stones, and I thought of those stolen from
the tomb of the Three Kings. Deep down in the sea, I saw
treasures of precious things, merchandise, chests, and even
whole ships. And I saw, also, the different parts of the world.
My guide pointed out Europe and, showing me a little sandy
patch in it, he uttered these remarkable words: 'Behold
hostile Prussia!'—then, pointing further north, he said:
'See mischief-making Moscovy!'"

10. Sufferings for the Church (May–June, 1821). St. Cunegundes.

Sister Emmerich's assistance was about this time
requested for an Ursuline nun, suffering from acute
rheumatism. "I was by her," she said. "I saw her
illness, and I suggested to her not to ask for a cure, but for
what would be most pleasing to God. She will be relieved,
but she will not entirely recover." Sister Emmerich's
prayer for this invalid was, as usual, a real physical participation in her sufferings as may be inferred from the
Pilgrim's notes of May 29th :—

"Sister Emmerich's malady is greatly aggravated. During the night, she vomited a whitish liquid and endured
sharp pains in her head and members, accompanied by re-

tention, burning thirst, and inability to drink. She looks like one in death agony. She can with extreme difficulty and only at long intervals pronounce a few words; but her soul is in peace. She is constantly in vision, laboring in a poor, neglected church. About noon she appeared to be dying. She lay stiff and cold, unable to ask assistance. Fortunately, her sister happened to approach her bed and, seeing her condition, raised her up, otherwise she would have strangled from the vomiting which came on suddenly. After this she again lay for awhile like one dead when she sat up suddenly without effort or support, joined her hands, and so remained for about six minutes in an attitude of earnest prayer. ' Ah! I have rested and thanked God for my difficult task !' She exclaimed, ' O that broom I used was a very heavy one !' Her words came slowly, but her breathing was easier, though at intervals her pains were still very intense. They lasted for about five minutes at a time, her feet trembling so violently as to shake the chair on which they rested. They are like so many sharp bones wrapped in bandages; a mere touch on them produces a quivering that communicates itself to the lower limbs. Her labor was not yet finished, as she said. When her confessor exhorted her to patience, she replied: 'Patience hovers yonder in a globe !' and fell again into her former suffering state."

May 30th—" Her vomitings have ceased; but there has come upon her so acute an ear-ache that she hides her head under the pillows to avoid hearing the least sound."

May 31st—" The headache and ear-ache lasted all night. They have become almost unendurable, nearly depriving her of consciousness. Her condition is pitiable."

June 1st—The Pilgrim found her this morning serene and singularly joyous, the pain in her head abated, though she could scarcely hear. "I have had," she said, "indescribable visions on the state of the Church both in general and particular. I saw the Church Militant under the symbol of a city like the Heavenly Jerusalem, though it was still on earth. In it were streets, palaces, and gardens through which I wandered and saw processions composed entirely of Bishops. I recognized the interior state of each. I saw their thoughts issuing from their mouths under the form of pictures. Their religious transgressions were represented by external deformity : for instance, there were some whose head seemed to be only a misty cloud ; others had a head, but a heart, a body of dark vapor ; others were lame or paralytic ; others sleeping or reeling. Once I saw a mitre floating in the air and a hand out of a dark cloud trying repeatedly, but vainly, to seize it. Under the mitre I beheld many persons not unknown to me, bearing on their shoulders amid tears and lamentations, crosses of all kinds— among them walked myself. I think I saw almost all the Bishops in the world, but only a very few were perfectly sound. I saw the Holy Father very prayerful and God-fearing, his figure perfect, though worn out by old age and manifold sufferings, his head sunk on his breast as if in sleep. He often fainted away and seemed to be dying. I often saw him supported by apparitions during his prayer, and then his head was upright. When it sank upon his breast, then were the minds of many turned quickly here and there ; that is, viewing things in a worldly light. When the hand out of the cloud tried to seize the mitre, I saw the Church of our country in a miserable state to which the learned young school-master had especially contributed. Protestantism was in the ascendancy and religion was falling to utter decay. I saw the majority of the clergy, dazzled by the false show of the young fellow, furthering the work of de-

struction, and one in particular taking part in it through
vanity and ignorance. He will see his error only when it will
be too late to retrieve it. The misery under him will be
great. Many simple-minded, enlightened men, and especially the school-master, are praying for the removal of this
pastor. I saw, at the most, only four ecclesiastics in the
whole country steadfast and faithful. These visions were
so frightful that I came near crying out. I see in the future
religion falling so low that it will be practised only here and
there in farm-houses and in families protected by God
during the horrors of war.

"I had another singular vision. St. Cunegundes brought
me a crown and a little piece of pure gold in which I
could see myself. She said : 'I have made thee this crown,
but the right side" (where Sister Emmerich's great pain
was) "is not quite finished. Thou must complete it with
this gold. I made thee this crown because thou didst
place a precious stone in my crown even before thou wert
born '—and then she pointed to a stone or pearl in one side
of her crown so dazzlingly bright that one could scarcely
look at it—and this I had put there! I thought that really
laughable, and so I said right out : ' How can this be ? It
would indeed be strange had I done that before my birth !
To which the saint replied that all my labors and sufferings,
as well as those of all mankind, were already portioned out
and divided among my ancestors ; and she showed me pictures of Jesus working in the person of David, our own
fall in Adam, of the good we do already existing in our ancestors, though obscurely, etc. She showed me my origin
on my mother's side (she was named Hillers) up through
several generations to her own ancestors where a thread
appeared connecting them. She explained to me how I
had put the jewel in the crown. I understood it all in

vision, but now I cannot explain it. It was as if the
property of patient suffering which sprang from the thread
of life connected with my existence, had been communicated to her ; and thus I, or something of mine in her had
gained a victory which was represented by the jewel in
her crown.—In the beginning of the vision I saw her in a
heavenly sphere or garden in company with kings and
princes. I saw the Emperor Henry, her holy spouse, in
a sphere. He appeared fresh and younger than she, as if
she had existed there a longer time in the persons of
her ancestors. But this I cannot explain, indeed I did not
understand it at the time, and so I let it alone.—There was,
above all, in this vision something unspeakably disengaged
from the conditions of time ; for, although wondering to find
that I had even before my birth labored at a pearl in Cunegundes's crown, yet it seemed very natural. I felt that
I had lived in her time—yes, that I was even anterior to
her, and I felt myself present to myself even in my earliest
origin.—St. Cunegundes showed me on her left her extraction according to the flesh and on the right her descendants
according to the spirit, for she had had no children. Her
spiritual posterity was very rich, very fruitful. I saw her
ancestors as well as my own far, far back to people who
were not Christians. Among them I saw some who had
received a merciful judgment. This astonished me, since
it is written : ' Whoever believes not and is not baptized
shall not enter into the kingdom of heaven.' But St.
Cunegundes explained it thus : ' They loved God as far as
they knew Him and their neighbor as themselves. They
knew nothing of Christianity, they were as if in a dark
pit into which light never penetrated. But they were such
as would have been perfect Christians had they known
Christ, consequently, they found mercy in His sight.'—

I had a vision of my being before my birth or that of my forefathers, not like one genealogical tree, but like numerous branches spread over all the earth and in all sorts of places. I saw rays extending from one to another which, after uniting in multiplied beams, branched out again in different directions. I saw many pious members among my ancestors, some high, some low. I saw a whole branch of them on an island; they were wealthy and owned large ships, but I know not where it was. I saw very many things in this vision. I received many clear lights upon the importance of transmitting to the world a pure posterity and of maintaining pure, or of purifying in ourselves that which our ancestors have handed down to us. I understood it to refer both to spiritual and to natural posterity.

"I saw, too, my father's parents. His mother was named Rensing. She was the daughter of a rich farmer. She was avaricious and, during the "Seven Years' War," she buried her money near our house. I knew almost the exact spot. It will be found long after my death when the house will have passed into other hands. I knew this long ago, even when a child.

June 2d—The Pilgrim found Sister Emmerich very much agitated. With agonizing tears she recounted the following: "I have had a frightful night! A cat came to my bed and sprang at my hand. I caught it by the hind legs, held it out of the bed, and tried to kill it; but it escaped from me and fled. I was wide awake, I saw everything. I saw the child lying asleep there disturbed, and I was afraid she would see what was going on. The whole night until three o'clock did the enemy under a horrible, black figure, maltreat me. He struck me, dragged me out of bed, hurled me forward with the pillows, and squeezed me terribly. He kicked me before him, threw the pillows on me, and tossed me up in the air to my indescribable anguish. I saw clearly it was no dream, and I did all I could think of to drive him away. I took my holy relics and the cross, but in vain. I implored God and His saints to say whether I were in sin or not, whether I had any ill-gotten goods; but I received no answer. I adjured the enemy in the name of all that is sacred, to say what power he had over me; but he answered not and went on tormenting me, grasping me by the neck and back with his icy cold hands, or claws. At last I crept to the wardrobe at the foot of my bed, took from it my confessor's stole which is kept there, and threw it about my neck. Then the devil touched me no more, and he even answered my questions. He always speaks with astonishing assurance and artfulness. I am sometimes tempted to think he is right in what he says, so confident does he appear. He reproached me with the failure of many of his designs saying that I did him great wrong. He said this with an injured air as if his rights were the best in the world. When I asked God if I possessed anything badly acquired, the enemy answered: 'Thou hast something of mine,' but I replied: ' From thee have I sin accursed along with thyself from the beginning! Jesus Christ has satisfied for us! Take sin for thy own portion, keep it, go off with it into the abyss of hell!' No words can say all that I endured!" and here she wept, trembling in every limb.

June 3d—"The violent pains in her head have decreased, though she still suffers in one ear, which has become so deaf that she raises her voice in speaking. 'St. Cunegundes,' she says, 'was with me a long time last night. During the last few days I have learned an infinity of things from her, chiefly concerning our origin and our participation in another life. I have

seen innumerable histories and details of our ancestors. To-
day she told me that, like myself, she had been freed from
her youth from all temptations of the flesh and had early
vowed herself to God. She did not dare to tell her mother;
but she informed her husband, who made with her the vow
of chastity. And yet, she was afterward subjected to frightful calumnies and sharp trials. I did not see last night the
cause of her subjection to the fiery ordeal, but I had already
seen it.—She was too good to one of her servants who also
had endured much from false accusations.—I saw her death
and that of her husband. The latter was interred in a
church he had built and dedicated to St. Peter (at Bamberg). I do not know whether it was in this church or in
another that Cunegundes in magnificent imperial robes assisted at a service for her husband. After it was over, in
the presence of five Bishops, she laid aside her crown and
royal attire for the humble habit of a religious, like that of
Sister Walburga, and covered her head with a veil. The
people who had witnessed her pompous entrance, were
moved to tears on seeing her leave the church in her lowly
garb. A few days before her death, her angel told her
that her husband would come for her at the last moment.
I beheld him doing so with crowds of souls, the poor
whom they had fed and others to whom they had done good.
I understood that they were their spiritual children. Her
husband presented them to her as the fruit of their union.' "

June 4th—"The invalid still suffers from ear-ache and
partial deafness. The pain is very acute, and she understands how truly it is the symbol of the finely-wrought
jewel that completed St. Cunegundes's crown."

June 5th—"The ear-ache continues, though at intervals
it is relieved by the confessor's imposition of hands. At such
moments, he feels sharp pains in his hand as if they had

been pricked by thorns.　Sister Emmerich knows well why this suffering was imposed upon her, and also that it was symbolized by the crown that St. Cunegundes gave her to finish.　And yet, what is very remarkable, she constantly speaks of inflammation and of deafness.　She even begs the physician for remedies which he prescribes, but which after all she does not use."

June 6th—" Sister Emmerich declares that this ear-ache will continue till Pentecost.—' God wants this labor,' she says. ' He will make use of it, there lies the secret.　St. Cunegundes is connected with me by a secret tie existing between those that from infancy have been freed from the concupiscence of the flesh.　It is impossible to explain this to the impure world. It is a secret of an unknown nature. I am, moreover, related to the saint through our ancestors.'"

June 8th—" Her deafness and pain still continue, and last night the tempter again appeared to her under the form of an angel.　He told her that, as Dean Overberg came not to her, it would be well for her to turn to *him* for he could help her.　But she, raising her heart to God, recognized Satan and boldly put him to flight."

June 9th—" As Sister Emmerich had predicted, the ear-ache left her to-day, though slight deafness still remains. She says she has finished and offered to God the crown given her by St. Cunegundes to complete.　The saint, moreover, showed her for whom the task was performed.—' I have seen an influential Protestant who has some idea of returning to the Church.　He would, indeed, be very useful to it, for even now he does much for the Catholics, though secretly.　He is known to the Pope.　My suffering will purchase his crown if he conquers human respect and follows the dictates of conscience.—By my labor united to the merits of Christ, the crown has been finished for him."

11. PENTECOST.—THE MOUNTAIN OF THE PROPHETS.

"I have seen as usual the Feast of Pentecost, and many pictures of the communication of the Holy Spirit throughout the whole world, also the twelve new Apostles and their connection with the Church. I saw from several parishes which received the Holy Ghost, a spiritual church formed, symbolical of the infusion of new life into the Church Militant, and I also saw numerous individuals receiving the Holy Spirit.

" Last night I made a long journey, chiefly to the Mountain of the Prophets and Paradise in its vicinity. All was as usual on the mountain, the man under the tent writing and arranging books and rolls of parchment, erasing many things, and burning others. I saw him giving leaves to doves which flew away with them. I had also a vision of the Holy Ghost, a winged figure in a triangle surrounded by bands of light of seven different colors which spread over the spiritual Church floating below and over all in communication with her. In this vision I felt that the effusion of the Holy Ghost exercises an influence over all nature. I stood above the earth near the Mountain of the Prophets and saw the waters that fall from it spread out like a transparent, many-colored veil above the earth, and I saw all sorts of things shining through it. One color sprang from another and produced a different effect.

When the veil is rent, the rain descends. These effusions take place at certain seasons commemorative of the saints and their victories. The feast of a saint is his true harvest-day. On it he dispenses his gifts as a tree does its fruits. What souls do not receive in this out-pouring of spiritual gifts falls upon the earth as rain and dew; in this way, does a superabundance of rain become a chastisement from God. I often see wicked people in fertile places nourished by the fruits of the earth, and good men in sterile regions receiving into their own souls the gifts of the Holy Spirit. Were man and the earth in perfect harmony, there would be Paradise here below. Prayer governs the weather, and the days marked in the old weather-tables are the days on which such distributions are made. When it says: 'If it rain on the third day of Pentecost, the harvest will not be gathered dry,' may mean, if the spiritual gifts poured out on mankind at Pentecost are received by them only in small measure, they will be changed into rain which will fall upon them as a chastisement. I see the life of nature intimately connected with that of the soul.

"Wind is something wonderful. I often see a storm bearing sickness from a far-off land; it looks like a globe full of evil spirits. Violent winds affect me painfully. I have always had a horror of them. And from my very childhood, shooting stars have been hateful to me; for wherever they fall, the air is full of bad spirits. When as a child I watched the rising and setting of the sun, I used to hail it as a creature endued with life. I thought: 'He weeps over the numerous sins he is forced to witness!' Moonlight would be agreeable to me on account of the peaceful silence, were it not that I know the sins it covers and its powerful influence over man's sensual nature; for the moon is more deeply enervating than the sun."

12. JUDITH IN AFRICA.

"I was with Judith in the Mountains of the Moon, and I saw many changes there. The ravine and bridge leading to her castle have disappeared as if an earth-slip had filled up the former. A level road now leads to the house.

Judith looked much older. She seems to be much nearer to Christianity, if not really a Christian in heart. I do not think she has yet been baptized ; but, were a priest at hand, it might be done immediately. In the room in which I once saw her taking coffee with several others stood something like a little altar ; above it was the picture of an infant in a manger, below which was a cavity in the altar, cut out like a basin, in which lay a small spoon and a white bone or stone knife. Lamps burned around and near by were desks with rolls of writings. Judith knelt there in prayer with many younger than herself and an old man, her assistant. All seemed to be suddenly convinced that the Messiah was already come ; but I saw as yet no cross. In the upper room in which were the old busts, the aged Jews were still assembled.—The treasure in the cellar was greatly diminished, for Judith gave much to the poor. Her abode is very wonderful ! Her house to the west faces a deep valley beyond which rises a mountain that shines and sparkles in the sun like stars ; on the opposite side,. far away in the distance, are seen strange high towers and long buildings on the mountains. They cannot be descried from the castle, but I saw them. I saw also the people on the Ganges. Their church is in beautiful order, and they have among them an old priest, a missionary, I think."

13. Sufferings for Five Bishoprics of the Upper-Rhine.

March, 1820.—" I passed through Frankfort (1) and saw in a large house not far from a great church, a society assembled for deliberation on evil projects ; among them

(1) Precisely at this moment the ecclesiastic and the lay delegates of the petty German States were convened for the second time to deliberate on the means to be adopted for the gradual extinction of Catholicity in the five dioceses.

were ecclesiastics, and devils were crouching under the chairs. . . . . . I went again to the large house at whose entrance lay sleeping, under the form of a black dog with red eyes, Satan himself. I roused him with my foot, saying : ' Up, Satan ! why sleepest thou here ?'—' I can sleep quietly here,' he replied, ' for the people inside are attending to my work.' "

Sister Emmerich saw also in a symbolical picture, the results following from this new way of establishing Churches :—" I found myself," she says, " lying in the only sound spot of a ship that was all punctured. The crew kicked and ill-treated me in many ways whilst I prayed earnestly for them that they might not fall into the deep from the sides of the vessel on which they were sitting. I saw the ship going to pieces, and I was sick unto death. At last they put me ashore where my friends were in waiting to convey me to some other place. I kept on praying that the unhappy people might also disembark ; but, scarcely had I reached the shore, before the ship capsized and to my great grief, all were lost.—There was an abundance of fruit where I was."

On Wednesday after Passion-Sunday, March 22, 1820, the Frankfort Convention held its first formal sitting to deliberate upon the means to be adopted *to seize Jesus by stealth and deliver Him to death.* Its members said : " Let it not be in daylight, lest the Pope perceive it and make opposition !" Whilst this was going on, Sister Emmerich's attention was attracted to them and she entered the lists against them. " I am bearing" she said, " an enormous weight on my right shoulder, for I am atoning by my many afflictions for the sins of others. I am almost sinking and my visions on the state of mankind, particularly of the clergy, are so sad that I cannot help taking still heavier

burdens upon myself (1).   I prayed God to touch the hard
hearts of His enemies that, during these Paschal Feasts,
they may return to better dispositions.   I begged to suffer
for the most hardened or for those for whom He knows it to be
most necessary.   Then I felt myself suddenly raised and
suspended in the air in a shining vessel.   There passed
through me a shower of keen, indefinable pains, which have
not yet ceased, and the oppression in my left side increased.
When I looked below me, I saw distinctly through a dark
veil the manifold errors, wanderings, and sins of mankind,
their stupidity and wickedness in acting against truth
and reason.— I saw pictures of all kinds.   Again I saw
the miserable old ship full of popular, self sufficient men,
sail by me on the stormy waves, and I waited to see it go
down at any moment.   I recognized some priests among the
crew, and with all my heart I offered my sufferings to bring
them to repentance.   Below I saw crowds of gray figures
moving sadly to and fro in certain places, in old cemeteries
long since forgotten.   Again I saw souls wandering alone
in solitary places either where they themselves had perished,
or where they had taken the life of others—I do not now
remember which, but I think their detention there had
something to do with the expiation of the crime.   I begged
for fresh sufferings that thus I might obtain relief and
pardon for them.—When I cast my eyes upward I saw, in
contrast to the abominations below, a heavenly sight so
beautiful as almost to dazzle me : the saints, the angels, and
the throne of the Most Holy Trinity.   I beheld Our Saviour
offering all His sufferings in detail to His Heavenly Father

(1) Once she said : " I see so many ecclesiastics under the ban of excommunication !
But they seem quite at their ease, almost unconscious of their state ; and yet, all who
join associations, take part in enterprises, or adhere to opinions condemned by the
Church, are really excommunicated by that fact itself.   I see such men hemmed in, as
it were, by a wall of fog.   By this we may clearly see what account God makes of the
decrees, orders, and prohibitions of the Head of the Church and how rigorously He
exacts their observance, whilst men coolly mock and scoff at them.

for us, Mary renewing the offering of her sorrows through
Jesus, and all the saints offering their merits and prayers
in like manner. It was a vision in which variety and unity,
action and repose, supreme magnificence, love, and peace
were inexpressibly blended. As I continued to gaze upon
it, I perceived all at once that I was lying in one side of a
pair of scales, for I saw the needle and beam above me. In
the other scale, hanging in darkness, lay God's most hardened enemies, around them many others seated on the rim,
as they had been on the sides of the ship. As at the sight
I redoubled my patience and my prayers, as my pains also
increased, the scale rose a very little; but it was too heavy
and most of the men fell off. All, however, for whom I had
given my sufferings as a counter-balance were saved. Above
me I saw heaven and the efficacious merits of Jesus, and I
rejoiced that with God's grace I had been able to gain
something by my pains.—These men are hard as rocks;
they fall from sin to sin, each more grievous than the last."

The cunning with which these plotters sought to hide
their intrigues was shown to Sister Emmerich under the
form of the tempter :

" After my examen," she says, " I was saluting the
Wounds of Jesus, when I suddenly fell into the greatest
mental agony. An ecclesiastic appeared before me saying that he had just returned from Rome with all sorts of
sacred objects for me ; but I felt intense repugnance both
for him and his gifts. He showed me all sorts of little
crosses and stars, but not one of them was perfect; all were
crooked and deformed. He told me in many words that he
had spoken of me to the Holy Father, that I had not a
suitable confessor, etc. His words were so plausible that,
although I still felt aversion for him, I thought : 'Perhaps I judge him too severely !'—I again examined his sin-

gular-looking sacred objects, remarking, with the hope that
he would not be offended, that I too had recently received
holy things from Rome and Jerusalem, though not indeed
artistically made ; but that his articles seemed to have been
picked up from some abominable old pit or tomb—whereupon, he asked how I could have so bad an opinion of an
innocent man.   I wanted no further parley with him, and
so I said : ' I have God and the relics of the saints ; I have
no need of thee !' and I turned away from him, when he instantly disappeared.   I was bathed in perspiration, I trembled in every limb, and I begged God not to subject me
again to such agony.—Some days later Satan again approached me, under the form of a priest.   He cunningly tried
to excite all sorts of scruples in my mind, saying principally
that I meddled too much in outside affairs, etc. ; but I soon
discovered him when he said that he met me everywhere,
that I gave him no peace."

The evil plottings, which kept the episcopal sees so long
vacant, were shown Sister Emmerich in a touching vision
of which, however, her terrible sufferings permitted her to
communicate only a part.   " In a journey to the Nuptial
House, I came to a cabin by a field where awaited a
bridegroom the coming of his bride.   The field belonged to the apostates.   Near by stood a large house
in which I found a very good bride.   She accompanied me,
apparently right well pleased.   Her brother, also, came
with us, but there was something singular about him (1)
and he turned back when we had gone only half-way.   I
took the bride to the bridegroom in the cabin.   He received her lovingly and joyfully, presenting her tempting refreshments apparently of a spiritual nature.   The bride
gave him her hand and appeared truly good, but she still

(1) The secular power.

put off the marriage and made some excuse to withdraw. The bridegroom, greatly distressed, looked after her tenderly, resolving to wait for her, to take no other in her place. I felt so sorry for him. I gave him some money I happened to have about me, which he accepted.—I felt that he was the Heavenly Bridegroom; that the bride was His flock; and that the money I gave Him was the prayer and labor which I offered as security for her. Ah! if the bride had seen the Bridegroom! Had she seen how He gazed and sighed after her, how He waited for her, she could not have left Him with such indifference! What has He not done for her! How easy has He not made things for her! And yet she abandons Him!"

The foregoing vision was repeated under various forms every time Sister Emmerich was commanded to pray for the appointment of Bishops to the vacant sees. In November, beginning with the Feast of St. Martin, she performed an eight days' labor for this end during which the spiritual nuptials were constantly before her. "I saw," she said, "a most beautiful and holy bride. I with four others was her bridemaid. The bridegroom was a dark, gloomy man. He had five groomsmen, and they drank all day long. In the evening, however, there appeared another bridegroom who put the dark one out-of-doors, saying: 'This bride is far too noble and holy for thee!' I spent these days in continual contemplation. I saw the bridal house as a church, and the bride so beautiful and holy that one could not approach her without fear and respect."

A FALSE ASPIRANT TO THE HAND OF THE BRIDE IS PUT OUT OF THE VINEYARD OF THE CHURCH.

One day Sister Emmerich was in a pitiable state. Her right arm and shoulder were paralyzed; profuse perspira-

tion flowed so copiously from her head and breast as to soak
the bed on which she lay ; and she was tormented by incessant attacks of whooping-cough which, she said, was to
last for six hours. At intervals she swooned away from the
violence of her sufferings. She afterward related the following : " I found lately at the Nuptial House hedges of wal-
nut-trees outside the choir of the church where there used
to be beautiful vines, and just behind the main altar was a
high nut-hedge full of ripe nuts. I saw a distinguished
ecclesiastic wearing a cross, (something like a Vicar-General) who went to the hedge with a nut-cracker in his hand.
I saw it distinctly. He cracked and ate numbers of nuts,
after which he hid the shells and went into the church. I
felt the great impropriety of his entering the church after
eating the nuts, for the act of cracking nuts is a symbol of
treachery and discord. He was from the unhappy house
connected by an outer staircase with the Nuptial House.
In it were assembled all who entered not by the true gate ;
but he was driven from the church. He was the cause of
my profuse perspiration, the sharp pain in my shoulder,
and the paralysis of my right side. Seeing him after he
had been chased away standing before a wall unable to advance or to go back, I grasped him by the shoulders and
drew him with incredible difficulty to the top of the wall.
I was told just to let him drop down on the other side. But
I saw that he would be dashed to pieces, and so with great
fatigue I carried him down and dragged him into a region
quite new to me. Here I met first a great river, then a
lake on whose banks stands a city (Constance). Around
lay towns and villages. As I carried my heavy load across
the lake, invisible hands placed under my feet two narrow
planks, one after the other, which as I stepped on them
rose and sank alternately. It was a difficult passage, but

I accomplished it. Before me arose high mountains.—I have more than once seen this ecclesiastic (Wessenberg) in the Nuptial House. He is a worldly man to whom the Protestants are as well inclined as he is to them. He will help them as far as he can. He intruded himself into his high position by all sorts of artful means, signified by the nut-cracker; he is strongly opposed to the Pope and he has many adherents. I prayed very much for the Church and the Holy Father, and then I was commissioned to perform this task. It would be well if this man could without scandal come to some terms with his partisans. The Protestants would thereby receive a severe blow, for they are continually exciting and defending him. They are getting the upper hand; but they will lose much, if this unworthy priest does not succeed."

The invalid was at this time continually engaged in repelling the attacks of the enemies of the Church; consequently, her state was most distressing. The Pilgrim writes: "She is sick, very sick, but quite supernaturally so! Her state is one of constant change: sometimes drenched with icy death-sweats; again radiant as if in full health; and shortly after falling from one swoon to another. But she rejoices in having already accomplished a great part of the task undertaken. When her sufferings become quite intolerable, she is so consoled and rejoiced by some beautiful vision that she often laughs with joy; for example, when sinking under her pains, St. Benedict appeared and said pleasantly to her: 'Ah! thou art always stumbling although so old!—' and St. Joseph took her to a beautiful meadow full of flowers, telling her to walk on them without bruising them. This feat, possible only to the Child Jesus, she could not accomplish, whereupon St. Joseph said: 'Now thou seest thou dost not belong here!'—There was shown her a rich treasure of pearls; viz., lost graces, which she by her sufferings was to gather up and pay off the debt of those who had squandered them. Her weakening, death-like sweats she offers for the poor souls whom she beholds hourly becoming brighter, and who thank her for the relief her charity affords them.—Again she saw the fatal intrigues of the false suitor in the Nuptial House. 'I met few ecclesiastics there according to my liking,' she said. 'I had to cook for them, that is, prepare spiritual nourishment for them. Many sat at table, and I saw him whom I had to drag so far enter and boldly seat himself with his five followers. I had prepared three dishes; but when I set them on the table, the insolent fellow cried out scornfully : " The Pope has given us a fine cook, indeed! now we'll get nothing but gray pease !"'"

In Easter week, 1820, Sister Emmerich had another vision in which was shown her the immense evil this man and his supporters would do the Church, as also the fatal consequences of the Frankfort convention :—"I saw," she said, "a field (1) full of people and hard by a circular building with a gray cupola like a new church. In it were some learned men, and such crowds were flocking into it that I wondered how it could contain them all ; it looked like the influx of a whole nation ! Then the air all around grew darker and darker. A black vapor filled the church and poured out of its windows spreading over meadows, fields, and parishes, till the whole country, far and wide, was changed to a bleak, wild moor. Then I saw numbers of well-meaning persons pressing toward one side of the

---

(1) The green field, or meadow, signifies the festivals of the Church, the ecclesiastical year, the communion of the faithful from which the friends and abettors of the " *new lights*" wished not to separate, despite their incredulity, their revolt against legitimate authority. Like the Jansenists, they directed their destructive darts against the Church from her very bosom ; therefore it was that, though in the meadow, they stood apart. They erected a church in the Church, spreading therein the night of unbelief, the horrors of spiritual death.

field where light and verdure were still to be found.—I cannot describe the dark, the frightful, the deadly influence of
this scene: fields withered, trees blasted, gardens
blighted, darkness spreading everywhere as far as the eye
could see, and encircling the country as if with a black chain.
I know not what became of the people in the church. They
seemed to be consumed with it (1) as it grew blacker and
blacker like a mountain of coal, and peeled off frightfully.
—I went afterward with three angels into a green enclosure about as large as the cemetery outside Dülmen, and it
appeared to me that I was laid on a high bench. I know
not whether I was dead or alive, but I was habited in a
long white robe. The greatest of the three angels said to
me: 'Thank God! it will now be fresh and light here!'
and then there fell between the black church and me a glittering shower of pearls and precious stones like a rain from
heaven. One of my three companions ordered me to gather
them up (2) and then left me. I know not whether all went
or not. I only remember that, in my anxiety about the
black church, I had not the courage to gather up the precious stones. When the angél returned, he asked me if
I had gathered them, and on my answering no, he bade
me to do so at once. I dragged around, and picked up
three little stones like crystals with ground edges that lay
all in a row, one blue, another light red, and the third white,
glittering, and transparent. I took them to my little companions who ran to and fro, rubbing them against one another until the loveliest colors and rays of light flashed
around, renewing the vegetation and bringing forth light
and life. Then on the other side, I saw the dark church
crumbling to pieces. Suddenly a great multitude streamed

(1) Depriving them of the life of grace by the destruction of faith and the Christian
life springing from it.

(2) The merits of her prayers and sufferings which arrest the progress of decay.

out of it into the bright green fields, and wended their way
to a luminous city. Behind the black church all remained
dark as night."

The following vision, though chiefly upon the ravages
made in the Church by the infidelity of Sister Emmerich's
own day, comprehends many other things and embraces
seven periods of time. This was indicated to her; but her
sufferings prevented her, unfortunately, from specifying
these periods or saying which among the events would be
realized in her own lifetime, or which would take place only
after her demise.

"I saw the earth's surface covered with darkness and
obscurity, all creation, trees and shrubs, plants and flowers,
withering and dying. The waters seemed to have flowed
back to their sources, brooks, fountains, rivers, and seas to
have returned to the waters above the firmament around
Paradise. I wandered over the desolate earth. I saw the
rivers like fine threads; the seas like black abysses with
here and there a tiny stream; and, wallowing in the slime,
lay huge animals struggling with death. I went so far that
I could distinctly see the shore on which St. Clement was
drowned. Mankind was in a sad state of confusion and, as
the earth became more arid and desolate, the deeds of darkness increased. I saw in detail many abominations. I recognized Rome, and I beheld the oppression of the Church,
as also her internal and external decadence. Then I saw
immense troops marching from various quarters to a certain
place near which was a great black spot like an enormous
abyss into which numbers of the troops seemed to fall, unnoticed by their companions. Again I saw in the midst of
these disasters the twelve new Apostles laboring in different countries, unknown to one another, each receiving
streams of living water from on high. They all did the

same work. They knew not whence they received their tasks; but as soon as one was finished, another was ready for them. They were twelve in number, not one over forty years; three were priests, and others aspired to that dignity. I have often met one of them; he is either known to me or he is near me. They were not dressed alike, but each according to the custom of his country and the fashion of his time. They received from God all the graces squandered by others; they did good everywhere; they were all Catholics.—Among the dark destroyers, I saw false prophets and people who labored against the writings of the twelve new Apostles. I often beheld the latter disappear in the tumult to reappear again, however, more courageous, more dauntless than ever. I saw also about a hundred women prophesying as if in rapture. By them were men who mesmerized them. They filled me with loathing and horror and, as I thought I beheld among them the clairvoyant of Münster, I reflected that, at all events, the *Father* would not be with her(1).—Whilst the ranks of the combatants around the dark abyss became thinner and thinner until a whole city (2) had disappeared, the twelve Apostles constantly gained new followers, and from the other city (Rome, the true city of God) there issued, as it were, a luminous wedge which pierced the dark disc. Above the little church stood a majestic lady in a flowing sky-blue mantle, a crown of stars on her head. From her streamed out light into the deep darkness. Wherever it penetrated, all things revived and flourished. In a large city I saw *a church once the smallest become the greatest* (3). The new Apostles entered into the light, and I thought I saw myself with

(1) See Vol. 1.

(2) The false church with its followers.

(3) The little church of Notre-Dame des Victoires, Paris, in which the Arch-confraternity of the Most Holy and Immaculate Heart of Mary took its rise.

others whom I recognized, in the first rank"—(that is, with others who like herself had contributed to the renewal of life).

" Now all is again flourishing. I saw a new, very resolute Pope, and the black abyss gradually closing until the opening was so small that a water-pail could cover it. Lastly, I saw again three troops or parishes uniting in the light under holy, enlightened men, and entering into the Church. The waters again gushed forth ; all was renewed, all was living and flourishing, churches and convents were rebuilt.— Whilst that frightful drought prevailed, I was taken over a verdant meadow full of those lovely white flowers I once had to gather, and I came to a thorn-hedge on which I scratched myself badly in the dark; but it also was full of buds and I pressed through joyously."

April 12, 1820.—" I have had another vision on the great tribulation everywhere reigning. It seemed as if something were exacted of the clergy, something that could not be granted. I saw many aged priests, some of them Franciscans, and one, in particular, a very old man, weeping bitterly and mingling their tears with those of others younger than themselves. I saw others, tepid souls, willingly acceding to conditions hurtful to religion. The old faithful in their distress submitted to the interdict and closed their churches. Numbers of their parishioners joined them; and so, two parties were formed, a good and a bad one."

As the supporters of the " new lights," the Illuminati, especially hated the devotion of the Rosary, the value of this popular form of prayer was shown Sister Emmerich in a very significant vision " I saw Mary's Rosary with all its mysteries. A pious hermit had thus honored the Mother of God, weaving in his childlike faith a garland of leaves and flowers for her ; and, as he understood their significa-

tion, his garlands were always profoundly symbolical. He
begged the Blessed Virgin to obtain for him some favor
from her Son, whereupon she gave him the Rosary." Then
Sister Emmerich described this Rosary ; but after the vision was over, neither she nor the Pilgrim could clearly repeat
what had been seen and heard. It seems that the Rosary
was surrounded by three rows of different colored notched
leaves, on which were represented in transparent figures all
the mysteries of the Church from both the Old and the New
Testament. In the centre of the Rosary stood Mary with
the Child surrounded by angels and virgins, hand in hand,
their colors and attributes expressive of the various mysteries. Sister Emmerich described each bead, beginning with
the coral cross on which is said the Creed. The cross
grew out of a fruit like the apple of the forbidden tree ;
it was carved, it had certain determinate colors, and it was
full of little nails. On it was the figure of a youth, in his
hand a vine which sprang from the cross, and sitting on
the vine were other figures eating the grapes. The beads
were joined by colored, spiral rays, like roots, each possessing some natural and mystical signification. Every Our
Father was enclosed in a wreath of leaves from whose centre sprang a flower in which was portrayed one of Mary's
joys or sorrows. The Hail Maries were stars of precious
stones on which were cut scenes from the lives of the patriarchs and Mary's ancestors relating to the Incarnation and
Redemption. Thus does the Rosary comprehend heaven
and earth, God and nature and history and the restoration of all things through the Redeemer born of Mary.
Every figure and color in its essential signification was
employed for the perfecting of this divine master-piece.
This Rosary, though inexpressibly profound in signification
was described by the invalid with deep feeling and child-

like simplicity. With trembling joy she went from leaf to leaf, from figure to figure, describing all with the eager and joyous readiness of a lively child. "This is the Rosary," she said, "that the Mother of God gave to man as the devotion dearest to her; but few have said it in this way! Mary also showed it to St. Dominic; but, in course of time, it became from neglect and disuse so soiled and sullied with dust that she covered it with her veil as with a cloud, through which, however, it still glimmers. Only by special grace, by great piety and simplicity can it now be understood. It is veiled and far away—only practice and meditation can bring it near!"

During the whole octave of Corpus Christi, 1821, Sister Emmerich had visions upon the state of devotion to the Blessed Sacrament throughout Germany, the sight of which drew from her tears and sighs of bitter grief. If, as she said, there were some portions of the country in a less lamentable condition than others, it was where that most august Sacrament was not altogether forgotten, where It was sometimes exposed for public veneration, sometimes borne in procession. Those districts which had fallen more or less under the influence of the new regime, *liberty, love, and toleration,* appeared under the form of a vineyard, withering and dying before the progress of *the lights.* In them she had to labor diligently, clearing and weeding until her hands were torn and bleeding. In December, though weighed down by all kinds of sufferings, she could not forbear asking Almighty God to send her still fresh ones; for the mental anguish she endured at the sight of the coldness, neglect, and irreverence offered the Blessed Sacrament was greater than any physical pain could be. Her prayer was heard but only on condition of her confessor's permission, that the merit of obedience might be added to that of suffering and supply the strength necessary for its patient endurance. The Pilgrim writes, Dec. 12, 1821, in the octave of the Immaculate Conception of Mary: "For several days, Sister Emmerich has had continual cramps, convulsive cough, spitting of blood. She swoons, she is perfectly prostrate, but her visions on the dangers threatening the faith are never interrupted. 'I must suffer it!' she exclaims in ecstasy, 'I have taken it upon myself, but I hope to be able to bear it!'—Once she seemed about to spring from her bed :—'I must find my confessor, I must ask his permission, I must open another fountain in the Heart of Jesus! It has already five sources, but they have been wholly obstructed by the sins of men. Alas! they permit not those fountains to flow upon them! I am to do it. I am to begin a new task, although my present one is not yet finished! I must get my confessor's permission!'—The confessor was absent, and Sister Emmerich several times repeated her petition to be allowed to open the obstructed sources." The Pilgrim at first thought her delirious, but he soon reported the following: "Her condition becomes more and more critical and inexplicable—torture, weakness, vomiting, bloody sweats, cramps, burning thirst, inability to drink, temptations to impatience and struggles against it."

Dec. 13th—"Sister Emmerich lies to-day in a state altogether different from that of the last few days—painful paralysis of her members accompanied with acute rheumatism. A touch brings forth a groan, and still she had to be raised to a sitting posture several times during the night, on account of sharp pains of retention. She is too weak to explain the connection between her sufferings and her spiritual labors." That afternoon as the Pilgrim and confessor sat in the adjoining room, they were not a little startled on seeing the invalid suddenly leave her bed, approach them with a firm step, and kneel before the latter, her hands joined, saying : ' Give me a blessing ! I need it for a certain person,' Father Limberg blessed her and, though looking like a skeleton, she returned to her bed as briskly as one in perfect health. At such moments her slightest motions are singularly striking and impressive ; she seems wholly unconscious of her movements. Like the turning of a flower to the light, they appear to be involuntary and they excite surprise in the beholder. After a short silence, she exclaimed: "They are strewing the road with rose leaves—some one must be coming!" and then she was shown how the sources of grace in the Sacred Heart were cut off from many souls of good-will by the suppression of devotional exercises, by the closing and profanation of churches. In reparation for the same, she was directed to make special exercises in honor of the Divine Heart. "Great periods of suffering," she said, "begin with visions of roses and flowers scattered over me ; they signify my different pains. When I was seized with rheumatism, I saw a pyramid of sharp thorns covered with roses. I groaned with fright at the thought of climbing it." Once she uttered these prophetic words : " I see the enemies of the Blessed Sacrament who close the churches and prevent Its adoration, rushing to their own destruction! They fall sick, they die without priest or Sacrament !"

From Quasimodo until the third Sunday after Easter, 1820, Sister Emmerich's state became so aggravated in consequence of the attacks made by Wessenberg and his party on the celibacy of the clergy and the scandals arising from the same, that her friends, though long accustomed to such scenes, could scarcely bear the sight of it.

Still, however, her physical pains were perhaps even more endurable to the poor invalid than were the ill-advised efforts to relieve her and the disturbance occasioned her little household. The Pilgrim's brother, Christian Brentano, was in Dülmen at the time and, finding a noisy game of nine-pins going on just beneath Sister Emmerich's window one day, he resolved to have her removed to a more retired neighborhood. For this end he sought to gain Father Limberg and Dr. Wesener's approval, hoping to win through the latter the consent of the old Abbé Lambert, then sick and confined to his bed. But the old priest, weighed down by infirmity and desirous of ending his days in peace, would by no means consent to the change. " Full of sadness," as the Pilgrim says, he dragged himself to the invalid's bedside and protested against a removal. Sister Emmerich, anxious and annoyed by the repetition of such scenes, fell into a most deplorable state. Then it was that all concerned urged the use of various ineffectual remedies. They forgot the supernatural character of her sufferings which, had they been other than they were, must have ended in death. In view of this irritating com-motion, we may readily understand the effort it cost the poor invalid to preserve her patience unruffled and the earnestness with which she longed for Dean Overberg's presence to lull the storm. The Pilgrim gives us the follow-ing details : —

April 15th—" I found Sister Emmerich quite unable to speak from excessive pain. She had lain all night unable to stir on account of the violent suffering in her left side. She could neither stretch out her hand to the tumbler at her side, nor move her feet from the bottle of hot water that had been placed in her bed ; and thus she spent the night, abandoning herself to the mercy of God. When her confessor visited her next morning, he ordered the dreaded brandy lotions, which only served to aggravate her misery."

April 16th—" The pains in the wound of her side are excruciating. They began by a vision on St. Thomas's incredulity. To-day, Sunday, as she was contemplating a scene from the Gospel, the wound bled and she felt that with every breath she drew the air blew through it. To prevent this she laid her hand over the wound. The retention from which she suffers is very severe. To crown all, there is a game of ninepins going on under her window. A friend is endeavoring to persuade her to change her lodgings."

April 17th—" Her pains increase ; she is all swollen, and the retention is so sharp as sometimes to deprive her of consciousness. She lies like a corpse, like one who had died from starvation. Sometimes her hunger for the Blessed Sacrament becomes intolerable ; her heart burns with desire, whilst her hands are icy cold.'

April 18th—" Her condition is truly pitiable! Father Limberg begged the Parish-priest of Haltern to come and give her his benediction, which he did apparently to her relief. This evening a brandy lotion was again prescribed, to which the poor invalid submitted with a groan. I have brought it upon myself!' she said, 'I have prayed for expiatory sufferings, and now the fire must burn out. I abandon all to God !' "

April 19th—' The whole night she lay consumed by fever and not allowed to drink for fear of retention. The Parish-priest of Haltern again prayed over and relieved her. When the Pilgrim visited her in the afternoon, he found her lying on the foot of the bed, her limbs gathered up ; she was groaning with agony, and her fever was high. The pain seems now to be centred in the left side of the

vertebral column. Although in this pitiable state, she
thanked God for all and, thinking herself in purgatory, she
rejoiced in the thought of never being able to offend Him
again."

April 20th—" Her pains still continue ; her bed is steeped with perspiration, and even Gertrude (not very easily
moved) shed tears at her sister's sufferings. The invalid
declares that, unless relieved, she must surely die ; she cannot longer support her pains. She is quite deformed. She
sent in haste for the Curé, who came at once. He prayed
and imposed hands upon her, when she instantly fell into a
gentle slumber. Afterward she said in allusion to this
crisis : 'I begged God earnestly to forgive me if I had
asked for sufferings beyond my strength, to pity me for
the sake of His Son's Precious Blood, and to help me
to do His holy will, if I can still be of any service on this
earth. I felt sure that, had I died this time, I should, in
some measure, have been guilty of my own death and
that I should have had to do penance in purgatory. As I
received no other answer than : " The fire thou thyself hast
lighted must burn to the end !"—I became discouraged, for
I saw myself in a very precarious state. I recommended
my affairs to God, since I should have to leave them behind me in disorder. When the Cure prayed and imposed
hands upon me, it seemed as if a gentle stream of light
passed through me. I fell asleep feeling that I was again a
little child being rocked to rest. A luminous ray rested upon
me which vanished when he withdrew his hand ; but I was
relieved, I was again full of courage ! "

Toward noon, Sister Emmerich had another attack
which the old Abbé Lambert relieved by the imposition of
hands and the recital of the Rosary. The Pilgrim put into
her hand the crusts that had fallen from her stigmata.

She smiled with a surprised air, and said : " There is a poor sick person in a most pitiable condition ! The Curé of Haltern must know her ! There she lies over there ! She is much worse off than I, but she is patient ! Ah ! she is in great danger, but the Curé has helped her. I cannot bear to see her suffering so ; it makes me worse ! I shall pray for her. She must have been shown me for my humiliation, for she is far better, far more patient than I, though much more suffering !"—and here the Pilgrim removed the crusts.

April 21st—"She appears better to-day. St. Walburga and Madeline von Hadamar have appeared and consoled her. She is in continual contemplation.'

April 22d—"Her pains are not so severe, but she is so weak as to be hardly able to speak. Her confessor told her to-day : 'You are averse to brandy lotions, yet I know they are good for the stomach and back.'"

April 23d—Second Sunday after Easter : " At the Abbé Lambert and Gertrude's request, the mistress of the house made Sister Emmerich a small cup of chicken broth without seasoning ; for, as they said, she would never get strong without nourishment. The poor invalid patiently yielded to their united solicitations, but no sooner had she done so than her stomach revolted and she lay until evening in a state calculated to draw tears from the beholders. Fever, chills, cramps, and total insensibility succeeded one another in rapid succession ; at last, the doctor pronounced mortification as having set in, and her death was momentarily expected. But after some time, she suddenly opened her eyes and said smilingly : 'I am no longer ill, I have no pain !' The confessor ordered her to go to sleep which, however, her burning fever prevented, and she replied in a deprecating tone : 'I want to, but I cannot,' and she be-

gan in a low voice to make tender acts of love to God.
'What do you want with the saints?' asked Father Limberg. 'Go to sleep! Fine obedience!' Again she replied:
'Ah! I want to, but I cannot!' At last she fell into
ecstasy, her whole body becoming rigid with no sign of
pulsation excepting under the touch of the priest's fingers
(1). The fever also left her."

April 24th—" The doctor and the confessor are anxious
about the invalid. They fear mortification. She herself
asks for Extreme Unction and begs them to send for Dean
Overberg. They delay, however, giving her Holy Communion, as they expect the Vicar-General this evening
and desire him to perform that office for her."

The Vicar-General came not, and Sister Emmerich lay
for hours without assistance; but God took compassion
on His faithful servant. The Pilgrim reports under date
of April 26th—"The invalid, who seemed to be in agony,
suddenly arose to a sitting posture, her hands joined, her
countenance radiant with youth and health and wearing an
expression of the tenderest piety; thus she remained for a
few minutes, made a motion as if swallowing, and then
sank back on her pillows entirely changed. Gaily and
with childlike simplicity she exclaimed: 'O I have obtained something! I have been so long begging at that magnificent table and, at last, I received a crumb which has en-·
tirely restored my strength. I am entirely changed! All
is well, all is in the hands of God. I have abandoned all to
Him, I am perfectly relieved! Something like a dark vapor
went out from me and floated upward.—It may stay away;
I don't want it!' Next day, she said: 'Although in contemplation, I saw what was going on around me, what was

---

(1) " This pulsation," says Brentano, " is a witness of the highest importance rendered by nature to the Church; but it is incomprehensible! Unfortunately, we do
not attach to it its proper value."

being done to assist me, to arrange things as is customary in this lower world. It struck me as being so very ridiculous that I had to laugh, though I was in such pain.'"

April 27th—"She was very weak this morning. When she received through the Pilgrim the announcement of Dean Overberg's inability to come just then she wept, but soon regained her composure and related a vision she had had the night before: 'I was a child again. I was home, sick unto death, and all alone, father and mother absent. But ever so many of the neighbors' children, those of the mayor and others, came in and waited on me, and were so sweet and kind! They got green branches, (it was in May) stuck them in the ground, and made a little hut. They carried leaves to it and made a bed for me. Then they brought me the most wonderful playthings, more beautiful than I could ever have dreamed of: dolls, cribs, animals, cooking utensils, little angels—and I played with them until morning. At times I feel as if some of them were still lying around.— I wept much this afternoon, and once I pressed the Mother of God right to my heart, saying over and over again: " Thou art my mother, my only mother!" and that did me good.'"

How often the poor sufferer had to struggle against the frightful evil that attacked the celibacy of the clergy may be seen by the following vision of August 16, 1821:— "I was taken to a flock (*a diocese*) at one end of the field by the Nuptial House (that is, a diocese surrounded by Protestant sects). Among the sheep were many good-for-nothing goats that injured them with their horns. I was ordered to drive them out, a task which proved both troublesome and difficult, as I knew not how to tell the good from the bad. Then appeared St. Stanislaus Kostka who helped me. First, I went to the banks of a swift, broad stream and called all the goats together. The saint told me that the worthless ones were those with long, stiff hairs behind their ears and on the nape of the neck. I seized seven such animals and cast them into the cold waters which swept them off."

August 19th—"I have had a frightful night! I was nailed, crucified by the world, the flesh, and the devil, and I had to struggle with an enormous ram; but I conquered him! I bent his horns over his neck, broke them, and laid them crosswise on his back. 'Thou, also, shalt bear the cross!' I said." In a subsequent vision the fruit of her sufferings was shown her: "I saw a number of young ecclesiastics in a seminary assembled for a repast and, as I came from a higher sphere, I had many things to provide for them. I collected all in various places, though not without great fatigue. All sorts of cripples and beggars helped me and also the souls of many deceased persons. My companions in religion were to assist me, but I had first to light them out of a dark cave (1). Reverend Mother remarked to them how wonderful it was that I should have been commissioned to lead them to such a task. I had to distribute a dozen sugar-loaves made by myself. I had to drag the sugar-cane from a great distance and put it through the necessary processes. I distributed eleven; the twelfth I laid aside for the poor. But Sister Eswig made such a fuss about it, saying that I had put it away for myself, that I replied: 'Very well! I shall divide it. But let every one give me back a part of hers for my trouble!' and so, I got more than I had at first.—This vision was very extended. I saw the revival of the priesthood and religious Orders after a period of great decadence. I saw too by what prayers, labors, and holy souls this will be brought about after my death. It seemed as if a band of pious workmen arose from

(1) Purgatory.

whom these good results were to emanate. The gifts bestowed upon the clergy were very varied ; each received what he most needed   There appeared to be very peculiar plants and flowers among them.   From the ecclesiastics the best were chosen."

Again we find Sister Emmerich's labors directed to the good of ecclesiastical seminaries, as the following vision shows :—

May, 1821.—"I was in a long hall, on either side of which at their desks were young men in long robes like seminarists ; passing up and down among them was a tall man.   I was in one corner.   All at once, the young men turned into horses and the tall man into an immense cud-chewing ox.   The horses showed their teeth behind him and made all sorts of mocking grimaces.   I was wishing the ox would show them his horns and make them behave, but all he did was to butt the wall every time he came to the end of the hall.   There was a hole in it already, and I thought the building would soon come down on top of us. I knew not how to get out when, all at once, one of the horses left his place to go to another.   I perceived a door behind the seat he had vacated, and by it I made my escape."

On the evening of Jan. 15, 1822, Sister Emmerich vomited blood freely, and then suddenly exclaimed : "Ah ! a pious, parish-priest has just died in Rome of old age ! I received the general absolution with him ! His soul went straight to purgatory, but he will very soon be released.   We must pray for him.   He was greatly attached to the Pope dur-ing whose captivity he did much good in secret.   The Pope himself has not long to live."   And again she said : "That good old priest was one of the twelve unknown Apostles whom I always see supporting the Church and of whom I have often spoken.   He is the second that has died.

There are now only ten ; but I see others growing up. He was a friend and counsellor of the Holy Father, but he would never give up his parish for a higher position."

19. CORONATION OF A POPE.

January 27, 1822, Feast of St. Paul's Conversion (Münster). Sister Emmerich suddenly fell into ecstasy during which she prayed fervently. That evening she said to the Pilgrim: "There has been a thanksgiving feast in the spiritual church. It was filled with glory, and a magnificent throne stood in the middle of it. Paul, Augustine, and other *converted* saints figured conspicuously. It was a feast in the Church Triumphant, a thanksgiving for a great, though still future grace, something like a future consecration. It referred to the conversion of a man whom I saw of slight figure and tolerably young, who was one day to be Pope. I saw him below in the church among other pious men ; he had been connected with the good old priest whose death I saw the other day in Rome. I saw many Christians returning to the bosom of the Church, entering through the walls. That Pope will be strict, he will remove from him lukewarm, tepid Bishops—but it will be a long time before this happens.—All whose prayers have been instrumental in obtaining this grace were present in the church. I saw also those men eminent in prayer whom I so often see. The young man was already in Orders and it seemed as if he were receiving some new dignity. He is not Roman, though an Italian from a place not far from Rome. I think he is of a pious noble family. He travels sometimes. But before his time there will be many struggles.—It was an indescribably beautiful and joyous festival, and I was so happy ! The church is still there—I want to go back to it !—" and at these words she relapsed into ecstasy, during which she rose in her bed to pray until ordered by her confessor to lie down.

Sister Emmerich spent the fall of 1822 in continual labors for the Church in Germany. She made nightly journeys to Rome ; averted dangers from couriers, whose dispatches robbers and assassins were lying in wait to seize ; assisted the sick and leprous whom she found on the road, and took charge of their disgusting packages; protected brides from false bridegrooms, that is opposed the illegitimate occupation of certain episcopal sees ; and all this she did with so much fatigue, with corporal sufferings so intense, as to be able to give very little account of them. The following vision, however, distinctly points to the object of these journeys ; viz., the ecclesiastical affairs of the Upper-Rhine province. Just at this epoch strenuous efforts were being made to gain the Holy See to renounce all right to certain bishoprics and to recognize as lawful incumbents men who had formally ratified an engagement with their patrons to betray the Catholic faith and to ignore for the future the laws and jurisdiction of the Church. Sister Emmerich was the instrument employed by God to oppose these iniquitous projects:—

Oct. 22, 1822.—"I was on my way to Rome, when I found a singular-looking child on a heath by the roadside. It seemed to be only one day old. It lay in the centre of a dark globe which looked like fog, but which in reality was formed of thousands of twisted threads proceeding from the most distant regions. I had to pierce this web to get at the child which I found closely enveloped in a beautiful little cloak with a large scalloped cape. I felt something under the cloak fastened to the child's back. I tried, though in vain, to remove it, for I suspected that it was nothing good, when this child of a day began to laugh ! I shrank from it unable to account for its mirth. I now know what it meant. The authors of the trick doubted not of its success. They had wrapped it (the book) up with the gentle child in order to have it secretly conveyed to Rome. I do not now remember to whom I confided the child, but I think it was to a secular. I saw many whom I knew exulting over my taking the child, for there are in Rome even among the prelates many whose sentiments are not Catholic, and who had connived at the success of the scheme. I saw in Germany among worldly-wise ecclesiastics, and *enlightened* Protestants, plans formed for the blending of religious creeds, the suppression of Papal authority, the appointment of more superiors, the diminishing of expenses and the number of ecclesiastics, etc., which projects found abettors in many of the Roman prelates. (I have often seen that C. C—is not of much account) (1). He does much harm, he hates his father; but he is so mixed up in affairs that they cannot get rid of him. He is perfectly entangled by the secret society, that wide-spread association which works more quickly and still more superficially than even the Freemasons."

The child in the globe of fog typifies the plan conceived for the suppression of Catholicity enveloped, as in a cloak, by beautiful figures of rhetoric ; the fog signifies imposture which works in the dark ; the laughing of the child, the premature triumph of the plotters (men devoted to the pleasures of the table) at having outwitted the Sovereign Pontiff despite his protests and briefs ! The book under the mantle represents the writings forwarded to Rome in favor of the projects. They were on their way, indeed, but they were incapable of preventing the discovery and defeat of the plot. Sister Emmerich saw the same wicked designers hunting up the decisions of

(1) (Ich habe oft gesehen, das C. C. nichts taugt, etc.)

the early Councils, on which occasion Pope Gelasius was shown her as opposing the Manicheans, prototypes of the modern *Illuminati.* The intention of annihilating the Pope and his authority really existed, as the Church-Councillor Werkmeister, the most active and influential of the sect, openly and cynically boasted. This man, once a monk at Neresheim, then a Church-Councillor at Stuttgard, boldly arrogated to himself the glory of having incontestably demonstrated that "The Papacy could and ought to be rooted out," setting forth, for the benefit of the secular powers, the surest means of attaining that end, a means which was afterward literally adopted by the Frankfort Assembly of which we have made mention (1). Whilst these agents of the evil one seemed to grow stronger day by day in numbers and influence; whilst flattering themselves that they had even smoothed the way in Rome for the success of their plans, the prayers and sufferings of the poor stigmatisée of Dülmen arrested their work of destruction. She so courageously resisted the enemies of God, besieging Him with prayers so ardent that, in a short time, she was able to say: " God ordained that the Holy Father should be ill at this moment, whereby he escaped the snare laid for him. The enemy has long been maturing his plans; but they will not succeed, they have been discovered. I had many visions on this head, but I only recall the following: I beheld the only daughter of the King of kings attacked and persecuted. She wept bitterly over the quantity of blood shed (2), and cast her eyes on a race of valiant virgins (3) who were to combat at her side. I had much to do with her. I begged her to remember my

(1) Plan for the Re-organization of the Catholic Church in the Germanic Confederation." Published in German, 1816.
(2) The numberless souls lost.
(3) Chaste priests, defenders of her rights.

country, as well as certain others that I named, and I petitioned for some of her treasures for the clergy. She responded: ' Yes; it is true that I have great treasures, but they tread them under foot.' She wore a sky-blue robe.— Then my guide exhorted me anew to pray and, as far as I could, to incite others to pray for sinners and especially for erring priests. ' Very evil times are coming,' he said. ' The non-Catholics will mislead many. They will use every possible means to entice them from the Church, and great disturbances will follow.'—I had then another vision in which I saw the King's daughter armed for the struggle. Multitudes contributed to this with prayers, good works, all sorts of labors and self-victories which passed from hand to hand up to heaven where each was wrought, according to its kind, into a piece of armor for the virgin-warrior. The perfect adjustment of the various pieces was most remarkable, as also their wonderful signification. She was armed from head to foot. I knew many of those who contributed the armor, and I saw with surprise that whole institutions and great and learned people furnished nothing. The contribution was made chiefly by the poor and lowly.—And now I saw the battle. The enemies' ranks were by far the more numerous ; but the little body of the faithful cut down whole rows of them. The armed virgin stood off on a hill. I ran to her, pleading for my country and those other places for which I had to pray. She was armed singularly, but significantly, with helmet, shield, and coat of mail, and the soldiers were like those of our own day. The battle was terrible ; only a handful of victorious champions survived !"

20. A DIOCESE SEPARATED FROM THE ROCK OF PETER.

"I saw a church sailing on the waters and in great danger of sinking, for it had no foundation ; it rolled **on the**

sea like a ship. With mighty efforts I had to help to restore its balance, and we sent many people into it, chiefly
children, stationing them around on the beams and planks
(1). In the three aisles of the church lay twelve men
prostrate and motionless in fervent prayer, and there were
crowds of children at the entrance prostrate before an altar. I saw no Pope, but a Bishop prostrate before the High
Altar. In this vision I saw the church bombarded by other
vessels, but we hung wet cloths before it and it received
no damage. It was threatened on all sides; it seemed
as if its enemies wanted to hinder its landing. When by
the help of extra weight it was again righted, it sank a
little in the sand. Then we laid down planks to the shore.
Instantly all sorts of bad ecclesiastics ran in with others,
who had given no assistance in time of need, (2) and began to mock the twelve men whom they found in prayer
and to box their ears; but the latter were silent and went
on praying.—Then we brought great stones which we
stuck all around for a foundation which began to increase
as if it were growing of itself. The stones came to
gether, and it seemed as if a rock sprang up and all
became solid. Crowds of people, among them some strangers, entered by the door, and the church was again on
land."

This vision lasted several nights and was accompanied by hard labor. Once Sr. Emmerich, still in ecstasy,
uttered the following words: "They want to take from the
shepherd his own pasture grounds! They want to fill his
place with one who will hand all over to the enemy!"—
Then she shook her hand indignantly, crying out: "O ye

(1) A symbol of the future. This church, tossed to and fro and about to be engulfed
by the waves, was to find by degrees a more solid foundation on the rock of Peter.
(2) The old liberal party who, when they could do so without danger or fatigue
sought to possess themselves of the rights of others,

German cheats! (1) Wait awhile! You will not succeed! The Shepherd stands upon a rock! O ye priests! You stir not, ye sleep, and the sheepfold is everywhere on fire! You do nothing! O how you will bewail this some day! If you had said only one *Our Father!* The whole night have I seen the enemies of the Lord Jesus drag Him around and maltreat him upon Calvary! I see so many traitors! They cannot bear to hear said: 'Things are going badly!'—All is well with them if only they can shine before the world!"

April, 1823.—" I almost killed myself working last night. I am full of pains! First, I had to drag a great man into the church. He had tried to prevent my adoring the Blessed Sacrament in a spiritual church and had seized me by the shoulders. When I caught him he resisted; but I held him firmly by the hands and, not being able to free himself, he dragged me backwards on my knees. At last, after much struggling, I succeeded in bringing him before the altar. The house from which he had come (the Nuptial House) was on fire, which it seems he himself had kindled. With infinite trouble, I had to save everything, to carry all to the sheep-fold. The fire had already mounted to the roof and there was no human being to help me, although I saw many priests, whom I knew, walking leisurely around. At last an ecclesiastic approached with one who looked like a lawyer, and they helped me. We rescued from all corners of the house chests, boxes, mantles, candlesticks, and church chandeliers, and took them to the sheep-fold. I worked myself to death!—As the flames darted out through the roof, the priest rushed in and snatched up *a son,* (2) *a child* from one

(1) The so-called German *patriots* who were opposed to the Latin tongue as the language of the Church. They sought to establish a national German Church, without God, without the Sacraments, without the Pope.

(2) The *son, the child* , viz., the plot to establish certain relations with the Greek schism. Sister Emmerich saw this *son* go to Russia.

of the rooms that he whom I had dragged into the church had tried to kill, but which was still alive. The servants slept over that room; but, fortunately, they were saved. The smoke and fumes soon cleared away. We three saved all."

Sister Emmerich about this period was also engaged in the conversion of N——— whom she saw surrounded by a fog, cut off by a wall of separation as if under the ban of excommunication. She begged God to cure him corporally and spiritually. " His condition is somewhat improved; his long illness has been a grace from God, and his sentiments on many points are quite changed. It is as if he died and came to life again an altered man. He confessed many things to the Holy Father, accused himself of many things, gave up all, died to all, and then lived again. I saw him lying on his bed surrounded by high Church dignitaries, and once too the Pope was by him. Around lay writings, many of which he gave up. They spoke, they questioned, and I often saw him raising his hand as if affirming something; perhaps he could no longer speak distinctly, but I know not for certain. He seemed to be declaring that he disengaged himself from everything, that he gave up everything. The Pope was with him alone for some time, perhaps hearing his confession. I know not, but he used his hand as before and I think he put his arm around the Pope's neck.—I know not whether he was merely embracing him, or bidding him adieu, or whether the Holy Father was forgiving him something.—Then the latter went out. Among the papers that N——— gave to the Pope was one in particular relating to our Church. It was not perfectly conformable to the Holy Father's sentiments; indeed he even seemed not to have had any previous knowledge of it. It is well that events fell out thus!

Affairs will now take a turn quite different from that which the enemy expected. N——— wept as did also the Pope and all the assistants. It looked as if they were taking leave of him.

"I have had much to do for the Church of this country, and I am now undergoing a frightful martyrdom! I am passing through horrible states! I have to work for the whole Church, I am quite bewildered by the disorder and distress I see all around and by my own pains and labors. I have had a vision on the fatal condition of students of the present day. I saw them going through the streets of Munster and Bonn with bundles of serpents in their hands. They drew them through their mouth, and sucked their heads, and I heard these words: '*These are philosopical serpents!*'—I have often seen that the simple, pious old schoolmasters, who are generally ignored as ignorant, form children to piety; whilst the skilful masters and mistresses put nothing into their heads because, by their pride and self-sufficiency, they deprive their labor of its fruit and, so to speak, consume it themselves. It is the same as with the blessing attached to good works which, when done in public or through motives of policy, have little efficacy.— Where charity and simplicity are wanting, there is no secret success. I saw many pastors cherishing dangerous ideas against the Church. Full of sadness, I turned my eyes away and prayed for Bishops; for if they become better, their priests will soon follow their example. I saw among other things that the house whence I had dragged that man, was the Church under N———. In all the rooms lay his children (that is, *his plans*) a full collection of his views. My dragging him to the altar signified his conversion, his confession. He had set fire to the house, and I with others had to save the goods and convey them to the sheep-fold.

"They built a large, singular, extravagant church which was to embrace all creeds with equal rights : Evangelicals, Catholics, and all denominations, a true communion of the unholy with one shepherd and one flock. There was to be a Pope, a salaried Pope, without possessions. All was made ready, many things finished ; but, in place of an altar, were only abomination and desolation. Such was the new church to be, and it was for it that he had set fire to the old one ; but God designed otherwise. He died with confession and satisfaction—and he lived again !"

Here the Pilgrim remarks : " Her state makes me shudder ! Her communications have ceased. She has been told that for the next fourteen days, that is until Pentecost, she will continue to suffer for the Church."

In the fall of 1823, Sister Emmerich related what follows: " I saw the Pope when he fell (1). Some persons had just left him. He had risen from his chair to reach something when he fell.—I could not believe that he was really dead. I felt that he was still governing, that all went on by his orders. I saw him lying dead, and yet I thought him still acting. Pius was constantly in prayer, always communing with God, and he often had divine illuminations; he was very sweet and condescending. Leo XII. cannot yet pray like Pius VII., but he has a resolute will.

" On the Feast of the Assumption I saw many things concerning N——. The Pope and some Cardinals seemed to be exhorting him to keep his promise and to devote himself in earnest to the good of the Church. N——— had in childhood learned from his mother a short invocation in honor of Mary. He frequently repeated it morning and evening, and so obtained Mary's intercession with Jesus. I saw her warning him and sending him grace to amend."

(1) Pius VII. died Aug. 20, 1823, of a fracture of the hip occasioned by a fall.

November.—"These last days, I had to urge a man employed in St. Peter's, at Rome, to make known to the Pope that he is a Free-mason. He did so with the excuse, however, that he was only a treasurer, that he saw no harm in it, and that he did not want to lose his place. But the Pope gravely represented to him that he must either resign the office immediately, or give up his employment in the church. I heard the whole interview."

With the month of January, 1823, began the spiritual task of collecting and distributing materials for sacerdotal ornaments whilst, at the same time, Sister Emmerich commenced to prepare her Christmas gifts for poor children. Her work was repeatedly delayed by the want of some indispensable article, by the awkwardness of an unskilful assistant, or by violent pains in her eyes. She had a thousand temptations to impatience ; but she overcame all, she triumphed by prayer and perseverance. She says : "I made a journey to Cyprus," (and here she accompanied Our Lord in His travels). "As I left the continent, I saw Marseilles on my right, and only once did I pass over a point of land. My guide and I moved along by the shore. I had various tasks to perform on the way : things to arrange, secret packages and letters which I carried under my arm, to deliver, often with great risk ; obstacles to surmount ; people to admonish in prayer ; sleepers to awaken, the wounded to bandage ; robbers and other evil-doers to disturb ; prisoners to console ; those in danger to warn ; and, for several days, I had to urge a man who was the bearer of a letter which, like that of Urias, contained instructions to those to whom it was addressed to make away with him. It was on this side of Rome. I whispered to him : 'Where are you going ? You are on the wrong road !'—'No,' said he. 'Here is the address on my letter.'—'Open it,' I said,

' there you will see.'—He did so, read the plot laid for him, and fled.

" Then I had an immense labor on all kinds of ecclesiastical vestments in the house I had seen on fire last spring. I had to make an alb for a Bishop whom I saw in the distance; but I had not wherewith to finish it, and so I asked alms from everybody. Dean Overberg said he could give only a groschen, and that mortified me. I had to make that alb because I must soon die. . . . Again, in Switzerland I had to beg materials for surplices. I rolled them into a large bundle and dragged it to Rome where they were to be made up.

" I was in Rome, in the midst of an assembly of ecclesiastics presided over by the Pope. There was question of re-establishing or organizing something, but the resources for it had been squandered. The ecclesiastics were for letting the affair drop, saying: ' Nothing can be made of nothing ;' but the Holy Father was for going on with it. Then I interposed : ' A good undertaking ought not to be abandoned. If there is nothing, God will supply.' The Pope told me that I had a good deal of courage for a nun, but that I was right.

" Again I went to Rome, and I was very much vexed to find a quantity of church linen that had been washed in the time of the last Pope and which had been hanging there ever since. I myself had made and brought many pieces. Much of it had never been used but had lain neglected, laces, ribands, borders torn off, even great holes in them. The ivory crucifixes I had taken there were now minus the figures, only the crosses and marble stands remained. On one they had even hung a little brass figure. In the midst of this wash, walked all sorts of distinguished ecclesiastics taking great notice of the school-examination and First-Communion dresses, and other unimportant articles, but paying no attention to the church linen which hung in such disorder. I was indignant at seeing five disgraceful chemises of costly and extravagant style conspicuous among the church linen. I was indignant, for they looked to me indecent and less proper for a bride and bridegroom than for adulterers. The upper part was miserably made, the shoulder straps of coarse pack-cloth; but the rest was of the finest, most transparent material, trimmed elaborately with lace and open-work embroidery. These chemises were provided with a hood to blindfold the eyes, as if shame and nakedness could be hidden under this infamous veil! I was deeply afflicted at such a scandal; and, grieving over my mutilated crucifixes, I packed the things I had brought in a long basket to take them back with me. One of the ecclesiastics wanted to hinder my packing the things, but another whom I knew took my part. I saw also the deceased Abbé Lambert in the distance." (It was the eve of his feast, St. Martin's). "I asked him to help me and also why he had not yet come for me. —He laughed, shook his finger, and said: 'Did I not tell you, you were still to suffer much?' and then he turned away. I insisted on having what belonged to me, succeeded in getting the marble stands of the naked crosses, and packed up everything. I asked how those vile chemises came there. I would have loved to tear them to pieces, and I found that, in compliment to some Protestant gentlemen, they had been received and tolerated. I took one down, and then only did I discover the hood; for, at first, I thought it a collar. I was so angry that I thought: 'Wait! I'll sew your fine trimmings with cobbler's thread that people may see what is wanting to you!'—The Pope, too, was very indignant at the sight of those shameful chemises. He tore one to shreds, and I saw that several Cardinals and secular princes were quite displeased at his act."

" The five vile chemises," says the Pilgrim, " signify
the occupation of the five vacant sees by men who, instead
of forming a chaste and lawful union with their bride, the
Church, founded on faith and fidelity, rested their adul-
terous claims upon treason and perjury under the patronage of the secular powers; men whose intrinsic vileness had
to be veiled by high sounding expressions, *peace, gratitude,
toleration,* etc. The picture could hardly be more striking
both upon this point and upon those that refer to school ex-
hibitions and to the theatrical costumes worn at First Communion. Such dresses banish from the souls of many hundreds of children that piety and recollection, that reverence
and devotion so necessary for the worthy reception of their
Eucharistic God. Sister Emmerich was so much the more
affected by this vision as she knew how important, how
decisive for after-life is the child's First Communion. One
day the Pilgrim found her consoling and instructing her little
niece who was in a flood of tears because the teacher had demanded from each pupil a sketch of the Sunday sermon.
The little thing had caught nothing of it, excepting a
few words relating to the justification of the Pharisees in
their own eyes. Her aunt told her that that would be quite
sufficient. She remarked at the same time that the task imposed upon children was already the fruit of the impetus
given by the mischievous young school-master of the Nuptial
House; for the sermons and instructions were given in High
German, whilst the poor little ones understood only the
Low German patois."

21. Journeys Undertaken for Her Neighbor.

" Last night I performed a wonderful task. I was
thinking yesterday evening of the misery of those who,
living in a state of impurity, make insincere confessions,

and I prayed earnestly for all such sinners. Then came the soul of a noble lady to my bedside, begging me to pray God for the conversion of her daughter, to pray for her with extended arms because His Son had so prayed. Her daughter lay dying after having concealed her sins in eighteen confessions. Then my guide took me a long journey, first to the east, afterward toward the west. I met on my road various cases requiring assistance. There were at least ten; but I only remember three:—In a beautiful city, more Lutheran than Catholic, I was taken by my guide to the house of a widow who was ill. Just as we entered, her confessor was leaving. The lady lay surrounded by friends and acquaintances, and I stood in the background, forgetting that I was there only as a spirit, as a messenger. I looked around and felt as an insignificant person would naturally do when treated with indifference by the great ones of the world. I soon saw the lady's state.—She was a Catholic, apparently pious, for she gave large alms. But she had fallen into manifold secret disorders which she had concealed eighteen times in the confessional, thinking she could repair all by alms; her disease also she kept secret. I was quite confused and abashed before all these grand people. I heard the sick lady say laughingly to her friends, as they raised her in the bed: 'I did not tell *him* (*the priest*) such or such a thing'—and then they all laughed. They withdrew as if to let her rest. My guide now bade me remember that I had come as God's messenger, and to step forward. I drew near the bed with him and spoke to her—my words passed before her as luminous writing, one line after another. I know not whether she beheld my guide or myself, but she turned pale and swooned from fright, in which state I saw that she read even more distinctly the words that appeared before her bodily eyes. My words were these: 'You laugh, and yet you have eighteen times abused the Sacraments to your own condemnation! You have. . . . . .,' and here I rehearsed her hidden sins. — 'Eighteen times have you concealed all these in false confessions! In a few hours will you stand before the judgment-seat of God! Have pity on your own soul! Confess and repent!'—She was perfectly overcome, the cold sweat ran down her forehead! I stepped back, and she cried out to her attendants that she wanted her confessor. They expressed great surprise, as he had just left the house; but she made no reply, she was in frightful anguish. The priest was called. She confessed all with plentiful tears; received the last Sacraments, and died. I know her name, but I cannot tell it; some members of her family are still living. It is with a joyful, and yet a heartrending feeling that I perform such tasks.

"I entered a country of vast swamps and bogs over which my guide and I floated. We came to a village and went into a peasant's house, the mistress of which lay very ill. There was no priest in the neighborhood. The woman was a hypocritical adulteress who lived apart from her husband, the more readily to sin with another. I brought up her wickedness before her eyes, and told her that she must confess it to her husband and crave his pardon. This she did with many tears. Her accomplice also was forced to appear. The husband opened the door for him, and the wife declared to him earnestly that their relations with each other must cease. She did not die; she recovered.

"I went to a large city and into a house with a beautiful garden full of groves, ponds, and pavilions. The parents were living; the mother, a pious, good woman. They had a daughter, a very discreet maiden apparently, but who was in the habit of meeting her lovers secretly and by appointment in the garden. There I found her last night awaiting one of them. I stood by, begging God to come to her aid. Suddenly I saw a figure trying, but in vain, to approach her. I recognized Satan. The girl grew agitated and withdrew into a summer-house. I followed and found another figure enveloped in a mantle whom she took for her expected sweetheart. She went up to him, drew aside the cloak that concealed him, and there she saw (*and I saw also*) the figure of the Saviour covered with blood and wounds, His hands bound, the crown of thorns upon His head!—The piteous figure spoke: ' Behold to what thou hast reduced Me!' and the girl fell to the ground as if dead. I took her in my arms, told her in what crime she was living, and urged her to confess and do penance. She recovered consciousness and thinking, no doubt, that I was a servant or perhaps some stranger who had come across her, she moaned plaintively : ' O if I were only in the house ! My father would kill me if he found me here !'—Then I told her that, if she would promise to confess and do penance, I would help her to regain her room ; otherwise, she would have to lie there until morning and steal in as best she could. She promised everything, her strength returned, and she slipped into the house as she was accustomed to do; but, when safe in her room, she again fell ill. The priest for whom she sent next morning was found by God's mercy ready to attend her. She confessed, repented sincerely, and died fortified by the Sacraments. Her parents had no suspicion of her sins.

"I saw ten such cases last night; but I am not successful in all, some will not give up their evil ways. It is horrible ! I still must weep, the devil holds them so fast !. . . . .

I have found it particularly difficult to convert ecclesiastics given to such sins.   I met some last night for whom prayer is the only hope."

November, 1820.—" I took a great journey on which I had much to do, but I only remember the following cases distinctly :—Near Paderborn, my guide took me to a house, saying: 'There is in this house a young girl immersed in frivolity. You must warn her. She will soon return from a dance. I shall give you the voice and language of a pious young neighbor and, whilst she prepares to retire, you will reproach her with her levity.'—Then I saw a picture of the girl's whole life—she was vain, giddy, fond of dress and dancing, in short, a practised flirt. And now I beheld her returning from the dance.—She went to her room without a light, and laid off her ornaments to go to bed. I drew near and said: ' It is time for you to think seriously of your life. In laying aside this toilette, abandon also your evil courses. Serve no longer the devil rather than your God who gave you body and soul, who redeemed you with His blood!' At these words, she grew angry, told me I had better go off home, what did I want there with my prattling. She needed no monitress, she knew very well what she was about, etc.—She jumped into bed without a prayer. When she had fallen asleep, my guide said :   Rouse her ! I shall show her some pictures of her life !'—I did not see the pictures, but I knew that she saw Satan, herself, and her lovers. My guide called Satan by another name, I think *the prince of this world.* I shook her. She arose trembling-ly upon her bed and, in great terror, hastily recited all the prayers she knew. I saw her run to her mother, and tell her how frightened she had been and that she would never again go to a dance. Her mother in vain tried to dissuade her from her resolution. Next morning she did as I had directed, and made a good confession of her whole life. I know for a certainty that she amended."

March 8, 1820.—" I went last night on a journey through the snow, and saw two poor travellers set upon and beaten by others with clubs. One fell dead and, as I ran to his assistance, the assassins seemed to be frightened and fled. The second was still alive. Some of his kinsmen came up and carried him to a physician's in the neighborhood. This I obtained by my prayers. I knew well that I ought not to add anything to my burden, and yet I was so anxious to suffer a part of his pains. I obtained my wish.—Then I made another long journey, and returning I again met snow. As I neared my home, I saw a poor famished man who, whilst trying to get bread for his children, had met with a serious fall. He could not extricate himself from the snow. I helped him to get free, as also to obtain food. I think we shall hear of him soon"—and, in effect, that very afternoon the Pilgrim found Sister Emmerich sick and drenched in perspiration, which state she said was to last till five o'clock. The profuse perspiration, a mixture of blood and water, had been imposed upon her for the relief of the wounded man. She said : " People may think as they please, but I know that it is God's will for me so to do, so to suffer. I have done so from my youth, I am called by Him to such works of mercy. When only four years old, I heard my mother groaning with pain at the birth of my sister. I slept with an old woman, and I began to pray to God, saying over and over : " I will take my mother's pains ! Give me my mother's pains !"

22. Journey to Palermo.

August, 1820.—" All yesterday afternoon I felt that I should have to set out somewhere. Some one called for prayers and help. and last night I had a vision. In the island south of Italy, during a period of frightful murders and robberies which happened there lately, I saw one of the ringleaders earnestly beseeching God and the Blessed Virgin to help him. He had resolved to change a life which, for too many years, had been a Godless one. He had a wife and children, but the former was among the most furious of the gang. During all his reckless life this man had worn a little picture of the Blessed Virgin painted on parchment or something similar, concealed in his coat between the button-holes. He never went without it, and he often thought of it. The picture was variegated blue and gold and quite neatly executed.—The man was a sort of subaltern over the armed insurgents. The latter wore no uniform. It seemed as if an attack was to be made before morning, for they were lying in the open air before a town. There was great misery throughout the whole country. Many good people had been murdered and many more are yet to perish in the same way, that they may not see the deluge of coming woes. The distress, rebellion, and disorder are truly frightful, and the people are very poor and superstitious. I saw that poor man in great agony of conscience unceasingly calling upon God and Mary : ' Ah ! if what religion teaches be true, then let the Blessed Virgin intercede for me that I may not die in my sins and be damned forever ! Send me help, for I know not how to free myself !'—(I had also a vision of St. Rosalia after whose feast these horrors began).—Hardly had I seen and *felt* the poor fellow's distress and anguish, than I earnestly begged God to pity him, to save him ; and instantly, without being conscious of having made a journey, I stood before him in the midst of his sleeping comrades. I cannot remember all I said to him, but only that he should rise and depart, for his place was not among them. I do not think he *saw* me ; he had only an interior perception of my presence. He left the rebels, fled to the sea, and embarked in a little sail-boat which had two cars. I went with him. We sailed rapidly and securely by the still moonlight and, in an extraordinarily short time, reached the capital of the island in which are the two little nuns who have the stigmata (Cagliari, in Sardinia). There I left him in safety. He wanted to reform, and lead a pious life unknown to the world.—I visited the nun of Cagliari who lives with a pious lady. I found her still tolerably well, praying for the cessation of those fearful calamities. I went also to see Rosa Serra in the Capuchine Convent of Ozieri. She is very old, sick, and emaciated and there is no mention made of her extraordinary graces. The nuns are good and very poor, their country at peace. On my return, I stopped at Rome and found the Holy Father in deep affliction. He had been directed in prayer to admit no one to his presence for the time being. The black church is gaining ground. There are numbers of unfortunate people ready to join it on the first sign of an outbreak. I saw the secret society from which all these plots emanate, working very actively."

23. Rescue of a French Family in Palermo.

" For several days I have had repeated visions of an affair which came to an end last night. A family was shown me in that unhappy place in which there has just been a massacre. It is a noble household, husband and wife, several grown children, and one especially attractive male servant (formerly a slave) with brown complexion and crispy hair. I was first shown how this family came to settle there. They are French. I saw them before the Revolution living piously and happily in France. They were truly good and especially devout to the Mother of God, before whose picture they burned a lamp every Saturday and said prayers in common. The slave was not then a Christian, though a good-natured, extremely active and intelligent man. He was very slight, well-proportioned, and so nimble and handy that it was a pleasure to see him serving the family. I cannot endure slow, stiff, *immovable* people! I often think that the souls of the active are more easily influenced by grace. I saw how fond the master and the whole family were of this slave and how all, by a special inspiration from God, longed for his conversion to Christianity. The gentleman and lady begged this favor of the Blessed Virgin. The slave fell sick. On the eve of the Assumption, his master took a picture of Mary to him, saying that, since he could do nothing else, he might make as lovely a garland for it as possible; that she whom it represented would sympathize with his sufferings and obtain mercy for him from God; and that he should make the garland with all the love of his heart. The servant joyfully undertook to fulfil his master's request, and skilfully twined an exquisite wreath around the picture. As he worked his heart was touched. The Mother of God appeared to him that night, cured him, told him that his garland was most pleasing to her, and that he must go to his master and ask for instructions and Baptism. The slave obeyed next morning; and his master, who had earnestly prayed for this result, was radiant with joy at the success of his pious scheme. The slave became a Christian, and his devotion to the Mother of God was very great. He twined a garland for all her festivals and, if he had no flowers, he used colored paper; he burned a light every Saturday before her picture, he was very pious. The Mother of God failed not to reward the piety of this family. They were in great danger during the Revolution. They embarked, and arrived safe in Sicily where the gentleman became very rich, the owner of magnificently furnished houses, lovely gardens and villas supported in grand style. But he was no longer as pious as he used to be. He was mixed up with all sorts of wicked undertakings, and his public office brought him into connection with the revolutionary faction. His position was such as to force him either to take part in the rebellion, or expose himself to the greatest risks; he could not draw back. Some of the old pious customs were still kept up in his family, and the light was burned on Saturdays in honor of the Mother of God. The good servant was now much better than his masters, and he wove his garlands as before. More than once I had to go to exhort the gentleman to amend his life and make his escape from the island. The first time (eve of the Assumption) I went by night to his bedside and reminded him and his wife of their pious, innocent days when, before this same feast, they had converted the sick slave through the garland in Mary's honor. This was now the anniversary of that happy day. I contrasted with it their present state. I exhorted the husband to make a garland of all his sins and evil inclinations as he had formerly done of flowers, burn it with sincere repentance before the Mother of God on her feast, and then leave the country as quickly as possible. I shook him by the arm; he awoke and aroused his wife. Both were deeply affected and related to each other the same dream. The slave had already placed the light before the picture for the feast. I had to return several times and urge the husband to depart, as it was a severe trial to them to leave their houses, their gardens, and all their wealth; but the last night I went I found them all ready to go. They took with them gold, more than sufficient for their wants, left all the rest, and embarked in a large ship for India. The gentleman chose that country, as he had heard that religion was highly prosperous on one of the islands. And so the good slave got back to his own country again. I saw shocking misery in the island they left (Sicily), the inhabitants living in mutual distrust. I saw also the wife of the man who had fled into Sardinia. She was furious enough to kill him, for it was principally owing to her that he had joined the conspirators ; but he was now thoroughly converted. He visited all the shrines in spirit on his journey, and went to confession as soon as he arrived in Sardinia. It seems strange, but I have been told that he will visit our country and I shall, perhaps, see him !"

October 14th—" I saw the family with the old Indian slave landing on the island for which they had set sail. They were well received."

September 2d—" I saw the Feast of St. Evodius, in Syracuse, and a pious man earnestly invoking the saint. He was in great anxiety respecting the troubled times and he wanted to leave the country ; but he had a large family and his wife refused her consent. I was commissioned to tell him to go. It was evening when I entered the courtyard of his house where he was walking troubled and anxious. He asked not who I was. We conversed together, and I told him he must go even without his wife; if she would not accompany him, she would follow him before long, and so he went."

October 13th—" Last night I met on the sea a vessel without oars or sails, tossed about by the tempest. It was full of refugees from Sicily. My guide gave me a blunt iron bar to push the ship forward ; but the bar kept slipping off, and so I thought it ought to have been pointed.

He told me, however, to go on pushing in spite of trouble
and fatigue, that it must be done in that way. Pointed instruments are for worldly affairs, and only too many of them
are now in use in Sicily. The ship reached land in safety."

24. A Theft Prevented.

" I was in a little town, a hundred leagues distant, and I
saw in a church a picture of Mary surrounded by silver
offerings which three men had planned to steal the following night. I recognized one of them. I had given him a
shirt just before he left home. He used to be a good young
man; it was hunger and misery that had driven him to sin.
I pitied him, but for the others I had no such feeling—
perhaps they were not Catholics, and I could not pray for
them fervently. They argued thus: ' We are starving,
the picture has need of nothing,' and so they thought they
were robbing no one. The poor parents of the one I knew
had, on bidding him adieu, recommended him to Jesus,
Mary, and Joseph, and I was now charged to dissuade him
from the robbery. They had planned to enter the church
that night through a window by a ladder. The one of
whom I speak was to keep watch whilst the others despoiled the shrine ; the whole affair was repugnant to him,
but hunger pressed. Fortunately, just at the moment for the
evil deed, a poor woman came to pray before the church.
She was the mother of a large family. Her wretched
husband had abandoned her, leaving her deeply in debt.
Her little household effects were about being seized and, in
her distress, she had recourse to the Mother of God. Her
presence frightened the unfortunate men, who put off their
design till next morning. I prayed for the poor woman"
(and here Sister Emmerich earnestly begged the Pilgrim
to unite with her in prayer for the miserable husband).

"At noon next day I saw the three comrades sauntering along and deliberating upon their projected theft, but the young man wanted to have nothing more to do with it. He said that he would rather pull up potatoes and roast them when hungry than rob the shrine. His two companions threatened to kill him if he did not join them, so he promised; but he left them, resolved to take no part in the affair. The church stands on the outskirts of the town.

"Once, years ago, I had to frighten a young man and thus prevent his committing sin. Later on, he married the person and I often had occasion to advise him and his wife. There was not much blessing on their union, and the husband was tempted to rob. More than once I saw him by night lurking around ovens, a sack on his back, with the intention of stealing bread of which he really had no need. I used to make a noise or frighten him off in some other way, and thus I had the happiness of several times preventing his thefts. One night, I saw him stealing into the house of one of my friends who had a batch of bread in his trough. I was as if spell-bound, I could not stop him. He had already filled his sack with dough when the owner, awakened by the barking of dogs, got up to strike a light. Now, if he did this the thief would be detected and his family forever disgraced, for in order to escape he would be obliged to pass the owner of the house. Not being able to prevent the theft, I sought to screen the thief that he might reform; consequently, I gathered up strength and slammed the door several times. The light went out, and the fellow escaped with his sack. Some weeks after the good man who had lost the dough, came to see me and related the whole affair. He knew not, he said, why he had not seized the thief, but he felt a sort of pity for him; perhaps, it was just as well that he had not discovered him, he could now amend, etc. He spoke very wisely. The thief's wife also came to see me and, as she reminded me that I had before her marriage preserved her from sin, I took occasion to speak to her of the facility with which one falls from small faults into great ones. She wept bitterly, for she knew of her husband's doings. Both have made restitution and corrected.—I acted thus by the direction of God."

January 22, 1820.—"I was suddenly called by an earnest prayer, and I saw on the shore across the sea an old man praying in great trouble. The country was covered with snow; there were pines and similar trees with prickly leaves growing around. The man wore a large fur coat and a rough cap trimmed with fur. He lived in a large house which stood by itself in the midst of smaller ones. I saw no church, but some buildings like schools. He seemed to be truly good. His son, who led a very disorderly life, had left the house in a violent passion, and gone to sea in a ship richly laden with silver and merchandise. The father had a presentiment of the great dangers she would encounter in a tempest and dreaded his son's being lost in his present state; therefore he began to pray, dispatched his servants in all directions with alms and requests for prayers, whilst he himself went to a wood where dwelt a holy solitary in whose intercession he placed great confidence. All this I saw across the sea; and on the stormy waves I saw the ship in ·imminent peril, tossed hither and thither by the tempest. It was an enormous ship, almost as large as a church. I saw the crew climbing and scrambling and shouting; few of them had any religion, and the son I saw was not good. Things seemed desperate. I prayed to God with all my power and, in various directions, I saw others in prayer for the same intention, especially the old man in the forest. I prayed fervently; I presented my petition to God boldly and persistently. I was, perhaps, too bold, for I received a rebuke; but I thought not of it. It seemed as if I were not to be heard; but the distress before me was heartrending. I ceased not to pray, to implore, to cry, until I beheld the ship enter a harbor in safety. The father received an interior assurance that tranquillized him, and I felt that the son would reform, for all which I thanked God. I did know the whole history of the widowed father and his son, but I have forgotten it."

July 16, 1820.—"I had to make a long journey with my guide to a city of the north where lived in a small isolated house a poor, miserable couple, seemingly farm-tenants. They were expecting to be driven from house and home and reduced to misery, though why I know not. They had confidence in me and, in their distress, they thought of me that I might intercede with God for them. Some of their children were quite young. In a distant country they had grown ones: a son, a fine young man, who travelled on business, and a daughter who seemed to be in my vicinity and pushing me on to her parents. The husband had not always been good, but he had reformed; his wife seemed older than he. *They drew me to them by prayer, I had to go to them,* and my guide ordered me to follow him. I carried something with me, what, I no longer know; it may have been real or only symbolical. I came to a steep rampart on the way over which to all appearances I could not possibly climb. I thought of the words of Jesus that faith can move mountains and, full of this truth, I set about penetrating it, when the steep mountain was levelled under my feet. I passed through the country where I had once seen the father of a family saved through prayer from a tempest which threatened his life. I saw in a mountainous district St. Hedwiges on my right, and I met other saints, patrons of the countries wherein their relics repose. It was night when I entered the cottage of the people to whom I had been called. The husband was up, roused by some noise, I think ; the wife lay in bed weeping. I no longer remember what I did for them or what I took to them, but they were relieved and consoled; the danger was passed when I left them. I was taken back by a different road more toward the west. I performed many tasks on the way ; among them I prevented a robbery."

March 2, 1822.—A large sum of money had been stolen from a poor tax-collector, a Protestant, who had in consequence lost his situation; his family were in need of the necessaries of life. The Pilgrim recommended the case to Sister Emmerich, who very willingly undertook to pray for him. Having done so several times, she remarked : " It is singular one can effect so little for such people by prayer! I see such tepid Protestants in a very strange state groping about in the dark, in a fog, perfectly blind and stupid ! They are, as it were, in the midst of a whirlwind whose gusts strip them naked. I know not whether God will help in this case or not ! "

October 16, 1820.—" In a large city with suburbs, smoke, and heaps of coal, where are many students, learned men, and Catholic churches, I saw in a public house a man who had nothing good in his intentions. He sat at table ; around him frisked a strange-looking black dog which seemed to be the devil. The man wanted to cheat the landlord and to get off without paying his bill, so he made his escape by a window whilst the latter was waiting for him at the door.—I saw him afterward in a fir-forest attacking a harmless foot-traveller who, to save his life, delivered to him a little roll of money and fled. The robber had a knife concealed at his side, and he tried to run

after the poor man to stab him in the back ; but my guide
and I obstructed his path. On whatever side he ran,
there we stood before him ; at the same time the money became so heavy that he could no longer carry it. He was
terror-stricken, his limbs trembled, and he cried out:
' Friend! Friend! wait! take back your money!' and
then he found himself free to advance. The traveller
paused. The robber ran up, restored the money, told him
all, even of his design to murder him, but that the sight of
two white figures had terrified him, and he resolved never
again to commit such a crime. He was a student and had
several accomplices whom he warned to follow his example
and amend their life. He continued his journey with the
traveller, who promised to take an interest in him."

25. Assistance in the Kingdom of Siam.

November 12, 1820.—" I went to a vast wilderness and
saw a man and woman savage and miserable, on their knees
and crying to God. I approached them and they asked
me what they should do, for that I was surely the person
who, in answer to their prayers, had been shown them in
a dream as the one who was to comfort them. I do not
remember whether I had seen their distress in vision, or
whether I learned it from themselves. They were thus
abandoned in this desert in punishment of a great crime
for which they would have had to undergo mutilation, had
not their guards in pity allowed them to escape. Their
great misery took the place of penance, but they knew
nothing of God. During their stay in the wilderness they
had prayed earnestly for instruction. Their angels had
told them in a dream that God would send them some one,
and what they were commanded that should they do. They
dwelt in a cave. A great hunt was annually held in

these parts. To avoid discovery, the outcasts covered the entrance of the cave with brush-wood and before it laid a carcass whose stench drove the sportsmen from that quarter. In conformity with an ancient tradition such places are regarded as impure, and so the poor creatures remained undiscovered. Distress and want had rendered them almost savage. I gave them such instruction and consolation as God inspired. I told them especially that the criminal connection in which they lived was an abomination in the eyes of God, that they must henceforth abstain from such intercourse until they had been instructed in the Christian faith and lawfully united. The poor creatures could scarcely understand me; compliance seemed to them very difficult. They had become like wild animals. I pointed out to them how they might reach a place in which I had seen Christianity making great progress and to which I had sent many persons from Sicily. There they could be instructed. I do not remember any more of this vision.

" I went also to that island in which the Christians are so well received by the heathen population, and there I saw many new buildings. The French gentleman from Palermo and his family were there; he had built a house for himself and was preparing another for priests. Catholic missionaries are, unhappily, but few, whilst the heterodox are numerous.

" On this journey I met in the open sea a ship in great distress; it was unable to advance, and was in danger of sinking. I saw crowds of evil spirits around it. A Sicilian family was on board, grandfather and grand-children. At the time of the pillage, they had appropriated immense treasures belonging to the Church for the erection of grand houses in the country to which they were going. This was the reason the vessel could not proceed on its course. I was commissioned to tell them that they would surely be lost unless they restored their ill-gotten goods. This they hardly knew how to do without betraying their guilt. I advised them to deposit the treasure on the shore, addressed to the rightful owners, where it would be found and taken back by some other ship.- I knew that God would take care of it. When they had done so, they were able to continue their voyage."

26. LABORS FOR CONVENTS.

August 13, 1820.—"I had to go to a distinguished ecclesiastic who allowed many very pressing affairs to lie neglected to the great detriment of all concerned. His whole interior was shown me—good judgment, humility, apparently a little exaggerated, but great negligence. I saw that once, in some business matter connected with a convent, he received letters from the Superioress which he threw among other papers and entirely forgot, thus giving rise to much confusion. I saw, too, that he took not sufficiently to heart the present state of the Church. I could hardly believe that I was to admonish so distinguished a man as he, one so humble. I looked upon it all as a dream, I was perfectly incredulous.— Then St. Thomas suddenly appeared before me and spoke against incredulity. I had several visions of him. I saw how he had doubted from the very first; but his disbelief of Christ's miracles had led him to Jesus and had ended in the conviction that made of him a disciple. I saw many other incidents of his life.—Then I was taken to the priest for whom I had to pray. He lay in a large room, reading by the light of a taper. I saw that he was anxious; his many oversights were like a weight on his heart. He arose, looked in his secretary for the long-neglected letter of the Superioress, and began to read it.

"I had, also, work to do for some future nuns. I saw
over thirty young girls conversing together in a convent.
They had not yet embraced the religious life. They seemed
to belong to three different classes : some to two institutions
still existing, devoted to the education of the young and the
care of the sick, but which were to be reformed; the others
were destined for a third not yet founded whose object
would be manual labor and education. It pained me to see
that these girls allowed so much disorder around them.
There was one among them destined to be a Superioress,
and some who wanted merely to be lay-sisters, although they
appeared to be of as good standing in society as the others.
My guide said to me : 'See! these girls are all hesitating,
they will and they will not! They say, *"This is God's will,
that is God's will, where is God's will? If it is the will of
God,"* &c.; but at the same time they are full of self-will!
They have out-doors some wild horses which thou art to
tame,' and he took me out. I saw a herd of wild horses,
symbolical of the passions of those aspirants to the religious
life, as also of some others, secular persons, who were opposed to the establishment of the convent. They were all
bound together by these passions and both parties concurred,
though in different ways, in marring the success of the undertaking. The horses were almost equal in number to those
inside. They went raging around the house, as if about to attack it.   It reminded me of the summer-time when the cattle, tormented by flies, try to run into houses. It seemed
strange that, weak as I was, I should be appointed to tame these
animals; besides I had never been accustomed to them, excepting when a little child I used to bring my father's horse to
him at daybreak. My guide said to me: 'By spiritual
means, thou must mount and tame them.' But I thought : How
could that ever be done?   He said : 'Thou canst do it and

thou wilt do it, but only by prayer and patience, by bearing
calmly and meekly what is still in store for thee ! Thou wilt
have to begin again and again.   Hast thou not so often declared thou wouldst begin anew a thousand times ?   Now,
so begin that at every instant thou mayest be ready to endure
new sufferings. Think always that as yet thou hast suffered
nothing, accomplished nothing, and thus thou wilt tame all
those horses ; for until thou hast mastered them, these young
girls will remain imperfect.   In this way also thou wilt influence all around thee.   Thou art the spiritual Superioress
of these young plants of the spiritual life.   By spiritual
means must thou cultivate them, purify them, urge them
on in the spiritual life !'   I replied that the task seemed
absolutely impossible, as some of the animals were perfectly
furious ; whereupon my guide said : 'The owners of those
horses will become the very best, the strongest columns of
the Nuptial House.   They have superior talents ; they will
be very influential when their horses are tamed.'   Then I
went out and began to chase the herd before me.   They
fled in all directions, and I saw all around me pictures of
those who, wittingly or unwittingly, opposed the success of
the house.   Among them were the malevolent and the good,
people with a good enough will, but with little judgment ;
and, to my sorrow, I saw these latter doing even more harm
to the undertaking than the former.   There were some very
respectable members of the clergy among the ill-affected.

"Again I had to pray for the re-establishment of a convent of women pointed out to me by two deceased nuns.
I saw the convent, and the meadow in which the linen was
washed and bleached.   There was more than enough linen
for a wash, but all in the greatest disorder.   At one end of
the garden ran a cool, limpid, sparkling stream ; but the
nuns made no use of it, they went rather to a muddy pool

nearer the house. My companions remarked : 'Notice, how difficult a task it would be to arrange all this disordered linen ! A much more difficult one will it be to restore regularity in the community. Try if thou canst do it !' I set to work at the linen and found it full of rents and old stains ; it will give me much trouble, and take a long time."

27. Prayer for Greece.

July 31, 1821— " All last night I worked at a singular task, praying for innocent Christians who endure such misery in Turkey, and I had to repel the attacks of the Turks. I invoked St. Ignatius Loyola, who gave me his staff and taught me how to use it. I hovered above a city situated tolerably high on a bay toward the west. Numberless ships lay before the city, like a forest of masts, and many of the citizens took refuge in them.—I saw in vision the holy martyr, St. Ignatius of Antioch brought there in chains on his way to Rome and receiving the visits of other Bishops.—The city was surrounded by Turks trying to enter it, sometimes at one point, sometimes at another, by the gardens or by breaches in the wall. All was confusion. I hovered in the air as if I were flying and, when I rose a little, I did indeed fly. I gathered my robe around my feet and, holding Ignatius's staff in my hand, I flew to meet the assailants. I repulsed them at every encounter, the bullets whizzing around me. Troops of white-robed figures accompanied me, but they often remained behind and let me go on alone. I was at times very much afraid of getting entangled in the high trees which bore great, broad leaves and black fruit shaped like grapes. I often thought : ' It is well that my folks cannot see me now flying in this way ! They would certainly think me a witch.' Whilst I fought now here, now there, I saw multitudes hastily

leaving the city, bag and baggage, and fleeing to the ships.
These vessels were surrounded by galleries from which
little bridges reached to the shore; they were full of citizens. All night did I thus labor. I saw the Greeks also,
and they appeared even more savage and cruel than
the Turks. In a vast field, far away to the north, I beheld
numerous troops marching to the rescue of the city, and I
felt that if they arrived things would go still worse.—
Then I had a picture in which it was shown me how widely
the Greeks are separated from the Church.—I saw it as a
running river, and the sight pained me greatly. The Turks
when thus invading a country, look not like regular soldiers;
they wear no uniform, they go half-naked in all sorts of
rags."

28. Labors for the Parish of Gallneukirchen, Upper Austria, Corrupted by Sectaries.

November 23, 1822.—" St. Odilia accompanied me on my
last night's journey to Ratisbon. On coming to a certain
house, she said; ' That's where Erhard lived; he gave me
sight of soul and body.' It seemed to me as if it had happened only yesterday. St. Walburga joined us. We entered
the house, and I had to argue some points in it—I am worn
out. Neither Walburga nor Odilia wanted me to dispute
so long; the latter especially was anxious to proceed, for
she said: ' We must go! There is a place in Austria from
which they are about to carry off a bride. You must
arouse her brothers, otherwise her posterity will be utterly
ruined. '—And she gave me no rest until we had set out.
We journeyed southward to a mountainous district in Austria, in which we saw beautiful spotted cows in magnificent meadows shut in by high rocks and large bodies of
standing water full of reeds. The inhabitants are a simple-

minded race, some of them apparently silly. They act like children. About two leagues from a large river stands a castle surrounded by other buildings. Here dwelt the bride. She had consented to elope with a stranger who was on the watch at the gate with a carriage and servants; she had packed up secretly, and was all ready to start. Her own bride-groom was away; he was too rigid, too severe for her. Urged by Odilia I went to arouse the brothers who were asleep in one of the neighboring houses, a difficult undertaking, for they were *sound* asleep. I shook them, I called them and, at last, I held to their nose a little herb I had gathered on the way. This awoke them. I told them all and made them come with me. As the bride stepped out of the courtyard, we seized her gently and bore her back. The seducer waited and waited, and at last, rode back home in a fury. He rushed into a beautiful apartment which was adorned with artificial flowers and hung with mirrors, all borrowed for the occasion. I saw some men bringing in still more. The man was fairly beside himself with rage; he would willingly have shattered everything in the room.—This labor cost me much. I found the roads all obstructed by rocks, stones, fallen trees, beams" (symbols of difficulties to be overcome), "but I received the explanation of it. The *bride* is a distant parish in which a certain preacher has led a large number into heresy, and they have formed a project to separate from the Church; the sleeping brothers are two of their priests, good enough, but negligent; the lawful bridegroom, living at some distance, is the parish priest, somewhat stern and careless also; the seducer symbolizes vain-boasting and frivolous joys. When this task was ended, Odilia went toward the east, Walburga to the west, for they still had others to perform."

November 24—"I have had more and very fatiguing work to do in that parish. My father's blessing was necessary, and to get it I was obliged to make a most painful journey beset with a thousand obstacles. But I found him, at last, in a lovely garden surrounded by beautiful dwellings. I spoke to him of my eldest brother's sternness toward the youngest one, and he replied that he knew from experience how grievous such a thing is. He gave me his benediction, and I ascended to a higher region and into a spiritual church. There I found holy Bishops of the early ages who had evangelized the country in which lay the infected parish : Maximus, Rupert, Vital, Erhard, Walburga's brothers, and some pious parish-priests who had died there. From them I received a large blessed candle which, through many difficulties, I had to carry lighted into the parish. The way was long and each instant I thought my light would be extinguished ; but I succeeded at last. I placed the candle on a candlestick in the centre of the parish whence it diffused all around rays as bright as the sun. There was a dirty old oil-lamp hanging near the ground from the end of a long pole. It cast around only a dull, dingy glare; it looked more like a hole in the ground than anything else. This I had to remove, though not without great trouble. I could not keep it at the end of the pole. The road was hilly and full of stones and rubbish. I hurt myself, bruised my knees, soiled my clothes with the grease, and became so tired and impatient that, at last, I ran to my mother. I found her lying in a beautiful bed in a fine house. She tried to console me ; but, as I still wept, she told me to put the lamp down, that I could not manage it, for it had to be twisted and hung out of a beam in the hall. Then the thought came to me that it could not be twisted, for it was made of iron ; whereupon my mother commanded me to try, and I found that I could twist it just like lead.   I hung it **out of** the beams in the unfinished hall, and my mother took me into bed with her and bound up my feet.   Then I saw all in the parish gathering around the light.   The two pastors labored earnestly among the people in union with a third, a very zealous man from a distance.   I saw also the rector of the parish about a quarter of a league away ; he was a little stiff.   I saw Rupert, one of the holy apostles of the country, giving instructions with his *spiritual voice*, and the light increasing wherever he went.   The stranger priest was enraptured. He asked the rector if he did not think the sermon admirable.   The latter answered that he did not hear a word of it.   But his two assistants heard it and led him up nearer to the preacher, when he could hear a little. Things are better now in that parish."

29. Voyage to an Island of Japan.

December 24, 1822.—"Last night I made a long journey, partly by land, partly by water, to an island of Japan. For a long time I sailed with both Christians and Jews, to the latter of whom I spoke of Jesus.   I saw that they were touched by my words.   It was somewhat similar to a case which happened lately here in Dülmen.   I had to speak in vision to some persons whom I convinced and who, after a few days, came to me asking if they ought not to do such and such a thing.   They could get no peace—it was the effect of my remonstrances.—The island on which I landed lay in the midst of others, large and small, and it is called *P-a-h-g-ä-i*." (Sister Emmerich pronounced each letter separately).   "The shores are steep and rocky.   It is dark and bleak all around. Ships seldom touch here. The island may be ten leagues in circumference ; it contains a city, but there are no Christians on it.   I saw the

inhabitants adoring something like a lion which they carry
in procession. I went to an old sick woman belonging to a
tribe, dark and ugly but well-disposed, who dwell in caves
around a high mountain. They build sheds before these
caves, lighter or heavier according to the season. It was
daylight when I arrived. The woman lay on a bed of very
white moss, a sort of shaggy skin around her shoulders and
a covering over her. On first seeing me she appeared
startled, but soon gained confidence. I told her all about
the little Christ-Child and urged her to make a crib; whereupon she recalled some confused traditions of her people's
ancestors. She was perfectly resigned to die. When I
asked if she did not want to be cured, she did not show any
anxiety that way but thought it was time for her now *to go
home,* as she expressed it. I told her to invoke the Infant
Jesus with all her heart that she might get well. She
obeyed most earnestly, and promised to make as beautiful
a crib as she could. She had always sighed for the true
religion. 'All my life,' she said, 'I have longed for white
people who could instruct me, and often in the fields I had
so strong a feeling that they were behind me that I looked
back to see them.' She had a son and daughter whom she
greatly lamented as they were in slavery, and she had no
hope of ever seeing them again. Ah! if they did but know
the true religion! If her son would only return and announce
it to his people! She had no other religion than that of making offerings of rice before a cross which she always carried with her, and which she stuck in the ground for that
purpose. She also lay upon three iron crosses placed side
by side in her bed of moss. Her people form a kind of
procession around the fields and burn rice in honor of the
Supreme Being. They gather the harvest three times a
year. I told her how I used to play with my little com-

panions when a child, how we used to make a crib in the
fields, say our prayers before it, and choose one of our number to preside as priest and keep order.   Her people weave
most beautifully.   They make lovely baskets and other
things out of fine rushes, grasses, and willows, and she had
woven a beautiful body for her cross.   I taught her all that
she should teach her people and all that they should do.
I prayed with her and, though with difficulty, prevailed
upon her to rise.   She thought she could not, that she was
still too ill, she must *now go home.*   But when I repeated
that the Infant Jesus can refuse nothing to earnest prayer,
she prayed and arose.   She wore a long cotton garment, a
fur skin about her neck, and around her head a colored
handkerchief which seemed to be padded with moss.   After
she arose, it appeared as if she no longer saw me.   She
called her people together, told them that she had been
cured by a person who had come to her from a star (I forget from what star or heaven), who had related to her the
history of a new-born Saviour whose feast occurred the
next day, and who had instructed her how to pray to Him,
the Infant Jesus.   She also informed them of her promise to
make a crib, for which she had received all necessary directions.   The joy of these simple-hearted, innocent people
was great on hearing the above; they believed all that she
said, for they both loved and esteemed her.—I learned
also that at a former period a Christian traveller had visited
the island, and found the pagans honoring for twenty days
in the year a child in a crib.   This was the sole remnant of
Christianity once existing among the natives."

December 25, 1822.—"I was again with the woman
on the island, and I saw the simple, beautiful crib she had
made.   The child was a doll in swathing bands, the features drawn in lines without relief, the body beautifully

woven. It lay in a basket of lovely flowers and moss in the centre of a garden and under a tent made of the best materials that could be produced. There was a figure dressed in finely plaited paper to represent the Blessed Virgin; but I thought the child rather large compared with the mother. St. Joseph, the Three Kings, and the shepherds were all dressed in paper. All around were long, hollow reeds stuck in the ground, furnished with oil and a wick ; around the stem was a ring to force the oil up. The effect of these lights under the trees was very b autiful. These flambeaux were trimmed off with colored paper folded to represent roses, stars, garlands, etc.— The people own flocks of very agile animals which they keep penned up. They are not sheep or goats like ours; they have long hair and run very swiftly. The whole scene was wonderfully beautiful ! Crowds of grown people and children came in procession with torches in their hands and bearing crowns and garlands; they knelt around the crib and offered all sorts of things as alms for the poor. The woman instructed them, explained all that had happened to her, all that had been told her of the Birth of Christ, His Childhood, doctrine, Passion and Ascension. Her hearers were full of joy and eager to know more. The woman was very old, but still uncommonly active and vigorous. I saw the Blessed Virgin and the Child Jesus assisting at this celebration, both clothed as they had been in the cave at Bethlehem. The infant wore a cap with a pointed fold on the forehead. The people did not see them.

" I spoke again with the old woman and learned that two centuries before in an island not far off, the inhabitants used to erect a tomb on the anniversary of St. Thomas's death, and go on a pilgrimage to it for the space of twenty days. (This number is usual in their festivals.) They used to lay fine white bread on the tomb, which, the Apostle appearing, blessed. It was then divided as a sacred thing. But something happened later on which deprived the people of this grace, and the Apostle came no more. They think that he was offended. Such is the tradition, such the belief of these people, handed down from father to son. As I listened to the old woman's earnest desires that her only son, who was at sea, might introduce into his country some ideas of Christianity, it was given me to glance at him. He was more than a common sailor, something like a pilot on the ship which had a mixed crew. He had spoken in some place with so much earnestness of his people's longing after Christianity, that two men resolved to visit them. I do not think they are priests, but they will report the case at Rome; perhaps they will ask for a priest. There dwells in another wild part of the island a darker race who are slaves. The people to whom my woman belongs wear long garments and pointed caps, larger or smaller; they are rich in rice and immense nut-trees. The monkeys climb the rocks like men, and leap around freely. The woman lives about two leagues from the sea."

30. Conversion of a Rabbi, at Maestricht.

February 26, 1821.—The Pilgrim began to read a letter to Sister Emmerich containing the news of the conversion of a Rabbi of Maestricht. But she interrupted him: " I know all about it. I have seen him several times. Once I saw him in a mail-coach with some devout persons who spoke of the Mother of God and of the miracles they had just witnessed before a miraculous picture, Our Lady of Good Counsel, I think, which they had just visited. The Jew interposed: 'Mother of God! Mother of God!

God has no Mother!'—and he mocked their faith. The good people were saddened. They prayed and asked the prayers of others for the Jew's conversion through Mary. All my life I have felt great compassion for the Jews and, through God's mercy, many things have been shown me in vision for which I had to pray; consequently, I saw this man also and prayed for him. After the incident related above he was shown me more frequently, and I perceived that he was unable to drive the thought of Mary from his mind. I used to see her approaching him and presenting the Infant Jesus to him with these words: 'This is the Messiah!'—I know not whether he really saw her, or if his inmost thoughts were thus shown me, symbolized as I am accustomed to see consolations and temptations. He looked upon them as temptations and struggled against them. He used to find out where processions of the Blessed Sacrament were to be made for the sole purpose of attending them, thus to excite in himself disgust and to mock at them in his heart. I saw him on such an occasion, I think it was Corpus Christi, fall involuntarily upon his knees. I know not whether it was through some inexplicable emotion, or whether he saw what I did; viz., the Mother of God in the Sacred Host holding toward him the Infant Jesus. Straightway he became a Christian. I am sure were he questioned on the subject, he would say that the thought of Mary pursued him constantly. I have heard nothing of this conversion and, indeed, I thought it only a dream."

31. An Infanticide Prevented.

On the evening of February 27, 1821, as Sister Emmerich lay in prayer, she suddenly cried out: " O it is well that I came! It is well that I came! The child is saved! I prayed that she might bless it, for I knew she could not then **throw it** into the pool. A wretched girl was about to drown her child not far from here. I have prayed so much lately for innocent babes that they might not die without Baptism, for the martyrdom of the innocents again draws nigh, we have no time to lose! I have just been able to save both child and mother. I may, perhaps, go again to see the child."—Such were the words just after the fact accomplished in vision, of which she gave a detailed account the next day. "I saw a miserable girl of Münster give birth to a child behind a hedge, and then carry it in her apron to a stagnant pool with the intention of drowning it. A tall, black spirit stood by her from whom radiated a sort of sinister light. I think it was the evil spirit. As I approached the girl and prayed, it withdrew. Then she took the child in her arms, blessed it, kissed it, and had not the heart to drown it. She sat down weeping bitterly, for she knew not what to do. I consoled her, and suggested to her to go to her confessor. She did not see me, but her angel told her. She seemed to belong to the middle class."

32. Sister Emmerich Assists a Dying Jansenist.

"Last night my mother appeared to me, telling me to go to a castle she pointed out in the distance where I was to assist a dying lady. These apparitions of my mother puzzle me. I cannot understand why she is so brief in her words, why she is so strange toward me; perhaps, it is because she is a spirit and I am not. I set out with my guide over a difficult road, to the Netherlands, I think. When we came in sight of the castle we met two roads leading to it: one smooth and pleasant; the other wild and marshy. My guide bade me choose between them. I was, at first, very undecided and, being very much fatigued, I greatly inclined toward the good one ; but, finally, I took the other for the sake of the poor souls in purgatory. The castle was old, dilapidated, and surrounded by trenches ; but the land was fertile, and there was a fir-forest near. I was at a loss how to enter. Again my mother appeared, and showed me an opening in the wall like a window through which I climbed. Inside I found a noble old lady in a most pitiable condition. She was at the point of death. She was a most disgusting object, covered with filth and sores. She lay off in a deserted part of the house, abandoned by every one excepting one old domestic who had been appointed to wait on her. By her, on oblong porcelain plates, lay several small slices of buttered bread. Not one in the house gave the poor lady a thought. The young people lived in another part of the castle ; they were just then having a feast, celebrating a name's day I think. The poor old lady had no priest, for they were no longer Catholics. An ecclesiastic, who had once attended her, had become a Jansenist, and she had followed his example.— Here I was shown something connected with the history of the Jansenists which, however, I do not remember very well. Their first separation from the Church was caused by an ill-regulated desire of greater piety, and they ended by becoming a sort of Calvanists. I saw, also, that that pious sect lately formed in Bavaria, will very likely fall into similar errors.—At my guide's command and to overcome myself, I had to kiss the poor old lady. As I entered, she seemed quite changed, sat up, thanked me joyously and heartily for coming, and expressed her desire for a Catholic priest. The nearest was three leagues away, but he was brought to her secretly by the old servant. She confessed, received the Sacraments, and died in peace shortly after her return to the Church."

August 28, 1822.—As Sister Emmerich was conversing with Father Limberg, her confessor, she suddenly paused, and fell into ecstasy, her countenance becoming unusually grave. When she returned to consciousness, she exclaimed: "I was called by my angel to pray for a man belonging to the middle class, who was just then dying in a fit!" Such cases were of frequent occurrence.

33. Affecting Death of a Converted Sinner in Münster.

September 2, 1820.—"I saw a poor, God-fearing man dying in sentiments of deep contrition, the Blessed Virgin and the Infant Jesus at his bedside. Then I saw his whole history. He belonged to a distinguished French family. At his birth he had been dedicated to the Blessed Virgin by his parents who were, I think, afterward guillotined. He grew up, became a soldier, and deserted; but, because of his secret veneration for the Blessed Virgin, he always escaped the greatest dangers. At last, he joined a band of robbers, or rather assassins, among whom he lead a debauched life; but as often as he passed an image of Mary, he was seized with shame and fear. For some crime or other, he was sentenced to imprisonment for life. His comrades found means to procure his escape, and he afterward led a wandering life until again committed to prison for robbery in a certain city. On an invasion of the French, he recovered his freedom. He again enlisted in the army, once more deserted, took foreign service, received a wound in his arm, and then settled down peaceably on his pension. He married and devoted himself to the care of the sick and similar charitable offices. He was again tempted to commit a robbery at Ueberwasser; but the Blessed Virgin appeared to him, told him of his con-

secration to her at his birth, and exhorted him to amend
his life. He entered into himself, reflected upon God's
patience toward him and began a new life, a life of rigorous penance, passing his nights in sharp disciplines and
prayer. I saw him die last night in peace and joy, assisted by Jesus and Mary. He had often changed his name
during his wild career."

November 28, 1822.—Sister Emmerich, though very ill,
related the following : "I have had much to do in the
Low-Countries. I was with a pastor who lay dying miserably. One could do nothing for him. He was a Free-
mason, and a crowd of the brethren gathered around him
like a strong chain, the padlock of which was another parish-priest who lived a scandalous life with a certain person.
He, too, was a Free-mason and in such disrepute that the
faithful would not receive the Sacraments from his hands.
He was now called upon to prepare his friend for death, the
latter being fully aware of his evil life.—It was altogether a
villainous affair. The chain was fast locked, but the two
went through the ceremonies with as much pomp and gravity as if it were a saint assisting a saint. With difficulty
I pushed my way to the dying man and, by prayer, obtained that he should live till the morrow and perhaps repent.
This nest of impiety must be cleared out. I had business
also with the Bishop and his affair at Rome. I went, likewise, to five beguines who are full of self-conceit, who live
perfectly at their ease. I had to send to them a devout man
to rouse them up and make them change their life. "

November 29th—"The pastor is still alive and even
getting better. He confesses all—many things will now
come to light !" (Sister Emmerich was herself very ill at
this time). "The other will also confess and amend his life,
and the persons seduced by him, as well as their children,

will receive a support." For several nights Sister Emmerich's sufferings were very intense, on account of the miserable state of this unhappy priest.

34. A Church Profaned and a Sacrilege Committed.

October, 1820.—" I was in an agony all last night at seeing a robbery committed in a church of this place, and I had no one to send to prevent it. It was between one and three o'clock. There were five or six men, three in the church, the others keeping watch outside. The watchman passed twice, but the robbers hid. I saw two go by here, and I think one remained concealed in the church to open it. For about two hours and a half, I saw them busy rummaging and breaking. In the street back of the choir was a woman on watch and another near the doctor's house; a boy, only eight years old, was stationed near the post-office. Once they had to interrupt their work, because people were passing through the cemetery. They had planned also to break open the Canon's house, and they watched their chance a long time. It is the same party that robbed the Dean. I think the mother of one of them lives here. As they poured out the Hosts on the altar-cloth, one of them said : 'I will lay Our Lord on a bed !' They did something also behind the main altar—the sight was horrible ! I saw a devil by each of the robbers helping him ; but the evil spirits could not approach the altar, they had to remain far off. I saw them running up to one another, and it looked to me as if a devil does not know of what his fellows are thinking. At times they flew to the miserable wretches whom they were instigating to crime, and whispered something into their ears. I saw angels hovering over the Body of the Lord and, when the robbers broke off the silver from the large crucifix, I saw Jesus in the form of a youth whom they struck and buffeted and trod under foot. It was horrible!—They did everything boldly, carelessly ; they have no religion. I cried out to Jesus to work a miracle, but received for answer that it was not the time. My heart was rent with anguish ! ''

December 30, 1821.—Lying in ecstasy this evening, Sister Emmerich began to recite gaily the following nursery rhyme :

" Down yonder, by the Rhine,
Stands a barrel full of wine,
Without bung, without tap—
Now, tell me what is that?"

The Pilgrim thought she had suddenly . recalled some childish sport and, when she returned to consciousness, he questioned her as to the meaning of it. She seemed, at first, not to know to what he referred ; but, after a little reflection, she remembered having been on the shores of the Rhine where smugglers had concealed a cask of liquor and then hid from the custom-house officers. " I had to go there and pray that they might not be caught," she said. " I saw what trouble they would get into if they were taken. I stood by the cask near the Rhine, and I almost froze in the storm. It was a large cask, and I thought : ' What a pity ! It will go to waste ! O if the Father only had it in his cellar !' Then that childish riddle came to my mind, and I recited it shivering with cold."

CHAPTER VI.

SISTER EMMERICH'S GIFT OF RECOGNIZING RELICS AND BLESSED OBJECTS.

With the gift of prophecy, Sister Emmerich had also received the power of discerning holy objects, even by the senses. Blessed bells had for her a melody all their own, a sound essentially different from every other that struck her ear; her taste detected the blessing imparted to holy water as readily as others can distinguish water from wine; her sense of smell aided her sight and touch in recognizing the relics of saints; and she had as lively a perception of the sacerdotal benediction sent her from afar as when given in her actual vicinity. Whether in ecstasy or the state of consciousness, she would involuntarily follow the consecrated fingers of a priest as if deriving from their influence strength and benediction. This keen perception of all that was holy, of virtues, of spiritual properties, was not conveyed to her senses by previous knowledge received in vision. It was perfectly independent of the activity of the mind and as involuntary as is the transmission of ideas to it through the medium of the senses. This faculty of realizing what the senses could not perceive had, like the gift of prophecy, its very foundation in the grace of Baptism and infused faith. Her angel once said to her: "Thou perceivest the light from the bones of the saints by the same power thou dost possess of realizing the communion of the faithful; but faith is the condition on which depends the power of receiving holy influences."

Sister Emmerich **saw all** that was holy radiant with light. " I sometimes see," she said, " when lying fully awake, a resplendent form hovering in the air, toward which rise thousands of brilliant rays, until the two lights unite. If one of these rays should happen to break, it falls back, as it were, and darkness takes its place." This is an image of the spiritual communion of the faithful by prayer and good works. She felt the influence of this light as of something that relieved and strengthened her, something that filled her with joy and powerfully attracted her to itself; whilst, on the contrary, she turned suddenly and involuntarily, filled with horror and disgust, from whatever was unholy, from whatever was tainted with sin.

" It is very difficult to explain this clearly," she once said to the Pilgrim. " I see the blessing and the blessed object endowed with a healing and helping power. I see them luminous and radiating light ; evil, crime and malediction appear before me as darkness radiating darkness and working destruction. I see light and darkness as living things enlightening or obscuring. For a long time I have had a perception of the authenticity of relics and, as I abhor the veneration of false ones, I have buried many such. My guide tells me that it is a great abuse to distribute as genuine relics objects that have only *touched* relics. One day whilst I was baking hosts in the convent, I felt suddenly attracted toward a certain cupboard, indeed, I was violently drawn to it. In it I found a round box containing relics, and I had no peace until I gave them a more honorable resting-place." On July 19, 1820, she spoke as follows : " I have been told that the gift of recognizing relics has never been bestowed upon any one in the same degree as God has given it to me, and this on account of their being so sadly neglected and because their

veneration is to be revived." These last words are fully
explained by Sister Emmerich's communications on the
Feast of the Holy Relics, 1819-1820. On the first Sunday
of July, 1819, she related what follows: "I had to go
with my guide into all parts of our country where lay
buried the bones of the saints (1). I saw entire bodies
over which buildings had been erected and places upon
which convents and churches had once stood. Here lay
whole rows of bodies, among them those of some saints.
In Dülmen, I saw sacred relics reposing between the church
and the school-house, and the saints to whom they belonged
appeared to me, saying: ' That is one of my bones!'—I
saw that these neglected treasures confer blessings wherever
they lie and ward off Satan's influence. I have seen
certain places preserved from serious calamities by them
whilst others of recent date suffered severely, because
possessing nothing of the kind. I cannot say in how many
strange, out-of-the-way places, under walls, houses, and
corners I have been where the richest treasures of relics
lie unhonored, covered up by rubbish. I venerated them
all and begged the dear saints not to withdraw their love
from the poor people. I went also to the place of martyrdom in Rome and saw the multitudes of saints who there
suffered death. My Heavenly Bridegroom there appeared
to me under the form in which I am so accustomed to see
Him ; viz., in His twelfth year. The saints seemed to me
innumerable ; they were divided into choirs headed respectively by him who had instructed and encouraged them.
They wore long white mantles with crosses and caps, from
either side of which hung long flaps down to the shoulders.

---

(1) " This vision appeared to me all the more remarkable," writes Brentano, "when
I discovered that the Feast of Holy Relics is celebrated at present in the diocese of
Münster, a fact wholly unknown to Sister Emmerich. Her obligation to satisfy for the
negligence committed in the Church is indeed wonderful !"

I went with them into underground caves full of passages, chambers, round apartments like chapels, into which several others opened, and in the centre of which stood a pillar supporting the roof. Many of these pillars were ornamented with beautiful figures. In the walls were deep, quadrangular excavations in which reposed the bones of the dead. As we passed along, sometimes one of my guides, sometimes another would say: 'See, here we lived in time of persecution, here we taught and celebrated the mysteries of Redemption!'—They showed me long stone altars projecting from the wall, and others round and beautifully sculptured upon which the Holy Sacrifice had been offered. 'See,' they said, 'we lived here for a time in poverty and obscurity, but the light and strength of faith were ours!' and after those words, the different leaders disappeared with their choir. Sometimes we came to daylight, but only again to plunge into the caves. I saw gardens, walls, and palaces overhead and I could not understand how the people up there knew nothing of what was going on below, how all these things had been brought down into the caves, how it was all done! At last, there remained with me of all the saints only one old man and a youth. We entered a spacious apartment whose form I could not determine, as I could not see its limits. It was supported by numerous pillars with sculptured capitals, and beautiful statues larger than life lay around on the ground. At one end the hall converged to a point where, standing out from the wall, was an altar and behind it other statues. The walls were full of tombs in which rested bones, but they were not luminous. In the corners lay numberless rolls, some short and thick, others as long as one's arm, like rolls of linen. I thought they were writings. When I saw everything so well preserved, the hall so neat and cheerful, I thought it would be very nice to stay awhile, to examine and arrange things, and I wondered that the people overhead guessed not of its existence. Then I had an assurance that all would come to light some day through a great catastrophe. Were I present at the time, I should try to bring it about without injuring anything. Nothing was said to me in this place; I had but to gaze. Why? I know not. And now the old man disappeared. He wore a cap like the others with lappets on the shoulders, and a long beard. Then the youth took me back home."

FEAST OF HOLY RELICS, 1820.

"I again visited innumerable places where lie relics under buildings buried and forgotten. I went through cellars in mud and dust, into old church crypts, sacristies, tombs, and I venerated the holy things lying there, scattered and unknown. I saw how they once shone with light, how they shed around a benediction, but their veneration ceased with the decline of the Church. The churches erected over them are dark and desolate, the saints under them are no longer honored. I saw that their veneration and that of their relics had decreased in the same measure as the adoration of the Most Blessed Sacrament, and then I was shown how evil a thing it is to receive the Holy Eucharist through mere habit. Grievous sufferings were imposed upon me for this contempt. In the spiritual Church I saw the value and efficacy of the holy relics now so little regarded on earth.

"I saw an octangular church arising like a lily from a stalk and surrounded by a vine. It had no altar; but in the centre, on a many-branched candlestick, reposed the richest treasures of the Church like bunches of opening flowers. I saw the holy things collected and honorably placed by the saints on this candlestick, this ornamental stand, which seemed constantly to increase in size. Whilst thus engaged, the saints very often saw their own relics brought in by those who lived after them. I saw the disciples of St. John bringing in his head and other relics of him and the Blessed Virgin with little crystal phials of the Blood of Jesus. In one of them the Blood was still clear and shining. All were in the costly reliquaries in which the Church preserves them. I saw saintly men and women of Mary's time depositing in precious vases, holy things that once belonged to her; they were given the place of honor on the right. There was a crystal vase shaped like a breast in which was some of her milk, also pieces of her clothing, and another vase with some of her hair. I saw a tree before the church, and I was shown how it had fallen and been fashioned into the Saviour's cross. I saw it now in the form in which I always see it, brought in by a woman wearing a crown. It hovered in the air over Mary's relics. The three nails were stuck in it, the little foot-ledge was in its place, as also the inscription, and, skilfully arranged around, were the instruments of the Passion: the ladder, the lance, the sponge, the rods, the whips, the crowbars, the pillar, the cords, the hammers, etc., whilst the Crown of Thorns hung from the centre· As the sacred objects were brought in and arranged, I had successive visions of the places in which these relics of the Passion were found, and I felt certain that of all I saw some particles are still preserved and honored. There must be many relics of the Crown of Thorns in different places. I discovered that my particle of the lance is from the haft. I saw in all directions, on altars, in chambers, churches, vaults, in walls, in rubbish, under the earth and on the earth, portions of the relics and bones which were brought

into the church. Many consecrated Hosts in chalices and
ciboriums were brought thither by Bishops and corporals
stained with the Precious Blood. They were placed on
high over the cross. Then came the relics of the Apostles
and the early martyrs followed by those of whole bands of
martyrs, Popes, priests, confessors, hermits, virgins, religious, etc. They were deposited at the foot of the cross,
in costly vases, ornamented caskets, towers, and shrines wonderfully wrought in precious metal. A mountain of treasures
arose under the cross which gradually ascended as
the mound increased and, finally, rested upon what might
be termed a transfigured Calvary. The relics were
brought by those who had themselves honored them and
exposed them to the veneration of the faithful; they were,
for the most part, holy personages whose own relics are
now held in benediction. All the saints whose relics were
present ranged in choirs, according to their rank and profession; the church became more and more crowded; the
heavens opened and the splendor of glory gleamed around.
—It was like the Heavenly Jerusalem! The relics were
surrounded by the aureolas of the saints to whom they
belonged, whilst the saints themselves sent forth rays of
the same colors, thus establishing a visible and marvellous
connection between them and their remains.

"After this I saw multitudes of well-dressed people
thronging around the church with marks of deep veneration. They wore the various costumes of their times;
of the present day, I saw but few. They were people who
honored the saints and their relics as they ought to be honored, as members of the Body of Jesus Christ, as holy vessels of divine grace through Jesus, in Jesus. On them I
saw falling like a celestial dew the beneficent influence of
those saints; prosperity crowned all their undertakings. I

rejoiced to see here and there, in these our days, some good souls (some of whom I know) still honoring relics in all simplicity. They belong chiefly to the peasantry. They salute simply and earnestly the relics in the church as they enter. To my great joy, I saw my brother among them. As he enters the church, he devoutly invokes the holy relics it contains. and I see that the saints give fertility to his fields. The veneration paid the saints and their relics in the present day, I saw symbolized by a ruined church in which they lay scattered, neglected, covered with dust, yes, even thrown among filth and dirt; and yet they still shed light around, still draw down a blessing. The church itself was in as pitiable a state as the relics. The faithful still frequented it, but they looked like grim shadows; only occasionally was a simple, devout soul to be seen who was clear and luminous. The worst of all were the priests themselves who seemed to be buried in mist, unable to take one step forward. They would not have been able to find the church door were it not that, in spite of their neglect, a few fine rays from the forgotten relics still reached them through the mist. Then I had distinct visions of the origin of the veneration of relics. I saw altars erected over the remains of the saints which, by the blessing of God, afterward became chapels and churches, but which were now in ruins owing to the neglect of their sacred treasures. I saw in the time in which all was misty and dark, the beautiful reliquaries broken up to make money and their contents scattered around, which latter desecration gave rise to greater evils than did even the selling of the caskets. The churches in which these sacrileges happened have fallen to decay, and many have even wholly disappeared. I have been to Rome, Cologne, and Aix-la-Chapelle, where I saw treasures of relics to which certain honors are paid."

In consequence of the dismantling of churches and the suppression of convents, innumerable sacred relics had been scattered and profaned and had finally fallen into irreverent hands. This was a source of deep sorrow to Sister Emmerich, who sought every opportunity to revive veneration toward these holy objects. People soon discovered that they could not give the poor invalid greater pleasure than by bringing her something of the kind, or asking her advice on the subject. In this way she accumulated quite a treasure of holy things (1). More than three hundred genuine relics, with whose whole history she was perfectly familiar, were in her possession at the time of her death. She had received them principally from Dean Overberg, Father Limberg, the Pilgrim, and others, who knew of her ability to recognize such things. If she found any spurious among those presented to her, she had them buried in consecrated ground. The others constituted her spiritual treasure upon which she had at various times lights more or less clear, as God ordained that the gift He had bestowed upon His servant should tend to the restoration of the honor due His saints. Sister Emmerich's recognition of relics was a grace which, in accordance with the designs of God, was intimately connected with the mission of her life; and it was for this reason that her angelic guide guarded it so jealously against the caprice. vain curiosity, or love of the marvellous, which might actuate those who submitted it to the test of trial.

---

(1) One day Clara Soentgen brought her a little package of relics. Sister Emmerich took it, saying: "O this is a great treasure! Here are relics of St. Peter, his step-daughter Petronilla, Lazarus, Martha, and Magdalen. It was brought from Rome long ago. This is the way the saints' bones lie around when they pass from the Church into private hands. This reliquary was first bequeathed as an inheritance, then given away among old worthless things, and at last it fell by chance into Clara Soentgen's possession. I must have the relics honored."

On another occasion, a Jewess found among some old clothing she had purchased a reliquary which she forcibly opened; but, terrified at her own act, she hurried with the relics to Sister Emmerich who had witnessed the whole affair in vision. She could not help smiling at the woman's fright.

It was only at the close of those investigations which so closely scrutinized Sister Emmerich's whole life, both interior and exterior, that God provided occasions for the manifestation of the extraordinary gifts of His servant. He willed the perfection of her virtue to prove the reality of her supernatural gifts, rather than that the latter should be made the touchstone of her holiness. The first trial made with false relics and condemned by her angel, is thus recorded by the Pilgrim under date of August 30, 1820 :—

"The parish-priest of N— had sent to Sister Emmerich three small packages of bones by Christian Brentano, the Pilgrim's brother. At the Pilgrim's request one of them was laid by her. The next day she related the following : ' I saw far away dark, desolate tombs full of black bones, and I did not feel that they were holy. I saw the Father take some of them, and then I found myself up high in a dark chapel around which all was cold and bleak and foggy. My guide left me, and I saw a stately figure approaching me with a most gracious air. At first I thought it was an angel, but soon I trembled with fright. I asked : " Who art thou ?"—The answer came in two unknown words. I thought of them all the morning, but now I cannot recall them They signified : *"Corruptor of Babylon, Seducer of Juda."* Then the figure said : " I am the spirit that reared Semiramis of Babylon and built up her empire! I am he who brought about thy Redemption, for I made Judas seize *Him !"*—(he named not Christ)—and this he said with an important air as if wishing to impress me with the greatness of his exploits. I made the sign of the cross on my forehead, whereupon he grew horrible to behold. He began to rage furiously against me for having once snatched a young girl from him, and then he disappeared uttering fearful threats. **As**

he pronounced the first of the unknown words, I saw Semiramis as a little girl under some beautiful trees, the same
spirit standing before her and offering her all kinds of
fruits. The child looked up at him unshrinkingly and,
although she was very beautiful, there was something repulsive about her; she seemed to be full of thorns, full of
talons. The spirit nourished her, and gave her all sorts
of gewgaws. The country around was lovely; it was
covered with tents, green meadows, whole herds of elephants
and other animals with their keepers. It was shown me
also how Semiramis raged against God's people, how she
drove Melchisedech from her realm and committed many
other abominations; and yet, she was almost adored!—
At the second word the spirit pronounced, I had a vision
of Christ on Mount Olivet, the treason of Judas, and the
whole of the bitter Passion. I do not understand why this
spirit appeared to me; perhaps these are pagan bones and,
consequently, the enemy has power to approach me. My
guide has strictly forbidden me ever to take such bones
again. "I tell thee," he said, "in the Name of Jesus, it is
a dangerous experiment! There is treachery in it. Thou
mightest be seriously injured by it. We must not cast
pearls before swine; that is, before the unbelieving, for
pearls should be set in gold. Attend to such relics only as
come to thee by the direction of God!"'"

In September following, some relics were sent to her by
a priest who had visited her in Dülmen. Sister Emmerich
remarked: "I have had no particular vision concerning
these relics. But I saw that the priest who sent them is a
good man, although there are in his parish certain souls
inclining to *pietism* not in accordance with the spirit of the
Church. He cannot detect them, he thinks them very
devout; but I have seen them spreading darkness all around.

They make little account of the ceremonies of our holy Church. They have not openly declared themselves as yet; the evil is, however, in them. Then I heard a voice repeating near me : ' Thou forgettest me ! Thou forgettest me !' It was a warning from the other relics, and I was again told not to accept any more unknown relics to recognize even if brought me by the holiest priest in the world, for serious harm might result to me from it. I must arrange what I have first."

Very little notice, however, was paid to the prohibition so earnestly repeated by the poor invalid. Curiosity triumphed over other considerations. The Pilgrim not long after presented her, whilst in ecstasy, a little package of relics from two Rhenish convents. They had been sent him by a friend. Sister Emmerich took them unsuspectingly, thinking them her own ; but the next day she said : "My guide has severely reprimanded me for taking those relics contrary to his orders and, consequently, I have quite forgotten all that I saw. He again repeated that it is not the time to recognize unknown relics and my too ready acceptance of them might entirely mislead me. The gift of recognizing such things is not a privilege to be called into play at every moment. It is a special grace. The time will soon come for me to use it, but not now. My guide also bade me remember the Curé N— and his package, the thoughtless remarks he had made somewhere about myself and my relics, and that such remarks might do much harm. I must for the future refuse such things and meddle with none but my own."

The same warning was again repeated, and she was told that the Pilgrim's friend, an enthusiastic supporter of the theory of mesmerism, was merely trying experiments on her which might have very serious consequences, as her gifts were not what he thought. They were not subject to her own good pleasure, not a natural faculty to be employed at the discretion of the curious. The Pilgrim submitted, but not so his friend, who still found excuses for testing her wonderful powers. On the 12th of December, she again declared: "Your friend's judgment of me and of what he sees in me is false! Consequently, I have been expressly forbidden by my guide to receive even a saint's relic from him. He only wants to make experiments which may prove very injurious to me; and besides, he speaks of them publicly and in a manner quite opposed to the real state of the case. My gifts, my means of knowing, are not what he imagines! I see the drift of his thoughts when he speaks with me. He is all wrong concerning me. I was long ago warned of it in vision."

On December 16th, Sister Emmerich said: "I have had a wonderfully clear vision on the subject of relics, which I saw all around me and in many churches on the banks of the Rhine. I saw a coach attacked by robbers, and a little box of relics thrown from it into a field on the roadside. The owner returned to seek it, but in vain; it was found by another person who kept it for some time. In it I saw the bone, brought here by *the friend*, but I must not name it. *The friend* must wait until his heart is changed. He is still surpassingly high and broad in his views.—Faith, also, is high and broad; but it must often pass through a key-hole! *The friend* is obstinate in his erroneous opinion of me and my mission, his ideas on this point are strange and unreasonable; therefore, have I received positive commands to have nothing to do with relics coming from *him.* His views are false, he publishes them unnecessarily, and he may thereby bring trouble upon me. My time is not yet come."

December 21st, St. Thomas's Day.—The Pilgrim, on entering to pay his accustomed visit, found Sister Emmerich busily engaged with her box of relics, *her church,* as she playfully called it. Among them she had discovered several very ancient ones. The Pilgrim was surprised to see in what beautiful order she had arranged them during the previous night. Although in a state of contemplation, she had lined the box with silk as neatly as if she had been wide awake. The five relics of St. James the Less, St. Simon the Chananean, St. Joseph of Arimathea, St. Denis the Areopagite, and a disciple of St. John, whom she called *Eliud* she had folded separately. "I had," she exclaimed, "a very bright night! I found out the names of all the bones by me and I saw all the journeys of St. Thomas, as also those of all the Apostles and disciples whose relics I have. I had a vision of a great festival and of how all these relics came to Münster. They were collected by a foreign Bishop at a very remote period, and they afterward fell into the hands of a Bishop of Münster.—I saw all with the dates and names, and I trust in God it will not be lost! . . . . . I received permission, also, to reveal to my confessor the name of the relic that *the friend* brought me that he may note it down; but I must not tell *the friend* himself."

The friend, however, would not understand these words so indicative of Sister Emmerich's bond with the Church and the supernatural origin of her marvellous gift; and she, seeing his ideas still unchanged, felt a lively desire to make known to him the secret name. She says most ingenuously: "Ah! I thought, if I could only tell him the name of that relic! and I had the word on my tongue when all at once a shining white hand was stretched forth from the closet there and laid on my lips to prevent my uttering it. It came so suddenly, so unexpectedly that I almost laughed out!" This scene was repeated under almost similar circumstances a few days later when she was again seized with desire to gratify *the friend's* curiosity on the score of the relic he had given her. "I was again tempted to name the saint whose relic had caused me so much annoyance; but just as I was about to pronounce it, I heard a rapping in the closet which checked me, and I dared not, I could not say it. More than once I have had the word on my tongue, but I could not speak it, although I wanted to do so." Her confessor and *the friend* had likewise heard the rapping in the closet and were unable to account for it. But when the former exclaimed: "The evil one shall play us no tricks!"— Sister Emmerich quietly took the relic from the closet, saying: "It is the saint the Pilgrim's *friend* brought."

We shall here subjoin some facts which clearly show the power of the priest over this chosen soul. On January 18, 1821, Father Limberg placed by Sister Emmerich a little sealed package, saying to the Pilgrim as he did so: "I do not know what it contains; but when she notices it, I shall tell her where I got it." Then, turning to the invalid he asked: "What is this? Is it good? Tell me what it is." Although interrupted in her vision, Sister Emmerich answered after a short pause: "It belongs to a pious man in the seminary at Paris. He brought it from Jerusalem and Rome. It contains various things: some hair belonging to a Pope; a particle of the body of a new saint who died in a convent in the Holy Land; a small stone from the Holy Sepulchre; some earth from the spot on which Our Lord's Body lay; and some hair belonging to another person." The Pilgrim remarked to Father Limberg: "You found it, I presume, among the Abbé Lambert's effects, for he received similar objects from Paris."—" Yes," replied Father Limberg. " In arranging his papers, I found the little parcel," and with these words he left the room.

" Who is that miserable little nun ?" exclaimed the invalid. " The Father said nothing to me about her ! He ought to go see her. She is much worse off than I ; she is lying in the midst of thorns !" Sister Emmerich saw herself under this figure, because the sealed parcel contained some of her own hair which the old Abbé intended to send to his friend.

One day she recognized a relic as belonging to a holy Pope whose name, however, she failed to recall. The Pilgrim begged the confessor to present it to her once more. He did so, and she held it but a few seconds when she exclaimed confidently : " It is a relic of Pope Boniface I."

August 9, 1821.—Sister Emmerich said : " I was busy all last night with the sacred bones. I saw all the saints, and I was told to say as many *Our Fathers* as there are relics, for the souls of all resting here in our cemetery."

The following fact will show in a most striking manner the powerful impression made upon Sister Emmerich by profane, as well as by holy objects. The Pilgrim records under date of May 9, 1820 :

" Dr. Wesener, whilst excavating a pagan tomb, found a vase of ashes with which were mingled some fragments of a human skull. The Pilgrim placed one on Sister Emmerich's couch as she lay absorbed in ecstatic prayer ; but she who was so powerfully attracted by the relics of the saints, as to move her head, her hands, her whole person trembling in every muscle after them, let this bone lie unnoticed on the coverlet near the fingers of her left hand. The Pilgrim thought it an object of indifference to her, when she suddenly exclaimed: " What does that old Rebecca want with me ?" and when he moved the bone a little nearer, she hid her hands under the coverlet, crying out that a swarthy old savage woman was running around the room followed by children naked like frogs. She could not look at her, she was afraid ; she had seen such dark, wild people in Egypt, but she knew not what this old woman wanted with her, etc. Then catching up her box of relics, she pressed it to her bosom with both hands saying, though still in ec- stasy : " Now she cannot hurt me !" and she slipped under the coverlet. The Pilgrim put the bone in his pock- et and stepped to the side of her bed toward which her face was turned ; but instantly she changed her posture. He returned to the opposite side, and again she as quickly averted her head; at last, he removed the unholy object from her presence, when she exclaimed with a sigh of re- lief that the saints had preserved her. During this scene, her confessor held out to her his consecrated finger toward which she moved her head so quickly as to seize it with her lips and press it eagerly. " What is that ?" he demanded. Instantly came the astonishing answer : " *It is more than thou dost comprehend !* " Then he withdrew his finger and laid his hand on the foot of the bed where, too, she tried to follow. Rigid in ecstasy and still clasping her box, she arose to a sitting posture and endeavored to reach the consecrated fingers with her lips. Then the Pil- grim laid near the hand that clasped the box of relics, a frag- ment of the fossil remains of some animal which the doctor had found in the Lippe. Sister Emmerich willingly received it, saying : " Ah ! this is all right ! There is nothing hurtful about this. It is a good animal ; it never committed sin !" Then she exhorted the Pilgrim not to meddle with heathen bones, not to bring them to her mixed up with the bones of the saints. "Go, throw that old women away! Take care, she might hurt you!" she exclaimed earnestly at intervals. Some days after when the Pilgrim alluded to the incidents just related, Sister Emmerich severely represented to him how improper, how dangerous it was for him to make such experiments upon her, to mingle thus the sacred with the profane, and to expose her to unbecoming impressions. "Pagan bones repel me, fill me with disgust and loathing! I cannot say that I actually felt that the woman is damned; but I perceived around her something sinister, something that turns away from God, that spreads around darkness, or rather that is darkness itself, quite contrary to the luminous, attractive, beneficent bones of the saints. The old woman glanced around furtively, as if in connection with the powers of evil, as if she herself could harm. All round her, forest and heath, lay in darkness; not in the darkness of night, but in spiritual darkness, the darkness of wicked doctrines, in the darkness of separation from the light of the world, in the covenant of darkness. I saw only the woman and her children, but there were miserable huts of various forms scattered here and there, sunk in the earth, surmounted, some by round sod roofs, others by square reed ones, and some again by conical ones; between most of these huts were underground passages. The unholy, heathenish influence of such remains may produce much evil if made use of for unlawful superstitious practices. They who so use them become thereby, though unknown to themselves, participators in their influence; they establish a communication with them, just as the veneration of holy relics imparts a share in the benediction, the sanctifying influence of what is redeemed and regenerated."

It was not only in vision, but also in the natural state of

consciousness that Sister Emmerich felt the attractive influence of holy relics, saw them shining, and knew their names ; a fact to which the Pilgrim testifies in his journal of Dec. 30, 1818 : " Sister Neuhaus," he says, " Sister Emmerich's former Mistress of Novices, came to see her bringing with her a small package. As she entered the room, the invalid experienced, as she herself said, a thrill of joy and an interior conviction that the package contained relics. ' Ah !' she exclaimed, ' you bring the treasure from your room and you keep there the dust !' and when Sister Neuhaus laid the parcel on the table near her, so great was her emotion that she feared every moment she would be ravished in ecstasy. It was with the greatest effort that she could entertain her visitor, her attention being powerfully drawn to the relics. Sister Neuhaus asked if she were unusually sick. ' Not perfectly well,' was the answer, and then she spoke of indifferent subjects, hoping to divert her mind from its all-absorbing object. An interior voice seemed to be calling out to her : ' There is Ludger ! There he is !'— After the sister left, the invalid said : ' I saw the whole time over the relic a glimmering of light, white as milk and brighter than the day ; and, when a particle fell on the floor, I saw, as it were, a bright spark drop under the box (1). As the Pilgrim looked over the relics, I was almost ravished and I heard a voice, exclaiming: " There is Ludger ! That is his bone !" and instantly I beheld the holy Bishop with mitre and crosier in the assembly of the saints. Then others were shown me, one by one : first, Scholastica above a troop of nuns, and her relic on the table ; then Afra surrounded by nuns, and her relic on the table ; Benedict over a crowd of monks, and his relic on the table ; Walburga with her nuns, and her relic below by the Pilgrim. Among

(1) " There I looked, poor blind man that I am, and found it !"—Brentano.

the nuns one was pointed out as Emerentiana, and I heard these words: " That is Emerentiana, and there is her bone !" I was surprised, for I had never heard that name before. Then I saw a maiden with a crown of double roses round her brow, holding in one hand a lovely garland of roses, in the other a bouquet, and I heard these words : ' That is Rosalie who did so much for the poor. She now holds the flower garland as she once did her pious gifts, and there lies her relic !' Then I saw a nun in a shining troop, and I was told : ' That is Ludovica, and there is her relic. See, how she scatters her gifts !'—and I saw that she had her apron full of loaves which she distributed to the poor. Then I saw a Bishop and heard the words: ' He lived in Ludger's time. They knew each other ; they labored to- gether,' and yet, I saw them far apart. And now, among other blessed maidens, I saw a very young secular clothed in a spiritual garment of the style of the Middle Ages. Her body had been found incorrupt and entire. Her sanctity had thus been recognized, and one of her bones was placed among other relics. At the same time, I saw her open tomb. Then I saw a delicate youth of the early ages and near him six others and a woman. The name *Felicitas* was pronounced and, immediately, a round place enclosed by walls and arches was shown me, and I was told that in the dens on one side were the wild beasts, and in the pris- ons opposite the martyrs in chains waiting to be torn to pieces. I saw also people digging by night and carrying off bones, and it was said to me : ' They do this secretly. They are the martyrs' friends. In this way their relics are carried to Rome and distributed.' I saw Felicitas near seven youths."

A week later, the Pilgrim presented Sister Emmerich with the rest of the relics in Sister Neuhaus's package. " I

gave her seven parcels," he says, " all of which she recognized as belonging to St. Elizabeth of Thuringia. 'I see
Elizabeth,' she exclaimed, 'a crown in one hand, in the
other a little basket from which fall golden roses, large and
small, on a poor beggar below.' Here she pointed to a
relic, saying, ' That is Barbara! I see her with a crown on
her head and in her hand a chalice with the Blessed Sacrament.' Then turning to another little paper, she said :
' These are from the place of martyrdom in Rome.' " With
these words she fell into ecstasy and described the places
she saw and the sufferings of the martyrs whilst, at the
same time, she named the relics and presented them to the
Pilgrim to fold and label. He was amazed at the rapidity
of her speech and movements. He expressed his astonishment in these words : " I must acknowledge, to my shame,
that of such things I know almost nothing! Fancy to yourself this poor peasant-girl gazing on ancient Rome, describing its manners and customs! She understands all that she
sees, even the moral state of the martyrs ; and yet, her inexperience is such that, for the most part, she knows not
how to name the objects, the localities, the instruments
that fall under her eyes!" At the close of her vision, she
asked her guide how these relics had come where they were,
and why they had not received the honor due them? He
answered that they had been exhumed long ago, had passed
from place to place, and had at last reached Münster.
Here they had been put aside to make way for other things.

"I was in a strange, wonderful city," she says. "I
stood on top of the round building enclosing the circular
place. Over the entrance, right and left, ran an inside
staircase to where I was. On one side were prisons opening into the enclosure ; on the other, the cages of the wild
beasts. Behind these were nooks into which the execu-

tioners slipped when they released the animals. Facing
the entrance against the wall, was a stone seat up to which
steps led on either side. Here sat the wife of the wicked
emperor with two tyrants. Just back of this seat, upon
the platform, sat a man who appeared to superintend affairs,
for he made gestures right and left as if commanding something. And now the door of one of the cages was thrown
open, and out dashed a spotted animal like a huge cat. The
executioners stood behind the door, slipped into the nook
for safety, and then mounted the steps to the platform.
Meanwhile, two other executioners had dragged a maiden
from the prison opposite and removed her white tunic.
Like all the martyrs she shone with light. She stood
calmly in the middle of the arena with raised eyes and
hands crossed on her breast; she showed no sign of
fear. The beast did her no harm but, crouching
before her, sprang upon the slaves who were urging it on
with spears and cries. As it would not attack her, they
got it back into its cage, I know not how. The maiden
was then led to another place of execution around which
there were only railings. She was fastened to a stone by
a stake, her hands bound behind her, and beheaded. I
saw her put her hands behind her back herself. Her hair
was braided round her head; she was lovely, and she
showed no fear. Then a man was led out into the arena;
his mantle was removed, and only an under-garment left
that reached to his knees. The beasts did him no harm,
and he, too, was beheaded. He was, like the maiden,
pushed from side to side and pricked with sharp iron rods.
These grievous tortures were borne with such joy that the
looker-on can but regret not sharing them. Sometimes the
executioners themselves are so wonderfully affected by the
sublime spectacle that they boldly join the martyrs, confess

Jesus Christ, and suffer with them.—I see a martyr in the
arena. A lioness pounces upon him, drags him from side to
side, and tears him to pieces. I see others burned alive,
and one from whom the flames turn away and seize upon
the executioners of whom numbers perish. A priest who
secretly consoled the sufferers has his limbs cut off one by
one and presented to him in the hope of making him ab-
jure his faith ; but the mutilated body, full of joy, praises
God until the head is struck off. I went, also, into the
catacombs. I saw men and women kneeling in prayer before a table on which were lights. One priest recited
prayers, and another burned incense in a vase. All
seemed to offer something in a dish placed on the table.
The prayers were like a preparation for martyrdom. Then
I saw a noble lady with three daughters, from sixteen to
twenty years of age, led into the arena. The judge seated
on high was not the same that I had last seen. Several
beasts were let loose upon the Christians, but they harmed
them not ; they even fawned upon the youngest. The
martyrs were now led before the judge, and then to the
other place of execution near by. The eldest was first burned
with black torches on the cheeks and breasts and under
the arms, and pincers applied to her whole body ; after
which she was conducted back before the judge. She noticed him not, however, for she was intent upon her sister
whom they were now torturing. The same happened to
all four, and then they were beheaded. The mother was
reserved for the last, her sufferings intensified by the sight
of her daughters' torments.—I saw a holy Pope betrayed,
dragged from the catacombs, and martyred, whilst one of
the most furious of the Romans, suddenly touched with repentance, rushed among the martyrs and perished with
them. I longed so for the same favor that I cried out ; but

a voice said to me : ' Every one goes his own way ! We suffered martyrdom but once, but thou art constantly martyred. We had one enemy, thou hast many !' "

On another occasion, the Pilgrim offered the invalid
some relics which she took, pressed to her heart, arranged
in order, again pressed to her heart, and regarded attentively. Then she gave them back separately, removing one
from the lot as spurious and exclaiming : "They are
grand! No words can describe their beauty !" To the
question as to what she experienced from the sacred bones,
she answered : ' I *see*, I *feel* the light ! It is like a ray that
pierces me, ravishes me. I *feel* its connection with the glorified spirit, with the whole world of light. I see pictures
from the life of the saint, and his place in the Church
Triumphant. There is a wonderful connection between
body and soul, a connection which ceases not with death ;
consequently, the blessed soul can continue its influence
over the faithful through particles of its earthly remains. It
will be very easy for the angels to separate the good from
the bad at the last day, for all will be either light or dark."

On July 31st, whilst rapt in contemplation, Sister Emmerich took her little box of relics and, from among more
than one hundred, chose out one particle which she
said belonged to St. Ignatius of Loyola. On returning to wakefulness, she began again to hunt up fragments
belonging to one another, and in about five minutes
she had made up six separate piles. Of one of them she
said : "I ought to have ten pieces." She counted again,
but found only nine. "There ought to be *ten*," she repeated. At last, she found the tenth. She fell back exhausted, saying : "I can do no more. I can see no more ! "
—After a pause, she exclaimed : "I felt irresistibly drawn
to look for these relics. They attracted me, and I sighed

for them ! It is easy to recognize them at such times, for
they shine with a different light. I see little pictures like
the faces of the saints to whom they belong, toward which
rays of light dart from the particles. I cannot express
it ! It was a wonderful state ! It is as if one felt something
confined in one's breast that strives to get free. The effort fatigues, exhausts." Opening a paper, she remarked :
" Here is a little stone," and she picked it out from among
many others precisely similar. She had no need of light
for this occupation ; indeed, she often performed it by
night.—The Vicar Hilgenberg, having arranged some relics very elegantly, brought them to show the invalid. She
was delighted with them. She said : " I see some of them
surrounded by an aureola of various colors. They shine with
light, they are perfectly transparent. On looking more
closely, I see a tiny figure which gradually increases in size
until I behold the form, the clothing, demeanor, life, history, and name of the saint. The names are always under
the feet for men, at the right side for women. Only the
first syllable is written, the rest I perceive interiorly (1).
The letters are surrounded by an aureola of the same colors
as the relics of the saints to whom they belong. It
seems as if the names were something essential, something
substantial ; there is a mystery in them. When I see the
saints in a general way, without reference to my recognizing them, they appear to be in hierarchies and choirs,
clothed according to their rank in the costume of the Church
Triumphant, and not in that of the time in which they
lived. Popes, Bishops, kings, all the anointed, the martyrs, the virgins, etc., are in heavenly garments surrounded by glory. The sexes are not separated. The virgins

(1) Whenever Sister Emmerich, in compliance with Brentano's request, tried to
trace the names of the relics as shown her in vision, she invariably wrote only the
first syllable and that in Roman characters.

have an entirely distinct, mystical rank. They were either voluntary virgins, or chaste married women, or martyrs to whom the executioners offered violence. I see Magdalen in a high rank, but not among the virgins. She was tall, beautiful, and so attractive that, had she not been converted to Jesus, she would have become a female monster. She gained a great victory!

" Sometimes I see only the saints' heads, sometimes the whole bust radiant with colored light. The glory of virgins and those who have led a tranquil life, whose combats have been only those of patience in daily trials, in domestic troubles, is white as snow, and it is the same for youths whom I often see with lilies in their hands. They who were martyred by secret sufferings for the honor of Jesus shine with a pale red light. The martyrs have bright red aureolas and palms in their hands. The confessors and doctors are yellow and green, like a rainbow, and they bear green branches. The martyrs are in different colored glory, according to the various degrees of torments they endured. Among my relics I see some saints who became martyrs by the interior martyrdom of the soul without the shedding of blood.

" I see the angels without aureolas. They appear to me, indeed, under a human form with faces and hair, but they are more delicate, more noble, more beautiful than men. They are immaterial, perfectly luminous and transparent, but in different degrees. I see blessed souls surrounded by a material light, rather white than resplendent, and around them a many-colored glory, an aureola whose tints correspond to their kind of purification. I see neither angels nor saints moving their feet, excepting in the historic scenes of their life upon earth, as men among men. I never see these apparitions in their real state speaking to

one another with the mouth; they turn to one another, in-
terpenetrate one another."

Among Sister Emmerich's relics were two of St. Hildegarde, one small, the other larger, a piece of the hip-bone.
One day she looked up with an air of surprise, as if some
one were approaching her: " Who is that in a long white
robe ?" she asked, and then, turning to the little closet
by her, she said : " O it is Hildegarde ! I have two relics of
her, one large which I do not often find, and a smaller one
which is always coming to hand. The large one is less
luminous. It belongs to a less noble part, for bones differ in
dignity. So, too, the garments worn by Magdalen before
her conversion shine less than the others. The members
lost by a saint before his second birth are relics, since all
mankind, even before the coming of Jesus, were redeemed
through Him. The relics, the holy bones of pure, chaste,
courageous souls are firmer, more solid than those of persons
agitated by passions ; consequently, the bones belonging to
the simple old times are firmer and more attractive than
those of a later period."

The Pilgrim brought her a little box containing about
fifty fragments of relics all lying together. As the invalid
was at the moment perfectly conscious, in the waking state,
he remarked that it would be a good time to sort and
arrange them. Sister Emmerich assented and set to work
earnestly, putting the particles of the same body by themselves, and even designating to what members they belonged. " These," she said, picking up some scraps, "were
once in fire. I now see people hunting for them in the
ashes. These were in the city church, and I see how they
cleaned and prepared them. Those there are very brilliant,
these less so; and there is one," pointing to it, " that sheds
around a particularly beautiful golden red light." Here she

fell into contemplation from which she soon returned with the words: " I see an old palsied man, lying on a bed in an open square.—A Bishop, with a crosier resting on his arm, is leaning over him, his head upon his shoulder, whilst his attendants stand around with lighted torches," and she pointed out the relic with the beautiful light as connected with this scene, naming it *Servulus.* She also named St. Quirinus in connection with one of these relics.

The Pilgrim brought her a small package of relics belonging to the Castle of Dülmen. It contained eight scraps of old stuff which she laid aside with the words : " It was once worn by a saint. It is a piece of a stole, a vestment which touched a holy thing." When asked how she knew that, she answered that ever since the package entered her room, she had seen four saints by her clothed in this stuff. They had cut and touched it, and again they appeared to her as she was picking out the shreds. The Pilgrim inquired if she did not see St. Thecla whose relic lay by her. "Yes," was the answer, " I see her, now here, now there, in a vision, as if on the watch near the prison in which St. Paul is confined. Sometimes I see her gliding along by a wall, sometimes under an arch, like a person anxiously seeking something." Picking up a splinter of brown wood wrapped in blue, she said : " This is a piece of the wood of which the cross Mary had at Ephesus was made. It is cedar-wood, and the scrap of blue silk belonged to a mantle that once clothed an image of Mary. It is very old."

On November 6, 1821, Sister Emmerich found among her relics a scrap of wood which she gave the Pilgrim, saying : " This was brought from the Holy Land long ago by a pilgrim. It was taken from a tree which stood in the little garden of an Essenian. Jesus was carried up over it by the tempter at the close of His forty days' fast." Then she handed another package to him: "Here," she said, "is some earth from Mt. Sinai. I see the mountain by it." Taking up a bone, she said: "It belongs to a saint of July; his name begins with *E*. I saw him in prison with two others whom starvation forced to suck the bones of the dead. When led forth to martyrdom, he was, on account of his wonderful discourse on God, looked upon as a fool, and they wanted to free him. But one of the soldiers cried out : 'Let us see if he can call his God down from heaven ! He is as worthy of martyrdom as the others !' and the blasphemous wretch was immediately struck by lightning. Then I saw the saint celebrating divine service in a church, after which he was martyred."

History of a Reliquary.

November 8, 1819.—When the Pilgrim visited Sister Emmerich on this day, he brought with him in his breast-pocket an old cross containing relics which she had never seen. As he approached her bed, she cried out : " O here comes a whole procession !" and she extended her hand toward the cross which he had not yet removed from his pocket. He handed it to her. Opening it eagerly, she exclaimed : " Here they all are, and one old man as up-right as the Swiss hermit !" The Pilgrim left the cross with her, and next day she related the following history :—

" As this reliquary approached I saw in the order in which the relics lie, the saints hovering in the air in the form of a cross. Below lay a wild, woody country with a mass of dense underwood. I saw also some people among whom was one old man like the old Swiss hermit. Then I had a vision referring to the cross. In a woody valley among mountains near the sea, I saw a hermitage of six female recluses, and I beheld their whole way of life. They were all young enough to help themselves ; they were very silent, retired, and poor, keeping by them no provisions whatever, but depending wholly upon alms. They lived under a superior and recited the Canonical Hours. They wore a coarse, brown habit with a cowl. In front of their cells were neat little gardens which they cultivated themselves ; each had its own entrance and contained orange trees. Here I saw the recluses. I saw them occupied also in some labor new to me. On a machine like a loom were stretched cords which they wove into various colored carpets, coarse but very neat; they also did beautiful basketwork out of fine white straw. They slept on the ground, on a plank with two coverlets and a poor pillow, and they ate scarcely anything cooked. They took their meals together off a table in which holes were hollowed out to serve for plates ; on either side swung leaves which could be raised to cover these stationary plates. I saw them eating a brownish-looking stew of vegetables. The greatest simplicity reigned also in the chapel. Whatever there was beautiful in it was of plaited straw. I thought : ' Here are golden prayers and straw ornaments; but we have prayers of straw and gilded ornaments !' The stone altar was covered with a beautiful straw matting, scalloped on either side and falling at the ends. In the centre stood a small tabernacle on which was that same cross that the Pilgrim has. Two wooden candlesticks and a pair of wooden vases, with bouquets very symmetrically arranged in the form of a monstrance, stood on either side. The little convent was a square, stone building with a shingle roof. The rooms were partitioned off by a box-wood wickerwork, the openings about as large as one's hand, and they were of various heights. In the chapel they were higher than a man, though they did not reach the roof; but in the cells they were lower, the recluses could see over them.

They were woven on rods fixed in the walls. The entrance, which faced the sea, led into the kitchen which opened into the refectory with its singular table; behind was the chapel. To the right and left were three cells before which lay the little gardens. The doors leading into them from the cells were in the form of an arch, low and narrow, and the windows were over the doors, so that the inmates could not look out. Before the windows were straw mats that could be raised on sticks like screens. The straw stools had no backs, only a wooden handle to raise them. The chapel was covered with the coarse striped carpet which the recluses made themselves. They did not have Mass every Sunday, but a hermit came from time to time to say it for them and give them Holy Communion. They kept the Blessed Sacrament, however, in their little chapel. I saw them one evening at prayer in their chapel when they were attacked by pirates. They had short, broad swords, wore turbans on their head, and they spoke a strange tongue; they often carried off people into slavery. They were very savage, almost like beasts. Their vessel was large and lay at some distance from the shore to which they came in a small boat. They destroyed the hermitage and dragged off the recluses, but without offering them insult. One of the religious, still young and robust, took the reliquary from the altar as a protection, fervently imploring God's assistance. Before the robbers reached the shore, they quarrelled over their prey and, during their struggle, the young girl crept into a thicket, vowing to serve God in the wilderness if He would deliver her. The pirates sought her long, but in vain. At daybreak she saw them embark. Kneeling before the cross, she thanked God. The wilderness lay in a narrow, deep valley, snow-capped mountains on either side, far

away from any road; no people, no hunters ever came
there. The recluse sought long for a suitable place, and
found deep in the forest a little clearing surrounded by trees
and thorn-bushes. It was sufficiently large for a small
house. The trees almost entirely hid it overhead, and
their roots spread over the ground. Here she resolved to
serve God far away from mankind, destitute of both
spiritual and human assistance. She built an altar of stones,
placed upon it the cross, her only treasure, and arranged
·a little place wherein to take repose. She had no fire ; she
needed none, for it burned in her own heart. For nearly
thirty years she never saw bread. High up in the mountains were animals like goats leaping among the crags, and
around the dwelling of the hermitess were white hares and
birds of the size of a chicken. At last, a hunter in the
service of a lord whose castle was some miles off, came
with his hounds into the neighborhood. (The castle was destroyed at a later period, only part of a moss-covered tower
now stands). The hunter wore a tight gray jacket, an embroidered belt as wide as one's hand, and a small round
cap; he carried a spear in one hand and a cross-bow under
his arm. His dogs pressed barking into the thicket in
which the hunter saw something shining as he came up.
It was the cross. Entering the enclosure, he began to call
aloud but the solitary had hidden. She hoped to remain
undiscovered ; but finally, having no alternative, she made
her appearance, bidding him not to be frightened at seeing
one who no longer bore the semblance of a human being.
As *we* looked at her, the hunter and I, we saw her surrounded by a bright light. She was tall, had a cincture
round her waist, and her long gray hair hung over her
breast and back ; her feet were rough, her arms quite brown,
and she walked bent down by years. In spite of her

singular exterior, there was something very noble and
imposing about her. She seemed, at first, unwilling to
disclose her story; but seeing in the hunter a good, pious
man, she said: ' I see that thou art a servant of God,' and
then explained to him how she had come there. She refused to go with him, but begged him to return in a year
with a priest who would bring her the Blessed Sacrament.—
At the time specified, I saw the hunter return with a hermit,
a priest, who gave her Holy Communion, after which she
asked to be left alone for awhile. When they returned,
she was dead. They tried to bear away her body, but
they could by no means move it; so they interred her on
the spot. The hunter secretly took the cross as a memento
of the affair. Later on, a chapel was erected over her grave
in honor of a saint whom she particularly venerated and
whom she had named; on all sides of it were doors. This
virgin had lived a life of extreme poverty and entirely hidden in God. Before the pirates' attack she had had a
dream in which she saw herself dragged into the water. In
her dream, she made a vow to Our Lady of the Hermits to
keep perpetual fast in solitude, if she were saved. Then
she suddenly found herself in a canal or sewer, along which
she crept until she reached the wilderness in which she
afterward really lived, and where she was told she should
remain. When she asked on what she should subsist, figs
and chestnuts fell from the trees. As she gathered them,
they turned to precious stones, the fruits of her penance
and mortification. As she related this prophetic dream to
the hunter, I saw every circumstance of it. She was a
Swiss by birth, and she had been just thirty years in the
wilderness when the hunter discovered her. She told him
that she was from Switzerland, as he might find on inquiry,
and she named her birthplace. She had always had great

confidence in Our Lady of the Hermits, and from her childhood she had heard a voice, urging her to leave her home
and serve God in solitude. To this, however, she had paid
little attention. At last, a youth appeared to her saying :
' What ! still here ? Not yet set out ?' and he led her
away. She thought it all a dream ; but on awaking, she
found herself in another country, far from her home. She
entered the little convent of recluses among whom she was
well received. The hunter kept the cross devoutly for
some time, and then gave it to a man who lived in a town
across the mountains. He too prized it very highly and
always prayed before it. He attributed to it his own preservation and that of his property during a tempest that
destroyed the whole town. At his death, it passed to his
heirs and, at last, fell into the hands of a peasant who sold
it with other effects ; but misfortune followed this transac-
tion, for the man lost all that he possessed. Then I saw
the precious cross thrown aside with all sorts of things
among people who thought little of the fear of God. A
stranger, with no fixed principles of faith, purchased it from
them not through piety, but through pure curiosity. He
knew not the treasure he acquired, and yet it brought him
great good."

Here the Pilgrim makes the following remark in his
journal :—" This last incident refers to the Pilgrim himself
who, at a time in which he lived in deplorable blindness,
purchased the reliquary at Landshut from an old-clothes'
dealer. Sister Emmerich knew nothing of this by human
means ; therefore, if her last remark is beyond questioning,
why should we hesitate to receive as authentic all that refers to this singular story ?" Then, as if deeply impressed
by the invalid's supernatural knowledge, he exclaimed :—
" How wonderfully are all things preserved in the

treasury of God! Nothing is lost, nothing annihilated, nothing comes to pass without design! All is eternal in the mind of God! Now do I understand why God must punish every idle word! The thought of my sins saddens me. Does this evil exist eternally? Are a man's sins visible after penance, after repentance?" And Sister Emmerich answers: "No, Jesus Christ atones for them; they no longer exist! I never see them, unless when they are intended to serve as an example; for instance, the sin of David. But sins that have never been expiated, sins that a man carries around with him shut up in his heart, I clearly see. The expiated are like foot-prints in the sand, which the next step, the step of repentance, effaces. The contrite confession of sin blots out sin!"

An Infant-Martyr of Sachsenhausen.

The Pilgrim presented a relic to Sister Emmerich which she had already designated as belonging to a hermit. After a few days, she related the following vision of a child, a relative of the old hermit, who had been martyred by the Jews. "I have had an apparition of a child about four years old, surrounded by the martyrs' rosy aureola. There was something wonderfully attractive about him; his words were few, but full of wisdom. I went a long journey with him, and I was deeply impressed on seeing the little boy so brilliant with light, so grave, and so wise! We passed over a city, and I was instantly conscious of its state, I felt that its pious souls were few. The child led me over a bridge and showed me the house in which he was born, a tolerably large, old-fashioned dwelling. All was still within. On our approach, the inmates thought of the little boy, a faint remembrance of their history recurred to them, and I was told that the sudden remembrance of the dead often arises from their proximity. The child showed me that, as the union between the soul and the body never ceases, not even after death, so the influence of a holy soul never ceases to be exerted over all belonging to it by ties of blood. A saint continues his influence over his family and, in proportion to their faith and piety, do they profit by it. He told me also of the salutary influence he had exercised over his relatives, and that he had attained by martyrdom to that perfection to which he would have arrived, if his life had not been cut short by man's wickedness ; yet more, his relatives had profited spiritually by the influence he would have exercised had he lived, instead of being snatched away in his fourth year. Evil happens not by the will of God, but only by His permission, and the accomplishment of good, prevented by another's sin, is not wholly frustrated ; it is effected most surely, but in a different way. Crime in its essential consequences attacks its author only. As to its innocent victims, martyrdom leads them all the more speedily to perfection. Though sin against another be an act directly opposed to the law of God, yet the designs of God are never frustrated, since all that the victim would have achieved during life, he accomplishes spiritually and with the same freedom of will.—Then I saw the history of the martyred child. His parents were very pious people who lived about three hundred years ago, at Sachsenhausen, near Frankfort. They had a near relative in Egypt, an anchoret, whom they regarded with great affection and veneration. They frequently remarked, as they looked on their child, how happy they would be if he, too, would one day lead a holy life and serve God in solitude. Surely, parents who could form such a desire for an only child, still in his first year, must have been persons of more than ordinary piety ! When the child had attained his first year, one of his parents died. The other married again, and still in the new family continued to speak of the hermit and of the child's following his example. The little fellow was often entertained with this plan for his future. At last his only surviving parent died, and the little boy was now an orphan. The hermit continued to be spoken of in the family and the child, now four years old, earnestly longed to see him. (He told me that he was a beautiful child, but by no means so beautiful as I now beheld him, and that, had he lived, he would have been-very good, perhaps a hermit.) His step-parents, who saw in him an heir of the family, were nothing loath to get rid of him. They secretly encouraged him in his desire to walk in his pious relative's footsteps; and, when not quite four years old, they intrusted him to some foreign Jews who were journeying to Egypt. This they did to make away with him; the plea of sending him to his relative was only a cloak for their treachery. Although this step led to his martyrdom, yet the child ever loved his family and country.—A feast was going on in the old-fashioned house. I thought it was a wedding, but the child told me that it was a local festival. I saw numbers of brilliantly lighted apartments filled with elegantly dressed people dancing and feasting. . . . . 'Thus they make merry,' said the child, ' over the bones of their ancestor who, by his piety, laid the foundation of their affluence.' Then he took me to a walled-up vault where lay a white, well-preserved skeleton on a neatly arranged couch in a double coffin; the inner one of lead, the outer of some kind of dark wood. This was the progenitor of the family and a near relative of the child. He had been a very pious man, and had amassed great wealth, without detriment to his piety. When the church in which he had been interred was destroyed.

his children deposited his body in this vault, where he now lay wholly forgotten. I went through the whole house.—In this city I saw numbers of sacred bones in vaults over which had once stood convents and churches, but whose sites were now occupied by dwellings. The child told me that the city would soon decline, for it had now reached the summit of pride. Then he left me. I travelled far across the sea into a hot sandy country where he again joined me in a ruined city whose houses seemed to be toppling down on one another. In a cave under a hill, he showed me the place of his martyrdom : it looked like a slaughter-house. In the walls were iron hooks from which the Jews had hung the child, as from a cross, and slowly bled him to death. On the ground yet lay the bones of many other martyred children, shining like sparks. It seemed as if no one knew of this place, and the martyrdom of the child had never been discovered or punished. There were no Christians there, only a few hermits who lived in the desert and occasionally visited the city. Then I went into the desert and again met the child-martyr under the palm-trees by the hermit's grave, in the same spot in which he had lived. He had died before his young relative had left Frankfort. His remains were luminous. Several others were buried in this desert, and around in the white sand lay pieces of some kind of black stuff, like broken pottery. Here the child again left me, and I was taken over the sea to another place, to a hill near the city which contains the *martyr-place* (Rome). On one side stand houses with grape-vines here and there, and under it is a spacious vault upheld by columns. The entrance is closed, no one knows of its existence. As I entered, the child-martyr again appeared to me and I found a rich treasure of holy bones; the whole cave was lighted up by them. There were entire bodies in coffins standing against the walls and numberless bones in smaller caskets. I set to work to dust and open them. In one of them I found a body whose winding-sheet was perfect wherever it had touched the holy remains, whilst all the rest was fallen to dust; and in others the bodies were thoroughly dried up and as white as snow. I saw by my visions of the life of these saints that most of them belonged to the early ages. Some had been martyred for making offerings to Christian priests and, I think, they were denounced by their pagan relatives. I saw them going along with little birds under their arms. I saw multitudes who had become religious by the vow of chastity, and married couples who, for the love of Jesus, had lived in continence. I turned to a square shallow casket to which I was irresistibly attracted. I felt as if it belonged to me for there I found all my own saints, all whose relics I have here. I wanted to bring it away with me, but the child said no, it must stay where it was, and so I covered it with a blue veil. The relics were all arranged on little cushions. The child told me that they had lain there concealed since the early ages and that there they were to stay. But the time will come when they will be brought to light."

Relics belonging to Churches in Münster sent by Dean Overberg.

Dean Overberg had sent to Münster at various times packages of relics, some encased and labelled, others without either label or wrapping. Sister Emmerich had first a general vision of them and afterward, as the feasts of the different saints occurred, she received more particular information concerning each. She says: "When I received those relics from Dean Overberg, I saw in vision with what solemnity they had been brought from Rome to Münster, mostly by Bishops, and with what veneration they had been received and distributed. I saw devout women assembling together to fold and ornament them, and I saw the priests who divided them. To be allowed to share this labor, one had to be most pure and holy. The relics were glued, surrounded by embroidery and flowers, and arranged in pyramids. The first time they were exposed for veneration was a grand festival; the whole city rejoiced. I saw that many sacred relics were put into the altars of the Ueberwasser church. I saw devout Canons of the Cathedral who, whenever they heard of a saint, or holy person, tried to get a relic of the same. This they honored as a great treasure. When the church was rebuilt, the relics of the different altars were mixed and the members of several of the holy bodies were scattered; thus it was that the remains of the holy maiden of whom I have a bone were discovered. The great blessings diffused around by relics I saw withdrawn when they are treated with neglect. It was not by chance that these bones fell into Dean Overberg's hands. Without knowing to whom they belong, he gave them the honor due them."—" How wonderful are the ways of God!" remarks the Pilgrim. "He willed that these relics should be scattered that they might fall under the supernaturally enlightened eyes of her who knows so well their value."

One day having taken up the box of relics, her *church* as she called it, the Apostle St. Thomas appeared to her, and she had a full vision of his journeys and apostolic labors in the Indies. He went from kingdom to kingdom, wrought many miracles, and uttered many prophecies. He set up a stone at a great distance from the sea, made a mark on it, and said : ' When the sea flows this far, another

will come to propagate the knowledge of Jesus!' I saw
that he referred to St. Francis Xavier. St. Thomas was
pierced with a lance, buried, and afterward disinterred.
I think Matthias and Barsabas are among those relics, for
I had a short vision of their election to the Apostleship.
Matthias, though more delicately constituted, had more
strength of soul, and he was, therefore, preferred by God
to Barsabas who was young and vigorous. I saw many
things concerning the latter. I had also a vision of St. Simeon,
a blood-relative of Jesus. He became Bishop of Jerusalem
after St. James, and suffered martyrdom when over a hundred years old. There must be a relic of him here.—"
Next day St. Thomas's relic was pointed out to her in vision.
She labelled it and wrapped it in paper.—" I had visions of
his journeys. I saw them as if on a map, and the bones of
Simon and Jude Thaddeus, his brother, were shown me.
Then I saw the whole family of St. Anne. She had three
husbands. Joachim died before the birth of Christ. After
his death Anne married twice and had two daughters. I
was greatly astonished to hear of these marriages, but I was
told the reason of her contracting them. Then I thought
of *Anna* whom I at once saw, as well as all the lodgings of
the widows and virgins in the Temple. St. Anne's first daughter was Mary Alpheus who at the birth of the Most Holy Virgin had a tolerably large daughter, Mary, afterward the wife
of Cleophas by whom she had four sons, James the Less,
Simon, Jude Thaddeus, and Joseph Barsabas. I have bones
of the last three. In the presence of their relics I felt that
they were united to Jesus by consanguinity. I had also a
vision of Jude's going to Abgarus, in Edessa. He carried
a writing in his hand which Thomas had given him. As
he entered I saw a radiant apparition of the Saviour at his
side, before which the sick king inclined, taking no notice

of the Apostle, whom he saw not. But the latter laid his hand upon him and cured him. After this he preached in the city and converted all the inhabitants.

"I have again had visions of different saints. I saw the martyrdom of one St. Evodius who, with Hermogenes, his brother, and a sister, suffered in Sicily. I saw also many pictures of a holy white-robed nun, the Cistercian, Catherine of Parcum. I saw her still a Jewess, reading from rolls of parchment things relating to Jesus which deeply affected her. Some Christian children told her of the Child Jesus, of Mary and the Crib, to which they took her secretly, and she was still more drawn to Jesus. She received instructions privately and, in consequence of an apparition of Mary, fled to a convent. I saw many other touching things concerning her, especially her longing to be despised."—This saint's relic was firmly sewed in red velvet, and when Sister Emmerich took it to label and wrap, she saw, being in contemplation, that it contained a scrap of stuff that touched the Saviour's Crib, some splinters of the same, and a ticket on which all was marked. This relic of the Crib was the one that had belonged to St. Catherine herself and had been particularly honored by her, for she had seen in a vision the Infant Saviour lying in His Crib, and she often had the honor of holding Him in her arms. All the above Sister Emmerich related to the Pilgrim before opening the little package. Judge of his satisfaction, then, when on removing the covering, he found just what she had described, some scraps of word, wrapped in a piece of brown stuff, with the inscription: "*De præsepio Christi.*" Sister Emmerich had fallen into ecstasy and, when the Pilgrim offered her the scraps of word, she took them smilingly, saying: "Ah! these belong to the Crib of Our Lord. The little nun used to venerate them!"—The Pilgrim, seized with a feeling of veneration for the favored being before him, made a movement as if to kiss her hand; but she suddenly withdrew it with the words: " Kiss St. Clare's relic. That is no longer of this earth ! This," raising her hand, " is still earthly." At these words he was still more astonished, for he had in his breast-pocket a relic of St. Clare which he had not yet shown her. He now presented it to her; she kissed it, exclaiming : " O there is Clare beside me !" When returned to consciousness, she said: " I had a little vision of St. Clare. War was raging round her convent and, although she was ill she had herself borne to the gate. She carried in her hands the Blessed Sacrament in an ivory box lined with silver. Here she knelt with all her nuns invoking God, when she heard an interior voice bidding her not to fear, and I saw the enemy departing from the city."

One day, the Pilgrim drew near her bed with a relic from the casket which she had not yet seen. " Afra !" she exclaimed joyously. " Have we St. Afra ? I see her bound hand and foot to a stake ! O how the flames dance around her ! She turns her head to look"—and with these words Sister Emmerich seized the relic, which she kissed and venerated as belonging to St. Afra.

Toward dusk that same day, the Pilgrim opened another of the little parcels on which were inscribed the words: " *From the clothing of a saint,*" and which contained also a bone and a label. It was almost dark and the objects were so very small that he did not imagine Sister Emmerich noticed his action. To his surprise, she called to him : " Take care of the label! The relic shines; it is authentic !" He handed her the particle of bone, when she instantly fell into contemplation. On returning to herself she said : " I have been far away to Bethany, Jerusalem, and France.

The bone belongs to Martha ; the clothing, to Magdalen.
It is blue with yellow flowers and green leaves, the remnants
of her vanity, which she wore under a mourning mantle, in
Bethania, at the raising of Lazarus. This dress remained
in Lazarus's house when he and his sisters went to France,
and pious friends took it as a memento. Some pilgrims
when visiting their tomb in France, wrapped this relic in a
part of the dress, thinking both belonged to Magdalen ; but
only the clothing is hers, the relic is Martha's." When
the Pilgrim closely examined the inscription, he, indeed,
found : " *Sancta Maria Magdalena.*" Among these relics of
Dean Overberg's, Sister Emmerich recognized "a bone of
Pope Sixtus VIII. and another of the third Pope after
Peter." She appeared pleased at having been able to de-
cipher the numbers ; but next day she said : " When I
again saw the saints to whom the relics belong, it was said
to me : 'Not the *third*, but the *thirteenth !* His name
signifies *Saviour.*'"—"How wonderful !" exclaims the
Pilgrim. "The *thirteenth* Pope is *Soter*, the Greek for
Saviour !"

Father Limberg presented her a little package marked :
" *St. Clement*," asking if it really was a relic of Pope St.
Clement. Sister Emmerich laid it by her and next day answered, no, it was not St. Clement's, but one of St. Marcella,
widow. The confessor asked for more precise details.
After some days, the invalid gave the following : " I have
again seen the life of St. Marcella. I saw her as a widow living very retired in a beautiful large house built in Roman
style, like St. Cecilia's ; around it were gardens, courtyards,
and fountains. I often saw St. Jerome with her opening
rolls of writings. Marcella gave all she had to the poor
and to prisoners whom she used to visit by night, the
prison doors opening of themselves to admit her. She **was**

so deeply impressed on reading the life of St. Antony that she put on a veil and the monastic dress, and influenced young maidens to do the same. I saw a strange people enter and pillage Rome. They tried to extort money from Marcella by blows; but she had given all to the poor. This is all I remember. The first time I saw her, she encouraged me respecting my visions on the Holy Scriptures and told me something for my confessor. But I have entirely forgotten it."

Another relic she recognized as belonging to St. Marcellus of whom she related the following : " I had a vision of the saint. He used to go with his companions by night to hunt up the bodies of the martyrs and give them Christian burial, inscribing their names over their resting places. I often saw him going around by night with bones in his mantle. He carried also many holy bodies into the catacombs, laid rolls of writings by them, principally the acts of their martyrdom, and marked them. I think it was he who brought many of the things into the great vault in which I once saw so many relics preserved. I remarked again that we have many precious relics here, for many belong to bodies that Marcellus labelled.—I have seen the holy widow Lucina. She begged him to bury two martyrs who had long before perished of hunger in prison. During the night he and Lucina bore the remains of a man and a woman to the place where Lawrence lay buried ; but, as they attempted to lay them by him, the bones of St. Lawrence recoiled, as if unwilling to have them near him, and so they buried them elsewhere.—I saw Marcellus led before the emperor. On his refusal to offer sacrifice, he was scourged to blood and sent to take charge of a large stable. The stable was circular, built around a court, and there were in it not only beasts of burden, but also cages for the beasts intended to be let loose upon the martyrs. These Marcellus had to feed, but they were tame and gentle with him. Here, too, he found means to assist his brethren in secret. Through the intervention of Lucina, who bribed the jailers, he often left the prison by night to bury the dead and encourage the faithful. I saw, too, that he received the Blessed Sacrament from other priests and distributed It by night. He was, at last, liberated, again imprisoned, and again liberated for having cured the wife of a great personage. After this he lived retired in the house of Lucina which he secretly converted into a church, and wherein he practised, as usual, his works of mercy. But his enemies again attacked him, turned the house into a stable, and condemned him to serve in it. As he still persevered in his spiritual labors for souls, they had him horribly scourged with the whips used for the beasts of burden. He died in a corner of the stable, on the ground, and the Christians gave him burial.—After this I had visions of Ambrose, Liborius, and of St. Gregory's pontificate. They referred chiefly to the communications of these saints with holy women, which had given rise to many calumnies. Gregory established numerous convents of nuns. On the ancient pagan festivals, public prayers were offered and penances performed by hundreds of their members clothed as penitents, to repair the scandals then committed. A great deal of good was thus effected and the number of festivals consecrated to the demon and sin was thereby diminished; but St. Gregory had much to suffer from it. . . . . I saw also a picture of a certain deacon *Cyriacus*, who suffered unspeakably. Once he lay hidden and almost starving in the catacombs not far from where St. Peter's now stands. He was, later on, martyred. I remember that the deacon Cyriacus received Orders from Marcellus, and that,

with two Christians, Largus and Smaragdus, he assisted
the faithful condemned to labor at the public-works. He
was himself afterward condemned to do tho same. He
delivered the daughter of his persecuter from the power of
the devil.

" I recognized the bones of Placidus and Donatus, the
former of whom was as elegant in appearance as St. Francis de Sales. He was martyred in Sicily with his brothers.
I saw many scenes of his life, particularly- of his infancy.
He was the youngest of five children, three brothers and
one sister older than himself. Even as a child, he was looked
upon as a saint. I saw him, an infant in his mother's arms,
seize a roll of writings and joyously lay his tiny hands upon
the names of Jesus and Mary. He was universally loved.
Often whole families gathered round him on his mother's
knee. Then I saw him as a boy in the garden with his pious
tutor, where he amused himself tracing crosses in the sand,
or weaving them of flowers and leaves, the birds
hopping familiarly about him. When older he was taken
to another place to make his studies, and afterward to the
convent of St. Benedict which still had a few scholars. He
was slender, handsome, and rapidly developing into a most
distinguished-looking youth.—At the same time, I had a
vision of another saint of very low condition in life, reared
as a herdsman, but who afterward became Pope. I saw
the life of each side by side.—-I spoke with Placidus and he
again promised me help, telling me that I had only to invoke him when I wanted him and he would surely come."

One day the Pilgrim drew Sister Emmerich's attention
to the fact that St. Teresa's Feast was at hand, adding:
" We have a relic of her here, also one of *Catherine of
Sienna*. There they lie among several others," whereupon she began and named in their order the saints whose

relics hung in a cross at the foot of her bed. "I see their names, either at their feet or by their side, and I see, too, their attributes. There is Ediltrudis with the crown she resigned, and there are *Teresa, Radegonda, Genevieve, Catherine, Phocas,* and *Mary Cleophas.* The last named is taller than Mary, but dressed in the same style; she is the daughter of Mary's eldest sister. And there I see *Ambrose, Urban,* and *Silvanus !"*—The Pilgrim asked: "Where is Pelagia ?" and she answered: "She is not by me any more, she is *there,*" pointing to the Pilgrim's breast-pocket, where indeed, the relic really was, he having taken it to fold and label as one already recognized. The same was the case with another which he still had about him for a similar purpose. As he approached her she cried out: "O I see *Engelbert !* Have we his relics too ?"—The Pilgrim handed her the relics and next day she said: "I recognized that relic. It belongs to Engelbert of Cologne. Last night I saw many incidents of his life. He was very influential at court, where he was occupied with important diplomatic affairs. He led an upright, fervent life ; but on account of his position, he was not so much given to interior things as other saints. His devotion to Mary was very great. I saw him busy in the Cathedral, arranging in caskets precious relics no longer known and burying them altogether under the altars. But that was not proper. I saw his death.—He was attacked whilst on a journey and horribly maltreated by a relative whom he had once been obliged to punish. I counted over seventy wounds on his body. He was sanctified by his earnest preparation for death, for he had shortly before made a fervent general confession. The unspeakable patience with which he endured his slow murder also contributed thereto, for he never ceased praying for his assassins. The Mother of God was with him visibly consoling and encouraging him to suffer and die patiently; he was indebted to her for his holy death. I have also recognized the relic of *St. Cunibert* of Cologne. I saw him as a boy sleeping near King Dagobert."

St. Agnes and St. Emerentiana.

"I saw a very lovely delicate maiden dragged through the streets by rude soldiers. She was wrapped in a long brown woollen mantle, her braided hair concealed under a veil. The soldiers seized her mantle by the sides and dragged her so violently forward that they tore it apart. They were followed by a crowd, among them a few women. She was led through a high gateway, across a square court, and into an apartment destitute of furniture, saving some long, cushioned chests. They pushed her in and dragged her from side to side, and tore from her both mantle and veil. Agnes was like an innocent patient lamb in their hands, and light and airy as a bird; she seemed to fly as they pulled her here and there. They took her mantle and left her. Agnes in a white, sleeveless undergarment open at the sides now stood back in the corner of the room praying calmly with outstretched hands and face upturned. The women who had followed her were not admitted into the court-yard. All sorts of men stood around the doors as if the saint were their common prey. I saw her white tunic bloody around the neck from a wound received, perhaps on the way.—First two or three youths entered and fell upon her, furiously dragging her hither and thither, and tearing from her person the open garment. I saw blood on her neck and breast. She did not attempt to defend herself, for, on the instant they deprived her of her garments, her long hair fell down around her, and I saw a shining figure just above her in the air, who spread over her, like

a garment, a stream of light. The wretches who had assaulted her fled terror-stricken. They encountered her insolent lover outside who began to mock their cowardice.
He rushed in himself to seize her; but Agnes grasped him
firmly by the hands and held him back. He fell to the
ground, but arose quickly, and again rushed madly upon
her.—Again did the virgin drive him back as far as the
door, and again did he fall; but this time motionless. She
stood calm as before, praying, shining, blooming, her face
like a brilliant rose. A loud cry was raised, and several
distinguished personages hastily entered the room. One
of them seemed to be the youth's father. He was furious,
indignant, he spoke of sorcery; but when Agnes told him that
she would pray for his son's restoration, if he would ask it
in the name of Jesus, he grew calm and begged her to do
so. Then Agnes turned toward the dead youth, and addressed a few words to him. He arose, and was led away
still weak and tottering. And now came other men toward
Agnes; but like the first they too retired in fright. Then I
saw the soldiers go into the room. They took with them a
brown robe, open at the side and fastened by a clasp, and an
old veil such as were generally given to the martyrs. Agnes
put the robe on, twisted her hair under the veil, and accompanied the soldiers to the judgment-hall. This was a square
place, surrounded by a wall in which were prisons, or chambers; one could stand on it and watch what was going on below. There were spectators on it at the time of which I
speak. Many Christians were led to the tribunal from a
prison which seemed not far from the place in which Agnes
had been so ill-used. I think they were a grandfather, his
two sons-in-law, and their children, all bound together with
cords. They were led before the judge who was seated on
a high stone seat in the square court-yard, and **Agnes with**

them. The judge spoke to them kindly, questioned them, and warned them ; but it was soon evident that the prisoners had been brought out only to be present at Agnes's death. Three times was she summoned before the tribunal. At last, she was condemned to be burned alive. She was led to a stake, made to mount three steps, and the faggots piled around her. They wanted to bind her, but this she would not allow. And now the torch was applied, and again I saw the shining youth shedding over her streams of light which enveloped her as with a screen whilst, at the same time, the flames turned upon her excutioner, leaving Agnes untouched. She was then taken down and led before the judge, at whose command she was placed upon a block, or stone. Again they wanted to bind her hands, but again she refused and crossed them on her bosom. The executioner seized her by the hair and cut off her head which, like Cecilia's, remained hanging upon one shoulder. Her body was thrown, clothed as it was, upon the funeral pile, and the other Christians were led back to their prisons. During the trial, I saw Agnes's friends standing afar off weeping. I often wondered that nothing was ever done to the friends who showed so much sympathy, assisting and consoling the martyrs. Agnes's body was not burned, nor her clothing neither, I think. Her soul went forth from her body white as the moon, and flew toward heaven. Her execution took place in the forenoon, I think, for it was still day when her friends took the body from the funeral pile and reverently buried it. Many were present, but enveloped in mantles, to avoid being known, I think. I saw at the tribunal the youth whom Agnes restored to life, but who was not yet converted.—I saw Agnes also apart from this vision, as an apparition near me, radiant and sparkling with light, a palm in her hand. The aureola which surrounded her whole person was rosy in the centre, the rays changing to blue. She was full of joy; she consoled me in my sharp pains, saying: ' With Jesus to suffer, in Jesus to suffer, is sweet!'—I cannot describe the great difference there is between these Romans and people of the present day. There was no mixture in them; they were wholly one thing or another. With us all is so indifferent, so complicated! It is as if there were in us a thousand compartments within a thousand compartments.

"I had another vision. I saw a maiden prostrate in prayer at Agnes's tomb whither she often went by night, wrapped in a long mantle, gliding along like Magdalen to the tomb of Our Lord. I saw the enemies of the Christians lying in wait for her; they fell upon her and dragged her off.—Then I saw a little church, a perfect octagon, and over its altar a feast among the saints, apparently a patronal feast, very simple, innocent, and yet solemn. A lovely young martyr sat on a throne whilst other Roman martyrs, youths and maidens of the early times, wreathed her with garlands. I saw St. Agnes and by her a little lamb."

Here the Pilgrim handed Sister Emmerich a relic under which in legible characters appeared the name of the *Apos tle St. Matthew*, but which she had already designated as belonging to *S^t. Emerentiana*. Scarcely had she touched it when she exclaimed: " O what a lovely child! Whence comes that beautiful child? And see, there's a woman with another child !"— Next morning she related what follows: —"Last night I saw two lovely children with a nurse. First, one about four years old, came out through a gate in a portico, followed by an old woman with a hooked nose, like a Jewess. She was dressed in a flowing garment, a scalloped collar, and lappets like maniples on her arms. She led another little girl of about five and a half years.

The old nurse walked up and down under the portico whilst the children played. The centre columns of the portico were round, capped by curled heads crowned with crisped leaves, and entwined by sculptured serpents with beautiful human faces which stretched out from the columns. The corner ones were square with huge masks cut on the inner side, like oxen's heads, below which were hollowed out three round holes one under the other. At certain distances in the inner wall stood pillars; above it was a platform to which steps led on either side. In the middle was an arrangement like a tabernacle by which something could be turned out from the wall. All around were seats sculptured like the lower part of the columns; below them were compartments in which the children could put their toys. Here the nurse sat and watched them. The two lovely children wore little knit or woven slips like shirts confined by a belt. Some other children from the neighborhood joined them and they played very nicely together, mostly near the tabernacle which they drew out and in which they put their toys, little puppets on wires very artistically made. They skipped around the steps by the tabernacle, and ran up and down to the platform. They had, also, some little vessels with which they played by the seats with the semi-circular boxes. I took a peevish little thing up into my lap, but she struggled and would not stay with me. This made me feel sad, for I thought it was because of my unworthiness. Then the strange children went home, and the servant, or nurse, took her two in through the gate, across a court-yard, and up a flight of steps to an apartment in which the mother of one was seated apparently reading from a book. She was a large woman, wore a robe with folds, walked heavily and languidly, had a grave air, and took little notice of

the children. She did not caress them although she gave them
little cakes of different shapes and colors. She took still
less notice of the strange child than of her own. The
seats in this room were like cushions, some leather, others
worsted, and they had something by which to lift them.
The ceiling and walls were covered with paintings. The
windows were not glass, but furnished with nets embroidered in all sorts of figures. In the corners of the room
stood statues on pedestals.—Then I saw the nurse and
children in a garden which lay like a court-yard in the
middle of the building, with rooms all around it and a
fountain in the centre. Here the children played and ate
fruit. I saw not the father.—And now I had another picture. I saw the two children a few years later alone and
in prayer, and I felt that their nurse was a Christian in
secret and that she directed their steps. I saw them going
by night stealthily with other maidens to one of the small
houses next the large mansion. I also saw persons cautiously approaching by night the house in which they lived,
and giving the inmates a sign through a hole in the wall,
whereupon the latter arose and came out. The nurse used
to lead the children out by a back passage and then return
I saw them wrapped in mantles and gliding with others by
an old wall to a subterranean apartment in which many
people were assembled. There were two such rooms. In
one was an altar on which all on entering deposited
an offering. In the other was no altar; it appeared
to be used only for prayer and instruction. To these
secret underground reunions, I saw the children going by
night.

"Again I stood before the house in which I had seen the
little ones at play, and I felt an eager desire for them to
come out. I saw one of their playmates, and I sent her in

to coax the nurse to bring the children out. She did so with Agnes in her arms, an infant of about eighteen months. She said that the other child was not there. I replied that she would certainly come soon, and we went together to a great shade tree like a linden. Sure enough, here came the other child in the arms of a young girl from a small, neighboring house. But the nurses could not stay; they had something to do. I begged them to leave the children with me a little while which they did. I took them both on my knees, kissed, and caressed them ; but they soon grew uneasy and began to cry. 1 had nothing to give them and, in my perplexity, I laid them on my breast when they became quiet. I threw around them my large mantle when suddenly, to my surprise and alarm, I felt that they were really receiving nourishment from me. I handed them to their nurses who soon returned followed by the children's mothers. Emerentiana's mother was the smaller, the more active, the more pleasing of the two. She carried her child home herself, whilst Agnes's mother let the nurse carry her. But now, to my great alarm, I noticed something strange about my breasts, as if by the children's suckling they had become swollen, full of nourishment, and I felt an oppression, a burning in them which gave me great anxiety. I was hardly half-way home, when two poor children of our neighborhood came and drained my breast, causing me much pain. Several others did the same. I noticed on these poor little ones swarms of vermin which I removed ; so they were fed and cleaned at the same time. I was relieved of the oppression in my breast ; but, as I thought it had all happened in consequence of the relics, I put them away in the closet." The following day as Sister Emmerich lay in ecstasy, the Pilgrim approached her bed with the relics of Sts. Agnes and Emerentiana. She turned quickly away, exclaiming : " No, No ! I cannot ! I love those children, but I cannot again ! "—

St. Paula.

Father Limberg handed the invalid a scrap of brown stuff from a package of relics, with the question : "What is this ?" Sister Emmerich looked at it attentively and then said in a decided tone : " It belongs to the veil of the lady who went from Rome to Jerusalem and Bethlehem ; it is a scrap of St. Paula's veil. I see the saint standing there in a long veil that falls over her face. She holds a gnarled stick in her hand." Then she recognized another scrap of silk as part of the curtain that hung before the manger in Paula's little chapel. " The saint," she said, " and her daughter often prayed behind this curtain. The Infant Jesus frequently appeared to them there." The Pilgrim asked : " Was it the curtain of the true Crib, the Grotto ?" She answered : " No ! it hung before the little representa-tion of the true Crib which St. Paula's nuns had in their chapel. The monastery was so near the Holy Grotto that the chapel seemed to join it. It was right next the spot in which Jesus was born. It was built only of wood and wicker-work, and the inside was hung with tapestry. From it ran four rows of cells lightly built, as the pilgrims' quarters always are in the Holy Land. Each had a little garden in front. Here it was that Paula and her daughter gathered together their first companions. In the chapel stood an altar with a tabernacle behind which, concealed by a red and white silk curtain, was the crib arranged by St. Paula. It was separated only by a wall from the true place of the birth of Jesus. The crib was a true represen-tation of the Holy Crib, only smaller and of white stone ; but so exact that even the straw was imitated. The little

child lay closely wrapped in blue swathing-bands; and
when Paula knelt before it, she used to take it up in her
arms. Where the crib rested against the wall hung a
curtain on which was wrought in colors the ass with his head
turned toward the crib, its hair done in thread. Over the
crib was fixed a star and before the curtain, on either side
of the altar, hung lamps."

St. Agatha.

" Last night I was in that city in which I saw the great
insurrection (*Palermo*). The churches and houses still bear
the marks of it. I saw a grand and wonderful festival. The
church was hung with tapestry and in the middle of it was a
curtain like our Lenten curtain, our *Hungertuch*.—In one
place I saw a great fire like our St. John's fires, to which the
priests all went in procession carrying a veil. It was a grand
festival, great pomp and parade. The people seem to join
in it eagerly, and brawls are of frequent occurrence. The
church was magnificent and, during the ceremonies, I saw
Agatha and other saints.

" I saw that Agatha was martyred in another city, Catana, though her parents lived in Palermo. Her mother, a
Christian in secret, had instructed her child in the faith;
but the father was a pagan. Agatha had two nurses. From
her earliest years, she enjoyed most familiar intercourse
with Jesus. I often saw her sitting in the garden, and
by her a shining, beautiful Boy playing and conversing
with her; it seemed as if they were growing up together.
I saw her make a seat for Him in the grass and listen to
Him thoughtfully, her hands in her lap. Sometimes they
played with flowers and little sticks. He seemed to grow
as she grew, but He only came when she was alone. I
think she saw Him, for her actions indicated consciousness

of His presence. I saw her increase wonderfully in interior purity and strength of soul. It is impossible to say
how one sees such things.—It is as if some object continually became more magnificent, like gold being purified,
a spark becoming a star, a fire becoming a sun! I
saw Agatha's extraordinary fidelity to grace. I saw her
constant turning-away from every shadow of impurity,
from every little imperfection for which she punished herself severely. When she would have wished to lie down
in the evening, her guardian-angel often stood visibly by her
side reminding her of something, some forgotten duty perhaps, which she would then hasten to perform : some prayer,
some alms, something relating to charity, purity, humility,
obedience, mercy, or some effort to prevent sin.—I often
saw her as a child gliding along unknown to her mother
with alms and food for the poor. She was so noble, so dear
to Jesus,—and yet she lived in a constant struggle!
I often saw her pinch and strike herself for the least faults,
the slightest inclinations ; but with it all, she was so open,
so frank, so courageous !—I saw her in her eighth year
taken in a carriage with several other maidens to Catana.—
This was by her father's orders, for he wanted her reared
in all the liberty of paganism. She was placed in the house
of a shameless woman who had five daughters. I cannot
say that she kept a public-house of infamy, such as I have
often seen in those times ; she seemed rather to be a bold
worldly woman of high position. Her house was beautifully situated, everything about it sumptuous. Here Agatha
remained a long time, but she was never allowed to go out.
I generally saw her with other little girls in a handsome room
before which lay a lake which reflected in its waters the
whole house ; the other sides of the dwelling were guarded.
The lady and her five daughters gave themselves the greatest

trouble imaginable to form Agatha to their kind of *virtue.* I saw them walking with her in the beautiful gardens and showing her all kinds of elegant clothes; but she turned away indifferently from such things. And here too I often saw the Heavenly Boy at her side, whilst she daily became more serious, more courageous. Agatha was a very beautiful child, not tall, but perfectly formed. She had dark hair, great black eyes, a beautiful nose, round face, a very mild but firm manner and an expression indicative of extraordinary strength of soul. Her mother died of grief during her child's absence.

"I saw Agatha in this house constantly and courageously overcoming herself and her natural inclinations, resisting every seduction. Quintianus, who afterward condemned her to death, often visited the house. He was a married man, but he could not endure his wife. He was a disagreeable, very vulgar, and insolent man, and he used to go prowling around the city spying out everything, annoying and tormenting the inhabitants. I used to see him with the lady of the house. He often looked at Agatha as one might gaze on a beautiful child; but he never offered her any improper attentions. I saw her Heavenly Bridegroom standing by her, visible to her alone, and I heard Him say to her: 'Our bride is little, she has no breasts (1). When she will have them, they will be cut off; for none shall ever drink thereof!'—The Youth spoke these words to Agatha in vision, and they mean that but few Christians, few priests were then in her country (Sicily) (2). I saw that the instruments of her martyrdom were shown her by her Bridegroom; indeed, I think they played with them.—

(1) Canticle viii., 8.

(2) Agatha was " *The Bride,*" the Church of Sicily, as yet young...... Her martyrdom was here foretold. by which she was to become the spiritual mother of innumerable souls, to whom the milk of her breasts ; viz., the rich blessings flowing from her martyrdom, was to procure the grace of salvation.

Later, I saw Agatha again in her native city, after her father's death when she was about thirteen years old. She made an open profession of Christianity and had only good people around her.—Then I saw her dragged from her house by men sent by Quintianus from Catana to arrest her. In passing out of the city-gate, she stooped to fasten her shoe and looking back, she perceived that all her friends had abandoned her and were hurrying back to the city. Agatha begged God to set up some sign as a memorial of their ingratitude, when instantly there arose on the spot a sterile olive-tree.

"I saw Agatha again with the wicked woman and her Heavenly Bridegroom by her. He said: 'When the serpent, formerly mute, began to speak, Eve should have known it was the devil.'—The woman tried again in every way to seduce her by flattery and amusements, but I heard Agatha applying to her the teachings of her Bridegroom. When she urged her to wantonness, Agatha replied: 'Thy flesh and blood are, like the serpent, creatures of God; but he who speaks through them is the devil!' I saw Quintianus's communications with this woman, and I knew very well two of his other friends there.—Then I saw Agatha thrown into prison, interrogated, beaten, and finally, her breasts cut off. One man held her whilst a second took off the breasts with an instrument shaped like a poppy-pod. It opened in three parts like a mouth, and bit off the breast in one piece. The executioners had the revolting cruelty to hold them up mockingly before the maiden, and then throw them on the ground at her feet. During the torture, Agatha said to Quintianus: 'Dost thou not shudder to tear from a woman that from which thy own mother once fed thee?' She stood firm, self-possessed, and once she exclaimed: My soul has breasts more noble than

those thou canst take from me !' Agatha was scarcely
more than a child, and her bosom was far from being developed. The wound was perfectly round; it was not
lacerated, the blood gushed out in little streams. I often
saw that same instrument used in torturing the martyrs.
They used to tear off whole pieces of flesh from their person with it. How wonderful were the help and strength
the martyrs received from Jesus Christ! I often see Him
by them strengthening them for the combat; they faint not
where another would die.—Then I saw Agatha in prison
where an aged man appeared to her, offering to heal her
wounds. She thanked him, but replied that she had never
had recourse to medicine; that she had her Lord Jesus
Christ who could heal her if He so willed. 'I am a Christian and a gray-haired old man,' said he, 'be not ashamed
of me!' She replied: 'My wounds have nothing about
them revolting to modesty! But Jesus will heal me, if He
sees fit. He created the whole world, and He can also restore my breasts!' Then the old man laughed and said: 'I
am His servant Peter! Behold! Thy breasts are healed!'
and he disappeared.—I saw that an angel fastened to the
roof of her prison something like a ticket on which was
writing, but I do not now remember what it was. Agatha's
breasts were perfectly restored. It was not merely a healing of the skin, it was a new, a perfect bosom.
Around each breast I saw circles of light, the inner
one composed of rainbow-colored rays. Again was Agatha
led forth to martyrdom. In a vault were rows of furnaces
like deep chests, stuck full of sharp points and potsherds ;
under them burned fires. There was room to pass between
the chests, and many poor victims were roasted at the same
time. As Agatha was thrown into one of these furnaces,
the earth quaked, and a falling wall crushed the two friends

of Quintianus. The latter had fled during a revolt of the people. Agatha was led back again to her prison where she died. I saw Quintianus, when on his way to seize Agatha's property, drowning miserably in a river.—I afterward saw a mountain vomiting forth fire, and people fleeing before the fiery wave. It rolled as far as Agatha's tomb, where it was extinguished."

St. Dorothea.

" Again I recognized this saint's relic and I saw a large city in a hill country. Playing in the garden of a house built in the Roman style, were three little girls between five and eight years old. They took hold of hands, danced in a ring, stood still, sang, and gathered flowers. After awhile the two eldest ran away from the youngest, tearing up their flowers as they went, and leaving the little one deeply hurt at their treatment of her. I saw her standing there all alone with a sharp pain in her heart, a pain which I also felt. Her face grew pale, her clothing became white as snow, and she fell to the ground as if dead. Then I heard an interior voice saying : ' That is Dorothea !' and I saw the apparition of a resplendent Boy approaching her with a bouquet of flowers in his hand. He raised her, led her to another part of the garden, gave her the bouquet, and disappeared. The little thing was delighted ; she ran to the other two, showed them her flowers, and told them who had given them to her. Her companions were amazed ; they pressed the child to their heart, appeared sorry for the pain they had caused her, and peace was restored. At this sight I felt an eager desire for some such flowers to strengthen me. All at once, Dorothea stood before me as a young maiden, and made me a beautiful discourse in preparation for Communion. ' Why sighest thou after flowers ?' she asked, 'thou who so often receivest the Flower of all flowers !'—Then she explained the vision I had just had of the children, the desertion and return of the two elder ones, and I had another vision referring to her martyrdom. I saw her imprisoned with her elder sisters, a contest going on among them. The two elder wished not to die for Jesus, and so they were set free. Dorothea was sent by the judge to the two apostates in the hope that she would follow their example and advice. But the contrary was the case ; she brought her sisters back to the faith. Then Dorothea was fastened to a stake, torn with hooks, burned with torches and, finally, beheaded. Whilst she was being tortured, I saw a youth, who had mocked at her on her way to martyrdom and to whom she had addressed a few words, suddenly converted. A resplendent boy appeared to him with roses and fruits. He entered into himself, confessed the faith, and suffered martyrdom by decapitation. With Dorothea suffered many others ; some by fire, some by being fastened to animals and quartered."

St. Apollonia.

"I had the saint's relic by me, and I saw the city in which she was martyred. It stands on a cape not far from the mouth of the Nile ; it is a large and beautiful city. The house of Apollonia's parents stood on an elevated spot surrounded by court-yards and gardens. Apollonia was, at the time of her martyrdom, an aged widow (1), very tall. Her parents were pagans. But she had been converted in childhood by her nurse, a Christian in secret, and had married a pagan in obedience to her parents, with whom she lived at home. She had much to suffer ; married life was for her a rude penance. I have seen her lying on the

(1) In the Roman Martyrology and Breviary she is designated as *V. M.*

ground, praying, weeping, her head covered with ashes. Her husband was very thin and pale, and he died long before her, leaving her childless. She survived him thirty years. Apollonia was extremely compassionate to the poor persecuted Christians ; she was the hope and consolation of all in suffering. Her nurse also suffered martyrdom shortly before her in an insurrection, during which the dwellings of Christians were plundered and burned, and many of the occupants put to death. —Later on, I saw Apollonia herself arrested in her house by the judge's orders, led before the tribunal, and cast into prison. Again I saw her brought before the judge and horribly maltreated, on account of her severe and resolute answers. It was a heart-rending sight and I cried bitterly, although I had witnessed with less emotion even more cruel punishments ; perhaps it was her age and dignified bearing that touched me. They beat her with clubs, and struck her on the face and head with stones until her nose was broken. Blood flowed from her head, her cheeks and chin were all torn, and her teeth shattered in her gums. She wore the open white robe in which I have so often seen the martyrs, and under it a colored woollen tunic. The executioners placed her on a stone seat without a back, her hands chained behind her to the stone, her feet in fetters. Her veil was torn off, and her long hair hung around her face, which was quite disfigured and covered with blood. One executioner stood behind and violently forced back her head, whilst another opened wide her torn mouth and pressed into it a small block of lead. Then with great pincers he drew out the broken teeth one after the other, tearing away with each a piece of the jaw-bone. Apollonia almost fainted under this torture, but I saw angels, souls of other martyrs, and Jesus Himself strengthening and consol-

ing her. At her own request, the power was conferred
upon her of relieving all pains of the teeth, head, or face.
As she still continued to glorify Jesus and insult the idols,
the judge ordered her to be thrown on the funeral pile.
She could not walk alone, she was half dead; consequently,
two executioners had to support her under the arms to a
high place where a fire burned in a pit. As she stood a
moment before it, she appeared to pray for something; she
could no longer hold up her head. The pagans thought
she was about to deny Jesus, that she was wavering, and so
they released their hold upon her. She sank on the ground
as if dying, lay there a moment, and then suddenly arose
praying, and leaped into the flames.—During the whole
time of her martyrdom, I saw crowds of the poor whom she
had befriended wringing their hands, weeping, and lamenting. Apollonia could never have leaped into the fire by
herself. Strength came to her with the inspiration from
God. She was not consumed, but only scorched. When
she was dead, the pagans withdrew; and the Christians,
approaching stealthily, took the holy body and buried it in
a vault."

St. Benedict and St. Scholastica.

" Through the relics of St. Scholastica, I saw many
scenes in her life and that of St. Benedict. I saw their paternal house in a great city, not far from Rome. It was
not built entirely in the Roman style; before it was a paved
court-yard whose low wall was surmounted by a red lattice-
work, and behind lay another court with a garden and a
fountain. In the garden was a beautiful summer-house
overrun by vines, and here I saw Benedict and his little
sister Scholastica, playing as loving, innocent children are
wont to amuse themselves. The flat ceiling of the summer-

house was painted all over with figures which I thought, at first, sculptured, so clearly were their outlines defined. The brother and sister were very fond of each other and so nearly of the same age that I thought them twins. The birds flew in familiarly at the windows with flowers and twigs in their beaks and sat gazing at the children who, also, were playing with flowers and leaves, planting sticks and making gardens. I saw them writing and cutting all sorts of figures out of colored stuffs. Occasionally their nurse came to look after them. Their parents seemed to be people of wealth who had much business on hand, for I saw about twenty persons employed in the house; but they did not seem to trouble themselves about their children. The father was a large, powerful man, clothed in the Roman style; he took his meals with his wife and some other members of the family in the lower part of the house, whilst the children lived entirely up-stairs in separate apartments. Benedict had for preceptor an old ecclesiastic with whom he stayed almost all the time, and Scholastica had a nurse near whom she slept. The brother and sister were not often allowed to be alone together; but whenever they could steal off for awhile, they were very gleeful and happy. I saw Scholastica by her nurse's side, learning some kind of work. In the room next that in which she slept stood a table on which lay in baskets the materials for her work, various colored stuff, from which she cut figures of birds, flowers, etc., to be sewed on other larger pieces. When finished they looked as if carved on the ground-work. The ceilings of the rooms, like that of the summer-house, were covered with different colored pictures. The windows were not glass; they were of some kind of stuff on which were embroidered all sorts of figures, trees, lines, and pointed ornaments. Scholastica slept on a low bed behind a curtain. I saw her in the morning when her nurse left the room, spring out of bed and prostrate in prayer before a crucifix on the wall. When she heard the nurse returning she used to slip quickly behind the curtain and be in bed again before she re-entered the room. I saw Benedict and Scholastica separately learning from the former's tutor. They read from great rolls of parchment, and they painted letters in red, gold, and an extraordinarily fine blue. As they wrote they rolled the parchment. They made use of an instrument about as long as one's finger. The older the children grew, the less were they allowed to be together.

" I saw Benedict at Rome, when about fourteen years old, in a large building in which there was a corridor with many rooms; it looked like a school, or a monastery. There were many young men and some old ecclesiastics in a large hall, as if at a holiday feast. The ceilings were adorned with the same kind of paintings as those in Benedict's home. The guests did not eat reclining. They sat on round seats so low that they were obliged to stretch out their feet; some sat on one side, back to back, at a very low table. There were holes hollowed in the massive table to receive the yellow plates and dishes; but I did not see much food, only three large plates of flat, yellow cakes in the centre of the table. When all had finished, I saw six females of different ages, relatives of the youths, enter the hall bearing something like sweetmeats and little flasks in baskets on their arms. The young men arose and conversed with their friends at one end of the hall, eating the dainties and drinking from the flasks. There was one woman of about thirty years of age, whom I had once before seen at Benedict's home. She approached the young man with marked affability : but he, perfectly pure and innocent, suspected nothing bad in her. I saw that she hated his purity and entertained a sinful love for him. She gave him a poisoned, an enchanted drink from a flask. Benedict suspected nothing, but I saw him that evening in his cell restless and tormented. He went, at last, to a man and asked permission to go down into the court-yard, for he never went out without leave. There he knelt in a corner of the yard, disciplining himself with long thorn branches and nettles.—I saw him, later on, when a hermit, helping this his would-be seducer who had fallen into deep distress precisely because she had sought to tempt him. Benedict had been interiorly warned of her guilt.

"Afterward I saw Benedict on a high, rocky mountain when, perhaps, in his twentieth year. He had hollowed out a cell for himself in the rock. To this he added a passage and another cell, and then several cells all cut in the rock ; but only the first opened outside. Before it he had planted a walk of trees. He arched them and ornamented the vaulted roof with pictures which seemed to be made of many small stones put together. In one cell I saw three such pictures : Heaven in the centre, the Nativity of Christ on one side, the Last Judgment on the other. In the last, Our Lord was represented sitting on an arch, a sword proceeding from His mouth ; below, between the elect and the reprobate, stood an angel with a pair of scales. Benedict had, besides, made a representation of a monastery with its abbot, and crowds of monks in the background. He seemed to have had a foresight of his own monastery.

"More than once I saw Benedict's sister, who lived at home, going on foot to visit her brother. He never allowed her to stay with him over night. Sometimes she brought him a roll of parchment which she had written. Then he showed her what he had done, and they conversed together on divine things. Benedict was always very grave in his sister's presence whilst she, in her innocence, was all mirth and joy. When she found him too serious, she turned to God in prayer, and he instantly became like herself, bright and gay. Later on, I saw her under her brother's direction, establishing a convent on a neighboring mountain distant only a short day's journey. To it flocked numbers of religious women. I saw her teaching them to chant; they had no organs. Organs have been very prejudicial to singing. They make of it only a secondary affair. The nuns prepared all the church ornaments themselves with the same kind of needlework that Scholastica had learned when a child at home. On the refectory table was a large cloth on which were all sorts of figures, pictures, and sentences, so that each religious always had before her that to which she was especially obliged. Scholastica spoke to me of the sweets and consolations of spiritual labor and the labor of ecclesiastics.

" I always saw Scholastica and Benedict surrounded by tame birds. Whilst the former was yet in her father's house, I used to see doves flying from her to Benedict in the desert; and in the monastery I saw around her doves and larks bringing her red, white, yellow, and violet-blue flowers. Once I saw a dove bringing her a rose with a leaf. I cannot repeat all the scenes of her life that were shown me, for I am so sick and miserable! Scholastica was purity itself. I see her in heaven as white as snow. With the exception of Mary and Magdalen, I know of no saint so loving."

St. Eulalia (1).

Among Sister Emmerich's relics were two teeth marked *St. Eulalia.* After some time, she said : "Only one of these teeth belongs to the holy virgin-martyr Eulalia of Barcelona. The other belongs to a priest who received Holy Orders at an advanced age, and whom I have seen journeying around helping widows and orphans. St. Eulalia's tooth was drawn about six months before her martyrdom. I saw the whole operation. The tooth caused her much suffering and she had it extracted at a young friend's house because her mother, through excessive tenderness, could not endure that it should be done at home. The old man who drew the tooth was a Christian. He sat on a low stool, Eulalia before him on the floor, her back to him. She rested her back against him and he quickly drew the tooth with an instrument which fitted closely around it.—The instrument had a transverse piece to the haft. When the tooth came out, he held it up in the pincers before the two girls, who both began to laugh. Eulalia's friend begged her to make her a present of it, which she readily did. All Eulalia's companions loved her and, after her martyrdom, the tooth became a more precious object, a sacred relic to the possessor. It passed successively into the hands of two other females. Later on, I saw it in a church enclosed in a silver box shaped like a little censer. It hung before a picture of St. Apollonia. In this picture Apollonia was represented not as old, but young with pincers in her hand and a pointed cap on her head. Then I saw that, when this church had been despoiled of its silver, the tooth fell into the possession of a pious maiden

Sister Emmerich had frequently felt and referred to the presence of this relic, saying : " There must be a *St. Culalia* in my church ! She belongs to Barcelona." She had seen the name in vision in small Roman letters, and had mistaken *C* for *E.*

far away from Eulalia's native land.   A little piece of one
of the roots had been broken off, which I also saw preserved
as a relic, but I cannot name the place.   The tooth shines,
but not with the glory of martyred bones.   It shines by
reason of Eulalia's innocence and the ardent desire to die
for Jesus which even then animated her ; and also on account of the intense pain she endured so patiently from it.
I do not see the bones that the saints lost before martyrdom
shining with the colors of the glory that distinguishes their
other relics.   To the light of this tooth was wanting the
martyrdom of the whole person.   Eulalia's parents were
very distinguished people.   They lived in a large house
surrounded by olive-trees and others with yellow fruits.
They were Christians, but not very zealous ones ; they
allowed nothing of their faith to be remarked in them.
Eulalia was intimate with a female older than herself, a
zealous Christian, who lived not far from Eulalia's home in
which she was often employed to do great pieces of embroidery.   I saw her and Eulalia making church-vestments
secretly by night, fastening in round-stitch figures on cloth.
They used a lamp with a transparent shade ; it gave a very
clear light.   I used to see Eulalia retired in her own chamber, praying before a simple cross which she had cut out of
box wood.   She was consumed with a desire to confess
Jesus openly, for he often showed her in vision the martyr's
crown.   I saw her walking with other maidens and expressing to them the longings which she dared not utter in her
father's house."

St. Walburga.

Sister Emmerich took from " *her church* " a finger-bone,
looked at it in silence for a moment, and then exclaimed :
"What a sweet little nun ! so clear, so beautiful, so trans-

parent! She is altogether angelic! It is Walburga!
I see her convent, too." Then followed visions of the
saint and of the disinterring of her sacred remains, which
Sister Emmerich gives as follows : "Two blessed nuns
took me into a church in which a grand festival was
being celebrated, either the translation of a saint's relics, or
a canonization. A Bishop was superintending everything,
and assigning places to the assistants. It was not the
church of the convent in which Walburga had lived; it was
another and a larger one, and the crowd was far greater
than I had ever seen around the crucifix at Coesfeld. Numbers were obliged to remain outside the doors. I stood
near the altar, not far from the sacristy, the two nuns by
me. On the steps of the altar was a plain white chest containing the holy body; the white linen cloth was raised and
hung at either side. The body was white as snow, and
one might have thought her alive, so rosy were her cheeks.
Walburga always had the pure, fair complexion of a delicate
little child. The feast began with High Mass. But I
could not stand any longer. I must have fainted, for I
found myself lying on the ground, my two companions at
my head and feet. I saw an abbess of Walburga's convent
in the sacristy preparing three kinds of dough for bread :
two fine ; the third coarser, of white flour indeed, but full
of chaff, and I began to wonder for whom they were. Here
I lost sight of the earthly festival and I entered a heavenly
garden in which I was shown Walburga's reward in heaven.
I saw her with Benedict, Scholastica, Maurus, Placidus,
and many holy virgins of Benedict's Rule, at a table spread
with marvellous dishes. At the head sat Walburga completely surrounded by garlands and arches of flowers.—
When I returned to the church, the feast was over; but I
received from the Bishop and abbess a loaf of coarse bread,

marked with the number IV. The fine bread was given
to my companions. The Bishop told me that my loaf was
for myself alone, that I must not give it away. Then
he led me out before the church door where St. Walburga's nuns had their little oratory, and I had another vision of Walburga. She had, a short time before her blessed
death, been found as if dead in her kneeling-place. Her
brother Willibald was sent for and, to his surprise, he saw
her face and hands covered with white dew-drops like
manna. He gathered it into a brown bowl and gave it to
the nuns as a holy thing. They wrought numerous cures
with it after Walburga's death. When she returned to
herself, Willibald gave her Holy Communion. The dew
prefigured Walburga's oil, which I saw had begun to flow
on a Thursday, because the saint bore so great a devotion to
the Blessed Sacrament and Our Saviour's agony in the
garden of Olives. As often as I take this oil, I feel
strengthened as by a heavenly dew ; it has helped me
greatly in severe sicknesses. Walburga was full of tenderest love for the poor. She used to see them in vision.
She knew even before they came to her how she should
distribute her bread among them. She gave to some whole
loaves, to others half, and to others pieces which she cut
herself. She gave them, also, a certain oil, thick poppy-
oil, I think, which she mixed with butter and spread on the
bread; besides which she gave them some for their cooking.
On account of her bounty and the soothing, consoling influence of her gentle, loving words, her relics have received
the property of distilling oil. Walburga also protects
against vicious dogs and wild beasts. I saw her going by
night to the sick daughter of a gentleman in the neighborhood of her convent. She was assailed by his dogs which,
however, she put to flight. She wore a narrow brown

habit, a broad girdle, and a black veil over a white one; it was more the dress of pious females of the time, than a regular religious habit. I saw a miracle which took place at the time of the great pilgrimage to her tomb. Two assassins joined a pilgrim on his way thither, the latter kindly sharing with them his bread; but they, in return, killed him as he slept. Then one took up the corpse on his back to bury it out of sight; but he could not lay it down again, it stuck to him as if it had grown fast. I saw him wandering around in despair with the corpse on his back until, at last, he plunged into the river to drown himself. But he could not sink, the waters would not have him; they cast him up on the opposite bank, the horrible load still clinging to him. Then I saw some one try to loosen the hands of the dead man with his sword; but, far from succeeding, he remained himself fastened to the corpse until he freed himself by prayer."—When the Pilgrim objected to this narrative, saying that it was strange she should see as true so many singular things which even pious priests denied, she replied: "One cannot say how simple, natural, and connected all such things appear in the state of contemplation; and, on the contrary, how perverse, unreasonable, and even insane are the intentions and actions of the enlightened world compared with them! People who think themselves very intelligent and who are esteemed such by others, often appear to me insane enough to be confined in a madhouse."

Sts. Paschal and Cyprian.

" As I took my church to arrange and venerate the holy relics, I recognized a splinter of an arm-bone as belonging to the holy martyr Paschal (1). He had been paralytic from childhood, though otherwise healthy. His father suffered in a persecution of the Christians, and young Paschal and his sister found a home with their elder brother who had a son, a priest also named Cyprian. I used to see the latter saying Mass underground, for the Christians all dwelt at that period in caves, ruined walls, and even in tombs. Cyprian was full of love and compassion for the poor cripple, who had not the use of his limbs; he was so deformed that his knees and chin met. When sixteen years old, Paschal begged to be taken to the tomb of a martyr; and about twenty persons, among them Cyprian, bore him on a litter to a place of martyrdom. They proceeded silently along by the prisons to a spot on which a saint had either been martyred or buried, I do not now remember which, and here they prayed. Paschal was in a kind of litter that could be raised or lowered at pleasure, and he prayed most fervently. Suddenly he sprang up, cast away his crutches, and joyfully thanked God for his perfect cure, which he had confidently expected in this place. I saw his friends eagerly embracing him; he returned with them perfectly cured. Then I saw in a series of pictures how pious and charitable he was, and how zealously he aided Cyprian, his brother's son, in the care of the sick and poor, carrying on his shoulders those who could not walk. His elder brother died, and I saw them burying him secretly. And now there broke out a great persecution, I think under the Emperor Nero. Multitudes of Christians, men, women, and maidens, were gathered together in a certain quarter of the city and, after a short examination, martyred in

(1) Sister Emmerich had this vision on Feb. 26, 1821; consequently, she looked upon this day as the anniversary of the martyrdom, or the miraculous discovery of the sacred remains of these two saints. According to the *Acta Sanctorum*, they were presented Feb. 26, 1646, by Cardinal Altieri, to the Jesuit College of Antwerp. St. Cyprian's body was given at a later period to the College of Mechlin.

many different ways. Trees opposite one another were bent down, and the martyrs bound to them by a leg or an arm. When the trees were allowed to resume their upright position, the Christians were torn asunder. I saw maidens hung up by the feet, their head almost touching the ground, their hands tied behind their back Whilst in this posture spotted animals, which looked like great cats, devoured the breasts of their still living body. Paschal's sister fled with many other Christians; but Paschal and Cyprian courageously repaired to the place of execution, to console and encourage their friends. They were, at first, driven off; but, having declared themselves Christians, they too were interrogated and martyred. The Christians were sometimes condemned to be crushed between immense stone plates which covered the whole body, with the exception of the arms and feet, which projected beyond them. Sometimes two were laid, one upon another, face to face, and crushed together. Paschal and Cyprian thus suffered, but side by side. Then my vision changed to a later period, one in which the Christians enjoyed more liberty, one in which they could visit and honor the tombs of the saints. I saw a father and mother carrying a lame boy about seven years old across a field in which many martyrs were interred. Monuments and little chapels stood here and there over the graves. At the end of the cemetery, which was named after Pope Calixtus, the parents halted with their afflicted children on a spot covered only with grass; for here, the boy said, lay two holy martyrs who would help him. They prayed. I think the child invoked them by name, and up he arose perfectly cured. Then I saw the mother and child kneeling to thank God, and the father running back to the city to proclaim the miracle. He returned with some men, among them

priests, who carefully dug around, until they came to the
bodies of the two saints. They lay arm in arm, well-preserved, perfectly white and dry. The tomb was quadrangular and, at the spot in which the saints' arms locked
there was a break in the low wall of partition between the
bodies. They were not entirely disinterred at this time,
but a festival was celebrated on the spot, the tomb was
beautifully repaired, and a writing deposited in it. It was
then closed, a roof supported by four or six columns raised
over it, and the whole sodded. I saw various kinds of
plants on it, one with very large leaves, a thick tuft like
the house-leek. Under the roof was a stone before which
was raised an altar with an opening on top which could be
closed at pleasure. On the vertical stone was an inscription. I saw the Holy Mass celebrated and Holy Communion
given, the communicants holding under the chin a plate and
white cloth. The sacred remains still lay buried there,though
the little edifice over their grave was destroyed at a later
period.—Then I had a vision of many graves in this cemetery
being opened and the holy remains removed, among them
those of Paschal and Cyprian, now mere skeletons, but still
lying in good condition. Then I saw them in two little
four-cornered caskets, in possession of the Jesuits of Antwerp, who with many solemn ceremonies and in grand procession richly encased the relics and laid them in beautiful
shrines."

Sts. Perpetua and Felicity.

On February 27, 1820, Sister Emmerich related the following: "Last night, as I began to bemoan before God my
pitiable state, I received this just reproach: 'How canst
thou complain, surrounded as thou art by so rich a treasure
of relics for which others had to journey so far? Thou

hast the privilege of living with these holy personages, of seeing all they did, of knowing all they were !' I felt then how wrong it was in me to repine, and I saw a whole troop of saints whose relics are here by me. In the life of St. Perpetua, I saw many scenes. Even as a child, she had visions of her future martyrdom.—It reminded me of a dream I had had in my childhood in which I thought I was to have nothing but black bread and water. I thought this signified that I was to be a beggar; but now I think Walburga's black bread which I received explains the dream.—I saw all the sufferings of Perpetua, Felicity, and others, martyred with and after them in the same country. They were hunted by beasts and put to the sword." At these words, Sister Emmerich took one of the relics, kissed it, laid it upon her heart, and said : "Perpetua is there by me !" then, taking another little particle, she exclaimed : "This is very precious. It is the bone of a little boy who courage-ously suffered martyrdom with his father, mother, and two sisters. He was imprisoned with Perpetua and he suffered by fire. There were little eminences in an enclosed place and on them stakes, or seats, on which the martyrs were placed, the fire being lighted all around them. The bone shines with wonderful brilliancy, a glory of the finest blue with golden rays, such as surrounded the child-martyr. The light is so wonderfully invigorating that no words can express it.--I thought at first that Perpetua and Felicity were martyred in Rome, because I saw them executed in a building similar to the one in that city ; but now I know that it was in a place far distant."

March 2d—" I had St. Perpetua's relic and I saw many pictures of her captivity and martyrdom ; but all will be more clear on her feast-day. I saw the captive Christ-ians in a round, subterranean prison under an old building.

They were separated from one another by gratings through which they could talk, and even pass the hand. It was very dark, excepting around the captives, where I saw a faint light glimmering. The only egress was by a trap-door in the roof, besides which there were four gratings to admit air. I saw four men imprisoned with Felicity and Perpetua, the latter of whom was suckling her child. Felicity, who had not yet given birth to hers, was in the adjoining cell. Perpetua was tall, robust, well-proportioned, and very dignified in all her actions. Felicity was much shorter, more delicate, more beautiful; both had black hair. Perpetua's confident, energetic words kept up the courage of all her companions. At some distance were many other prisoners. The courageous little boy-martyr was with his father in one cell, and the mother with her two little girls in another. They were separated by a wall through which their friends conversed with them. Before the grating of Perpetua's cell, I saw a disconsolate old man tearing his hair and weeping bitterly. He was not a Christian. I think it was her father. There was a kind officer among the guards who often brought bread or other things to Perpetua, who divided the provisions among her companions. She kept carefully hidden by her a roll of parchment. All wore the long, narrow prison-costume; the women's of coarse white wool, the men's brown. The prison of the latter was near the entrance, that of the women further back. I saw a young man die here and his body taken and buried by his friends. One evening I saw Perpetua conversing with a man. That night as she lay on her side asleep, she had a wonderful vision. The whole prison was lighted up, and I saw all its inmates either asleep or in prayer. In this light I beheld a marvellous ladder reaching up to the sky, leading, as it were, into the heavenly gardens; at the foot of it lay right and left, two dragons, with outstretched heads. The ladder was only a pole, far too slender, one would say, considering its great height. I wondered it did not snap. The rounds stood out on either side, long and short alternately. Where a short one jutted out to the left, to the right was a long one bristling with hatchets, spears, and other sharp instruments of torture, and so on all the way up. How any one could mount was perfectly incomprehensible ; and yet, I saw a figure ascending on one side and descending on the other, as if to help some one up. Then I saw Perpetua, who lay there asleep, stepping over the head of the dragon which meekly bent its neck. She mounted the ladder followed by others, and entered the garden where several blessed spirits awaited to encourage and strengthen them. Again, I saw by the sleeping Perpetua a vision of her little deceased brother. I saw a large, dark abode and in it a boy seemingly very miserable ; he was parching with thirst. He stood by a vessel of water from which, however, he could not drink as it was beyond his reach. When Perpetua had the vision of the ladder, I saw by the light that filled the prison that Felicity, her neighbor, had not yet been delivered. Suddenly I saw all the captives prostrating on the ground in prayer ; and soon after I saw a little child lying on Felicity's lap. A woman in tears, in great trouble, took the child, which the young mother joyfully resigned to her.

" And now I saw the martyrs led to death. They left the prison between two files of soldiers who cruelly pushed them from side to side on their way to the place of execution. This place consisted of several communicating enclosures not exactly like that of Rome. Twice on the way did persons approach the procession and hold up Perpetua's child for her to see : first, at the gate where a halt was made and a contest arose between the soldiers and their prisoners about something which the latter refused to do ; and secondly, at a cross-road where they ran to meet her. All the other Christian ·captives had been brought out merely to witness the martyrdom, for only Perpetua, Felicity, and three men suffered at this time. 1 cannot say how unspeakably noble these martyrs appeared ! The two women looked perfectly glorious, whilst the men boldly exhorted the spectators. They were forced to pass slowly between two files of executioners who struck them on the back with whips. Then the two men were stationed opposite the cage of a wild beast which looked like an enormous spotted cat. It sprang forth furiously but did not harm them much ; after this they were set upon by a bear. A wild boar was let loose upon the third ; but it turned upon the executioner, whom I saw borne off covered with blood."

March 3d—" Perpetua and Felicity came and gave me a drink, and then I had a vision of their youth. I saw them with other little girls playing in a circular garden enclosed by a wall. In it were numbers of slender trees higher than a man and so close together that their top branches interlaced In the centre stood a round summer house, on the roof of which was a walk protected by a railing. In the centre stood a white statue, the size of a child, one hand raised, the other lowered, and holding something between the two. Near by played a fountain which was surrounded by a railing stuck with sharp points, to prevent the children from climbing it. By means of an opening, they could make the water flow into a shallow stone basin like a shell in which they played. Here they amused themselves with puppets on wires and little wooden animals. I often saw the two saints withdrawing from the other children and

tenderly embracing each other, by which I knew that their
love began in childhood. I was told that they had promised never to separate. They often played that they were
Christians and were being martyred; but even then they
would not be separated. St. Monica (of whom I had a
relic) told me that the city is called Carthage."

March 6th—"I was until two o'clock with Perpetua and
Felicity, and I saw successive pictures of their youth up to
the time of their imprisonment. They did not reside in the
place in which they were imprisoned and martyred, but
about half a league distant, in the suburbs where the
houses stood far apart. It was connected with the city by
a road running between two low walls and several high archways. Perpetua's home stood by itself. It was tolerably
large, and her parents seemed to be people of distinction.
It had an enclosed court and inner colonnade, though not exactly like that of Agnes's house in Rome, and there were
statues in the walks. In front was an open space, and behind, though at some distance, the circular garden I lately
saw. Perpetua's mother was a Christian, but in secret, and
she knew that her children were the same. The father
alone was a pagan. I saw some young men in the house.—
Felicity was younger than Perpetua. She was the child of
very poor people who lived in another part of the city, in a
miserable little house built in the city-wall. The mother
was a stout, active, dark-complexioned woman; the father
was already old at the time of the martyrdom. I saw them
as they carried fruit and vegetables to the market in baskets, and I often saw Perpetua going to visit them. As a
little girl, she was very much attached to Felicity, with
whom she and her brothers and other little boys used to play
together most innocently. I often saw them in the garden.
In their childish games, Perpetua and Felicity were always

Christians and martyrs ; the former was wonderfully courageous even from childhood, boldly promoting good and the
Christian faith, on which account she often ran great risks.
Felicity was pretty and delicate, and altogether more beautiful than Perpetua.   The features of the latter were more
strongly marked ; her manners rather independent and masculine.   Both were dark, like all the people of that country,
and they had black hair.   I saw Perpetua when a young
girl often going to Felicity's home ; and once I saw their
future husbands, good, pious men, Christians in secret.
Perpetua had seen in vision that, if she married, she would
attain martyrdom more speedily.   In the same vision, she
had also seen her father's displeasure and the greater part of
her own sufferings.   After her own marriage she forwarded
that of Felicity and assisted her in her poverty.   Perpetua's
husband seemed to me to be far beneath her in station; she
accepted him only through respect for his virtue.   When
she left the house of her father, who was greatly dissatisfied
with his daughter's marriage, her friends neglected her, and
she lived a retired life with her husband.   Felicity's husband was also a pious Christian, but very poor.   I used to
see them going by night to a distant, retired place, like a
large under-ground cave, supported on square pillars.   It
lay beyond the walls under a ruined building.   Here about
thirty Christians met quietly, closed all the entrances, lighted flambeaux, and ranged in groups.   I saw no divine service, but only instructions."

March 7th—"I saw two holy men approach my bed on one
side, and three holy women on the other. They were the two
husbands, and Perpetua, Felicity, and Perpetua's mother-in-
law, a dark-complexioned old woman. Perpetua and Felicity
took me up and laid me in a bed with blue curtains bound
with red, and the mother-in-law moved a round table up to it

on which she laid all sorts of marvellous food. It seemed as
if she did it in Perpetua's name. The table stood in the air
near my bed without any support. Then the two holy women
passed into another and larger apartment and, as I fancied
that their silent departure betokened some trouble for me, I
became sad. The mother-in-law followed them and the
two men, likewise, disappeared. Then I perceived that
my hands and feet were bleeding. Suddenly several men
rushed toward me, crying out: ' Ah ! Ah ! she is eating !'
and the alarm was soon spread. The saints returned. The
mother-in-law told me that I should have had a cruel persecution to endure on account of the bleeding of my wounds,
if the prayers of the saints had not averted or mitigated it ;
that the three children whom I had clothed for Communion
would by their prayers ward off many trials from me ; and
that, instead of a new persecution, I should endure a painful illness. It was in view of this that I had received the
nourishment of fruits and flowers and fine bread on the
golden plates with blue inscriptions. The holy woman, the
mother-in-law, stayed by me and told me many things. She
was surrounded by a white aureola which dissolved into
gray. She told me that she was the mother of Perpetua's
husband and that she had lived near them. She had
neither been imprisoned nor martyred with them, but she
now enjoyed their companionship because, like so many
others during the persecution, she had died of grief and
want in her place of concealment. This circumstance God
rewarded as martyrdom. Perpetua and Felicity could have
escaped very easily, but the former longed for martyrdom.
She had openly declared herself a Christian when the persecution broke out. She told me also that Perpetua had
married in consequence of a vision she had had, and also
that she might more easily leave her father's house. I saw

the father, a short, stout old man ; he was seldom at home.
When I saw him, he was standing in the second story of
his house, in an apartment next his wife's. He could see all
she did, for there was only a light wicker partition between
the rooms, at the upper part of which was an opening with
a slide. Although he busied himself but little with her,
yet he seemed to regard her with suspicion, as she was a
Christian. I often saw her in this room. She was rather
stout, not very active, and she generally sat or reclined in
her oratory, doing some kind of coarse knitting with wood-
en needles. The walls of the room, like those of
the houses in Rome, were colored, but not so delicately. When the father was at home, the whole
house was silent and restrained ; but, when he was away,
the mother was bright and cheerful among her children.
Besides Perpetua, I saw two youths in the family. When
the former was about seventeen, I saw her in a room nursing and bandaging a sick boy of seven years. He had a
horrible ulcer in his face, and he was not very patient in
his sickness. His parents came not near him. I saw him
die in Perpetua's arms. She wrapped the body in linen
and concealed it. The father and mother saw him no
more.

" Felicity was a servant in the same house as one of her
fellow-martyrs, but she often went to her parent's house to
spend the night. Perpetua frequently carried thither at
dusk something in a little basket or under her mantle,
which they either used themselves, or took to the Christians
in concealment. Many of the latter died of hunger. All
these goings and comings went on before my eyes.—Perpetua was not beautiful in face. Her nose was rather short
and flat ; her cheek-bones high ; her lips a little too full,
like those of the people of her country ; her long black hair

was braided around her head. Her dress was in the Roman style, though not quite so simple, being scalloped round the neck and skirt, the upper garment laced. Her figure was tall and imposing; her whole air fearless and confident.—I saw in Perpetua's house the two husbands taking leave of their wives before their flight from persecution. When they had gone, I saw Perpetua and Felicity tenderly embracing each other as if they were now right joyful. Perpetua's home was plainer than that of her parents. It was only one story high, the yard enclosed by a wooden paling. At daybreak next morning the house was attacked by a troop of soldiers who had already taken two young men into custody. Perpetua and Felicity were led away full of joy; the mother-in-law had the child, and no one molested her. The four were now dragged with many cruel blows and much ill-usage, not by the ordinary way along the walls and under the arches, but by another route across the fields to a distant part of the city, where they entered a miserable old building that stood by itself, like a temporary fortress. Here they were to stay until taken to the ordinary prison. I saw a young man rapping at the prison gate. The soldiers let him in and put him with the other captives. Perpetua's father followed her here, praying, beseeching, conjuring her to renounce her faith; he even struck her in the face, but she answered in a few earnest words and bore all patiently. Then I saw the prisoners conducted through a section of the city and along many walls to an underground prison where there were already many captives. Here I again saw Perpetua's vision of the ladder. She ascended to the top, received strength, and then descended, in doing which she glanced to one side, caught her dress below the waist on one of the spears, and tore it. It was exactly the same spot that was afterward torn when she was tossed by the cow. I saw her lying on the ground, and then suddenly rising to arrange her dress. This was what the torn dress of the vision signified. I often saw her whilst in prison, speaking undauntedly to the guards, defending her companions, and gaining for herself universal esteem. During her torture, when being tossed by the cow, she seemed to be in vision, utterly unconscious of pain. She was dragged horribly from side to side and hurled up into the air in a frightful manner ; on falling she arranged her dress and seemed, for an instant, to have some consciousness of her position. As they were leading her across to another court, I heard her asking if she would soon be martyred now. She was in continual contemplation, conscious of nothing. In the middle of this second court, were little seats to which the martyrs were dragged and their throats pierced. Perpetua's death was horrible to behold ! she could not die ! The executioner pierced her through the ribs and then through the right shoulder to the neck, she herself guiding his hand ; and, when lying on the ground apparently dead, she still stretched forth one hand. She was the last to die and only after a long and hard agony. The two women had been stripped and put into a net and, owing to the tossing and scourging, their whole body was covered with blood. Their remains were taken away secretly and buried by the people of Carthage. I saw that many were converted by Perpetua's heroic behavior, and the prison was soon filled again."

March 8th —"I had the relics of Perpetua and Felicity by me all night : but, to my great surprise, I saw nothing of the two saints ! I had hoped for some pictures of their life, but I got not even a glance ; therefore, I see that such visions are very special, one cannot have them at pleasure."

St. Thomas Aquinas.

" My sister received from a poor woman the present of
a relic in a case. She put it away in her chest ; but I felt
its presence and gave her in exchange for it a picture of
the saint. The relic shone with a beautiful light, and I laid
it in my little closet. Now, last night after having endured
all the pains, all the tortures that a human body can undergo, I had a vision of St. Thomas. I saw a large mansion
in which was a nurse with a child in her arms, to whom
she gave a scrap of paper on which was written *Ave Maria.*
The little fellow held it fast, put it to his lips, and would
not give it up. His mother entered the room and tried to
take the writing from him, but the child struggled. He
cried bitterly when she succeeded in opening his little hand
and getting the paper. At last, however, seeing him so distressed, she gave it back to him, when he quickly swallowed
it. Then I heard an interior voice saying : ' That is
Thomas of Aquin ! '—and the saint appeared to me several
times from the little closet, but each time at a different period of his life. He told me that he would cure me of the
pain in my side, and the thought struck me : *My confessor
belongs to his Order ! Now, if I can only tell him that
Thomas cured me, he will readily believe that that is his relic !*—whereupon the saint replied in answer to my thought :
' Thou mayest tell him. I will cure thee ! ' and he laid his
girdle on my head."

The confessor relates on this point the following : " Sister
Emmerich spoke of St. Thomas. She said that he was by
her, that he would certainly cure her, if I thought well of
it. I ordered her to look for the relic. She did so and
handed it to me ; but the pain in her side was so intense
that she could, so to speak, neither live nor die. I touched

the relic to her side, telling her to pray and to have confidence in Jesus Christ. I prayed with her thinking, if it really were St. Thomas, she might indeed rise quite cured. Suddenly she sprang lightly to her feet and wanted to leave her bed. 'I feel no pain, no pain in my side!' she exclaimed. 'The saint has cured it; but he says I must bear my other sufferings!' Then she went on: 'I have seen various incidents of his life. Even as a little child, he loved to turn over the leaves of a book; he was unwilling to relinquish it even during his bath. I have seen that this relic was presented to our convent by an Augustinian, its first Superior, of whose life I also saw many incidents. He had all the relics belonging to the convent rearranged and freshly ornamented. There lived at that time in our convent a very holy young lady whom I have often seen.' Once again that day, Sister Emmerich, being in ecstasy, wanted to rise and take the relic to the Pilgrim. She appeared to be very much preoccupied with the saint."

HERMANN JOSEPH.

" I had visions of his childhood's years. He had a tiny picture of Mary on parchment. He made a case for it, attached a plain string, and hung it around his neck. This he did with the utmost faith and simplicity, and he never forgot to honor it. When Hermann played alone in his garden, two other boys always joined him. They were not the children of men, but this the child suspected not. He played with them quite simply and oftentimes sought, but never found them among the other children of the city. Even when he left his other companions to seek them, they came not; they only came when he was all alone. Once I saw him playing in a meadow near Cologne, by a brook which flows through St. Ursula's martyr-field. He fell into the stream; but, with child-like trust, he held his little picture of the Mother of God above the water that it might not get wet. The Blessed Virgin appeared, caught him by the shoulder, and drew him out. I saw many other incidents indicative of his great familiarity with Mary and the Infant Jesus in his childhood: for instance, once I saw him in church, reaching an apple to Mary which she graciously accepted; and, again, I saw him when he found the money under a stone (which had been pointed out by her) with which to buy himself a pair of shoes. I saw Mary helping him also in his studies."

St. Isidore.

" I saw the saintly peasant in many scenes of his domestic life. His costume was quite gay: a short brown jacket with buttons before and behind, a scalloped trimming on the shoulders, and scalloped cuffs; his small-clothes short and wide trimmed with ribands, his feet laced His low cap was of four pieces turned up and caught together by a button on the crown; it looked a little like a biretta. Isidore was a tall, handsome man, with nothing of the peasant in his appearance; his features and his whole demeanor were very distinguished. His wife too was tall, beautiful and, like himself, holy. They had one son whom I saw with them, once as a very young child, and again when about twelve years old. Their house stood near an open field about half a league from the city, which they could distinctly see. In it reigned order and neatness. I saw that it had other occupants beside Isidore and his family, but they were not his servants. Isidore and his wife accompanied all their actions with prayer; they blessed each particular kind of food. Isidore never knelt long in prayer before he was rapt in contemplation. I saw him, as he passed along the fields before beginning his work, blessing the earth, and he always received supernatural assistance in his husbandry. I often saw several ploughs with white oxen and driven by shining apparitions, breaking up the ground before him. His work was always finished before he had hardly thought of it; which circumstance, however, he appeared not to notice, as his mind was ever fixed on God. When he heard the bells in the city, he used to leave everything standing just as it was in the fields, and run to Holy Mass or other devotions, at which he assisted ravished in spirit. When the service was over, he would return joyously to find his work finished. Once I saw his little boy driving the plough to the field. The oxen appeared rather unmanageable. Suddenly, the bells rang for Mass, and off ran Isidore to the church. The restive animals became calm and, guided by the weak child, went on quietly with the work until their master's return. On another occasion, as Isidore was praying before the Blessed Sacrament, a messenger hurried in to tell him that a wolf was tearing his horse to pieces. But Isidore stirred not; he recommended the affair to God and, when he returned to the field, he found the wolf stretched dead before the horse. I often saw his wife in the fields with him, at morning and noon, hoeing the ground, invisible workmen laboring by them. Their task was soon accomplished. Isidore's field was more luxuriant, more productive than any others; its fruits appeared to be of superior quality. He and his wife gave all they had to the poor and sometimes, when they had nothing at all in the house, they recurred to God with great confidence. Then they sought again and found abundant provisions. I often saw Isidore's enemies trying to injure his cattle when he left them to go

to Mass ; but they were always hindered and put to flight.
I had many other pictures of his holy life, and then I saw
him among the saints ; once in his odd-looking peasant
costume, and again, as a blessed, shining soul."

Sts. Stephen, Lawrence, and Hippolyte.

On August 3, 1820, Sister Emmerich addressed these
words to the Pilgrim : "I feel that there is among
my relics one of St. Lawrence. It is just a tiny splinter
of bone." The Pilgrim hunted in the box of relics and
found a small parcel containing two scraps of bone in a
brown envelope tied with gold thread. He handed her
both. Scarcely had she touched them, when she exclaimed : O one is Stephen's ! O what a treasure !—This
belongs to Lawrence," and, becoming more profoundly
absorbed, she continued : "See, there they both stand !
Lawrence is behind Stephen. Stephen wears the white
robe of a Jewish priest with lappets on the shoulders, and
a broad girdle. He is a beautiful youth, taller than Lawrence. Lawrence wears the flowing robe of a deacon.'
Sister Emmerich's joy at having found this treasure was
very great. The vision she beheld seemed so real
that, all at once, she exclaimed : "But we have none of
their bones ; they are still alive ! There they are ! It is truly
laughable ! How could I think we had their relics, when they
are yet alive !" Later on, she said : "Besides the white
priestly robe and broad cincture, Stephen wears on his shoulders a scalloped cape, woven in red and white, and carries
a palm branch in his hand. Lawrence appeared in a long
plaited robe of bluish white with a wide cincture ; he wore a
stole around his neck. He was not so tall as Stephen ; but
he was young, beautiful, fearless like him. His relic must
have been scorched by fire ; it is wrapped in a scrap of

black stuff." The Pilgrim here opened the cover, and found the relic just as described. "The gridiron," Sister Emmerich continued, " had a rim around it like a pan, and in the middle of each side was a handle by which to lift it; it had six feet and four flat cross-bars. When the saint was stretched on it, a bar was placed over him from right to left. When Lawrence appeared to me, the gridiron was near him."

On the Feast of St. Lawrence, she related the following: " I saw that Lawrence was a Spaniard, a native of the city of Huesca. His parents were pious Christians, the mother's name Patience, the father's I have forgotten. All the inhabitants were not Christians, and the houses of the latter were marked with a cross cut in stone, of which some had a single, others a double transverse arm. Lawrence had a special devotion to the Blessed Sacrament. When about eleven years old, he was endowed with a supernatural consciousness of Its presence, so that he *felt* Its approach even if It were carried concealed. Wherever It was borne he followed with liveliest veneration. His pious parents had not so great a devotion themselves, and they blamed his zeal as excessive. I saw him give a touching proof of his love for the Blessed Sacrament. He once saw a priest carrying the Blessed Sacrament secretly to a leprous woman, a most disgusting object, who lived in a miserable hovel near the city-wall. Impelled by devotion, Lawrence stealthily followed the priest and prayerfully watched all the ceremonies. Just as the priest laid the Sacred Host on the poor creature's tongue, she vomited, ejecting the Sacred Species at the same time. The priest, whose name I knew, was a holy man ; he became a saint. But just at this moment, he was perfectly bewildered, not knowing how to withdraw the Sacred Host from the filth in which It lay. From his hiding-place, the boy Lawrence saw all. Unable to control the ardor of his love for Jesus in the Blessed Sacrament, he rushed into the room and, conquering every sentiment of disgust, threw himself on his knees and reverently took up the Body of his Lord with his lips. For this heroic self-victory he received from God indomitable strength and fortitude of soul. I saw, also, in an indescribable manner, that Lawrence was not *born of the blood nor of the will of man*, but of God. He was shown me as a new-born babe, and it was told me that he had been begotten in the spirit of renunciation with sentiments of confusion and penitence. His parents were in the state of grace, having devoutly received Holy Communion; so that, in his very conception, Lawrence had been consecrated to God, thereby receiving as an inheritance his early veneration for the Blessed Sacrament and the con- sciousness of Its presence. I was filled with joy on be- holding a child begotten as I have always thought it should be in Christian marriage, a state which ought to be looked upon as one of humiliating penance. Soon after his heroic act, Lawrence with his parents' consent went to Rome. There I saw him visiting the sick and prisoners in company with the holiest priests. He soon became especially dear to Pope Sixtus, who ordained him deacon. Lawrence always served the Pope's Mass. I saw the Pope communicating him under both forms after his own Communion, and then Lawrence distributing the Sacrament to the Christians. There was no Communion Table such as we have; but to the right of the altar was a railing with a swinging ledge, behind which the communicants knelt. The deacons gener- ally took turns in administering the Sacrament, but Lawrence always discharged that duty for Sixtus. When the latter was led to prison, I saw Lawrence running and calling after him not to leave him behind. Sixtus, divinely inspired, predicted his deacon's approaching martyrdom, and ordered him to distribute the treasures of the Church to the poor. Then I saw Lawrence hurrying with a large sum of money in his bosom to the widow Cyriaca, with whom were concealed numbers of Christians and sick people. He humbly washed the feet of all; relieved by the imposition of hands the widow, who had long suffered from violent headache; healed the lame, the sick, the blind; and distributed alms. Cyriaca aided him in every way, especially in converting the sacred vessels into money. That night I saw him entering a vault, penetrating deep into the catacombs, giving alms and other relief, distributing the Sacrament, and inspiring all with extraordinary courage. He was radiant with joy, full of supernatural fortitude and earnestness. Then I saw him with Cyriaca hastening to the Pope's prison. As the latter was led forth to death, Lawrence told him that he had distributed the treasure, and that he was now ready to follow him to death as his deacon. The Pope again foretold his martyrdom, and Lawrence was arrested on the spot by the soldiers, who had heard him speaking of *treasures*."

Sister Emmerich here saw every detail of St. Lawrence's imprisonment and martyrdom, just as related in the legend of the former and the Acts of the latter. She saw also the cures he wrought in prison, the conversion of Romain and Hippolytus, etc. She says:—

" Lawrence's tortures were long; they were continued all night with uncommon cruelty. Between two courtyards used as places of execution, ran a colonnade in which were kept the instruments of torture and in which all the preparations for the same were made. It was thrown open to spectators, and here Lawrence was stretched on the gridiron. Strengthened by his angel, he stepped lightly toward it with a gay remark, and laid himself upon it, refusing, however, to allow himself to be bound. I felt that, by divine assistance, he was insensible to the greater part of his torments; he lay as if upon roses. Other martyrs have had more terrible sufferings to endure. He wore the white robe of a deacon, a girdle, a stole, a scalloped cape, and a kind of upper garment like Stephen's. I saw him buried by Hippolytus and the priest Justin. Many wept over his grave and Mass was said there. Lawrence once appeared to me when I had scruples about receiving Holy Communion. He questioned me upon the state of my soul. When I had answered him, he said that I might communicate every other day."

On recognizing a relic of St. Hippolytus, Sister Emmerich spoke as follows: "I have had visions of his life. I saw him the child of indigent parents. His father died young; and his mother, a quarrelsome woman, was, although poor and mean herself, hard and proud toward others of her class. Several incidents of Hippolytus's youth were shown me which, as I was told, were the germs of future grace in store for him as a Christian, a martyr for Christ. I was then informed that graces are ever the reward of generous deeds, even those of pagans. I saw his mother quarrelling with another poor woman whom she treated shamefully, scornfully driving her out of the house. This greatly grieved the young Hippolytus, and he secretly took one of his under-garments and gave it to the poor woman, as if his mother had sent it to her in token of reconciliation. Hippolytus did not say this to the woman in express terms, but she naturally inferred it. She returned to his mother who, surprised at her bright, cordial manner after such treatment, now received her kindly. More than one of

these charitable acts were shown me in the boy's life.
Hippolytus became a soldier.   One of his companions was
sentenced to severe chastisement for some   fault, but Hippolytus presented himself before the judge instead of the
guilty one.   His generosity led to a mitigation of the punishment, which he suffered in the place of his friend. The latter was so deeply impressed by this act of charity that with
Hippolytus he became a Christian, a martyr.   I learned
from this that kind acts and good works inspired by disinterested love are never overlooked by the Lord ; they prepare
the way for future graces. Hippolytus was one of Lawrence's
guards. He was greatly touched on seeing the saint present
the poor to the emperor as the treasures of the Church. He
was upright, a pagan in the same sense as Paul was a Jew. I
saw him converted in the prison and after Lawrence's martyrdom, weeping and praying with the other Christians for
three days and three nights over his grave.   Justin celebrated Holy Mass on the tomb and gave Holy Communion.
All did not receive, but over those who did not I saw shining the flames of desire.   Justin sprinkled the Christians
with water. The martyr's tomb stood by itself in a retired
spot behind a hill.   Hippolytus was soon after arrested
with many of his companions, and dragged by horses in a
deserted spot not far from the grave of St. Lawrence.   The
horses were unwilling to move ; but the executioners struck
them, pricked them, and goaded them on with lighted
torches, so that Hippolytus was rather quartered than
dragged. In many spots were prepared stones, holes, and
thorns to tear the body. About twenty others suffered with
him, among them his friend. He wore the white baptismal
robe."

St. Nicodemus.

Sister Emmerich had several times declared that there ought to be in " *her church*" a relic of Nicodemus, for she had seen him in vision visiting Jesus by night. At last she found it and then had the following vision :—"When Nicodemus returned with Joseph and the others from the burial of the Lord, he went not to the Cenacle where some of the Apostles lay concealed, but proceeded alone to his own house, carrying with him the linen used in taking Jesus down from the cross. But the Jews, who were on the watch for him, seized him and confined him in a room intending to bring him to trial after the Sabbath. That night I saw an angel delivering him. There was no window in the room ; it appeared as if the angel raised the roof and took him out over the wall. Then I saw him going by night to join the Apostles in the Cenacle. They hid him ; and two days after, when he also knew of Christ's resurrection, Joseph of Arimathea concealed him in his own house, until they undertook to destribute alms. It was then that these linens, used for the descent from the cross, fell into the hands of the Jews. I also saw in vision that the Roman Emperor, in the third year after Christ's ascension, allowed Veronica, Nicodemus and a disciple named Epaphras, a relative of Joanna Chusa, to come to Rome, for he wanted to see some witnesses of Christ's death and resurrection. Epaphras was a simple-hearted man, and a very zealous, useful disciple. He had been a servant in the Temple and a messenger of the priests, and had with the Apostles seen Jesus in the first days of His resurrection and frequently after.—I saw Veronica in the emperor's presence. He was sick, and he lay on a raised couch before which hung a curtain. It was a small square room with no window in it, the light being admitted through the roof, from which hung cords attached to valves which could be opened or closed at pleasure. Veronica was alone with the emperor, his attendants having withdrawn into the ante-chamber. She had the sacred napkin and one of the linens of the tomb. The napkin was a long strip of stuff, a veil that Veronica used to wear around her head and neck. She now spread it out before the sick emperor, the impression of the Sacred Face being on one side of it. The face of Christ here depicted was not like a painting. It was impressed in blood, and broader than a portrait, because the napkin had been applied all around the face. On the other cloth was the bloody imprint of Our Lord's torn Body. I think it was the one on which the Sacred Body had been washed before burial. I did not see the emperor touch these linens, or that they were applied to him in any way. He was cured by the mere sight of them. In gratitude for this favor, he wanted to keep Veronica in Rome, make her rich presents, give her a house, faithful servants, etc.; but all the reward she asked was permission to return to Jerusalem and to die where Jesus had died.—I saw Pilate also in my vision. He was summoned to the presence of the angry emperor; but before obeying, he laid upon his breast, under his own robe, a piece of Christ's mantle which he had received from the soldiers. I saw him standing among the guards, awaiting the emperor, and it seemed as if he already knew how irritated the latter was against him. At last the emperor arrived full of rage, but as soon as he approached Pilate's vicinity, he became calm and listened to him kindly. But when Pilate withdrew, the emperor again fell into a rage and ordered him to be recalled. He was obeyed and again grew calm on Pilate's approach. I saw that this was owing to the scrap of Jesus' mantle which Pilate wore on his breast. —I think, however, that I afterward saw Pilate exiled and in misery.—Nicodemus was maltreated by the Jews and left for dead. Gamaliel took him to his home where Stephen lay buried, and here he died and was interred."

THE HOLY MARTYR SUSANNA.

"I have a relic of St. Susanna. She kept me company all last night. I saw many scenes in her life, but I only remember some of them. I saw her in a large house with courtyard and colonnade in Rome. Her father was called Gabinus; he was a Christian and brother to the Pope who dwelt not far away. Susanna's mother must have been dead, for I never saw her. There were other Christians in the family of Gabinus. Like his daughter he was very charitable to the poor; he secretly shared his wealth with them. I saw a messenger sent from the Emperor Diocletian to Gabinus, who was his relative, proposing a marriage between Susanna and his own widowed son-in-law. Gabinus, seemed, at first, well pleased with the offer; but Susanna met it with extreme repugnance. She said that, having espoused Christ, she could never marry a pagan. On receiving this answer, Diocletian caused her to be removed from her father's house and brought to the court of his wife (Serena). He hoped by this to change her sentiments. The empress was a Christian in secret, and Susanna laid her case before her; they prayed together, and then she was reconducted to her father's house. And now came another messenger from the emperor, one Claudius, a relative of his own, who on saluting Susanna, attempted to kiss her, not impertinently, but either through custom, or because they were relatives. But Susanna kept him off

with her hand and, on his declaring his intention innocent,
she replied that lips sullied with praises of the false gods
should never touch hers. She then spoke to him earnestly, and pointed out his errors. Then I saw him, with his
wife and children, instructed and baptized by the Pope,
Susanna's uncle. As Claudius did not return with an answer, the emperor sent a brother of the same to see what
detained him. On entering he found Claudius and his family kneeling in prayer. Concealing his amazement, he
asked his brother what was Susanna's reply to the marriage proposal. Claudius evaded a direct answer, but persuaded his brother to accompany him to Susanna and convince himself that such a person could never espouse an
idolater. They went together to her presence, and lo! this
second messenger was converted by Susanna and her uncle
the Pope! The Empress Serena had three Christians in her
service, two men and one woman. I saw them all going together by night, Susanna along with them, into a subterranean apartment beneath the palace. In it stood an altar
before which a lamp constantly burned. Here they prayed,
and sometimes a priest came secretly to consecrate and administer to them the Blessed Sacrament. The emperor
was furious when he heard of the two brothers' conversion.
He ordered both to be imprisoned with their families; they
were afterward martyred. Susanna's father also was imprisoned.—Then I had another vision in which I saw Susanna sitting alone in a large hall, by a little round table
ornamented with gilded figures; her hands were joined, her
face raised in prayer. Round apertures in the roof admitted air, and in the corners of the apartment stood white
statues as large as a child. Here and there were animals' heads, especially on the feet of the furniture. Some
winged figures with long tails were sitting back on their

hind legs; others held scrolls in their fore-paws, etc."
(Probably sculptured ornaments, winged lions, griffins, etc.)
" As Susanna sat thus in prayer, I saw that the emperor
sent his son himself to offer her violence. I saw the man
leave his attendants outside and enter a door at Susanna's
back, when lo ! a figure stood before her and confronted
the bold intruder ! The latter instantly fell to the ground
like one dead. Then only did the maiden turn. Seeing a
man lying behind her, she cried out for assistance. His
friends rushed in astounded, raised him up, and bore him
from the room. The apparition stood before Susanna, her
enemy approached her from behind and, when she was half-
way between the two, the latter fell to the ground.—Then
I had another vision. I saw a man with twenty others going
to her, and two pagan priests who carried between them on a
platform furnished with handles, a gilded idol which must have
been hollow, for it was very light. They placed it in a
niche under the colonnade of the court-yard and stood before it a little round three-legged table which they had
brought from the house. Then several went in for Susanna, who was still in the upper hall. They dragged her out
to sacrifice to the idol. She prayed fervently to God and,
even before she reached the spot, I saw a miracle. The
idol, as if hurled by an invisible power, shot across the
court and colonnade far out into the street, where it fell
shattered into a thousand pieces ! At the same time I saw a
man running to spread the news. Then they tore off Susanna's upper-garment, leaving only a little covering on her
breast. Her back and shoulders were bare. In this state,
she had to cross the crowded vestibule where the soldiers
pricked and wounded her with their sharp spears, until
she sank down apparently dead. They then dragged her
into a side room and left her lying there on the floor. Again

I saw them trying to force her to offer sacrifice in a temple, but the idol fell to the ground; lastly, she was dragged by the hair into the court-yard of her own house and beheaded. The empress and Susanna's nurse came by night, washed the body, wrapped it in a winding-sheet, and buried it. The empress had first cut off one of her fingers and some of her hair. I afterward saw the Pope saying Mass on the spot of her martyrdom. Susanna had a round face, a resolute expression, and black hair braided around her head. She was dressed in white with a veil which fastened under the chin and fell behind in two ends. "

St. Clare.

" I had St. Clare's relic by me and I saw her life. Her pious mother when devoutly praying before the Blessed Sacrament for a happy delivery, was interiorly warned that she would give birth to a daughter brighter than the sun; hence, the child was named Clare. Before the event the mother went on a pilgrimage to Rome, Jerusalem, and the other Holy Places. The parents were noble and very pious. From her earliest infancy Clare was wonderfully attracted by whatever was holy. If she were taken into a church, she stretched out her tiny hands to the Blessed Sacrament; but other objects, no matter how highly colored, such as pictures, etc., made no impression upon her. I saw the mother teaching the child to pray and the little one zealously practising self-renunciation. The devotion of the Rosary must have been in use at the time, for I saw Clare's parents reciting every evening with their whole household, a certain number of *Our Fathers* and *Hail Maries*. I also saw the child seeking little smooth stones of various sizes which she carried around her in a leathern pouch with two pockets into which she dropped the stones

alternately as she prayed. Sometimes she laid them in a
row or circle as she prayed ; and she always observed a
certain number in her meditation or contemplation. Did
she fear having prayed inattentively, she imposed a penance
on herself. She wove very beautiful little crosses out of
straw. She was about six years old, when I saw her in
the yard in which the servants were slaughtering hogs.
She took the bristles, cut them small, and put them around
her neck, thus occasioning herself great suffering. Later
on, her extraordinary piety began to be noised abroad, and
St. Francis, divinely inspired, came to visit her parents.
Clare was called to see him and was deeply impressed by
the earnest words the saint spoke to her. After this a
youth sued for Clare's hand. Her parents did not flatly
discourage him, although they had not yet consulted their
child. But she, interiorly warned of what was pending,
ran to her chamber and, kneeling before her oratory, vowed
her virginity to God, which vow she solemnly made known
when her parents introduced her suitor. They were truly
amazed ; but they ceased to urge her. She now engaged
in all kinds of good works, exercising great charity toward
the poor, to whom she gave her own meals whenever she
could abstain from them unnoticed. I saw her visiting
Francis at Portiuncula and becoming more and more firm
in her determination to serve God alone. On Palm-Sunday
she went to church in her best attire. She remained standing in the lower part of the church whilst the Bishop distributed the palms at the altar. Suddenly, he saw a beam of
light shining over her head ; he went down himself
to where she stood and gave her a branch. Then
I saw the light spreading over many others around her.—
I saw her leave her parent's house by night for the church
of Portiuncula where Francis and his brethren received

her with lighted candles, chanting the *Veni Creator.* I saw
her in the church, receiving a penitential habit and cutting
off her hair, after which Francis took her to a convent in
the city. She already wore a horse-hair girdle with thirteen knots, which she now changed for one of boar skin,
the bristles turned next to her person. I saw a nun in her
convent who had conceived bitter hatred for her and who
would not be reconciled to her. This religious had been
sick for some time when Clare lay on her death-bed. The
dying saint sent to be reconciled to the sister, but the latter
refused. Then Clare prayed fervently and bade some of the
nuns bring the sick sister to her. They went to her, raised
her up, and lo! she was cured! She was so deeply affected
by this that she hastened to Clare and begged her pardon.
The saint responded by begging hers in return.—I saw the
Mother of God present at her death with a troop of holy
virgins."

Visions of St. Augustine, St. Francis de Sales and St. Jane Frances de Chantal.

Among the relics sent to Sister Emmerich by Dean
Overberg, was one of St. Augustine, St. Francis de Sales,
and St. Jane Frances respectively, all which Sister Emmerich had indeed recognized, but which the Pilgrim had
inadvertently changed, marking St. Augustine's as St.
Francis de Sales's, and vice versa. One he took away
with him, leaving the one marked as St. Augustine's with
the invalid. More than once she declared that she felt the
presence of St. Francis de Sales. She said: "I saw a holy
Bishop and a saintly woman. Their relics must be here, for
the apparitions descended and ascended by me. Whenever I see the apparition of a saint whose relic is by me, a
light issues from the latter and unites with that surrounding

the former; but when I have no relic, both the light and the apparition come from above." On hearing the above, the Pilgrim thought he would return her the little parcel in which was the relic marked by him St. Francis de Sales. She was at the moment in ecstasy, but seizing the package she pressed it joyously and smilingly to her heart, exclaiming: "O I have my dear Father Augustine by me!"—and afterward she related the following: "I saw the saint in his episcopal robes, at his feet his name in angular characters. What seemed strange to me was that I thought I saw his holy relics in a curiously twisted house, like a snail's shell. I could not imagine what it meant, when, suddenly, I saw the house under a more beautiful form, polished like marble; inside lay the relic."—St. Augustine's relic, of which Sister Emmerich here speaks, was inclosed in a box of mother-of-pearl! The visions of his life run as follows:—

" I saw the saint, a boy in his father's house, not far from a tolerably large city. It was built in the Roman style with a court-yard and colonnade, around it other buildings with gardens and fields; it looked to me like a villa. The father was a tall, vigorous man with something morose and severe about him. He must have had many orders to give, for I saw him speaking earnestly to people who looked like his inferiors. I saw others kneeling before him as if presenting petitions; they may have been servants or peasants. In little Augustine's presence he was more affable and gracious toward Monica, his wife, as if he were fond of the boy; he did not seem to have much to do with him, however, for Augustine was generally with his mother and two men. Monica was a little woman already advanced in years, slightly stooped in her carriage, and of very dark complexion. She was exceedingly gentle and God-fearing and in

constant dread and anxiety on Augustine's account. She followed him everywhere, for he was restless and mischievous.
I saw him climbing perilous heights and scampering recklessly around on the very edge of the flat roof.   Of the two men,
one seemed to be his preceptor, the other his servant ; the
former used to take him to a school in the neighboring city
which many little boys a tended, and bring him home again.
Augustine was at all sorts of tricks when out of school.   I
saw him beating animals, throwing stones at them, quarrelling with other boys, running into people's houses, ransacking
cupboards, and eating the good things. Still, there was something very generous in him, for he always divided what he
found with his companions ; sometimes he even threw it
away.   There lived also in his father's house a female who
was, perhaps, a nurse, or servant of some kind.   Later on,
I saw Augustine placed at school in a larger and more distant city, to which he went in a low chariot on small heavy
wheels, drawn by two beasts. He was always accompanied
by two persons.   Then I saw him in school with many
other boys.   He slept with several of them in a large hall,
their beds separated by a reed, or light wooden partition.
The school-room was larger than the sleeping-hall.   It had
stone benches all around the wall.   On these the scholars
sat holding little brown boards on their knees for writing,
rolls of parchment and pencils in their hands.   The master
stood in a little pulpit raised about two steps, behind which
was a larger board on which he drew numerous figures. He
called his pupils, now this one, now that one into the middle
of the floor, where they stood facing each other and reading
from their parchment rolls, gesticulating, at the same time,
as if they were preaching, and again as if disputing.   In
school Augustine was well-behaved and almost always stood
first ; but out-doors he carried on all sorts of pranks with

the other boys, damaging and destroying whatever fell in his way. I saw him, out of pure mischief, beating and stoning to death certain long-necked birds, the domestic fowl of that country, and then carrying away the dead bodies with tears of pity. I saw him running and wrestling with other boys in the shady walks of a circular garden, and stealing, injuring, wasting many things.

" I saw him return home from this school and give himself up to all kinds of mad pranks and disorders. One night I saw him robbing an orchard with companions like himself, and afterward throwing away a whole mantleful of the fruit. I saw Monica incessantly remonstrating with him, praying and shedding many tears. Then I saw him crossing a bridge over a broad river, on his way to the great city in which Perpetua was martyred. I soon recognized it. On one side arose rocks with walls and towers jutting out into the sea where lay many ships. A smaller city stood at no great distance from the large one. There were many great buildings as in ancient Rome, and also a large Christian church. I had numerous visions of Augustine's follies committed here with other young people. He dwelt alone in a house and held constant disputations with other young men. I used to see him going by himself to visit a certain female ; but he did not remain long in any one place, he was constantly on the go. I often saw him at public shows, in my eyes, truly diabolical. They were held in a great round building. On one side seats arose, one above the other, like steps and below were numerous entrances opening on the stairways which led to the seats. The building had no roof, only a tent-like covering. The place was crowded, and opposite the spectators, on an elevated platform, were enacted abominable scenes. In the background were all sorts of pictures which, at certain times, suddenly disappeared, as if swallowed up by the earth. Once there unfolded a large beautiful place in a great city; and yet, the whole scene occupied in reality but a very small space. Then men and women appeared, two by two, talking together and behaving wantonly. It was all horrible to me! The actors had frightful, colored faces with huge mouths; they wore on their feet broad-soled socks with pointed toes, red, yellow, and other colors. Below these were whole troops, talking and singing alternately with those above. I saw boys, eight or twelve years old, who played on straight and twisted flutes and also upon stringed instruments. Once several of them precipitated themselves head foremost from on high with outspread limbs. They must certainly have been fastened to something; but it looked very frightful. Then, again, there was a wrestling match in which one of the combatants received two cuts across his face, which a surgeon came and bandaged. I cannot describe the horrors, the confusion of the scene. The women among the actors were men in disguise. Augustine himself used to appear in public, though not in such performances as these. He entered with zest into all sorts of amusements, indulged in all sorts of sins. He was the leader everywhere, a distinction which he seemed to seek out of pure ostentation, for it gave him no real satisfaction; he was always sad and discontented when alone. I saw also that the woman with whom he lived brought a child to his house, which circumstance, however, did not seem to disconcert him in the least. I most frequently beheld him in halls and public places, disputing with others, speaking or listening, unfolding and reading rolls of parchment, etc. I saw his mother visit him in Carthage. She spoke to him earnestly and shed many

tears, but she did not stay with him whilst in the city.—
I never saw in Monica's house either cross or holy picture.
There were all kinds of pagan statues, but neither she nor
her husband took any notice of them. I constantly saw
her in some secluded corner of the house or garden, bent
in two praying and weeping; and yet, with all this, I saw
that she was not without her own faults. Whilst lamenting her son's thefts of sweetmeats, etc., she herself loved
dainties; it was from her that he had inherited his inclination. Whenever she went to the cellar to draw wine
for her husband, she used to sip a little herself from the
cask and eat good things; but she greatly regretted this
inclination and struggled against it. Then many of her
pious customs were shown me : for instance, at certain
seasons she used to take baskets of bread and other provisions to the cemetery which was surrounded by strong
walls. She laid the food on the tombstones with a pious
intention; the poor afterward came and took it away. I
saw her once, her son having now attained the age of manhood, journeying on foot with a servant, who carried a
small package. She was going to visit a Bishop who spoke
to her a long time and encouraged her on the score of her
son. She shed abundant tears, but he said something to
her that calmed her. Again, I saw Augustine returned
from Carthage after his father's death, and teaching in the
little city, where his life was as restless and disorderly as
ever. I saw him at the bedside of a sick friend who,
shortly before death, received Baptism, at which Augustine
hooted, although deeply afflicted at his friend's death.
Then I saw him again at Carthage, living as before."

The Pilgrim now saw the mistake he had made in
marking the relics, and the invalid promised to look in
" *her church* " for those of St. Francis de Sales and St.

Jane de Chantal. On May 29, 1820, he records, as follows : " This afternoon, I found Sister Emmerich in
ecstasy. I offered her the box of relics, which she took
and pressed to the bosom, her features, drawn by pain,
immediately becoming serene. I asked if St. Francis de
Sales were not in " *the church?* " She answered with an
effort, as if speaking from a great height: ' There they
are!' pointing meanwhile to the shelf before her
closet. Surprised, I hunted for the relic, but in vain ;
when she, tearing, so to speak, her right hand from its
ecstatic rigidity, removed quickly and in the greatest order, the books from the shelf. With anxious curiosity, I
glanced at the empty shelf, whilst that wonderfully endowed
hand went groping between the shelf and the panel, until
it grasped the missing treasure, a particle of bone wrapped
in green silk. She pressed it reverently to her lips,
and handed it to me as the relic of St. Francis de Sales.
I must not neglect to state that during this search she,
with the exception of the right hand and arm, remained
perfectly rigid, her head immovable, her eyes closed, her
left hand firmly pressing the box of relics to her breast.
Whilst I wrapped and labelled the relic, she replaced in
the same mechanical way all that she had removed from
the shelf and then opening her eyes, she glanced into the
box of relics, and allowed her hand to rest some moments
on a tiny parcel which she afterward presented to me as
the relic of St. Jane de Chantal. I asked her how it was
that these relics had got mixed up with those of the early
Roman martyrs. She answered : " Long ago, repairs were
made in the Church of Ueberwasser, Münster, when all the
relics of the different altars and shrines were thrown together
indiscriminately." Sister Emmerich afterward saw at various times the following symbolical figures of St. Francis de

Sales's apostolic ministry : " I saw," she said, " a young ecclesiastic of high rank, zealously laboring in a mountainous country between France and Italy, and I accompanied him in his numerous journeys. I saw him in his youth an earnest student. One day with a firebrand he put a shameless woman to flight. Then I saw him going from village to village with a burning torch enkindling a fire everywhere ; the flames leaped from one to the other and finally reached a large city on a lake. When the fire ceased to burn, there fell a gentle rain which lay on the ground like pearls and sparkling stones. The people gathered them up and took them into their houses. Wherever they were carried, prosperity followed, all became bright. I was amazed to see St. Francis so indescribably gentle and, at the same time, so zealous in his undertakings, so vigorous in pushing things forward. He went everywhere himself, climbing over snow and ice. I saw him with the king in France, with the Pope, and then at another court between the two. Day and night did he journey on foot from place to place, teaching and doing good, often passing the nights in a wood. Through him I was introduced to a noble lady, Frances de Chantal, who took me over all his journeys, showing me all he did. I travelled with her here and there, and spoke much with her. She was a widow and had children ; once I saw them with her. I received an account of something concerning her and all the sorrow it caused her, and I saw many scenes of the same. A little frivolous lady of distinction, seemingly penitent, was introduced by her to the Bishop; but she constantly relapsed into her evil ways. Frances said that this lady had caused her much trouble; indeed, she thought she had been bewitched by her. Later on, the Bishop founded a convent in concert with Frances, and the bad person, who seemed to have corrected, did penance in a small house

near by. I remember Frances's showing me the present
state of this person in a dark place.

"I saw the Bishop saying Mass in a place in which
many of the inhabitants doubted the real change wrought
in the Blessed Sacrament. During his Mass he saw in vision
a woman who had come to the church merely to please her
husband; she believed not in transubstantiation and she
had a piece of bread in her pocket. In his sermon the
Bishop remarked that the Lord could as truly change the
bread of the Holy Sacrifice into His Body as he could
change bread in the pocket of an unbeliever into stone.
On leaving the church, the woman found the bread in her
pocket turned into stone. The holy Bishop was always
neatly and properly dressed. I saw him surrounded by
enemies, and I also saw him concealed in a hut to which
about twenty persons came by night for instruction. His
life was sought and snares were laid for him in the forest
to which he had fled.— I went with the lady (St. Frances)
to a large city where, as she told me, the Bishop had disputed with a heretic, who in his arguments never kept to
the points under discussion. The saint, without losing
sight of the truth, had followed him in all his windings in
order to bring him back to the right road; but the man
would not be saved. The lady and I had to cross a large
square in this city. It was crowded with citizens and
peasants who were being drilled in separate troops. I was
dreadfully afraid of their attacking us and, besides, the
good lady said she could not possibly remain longer without food; she would faint from hunger. I looked around
and saw a man eating bread and meat from a paper. I
begged him for just one mouthful, and he gave me some
bread and a piece of chicken. When the lady had eaten
it, she was able to proceed to her convent.—With regard

to those visions in which I exercise some act of charity toward the apparition of a saint, I have from my childhood been interiorly instructed that they are works which the saints demand of us with the design of turning them over to others; they are good works which they cause to be performed for themselves, but which are, in reality, for the benefit of others. ' We do for the Lord what we do for the neighbor,' is here reversed; for here we do for the neighbor what we do for the saints.—I went to the convent which the lady had founded in concert with the Bishop. I went all through it. It was a singular old building; I saw every nook of it. In many of the rooms were large stores of various kinds of fruits and grains, quantities of clothing, and odd-looking caps. The religious must have given away much to the poor. I put everything in order. A saucy young nun continually followed me, reproaching me and accusing me of trying to steal. She said I was avaricious; for, though declaring money to be mire, yet I turned over every penny ; that I mixed myself up unnecessarily in worldly affairs ; that I wanted to accomplish so many things, and yet never finished any, etc. She kept at my back, not having the courage to face me. I told her to stand out before me, if she could. But she was, in fact, the tempter who tormented me greatly during those days. Away off in a remote corner of the convent I found a nun with a pair of scales. She had been placed there by the Foundress. On a plate by her side were heaps of mixed pease, little yellow seeds, of what kind I know not, pearls, and dust— all which she was to pick out and clean. Then she was to carry half the good seed to the front of the convent for seed-corn. But she would not do it; she refused to obey. Then came another in her place, but she was no better than the first ; and, at last, I undertook to sort and separate the mixture. It signified that from the spiritual harvest of this monastery clean, fresh seed-corn would be taken to the front of the house: that is, that the end and blessing of the saint's institution were to be renewed by the merits proceeding from the good discipline of former times; that what was injured by the faults of the last superioresses was to be repaired."

At a later period Sister Emmerich was given to see the entire life of St. Francis de Sales from his infancy to his death, but she had neither the strength nor opportunity to relate even a few of its details. St. Jane Frances again appeared to her at different times, claiming her prayers and sufferings for the renewal of her Order. On July 2d, 1821, she related the following: " Last night I was at Annecy, in the convent of the daughters of the holy Lady de Chantal. I lay very sick in bed, and saw all the preparations for the Feast of the Visitation. I seemed to be in a choir from which I could look down on the altar which was being dressed for the feast, I was very sick and about to swoon, when St. Francis de Sales came to me quickly with something that relieved me. He wore a long, yellow festal robe corded. St. Chantal also was by me."

St. Justina and St. Cyprian.

" I saw Justina, a child in the court-yard of her father's residence, which was only a square from the pagan temple of which he was a priest. She was with her nurse. She went down into a cistern where she stood on a stone in the middle of the water. Underneath were numerous holes in which different kinds of serpents and horrible-looking creatures lurked. They were kept and fed there. I saw Justina coolly take up a large serpent in one hand and several smaller ones in the other. She held them by the tail and amused herself watching them straightening themselves up like tapers, their head moving from side to side. They did not hurt her; they were quite at home with her. Among them were some about a foot long, like those we call chubs (salamanders); they were used in the worship of the idols. Justina once heard in a Christian church a sermon on the Fall of Man and the Redemption. She was so impressed by it that she received Baptism and converted her mother. The latter informed her husband who, having been very much troubled by an apparition, was baptized also with his wife, and they afterward lived most piously and happily. One scene struck me especially. Justina had a lovely round face and the most beautiful yellow hair that shone like gold. It was wound round her head in exquisite silken braids, or fell on her shoulders in luxuriant curls. I saw her standing at table by her father and mother, eating little loaves. The father, glancing with admiration at her hair, said : 'I fear, my child, you will not be able to pass through the world. Like Absalom, you will remain hanging in it by your hair.' Justina had never thought of her hair, and these words made her very grave. She withdrew, and I know not what she did to her beautiful hair, but she completely disfigured it as well as her eyebrows. They looked as if she had singed them. In this trim she went through the city to her father, who scarcely recognized her. I saw a youth in love with her. He was about to carry her off by force, as he could not hope to win her. He waited for her with armed companions in a lonely road between walls ; but when he seized her, she repulsed him with both hands, commanding him to remain standing where he was. And there he stood until she was out of danger. Then I saw the same youth engaging the assistance of the magician Cyprian, who confidently promised him success.

" This Cyprian, though naturally noble and generous, was entirely given up to necromancy. In his youth he had been instructed in sorcery. He had journeyed afar in pursuit of knowledge ; and had finally settled with great renown in Antioch where Justina and her parents had been converted. He was a bitter pagan. He had gone so far as often to revile Jesus in the Christian churches and to chase the people out by his sorcery. I used to see him calling to the demon. He had in his house a semi-subterranean vaulted cellar which was lighted from above. Around the walls stood hideous idols in the form of animals and serpents. In one corner was a hollow statue the size of a man, the open jaws resting on the edge of a round altar on which was a pan of live coals. When Cyprian invoked the demon he put on a particular costume, lighted the fire on the altar, read certain names from a roll of parchment, mounted upon the altar, and pronounced the same in the jaws of the idol. Instantly the spirit stood in human form beside him, under the appearance of a servant. There was something sinister and frightful, like a bad conscience, in the features of these apparitions. The spirit twice attempted to seduce Justina under the form of a youth, waylaying her in the courtyard ; but she put him to flight by the sign of the cross and escaped his influence by the crosses she erected in the corners of her room.—Then I saw her in a secret vault of her house, kneeling in prayer before a niche in which were a cross and a little white Infant. The latter seemed to be in a case, the upper part of the body free, its tiny hands crossed. Whilst Justina thus knelt, a youth approached her from behind with evil intentions; when suddenly I saw the apparition of a lady, as if coming out of the wall, and the youth sank to the earth even before Justina had perceived his presence. She turned and fled.—I saw her completely destroy her beauty with ointment. I saw Cyprian gliding around and sprinkling Justina's house, at an unguarded moment for her when she was not in prayer. She became violently agitated, ran around the house, and at last fled to her chamber, where before the crosses she had herself set up, she knelt in prayer until the charm was broken. When Cyprian made his third attempt, the enemy appeared under the form of a pious young girl who conversed with Justina on the subject of chastity. The latter was at first very much pleased; but when her companion began to speak of Adam, Eve, and marriage, Justina recognized the tempter and fled to her crosses. Cyprian saw all this in spirit, and became a Christian. I saw him lying prostrate in a church, even allowing himself to be trodden under foot as a fool. He was deeply penitent, and he burned all his books on magic. He afterward became a Bishop and placed Justina among the deaconesses. She dwelt next the the church. She made and embroidered grand church vestments.—Later I saw both Cyprian and Justina martyred. They were hung by one hand to a tree and torn with hooks."

St. Dionysius, the Areopagite (1).

"I saw this saint in his boyhood. He was the child of pagan parents, and of an inquiring turn of mind. He always recommended himself to the Supreme God who enlightened him by visions in sleep. I saw his parents reproving him for his neglect of the gods and placing him under the charge of a stern preceptor ; but an apparition came to him by night and bade him flee whilst his preceptor slept. He obeyed, and I saw him traversing Palestine and listening eagerly to whatever he could hear concerning Jesus. Again I saw him in Egypt where he studied astronomy in the

(1) This was the saint whose name she was not permitted to mention when the Pilgrim's friend tested her miraculous faculty.

place in which the Holy Family had sojourned. Here I saw
him, standing with several others before the school, observ-
ing the sun's eclipse at the death of Jesus. He said:
'This is not in accordance with nature's laws. Either a
God is dying, or the world is coming to an end!'—
I saw the preceptor himself, a man of upright inten-
tions, warned to seek his scholar. He did so, found
him, and went with him to Heliopolis. It was long before
Dionysius could reconcile himself to the idea of a crucified
God. After his conversion, he often travelled with Paul.
He journeyed with him to Ephesus to see Mary. Pope
Clement sent him to Paris where I saw his martyrdom.
He took his head in his hands, crossed them on his breast,
and walked around the mountain, a great light shining
forth from him. The executioners fled at the sight, and
a woman gave him sepulture. He was then very old. He
had had many celestial visions besides which, Paul had revealed to him what he himself had seen. He wrote magnificent
works of which many are still extan'. His book on the
Sacraments was not finished by himself, but by another."

A RELIC OF ST. LUKE.

On March 11, 1821, Sister Emmerich said : " For some
time past, I have frequently seen near me a beautiful
white particle of Luke's skull. I see it distinctly ; but, as
I would not believe it in vision, I was punished when
awake by forgetting it. Last night I saw its whole history.
Gregory the Great brought from Constantinople to
Rome the skull of St. Luke and an arm of St. Andrew, which
drew down upon him so many blessings that he made large
gifts to the poor. The holy relics were placed in his
monastery of St. Andrew. Afterward Cologne also was
enriched with a portion of them, to the great joy of its

Bishop. Later on, Mayence, Paderborn, and Münster received part of these relics, and now they are both with me.
The relic of St. Andrew is encased, and that of St. Luke
must be in a corner under some pieces. Just now I know
not exactly where."

The next day, the Pilgrim begged her to look for the
above-mentioned relics ; and, though in ecstasy, she complied with his request. She found that of St. Luke, a small,
three-cornered fragment of skull, hidden under a heap of
scraps in a corner of her press. She said : " I again saw
that this body was found in a ruined church of Constantinople, and its authenticity proved by its being applied
to the sick. The bones were washed and the water given
to a leper who drank of it and was cured. I saw many things
of St. Gregory, how highly he esteemed relics, and how
many cures he effected by them ; the first was that of an
insane woman, the second a young girl possessed of an unclean spirit. He laid the relics on their head. I saw how
some of the relics were brought to Cologne by a holy Bishop,
then to Treves, Mayence, Paderborn, and finally, to Münster, I think under a Bishop Fürstenberg."

St. Ursula.

" Ursula and her companions were massacred by the
Huns, about the year 450, near Cologne and in other
places. Ursula was raised up by God to preserve the
maidens and widows of her time from seduction and dishonor, and to enrol them in the celestial army of crowned
martyrs. She accomplished her mission with extraordinary
energy and constancy. The archangel Raphael was given
her as a guide. He announced to her her task, saying
that the mercy of God willed not that, at this frightful epoch
of destruction, so many virgins and widows left defenceless

and deprived of protectors by the bloody wars should fall
a prey to the savage Huns ; rather should they die as innocent children than live to fall into sin.   Ursula was not
exactly beautiful ; she was tall and strong, resolute and
energetic, of a very grave countenance and masculine bearing.   She was, at the time of her martyrdom, thirty-three
years old.   I saw her as a little girl in the house of her
parents, Deonotus and Geruma, in a city of England.
The house stood on a broad street ; it had steps before the
door, and a metal railing with yellow knobs.   It looked
like the paternal house of St. Benedict, in Italy, which too
had brass railings surmounting a low wall. Ursula had ten
playmates who joined her every morning and evening in
an inclosed field where, divided into two bands, they exercised in running, wrestling, and even in the use of the lance.
They were not all Christians, though Ursula and her parents
were.   Ursula was the instructress of her companions,
and she exercised them thus by order of her angel.   Her
parents often watched their games well-pleased.   Maximian,
a pagan, was then lord over England, and I am not
now sure that he was not the husband of Ursula's eldest
sister, Ottilia.   Ursula had vowed herself to God.   A
warrior, powerful and renowned, requested of her father
the privilege of witnessing the exercises of the maidens of
whom he had heard so much.   Though embarrassed by the
request, Ursula's father dared not refuse.   He tried, at
first, to put him off ; but the man insisted until he gained
his point.   He was charmed with Ursula's skill and beauty
and at once, asked her in marriage, saying that her young
companions should espouse his officers in a country beyond
the sea not yet peopled. I thought of Bonaparte, who made
matches for his officers.   I saw the father's deep affliction
and the daughter's fright when apprised of this offer

which could not be declined. Ursula went by night to the play-ground and besought God in earnest prayer. The archangel Raphael appeared to her, consoled her, and instructed her to request that each of her companions might be allowed to choose ten other maidens, and to demand a delay of three years in which to practise all sorts of naval combats and manœuvres. He exhorted her to confidence in God, who would not permit her vow of virginity to be violated. In these three years she was, with God's help, to convert her companions to Christianity. Ursula delivered these conditions to her father who, in turn, proposed them to the suitor. He accepted them. Ursula and her ten companions chose respectively ten other maidens, who became their pupils. The father had five small vessels fitted out for them, upon each of which were about twenty girls and also a few sailors to teach them how to manage the sails and fight at sea. And now I saw them exercising daily, first in a river, then along the sea-shore. They sailed along quietly, gave one another chase, separated, leaped from ship to ship, etc. I often saw a crowd on the shore watching them, especially the father and suitor, the latter rejoicing in the prospect of soon having so valorous and skilful a wife; for he thought with such a·one by his side, he would be able to overcome every obstacle. After awhile I saw the maidens practising alone without the sailors, Bertrand, the confessor, and two other ecclesiastics being upon the vessels. Ursula had, by this time, converted all her maidens, among whom were some only twelve years old. They were baptized by the priests. Ursula's courage and confidence in God increased every day. I saw them landing on small islands and practising their naval exercises, all accompanied with prayer and the chanting of the psalms, all performed with great freedom and boldness. Ursula's wonderful earnestness and courage are quite indescribable. The maidens wore short dresses, descending a little below the knee; they were quite plain on the hips and had close-fitting bodies. Their feet were laced. Some had their hair uncovered and braided around the head, whilst others wore a sort of head-dress with ends hanging behind. In their exercises they used light, blunt spears. When the three years agreed upon drew to a close, I saw that the maidens were one heart and one soul. When, having already taken leave of their parents, they were about to embark to go to their future husbands, I saw Ursula in prayer. A luminous figure stood before her bidding her trust all to God, the Lord, who would give them the martyr's crown as His own brides, pure virgins; that she herself should propagate Christianity wherever the Lord would lead her; and that many virgins should through her be saved from dishonor and enter heaven adorned with the crown of martyrdom. The angel ordered her also to proceed to Rome with part of her virgins. Ursula confided all this to her ten assistants whom it greatly encouraged. But as many of the others murmured against her because, having started for their nuptials as they thought, she now wanted them to be brides of Christ, Ursula went from ship to ship, reminding them of Abraham, of the sacrifice of his son, and of the miraculous help he had received from God. She told them that they, too, should receive similar strength to offer Him a pure and perfect sacrifice. Then she ordered the cowardly to leave the vessels and return home; but all were encouraged by her words to remain faithful. As they sailed from England under pretence of joining their destined husbands, a great storm arose which separated their vessels from those of their attendants, and drove them toward the Nether-

lands. They could make use of neither sails nor oars, and the
sea miraculously arose as they neared the land. As soon as
they disembarked, their dangers began. A savage nation
tried to oppose their progress; but at Ursula's words, the
maidens were allowed to return unmolested to their ships.
A city lay at the point at which they quitted the open sea
to sail up the Rhine, and here they encountered great troubles; but Ursula spoke for all, answered all. When violent hands were about to be laid on the virgins, they boldly flew to arms and received supernatural assistance which
paralyzed their aggressors, rendered them powerless to
harm them. Many maidens, as also widows and their children joined them on their journey. Before reaching Cologne, they were more than once challenged, interrogated,
and threatened by the barbarous tribes along the shores. It
was Ursula who always responded, and who urged her
companions to ply their oars. They arrived safe at Cologne where they found a Christian community and a little
church. Here they sojourned for a time. The widows
who had joined them on the journey and many young girls
remained behind when Ursula proceeded further on her
way. Before setting out, however, she earnestly exhorted
them to martyrdom as Christian matrons and virgins, rather than suffer violence from the pagan barbarians. They
scattered throughout the surrounding district, spreading
everywhere the teachings and heroic spirit of Ursula, who
had departed with five vessels. On reaching Bâsle, some of
her little company remained there with the ships whilst she
herself set out for Rome with about forty of her maidens,
accompanied by the priests and guides. They went processionally like pilgrims, through wildernesses and mountainous districts, praying and chanting psalms. Wherever they halted, Ursula spoke of the espousals with Jesus

and of the pure, immaculate death of virgins. Everywhere were they joined by recruits, whilst some of their number remained behind to diffuse their own spirit among the people.

"At Rome they visited the tombs of the martyrs and the different places sanctified by their death. As they were informed that their short dresses and freedom of demeanor attracted attention, they procured mantles. The Pope, Leo the Great, sent for Ursula who disclosed to him the secret of her mission, related her visions, and received his advice with humility and submission. He gave her his benediction and presented her with some relics. On their departure, they were joined by Bishop Cyriacus and two priests, one Peter of Egypt, and the other from St. Augustine's birth-place, a nephew of the one who had bestowed lands on the saint for his monastery. Reverence for the holy relics was their chief motive in following Ursula. She took with her to Cologne a relic of St. Peter which is still venerated as such, though none know whence it came ; one of St. Paul ; some hair of St. John the Evangelist, and a scrap of the garment he wore when cast into the boiling oil. On the return of the pilgrims to Bâsle, they were joined by so many recruits that eleven vessels were necessary to convey them to Cologne. Meantime, the Huns had made an irruption into the country, bringing with them misery and confusion. At some distance from the city, the angel Raphael appeared to Ursula in a vision, made known the approach of her martyr's crown, and told her all that she was to do; among other things, that she was to oppose resistance until her little army had been duly prepared and baptized. This vision Ursula communicated to her assistants, and all turn-ed their thoughts to God. As they approached Cologne, they were saluted by the shouts and darts of the Huns;

but they rowed vigorously and passed the city. They would not have disembarked at all in its vicinity, were it not that so many of their party were there awaiting their arrival. They landed, therefore, about a league and a half above Cologne and halted in a field between two thickets where they pitched a sort of camp. Here I saw those that had remained behind hurrying to join them with their recruits. Ursula and the priests addressed the different bands and prepared them for the struggle. The Huns approached and their leaders accosted Ursula; they insisted on being allowed to choose among the maidens. The latter, however, courageously prepared to defend themselves, whilst some of the inhabitants of the city and the country around who had suffered from the Huns, and others who had become acquainted with the virgins that had remained in Cologne, joined the pious little army armed with poles, clubs, and whatever else they could find. This was what had been commanded Ursula by the angel, that time might be gained until all were prepared for martyrdom. During the engagement, I saw Ursula running hither and thither, zealously exhorting the bands in the rear and ardently praying. The priests were everywhere busily baptizing, for numbers of pagan women and girls had come over to them. By the time all were prepared for death, the Huns had surrounded them on all sides. They now ceased defending themselves and gave themselves up to martyrdom, singing the praises of God. Then the Huns fell upon them and slew them with axe and spear. I saw a whole row of virgins fall at one time under the darts of the barbarians; among them was one named Editha, of whom we have a relic. Ursula herself fell pierced by a lance. Among the bodies that strewed the field of martyrdom there were, besides the British virgins, great numbers of those that had joined them at various places, also the priests from Rome, some other men, and some of their enemies. Many more were massacred on board the ships. Cordula was not among those who had accompanied Ursula to Rome. She remained at Cologne where many joined her. When the slaughter began, she hid at first through fear; but she afterward gave herself up with all her companions, requesting to be put to death. The Huns were eager to spare them; but they offered so sturdy a resistance that, after a long delay, they were placed in a line, bound together by the arms, and shot with arrows. They went joyfully singing and dancing to martyrdom as if to a marriage-feast. Later on many others gave themselves up and were put to death in different parts of the country. Shortly after, the Huns withdrew from the district. The bodies of the virgins and other martyrs were soon after interred in an enclosed field near Cologne. Deep pits were dug and walled in, and there the bodies were devoutly laid in rows.

" The ships of the virgins were open, beautiful, and very light, with galleries around them from which floated little standards; they had masts and projecting sides. By the oars ran benches used both for seats and births. I have never seen vessels so well ordered. About the time that Ursula left England, the saintly Bishops, Germain and Lupus, lived in France; the former visited St. Genevieve, in Paris. She was then about twelve years old. When he crossed over to England with Lupus to combat the heretics, he consoled the parents of Ursula and those of the other maidens.—The Huns mostly went bare-legged; they had leathern thongs hanging around the lower part of their body, and wore wide jackets and long mantles. These last they often rolled up and carried on their shoulders."

St. Hubert.

" As I took up his relics, I saw the holy Bishop. He said : ' That is my bone. I am Hubert!'—Then I had visions of his life, and I saw him as a boy in a solitary old castle surrounded by a moat. He wore a close-fitting suit and roamed with his cross-bow in forest and field shooting birds, which he afterward gave to the sick around the castle. I often saw him cautiously crossing the moat on a floating plank to distribute his alms.—Then I saw him a young married man in a distant country, joining with many others in a great hunt. He wore a leathern cap; on his breast hung a bent tube, over his shoulder a cross-bow, and in his hand he carried a light spear. The huntsmen all had little tawny dogs. I saw a large one at Hubert's side; he also had a sort of barrow between two asses on which to take home the game. The hunters crossed a vast, wild district to the scene of action, a broad plain near a running stream. Hubert and his dogs followed a small yellow stag for a long time; but, when the dogs had nearly overtaken it, they ran back to their master whining as if to tell him something. The stag paused, looked at Hubert, started on again pursued by the dogs until the latter, as before, ran back to their master. This they repeated several times. At last, Hubert set the hounds of his fellow-sportsmen on it; but they, too, came running back whining. Hubert's eagerness increased, and he noticed now that the stag grew larger and larger. He renewed the chase more ·ardently than before until he was far ahead of his companions, following the stag, which still seemed to increase in size. He pursued it to a dense thicket. Here he thought it would entangle its horns and be unable to proceed but, to his surprise, the animal pressed through without difficulty whilst he himself, accustomed to clear all sorts of hedges, followed only with effort. And now the stag paused. There he stood large and beautiful, in color like a yellow horse, with long silken hair on his neck. Hubert stood on his right, his spear raised to strike, when suddenly the animal cast upon him a glance full of gentleness, and behold, right between its antlers, shone a dazzling crucifix! Hubert sank on his knees and sounded his horn. When his companions came up, they found him unconscious. The apparition was still visible; but soon the crucifix vanished, the stag resumed its original size and disappeared. Then I saw Hubert borne back to the house on the barrow between the asses. He was a Christian. His father seemed to be an impoverished duke for his castle was greatly out of repair. When a boy Hubert had had in a wilderness an apparition of a youth who invited him to follow Him alone; but the happy impression then produced had been dispelled by his love for the chase. On another occasion he pursued a lamb until the little creature took shelter in a thornbush. Hubert built a fire around it; but the flames and smoke turned upon himself, leaving the lamb unharmed.— Hubert was taken back so ill that it was thought he would die. He was deeply contrite and he promised, if God would prolong his life, he would hereafter serve Him faithfully. He recovered, his wife died, and I saw him clothed in a hermit's garb. He was favored with a vision in which he received as a reward for his self-victory that all the ardor and energy of his baneful passions should be changed into the gift of healing. By the imposition of hands he cured both soul and body of all maladies engendered by wrath, fury, or thirst for blood; he even cured brute animals. He laid his girdle in the jaws of mad dogs, and they were instantly cured. I saw him baking and blessing little loaves, round for men, oblong for brutes, with which he cured madness. I saw, as a certain fact, that whoever confidently invokes this saint will be protected by his merits and healing power against the attacks of rage and madness.—I saw Hubert also in Rome, and the Pope, in consequence of a vision, consecrating him Bishop.'"

St. Nicostratus.

" The bone marked *N*, belongs to *Nicostratus*, a Greek, who, when a child, was led captive to Rome along with his mother and other Christians. The mother with many others was martyred, and the child was reared in paganism. He was a sculptor. I saw him at work with three companions. The sculptors used to dwell in a certain quarter of the city where lay numerous blocks of marble, and they worked in upper halls into which the light entered from above. They wore hoods, apparently of brown leather, to protect the face from the scraps of stone and splinters flying around. I saw Nicostratus and his companions getting marble from the quarries in which the Christians lived concealed. In this way they became acquainted with the old priest Cyril, who was full of cordiality and good-humor. There was something about Cyril that reminded me of Dean Overberg, affable, kind toward every one, even jocose, yet at the same time full of dignity. He converted numbers by his winning manners. Nicostratus and his fellow-workmen had heard from Cyril and other Christians the history of Jesus and Mary ; so they made a most beautiful statue—a veiled lady in long robes, who seemed to be sorrowfully seeking something. It was exquisitely lovely ! Nicostratus and Symphorian put it upon a wagon drawn by an ass, and took it to Cyril. ' Here,' said they, smiling, ' here is the Mother of your God

seeking her Son,' and they set down the statue before him.
Cyril was charmed with its beauty. He thanked them
adding words to this effect that he would pray that she
would also seek and find them; then their joking would be
changed to seriousness. This he said with his kindly
smile, and the youths took it, as usual, in jest. But,
as they returned home a strange fear and emotion took possession of both, of which however they said nothing to each
other. Some time after, they set to work on a statue of
Venus when, by a miracle which I do not now recollect,
they made instead of a Venus an inconceivably beautiful
and modest statue of a female martyr. In consequence of
this four of the young sculptors received instructions and
Baptism from Cyril. After this they made no more idols,
though they still continued their occupation as sculptors.
Actuated by faith and piety, they marked all the stone before using it with a cross, which wonderfully facilitated
the success of their labors. I saw a statue of a holy youth
bound to a column and pierced with arrows; a virgin kneeling before a block, her throat pierced by a sword; and a
stone coffin in which lay the remains of a holy martyr who
had been crushed to death under a marble slab. I saw a
fifth sculptor, still a pagan, Simplicius by name, who said
to them: 'I adjure you by the sun, how is it that your work
succeeds so well?'—They told him of Jesus and how they
always marked their stone with the sign of the cross;
whereupon, Simplicius, also, asked for instruction and Baptism. The Emperor Diocletian highly prized the skill of
these workmen but, when it became noised around that
they were Christians, he ordered them to make an idol of
Æsculapius. On their refusal to do so, he commanded
their arrest. They were taken before the judge and martyred. Their bodies were enclosed in leaden cases and

sunk in the river. But after some days they were miraculously found by a pious man and buried, an inscription with
their names being interred with them. These leaden cases
did not sink near the shore, for fine holes were bored in
them that the water might enter only gradually. A clay
mould, about the size of a man, was put into a hole and a
thin layer of molten lead poured around it. The mould
was then withdrawn and in its stead the holy martyrs were
put into the hot case and covered up, the holes were
pierced, and it was thrown into the water. I saw the
feast of these martyrs to-day (Nov. 8, 1821), but I think
the 7th is the real anniversary of their martyrdom. "

St. Theoctista.

" Whilst on my way to the Holy Land, I saw the life
of this holy virgin, hitherto perfectly unknown to me. She
belonged to the Isle of Lesbos. Before the city of her
birth arose a chapel of the Mother of God in which was a
statue of Mary without the Infant Jesus; it had been
chiselled from her portrait by St. Luke. The sculptor
was a holy confessor of the faith belonging to Jerusalem,
who afterward lost both his arms and legs in one of the
persecutions. Around the chapel were cells in which
dwelt pious women who followed a Rule founded on the
life of Mary and the holy women at Ephesus. They had
erected on the mountain a " Way of the Cross," like that
planned by Mary at Ephesus. They reared and instructed
little girls and, as their Rule ordained, examined their inclinations and dispositions, in order to choose for them a
state of life. Theoctista had been with them from childhood and her only desire was to remain with them. Her
parents were dead. The chapel and convent being destroyed in war, Theoctista entered another community on

the same island. The religious dwelt in caves on a mountain under the Rule of a holy woman who, in consequence of a vision, recognized the chain of St. Peter; but I have forgotten her name. Here Theoctista remained until her twenty-fifth year, when she went to visit her sister who lived at a distance. But the ship on which she was fell into the hands of Arab pirates when sailing from the Isle of Crete, and the whole crew was dragged into captivity. The pirates landed on the Isle of Paros, which contained many marble quarries. Whilst they were disputing over the ransom for their captives, Theoctista made her escape and hid in the quarries. Here she lived as a hermitess for fifteen years without human aid, until discovered one day by a hunter. She related to him her history and implored him to return with the Holy Eucharist in a pyx. This was permitted to laics at that time, as the Christians were often scattered and priests were few. At the end of a year, he returned with the Blessed Sacrament which she received as Viaticum. She died the same day. The hunter buried her, after first removing one of her hands and a piece of her clothing which he carried away with him. Through that blessed hand he happily accomplished his voyage home, in spite of the imminent risks he ran from pirates. When he related the affair to his Bishop, the latter reproached him for not having brought away the whole body of the saint."

St. Gertrude.

" I saw that Gertrude's mother had a prophetic dream before her child's birth. It appeared to her that she brought forth a little daughter who held in her hand the crosier of an abbess from which sprang a vine. The mother dwelt in an old castle, and once she and all her neighbors were greatly annoyed by mice which destroyed the crops and provisions. She had a great horror of these pests. Once I saw her in tears, recounting to her little Gertrude the ravages they had made. Gertrude instantly knelt down and fervently begged God for deliverance from the plague. Instantly, I saw all the mice scampering out of the castle and drowning in the waters of the moat. Gertrude by her childlike faith obtained great power against these and other noxious animals. She had some pet mice which she fed and which obeyed her call; she had also birds and hares. She was asked in marriage, but she rejected the proposal, and exhorted her suitor to choose the Church for his spouse, that is to become a priest. He did so in effect, but only after having seen the other maidens whom he sought die suddenly. I saw Gertrude as a religious, her mother as abbess; later on, she herself held that office. At the instant the crosier was presented her, there sprang from its top a vine-branch with a bunch on which were nineteen grapes, which she gave to her mother and her eighteen religious. Two mice ran around the crosier, as if paying homage to her authority. Thus was the mother's prophetic dream realized."

St. Cecilia.

November 22, 1819–'20.—"I saw the saint sitting in a very plain four-cornered room, on her knees a flat triangular box, about an inch high, over which were stretched strings which she touched with both hands. Her face was upturned and over her hovered bright, shining spirits like angels or blessed children. Cecilia seemed conscious of their presence. I often beheld her in this posture.—There was also a youth standing by her, of singularly pure and delicate appearence; he was taller than she, and full of de-

ference for her. He seemed to obey her orders. I think it
was *Valerian*, for I afterward saw him bound with another
to a stake, struck with rods, and then beheaded. But this
did not happen in the great circular martyr-place; it was
in a more remote, a more solitary spot. St. Cecilia's house
was square with a roof almost flat, around which one could
walk. On the four corners were stone globes, and in the
centre there was something like a figure. Before the house
lay a circular court-yard, the scene of Cecilia's own execution. Here burned a fire under an immense cauldron in
which sat Cecilia, full of joy, clothed in a shining white robe,
her arms outstretched; one angel, surrounded by a rosy
light, held out to her his hand, whilst another held a crown
of flowers above her head.—I have an indistinct remembrance of having seen a horned animal, like a wild cow,
though not such as we have, led in by the gate and through
the court to a dark recess. Cecilia was then removed from
the cauldron and struck three times on the neck with a
short, broad sword. I did not witness this scene, but I saw
the sword. I also saw Cecilia wounded, but still alive,
conversing with an old priest whom I had formerly seen in
her house. I afterward saw that same house changed into
a church and divine service celebrated in it. Many relics
were there preserved, among them Cecilia's body, from the
side of which some portions had been removed. This is
what I recollect just now of my many visions of Cecilia's
life."

November 22, 1820.—" Cecilia's paternal home stood on
one side of Rome and like Agnes's house, it had courts,
colonnades, and fountains. I rarely saw her parents.
Cecilia was very beautiful, gentle though active, with rosy
cheeks and a countenance almost as lovely as Mary's. I
saw her playing in the court with other children and almost

always by her side an angel under the form of a lovely boy.
He conversed with her and she saw him, although he was
invisible to others to whom he forbade her to speak of him.
I often saw him withdraw when the other children gathered
around her. Cecilia was then about seven years old. I
saw her again sitting alone in her chamber, and the angel
standing by her teaching her how to play on a musical instrument. He laid her fingers on the right strings and
held a sheet of music before her. At times she rested on
her knees something like a box over which strings were
stretched, whilst the angel floated before her with a paper
to which she occasionally raised her eyes; or again she
supported against her neck an instrument like a violin, the
chords of which she touched with her right hand, whilst
at the same time she sang into the mouth-piece which was
covered with skin. It produced a very sweet sound. I
often saw a little boy (*Valerian*) by her, along with his elder brother and a man in a long white mantle who lived
not far off and who seemed to be their preceptor. Valerian played with her; it seemed as if they were being reared together, as if destined for each other. Cecilia had a
Christian servant through whom she became acquainted
with Pope Urban. I often saw Cecilia and her playmates
filling their dresses with fruit and all kinds of provisions.
Then hooking them up at the sides like pockets and wrapping their mantles around them, they slipped stealthily
with their loads to a gate of the city. The angel was always at Cecilia's side. It was a charming sight! I saw
the children hurrying along the high-road to a building
made up of heavy towers, walls, and fortifications. Poor
people dwelt in the walls. In the underground caves and
vaults were Christians; whether imprisoned or only
concealed there, I do not know, but the poor creatures

nearest the entrance seemed to be always on their guard against discovery. Here it was that the children secretly distributed their alms. Cecilia used to fasten her robe around her feet with a cord and then roll down a steep bank. She passed into the vaults, and thence through a round opening into a cave where a man led her to St. Urban, who instructed her from rolls of parchment. Some of these rolls she brought to him concealed in her garments. She took others back home with her. I have an indistinct remembrance of her being baptized there. Once I saw the youth Valerian and his preceptor with the little girls as they were at play. Valerian tried to throw his arms around Cecilia, but she pushed him off. He complained of it to his preceptor, who reported the affair to her parents. I do not know what they said to Cecilia, but she was punished by being confined to her own room. There I saw the angel always with her teaching her to sing and play. Valerian was often allowed to visit and remain with her; at such times, she invariably began to play and sing. Whenever he wanted to press her in a loving embrace, the angel instantly flung around her a glittering, white garment of light. This had the effect of gaining Valerian over to Cecilia's way of thinking. After that he often remained in her room alone, whilst she went to St. Urban; her parents, meanwhile, imagining them together. Lastly, I had a vision of their betrothal. I saw the parents of both and a numerous company of people young and old in a hall magnificently adorned with statues; in the centre stood a table laden with dainties. Cecilia and Valerian wore festive suits of many colors and crowns and garlands of flowers. They were led to each other by their parents who presented them, one after the other, with a glass of thick red wine, or something of the kind. Some words were pronounced,

some passages read from manuscripts, something was
written, and then all partook of the refreshments standing.
I saw the angel ever at his post between Cecilia and her
bridegroom. Then they went in festal procession to the
back of the house where, in an open court, stood a round
building supported by columns; high up in the centre were
two figures embracing each other. In the procession
little girls, two by two, carried a long chain of flowers
suspended on white drapery. As the betrothed stood
before the statues in the temple, I saw the figure of a boy
which seemed to be inflated with air, flying down, moved
by some kind of machinery, first to Valerian's lips, then to
Cecilia's, to receive from each a kiss; but, when it flew to
Cecilia, the angel laid his hand over her lips. Then
Cecilia and Valerian were entwined in the flower-chain by
the little girls so that the two ends should meet around and
enclose both; but the angel still stood between them,
thus preventing Valerian's reaching Cecilia, or the
chain's being closed. Cecilia said some words to Valerian
like these: *Did he see nothing? She had another friend
and he, Valerian, should not touch her!* Then Valerian
grew very grave, and asked if she loved any other of
the youths present. To this Cecilia only answered that,
if he touched her, her friend would strike him with
leprosy. Valerian replied that, if she loved another, he
would kill them both. All this passed between them
in a low tone, one would have thought it only modesty
on Cecilia's part. She told Valerian that she would
explain herself later.—Then I saw them alone together in
an apartment. Cecilia told him that she had an angel by
her. Valerian insisted on seeing him too. She replied
that he could not do so until he was baptized, and
she sent him to St. Urban. At this time Valerian and
Cecilia were married and in their own home."

St. Catherine.

"St. Catherine's father was named Costa. He belonged
to a royal race and was a descendant of Hazael whom Elias,
by God's command, anointed king of Syria. I saw the prophet with the box of ointment, crossing the Jordan and
anointing Hazael, with whom after that all went well.
Costa's immediate ancestors emigrated to Cyprus with the
Persians or Medes, and there obtained possessions. They
were like Costa himself star and fire-worshippers, and
held also to the Syro-Phœnician worship of idols. Catherine, on her mother's side, was descended from the family
of the pagan priestess Mercuria, who had been converted by Jesus at Salamis. She had after her conversion
emigrated to the Holy Land, received in Baptism the name
of Famula and, in the persecution that broke out after the
stoning of Stephen, she had gained the martyr's crown.
There had long existed in her family the oft-told prediction that a great prophet would come from Judea to change
all things, to overturn the idols, to announce the true God,
and that he would come in contact with this family. When
Mercuria fled to Palestine with her two daughters, she left
behind in Cyprus an illegitimate son whose father was then
the Roman Consul. He had been baptized as early as the
time of Jesus, and he afterward left the island with Paul
and Barnaby. This son married his mother's youngest
sister, from which union was born Catherine's mother.
Catherine was Costa's only daughter. Like her mother,
she had yellow hair, was very sprightly and fearless, and
had always to suffer and to struggle. She had a nurse
and, at an early age, she was provided with male precep-
tors. I saw her making toys out of the inner bark of trees
and giving them to poor children. As she grew older, she

wrote a great deal upon tablets and parchment which she
gave to other maidens to copy.   She was well acquainted
with the nurse of St. Barbara, who was a Christian in secret.
She possessed in a high degree the prophetic spirit of her
maternal ancestors, and the prediction of the great prophet was shown her in vision when she was scarcely six
years old.   At the mid-day repast, she related it to her
parents to whom Mercuria's history was not unknown ; but
her father, a very cold, stern man, shut her up, as a punishment, in a dark vault.   There I saw her, a bright light
shining around her and the mice and other little creatures
playing tamely by her.   Catherine sighed earnestly after
that promised Redeemer of mankind ; she begged Him to
come to her, and she had numerous lights and visions.
From that time she conceived deep hatred toward the idols.
She broke, she hid, she buried all she could lay her hands on.
For this reason, as also for her singular and deeply-signifi-
cant words against the gods, she was often imprisoned by her
father.   She was instructed in all knowledge, and I saw
her during her walks scribbling in the sand and on the
walls of the castle, her playmates copying what she wrote.
When she was about eight years old, her father took her to
Alexandria, where she became acquainted with him who
was one day to aspire to her hand.   After some time she
returned with her father to Cyprus.   There were no longer
any Jews on the island, only here and there a few in slavery, and only a small number of Christians, who practised
their faith in secret.   Catherine was instructed by God
Himself; she prayed and sighed for holy Baptism, which
was given her in her tenth year.   The Bishop of Diospolis
sent three priests secretly to Cyprus to encourage and
strengthen the Christians, and on an interior admonition,
he also allowed the child to be baptized.   She was, at the

time, again in prison, her jailer being a Christian in secret. He took her by night to the secret meeting place of the Christians outside the city in a subterranean cave, whither she often went for instructions to the priests by whom she was finally baptized. She received with the Sacrament of Baptism the gift of extraordinary wisdom. The priest, in performing the ceremony, poured water over the neophytes out of a bowl. Catherine gave utterance to many wonderful things, though like all the other Christians she still kept her religion secret. But her father, though fondly attached to his beautiful and intelligent little girl, was unable longer to endure her persistent aversion to idolatry, her discourses, and her prophecies. He took her to Paphos and left her there in confinement, hoping thus to cut off all communication between her and her co-religionists. Her servants, both male and female, were by his orders frequently changed, as many among them were found to be Christians in secret. Catherine had already had at this time an apparition of Jesus as her Heavenly Affianced. He was always present to her, and she would hear of no other spouse. She returned home from Paphos. Her father now wanted to marry her to a youth of Alexandria, named Maximin, a descendant of an ancient royal house and nephew to the governor of Alexandria who, being childless, had adopted him as his heir. But Catherine would not listen to such a thing. She smilingly but fearlessly repelled all their advances, warded off every temptation. So great were her wisdom and learning that few could be found who were not forced to acknowledge her superiority. Before these marriage-proposals, she had, at the age of twelve years, seen her mother die in her arms. Catherine told her mother that she was a Christian, instructed her, and prevailed upon her to receive Baptism. I saw her with a little

green sprig, sprinkling water from a golden bowl on her
mother's head, forehead, mouth, and breast.

" There was always frequent intercourse between
Cyprus and Alexandria. Catherine's father took her to
a relative in that city, hoping she would at last yield to
his wishes concerning her marriage. She was then thirteen.
Her suitor went out in a vessel to meet her and, again, I
heard her uttering admirable, profound, and Christian
sentiments. She inveighed against the idols, whereupon
the suitor playfully struck her several times on the mouth.
Catherine laughed, and spoke more enthusiastically than
before. On disembarking, he took her to his father's house,
in which everything breathed of the world and its delights.
All hoped that Catherine's feelings would soon change ; but
here, too, she showed herself fearless and dignified, though
affable as before. Her suitor, who lived in another wing
of the house, was as if mad from love and disappointment ;
for Catherine spoke incessantly of her other Affianced.
Every means was taken to change her, learned men were
sent to argue with her and turn her from the Christian
faith ; but she confounded them all, put them all to
shame.

" At this time, the Patriarch Theonas was in Alexandria.
He had obtained by his great sweetness that the poor
Christians should not be persecuted by the pagans ; but
still they were greatly oppressed, they had to keep very
quiet, and carefully repress every word against idolatry.
From this state of affairs resulted very dangerous communications with the pagans and great lukewarmness
among the Christians, for which reason God ordained that
Catherine, by her superior intelligence and burning zeal,
should rouse them to renewed fervor in His service. I saw
Theonas give her the Holy Eucharist, which she carried home

on her breast in a golden pyx ; but she did not receive the
Precious Blood. I saw at that time in Alexandria, many poor
men, apparently hermits, and who were now prisoners. They
were frightfully treated, forced to labor at buildings, draw
heavy stones, and carry great burdens. I think they were
converted Jews who had established themselves on Mt.
Sinai, but who had been forcibly dragged into the city. They
wore brown robes woven of cords almost as thick as one's
finger, and a cowl of the same color, which fell on the
shoulders. I saw that the Blessed Sacrament was also secretly administered to them. Catherine's suitor set out
on a journey to Persia and she herself returned to Cyprus,
hoping now to be left in peace ; but her father was greatly
displeased at not seeing her married. Again did he send
her to Alexandria, and again was she the victim of new
attacks. Later on she joined her father at Salamis, where.
she was triumphantly received by the young pagan girls,
who loaded her with attentions and prepared all sorts of
diversions for her ; but all to no purpose. Then she was
taken back to Alexandria to be the object of redoubled importunities. Here I saw a great pagan festival at which
Catherine was compelled by her relatives to assist. But
though forced to appear in the temple, nothing could induce
her to offer sacrifice ; yet more, as the idolatrous ceremony
was being performed with great pomp, Catherine inflamed
with zeal, stepped up to the priests, overthrew the altar of
incense with the vessels, and exclaimed aloud against the
abominations of idolatry. A tumult arose. Catherine was
seized as mad and examined in the court-yard, but she
only spoke more vehemently than before ; whereupon she
was led away to prison. On the way thither, she adjured
the followers of Jesus Christ to join her and give their
blood for Him who had given His for their Redemption,

She was imprisoned, beaten with scorpions, and exposed to the beasts. Here the thought struck me : ' It is not lawful thus to provoke martyrdom !'—but there are exceptions to every rule, and God has His own instruments. Violence had always been employed to force Catherine into idolatry and a marriage abhorrent to her. Immediately after her mother's death, her father frequently took her to the abominable festivals of Venus, in Salamis, at which, however, she constantly kept her eyes closed. At Alexandria, Christian faith lay dormant. The pagans were well pleased that Theonas should console their ill-treated Christian slaves and exhort them to serve their barbarous masters faithfully. They were so friendly toward him that many weak Christians thought paganism not so bad, perhaps, after all ; therefore did God raise up this fearless, intrepid, enlightened virgin to convert by word and example, above all by her admirable martyrdom, many who would not otherwise have been saved. She made so little concealment of her faith that she went among the Christian slaves and laborers in the public squares, consoling and exhorting them to remain firm in their religion ; for she knew that many of them had grown tepid and fallen off, owing to the general toleration. She had seen some of these apostates in the temple, taking part in the sacrifices, and hence her holy indignation. The beasts to which she was exposed after her scourging, licked her wounds, which were miraculously healed when she was taken back to prison. Here her suitor attempted to offer her violence, but he was put to shame and withdrew utterly powerless. Her father returned from Salamis. Once more was Catherine taken from her prison to the house of her lover, and all possible means employed to make her apostatize ; but the young pagan girls sent to persuade her were converted by her to

Christ, and even the philosophers who came to dispute with her were won over. Her father was mad with rage; he called the whole affair sorcery, and had Catherine beaten and imprisoned again. The wife of the tyrant visited her in prison and she, too, was converted as also one of her officers. As she approached Catherine, I saw an angel holding a crown over her and another presenting her with a palm-branch; but I cannot say whether the lady saw it or not.

"Catherine was next taken to the circus and seated on a high platform between two broad wheels, stuck full of sharp iron points like a ploughshare. When the executioners attempted to turn the wheels, they were shivered by a thunderbolt and hurled among the pagan crowd, about thirty of whom were wounded or killed. A terrible hailstorm followed; but Catherine remained quietly seated with outstretched arms amid the shattered wheels. She was reconducted to her prison where she remained for several days. More than one pagan tried to offer her violence, but she drove them back with her hand, and they stood spellbound, motionless as statues. When others attempted similar violence, she pointed to those victims of her power, and thus averted further attacks. All this was regarded as sorcery, and Catherine was again led to the place of execution. She knelt before the block, laid her head on it sideways, and was beheaded with a piece of the iron from the broken wheels. An extraordinary quantity of blood flowed from the wound, spouting up into the air in one continuous jet until, at last, the flow became colorless as water. The head had been completely severed. The body was thrown upon a burning pile; but the flames turned against the executioners, leaving the holy remains enveloped in a cloud of smoke. It was then taken from the pile and thrown to the ravenous beasts which, however, would not touch it. Next day it was cast into a filthy ditch and covered over with elder-branches. But that night I saw two angels, in priestly vestments, wrapping the luminous body in bark and flying away with it.—Catherine was sixteen years old at the time of her martyrdom, A. D. 299. Of the crowd of maidens who had followed her in tears to the place of execution, some fell away; but the tyrant's wife and the officer bravely suffered martyrdom.—The two angels bore the virgin's body to an inaccessible peak on Mt. Sinai, on which was a level space sufficiently large for a small house. The peak was a mass of colored stone which bore the imprint of entire plants. Here they placed the remains the face downward. The stone seemed to be soft like wax, for the body left its impress on it as if in a mould. I could see the distinct imprint of the backs of the hands. Then they placed a shining cover over the whole. It arose a little above the surface of the rock. Here the saint's body lay concealed for hundreds of years, until God showed it in a vision to a hermit of Mt. Horeb, who lived with many others on the mountain under the conduct of an abbot. The hermit related the vision, which he had several times, to his Superior and found that another of the brethren had had a similar one. The abbot ordered them in obedience to remove the holy body. This was an undertaking not to be accomplished by natural means, for the peak was absolutely inaccessible, overhanging and craggy on all sides. But I saw the hermets set out and, in one night, make a journey which, under ordinary circumstances, would have required many days; they were, however, in a supernatural state. The night was cloudy and dark, but brightness shone around them. An angel carried each in his arms up the steep peak. The angels opened the tomb and one of the hermits took the head, the other the light, shrunken body with its winding-sheet in his arms, and both were borne down again by the angels. At the foot of Mt. Sinai I saw the chapel, supported by twelve columns, wherein rests the holy body. The monks seemed to be Greeks; they wear coarse habits made by themselves. I saw St. Catherine's bones in a small coffin, the snow white skull and one entire arm, but nothing more. All things around this spot have fallen to decay. Near the sacristy is a little vault hollowed in the rock; in it are excavations containing holy bones, most of them wrapped in wool or silk and well preserved. There are among them some bones of the prophets who once lived on the mountain. They were venerated even by the Essenians in their caves. I saw the bones of Jacob, and those of Joseph and his family which the Israelites brought with them from Egypt. These sacred objects seemed to be unknown, venerated only by the devout monks. The chapel is built on the side of the mountain facing Arabia."

The Stigmatisees Madeline of Hadamar, and Colomba Schanolt of Bamberg.

January 19, 1820.--The Pilgrim presented Sister Emmerich a scrap of cloth stained with blood from the wounded side of Madeline of Hadamar. She was in ecstasy at the time, but she instantly exclaimed: "What shall I do with this long garment? I cannot go to the nun; it is too far away! They tormented her so that she could not finish her task; she died before it was fully accomplished." These words were incomprehensible to the Pilgrim; but the following more extended vision which she had later on, explained all. "I have seen little Madeline to whom the garment once belonged. But I saw her only at a distance;

she could not come to me. I saw her in the cemetery of her convent. In one corner stands a little ossuary with the Station of Our Saviour carrying the Cross. Near by, on the churchyard wall there is another Station of the Via Crucis. An elder-tree and a nut-hedge make it a shady, retired spot. All around lay piles of unfinished work, sewing, etc., which I was to arrange and finish. I fell earnestly to work, making, mending, and, at the same time, saying my breviary, until I began to perspire profusely and feel violent pains in my hair. Every hair seemed to have its own peculiar pain. The good little Madeline had indulged her devotion too much in this pleasant nook, so well suited to prayer; consequently, she had neglected much work begun for the poor. When, at last, I had levelled the mountain, I found myself standing before a cupboard in a small house. Madeline came forward joyously thanking me as if she had not seen any one for a long time. She opened the cupboard, and there I saw stowed away all the morsels of which she had deprived herself for the poor. As she thanked me for arranging and finishing her work, she said: ' In life we can do in one hour what we can, by no means, make amends for in the other world, if left undone here!'— and she promised me some pieces for my poor children. She told me that through kind heartedness, she had undertaken more than she could accomplish; and that order and discretion are very essential in time of suffering, else confusion arises. Madeline was not tall; she was very thin, though her face was full and rosy. She showed me her parents' house and even the door through which she had left it on going to the convent. I saw then many scenes of her cloistered life. She was exceedingly kind and obliging, doing the work of others whenever she could. I saw her also sick in bed, suddenly attacked by different maladies and just as suddenly cured. I saw her wounds bleeding, and I saw the supernatural relief she received in her sufferings. When the prioress or any other nun stood by her, I beheld on the opposite side of the bed the forms of angels or deceased religious, floating down to her, consoling her, supporting her, or giving her a drink. She was well treated by her fellow-sisters; but her state became too public and she had to endure much from visits and false veneration. Her case was imprudently exaggerated, and this caused her great vexation, as she told me herself. Her confessor published an account of her state, rather expressive of his own admiration than a faithful record of facts. After the suppression of her convent, she was subjected to an inquiry in which both ecclesiastics and surgeons took part; but the former were indifferent and left everything to the physicians. I saw nothing improper, but these men were very rude and coarse, though far less false and crafty than those with whom I had to deal. They tormented her exceedingly, trying above all to make her eat. Such attempts always brought on vomiting. Even as a child, Madeline had been accustomed to privation, her parents being very poor, though very good people. Her mother particularly used often to say to her child at meals: ' Now, one bite less, one mouthful less for the poor, for the suffering souls !' — There were many wonderful things about Madeline, but she had become too public. She died before her time. She fretted and kept her sorrows to herself, consequently her life was shortened. I saw her death, not the ceremonies nor the obsequies, but the soul departing from her body."

When the Pilgrim again approached Sister Emmerich with the stained linen, she cried out: " Why, there thou art, little darling ! O she is so active and kind, so obliging and charitable !"—Then, after a long silence, she asked in a quick, animated tone : " Why did Jesus say to Magdalen, ' Woman, why weepest thou ? '—*I* know, my Affianced told me why He thus spoke ! Magdalen had sought Him so eagerly and impetuously that, when she *did* meet Him, she took Him for a gardener. Then said He : ' Woman, why weepest thou ? '—But when she exclaimed: ' Master !' and recognized Him, He said to her : ' Mary ! '—As we seek, so we find !

" I saw all this by little Madeline. I saw her lying in a small, dark room into which many persons entered; they were going to examine her case. They were rough, but not wicked like those who examined into mine. They spoke of an enema at which Madeline showed too great unwillingness. She began to complain ; but, when she resigned herself to their treatment, her vexation vanished. It was at this moment that I had the vision of the garden before her window. Perhaps she had had the same herself, since she despaired of finding her Affianced, although He was at her side. Madeline still owes me the pieces she promised me.

" I saw also the Dominicaness, Colomba Schanolt of Bamberg. She was inexpressibly humble, simple-hearted, and unaffected ; and, notwithstanding her stigmata, she was ever active and laborious. I saw her in her cell, praying prostrate on the ground as if dead. Again, I saw her in bed, her hands bleeding and blood flowing down from under her veil. I saw her receiving the Holy Eucharist, the form of a little luminous Child escaping to her from the hand of the priest ; and I, also, saw the visions she had had. They passed before her in pictures as she lay in her bed, or knelt in prayer. They were scenes from the life of Our

Lord, or others for her own direction and consolation. She wore a haircloth and round her waist a chain until forbidden to do so. Colomba was very well off in her convent, much less importuned than Madeline. She was consequently further advanced in the interior life, more simple, more re-collected. I saw her also occupying a higher rank in the other world. But the way in which one sees such things cannot be explained. The clearest manner of expressing it is, that she *travelled farther."*

A RELIC OF THE PRECIOUS BLOOD AND OF OUR LADY'S HAIR (1).

In June, 1822, the Pilgrim received from a suppressed Carmelite convent of Cologne, a little package inscribed: *" De Cruore Jesu Christi,"* which he hid, unknown to Sister Emmerich, in the closet at the head of her bed. The next day she said: "I have had a very uneasy night, I was in a most singular state! I was attracted in this direction," pointing toward the closet, "by a sweet feeling of hunger, a feeling of thirst, an insatiable longing! It was as

(1) With this relic was the following document: " I, John Verdunckh, Chamberlain and Master-of-the-Robes to His Electoral Highness Maximilian, Duke of Bavaria, etc., hereby attest that his Most Serene Princess and Lady, Countess-Palati..e of the Rhine, Duchess of Upper and Lower Bavaria, etc., nee Duchess of Lorraine, having died in the convent of Randshoffen, bequeathed her effects to her heirs. On the occasion of their being put in possession of them, the Marechal of the Court of His Electoral Highness, Count Maximilian Kurz von Senfftenan, etc., presented some tokens of remembrance to many connected with the execution of said bequests, whereby there happily fell to me a golden *Agnus Dei* with diamond pendant, enclosing a relic of Our Dear Lady's hair. I know not whether the Countess was aware of its containing this relic, but I kept it carefully and reverently, and gave it to my daughter Anne of Jesus, Carmelite religious, on the day of her profession in the convent of Cologne. Three or four years after, my gracious master, His Electoral Highness, after the birth of his heirs by his second wife, caused the holy relics to be exposed. Among them was a large piece of the *Terra madefacta Sanguine Christi,'* of which he put three particles into an *Agnus Dei* for Madame, his Countess, and the two young princes respectively. On the paper on which it had been divided there still remained two or three particles, so small that His Highness could not pick them up. He ordered me to burn them for fear of desecration. I folded them in the fine paper, but did not burn them as ordered. I preserved them most honorably and, at the request of my dear daughter, Anne of Jesus, I gave them to her.

"This I attest upon my conscience and as I hope for salvation! I declare the above statement true and exact, and in proof of the same, I have marked the relics with my private seal. I have written the above, I sign it, and I affix thereunto my seal, Given at Munich, the 30th day of May, A.D. 1643.

L. ✝ S.   " JOHN VERDUNCKH,
                                          " Electoral Chamberlain and Master-of-the-Robes,"

if I were forced to fly thither whilst drawn at the same
time in a contrary direction. In this excited state, I saw
numerous successive scenes. I saw over there the whole
of Christ's agony in the garden of Olives. I saw Him
kneeling on the rock in the grotto and sweating blood.
I saw the disciples sleeping near, whilst the sins of mankind were crushing their Lord. I saw the rock sprinkled
with the drops of congealed blood, which were in time completely hidden by the overlying dust and earth. It seemed as if that covering had been removed, that I might see
those drops. I seemed to see it all in the far, far past.
Then I had a vision of the Most Blessed Virgin who, whilst
her Son agonized in the grotto, knelt on a stone in the
court-yard of Mary Marcus's house. She left upon it the
imprint of her knees. She suffered the agony of Jesus with
Him ; she became unconscious, and her friends supported
her. These two scenes were presented to me at one and
the same time.—Then I had a vision of Mary's hair, and I
saw again that it had been divided into three parts and that
the Apostles cut some off after her death."—Here the Pilgrim
produced the little bag with the above-named relics, which
the invalid regarded devoutly for a few moments. She
then said :—

" Mary's hair is in it also. I see it again, and that is
really the Blood of Christ ! There are three tiny particles,
and they exert an influence totally different from the bones
of the saints. They attract me most wonderfully ; they excite in my soul a sweet, longing desire ! Other relics shine
with a light which, compared to this, is as a fire compared
to the splendor of the noonday sun." At intervals, she repeated : "It is the Blood of Christ ! Once before I saw
some that had flowed from a Host. This is truly some of the
Blood of Christ that remained on the earth. It is not the

substance of blood, but it is like it in color. I cannot explain it. I saw the angels gathering up only what flowed to the earth during the Passion and on the road to Calvary."

And now, Sister Emmerich had repeated visions upon the discovery, the worship, the whole history of this relic. She related them at intervals, as follows:—"I saw a devout princess in pilgrim's garb, going to Jerusalem with a numerous train. She belonged to the Isle of Crete. She was not yet baptized, though she ardently sighed for that grace. I saw her first in pagan Rome in a time of peace just before a persecution; for the Pope, who instructed her, dwelt in an old ruined edifice, and the Christians held secret assemblies here and there.—The Christians were tolerably secure in the Holy Land, though a journey to Jerusalem was attended by many dangers. The city was very much changed: hills had been levelled, valleys filled up, and streets built over the principal Holy Places. I think, too, that the Jews were confined to one quarter of the city, and only the ruins of the Temple were to be seen. The site of the Holy Sepulchre was near Calvary and still beyond the city limits; but it could not now be reached. The road leading to it had been closed, and buildings had been raised over and around it. There dwelt in caves hard by, many holy personages who venerated the sacred spot, and who seemed to belong to a community established by the first Bishops of Apostolic times. They could not visit the Holy Sepulchre in body, but they often did so in spirit. Few of the inhabitants seemed to trouble themselves about these Christians. They could, by using some precautions, freely visit the Holy Places around the country. They could also dig in search of, and collect precious things. It was at this period that many bodies of the saints of the early ages were found and preserved.

" The pilgrim-princess, whilst praying on Mt. Olivet, saw in vision the Precious Blood. She pointed it out to a priest of the Holy Sepulchre. With five companions he went to the spot indicated, turned up the earth, and found part of the colored rock upon which Jesus had knelt sprinkled with blood. As they could not remove the whole stone which formed a part of the solid rock, they detached from its surface a piece as large as one's hand. Of this the princess received a part, as also some relics of the garments of St. Lazarus and the old Simeon, whose tomb not far from the Temple lay in ruins. I think the princess is inscribed in the calendar, although she is not known among us. The piece of stone was three-cornered with various colored veins. At first it was placed in an altar, and afterward in the foot of a monstrance."

July 8th—"The father of the princess was descended from the Cretan kings; but Crete was, at this time, in the hands of the Romans. He still had vast possessions and lived in a castle near a city in the western part of the island, Cydon, or Kanea (or something of the kind) where grow quantities of yellow, ribbed fruit, broad at the stem and flat at the top (1). Between the city and the castle was a great arch through which one could see right into the former. A long avenue led to it. The father had five sons living. The mother died whilst the daughter was still young. The father had been to the Holy Land and Jerusalem. One of his ancestors had been an acquaintance of that Lentulus who had loved Jesus so much and who had been a friend of Peter, from whom he had learned the doctrines of Christianity. Hence it was that he was not unfavorable to the new religion. Once he was in Rome with his daughter's future husband. They conversed to-

(1) Doubtless, she meant quinces, known as *malum Cydonium.*

gether of Christianity, the young man expressing his hope
of one day embracing its teachings.   It was on this occasion, I think, that they agreed upon the marriage or, at
least, became acquainted.   They received from a priest more
detailed instructions.   The affianced, a count, was, in fact,
of Roman extraction though born in Gaul.   The Cretan
prince became more and more estranged from paganism.
His daughter and other children, whom he had reared as
well as he knew how, often heard him lauding Christianity.
He had a right and claim over the Labyrinth of Crete
which, however, owing to the change in his sentiments, he
resigned to his son-in-law.   The labyrinth and temple
were no longer used as formerly.   Men were no longer
brought there to be torn to pieces by wild beasts, though
idolatry was still practised.   Numbers flocked to them out
of curiosity, and they were the scene of many shameful observances.   At a distance, the labyrinth looked like a
verdant mountain.

" When the young princess was in Rome to be instructed,
she may have been seventeen years old ; and when, in the
following year, she made her pilgrimage to Jerusalem, it
seemed as if her father was dead and she was her own mistress.—She carried the Precious Blood on her person in a
richly embroidered girdle in which were several little pockets.
All the pilgrims wore such girdles crossed on the breast.—
She returned to Crete, but it was not long before the count
took her away again.   They embarked in a ship for Rome
where they stayed until secretly baptized.   The papal
chair had long been vacant ; for there had been confusion,
a schism, and a secret massacre of Christians.   From Rome
they embarked for Gaul with a numerous retinue of soldiers,
having lived about six months after their marriage, partly
in Rome, and partly in Crete.   The count now wore the

Precious Blood in a girdle, for the princess had given It him as a pledge of her fidelity. His castle was on an island in the Rhone about seven leagues from Avignon and Nimes, near a little village later known as St. Gabriel's. It owed its origin to a miracle by which a man had been saved during a storm on the lake. Tarascon and Martha's Solitude were not far off, St. Martha's monastery being situated on a mountain lying between the Rhone and a lake. There were at that period in Nimes some Christian catechists living together secretly, and the count received from time to time the visit of a holy hermit, a priest. The Precious Blood was, at first, preserved in a dark, underground vault whose entrance lay through many others, in one of which were stored plants and provisions; in winter even green trees were there preserved. It was kept in a vase like a chalice on an altar which had a little tabernacle with a locked door. Before it burned a lamp. I often saw the count and his lady praying before this tabernacle.

" I saw that, at a later period, they lived apart like hermits and at a distance from their castle. They went to it only to make their devotions before the Precious Blood. Once they heard a voice enjoining on them to place the relic in a chapel; whereupon they prepared a suitable place for It near the dining-hall. Their devotion toward It ever increased, though they continued to venerate It only in secret. The relic was afterward transmitted to their heirs with numerous precautions and duplicate documents.

" I saw at this time something connected with St. Trophimus of Arles: but I can now recall only the names. Before the count's marriage some Christians had immigrated to that country from Palestine; they were supported by him and they lived there in little communities.—The **countess's father had** concealed his sentiments from his eldest sons whose ideas differed from his ; but the younger ones held the same faith as their sister and, I think, there were martyrs among them.

July 11th—" Whilst thinking of the Precious Blood, I had a glimpse of the altar in the count's castle, and then I saw the countess herself, first as a maiden with her father on the Isle of Crete, then with her husband in Rome. At the same time, I saw St. Moses in Rome I saw him as a boy eight or ten years old, giving all kinds of nourishment to the Christians, sick and in prison. I saw the count and countess with other Christians in a subterranean vault, lit up by lamps, where priests seemed to be instructing them from rolls of writings. There were at that period, many distinguished personages secretly baptized in Rome ; there was, indeed, no open persecution, but from time to time one or other of the Christians was seized.

" I have said the Christians from Palestine had already settled near the count's domains and with them he kept up secret communications. They did not have Holy Mass at first, only prayer and reading ; but later on, a hermit came about every six weeks, and afterward a priest from Nimes to offer the Holy Sacrifice. The faithful were still allowed to carry the Blessed Eucharist to their homes.

" When the count and countess separated to live in solitude, they had grown children, two sons and a daughter. Their caves or hermitages were about half a league from each other and the same distance from the castle ; they were however on its lands. To reach them, one had to cross a bridge over a small stream. Other Christians throughout the country lived in the same way, mutually assisting one another. At one time it was like a monastery. They did not end their days there, however, nor were they martyred ; but when danger threatened, they fled."

July 13th—Sister Emmerich designated a relic as belonging to *Pope Anacletus*, saying that he had been the
fifth Pope, had succeeded St. Clement, and had been
martyred. At the same time she remarked in allusion to
the relic of the Precious Blood : " The priest who searched
for the Precious Blood was the saintly Bishop Narcissus of
the race of the Three Holy Kings with whom his ancestors
had journeyed to the Holy Land. It was perfectly light
when he dug that night upon the Mount of Olives and the
young princess was present. Narcissus was dressed like
the Apostles.—Jerusalem was then scarcely recognizable
for, when it was destroyed, valleys had been filled up and
hills levelled. The Christians still had a church at the
pool of Bethesda between Sion and the temple. They had
had one there even in the Apostles' time ; but it was not
now in existence. They dwelt around it in huts and although perfectly isolated from the other inhabitants, they
were obliged to pay a tax for the privilege of entering their
own church. A man and a woman sat at the gate to receive
from the faithful five small pieces of money as toll. This
regulation lasted some time.—The pool of Bethesda with
its porches was no more, all was closed up ; but there was
a covered well whose waters were regarded as sacred
and used by the people in time of sickness, just as we use
holy water.

" The count's name was the same as that of one of St.
Augustine's friends, *Pontianus*; that of the countess was
Tatula, or Datula, I cannot give it correctly. There is
such a saint toward the close of May, or the beginning of
June." On the afternoon of July 18th, Sister Emmerich
suddenly exclaimed : "There was a man here just now, a
Cardinal, the confessor of a holy queen named Isabella.
He was a very able director of souls. He told me that I

must accuse myself of the good I neglect to do, and do penance for the sins of others. He showed me St. Datula, who possessed the relic of the Precious Blood. For Its sake she had abandoned all her wealth and retired with her husband to grieve over their sins. The Cardinal was called *Ximenes*, a name I never heard before. He is not canonized."—One day, having seen several things in St. Martha's life, Sister Emmerich pointed out more precisely the abode of Pontianus and Datula. " The island with the castle," she said, " lay at the mouth of the eastern branch of the Rhone, and was about half a league in circumference. Pontianus had soldiers under him; his castle looked like a strong fortress. Seven leagues further up the river lay the city of Arles, and at about eight leagues distance was St. Martha's Monastery in a rocky, mountainous district."

On June 24th, Sister Emmerich had a vision, occasioned by what, or referring to what, she did not know. She recounted it with all the simplicity and astonishment of a peasant-girl beholding the march of a grand procession. She constantly interrupted her recital to give expression to her admiration at the magnificence, order, and propriety displayed in every part of it. " Crete," she began, " is a long, narrow island, with numerous indentations, the centre traversed by a mountain-ridge. The castle of St. Datula's father was a very handsome, spacious building apparently terraced out of a marble rock ; on the different terraces were colonnades and porticoes, on top of which were gardens. After embracing Christianity, Datula's father had built these porticoes and hanging gardens, as a screen to cut off his home altogether from the abominable, idolatrous temple and its labyrinths. He was a very skilful man ; he could do almost anything ; and he constantly superintended the architects and workmen himself. He was bald and stooped in the shoulders, but still very active and most benevolent. He owned other large property on the island, and he also exercised some kind of authority. The wall mentioned above was built in terraces which were full of well-kept plants. They opened into rooms and passages.

"To-day is the anniversary of the day on which Pontianus led his bride Datula from her brothers' castle, the father being then no more. All night I saw the grand feast, so distinctly that I still have the servants and children under my eyes. Two of Datula's brothers lived in the castle with their respective families. There were many children, boys and girls, and crowds of domestics ; for every child had, besides its tutors, several attendants, both male and female, each with a special duty. All the relatives of the family with their children and servants were then at the castle for the marriage. The road for half a league was adorned with triumphal arches and seats erected on either side, artistically twined with flowers, and ornamented with statues and rich hangings. Here sat the young musicians. At the gate of the castle was a raised throne for the bride and her attendants. Pontianus had arrived at a neighboring port the day before with a numerous retinue of ladies, soldiers, servants, and presents. He repaired to another castle at no great distance and there marshalled his procession. The joy of the bride's domestics and slaves was most touching. They had always been most lovingly treated and rewarded and now they were all delight. They were stationed in order on the road, the highest grades nearest the castle, the children with their attendants on raised seats. Pontianus appeared in sight with a grand cortege. Before and around him marched his soldiers, and servants in rich

dresses leading asses and little nimble horses laden with baskets of clothing and pastry. Pontianus himself rode in
an elegant large car, like a great canopied throne. It was
surrounded by lighted torches in stands transparent as
glass, the canopy surmounted by a flambeau. The whole
car was covered with gold and ivory, adorned with rich
hangings, and drawn by an elephant. In Pontianus's suite
was a long train of ladies.

" All moved so orderly, so joyously through the lovely
country with its charming walks of golden fruits, beautiful
flowers, and happy people—it was a real jubilee, but without any disorderly shouting. When the procession reached
the first row of servants, clothing and flat cakes, some of
the latter stuck full of little shrubs, were distributed to every
one by Pontianus's servants, and so they advanced, distributing gifts to the joyous crowd. When the bridegroom
reached the seats of the children of the family, they
stretched silken draperies with fringes and long streamers
across the road before him, whilst the choir of children
saluted him with music. Pontianus arose, presented them
with gifts, and the procession moved on toward the brothers
and sisters-in-law of the bride. At last, it passed through
an immense arched avenue of trees elegantly decorated,
and across a bridge. And now appeared between the
magnificent buildings and gardens a kind of stage in tiers,
covered with rich carpets and ornamented with garlands
and beautiful statues transparent and glittering. I remember among others the representation of a whole chase;
the eyes of the animals sparkled like fire. The procession
took place in the day-time; but the throne of the bride
was placed in a recess lighted partly from behind, partly
from the sides by flambeaux such as surrounded the bridegroom's car. Around it was raised a semi-circle of little

balconies whence burst forth at the instant of Pontianus's arrival a chorus of voices accompanied by flutes—it was all wondrously charming !

" But loveliest of all was Datula, the bride, seated high on her throne, and below her, in double rows, her young companions and attendants all in white with long veils, their hair braided artistically around their head and adorned with rich ornaments. Datula wore a glistening white robe, I think of silk, which fell in full, long folds, and her hair was entwined with most beautiful pearls. I cannot say how powerfully I was touched when I beheld through her cloth- ing the gleaming of the relic of the Precious Blood. It lay on her heart in Its richly embroidered girdle, shedding rays of celestial glory over the magnificent scene. Her heart was perfectly absorbed in the thought of the sacred object she bore about her. She looked like a living mon- strance when her betrothed appeared before the throne, his attendants, male and female, in a semi-circle around him. They bore upon a great silken cushion under a beautiful cover presents of costly dresses, jewels, and ornaments of all kinds. The cushion was presented to the female at- tendants and then to Datula, who with her suite now de- scended from the throne. Veiling her face, she knelt humbly before Pontianus, who raised her up, lifted her veil and led her by the hand first to the right and then to the left, the whole length of the semi-circle, presenting her to his followers as their future mistress.— It was a touching sight, the Precious Blood borne on Datula's person in the midst of these pagans! I think Pontianus knew of Its presence, so respectful, so reverential was he. At last, they all entered the castle with the family.

" No words can describe the order that reigned through- out the joyous multitude scattered in the chambers, the courtyards, the terraces and groves, or under tents, eating, singing, jesting. I saw no dancing. There was a grand banquet in a spacious, circular hall into which one could see from all points. The bride sat by Pontianus at a table higher than those in use among the Jews. The men reclined on couches, the women sat cross-legged. Most wonderful looking things were set on the table : great animals and figures with the meats in their sides, in their backs, or in baskets held in their mouth. It was droll and fantastic, and drew forth many pleasantries from the guests. The drinking vessels shone like mother-of-pearl. I gazed upon this scene all night; but yet, I did not see any nuptial ceremony, though I saw Datula's departure with Pontianus. A great deal of baggage was sent on before to the ship, and amid tears and good wishes they proceeded in festal procession to the port. Pontianus, Datula, and several others rode in a long, narrow chariot on many wheels and built in sections. At the turns in the road, sometimes it wheeled so as to bring the occupants into a semi-circle. It was drawn by little frisky horses. I saw nothing disorderly during the whole feast, nothing even slightly improper ; and, although these people were not all Christians, there was nothing idolatrous about them. They seemed to be pleasing to God, as if all were inclining toward Christianity. The men were remarkably handsome, and I cannot forget those tall, beautiful, healthy-looking women and girls. Datula took some of them with her, among them her nurse, or governess also, whose sentiments were very Christian. I did not see them embark."

On February 11, 1821, as Sister Emmerich lay in ecstasy, the Pilgrim dropped from a prayer-book a little picture of Jesus Crucified which fell on the coverlet of her bed. She seized it quickly, her eyes still closed, ran her fingers over it several times, and exclaimed : " It must be venerated ! It is very precious ! It has touched some sacred object ; it shines brilliantly !" Then laying it on her breast, she said : " It has touched Christ's robe on the neck of which is a stain of the Precious Blood of which no one knows !"

April 8, 1823.—" I have had to perform a wearisome task connected with relics of the earliest ages, in a country beyond the Holy Land where the priests do not dress exactly like Catholic priests. They wear very antique vestments something like those I saw on Mt. Sinai. It seemed to be in the country I always see next to that of the Three Kings ; the city in which was the old book of prophesies on copper plates (*Ctesiphon*) lay to the left of it. Here I had much to do with the Blood of Christ, and I had to discover a treasure of relics to the priests. I saw seven old priests digging under ruined walls in an underground cave ; they first propped the wall up for fear of its falling in. There they found holy relics sealed up in a great stone seemingly of one piece, but really formed of many three-cornered pieces skilfully put together. When it was opened, first appeared a thick hair-cloth under which reposed the treasure, the principal relics of the Passion and the Holy Family, all preserved in three-cornered vases placed side by side : sand from the foot of the cross, moistened and tinged with the Blood of Jesus ; and, in little phials, some of the water from His Side, clear, consistent, no longer liquid ; thorns from the Crown ; a piece of the purple mantle of derision ; some scraps of the Blessed Virgin's clothing ; some relics of St. Anne, and many others. Seven priests were there at work whilst deacons held torches, and I think they placed the Blessed Sacrament above them. I had much to do there and many poor prisoners, that is poor souls, to deliver, in which work the Precious Blood helped me. I think the Apostles had to say Mass in that cave."

October 9, 1821, Sister Emmerich related the following : " I saw many things in the life of St Francis Borgia, both as a man of the world and as a religious. I remember his having scruples about daily Communion and his praying before a picture of the Mother of God, where he received a stream of Blood from the Child Jesus and another of milk from Mary. He was told not to deprive himself of that oñ which he lived, daily Communion. This reception of milk from Mary I have often seen represented in the pictures of saints where they are painted in the act of suckling at her breast, like children, or the milk flowing from her breast to them ; but all that is wrong and absurd ! I saw it in an entirely different way : from Mary's breasts, or from the region of the breasts, something like a little white vapor streamed out to them and was breathed in by them. It was like a stream of manna from her, whilst from the Side of Jesus shone upon them a ray of rosy light. It is like wheat and wine, like flesh and blood—but quite unspeakable ! "

EFFECTS OF THE SACRED LANCE.

In July, 1820, Sister Emmerich's confessor, Father Limberg, received some relics without labels that had once belonged to the house of Dülmen ; among them was a particle of the Sacred Lance. When he presented it to the invalid, she exclaimed : " It pricks ! that's a sign ! I have received a thrust !"—and the wound in her side became red. Then she had the following vision of St. Longinus : "I saw the Lord dead on the cross. I saw all the people standing around in just the same position as on Good-Fri-

day. It was at the instant in which the legs of the crucified were to be broken. Longinus rode a horse or mule,
but it was not like our horses ; it had a thick neck. He
dismounted outside the circle of soldiers, and went in on
foot,his lance in his hand. He stepped upon the little mound
at the foot of the cross, and drove the lance into the right
Side of Our Lord. When he saw the stream of blood and
water, he was most powerfully affected. He hastily descended the mountain, rode quickly to the city, and went
to tell Pilate that he looked upon Jesus as the Son of God,
and that he resigned his appointment in the army, He
laid down his lance at Pilate's feet and left him. I think it
was Nicodemus whom he next met and to him he made the
same declaration, after which he joined the other disciples.
Pilate esteemed the lance dishonored, inasmuch as it had
been used as an instrument of punishment, and I think he
gave it to Nicodemus."—Here Sister Emmerich laid the
relic away in the little closet by her bed ; but after some
time, she turned to it in ecstasy, saying : " There are the
soldiers with the lance ! Some of Christ's lance is in there !
That is Victor. He carries a particle of it in his lance, but
only three know of it."—That evening she lay insensible
from excess of pain ; she was in such a state that neither
her confessor's benediction nor command seemed to have
any effect upon her. Later, she related what follows :
" After midday, I felt that the cross of Jesus was laid upon me and that His Sacred Body lay dead on my right arm;
at some distance lay the lance, first a large piece, then a
tiny particle. Which should I choose for my consolation ?
I took the Holy Body, and the lance was taken from me.—
Then I could speak again."

Again she exclaimed : " I still saw the Sacred Lance
sticking in my right side, and I felt it passing through to

my left ribs. I held it in the wound to direct it through between the ribs." Sister Emmerich, on this occasion, vomited blood and her side bled freely.

A Particle of the True Cross.

Dr. Wesener's journal contains the following, dated Oct. 16, 1816. It is the first fact reported by an ocular witness respecting Sister Emmerich's power of recognizing relics : " I found the invalid in profound ecstasy. Father Limberg was in her room. I showed him a little case I had found among some objects left me by my mother-in-law, lately deceased. Among other relics it contained two tolerably large particles of the True Cross. Father Limberg made no remark, but took the case. Approaching to within some distance of the bed, he held it out to the invalid. She arose instantly, eagerly stretched out her hands toward it and, on obtaining possession of it, pressed it closely to her heart; whereupon Father Limberg inquired : ' What is that ?' ' Something very precious ! some of the Holy Cross !'—she answered and, when withdrawn from her ecstasy by a command from the Father, she expressed her astonishment on finding that the relic was mine. She thought it had come among some pieces of old silk sent her from Coesfeld for her poor, and she wondered much that the pious donor had not taken better care of the precious case."

Five years later, the Pilgrim writes : " To-day they presented to Sister Emmerich a piece of the True Cross, belonging to Dr. Wesener. She grasped it eagerly, exclaiming : " I, too, have that ! I have it in my heart and on my breast !" (She always wore a relic of the True Cross sent her by Dean Overberg). " I have a piece of the lance also. On the cross hung the Body, in the Body was the lance! Which shall I love the more? The cross is the instrument of Redemption, the lance opened a wide door to love. O yesterday, I was far, far in!" The *yesterday* alluded to was a Friday. "The particle of the True Cross renders my sufferings sweet, the relic chases them away. I have often said to Our Lord, when the particle of the True Cross sweetened my pains, 'Lord, if it had been so sweet for *Thee* to suffer upon this cross, this little piece of it would not now make *my pains* so sweet!'"

In August, 1820, Sister Emmerich was moved to other lodgings, and the particle of the True Cross was lost in the confusion consequent on such a change. She was greatly distressed; she prayed to St. Anthony of Padua and had a Mass said in his honor for the recovery of her treasure. On returning from vision a few days later, she found it in her hand: "St. Joseph and St. Anthony," she exclaimed, "have both been with me, and St. Anthony put the cross in my hand!"

RELICS OF THE BLESSED VIRGIN'S CLOTHING.

July 30, 1820.—"In the little package of relics which my confessor gave me, I have more than once come across a small piece of brownish stuff belonging to a garment of the Mother of God. I had, in consequence, a vision of Mary. I saw her, after the death of Jesus, living with one servant in a small house off by itself. In a glimpse at the marriage-feast of Cana, I saw that Mary wore this dress there; it was a holiday dress. When she lived alone with her servant, she was frequently visited by John, or some other Apostle or disciple, but no man lived in the house. The servant provided the little that was needed for their support. The country around was still and tranquil; a forest stood not far from the house. I saw Mary in this dress following a road which she herself had laid out near her dwelling in memory of the last sorrowful journey of Jesus. At first, she went all alone, measuring each step of the dolorous Passion which she had so often retraced in spirit since the death of her Son. Wherever anything remarkable had happened to Jesus, there she set up a memorial with stones, or made a mark on a tree if one stood near. The road led into a little thicket which contained a hillock in which was a grotto ; and here was represented the tomb of Jesus. When she had thus laid off the different stations, she went from one to the other with her maid in silent contemplation, sat down at the places marked, meditated upon the mystery it recalled, prayed, and often arranged things still better. I saw her engraving on a stone with a stylus the particular circumstance of each station, or something of the kind. She and her maid cleaned out the grotto, and made it fit for the tomb and for prayer. I saw no pictures nor crosses, but only monuments with inscriptions, all very simple. This first attempt of Mary to perpetuate the remembrance of her Son's sufferings became, in consequence of frequent visits and improvements, a very beautiful road to which long after her death, pious Christians went to pray. Here and there they used to kiss the ground. The house in which Mary dwelt was, like the house of Nazareth, divided off by light partitions.

"The garment to which the relic belonged was an upper one ; it covered only the back where it fell in a fold down to the feet. A piece passed around the neck from one shoulder to the other where it fastened by a button, thus forming an opening for the neck. At the waist it was confined by a girdle ; thence it descended to the feet over the brown underskirt, and turned back at the sides to show the striped red and yellow lining. The relic does not belong to the lining, but to the outside stuff. It seemed to be a holiday dress of ancient Jewish style. Anna had one like it. She wore an under-robe, the bodice shaped like a heart. The front and sleeves were not concealed by the upper-robe; the latter were narrow and gathered in around the elbows and wrists. The hair was concealed by a yellow cap which fell on the forehead and which was caught in folds at the back of the head; over this was a veil of black stuff which fell half-way down the back.

"I beheld Mary in her last years, making the Way of the Cross in this robe. I know not whether she wore it because it was a holiday dress, or because she had worn it at the time of Christ's Crucifixion under the mantle of prayer and mourning which completely enveloped her. She was, at this time, advanced in years, though there was visible in her no other sign of age than an ardent desire for her transfiguration. She was remarkably grave. I never saw her laugh, and the older she grew, the fairer and more transparent became her countenance. She was thin, but I saw no wrinkle, no trace of decay about her; she was like a spirit.

"I have examined the relic; it is a piece of stuff about the length of one's finger."

Other Relics of Mary.

Nov. 14, 1821.—"I made my usual journey into the Holy Land and to many places in which I saw all sorts of relics of Mary and learned their history. I was also in Rome with St. Paula. It appeared to be on the day of her departure for the Holy Land, and she visited the Holy Places with me. I know not why I saw so many relics of the Blessed Virgin.

"I have been to that place, (I think Chiusi) where was

once the ring of Mary which is now at Perugia. They still exhibit there a white stone in a vase, but the ring is gone. Of this ring I still remember that a youth before his burial, arose in his coffin, declaring that he could not rest until his mother, a worldly woman named Judith, would give to the Church Mary's wedding ring which she had in her possession. After these words he lay down again.

" I have been some place. I know not whether it is the same in which the House of Loretto first stood, or whether only the vessels I saw came from it. They were not in an orthodox Christian church ; the people looked like Turks. There were bowls and earthen vessels like those in the Holy House when it came to Loretto, but I know not whether they were genuine, or only the models that St. Helena had made. There are still many of them at Loretto, but St. Helena had both the original and the copies covered with a thick coat of glazing to preserve them. I think those at Loretto are genuine. Those that I saw in the place of which I speak were carefully kept under an altar.

" I saw also in a Greek church somewhere in Asia a piece of faded blue stuff, a part of Mary's veil. It was once very large ; but so much had been given away that only this small piece remained. Through St. John's influence, it was presented to the church in which I saw it. I saw in a vision people disputing its authenticity. One rash man, attempting to seize it, boldly reached out his hand which was instantly paralyzed. His wife began to pray earnestly for her husband's cure. Luke, who was present, proved its authenticity by laying it on the man's hand, which was instantly cured. He also gave them something in writing concerning it which is still preserved there. He spoke to them of his own life, of his travels, of his having frequently seen Mary when he was with John at Ephesus, and of his own connection with the liberal arts. He mentioned the portraits he had painted.

"I went also to a place where was preserved an undergarment of Mary. I think it was in Syria, near Palestine. The garment was one that Mary had given to two women before her death. The people of the country were not Roman Catholics, but Greeks, I think; they held the relic in high veneration and were very proud of it. I think St. Francis of Assisi went there once and wrought a miracle in confirmation of its authenticity. I saw in the place in which are Mary's veil and Luke's writing, a letter written by the Mother of God. It is very short, but not even slightly discolored by age. I heard it read and, perhaps, I shall remember some of it. John wished her to write it to the people because they were incredulous about many things concerning Jesus.

"I had a vision of the cincture of Mary and the swathing-bands of Christ which were once preserved in a magnificent church at Constantinople. Where they now are, they are not known. I had another great vision of a pilgrim bringing from the Holy Land all sorts of relics of Mary, her clothing and also some of her hair. He was attacked and wounded by robbers who cast the sacred objects into the fire. But the holy man afterward crept to it, found the relics uninjured, and was healed.

"Where Mary's house at Ephesus stood, there still lies hidden under the ground, a stone upon which both Peter and John used to say Mass. Whenever they went into Palestine, they visited the House of Nazareth, and offered there the Holy Sacrifice on an altar raised where the fire-place once was. A little stand which Mary had used stood on the altar for a tabernacle. Anne's house was in the country about half a league from Nazareth. From it one could go, by a short cut and without being remarked, to the house of Mary and Joseph which stood near a hill, not on the hill but on the opposite side, a narrow path running between it and the house. Though it had a small window on that side, it was dark. The back of the house was, like that of Ephesus, triangular. Here, in this corner was Mary's sleeping apartment; here she received the angelic message. Her room was cut off from the rest of the house by the fireplace which, like that at Ephesus, was provided with a pipe terminating in a tube above the roof. At a later period, I saw two bells hanging from it. Right and left of the chimney, were doors opening into Mary's room. In the chimney walls were niches in which were placed the dishes. Mary's sleeping-place was on the right, a little wardrobe stood on the left and also an oratory with a low kneeling-stool. The window was opposite. The rough walls seemed to be covered with large leaves over which hung mats. The ceiling appeared to be woven out of sap-wood. In the three corners shone a star, the largest in the middle one. When Mary went to Capharnaum, she left the house beautifully adorned as a sacred oratory. She often returned to visit the scene of the Incarnation and pray there. Time rolled on, and more stars adorned the ceiling.

" I remember that the rear of the house, the chimney, and the little window were transported to Europe and, it seems to me when I think of it, that I saw the front in ruins. The roof was not high and conical, but level in the centre and sloping toward the edges, not so much so, however, that one could not take a turn on it. There was no turret, only the chimney and projecting pipe covered by a little roof. At Loretto I saw many lights burning. At the moment of the Annunciation, Anne was sleeping in an alcove to the left near the fireplace."

Spurious Relics of Mary's Hair.

Sister Emmerich had received from the convent of Notteln through one of her former fellow-religious, some hair said to have been brought into the country by St. Ludger as the hair of the Blessed Virgin. It was not long before she had the following vision concerning it: "From the foot of my bed there to the right, an uncommonly lovely maiden approached me. She wore a shining white robe and yellow veil; the latter fell down to her eyes, and through it I could see her golden hair. The whole room was suddenly lighted up around her, not as by reflected light, but as if by a sunbeam. Her whole appearance and her surpassing loveliness reminded me of the Mother of God; and, as this thought passed through my mind, she addressed me pretty much as follows:—'Ah! I am far, far from being Mary, though I sprang from her race about thirty or forty years after her. I am of her country, but I did not know her, nor did I ever visit the places of her sufferings; for I could not make known my religion at a time in which the Christians were very much persecuted. But the memory of the Lord and His Mother was so greatly revered in my family that I strove in every way to imitate their virtues. In spirit I followed the footsteps of the Saviour as other Christians do the " Way of the Cross." I received the grace of realizing Mary's secret sufferings, and that formed my martyrdom. A successor of the Apostles, a priest, was my friend and guide' (here she told me the name, but I have forgotten it; it was not one of the Apostles, nor is it in the Litanies. It is an ancient, foreign name which, it seems to me, I have heard more than once).

'This man was the cause of my being known; only for him I should have remained wholly unknown. He sent some of my hair to Rome and a Bishop of the country obtained possession of it. He brought it here with many other things; but the circumstance has long been forgotten. Many relics of my time were sent to Rome, though no relics of martyrs.'—This is about all I learned from the apparition. The way in which such communications are received cannot be explained. What is said is singularly brief, though one single word then imparts more knowledge than thirty would at another time. One sees the speaker's thoughts, though not with the eyes, and all is clearer, more distinct than any ordinary impression. The recipient experiences such pleasure as is produced by a cool breeze in the heat of summer; but words cannot express it! Then the vision disappeared."

Blessed Objects.

" I never saw miraculous pictures shining, though I have seen before them a beam of light from which they receive the rays which fall upon those praying below. I never saw the crucifix of Coesfeld shining, but only the particle of the True Cross in the upper part of it. I have also seen rays darting from the relic toward the devout suppliants kneeling before it. I think every picture that recalls God or one of His instruments may receive the power of working miracles by virtue of prayers said in common and with lively confidence. In this faith triumphs victoriously over the weakness of nature."

One day the Pilgrim presented Sister Emmerich an *Agnus Dei,* which she took with the words : " This is good and endued with strength. It is blessed. But here, in these relics" (she was at the time arranging some) '' I have

strength itself." Of a *blessed crucifix*, she said : "The
blessing shines upon it like a star! Keep it reverently.
But the consecrated fingers of the priest" (turning toward
her confessor) "are still holier. This crucifix is perishable, but the sacerdotal consecration is ineffaceable ; it will
last for all eternity, neither death nor hell can annihilate it!
It will shine forth in heaven! It is from Jesus who has
redeemed us." Some one brought her a little picture of
the Mother of God which had been blessed. "It is blessed !"
she said. "Keep it carefully. Do not let it lie among
profane things. He who honors the Mother of God is
honored by her before her Son. It is good in time of temptations to press such things to our heart. Keep them carefully!" Another little picture given her she laid on her
heart, saying, "Ah! the strong woman! This picture has
touched the miraculous picture."

St. Benedict's Medal.

The Pilgrim gave Sister Emmerich a reliquary inclosing
a medal on a scrap of velvet; she said : "This is a
blessed medal of St. Benedict, blessed with the benediction
that Benedict left to his Order by virtue of the miracle
which took place when his monks presented him a poisoned draught. The glass fell to pieces when he made the
sign of the cross over it. It is a preservative against
poison, pestilence, sorcery, and the attacks of the devil.
The red velvet on which the medal is sewed is also blessed ;
it once rested on the tomb of Willibald and Walburga, the
place where oil flows from the bones of the latter. I saw
the priests carrying it there barefoot, and then cutting it
up for such purposes as this. The medal was blessed in
that monastery."

One day, the Pilgrim laid near the invalid's hand a

little picture of St. Rita of Cassia which, some time previously, had been moistened by a drop of blood from her own stigmata. She took it, saying: "There, I see a sick nun without flesh or bones! I cannot touch her."

July 11, 1821.—Whilst Sister Emmerich was relating something she had seen in vision, the Pilgrim quietly slipped into her hand a book opened at a page stained with her own blood. Instantly a bright smile played over her countenance and she exclaimed: "What a beautiful flower! red and white streaked. It has fallen from the book into the palm of my hand."

Again the Pilgrim laid the same leaf in her hand with the question: "Has is touched anything?"—She felt it a moment and answered: "Yes, the Wounds of Jesus!"

In October, 1821, a lady sent her from Paris a little picture that had touched the bones of St. Bobadilla. Sister Emmerich was at the moment suffering from intense headache. She raised the picture to her forehead, when the saint appeared to her, relieved her pain, and she saw the whole scene of his martyrdom.—As she lay in ecstasy one day, the Pilgrim offered her a broken silver ring blessed in honor of Blessed Nicholas von der Flue, at his tomb in Sachseln. When returned to consciousness, she said: 'I saw how Brother Klaus separated from his family and how, in his conjugal union, by suppressing the material, he rendered the spiritual bond so much the stronger. I saw the mortifying of the flesh figured by the breaking of a ring, and I received an instruction on carnal and spiritual marriage. The ring which brought me this vision was blessed in honor of Brother Klaus."

A GLANCE AT PARADISE.

February 13, 1821.—As Sister Emmerich lay, as usual, absorbed in ecstatic contemplation in presence of Father Limberg and Christian Brentano, the brother of the Pilgrim, the latter entered the room with a piece of petrified bone in his hand. It was about the size of an egg and had been found in the Lippe. He laid it gently on her bed. Still in ecstasy, she took it into her left hand and held it for a few moments; then she opened her eyes and looked steadily at the Pilgrim who fully expected to receive a rebuke for having given her the bone of a brute animal instead of a holy relic. But still absorbed in contemplation, she exclaimed: "How did the Pilgrim get into that wonderful, that beautiful garden into which I can only look? There he is with that great animal! How can it be? O how beautiful is all I see! I cannot express it, I cannot describe it! O God, how wonderful, how incomprehensible, how powerful, how magnificent, how lovely art Thou in all Thy works! O here is something far above nature! for here there is nothing touched by sin! here is nothing bad, here all things seem to have just come from the hand of God! —I see a whole herd of white animals, with hair like masses of curls falling over their backs; they are much taller than men, and yet they run as lightly and nimbly as horses. Their legs are like pillars, and yet they tread so softly! They have a long trunk which they can raise and lower, and turn on all sides like an arm, and long snow-white teeth protrude from their mouth. How elegant, how clean they are! These animals are enormous, but so handsome! their eyes are small, but so intelligent, so bright, so mild— I cannot describe it! They have broad, hanging ears, a tail fine as silk, but so short, they cannot reach it with their trunk. O they must be very old, their hair is so long! They have young ones which they love tenderly, they play with them like children. They are so intelligent, so gentle, so mild! They go together in such order, as if on some business. Then there are other animals! They are not dogs —they are yellow as gold and have long manes, and faces almost human! O they are lions, but so gentle! They catch one another by the mane and frolic around. And there are sheep and camels, oxen and horses, all white and shining like silk, and wonderfully beautiful white asses! Words cannot say how lovely it all is, or what order and peace and love reign here! They do no harm to one another, they mutually help one another. Most are white, or golden; I see very few dark ones. And what is most astonishing is, that all have abodes so well arranged, so beautifully divided off into passages and apartments—and all so neat! One can form no idea of it. I see no men ; there are none here! Spirits must come and put things in order—we cannot imagine that the animals do it themselves."

Here Sister Emmerich paused as if attentively regarding something, and then exclaimed : " There's Frances of Rome! and there's Catherine of Ricci!—High over the beautiful garden floats something like a sun in whose rays the saints are hovering and looking down; there are ever so many of them up above me, and the sun is dazzlingly white. Its rays look like a great white silken carpet on which the saints float, or it is like a great white silk cover shining in the sun's rays. The saints are standing on it and looking down—O now I know it all! All the water comes from up there, and the lovely garden is the garden of Paradise! There are the animals kept, there all

is still as God created it, though the garden seems to me
much larger now than Paradise was at first. No man can
enter therein! The wonderfully clear, the magnificent,
holy water which there springs forth and flows in limpid
streams through the garden of the animals, forms around
the whole of Paradise a great liquid wall, not a lake—a
wall! and O what a wonderful, sparkling wall it is! The
top is formed of clear drops like precious stones, like the
morning dew on the hedges—such is this wall at the top,
but clear, transparent as crystal. At the base it flows in
tiny rivulets which unite and form further down an immense cataract. O how it roars! No one can hear it
without being deafened! All the waters of our earth
come from there ; but when they reach us they are altogether changed, they are quite impure!—The Mountain of the
Prophets also receives its water and moisture from Paradise,
which is situated as far above it as the sky is far above our
earth ; and the place in which I see the saints is as far above
Paradise as Paradise is above the Mountain of the Prophets.
By the time the great cataract, formed by the waters of Paradise, reaches the mountain, it is changed into clouds. No human being can reach that mountain, nothing is seen above it
but clouds.—In Paradise there are no buildings of stone, but
only green groves, and alleys, and walks for the animals.
The trees are enormously high, their trunks so straight
and elegant! I see white, yellow, red, brown, and black—
no not *black*, but shining steel-blue. And what wonderful
flowers! I see quantities of roses, chiefly white, very
large, growing on high bushes, some of them running up
into the trees; and there are also red ones and tall white
lilies. The grass looks soft as silk. But I can only see it.
I cannot feel it, it is too far away. O what beautiful
apples! so large and yellow! And how long the leaves of

the trees are! The fruits in the garden of the Nuptial House look perfectly deformed in comparison with these; and yet, they are unspeakably beautiful when compared with those of earth. I see numbers of birds, but no words could tell their beauty, their brilliancy of color, their variety! They build their nests in flowers, in clusters of the loveliest flowers. I see doves flying over the wall with tiny leaves and branches in their beak. I think the leaves and flowers I sometimes received for relief in my pains must have come from this garden. I see no serpents like those that crawl the earth, but there is a beautiful little yellow animal with a serpent's head. It is large around the body and tapering off toward the tail; it has four legs, and when it sits up on its hind feet, it is as tall as a child. Its fore feet are short, its eyes bright and intelligent, and it is uncommonly swift and graceful. I only see a few of them. It was an animal like this that seduced Eve.

" How wonderful! There is a gateway in the water wall and there lie two men! They are asleep, their back resting on the glittering water wall, their hands joined on their breast, their feet turned, one toward the other. They have long fair curls. They are spirits clothed in long white mantles, and they have under their arms small rolls of shining writings; their crooks lie near them. They are prophets! Yes, I feel it! they are in communication with the man on the Mountain of the Prophets. And on what wondrous couches they repose! Flowers grow around them in brilliant, regular forms, and surround their head, white, yellow, red, green, blue, shining like the rainbow." At this moment Father Limberg held out his consecrated fingers toward Sister Emmerich when she exclaimed: " And now, see, a priest! How came he here? Ah! it is well! He ought to see the wonders of God!"

On the following day, the Pilgrim found Sister Emmerich a little troubled at her confessor's having laughed at her vision of the preceding evening, as at things unreasonable and impossible. He chided her for her uneasiness, asking how she could complain of her enemies' looking upon her as an impostor, since she herself was so ready to treat as extravagant the wonders shown her by God. At this she repeated the above recital, adding thereto the following details : " I stood high up, outside the walls of Paradise, over which and through which I could see. In several parts of it I caught a glimpse of myself, and I looked incredibly large. Paradise is surrounded by drops of water (1) round, three-cornered, and of various shapes, which touch one another without mingling and form all kinds of figures and flowers like pictures woven in linen. One could see through it, though not so distinctly as over it. The extreme top was colored like the rainbow, but it had no figures ; it arose toward the heavens as does the rainbow that we see on earth. Toward the lower part of this wall are seen crystals melting into tiny streams like silver threads which unite to form the huge cataract. So great was its roar that I think to hear it, would be to die. It still sounds in my ears ! At a vast distance below, it vaporizes and forms clouds from which the Mountain of the Prophets receives all its waters. The top of the gate-way was arched and colored, but down toward the middle of the wall the light was not so clear. It was as when we see one thing through another.—The sides of the wall against which the prophets leaned were neither drops nor crystal, but one solid surface, snow-white like milk, like the finest silk. The prophets had long, yellowish white hair. Their eyes

---

(1) Calderon in his drama : " *La Vie est un Songe*," makes the Eternal Wisdom address the waters in these words : " Divide, ye waters, divide ! Rise up to heaven and form the crystal firmament that the fire, which there sits on a throne of light, may temper its heat in thy limpid waves !" etc.

were closed, and they lay as if on flower-beds; their hands were crossed on their breast, and they were wrapped in long, bright mantles. Their faces were turned earthward and encircling their brows was a halo of many colors, like the glory of the saints, the extremities paling off into light. Their rolls of writings had no knobs; they were thin and brilliant, with blue and gold lettering. Their crooks were white and slender, and variegated flowers seemed to be growing around them. The gate opened toward the east.— Some of the elephants had smooth skins, not thick curls like the others, and the little ones ran like lambs between their feet. They paired off with their young into great groves. I saw also white-haired camels, very beautiful, bluish asses striped, and animals like large white cats, spotted yellow and blue. The yellow serpent seemed to serve the other animals.

" In the limpid streams I saw shining fish and other animals; but I saw no vermin, no disgusting things, such as frogs. All the animals had separate abodes which were approached by different roads. Paradise is as large as our earth. It has round, smooth hills planted with beautiful trees; the highest I thought the one on which Adam rested. Toward the north was an egress, but not through a gate; it was like a gleam of twilight, like an aperture, like a steep descent, and it seemed to me that the waters of the deluge had been there poured forth. Near the great waters from which the cataract fell, I saw a broad green field scattered over with enormous bones bleached white, which seemed to have been cast up by the waters. Highest of all is the crystal wall; a little lower down run the silvery threads; and then appears the vast body of waters whence dashes the cataract with its deafening roar. This last is lost in the clouds which supply the Mountain of the Prophets with its waters. The mountain is much lower than Paradise and lies toward the east; even there everything is more like our earth."

November 1, 1823.—"Of the mammoths, those immense animals so numerous before the Deluge, a very young pair entered the Ark last and remained near the entrance. In the times of Nimrod, Dschemschids, and Semiramis, I still saw many. But they were constantly being hunted and soon they became extinct. Unicorns still exist and herd together. I know of a piece of the horn of one of these animals which is for sick beasts what blessed objects are for men. I have often seen that unicorns still exist, but far remote from the abodes of men, away up in the valleys around the Mountain of the Prophets. In size, they are something like a colt with slender legs; they can climb steep heights and stand on a very narrow ledge, their feet drawn close together. They cast their hoofs like shells or shoes, for I have often seen them scattered around. They have long yellowish hair, very thick and long around the neck and breast; it looks like wreathes. They live to a great age. On their forehead is a single horn, an ell in length, which curls up toward the back of the head, and which they shed at certain periods. It is sought after and preserved as something very precious. The unicorns are very timid, so shy that one cannot approach them, and they live at peace among themselves and with other animals. The males and females dwell apart and come together only at certain times, for they are chaste and produce not many young. It is very difficult to see or catch them, as they live far back behind the other animals over which they exercise a wonderful empire; even the most venomous, the most horrible seem to regard them with a species of respect. Serpents and other frightful things

coil themselves up and lie humbly on their backs
when a unicorn approaches and breathes on them.
They have a kind of alliance with the most savage beasts,
they mutually protect one another. When danger threatens
a unicorn, the others spread terror on all sides whilst the
unicorn hides behind them but it, in its turn, protects them
from their enemies, for all withdraw in affright from the
secret and marvellous power of the unicorn's breath. It
must be the purest of the lower animals, since all have so
great reverence for it. Wherever it feeds, wherever it
drinks, all venomous things withdraw. It seems to me that
it is looked upon as something holy, since it is said that the
unicorn rests its head only upon the bosom of a pure virgin.
This signifies that flesh issued pure and holy only from the
bosom of the Blessed Virgin Mary; that degenerate flesh
was regenerated in her, or that in her for the first time flesh
became pure; in her, the ungovernable was vanquished; in
her, what was savage was subdued; in her, unrestrained humanity became pure and tractable; in her bosom was the
poison withdrawn from the earth.—I saw these animals also
in Paradise, but much more beautiful. Once I saw them
harnessed to the chariot of Elias when he appeared to a
man of the Old Testament.—I have seen them on wild,
raging torrents, and running swiftly in deep, narrow, rugged
valleys; and I have also seen far distant places where lie
heaps of their bones on shores and in underground caves."

CHAPTER VII.

SISTER EMMERICH'S SITUATION FROM 1820-1824.—THE
LIFE OF OUR LORD —CLEMENT BRENTANO'S NOTES.—
FATHER LIMBERG'S POSITION.—DEATH OF THE
ABBÉ LAMBERT.

In the spring of 1820, Sister Emmerich was shown in
vision the crowd of petty annoyances soon to assail her,
chiefly on the part of her devoted and zealous amanuensis,
Clement Brentano, or the Pilgrim, as she herself styled him.
She saw that they were to last until her death, a period of
almost four years. She knew from experience the vexations
in store for her, as soon as the recital of the "Life of Jesus"
should be commenced ; and yet, this was the task still remaining to be accomplished, the only object for which her
life was now prolonged. "*My time is up,*" did she declare to
her confessor, March 11, 1820, "*and, if I still live, it is
only that I may fulfil a task for which but a short time is
granted!*" And the confessor also adds the weight of his
testimony to this declaration: "*Though none knew it,
yet her mission was ended. I know that for a certain fact !*"—
that is, she could now die, were it not that she was still
willing to suffer for the glory of God and the salvation of
souls. It is to the Pilgrim's journal, that faithful record of
Sister Emmerich's last six years on earth, that we are indebted for the following pages. As we read, we cannot but
feel impressed by the truth and uprightness of the man,
the conscientious fidelity with which he noted down every
circumstance in that wonderful life, every word that fell

from the invalid's lips, whilst we are sometimes tempted to smile at the little outbursts of vexation that meet us at almost every page, for Brentano was accustomed freely to intersperse his records with the passing emotions of his own soul. And, truly, his share in Sister Emmerich's task was neither light nor easy. Though devoting to it his time and his talents; though sacrificing for it his friends, his home, the legitimate pursuits of a life passed in the refined circles of the best society; he was at the invalid's bedside to all but the invalid herself an object of dislike and suspicion, an importunate intruder. He had to be willing to be pushed aside for very insignificant reason, for every trifle that sprang up to engage her attention; for she was ever ready to discontinue her communications at the call of charity, or for the exercise of patience, humility, or support of the neighbor. Under such circumstances we can better appreciate the fidelity with which he performed the task assigned him, and we can forgive his frequent complaints of endless and vexatious interruptions. We can admire the extraordinary candor and self-forgetfulness which, years after when revising his notes, made him scorn to change or modify any of those expressions which, though indicative of his own impatience, give us nevertheless so true a picture of the invalid and her surroundings.

"Daily she becomes weaker, sicker," he writes, "and she sacrifices all that is shown her by God! It would seem that her visions are for *herself*, and not for *others!* She does nothing but groan and vomit; she experiences naught but sickness and annoyances! She does not trouble herself about her visions; consequently, she forgets them! She allows them to be effaced from her mind by unnecessary concerns, by cares still more unnecessary! Did she herself derive strength and consolation from them, one might

excuse her! They are given'her that she may make them
known—and yet, she makes no account of them!" Dr.
Wesener came in for his share of the Pilgrim's strictures :
" He has fought a good fight with many bodily ills, but he
is not humble enough to acknowledge that this patient is
very different from any he has hitherto met. He is not
willing to own the inefficiency in her case of his treatment
and scribbling."

Now it is Father Limberg, Sister Emmerich's confessor,
who falls under the lash :—" As *the confessor* never wants to
acknowledge his mistakes, he can have no true charity;
and he never will have it, as long as he holds to such ideas.
The Pilgrim is convinced that, if the confessor would
only introduce some kind of order into Sister Emmerich's
life, none of her visions would be lost. It could be effected
without the slightest inconvenience, and how great would
be the peace and tranquillity it would procure her! But it
is impossible in the way in which she is directed! If she
begins a communication, the writer is at every moment exposed to the mortification of being forced to yield his place
by her to an insignificant visitor, some servant-girl, or gossiping old woman! Serious, important things are counted
for nothing; they must be pushed aside together with the
poor writer who sacrifices to them the last precious years of
his life. But it is useless and tiresome to speak of it! . . . . .
One thing is certain, no true idea will ever be had of the
harmony of her interior life!—She herself lives in ignorance of it.—The Pilgrim has no power over her and the
confessor, who holds the key to the great mystery of her
life, does not interest himself in it, nor, indeed, is he *capable*
of understanding it!—And yet in a certain sense, it is well
that it is so; for, if this abyss of separation existed not between the confessor's involuntary power over her and the

supernatural sphere of her visions, we should never know
how all these wonders are produced in her. Now the little that she does communicate is reflected from the mirror
of her own soul; we cannot reproach her with having altered the coloring."

The very reproaches made against Father Limberg by
the Pilgrim furnish conclusive proof that no more suitable
director could have been found for Sister Emmerich than
that simple-minded, humble priest, whose faith and morals
raised him high above suspicion; in whose eyes, not her
visions and extraordinary gifts, but the perfection attained
by suffering and the practice of virtue, formed the end
toward which he aimed in the conduct of his penitent. Not
from want of intelligence, not from indifference, or lack of
sympathy; but from a deep sense of duty, from a just appreciation of the power imparted to him by his sacerdotal
character, was he so laconic, so stern in his words, so prudent, so reserved in his communications with Sister Emmerich. He knew well that by such a course he was
grounding her in humility and utter forgetfulness of self
Never did he free her from her domestic cares, or the annoyances daily experienced from her insupportable sister
Gertrude; never did he close her door to the poor, the
sick, the afflicted, that at all hours she might have some
occasion of exercising humility, charity, and patience; and
never did he extol her visions, send her to seek supernatural relief, deny the influence of natural causes in her maladies, or prohibit her the assistance of a physician and his
remedies. Far from glorying in his charge of so wonderful a soul, gladly would he have resigned it if such had
been the will of God, as he testifies in these words let fall
one day before the Pilgrim: "I would I were back
in my convent! Were I not obliged to do so, I would never

visit Sister Emmerich." In 1813, he had proposed to the
Vicar-General to supply his place at the invalid's bedside
by another priest ; but he had been reinstated in his office of
confessor at the close of the first inquiry. For eight
long years he trod, in consequence of his spiritual relations
with Sister Emmerich, the bitter road of suffering, an object
of calumny to the ignorant public, and of distrust even
to his Ecclesiastical Superiors. It was only in August, 1820,
that he received marks of confidence in the shape of letters
from the Vicar-General; then only was his position defined
relatively to the pastor, Dean Rensing. As in the last
years of Sister Emmerich's life, her sufferings increased
and with them her need of spiritual succor, the Pilgrim
could not refrain from rendering the following testimony to
Father Limberg's zeal and devotedness :—"Truly, the
confessor exercises by the invalid, night and day, a most
painful spiritual ministry which, along with his other duties
performed in all kinds of wind and weather, he discharges
with untiring zeal, patience, and sweetness. He cannot be
sufficiently praised."—The above was penned after a little
scene between the good Father and Sister Emmerich's impetuous and exacting friend, when even F. Niesing, the
chaplain, had been appealed to by her to represent to
the latter his unreasonableness. In a subsequent conversation
with the Pilgrim, Father Limberg expressed himself in the
following words which the former, as usual, faithfully recorded :—

"I am," said Father Limberg, "ready at any moment
to resign my charge ; for, without God's help, I could not
endure it. I never question Sister Emmerich on her visions. I attend exclusively to what regards her conscience,
concerning which she involuntarily, as it were, communicates the least things. I never speak of her. As her con-

fessor, I *dare* not, nor do I ever write anything about her. Still, I know all that is necessary for me to know; and if God wills me to render testimony of her, it will all recur to my memory. I never question her on her affairs, though not through indifference. I often think the Pilgrim imagines I do things covertly, give secret orders, etc.; but it is not so. I have always found Sister Emmerich, whether waking or in ecstasy, most careful and exact in her words, and she has often reproached me when, in spiritual direction, I have spoken shortly to any one or failed to listen patiently. Once she told me my very thoughts, though she begged God not to give her such knowledge any more." The Pilgrim appended the following remark to the above: " May the Lord keep us all in the way of truth and charity, and lead us not into temptation!"

Dec. 14, 1821.—" The last three days and nights have been one succession of cramps, hemorrhages, nausea, and swoons, though her visions continue and she gently exclaims: ' I *must* suffer! I have taken it upon myself, I will endure it all!'—It is wonderfully affecting to behold her in such a state. Rapt in contemplation, she calls for her confessor, thinking she has something of the highest importance to say to him. But he troubles not himself about such things, he never truly enters into her visions. When in ecstasy, however, she seems ignorant of his indifference. She is attracted toward him by a spiritual force quite unknown to him, although in her waking state, she is usually silent before him upon many little domestic incidents for fear of vexatious results. If she falls into vision in his presence, she involuntarily inclines toward him, though he relishes not her narrations and treats them in his usual summary way. Is she worse than usual, her desire for his presence increases, though she seldom experiences relief,

unless, when in great need, he imposes upon her his priestly hand."

Daily experience taught the Pilgrim how great was the
distance between Father Limberg and himself in the invalid's estimation, a distance which he sought in vain to diminish. He jealously watched every word, every sign, with
the hope of reading some trace of her preference for himself
over the confessor, or even that she placed him on an
equality with the latter; but he watched in vain, and all illusion vanished on beholding "the immense power of obedience to his priestly word" or when he heard her exclaim
in ecstasy : "I must have my confessor. The Pilgrim
cannot help me, he cannot tell me. I must ask my confessor!" Sister Emmerich did, indeed, willingly consult the
Pilgrim on all her affairs both within and without the house,
her alms to the poor and sick, etc. But her interior was
open only to the eye of Father Limberg; he alone was the
representative of God for her who, in waking or in ecstasy,
knew but one law of action, viz., *faith and obedience.* As
nothing was further removed from her heart than the desire of being treated by her confessor otherwise than as an
ordinary Christian, so, too, was it utterly impossible for
her to prefer contemplation to the practice of charity or
any other virtue.

May 9, 1820.—"Sister Emmerich had a vision last
night which she distinctly remembered this morning. But,
about eight o'clock, in came the mistress of the house with
her baby and prattled until it was almost all forgotten.
Since her last serious attack, she has suffered from great
weakness of the head, which is aggravated by the noise of
the workmen. The fragments preserved in these pages
render sad testimony to the graces, the treasures, the richest and most abundant in fruits of salvation of any known

for ages, which are here daily, nightly, hourly sacrificed, and that without the least necessity, to annoyances from which even a child studying his lesson would be shielded. They who might prevent it, though conscious of their value, have let these graces go to waste for years, as if sporting with them, burying them. It breaks the writer's heart, but it is so! Posterity will mourn over a mission so badly seconded."

Easter-Sunday, 1821.—"This is the first Easter morn that has brought no real joy to Sister Emmerich; she was never before so sad on this feast.—'I received last night,' she said, 'no hope of relief. After the vision of the Resurrection, I had another of the Way of the Cross, in which Jesus laid a great white cross upon me, saying: *Take it up again and carry it on further!*—It was heavy enough to crush me, and I asked: " Am I, then, to have no help?" and He answered me briefly: " Take it! it is enough that I help thee!"—Still I thought, " It is well that there is only one of them!" and it seemed that I would have to carry it—I am very sad!'—And the Pilgrim, too, is very sad! He is weary of this vexatious life, so full of irritating and absurd events! He is almost in despair!"

" This morning, the Pilgrim found Sister Emmerich with tear-stained cheeks, the effects of the announcement of a spiritual trial for the interval between the Feast of St. Anthony of Padua and the Visitation of the Blessed Virgin. She dreads future trials, though actually present ones she entirely disregards. *The Pilgrim is nobody; he must yield to every old woman, to every trifle! Nothing seems to cost her so much as her communications to him!*—She complains of importunate visits; and yet, she treats her visitors with marked affability!"

From the foregoing extracts, the reader may readily perceive what a sea of bitterness surrounded the weary, suffering couch of Sister Emmerich's last years. The author of the present biography hesitates not to mention these facts, as they contain a faithful testimony to the ways by which it pleased Divine Providence to raise His servant to so high a degree of perfection. The habitual presence of the Pilgrim and the occasional sojourn of his brother, Christian Brentano, formed the school in which, in the midst of cruel sufferings, Sister Emmerich practised those eminent virtues that distinguished her: charity, forbearance, resignation. Christian Brentano looked upon her as a phenomenon in which he hoped to discover a confirmation of his pet theory, mesmerism; whilst to Clement she was a pure mirror whose lustre should be tarnished by no exterior influence, upon which he alone was to gaze. However different the light in which the two brothers regarded her, yet both agreed in this, that she should be withdrawn from every special contact with the outer world and become inaccessible to all but themselves. It was the working out of this scheme, though with the very best intentions on the part of its authors, that was to put the finishing stroke to Sister Emmerich's sanctification.

VISIONS FORESHADOWING SISTER EMMERICH'S DEATH.

February 28, 1820.—"Four sufferings have been announced to me," said the invalid, "one of which and the most painful of all will arise from a misunderstanding between the Pilgrim and his brother. I had also another vision which tormented me. I was in the greatest distress, I felt as if about to swoon, and I wanted some water; but it was so muddy that I could not drink it. Then appeared two men. One wanted to relieve me by giving me cherries from a tree that stood in shifting, marshy soil in which it

swayed two and fro with its fruit on the extremities of the
lower branches; there were no cherries high up. He
climbed the tree with difficulty to get the fruit because the
water was bad. Then the other began to reproach him, to
quarrel with him about the trouble he was giving himself.
He would fatigue himself, he said, he should have done so
and so, etc.; and they disputed the point so warmly that
the first came down from the tree and both went off in
opposite directions, leaving me there in my great need
abandoned and alone. I have been thinking all day of that
distressing scene, and I feared it might mean the Pilgrim
and his brother."—The cherries produced by the tree
growing in marshy ground, denote good intentions, benevolent assistance, springing not from motives of faith, but
from human considerations and preconceived opinions, none
of which were based on very reliable foundations (1). The
marshy water signifies water flowing not from the pure
source of divine love, but rendered turbid by self-love and
an obstinate attachment to one's own views, which cannot
furnish a just appreciation of the invalid's state nor afford
real refreshment.

March 4th—The Pilgrim writes: "Sister Emmerich did
not, at first, want to relate what she had seen, but after
awhile she yielded—*trouble with the Pilgrim !* It has been
shown her now for the third time.—'I saw myself,' she
says, 'laid by my confessor and the Pilgrim in a wheat-
field in which the ears were ripe. I wanted to rest there
awhile; but no, they hurried me off into a gloomy dark
room. The Pilgrim was very angry with me, although I
had done nothing.—We were widely separated. When he
spoke to me so harshly, I saw the devil behind him with

(1) January 10, 1820, Sister Emmerich remarked to the Pilgrim : " I have had a vision relating to your brother. He will cause disturbance here. He has false ideas of
my case, and I saw the Abbé Lambert much annoyed by him. I thank God for showing me this, for preparing me for it. I shall bear it all for my humiliation."

one hand on his shoulder. It seemed as if the Stations of the Cross passed before me, at each of which I found myself still further from the Pilgrim. Behind the Crucifixion, I saw the devil about to attack me. I drove him away and continued to gaze after the Pilgrim, who at last began to return. I resolved to receive him more kindly than ever."

Sister Emmerich's humility led her to take all the blame upon herself and to redouble her kindness and patience toward the Pilgrim. She hoped thus to finish the task undertaken with his assistance. His withdrawal from her in proportion as she followed the Stations of the Cross signifies his ever-increasing discontent and coldness with the vexatious consequences resulting therefrom. Like new and sorrowful stations, they strewed the pathway of her life. But he would not understand her admonition. In his journal we find the following note : " She has become ridiculously faint-hearted and self-reproachful, as if seeking to annoy her hearer ! She weeps and torments herself about faults she may *possibly* commit, and she cannot arise from her pitiable state of discouragement."

Shortly after we find the following record of Sister Emmerich's words : " My Heavenly Spouse has told me not to torment myself. He will not impute the fault to me. I must follow the middle course," words which, though carrying with them a most striking signification, the Pilgrim declares imcomprehensible. The invalid was placed between her confessor and the Pilgrim. She had to maintain peace between them, exhorting the former to forbearance and the latter to the restraint of his fiery, impetuous nature. It was with good reason she responds to his impatient strictures : " The Pilgrim has not understood me since Christmas. He is against me !"

Easter of 1820 brought Sister Emmerich the last joyful
Paschal solemnity she was to have on earth. The Pilgrim
thus describes it : " On Easter morn, I found the invalid,
who only the day before was a picture of woe, truly resuscitated. She was beaming with peace and joy ; her words,
her whole demeanor breathed fervor and the inward sentiment of the Redeemer's resurrection. The sentiments of
her soul imparted an indescribably noble air to her every
look and gesture. She had heard the songs of the parishioners as, toward one in the morning,they marched through
the streets of Dülmen. They were headed by the burgomaster, who bore the crucifix which had lain in the church
on Good-Friday and which the pastor had placed in his
hands for the nocturnal procession by virtue of an ancient
privilege. Those canticles of joy were repeated by thousands of peasants and their children, many of whom from
Good-Friday had neither eaten nor drunk, and who after
their hard day's work had spent most of the night in making the ' Way of the Cross.' These sounds had reached
her bed of pain, and in vision she had followed the praying
and chanting multitude. She afterward explained with
deep emotion this custom of olden times.   It seems that an
epidemic having once carried off all the priests, the burgomaster on this sacred night took the crucifix from the
Holy Sepulchre and bore it processionally around the city followed by the citizens. The pestilence ceased. From that
time the privilege of carrying the crucifix belonged by
right to that functionary. It is also the custom on Holy Saturday when the new fire is blessed,for the sacristan to light
little fagots at it and distribute them to the people. The
Pilgrim, having brought one home with him, placed it on the
invalid's bed as she lay in vision. In a moment or two, she
exclaimed : ' How came that charred wood on my bed ?'

and then, holding her hand over it as if warming herself, she said : ' That is holy fire, just kindled in the Church. She has a new light to-day, a new fire, though many, alas! are not warmed by it !"

A few days later, we find recorded in the ever-faithful journal the following instruction given her by her angel : —"I was very sick, and I laid before God my distress and desire to be freed from household cares and visitors : for instance, the Abbé had yesterday six guests to dinner, some priests who are visiting him and my brother's chidren. But my guide reproved me, saying that I should remain on my cross, for Jesus came not down from His. The less I worry about such things, the more surely shall I receive assistance. I had a long instruction on this point." Shortly after follows some intimation of the old Abbé's state :—

" The Abbé Lambert daily grows worse and needs many attentions. Sister Emmerich regards his state as critical and looks forward to the worst. She has had a vision of his interment. She saw a corpse borne out with lighted candles. She ran to see where it would be laid and found it to be in the neighboring cemetery. At the entrance two souls clothed in white stopped her ; they extended before her a white veil through which she could not pass. Then she begged to be allowed to take upon her the Abbé's pains. She was fully aware of their nature and grievousness, the good old priest being threatened with inflammation of the bowels. She spoke of the debt of gratitude she owed him. The Pilgrim and his brother found her very miserable, the noise of the ninepin-alley under her window distressing her greatly. Christian Brentano thought she ought to be moved to another house. He is convinced that all might be satisfactorily arranged by earnest remonstrances."

April 24th—"The Abbé is better; he is more cheerful and his foot less swollen. 'I must,' says Sister Emmerich, 'leave the rest to God. I cannot free him entirely from suffering. When he came weeping and afflicted at the prospect of moving I saw that if mortification set in, he could not live more than four days; so I begged God to send me his sufferings, that he might not die unresignedly. Instantly my pains increased and the Abbé was relieved. I hope he will soon be able to say Mass again.'—But she herself has scarcely strength to speak. When the Pilgrim told her that a decree had been issued at Berlin forbidding the professors of Münster to lecture, because the Vicar-General had prohibted the students from frequenting Bonn, she was deeply distressed. She said : 'Not what I now hear afflicts me most, but the far worse things in store for the future ! I see them in vision, but I cannot describe them. I have earnestly prayed for this affair, for I have been expecting it ; but it will yet be worse !'—And falling into contemplation, she exclaimed : 'Liborius defends me at Paderborn where they are abusing me !' "

April 25th—"The Pilgrim asked the invalid if she would not consent to a change of lodgings and separate from her sister Gertrude; but her only answer was that she could not. He would not accept her excuse, feeling convinced that, were she so disposed, the change might be easily effected." Sister Emmerich was, on this occasion, very much dejected by the pertinacity of the Pilgrim and his brother so anxious to carry out what they looked upon as benevolent intentions in her regard. She had the following vision on the subject: "Quantities of flowers lay scattered around me. With them I had to twine a garland. I had already advanced far in my task when there arose around me a green thorn-hedge, the thorns turned outward as if to form a barrier of protection. It was covered with numbers of tiny flowers on pedicles as fine as linen thread ; they were sky-blue with red centres. They had five stamens like a silver hammer on which rested dew of marvellous sweetness. The flowers grew among other plants and I wanted to gather them. But the Pilgrim and his brother opposed it. They said that it was not worth the trouble; however, I snapped off a thorn from the hedge and drew some of the flowers out with it."—The tiny blue flowers signified the little virtues of patience and meekness which she was then practising in the midst of her friends and her domestic cares. Of their merit she would be deprived if, in accordance with the Pilgrim's advice, she changed her abode and manner of life. The thorn-hedge, the living barrier around her, symbolized the prohibition of her angelic guide and the sufferings of her daily life. The Pilgrim, however, was unwilling to comprehend the lovely vision in this way. He objected that the flowers signified her complaints under trifling sufferings to which she ought not to be so sensitive. His remarks greatly troubled the poor invalid who, as the journal informs us, " wept bitterly, calling God and His Holy Mother to witness her affliction, since she knew not how to help herself, how to rise above her misery. They might, she said, represent her faults to her without disguise." That the Pilgrim understood not the drift of this prayer, his journal testifies in these words : "She was quite overcome by sadness and desolation, though seemingly without cause. It was only a temptation, which, alas ! she bore so impatiently that the Pilgrim was a little tried with her."

On May 1st—Sister Emmerich related the following : " Again I saw the little flowers, but they were all trodden down and destroyed by the Pilgrim and his brother. I wept at the sight. I stuck among them the cross of my gray robe, and, to my great joy, up sprang a thick sod all around. I had also a vision of a fire in the Abbé Lambert's room; it burned over him in his bed. It was formed of many tongues of flame which suddenly uniting rushed down the kitchen toward the staircase. I saw, too, many things connected with him, different people and details which however I no longer remember. I was so alarmed that I awoke. There flew out of the fire upon me a cloud of little crosses that quite covered my gray robe; that, too, frightened me greatly. But two blessed spirits like the Apostles appeared and told me not to be alarmed, that I had already consumed the most of these crosses; and indeed, they were perfectly black and only a few were left. I awoke from this vision in fright."

May 2d—" Sister Emmerich changed her room to-day for another further removed from the noise of the carpenters. Into it her canary had previously been taken. For three years she had raised the little creature in a nest on her bed. It had become so tame, so fond of its mistress, that it never left her. Whenever she was sick, its whole body swelled up and it fell down by her side as if dead. When it saw her enter the new room, its excitement was something remarkable; it hopped joyfully over the bed and gave every sign of satisfaction. But when it perceived her suffering state down it fell on its side; one would have thought it dying. After some moments Sister Emmerich made a sign with her hand for it to enter its cage. Its liveliness returned, it pecked at its feathers for joy, and swung itself in its ring. A lark, which had been tamed in the same way, unfortunately met its death one day in the kitchen fire. It used to sing its song on Sister Emmerich's bed, and hop from side to side; even if chased in that direction, it would not fly toward the window. If any one spoke unkindly to its mistress, it would pursue the unlucky individual to the door, screaming around his head. Sister Emmerich often spoke feelingly of the bird's wonderful attachment."

May 6th—" I have had a vision of the martyrdom of St. John the Baptist and I saw several scenes illustrative of his relations with the Lord. He asked me : ' If the Lord were now to visit thee and wanted to eat with thee, what wouldst thou set before Him, for thou hast nothing ?' I answered : ' I would give Him myself, I have nothing else.' And then, indeed, the Lord did come to me and my whole soul melted into sweetness. Next morning, when I received Holy Communion, with ardent desires I offered myself to Him in sacrifice !"

May 17th—" I have had a short vision of St. Paschal. I saw that he had a vehement love for the Blessed Sacrament which he went to adore whenever he possibly could. He was deprived of It for a time as a trial, from which privation he suffered much, although he received spiritually in his cell. This vision was vouchsafed me for my own consolation, since Dean Overberg gave me little hope of permission to communicate daily. I would often languish, did I not receive spiritually. Once, when my unworthiness prevented my approaching the Holy Table, I saw St. Gereon, in his military dress, going to church on Christmas day. He had intended to communicate ; but beholding over the altar an apparition of Jesus on the cross, the Blood from His Side dripping into the chalice, he was filled with fear at his own unworthiness, and dared not receive the Holy Sacrament. I saw that for a long time he dared not communicate ; at last, Mary appeared to him. She told him that, if he allowed himself to be deterred by the vision he had seen, if he waited until he became *worthy,* it would be very difficult for him to resume his Communions.   Who is worthy to receive so great a favor ?   Gereon communicated the very next day."

" The hunger that she experiences for the Holy Euchar- ist," adds the Pilgrim, " is often intolerable ; she even swoons away from it.   She weeps at being deprived of daily Communion, although at the time of the first investigation she had been promised the privilege of Mass in her room Formerly, when she received more frequently, her pre- paration and thanksgiving so occupied her mind that many petty annoyances were allowed to pass unheeded ; but now, all is changed, and she is obliged to support herself on her own strength.   She had had a presentiment that she would one day have to endure this privation of the Holy Euchar- ist, but neither the Dean nor her confessor would listen to it."

The next day the Pilgrim found Sister Emmerich in tears at the announcement of some expected visits.   She was a prey also to sufferings so intense as to render her quite un- able to make any communications to him ; consequently, instead of visions we find the following entry in his journal: "All that takes place in this house connected with outside affairs, is carried on without plan, order, or foresight.—It is absolutely unreasonable, absurd, shocking !   But on account of the indifference of all around, the absence of direction, the false ideas concerning things, one can remedy nothing.) —Her sufferings are almost intolerable to-day, violent shoot- ings in the wound of her side, pains all through her body, general debility and languishing for *Jesus!* "—The Pilgrim's vexation did not escape the invalid and, on his return that evening, she tried to banish it with these words : "I saw how dissatisfied you were this morning, because I was not able to relate anything.—You sang, and that is a sure sign !

I had a long talk about you with my confessor." Then she laid before him many reasons why he should overcome his impatience, treatFather Limberg with greater consideration, and try to suit himself to her position, as it was not in her power to change it. He assured her that she mistook the cause of his chagrin ; that it was the confusion and disorder that distressed him ; that he had indeed hummed an air, but only to repress his vexation, etc. " Nevertheless," he continues, "she would have the last word and ended by bursting into tears. She has thought the Pilgrim unreasonable all this Lent, whilst he is only distressed that the most magnificent visions are not recorded. If the confessor is worried by him, it is all his own fault. He is incessantly repeating that the Pilgrim and his brother are too learned for him, that they judge too severely, etc. It is all his own distrustful spirit, his unwillingness to accept advice ! "

Sister Emmerich having remarked that she had seen many things which her weak state and domestic affairs forbade her communicating, as for instance, a long vision on the *Magnificat* and the ancestors of Mary, her words fell like burning coals upon the Pilgrim. He exclaims bitterly : "Yes, those people torment her, beset her, smother her like wool sacks ! And thus are lost things more wonderful than were ever before revealed ! Those miserable trifles for which all is sacrificed drive one to desperation ! "

June 19, 1820.—" The invalid received the following instructions from her angelic guide : " 'Be not distressed, if thou now seest fewer details on the relics of the saints. Thou hast now another task before thee. It will be enough for thee to recognize them in a short vision; thou canst no longer spend so much time in it. There is something else now to be done. Relate thy visions as before. Hold for truth what thou seest, and repeat all to thy confessor, whether he be inclined to listen or not.'—My angel spoke to me in words like the above. They consoled me, and I think I shall not die yet." It soon became evident that her angel's words referred to the communication of her visions on the ' Life of Christ,' her last and most painful task. She had had all her life the clearest intuition of the earthly career of her Divine Spouse, she had imitated Him most faithfully, conformed her every action most closely to His ; but now, she was to contemplate Him, no longer for herself alone, but that she might make to her contemporaries a recital which by its fidelity to life, its unadorned simplicity, its perfect concordance with the holy Apostles and Doctors, would lead numbers of souls to the knowledge of the truth, and increase in others the fervor of piety. As this Divine Life has already appeared in German and French, mention will be made in the following pages of only the circumstances attendant on its recital. Her task began toward the latter part of July, 1820, and by the end of August, the Pilgrim rejoiced over the rich harvest he had been able to gather. September brought with it increased sufferings and domestic cares, to the infinite disgust of her amanuensis, and we again find his journal teeming with such words as the following: " She thinks her pains have caused her to forget everything, she has nothing to communicate; but the real cause is anxiety about her nephew who has been enrolled for military service.—All these vexations fall upon her. He was here last evening and this morning and, as she interests herself in his affairs, woful disorder necessarily follows. This is the reason of her inability to relate her visions. When the Pilgrim expressed his regret, she was troubled. If he very naturally feels impatience at her waste of time and strength on such things, she is ever ready to tax him with injustice; and yet, his only motives are those of duty and charity."

Some days later, three of her fellow-religious visited the invalid. The journal remarks : "By their empty talk they made her forget her visions."—And again : "The Pilgrim is very sad at being able to gather so little in the celestial garden opened by God in this soul, but which is carelessly, stupidly, ignorantly allowed to go to waste. O how heavy is the heart of him who records this ! And yet, it must be done ! Where lies the fault, the Pilgrim knows not. Of one thing, however, he is certain : the confessor could remedy much, yes, *all* of it—but he cares not ! The Pilgrim complained to him of the disorder around Sister Emmerich's sick-bed ; but he soon saw that his words gave offence."

From these records we may easily form some idea of the difficulties the poor invalid had to contend against in her communications with her impetuous, but highly appreciative friend. Whilst sympathizing largely with her, we cannot wholly ignore the fact that Brentano, also, held a most unenviable position near her. It must certainly have been most grievous to him to witness what he terms the loss of treasures so rich. We feel inclined to forgive his chagrin and impatience in consideration of the motives from which they spring. In September, the confessor found it necessary for the sake of peace to withdraw the permission accorded the invalid to recount her visions. The result of his prohibition was the following touching picture which deeply affected the Pilgrim :

The Dying Nightingale.

"I saw a shining table on which lay a number of groschens in a semi-circle. Just below the empty space I stood
with my guide. Behind the table was a row of magnificent flowers. The flowers were mine, the table was mine,
the treasure, the groschens, were mine; but, where I stood,
there was nothing. I could touch neither the table, the
flowers, nor the money. Then my guide stepped before
me, a dying nightingale in his hand, and said : 'Thou shalt
no longer have these flowers, these pictures, these treasures,
since the means of making them known (for which end
alone they were given thee) have been withdrawn. As a
proof of what I say restore life to this bird with the breath
of thy mouth.'—He held the bird to my lips and I breathed
into its beak. Life and strength and song returned, after
which my guide took it away. Then all vanished, all became dead and mute. I saw nothing more."

And now the journal laments : "Her memory is almost
entirely gone; she can relate nothing ! Things seem to her
as if they happened long ago. 'Because,' she says, 'my
misery increases and they leave me no peace to recount the
holy things shown me as I should, God has withdrawn them
from me. When peace returns, my visions also will return.'
She begged the Pilgrim with tears not to render her sufferings
intolerable : 'You think not of the pain you inflict ! God
alone knows it, to Him alone can I complain ! I have constantly before me the dread of some new suffering.'—She
speaks incessantly of her unknown sufferings. Her expressions are fretful, she is captious and easily wounded.
The Pilgrim ascribes it to the loss of her sublime visions and
consolations,"— so runs the journal. As on similar occa-

sions, Sister Emmerich now had recourse to her spiritual director, Dean Overberg (1). She wrote to him and deputed F. Niesing, the chaplain, to describe to him her situation and receive advice ; for, as she declared to the Pilgrim, it was only in obedience that she found the strength necessary for the task of communicating her visions. She took this step with Father Limberg's approbation. " Dean Overberg," she said, " was the first to tell me to communicate all to the Pilgrim, and he often reiterated the injunction. But the permission was given some time ago ; it must be renewed to be effective."

The Pilgrim could not hide from himself the gravity of the affair. He writes : " She is still deprived of her high contemplations, still without memory, very suffering, and apparently very anxious about some impending evil. What it is, one cannot imagine, and it is useless to torment one's self about it." He went himself to Münster to demand of the Dean a renewal of his powers which the latter granted, exhorting him, at the same time, to patience in the midst of the incessant and exceedingly vexatious interruptions of which he so bitterly complained. Father Limberg likewise withdrew his interdict, and Sister Emmerich could again relate her visions. Some days before, being in ecstasy, she exclaimed : " I see a heavenly garden full of magnificent fruits, but it is closed to me. My guide says I am not now able to bear the fruit."

" I have had a vision of my death, I saw myself dying, not here but out in the fields. I fell from swoon to swoon. St. Teresa was by me, as also the holy little nuns who are always with me. It seemed to me that I was again able to

(1) When the noble old man heard of the Abbé's illness, he at once offered assistance " See," he writes to Sister Emmerich " that the Abbé Lambert wants for nothing that could strengthen, relieve, or recreate him in his sickness. I shall be responsible for all extra expenses."

walk. All thought I **was** getting better, though, in reality, I **was** about to die. The Pilgrim was near, but he could not approach me, as I was not where I ought to be. I often glanced toward him. It was the third and last time that my death seemed inevitable, but I was full of courage. My guide asked me if, having suffered so much, I wanted still to live. I thought *yes*, if I could be of any use, although I saw much work before me."—Soon after this, a great task was announced to her: "I saw," she said, "Ignatius and Augustine, who both said to me: ' Arise, console thy friend and prepare for him a white robe that he may only pass through purgatory.'—I arose. I had a blue apron over my jacket My feet were bare, and I feared to step in the mud. I went to the Abbé Lambert and encouraged him to meet death; he became joyous, even anxious to die."

" I lay consumed by inward fever, I was in great pain, and I had a vision of a white man who threw on a little funeral pile all kinds of fuel, fruits, branches, twigs, tendrils, all purely symbolical (1). I stood by. He lit it on the four sides, and threw me on it. Whilst being burned alive, I saw the whole transformed into a little heap of snow-white ashes which the man scattered over the fields, and they became fertile."

November 19, 1820.—Sister Emmerich labored and prayed all night for the Abbé Lambert, who had an abscess in his side. She had a vision of his death and received from her Spouse the consoling assurance that his sufferings and her compassion would all be accounted in his behalf at the supreme hour. St. Elizabeth of Thuringia appeared to her, as she tells us: " Whilst I sewed at the children's caps, I suddenly saw her standing by me with the Child Jesus by

(1) This very significant vision refers to purgatory. It is **explained** in St. Paul, I, Cor., iii. 13.

the hand. I was going to stop my work and turn to her. But she put her hand on me and told me to go on sewing, for my labor was more useful than veneration; it was serving the Infant Jesus. Then she showed me a scene from her own life, the Infant Jesus sitting on her robe one day whilst she was working for the poor. He did not say a word until she had finished. She helped me."

Dec. 5, 1820.—I have had a sad vision. I saw that after the Abbé's death, my enemies tried to steal me away and shut me up; but they were prevented by some unforeseen obstacles. I was in great fear on seeing them around me again.—Then, in another vision, I saw that I shall be moved by my friends, the Pilgrim insisting on one place, his brother on another. I suffered much from their discord." (This vision was literally fulfilled on the day of the Abbé's interment).

December 9th—" Last night I gave the Mother of God no rest. I sat by her busily sewing on a cap. I showed it to her, telling her it was for her Child, and that she must give some relief to the Abbe Lambert. I gave her no peace! It was very hard, but I kept on saying: ' You must! You must!'—I only begged for him to suffer patiently, that nothing might prejudice his soul, only a little relief! But I had to take much upon myself, for I was answered: 'Sufferings must be endured!' As I thus pleaded, I saw all at once numbers of sick throughout the world. Again I was told: ' This one thou must help and that one,' and they passed before me in succession. Thus I spent the greater part of the night in prayer, labor, and visiting the sick; but at noon, when the Abbé sent me his greetings, saying that he felt better, that he had eaten with appetite, I was truly rejoiced."

December 10th—" Again did Mary speak to me in confidence. She told-me that her pregnancy had not been burdensome to her; that she had felt, at times, interiorly elevated, transported out of herself. She encompassed God and man, and He whom she bore carried her. I must make Him a little crib. Mary told me to recite daily nine *Aves* in honor of the nine months she bore the Saviour under her heart."

December 14th—" The Pilgrim found the invalid preparing bandages for the Abbé. She had seen in vision that he had had a profuse hemorrhage; in fact, when he attempted to rise this morning, blood gushed from his mouth, and he was obliged to remain in bed. She wants to get a man to sit up with him, but he is not willing for it. She herself lay all night in frightful convulsions with none to assist her."

" It is astonishing that, in her miserable state, she can remember anything. In the midst of the cruel sufferings which she shares with the sick Abbé, she was besieged by visitors and in the afternoon she took so much trouble with the newly-washed linen that her cramps returned."

" She is so taken up with the Abbé that she forgets all else; she related very little to-day. The thought of all these wonderful visions on the mystery of Redemption, so badly preserved, so lightly esteemed, breaks one's heart! Jesus was, indeed, sold for thirty pieces of silver!"

December 16th—"She has been sewing for the sick Abbé and her countenance wears an expression of suffering and annoyance. Her cheeks are wet with tears, her head aches violently, she vomits blood, her side bleeds, and again does she endure the pains of retention. When asked if these are not some of the Abbé's pains, she does not deny that they are. Advent is for her ordinarily the most joyous season of the year. Last year she was in constant contemplation, singing canticles of praise in Mary's honor; but now sufferings and annoyances overwhelm her. She communicates only fragmentary visions."

December 17th—" The Pilgrim found her to-day very much affected, the Abbé Lambert having dragged himself on his crutches to see her for the last time, to bid her adieu. The poor old man wept, and said he would never see her again. Father Limberg looked on with compassion. 'Sister Emmerich,' he remarked, 'will never again find so faithful a friend,' and he begged God not to let her survive him long."

December 19th—" She was very much exhausted to-day. She spent it in attending to the linen of the Abbé. At night she takes his sufferings upon herself as they are generally worse then. She has been accustomed to do this from her earliest childhood, curing ulcers by sucking them, etc. Compassion urges her thereto. She once cured her mother of erysipelas by her prayers and simple remedies. Her confessor sometimes dissuades her from such things, telling her that all is purely natural, that only ordinary remedies ought to be applied."

December 20th—" Sufferings, annoyances, graces, and great patience. She is worn out by her labors of last night. 'I was,' she said, 'in the garden of the Nuptial House where all that is beneficial to mankind may be found. Five roads lead thereto from all parts of the world; in the midst of it stands a building with many gates from which are distributed all kinds of good and salutary things. I saw many people there, among whom I recognized the three young girls and the four men who labor with me. There was also a Crib with pictures of the Holy Innocents and of Herod's punishment for having tried to frustrate the coming of the Saviour. I was told how they apply to the present;

viz., to those who seek to destroy in the world the fruit of His coming. I had to pray for all who are preparing to celebrate the Holy Feast of Christmas, that they may cast out the old leaven and with Christ become new men in the Church. I saw all around in the distance numbers of men whom I had to take up and carry ; they were all hindered, opposed in various ways. I had to carry and drag many ecclesiastics and heavy people. I would have been willing to carry the old Abbé, but I was told that he must creep along by himself. I had to carry the Pilgrim, though I could not see why he was unable to get along; he was on a very smooth road. Then the vision changed into a church and a magnificent festival; but I cannot describe it, I am worn out! The scenes followed one another in rapid succession."

This vision was followed by a great increase of suffering. For several days with frightful retchings she vomited blood and water almost every half hour, which weakened her so that she could scarcely speak. In this she clearly recognized her mission to obtain for impenitent sinners the grace of conversion.

December 23d—"Sister Emmerich was found this morning perfectly insensible and Father Limberg, who was obliged to go to the country, sent Father Niesing to recite over her the prayers for the sick. This Father Niesing did from the ' Little Book of Benedictions,' by Martin Cochem, and the invalid returned to consciousness ; or, as she herself expressed it, *she could again think.* Her pulse was hardly perceptible, she was stiff and cold, she could not speak. An hour after, Father Niesing repeated the prayers, when she opened her eyes, moved a little and, at last, sat up in bed exclaiming : ' See, what prayer and the hand of the priest can do ! Last night I suffered

everything. I had pains all over me and burning thirst.
I did not dare to drink, and indeed, I cannot do so yet.
At last, I fainted. I thought I should surely die, for all
night I was like one in agony. I wanted only *to think* the
holy names *Jesus, Mary, Joseph ;* but I could not even
remember the words. Then I felt how little man can do of
himself; he cannot even think on God, unless God give
him grace to do so. My very desire, however, was an
effect of that same divine grace. I knew when Father
Niesing came, yet I could neither move nor speak. I knew,
likewise, that he had the little book with him and I hoped
he would pray. When he began, his compassion penetrated me like warmth. I regained consciousness, and with
deep emotion I felt that I could again remember the names
Jesus, Mary, Joseph ! Life was a gift of the priestly blessing." That evening she again begged a benediction and
asked also for the relic of St. Cosmas. Next day, she
relapsed into a miserable state, though she was able to
articulate. 'I pressed the relic to my heart,' she said :
' I saw the saint by me and a stream of warmth passed
over me. I have now a little more life, though I am full of
racking pains. My greatest torment is thirst, but I dare
not drink.' All Christmas Eve she lay like a corpse ; but
since her increase of suffering the Abbé Lambert is better."

Sister Emmerich begged the Pilgrim to defer his visit
next day till noon, as she had need of repose, which request
gave rise to the following lines in his journal :—

" Her request is like an insinuation that the Pilgrim is
troublesome, as if he were ever willing to prove such to
her. He cannot understand it ! It saddened him during
the holy night ; he knows not why he should be made to
suffer so ! At noon, when he saw her, she was cured,
cheerful, though weak. ' I received at the Crib,' she said,

an order to distribute seven loaves to-day for the Abbé,
since he is still of this world (1). The order was repeated
thrice, and I begged God to show me the poor for whom they
were destined. Some came of themselves and received the
loaf with tears of gratitude ; the others I saw in spirit.' To
the Pilgrim's remark that, after the Abbé's death, she could
send away Gertrude and remove to more retired lodgings,
she replied that Dean Overberg would never permit either
change. The Pilgrim cannot understand how the Dean
could object.—It is either through a want of judgment on
the part of some, or an inexplicable disposition of Divine
Providence."

December 27th—Sister Emmerich has been busy making bandages and lint for the Abbé, and the severe cough
of her little niece gives her trouble; but she was untiring in
her efforts to relate what she could of her visions. What
little she gives is deserving of thanks, for she deals out
with a hand always beneficent, although dying. She is
again worse." These grateful acknowledgments were
drawn from the Pilgrim by the great vision of St. John
the Evangelist related on this occasion.

December 28th—" Fresh annoyances, unsatisfactory
communications, or none at all. She lies, as it were, in
the midst of disgusting torments; she is sick unto death,
her good will counts for nothing ! In tears and anxiety
she sews for the Abbé, to whose sick room she had herself
carried. She saw the need he is in of many things which
she is now trying to supply. He wept freely on seeing
her. She put off the recital of her visions until the evening, when she was very much fatigued and visibly struggling against temptations to complain. The confessor
came in, and the Pilgrim read to her a prayer in honor of

(1) The good old Abbé died the seventh week after.

Jesus Crucified. In a few instants she was deep in ecstasy, her whole person became light as a feather, and to the marks of pain on her countenance succeeded a radiant expression of peace and joy. The Pilgrim can express the brightness, the beauty that shone on her features only by one word, she was perfectly luminous. Her confessor presented the prayer-book to her; she took it and, her eyes still closed, continued reading the prayer to the end."

December 29th —" She has been taking a little barley broth every evening since Christmas, but she throws it off immediately. She cuts out and distributes clothes for poor children. She is very anxious about the Abbé."

December 31st—" Sunday. She confessed yesterday and was to have communicated to-day; but her confessor went on a mission to the country and forgot to engage some other priest to carry her Holy Communion. Her countenance wears the distressed expression of one who languishes with weakness. She shed tears, and she was not disposed to relate her visions—in truth, that is no rare thing now! She seems to attach very little weight to the admonition she receives from her angel to relate all, and the visions themselves seem to be a worry to her; she is always praying to be delivered from them. She still declares to the confessor that her guide has told her to send for the Pilgrim's brother, as she has something to tell him; but Father Limberg wants her to wait until he comes of his own accord. This brother sees in her state only a case of mesmerism; he judges whatever he beholds in her by this erroneous standard. ' But,' she says, ' it is not my affair; it is God's. I see how much annoyance that person will yet cause me. My guide told me that even the ignorant Landrath had more correct ideas of me.' "

January 1, 1821.—"I was at the Crib last night and I

begged for just a little relief—that God would, at least, take off one burden, free the poor child from its dreadful cough; but I was not heard, I received no encouragement. I had a real struggle with God. *I laid before Him His promises. I named those to whom they had been made, those to whose prayers He had listened*; but I was not heard! I learned that I should be still more severely tried this coming year. I implored God *to withdraw my visions*, that I may be relieved of the responsibility of communicating them. In this, also, I was not heard. I received, as usual, the injunction *to relate what I could*, even if I should be ridiculed for it, even if I saw no utility in it. I was told again that no one had ever had visions of the same kind or in the same measure as I; but it is not for myself, it is for the Church. I saw St. Joseph clearly, distinctly.—He was old, thin, and bald, but with ruddy cheeks. I entered into conversation with him, laid before him all my needs, and he told me to abandon myself entirely to God; that he, too, had had great trials before the angel told him that the Infant was of the Holy Spirit and that he was to be the Mother's protector; again when he had to go unexpectedly to Bethlehem and found there no lodgings; and, when from Nazareth where he had hardly begun to feel at home, he had to flee into Egypt, the Child scarcely nine months old. He uttered not a word, but hastily got together some clothing, some bread and a pair of small flasks, laid them on the ass and set out by night, thinking: *God has ordered it. He will direct all things.* Once he met numbers of serpents in the wilderness, and he thought: *Now it is time for God to help*, and he prayed for assistance. An angel appeared, and the serpents fled. I saw the whole scene, great serpents crawling out from among the bushes.—But, I interrupted, it was easy for him to endure such trials, since he had Jesus with him. He answered only by a look that silenced me, and he bade me prepare to be well tried this year. I thought yesterday I should have much to suffer in three weeks, or for three weeks."

To this communication are appended the Pilgrim's own remarks which we give in all their ingenuousness, as he himself would have us do: " In praying for a withdrawal of her visions, the good Sister has made a very unwise demand which clearly proves her non-appreciation of what she sees ; for the only support and relief in her miserable state, in the midst of the disorder that surrounds her, is that highest prerogative of hers, the faculty of vision—and from it she begs to be freed ! It looks, indeed, as if she hardly knew what she requested. The refusal of her petition is the greatest favor shown her. She would like to occupy herself exclusively with the poor—and yet, she could hardly give them more time than she does. She devotes scarcely two hours a day to the Pilgrim, notwithstanding the order to recount all she knows (1). As an instance of what he has to endure, behold the following :—The miller's wife brought some flour the other day for the Abbé Lambert and asked, at the same time, to see the invalid, Sister Emmerich. The Pilgrim was at the moment writing by her bedside and the woman was kept waiting a minute or two in the ante-room ; but as soon as the Sister spied her, she got a scruple. ' We must not give scandal,' she said. 'The woman might make reflections on what she was saying to the Pilgrim ; she might hear something,' etc., and she was all anxiety. The Pilgrim was, consequently, sent away till the afternoon, when very likely some new obstacle will arise to frustrate his work."

" She is suffering with Lambert. Every evening brings

(1) No, not all that *she knows*, but all that she *is able* to relate.

fever and hemorrhages ; and several times in the day she is obliged to hold the sick child half an hour at a time, lest it stifle whilst coughing. 'I have,' she said, 'continual visions of coming troubles. A white robe has been put on me and over it a black one, a black veil over a white one. There are many little crosses on the robe which I can put together ; among them three black ones tipped with gold and united into one. They lay on the robe, but when touched they sank in. I had also successive visions of great trials, no one any longer able to understand me. I was abandoned and ridiculed. I learned also that I should again take nourishment and be able to walk. My sister was not allowed to stay with me ; I was attended by some one else, and I was in another place. The Pilgrim brought me something to eat, but I could take only porridge, coarse bread, a couple of beans, and water. I was told that fruits, sweetmeats, and wines are poisonous to me. I saw, too, the experiments made upon me (1).

"'To-day her countenance is unusually calm and serene. She had herself carried to the Abbé, whom she found very weak. He wept on seeing her and again bade her farewell. She was so affected that she fell from swoon to swoon."

" She is again bright and cheerful, though very sad at the approaching death of the good Abbé. God gives her courage and consolation ; her resignation is His pure gift. She had a vison of Lambert's death : 'I thought I was by him, and I saw over him a great fire which vanished by degrees in a tiny flame.' She recounted also a vision of a child sacrificed by the Three Kings before they had received the divine light. 'When I saw on my right the horrible vision of the child's martyrdom, I turned away, but

(1). All this we shall see literally verified.

there it was again on my left! I begged God to deliver me from the awful spectacle, and my Spouse answered me: " There are still worse sights! See how they daily treat Me all over the world !"--and then I saw priests in mortal sin saying Mass the Host like a little live child on the altar before them. They cut It and gashed It horribly with the patena! Their sacrifice was murder. I saw in many places at the present day numbers of good people oppressed, tormented, persecuted--It is to Jesus Christ Himself such injuries are offered. This is an evil age. I see no refuge anywhere. A dense cloud of sin hangs over the whole world, tepidity and indifference everywhere! Even in Rome, I see wicked priests murdering the Child Jesus in their Mass. They want to exact something very pernicious from the Pope; but he sees what I do and, whenever they try to approach him, an angel with a drawn sword repulses them.' "

January 7th—" This morning calm and peaceful, toward noon anxious about the Abbé. When the Pilgrim returned about four o'clock, he found six children praying around the invalid's bed, on which was her little niece in one of the most frightful spells of convulsive coughing. Sister Emmerich's countenance had lost its serene expression; she asked for her confessor. As the Pilgrim could do nothing, he left perplexed and worried."

The next day, the 8th, she recounted the following: " All day long, even when talking or doing my work, I see before me the sick Abbé with all his sufferings and interior dispositions. I see the temptations by which the evil one tries to drive him to despair. He reads him a long list of faults and omissions, and conjures up visions of his failings. This renders him more cowardly and impatient, makes him more sick. Then I pray, I labor, I make all kinds of representations to God   I take upon myself the

Abbé's pains, and then I see his angel approach. St. Martin, his patron, helps him, and his faith, hope, and love increase. When he is freed from the temptation, there suddenly rises up some exterior affair, some contradiction, or accident to make me lose my presence of mind and pray no more for the sick Abbé. If happily I triumph over this, some other suffering is offered to my patient endurance. Yesterday I saw the Abbé at the point of death; he lost consciousness, his temptations were multiplied, his hands wandered over the coverlet. I turned to God, praying that he might still suffer, do penance in this world, but I was told that he must die, and that I must now examine whether I were willing to resign him to the will of God.— Then came a strange picture before me. Some one appeared and spoke in sorrowful terms of my loss if the Abbé died. This was done to drive me to complain and lament, to make me lose patience and resignation. It was a hard struggle! Besides, I was not alone one instant; they were constantly talking to me and the child was coughing. But I overcame the enemy and I said in my heart: *Thy will, O Lord, be done !*—Hardly had I uttered the words, when I saw the Abbé better and more cheerful. As lately he has suffered much from his wound, I prayed for him earnestly, and I was asked if I were willing to relieve him by sucking the wound. When I answered *yes,* I was immediately transported to his bedside. I sucked the wound, the pain was relieved, and he said to the doctor : ' I think *ma sœur* has helped me !'"

January 9th—"In a violent spell of coughing, she vomited at least two pints of blood, but she still went on working and praying for her sick friend. She related also her visions of the arrival at Bethlehem and the adoration of the Three Kings."

January 11th—" Lambert's sickness increases, and Sister Emmerich is worn out with anxiety. She says the Abbé has still some distance to go through the darkness. She has gained a respite for him from death, that he may not have to remain long in purgatory. The child's fearful coughing-spells will help to obtain for him a peaceful death."

January 12th—" She is very calm, thank God! although in a pitiable state and in expectation of the Abbé's death. His strength has greatly diminished, and she is constantly praying for him. She is making a chemise for a poor child who was shown her as needing one."

January 13th—" The efforts she makes and the cares devolving on her, greatly tax her strength. She says herself that her burden is a heavy one. She looks perfectly exhausted and the perspiration rolls down her pallid face. She still supports the child in its spells of coughing."

January 14th— " She related what follows : ' My mother appeared whilst the child was coughing, and consoled me. As long as she stayed, the child was relieved. She was more beautiful and luminous than usual, and I felt a certain awe in speaking to her. I did not see her all the time ; she vanished and reappeared. She promised me no help. I must suffer. The child also suffers and merits by it. I must persevere to the end. She showed me my sufferings and struggles as so many flowers, fruits, and crowns, and then as gardens and palaces, saying that what is there tasted and enjoyed is infinitely sweeter than mortal can conceive.—I am making in vision a painful journey with the Abbé. Sometimes he is quite near the Heavenly Jerusalem ; then he pauses, he has lost something which I have to take to him. I often pass over cemeteries where lies some one who has forgotten something which, with infinite toil and fatigue, I have to take to him over bad roads, the mud up to my waist. I have a thousand such tasks, and near by there is always some one to contradict me, to prevent my accomplishing anything.'"

January 15th—"The Pilgrim found her in ecstasy. She had had herself carried to the Abbé Lambert's room. As soon as she saw him, she fell into ecstasy, in which state she was borne back to her own room. When the Pilgrim entered, she seemed to be engaged in a very fatiguing spiritual labor. On returning to consciousness, she knew not where she was. 'How did I get here?' she asked. At last, recalling what had happened, she said : 'I saw, when with the Abbé, that his soul still needed something and so, I went barefoot through the snow to the chapel to make the Way of the Cross for him. I saw that that would pay off all his debt. The road was difficult, my feet cold.'—The Pilgrim saw that the whole day was as good as lost. What could benefit mankind is thrown away uselessly, for she remembers very little compared with what she might were she more favorably situated. It grieves him to record these lines, for it would be very easy to preserve all, were there ever so little order in the house. She breathes painfully and says : 'I feel that the Pilgrim is again dissatisfied, but I am not in fault.'—He would, indeed, be callous, were he not chagrined by this woful waste !—That afternoon the Pilgrim found her in conversation with one of her old convent companions, a Miss Woltermann. He cannot understand how she can wear herself out entertaining such a person, especially as it makes her forget her visions. Whilst he sat lamenting the irreparable loss, in came her unmarried brother and the Pilgrim had to withdraw to the adjoining room, whence he could hear the tones of her voice in animated conversation. She did most of the talking.

When, at last, the brother took his leave, the Pilgrim again returned to his post, remarking that she had held a long and brisk conversation. ' Yes,' she said, ' I spoke a little too much, for I said: *What would have become of the poor Abbé Lambert, had he not fallen among strangers ? An ecclesiastic in the hands of his relatives, is like a bird in the hands of children !* I ought not to have said that to my brother.' "

In the midst of her trials, Sister Emmerich was consoled by visions of her own childhood. "My deceased playmates took me with them to our old play-ground and to our crib. The ass was standing outside the grotto. I climbed on a mound and got on his back. ' See,' said I to the children, ' the Mother of God sat this way !'—The ass allowed itself to be stroked and held around the neck. Then we all went to the crib and prayed. The children gave me apples and flowers and a rose-bush surrounded by thorns; but I refused them all. They asked me why I never invoked them in my needs, for they were ready to help me. ' Men call so little upon the children, and yet they are very powerful with God, especially such as die shortly after Baptism.' There was one such among them who told me that I had obtained his blessed death for him. If his parents knew it they would be displeased with me. Then I remembered his having been brought to me directly after Baptism, when I held him up and prayed God with all my heart rather to take him in his innocence than let him live to lose it. He thanked me now for having asked heaven for him and promised to pray for me. They told me to pray particularly that new-born infants may not die without Baptism ; for, when we so pray, God promptly sends help. I often have visions of assistance so obtained." After some time, being in ecstasy, she called her confessor, saying :—

" About five thousand are dying at this moment, among them many priests. We must pray that we may meet in the valley of Josaphat, and they will pray for us in heaven. The valley of Josaphat is not now far away, only a short distance—a broad wall black and gloomy! God grant them eternal rest and may the Lord enlighten them! I see an amazing multitude in various situations. I am standing on an arch above the earth. From all points come rays to me through which I look as through a tube. I see the couches of the dying with their attendant circumstances; some are quite lonely and abandoned."

January 17th—" Lambert had a hemorrhage last night to the fright of the invalid and the whole household. She has, consequently, been very much exhausted the whole day, and the confessor is on the watch that she may not be disturbed. As I write, she is coughing and vomiting blood; but, for the rest, she is, day and night, in almost continual ecstasy, though of different degrees of absorption; she lives in one succession of marvellous visions. On no day yet, even amidst the most varied and complicated sufferings, have they failed; besides those now usual to her on the ' Life of Jesus,' she has others as the feasts of the saints recur, not to mention her spiritual journeys, etc. Her courage seems to have increased with her pains, for she is calm and serene. After one of her severe spells of coughing, she exclaimed : ' I have to travel so quickly from country to country, the air makes me cough !' On another occasion, she started up suddenly and looked around her for something; then, having found her crucifix, she said : ' There is a bear lying in wait for me in a thicket through which I have to pass. If I have my crucifix, I can chase him away.' One could see she was on her way to the Holy Land for she spoke of the Life of Jesus and of the Jordan."

January 18th—"Lambert thought he was dying last evening and said to the Pilgrim : ' I am waiting God's call! I pray Him, my dear sir, to reward you for what you have done for us ! I cannot do it myself !' and, at the Pilgrim's request, he gave him his blessing. His countenance was full of quiet dignity. He is a little better now. In the morning in came the old sister-in-law for a visit, but the Pilgrim proposed to her to go make the Way of the Cross. Sister Emmerich is miserable, but always in contemplation. On the Abbé Lambert's condition, she says : ' I cannot say how clear, how bright it looks to me. I see his soul like a little human figure of light hovering over his heart trying to go, trying to escape from the bonds that clasp it on all sides. It seems to be opening a way for itself, to be separating from the body, which is like a cloud torn asunder. I see its anxiety to get loose and the struggle to retain it. The body embraces it more closely, enfolds it more tightly ; it is again caught on one, or perhaps, on all sides. Sometimes it is surrounded by darkness, then by a fog, or again a ray of light breaks through to it, whilst a fire burns over the sick man all the time. And there, in the midst of it all, is the evil one constantly approaching with all kinds of torturing pictures. On the other side is his angel defending him, whilst bright rays fall upon him from his patron and other saints.' "

On this same day, the Pilgrim wrote to Dean Overberg : " By the time these lines reach you, the Abbé Lambert may be no more. With full consciousness, he has received the Last Sacraments and general absolution. Up to the week before last, he recited his Breviary and, until the day before yesterday, he said the Rosary, a practice which he began as a student and never omitted a single day since. He now clasps it in his hands, his scapular on his breast.

Of Sister Emmerich I can say, with full and calm conviction, that of all the souls favored by God (and I have read the lives of very many) *not one appears to me to have been so privileged and, at the same time, so neglected, so abandoned, so tormented, so tempted as she!* But I still continue to gather roses on thorns, to collect the leaves so ruthlessly scattered, and to weep over others borne lightly away on the sudden breeze."

January 19th—" As the Pilgrim entered to-day, the invalid awoke from vision, her countenance like that of a little child, half crying, half smiling, and she said plaintively: 'Now begins my misery! The little Child has gone away! Now it will begin! The Child told me all, He spoke earnestly.—I was at the Crib and I felt a great desire to have the Infant Jesus, to talk with Him. When I left the grotto, I was taken up a little hill which stood in the midst of limpid water. The hill was covered with the finest grass, as soft as silk. I thought: How soft it is! just like that under trees, and yet there are no trees here! I was a little thing in my baby-clothes. I remembered them well—a little blue frock, and I had a switch in my hand. After I had sat there awhile, the Christ-Child came. I spread out my frock and He sat down on it. I cannot say how lovely, how charming the vision was! I cannot forget it and sometimes, even in my pains, I have to laugh for joy. The Child spoke to me so sweetly, told me all about His Incarnation and His parents; but He reproached me very gravely for having complained, for being so cowardly. I should think, He said, of how things used to be with Him, what glory He had quitted, what snares had been laid for Him even in His earliest years, and to what a depth He had humbled Himself. Then He went over His whole childhood. O He told me so many things! He told me how

His coming on earth was retarded, because men opposed obstacles to it, blocked up the way. He spoke of St. Anne's great merit, how high she stands before God, and that she had become the Ark of the Covenant. He told me of Mary and Joseph's hidden, unknown, and despised life; and then I saw numerous pictures of it all. He related something relative to the Three Kings, of their wanting to take Him and His parents with them when they learned in a dream of Herod's rage. He showed me the treasures they had given Him, the beautiful gold pieces, the pure gold, and all sorts of things, particularly the lovely covers. He spoke of Herod's fury which had blinded him, had driven him to madness, and had made him despatch officers to seek the Child. But, as they sought only the son of a king, they passed over the poor little Jewish Babe in the grotto. When Jesus was nine months old, Herod, being still more disquieted and tormented, caused all the infants to be slain.'—Lambert rallies wonderfully from each attack, his wounds have lost their offensive odor and are now healed. He is more calm and serene, whilst Sister Emmerich's malady is greatly aggravated, her cough and hemorrhages more frequent."

January 21st—"Lambert's improved condition continues, whilst Sister Emmerich evidently grows worse. She had herself carried to his room and, in spite of her cough, had a long talk with him. St. Agnes appeared to her, consoled and exhorted her to suffer, for no pain is lost."

January 24th—" Sister Emmerich's cough and oppression have so increased that she cannot speak; she seems to be strangling. The confessor prayed over her. He laid his folded stole on her throat and breast, when she instantly fell into ecstasy, her face beaming and luminous, full of devotion, and innocent as a little child's. As often

as the confessor made the sign of the cross over her, she
took the posture of a devout worshipper in church, crossing
himself at the blessing. Though perfectly rigid, she assumed this attitude each time the sign of the cross was
made. When an action ceases in this state, the hand
often remains immovable where the act ended ; for example, if making the sign of the cross, the hand sometimes
remains resting on the right shoulder, but if the devotion
continues, then the hands are laid one in the other, the
fingers never clasped. When the blessing ended, she fell
back gently on her bed, obeying in that movement a spiritual rather than a physical law. Attracted by the stole
and the priest's hands, she moved toward the latter,
until some one replaced her in her proper position when
she became calmer and easier."

Although Sister Emmerich, in the midst of her trials and
sufferings, interrupted not the recital of her visions, yet we
still find such words as the following in the Pilgrim's
journal: "The greater part of these immense graces is
going to waste, no importance is attached to them, etc.! It
was to some such exclamation, we may imagine, that the
invalid quietly replied : "Yes, that is what my Spouse told
me last night when I complained to Him of my wants and
misery, of my seeing so many unintelligible things, etc.
He replied: 'I give thee visions, but not for thyself. Thou
must communicate them that they may be committed to
writing.' He added that this is not the time for miracles ;
therefore He gives visions, to prove that He is with His
Church till the consummation of ages. *But visions save
no one. Charity, patience, and the other virtues insure salvation!* Then He showed me a whole row of saints who
had had visions of different kinds, but who attained beatitude only by the good use they made of them.'"

February 6th—"She is in a pitiable state, her suffering and inquietude increasing with the increasing weakness of the Abbé. She wanted to be taken to his room this evening, but she was not gratified. The Pilgrim found her almost unable to speak from weakness."

February 7th, 1821.—"*Lambert died this morning at a quarter after ten.*" Such are the words that record the death of this faithful friend of Sister Emmerich, and we cannot but regret their brevity on an occasion so painful to her. The obsequies of the Abbé Lambert were performed on the morning of February 9th. The former Superioress of the Augustinians, Mother Hackebram, purposed remaining with Sister Emmerich during the ceremony. She it was who had received the good Abbé as chaplain to the convent, thus giving rise to the spiritual tie which afterward bound him so closely to their common child, the favored stigmatisée, who ever regarded the good lady as her revered Superioress and Mother. The journal tells us:—

"Whilst the funeral of the Abbé was taking place, the Pilgrim found the former Superioress by Sister Emmerich's bedside. Fearing her presence might incommode the invalid, he persuaded her to withdraw to the adjoining room, where he sat and entertained her. She is a good, simple-hearted person. Through the open doorway he could see the invalid. As he gazed, she suddenly became rigid, her hands joined, her face expressive of fervent piety, the blood trickling from under her forehead-binder. ' It comes from the plain chant!' she exclaimed. 'We are sitting as we used to do, facing choir and choir.'—And later, she said : ' I had made the Way of the Cross, and I met the funeral near the churchyard. I saw many souls accompanying the procession, one of whom had a lighted taper. I assisted at the services and joined with great effort in the Office. I now see the Abbé in a celestial garden with other priests and souls like himself. In it are things corresponding to the pure root, to the spirit of their inclinations here below, without earthly admixture or deformity. I saw by him at his last hour St. Martin and St. Barbara, whose assistance I had invoked."

Thus did Sister Emmerich perfectly fulfil the task announced to her by Sts. Augustine and Ignatius, thus had she prepared her worthy friend for a peaceful, blessed death! How admirable are the ways of God! The Abbé Lambert had been called from the heart of France to be the guardian of the soul who, perhaps, more than any other of her age, struggled and suffered for the most precious treasure of mankind, the Christian faith. Who was more worthy to stand by her side than the generous confessor who preferred exile and poverty to the betrayal of the Church? From the very first, he had divined the mystery of Sister Emmerich's life and hence his great desire to conceal its treasures as well from herself as from the world at large. What must not the noble old man have suffered when he beheld her suspected, maltreated, branded as an impostor? What must have been his feelings to hear himself denounced as the author of those mysterious marks, declared guilty by the Illuminati " of having made her wounds by artificial means, of having bound his victim to lifelong secrecy by most terrible oaths?" Did his enemies believe their own calumnies? This will be known only on the Judgment Day. Of one thing we are certain, the names of Lambert and Limberg will be pronounced with respect as long as the memory of Sister Emmerich shall be held in love and veneration by the faithful.

On February 8th, Friday before Sexagesima, Sister Emmerich was shown in vision her task for the coming Lent. "My Celestial Spouse has clothed me in a new black garment all strewn with little crosses. He presented them one by one, asking me so sweetly if I would accept them. 'For,' said He, 'there are so few willing to suffer; and yet, so much sin to expiate, so many souls to be saved!'—Then I silently took all the crosses. I was told that I should wear the robe for ten weeks and that it would become a help to me. I was also told that *the want of intelligence in those around me respecting my state, is alone sufficient to cause my death; but I must suffer all patiently.*"

The fulfilment of the preceding vision was not long delayed. Hardly was the Abbé buried when Sister Emmerich was amazed by the demand of Christian Brentano to change her lodgings and dismiss her sister Gertrude. The Abbé being no more, Christian Brentano thought the chief, if not the only obstacle to his cherished scheme was now removed. He and the Pilgrim were so sure of success that the latter enters into his journal the following lines: "Everything is arranged for the invalid's removal, a lodging hired at the house of the school-master, and measures agreed upon with Dean Rensing and the burgomaster. All is ready!"—But now arose opposition in another quarter as we see by the words: "The confessor will come to no decision, although he can give no good reason for thwarting the plan. At last, he resolves to apply to Dean Overberg, wants to go himself to Münster to take advice where never yet has advice been given. Sister Emmerich declares her inability to act without her confessor's co-operation. Things are in horrible confusion! The whole affair is tiresome, perplexing, incomprehensible!"

Sister Emmerich seeing the storm gathering around her

felt the necessity of coming to some decision and, on Sexagesima Sunday, having received strength in Holy Communion, she resolved to have an explanation with the two brothers, Christian and Clement Brentano, the latter of whom reports : " She has communicated ; she is strengthened and full of serenity. Past sufferings seem to her as nothing ; for, however miserable her physical condition may be, she is all day long in ecstasy. Her increase of strength to-day is a magical effect of Christ's presence within her ! My brother Christian visited her in the afternoon ; the Pilgrim followed him later. She was full of peace, mild, and kind. She made some remarks about certain things which she had to endure and of which complaints have already been made to her. But they were mere trifles, things for which we could make no satisfaction, as they were wholly without foundation. She said, for instance : ' When the Pilgrim is here, he sends visitors away under the pretext that I am asleep, and many are vexed by it. My own relations complain that he prevents their seeing me, and even my good brother says he was sent away by him. The Abbé Lambert told the confessor how hard it was to put up with the Pilgrim. He is like a spy, he watches everything that goes on.' This must have been one of Lambert's last temptations ! It was, however, very humiliating to the Pilgrim to hear such things. Unfortunately, he cannot with truth promise amendment, though the invalid thinks all might be easily rectified. The confessor also had a word to say to the same effect, but he was very friendly, very kind and affable."

The Pilgrim, however, despite the gentle remonstrance of the invalid and her confessor, seems to have insisted on a change of residence, as we may glean from the following entry in his journal :—

" She has been ill, all night in convulsions. The Pilgrim found her in a pitiable state, though her soul is calm. She said to him : ' My confessor bade me tell you that I am willing to change my abode ; but last night I received very clear and repeated warnings against it. The Abbé Lambert appeared and told me earnestly and decidedly that, if I did so, I would die before my time, after enduring unspeakable misery from the weakness of those around me. He chided me severely for having consented to the change. When about to excuse myself and speak to him as I used to do, he said shortly : ' *Be silent and obey! We judge of things differently where I am.*' Then falling into ecstasy, she said in a clear, firm voice which seemed to proceed from another, a very resolute person : ' God must help me, or I shall die ! Since I put on the black robe, I have been pierced through and through. I have seen all, I have heard all that, up to the present, has been said about my moving, as well as the sentiments of the individuals concerned. It is a terrible sight for me ! The wrath excited on my account and for which I really am not responsible, is for me a hell ! It may cause my death !' "

" The next day the Pilgrim did, indeed, find her perfectly disfigured in countenance and apparently at the point of death. All night she had had hemorrhages and during the day chills and fever. Once she held up her burning hands to her confessor, exclaiming : ' Take away these hands ! They are not mine ; they belong to *Francis !*' She became so much worse toward evening that, persuaded she was going to die, she sent, notwithstanding the late hour, for the Pilgrim's brother."

February 14th—" Next morning she was deathly weak, but calm and peaceful. She could speak only in a whisper. ' I am still alive,' she said, ' by the mercy of God ! Last night I saw above me two choirs of saints and angels, reaching to one another flowers, fruits, and writings. It seemed as if some wanted my death, whilst others were for my living longer. I thought myself that my hour had come. I was no longer in the body. I saw it lying here, whilst I was gently raised above it. I still had strength enough to confess and send for your brother, who has been displeased with me. After speaking to him, I had nothing more to trouble me, though what I said, I cannot now recall. It was nothing of my own ; my guide stood by me suggesting the words (1). I was raised up and I saw myself surrounded by saints, some praying that I might die, others that I might live, and they presented to me their prayers and merits. One of them showed me a man dying in Münster, his soul in a bad state. The saint told me to kneel and pray for him. I bestowed upon the dying man the prayers the saints had made for me; but, as I did not know whether my confessor would allow me to pray kneeling, since he often forbids it in the daytime, I sent the saint to ask him. He returned with the permission. I knelt and prayed, and saw a priest go to the dying man.' "

Father Limberg spoke of this night of agony, as follows : " Sister Emmerich had all the symptoms of approaching dissolution. After her confession, she sent for Mr. Christian Brentano, with whom she spoke in a low tone, after which he knelt down near her bed and prayed. I was in the adjoining room thinking : God grant that she may give me some sign by which I may know whether to administer to her the Last Sacraments!—when she suddenly arose on her knees, extended her arms, said an *Our Father*

(1) Christian Brentano afterward told his brother that Sister Emmerich had spoken to him very beautifully after her confession ; that, if things were as she said, they were of great importance ; but that he was resolved not to be hasty in changing his opinion. And, in truth, though now reconciled to her, he did not change his preconceived ideas of her case.—(Brentano's Notes).

in a loud voice, and spoke of some man who had just died in Münster. She seemed not to touch the bed. She told me that the Abbé Lambert would have had to suffer ten weeks longer, had she not averted it by her prayers; but she now had to supply for him, and another short period of life had been granted her."

February 17th, Quinquagesima Sunday.—" I have had a frightful night! Three times did Satan attack and horribly maltreat me! He stood at the left side of the bed, a dark figure full of rage, and assailed me with horrible menaces; but I drove him off by prayer, though not until after he had struck me and dragged me around cruelly.— Again he appeared, beat me, and dashed me about; but again I overcame him by calling on God for aid. When he disappeared, I lay a long time trembling with pain.— Toward morning, he came again for the third time and beat me, as if he wanted to break all my bones. Wherever his hot, fiery blows fell, my bones cracked. I grasped my relics and the particle of the True Cross. At last, Satan retired. Then my Heavenly Spouse appeared and said: *Thou art my bride!* and I became calm. When day dawned, I saw that the evil one had upset everything in my room."

Satan's attacks were renewed the following night. " The evil one appeared to me under different forms; he seized me by the shoulders, and loaded me with angry reproaches He often assumes a grand and imposing air as if he were very important, as if he had orders to give; or, again, he puts on a sanctified demeanor and gravely represents to me as a great fault that I have assisted some soul in purgatory, or prevented the commission of some sin, etc.,—as if such things were great crimes! Sometimes he appears in a frightful form, dwarfish and foxy with a broad, horrible face and twisted limbs. He abuses me, pinches me, pulls me

about,and occasionally he tries flattery. I often see him running around with a little horn on his head, very short arms
without elbows, and legs with the knees turned backward.''

The mental and physical sufferings which overwhelmed
Sister Emmerich just after the decease of her good old
friend, the Abbé, reduced her to such a state that it became exceedingly difficult for her to satisfy the Pilgrim
with respect to the communication of her much-prized visions.   He writes : '' We hear now only of her misery, her
torments, her vexations, of all she has done, etc., until one
feels inclined to accuse himself of having caused her annoyance.   Then in come a couple of old women or the
master of the house, or some old maid—all insignificant people, by whom, however, she permits herself to be annoyed.
She never rids herself of such people ; and so, these old
nobodies repeat visits which she looks upon as the greatest
torment, and which cause her to forget her visions. Those
precious graces, for which the Pilgrim is sacrificing a most
important period of his life, are stifled, so to say, neath the
filth of a few common flies, for it is nothing more nor less
than that !''

CHAPTER VIII.

Sister Emmerich is taken to a New Abode.—Sufferings for Souls in Temptation, for the Agonizing, etc.

After the Abbé Lambert's death, in February, 1821, Sister Emmerich received from Chancellor Diepenbrock, of the Chamber of Finances, father of Cardinal Melchior Diepenbrock, a kind invitation to come to Bocholt and spend the rest of her life in the bosom of his family. That she might not be deprived of his spiritual assistance, the position of almoner was offered to Father Limberg. Both the invalid and her confessor received this mark of benevolent sympathy with sentiments of liveliest gratitude. The Sister declared after reading the letter :—" Years ago when, in extreme distress, I cried out to God that I could not preserve my soul pure in the midst of my continued embarrassments, He told me to persevere to the end ; that when abandoned and despised by even my best friends, He would help me, I should have a short period of peace. I have always looked forward to this help." These words expressed a certain degree of willingness to accept the invitation. To her glance of inquiry, Father Limberg answered : "We will pray to know the will of God." Some weeks later Mr. Diepenbrock renewed his offer through his daughter Apollonia who had come to Dülmen to visit Sister Emmerich, accompanied by Miss Louise Hensel. In former years these ladies had spent some time with the invalid. Both were of the small number of intimate friends

with whom she was ever spiritually united, interesting herself in their soul's affairs and following them with her
prayers through all the paths of life.   That Sister Emmerich made no attempt to conceal her joyful emotions at the
generous offers made her ; that she should frequently and
earnestly repeat words of gratitude ; that she should dwell
with pleasure upon the thought of the cordial reception she
would meet, was perfectly natural ; nor did such words mil-
itate against her settled conviction, her interior assurance
that in the designs of God she would never quit Dülmen to
end her days in a more agreeable or tranquil position.   This
conviction she succeeded in insinuating into Father Limberg's mind, though the Pilgrim and his brother were slow to
relinquish the idea that her removal to Bocholt would be the
greatest benefit to her.   It would free her, as they so much
desired, from those endless annoyances which opposed their
own designs.   Firmly persuaded that they were furthering
her spiritual and temporal interests, these high-toned men,
following the impulse of poetic and scientific tastes rather
than a solid vocation to a more elevated life, perfectly ignored
the fact that her departure for Bocholt could be a step more
serious than a change of inns to a traveller.   The Pilgrim
says in his journal : " In the midst of the confusion that
surrounds her (1) and the phenomena wrought in her,
phenomena which demand absolute retirement and the care
of intelligent friends, her inveterate condescension leads her
to entertain all sorts of people.   They are good without doubt, but perfectly incapable of understanding her case.
They are scandalized that others (the Pilgrim and his
brother) should interest themselves in ameliorating her condition ; they stir up enmity and vain talk, whilst the invalid herself attributes all such annoyances to those who assist

(1) Her exterior situation such as it appeared to him.

without troubling her. If she is not entirely sequestered; if worldly affairs are not wholly retrenched; if she dies not perfectly to the outer world, and ceases not to give long, private interviews, the disorder will never be remedied. The Pilgrim told her lately that she often speaks confusedly. She took his words very much to heart; her tears began to flow, and a copious hemorrhage followed."

In July, Dean Overberg came to Dülmen and Sister Emmerich laid before him the whole state of affairs. She gave him an account of conscience, and received in return consolation and advice. She said: "He has taken all my scruples on himself, and nothing more has been said of a change of lodgings."—Some days after she repeated several times: "The devil tries to hinder what God demands of me. I see before me a large cross which seems to be constantly increasing. . . . . . I saw myself dying on a heath which I was crossing in a vehicle. To Bocholt I will go only in spirit. . . . . . They want to seize me and carry me off. . . . . ." On the first of August, she exclaimed: "I feel such dread. I feel as if great suffering were coming upon me. . . ." But the Pilgrim remarks after the above: "These are only the pictures of a fevered imagination. They are of no account whatever. . . ." and again: "She has been in a miserable state all day, a prey to feverish delirium."

On August 6th, however, it became evident that her agonizing presentiment was only too well founded. A carriage drew up before her abode with the Pilgrim and his brother to convey her to Bocholt. We find the incident recorded in the journal, as follows: "Madam Hirn and Dr. von Druffel arrived at noon (1). There was much talk of the measures taken with His Excellency, the Prince-Bishop of Münster, and the Dean. Every obstacle to the journey

(1) On Brentano's invitation.

seemed removed, and various plans were proposed. The invalid became worse; whereupon the confessor, contrary to expectation, opposed her being borne to the carriage. In his excitement, he had recourse to the strangest subterfuges. Dr. von Druffel and Madam Hirn represented to him that they had a written authorization from the Bishop for the invalid's removal. But even after it was produced, he would not yield. Dr. von Druffel retired in disgust. Madam Hirn imprudently mentioned to the invalid's simple brother that his sister was going away and he, naturally averse to such a step, repeated it to the perverse Gertrude—an explosion followed and the whole plan was frustrated !"

Sister Emmerich was greatly distressed at beholding such discord on her account. To prevent further dissensions, she resolved to accede to the wishes of the two brothers as far as she could in accordance with the divine direction. Father Limberg, too, influenced by the fact of the Prince-Bishop's having lent his authority to a change of domicile, at last declared, in the name of God, that his penitent might remove to another lodging and dismiss her sister Gertrude. Sister Emmerich, wishing to have the approbation of her former Superioress in religion, Mother Hackebram, sent for her to this effect; but she being absent from Dülmen at the time, Sister Neuhaus, the Mistress of Novices, responded to the call. In her presence and that of her confessor, the Sister declared to the two brothers that she was now ready to obey any command laid upon her. Let us listen to the Pilgrim's account of the interview :—" That silly old Sister Neuhaus stormed at the Pilgrim's brother and would not let the invalid be removed. But he soon silenced her. The invalid said not a word to relieve his embarrassment, never hinted that it was her own wish to be moved. Such weakness and dissimulation wounded him, confirmed him in his bad opinion of her. Then the mistress of the house joined her reproaches to those of Sister Neuhaus. She declared that the Pilgrim was a constant annoyance to the invalid, etc. Here, again, the latter ventured not a dissenting word, which second evidence of dissimulation hurt the Pilgrim's brother still more deeply. Then came the sister and the child to swell the chorus. Madam Hirn declared that she would not leave the house until the invalid had been removed (1). At last, on the evening of the 6th, Sister Emmerich was taken from this abode of confusion (2). Although wholly unconscious, she inclined profoundly to the Blessed Sacrament when passing the church, and next day she said that she thought she had been carried through it. This fact is most impressive, and to the unbeliever instructive. When installed in her new abode on the first floor, the Pilgrim and his brother reproached her with not having seconded their efforts in her behalf. The latter told her in plain terms what he thought of her moral state (3) ; whereupon she fell into trouble and doubt and told all to her confessor, who likewise became monstrously uneasy !—And so her misery recommenced and ended in renewed hemorrhages. *But the expression of her countenance denotes the highest peace of soul."*

August 9th—"Sister Emmerich is extremely troubled by what the Pilgrim's brother said to her. Very probably, she

(1) This good lady never had had any special relations with Sister Emmerich. That she should assume such authority over her is an additional proof of the way in which all believed themselves authorized to control this chosen soul.

(2) And yet in this so called *abode of confusion,* Sister Emmerich was so loved and venerated that up to the year 1859, the owner, Clement Limberg, kept the two small rooms she had occupied in the same condition as she had left them. After the publication of the first volume of her biography he sent to the author a written statement of his reminiscences of her which he retained unimpaired to an advanced age.

(3) For a layman but lately returned to the practice of his religion, to pass so severe a judgment upon one who had ever been scrupulously faithful to her religious vows and to the direction of enlightened guides, was revolting injustice. Sister Emmerich's silence, so odious to Christian Brentano, was dictated by her sense of truth. She could no more contradict the statements of her friends respecting the annoyance to which the Pilgrim's exactions subjected her, than she could declare a forced assent to her removal for the sake of peace to be her own free will and desire.

does not fully understand the nature of his remarks, for she calls upon God and His justice. *Still she is at times unspeakably calm, a very picture of peace.*"

August 10th—" To-day she was very sick; she was covered with a copious sweat of blood and water. She is, consequently, unable either to speak or to move. But her countenance is indescribably peaceful, bespeaking the sweetest tranquillity and purity of soul. No words can say how gentle she is in her utter prostration! Once she murmured: 'I am better now. I am always better when I am sick. Ignatius had ordered me to ask God for the true spirit of peace and understanding. I often received consolation through him, but we can never know how we stand with God."

Sister Emmerich's deep and solid humility made her ever accept as true and deserved the accusations brought against her. She looked upon herself as the real cause of the " discord and irritation going on around her," as Mr. Christian Brentano expressed it. Just at this time, Almighty God recompensed her by the consoling view of her own manner of contemplation, as mentioned in Vol I., Chap. VIII., in the vision beginning with these words : " When I saw these annoyances arise, etc." She was so strengthened and comforted by this sight that the Pilgrim remarks: " I found her this morning in vision softly singing canticles in Mary's praise. On awaking, she said : 'I have been in a procession. . . . . . . ,' and *her countenance wore an expression of happy, peaceful gravity.* This proves how detrimental it is to her soul to meddle in exterior affairs."

Although Gertrude had been banished from the invalid's new abode and all the Pilgrim's plans seemed to succeed, yet she was not sufficiently isolated, he thought, as long as her little niece remained under her care. " The Pilgrim asked her quite innocently," he writes, "if she did not intend the child to return to its parents—whereupon she complained that even the child would not be allowed to remain near her. Then he said jestingly : ' I know you so well that I venture to say, if you could, you would take your sister back again,' at which she began to weep." He was not, however, deceived in counting upon her submission ; for Gertrude was not recalled, and the little niece was sent home to her parents.

"The child's return home," he writes, "gives the invalid so much anxiety that her visions are laid aside for the sake of a couple of linen caps; and so, once more, all is lost ! Since she has had perfect repose her communications have, in general, become dull and languid—a most singular thing since her confessor instead of opposing obstacles to them, seems now even anxious to encourage them."— Again, we read : "She is exhausted, but calm. Her communications are very unconnected, on account of the great effort it costs her to make them. This inability seems to have increased since her removal to her present peaceful abode. . . . . She had beautiful visions of the angelic host, but their communication was postponed for some domestic trifle, the wash, perhaps; and others very important have also been passed over in consequence of a very useless conversation with the Chaplain Niesing." In complaints such as the above closes the month of August which, however, had given an unusually rich harvest to her amanuensis.

Sister Emmerich's almost passive submission to the Pilgrim's demands may, at first sight, seem inexplicable to the reader as it did to the writer of these pages ; but serious reflection upon the way followed by this favored soul presents her conduct under a different aspect. All that she endured from the communications of her visions had been

ordained by God, even the petty annoyances springing
from the Pilgrim's eagerness to record everything she saw
and his impatience at trivial interruptions. Never did she
receive from her angelic guide an injunction to dismiss
him, or to offer positive resistance to his plans. In previous visions she had, it is true, been prepared for what was
in store for her through his intervention, not that she might
escape those trials, but that she might virtuously triumph
over them. Once she remarked: " I have had, in vision,
to busy myself more than usual with the Pilgrim. He had
to show me his journal. I could not conceive how he arrogated to himself so many rights over me and took so many
liberties; yet I was ordered to tell him everything. It
seemed strange and I wondered at it since, after all, the
Pilgrim is *not a priest !*" She was, then, convinced that,
in bearing with the Pilgrim, she was obeying the will of
Divine Providence. If there are any facts which prove to
our limited understanding how far removed are the ways
of God from those of human calculations, they are precisely
those daily events in the lives of souls favored with extraordinary graces and who have arrived at high sanctity. Our
miserable shortsightedness would have their outer in perfect conformity with their inner life; but there lies the
great mistake, and into it the Pilgrim fell. He wished
not to recognize the fact that Sister Emmerich's sublime
gifts were not the end of her existence. He failed to understand that they were only the recompense of her fidelity
in little things; of her daily, hourly practices of virtue, of
her self-victories; her acts of humility and perfect charity
which, though hidden in the depths of her own heart, glorified God more than public miracles and wonders. When
we apply this rule to the direction given to Sister Emmerich, to her gentleness and patience toward her impetuous

amanuensis, her sweet condescension to his importunate demands, we behold in her actions a chain of sublime virtues,
and a pledge of her fidelity to God. The Pilgrim himself,
when viewed in this light, appears but as an instrument of
Divine Providence. His proceedings lose much of their
apparent severity, when we consider the zeal, the intentions that prompted them. Sister Emmerich saw in him
only the instrument of God's inscrutable designs, by whose
aid she was to attain perfection through the unremitting
exercise of the most difficult virtues. She neither could
nor would dismiss him. His presence was necessary for
the perfect accomplishment of her mission.

"The Pilgrim had now obtained what he had so long
sighed for; and yet, he was soon as dissatisfied as ever.
A few days after the Abbé Lambert's demise, he renewed
his complaints against Father Limberg for not discounten-
ancing the visits of Sister Emmerich's former companions
in the convent :—

"After the death of the troublesome old Abbé," he writes,
"the house became a perfect rendezvous for gossips and the
most tiresome disorder reigned, instead of the peace that
should have ensued. No measures were taken to secure
rest to the invalid, and her sister became simply unendurable. It was not the Abbé who had disturbed the
good arrangement of the household. He was, on the contrary, like a prop to support the pile of ruins 'neath
which the poor little child of Mary struggles. When he
was taken away, all fell upon her. There is no order, no
discretion, only stupid eagerness in all that is done for her,
whilst she herself receives visitors kindly, sends no one
away, though wishing all the time that none would come !"

A year after the Abbé's death, we read : "She often
laments Lambert's loss, because whilst he lived, she could

more frequently receive Holy Communion, the privation of which is most painful to her. She cares only for priests who can bless her, and give her the Bread of Life. He who would bring her Communion daily would be her best and only friend; other kind services seem to make no impression on her. As the Pilgrim is *not a priest,* as he cannot bring her the Blessed Sacrament, she has no sympathy with him or his efforts in her behalf. Regardless of his feelings she exclaims in her spiritual hunger and weakness : 'I have no help, no consolation! Even the Pilgrim is tired of me. I feel it more and more! '—All that know her must truly say that she never had more consolation than she has at present. How could she, surrounded as she was by endless cares? Her complaints proceed only from the privation of the Blessed Sacrament, after which she hungers."

Dr. Wesener also kept aloof at this period in which, as her visions, her interior direction, and exterior events indicate, began a new era in Sister Emmerich's existence. The Pilgrim writes : " Dr. Wesener's absence saddens the confessor. The invalid was exhausted from her sufferings of the previous night. She says she abandons herself wholly to God. She does nothing to procure relief; but she seems to be in temptation, owing to old habits. She worries about the confessor, as also over the discontinuance of Wesener's visits, which, perhaps, God allows for some greater good." If the truth must be told, the good doctor came rarely now, that he might not encounter Brentano at the invalid's bedside.

The wilful Gertrude was, at last, got rid of and her place near her sister supplied by a strange nurse ; yet the former had not left Dülmen and she came every week to see the invalid who, to the Pilgrim's intense disgust, received her kindly and even shed tears on seeing her. The nurse, too, soon

came in for her share of his animadversion when he found
her not only disinclined to vanish noiselessly on his approach,
but even presuming to address herself to Sister Emmerich
for advice, etc. He denominates her "*Very unskilful, quite
awkward and useless;*" but the "*unwearying condescension*"
of Sister Emmerich made her not only endure her patiently,
but even "*work, sew for the old creature who can never
finish anything herself; consequently the most important visions are laid aside.*" And again, "The invalid, alas! is miserable to-day, full of care and anxiety, her wounds very painful, her hands constantly quivering. She wore herself out
sewing and chatting with the old nurse. The minute or
two granted to the Pilgrim were not seriously utilized.—
She has neither will nor desire to communicate her visions!
One has actually to beg for them! The Pilgrim asks for
them only when he finds her ready to talk of other things
wholly unworthy her attention. Each day brings irreparable loss. She is simply a mirror and, when speaking in
vision, reflects perfectly all she sees. In her waking
moments she passes over many points, through her disinclination to talk, and over other very important ones, through
a thousand scruples and prejudices. She is always ready
with her convenient remark: ' *You'll find that in the Holy
Scriptures.*' And if the Pilgrim replies *no* a thousand times,
back she comes to her point! She seems not to weigh the
trouble she gives him.—Things are all just as they used to
be in her old lodgings. Yes, she even complained to the
Chaplain Niesing that the Pilgrim fatigues her by his importunities though, in truth, he is scrupulously careful
about pressing her too much. Her complaints are pure
fancies! Ought he not to grieve at so great a loss?—She
feels that his heart is troubled, and that increases her difficulty in relating her visions to him."

Lastly, Brentano is as much provoked at the poor old nurse as he had formerly been at Gertrude:—"The confusion and disorder around the invalid are disgusting! Through her total inability to help herself; her various interior sufferings; the exterior neglect resulting from the ignorance and stupidity of the old nurse, she is, with her sore eyes and dreadful vomiting, a true picture of woe. And the more easily all this could be remedied, the more painful does its continuance become to the beholder. The best way would be to discharge this stupid old woman and hire an humble, orderly servant-girl; but the confessor objects to any further change."

The Pilgrim betrays the secret motives of his efforts to banish from the invalid's vicinity whatever could disturb her ecstatic contemplations when he remarks: "In ecstasy she resembles a pure mirror which reflects truly every image presented before it; whilst, in the state of consciousness, she passes over many things unheeded." His zeal for the preservation of those visions, so precious in his eyes, made him forget that, not by them, but by the daily practice of the love of God and the neighbor was Sister Emmerich to sanctify herself. He failed to perceive that he was struggling against the ordinance of God Himself; therefore the failure of his cherished plans rendered him, though naturally compassionate and kind-hearted, irritable and severe toward all whom he looked upon as an obstacle to the communication of her visions during the actual period of her ecstatic prayer. Nor did he spare the invalid herself when she cordially welcomed intrusive visitors: the sick, the poor, the sorrow-stricken were all received with kindness so sincere that no one left her unconsoled. If, under the pressure of more than ordinary suffering, a feeling of repugnance arose in her soul, she instantly surmounted it

for the love of God, received the strength requisite to serve
Him in her neighbor, and thus accomplished something incomparably greater than the contemplation of her visions.
This was precisely the point that the Pilgrim could not
comprehend; and hence arose the vexation which found
utterance in such complaints as the following:—

"All has been lost to-day! Sister Emmerich, though
ill unto death, has been besieged by visitors. No one has
been denied admittance. She receives all kindly but, no
sooner are they gone, than she almost dies of pain, torture,
and sickness. One cannot answer for all this! These
people have nothing to say, so she has to gather up her
strength to entertain them; and, in the end, they fancy
themselves most welcome. What follows? The loss of all
her visions, though she sighs in the evening at not having
related them! The Pilgrim has never yet known her to
excuse herself from the most insignificant visit for the sake
of communicating her visions."

"Sick and in a most pitiable state, she wept because visitors were expected; and yet, when they came, she received
them graciously, chatted with them, and even gave them
presents." Sister Emmerich's relations came but seldom
during the year to spend a few days at Dülmen and, in their
intercourse with her, they observed the strictest reserve.
But it was on such occasions more than any other that the
Pilgrim looked upon himself as a truly unfortunate man.
He considered the interest she manifested in their affairs
an unpardonable infidelity to the mission of her life. Her
eldest brother had a son studying for the priesthood.
Every year the young man was allowed to spend part of
his vacation with his aunt, who felt for him the tender
solicitude of a spiritual mother. Her only desire was that
he might one day become a holy priest. But as long as

the poor young student remained in Dülmen, both he and his aunt lived in continual dread of the Pilgrim who could ill-brook such *"interruptions."*

" Her nephew and niece," he writes, " are here again and she is unnecessarily busy, anxious, preoccupied about them.—She butters bread, cuts ham, pours out coffee for them !—and for such duties graver ones are neglected. The more she sees of her relatives, the less she has to relate. The Pilgrim should have *iron* patience to preserve calmness in such disorder. There is neither foresight nor regularity in her household !"

Sister Emmerich wept over the Pilgrim's unjust remarks and exclaimed : " I am always told in vision how to act. I must keep my nephew near me that he may not fall into sin, that feeling his poverty, he may not grow proud. And I dare not send my niece among the peasants, for I see her dispositions ; I know what would befall her in Flamske. I have had visions of her future life, and I have to pray and labor that she may escape the dangers that menace her soul. The Countess Galen would kindly take the child ; but I know not yet whether I ought to accept the offer."—To the above the Pilgrim adds a few of his remarks :—" That the niece and nephew wish not to stay with their parents is conceited ignorance in the one and self-will in the other."

September 8, 1822.—" This is Sister Emmerich's birthday. She is worried over the faults of her rustic nephew. She speaks of them freely herself, but let the Pilgrim gently suggest a remedy, and she instantly appears mortified. Whilst he, the nephew, was tramping around her room, she said she could communicate nothing to-day. The Pilgrim annoyed reminded her of her promise and withdrew, when she became very ill. That evening, through the confessor's intervention, the Pilgrim persuaded the nephew *to make a little excursion on foot.*"

September 9th—"*The nephew is gone*, but the invalid is still taken up with the thought of him and the niece. She is distracted and overwhelmed with useless cares."

Oct. 13th—"The niece is going home. Great interior trouble."

Oct. 14th—"Somewhat calmer, though still thinking of the niece."

After-years proved that Sister Emmerich was right in the course she pursued relative to the young student, her nephew, and that she clearly recognized the designs of God in his regard. He became one of the ornaments of the Münster clergy from whom, to the regret of all, he was snatched away by a premature death.

Oct. 20, 1822.—"Violent vomiting with convulsive cough. As she began to relate the 'Life of Jesus,' in came her brother, the tailor; and, though the visit was inopportune, and perfectly useless, the Pilgrim had to retire, as if for *the Pope!* When her sister comes, the invalid generally signs for him to withdraw, and thus the most serious work of his life has to give way before every servant-girl, every old gossip, without his daring to show a sign of vexation. Another peasant followed the brother, and there they sat until after mid-day! In the evening she had a visit from Mrs. Wesener. This left the Pilgrim but a few moments to finish taking down the oft-interrupted vision. This is a sample of her exterior life, which for years nothing has been done to regulate. She has never, for the sake of her communications to the Pilgrim, kept the most insignificant visitor waiting an instant. Serious affairs must be cast aside for every trifle; but, notwithstanding these interruptions, her spiritual, contemplative life pursues its even tenor."

"A pious old aunt visited Sister Emmerich to-day. She was very much distressed at not being able to offer her some coffee, as the nurse was at church. The aunt, however, consoled her, saying that she was glad to be able to make the stations fasting. Sister Emmerich still chats with the young peasant, her nephew, and allows her precious visions to go to waste. Yes and she can prattle gayly with the old nurse, too! It's a wonder she has anything at all left for the Pilgrim!....."

"To-day she began by a confused recital of her cares and sufferings (all perfectly unintelligible, as she mentions not the interior cause) and the Pilgrim was listening with ill-restrained impatience, when in came Vicar Hilgenberg with whom she chatted over nothings and—*another day was lost!.....*"

When the Pilgrim introduces visitors himself at the couch of his friend, his remarks are made in quite a different tone :—

"It was remarkable how, though hardly able to open her lips before, she brightened up on the arrival of N. N. and talked to him for an hour. When he left, she was more dead than alive from fatigue."

"The Pilgrim's brother came and, by the singular stories he told, troubled a little the peaceful current of her communications."

"The visions of the night are lost, in consequence of the morning visit of the Pilgrim's brother. Her efforts to talk with him so exhausted her that, on his departure, she had a hemorrhage. Thank God, her interior was not thereby disturbed, *nor that of the Pilgrim neither!*"

The remaining part of Sister Emmerich's life, as signified by the vision pointing to its prolongation, was to be employed principally in preparing the agonizing for a good death by taking upon herself their corporal and spiritual suffering. For this end, the assistance of the saints, whose relics were in her *"church,"* was promised her.

August 30, 1821.—"I have had a wonderful vision of all my relics. I saw them all just as they are, the color of their wrappings and the number of particles. The saints issued from them and ranged around me in their rank. I recognized all and saw pictures of the life of each. Between them and me stood a large table (1) covered with celestial viands, and the relics disappeared. I sang with the saints the *Lauda Sion* (2) with celestial accompaniment. I saw the instruments on which many of them played. In the crowd of heavenly visitors were many blessed children ; but the vision made me sad, for I felt that the saints were bidding me farewell. They were so affectionate to me, because I had loved and honored them. I understood interiorly that I was no longer to have the visions of relics, as other work was in store for me. The saints withdrew to the sound of celestial harmony, wheeling around and turning their back upon me. I ran after them and tried to catch a glimpse of the last one's features, St. Rose; but I could not. Then the Mother of God, Augustine, and Ignatius of Loyola appeared and gave me such consolation and instruction as I may not repeat."

The instructions referred to concerned her new labors of

---

(1) The consolations the saints were to afford her.

(2) The chant of the *Lauda Sion* is connected with the task intrusted to Anne Catherine. She had to contribute to the accomplishment in many dying souls of the following words of the hymn :

> Bone pastor, panis vere,
> Jesu, nostri miserere ;
> Tu nos pasce, nos tuere,
> Tu nos bona fac videre
> In terra viventium.

suffering; for shortly after the Pilgrim had to record a
state of the invalid such as he had never before beheld in
her:—

"Since the 29th of August," he writes, "she has
passed from sickness to sickness, a series of convulsions,
pains in her limbs and wounds, profuse sweats, etc.; she often appears to be at the point of death. Between these attacks, she has had to struggle with the strangest temptations, such as anxiety about food, etc. On the afternoon of
September the 2d, this mental disorder took the form of
well-defined delirium, followed by a new attack of physical
sufferings. She was, at one and the same time, awake
and in vision, and she incessantly groaned: 'This cannot
last much longer. I never was so poor before. I cannot
pay my debts; all is lost,' etc.—And yet she did not seem
dejected; on the contrary, she was almost gay. She shook
her head, bade the silly thoughts be off, and looked upon
her own talk as foolish. When she uttered such extrava-
gance before the mistress of the house, she instantly begged
pardon with the excuse that she was in pain and trouble.
A night of cruel suffering followed. These attacks lasted
day and night until the evening of the 4th, when she struggled so vigorously against them as to lose consciousness.
Her wanderings all bore upon the point of her penniless
condition; she thought that she could not supply her wants,
and she had no one on whom she could rely.—It is frightful to see one so favored by God in such a state of misery
and weakness when grace is withdrawn! Of course, there
is now no record of visions. What a frail vessel is man,
and how patient, how merciful is God toward him!"

Grace had not been withdrawn from Sister Emmerich,
as the Pilgrim erroneously thought, nor had she been delirious. She had taken the place of a dying man, and had

vigorously combated against the passions that had held him captive all his life. The terrible task was first announced to her on the Feast of the Assumption. "I saw in the heavenly Church the Feast of Mary's Assumption. I saw the Mother of God taken up from the low earthly Church by innumerable angels, borne, as it were, on a crown of five arches, on which she hovered over the altar. The Holy Trinity descended from the highest heavens and laid a crown on Mary's head. The choirs of angels and saints surrounded the altar at which the Apostles celebrated the divine service. These choirs were ranged like the side-chapels in a church. I received the Blessed Sacrament and Mary came to me, and, as if from one of the side-chapels, approached St. Ignatius, to whom I had just made special devotions. I was told that, if my confessor ordered me in the name of Jesus, to rise and walk, I should be able to do so, even were I ill and in the most miserable state. I was so impatient for this that I exclaimed: 'Why not now, right away?' (1) And I heard a voice like that of my Heavenly Spouse, saying: 'Thou art mine! Why this questioning, if I wish it thus and not otherwise?'"--

Father Limberg would not act on this vision. He declined giving any command before further manifestation of God's will. The promise was fulfilled, however, on the Feast of Mary's Nativity, as Sister Emmerich herself tells us:—

" On the eve of the feast, I lay in intense pain and violent cramps, notwithstanding which I was full of inward joy. The night was a weary one, but at three o'clock in the morning, the hour of Our Lady's birth, she appeared

(1) Her impatience is the joyful longing for the task connected with the power of walking. This task consisted in preparing sinners for a happy death, a task which, like all others, can be accomplished only by the means marked out by the Church : viz., *obedience to her confessor.*

to me, telling me to rise and walk a little. I should have done so on the Feast of the Assumption or on that of St. Augustine, had my confessor ordered me to that effect; but now it was through Mary I was to do it. She told me that I should in this state do and suffer in her honor whatever befell me; I should never again be perfectly well, nor able to eat and drink like other people, and that I should still have much sickness and suffering. She told me also that the graces imparted to mankind on the day of her birth still continue to be poured upon them, and she urged me to pray for the conversion of sinners. I should not, she said, try to walk until my confessor came, though I was not to entertain the slightest doubt on the subject. I was full of joy, though more sick and miserable than ever, with cramps and pains chiefly in my breast. The Blessed Virgin said: 'I give thee strength,' and as she spoke, the words left her lips in a substantial form and entered mine as a sweet morsel. I began right off, in obedience to her command, to pray for the conversion of the sinners she pointed out to me, some of whom I saw becoming contrite. In the morning after Communion, I had another vision. I saw the Blessed Virgin, St. Anne, St. Joachim, Joseph, Augustine, and Ignatius. The Blessed Virgin helped me up, and I thought I walked around the room supported by the saints. It seemed as if everything helped me, the floor, the table, the walls. Still I know not whether it was real or only in vision."

Toward noon Sister Emmerich asked her confessor's permission to rise and walk. He hesitated, reminding her of her extreme weakness; but when she recalled the promise she had received, he yielded. With joyous alacrity she threw her wrapper around her, slipped out of bed, tottered across the room like a child learning to walk, and sank upon a chair. She was exhausted by the effort, but radiant with delight. She was not accustomed to the light which now falling full upon her, dazzled her weak eyes. With assistance she took a few more steps around the room, and then sat in an arm-chair until evening, when she returned to her bed full of joyous emotion. The wounds in her hands, feet, and side caused her much pain.

From this time, Sister Emmerich began to rise and walk around regularly, though at the cost of great fatigue. She regarded it as a duty to be daily fulfilled as far as she was able, in obedience to Our Lady's commands. The Pilgrim, seeing her painful efforts procured her a pair of crutches. This he seems afterward to have regretted, as he feared such exertions would interfere with the narration of her much-prized visions. Impelled by this fear, he addressed her one day:

"Strange that one prevented by so many graces should be so eager for a few perilous, miserable steps on crutches!"—to which she replied: "More than once I have seen the most perfect of creatures, the Blessed Virgin Mary, in the Temple impatiently asking holy Anna: 'Ah! will the Child be born soon? Ah! if I could only see Him! Ah! If I could only live until He is born!'—Then Anna almost annoyed would say: 'Do not interrupt my work! I have already been here seventy years, and I must await the Child's coming nearly a hundred!—And thou, thou art so young, canst thou not wait?'—and Mary often wept with desire."

The Pilgrim did not understand the deep significance of her touching reply. She was not impatient for her poor walk on crutches, but she *was* impatient to help souls, for which end alone had the power of eating and walking been restored to her. He remarks, November 1st—"For several weeks the invalid has found more facility in rising, walking with the crutches, and sitting up to sew. She can now dress herself slowly, and take a little broth and coffee. Her vomiting has decreased. Toward tne last of October, she took a little carrot juice."

Whilst her friends looked upon this change as a purely natural amelioration in her physical condition, and her eagerness to walk as a sign of her desire to be cured, it was, in fact, a work of painful expiation for poor sinful souls. She no longer simply prays for them, endures great bodily sufferings for them—she now becomes their actual substitute, taking upon herself and vigorously combating their spiritual evils, their temptations, and vicious inclinations. She had a great vision on this sort of substitution from which she related what follows:—"I had a vision in which it was given me to see why I had so much sickness. I saw a gigantic apparition of Jesus Christ between earth and heaven in the same form and dress as when He bore the insults of the Jews. But His hands were outstretched and pressed down upon the world—it was the hand of God that pressed! I saw many colored rays of woe and suffering and pain falling upon people of every condition. When, through compassion, I began to pray, whole torrents of pains were diverted from their course and pressed heavily upon me in a thousand different ways, the greater part coming from my friends. The apparition was of Jesus, and yet the Three Divine Persons were also included. I saw them not, but I *felt* them."

The following fact, related by Sister Emmerich, February 18th, shows how the strength given her for her present task was increased by her sufferings and struggles.—"I was fully conscious and speaking to my confessor, when suddenly I felt faint and about to die. He noticed the

change and asked : ' What does this mean ?'—I answered
that I felt that strength had gone out from me. I saw it
under the form of rays streaming over twenty different individuals, some in Rome, some in Germany, others in our own
immediate country. They were thereby strengthened to
struggle against a mighty power, a fact which greatly pleased me. Then I saw the harlot of Babylon under a scandalous form, in her hand a colored jacket with its ribands.
The strength that still remained to me went out against her,
much to my dissatisfaction at first ; but it forced her to
cover herself with her jacket. With each ray of strength
I laced the ribands tighter and tighter, until all within her,
all the different impious plots against the Church conceived
by her connection with the spirits of the world and
the age, were smothered and stifled."

In this state of substitution for others, Sister Emmerich
appeared to possess a two-fold existence. One might read
in her countenance, her speech, her gestures, her tone of
voice, the character of the individual whose struggles she
took upon herself. Her own purity of soul shone like a
sunbeam through the clouds, proving that nothing could tarn-
ish its brilliancy. Let us picture to ourselves a saint given to
austerity and penance, yet who, in spite of his disgust and
horror, takes upon himself the miserable state of a drunkard in order to save him from hell's abyss, and we may be
able to form some idea of this double state. Without losing
consciousness, he struggles against the strange power that
is benumbing his senses, a power which creates in him but
loathing and disgust ; thus are simultaneously manifested
in him the two states of sobriety and inebriety. When Sister Emmerich tried to explain this, she said : " It seems to
me then that I am two-fold, as if there lay on my breast a
wooden image of myself which speaks without my power to

prevent or direct it." (That is by which her assumed state
of despair, impatience, intemperance, etc., expresses itself). "Then I reflect that I must endure it, that the
image must know better than I what it ought to do, what
it ought to answer for me. Consciousness is then in me
like a smothered voice."

"Sometimes I know not how to resist my numerous visions
of terror and anguish. They are not sudden thoughts or
attacks, but whole scenes in which I both see and hear,
which attract me violently, affright me, irritate me. I have
to resist with all my strength not to be overcome. Persons
and future events are shown me, and the intentions with
which such or such a thing is done against me. I hear the
scoffs of the wicked fiend, and it is not without a struggle
that I recognize the permission of God and repel the enemy
with his lies. When these crowds of pictures incite me to
impatience, my confessor's approach, a word of consolation
from him or his blessing are an immediate relief; but the
irritation of some around me is, in such moments more
painful than at other times."

"Once a great mirror with a magnificent golden frame
was held before me in which I could see only such things
as were calculated to irritate me. The very sight of the
vain thing vexed me, and I hid my face in the pillows so
that I might not see it; but still it was there, always before
me. At last I seized it and dashed it to the floor, crying:
'What have I to do with such vanity, with such a mirror?'—but it fell gently without breaking. It disappeared
only when, with contempt of its magnificence, the feeling
of my own lowliness and misery also increased. Then I
was permitted to visit Mary in the Grotto of the Crib."

The most humiliating of these assumed states was that
of the gluttonous. In it she experienced sudden and

devouring hunger which gave way to the most intense disgust, as soon as satisfied. The Pilgrim wrote in 1823 :—
" She is sick all the time, without consolation, overwhelmed
with pains, and struggling against the temptations and attacks of the enemy. We hear only coughing, vomiting,
and sighing to eat, and yet she is unable to take food.
Hunger suddenly seizes upon her and she faints.—She eats
and vomits. She craves all sorts of coarse, unsuitable food,
and then moans and weeps for having eaten against her
will.—All this refers to the state of an old companion, Sr.
M. . . . ., who is at the point of death and for whom she
is praying and suffering. Sr. M— is afflicted with dropsy
of the chest and in this her last illness she is, as Dr.
Wesener says, still a victim to her capital fault, gourmand-
izing."

In this state of substitution, Sister Emmerich endured
in turn the various symptoms and sufferings of dropsy,
rheumatism, consumption, internal diseases, etc., as well
as the desolation, weariness, impatience, and temptations of
the poor dying one. All this suffering for individuals added
to that which she underwent for the Church in general,
rendered her condition truly pitiable. From her words
dropped in ecstasy, the Pilgrim recognized the elevated
spiritual character of her various maladies, but he would
have wished for more precise information : for instance,
he would have desired a special explanation as to what
particular faults were expiated by each particular pain.
But in this he proposed to himself an unattainable end.
He resembled a physician who sympathizes with his
patient only in proportion as the latter describes mi-
nutely the symptoms of his disease. He is thus enabled to
observe more perfectly a particularly interesting case, the
study of which is likely to enrich his pathological knowl-

edge and experience. In December, 1821, he writes:—
" The last three days have been one succession of fearful
pains which ended in death-like prostration. They did
not, however, interfere with her visions. Sometimes she
declares calmly and confidently : 'I must suffer this. I have
taken it upon myself. I must endure it !'—but soon comes
a temptation to impatience, and thus she alternates between war and peace. One becomes so accustomed to these
exterior sufferings as to appear almost barbarous to a
spectator who witnesses them for the first time. Thus did
those around her appear to the Pilgrim during the early
days of his sojourn in Dülmen. But when something of
their interior signification is known, they excite the greatest
astonishment, they afford a solution to the strangest enigma
of life, of Christianity, although their study is rendered
impossible by a thousand trifles of every day occurrence...." " Though her sufferings are closely linked
with spiritual labors and she herself knows it well, she
speaks of the fact only superficially and without attaching
due importance to it. She esteems another's calm, deep
reflection on it a want of sympathy."

January, 1822.—" Her maladies would be most instructive were she ordered to explain their end and design, for
she always has as their forerunner a vision so much the
more remarkable as it is wonderfully allegorical. It is
like a deeply significant parable. What she will have to
suffer and the end for which she suffers are generally shown
her in visons of gardening and agriculture : first, a general
view of existing evils, under the symbol of crumbling
churches, flocks with their shepherds, etc.; next she has
to run, carry, dig, warn, etc.; or again, she makes painful
journeys to bring souls back to their duties and prevent
sin. In all these various tasks she is assisted by the saints

of the day. But all this is lost to the writer ! Nothing
remains but the signs of the temptations to which the fiend
subjects her during her task. Her sufferings render her,
it is true, an object of compassion; but, being inundated
with graces and visions so real and fruitful, she is, after
all, more deserving of envy than pity. Her negligence in
communicating them, the endless histories she retails after
her periods of actual ecstasy, make one rather inclined to
sympathize with posterity than to pity her. The continual
danger of death which, however, never occurs, tends to reassure the beholder with regard to her frightful, unaccountable maladies. One grows used to them, looks upon them
with a sort of compassion, it is true, a kind of endurance,
neither improving nor elevating, but which begets a species
of policy, a secret desire to extricate one's self from the
whole affair."

February 4, 1822.—" Although Sister Emmerich relates
less and less every day; although she consumes much
time in describing her maladies and pains, which are
very obscure, on account of her silence as to their interior
cause; yet she remarks: 'Since the beginning of my pains
last Christmas, I have suffered much from the Pilgrim's
dissatisfaction at my not communicating everything to suit
him. My heart has been well-nigh crushed with sorrow.
I would willingly have satisfied him, but I could not. I
have often been so depressed by his appearance as to be
unable to speak. I have made special devotions to know
what I should do, but I have received no answer. I hoped
God would take me in this last illness, that I might have
nothing more to communicate. The Pilgrim will one day understand how willingly I would have made all known to him,
were it in my power.' This she said with a good intention.
Such prayers for release from the duty of relating her vis-

ions are usual to her; but the only answer she receives is a formal order to communicate everything."

February 23, 1822.—"The Pilgrim found her sick unto death, and the confessor told him that she had been insensible all the morning from excess of pain. She had abandoned herself wholly into the hands of the Mother of God, and had taken upon herself sufferings for the conversion of souls given to impurity. Later she said that she had been troubled at the thought of the Pilgrim's having left all and settled in Dülmen on her account; and yet, she could now be of no service to him. The Pilgrim consoled her. Would that she always looked upon her communications as a serious rather than a light and painful task!"

"She received the Pilgrim quite graciously to-day, though her words showed that she is wholly incapable of appreciating her celestial favors at their just value. She thought that during his absence of three days, she had been a little more composed, had had a little rest!'—as if his presence could disturb her peace! But such words signify nothing—they are the expression of merely stereotyped ideas!"

Two months before her death, Sister Emmerich uttered these earnest words to her confessor: "The Pilgrim will one day see that he had no reason to boast his patience over mine. I have had as much patience with him as with my sister!"

April 3, 1823.—"Sister Emmerich is suffering a share of her neighbor, Mrs. B—'s pains, who is at the point of death from dropsy of the chest. Sister Emmerich is suffocating and in constant agitation. The sick lady is relieved, she calmly begins to pray."

April 5th.—"She, Sister Emmerich, complains of confusion in her ideas, and she has a feeling of not having made her Easter. The oppression on her chest increases."

April 7th—"Sister Emmerich's sufferings increase as the good lady's end draws near. She bears a whole half of her pains and her state is precisely similar; though, as a general thing, Mrs. B—is easier when Sister Emmerich suffers most. The Pilgrim verified this by daily comparison. He found that the feeling Sister Emmerich had of not having made her Easter, proceeds from the dying woman's own state; for she, in effect, has not made hers. Sister Emmerich has engaged her confessor to go again and remind the family of it."

April 9th and 10th.—" All the symptoms and pains of a person dying of dropsy were still seen in our invalid this morning, and during the night she struggled in death agony; but the restless, agonizing lady has grown calm and resigned to death, much to the consolation of her family. Toward noon the Pilgrim found Sister Emmerich deathly weak, scarcely able to give a sign of life; whilst Madam B— slumbered sweetly, repeating at intervals the pious little prayers of her youth. At half-past three, Sister Emmerich grew suddenly strong, sat up in bed, and recited in a low voice the Litanies of the Passion. At the same instant, Madam B — expired sweetly as a child falling asleep. Sister Emmerich's oppression instantly ceased, all symptoms of dropsy disappeared, and she again breathed freely. But her clear-sighted compassion allowed her no repose. Her malady suddenly assumed the character of inflammation of the chest and fever as indicated by her pulse. Another sick person, a Madam S — with whom Sister Emmerich was only slightly acquainted, took the place of Madam B — She suffered intensely for her until the following day, when she died. And now another poor creature in the last stage of consumption, the wife of W—, the basket-maker, claimed her aid. Sister Emmerich suffered incredibly for this poor woman, to whom she sent all sorts of comforts, drinks, and nourishment. The poor thing, who had been very harshly treated by her husband and relatives, was thus preserved from resentment and despair. She prepared for death in sentiments of charity and forgiveness. Sister Emmerich often deplored the spiritual abandonment in which such persons are left. ' They are,' she said, ' for the most part, uninstructed. In a long illness they are bereft of all consolation ; they are left to their miseries, deprived of proper assistance, and seldom receive the visit of a priest.' "

" On the 20th, the Pilgrim found Sister Emmerich very much troubled, her countenance gloomy. She was a prey to interior anguish and chagrin against certain priests who were neglectful of their charge and sparing of their consolations. This was also a phase in the poor, sick woman's state. After a long absence, the priest had, at last, visited her ; but he could not give her strength and courage, as her mind wandered a little. He left her more agitated than he found her, and she was seized with so violent an aversion for him that she would not again hear of a priest. 'What a priest!' she cried. 'I will not see him!'— Such was the change wrought in the sentiments of the poor dying woman, once so gentle and submissive. Sister Emmerich took upon herself the poor woman's struggles. She endured them all day Sunday ; she experienced intense resentment against a certain negligent priest. On the evening of the 20th, the poor woman's family thought her dying. But Sister Emmerich prayed all night that God would keep her alive until she had regained her peace of soul. The morning of the 21st found her, indeed, still alive, sweetly pardoning every one and welcoming death.

Toward noon Sister Emmerich appeared to be in **her**
agony, and the Pilgrim recited with her several litanies
for the sick. In this state she remained with various alter-
nations of suffering until the following morning at half **after**
eight, when she experienced relief—but her patient **was**
dead! All that day she spent in great dejection, for she **saw**
a new labor approaching. In the evening the Pilgrim found
her condition quite changed; she had pains in her limbs **and**
a cold, empty feeling in her stomach, etc. She was now assisting the pious wife of poor H—, the tailor. She had said :
"When I shall have finished with the basket-maker's **wife,**
I must pray for her. These people are so pious and humble, perhaps the wife may still recover. She has no medicine and only very poor nourishment.'—The Pilgrim **did**
not know the family, but he hunted them up to give them
alms, and found the wife's sufferings precisely similar to
those of Sister Emmerich. He had heard the latter **say :**
' Some days ago, this woman appeared before me. I
thought I should have to pray for her, as soon as the basket-maker's wife dies.'—The sick woman remarked, to the
great surprise of the Pilgrim : 'Ah! I dreamed some **days**
ago that I was standing at the door, when Sister Emmer
ich approached me from the Coesfeld gate. She gave **me**
her hand, saying, *Well, Gertrude, how are you ? You* **must**
get well !—I saw her distinctly.'—The Pilgrim asked Sister
Emmerich if she remembered this walk in vision. She answered : ' No, I cannot recall it, but I have often been
near her lately and I have seen all she did. I do not remember anything particular in this instance, for I go to so
many places.' "

April 25th—" Sister Emmerich is miserable and dejected. Every night since the death of the basket-maker's
wife, she has had visions in which she had to wheel heavy

loads of corn for her on a barrow, a labor in which the poor creature had constantly been engaged. These were loads that she had wheeled unwillingly and angrily; or had, perhaps, altogether neglected. Sister Emmerich declared herself unable to continue the work longer, and told the Pilgrim to have a Mass said instead of it. He did so, and thus ended her wheeling of corn."

DELIVERANCE FROM DANGER.

One day in August, 1821, the confessor informed the Pilgrim at the invalid's bedside that, since the preceding evening, she had had headache so violent as to render her delirious. She insisted that she had been shot in the head, and she begged to have it bandaged. Soon after she related the following facts:—

"Last night I offered my pains for the deliverance of souls in danger. As I started on my accustomed journey to the Nuptial House, my guide took me to a high mountain, where I found a learned scholar who, whilst clambering over the rocks, a tablet in his hand, had fallen down a steep precipice. As he fell, he invoked Almighty God. I appeared, and carried him on my back to a wagon that was following him. I suffered much from that labor.—Then I saw people with poles in their hands and hooks on their shoes, climbing the cliffs and firing at a flock of birds. A bullet went whizzing straight toward the head of one of the hunters. I threw myself before it and received the whole charge right in my head. The pain was terrible. My head felt as if it were cleft in twain and I saw, at the close of the vision, that the bullets were pure pearls (*merits*). I thought, 'If the Prussians take me now, they will soon extract them,' though I know not how such an idea came into my mind. My broken head made me cry."

In November and December, 1822.—Sister Emmerich suffered much for the Church. " My present sufferings," did she say on the Feast of St. Thomas of Canterbury, " were imposed on St. Catherine's Day for the Church and her prelates. To-day I saw the life of the holy martyr Thomas and the sharp persecution he endured, opposed to which were portrayed the weakness and tepidity of pastors of the present day. My heart was torn at the sight !" The Pilgrim here remarks : " Her sufferings increase and she cannot speak, on account of her insupportable cough ; but her patience is wonderful ! Notwithstanding her frightful tortures, she is all courage and peace. The wound of her side and the crown of thorns cause her incessant pain ; she cannot rest her head an instant. She has a continual feeling of the great sharp crown. She often speaks of the severe, though salutary pains she is enduring."

In the early part of 1823, her sufferings were simply intense, accompanied by uninterrupted visions on the state of the Church. On the evening of January 11th, the Pilgrim found her in ecstasy. She asked for a poultice of boiled figs and barley for her right side. Its application gave relief and when returned to consciousness, she said :

" There is inflammation in my side ; it has been pierced. I heard it crack. I feel the internal dislocation, and I can recover only by a miracle." Father Limberg replied : " You have been delirious the whole afternoon." But the Pilgrim on close observation found her perfectly sensible and consistent, speaking and acting comformably to her interior and exterior direction, her ideas clear, her soul at peace. She directed a plaster to be prepared, asked all to pray, and next day was in a state to account for what had happened.

" I had to go to the Pastor's city (*Rome*), for danger

threatened the faithful chief-servant who has the little dog. They were about to murder him (1). I threw myself before him, and the knife pierced my right side through to the back. The good chief-servant was returning home and on a lonely part of the road where escape would be easy, a traitor met him with a three-cornered knife concealed under his cloak. In mock friendship, he was about to embrace him, but I cast myself between them and received the thrust in my back. It cracked. I think the knife must have broken in it. The chief-servant parried the blow and fell senseless; people came up, and the assassin fled. I think the villain on meeting such resistance, thought the chief servant wore a cuirass   As I warded off the blow, the devil turned on me in a rage, mocked me, and dashed me from side to side.—'What dost thou here ?' he cried. ' Must I meet thee everywhere ? But I'll catch thee yet!'" Sister Emmerich's wound did not heal the whole of January, and she passed through the different stages of fever and inflammation consequent upon such wounds.

January 17th—" She still suffers severe pains in her wounded side; sometimes even she loses consciousness. Her side is much inflamed and a violent cough torments her; but she is otherwise patient and cheerful."

January 18th—" She had a glimpse into the anatomical nature of her wound, of which she gives a minute description. Her pains are intense."

January 22d—" Her sufferings have decreased but, unfortunately, she speaks of insignificant things, such as household affairs and the sick child of one of the townsmen. It is unaccountable to the Pilgrim how such things can so interest her !"

(1) "*Canis et coluber*," emblem of Pope Leo XII. in St. Malachy's prophecy. (Father Schmöger.)

Cardinal Wiseman says, in his " Recollections of the Last Four Popes," that Leo XII. had habitually in his apartments a faithful companion, a very intelligent little dog.

January 27th—"There seems to be a change in her; she is livelier, more energetic and resolute in her bearing and words. She says she is struggling against involuntary anger and resentment against certain individuals, especially against the would-be assassin. Her hemorrhages are more copious. The abscess in her side has softened and is discharging internally. She describes it as a *mushroom,* alternately gathering and discharging. She feels it between the ribs. She declares that her hemorrhages come not from the lungs, for they discharge into the stomach."

February 10th—"Last night her hemorrhages of blood and pus were so copions, that she now lies like one dead. She asserts that she has now vomited the so-called pus-sack, and feels in its stead a void, a wound not yet healed."

Singular Share in an Accident.

March, 1822. —"I have had intense pains in my left foot. I had to go to a hospital where lay a poor woman dangerously injured in one limb by a fall down stairs," said Sister Emmerich one day; but no attention was paid to her words at the time. Some weeks later however it became evident that she had, indeed, endured for the injured woman the pains of the first bandage. An operation had become necessary. In the following mon..h, April, Sister Emmerich suddenly interrupted a conversation with her confessor—"They have taken a splinter from my left foot!" —and she seemed to have a far off vision and to experience the painful application of a bandage. "I cannot understand," she exclaimed, "how that piece of my small bone can fit the limb of that great, tall woman! How sharp the pain was when they reached the bone!—The poor woman, a pious Catholic, was shown me lately; but she must be far away from here in a hospital full of disagreeable sick people.

She has much to suffer, I feel very sorry for her. I have prayed for her and asked for her pains. The doctors are Lutherans. At noon to-day they extracted a large piece of her thigh-bone, and I let them have a piece of mine to insert in its stead, though I cannot see how my small bone can suit—she is so tall and large!—Now they have bandaged our wounds! The pain is excruciating!" Sister Emmerich uttered the above with many minor details whilst conversing with those around her.

EYE-AFFECTIONS.

A father begged Sister Emmerich's prayers for his little child who had been attacked by a very serious eye-affection. Scarcely had he made the request when the invalid was seized with sharp pains in her eyes which lasted several days. One eye was quite inflamed, the same which was believed to be almost lost to the child. In her loving compassion, she had the little sufferer brought to her and, hoping the eye was not beyond recovery, she applied her lips to it and drew out the pus. It was a whole week before she regained the use of her eye. During that time she performed many labors in the fields around the Nuptial House, rooting up stumps of trees, etc., and praying and suffering for many poor creatures attacked with disease similar to that which then assailed herself. She remembered one in particular, a poor tailor who had already lost one eye. When she prayed for sick children, she generally felt them by her on the bed, and she did what she could for them, sending to their homes linen and nourishment for them.

TEMPTATIONS ASSUMED.

On Holy Saturday, 1822, Father Limberg recommended to his penitent's prayers a poor peasant, who, having lost two horses, had fallen into melancholy bordering on despair. On Easter-Sunday morning, Sister Emmerich was assailed by visions which became so horrible during the celebration of High Mass that she thought she should die of fright. After Divine Service, Father Limberg visited her and told her that the man had been so violently agitated just at the moment of Consecration, that groaning and weeping, he had to be removed from the church. Sister Emmerich shuddered involuntarily at this confirmation of what had been shown her in vision. She lay till Tuesday evening struggling against rage, anguish, and despair, and complaining of the sad Easter festivals she had spent. When her struggle ceased, Father Limberg found the poor man calm and in better dispositions; but, before he could acquaint Sister Emmerich of the change, she exclaimed joyfully and thankfully: "St. Ann did it! I invoked her all the time for the poor fellow! She obtained this grace! She is the patroness of the despairing, of all who are tormented by the evil spirit. For days I have suffered terribly for this man who was shown me some time ago. He has no religion. He is not in the state which renders a Christian invulnerable, the state of grace; therefore, a malediction fell upon him. By superstitiously cooking a horse's heart, he put himself in relation with the demon. Despair seized him, and on Easter-Sunday, with rage and hatred in his heart, he assisted at the Most Holy Sacrifice of the Son of God who gave His life for His enemies. St. Ann has delivered him. But if he does not now thoroughly amend, something worse will befall him!"

Dr. Wesener, who visited the man professionally, heard him acknowledge having cooked the heart of one of the dead horses whilst uttering imprecations against him whom he suspected of having caused their death. At the same time, he resolved to shoot the first person he met after his magical incantations. Some weeks later, the same man, threatened with the loss of another horse, seemed about to relapse into his miserable state. Sister Emmerich was greatly distressed. She said to Father Limberg:—"It must not be! The man will again fall into despair. We must pray that the horse may not die,"—and for two days she again sustained a struggle in the poor man's behalf. Her manner became nervous and agitated, her countenance dark and gloomy, her glance wandering and timorous; but the horse was cured.

May, 1823.—Sister Emmerich about this time supplied clothes and baby-linen to a poor woman whose brutal husband treated her shockingly. He had not been to the Sacraments for years, and he lived in enmity with his neighbor. Sister Emmerich had often prayed for his conversion. She now renewed her efforts for him, assuming his miserable state of anger and resentment to such a degree that her countenance became quite distorted. The wretched object of her prayers was seized with anxiety and trouble, as he himself acknowledged to his ill-used wife. At last he went to Father Limberg and made his confession. But Sister Emmerich's struggles, far from abating, became still more severe, and it was evident that this poor man had furnished her an occasion for obtaining similar graces for numerous others. She said: "I thought I should die of pain. I received no help, and I offered it up for all those miserable creatures who languish without the consolation of the Sacraments. I was wide awake when I suddenly saw around

me, far and near, over the whole earth, countless scenes of
sorrow and desolation: the sick and the dying, the wandering and the imprisoned, all without priests, without Sacraments. I cried aloud for help ; I besought God to aid them ;
and I heard the words : ' Thou canst not have it without
cost...It must be purchased by labor !'—Then I offered
myself for the task and fell into a frightful state.—Cords
were tightly bound around my upper and lower limbs, which
were then stretched so violently that I thought all my
nerves were torn asunder. My neck was throttled, my
breast-bones protruded, and my stiffened tongue fell back
in my throat. I was in agony ; but, to my great joy, I saw
that many souls were saved."

These excruciating tortures were renewed the following
night when she saw herself actually crucified. The Pilgrim found her throat and tongue very much swollen next
day, and it was only with difficulty she could relate the fol
lowing :—

" I have seen that the Church's distress springs from
treason, omissions, and negligences ; and, though great is
the misery here among us, it is still greater in other places.
I saw priests in taverns, in bad company, and their parishioners dying without the Sacraments ; and again I had a
vision of how the secret sect cunningly attacks the Church
of Peter on all sides. They used all sorts of tools and ran here
and there with the broken stones ; but they had to leave
the altar standing, they could not carry it off. I saw
them profane and rob a statue of Mary. I complained to
the Pope of his tolerating so many priests among the destroyers, and I saw why the Church was founded in Rome.
It was because Rome was at that time the centre of the
world, the metropolis of nations. It will stand like an
island, like a rock in the sea, when all around it goes to

ruin. Jesus gave this power to Peter and set him over all His Church, because of his fidelity and uprightness. When Jesus said to him, 'Follow Me,' Peter understood that he, too, would be crucified. As I watched the destroyers, I marvelled at their great skill. They had all kinds of machinery; they did everything according to a given plan. They made no noise, they noticed everything, profited by everything, had recourse to all kinds of artifice, and the building seemed to disappear under their touch, though nothing crumbled of itself. Some among them were engaged in reconstructing. They destroyed the holy and the great, and they built up the empty, the hollow, the superfluous! From some of the altar stones, they made steps at the entrance."

Father Limberg was deeply affected at the sight of the invalid's cruel sufferings. He sought to relieve her by the invocation of the Holy Name and by exorcisms. He had read of Father Gassner, the Exorcist's, doing the same among the sick in Bavaria, especially if he suspected the malady to come from the evil one. But Sister Emmerich said to him: "Exorcisms will have no effect upon me. I know well that my sufferings do not come from the devil. I can be relieved only by your benediction, by patient compassion, and by prayer for the cause of my misery. As long as I can remember, I have always had firm faith in the name of Jesus, and I have helped others, as well as myself, by its invocation. But what I am now enduring I know. I have taken it upon myself in the same Holy Name! I have seen many of those who were cured by Father Gassner but none of them pleased me. The cause of their maladies was *sin*."

A year previously, Jan. 20th, the Pilgrim recorded a remarkable fact in reference to the relief Sister Emmerich had derived from the name of Jesus:—" I earnestly begged

God to relieve my greatest pain, that caused by the trouble
in my bowels, when He answered me gravely : ' Why to-
day ? Will not to-morrow do ? Hast thou not given thyself to Me ? May I not do with thee as I will ?'—Then I
abandoned myself entirely to Him ! May it be done according to His will ! O what a grace to be able still to
suffer ! Blessed is he who is mocked and despised ! It is
all that I deserve. Hitherto I have been only too much
honored. Ah ! if I were spit upon in the public street, if
I were trodden under foot, I should gratefully kiss the feet
of all ! St. Agnes also suffered. I have seen what she endured."

On the evening of this day, Dr. Lutterbeck came to Dülmen and received from the Pilgrim, though not in her
presence or hearing, a full account of the invalid's state.
She cried out of her ecstasy : " How can you tread among
my flowers ! You are trampling down my beautiful
flowers ! " She had seen him who revealed her secret tortures under the symbol of one carelessly crushing the flower-
beds of her garden. The next day the pains in her abdomen
were so intense that Father Limberg in pity gave her some
blessed oil, and commanded them in the name of Jesus to
leave her. She was instantaneously and entirely relieved.
The words : " Will not *to-morrow* do ?" were then verified.
During this sickness Sister Emmerich made the following
declaration :

" The sufferings of the impatient are far harder for me
to bear than those of others ; for with them I experience an
irresistible inclination to impatience, and I have to struggle
hard against it. Through the whole course of this illness,
I have been wonderfully sustained. Almost . all night and
frequently by day, I see a table white like marble floating
near me full of vessels of juices and dishes of herbs.

Now one saint or martyr, now another, male or female, approaches and prepares medicine for me, sometimes a compound weighed in golden scales, but oftener the juices of herbs. Sometimes tiny bunches of flowers are presented for me to smell or taste. They often relieve my pains, though more frequently they increase my strength to bear the more extraordinary and complicated sufferings that immediately follow. I see all this going on so clearly and orderly that I sometimes fear my confessor, in passing in and out, will overturn the heavenly dispensatory."

This table suddenly vanished one day, when, by an unguarded word, Sister Emmerich afforded some one a chance to praise her. She was giving the person in question advice upon the best way to lead a retired life, and she happened to conclude with the words : " It was thus I acted in my youth and I derived benefit from it." Some words of commendation were uttered in reply, and the table disappeared.

SUFFERING FOR PENITENTS.

" When I see people going to confession, I often have frightful visions of the necessity of praying for them : for instance, I sometimes see the penitent spitting out a serpent and taking it back again, often indeed, even before Communion. They who hide sins appear with a hideous countenance and near them a horrible beast seizing their breast with its claws. I often see a figure whispering into the ear of those who live in criminal connections. He urges them to say nothing about it. I behold others pressing to their hearts whilst they confess a figure like a dragon. I have always understood that disgusting things, such as worms and certain insects, rise from sin and are images of sin. Near such as conceal secret sins, but who are exteriorly modest and pious, I see horrible things either at their side, or on their clothing, or often covered up and secretly caressed and fed. I have often seen such things so distinctly near certain persons that I tried to remove them, and desisted only when I perceived their amazement at my efforts. The cricket is an image of sin, restless, greedy, shrill, noisy. It moves all its hairs, cleans itself, and flaps its wings when it chirps, as do they who cherish such sins as those that it symbolizes."

One day, Sister Emmerich related the following:—"I was praying, at his own request, for a certain priest's penitents and I had a very painful labor to perform. I saw two boats about to sink. In one were men, in the other women, the latter the more numerous. Their confessor was on the shore, trying to draw the boats to land, first one, then the other. The men's boat was easily managed. But many, or rather almost all the women had, in disobedince to their confessor and partly unknown to him, cats hidden under their kerchiefs which were the cause of the boat's sinking. The cats held fast; they would not let go; they clawed right and left. I rowed out on a plank to the boat, and urged the women to throw the cats overboard. They obeyed very reluctantly, and began to quarrel with me. The confessor pulled with all his might, though not always in the right way. I had to call out to him to pull in the opposite direction."

Sister Emmerich, though eating absolutely nothing, was subject at intervals, for two days at a time, to violent spells of retching. These efforts reduced her to such weakness that she frequently swooned, unconsciously uttering the words: "Sins must be cast out; they must be confessed!" which bore evidence to the fact that she was expiating sacrilegious confessions.

She had a special devotion to St. Anthony of Padua.

On his feast and during the octave she received the commission to urge sinners to repentance. On such days she
lay a victim to rapidly changing maladies, convulsions, interior anguish, and spiritual abandonment. One day she
related what follows :—"The saint (*St. Anthony*) showed
me some people whom I was to urge to make a general
confession, which they actually did to Dean Overberg and
Father Limberg. I did not know them except in vision.
Such affairs are carried on as if the saint sent a message,
or an order to my guide who said to me :—' Arise ! Follow
me, if thou dost wish to aid such or such a one !' Then
comes a tiresome journey full of difficulties, typical of the
spiritual obstacles in the souls of penitents: perverse ideas,
passions, and struggles against a sincere and contrite confession.

Some of these souls seem very small, very far off ; others
appear to be nearer, and this signifies their dispositions for
confession. Some who are really near me seem to be very
small, and far away ; whilst others, who are actually at a
distance, appear large and spiritually near. To reach some
who are near me, I have to climb rugged mountains down
which I incessantly stumble. When by the help of God's
grace and the saint's (St. Anthony's) assistance I succeed
in crossing it, I find their heart changed."

On November 29, 1822, six fierce outlaws condemned to
imprisonment passed through Dülmen. They spent the night
in the city jail. This was shown Sister Emmerich in vision,
and she immediately set to work to pray for the miserable
wretches. Next morning she said : " I visited the prisoners
for whom I was praying and, as I drew near the prison
I found it surrounded by thorns which grew even over the
walls. I got my hands all torn by them. The enclosure
had no roof and I descended ; but I could not reach the

prisoners. They seemed to be in holes and windings with beams and rafters over and in front of them. All was dark and desolate, as if turned to stone. I labored hard, but reached none of them ; they were perfectly hardened. Then came N——, the police officer, and I hurried away for fear, if he saw me, he might think I wanted to set the prisoners free."

April, 1820.—Sister Emmerich was suddenly seized with violent pains in her left side. She could lie only on her right, she could not speak ; she frequently swooned and she thought surely she was going to die. But she said calmly: " This is the remains of Lent. I burdened myself too heavily. I thought it would come ! I took it upon myself for a stranger who wanted to make his Easter confession here. I saw him at the confessional in bad dispositions ; he was not sincere, and so he became more culpable. I begged Our Lord to let me suffer for him, to satisfy Divine Justice, and to change his heart. Then this intense pain came on, but I can scarcely bear it !" The Abbé Lambert prayed over her and she was, for the time, somewhat relieved; but when he left her, the pain returned so violently that she swooned away, the cold perspiration rolling in great drops down her forehead. Her confessor was sent for. He came, blessed her, and commanded the pain to depart in the name of Jesus, when she instantly fell into a gentle sleep.

Easter-tide, 1823.—" I had to drag a man by force into the church and up to the Communion rail. He resisted and almost threw me to the ground. I suffered fearfully and received so severe blows on my heart that I felt as if it were being crushed." Such was the invalid's task at this time and the foregoing scene was frequently renewed until the week before Pentecost, when she said one day to

her confessor: " I am worn out on that same man's account !"
—Soon the very individual of whom she spoke presented
himself, begging the Father to hear his general confession.
Father Limberg received him most kindly and introduced
him, at his own request, to Sister Emmerich.   He begged
her pardon with tears for having calumniated her.

The carnival was annually for Sister Emmerich a time
of excruciating suffering, because of the excesses then
committed.   " I have to behold all the abominations of the
dissolute : the thoughts, the inward wickedness of hearts ;
the snares of the devil; the sloth, the wavering, the
wandering of souls ; and lastly, their unhappy fall.   I see
Satan everywhere, and I have to run, to fly, to suffer and
exhort, to beseech God and deliver myself over to chastisement.   I see at the same time the injury these insensates
offer their Redeemer, my Saviour, whom I behold all
covered with spittle, torn, and bloody.   The so-called
innocent amusements I see in their frightful nakedness, in
their deplorable consequences ! I am seized with horror and
compassion.   I pass from martyrdom to martyrdom to obtain
for this or that sinner time and grace.   I see this among
laics and priests ; but the latter make me suffer more.   At
last, I was so exhausted that I could do no more, and I asked
my angel and the other guardian-angels to take my place for
some poor creatures whose state touched me deeply."—She
was at this time so utterly prostrate as to be unable to move,
her very breathing was agonizing; yet she lay sweet and
calm and patient as ever.   The evil one assaults her day
and night.

Ash-Wednesday, March, 1821.-" The Pilgrim found her
this morning bruised, pale, and exhausted, her countenance
peaceful, her soul calm ; she was all kindness and
charity.   She said :—" I think I had last night all the pains

and tortures a human being can possibly endure. I found some relief for my intense ear-ache from a little blessed oil on cotton.'—Then suddenly exclaiming : ' Now, there's a dance !' she writhed on her bed, her feet quivering with pain, whilst in terror and as if defending herself she cried out : ' They have set a furious cur on me !'— Later on she explained as follows : 'I was sent to a village in which the peasants were dancing again to-day. I had to reprove them for their levity. They became en- raged, and it seemed as if they let a mad dog loose against me. I was, at first, terrified, but then came the thought : *Thou art not here in body, so he cannot bite thee!*—and I squeezed into a little corner and discovered that the dog was the devil. He had horrible claws and fiery eyes. Just at that moment, a saint reached me from above a large iron club which seemed to be hollow, it was so light. He said : ' Here, I often drubbed Satan with this !'—I took it and held it out to the dog. He bit it and tugged at it until, at last, he ran off with it. Then I was able to execute my commission and the dance was broken up.' "

April, 1822.—" The invalid is in a most pitiable state, though singularly patient, even joyous in her pains which seem ever to increase. To her cough, vomiting, and reten- tion, are added sharp pains in her face and swelling of the lips which are covered with white blisters ; she can neither speak nor drink. The doctor prescribed external applica- tions, but the only relief she experiences is from St. Walburga's oil. Her angelic guide told her to leave her- self to God, as she was expiating sins of the tongue. This state lasted about seven days, during which, at her angel's bidding, she recited long vocal prayers almost all night, a hundred Our Fathers, Hail Maries, and Litanies."

CHAPTER IX.

Last Days and Death of Sister Emmerich.

On Good-Friday, 1823, Sister Emmerich remarked : "I shall not see another Easter. I am hungering for the Blessed Sacrament. I have been told that, if there is no change, I shall soon die." And shortly before the Feast of Corpus Christi of the same year, the Pilgrim wrote : "Her labors for the Church are now, as she says, so painful and demand such efforts on her part that she thinks her end is approaching ; should she survive this feast, she may hope for a little more time."

The feast alluded to found her in a most miserable state which, however, did not prevent her having a magnificent vision on the Blessed Sacrament. She feared on account of frequent vomiting, that she should not be able to communicate, and she prayed God in agony not to deprive her of this consolation. Her prayer was graciously heard. A sudden change appeared in her, and she was able to receive the Blessed Sacrament. " I saw," she said, " Jesus with Walburga, His beautiful bride, whilst I was so miserable, like a poor worm, and I begged to be a bride like her. Jesus asked me : 'What dost thou desire ?' and I answered suppliantly : ' Ah ! grant that I may never offend Thee by any sin ! '—I received no answer, and they withdrew."

Sister Emmerich now barely lived. Her sufferings were intensified from month to month, as we see by the Pilgrim's journal:

" She has entered upon a frightful martyrdom for the

Church. She is tortured, crucified! Her throat and tongue are swollen, and she lies as if crushed by woe.— She is suffering for the impenitent. Barbara and Cecilia show her what she must do. She must not grow discouraged. She has imposed these sufferings upon herself; she must endure them till the end. . . . . . Terrible pains in her eyes endured for a Cardinal, render her almost blind. She is ready to succumb, and she groans: 'It strikes like hammers on my eyes!'—She begged for and received some mitigation of her sufferings, but they soon returned. She is, indeed, very ill, and to these eye-troubles are added constant vomiting. She can neither speak nor see; pain has robbed her of her senses."

During the octave of the Immaculate Conception, the Superioress of the Ladies of the Sacred Heart of Amiens, Madam G. Duhayet, wrote to beg Sister Emmerich's prayers for her community. Father Limberg hesitated about reading the letter to her, as she was so ill. He thought it would suffice to mention the intention to her; but the Pilgrim was of the contrary opinion and persuaded him to communicate to her its contents. He did so, when she exclaimed: "I have seen that little nun; she needs spiritual assistance. They do not understand her, but she has a strong and vigorous soul. I love her much, I shall establish a bond of prayer with her." Some days later, she related part of a vision she had had and a symbolical spiritual labor she had performed for the good lady. "I was in a garden with the little nun who was very skilful in sowing seeds. She had a little basket divided into compartments. It contained numbers of neat little bags which held seeds of all the different flowers and plants. Whenever she discovered a new plant, she gathered the seed into one of her little bags; some had a great many, others only a few, and in some the seeds were mixed. We spoke not, but I worked and planted diligently. The garden was laid off in small beds. The nun had worked here and there, but the greater part was still uncultivated, the ground hard. She had no help and sometimes she knew not what to do."

This was Sister Emmerich's last communication, for at Christmas the Pilgrim made the following entry in his journal: "The invalid, generally bright and joyous on this festival, continues in a dying state, in consequence of her sympathetic sufferings with rheumatic and other sick people. She cannot speak ; she groans and coughs, and is indescribably weak. A young person was shown her who had procured for herself a very showy breast-pin. To shield her from the danger to which her vanity exposes her, Sister Emmerich has to endure in her neck and breast as many different pains as the goldsmith gave blows and cuts in making the pin. She had to pray also for such as approach the Sacraments on these feasts out of mere custom and laden with sins of frivolity."

January 6, 1824.—"She has began the New-Year very miserably, fever, cramps, rheumatism, but still she is actively employed in spirit for the Church and the dying. Once she said: 'The Pope has laid his terrible burden upon me. He was very ill. He suffered so much from the interference of Protestants! I heard him say once that he would rather be executed before St. Peter's than tolerate such encroachments longer. The See of Peter must be free!'"

January 9, 1824.—"Her confessor thinks her mission will soon end, for she exclaimed earnestly in vision: 'I can undertake no new labors! I have reached the goal!'"

January 10th—"She sighs and groans with pain. She

writhes like a worm, or like one stretched on a rack. She remarked to Father Limberg, 'Hitherto I suffered for others; now I am suffering for myself.' With a dying voice she calls upon the name of Jesus.' "

January 11th—"To-day she said: 'The Christ-Child brought me many pains this Christmas, and He came again last night with many more.'"

January 12th—" What pen can describe her terrible suffering! Her stifled groans and sighs to God, her broken entreaties to Him for help (she who used to endure the greatest pains in silence) declare it. Dr. W— says we may expect her death at any hour, and she herself often asks to confess. She has explained to Father Limberg how to dispose of her little effects. Inflammation of the bowels has set in, in consequence of her constant coughing and vomiting. Day and night she sits swaying and groaning with pain, *her expression sweet and patient, perfectly resigned to the frightful rigor of her martyrdom.* This state is only interrupted by frequent swoons and death-like sweats."

January 15th—"She said to-day with trembling earnestness: ' The Child Jesus brought me great suffering after His Circumcision when He had fever caused by His wound. He told me all His own and His Mother's sufferings, their hunger and thirst. He told me everything.—They had only a little crust of dry bread. He said to me: "Thou art Mine! Thou art My bride! suffer what I suffered! Ask not why; it is life and death!"—I know not how long I shall have to suffer, nor how, nor where. I am handed over blindfolded to a terrible martyrdom, I know not whether I shall live or die. It is as when we say in prayer, *I abandon myself to God! May His secret will be done in me!*—But I am calm and resigned. I have many consolations in my pains. Even this morning I was very happy.'—Then she inquired : 'What is the date? Ah! I should soon have finished the Life of Jesus but now I am in a miserable state!'"

January 16th—"The Pilgrim sat by her bedside a few moments to-day; but she spoke not, moved not save in convulsive pain, her hands quivering incessantly, her pitiful groans heard by day and by night. One cannot restrain his tears at such a spectacle! Her eyes are closed, her face wears the solemn impress of untold sufferings. The confessor thinks she has gangrene ; the docter gives no hope. 'Judging humanly,' he says, 'she may die at any instant.' When the Pilgrim asked him if there was room for hope, he shook his head gravely. Her condition is heartrending."

January 18th—"Just the same. To the question, 'Are you patient?' she answered by a sweet smile of thanksgiving to God breaking over her countenance through the terrible gravity of pain and weakness. There are frequent, nay constant changes in her state, though all do not perceive it. She said to the Vicar Hilgenberg this morning, although no bells were ringing : 'What sweet bells! They are ringing for to-day's festival.' " (Feast of the Holy Name of Jesus.)

January 20th—The Vicar and the Pilgrim were conversing on the nature of Sister Emmerich's sufferings, but at a distance where she could not possibly hear, when she exclaimed in a broken voice, 'Ah! do not praise me! It makes me worse!' Father Limberg says she has used these words several times since yesterday (1)."

January 21st— " She grows worse daily. She moans and

(1) On the 20th of January, Father Limberg wrote to Sister Soentgen, as follows : "As I know the interest you feel in your old companion, Sister Emmerich, I take the liberty of informing you of her present condition. The inflammation of the eyes from which she had been suffering for months was allayed about Christmas, when she was attacked by a violent cough that so weakened and wasted her that she seems but skin and bone. She cannot now last long, if God does not prolong her life miraculously. Eight

the death-rattle sounds day and night. She can scarcely hear. Her countenance expresses gravity mingled with peace; it is truly awe-inspiring. Seldom, excepting when in absolute need of assistance, does she stammer a few almost unintelligible words in a hollow voice. Her back from constantly lying on it is covered with sores; if turned on her side, she begins to suffocate. The Pilgrim gives her morning and evening St. Walburga's oil. Sometimes when taking it she exclaims faintly, 'O how sweet!' She never sleeps, but rests in a half-reclining posture, groaning and breathing heavily, her eyes constantly closed."

January 22-26.—"Her sufferings are the same. She has no hope of life. She sent for her brothers and their children, also for her nephew, the student at Münster· Though she can say but a few words to them, yet she wishes them to remain by her a little while, a thing she never did in any former illness, even apparently mortal. When her brother's second son, a fine young peasant, took leave of her this morning, she told him, as her confessor says, in an unusually distinct tone to lead a good life and to keep God ever before his eyes. After that she requested that her relations would not come again to see her."

January 27th—"Sister Emmerich is more dead than alive, scarcely able to swallow the Walburga oil the Pilgrim offered her. Her cheeks glow with fever, her hands are deathly white, and the stigmata shine like silver through the parched skin. She wishes to die as a religious, so in the afternoon she begged Madam Hackebram, through her confessor, to be present as her Superioress, the representative of her former community, when Extreme Unction

days ago Dr. Wesener declared from the state of her pulse that she might die at any moment. Thank God, she has had up to the present the grace to endure with patience! Pray, nevertheless, for your afflicted fellow-sister that the will of God may be done in her; that He may be glorified by the trial to which He subjects her; and that she may persevere to the end. . .Have the kindness to acquaint her cousin Bernard Emmerich of her state, that he may redouble his prayers for her."

would be administered. She received the Sacrament calmly, in full consciousness, and sent the Chaplain, Father Niesing, and Madam Hackebram to Dean Rensing to ask pardon in her name for any offence she might have given him, although involuntarily and unwillingly. They fulfilled their commission. But the Dean still absents himself."

January 31st—" She speaks now only to her confessor and an occasional word to her niece."

February 1st—The Pilgrim visited her in the evening and found her breathing with great difficulty. Suddenly she seemed to recollect herself. The evening bells were ringing for the morrow's feast, the Purification of the Blessed Virgin."

February 2d—" To-day she whispered softly: 'It is a long time since I felt so well. The Mother of God has done so much for me! I have been sick eight days, have I not? I know nothing of what has been going on. O what has the Mother of God not done for me! She took me with her, and I wanted to stay with her.' Then, as if reflecting, she said with raised finger: 'Hush! I dare not tell all!' She is ever on her guard against praise; it makes her suffer more."

February 6th—" She requested a Mass to be said to-morrow for the Abbé Lambert. It is his anniversary."

February 7th—" She constantly sighs to God for help; her sufferings do not abate. She often prays: 'Ah! Lord Jesus, a thousand thanks for my whole life! Lord, not as I will, no, but as Thou wilt!' And once she uttered these touching words: 'Ah! the lovely little basket of flowers there! Take care of it! And that young laurel-tree, take care of it also. I have tended it long, but I can do so no more.' Probably she alluded to her niece and her nephew, the student."

February 8th—" Toward evening, the Vicar Hilgenberg prayed by her. Through gratitude she wanted to kiss his hands which, however, he humbly withdrew. She begged him to stay by her at the hour of death, relapsed into silence awhile, and then said: ' Jesus, for Thee I live, for Thee I die !' and again: ' Thanks to God, I can no longer hear,I can no longer see !' She appeared unconscious from pain as the Pilgrim knelt by her bed in prayer. He slipped into her hand a little reliquary which she once used to wear and which she had given him four years previously. She clasped it firmly for a moment, and then he took it from her. Next day he found the silver ring snapped in two—it was the day of Sister Emmerich's death."

February 9th—Father Limberg states :—" I gave Sister Emmerich Holy Communion before daybreak. She received with her accustomed fervor. During the night she remarked that she knew the signification of her illness and that she would tell me as her confessor,had she the strength. Toward two P. M., the death struggle came on, and she groaned in agony from the wounds on her back. Some one offered to re-arrange her pillows, but she declined with the words : ' It will soon be over. I am on the cross !'— which words affected me deeply. I gave her the general absolution and recited the prayers for the dying at the conclusion of which she seized my hand, pressed it, thanked me, and bade me farewell. Shortly after her sister entered and begged her pardon. The dying one turned toward her, gazed at her fixedly, and said to me : ' What does she say ?' ' She asks your pardon,' I answered. She replied solemnly : ' There is no one on earth whom I have not forgiven.'

"She ardently longed for death and frequently sighed : ' Come, Lord Jesus !'—I encouraged her to suffer with her

Saviour who forgave the thief on the cross, and she uttered these significant words: 'The people of that time, even
the murderer on the cross, had not so much to answer for,
they received not so many graces as we. I am far worse
than the murderer on the cross!'—And again, 'I cannot
die, because some good people are deceived in me; they
think too well of me. Tell them all that I am a miserable
sinner!'—As I again tried to reassure her, she replied en-
ergetically: 'Ah! that I could cry out loud enough for all
to hear that I am nothing but a miserable sinner far worse
than the murderer on the cross!'— after which she grew
calm just as the Vicar Hilgenberg arrived. The good old
man knelt by her a whole hour in prayer."

The closing scene of Sister Emmerich's life we take
from the Pilgrim's ever-faithful journal :—

"The Pilgrim arrived at about half-past six, just as
Father Limberg drew the blinds of her little room, saying
in low tones, ' The end has come ! '—Kneeling around were
her sister, her brother, and her niece, the Vicar Hilgenberg, Father Limberg's sister and sister-in-law, Madam
Clement Limberg, with the latter of whom Sister Emmerich
had formerly lodged. The door was open to admit air to
the dying one. She lay half reclining in her little willow bed,
her breathing short, her countenance imposing, her eyes
raised to the crucifix. The blessed candle had burned
low. After a few moments, she drew her right hand from
under the bed-clothes and laid it upon the coverlet. Father
Limberg spoke words of comfort and repeatedly presented
to her the crucifix to kiss; her lips invariably sought and
pressed the feet with lingering love. She never touched
the head or breast. And now she seemed desirous of communicating something to her confessor. Obedient to the
last, she responded instantly to his question regarding her

wish to speak to him. All left the room, and the Pilgrim
saw her no more alive. It was then just eight o'clock.
Father Limberg afterward told us that she spoke of a trifle
already confessed and then remarked: ' *I am now as
peaceful and confident as if I had never sinned.*' She kissed
the crucifix and again Father Limberg recited the prayers
for the agonizing. At intervals she sighed: 'O Lord,
help! Help, O Lord Jesus!'—Father Limberg placed the
blessed candle in her right hand and rang a little Loretto
bell, which had formerly been used in the Agnetenberg
convent on the death of the religious, saying: 'She is dying.' It was now half after eight (1). The Pilgrim approached the bed just as she sank down on the left side, her
head upon her breast, and her right hand upon the coverlet, that miraculous hand to which the Giver of celestial
gifts had attached the unheard of privilege of recognizing
whatever was holy, whatever was blessed by the Church.
No one before her, perhaps, had ever possessed that grace
in so high a degree. The Pilgrim took that blessed hand, that
organ of spiritualized sense which could discover the sanctified substance even in a grain of dust—it was cold and lifeless! Yes, that humble, beneficent hand which had so often fed the hungry and clothed the naked, now lay cold
and dead! The gift was withdrawn from earth, and with
us lies the blame! Some years previously she had in vision
told her confessor that he should remove her right hand
from her body after death (2), and the Pilgrim remembers
her assuring him that even after death, if ordered to do so,
she would still be able to discern whatever is blessed.
Once she saw herself lying in her coffin before the church
without her hands, which were floating up in the air toward

(1) Sister Emmerich died on the Monday before Septuagésima.
(2) See Vol. I, 39.

the holy things in the church. Father Limberg trembled till the last moment with the fear of the invalid's repeating her request of previous years. 'Perhaps,' he said, 'seeing my dread, she refrained from doing so.'"

The next day, February 10th, the Pilgrim went to Haltern and Bocholt, returning only toward the close of the month. Father Limberg and Dr. Wesener conformed scrupulously to Sister Emmerich's dying request that her body should not be subjected to examination. The care of preparing her blessèd remains for burial was intrusted by Father Limberg to his brother Clement's wife, to whom the Pilgrim renders the following testimony : "Humbler hands could not have been found for the task, which she reverentially regarded as a favor, a high distinction conferred upon her."

This good lady gives us the following account of her labor of love : "On Wednesday afternoon, the 11th, in accordance with the wish of the deceased, I wrapped the body in a large winding-sheet, and removed it from the bed on which she died to a mattress. The feet were firm-ly crossed one over the other, the wounds of which, as well as those of the hands, being of a deeper red and more distinct than usual. As I raised the body, blood and water flowed from the mouth. All the members were perfectly supple. Our Sister looked very lovely. Contrary to her wish for a poor, plain coffin, they furnished a handsome one, and in it she was placed on Thursday at noon. The funeral took place Friday, at half-past eight A. M., the concourse of people being so large that never before had the like been seen in Dülmen : clergymen, citizens, the school-children, the poor, all took part in it."

On February 11th, Father Limberg gave alms to a poor woman to make with her children the Way of the Cross for the deceased during nine days. He afterward told the Pilgrim what follows :

" Several days before her death Sister Emmerich charged me to have a Mass said for her by Vicar Hilgenberg, for nine days in St. Anne's chapel, and to burn a candle before the saint's picture. She likewise requested that the poor woman and her children would make the Stations for the same time. The last part of the commission I did not fulfil, on account of the bad weather. Though Sister Emmerich could naturally know nothing of the omission, yet shortly before her death she said to me : ' You have deprived me of one consolation. You have not sent the woman to make the Stations for me."

Dr. Wesener was another witness of Sister Emmerich's last hours. From his notes we cull the following :—

" All winter Sister Emmerich suffered intensely from her eyes. When, by applications customary in such cases, external inflammation was allayed, the disease attacked the interior of the eye-ball. Remedies proved vain, as she herself declared whilst in ecstasy, for it was a spiritual labor, imposed in the form of suffering, which had to be finished at Christmas. In effect, the malady ceased on the day after that feast, only to be succeeded, however, by a most painful convulsive cough. For several weeks she clearly foresaw her death. Fourteen days before it actually happened, she sent for her nearest relations and took a most edifying leave of them, consoling them with the hope of a speedy reunion and begging them not to visit her again. The last eight days she spoke but little excepting to her confessor, the few remaining hours of life being wholly consecrated to prayer. Up to the last sigh she preserved, though in the greatest pain, her unalterable patience, and gracious demeanor. When unable to speak she pressed our hands. On my morning visit of Feb. 9th, I found her in a pitiable state. Her copious expectoration

had ceased, and she complained of pains in her side. I
was convinced that a fresh attack of pleurisy had come on
in the night. She suffered indescribably till four P. M.,
when the struggle appeared to come to an end, pulmonary
paralysis having set in. Her countenance fell, her pulse vanished, and her extremities became icy cold. She regained her
serenity and spoke up to a few moments before her death,
which occurred at half-past eight P. M. She died in full
consciousness."

On February 10th, the Vicar Hilgenberg penned the following lines to Sister Soentgen :—

"Our dear friend has finished her course. Having kept
the faith, we may rightly believe that she now wears the
crown. Her death was edifying as her life. During the
whole winter she suffered more than usual. Eight days
ago she said to me : ' Stay by me when I am dying!'—
Yesterday evening she sent for me about six o'clock, and
at half-past eight she sweetly expired after kissing the
crucifix repeatedly. Father Limberg, her confessor,
never left her. Brentano, too, was there, with Madam
Clement Limberg, her sister Gertrude, her brother, her
niece, and the nurse, Wissing.—All were silently praying
in the adjoining room. Some moments before her death,
she signified her desire to speak with Father Limberg, after
which he called us in, saying, ' She is dying!'—Sweet was
her death and most sensibly do we feel her loss! Still, I
must say that I experienced real joy at seeing her triumph,
her victory over the world. Pray with the friends around
you for our glorified one if, perchance, she have need of
such help, though I feel that she is now praying for us."

Again the Vicar wrote on February 16th—" In reply to
your questions, I inform you that Sister Emmerich's obsequies took place on Friday, the 13th. No examination

of the body was made; such a step would have been a most
painful one to good Dr. Wesener. It was not removed from
the bed of death till the afternoon of the 11th, when her cheeks
were still flushed. The water which, on her deathbed, she
had taken more freely than usual, flowed from her mouth and
nostrils and her head was covered with a bloody moisture.
The body was immediately enclosed in the coffin on account of the crowds that flocked to see her, a favor granted
only to few. Although she had expressed a desire for an
humble, simple funeral, without the pomp of a High Mass,
and the attendance of the confraternity and school-children,
yet the concourse of mourners was so great that the oldest
inhabitants of Dülmen remember nothing like it. The
church was crowded as on a Sunday. All Dülmen mourns
her loss. I have made known your request to Father
Limberg, who sends cordial greetings to you. He promises to be in Münster soon. On Saturday, the 14th, Dean
Rensing received a visit from a person who offered on the
part of the Hollanders, 4000 florins for Sister Emmerich's
remains. He alleged that he was authorized to do so by
the Pro-vicar and the Chief-President Vinke; but the offer
was very justly rejected. God grant that she, whose life
was one of such annoyance, may now rest in peace!"

The Pilgrim visited the Dean for the purpose of obtaining
a full explanation of the proposed purchase. The following is his statement of the affair:—"On Sunday, February 29th, the Pilgrim went to see Dean Rensing about a
tombstone for the deceased; he spoke to him also concerning the offers to purchase the body upon which he received
the following account.—' The evening after the funeral the
merchant, Mr. H— of Münster, came to see me. He had
been commissioned by a Hollander to pay 4000 florins to
Sister Emmerich's family or to the parish church of Dül-

men for her body. He likewise stated what seemed to me rather doubtful, that the Pro-vicar and the Chief-President Vinke had no objection to the bargain's being made. But, when I asked what he wanted with the body which had already begun to decompose, he withdrew his offer."

The Pilgrim went on to speak of the extraordinary graces granted the deceased, when the Dean remarked : ' *Yes, she certainly was one of the most remarkable personages of the age.*'—And yet he had not taken one step to console this member of his own flock who, when dying, had craved his pardon, though she had never offended him.

It did not escape the Pilgrim that the Dean, after declaring in the beginning of the conversation that a tombstone could not be placed over the grave without the authorization of Ecclesiastical Superiors, and that the grave could not be opened without the same, yet ended by saying : ' Before a tombstone is erected, it would be well to see whether the body is still there or not.' "

After the foregoing speech, it would seem as if Dean Rensing also gave some faith to the report that a Hollander had secretly carried off the body, a report which spread rapidly and raised so great excitement in Dülmen that the authorities found it expedient to open the grave to assure themselves of the truth. On March 26. 1824, the Vicar Hilgenberg again wrote to Sister Soentgen :—

" I write to inform you that, on the night of the 21-22d of March, the Burgomaster Moellmann, in presence of the police and Witte, the carpenter, had Sister Emmerich's grave opened by two grave-diggers (as she had herself predicted). They found the body lying in precisely the same condition as at the time of burial, the winding-sheet enveloping it in such a way that only the face and forepart of the head could be seen. A reddish liquid had flowed from her mouth and her cheeks were tinged with red. She looked even more beautiful than on the bed of death, without a sign of corruption, though six weeks in the grave. The wounds of the feet were still plainly visible, but those of the hands could not be seen as they were enveloped in the folds of the winding-sheet. Around the top of the head, as also at the sides of the body, could be seen a bloody moisture. The police officers, fearing an offensive exhalation, had lighted their pipes and the burgomaster held his handkerchief to his face. But no such precautions were necessary ; there was not the slightest odor. The burgomaster, who was commissioned to make the investigation will now send in his report, and false rumors will cease. Miss Hensel has planted a rose-bush and other flowers on the grave. I feel confident that Our Lord will reward the deceased with an unfading crown, and that He will accept her prayers for us."

Some days previously Miss Hensel had had her friend's grave opened, but secretly, as much through disquiet at the alarming reports current, as through desire to gaze once again on the features of her whom she so greatly revered.

" She had been buried five weeks," she wrote to the author of this biography. " The straw on which she lay was already full of mold, and yet there was not the slightest disagreeable odor. The winding-sheet was damp, as if lately washed, and it clung close to the limbs. Her features were lovely, not the least change in them. Her remains in their linen winding-sheet left upon me an ineffaceable impression. I slipped under her head a leaden plate inscribed with her name and date of decease."

On October 6, 1858, Sister Emmerich's grave was opened for the third time, as may be seen by the following interesting and circumstantial letter written to the author by Canon Krabbe, Dean of the Cathedral, Münster:—"On the 6th of October, 1858, in presence of Mr. Bernard Schweling, Episcopal Commissioner and Notary Apostolic, Mr. Cramer, Dean of Dülmen, and several other reverend gentlemen, the grave of the late Sister Emmerich was opened, the third time since her interment, February 13, 1824. Father Pellicia, Order of the Brothers of Mercy, had visited his aged mother in Münster a few years previously, which circumstance led indirectly to the subsequent examination into the state of Sister Emmerich's remains. He spoke often of the great veneration in which she was held in Rome and expressed his astonishment at hearing so little mention made of her in Westphalia, her native country. He went to Dülmen to visit her grave, and there, again, was he surprised to find it destitute of even a memorial cross. He declared his intention to raise a collection on his return to Rome among those who venerated her memory, for the purpose of erecting a tomb to her honor. The collection was, in effect, made among the most distinguished of the Roman nobility and sent to Münster for the purpose signified. Mgr., the Bishop, authorized the erection of a Gothic cross over the grave and the opening of the latter in presence of responsible witnesses, in order to lay a foundation of brick-work. No trace of the coffin was visible, excepting one nail. After carefully removing the earth from the remains, two Sisters of Charity from the neighboring hospital lifted them out, one by one, and handed them to the physicians, Drs. Wiesmann and Wesener, the latter the son of him who had so faithfully attended the stigmatisée during the last ten years of her miraculous life. The bones were recognized by the two physicians as those of a female, and placed by the Sisters in an oak coffin. The whole skeleton was, at last, found in a natural position, only a small part, which had dissolved and mingled with the dust, was wanting. The coffin was then conveyed by the Sisters, followed by the assistants, to the hospital where it was hermetically sealed. When the tomb was ready to receive it, the coffin was again borne processionally to its final resting-place in which it was solemnly deposited with the accustomed blessings and prayers. A brick vault now holds the remains and on it lies the old marble slab, surmounted by a handsome Gothic cross."

Some years later the grave was inclosed by a beautiful iron railing and surrounded by kneeling-benches on which devout souls may often be seen in silent prayer.

In March, 1824, Mr. Clement Brentano, "the Pilgrim," as the good Sister herself taught us to style him, bade a final farewell to Dülmen. He took with him the precious harvest he had zealously gleaned and which he has transmitted to us in his journal, that ingenuous record of over five years spent by the invalid's bedside. All feelings of bitterness had been effaced from his heart by the loss of her to whom he owed so much, and all remembrance of past annoyance perfectly obliterated. His farewells to the Vicars Hilgenberg and Niesing, to Father Limberg, Dr. Wesener, and others were so sincere and cordial, that the kindest feelings ever afterward existed between him and his friends in Dülmen. The numerous letters which he annually received from them testify to this.

Dr. Wesener wrote to him the following lines, March 18, 1825 :—" You have learned through our friends here that I have been to the gates of the tomb. I allude to it, that I may make mention of one fact which with me you will esteem the most important of my illness ; viz., my perfect peace of soul in the severest sufferings. This peace I owe to close union with Our Lord Jesus Christ and the use of His spiritual remedies. Father Limberg and the Vicar Niesing were my faithful supporters; both rejoiced on beholding the consolations of faith sweetening my great pain and enabling me to bear it with patience. My cure was wrought at the moment in which all, including myself, thought me dying. It was on a January morning about four o'clock. In her distress, my wife ran to the cemetery and invoked the intercession of our dear Sister Emmerich. O dear, good soul, how often in my illness did I not call to mind thy nameless sufferings!"

Mr. Brentano wrote to one of his intimate friends in the early part of the year 1832:—"I am working diligently on my journal of the first three months of my sojourn near Sister Emmerich; but on account of its personal connections, it is a difficult task."

Another letter to the same friend ends with these words: "I beg you earnestly and in all confidence to pray for my intentions; namely, that God may still have mercy on me, and give me grace and strength not to offend Him so often and so grievously by my words. I am so frequently and easily led to speak imprudently and uncharitably of others without necessity or utility; it is for me a subject of daily discouragement. Pray, too, that God may prolong my life until I finish my task and dispose of what I possess in favor of the poor."

Some months later, Mr. Brentano published from his journal, "*The Dolorous Passion of Our Lord Jesus Christ, with a Short Sketch of the Life of the Servant of God, A. C. Emmerich* (1)." Notwithstanding the rapid sale of the "*Dolorous Passion,*" and the blessed fruits it produced, he

(1) Salzbach, 1833.

could not resolve upon publishing anything else from the same source. He sought the aid of younger, more vigorous workmen than himself to whom he might confidently confide the publication of his manuscripts. Writing to Guido Gœrres, he says: " Would that you and I were not so far apart! I would intrust to you, to you and Frederick Windischmann, my journal with the sum necessary for its publication; but that cannot be done at so great a distance. Order in arrangement of the notes is indispensable. And for this much reflection and many oral explanations would be absolutely requisite; for what there is of good in them is as delicate as the dust that paints the butterfly's wing. I sit alone as in a desert of shifting sand, eagerly bending over my treasure of fugitive leaves, and languishing in the noise and bustle of the careless world."

But the labors of their profession allowed not these chosen friends to assume the arduous task of publication, and two other attempts to find an associate in the work were equally unsuccessful.

Clement Brentano, the faithful friend and zealous amanuensis of Sister Emmerich, died July 28, 1842, with the unshaken conviction that God would not permit the precious treasure of his manuscripts, the fruit of so much toil and suffering, to lie hidden. His generous, magnanimous soul could never resolve to efface a single line of the endless complaints against the invalid and her surroundings that fill its pages. Ignoring self, he preferred leaving it as it fell from his pen under the impulse of passing impressions, that the future laborer at the work of its arrangement might have as exact an idea of every incident recorded, as if he had been an eye-witness of the same, and consequently be enabled to judge of it impartially, with truth and justice. Christian Brentano survived his brother Clement ten years.   He had the journal in his possession for a long time ; but, though he examined it most carefully, he also scrupulously refrained from retrenching a word therein recorded.   Animated by the same liberal spirit as his brother, he desired it to stand as a faithful witness to the situation in which Sister Emmerich was placed by Divine Providence and the circumstances under which she accomplished the daily task allotted her.

J. M. J.

A profoundly soul-stirring, unforgettable book . . .

THE PASSION
—Catholic Edition—

A Pictorial Coffee-Table Book Based on Mel Gibson's Film *The Passion of the Christ*

Foreword by Mel Gibson

No. 1942. 143 Pp.
123 Full-Color Pictures.
9 x 11½ Hardbound.
Jacket.
ISBN 0-89555-781-9.

25.00

Prices subject to change.

A beautiful pictorial book depicting the Passion and Death of Our Lord Jesus Christ in stunning color photographs, taken by professional photographers during the filming of Mel Gibson's movie on the Passion of Our Lord. This book retells the whole story of Our Lord's Passion. The printed text is minimal and taken from the edifying, traditional *Douay-Rheims Bible*, the classic Catholic Bible in English. Ten, twenty or thirty years from now, this book will still powerfully tell the story of Our Lord's Passion to one's children and grandchildren. Striking photos depicting Our Lord in His Agony and Death, as well as the Blessed Mother, St. John, St. Peter, St. Veronica, Simon of Cyrene, Judas, Pontius Pilate, the Jewish leaders, the Roman soldiers, etc. An unforgettable book that will make you want to see the movie and read *The Dolorous Passion* by Ven. Anne Catherine Emmerich.

Beautiful Gift Edition!

TAN BOOKS AND PUBLISHERS, INC.
P.O. Box 424 • Rockford, Illinois 61105

Toll Free 1-800-437-5876
Tel 815-226-7777

Fax 815-226-7770
www.tanbooks.com

THE LIFE OF JESUS CHRIST
And Biblical Revelations of
Anne Catherine Emmerich
From the Journals of Clemens Brentano
Edited by V. Rev. C. E. Schmöger, C.SS.R.

**No. 1943. 2,088 Pp. PB.
4 Vols. Impr. ISBN-7916.
Large Ed. (5 1/2 x 8 1/2")
Reg. 75.00**

Now only 60.00

Prices subject to change.

Begins with the Fall of the angels, creation of the earth, Adam and Eve, the Fall, Noe, Abraham, Melchisedech, the Ark of the Covenant, etc. Includes a day-by-day account of the public life of Christ—His teachings and miracles—plus a rendition of the lives of Mary and Joseph, John the Baptist, St. Anne and St. Joachim, and many ancestors of Our Lord. Describes Our Lord's founding of the Catholic Church and institution of the Sacraments, the Apostles' early missionary work, plus the death of the Blessed Mother. Researchers, using Sister Emmerich's descriptions of biblical sites, actually found the ruins of the places she had mentioned. A treasure trove of information obtainable from no other source. Seems an act of God these visions were permitted and recorded.

Testimonies of Famous People about this Book

"The books which proved very helpful during that period [of his conversion] were . . . Pascal . . . Bossuet . . . Dante . . . not to mention the marvelous private revelations of Catherine Emmerich."　　—Paul Claudel

"One day in the Long Retreat they were reading in the refectory Sister Emmerich's account of the Agony in the Garden and I suddenly began to cry and sob and could not stop . . ."　　—Fr. Gerard M. Hopkins, S.J.

"At the very beginning [of the conversion of the Maritains] Leon Bloy made us read Schmoger's three thick volumes of the life and visions of Anne Catherine Emmerich . . . one of the greatest mystics of the nineteenth century . . ."　　—Raissa Maritain

"From our own deep conviction of the great advantage to be derived from the pious perusal of this work . . . we do not hesitate in its approval to add our signature . . ."　　—James Cardinal Gibbons

If you have enjoyed this book, consider making your next selection from among the following . . .

Christian Perfection and Contemplation. *Garrigou-Lagrange, O.P.* 21.00
Practical Commentary on Holy Scripture. *Bishop Knecht.* 40.00
The Ways of Mental Prayer. *Dom Vitalis Lehodey* 16.50
The 33 Doctors of the Church. *Fr. Christopher Rengers, O.F.M. Cap.* 33.00
Pope Pius VII. *Prof. Robin Anderson* 16.50
Life Everlasting. *Garrigou-Lagrange, O.P.* 16.50
Mother of the Saviour/Our Int. Life. *Garrigou-Lagrange, O.P.*. 16.50
Three Ages/Int. Life. *Garrigou-Lagrange, O.P. 2 vol.* 48.00
Ven. Francisco Marto of Fatima. *Cirrincione,* comp. 2.50
Ven. Jacinta Marto of Fatima. *Cirrincione* 3.00
St. Philomena—The Wonder-Worker. *O'Sullivan* 9.00
The Facts About Luther. *Msgr. Patrick O'Hare* 18.50
Little Catechism of the Curé of Ars. *St. John Vianney.* 8.00
The Curé of Ars—Patron Saint of Parish Priests. *Fr. B. O'Brien* 7.50
Saint Teresa of Avila. *William Thomas Walsh* 24.00
Isabella of Spain: The Last Crusader. *William Thomas Walsh* 24.00
Characters of the Inquisition. *William Thomas Walsh* 16.50
Blood-Drenched Altars—Cath. Comment. on Hist. Mexico. *Kelley* 21.50
The Four Last Things—Death, Judgment, Hell, Heaven. *Fr. von Cochem* . . . 9.00
Confession of a Roman Catholic. *Paul Whitcomb* 2.50
The Catholic Church Has the Answer. *Paul Whitcomb* 2.50
The Sinner's Guide. *Ven. Louis of Granada* 15.00
True Devotion to Mary. *St. Louis De Montfort* 9.00
Life of St. Anthony Mary Claret. *Fanchón Royer* 16.50
Autobiography of St. Anthony Mary Claret. 13.00
I Wait for You. *Sr. Josefa Menendez* 1.50
Words of Love. *Menendez, Betrone, Mary of the Trinity.* 8.00
Little Lives of the Great Saints. *John O'Kane Murray* 20.00
Prayer—The Key to Salvation. *Fr. Michael Müller.* 9.00
Passion of Jesus and Its Hidden Meaning. *Fr. Groenings, S.J.* 15.00
The Victories of the Martyrs. *St. Alphonsus Liguori* 13.50
Canons and Decrees of the Council of Trent. *Transl. Schroeder* 16.50
Sermons of St. Alphonsus Liguori for Every Sunday. 18.50
A Catechism of Modernism. *Fr. J. B. Lemius* 7.50
Alexandrina—The Agony and the Glory. *Johnston.* 7.00
Life of Blessed Margaret of Castello. *Fr. William Bonniwell* 9.00
Catechism of Mental Prayer. *Simler* 3.00
St. Francis of Paola. *Simi and Segreti.* 9.00
St. Martin de Porres. *Giuliana Cavallini.* 15.00
The Story of the Church. *Johnson, Hannan, Dominica.* 22.50
Hell Quizzes. *Radio Replies Press* 2.50
Purgatory Quizzes. *Radio Replies Press* 2.50
Virgin and Statue Worship Quizzes. *Radio Replies Press* 2.50
Meditation Prayer on Mary Immaculate. *Padre Pio* 2.50
Little Book of the Work of Infinite Love. *de la Touche* 3.50
Textual Concordance of The Holy Scriptures. *Williams. pb.* 35.00
Douay-Rheims Bible. *Hardbound* 55.00
The Way of Divine Love. *Sister Josefa Menendez* 21.00
The Way of Divine Love. (pocket, unabr.). *Menendez* 12.50
Mystical City of God—Abridged. *Ven. Mary of Agreda* 21.00

Prices subject to change.

At your Bookdealer or direct from the Publisher.
Toll-Free 1-800-437-5876   **Fax 815-226-7770**
Tel. 815-229-7777   **www.tanbooks.com**

Prices subject to change.